Oscar L. Loudenslager

A COMPILATION

OF THE

MESSAGES AND PAPERS

OF THE

PRESIDENTS

Prepared Under the Direction of the Joint Committee
on Printing, of the House and Senate,
Pursuant to an Act of the Fifty-Second Congress
of the United States

(With Additions and Encyclopedic Index
by Private Enterprise)

VOLUME VI

PUBLISHED BY

BUREAU OF NATIONAL LITERATURE

1913

Copyright, 1897,
BY
JAMES D. RICHARDSON

Prefatory Note

The Presidential papers during the period from March 4, 1861, to March 4, 1869, are contained in this volume. No other period of American history since the Revolution comprises so many events of surpassing importance. The Administrations of Presidents Lincoln and Johnson represent two distinct epochs. That of Abraham Lincoln was dedicated to the successful prosecution of the most stupendous war of modern times, while that of Andrew Johnson was dedicated to the reestablishment of peace and the restoration of the Union as it had existed prior to the war. Strange to say, it fell to the lot of the kind-hearted humanitarian, who loved peace and his fellow-man, to wage the bloody conflict of civil war, and the more aggressive, combative character directed the affairs of the Government while the land took upon itself the conditions of peace. Yet who can say that each was not best suited for his particular sphere of action? A greater lover of his kind has not filled the office of President since Thomas Jefferson, and no public servant ever left with the people a gentler memory than Abraham Lincoln. A more self-willed and determined Chief Executive has not held that office since Andrew Jackson, and no public servant ever left with the people a higher character for honesty, integrity, and sincerity of purpose and action than Andrew Johnson. The life of each of these two great men had been a series of obscure but heroic struggles; each had experienced a varied and checkered career; each reached the highest political station of earth. Their official state papers are of supreme interest, and comprise the utterances of President Lincoln while he in four years placed in the field nearly three millions of soldiers; what he said when victories were won or when his armies went down in defeat; what treasures of blood and money it cost to triumph; also, the utterances of President Johnson as he through his eventful term waged the fiercest political battle of our country's history in his efforts, along his own lines, for the restoration of peace and the reunion of the States.

Interesting papers relating to the death and funeral obsequies of President Lincoln have been inserted, as also the more important papers and proceedings connected with the impeachment of President Johnson.

Much time and labor have been expended in the compilation of this volume—more than on any one of the preceding—to the end that all papers of importance that could be found should be published; and I feel sure that no other collection of Presidential papers is so thorough and complete.

The perusal of these papers should enkindle within the heart of every citizen of the American Republic, whether he fought on the one side or the other in that unparalleled struggle, or whether he has come upon the scene since its closing, a greater love of country, a greater devotion to the cause of true liberty, and an undying resolve that all the blessings of a free government and the fullest liberty of the individual shall be perpetuated.

JAMES D. RICHARDSON.

NOTE.

The pages of "The Messages and Papers of the Presidents" have been renumbered from page one to the end, and the division into volumes has been altered. This plan is required by the addition of new matter and the desirability of keeping the volumes as nearly uniform in size as possible.

ILLUSTRATIONS IN VOLUME SIX

Each voter will be allowed to cast a separate ballot for or against either or both of the provisions above quoted.

In testimony whereof I have hereunto set my hand and caused the seal of the United States to be affixed.

[SEAL.] Done at the city of Washington, this 14th day of May, A. D. 1869, and of the Independence of the United States of America the ninety-third.

U. S. GRANT.

By the President:

HAMILTON FISH, *Secretary of State.*

BY THE PRESIDENT OF THE UNITED STATES OF AMERICA.

A PROCLAMATION.

Whereas the act of Congress approved June 25, 1868, constituted, on and after that date, eight hours a day's work for all laborers, workmen, and mechanics employed by or on behalf of the Government of the United States, and repealed all acts and parts of acts inconsistent therewith:

Now, therefore, I, Ulysses S. Grant, President of the United States, do hereby direct that from and after this date no reduction shall be made in the wages paid by the Government by the day to such laborers, workmen, and mechanics on account of such reduction of the hours of labor.

In testimony whereof I have hereto set my hand and caused the seal of the United States to be affixed.

[SEAL.] Done at the city of Washington, this 19th day of May, A. D. 1869, and of the Independence of the United States the ninety-third.

U. S. GRANT.

By the President:

HAMILTON FISH, *Secretary of State.*

BY THE PRESIDENT OF THE UNITED STATES OF AMERICA.

A PROCLAMATION.

Whereas satisfactory evidence has been received by me from His Majesty the Emperor of France, through the Count Faverney, his chargé d'affaires, that on and after this date the discriminating duties heretofore levied in French ports upon merchandise imported from the countries of its origin in vessels of the United States are to be discontinued and abolished:

Now, therefore, I, U. S. Grant, President of the United States of America, by virtue of the authority vested in me by an act of Congress of the 7th day of January, 1824, and by an act in addition thereto of the 24th day of May, 1828, do hereby declare and proclaim that on and after this date, so long as merchandise imported from the countries of its origin into French ports in vessels belonging to citizens of the United States is admitted into French ports on the terms aforesaid, the discriminating duties heretofore levied upon merchandise imported from the countries of its origin into ports of the United States in French vessels shall be, and are hereby, discontinued and abolished.

In testimony whereof I have hereunto set my hand and caused the seal of the United States to be affixed.

[SEAL.]   Done at the city of Washington, this 12th day of June, A. D. 1869, and of the Independence of the United States of America the ninety-third.

U. S. GRANT.

By the President:

HAMILTON FISH, *Secretary of State*.

BY THE PRESIDENT OF THE UNITED STATES OF AMERICA.

A PROCLAMATION.

In pursuance of the provisions of the act of Congress approved April 10, 1869, I hereby designate Tuesday, the 30th day of November, 1869, as the time for submitting the constitution adopted on the 15th day of May, 1868, by the convention which met in Jackson, Miss., to the voters of said State registered at the date of such submission, viz, November 30, 1869.

And I submit to a separate vote that part of section 3 of Article VII of said constitution which is in the following words:

That I am not disfranchised in any of the provisions of the acts known as the reconstruction acts of the Thirty-ninth and Fortieth Congress, and that I admit the political and civil equality of all men. So help me God: *Provided*, If Congress shall at any time remove the disabilities of any person disfranchised in said reconstruction acts of the said Thirty-ninth and Fortieth Congress (and the legislature of this State shall concur therein), then so much of this oath, and so much only, as refers to the said reconstruction acts shall not be required of such person so pardoned to entitle him to be registered.

And I further submit to a separate vote section 5 of the same article of said constitution, which is in the following words:

No person shall be eligible to any office of profit or trust, civil or military, in this State who, as a member of the legislature, voted for the call of the convention that passed the ordinance of secession, or who, as a delegate to any convention, voted for or signed any ordinance of secession, or who gave voluntary aid, countenance, counsel, or encouragement to persons engaged in armed hostility to the United States, or who accepted or attempted to exercise the functions of any office, civil or military, under any authority or pretended government, authority, power, or constitution within the United States hostile or inimical thereto, except all persons who aided reconstruction by voting for this convention or who have continuously advocated the assembling of this convention and shall continuously and in good faith advocate the acts of the same; but the legislature may remove such disability: *Provided*, That nothing in this section, except voting for or signing the ordinance of secession, shall be so construed as to exclude from office the private soldier of the late so-called Confederate States army.

And I further submit to a separate vote section 5 of Article XII of the said constitution, which is in the following words:

The credit of the State shall not be pledged or loaned in aid of any person, association, or corporation; nor shall the State hereafter become a stockholder in any corporation or association.

And I further submit to a separate vote part of the oath of office prescribed in section 26 of Article XII of the said constitution, which is in the following words:

That I have never, as a member of any convention, voted for or signed any ordinance of secession; that I have never, as a member of any State legislature, voted for the call of any convention that passed any such ordinance.

The above oath shall also be taken by all the city and county officers before entering upon their duties, and by all other State officials not included in the above provision. I direct the vote to be taken upon each of the above-cited provisions alone, and upon the other portions of the said constitution in the following manner, viz:

Each voter favoring the ratification of the constitution (excluding the provisions above quoted), as adopted by the convention of May 15, 1868, shall express his judgment by voting for the constitution.

Each voter favoring the rejection of the constitution (excluding the provisions above quoted) shall express his judgment by voting against the constitution.

Each voter will be allowed to cast a separate ballot for or against either · or both of the provisions above quoted.

It is understood that sections 4, 5, 6, 7, 8, 9, 10, 11, 12, 13, 14, and 15 of Article XIII, under the head of "Ordinance," are considered as forming no part of the said constitution.

In testimony whereof I have hereunto set my hand and caused the seal of the United States to be affixed.

[SEAL.]   Done at the city of Washington, this 13th day of July, A. D. 1869, and of the Independence of the United States of America the ninety-fourth.

U. S. GRANT.

By the President:

HAMILTON FISH, *Secretary of State.*

BY THE PRESIDENT OF THE UNITED STATES OF AMERICA.

A PROCLAMATION.

In pursuance of the provisions of the act of Congress approved April 10, 1869, I hereby designate Tuesday, the 30th day of November, 1869, as the time for submitting the constitution adopted by the convention which met in Austin, Tex., on the 15th day of June, 1868, to the voters of said State registered at the date of such submission, viz:

I direct the vote to be taken upon the said constitution in the following manner, viz:

Each voter favoring the ratification of the constitution as adopted by the convention of the 15th of June, 1868, shall express his judgment by voting for the constitution.

Each voter favoring the rejection of the constitution shall express his judgment by voting against the constitution.

In testimony whereof I have hereunto set my hand and caused the seal of the United States to be affixed.

[SEAL.]   Done at the city of Washington, this 15th day of July, A. D. 1869, and of the Independence of the United States of America the ninety-fourth.

U. S. GRANT.

By the President:

HAMILTON FISH, *Secretary of State.*

BY THE PRESIDENT OF THE UNITED STATES OF AMERICA.

A PROCLAMATION.

The year which is drawing to a close has been free from pestilence; health has prevailed throughout the land; abundant crops reward the labors of the husbandman; commerce and manufactures have successfully prosecuted their peaceful paths; the mines and forests have yielded liberally; the nation has increased in wealth and in strength; peace has prevailed, and its blessings have advanced every interest of the people in every part of the Union; harmony and fraternal intercourse restored are obliterating the marks of past conflict and estrangement; burdens have been lightened; means have been increased; civil and religious liberty are secured to every inhabitant of the land, whose soil is trod by none but freemen.

It becomes a people thus favored to make acknowledgment to the Supreme Author from whom such blessings flow of their gratitude and their dependence, to render praise and thanksgiving for the same, and devoutly to implore a continuance of God's mercies.

Therefore I, Ulysses S. Grant, President of the United States, do recommend that Thursday, the 18th day of November next, be observed as a day of thanksgiving and of praise and of prayer to Almighty God, the creator and the ruler of the universe; and I do further recommend to all the people of the United States to assemble on that day in their accustomed places of public worship and to unite in the homage and praise due to the bountiful Father of All Mercies and in fervent prayer for the continuance of the manifold blessings he has vouchsafed to us as a people.

In testimony whereof I have hereunto set my hand and caused the seal of the United States to be affixed, this 5th day of October, A. D. 1869, and of the Independence of the United States of America the ninety-fourth.

[SEAL.]

U. S. GRANT.

By the President:

HAMILTON FISH, *Secretary of State.*

By the President of the United States of America.

A PROCLAMATION.

Whereas by the proclamation of the President of the United States of the 12th day of June last the levying of discriminating duties on merchandise imported into the United States in French vessels from the countries of its origin was discontinued; and

Whereas satisfactory information has since been received by me that the levying of such duties on all merchandise imported into France in vessels of the United States, whether from the countries of its origin or from other countries, has been discontinued:

Now, therefore, I, U. S. Grant, President of the United States of America, by virtue of the authority vested in me by an act of Congress of the 7th day of January, 1824, and by an act in addition thereto of the 24th day of May, 1828, do hereby declare and proclaim that on and after this date, so long as merchandise imported into France in vessels of the United States, whether from the countries of its origin or from other countries, shall be admitted into the ports of France on the terms aforesaid, the discriminating duties heretofore levied upon merchandise imported into the United States in French vessels, either from the countries of its origin or from any other country, shall be, and are, discontinued and abolished.

In testimony whereof I have hereunto set my hand and caused the seal of the United States to be affixed.

[SEAL.]   Done at the city of Washington, this 20th day of November, A. D. 1869, and of the Independence of the United States of America the ninety-fourth.

U. S. GRANT.

By the President:

HAMILTON FISH,
Secretary of State.

EXECUTIVE ORDERS.

GENERAL ORDERS, NO. 10.

HEADQUARTERS OF THE ARMY,
ADJUTANT-GENERAL'S OFFICE,
Washington, March 5, 1869.

The President of the United States directs that the following orders be carried into execution as soon as practicable:

1. The Department of the South will be commanded by Brigadier and Brevet Major General A. H. Terry.

2. Major-General G. G. Meade is assigned to command the Military Division of the Atlantic, and will transfer his headquarters to Philadelphia, Pa. He will turn over his present command temporarily to Brevet Major-General T. H. Ruger, colonel Thirty-third Infantry, who is assigned to duty according to his brevet of major-general while in the exercise of this command.

3. Major-General P. H. Sheridan is assigned to command the Department of Louisiana, and will turn over the command of the Department of the Missouri temporarily to the next senior officer.

4. Major-General W. S. Hancock is assigned to command the Department of Dakota.

5. Brigadier and Brevet Major General E. R. S. Canby is assigned to command the First Military District, and will proceed to his post as soon as relieved by Brevet Major-General Reynolds.

6. Brevet Major-General A. C. Gillem, colonel Twenty-fourth Infantry, will turn over the command of the Fourth Military District to the next senior officer and join his regiment.

7. Brevet Major-General J. J. Reynolds, colonel Twenty-sixth Infantry, is assigned to command the Fifth Military District, according to his brevet of major-general.

8. Brevet Major-General W. H. Emory, colonel Fifth Cavalry, is assigned to command the Department of Washington, according to his brevet of major-general.

By command of the General of the Army:

E. D. TOWNSEND,
Assistant Adjutant-General.

GENERAL ORDERS, No. 11.

HEADQUARTERS OF THE ARMY,
ADJUTANT-GENERAL'S OFFICE,
Washington, March 8, 1869.

The following orders of the President of the United States are published for the information and government of all concerned:

WAR DEPARTMENT,
Washington City, March 5, 1869.

By direction of the President, General William T. Sherman will assume command of the Army of the United States.

The chiefs of staff corps, departments, and bureaus will report to and act under the immediate orders of the General Commanding the Army.

All official business which by law or regulations requires the action of the President or Secretary of War will be submitted by the General of the Army to the Secretary of War, and in general all orders from the

President or Secretary of War to any portion of the Army, line or staff, will be transmitted through the General of the Army.

J. M. SCHOFIELD, *Secretary of War.*

By command of the General of the Army:

E. D. TOWNSEND,
Assistant Adjutant-General.

SPECIAL ORDERS, NO. 55.

HEADQUARTERS OF THE ARMY,
ADJUTANT-GENERAL'S OFFICE,
Washington, March 9, 1869.

*   *   *   *   *   *   *

6. By direction of the President, Brevet Major-General Adelbert Ames, lieutenant-colonel Twenty-fourth United States Infantry, is hereby assigned to command the Fourth Military District, according to his brevet rank.

*   *   *   *   *   *   *

By command of General Sherman:

E. D. TOWNSEND,
Assistant Adjutant-General.

GENERAL ORDERS, NO. 18.

HEADQUARTERS OF THE ARMY,
ADJUTANT-GENERAL'S OFFICE,
Washington, March 16, 1869.

By direction of the President of the United States, the following changes are made in military divisions and department commands:

I. Lieutenant-General P. H. Sheridan is assigned to command the Military Division of the Missouri.

II. Major-General H. W. Halleck is assigned to the command of the Military Division of the South, to be composed of the Departments of the South and Louisiana, of the Fourth Military District, and of the States composing the present Department of the Cumberland; headquarters, Louisville, Ky. Major-General Halleck will proceed to his new command as soon as relieved by Major-General Thomas.

III. Major-General G. H. Thomas is assigned to command the Military Division of the Pacific.

IV. Major-General J. M. Schofield is assigned to command the Department of the Missouri. The State of Illinois and post of Fort Smith, Ark., are transferred to this department.

V. Brigadier and Brevet Major General O. O. Howard is assigned to command the Department of Louisiana. Until his arrival the senior officer, Brevet Major-General J. A. Mower, will command, according to his brevet of major-general.

VI. The Department of Washington will be discontinued and merged in the Department of the East. The records will be sent to the Adjutant-General of the Army.

VII. The First Military District will be added to the Military Division of the Atlantic.

VIII. As soon as Major-General Thomas is ready to relinquish command of the Department of the Cumberland, the department will be discontinued, and the States composing it will be added to other departments, to be hereafter designated. The records will be forwarded to the Adjutant-General of the Army.

By command of General Sherman :

E. D. TOWNSEND,
Assistant Adjutant-General.

WAR DEPARTMENT,
Washington City, March 26, 1869.

By direction of the President, the order of the Secretary of War dated War Department, March 5, 1869, and published in General Orders, No. 11, Headquarters of the Army, Adjutant-General's Office, dated March 8, 1869, except so much as directs General W. T. Sherman to "assume command of the Army of the United States," is hereby rescinded.

All official business which by law or regulations requires the action of the President or Secretary of War will be submitted by the chiefs of staff corps, departments, and bureaus to the Secretary of War.

All orders and instructions relating to military operations issued by the President or Secretary of War will be issued through the General of the Army.

JNO. A. RAWLINS,
Secretary of War.

SPECIAL ORDERS, No. 75.

HEADQUARTERS OF THE ARMY,
ADJUTANT-GENERAL'S OFFICE,
Washington, March 31, 1869.

*   *   *   *   *   *   *

16. By direction of the President of the United States, Brevet Major-General A. S. Webb, United States Army, is assigned to command the First Military District, according to his brevet of major-general, until the arrival of Brevet Major-General Canby to relieve him. He will accordingly repair to Richmond, Va., without delay.

17. By direction of the President, Brevet Major-General George Stoneman, colonel Twenty-first United States Infantry, is hereby relieved from

the temporary command of the First Military District, and will accompany his regiment to the Military Division of the Pacific.

* * * * * * *

By command of General Sherman:

E. D. TOWNSEND,
Assistant Adjutant-General.

EXECUTIVE MANSION,
Washington, D. C., June 3, 1869.

A commission of citizens having been appointed under the authority of law to cooperate with the administrative departments in the management of Indian affairs, consisting of William Welsh, of Philadelphia; John V. Farwell, of Chicago; George H. Stuart, of Philadelphia; Robert Campbell, St. Louis; W. E. Dodge, New York; E. S. Tobey, Boston; Felix R. Brunot, Pittsburg; Nathan Bishop, New York, and Henry S. Lane, of Indiana, the following regulations will till further directions control the action of said commission and of the Bureau of Indian Affairs in matters coming under their joint supervision:

1. The commission will make its own organization and employ its own clerical assistants, keeping its "necessary expenses of transportation, subsistence, and clerk hire when actually engaged in said service" within the amount appropriated therefor by Congress.

2. The commission shall be furnished with full opportunity to inspect the records of the Indian Office and to obtain full information as to the conduct of all parts of the affairs thereof.

3. They shall have full power to inspect, in person or by subcommittee, the various Indian superintendencies and agencies in the Indian country, to be present at payment of annuities, at consultations or councils with the Indians, and when on the ground to advise superintendents and agents in the performance of their duties.

4. They are authorized to be present, in person or by subcommittee, at purchases of goods for Indian purposes, and inspect said purchases, advising the Commissioner of Indian Affairs in regard thereto.

5. Whenever they shall deem it necessary or advisable that instructions of superintendents or agents be changed or modified, they will communicate such advice through the office of Commissioner of Indian Affairs to the Secretary of the Interior, and in like manner their advice as to changes in modes of purchasing goods or conducting the affairs of the Indian Bureau proper. Complaints against superintendents or agents or other officers will in the same manner be forwarded to the Indian Bureau or Department of the Interior for action.

6. The commission will at their board meetings determine upon the recommendations to be made as to the plans of civilizing or dealing with the Indians, and submit the same for action in the manner above indicated, and all plans involving the expenditure of public money will

be acted upon by the Executive or the Secretary of the Interior before expenditure is made under the same.

7. The usual modes of accounting with the Treasury can not be changed, and all expenditures, therefore, must be subject to the approvals now required by law and the regulations of the Treasury Department, and all vouchers must conform to the same laws and requirements and pass through the ordinary channels.

8. All the officers of the Government connected with the Indian service are enjoined to afford every facility and opportunity to said commission and their subcommittees in the performance of their duties, and to give the most respectful heed to their advice within the limits of such officers' positive instructions from their superiors; to allow such commissioners full access to their records and accounts, and to cooperate with them in the most earnest manner to the extent of their proper powers in the general work of civilizing the Indians, protecting them in their legal rights, and stimulating them to become industrious citizens in permanent homes, instead of following a roving and savage life.

9. The commission will keep such records or minutes of their proceedings as may be necessary to afford evidence of their action, and will provide for the manner in which their communications with and advice to the Government shall be made and authenticated.

U. S. GRANT.

[From the Daily Morning Chronicle, Washington, September 8, 1869.]

DEPARTMENT OF STATE,
*Washington, September 7, 1869.**

It is my melancholy duty to inform you that the Hon. John A. Rawlins, Secretary of War, departed this life at twelve minutes past 4 o'clock on yesterday afternoon. In consequence of this afflicting event the President directs that the Executive Departments of the Government will be careful to manifest every observance of honor which custom has established as appropriate to the memory of one so eminent as a public functionary and so distinguished as a citizen.

I am, sir, very respectfully, your obedient servant,

HAMILTON FISH.

[From the Daily Morning Chronicle, Washington, September 8, 1869.]

DEPARTMENT OF STATE,
Washington, September 7, 1869.

SIR:* I have the honor to inform you that the President directs me to communicate to you his order that in honor of the memory of the Hon. John A. Rawlins, late Secretary of War, who died yesterday at twelve minutes past 4 o'clock p. m., the Executive Departments shall be draped

*Addressed to the heads of the Executive Departments.

in mourning for a period of thirty days, and that they be closed from the morning of the 8th instant until after the obsequies of the deceased shall have been solemnized.

I have the honor to be, your obedient servant,

HAMILTON FISH.

DEPARTMENT OF STATE, *Washington, September 7, 1869.*

The remains of the Hon. John A. Rawlins, late Secretary of War, will be interred with military honors, under the direction of the General of the Army, on Thursday, the 9th instant, at 10 o'clock a. m. The following persons will officiate as pallbearers on the occasion:

Brevet Major-General Edward D. Townsend, Adjutant-General; Brevet Major-General Randolph B. Marcy, Inspector-General; Brevet Major-General Joseph Holt, Judge-Advocate-General; Brevet Major-General Montgomery C. Meigs, Quartermaster-General; Brevet Major-General Amos B. Eaton, Commissary-General; Brevet Major-General Joseph K. Barnes, Surgeon-General; Brevet Major-General B. W. Brice, Paymaster-General; Brevet Major-General A. A. Humphreys, Chief of Engineers; Brevet Major-General Alexander B. Dyer, Chief of Ordnance; Brevet Brigadier-General Albert J. Myer, Chief Signal Officer; Brevet Major-General O. O. Howard; Brevet Major-General John E. Smith; Commodore Melancton Smith, Chief Bureau Equipment; Brigadier-General Jacob Zeilin, Marine Corps; Brigadier-General Giles A. Smith, Second Assistant Postmaster-General; Hon. Sayles J. Bowen, mayor of Washington.

On the day of the funeral the customary number of guns will be fired from all arsenals, forts, and navy-yards in the United States and from the Military and Naval Academies. Flags will be kept at half-mast, custom-houses closed, and all public work suspended during the day.

The General of the Army and heads of the several Executive Departments will issue the orders necessary for carrying these directions into effect.

By order of the President:

HAMILTON FISH, *Secretary of State.*

GENERAL ORDERS, No. 69.

HEADQUARTERS OF THE ARMY,
ADJUTANT-GENERAL'S OFFICE,
Washington, October 9, 1869.

I. The following order of the President has been received from the War Department:

EXECUTIVE MANSION, *Washington, October 8, 1869.*

The painful duty devolves upon the President of announcing to the people of the United States the death of one of his honored predecessors, Franklin Pierce, which occurred at Concord early this morning.

Eminent in the public councils and universally beloved in private life, his death will be mourned with a sorrow befitting the loss which his country sustains in his decease.

As a mark of respect to his memory, it is ordered that the Executive Mansion and the several Departments at Washington be draped in mourning, and all business suspended on the day of the funeral.

It is further ordered that the War and Navy Departments cause suitable military and naval honors to be paid on the occasion to the memory of this illustrious citizen who has passed from us.

U. S. GRANT.

II. In compliance with the instructions of the President and of the Secretary of War, on the day after the receipt of this order at each military post the troops will be paraded at 10 o'clock a. m. and the order read to them, after which all labors for the day will cease.

The national flag will be displayed at half-staff.

At dawn of day thirteen guns will be fired, and afterwards at intervals of thirty minutes between the rising and setting sun a single gun, and at the close of the day a national salute of thirty-seven guns.

The officers of the Army will wear crape on the left arm and on their swords and the colors of the several regiments will be put in mourning for the period of thirty days.

By command of General Sherman:

J. C. KELTON,
Assistant Adjutant-General.

GENERAL ORDER.

NAVY DEPARTMENT,
Washington, October 9, 1869.

The death of ex-President Franklin Pierce is announced in the following order of the President of the United States:

[For order see preceding page.]

In pursuance of the foregoing order, it is hereby directed that twenty-one guns be fired, at intervals of one minute each, at the several navy-yards and stations, on the day of the funeral where this order may be received in time, otherwise on the day after its receipt, commencing at noon, and also on board the flagships in each fleet. The flags at the several navy-yards, naval stations, marine barracks, and vessels in commission will be placed at half-mast from sunrise to sunset on the day when the minute guns are fired.

All officers of the Navy and Marine Corps will wear the usual badge of mourning attached to the sword hilt and on the left arm for thirty days.

GEO. M. ROBESON,
Secretary of the Navy.

BY THE PRESIDENT OF THE UNITED STATES.

EXECUTIVE ORDER.

WASHINGTON, *October 19, 1869.*

All communications in writing intended for the executive department of this Government and relating to public business of whatever kind, including suggestions for legislation, claims, contracts, employment, appointments, and removals from office, and pardons, must be transmitted through the Department to which the care of the subject-matter of the communication properly belongs. Communications otherwise transmitted will not receive attention.

By order of the President:

HAMILTON FISH,
Secretary of State.

FIRST ANNUAL MESSAGE.

EXECUTIVE MANSION,
Washington, D. C., December 6, 1869.

To the Senate and House of Representatives:

In coming before you for the first time as Chief Magistrate of this great nation, it is with gratitude to the Giver of All Good for the many benefits we enjoy. We are blessed with peace at home, and are without entangling alliances abroad to forebode trouble; with a territory unsurpassed in fertility, of an area equal to the abundant support of 500,000,000 people, and abounding in every variety of useful mineral in quantity sufficient to supply the world for generations; with exuberant crops; with a variety of climate adapted to the production of every species of earth's riches and suited to the habits, tastes, and requirements of every living thing; with a population of 40,000,000 free people, all speaking one language; with facilities for every mortal to acquire an education; with institutions closing to none the avenues to fame or any blessing of fortune that may be coveted; with freedom of the pulpit, the press, and the school; with a revenue flowing into the National Treasury beyond the requirements of the Government. Happily, harmony is being rapidly restored within our own borders. Manufactures hitherto unknown in our country are springing up in all sections, producing a degree of national independence unequaled by that of any other power.

These blessings and countless others are intrusted to your care and mine for safe-keeping for the brief period of our tenure of office. In a short time we must, each of us, return to the ranks of the people, who have conferred upon us our honors, and account to them for our stewardship. I earnestly desire that neither you nor I may be condemned by a free and enlightened constituency nor by our own consciences.

Emerging from a rebellion of gigantic magnitude, aided, as it was, by the sympathies and assistance of nations with which we were at peace, eleven States of the Union were, four years ago, left without legal State governments. A national debt had been contracted; American commerce was almost driven from the seas; the industry of one-half of the country had been taken from the control of the capitalist and placed where all labor rightfully belongs—in the keeping of the laborer. The work of restoring State governments loyal to the Union, of protecting and fostering free labor, and providing means for paying the interest on the public debt has received ample attention from Congress. Although your efforts have not met with the success in all particulars that might have been desired, yet on the whole they have been more successful than could have been reasonably anticipated.

Seven States which passed ordinances of secession have been fully restored to their places in the Union. The eighth (Georgia) held an election at which she ratified her constitution, republican in form, elected a governor, Members of Congress, a State legislature, and all other officers required. The governor was duly installed, and the legislature met and performed all the acts then required of them by the reconstruction acts of Congress. Subsequently, however, in violation of the constitution which they had just ratified (as since decided by the supreme court of the State), they unseated the colored members of the legislature and admitted to seats some members who are disqualified by the third clause of the fourteenth amendment to the Constitution—an article which they themselves had contributed to ratify. Under these circumstances I would submit to you whether it would not be wise, without delay, to enact a law authorizing the governor of Georgia to convene the members originally elected to the legislature, requiring each member to take the oath prescribed by the reconstruction acts, and none to be admitted who are ineligible under the third clause of the fourteenth amendment.

The freedmen, under the protection which they have received, are making rapid progress in learning, and no complaints are heard of lack of industry on their part where they receive fair remuneration for their labor. The means provided for paying the interest on the public debt, with all other expenses of Government, are more than ample. The loss of our commerce is the only result of the late rebellion which has not received sufficient attention from you. To this subject I call your earnest

By the President of the United States of America,

A Proclamation

Whereas objects of interest to the United States require that the Senate should be convened at twelve o'clock on the Twelfth day of April 1869 to receive and act upon such communications as may be made to it on the part of the Executive:

Now therefore, I, U. S. Grant, President of the United States, have considered it to be my duty to issue this, my Proclamation, declaring that an extraordinary occasion requires the Senate of the United States to convene for the transaction of business at the Capitol in the City of Washington on the Twelfth day of April 1869, at twelve o'clock noon on that day, of which all who shall at that time be entitled to act as members of that body are hereby required to take notice.

Given under my hand and the Seal of the United States at Washington the eighth day of April in the year of our Lord one thousand Eight hundred and sixty nine, and of the Independence of the United States of America the ninety third.

U. S. Grant

By the President
Hamilton Fish
Secretary of State.

PRESIDENT GRANT'S PROCLAMATION CALLING FOR AN
EXTRA SESSION OF THE SENATE.

attention. I will not now suggest plans by which this object may be effected, but will, if necessary, make it the subject of a special message during the session of Congress.

At the March term Congress by joint resolution authorized the Executive to order elections in the States of Virginia, Mississippi, and Texas, to submit to them the constitutions which each had previously, in convention, framed, and submit the constitutions, either entire or in separate parts, to be voted upon, at the discretion of the Executive. Under this authority elections were called. In Virginia the election took place on the 6th of July, 1869. The governor and lieutenant-governor elected have been installed. The legislature met and did all required by this resolution and by all the reconstruction acts of Congress, and abstained from all doubtful authority. I recommend that her Senators and Representatives be promptly admitted to their seats, and that the State be fully restored to its place in the family of States. Elections were called in Mississippi and Texas, to commence on the 30th of November, 1869, and to last two days in Mississippi and four days in Texas. The elections have taken place, but the result is not known. It is to be hoped that the acts of the legislatures of these States, when they meet, will be such as to receive your approval, and thus close the work of reconstruction.

Among the evils growing out of the rebellion, and not yet referred to, is that of an irredeemable currency. It is an evil which I hope will receive your most earnest attention. It is a duty, and one of the highest duties, of Government to secure to the citizen a medium of exchange of fixed, unvarying value. This implies a return to a specie basis, and no substitute for it can be devised. It should be commenced now and reached at the earliest practicable moment consistent with a fair regard to the interests of the debtor class. Immediate resumption, if practicable, would not be desirable. It would compel the debtor class to pay, beyond their contracts, the premium on gold at the date of their purchase, and would bring bankruptcy and ruin to thousands. Fluctuation, however, in the paper value of the measure of all values (gold) is detrimental to the interests of trade. It makes the man of business an involuntary gambler, for in all sales where future payment is to be made both parties speculate as to what will be the value of the currency to be paid and received. I earnestly recommend to you, then, such legislation as will insure a gradual return to specie payments and put an immediate stop to fluctuations in the value of currency.

The methods to secure the former of these results are as numerous as are the speculators on political economy. To secure the latter I see but one way, and that is to authorize the Treasury to redeem its own paper, at a fixed price, whenever presented, and to withhold from circulation all currency so redeemed until sold again for gold.

The vast resources of the nation, both developed and undeveloped, ought to make our credit the best on earth. With a less burden of taxation than the citizen has endured for six years past, the entire public debt could be paid in ten years. But it is not desirable that the people should be taxed to pay it in that time. Year by year the ability to pay increases in a rapid ratio. But the burden of interest ought to be reduced as rapidly as can be done without the violation of contract. The public debt is represented in great part by bonds having from five to twenty and from ten to forty years to run, bearing interest at the rate of 6 per cent and 5 per cent, respectively. It is optional with the Government to pay these bonds at any period after the expiration of the least time mentioned upon their face. The time has already expired when a great part of them may be taken up, and is rapidly approaching when all may be. It is believed that all which are now due may be replaced by bonds bearing a rate of interest not exceeding 4½ per cent, and as rapidly as the remainder become due that they may be replaced in the same way. To accomplish this it may be necessary to authorize the interest to be paid at either of three or four of the money centers of Europe, or by any assistant treasurer of the United States, at the option of the holder of the bond. I suggest this subject for the consideration of Congress, and also, simultaneously with this, the propriety of redeeming our currency, as before suggested, at its market value at the time the law goes into effect, increasing the rate at which currency shall be bought and sold from day to day or week to week, at the same rate of interest as Government pays upon its bonds.

The subjects of tariff and internal taxation will necessarily receive your attention. The revenues of the country are greater than the requirements, and may with safety be reduced. But as the funding of the debt in a 4 or a 4½ per cent loan would reduce annual current expenses largely, thus, after funding, justifying a greater reduction of taxation than would be now expedient, I suggest postponement of this question until the next meeting of Congress.

It may be advisable to modify taxation and tariff in instances where unjust or burdensome discriminations are made by the present laws, but a general revision of the laws regulating this subject I recommend the postponement of for the present. I also suggest the renewal of the tax on incomes, but at a reduced rate, say of 3 per cent, and this tax to expire in three years.

With the funding of the national debt, as here suggested, I feel safe in saying that taxes and the revenue from imports may be reduced safely from sixty to eighty millions per annum at once, and may be still further reduced from year to year, as the resources of the country are developed.

The report of the Secretary of the Treasury shows the receipts of the Government for the fiscal year ending June 30, 1869, to be $370,943,747, and the expenditures, including interest, bounties, etc., to be $321,490,597. The estimates for the ensuing year are more favorable to the Government, and will no doubt show a much larger decrease of the public debt.

The receipts in the Treasury beyond expenditures have exceeded the amount necessary to place to the credit of the sinking fund, as provided by law. To lock up the surplus in the Treasury and withhold it from circulation would lead to such a contraction of the currency as to cripple trade and seriously affect the prosperity of the country. Under these circumstances the Secretary of the Treasury and myself heartily concurred in the propriety of using all the surplus currency in the Treasury in the purchase of Government bonds, thus reducing the interest-bearing indebtedness of the country, and of submitting to Congress the question of the disposition to be made of the bonds so purchased. The bonds now held by the Treasury amount to about seventy-five millions, including those belonging to the sinking fund. I recommend that the whole be placed to the credit of the sinking fund.

Your attention is respectfully invited to the recommendations of the Secretary of the Treasury for the creation of the office of commissioner of customs revenue; for the increase of salaries to certain classes of officials; the substitution of increased national-bank circulation to replace the outstanding 3 per cent certificates; and most especially to his recommendation for the repeal of laws allowing shares of fines, penalties, forfeitures, etc., to officers of the Government or to informers.

The office of Commissioner of Internal Revenue is one of the most arduous and responsible under the Government. It falls but little, if any, short of a Cabinet position in its importance and responsibilities. I would ask for it, therefore, such legislation as in your judgment will place the office upon a footing of dignity commensurate with its importance and with the character and qualifications of the class of men required to fill it properly.

As the United States is the freest of all nations, so, too, its people sympathize with all people struggling for liberty and self-government; but while so sympathizing it is due to our honor that we should abstain from enforcing our views upon unwilling nations and from taking an interested part, *without invitation*, in the quarrels between different nations or between governments and their subjects. Our course should always be in conformity with strict justice and law, international and local. Such has been the policy of the Administration in dealing with these questions. For more than a year a valuable province of Spain, and a near neighbor of ours, in whom all our people can not but feel a deep interest, has been struggling for independence and freedom. The people and Government of the United States entertain the same warm feelings and sympathies for the people of Cuba in their pending struggle that they manifested throughout the previous struggles between Spain and her former colonies in behalf of the latter. But the contest has at no time assumed the conditions which amount to a war in the sense of international law, or which would show the existence of a *de facto* political organization of the insurgents sufficient to justify a recognition of belligerency.

The principle is maintained, however, that this nation is its own judge when to accord the rights of belligerency, either to a people struggling to free themselves from a government they believe to be oppressive or to independent nations at war with each other.

The United States have no disposition to interfere with the existing relations of Spain to her colonial possessions on this continent. They believe that in due time Spain and other European powers will find their interest in terminating those relations and establishing their present dependencies as independent powers—members of the family of nations. These dependencies are no longer regarded as subject to transfer from one European power to another. When the present relation of colonies ceases, they are to become independent powers, exercising the right of choice and of self-control in the determination of their future condition and relations with other powers.

The United States, in order to put a stop to bloodshed in Cuba, and in the interest of a neighboring people, proposed their good offices to bring the existing contest to a termination. The offer, not being accepted by Spain on a basis which we believed could be received by Cuba, was withdrawn. It is hoped that the good offices of the United States may yet prove advantageous for the settlement of this unhappy strife. Meanwhile a number of illegal expeditions against Cuba have been broken up. It has been the endeavor of the Administration to execute the neutrality laws in good faith, no matter how unpleasant the task, made so by the sufferings we have endured from lack of like good faith toward us by other nations.

On the 26th of March last the United States schooner *Lizzie Major* was arrested on the high seas by a Spanish frigate, and two passengers taken from it and carried as prisoners to Cuba. Representations of these facts were made to the Spanish Government as soon as official information of them reached Washington. The two passengers were set at liberty, and the Spanish Government assured the United States that the captain of the frigate in making the capture had acted without law, that he had been reprimanded for the irregularity of his conduct, and that the Spanish authorities in Cuba would not sanction any act that could violate the rights or treat with disrespect the sovereignty of this nation.

The question of the seizure of the brig *Mary Lowell* at one of the Bahama Islands by Spanish authorities is now the subject of correspondence between this Government and those of Spain and Great Britain.

The Captain-General of Cuba about May last issued a proclamation authorizing search to be made of vessels on the high seas. Immediate remonstrance was made against this, whereupon the Captain-General issued a new proclamation limiting the right of search to vessels of the United States so far as authorized under the treaty of 1795. This proclamation, however, was immediately withdrawn.

I have always felt that the most intimate relations should be cultivated

EARLY ATTEMPTS AT AN ISTHMIAN CANAL

EARLY ATTEMPTS AT A PANAMA CANAL

It seems strange to credit the project of a canal across the Isthmus of Darien, connecting the Atlantic with the Pacific, to a Spaniard, but according to the account in the index (volume eleven), entitled "Panama Canal," the idea was first broached in 1527 by de la Serna, who even surveyed a route from Chagres to Panama.

The illustration shows the Selfridge expedition of 1870 making surveys.

between the Republic of the United States and all independent nations on this continent. It may be well worth considering whether new treaties between us and them may not be profitably entered into, to secure more intimate relations—friendly, commercial, and otherwise.

The subject of an interoceanic canal to connect the Atlantic and Pacific oceans through the Isthmus of Darien is one in which commerce is greatly interested. Instructions have been given to our minister to the Republic of the United States of Colombia to endeavor to obtain authority for a survey by this Government, in order to determine the practicability of such an undertaking, and a charter for the right of way to build, by private enterprise, such a work, if the survey proves it to be practicable.

In order to comply with the agreement of the United States as to a mixed commission at Lima for the adjustment of claims, it became necessary to send a commissioner and secretary to Lima in August last. No appropriation having been made by Congress for this purpose, it is now asked that one be made covering the past and future expenses of the commission.

The good offices of the United States to bring about a peace between Spain and the South American Republics with which she is at war having been accepted by Spain, Peru, and Chile, a congress has been invited to be held in Washington during the present winter.

A grant has been given to Europeans of an exclusive right of transit over the territory of Nicaragua, to which Costa Rica has given its assent, which, it is alleged, conflicts with vested rights of citizens of the United States. The Department of State has now this subject under consideration.

The minister of Peru having made representations that there was a state of war between Peru and Spain, and that Spain was constructing, in and near New York, thirty gunboats, which might be used by Spain in such a way as to relieve the naval force at Cuba, so as to operate against Peru, orders were given to prevent their departure. No further steps having been taken by the representative of the Peruvian Government to prevent the departure of these vessels, and I not feeling authorized to detain the property of a nation with which we are at peace on a mere Executive order, the matter has been referred to the courts to decide.

The conduct of the war between the allies and the Republic of Paraguay has made the intercourse with that country so difficult that it has been deemed advisable to withdraw our representative from there.

Toward the close of the last Administration a convention was signed at London for the settlement of all outstanding claims between Great Britain and the United States, which failed to receive the advice and consent of the Senate to its ratification. The time and the circumstances attending the negotiation of that treaty were unfavorable to its acceptance by the people of the United States, and its provisions were wholly inadequate for the settlement of the grave wrongs that had been sustained by this

Government, as well as by its citizens. The injuries resulting to the United States by reason of the course adopted by Great Britain during our late civil war—in the increased rates of insurance; in the diminution of exports and imports, and other obstructions to domestic industry and production; in its effect upon the foreign commerce of the country; in the decrease and transfer to Great Britain of our commercial marine; in the prolongation of the war and the increased cost (both in treasure and in lives) of its suppression—could not be adjusted and satisfied as ordinary commercial claims, which continually arise between commercial nations; and yet the convention treated them simply as such ordinary claims, from which they differ more widely in the gravity of their character than in the magnitude of their amount, great even as is that difference. Not a word was found in the treaty, and not an inference could be drawn from it, to remove the sense of the unfriendliness of the course of Great Britain in our struggle for existence, which had so deeply and universally impressed itself upon the people of this country.

Believing that a convention thus misconceived in its scope and inadequate in its provisions would not have produced the hearty, cordial settlement of pending questions, which alone is consistent with the relations which I desire to have firmly established between the United States and Great Britain, I regarded the action of the Senate in rejecting the treaty to have been wisely taken in the interest of peace and as a necessary step in the direction of a perfect and cordial friendship between the two countries. A sensitive people, conscious of their power, are more at ease under a great wrong wholly unatoned than under the restraint of a settlement which satisfies neither their ideas of justice nor their grave sense of the grievance they have sustained. The rejection of the treaty was followed by a state of public feeling on both sides which I thought not favorable to an immediate attempt at renewed negotiations. I accordingly so instructed the minister of the United States to Great Britain, and found that my views in this regard were shared by Her Majesty's ministers. I hope that the time may soon arrive when the two Governments can approach the solution of this momentous question with an appreciation of what is due to the rights, dignity, and honor of each, and with the determination not only to remove the causes of complaint in the past, but to lay the foundation of a broad principle of public law which will prevent future differences and tend to firm and continued peace and friendship.

This is now the only grave question which the United States has with any foreign nation.

The question of renewing a treaty for reciprocal trade between the United States and the British Provinces on this continent has not been favorably considered by the Administration. The advantages of such a treaty would be wholly in favor of the British producer. Except, possibly, a few engaged in the trade between the two sections, no citizen of

the United States would be benefited by reciprocity. Our internal taxation would prove a protection to the British producer almost equal to
the protection which our manufacturers now receive from the tariff.
Some arrangement, however, for the regulation of commercial intercourse between the United States and the Dominion of Canada may be
desirable.

The commission for adjusting the claims of the "Hudsons Bay and
Puget Sound Agricultural Company" upon the United States has terminated its labors. The award of $650,000 has been made and all rights
and titles of the company on the territory of the United States have been
extinguished. Deeds for the property of the company have been delivered. An appropriation by Congress to meet this sum is asked.

The commissioners for determining the northwestern land boundary
between the United States and the British possessions under the treaty
of 1856 have completed their labors, and the commission has been dis-
solved.

In conformity with the recommendation of Congress, a proposition was
early made to the British Government to abolish the mixed courts created
under the treaty of April 7, 1862, for the suppression of the slave trade.
The subject is still under negotiation.

It having come to my knowledge that a corporate company, organized
under British laws, proposed to land upon the shores of the United States
and to operate there a submarine cable, under a concession from His
Majesty the Emperor of the French of an exclusive right for twenty
years of telegraphic communication between the shores of France and
the United States, with the very objectionable feature of subjecting all
messages conveyed thereby to the scrutiny and control of the French
Government, I caused the French and British legations at Washington
to be made acquainted with the probable policy of Congress on this subject, as foreshadowed by the bill which passed the Senate in March last.
This drew from the representatives of the company an agreement to
accept as the basis of their operations the provisions of that bill, or of
such other enactment on the subject as might be passed during the
approaching session of Congress; also, to use their influence to secure
from the French Government a modification of their concession, so as to
permit the landing upon French soil of any cable belonging to any company incorporated by the authority of the United States or of any State
in the Union, and, on their part, not to oppose the establishment of any
such cable. In consideration of this agreement I directed the withdrawal of all opposition by the United States authorities to the landing
of the cable and to the working of it until the meeting of Congress. I
regret to say that there has been no modification made in the company's
concession, nor, so far as I can learn, have they attempted to secure one.
Their concession excludes the capital and the citizens of the United
States from competition upon the shores of France. I recommend

legislation to protect the rights of citizens of the United States, as well as the dignity and sovereignty of the nation, against such an assumption. I shall also endeavor to secure, by negotiation, an abandonment of the principle of monopolies in ocean telegraphic cables. Copies of this correspondence are herewith furnished.

The unsettled political condition of other countries, less fortunate than our own, sometimes induces their citizens to come to the United States for the sole purpose of becoming naturalized. Having secured this, they return to their native country and reside there, without disclosing their change of allegiance. They accept official positions of trust or honor, which can only be held by citizens of their native land; they journey under passports describing them as such citizens; and it is only when civil discord, after perhaps years of quiet, threatens their persons or their property, or when their native state drafts them into its military service, that the fact of their change of allegiance is made known. They reside permanently away from the United States, they contribute nothing to its revenues, they avoid the duties of its citizenship, and they only make themselves known by a claim of protection. I have directed the diplomatic and consular officers of the United States to scrutinize carefully all such claims for protection. The citizen of the United States, whether native or adopted, who discharges his duty to his country, is entitled to its complete protection. While I have a voice in the direction of affairs I shall not consent to imperil this sacred right by conferring it upon fictitious or fraudulent claimants.

On the accession of the present Administration it was found that the minister for North Germany had made propositions for the negotiation of a convention for the protection of emigrant passengers, to which no response had been given. It was concluded that to be effectual all the maritime powers engaged in the trade should join in such a measure. Invitations have been extended to the cabinets of London, Paris, Florence, Berlin, Brussels, The Hague, Copenhagen, and Stockholm to empower their representatives at Washington to simultaneously enter into negotiations and to conclude with the United States conventions identical in form, making uniform regulations as to the construction of the parts of vessels to be devoted to the use of emigrant passengers, as to the quality and quantity of food, as to the medical treatment of the sick, and as to the rules to be observed during the voyage, in order to secure ventilation, to promote health, to prevent intrusion, and to protect the females; and providing for the establishment of tribunals in the several countries for enforcing such regulations by summary process.

Your attention is respectfully called to the law regulating the tariff on Russian hemp, and to the question whether to fix the charges on Russian hemp higher than they are fixed upon manila is not a violation of our treaty with Russia placing her products upon the same footing with those of the most favored nations.

Our manufactures are increasing with wonderful rapidity under the encouragement which they now receive. With the improvements in machinery already effected, and still increasing, causing machinery to take the place of skilled labor to a large extent, our imports of many articles must fall off largely within a very few years. Fortunately, too, manufactures are not confined to a few localities, as formerly, and it is to be hoped will become more and more diffused, making the interest in them equal in all sections. They give employment and support to hundreds of thousands of people at home, and retain with us the means which otherwise would be shipped abroad. The extension of railroads in Europe and the East is bringing into competition with our agricultural products like products of other countries. Self-interest, if not self-preservation, therefore dictates caution against disturbing any industrial interest of the country. It teaches us also the necessity of looking to other markets for the sale of our surplus. Our neighbors south of us, and China and Japan, should receive our special attention. It will be the endeavor of the Administration to cultivate such relations with all these nations as to entitle us to their confidence and make it their interest, as well as ours, to establish better commercial relations.

Through the agency of a more enlightened policy than that heretofore pursued toward China, largely due to the sagacity and efforts of one of our own distinguished citizens, the world is about to commence largely increased relations with that populous and hitherto exclusive nation. As the United States have been the initiators in this new policy, so they should be the most earnest in showing their good faith in making it a success. In this connection I advise such legislation as will forever preclude the enslavement of the Chinese upon our soil under the name of coolies, and also prevent American vessels from engaging in the transportation of coolies to any country tolerating the system. I also recommend that the mission to China be raised to one of the first class.

On my assuming the responsible duties of Chief Magistrate of the United States it was with the conviction that three things were essential to its peace, prosperity, and fullest development. First among these is strict integrity in fulfilling all our obligations; second, to secure protection to the person and property of the citizen of the United States in each and every portion of our common country, wherever he may choose to move, without reference to original nationality, religion, color, or politics, demanding of him only obedience to the laws and proper respect for the rights of others; third, union of all the States, with equal rights, indestructible by any constitutional means.

To secure the first of these, Congress has taken two essential steps: First, in declaring by joint resolution that the public debt shall be paid, principal and interest, in coin; and, second, by providing the means for paying. Providing the means, however, could not secure the object desired without a proper administration of the laws for the collection of the revenues and an economical disbursement of them. To this, subject the Administration has most earnestly addressed itself, with results, I hope, satisfactory to the country. There has been no hesitation in changing officials in order to secure an efficient execution of the laws, sometimes, too, when, in a mere party view, undesirable political results were likely to follow; nor any hesitation in sustaining efficient officials against remonstrances wholly political.

It may be well to mention here the embarrassment possible to arise from leaving on the statute books the so-called "tenure-of-office acts," and to earnestly recommend their total repeal. It could not have been the intention of the framers of the Constitution, when providing that appointments made by the President should receive the consent of the Senate, that the latter should have the power to retain in office persons placed there by Federal appointment against the will of the President. The law is inconsistent with a faithful and efficient administration of the Government. What faith can an Executive put in officials forced upon him, and those, too, whom he has suspended for reason? How will such officials be likely to serve an Administration which they know does not trust them?

For the second requisite to our growth and prosperity time and a firm but humane administration of existing laws (amended from time to time as they may prove ineffective or prove harsh and unnecessary) are probably all that are required.

The third can not be attained by special legislation, but must be regarded as fixed by the Constitution itself and gradually acquiesced in by force of public opinion.

From the foundation of the Government to the present the management of the original inhabitants of this continent—the Indians—has been a subject of embarrassment and expense, and has been attended with continuous robberies, murders, and wars. From my own experience upon the frontiers and in Indian countries, I do not hold either legislation or the conduct of the whites who come most in contact with the Indian blameless for these hostilities. The past, however, can not be undone, and the question must be met as we now find it. I have attempted a new policy toward these wards of the nation (they can not be regarded in any other light than as wards), with fair results so far as tried, and which I hope will be attended ultimately with great success. The Society of Friends is well known as having succeeded in living in peace with the Indians in the early settlement of Pennsylvania, while their white neighbors of other sects in other sections were constantly embroiled. They are also known for their opposition to all strife, violence, and war, and are generally noted for their strict integrity and fair dealings. These considerations induced me to give the management of a few reservations of Indians to them and to throw the burden of the selection of agents upon the society itself. The result has proven most satisfactory. It will be found more fully set forth in the report of the Commissioner of Indian Affairs. For superintendents and Indian agents not on the reservations, officers of the Army were selected. The reasons for this are numerous. Where Indian agents are sent, there, or near there, troops must be sent also. The agent and the commander of troops are independent of each other, and are subject to orders from different Departments of the Government. The army officer holds a position for life; the agent, one at the will of the President. The former is personally interested in living in harmony with the Indian and in establishing a permanent peace, to the end that some portion of his life may be spent within the limits of civilized society; the latter has no such personal interest. Another reason is an economic one; and still another, the hold which the Government has upon a life officer to secure a faithful discharge of duties in carrying out a given policy.

The building of railroads, and the access thereby given to all the agricultural and mineral regions of the country, is rapidly bringing civilized settlements into contact with all the tribes of Indians. No matter what ought to be the relations between such settlements and the aborigines, the fact is they do not harmonize well, and one or the other has to give way in the end. A system which looks to the extinction of a race is too horrible for a nation to adopt without entailing upon itself the wrath of all Christendom and engendering in the citizen a disregard for human life and the rights of others, dangerous to society. I see no substitute for such a system, except in placing all the Indians on large reservations, as rapidly as it can be done, and giving them absolute protection there. As soon as they are fitted for it they should be induced to take their lands in severalty and to set up Territorial governments for their own protection. For full details on this subject I call your special attention to the reports of the Secretary of the Interior and the Commissioner of Indian Affairs.

The report of the Secretary of War shows the expenditures of the War Department for the year ending June 30, 1869, to be $80,644,042, of which $23,882,310 was disbursed in the payment of debts contracted during the war, and is not chargeable to current army expenses. His estimate of $34,531,031 for the expenses of the Army for the next fiscal year is as low as it is believed can be relied on. The estimates of bureau officers have been carefully scrutinized, and reduced wherever it has been deemed practicable. If, however, the condition of the country should be such by the beginning of the next fiscal year as to admit of a greater concentration of troops, the appropriation asked for will not be expended.

The appropriations estimated for river and harbor improvements and for fortifications are submitted separately. Whatever amount Congress may deem proper to appropriate for these purposes will be expended.

The recommendation of the General of the Army that appropriations be made for the forts at Boston. Portland, New York, Philadelphia, New

Orleans, and San Francisco, if for no other, is concurred in. I also ask your special attention to the recommendation of the general commanding the Military Division of the Pacific for the sale of the seal islands of St. Paul and St. George, Alaska Territory, and suggest that it either be complied with or that legislation be had for the protection of the seal fisheries from which a revenue should be derived.

The report of the Secretary of War contains a synopsis of the reports of the heads of bureaus, of the commanders of military divisions, and of the districts of Virginia, Mississippi, and Texas, and the report of the General of the Army in full. The recommendations therein contained have been well considered, and are submitted for your action. I, however, call special attention to the recommendation of the Chief of Ordnance for the sale of arsenals and lands no longer of use to the Government; also, to the recommendation of the Secretary of War that the act of 3d March, 1869, prohibiting promotions and appointments in the staff corps of the Army, be repealed. The extent of country to be garrisoned and the number of military posts to be occupied is the same with a reduced Army as with a large one. The number of staff officers required is more dependent upon the latter than the former condition.

The report of the Secretary of the Navy accompanying this shows the condition of the Navy when this Administration came into office and the changes made since. Strenuous efforts have been made to place as many vessels "in commission," or render them fit for service if required, as possible, and to substitute the sail for steam while cruising, thus materially reducing the expenses of the Navy and adding greatly to its efficiency. Looking to our future, I recommend a liberal, though not extravagant, policy toward this branch of the public service.

The report of the Postmaster-General furnishes a clear and comprehensive exhibit of the operations of the postal service and of the financial condition of the Post-Office Department. The ordinary postal revenues for the year ending the 30th of June, 1869, amounted to $18,344,510, and the expenditures to $23,698,131, showing an excess of expenditures over receipts of $5,353,620. The excess of expenditures over receipts for the previous year amounted to $6,437,992. The increase of revenues for 1869 over those of 1868 was $2,051,909, and the increase of expenditures was $967,538. The increased revenue in 1869 exceeded the increased revenue in 1868 by $996,336, and the increased expenditure in 1869 was $2,527,570 less than the increased expenditure in 1868, showing by comparison this gratifying feature of improvement, that while the increase of expenditures over the increase of receipts in 1868 was $2,439,535, the increase of receipts over the increase of expenditures in 1869 was $1,084,371.

Your attention is respectfully called to the recommendations made by the Postmaster-General for authority to change the rate of compensation to the main trunk railroad lines for their services in carrying the mails;

for having post-route maps executed; for reorganizing and increasing the efficiency of the special-agency service; for increase of the mail service on the Pacific, and for establishing mail service, under the flag of the Union, on the Atlantic; and most especially do I call your attention to his recommendation for the total abolition of the franking privilege. This is an abuse from which no one receives a commensurate advantage; it reduces the receipts for postal service from 25 to 30 per cent and largely increases the service to be performed. The method by which postage should be paid upon public matter is set forth fully in the report of the Postmaster-General.

The report of the Secretary of the Interior shows that the quantity of public lands disposed of during the year ending the 30th of June, 1869, was 7,666,152 acres, exceeding that of the preceding year by 1,010,409 acres. Of this amount 2,899,544 acres were sold for cash and 2,737,365 acres entered under the homestead laws. The remainder was granted to aid in the construction of works of internal improvement, approved to the States as swamp land, and located with warrants and scrip. The cash receipts from all sources were $4,472,886, exceeding those of the preceding year $2,840,140.

During the last fiscal year 23,196 names were added to the pension rolls and 4,876 dropped therefrom, leaving at its close 187,963. The amount paid to pensioners, including the compensation of disbursing agents, was $28,422,884, an increase of $4,411,902 on that of the previous year. The munificence of Congress has been conspicuously manifested in its legislation for the soldiers and sailors who suffered in the recent struggle to maintain "that unity of government which makes us one people." The additions to the pension rolls of each successive year since the conclusion of hostilities result in a great degree from the repeated amendments of the act of the 14th of July, 1862, which extended its provisions to cases not falling within its original scope. The large outlay which is thus occasioned is further increased by the more liberal allowance bestowed since that date upon those who in the line of duty were wholly or permanently disabled. Public opinion has given an emphatic sanction to these measures of Congress, and it will be conceded that no part of our public burden is more cheerfully borne than that which is imposed by this branch of the service. It necessitates for the next fiscal year, in addition to the amount justly chargeable to the naval pension fund, an appropriation of $30,000,000.

During the year ending the 30th of September, 1869, the Patent Office issued 13,762 patents, and its receipts were $686,389, being $213,926 more than the expenditures.

I would respectfully call your attention to the recommendation of the Secretary of the Interior for uniting the duties of supervising the education of freedmen with the other duties devolving upon the Commissioner of Education.

If it is the desire of Congress to make the census which must be taken during the year 1870 more complete and perfect than heretofore, I would suggest early action upon any plan that may be agreed upon. As Congress at the last session appointed a committee to take into consideration such measures as might be deemed proper in reference to the census and report a plan, I desist from saying more.

I recommend to your favorable consideration the claims of the Agricultural Bureau for liberal apppropriations. In a country so diversified in climate and soil as ours, and with a population so largely dependent upon agriculture, the benefits that can be conferred by properly fostering this Bureau are incalculable.

I desire respectfully to call the attention of Congress to the inadequate salaries of a number of the most important offices of the Government. In this message I will not enumerate them, but will specify only the justices of the Supreme Court. No change has been made in their salaries for fifteen years. Within that time the labors of the court have largely increased and the expenses of living have at least doubled. During the same time Congress has twice found it necessary to increase largely the compensation of its own members, and the duty which it owes to another department of the Government deserves, and will undoubtedly receive, its due consideration.

There are many subjects not alluded to in this message which might with propriety be introduced, but I abstain, believing that your patriotism and statesmanship will suggest the topics and the legislation most conducive to the interests of the whole people. On my part I promise a rigid adherence to the laws and their strict enforcement.

U. S. GRANT.

SPECIAL MESSAGES.

WASHINGTON, *December 6, 1869.*

To the Senate of the United States:

I submit to the Senate, for its consideration with a view to ratification, an additional article to the convention of the 24th of October, 1867, between the United States of America and His Majesty the King of Denmark.

U. S. GRANT.

WASHINGTON, *December 6, 1869.*

To the Senate of the United States:

I submit to the Senate, for its consideration with a view to ratification, a convention between the United States and His Hawaiian Majesty, signed in this city on the 8th day of May last, providing for the extension of the term for the exchange of the ratifications of the convention for commercial reciprocity between the same parties, signed on the 21st day of May, 1867.

U. S. GRANT.

WASHINGTON, *December 6, 1869.*

To the Senate of the United States:

I submit to the Senate, for its consideration with a view to ratification, a protocol, signed in this city on the 23d of October last, to the convention upon the subject of claims between the United States and the Mexican Republic, signed the 4th of July, 1868.

U. S. GRANT

WASHINGTON, *December 7, 1869.*

To the Senate of the United States:

I transmit, for the consideration of the Senate, the accompanying copy of a correspondence between the Secretary of State and the minister of the United States at Berlin, in relation to the exchange of the ratifications of the naturalization convention dated July 27, 1868, between the United States and the Government of Wurtemberg, which was not effected within the time named in the convention.

U. S. GRANT.

WASHINGTON, *December 7, 1869.*

To the Senate of the United States:

I transmit, for the consideration of the Senate, the accompanying copy of a correspondence between the Secretary of State and the legation of the United States at Brussels, in relation to the exchange of the ratifications of the consular convention with Belgium signed on the 5th of December, 1868, which was not effected within the time named in the convention.

U. S. GRANT.

WASHINGTON, *December 7, 1869.*

To the Senate of the United States:

I transmit to the Senate a copy of a correspondence, a list of which is hereto annexed, between the Secretary of State and the minister resident of the United States at Constantinople, and invite its consideration of the question as to the correct meaning of the fourth article of the treaty of 1830 between the United States and Turkey.

U. S. GRANT.

WASHINGTON, D. C., *December 9, 1869.*

To the Senate of the United States:

In compliance with the resolution of the Senate of the 6th instant, requesting reports of the military commander of the district of which Georgia is a part in regard to the political and civil condition of that State, the accompanying papers are submitted.

U. S. GRANT.

WASHINGTON, *December 9, 1869.*

To the House of Representatives:

I transmit a report from the Secretary of State, in answer to a resolution of the House of Representatives of yesterday, asking to be informed what legislatures have ratified the proposed fifteenth amendment of the Constitution of the United States.

U. S. GRANT.

WASHINGTON, *December 15, 1869.*

To the House of Representatives:

I transmit a further report from the Secretary of State in answer to the resolution of the House of Representatives of the 9th instant, making known that official notice has been received at the Department of State of the ratification by the legislature of the State of Alabama of the amendment to the Constitution recently proposed by Congress as Article XV.

U. S. GRANT.

WASHINGTON, *December 15, 1869*

To the House of Representatives:

In answer to the resolution of the House of Representatives of the 13th instant, requesting a copy of official correspondence on the subject of Cuba, I transmit a report from the Secretary of State, to whom the resolution was referred.

U. S. GRANT.

EXECUTIVE MANSION,
Washington, D. C., December 15, 1869.

To the House of Representatives:

In answer to the resolution of December 9, 1869, requesting a copy of the charges, testimony, findings, and sentence in the trial by court-martial of Passed Assistant Surgeon Charles L. Green, United States Navy, I transmit herewith a report from the Secretary of the Navy, to whom the resolution was referred.

U. S. GRANT.

EXECUTIVE MANSION,
Washington, D. C., December 20, 1869.

To the Senate of the United States:

I hereby request the return of such part of my message of December 9, in response to Senate resolution of December 6, requesting the reports of the military commander of the district of which Georgia is a part, to wit, an anonymous letter purporting to be from "a Georgia woman." By accident the paper got with those called for by the resolution, instead of in the wastebasket, where it was intended it should go.

U. S. GRANT.

WASHINGTON, *December 20, 1869.*

To the Senate of the United States:

I transmit to the Senate, in relation to their resolution of the 8th instant, a report from the Secretary of State, with accompanying documents.*

U. S. GRANT.

WASHINGTON, *December 22, 1869.*

To the Senate:

In answer to the resolution of the Senate of the 20th instant, in relation to correspondence between the United States and Great Britain concerning questions pending between the two countries since the rejection of the claims convention by the Senate, I transmit a report from the Secretary of State upon the subject and the papers by which it was accompanied.

U. S. GRANT.

WASHINGTON, *December 22, 1869.*

To the Senate of the United States:

I transmit to the Senate, in answer to their resolution of the 8th instant, a report † from the Secretary of State.

U. S. GRANT.

WASHINGTON, *January 10, 1870.*

To the Senate of the United States:

I transmit to the Senate, for consideration with a view to its ratification, a convention between the United States and the Dominican Republic for a lease to the former of the bay and peninsula of Samana.

U. S. GRANT.

---

*Relating to the revolution in Cuba and the political and civil condition of that island.

†Stating that neither correspondence nor negotiation upon the subject of trade and commerce between the United States and Canada had been entered into.

WASHINGTON, *January 10. 1870.*

To the Senate of the United States:

I transmit to the Senate, for consideration with a view to its ratification, a treaty for the annexation of the Dominican Republic to the United States, signed by the plenipotentiaries of the parties on the 29th of November last.

U. S. GRANT.

EXECUTIVE MANSION,
Washington, D. C., January 10, 1870.

To the Senate of the United States:

In response to the resolution of the Senate of December 9, 1869, requesting the information in possession of the President or any of the Departments relating to the action which has been had in the District of Virginia under the act "authorizing the submission of the constitutions of Virginia, Mississippi, and Texas to a vote of the people, and authorizing the election of State officers provided by the said constitutions, and Members of Congress," approved April 10, 1869, I have the honor to transmit herewith the reports of the Secretary of State, the Secretary of War, and the Attorney-General, to whom, severally, the resolution was referred.

U. S. GRANT.

EXECUTIVE MANSION,
Washington, D. C., January 21, 1870.

To the House of Representatives:

In answer to the resolution passed by the House of Representatives on the 17th instant, requesting to be informed "under what act of Congress or by other authority appropriations for the Navy are diverted to the survey of the Isthmus of Darien," I transmit a report by the Secretary of the Navy, to whom the resolution was referred.

U. S. GRANT.

EXECUTIVE MANSION,
Washington, D. C., January 29, 1870.

To the Senate and House of Representatives:

I herewith transmit to Congress a report, dated 29th instant, with the accompanying papers,* received from the Secretary of State, in compliance with the requirements of the eighteenth section of the act entitled "An act to regulate the diplomatic and consular systems of the United States," approved August 18, 1856.

U. S. GRANT.

* Report of fees collected, etc., by consular officers of the United States for 1868, and tariff of consular fees.

WASHINGTON, *February 1, 1870.*

To the Senate of the United States:

I transmit to the Senate, in compliance with its resolution of the 31st ultimo, a report from the Secretary of State, communicating information in relation to the action of the legislature of the State of Mississippi on the proposed fifteenth amendment to the Constitution of the United States.

U. S. GRANT.

WASHINGTON, *February 2, 1870.*

To the Senate of the United States:

In answer to the resolution of the Senate of the 8th ultimo, I transmit a report* from the Secretary of State and the papers which accompanied it.

U. S. GRANT.

EXECUTIVE MANSION, *February 4, 1870.*

To the Senate of the United States:

I herewith lay before the Senate, for the consideration and action of that body in connection with a treaty of December 4, 1868, with the Seneca Nation of Indians, now pending, amendments to said treaty proposed at a council of said Indians held at their council house on the Cattaraugus Reservation, in New York, on the 26th ultimo.

A letter of the Secretary of the Interior, of the 3d instant, accompanies the papers.

U. S. GRANT.

EXECUTIVE MANSION, *February 4, 1870.*

To the Senate of the United States:

For the reasons stated in the accompanying communication from the Secretary of the Interior, I respectfully request to withdraw the treaties hereinafter mentioned, which are now pending before the Senate:

First. Treaty concluded with the Great and Little Osages May 27, 1868.

Second. Treaty concluded with the Sacs and Foxes of the Missouri and Iowa tribes of Indians February 11, 1869.

Third. Treaty concluded with the Otoe and Missouria Indians February 13, 1869.

Fourth. Treaty concluded with the Kansas or Kaw Indians March 13 1869.

U. S. GRANT.

WASHINGTON, *February 8, 1870.*

To the House of Representatives:

In answer to the resolution of the House of Representatives of the 3d instant, calling for the number of copies of the tributes of the nations to

* Relating to the insurrection in the Red River settlement, in British North America.

Abraham Lincoln now in possession of the Department of State, I transmit a report from the Secretary of State and the paper which accompanied it.

U. S. GRANT.

WASHINGTON, *February 11, 1870.*

To the House of Representatives:

In compliance with the resolution of the House of Representatives requesting me to furnish any information which may have been received by the Government in relation to the recent assault upon and reported murder of one or more American citizens in Cuba, I communicate a report from the Secretary of State, with the papers accompanying it.

U. S. GRANT.

WASHINGTON CITY, *February 11, 1870.*

To the Senate of the United States:

The papers in the case of Commander Jonathan Young. of the United States Navy, show—

That when the naval promotions were made in 1866 the name of Commander Jonathan Young was not included among them, and he was passed over, while Commander George W. Young was not passed over; that among other testimonials is one from Vice-Admiral D. D. Porter stating that "Commander Jonathan Young was passed over by mistake; that he was recommended for promotion, while Commander George W. Young was not recommended for promotion, and by some singular mistake the latter was promoted, while the former was passed over."

That eminent officers, formerly *junior* to Commander Young, but promoted over his head, desire his restoration to his former position, because they consider such restoration due to his character, ability, and services.

In view, therefore, of these facts, and of the general good standing of Commander Jonathan Young, and of his gallant and efficient services during the war, and to remedy so far as is now possible what is believed to have been a clerical error of the Department, which has worked to his injury, the Department now recommends that he be restored to his original standing upon the navy list.

For these reasons I nominate Commander Jonathan Young to be restored to his original position, to take rank from the 25th July, 1866, and next after Commander William T. Truxtun.

U. S. GRANT.

WASHINGTON, D. C., *February 11, 1870.*

To the Senate of the United States:

In reply to the resolution of the Senate of the 4th instant, requesting information in regard to the proceedings had in the State of Georgia in pursuance of the recent act of Congress entitled "An act to promote the reconstruction of the State of Georgia," and in relation to the organization of the legislature of that State since the passage of that act, I herewith transmit the report of the Secretary of War, to whom the resolution was referred.

U. S. GRANT.

WASHINGTON, *February 15, 1870.*

To the Senate of the United States:

In reply to a resolution of the Senate of the 9th instant, in relation to the Central Branch, Union Pacific Railroad Company, I transmit a copy of a letter addressed to me on the 27th ultimo by the Secretary of the Interior. It contains all the information in my possession touching the action of any of the Departments on the claim of that company to continue and extend its road and to receive in aid of the construction thereof lands and bonds from the United States.

U. S. GRANT.

WASHINGTON, *February 16, 1870.*

To the Senate of the United States:

In response to the resolution of the Senate of the 8th instant, asking "how much of the appropriations heretofore made, amounting to $100,000, to provide for the defense of certain suits now pending in the Court of Claims, known as the cotton cases, has been expended, and to whom the same has been paid; for what services rendered, and the amount paid to each of said persons; and also the number of clerks in the Treasury Department, and other persons, with their names, engaged or occupied in the defense of said suits," I herewith transmit the report of the Secretary of the Treasury, to whom the resolution was referred.

U. S. GRANT.

WASHINGTON, *February 16, 1870.*

To the House of Representatives:

In answer to the resolution of the House of Representatives of the 10th instant, I transmit a report* from the Secretary of State, with accompanying documents.

U. S. GRANT.

WASHINGTON, *February 17, 1870.*

To the Senate of the United States:

I transmit to the Senate, in answer to their resolution of the 24th ultimo, the report from the Secretary of State, with accompaniments.†

U. S. GRANT.

---

* Relating to the payment in currency, instead of coin, of the semiannual installments of interest due to the United States under the convention with Spain concluded February 17, 1834, and opinion of the Attorney-General relative thereto.

† Lists of officers commissioned by the Department of State, their compensation, etc.

WASHINGTON, *February 18, 1870.*

To the House of Representatives:

I transmit to the House of Representatives, in further answer to their resolution requesting information in relation to the recent assault upon and reported murder of one or more American citizens in Cuba, a report from the Secretary of State, with accompanying papers.

U. S. GRANT.

WASHINGTON, *February 19, 1870.*

To the Senate of the United States:

In reply to the resolution of the Senate of the 11th instant, requesting "any information which may have been received by the Government of the recently reported engagement of Colonel Baker with the Indians,* with copies of all orders which led to the same," I transmit a report from the Secretary of War, to whom the resolution was referred.

U. S. GRANT.

EXECUTIVE MANSION,
Washington, D. C., February 21, 1870.

To the House of Representatives:

I transmit to the House of Representatives, in answer to their resolution of the 7th instant, a report from the Secretary of State, with accompanying documents.†

U. S. GRANT.

WASHINGTON, *February 23, 1870.*

To the Senate of the United States:

I transmit to the Senate, in answer to their resolution of the 14th instant, a report from the Secretary of State, with accompanying documents.‡

U. S. GRANT.

WASHINGTON, *February 24, 1870.*

To the Senate of the United States:

In answer to the resolution of the Senate of the 21st instant, directing the Secretary of State to furnish the Senate with copies of all correspondence relating to the imprisonment of Mr. Davis Hatch by the Dominican Government, I transmit a report of the Secretary of State upon the subject.

U. S. GRANT.

---

* Piegan in Montana.

† Correspondence relative to affairs connected with Cuba and to the struggle for independence in that island.

‡ Correspondence of the United States minister to Japan relative to American interests in that country.

WASHINGTON, *February 28, 1870.*

To the Senate of the United States:

In answer to the resolution of the Senate of the 19th instant, requesting to be informed "if any officer of the Government has, contrary to the treaty of July 19, 1866, with the Cherokee Nation, enforced or sought to enforce the payment of taxes by Cherokees on products manufactured in the Cherokee Nation and sold within the Indian Territory," I transmit a report from the Secretary of the Treasury, to whom the resolution was referred.

U. S. GRANT.

WASHINGTON, *February 28, 1870.*

To the House of Representatives:

In answer to the resolution of the House of Representatives of the 15th instant, I transmit a report from the Secretary of State upon the subject,* and the papers by which it was accompanied.

U. S. GRANT.

WASHINGTON, *March 1, 1870.*

To the Senate and House of Representatives:

I transmit to Congress a communication from the Secretary of State, with the accompanying documents, relative to the claims of citizens of the United States on the Government of Venezuela which were adjusted by the commission provided for by the convention with that Republic of April 25, 1866.

U. S. GRANT.

EXECUTIVE MANSION,
Washington, D. C., March 3, 1870.

To the House of Representatives:

I transmit herewith, in response to the resolution of the House asking for information in relation to the repairs of Spanish war vessels at the docks of the United States, the report of the Secretary of the Navy, to whom the resolution was referred.

U. S. GRANT.

EXECUTIVE MANSION,
Washington, D. C., March 8, 1870.

To the Senate and House of Representatives:

Herewith I have the honor to transmit a communication from the Secretary of the Interior, relative to the obligation of Congress to make the necessary appropriations to carry out the Indian treaties made by what is known as the Peace Commission of 1867.

*Imprisonment of American citizens in Great Britain for political offenses.

The history of those treaties and the consequences of noncompliance with them by the Government are so clearly set forth in this statement that I deem it better to communicate it in full than to ask the necessary appropriation in a shorter statement of the reasons for it. I earnestly desire that if an Indian war becomes inevitable the Government of the United States at least should not be responsible for it. Pains will be taken, and force used if necessary, to prevent the departure of the expeditions referred to by the Secretary of the Interior.

U. S. GRANT.

WASHINGTON, *March 10, 1870.*

To the Senate of the United States:

In answer to the resolution of the Senate of the 4th instant, in relation to the "Transcontinental, Memphis, El Paso and Pacific Railroad Company," I transmit reports from the Secretary of State and the Secretary of the Interior, with accompanying papers. U. S. GRANT.

WASHINGTON, *March 10, 1870.*

To the Senate of the United States:

I transmit to the Senate, in answer to their resolution of the 28th ultimo, a report * from the Secretary of State, with accompanying documents. U. S. GRANT.

EXECUTIVE MANSION,
Washington, D. C., March 14, 1870.

To the Senate of the United States:

In reply to your resolution of the 14th of February, requesting to be informed whether I desire that any of the Indian treaties now pending before you be considered confidentially, I have to inform you that there are none of them which I object to having discussed in open session.

U. S. GRANT.

EXECUTIVE MANSION,
Washington, D. C., March 14, 1870.

To the Senate of the United States:

I would respectfully call your attention to a treaty now before you for the acquisition of the Republic of St. Domingo, entered into between the agents of the two Governments on the 29th of November, 1869, and by its terms to be finally acted upon by the people of St. Domingo and the Senate of the United States within four months from the date of signing

---

* Relating to legislation necessary to insure the administration of justice and the protection of American interests in China and Japan.

the treaty. The time for action expires on the 29th instant, a fact to which I desire expressly to call your attention. I would also direct your notice to the fact that the Government of St. Domingo has no agent in the United States who is authorized to extend the time for further deliberation upon its merits.

The people of St. Domingo have already, so far as their action can go, ratified the treaty, and I express the earnest wish that you will not permit it to expire by limitation. I also entertain the sincere hope that your action may be favorable to the ratification of the treaty.

U. S. GRANT.

WASHINGTON, *March 15, 1870.*

To the Senate of the United States:

I transmit a report from the Secretary of State, in answer to a resolution of the Senate of the 3d instant, asking to be informed what States have ratified the amendment known as the fifteenth amendment to the Constitution of the United States, so far as official notice thereof has been transmitted to the Department of State, and that information from time to time may be communicated to that body, as soon as practicable, of such ratification hereafter by any State.

U. S. GRANT.

EXECUTIVE MANSION,
Washington, D. C., March 23, 1870.

To the Senate and House of Representatives:

In the Executive message of December 6, 1869, to Congress the importance of taking steps to revive our drooping merchant marine was urged, and a special message promised at a future day during the present session, recommending more specifically plans to accomplish this result. Now that the committee of the House of Representatives intrusted with the labor of ascertaining "the cause of the decline of American commerce" has completed its work and submitted its report to the legislative branch of the Government, I deem this a fitting time to execute that promise.

The very able, calm, and exhaustive report of the committee points out the grave wrongs which have produced the decline in our commerce. It is a national humiliation that we are now compelled to pay from twenty to thirty million dollars annually (exclusive of passage money, which we should share with vessels of other nations) to foreigners for doing the work which should be done by American vessels, American built, American owned, and American manned. This is a direct drain upon the resources of the country of just so much money, equal to casting it into the sea, so far as this nation is concerned.

A nation of the vast and ever-increasing interior resources of the

United States, extending, as it does, from one to the other of the great oceans of the world, with an industrious, intelligent, energetic population, must one day possess its full share of the commerce of these oceans, no matter what the cost. Delay will only increase this cost and enhance the difficulty of attaining the result.

I therefore put in an earnest plea for early action in this matter, in a way to secure the desired increase of American commerce. The advanced period of the year and the fact that no contracts for shipbuilding will probably be entered into until this question is settled by Congress, and the further fact that if there should be much delay all large vessels contracted for this year will fail of completion before winter sets in, and will therefore be carried over for another year, induces me to request your early consideration of this subject.

I regard it of such grave importance, affecting every interest of the country to so great an extent, that any method which will gain the end will secure a rich national blessing. Building ships and navigating them utilizes vast capital at home; it employs thousands of workmen in their construction and manning; it creates a home market for the products of the farm and the shop; it diminishes the balance of trade against us precisely to the extent of freights and passage money paid to American vessels, and gives us a supremacy upon the seas of inestimable value in case of foreign war.

Our Navy at the commencement of the late war consisted of less than 100 vessels, of about 150,000 tons and a force of about 8,000 men. We drew from the merchant marine, which had cost the Government nothing, but which had been a source of national wealth, 600 vessels, exceeding 1,000,000 tons, and about 70,000 men, to aid in the suppression of the rebellion.

This statement demonstrates the value of the merchant marine as a means of national defense in time of need.

The Committee on the Causes of the Reduction of American Tonnage, after tracing the causes of its decline, submit two bills, which, if adopted, they believe will restore to the nation its maritime power. Their report shows with great minuteness the actual and comparative American tonnage at the time of its greatest prosperity; the actual and comparative decline since, together with the causes; and exhibits all other statistics of material interest in reference to the subject. As the report is before Congress, I will not recapitulate any of its statistics, but refer only to the methods recommended by the committee to give back to us our lost commerce.

As a general rule, when it can be adopted, I believe a direct money subsidy is less liable to abuse than an indirect aid given to the same enterprise. In this case, however, my opinion is that subsidies, while they may be given to specified lines of steamers or other vessels, should not be exclusively adopted, but, in addition to subsidizing very desirable lines of ocean traffic, a general assistance should be given in an effective way. I therefore commend to your favorable consideration the two bills proposed by the committee and referred to in this message.

U. S. GRANT.

EXECUTIVE MANSION, *March 25, 1870.*
To the Senate of the United States:

In reply to a Senate resolution of the 24th instant, requesting to be furnished with a report, written by Captain Selfridge, upon the resources and condition of things in the Dominican Republic, I have to state that no such report has been received.

U. S. GRANT.

WASHINGTON, *March 25, 1870.*
To the Senate of the United States:

In answer to the resolution of the Senate of the 15th ultimo, I transmit a report, with accompanying paper,* from the Secretary of the Navy, to whom the resolution was referred.

U. S. GRANT.

EXECUTIVE MANSION, *March 29, 1870.*
To the House of Representatives:

In reply to your resolution of December 20, 1869, asking "whether any citizens of the United States are imprisoned or detained in military custody by officers of the Army of the United States, and, if any, to furnish their names, date of arrest, the offenses charged, together with a statement of what measures have been taken for the trial and punishment of the offenders," I transmit herewith the report of the Secretary of War, to whom the resolution was referred.

U. S. GRANT.

EXECUTIVE MANSION, *March 30, 1870.*
To the Senate and House of Representatives:

It is unusual to notify the two Houses of Congress by message of the promulgation, by proclamation of the Secretary of State, of the ratification of a constitutional amendment. In view, however, of the vast importance of the fifteenth amendment to the Constitution, this day declared a part of that revered instrument, I deem a departure from the usual custom justifiable. A measure which makes at once 4,000,000 people voters who were heretofore declared by the highest tribunal in the land not citizens of the United States, nor eligible to become so (with the assertion that "at the time of the Declaration of Independence the opinion

*Statement of the number and character of the ironclad vessels of the Navy, their cost, by whom designed, who recommended their construction, and their condition.

was fixed and universal in the civilized portion of the white race, regarded as an axiom in morals as well as in politics, that black men had no rights which the white man was bound to respect''), is indeed a measure of grander importance than any other one act of the kind from the foundation of our free Government to the present day.

Institutions like ours, in which all power is derived directly from the people, must depend mainly upon their intelligence, patriotism, and industry. I call the attention, therefore, of the newly enfranchised race to the importance of their striving in every honorable manner to make themselves worthy of their new privilege. To the race more favored heretofore by our laws I would say, Withhold no legal privilege of advancement to the new citizen. The framers of our Constitution firmly believed that a republican government could not endure without intelligence and education generally diffused among the people. The Father of his Country, in his Farewell Address, uses this language:

Promote, then, as an object of primary importance, institutions for the general diffusion of knowledge. In proportion as the structure of a government gives force to public opinion, it is essential that public opinion should be enlightened.

In his first annual message to Congress the same views are forcibly presented, and are again urged in his eighth message.

I repeat that the adoption of the fifteenth amendment to the Constitution completes the greatest civil change and constitutes the most important event that has occurred since the nation came into life. The change will be beneficial in proportion to the heed that is given to the urgent recommendations of Washington. If these recommendations were important then, with a population of but a few millions, how much more important now, with a population of 40,000,000, and increasing in a rapid ratio. I would therefore call upon Congress to take all the means within their constitutional powers to promote and encourage popular education throughout the country, and upon the people everywhere to see to it that all who possess and exercise political rights shall have the opportunity to acquire the knowledge which will make their share in the Government a blessing and not a danger. By such means only can the benefits contemplated by this amendment to the Constitution be secured.

U. S. GRANT.

HAMILTON FISH, SECRETARY OF STATE OF THE UNITED STATES.

To all to whom these presents may come, greeting:

Know ye that the Congress of the United States, on or about the 27th day of February, in the year 1869, passed a resolution in the words and figures following, to wit:

A RESOLUTION proposing an amendment to the Constitution of the United States.

Resolved by the Senate and House of Representatives of the United States of America in Congress assembled (two-thirds of both Houses concurring), That the following article be proposed to the legislatures of the several States as an amendment to the

Constitution of the United States, which, when ratified by three-fourths of said legislatures, shall be valid as a part of the Constitution, viz:

ARTICLE XV.

SECTION 1. The right of citizens of the United States to vote shall not be denied or abridged by the United States, or by any State, on account of race, color, or previous condition of servitude.

SEC. 2. The Congress shall have power to enforce this article by appropriate legislation.

And further, that it appears from official documents on file in this Department that the amendment to the Constitution of the United States, proposed as aforesaid, has been ratified by the legislatures of the States of North Carolina, West Virginia, Massachusetts, Wisconsin, Maine, Louisiana, Michigan, South Carolina, Pennsylvania, Arkansas, Connecticut, Florida, Illinois, Indiana, New York, New Hampshire, Nevada, Vermont, Virginia, Alabama, Missouri, Mississippi, Ohio, Iowa, Kansas, Minnesota, Rhode Island, Nebraska, and Texas; in all, twenty-nine States;

And further, that the States whose legislatures have so ratified the said proposed amendment constitute three-fourths of the whole number of States in the United States;

And further, that it appears from an official document on file in this Department that the legislature of the State of New York has since passed resolutions claiming to withdraw the said ratification of the said amendment, which had been made by the legislature of that State, and of which official notice had been filed in this Department;

And further, that it appears from an official document on file in this Department that the legislature of Georgia has by resolution ratified the said proposed amendment:

Now, therefore, be it known that I, Hamilton Fish, Secretary of State of the United States, by virtue and in pursuance of the second section of the act of Congress approved the 20th day of April, in the year 1818, entitled "An act to provide for the publication of the laws of the United States, and for other purposes," do hereby certify that the amendment aforesaid has become valid to all intents and purposes as part of the Constitution of the United States.

In testimony whereof I have hereunto set my hand and caused the seal of the Department of State to be affixed.

[SEAL.]   Done at the city of Washington this 30th day of March, A. D. 1870, and of the Independence of the United States the ninety-fourth.

HAMILTON FISH.

WASHINGTON, *March 31, 1870.*

To the Senate of the United States:

I transmit, for consideration with a view to its ratification, a treaty between the United States and the United States of Colombia for the construction of an interoceanic canal across the Isthmus of Panama or Darien, signed at Bogota on the 26th of January last.

A copy of a dispatch of the 1st ultimo to the Secretary of State from General Hurlbut, the United States minister at Bogota, relative to the treaty, is also transmitted for the information of the Senate.

U. S. GRANT.

WASHINGTON, *March 31, 1870.*

To the Senate and House of Representatives:

I transmit to Congress a further communication from the Secretary of State, with the accompanying documents, relative to the claims of citizens of the United States on the Government of Venezuela which were adjusted by the commission provided for by the convention with that Republic of April 25, 1866.

U. S. GRANT.

WASHINGTON, *March 31, 1870.*

To the House of Representatives:

In answer to the resolution of the House of Representatives of the 7th instant, relating to fisheries in British waters, I transmit a report from the Secretary of State and the papers which accompanied it, and I have to state that the commanding officer of the naval steamer ordered to the fishing grounds will be instructed to give his attention, should circumstances require it, to cases which may arise under any change which may be made in the British laws affecting fisheries within British jurisdiction, with a view to preventing, so far as it may be in his power, infractions by citizens of the United States of the first article of the treaty between the United States and Great Britain of 1818, the laws in force relating to fisheries within British jurisdiction, or any illegal interference with the pursuits of the fishermen of the United States.

U. S. GRANT.

WASHINGTON, *April 5, 1870.*

To the House of Representatives:

In answer to the resolution of the House of Representatives of the 28th ultimo, I transmit a report* from the Secretary of State, to whom the resolution was referred.

U. S. GRANT.

EXECUTIVE MANSION, *April 6, 1870.*

To the House of Representatives:

In answer to your resolution of the 7th ultimo, requesting to be furnished with a copy of orders, correspondence, reports of councils with Indians by military and civil officers of the Government, in possession of the Interior and War Departments, relating to difficulties with the Cheyenne, Comanche, Arapahoe, Apache, and Kiowa tribes of Indians during the year 1867, etc., I herewith transmit the reports received from those Departments.

U. S. GRANT.

* Declining to communicate a copy of the list of privileges accompanying or relating to the San Domingo treaty while the subject is pending before the Senate in executive session.

WASHINGTON, *April 14, 1870.*

To the Senate and House of Representatives:

I transmit to Congress a report from the Secretary of State, relative to results of the proceedings of the joint commission at Lima under the convention between the United States and Peru of 4th of December, 1868, and recommend that an appropriation be made to discharge the obligation of the United States in the case of the claim of Esteban G. Montano, to which the report refers.

U. S. GRANT.

EXECUTIVE MANSION, *April 20, 1870.*

To the House of Representatives:

In answer to your resolution of the 21st ultimo, requesting to be informed "whether any portion of the military forces of the United States has been sent into the counties of Bourbon, Crawford, and Cherokee, in the State of Kansas, and, if so, when, what number, for what purpose, and on whose procurement; and also whether they have been required to erect there any winter quarters, forts, fortifications, or earthworks, and, if so, what, for what purpose, and at whose expense, and at what probable expense to the Government have all said acts been done," I transmit herewith a report, dated 18th instant, from the Secretary of War, to whom the resolution was referred.

U. S. GRANT.

WASHINGTON, *April 26, 1870.*

To the House of Representatives:

In answer to the resolution of the House of Representatives of the 9th instant, I transmit a report from the Secretary of State and the paper* which accompanied it.

U. S. GRANT.

WASHINGTON, *May 6, 1870.*

To the Senate of the United States:

In answer to the resolution of the Senate of the 26th ultimo, I transmit a report from the Secretary of State and the papers† by which it was accompanied.

U. S. GRANT.

WASHINGTON, *May 21, 1870.*

To the Senate of the United States:

I transmit to the Senate, in answer to their resolution of the 18th instant, calling for information relative to the passage of any English or

*Supplemental report to the Department of State by Samuel B. Ruggles, United States delegate to the International Monetary Conference at Paris, 1867.

† Dispatches of J. Somers Smith, commercial agent of the United States at San Domingo, relative to the imprisonment of Davis Hatch by the Dominican Government.

Canadian steamer through the canal of Sault Ste. Marie, a report from the Secretary of State, with accompanying papers.

U. S. GRANT.

WASHINGTON, *May 23, 1870.*

To the Senate of the United States:

In response to your resolution of the 12th instant, requesting information "in relation to an organized band of persons at Cheyenne, in the Territory of Wyoming, or vicinity, the number and designs of such persons," I transmit herewith the reports of the Secretary of War and the Secretary of the Interior, to whom the resolution was referred.

U. S. GRANT.

WASHINGTON, *May 23, 1870.*

To the House of Representatives:

I transmit to the House of Representatives, in answer to their resolution of the 5th instant, a report from the Secretary of State and its accompanying papers.*

U. S. GRANT.

WASHINGTON, *May 26, 1870.*

To the Senate of the United States:

I have the satisfaction of transmitting to the Senate, for consideration with a view to its ratification, a convention between the United States and Her Britannic Majesty, relative to naturalization, signed in London on the 13th instant.

The convention is substantially the same as the protocol on the subject signed by Mr. Reverdy Johnson and Lord Stanley on the 9th of October, 1868, and approved by the Senate on the 13th April, 1869.

If the instrument should go into effect, it will relieve the parties from a grievance which has hitherto been a cause of frequent annoyance and sometimes of dangerous irritation.

A copy of Mr. Motley's dispatch on the subject and of the act of Parliament of May 12, 1870, are also transmitted.

U. S. GRANT.

WASHINGTON, *May 28, 1870.*

To the Senate of the United States:

In answer to the resolution of the Senate of the 24th instant, I transmit a report from the Secretary of State and the document† by which it was accompanied.

U. S. GRANT.

* Relating to the claims of United States citizens against Venezuela.

† Dispatch from Henry T. Blow, United States minister to Brazil, relative to the commercial interests of the United States with South America.

EXECUTIVE MANSION, *May 31, 1870.*

To the Senate of the United States:

I transmit to the Senate, for consideration with a view to its ratification, an additional article to the treaty of the 29th of November last, for the annexation of the Dominican Republic to the United States, stipulating for an extension of the time for exchanging the ratifications thereof, signed in this city on the 14th instant by the plenipotentiaries of the parties.

It was my intention to have also negotiated with the plenipotentiary of San Domingo amendments to the treaty of annexation to obviate objections which may be urged against the treaty as it is now worded; but on reflection I deem it better to submit to the Senate the propriety of their amending the treaty as follows: First, to specify that the obligations of this Government shall not exceed the $1,500,000 stipulated in the treaty; secondly, to determine the manner of appointing the agents to receive and disburse the same; thirdly, to determine the class of creditors who shall take precedence in the settlement of their claims; and, finally, to insert such amendments as may suggest themselves to the minds of Senators to carry out in good faith the conditions of the treaty submitted to the Senate of the United States in January last, according to the spirit and intent of that treaty. From the most reliable information I can obtain, the sum specified in the treaty will pay every just claim against the Republic of San Domingo and leave a balance sufficient to carry on a Territorial government until such time as new laws for providing a Territorial revenue can be enacted and put in force.

I feel an unusual anxiety for the ratification of this treaty, because I believe it will redound greatly to the glory of the two countries interested, to civilization, and to the extirpation of the institution of slavery.

The doctrine promulgated by President Monroe has been adhered to by all political parties, and I now deem it proper to assert the equally important principle that hereafter no territory on this continent shall be regarded as subject of transfer to a European power.

The Government of San Domingo has voluntarily sought this annexation. It is a weak power, numbering probably less than 120,000 souls, and yet possessing one of the richest territories under the sun, capable of supporting a population of 10,000,000 people in luxury. The people of San Domingo are not capable of maintaining themselves in their present condition, and must look for outside support.

They yearn for the protection of our free institutions and laws, our progress and civilization. Shall we refuse them?

I have information which I believe reliable that a European power stands ready now to offer $2,000,000 for the possession of Samana Bay alone. If refused by us, with what grace can we prevent a foreign power from attempting to secure the prize?

The acquisition of San Domingo is desirable because of its geographical position. It commands the entrance to the Caribbean Sea and the Isthmus transit of commerce. It possesses the richest soil, best and most capacious harbors, most salubrious climate, and the most valuable products of the forests, mine, and soil of any of the West India Islands. Its possession by us will in a few years build up a coastwise commerce of immense magnitude, which will go far toward restoring to us our lost merchant marine. It will give to us those articles which we consume so largely and do not produce, thus equalizing our exports and imports.

In case of foreign war it will give us command of all the islands referred to, and thus prevent an enemy from ever again possessing himself of rendezvous upon our very coast.

At present our coast trade between the States bordering on the Atlantic and those bordering on the Gulf of Mexico is cut into by the Bahamas and the Antilles. Twice we must, as it were, pass through foreign countries to get by sea from Georgia to the west coast of Florida.

San Domingo, with a stable government, under which her immense resources can be developed, will give remunerative wages to tens of thousands of laborers not now on the island.

This labor will take advantage of every available means of transportation to abandon the adjacent islands and seek the blessings of freedom and its sequence—each inhabitant receiving the reward of his own labor. Porto Rico and Cuba will have to abolish slavery, as a measure of self-preservation to retain their laborers.

San Domingo will become a large consumer of the products of Northern farms and manufactories. The cheap rate at which her citizens can be furnished with food, tools, and machinery will make it necessary that the contiguous islands should have the same advantages in order to compete in the production of sugar, coffee, tobacco, tropical fruits, etc. This will open to us a still wider market for our products.

The production of our own supply of these articles will cut off more than one hundred millions of our annual imports, besides largely increasing our exports. With such a picture it is easy to see how our large debt abroad is ultimately to be extinguished. With a balance of trade against us (including interest on bonds held by foreigners and money spent by our citizens traveling in foreign lands) equal to the entire yield of the precious metals in this country, it is not so easy to see how this result is to be otherwise accomplished.

The acquisition of San Domingo is an adherence to the "Monroe doctrine;" it is a measure of national protection; it is asserting our just claim to a controlling influence over the great commercial traffic soon to flow from east to west by the way of the Isthmus of Darien; it is to build up our merchant marine; it is to furnish new markets for the products of our farms, shops, and manufactories; it is to make slavery insupportable in Cuba and Porto Rico at once and ultimately so in Brazil; it is to settle the unhappy condition of Cuba, and end an exterminating conflict; it is to provide honest means of paying our honest debts, without overtaxing the people; it is to furnish our citizens with the necessaries of everyday life at cheaper rates than ever before; and it is, in fine, a rapid stride toward that greatness which the intelligence, industry, and enterprise of the citizens of the United States entitle this country to assume among nations.

U. S. GRANT.

EXECUTIVE MANSION,
Washington, D. C., June 2, 1870

To the Senate of the United States:

In reply to your resolution of the 1st instant, requesting, "in confidence," any information in possession of the President "touching any proposition, offer, or design of any foreign power to purchase or obtain any part of the territory of San Domingo or any right to the Bay of Samana," I transmit herewith a copy of a letter, dated 27th of April, 1870, addressed to "Colonel J. W. Fabens, Dominican minister, Washington," by "E. Herzberg Hartmount, Dominican consul-general in London."

U. S. GRANT.

WASHINGTON, *June 3, 1870.*

To the Senate of the United States:

I transmit to the Senate, in answer to their resolution of the 18th ultimo, a report from the Secretary of State, with an accompanying paper.*

U. S. GRANT.

WASHINGTON, *June 3, 1870.*

To the Senate of the United States:

I transmit to the Senate, for consideration with a view to its ratification, an additional convention to the treaty of the 7th of April, 1862, for the suppression of the African slave trade, which additional convention was signed on this day in the city of Washington by the plenipotentiaries of the high contracting parties.

U. S. GRANT.

WASHINGTON, *June 6, 1870.*

To the Senate of the United States:

I transmit to the Senate, in answer to their resolution of the 3d instant, the accompanying report † from the Secretary of State.

U. S. GRANT.

* Communication from George Bancroft, United States minister at Berlin, relative to political questions in Germany.

† Stating that he has received no official information relative to a reported persecution and massacre of Israelites in Roumania.

EXECUTIVE MANSION, *June 13, 1870.*

To the Senate and House of Representatives:

In my annual message to Congress at the beginning of its present session I referred to the contest which had then for more than a year existed in the island of Cuba between a portion of its inhabitants and the Government of Spain, and the feelings and sympathies of the people and Government of the United States for the people of Cuba, as for all peoples struggling for liberty and self-government, and said that "the contest has at no time assumed the conditions which amount to war in the sense of international law, or which would show the existence of a *de facto* political organization of the insurgents sufficient to justify a recognition of belligerency."

During the six months which have passed since the date of that message the condition of the insurgents has not improved, and the insurrection itself, although not subdued, exhibits no signs of advance, but seems to be confined to an irregular system of hostilities, carried on by small and illy armed bands of men, roaming without concentration through the woods and the sparsely populated regions of the island, attacking from ambush convoys and small bands of troops, burning plantations and the estates of those not sympathizing with their cause.

But if the insurrection has not gained ground, it is equally true that Spain has not suppressed it. Climate, disease, and the occasional bullet have worked destruction among the soldiers of Spain; and although the Spanish authorities have possession of every seaport and every town on the island, they have not been able to subdue the hostile feeling which has driven a considerable number of the native inhabitants of the island to armed resistance against Spain, and still leads them to endure the dangers and the privations of a roaming life of guerrilla warfare.

On either side the contest has been conducted, and is still carried on, with a lamentable disregard of human life and of the rules and practices which modern civilization has prescribed in mitigation of the necessary horrors of war. The torch of Spaniard and of Cuban is alike busy in carrying devastation over fertile regions; murderous and revengeful decrees are issued and executed by both parties. Count Valmaseda and Colonel Boet, on the part of Spain, have each startled humanity and aroused the indignation of the civilized world by the execution, each, of a score of prisoners at a time, while General Quesada, the Cuban chief, coolly and with apparent unconsciousness of aught else than a proper act, has admitted the slaughter, by his own deliberate order, in one day, of upward of 650 prisoners of war.

A summary trial, with few, if any, escapes from conviction, followed by immediate execution, is the fate of those arrested on either side on suspicion of infidelity to the cause of the party making the arrest.

Whatever may be the sympathies of the people or of the Government

THE PERPETUAL CUBAN REVOLUTION

THE PERPETUAL CUBAN REVOLUTION

Cuba has played a large and interesting part in our history from the very earliest days. The article "Cuba," in the index (volume eleven), succinctly presents the salient facts regarding her natural resources, her history and her present condition. She was a bone of contention in our domestic politics. The South, represented by the Democratic party, was bent on annexing her; proffers were made of money to insolvent Spain, only to be spurned; if gold will not buy, force of arms must conquer, was the motto. With the encouragement of the South, filibustering expeditions were fitted out, and with the connivance of traitorous Southern agents of the Federal Government, escaped the vigilance of our cruisers only to be snapped up by the watchful Spaniards. Such violations of our treaties were likely to bring on war; far from dreading such a result, the South would have welcomed it with glee, for then the doctrine of "manifest destiny" with which they sought to palliate our unjust war on Mexico, would cloak the robbing of Cuba from Spain. Why did the South want Cuba? Simply because if annexed two or three new slave states could be created, four or six new slave Senators be elected, and their vanishing domination in Congress be restored. The illustrations are contemporary and truthful representations of scenes in the Cuban insurrection of 1868–1877. The post-bellum view of Cuban affairs will be found by consulting the discussions of the matter by the Presidents from Grant to McKinley, on the pages cited by the index under the heading "Cuba." On page 2701 President Fillmore states the reasons against annexation, and on page 3041 President Buchanan recommends it.

of the United States for the cause or objects for which a part of the people of Cuba are understood to have put themselves in armed resistance to the Government of Spain, there can be no just sympathy in a conflict carried on by both parties alike in such barbarous violation of the rules of civilized nations and with such continued outrage upon the plainest principles of humanity.

We can not discriminate in our censure of their mode of conducting their contest between the Spaniards and the Cubans. Each commit the same atrocities and outrage alike the established rules of war.

The properties of many of our citizens have been destroyed or embargoed, the lives of several have been sacrificed, and the liberty of others has been restrained. In every case that has come to the knowledge of the Government an early and earnest demand for reparation and indemnity has been made, and most emphatic remonstrance has been presented against the manner in which the strife is conducted and against the reckless disregard of human life, the wanton destruction of material wealth, and the cruel disregard of the established rules of civilized warfare.

I have, since the beginning of the present session of Congress, communicated to the House of Representatives, upon their request, an account of the steps which I had taken in the hope of bringing this sad conflict to an end and of securing to the people of Cuba the blessings and the right of independent self-government. The efforts thus made failed, but not without an assurance from Spain that the good offices of this Government might still avail for the objects to which they had been addressed.

During the whole contest the remarkable exhibition has been made of large numbers of Cubans escaping from the island and avoiding the risks of war; congregating in this country, at a safe distance from the scene of danger, and endeavoring to make war from our shores, to urge our people into the fight which they avoid, and to embroil this Government in complications and possible hostilities with Spain. It can scarce be doubted that this last result is the real object of these parties, although carefully covered under the deceptive and apparently plausible demand for a mere recognition of belligerency.

It is stated on what I have reason to regard as good authority that Cuban bonds have been prepared to a large amount, whose payment is made dependent upon the recognition by the United States of either Cuban belligerency or independence. The object of making their value thus contingent upon the action of this Government is a subject for serious reflection.

In determining the course to be adopted on the demand thus made for a recognition of belligerency the liberal and peaceful principles adopted by the Father of his Country and the eminent statesmen of his day, and followed by succeeding Chief Magistrates and the men of their day, may furnish a safe guide to those of us now charged with the direction and control of the public safety.

From 1789 to 1815 the dominant thought of our statesmen was to keep the United States out of the wars which were devastating Europe. The discussion of measures of neutrality begins with the State papers of Mr. Jefferson when Secretary of State. He shows that they are measures of national right as well as of national duty; that misguided individual citizens can not be tolerated in making war according to their own caprice, passions, interests, or foreign sympathies; that the agents of foreign governments, recognized or unrecognized, can not be permitted to abuse our hospitality by usurping the functions of enlisting or equipping military or naval forces within our territory. Washington inaugurated the policy of neutrality and of absolute abstinence from all foreign entangling alliances, which resulted, in 1794, in the first municipal enactment for the observance of neutrality.

The duty of opposition to filibustering has been admitted by every President. Washington encountered the efforts of Genêt and of the French revolutionists; John Adams, the projects of Miranda; Jefferson, the schemes of Aaron Burr. Madison and subsequent Presidents had to deal with the question of foreign enlistment or equipment in the United States, and since the days of John Quincy Adams it has been one of the constant cares of Government in the United States to prevent piratical expeditions against the feeble Spanish American Republics from leaving our shores. In no country are men wanting for any enterprise that holds out promise of adventure or of gain.

In the early days of our national existence the whole continent of America (outside of the limits of the United States) and all its islands were in colonial dependence upon European powers.

The revolutions which from 1810 spread almost simultaneously through all the Spanish American continental colonies resulted in the establishment of new States, like ourselves, of European origin, and interested in excluding European politics and the questions of dynasty and of balances of power from further influence in the New World.

The American policy of neutrality, important before, became doubly so from the fact that it became applicable to the new Republics as well as to the mother country.

It then devolved upon us to determine the great international question at what time and under what circumstances to recognize a new power as entitled to a place among the family of nations, as well as the preliminary question of the attitude to be observed by this Government toward the insurrectionary party pending the contest.

Mr. Monroe concisely expressed the rule which has controlled the action of this Government with reference to revolting colonies pending their struggle by saying:

As soon as the movement assumed such a steady and consistent form as to make the success of the Provinces probable, the rights to which they were entitled by the laws of nations as equal parties to a civil war were extended to them.

The strict adherence to this rule of public policy has been one of the highest honors of American statesmanship, and has secured to this Government the confidence of the feeble powers on this continent, which induces them to rely upon its friendship and absence of designs of conquest and to look to the United States for example and moral protection. It has given to this Government a position of prominence and of influence which it should not abdicate, but which imposes upon it the most delicate duties of right and of honor regarding American questions, whether those questions affect emancipated colonies or colonies still subject to European dominion.

The question of belligerency is one of fact, not to be decided by sympathies for or prejudices against either party. The relations between the parent state and the insurgents must amount in fact to war in the sense of international law. Fighting, though fierce and protracted, does not alone constitute war. There must be military forces acting in accordance with the rules and customs of war, flags of truce, cartels, exchange of prisoners, etc.; and to justify a recognition of belligerency there must be, above all, a *de facto* political organization of the insurgents sufficient in character and resources to constitute it, if left to itself, a state among nations capable of discharging the duties of a state and of meeting the just responsibilities it may incur as such toward other powers in the discharge of its national duties.

Applying the best information which I have been enabled to gather, whether from official or unofficial sources, including the very exaggerated statements which each party gives to all that may prejudice the opposite or give credit to its own side of the question, I am unable to see in the present condition of the contest in Cuba those elements which are requisite to constitute war in the sense of international law.

The insurgents hold no town or city; have no established seat of government; they have no prize courts; no organization for the receiving and collecting of revenue; no seaport to which a prize may be carried or through which access can be had by a foreign power to the limited interior territory and mountain fastnesses which they occupy. The existence of a legislature representing any popular constituency is more than doubtful.

In the uncertainty that hangs around the entire insurrection there is no palpable evidence of an election, of any delegated authority, or of any government outside the limits of the camps occupied from day to day by the roving companies of insurgent troops; there is no commerce, no trade, either internal or foreign, no manufactures.

The late commander in chief of the insurgents, having recently come to the United States, publicly declared that "all commercial intercourse or trade with the exterior world has been utterly cut off;" and he further added: "To-day we have not 10,000 arms in Cuba."

It is a well-established principle of public law that a recognition by a foreign state of belligerent rights to insurgents under circumstances such as now exist in Cuba, if not justified by necessity, is a gratuitous demonstration of moral support to the rebellion. Such necessity may yet hereafter arrive, but it has not yet arrived, nor is its probability clearly to be seen.

If it be war between Spain and Cuba, and be so recognized, it is our duty to provide for the consequences which may ensue in the embarrassment to our commerce and the interference with our revenue.

If belligerency be recognized, the commercial marine of the United States becomes liable to search and to seizure by the commissioned cruisers of both parties; they become subject to the adjudication of prize courts.

Our large coastwise trade between the Atlantic and the Gulf States and between both and the Isthmus of Panama and the States of South America (engaging the larger part of our commercial marine) passes of necessity almost in sight of the island of Cuba. Under the treaty with Spain of 1795, as well as by the law of nations, our vessels will be liable to visit on the high seas. In case of belligerency the carrying of contraband, which now is lawful, becomes liable to the risks of seizure and condemnation. The parent Government becomes relieved from responsibility for acts done in the insurgent territory, and acquires the right to exercise against neutral commerce all the powers of a party to a maritime war. To what consequences the exercise of those powers may lead is a question which I desire to commend to the serious consideration of Congress.

In view of the gravity of this question, I have deemed it my duty to invite the attention of the war-making power of the country to all the relations and bearings of the question in connection with the declaration of neutrality and granting of belligerent rights.

There is not a *de facto* government in the island of Cuba sufficient to execute law and maintain just relations with other nations. Spain has not been able to suppress the opposition to Spanish rule on the island, nor to award speedy justice to other nations, or citizens of other nations, when their rights have been invaded.

There are serious complications growing out of the seizure of American vessels upon the high seas, executing American citizens without proper trial, and confiscating or embargoing the property of American citizens. Solemn protests have been made against every infraction of the rights either of individual citizens of the United States or the rights of our flag upon the high seas, and all proper steps have been taken and are being pressed for the proper reparation of every indignity complained of.

The question of belligerency, however, which is to be decided upon definite principles and according to ascertained facts, is entirely different from and unconnected with the other questions of the manner in which the strife is carried on on both sides and the treatment of our citizens entitled to our protection.

The questions concern our own dignity and responsibility, and they have been made, as I have said, the subjects of repeated communications with Spain and of protests and demands for redress on our part. It is hoped that these will not be disregarded, but should they be these questions will be made the subject of a further communication to Congress.

U. S. GRANT.

EXECUTIVE MANSION, *June 17, 1870.*

To the Senate of the United States:

In answer to the resolution of the Senate of the 8th instant, requesting the President "to communicate, in confidence, the instructions of the Navy Department to the navy officers in command on the coast of Dominica and Hayti, and the reports of such officers to the Navy Department, from the commencement of the negotiation of the treaty with Dominica," I herewith transmit the papers received from the Secretary of the Navy, to whom the resolution was referred.

U. S. GRANT.

EXECUTIVE MANSION, *June 25, 1870.*

To the Senate of the United States:

In answer to the resolution of the 22d instant, requesting to be furnished with "proposals received from any company or citizens of the United States for constructing and placing iron steamships in transatlantic service," I transmit herewith the only proposal of that nature received by me.

U. S. GRANT.

WASHINGTON, *July 9, 1870.*

To the Senate of the United States:

In answer to the resolutions of the Senate of the 26th of May and of the 14th of June last, I transmit a report from the Secretary of State thereupon, and the papers* by which it was accompanied.

U. S. GRANT.

WASHINGTON, *July 12, 1870.*

To the Senate of the United States:

I transmit to the Senate, for consideration with a view to ratification, a convention between the United States and Austria, concerning the

---

*Lists of American vessels seized by Spanish authorities in Cuba; of American citizens executed and imprisoned in Cuba; of American citizens whose property was confiscated or embargoed in Cuba, and of decrees under which the Spanish authorities acted, and correspondence showing steps taken by the United States Government in reference thereto.

rights, privileges, and immunities of consuls in the two countries, signed at Washington on the 11th instant.

                                               U. S. GRANT.

WASHINGTON, *July 13, 1870.*

To the Senate of the United States:

I transmit to the Senate, in answer to their resolution of the 8th instant, a report from the Secretary of State and the papers* which accompanied it.

                                               U. S. GRANT.

WASHINGTON, *July 13, 1870.*

To the Senate of the United States:

In answer to their resolution of the 8th instant, I transmit to the Senate a report from the Secretary of State and the papers† which accompanied it.

                                               U. S. GRANT.

WASHINGTON, *July 14, 1870.*

To the Senate of the United States:

I transmit to the Senate, in answer to their resolution of the 7th instant, a report from the Secretary of State, with accompanying documents.

                                               U. S. GRANT.

DEPARTMENT OF STATE,
Washington, July 14, 1870.

The Secretary of State, to whom was referred the resolution of the Senate requesting the President "to institute an inquiry, by such means as in his judgment shall be deemed proper, into the present condition of the commercial relations between the United States and the Spanish American States on this continent, and between those countries and other nations, and to communicate to the Senate full and complete statements regarding the same, together with such recommendations as he may think necessary to promote the development and increase of our commerce with those regions and to secure to the United States that proportionate share of the trade of this continent to which their close relations of geographical contiguity and political friendship with all the States of America justly entitle them," has the honor to report:

The resolution justly regards the commercial and the political relations of the United States with the American States of Spanish origin as necessarily dependent upon each other. If the commerce of those countries has been diverted from its natural connection with the United States, the fact may probably be partly traced to political causes, which have been swept away by the great civil convulsion in this country.

For the just comprehension of the position of this Government in the American political system, and for the causes which have failed to give it hitherto the influence

---

* Instructions to the minister to Spain stating the basis on which the United States offered its good offices for the purpose of terminating the war in Cuba, correspondence relative thereto, etc.

† Correspondence between the United States and Great Britain concerning questions pending between the two countries.

to which it is properly entitled by reason of its democratic system and of the moderation and sense of justice which have distinguished its foreign policy through successive Administrations from the birth of the nation until now, it is necessary to make a brief notice of such measures as affect our present relations to the other parts of this continent.

The United States were the first of the European colonies in America to arrive at maturity as a people and assume the position of an independent republic. Since then important changes have taken place in various nations and in every part of the world. Our own growth in power has been not the least remarkable of all the great events of modern history.

When, at the conclusion of the Revolutionary War, having conquered by arms our right to exist as a sovereign state, that right was at length recognized by treaties, we occupied only a narrow belt of land along the Atlantic coast, hemmed in at the north, the west, and the south by the possessions of European Governments, or by uncultivated wastes beyond the Alleghanies, inhabited only by the aborigines. But in the very infancy of the United States far-sighted statesmen saw and predicted that, weak in population and apparently restricted in available territory as the new Republic then was, it had within it the germs of colossal grandeur, and would at no remote day occupy the continent of America with its institutions, its authority, and its peaceful influence.

That expectation has been thus far signally verified. The United States entered at once into the occupation of their rightful possessions westward to the banks of the Mississippi. Next, by the spontaneous proffer of France, they acquired Louisiana and its territorial extension, or right of extension, north to the line of the treaty demarcation between France and Great Britain, and west to the Pacific Ocean. Next, by amicable arrangement with Spain, they acquired the Floridas, and complete southern maritime frontiers upon the Gulf of Mexico. Then came the union with the independent State of Texas, followed by the acquisitions of California and New Mexico, and then of Arizona. Finally, Russia has ceded to us Alaska, and the continent of North America has become independent of Europe, except so much of it as continues to maintain political relations with Great Britain.

Meanwhile, partly by natural increase and partly by voluntary immigration from Europe, our population has risen from 3,000,000 to nearly 40,000,000; the number of States and Territories united under the Constitution has been augmented from thirteen to forty-seven; the development of internal wealth and power has kept pace with political expansion; we have occupied in part and peopled the vast interior of the continent; we have bound the Pacific to the Atlantic by a chain of intervening States and organized Territories; we have delivered the Republic from the anomaly and the ignominy of domestic servitude; we have constitutionally fixed the equality of all races and of all men before the law; and we have established, at the cost of a great civil war—a cost, however, not beyond the value of such a result—the indissoluble national unity of the United States.

In all these marked stages of national progress, from the Declaration of Independence to the recent amendments of the Constitution, it is impossible not to perceive a providential series and succession of events, intimately attached one to the other, and possessed of definite character as a whole, whatever incidental departures from such uniformity may have marked, or seemed to mark, our foreign policy under the influence of temporary causes or of the conflicting opinions of statesmen.

In the time of Washington, of the first Adams, of Jefferson, and of Madison the condition of Europe, engaged in the gigantic wars of the French Revolution and of the Empire, produced its series of public questions and gave tone and color to our foreign policy. In the time of Monroe, of the second Adams, and of Jackson, and subsequently thereto, the independence of the Spanish and Portuguese colonies of America produced its series of questions and its apparent modification of our public policy. Domestic questions of territorial organization, of social emancipation, and of national unity have also largely occupied the minds and the attention of the later Administrations.

The treaties of alliance and guaranty with France, which contributed so much to our independence, were one source of solicitude to the early Administrations, which were endeavoring to protect our commerce from the depredations and wrongs to which the maritime policy of England and the reaction of that policy on France subjected it. For twenty years we struggled in vain to accomplish this, and at last drifted into war.

The avoidance of entangling alliances, the characteristic feature of the foreign policy of Washington, sprang from this condition of things. But the entangling alliances which then existed were engagements made with France as a part of the general contract under which aid was furnished to us for the achievement of our independence. France was willing to waive the letter of the obligation as to her West India possessions, but demanded in its stead privileges in our ports which the Administration was unwilling to concede. To make its refusal acceptable to a public which sympathized with France, the Cabinet of General Washington exaggerated the principle into a theory tending to national isolation.

The public measures designed to maintain unimpaired the domestic sovereignty and the international neutrality of the United States were independent of this policy, though apparently incidental to it. The municipal laws enacted by Congress then and since have been but declarations of the law of nations. They are essential to the preservation of our national dignity and honor; they have for their object to repress and punish all enterprises of private war, one of the last relics of mediæval barbarism; and they have descended to us from the fathers of the Republic, supported and enforced by every succeeding President of the United States.

The foreign policy of these early days was not a narrow one. During this period we secured the evacuation by Great Britain of the country wrongfully occupied by her on the Lakes; we acquired Louisiana; we measured forces on the sea with France, and on the land and sea with England; we set the example of resisting and chastising the piracies of the Barbary States; we initiated in negotiations with Prussia the long line of treaties for the liberalization of war and the promotion of international intercourse; and we steadily demanded, and at length obtained, indemnification from various governments for the losses we had suffered by foreign spoliations in the wars of Europe.

To this point in our foreign policy we had arrived when the revolutionary movements in Spanish and Portuguese America compelled a modification of our relations with Europe, in consequence of the rise of new and independent states in America.

The revolution which commenced in 1810, and extended through all the Spanish American continental colonies, after vain efforts of repression on the part of Spain, protracted through twenty years, terminated in the establishment of the independent States of Mexico, Guatemala, San Salvador, Honduras, Nicaragua, Costa Rica, Venezuela, Colombia, Ecuador, Peru, Chile, Bolivia, the Argentine Republic, Uruguay, and Paraguay, to which the Empire of Brazil came in time to be added. These events necessarily enlarged the sphere of action of the United States, and essentially modified our relations with Europe and our attitude to the rest of this continent.

The new States were, like ourselves, revolted colonies. They continued the precedent we had set, of separating from Europe. Their assumption of independence was stimulated by our example. They professedly imitated us, and copied our National Constitution, sometimes even to their inconvenience.

The Spanish American colonies had not the same preparation for independence that we had. Each of the British colonies possessed complete local autonomy. Its formal transition from dependence to independence consisted chiefly in expelling the British governor of the colony and electing a governor of the State, from which to the organized Union was but a step. All these conditions of success were wanting in Spanish America, and hence many of the difficulties in their career as independent states; and, further, while the revolution in British America was the exclusive result of the march of opinion in the British colonies, the simultaneous action of the separate Spanish colonies, though showing a desire for independence, was principally produced by the accident of the invasion of Spain by France.

The formation of these new sovereignties in America was important to us, not only because of the cessation of colonial monopolies to that extent, but because of the geographical relations to us held by so many new nations, all, like ourselves, created from European stock and interested in excluding European politics, dynastic questions, and balances of power from further influence in the New World.

Thus the United States were forced into new lines of action, which, though apparently in some respects conflicting, were really in harmony with the line marked out by Washington. The avoidance of entangling political alliances and the maintenance of our own independent neutrality became doubly important from the fact that they became applicable to the new Republics as well as to the mother country. The duty of noninterference had been admitted by every President. The question came up in the time of the first Adams, on the occasion of the enlistment projects of Miranda. It appeared again under Jefferson (anterior to the revolt of the Spanish colonies) in the schemes of Aaron Burr. It was an ever-present question in the Administrations of Madison, Monroe, and the younger Adams, in reference to the questions of foreign enlistment or equipment in the United States, and when these new Republics entered the family of nations, many of them very feeble, and all too much subject to internal revolution and civil war, a strict adherence to our previous policy and a strict enforcement of our laws became essential to the preservation of friendly relations with them; for since that time it has been one of the principal cares of those intrusted with the administration of the Government to prevent piratical expeditions against these sister Republics from leaving our ports. And thus the changed condition of the New World made no change in the traditional and peaceful policy of the United States in this respect.

In one respect, however, the advent of these new States in America did compel an apparent change of foreign policy on our part. It devolved upon us the determination of the great international question at what time and under what circumstances to recognize a new power as entitled to a place among the family of nations. There was but little of precedent to guide us, except our own case. Something, indeed, could be inferred from the historical origin of the Netherlands and Switzerland. But our own case, carefully and conscientiously considered, was sufficient to guide us to right conclusions. We maintained our position of international friendship and of treaty obligations toward Spain, but we did not consider that we were bound to wait for its recognition of the new Republics before admitting them into treaty relations with us as sovereign states. We held that it was for us to judge whether or not they had attained to the condition of actual independence, and the consequent right of recognition by us. We considered this question of fact deliberately and coolly. We sent commissioners to Spanish America to ascertain and report for our information concerning their actual circumstances, and in the fullness of time we acknowledged their independence; we exchanged diplomatic ministers, and made treaties of amity with them, the earliest of which, negotiated by Mr. John Quincy Adams, served as the model for the subsequent treaties with the Spanish American Republics. We also, simultaneously therewith, exerted our good offices with Spain to induce her to submit to the inevitable result and herself to accept and acknowledge the independence of her late colonies. We endeavored to induce Russia to join us in these representations. In all this our action was positive, in the direction of promoting the complete political separation of America from Europe.

A vast field was thus opened to the statesmen of the United States for the peaceful

Messages and Papers of the Presidents

introduction, the spread, and the permanent establishment of the American ideas of republican government, of modification of the laws of war, of liberalization of commerce, of religious freedom and toleration, and of the emancipation of the New World from the dynastic and balance of power controversies of Europe.

Mr. John Quincy Adams, beyond any other statesman of the time in this country, had the knowledge and experience, both European and American, the comprehension of thought and purpose, and the moral convictions which peculiarly fitted him to introduce our country into this new field and to lay the foundation of an American policy. The declaration known as the Monroe doctrine, and the objects and purposes of the congress of Panama, both supposed to have been largely inspired by Mr. Adams, have influenced public events from that day to this as a principle of government for this continent and its adjacent islands.

It was at the period of the congress of Aix-la-Chapelle and of Laybach, when the "Holy Alliance" was combined to arrest all political changes in Europe in the sense of liberty, when they were intervening in southern Europe for the reestablishment of absolutism, and when they were meditating interference to check the progress of free government in America, that Mr. Monroe, in his annual message of December, 1823, declared that the United States would consider any attempt to extend the European system to any portion of this hemisphere as dangerous to our peace and safety. "With the existing colonies or dependencies of any European power," he said, "we have not interfered and shall not interfere; but with the governments who have declared their independence and maintained it, and whose independence we have, on great consideration and on just principles, acknowledged, we could not view any interposition for the purpose of oppressing them, or controlling in any other manner their destiny, by any European power in any other light than as the manifestation of an unfriendly disposition toward the United States."

This declaration resolved the solution of the immediate question of the independence of the Spanish American colonies, and is supposed to have exercised some influence upon the course of the British cabinet in regard to the absolutist schemes in Europe as well as in America.

It has also exercised a permanent influence on this continent. It was at once invoked in consequence of the supposed peril of Cuba on the side of Europe; it was applied to a similar danger threatening Yucatan; it was embodied in the treaty of the United States and Great Britain as to Central America; it produced the successful opposition of the United States to the attempt of Great Britain to exercise dominion in Nicaragua under the cover of the Mosquito Indians; and it operated in like manner to prevent the establishment of a European dynasty in Mexico.

The United States stand solemnly committed by repeated declarations and repeated acts to this doctrine, and its application to the affairs of this continent. In his message to the two Houses of Congress at the commencement of the present session the President, following the teachings of all our history, said that the existing "dependencies are no longer regarded as subject to transfer from one European power to another. When the present relation of colonies ceases, they are to become independent powers, exercising the right of choice and of self-control in the determination of their future condition and relations with other powers."

This policy is not a policy of aggression; but it opposes the creation of European dominion on American soil, or its transfer to other European powers, and it looks hopefully to the time when, by the voluntary departure of European Governments from this continent and the adjacent islands, America shall be wholly American.

It does not contemplate forcible intervention in any legitimate contest, but it protests against permitting such a contest to result in the increase of European power or influence; and it ever impels this Government, as in the late contest between the South American Republics and Spain, to interpose its good offices to secure an honorable peace.

The congress of Panama was planned by Bolivar to secure the union of Spanish America against Spain. It had originally military as well as political purposes. In the military objects the United States could take no part; and, indeed, the necessity for such objects ceased when the full effects of Mr. Monroe's declarations were felt. But the pacific objects of the congress—the establishment of close and cordial relations of amity, the creation of commercial intercourse, of interchange of political thought, and of habits of good understanding between the new Republics and the United States and their respective citizens—might perhaps have been attained had the Administration of that day received the united support of the country. Unhappily, they were lost; the new States were removed from the sympathetic and protecting influence of our example, and their commerce, which we might then have secured, passed into other hands, unfriendly to the United States.

In looking back upon the Panama congress from this length of time it is easy to understand why the earnest and patriotic men who endeavored to crystallize an American system for this continent failed.

Mr. Clay and Mr. Adams were far-sighted statesmen, but, unfortunately, they struck against the rock of African slavery. One of the questions proposed for discussion in the conference was "the consideration of the means to be adopted for the entire abolition of the African slave trade," to which proposition the committee of the United States Senate of that day replied: "The United States have not certainly the right, and ought never to feel the inclination, to dictate to others who may differ with them upon this subject; nor do the committee see the expediency of insulting other states with whom we are maintaining relations of perfect amity by ascending the moral chair and proclaiming from thence mere abstract principles, of the rectitude of which each nation enjoys the perfect right of deciding for itself." The same committee also alluded to the possibility that the condition of the islands of Cuba and Porto Rico, still the possessions of Spain and still slaveholding, might be made the subject of discussion and of contemplated action by the Panama congress. "If ever the United States," they said, "permit themselves to be associated with these nations in any general congress assembled for the discussion of common plans in any way affecting European interests, they will by such act not only deprive themselves of the ability they now possess of rendering useful assistance to the other American States, but also produce other effects prejudicial to their own interests."

Thus the necessity at that day of preserving the great interest of the Southern States in African slavery, and of preventing a change in the character of labor in the islands of Cuba and Porto Rico, lost to the United States the opportunity of giving a permanent direction to the political and commercial connections of the newly enfranchised Spanish American States, and their trade passed into hands unfriendly to the United States, and has remained there ever since.

Events subsequent to that date have tended to place us in a position to retrieve our mistakes, among which events may be particularly named the suppression of the rebellion, the manifestation of our undeveloped and unexpected military power, the retirement of the French from Mexico, and the abolition of slavery in the United States.

There is good reason to believe that the latter fact has had an important influence in our favor in Spanish America. It has caused us to be regarded there with more sympathetic as well as more respectful consideration. It has relieved those Republics from the fear of filibusterism which had been formerly incited against Central America and Mexico in the interest of slave extension, and it has produced an impression of the stability of our institutions and of our public strength sufficient to dissipate the fears of our friends or the hopes of those who wish us ill.

Thus there exists in the Spanish American Republics confidence toward the United States. On our side they find a feeling of cordial amity and friendship, and a desire to cultivate and develop our common interests on this continent. With some of these States our relations are more intimate than with others, either by reason of closer similarity of constitutional forms, of greater commercial intercourse, of proximity in fact, or of the construction or contemplated construction of lines of transit for our trade and commerce between the Atlantic and the Pacific. With several of them we have peculiar treaty relations. The treaty of 1846 between the United States and New Granada contains stipulations of guaranty for the neutrality of that part of the Isthmus within the present territory of Colombia, and for the protection of the rights of sovereignty and property therein belonging to Colombia. Similar stipulations appear in the treaty of 1867 with Nicaragua, and of July, 1864, with Honduras. Those treaties (like the treaty of alliance made with France in 1778 by Dr. Franklin, Silas Deane, and Arthur Lee) constitute *pro tanto* a true protective alliance between the United States and each of those Republics. Provisions of like effect appear in the treaty of April 19, 1850, between Great Britain and the United States.

Brazil, with her imperial semblance and constitutional reality, has always held relations of amity with us, which have been fortified by the opening of her great rivers to commerce. It needs only that, in emulation of Russia and the United States, she should emancipate her slaves to place her in more complete sympathy with the rest of America.

It will not be presumptuous, after the foregoing sketch, to say, with entire consideration for the sovereignty and national pride of the Spanish American Republics, that the United States, by the priority of their independence, by the stability of their institutions, by the regard of their people for the forms of law, by their resources as a government, by their naval power, by their commercial enterprise, by the attractions which they offer to European immigration, by the prodigious internal development of their resources and wealth, and by the intellectual life of their population, occupy of necessity a prominent position on this continent, which they neither can nor should abdicate, which entitles them to a leading voice, and which imposes upon them duties of right and of honor regarding American questions, whether those questions affect emancipated colonies or colonies still subject to European dominion.

The public questions which existed as to all European colonies prior to and during the revolutions in the continental colonies of Spain and Portugal still exist with reference to the European colonies which remain; and they now return upon us in full force, as we watch events in Cuba and Porto Rico.

Whatever may be the result of the pending contest in Cuba, it appears to be the belief of some of the leading statesmen of Spain that the relations which now exist between the island and the mother country can not be long continued. It is understood that the resources for carrying on the struggle have been supplied mainly from Cuba, by the aid of that portion of the population which does not desire to see its political destinies intrusted to the persons who direct the movements of the insurgents; but it does not follow that its political relations with Spain are to remain unchanged, or that even the party which is now dominant in the island will wish to forever continue colonists.

These facts give reason to think that when the contest shall close, Cuba, with her resources strained, but unexhausted (whatever may be her political relations), will resume and continue her old commercial relations with the United States; and it is not impossible that at some day, not far distant when measured by the course of history, she will be called upon to elect her position in the family of nations.

Although the resolution of the Senate does not in terms apply to the islands of the Antilles, it is impossible to answer it without speaking of them. They outlie the southern coast of the United States and guard the approaches to the ports of Mexico, Venezuela, and the Isthmus, by which we reach from the east the western coasts of Mexico and of the Spanish States. The people of the Spanish islands speak the language and share the traditions, customs, ideas, and religion of the Spanish American States of the continent, and will probably, like them, become at some time independent of the mother country. It would, therefore, be unwise, while shaping a commercial policy for the continent, to disregard the islands which lie so much nearer to our seaports.

With the Spanish islands of Cuba and Porto Rico we maintain, in spite of their adverse legislation, a large commerce by reason of our necessities and of their proximity. In the year ending June 30, 1869, we imported from them merchandise valued at $65,609,274. During the same time we sent them goods to the value only of $15,313,919.

The prohibitory duties forced upon them by the policy of Spain shut out much that we might supply. Their tropical productions, for instance, are too valuable to allow their lands to be given up to the growth of breadstuffs; yet, instead of taking these articles from the superabundant fields of their nearest neighbors, they are forced to go to the distant plains of Spain. It will be for the interest of the United States to shape its general policy so that this relation of imports and exports shall be altered in Cuba when peace is restored and its political condition is satisfactorily established.

With none of the other Spanish American States in North and South America are our commercial relations what they should be. Our total imports in the year ending June 30, 1869, from these countries were less than $25,000,000 (or not one-half the amount from Cuba alone), and our exports for the same time to them were only $17,850,313; and yet these countries have an aggregate population nearly or quite as great as that of the United States; they have republican forms of government, and they profess to be, and probably really are, in political sympathy with us.

This Department is not able to give with entire accuracy the imports and exports of Great Britain with the same countries during the corresponding period. It is believed, however, the following figures will be found to be not far from correct: Imports to Great Britain, $42,820,942; exports from Great Britain, $40,682,102.

It thus appears that notwithstanding the greater distance which the commerce has to travel in coming to and from Great Britain, notwithstanding the political sympathy which ought naturally to exist between republics, notwithstanding the American idea which has been so prominently and so constantly put forward by the Government of the United States, notwithstanding the acknowledged skill of American manufacturers, notwithstanding the ready markets which the great cities of the United States afford for the consumption of tropical productions, the inhabitants of the Spanish American continent consume of the products of Great Britain more than twice the quantity they take of the products of the United States, and that they sell to us only three-fifths of the amount they sell to Great Britain.

The Secretary of State appends to this report the tables on which these statements are founded. That their commerce with the United States is not large may be partially explained by the fact that these States have been subject to many successive revolutions since the failure of the congress of Panama. These revolutions not only exhaust their resources and burden them with debt, but they check emigration, prevent the flow of foreign capital into the country, and stop the enterprise which needs a stable government for its development.

These suggestions are, however, applicable to the British commerce as well as to our own, and they do not explain why we, with the natural advantages in our favor, fall so far behind. The Isthmus of Panama is the common point where the commerce of the western coasts of Mexico and South America meets. When it arrives there, why should it seek Liverpool and London rather than New York?

The political causes which have operated to divert this commerce from us the Secretary of State has endeavored to explain. A favorable time has now come for removing them—for laying the foundation of an American policy which shall bind in closer union the American Republics. Let them understand that the United States do not covet their territories; that our only desire is to see them peaceful, with free and stable governments, increasing in wealth and population, and developing in the lines in which their own traditions, customs, habits, laws, and modes of thought will naturally take them. Let them feel that, as in 1826, so now, this Government is ready to aid them to the full extent of its constitutional power in any steps which they may take for their better protection against anarchy. Let them be convinced that the United States is prepared, in good faith and without ulterior purposes, to join them in the development of a peaceful American commercial policy that may in time include this continent and the West Indian Islands. Let this be comprehended, and there will be no political reason why we may not "secure to the United States that proportionate share of the trade of this continent to which their close relations of geographical contiguity and political friendship with all the States of America justly entitle them."

It may not be enough to remove the political obstacles only. The financial policy which the war made necessary may have operated injuriously upon our commerce with these States. The resolution of the Senate calls, on these points, for detailed information which is not within the control of the Secretary of State, and for recommendations for the future which he is not prepared to give without that information. To fully answer the Senate's call, it would probably be necessary to employ some competent agent, familiar with the Spanish American States, to collate and arrange the information asked for. For this there is no appropriation by Congress.

Respectfully submitted.

HAMILTON FISH.

Commerce of the United States with the countries on this continent and adjacent islands for the year ended June 30, 1869.

[Compiled from the Annual Report on Commerce and Navigation.]

Countries.	Imports.	Exports.	Reexports.	Total exports.	Total commerce.
Dominion of Canada......	$30,353,010	$18,188,613	$2,858,782	$21,047,395	$51,400,405
All other British possessions in North America.	1,737,304	2,703,173	446,664	3,149,837	4,887,141
British West Indies	6,682,391	9,142,344	101,760	9,244,104	15,926,495
Total...............	38,772,705	30,034,130	3,407,206	33,441,336	72,214,041
Cuba.....................	58,201,374	12,643,955	7,064,787	19,708,742	77,910,116
Porto Rico	7,407,900	2,669,964	114,037	2,784,001	10,191,901
Total...............	65,609,274	15,313,919	7,178,824	22,492,743	88,102,017
French possessions in America.................	696,952	1,174,056	45,514	1,219,570	1,916,522
Danish West Indies.......	638,550	1,500,000	39,121	1,539,121	2,177,671
Dutch West Indies and Guiana..................	999,099	926,051	29,595	955,646	1,954,745
Hayti and San Domingo..	729,632	1,349,438	129,462	1,478,900	2,208,532
Sandwich Islands.........	1,298,065	700,962	86,665	787,627	2,085,712
Total...............	4,362,318	5,650,507	330,357	5,980,864	10,343,182
Mexico...................	7,232,006	3,836,699	1,047,408	4,884,107	12,116,113
Central American States.	733,296	1,324,336	52,146	1,376,482	2,109,778
Colombia.................	5,291,706	4,900,075	180,267	5,080,342	10,372,048
Peru	1,386,310	1,556,434	116,911	1,673,445	3,059,755
Chile....................	1,186,982	1,969,580	115,905	2,085,485	3,272,467
Argentine Republic	5,162,966	2,235,089	272,425	2,507,514	7,670,480
Uruguay	1,472,608	835,112	58,270	894,382	2,366,990
Brazil	24,912,450	5,910,565	158,514	6,069,079	30,981,529
Venezuela................	2,431,760	1,191,888	29,176	1,221,064	3,652,824
Total...............	49,810,084	23,760,878	2,031,022	25,791,900	75,601,984
Grand total	158,554,381	74,759,434	12,947,409	87,706,843	246,261,224
Total commerce of United States	437,314,255	413,954,615	25,173,414	439,128,029	876,442,284

Imports and exports of Great Britain with Spanish America and some of the West India Islands for parts of the years 1868 and 1869.

	Year.	Imports.	Exports.
Cuba and Porto Rico...................	1869	£3, 228, 292	£1, 374, 242
French possessions in America.......	1868	4, 252	3, 002
Danish West Indies...................	1868	295, 102	9, 211
Dutch West Indies and Guiana.......	1868	148, 882	4, 444
Hayti and San Domingo..............	1868	220, 806	6, 043
Sandwich Islands	1868	33, 336	917
Mexico	1868	350, 664	92, 077
Central American States..............	1868	939, 827	173, 611
Colombia	1869	971, 396	2, 500, 039
Peru	1869	2, 734, 784	1, 180, 931
Chile	1869	3, 211, 174	1, 596, 905
Argentine Republic..................	1869	1, 034, 445	1, 841, 953
Uruguay.............................	1869	535, 015	1, 009, 425
Brazil...............................	1869	7, 754, 526	5, 477, 439
Venezuela	1868	69, 997	10, 452

WASHINGTON, *July 14, 1870.*

To the Senate of the United States:

I transmit, for the consideration of the Senate with a view to ratification, a convention between the United States and His Majesty the King of Sweden and Norway, relative to the citizenship of natives of the one country who may emigrate to the other. A protocol on the subject is also herewith transmitted.

U. S. GRANT.

WASHINGTON, *July 14, 1870.*

To the Senate of the United States:

I transmit, for consideration with a view to its ratification, a convention between the United States and the Republic of Salvador for the surrender of fugitive criminals, signed at San Salvador on the 23d day of May last.

U. S. GRANT.

WASHINGTON, D. C., *July 15, 1870.*

To the Senate and House of Representatives:

Your attention is respectfully called to the necessity of passing an Indian appropriation bill before the members of Congress separate. Without such appropriation Indian hostilities are sure to ensue, and with them suffering, loss of life, and expenditures vast as compared with the amount asked for.

The latest intelligence from Europe indicates the imminence of a war between France and North Germany. In view of this a sound policy indicates the importance of some legislation tending to enlarge the commercial marine of this country. The vessels of this country at the present time are insufficient to meet the demand which the existence of a war in Europe will impose upon the commerce of the United States, and I submit to the consideration of Congress that the interests of the country will be advanced by the opportunity afforded to our citizens to purchase vessels of foreign construction for the foreign trade of the country. An act to this effect may be limited in its duration to meet the immediate exigency.

The foreign-mail service of the United States is in a large degree dependent upon the Bremen and Hamburg lines of steamers. The Post-Office Department has entered into contracts in writing with the two companies above named, and with the Williams and Guion lines, respectively, for a regular and continuous service of two years. The only arrangement that could be made with the Inman and Cunard lines is temporary, and may be broken off at any time.

The North German lines are first class in point of speed and equipment, their steamers usually making the trip across the Atlantic in from twenty-four to thirty-six hours in advance of the Williams and Guion lines.

Should the North German steamers be blockaded or impeded by France, our postal intercourse with foreign nations will be greatly embarrassed unless Congress shall interpose for its relief.

I suggest to Congress the propriety of further postponing the time for adjournment, with the view of considering the questions herein communicated.

U. S. GRANT.

WASHINGTON, *July 15, 1870.*

To the Senate of the United States:

In answer to their resolution of the 9th instant, I transmit a report* from the Secretary of State and the papers which accompanied it.

U. S. GRANT.

VETO MESSAGES.

EXECUTIVE MANSION,
Washington, D. C., January 11, 1870.

To the Senate of the United States:

I return herewith without my approval Senate bill No. 273, entitled "An act for the relief of Rollin White," for the reasons set forth in the accompanying communication, dated December 11, 1869, from the Chief of Ordnance.

U. S. GRANT

*Relating to the importation of Chinese coolies into the United States

ORDNANCE OFFICE, WAR DEPARTMENT,
Washington, December 11, 1869.

Hon. W. W. BELKNAP,
    Secretary of War.

SIR: In the year 1855 Rollin White obtained letters patent for improvements in repeating pistols, in (among other things) extending the chambers of the rotating cylinder through to the rear, so as to enable the chambers to be charged at the rear by hand or by a self-acting charger.

Some time afterwards, and prior to the breaking out of the rebellion, he assigned this patent to Smith & Wesson, of Springfield, Mass., for the sum of $500 in cash and their obligation to pay him 25 cents royalty on each pistol manufactured under the patent, binding himself to apply for and to use his influence to procure a renewal of the patent. He afterwards surrendered this original patent and obtained a reissue in three divisions. Two years before the expiration of the latter he applied to the Commissioner of Patents for an extension, upon the ground of insufficiency of compensation. The Commissioner rejected the application for an extension, without assigning any reason, and the patents expired by limitation on the 3d of April, 1869, and the invention became public property.

On the 9th of April, 1869, a bill authorizing the Commissioner of Patents to reconsider the application of Rollin White for extension of his patents was introduced in the Senate and passed without debate. It passed the House without debate on the 10th of April, but failed to receive the signature of the Vice-President before Congress adjourned. It is understood that it has now been signed by that officer, and only awaits the approval of the President to become a law.

Unless the ends of justice require the extension of this patent, it should not be renewed. So far as I have been able to ascertain, justice to the Government and to the public forbids this patent from being renewed.

The validity of the patent has been questioned for many years, and it is understood that it was only affirmed by the Supreme Court by a tie vote, four of the justices voting affirmatively and an equal number negatively.

Its renewal is urged by Rollin White upon the ground that he has not been sufficiently compensated for his invention. Rollin White has received nearly $71,000 as royalty. Smith & Wesson, for the years 1862, 1863, 1864, 1865, 1866, 1867, and 1868, returned incomes amounting in the aggregate to about $1,000,000. This was derived chiefly from the manufacture of firearms under Rollin White's patent, that firm holding the exclusive right to manufacture under it and being engaged almost exclusively in their manufacture.

It is believed that the Government suffered inconvenience and embarrassment enough during the war in consequence of the inability of manufacturers to use this patent, and that its further extension will operate prejudicially to its interest by compelling it to pay to parties already well paid a large royalty for altering its revolvers to use metallic cartridges.

For these reasons I respectfully request that you will call the attention of the President of the United States to this subject before he acts upon the bill which is now before him.

Respectfully, your obedient servant,

A. B. DYER,
Brevet Major-General, Chief of Ordnance

EXECUTIVE MANSION, *July 14, 1870.*

To the Senate of the United States:

I herewith return without my approval Senate bill No. 476, "An act to fix the status of certain Federal soldiers enlisting in the Union Army from the States of Alabama and Florida," for the reasons embodied in the following facts, which have been obtained from the office of the Second Comptroller:

The First Regiment of Florida Cavalry, composed of six companies, was organized from December, 1862, to August, 1864, to serve three years. It was mustered out of service November 17, 1865, by reason of general order from the War Department discharging all cavalry organizations east of the Mississippi.

The men of this regiment enlisting prior to July 18, 1864, received $25 advance bounty at muster-in, and the discharged soldiers and heirs of those deceased have been paid the same bounty under act of July 22, 1861, joint resolution of January 13, 1864, an act of July 28, 1866, as men enlisted at the same time in other volunteer organizations.

The Second Regiment of Florida Cavalry, composed of seven companies, was organized from December, 1863, to June, 1864, to serve three years. It was mustered out November 29, 1865, by reason of the order discharging cavalry organizations east of the Mississippi. Most of the men received the $25 advance bounty at muster-in, and the discharged men and heirs of deceased men have received bounty under the several acts of Congress cited above, subject to the same conditions which apply to men who enlisted at the same time in other volunteer organizations.

The First Alabama Cavalry was originally organized as a one-year regiment from December, 1862, to September, 1863, and two companies of three-years men (Companies I and K) were added to complete its organization. These companies were formerly Companies D and E of the First Middle Tennessee Cavalry. Prior to the expiration of the term of the one-year men, the Adjutant-General of the Army, of date May 15, 1863, authorized General Dodge to fill up this command, and in accordance therewith the places of the companies discharged by reason of expiration of term were filled by companies of men enlisted for three years. The original companies, A, B, C, D, E, F, G, H, and L, were organized from December, 1862, to September 25, 1863, and were discharged by companies from December 22, 1863, to September 28, 1864, in order as the term (one year) of each company expired. Companies I and K, mustered in August, 1862, to serve three years, were discharged in July, 1865, by reason of expiration of term of service. As reorganized under the order above mentioned, the regiment consisted of Companies A, B, C, D, E, and G, organized from February 5, 1864, to October, 1864, to serve three years; Companies F, L, and M, organized from December 28, 1863, to October 31, 1864, to serve one and three years; Company H, organized in March and April, 1865, to serve three years, and Companies I and K, of the old organization described above. The men of the First Alabama Cavalry who enlisted for three years have been paid bounty under the several acts of Congress upon the same principles which apply to other three-years volunteers. The one-year men enlisted prior to July 18, 1864, received no bounty, but $100 bounty has been paid the proper heirs of the one-year men of this organization who died in the service, in accordance with the act of July 22, 1861, under which the regiment was originally organized.

Some of the men of these organizations were erroneously paid by the Pay Department at the time of their muster out of service, they having been paid but $100, when they should have been allowed $300 under the joint resolution of January 13, 1864. The balance of bounty due these men is being paid by the proper accounting officers. It will be seen by comparing the above statement with the act under consideration that the effect of the act will be to give the one-year men of the First Alabama Cavalry, nearly all of whom enlisted in 1862 and 1863, a bounty of $100 each, or a proportionate part, according to the time served. It would give each man of Companies I and K of the First Alabama Cavalry $100 more bounty. The bounty of the other three-years men of the First Alabama Cavalry, First Florida Cavalry, and Second Florida Cavalry, who enlisted prior to December 25, 1863, and from April 1, 1864, to July 17, 1864, inclusive, and who were discharged by reason of orders from the War Department, will not be affected.

The men enlisting in these organizations under joint resolution of January 13, 1864, receive under existing laws $100 more bounty than they would be entitled to receive if the act under consideration becomes a law.

In case of deceased men the working of the act is still more perplexing, as the prescribed order of inheritance under the act of July 4, 1864, is entirely different from that under all other acts.

A large proportion of the claims in case of the deceased men have been settled, and the bounties have been paid fathers, mothers, brothers, and sisters, the proper heirs under existing laws, which under this act would go only to the widow, children, and widowed mother. Bounty has also been paid to parents under act of July 28, 1866, which this act would require to be paid to the widow, although she may have remarried.

Under the act of July 28, 1866, children of age are not entitled, but this act makes them joint heirs with the minor children.

In case of the deceased one-year men, and the three-years men enlisted under joint resolution of January 13, 1864, the effect of this act would only be to change the prescribed order of inheritance.

In case of the three-years men enlisted under act of July 22, 1861, the order of inheritance is changed by this act, and the heirs entitled (widow, children, and widowed mother) will receive $100 more bounty than they are now entitled to receive.

It may be well to state that November 14, 1864, the War Department gave authority to enlist men who had deserted from the rebel army as recruits for the First Alabama Cavalry, with the distinct understanding that they were to receive no bounty. Such recruits have not been paid bounty, and it may be a question whether the act under consideration would entitle them to any.

U. S. GRANT.

PROCLAMATIONS.

By the President of the United States of America.

A PROCLAMATION.

Whereas, pursuant to the first section of the act of Congress approved the 11th day of June, 1864, entitled "An act to provide for the execution of treaties between the United States and foreign nations respecting consular jurisdiction over the crews of vessels of such foreign nations in the waters and ports of the United States," it is provided that before that act shall take effect as to the ships and vessels of any particular nation having such treaty with the United States the President of the United States shall have been satisfied that similar provisions have been made for the execution of such treaty by the other contracting party, and shall have issued his proclamation to that effect, declaring that act to be in force as to such nation; and

Whereas due inquiry having been made and satisfactory answers having been received that similar provisions are in force in France, Prussia and the other States of the North German Union, and Italy:

Now, therefore, be it known that I, Ulysses S. Grant, President of the United States of America, do hereby proclaim the same accordingly.

Done at the city of Washington, this 10th day of February, A. D.
[SEAL.]   1870, and of the Independence of the United States of America the ninety-fourth.

U. S. GRANT.

By the President:
    HAMILTON FISH,
        Secretary of State.

Ulysses S. Grant, President of the United States of America.

To all whom it may concern:

An exequatur, bearing date the 17th day of June, 1865, having been issued to Joaquin de Palma, recognizing him as vice-consul of Portugal at Savannah, Ga., and declaring him free to exercise and enjoy such functions, powers, and privileges as are allowed to vice-consuls by the law of nations or by the laws of the United States and existing treaty stipulations between the Government of Portugal and the United States; but for satisfactory reasons it is deemed advisable that the said Joaquin de Palma should no longer be permitted to continue in the exercise of said functions, powers, and privileges:

These are therefore to declare that I no longer recognize the said Joaquin de Palma as vice-consul of Portugal at Savannah, Ga., and will not permit him to exercise or enjoy any of the functions, powers, or privileges allowed to a consular officer of that nation; and that I do hereby wholly revoke and annul the said exequatur heretofore given, and do declare the same to be absolutely null and void from this day forward.

In testimony whereof I have caused these letters to be made patent and the seal of the United States of America to be hereunto affixed.

[SEAL.]   Given under my hand, at Washington, this 12th day of May, A. D. 1870, and of the Independence of the United States of America the ninety-fourth.

U. S. GRANT.

By the President:
    HAMILTON FISH,
        Secretary of State.

BY THE PRESIDENT OF THE UNITED STATES OF AMERICA.

A PROCLAMATION.

Whereas it has come to my knowledge that sundry illegal military enterprises and expeditions are being set on foot within the territory and jurisdiction of the United States with a view to carry on the same from such territory and jurisdiction against the people and district of the Dominion of Canada, within the dominions of Her Majesty the Queen of the United Kingdom of Great Britain and Ireland, with whom the United States are at peace:

Now, therefore, I, Ulysses S. Grant, President of the United States, do hereby admonish all good citizens of the United States and all persons within the territory and jurisdiction of the United States against aiding, countenancing, abetting, or taking part in such unlawful proceedings; and I do hereby warn all persons that by committing such illegal acts they will forfeit all right to the protection of the Government or to its interference in their behalf to rescue them from the consequences of their own acts; and I do hereby enjoin all officers in the service of the United States to employ all their lawful authority and power to prevent and defeat the aforesaid unlawful proceedings and to arrest and bring to justice all persons who may be engaged therein.

In testimony whereof I have hereunto set my hand and caused the seal of the United States to be affixed.

[SEAL.]   Done at the city of Washington, this 24th day of May, A. D. 1870, and of the Independence of the United States the ninety-fourth.

U. S. GRANT.

By the President:
    HAMILTON FISH,
        Secretary of State.

BY THE PRESIDENT OF THE UNITED STATES OF AMERICA.

A PROCLAMATION.

Whereas a state of war unhappily exists between France on the one side and the North German Confederation and its allies on the other side; and

Whereas the United States are on terms of friendship and amity with all the contending powers and with the persons inhabiting their several dominions; and

Whereas great numbers of the citizens of the United States reside within the territories or dominions of each of the said belligerents and carry on commerce, trade, or other business or pursuits therein, protected by the faith of treaties; and

Whereas great numbers of the subjects or citizens of each of the said belligerents reside within the territory or jurisdiction of the United States and carry on commerce, trade, or other business or pursuits therein; and

Whereas the laws of the United States, without interfering with the free expression of opinion and sympathy, or with the open manufacture or sale of arms or munitions of war, nevertheless impose upon all persons who may be within their territory and jurisdiction the duty of an impartial neutrality during the existence of the contest:

Now, therefore, I, Ulysses S. Grant, President of the United States, in order to preserve the neutrality of the United States and of their citizens and of persons within their territory and jurisdiction, and to enforce their laws, and in order that all persons, being warned of the general tenor of the laws and treaties of the United States in this behalf and of the law of nations, may thus be prevented from an unintentional violation of the same, do hereby declare and proclaim that by the act passed on the 20th day of April, A. D. 1818, commonly known as the "neutrality law," the following acts are forbidden to be done, under severe penalties, within the territory and jurisdiction of the United States, to wit:

1. Accepting and exercising a commission to serve either of the said belligerents, by land or by sea, against the other belligerent.

2. Enlisting or entering into the service of either of the said belligerents as a soldier or as a marine or seaman on board of any vessel of war, letter of marque, or privateer.

3. Hiring or retaining another person to enlist or enter himself in the service of either of the said belligerents as a soldier or as a marine or seaman on board of any vessel of war, letter of marque, or privateer.

4. Hiring another person to go beyond the limits or jurisdiction of the United States with intent to be enlisted as aforesaid.

5. Hiring another person to go beyond the limits of the United States with intent to be entered into service as aforesaid.

6. Retaining another person to go beyond the limits of the United States with intent to be enlisted as aforesaid.

7. Retaining another person to go beyond the limits of the United States with intent to be entered into service as aforesaid. (But the said act is not to be construed to extend to a citizen or subject of either belligerent who, being transiently within the United States, shall, on board of any vessel of war which at the time of its arrival within the United States was fitted and equipped as such vessel of war, enlist or enter himself, or hire or retain another subject or citizen of the same belligerent who is transiently within the United States to enlist or enter himself, to serve such belligerent on board such vessel of war, if the United States shall then be at peace with such belligerent.)

8. Fitting out and arming, or attempting to fit out and arm, or procuring to be fitted out and armed, or knowingly being concerned in the furnishing, fitting out, or arming of any ship or vessel with intent that such ship or vessel shall be employed in the service of either of the said belligerents.

9. Issuing or delivering a commission within the territory or jurisdiction of the United States for any ship or vessel to the intent that she may be employed as aforesaid.

10. Increasing or augmenting, or procuring to be increased or augmented, or knowingly being concerned in increasing or augmenting, the force of any ship of war, cruiser, or other armed vessel which at the time of her arrival within the United States was a ship of war, cruiser, or armed vessel in the service of either of the said belligerents, or belonging to the subjects or citizens of either, by adding to the number of guns of such vessel, or by changing those on board of her for guns of a larger caliber, or by the addition thereto of any equipment solely applicable to war.

11. Beginning or setting on foot or providing or preparing the means for any military expedition or enterprise to be carried on from the territory or jurisdiction of the United States against the territories or dominions of either of the said belligerents.

And I do further declare and proclaim that by the nineteenth article of the treaty of amity and commerce which was concluded between His Majesty the King of Prussia and the United States of America on the 11th day of July, A. D. 1799, which article was revived by the treaty of May 1, A. D. 1828, between the same parties, and is still in force, it was agreed that "the vessels of war, public and private, of both parties shall carry freely, wheresoever they please, the vessels and effects taken from their enemies, without being obliged to pay any duties, charges, or fees to officers of admiralty, of the customs, or any others; nor shall such prizes be arrested, searched, or put under legal process when they come to and enter the ports of the other party, but may freely be carried out again at any time by their captors to the places expressed in their commissions, which the commanding officer of such vessel shall be obliged to show."

And I do further declare and proclaim that it has been officially communicated to the Government of the United States by the envoy extraordinary and minister plenipotentiary of the North German Confederation at Washington that private property on the high seas will be exempted from seizure by the ships of His Majesty the King of Prussia, without regard to reciprocity.

And I do further declare and proclaim that it has been officially communicated to the Government of the United States by the envoy extraordinary and minister plenipotentiary of His Majesty the Emperor of the French at Washington that orders have been given that in the conduct of the war the commanders of the French forces on land and on the seas shall scrupulously observe toward neutral powers the rules of international law and that they shall strictly adhere to the principles set forth in the declaration of the congress of Paris of the 16th of April, 1856; that is to say:

First. That privateering is and remains abolished.

Second. That the neutral flag covers enemy's goods, with the exception of contraband of war.

Third. That neutral goods, with the exception of contraband of war, are not liable to capture under the enemy's flag.

Fourth. That blockades, in order to be binding, must be effective—that is to say, maintained by a force sufficient really to prevent access to the coast of the enemy; and that, although the United States have not adhered to the declaration of 1856, the vessels of His Majesty will not seize enemy's property found on board of a vessel of the United States, provided that property is not contraband of war.

And I do further declare and proclaim that the statutes of the United States and the law of nations alike require that no person within the territory and jurisdiction of the United States shall take part, directly or indirectly, in the said war, but shall remain at peace with each of the said belligerents and shall maintain a strict and impartial neutrality, and that whatever privileges shall be accorded to one belligerent within the ports of the United States shall be in like manner accorded to the other.

And I do hereby enjoin all the good citizens of the United States and all persons residing or being within the territory or jurisdiction of the United States to observe the laws thereof and to commit no act contrary to the provisions of the said statutes or in violation of the law of nations in that behalf.

And I do hereby warn all citizens of the United States and all persons residing or being within their territory or jurisdiction that while the free and full expression of sympathies in public and private is not restricted by the laws of the United States, military forces in aid of either belligerent can not lawfully be originated or organized within their jurisdiction; and that while all persons may lawfully and without restriction, by reason of the aforesaid state of war, manufacture and sell within the United States arms and munitions of war and other articles ordinarily known as "contraband of war," yet they can not carry such articles upon the high seas for the use or service of either belligerent, nor can they transport soldiers and officers of either, or attempt to break any blockade which may be lawfully established and maintained during the war, without incurring the risk of hostile capture and the penalties denounced by the law of nations in that behalf.

And I do hereby give notice that all citizens of the United States and others who may claim the protection of this Government who may misconduct themselves in the premises will do so at their peril, and that they can in no wise obtain any protection from the Government of the United States against the consequences of their misconduct.

In witness whereof I have hereunto set my hand and caused the seal of the United States to be affixed.

[SEAL.] Done at the city of Washington, this 22d day of August, A. D. 1870, and of the Independence of the United States of America the ninety-fifth.

U. S. GRANT.

By the President:

HAMILTON FISH,
Secretary of State.

BY THE PRESIDENT OF THE UNITED STATES OF AMERICA.

A PROCLAMATION.

Whereas on the 22d day of August, 1870, my proclamation was issued enjoining neutrality in the present war between France and the North German Confederation and its allies, and declaring, so far as then seemed to be necessary, the respective rights and obligations of the belligerent parties and of the citizens of the United States; and

Whereas subsequent information gives reason to apprehend that armed cruisers of the belligerents may be tempted to abuse the hospitality accorded to them in the ports, harbors, roadsteads, and other waters of the United States, by making such waters subservient to the purposes of war:

Now, therefore, I, Ulysses S. Grant, President of the United States of America, do hereby proclaim and declare that any frequenting and use of the waters within the territorial jurisdiction of the United States by the armed vessels of either belligerent, whether public ships or privateers, for the purpose of preparing for hostile operations or as posts of observation upon the ships of war or privateers or merchant vessels of the other belligerent lying within or being about to enter the jurisdiction of the United States, must be regarded as unfriendly and offensive and in violation of that neutrality which it is the determination of this Government to observe; and to the end that the hazard and inconvenience of such apprehended practices may be avoided, I further proclaim and declare that from and after the 12th day of October instant, and during the continuance of the present hostilities between France and the North German Confederation and its allies, no ship of war or privateer of either belligerent shall be permitted to make use of any port, harbor, roadstead, or other waters within the jurisdiction of the United States as a station or place of resort for any warlike purpose or for the purpose of obtaining any facilities of warlike equipment; and no ship of war or privateer of either belligerent shall be permitted to sail out of or leave any port, harbor, roadstead, or waters subject to the jurisdiction of the United States from which a vessel of the other belligerent (whether the same shall be a ship of war, a privateer, or a merchant ship) shall have previously departed until after the expiration of at least twenty-four hours from the departure of such last-mentioned vessel beyond the jurisdiction of the United States. If any ship of war or privateer of either belligerent shall, after the time this notification takes effect, enter any port, harbor, roadstead, or waters of the United States, such vessel shall be required to depart and to put to sea within twenty-four hours after her entrance into such port, harbor, roadstead, or waters, except in case of stress of weather or of her requiring provisions or things necessary for the subsistence of her crew or for repairs, in either of which cases the authorities of the port or of the nearest port (as the case may be) shall require her to put to sea as soon as possible after the expiration of such period of twenty-four hours, without permitting her to take in supplies beyond what may be necessary for her immediate use; and no such vessel which may have been permitted to remain within the waters of the United States for the purpose of repair shall continue within such port, harbor, roadstead, or waters for a longer period than twenty-four hours after her necessary repairs shall have been completed, unless within such twenty-four hours a vessel, whether ship of war, privateer, or merchant ship, of the other belligerent shall have departed therefrom, in which case the time limited for the departure of such ship of war or privateer shall be extended so far as may be necessary to secure an interval of not less than twenty-four hours between such departure and that of any ship of war, privateer, or merchant ship of the other belligerent which may have previously quit the same port, harbor, roadstead, or waters. No ship of war or privateer of either belligerent shall be detained in any port, harbor, roadstead, or waters of the United States more than twenty-four hours by reason of the successive departures from such port, harbor, roadstead, or waters of more than one vessel of the other belligerent. But if there be several vessels of each or either of the two belligerents in the same port, harbor, roadstead, or waters, the order of their departure therefrom shall be so arranged as to afford the opportunity of leaving alternately to the vessels of the respective belligerents and to cause the least detention consistent with the objects of this proclamation. No ship of war or privateer of either belligerent shall be permitted, while in any port, harbor, roadstead, or waters within the jurisdiction of the United

States, to take in any supplies except provisions and such other things as may be requisite for the subsistence of her crew, and except so much coal only as may be sufficient to carry such vessel, if without sail power, to the nearest European port of her own country, or, in case the vessel is rigged to go under sail and may also be propelled by steam power, then with half the quantity of coal which she would be entitled to receive if dependent upon steam alone; and no coal shall be again supplied to any such ship of war or privateer in the same or any other port, harbor, roadstead, or waters of the United States, without special permission, until after the expiration of three months from the time when such coal may have been last supplied to her within the waters of the United States, unless such ship of war or privateer shall, since last thus supplied, have entered a European port of the Government to which she belongs.

In testimony whereof I have hereunto set my hand and caused the seal of the United States to be affixed.

[SEAL.]   Done at the city of Washington, this 8th day of October, A. D. 1870, and of the Independence of the United States of America the ninety-fifth.

U. S. GRANT.

By the President:

HAMILTON FISH,
Secretary of State.

BY THE PRESIDENT OF THE UNITED STATES OF AMERICA.

A PROCLAMATION.

Whereas divers evil-disposed persons have at sundry times within the territory or jurisdiction of the United States begun or set on foot, or provided or prepared the means for, military expeditions or enterprises to be carried on thence against the territories or dominions of powers with whom the United States are at peace, by organizing bodies pretending to have powers of government over portions of the territories or dominions of powers with whom the United States are at peace, or, by being or assuming to be members of such bodies, by levying or collecting money for the purpose or for the alleged purpose of using the same in carrying on military enterprises against such territories or dominions by enlisting and organizing armed forces to be used against such powers, and by fitting out, equipping, and arming vessels to transport such organized armed forces to be employed in hostilities against such powers; and

Whereas it is alleged and there is reason to apprehend that such evil-disposed persons have also at sundry times within the territory and jurisdiction of the United States violated the laws thereof by accepting and exercising commissions to serve by land or by sea against powers with whom the United States are at peace by enlisting themselves or other persons to carry on war against such powers by fitting out and arming vessels with intent that the same shall be employed to cruise or commit hostilities against such powers, or by delivering commissions within the territory or jurisdiction of the United States for such vessels to the intent that they might be employed as aforesaid; and

Whereas such acts are in violation of the laws of the United States in such case made and provided, and are done in disregard of the duties and obligations which all persons residing or being within the territory or jurisdiction of the United States owe thereto, and are condemned by all right-minded and law-abiding citizens:

Now, therefore, I, Ulysses S. Grant, President of the United States of America, do hereby declare and proclaim that all persons hereafter found within the territory or jurisdiction of the United States committing any of the aforerecited violations of law or any similar violations of the sovereignty of the United States for which punishment is provided by law will be rigorously prosecuted therefor, and, upon conviction and sentence to punishment, will not be entitled to expect or receive the clemency of the Executive to save them from the consequences of their guilt; and I enjoin upon every officer of this Government, civil or military or naval, to use all efforts in his power to arrest for trial and punishment every such offender against the laws providing for the performance of our sacred obligations to friendly powers.

In testimony whereof I have hereunto set my hand and caused the seal of the United States to be affixed.

[SEAL.]   Done at the city of Washington, this 12th day of October, A. D. 1870, and of the Independence of the United States of America the ninety-fifth.

U. S. GRANT.

By the President:

HAMILTON FISH, *Secretary of State.*

BY THE PRESIDENT OF THE UNITED STATES OF AMERICA.

A PROCLAMATION.

Whereas it behooves a people sensible of their dependence on the Almighty publicly and collectively to acknowledge their gratitude for his favors and mercies and humbly to beseech for their continuance; and

Whereas the people of the United States during the year now about to end have special cause to be thankful for general prosperity, abundant harvests, exemption from pestilence, foreign war, and civil strife:

Now, therefore, be it known that I, Ulysses S. Grant, President of the United States, concurring in any similar recommendations from chief magistrates of States, do hereby recommend to all citizens to meet in their respective places of worship on Thursday, the 24th day of November next, there to give thanks for the bounty of God during the year about to close and to supplicate for its continuance hereafter.

In witness whereof I have hereunto set my hand and caused the seal of the United States to be affixed.

[SEAL.]   Done at the city of Washington, this 21st day of October, A. D. 1870, and of the Independence of the United States the ninety-fifth.

         U. S. GRANT.

By the President:
     HAMILTON FISH,
        Secretary of State.

EXECUTIVE ORDERS.

GENERAL ORDERS, NO. 83.

HEADQUARTERS OF THE ARMY,
ADJUTANT-GENERAL'S OFFICE,
Washington, December 24, 1869.

Brevet Major-General A. H. Terry, in addition to his duties as commander of the Department of the South, is, by order of the President of the United States, appointed to exercise the duties of commanding general of the District of Georgia, as defined by the act of Congress approved December 22, 1869.

By command of General Sherman:

         E. D. TOWNSEND,
           Adjutant-General.

EXECUTIVE MANSION,
Washington, D. C., December 24, 1869.

The painful duty devolves upon the President of announcing to the people of the United States the death of one of her most distinguished citizens and faithful public servants, the Hon. Edwin M. Stanton, which occurred in this city at an early hour this morning.

He was distinguished in the councils of the nation during the entire period of its recent struggle for national existence—first as Attorney-General, then as Secretary of War. He was unceasing in his labors, earnest and fearless in the assumption of responsibilities necessary to his country's success, respected by all good men, and feared by wrongdoers. In his death the bar, the bench, and the nation sustain a great loss, which will be mourned by all.

As a mark of respect to his memory it is ordered that the Executive Mansion and the several Departments at Washington be draped in mourning, and that all business be suspended on the day of the funeral.

         U. S. GRANT.

GENERAL ORDERS, NO. 1.

HEADQUARTERS OF THE ARMY,
ADJUTANT-GENERAL'S OFFICE,
Washington, January 4, 1870.

By direction of the President of the United States, so much of General Orders, No. 103, dated Headquarters Third Military District (Department of Georgia, Florida, and Alabama), Atlanta, Ga., July 22, 1868, and so much of General Orders, No. 55, dated Headquarters of the Army, Adjutant-General's Office, Washington, July 28, 1868, as refers to the State of Georgia is hereby countermanded. Brevet Major-General Terry will until further orders exercise within that State the powers of the commander of a military district, as provided by the act of March 2, 1867, and the acts supplementary thereto, under his assignment by General Orders, No. 83, dated Headquarters of the Army, Adjutant-General's Office Washington, December 24, 1869.

By command of General Sherman:

E. D. TOWNSEND,
Adjutant-General

GENERAL ORDERS, NO. 11.

HEADQUARTERS OF THE ARMY,
ADJUTANT-GENERAL'S OFFICE,
Washington, January 29, 1870.

I. The Senators and Representatives from the State of Virginia having been admitted to their respective Houses of Congress, the command known as the First Military District has ceased to exist.

II. By direction of the President, the States of Maryland, Virginia, West Virginia, and North Carolina will compose the Department of Virginia, under the command of Brevet Major-General E. R. S. Canby, headquarters at Richmond, Va., and will form a part of the Military Division of the Atlantic.

III. Commanding officers of all posts and detachments now serving in the limits of the new department will report to General Canby for instructions. The companies of the Eighth Infantry now serving in the State of North Carolina will be relieved as early as possible, and report to Brevet Major-General A. H. Terry, commanding Department of the South, for orders.

By command of General Sherman:

E. D. TOWNSEND,
Adjutant-General.

GENERAL ORDERS, No. 25.

HEADQUARTERS OF THE ARMY,
ADJUTANT-GENERAL'S OFFICE,
Washington, February 26, 1870.

I. The Senators and Representatives from the State of Mississippi having been admitted to their respective Houses of Congress, the command known as the Fourth Military District has ceased to exist.

II. By direction of the President, the State of Mississippi is attached to the Department of the Cumberland, and the officers and troops within the late Fourth Military District will accordingly report to Brevet Major-General Cooke, commanding the department.

III. The general commanding the late Fourth Military District will complete the records of that district as soon as practicable and send them to the Adjutant-General of the Army, except such military records as should properly be retained at the headquarters of the department, which he will send there.

By command of General Sherman:

E. D. TOWNSEND,
Adjutant-General.

GENERAL ORDERS, No. 35.

HEADQUARTERS OF THE ARMY,
ADJUTANT-GENERAL'S OFFICE,
Washington, March 31, 1870.

I. By order of the President of the United States, the State of Texas having been admitted to representation in Congress, the command heretofore known as the Fifth Military District will cease to exist, and will hereafter constitute a separate military department, headquarters Austin, Tex., Brevet Major-General J. J. Reynolds commanding.

II. The department known as the Department of Louisiana will be broken up; the State of Louisiana is hereby added to the Department of Texas, and the State of Arkansas to the Department of the Missouri. The commanding general Department of the Missouri will, as soon as convenient, relieve the garrison at Little Rock by a detachment from the Sixth Infantry, and the commanding officer of the troops now in Arkansas will report to General J. J. Reynolds for orders, to take effect as soon as replaced.

III. The new Department of Texas will form a part of the Military Division of the South.

By command of General Sherman:

E. D. TOWNSEND,
Adjutant-General

SECOND ANNUAL MESSAGE.

EXECUTIVE MANSION, *December 5, 1870.*

To the Senate and House of Representatives:

A year of peace and general prosperity to this nation has passed since the last assembling of Congress. We have, through a kind Providence, been blessed with abundant crops, and have been spared from complications and war with foreign nations. In our midst comparative harmony has been restored. It is to be regretted, however, that a free exercise of the elective franchise has by violence and intimidation been denied to citizens in exceptional cases in several of the States lately in rebellion, and the verdict of the people has thereby been reversed. The States of Virginia, Mississippi, and Texas have been restored to representation in our national councils. Georgia, the only State now without representation, may confidently be expected to take her place there also at the beginning of the new year, and then, let us hope, will be completed the work of reconstruction. With an acquiescence on the part of the whole people in the national obligation to pay the public debt created as the price of our Union, the pensions to our disabled soldiers and sailors and their widows and orphans, and in the changes to the Constitution which have been made necessary by a great rebellion, there is no reason why we should not advance in material prosperity and happiness as no other nation ever did after so protracted and devastating a war.

Soon after the existing war broke out in Europe the protection of the United States minister in Paris was invoked in favor of North Germans domiciled in French territory. Instructions were issued to grant the protection. This has been followed by an extension of American protection to citizens of Saxony, Hesse and Saxe-Coburg, Gotha, Colombia, Portugal, Uruguay, the Dominican Republic, Ecuador, Chile, Paraguay, and Venezuela in Paris. The charge was an onerous one, requiring constant and severe labor, as well as the exercise of patience, prudence, and good judgment. It has been performed to the entire satisfaction of this Government, and, as I am officially informed, equally so to the satisfaction of the Government of North Germany.

As soon as I learned that a republic had been proclaimed at Paris and that the people of France had acquiesced in the change, the minister of the United States was directed by telegraph to recognize it and to tender my congratulations and those of the people of the United States. The reestablishment in France of a system of government disconnected with the dynastic traditions of Europe appeared to be a proper subject for the felicitations of Americans. Should the present struggle result in attaching the hearts of the French to our simpler forms of representative government, it will be a subject of still further satisfaction to our people.

While we make no effort to impose our institutions upon the inhabitants of other countries, and while we adhere to our traditional neutrality in civil contests elsewhere, we can not be indifferent to the spread of American political ideas in a great and highly civilized country like France.

We were asked by the new Government to use our good offices, jointly with those of European powers, in the interests of peace. Answer was made that the established policy and the true interests of the United States forbade them to interfere in European questions jointly with European powers. I ascertained, informally and unofficially, that the Government of North Germany was not then disposed to listen to such representations from any power, and though earnestly wishing to see the blessings of peace restored to the belligerents, with all of whom the United States are on terms of friendship, I declined on the part of this Government to take a step which could only result in injury to our true interests without advancing the object for which our intervention was invoked. Should the time come when the action of the United States can hasten the return of peace by a single hour, that action will be heartily taken. I deemed it prudent, in view of the number of persons of German and French birth living in the United States, to issue, soon after official notice of a state of war had been received from both belligerents, a proclamation* defining the duties of the United States as a neutral and the obligations of persons residing within their territory to observe their laws and the laws of nations. This proclamation was followed by others,† as circumstances seemed to call for them. The people, thus acquainted in advance of their duties and obligations, have assisted in preventing violations of the neutrality of the United States.

It is not understood that the condition of the insurrection in Cuba has materially changed since the close of the last session of Congress. In an early stage of the contest the authorities of Spain inaugurated a system of arbitrary arrests, of close confinement, and of military trial and execution of persons suspected of complicity with the insurgents, and of summary embargo of their properties, and sequestration of their revenues by executive warrant. Such proceedings, so far as they affected the persons or property of citizens of the United States, were in violation of the provisions of the treaty of 1795 between the United States and Spain.

Representations of injuries resulting to several persons claiming to be citizens of the United States by reason of such violations were made to the Spanish Government. From April, 1869, to June last the Spanish minister at Washington had been clothed with a limited power to aid in redressing such wrongs. That power was found to be withdrawn, "in view," as it was said, "of the favorable situation in which the island of Cuba" then "was," which, however, did not lead to a revocation or suspension of the **extraordinary** and arbitrary functions **exercised** by the **ex**ecutive power in Cuba, and we were obliged to make our complaints

* See pp. 4040–4043.   † See pp. 4043–4046.

at Madrid. In the negotiations thus opened, and still pending there, the United States only claimed that for the future the rights secured to their citizens by treaty should be respected in Cuba, and that as to the past a joint tribunal should be established in the United States with full jurisdiction over all such claims. Before such an impartial tribunal each claimant would be required to prove his case. On the other hand, Spain would be at liberty to traverse every material fact, and thus complete equity would be done. A case which at one time threatened seriously to affect the relations between the United States and Spain has already been disposed of in this way. The claim of the owners of the *Colonel Lloyd Aspinwall* for the illegal seizure and detention of that vessel was referred to arbitration by mutual consent, and has resulted in an award to the United States, for the owners, of the sum of $19,702.50 in gold. Another and long-pending claim of like nature, that of the whaleship *Canada*, has been disposed of by friendly arbitrament during the present year. It was referred, by the joint consent of Brazil and the United States, to the decision of Sir Edward Thornton, Her Britannic Majesty's minister at Washington, who kindly undertook the laborious task of examining the voluminous mass of correspondence and testimony submitted by the two Governments, and awarded to the United States the sum of $100,740.09 in gold, which has since been paid by the Imperial Government. These recent examples show that the mode which the United States have proposed to Spain for adjusting the pending claims is just and feasible, and that it may be agreed to by either nation without dishonor. It is to be hoped that this moderate demand may be acceded to by Spain without further delay. Should the pending negotiations, unfortunately and unexpectedly, be without result, it will then become my duty to communicate that fact to Congress and invite its action on the subject.

The long-deferred peace conference between Spain and the allied South American Republics has been inaugurated in Washington under the auspices of the United States. Pursuant to the recommendation contained in the resolution of the House of Representatives of the 17th of December, 1866, the executive department of the Government offered its friendly offices for the promotion of peace and harmony between Spain and the allied Republics. Hesitations and obstacles occurred to the acceptance of the offer. Ultimately, however, a conference was arranged, and was opened in this city on the 29th of October last, at which I authorized the Secretary of State to preside. It was attended by the ministers of Spain, Peru, Chile, and Ecuador. In consequence of the absence of a representative from Bolivia, the conference was adjourned until the attendance of a plenipotentiary from that Republic could be secured or other measures could be adopted toward compassing its objects.

The allied and other Republics of Spanish origin on this continent may see in this fact a new proof of our sincere interest in their welfare, of our desire to see them blessed with good governments, capable of maintaining order and of preserving their respective territorial integrity, and of our sincere wish to extend our own commercial and social relations with them. The time is not probably far distant when, in the natural course of events, the European political connection with this continent will cease. Our policy should be shaped, in view of this probability, so as to ally the commercial interests of the Spanish American States more closely to our own, and thus give the United States all the preeminence and all the advantage which Mr. Monroe, Mr. Adams, and Mr. Clay contemplated when they proposed to join in the congress of Panama.

During the last session of Congress a treaty for the annexation of the Republic of San Domingo to the United States failed to receive the requisite two-thirds vote of the Senate. I was thoroughly convinced then that the best interests of this country, commercially and materially, demanded its ratification. Time has only confirmed me in this view. I now firmly believe that the moment it is known that the United States have entirely abandoned the project of accepting as a part of its territory the island of San Domingo a free port will be negotiated for by European nations in the Bay of Samana. A large commercial city will spring up, to which we will be tributary without receiving corresponding benefits, and then will be seen the folly of our rejecting so great a prize. The Government of San Domingo has voluntarily sought this annexation. It is a weak power, numbering probably less than 120,000 souls, and yet possessing one of the richest territories under the sun, capable of supporting a population of 10,000,000 people in luxury. The people of San Domingo are not capable of maintaining themselves in their present condition, and must look for outside support. They yearn for the protection of our free institutions and laws, our progress and civilization. Shall we refuse them?

The acquisition of San Domingo is desirable because of its geographical position. It commands the entrance to the Caribbean Sea and the Isthmus transit of commerce. It possesses the richest soil, best and most capacious harbors, most salubrious climate, and the most valuable products of the forests, mine, and soil of any of the West India Islands. Its possession by us will in a few years build up a coastwise commerce of immense magnitude, which will go far toward restoring to us our lost merchant marine. It will give to us those articles which we consume so largely and do not produce, thus equalizing our exports and imports. In case of foreign war it will give us command of all the islands referred to, and thus prevent an enemy from ever again possessing himself of rendezvous upon our very coast. At present our coast trade between the States bordering on the Atlantic and those bordering on the Gulf of Mexico is cut into by the Bahamas and the Antilles. Twice we must as it were, pass through foreign countries to get by sea from Georgia to the west coast of Florida.

San Domingo, with a stable government, under which her immense resources can be developed, will give remunerative wages to tens of thousands of laborers not now upon the island. This labor will take advantage of every available means of transportation to abandon the adjacent islands and seek the blessings of freedom and its sequence—each inhabitant receiving the reward of his own labor. Porto Rico and Cuba will have to abolish slavery, as a measure of self-preservation, to retain their laborers.

San Domingo will become a large consumer of the products of Northern farms and manufactories. The cheap rate at which her citizens can be furnished with food, tools, and machinery will make it necessary that contiguous islands should have the same advantages in order to compete in the production of sugar, coffee, tobacco, tropical fruits, etc. This will open to us a still wider market for our products. The production of our own supply of these articles will cut off more than one hundred millions of our annual imports, besides largely increasing our exports. With such a picture it is easy to see how our large debt abroad is ultimately to be extinguished. With a balance of trade against us (including interest on bonds held by foreigners and money spent by our citizens traveling in foreign lands) equal to the entire yield of the precious metals in this country, it is not so easy to see how this result is to be otherwise accomplished.

The acquisition of San Domingo is an adherence to the "Monroe doctrine;" it is a measure of national protection; it is asserting our just claim to a controlling influence over the great commercial traffic soon to flow from west to east by way of the Isthmus of Darien; it is to build up our merchant marine; it is to furnish new markets for the products of our farms, shops, and manufactories; it is to make slavery insupportable in Cuba and Porto Rico at once, and ultimately so in Brazil; it is to settle the unhappy condition of Cuba and end an exterminating conflict; it is to provide honest means of paying our honest debts without overtaxing the people; it is to furnish our citizens with the necessaries of everyday life at cheaper rates than ever before; and it is, in fine, a rapid stride toward that greatness which the intelligence, industry, and enterprise of the citizens of the United States entitle this country to assume among nations.

In view of the importance of this question, I earnestly urge upon Congress early action expressive of its views as to the best means of acquiring San Domingo. My suggestion is that by joint resolution of the two Houses of Congress the Executive be authorized to appoint a commission to negotiate a treaty with the authorities of San Domingo for the acquisition of that island, and that an appropriation be made to defray the expenses of such a commission. The question may then be determined, either by the action of the Senate upon the treaty or the joint action of the two Houses of Congress upon a resolution of annexation, as in the case of the acquisition of Texas. So convinced am I of the advantages to flow from the acquisition of San Domingo, and of the great disadvantages—I might almost say calamities—to flow from nonacquisition, that I believe the subject has only to be investigated to be approved.

It is to be regretted that our representations in regard to the injurious effects, especially upon the revenue of the United States, of the policy of the Mexican Government in exempting from impost duties a large tract of its territory on our borders have not only been fruitless, but that it is even proposed in that country to extend the limits within which the privilege adverted to has hitherto been enjoyed. The expediency of taking into your serious consideration proper measures for countervailing the policy referred to will, it is presumed, engage your earnest attention.

It is the obvious interest, especially of neighboring nations, to provide against impunity to those who may have committed high crimes within their borders and who may have sought refuge abroad. For this purpose extradition treaties have been concluded with several of the Central American Republics, and others are in progress.

The sense of Congress is desired, as early as may be convenient, upon the proceedings of the commission on claims against Venezuela, as communicated in my messages of March 16, 1869, March 1, 1870, and March 31, 1870. It has not been deemed advisable to distribute any of the money which has been received from that Government until Congress shall have acted on the subject.

The massacres of French and Russian residents at Tien-Tsin, under circumstances of great barbarity, was supposed by some to have been premeditated, and to indicate a purpose among the populace to exterminate foreigners in the Chinese Empire. The evidence fails to establish such a supposition, but shows a complicity between the local authorities and the mob. The Government at Peking, however, seems to have been disposed to fulfill its treaty obligations so far as it was able to do so. Unfortunately, the news of the war between the German States and France reached China soon after the massacre. It would appear that the popular mind became possessed with the idea that this contest, extending to Chinese waters, would neutralize the Christian influence and power, and that the time was coming when the superstitious masses might expel all foreigners and restore mandarin influence. Anticipating trouble from this cause, I invited France and North Germany to make an authorized suspension of hostilities in the East (where they were temporarily suspended by act of the commanders), and to act together for the future protection in China of the lives and properties of Americans and Europeans.

Since the adjournment of Congress the ratifications of the treaty with Great Britain for abolishing the mixed courts for the suppression of the slave trade have been exchanged. It is believed that the slave trade is now confined to the eastern coast of Africa, whence the slaves are taken to Arabian markets.

The ratifications of the naturalization convention between Great Britain and the United States have also been exchanged during the recess, and thus a long-standing dispute between the two Governments has been settled in accordance with the principles always contended for by the United States.

In April last, while engaged in locating a military reservation near Pembina, a corps of engineers discovered that the commonly received boundary line between the United States and the British possessions at that place is about 4,700 feet south of the true position of the forty-ninth parallel, and that the line, when run on what is now supposed to be the true position of that parallel, would leave the fort of the Hudsons Bay Company at Pembina within the territory of the United States. This information being communicated to the British Government, I was requested to consent, and did consent, that the British occupation of the fort of the Hudsons Bay Company should continue for the present. I deem it important, however, that this part of the boundary line should be definitely fixed by a joint commission of the two Governments, and I submit herewith estimates of the expense of such a commission on the part of the United States and recommend that an appropriation be made for that purpose. The land boundary has already been fixed and marked from the summit of the Rocky Mountains to the Georgian Bay. It should now be in like manner marked from the Lake of the Woods to the summit of the Rocky Mountains.

I regret to say that no conclusion has been reached for the adjustment of the claims against Great Britain growing out of the course adopted by that Government during the rebellion. The cabinet of London, so far as its views have been expressed, does not appear to be willing to concede that Her Majesty's Government was guilty of any negligence, or did or permitted any act during the war by which the United States has just cause of complaint. Our firm and unalterable convictions are directly the reverse. I therefore recommend to Congress to authorize the appointment of a commission to take proof of the amount and the ownership of these several claims, on notice to the representative of Her Majesty at Washington, and that authority be given for the settlement of these claims by the United States, so that the Government shall have the ownership of the private claims, as well as the responsible control of all the demands against Great Britain. It can not be necessary to add that whenever Her Majesty's Government shall entertain a desire for a full and friendly adjustment of these claims the United States will enter upon their consideration with an earnest desire for a conclusion consistent with the honor and dignity of both nations.

The course pursued by the Canadian authorities toward the fishermen of the United States during the past season has not been marked by a friendly feeling. By the first article of the convention of 1818 between Great Britain and the United States it was agreed that the inhabitants of the United States should have forever, in common with British subjects, the right of taking fish in certain waters therein defined. In the waters not included in the limits named in the convention (within 3 miles of parts of the British coast) it has been the custom for many years to give to intruding fishermen of the United States a reasonable warning of their violation of the technical rights of Great Britain. The Imperial Government is understood to have delegated the whole or a share of its jurisdiction or control of these inshore fishing grounds to the colonial authority known as the Dominion of Canada, and this semi-independent but irresponsible agent has exercised its delegated powers in an unfriendly way. Vessels have been seized without notice or warning, in violation of the custom previously prevailing, and have been taken into the colonial ports, their voyages broken up, and the vessels condemned. There is reason to believe that this unfriendly and vexatious treatment was designed to bear harshly upon the hardy fishermen of the United States, with a view to political effect upon this Government. The statutes of the Dominion of Canada assume a still broader and more untenable jurisdiction over the vessels of the United States. They authorize officers or persons to bring vessels hovering within 3 marine miles of any of the coasts, bays, creeks, or harbors of Canada into port, to search the cargo, to examine the master on oath touching the cargo and voyage, and to inflict upon him a heavy pecuniary penalty if true answers are not given; and if such a vessel is found "preparing to fish" within 3 marine miles of any of such coasts, bays, creeks, or harbors without a license, or after the expiration of the period named in the last license granted to it, they provide that the vessel, with her tackle, etc., shall be forfeited. It is not known that any condemnations have been made under this statute. Should the authorities of Canada attempt to enforce it, it will become my duty to take such steps as may be necessary to protect the rights of the citizens of the United States.

It has been claimed by Her Majesty's officers that the fishing vessels of the United States have no right to enter the open ports of the British possessions in North America, except for the purposes of shelter and repairing damages, of purchasing wood and obtaining water; that they have no right to enter at the British custom-houses or to trade there except in the purchase of wood and water, and that they must depart within twenty-four hours after notice to leave. It is not known that any seizure of a fishing vessel carrying the flag of the United States has been made under this claim. So far as the claim is founded on an alleged construction of the convention of 1818, it can not be acquiesced in by the United States. It is hoped that it will not be insisted on by Her Majesty's Government.

During the conferences which preceded the negotiation of the convention of 1818 the British commissioners proposed to expressly exclude the fishermen of the United States from "the privilege of carrying on trade with any of His Britannic Majesty's subjects residing within the limits assigned for their use;" and also that it should not be "lawful for the vessels of the United States engaged in said fishery to have on board any goods, wares, or merchandise whatever, except such as may be necessary for the prosecution of their voyages to and from the said fishing grounds: and any vessel of the United States which shall contravene this regulation may be seized, condemned, and confiscated, with her cargo."

This proposition, which is identical with the construction now put upon the language of the convention, was emphatically rejected by the American commissioners, and thereupon was abandoned by the British plenipotentiaries, and Article I, as it stands in the convention, was substituted.

If, however, it be said that this claim is founded on provincial or colonial statutes, and not upon the convention, this Government can not but regard them as unfriendly, and in contravention of the spirit, if not of the letter, of the treaty, for the faithful execution of which the Imperial Government is alone responsible.

Anticipating that an attempt may possibly be made by the Canadian authorities in the coming season to repeat their unneighborly acts toward our fishermen, I recommend you to confer upon the Executive the power to suspend by proclamation the operation of the laws authorizing the transit of goods, wares, and merchandise in bond across the territory of the United States to Canada, and, further, should such an extreme measure become necessary, to suspend the operation of any laws whereby the vessels of the Dominion of Canada are permitted to enter the waters of the United States.

A like unfriendly disposition has been manifested on the part of Canada in the maintenance of a claim of right to exclude the citizens of the United States from the navigation of the St. Lawrence. This river constitutes a natural outlet to the ocean for eight States, with an aggregate population of about 17,600,000 inhabitants, and with an aggregate tonnage of 651,367 tons upon the waters which discharge into it. The foreign commerce of our ports on these waters is open to British competition, and the major part of it is done in British bottoms.

If the American seamen be excluded from this natural avenue to the ocean, the monopoly of the direct commerce of the lake ports with the Atlantic would be in foreign hands, their vessels on transatlantic voyages having an access to our lake ports which would be denied to American vessels on similar voyages. To state such a proposition is to refute its justice.

During the Administration of Mr. John Quincy Adams Mr. Clay unanswerably demonstrated the natural right of the citizens of the United States to the navigation of this river, claiming that the act of the congress of Vienna in opening the Rhine and other rivers to all nations showed the judgment of European jurists and statesmen that the inhabitants of a country through which a navigable river passes have a natural right to enjoy the navigation of that river to and into the sea, even though passing through the territories of another power. This right does not exclude the coequal right of the sovereign possessing the territory through which the river debouches into the sea to make such regulations relative to the police of the navigation as may be reasonably necessary; but those regulations should be framed in a liberal spirit of comity, and should not impose needless burdens upon the commerce which has the right of transit. It has been found in practice more advantageous to arrange these regulations by mutual agreement. The United States are ready to make any reasonable arrangement as to the police of the St. Lawrence which may be suggested by Great Britain.

If the claim made by Mr. Clay was just when the population of States bordering on the shores of the Lakes was only 3,400,000, it now derives greater force and equity from the increased population, wealth, production, and tonnage of the States on the Canadian frontier. Since Mr. Clay advanced his argument in behalf of our right the principle for which he contended has been frequently, and by various nations, recognized by law or by treaty, and has been extended to several other great rivers. By the treaty concluded at Mayence in 1831 the Rhine was declared free from the point where it is first navigable into the sea. By the convention between Spain and Portugal concluded in 1835 the navigation of the Douro throughout its whole extent was made free for the subjects of both Crowns. In 1853 the Argentine Confederation by treaty threw open the free navigation of the Parana and the Uruguay to the merchant vessels of all nations. In 1856 the Crimean War was closed by a treaty which provided for the free navigation of the Danube. In 1858 Bolivia by treaty declared that it regarded the rivers Amazon and La Plata, in accordance with fixed principles of national law, as highways or channels opened by nature for the commerce of all nations. In 1859 the Paraguay was made free by treaty, and in December, 1866, the Emperor of Brazil by imperial decree declared the Amazon to be open to the frontier of Brazil to the merchant ships of all nations. The greatest living British authority on this subject, while asserting the abstract right of the British claim, says:

It seems difficult to deny that Great Britain may ground her refusal upon strict *law*, but it is equally difficult to deny, first, that in so doing she exercises harshly an extreme and hard law; secondly, that her conduct with respect to the navigation of the St. Lawrence is in glaring and discreditable inconsistency with her conduct with respect to the navigation of the Mississippi. On the ground that she possessed a small domain in which the Mississippi took its rise, she insisted on the right to navigate the entire volume of its waters. On the ground that she possesses both banks of the St. Lawrence, where it disembogues itself into the sea, she denies to the United States the right of navigation, though about one-half of the waters of Lakes Ontario, Erie. Huron, and Superior, and the whole of Lake Michigan, through which the river flows, are the property of the United States.

The whole nation is interested in securing cheap transportation from the agricultural States of the West to the Atlantic Seaboard. To the citizens of those States it secures a greater return for their labor; to the inhabitants of the seaboard it affords cheaper food; to the nation, an increase in the annual surplus of wealth. It is hoped that the Government of Great Britain will see the justice of abandoning the narrow and inconsistent claim to which her Canadian Provinces have urged her adherence.

Our depressed commerce is a subject to which I called your special attention at the last session, and suggested that we will in the future have to look more to the countries south of us, and to China and Japan, for its revival. Our representatives to all these Governments have exerted their influence to encourage trade between the United States and the countries to which they are accredited. But the fact exists that the carrying is done almost entirely in foreign bottoms, and while this state of affairs exists we can not control our due share of the commerce of the world; that between the Pacific States and China and Japan is about all the carrying trade now conducted in American vessels. I would recommend a liberal policy toward that line of American steamers—one that will insure its success, and even increased usefulness.

The cost of building iron vessels, the only ones that can compete with foreign ships in the carrying trade, is so much greater in the United States than in foreign countries that without some assistance from the Government they can not be successfully built here. There will be several propositions laid before Congress in the course of the present session looking to a remedy for this evil. Even if it should be at some cost to the National Treasury, I hope such encouragement will be given as will secure American shipping on the high seas and American shipbuilding at home.

The condition of the archives at the Department of State calls for the early action of Congress. The building now rented by that Department is a frail structure, at an inconvenient distance from the Executive Mansion and from the other Departments, is ill adapted to the purpose for which it is used, has not capacity to accommodate the archives, and is not fireproof. Its remote situation, its slender construction, and the absence of a supply of water in the neighborhood leave but little hope of safety for either the building or its contents in case of the accident of a fire. Its destruction would involve the loss of the rolls containing the original acts and resolutions of Congress, of the historic records of the Revolution and of the Confederation, of the whole series of diplomatic and consular archives since the adoption of the Constitution, and of the many other valuable records and papers left with that Department when it was the principal depository of the governmental archives. I recommend an appropriation for the construction of a building for the Department of State.

I recommend to your consideration the propriety of transferring to the Department of the Interior, to which they seem more appropriately

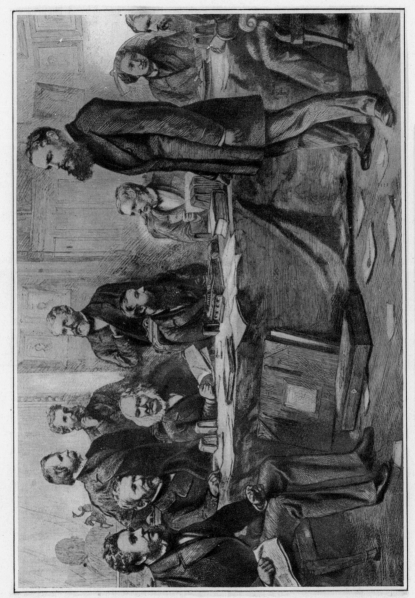

A SESSION OF THE *ALABAMA* CLAIMS ARBITRATORS

SETTLEMENT OF ALABAMA CLAIMS

The modern world, up to 1872, had not beheld any example of the settlement of international disputes by peaceful process of law. When the irritating nature of the controversy and the popular readiness for war in both countries are considered, the glory of the achievement is increased. The maintenance of peace between the United States and Great Britain and the exclusion of all but friendly rivalry between them is of vast importance to our race and to all the world. One of the most valuable results, therefore, of the Geneva Arbitration was the code of rules there devised to govern Anglo-American relations.

The two men most closely associated with the event are President Grant and Hamilton Fish, his Secretary of State. Their narrative of the negotiations will be found by consulting the heading " Alabama Claims," in the index (volume eleven), where are cited the pages on which discussions of the matter occur. The article on the Alabama Claims which precedes the page citations, presents a brief summary of the case.

to belong, all powers and duties in relation to the Territories with which the Department of State is now charged by law or usage; and from the Interior Department to the War Department the Pension Bureau, so far as it regulates the payment of soldiers' pensions. I would further recommend that the payment of naval pensions be transferred to one of the bureaus of the Navy Department.

The estimates for the expenses of the Government for the next fiscal year are $18,244,346.01 less than for the current one, but exceed the appropriations for the present year for the same items $8,972,127.56. In this estimate, however, is included $22,338,278.37 for public works heretofore begun under Congressional provision, and of which only so much is asked as Congress may choose to give. The appropriation for the same works for the present fiscal year was $11,984,518.08.

The average value of gold, as compared with national currency, for the whole of the year 1869 was about 134, and for eleven months of 1870 the same relative value has been about 115. The approach to a specie basis is very gratifying, but the fact can not be denied that the instability of the value of our currency is prejudicial to our prosperity, and tends to keep up prices, to the detriment of trade. The evils of a depreciated and fluctuating currency are so great that now, when the premium on gold has fallen so much, it would seem that the time has arrived when by wise and prudent legislation Congress should look to a policy which would place our currency at par with gold at no distant day.

The tax collected from the people has been reduced more than $80,-000,000 per annum. By steadiness in our present course there is no reason why in a few short years the national taxgatherer may not disappear from the door of the citizen almost entirely. With the revenue stamp dispensed by postmasters in every community, a tax upon liquors of all sorts and tobacco in all its forms, and by a wise adjustment of the tariff, which will put a duty only upon those articles which we could dispense with, known as luxuries, and on those which we use more of than we produce, revenue enough may be raised after a few years of peace and consequent reduction of indebtedness to fulfill all our obligations. A further reduction of expenses, in addition to a reduction of interest account, may be relied on to make this practicable. Revenue reform, if it means this, has my hearty support. If it implies a collection of all the revenue for the support of the Government, for the payment of principal and interest of the public debt, pensions, etc., by directly taxing the people, then I am against revenue reform, and confidently believe the people are with me. If it means failure to provide the necessary means to defray all the expenses of Government, and thereby repudiation of the public debt and pensions, then I am still more opposed to such kind of revenue reform. Revenue reform has not been defined by any of its advocates to my knowledge, but seems to be accepted as something which is to supply every man's wants without any cost or effort on his part.

A true revenue reform can not be made in a day, but must be the work of national legislation and of time. As soon as the revenue can be dispensed with, all duty should be removed from coffee, tea and other articles of universal use not produced by ourselves. The necessities of the country compel us to collect revenue from our imports. An army of assessors and collectors is not a pleasant sight to the citizen, but that of a tariff for revenue is necessary. Such a tariff, so far as it acts as an encouragement to home production, affords employment to labor at living wages, in contrast to the pauper labor of the Old World, and also in the development of home resources.

Under the act of Congress of the 15th day of July, 1870, the Army has gradually been reduced, so that on the 1st day of January, 1871, the number of commissioned officers and men will not exceed the number contemplated by that law.

The War Department building is an old structure, not fireproof, and entirely inadequate in dimensions to our present wants. Many thousands of dollars are now paid annually for rent of private buildings to accommodate the various bureaus of the Department. I recommend an appropriation for a new War Department building, suited to the present and growing wants of the nation.

The report of the Secretary of War shows a very satisfactory reduction in the expenses of the Army for the last fiscal year. For details you are referred to his accompanying report.

The expenses of the Navy for the whole of the last year—*i. e.*, from December 1, 1869, the date of the last report—are less than $19,000,000, or about $1,000,000 less than they were the previous year. The expenses since the commencement of this fiscal year— *i. e.*, since July 1—show for the five months a decrease of over $2,400,000 from those of the corresponding months last year. The estimates for the current year were $28,205,671.37. Those for next year are $20,683,317, with $955,100 additional for necessary permanent improvements. These estimates are made closely for the mere maintenance of the naval establishment as it now is, without much in the nature of permanent improvement. The appropriations made for the last and current years were evidently intended by Congress, and are sufficient only, to keep the Navy on its present footing by the repairing and refitting of our old ships.

This policy must, of course, gradually but surely destroy the Navy, and it is in itself far from economical, as each year that it is pursued the necessity for mere repairs in ships and navy-yards becomes more imperative and more costly, and our current expenses are annually increased for the mere repair of ships, many of which must soon become unsafe and useless. I hope during the present session of Congress to be able to submit to it a plan by which naval vessels can be built and repairs made with great saving upon the present cost.

It can hardly be wise statesmanship in a Government which represents a country with over 5,000 miles of coast line on both oceans, exclusive of Alaska, and containing 40,000,000 progressive people, with relations of every nature with almost every foreign country, to rest with such inadequate means of enforcing any foreign policy, either of protection or re-dress. Separated by the ocean from the nations of the Eastern Continent, our Navy is our only means of direct protection to our citizens abroad or for the enforcement of any foreign policy.

The accompanying report of the Postmaster-General shows a most satisfactory working of that Department. With the adoption of the recommendations contained therein, particularly those relating to a reform in the franking privilege and the adoption of the "correspondence cards," a self-sustaining postal system may speedily be looked for, and at no distant day a further reduction of the rate of postage be attained.

I recommend authorization by Congress to the Postmaster-General and Attorney-General to issue all commissions to officials appointed through their respective Departments. At present these commissions, where appointments are Presidential, are issued by the State Department. The law in all the Departments of Government, except those of the Post-Office and of Justice, authorizes each to issue its own commissions.

Always favoring practical reforms, I respectfully call your attention to one abuse of long standing which I would like to see remedied by this Congress. It is a reform in the civil service of the country. I would have it go beyond the mere fixing of the tenure of office of clerks and employees who do not require "the advice and consent of the Senate" to make their appointments complete. I would have it govern, not the tenure, but the manner of making all appointments. There is no duty which so much embarrasses the Executive and heads of Departments as that of appointments, nor is there any such arduous and thankless labor imposed on Senators and Representatives as that of finding places for constituents. The present system does not secure the best men, and often not even fit men, for public place. The elevation and purification of the civil service of the Government will be hailed with approval by the whole people of the United States.

Reform in the management of Indian affairs has received the special attention of the Administration from its inauguration to the present day. The experiment of making it a missionary work was tried with a few agencies given to the denomination of Friends, and has been found to work most advantageously. All agencies and superintendencies not so disposed of were given to officers of the Army. The act of Congress reducing the Army renders army officers ineligible for civil positions. Indian agencies being civil offices, I determined to give all the agencies to such religious denominations as had heretofore established missionaries among the Indians, and perhaps to some other denominations who would undertake the work on the same terms—*i. e.*, as a missionary work. The societies selected are allowed to name their own agents, subject to the approval of the Executive, and are expected to watch over them and aid them as missionaries, to Christianize and civilize the Indian, and to train him in the arts of peace. The Government watches over the official acts of these agents, and requires of them as strict an accountability as if they were appointed in any other manner. I entertain the confident hope that the policy now pursued will in a few years bring all the Indians upon reservations, where they will live in houses, and have schoolhouses and churches, and will be pursuing peaceful and self-sustaining avocations, and where they may be visited by the law-abiding white man with the same impunity that he now visits the civilized white settlements. I call your special attention to the report of the Commissioner of Indian Affairs for full information on this subject.

During the last fiscal year 8,095,413 acres of public land were disposed of. Of this quantity 3,698,910.05 acres were taken under the homestead law and 2,159,515.81 acres sold for cash. The remainder was located with military warrants, college or Indian scrip, or applied in satisfaction of grants to railroads or for other public uses. The entries under the homestead law during the last year covered 961,545 acres more than those during the preceding year. Surveys have been vigorously prosecuted to the full extent of the means applicable to the purpose. The quantity of land in market will amply supply the present demand. The claim of the settler under the homestead or the preemption laws is not, however, limited to lands subject to sale at private entry. Any unappropriated surveyed public land may, to a limited amount, be acquired under the former laws if the party entitled to enter under them will comply with the requirements they prescribe in regard to the residence and cultivation. The actual settler's preference right of purchase is even broader, and extends to lands which were unsurveyed at the time of his settlement. His right was formerly confined within much narrower limits, and at one period of our history was conferred only by special statutes. They were enacted from time to time to legalize what was then regarded as an unauthorized intrusion upon the national domain. The opinion that the public lands should be regarded chiefly as a source of revenue is no longer maintained. The rapid settlement and successful cultivation of them are now justly considered of more importance to our well-being than is the fund which the sale of them would produce. The remarkable growth and prosperity of our new States and Territories attest the wisdom of the legislation which invites the tiller of the soil to secure a permanent home on terms within the reach of all. The pioneer who incurs the dangers and privations of a frontier life, and thus aids in laying the foundation of new commonwealths, renders a signal service to his country, and is entitled to its special favor and protection. These laws secure that object and largely promote the general welfare. They should therefore be cherished as a permanent feature of our land system.

Good faith requires us to give full effect to existing grants. The time-honored and beneficent policy of setting apart certain sections of public land for educational purposes in the new States should be continued. When ample provision shall have been made for these objects, I submit as a question worthy of serious consideration whether the residue of our national domain should not be wholly disposed of under the provisions of the homestead and preemption laws.

In addition to the swamp and overflowed lands granted to the States in which they are situated, the lands taken under the agricultural-college acts and for internal-improvement purposes under the act of September, 1841, and the acts supplemental thereto, there had been conveyed up to the close of the last fiscal year, by patent or other equivalent title, to States and corporations 27,836,257.63 acres for railways, canals, and wagon roads. It is estimated that an additional quantity of 174,735,523 acres is still due under grants for like uses. The policy of thus aiding the States in building works of internal improvement was inaugurated more than forty years since in the grants to Indiana and Illinois, to aid those States in opening canals to connect the waters of the Wabash with those of Lake Erie and the waters of the Illinois with those of Lake Michigan. It was followed, with some modifications, in the grant to Illinois of alternate sections of public land within certain limits of the Illinois Central Railway. Fourteen States and sundry corporations have received similar subsidies in connection with railways completed or in process of construction. As the reserved sections are rated at the double minimum, the sale of them at the enhanced price has thus in many instances indemnified the Treasury for the granted lands. The construction of some of these thoroughfares has undoubtedly given a vigorous impulse to the development of our resources and the settlement of the more distant portions of the country. It may, however, be well insisted that much of our legislation in this regard has been characterized by indiscriminate and profuse liberality. The United States should not loan their credit in aid of any enterprise undertaken by States or corporations, nor grant lands in any instance, unless the projected work is of acknowledged national importance. I am strongly inclined to the opinion that it is inexpedient and unnecessary to bestow subsidies of either description; but should Congress determine otherwise I earnestly recommend that the right of settlers and of the public be more effectually secured and protected by appropriate legislation.

During the year ending September 30, 1870, there were filed in the Patent Office 19,411 applications for patents, 3,374 caveats, and 160 applications for the extension of patents. Thirteen thousand six hundred and twenty-two patents, including reissues and designs, were issued, 1,010 extended, and 1,089 allowed, but not issued by reason of the non-payment of the final fees. The receipts of the office during the fiscal year were $136,304.29 in excess of its expenditures.

The work of the Census Bureau has been energetically prosecuted. The preliminary report, containing much information of special value and interest, will be ready for delivery during the present session. The remaining volumes will be completed with all the dispatch consistent with perfect accuracy in arranging and classifying the returns. We shall thus at no distant day be furnished with an authentic record of our condition and resources. It will, I doubt not, attest the growing prosperity of the country, although during the decade which has just closed it was so severely tried by the great war waged to maintain its integrity and to secure and perpetuate our free institutions.

During the last fiscal year the sum paid to pensioners, including the cost of disbursement, was $27,780,811.11, and 1,758 bounty-land warrants were issued. At its close 198,686 names were on the pension rolls.

The labors of the Pension Office have been directed to the severe scrutiny of the evidence submitted in favor of new claims and to the discovery of fictitious claims which have been heretofore allowed. The appropriation for the employment of special agents for the investigation of frauds has been judiciously used, and the results obtained have been of unquestionable benefit to the service.

The subjects of education and agriculture are of great interest to the success of our republican institutions, happiness, and grandeur as a nation. In the interest of one a bureau has been established in the Interior Department—the Bureau of Education; and in the interest of the other, a separate Department, that of Agriculture. I believe great general good is to flow from the operations of both these Bureaus if properly fostered. I can not commend to your careful consideration too highly the reports of the Commissioners of Education and of Agriculture, nor urge too strongly such liberal legislation as to secure their efficiency.

In conclusion I would sum up the policy of the Administration to be a thorough enforcement of every law; a faithful collection of every tax provided for; economy in the disbursement of the same; a prompt payment of every debt of the nation; a reduction of taxes as rapidly as the requirements of the country will admit; reductions of taxation and tariff, to be so arranged as to afford the greatest relief to the greatest number; honest and fair dealings with all other peoples, to the end that war, with all its blighting consequences, may be avoided, but without surrendering any right or obligation due to us; a reform in the treatment of Indians and in the whole civil service of the country; and, finally, in securing a pure, untrammeled ballot, where every man entitled to cast a vote may do so, just once at each election, without fear of molestation or proscription on account of his political faith, nativity, or color.

U. S. GRANT.

SPECIAL MESSAGES.

DECEMBER 6, 1870.

To the Senate and House of Representatives:

In pursuance of the provisions of the second section of an act approved June 20, 1864, entitled "An act making appropriations for the consular and diplomatic expenses of the Government for the year ending June 30, 1865, and for other purposes," I inform Congress that Louis W. Viollier, a consular clerk, was, on the 26th day of September last, removed from office for the following causes, namely: For disobedience of orders and continued absence from duty after orders to proceed to his post.

U. S. GRANT.

WASHINGTON, *December 6, 1870.*

To the Senate and House of Representatives:

I herewith transmit to Congress a report, dated the 5th instant, with the accompanying papers,* received from the Secretary of State, in compliance with the requirements of the eighteenth section of the act entitled "An act to regulate the diplomatic and consular systems of the United States," approved August 18, 1856.

U. S. GRANT.

WASHINGTON, *December 6, 1870.*

To the Senate of the United States:

I transmit to the Senate, for its consideration with a view to ratification, a convention for the surrender of criminals between the United States of America and the Republic of Guatemala, signed on the 11th day of October last, together with correspondence on the subject, a list of which is given.

U. S. GRANT.

WASHINGTON, *December 6, 1870.*

To the Senate of the United States:

I transmit to the Senate, for its consideration with a view to ratification, a convention for the extradition of criminals fugitives from justice between the United States of America and the Republic of Nicaragua, signed at the city of Nicaragua on the 5th day of June last, together with correspondence upon the subject, of which a list is annexed.

U. S. GRANT.

* Report of fees collected, etc., by consular officers of the United States for 1868, and tariff of consular fees prescribed by the President October 1, 1870.

WASHINGTON, *December 6, 1870.*

To the Senate of the United States:

I transmit to the Senate, for its consideration with a view to ratification, a treaty for the extradition of criminals fugitives from justice between the United States and the Republic of Peru, signed at Lima on the 12th day of September last. As this treaty contains some stipulations of an unusual character, the special attention of the Senate is called to them.

U. S. GRANT.

WASHINGTON, *December 6, 1870.*

To the Senate of the United States:

I transmit to the Senate, for its consideration with a view to ratification, a treaty of friendship, commerce, and navigation between the United States of America and the Republic of Peru, signed at the city of Lima on the 6th day of September last, together with the correspondence in relation thereto, a list of which is annexed.

U. S. GRANT.

WASHINGTON, *December 6, 1870.*

To the Senate of the United States:

Referring to my message of the 1st of February last, transmitting to the Senate, for its consideration with a view to ratification, a treaty between the United States and the United States of Colombia for the construction of an interoceanic canal across the Isthmus of Panama or Darien, signed at Bogota on the 26th of January last, I herewith submit correspondence upon the subject between the Secretary of State and the minister of the United States at Bogota, a list of which is hereto appended.

U. S. GRANT.

WASHINGTON, *December 8, 1870.*

To the House of Representatives of the United States:

In answer to its resolution of the 1st of July, 1870, I transmit to the House of Representatives a report* from the Secretary of State.

U. S. GRANT.

WASHINGTON, *December 8, 1870.*

To the Senate of the United States:

In answer to a resolution of the 5th instant, I transmit to the Senate a report † from the Secretary of State.

U. S. GRANT.

---

*Stating that the correspondence relative to the arrest and detention of American fishing vessels in the Straits of Canso by armed vessels flying the British flag had been communicated to Congress with the President's annual message on the 5th instant.

† Stating that the correspondence with the United States minister at Paris relative to the Franco-Prussian war had been communicated with the President's annual message on the 5th instant.

WASHINGTON, *December 12, 1870.*

To the Senate of the United States:

I submit to the Senate, for their consideration with a view to ratification, a convention relating to naturalization between the United States and the Austro-Hungarian Empire, signed at Vienna on the 20th of September, 1870, which is accompanied by the papers mentioned in the subjoined list.

U. S. GRANT.

WASHINGTON, *December 13, 1870.*

To the Senate of the United States:

I transmit, in answer to the resolution of the Senate of June 14, 1870, a report from the Secretary of State and the papers * by which it was accompanied.

U. S. GRANT.

WASHINGTON, *December 15, 1870.*

To the House of Representatives:

In answer to the resolution of the House of Representatives of the 9th of April, 1869, I herewith transmit a report † from the Secretary of State.

U. S. GRANT.

WASHINGTON, *December 15, 1870.*

To the House of Representatives:

In answer to the resolution of the House of Representatives of the 20th of January last, I herewith transmit a report ‡ from the Secretary of State, with accompanying documents.

U. S. GRANT.

EXECUTIVE MANSION, *December 19, 1870.*

To the Senate and House of Representatives of the United States:

I transmit herewith a report § of the Secretary of the Treasury, made in compliance with section 2 of the act approved July 11, 1870, "making appropriations for the consular and diplomatic expenses of the Government for the year ending June 30, 1871, and for other purposes."

U. S. GRANT.

* Relating to charges for messages made by the International Ocean Telegraph Company.

† Stating that all the correspondence relative to the condition of affairs in Paraguay believed to be required by the public interest had been made public.

‡ Stating that the claim for indemnity in the case of the ship *Canada*, wrecked on the coast of Brazil in 1865, had been referred to the British minister as arbiter, and submitting a summary of the case, correspondence connected with it, and a copy of the award of the arbiter.

§ Transmitting reports of consular agents.

WASHINGTON, *December 19, 1870.*

To the House of Representatives:

I transmit to the House of Representatives a report of the Secretary of State and the papers* by which it was accompanied, in answer to its resolution of the 7th instant.

U. S. GRANT.

EXECUTIVE MANSION, *January 4, 1871.*

To the House of Representatives:

I transmit to the House of Representatives, in answer to their resolution of the 12th of December, 1870, a report from the Secretary of State, with accompanying documents.†

U. S. GRANT.

WASHINGTON, *January 9, 1871.*

To the Senate of the United States:

I transmit to the Senate, in answer to their resolution of the 5th instant, a report from the Secretary of State, with accompanying documents.‡

U. S. GRANT.

WASHINGTON, *January 9, 1871.*

To the House of Representatives:

I transmit to the House of Representatives, in answer to their resolution of the 5th instant, a report from the Secretary of State, with the accompanying documents.§

U. S. GRANT.

WASHINGTON, D. C.,
January 9, 1871.

To the Senate of the United States:

I transmit, for consideration with a view to its ratification, a treaty of amity, commerce, and consular privileges between the United States and the Republic of Salvador, signed at the city of San Salvador on the 6th of December last.

A copy of the official correspondence relating to the instrument is also herewith transmitted.

U. S. GRANT.

*Relating to the seizure at Port Hood, Nova Scotia, by a Canadian revenue cutter, of the schooner *Granada*, of Provincetown, Mass.

†Correspondence relative to public documents or libraries in the care of legations of the United States.

‡ The last correspondence with Mr. Motley, including telegraphic dispatches, etc., relative to his recall as minister to the Court of St. James.

§ Correspondence, etc., in 1844 and 1845 relative to the resources and condition of the Dominican Republic.

EXECUTIVE MANSION, *January 11, 1871.*

To the Senate of the United States:

In view of a proclamation having been published in newspapers of the United States purporting to emanate from Cabral, a chieftain who opposed the constitutional authorities of the Republic of San Domingo, I deem it but just to communicate to the Senate of the United States the views of that chieftain and his followers, as voluntarily communicated by him through the United States minister to the Republic of Hayti in June last. It will be observed by the letter of Minister Bassett that Cabral did not wish his views to be made public before the question of annexation was disposed of, in a way to work prejudice to his interest. But as the object which Cabral had already in view was to declare to the treaty-making power of the United States his views and those of his followers upon the subject of annexation of the Republic of San Domingo, and as the Senate is a branch of that power, I deem it no breach of confidence to communicate this letter to the Senate. I ask, however, that it may be read in executive session and that the request of Cabral be observed, so that in no case they shall be made public or used against him until the question of annexation is disposed of.

U. S. GRANT.

EXECUTIVE MANSION, *January 11, 1871.*

To the House of Representatives:

I transmit herewith, in reply to the resolution of the House of Representatives of the 5th instant, copies of the reports of Captain George B. McClellan upon the Dominican Republic, made in the year 1854.

U. S. GRANT.

EXECUTIVE MANSION, *January 13, 1871.*

To the Senate of the United States:

In reply to the resolution of the Senate of the 16th of December, 1870, requesting to be furnished with information relative to the organization of disloyal persons in North Carolina having in view resistance of the United States laws, denial of protection, and the enjoyment of the rights and liberties secured under the United States, etc., I transmit herewith abstracts of reports and other papers on file in the War Department relative to outrages in North Carolina, and also, for the information of the Senate, those relative to outrages in the other Southern States. The original reports and papers are too voluminous to be copied in season to be used by the present Congress, but are easily accessible for reference, and copies of such papers can be furnished as the Senate may deem necessary.

U. S. GRANT.

WASHINGTON, *January 16, 1871.*

To the Senate of the United States:

I transmit to the Senate, in answer to their resolution of 4th instant, a report from the Secretary of State, with accompanying documents, relating to the proposed annexation of the Dominican portion of the island of San Domingo.

U. S. GRANT.

EXECUTIVE MANSION, *January 17, 1871.*

To the Senate of the United States:

In answer to their resolution of the 16th of December, 1870, I herewith transmit copies of certain reports received at the War Department relative to disloyal organizations in the State of North Carolina, intended to resist the laws or to deprive the citizens of the United States of the protection of law or the enjoyment of their rights under the Constitution of the United States. These reports are in addition to the abstracts of those sent to the Senate on the 13th instant.

U. S. GRANT.

EXECUTIVE MANSION, *January 24, 1871.*

To the Senate of the United States:

In answer to your resolution of the 21st December, 1870, requesting the President "to furnish the Senate with the amount of money expended by the United States for freight and passage to the Pacific Coast by the way of the Isthmus and Cape Horn during the twelve months now last past," I herewith transmit reports from the Secretary of the Treasury, of War, and of the Navy, to whom, respectively, the resolution was referred.

U. S. GRANT.

WASHINGTON, *January 27, 1871.*

To the Senate and House of Representatives:

I transmit herewith, for the consideration of Congress, a report of the Secretary of State and the papers which accompanied it, concerning regulations for the consular courts of the United States in Japan.

U. S. GRANT.

WASHINGTON, *January 27, 1871.*

To the Senate of the United States:

I transmit, for consideration with a view to its ratification, a treaty of friendship, commerce, and navigation between the United States and the Oriental Republic of Uruguay, which was signed at Montevideo, it is presumed, in the course of last month, though the precise date has inadvertently been omitted.

A copy of the correspondence relating to the instrument is also herewith transmitted. From this it will be seen that the treaty is substantially the same as one between the same parties which has already been approved by the Senate and ratified by the President of the United States, but the ratifications of which have never been exchanged. If the Senate should approve the new treaty, it is suggested that their resolution to that effect should include authority to insert the precise date when that shall have been ascertained.

U. S. GRANT.

EXECUTIVE MANSION, *January 30, 1871.*

To the Senate and House of Representatives:

I transmit herewith an official copy of the proceedings of the council of Indian tribes held at Ocmulgee in December last, which resulted in the adoption of a declaration of rights and a constitution for their government, together with a copy of the report of the Commissioner of Indian Affairs and the views of the Secretary of the Interior thereon.

It would seem highly desirable that the civilized Indians of the country should be encouraged in establishing for themselves forms of Territorial government compatible with the Constitution of the United States and with the previous customs toward communities lying outside of State limits.

I concur in the views expressed by the Secretary of the Interior, that it would not be advisable to receive the new Territory with the constitution precisely as it is now framed. As long as a Territorial form of government is preserved, Congress should hold the power of approving or disapproving of all legislative action of the Territory, and the Executive should, with "the advice and consent of the Senate," have the power to appoint the governor and judicial officers (and possibly some others) of the Territory.

This is the first indication of the aborigines desiring to adopt our form of government, and it is highly desirable that they become self-sustaining, self-relying, Christianized, and civilized. If successful in this their first attempt at Territorial government, we may hope for a gradual concentration of other Indians in the new Territory. I therefore recommend as close an adherence to their wishes as is consistent with safety.

It might be well to limit the appointment of all Territorial officials appointed by the Executive to native citizens of the Territory. If any exception is made to this rule, I would recommend that it should be limited to the judiciary.

It is confidently hoped that the policy now being pursued toward the Indian will fit him for self-government and make him desire to settle among people of his own race where he can enjoy the full privileges of civil and enlightened government.

U. S. GRANT.

EXECUTIVE MANSION, *February 7, 1871.*

To the Senate and House of Representatives:

The union of the States of Germany into a form of government similar in many respects to that of the American Union is an event that can not fail to touch deeply the sympathies of the people of the United States.

This union has been brought about by the long-continued, persistent efforts of the people, with the deliberate approval of the governments and people of twenty-four of the German States, through their regularly constituted representatives.

In it the American people see an attempt to reproduce in Europe some of the best features of our own Constitution, with such modifications as the history and condition of Germany seem to require. The local governments of the several members of the union are preserved, while the power conferred upon the chief imparts strength for the purposes of self-defense, without authority to enter upon wars of conquest and ambition.

The cherished aspiration for national unity which for ages has inspired the many millions of people speaking the same language, inhabiting a contiguous and compact territory, but unnaturally separated and divided by dynastic jealousies and the ambition of short-sighted rulers, has been attained, and Germany now contains a population of about 34,000,000, united, like our own, under one Government for its relations with other powers, but retaining in its several members the right and power of control of their local interests, habits, and institutions.

The bringing of great masses of thoughtful and free people under a single government must tend to make governments what alone they should be—the representatives of the will and the organization of the power of the people.

The adoption in Europe of the American system of union under the control and direction of a free people, educated to self-restraint, can not fail to extend popular institutions and to enlarge the peaceful influence of American ideas.

The relations of the United States with Germany are intimate and cordial. The commercial intercourse between the two countries is extensive and is increasing from year to year; and the large number of citizens and residents in the United States of German extraction and the continued flow of emigration thence to this country have produced an intimacy of personal and political intercourse approaching, if not equal to, that with the country from which the founders of our Government derived their origin.

The extent of these interests and the greatness of the German Union seem to require that in the classification of the representatives of this Government to foreign powers there should no longer be an apparent undervaluation of the importance of the German mission, such as is made in the difference between the compensation allowed by law to the minister to

Germany and those to Great Britain and France. There would seem to be a great propriety in placing the representative of this Government at Berlin on the same footing with that of its representatives at London and Paris. The union of the several States of Germany under one Government and the increasing commercial and personal intercourse between the two countries will also add to the labors and the responsibilities of the legation.

I therefore recommend that the salaries of the minister and of the secretary of legation at Berlin be respectively increased to the same amounts as are allowed to those at London and Paris.

U. S. GRANT.

EXECUTIVE MANSION, *February 7, 1871.*

To the Senate of the United States:

In answer to that part of your resolution of the 4th of January last requesting copies of "instructions to the commander of our naval squadron in the waters of the island [of San Domingo] since the commencement of the late negotiations, with the reports and correspondence of such commander," I herewith transmit a report, with accompanying papers, received from the Secretary of the Navy.

U. S. GRANT.

EXECUTIVE MANSION, *February 8, 1871.*

To the Senate and House of Representatives:

I transmit herewith an extract of a paper addressed to the President, the Secretary of the Interior, and the Commissioner of Indian Affairs by the committee of Friends on Indian affairs having charge of the northern superintendency, in relation to a desire of certain Indian tribes to sell a portion of the lands owned by them, with a view of locating on other lands that they may be able to purchase, together with the report of the Commissioner of Indian Affairs thereon and a letter of the Secretary of the Interior Department approving the report of the Commissioner.

I submit the draft of a bill which has been prepared, and which it is believed will effect the object desired by the committee, and request the consideration thereof by Congress.

U. S. GRANT.

WASHINGTON, *February 9, 1871.*

To the Senate:

The British minister accredited to this Government recently, in compliance with instructions from his Government, submitted a proposal for the appointment of a "joint high commission," to be composed of members to be named by each Government, to hold its session at Washington, and to treat and discuss the mode of settling the different questions which have arisen out of the fisheries, as well as those which affect the relations of the United States toward the British possessions in North America.

I did not deem it expedient to agree to the proposal unless the consideration of the questions growing out of the acts committed by the vessels which have given rise to the claims known as the "Alabama claims" were to be within the subject of discussion and settlement by the commission. The British Government having assented to this, the commission is expected shortly to meet. I therefore nominate as such commissioners, jointly and separately, on the part of the United States:

Hamilton Fish, Secretary of State.

Robert C. Schenck, envoy extraordinary and minister plenipotentiary to Great Britain.

Samuel Nelson, an associate justice of the Supreme Court of the United States.

Ebenezer R. Hoar, of Massachusetts.

George H. Williams, of Oregon.

I communicate herewith the correspondence which has passed on this subject between the Secretary of State and the British minister.

U. S. GRANT.

EXECUTIVE MANSION, *February 10, 1871.*

To the Senate and House of Representatives:

I submit herewith, for the information of Congress, the second annual report of the Board of Indian Commissioners to the Secretary of the Interior.

U. S. GRANT.

EXECUTIVE MANSION, *February 13, 1871*

To the House of Representatives:

I transmit herewith, in answer to the resolution of the House of the 6th instant, copies of the correspondence between the governor of the State of California and the President of the United States in the month of October, 1868, relative to the use of the military forces of the National Government in preserving the peace at the approaching State election.

U. S. GRANT.

EXECUTIVE MANSION, *February 15, 1871.*

To the Senate and House of Representatives:

I have this day transmitted to the Senate the announcement that Senate bill No. 218, "An act prescribing an oath of office to be taken by persons who participated in the late rebellion, but who are not disqualified from holding office by the fourteenth amendment to the Constitution of the United States," has become a law in the manner prescribed by the Constitution, without the signature of the President.

If this were a bill for the repeal of the "test oath" required of persons "selected or appointed to offices of honor or trust," it would meet my approval. The effect of the law, however, is to relieve from taking a prescribed oath all those persons whom it was intended to exclude from such offices and to require it from all others. By this law the soldier who fought and bled for his country is to swear to his loyalty before assuming official functions, while the general who commanded hosts for the overthrow of his Government is admitted to place without it. I can not affix my name to a law which discriminates against the upholder of his Government.

I believe, however, that it is not wise policy to keep from office by an oath those who are not disqualified by the Constitution, and who are the choice of legal voters; but while relieving them from an oath which they can not take, I recommend the release also of those to whom the oath has no application.

U. S. GRANT.

EXECUTIVE MANSION, *February 17, 1871.*

To the Senate of the United States:

In answer to your resolution of the 19th of December last, requesting the President "to furnish the Senate with the entire cost of transportation of mails and freights of every description to the Pacific Coast, also to all intermediate points west of the Missouri River, from the annexation of California to July 1, 1864; and also the expenses of the War Department and Indian Bureau during the same period in guarding the overland route from the Missouri River to California against Indians and Mormons, and the cost of the Indian service on the same line, including in all cases freights and all other expenditures," I transmit herewith reports received from the Secretary of the Interior, the Secretary of War, and the Postmaster-General.

U. S. GRANT.

WASHINGTON, *February 27, 1871.*

To the Senate of the United States:

I transmit to the Senate, for its consideration with a view to ratification, a convention between the United States and Great Britain, concluded at Washington on the 23d instant, supplemental to the convention between the two countries concluded May 13, 1870, concerning the citizenship of citizens or subjects of either country emigrating to the other.

The conclusion of the supplemental convention now submitted was found to be expedient in view of the stipulation contained in Article II of the before-named convention of May 13, 1870, that the two Govern ments should agree upon the manner in which the renunciation within the periods specified, by naturalized citizens and subjects of either coun-try, of their naturalization should be effected.

U. S. GRANT.

WASHINGTON, March 3, 1871.

To the Senate of the United States:

I transmit to the Senate, in answer to their resolution of the 2d instant a report of the Secretary of State, with accompanying documents.*

U. S. GRANT.

WASHINGTON, March 3, 1871.

To the Senate of the United States:

I transmit to the Senate, in answer to their resolution of February 1, 1871, a report from the Secretary of State, with accompanying documents.†

U. S. GRANT.

VETO MESSAGES.

EXECUTIVE MANSION, January 4, 1871.

To the House of Representatives:

I herewith return without my approval House bill No. 1395, entitled "An act for the relief of Charles Cooper, Goshorn A. Jones, Jerome Rowley, William Hannegan, and John Hannegan," for the following reasons:

The act directs the discontinuance of an action at law said to be now pending in the United States district court for the northern district of Ohio for the enforcement of the bond executed by said parties to the United States, whereas in fact no such suit is pending in the district court, but such a suit is now pending in the circuit court of the United States for the sixth circuit and northern district of Ohio.

Neither the body of said act nor the proviso requires the obligors in said bond, who are released from all liability to the United States on account thereof, to abandon or release their pretended claim against the Government.

Since these parties have gone to Congress to ask relief from liability for a large sum of money on account of the failure of the principals in

---

* Correspondence from the United States legation at Constantinople relative to restrictions on the passage of the straits of the Dardanelles and the Bosphorus by the ships of other nations.

† Dispatches, etc., from the United States minister to the Court of Brazil relative to the Paraguayan war, the culture of cotton in Brazil, trade with Brazil, etc.

the bond to execute their contract, it is but just and proper that they at the same time should abandon the claim heretofore asserted by them against the Government growing out of the same transaction.

U. S. GRANT.

EXECUTIVE MANSION, *February 7, 1871.*

To the Senate of the United States:

I hereby return without my approval Senate resolution No. 92, entitled "A resolution for the relief of certain contractors for the construction of vessels of war and steam machinery," for the following reasons:

The act of March 2, 1867 (14 U. S. Statutes at Large, p. 424), directs the Secretary of the Navy—

to investigate the claims of all contractors for building vessels of war and steam machinery for the same under contracts made after the 1st day of May, 1861, and prior to the first day of January, 1864; and said investigation to be made upon the following basis: He shall ascertain the additional cost which was necessarily incurred by each contractor in the completion of his work by reason of any changes or alterations in the plans and specifications required, and delays in the prosecution of the work occasioned by the Government, which were not provided for in the original contract; but no allowance for any advance in the price of labor or material shall be considered unless such advance occurred during the prolonged time for completing the work rendered necessary by the delay resulting from the action of the Government aforesaid, and then only when such advance could not have been avoided by the exercise of ordinary prudence and diligence on the part of the contractor. * * *

The present joint resolution transfers the investigation to the Court of Claims, and repeals "so much of said act as provides against considering any allowance in favor of any such parties for any advance in the price of labor or material, unless such advance could have been avoided by the exercise of ordinary diligence and prudence on the part of the contractor." It seems to me that the provision thus repealed is a very reasonable one. It prevents the contractor from receiving any allowance for an advance in the price of labor and material when he could have avoided that advance by the exercise of ordinary prudence and diligence. The effect of the repeal will be to relieve contractors from the consequences of their own imprudence and negligence. I see no good reason for thus relieving contractors who have not exercised ordinary prudence and diligence in their business transactions.

U. S. GRANT.

EXECUTIVE MANSION, *February 28, 1871.*

To the House of Representatives:

I herewith return without my approval House bill No. 2566, entitled "An act for the relief of Henry Willman, late a private in the Third Regiment of Indiana Cavalry," for the following reasons:

The records of the War Department show that Henry Willman was mustered into the military service April 4, 1862, and that he was mounted on a private horse. It appears from evidence presented by himself **that** his horse died May 18, 1862; that he remounted himself on June 8, 1862, and so continued mounted till October 1, 1862, when his horse was killed by the enemy, and that he was not afterwards mounted upon a private horse.

Upon presenting a claim against the United States for the legal value of the two horses lost by him in the public service, the claim, after investigation, was allowed; but it being discovered that he had erroneously been paid for the use and risk of a private horse from May 18 to June 8, 1862, and from October 1, 1862, to April 30, 1864, during which periods he had no horse in the public service, the amount so overpaid was offset against his claim, leaving the latter fully liquidated and the claimant indebted to the United States in an amount not yet refunded.

The person named in the act is not, in law or equity, entitled to the relief therein provided, and has no unsatisfied demands against the United States.

U. S. GRANT.

PROCLAMATION.

By the President of the United States of America.

A PROCLAMATION.

Whereas satisfactory evidence was given to me on the 17th day of this month by the Government of Portugal that the discriminating duties heretofore levied in the ports of Portugal on merchandise imported in vessels of the United States into said ports from other countries than those of which said merchandise was the growth, production, or manufacture have been abolished:

Now, therefore, I, Ulysses S. Grant, President of the United States of America, by virtue of the authority vested in me by an act of Congress of January 7, 1824, and by an act in addition thereto of May 24, 1828, do hereby declare and proclaim that the discriminating duties heretofore levied in ports of the United States upon merchandise imported in Portuguese vessels from countries other than those of which such merchandise is the growth, produce, or manufacture shall be, and are hereby, suspended and discontinued, this suspension or discontinuance to take effect on and after the said 17th day of this month and to continue so long as the reciprocal exemption of merchandise belonging to citizens of the United States from such discriminating duties shall be granted in the ports of Portugal.

In testimony whereof I have hereunto set my hand and caused the seal of the United States to be affixed.

[SEAL.]   Done at the city of Washington, this 25th day of February, A. D. 1871, and of the Independence of the United States of America the ninety-fifth.

U. S. GRANT.

By the President:

HAMILTON FISH,
Secretary of State.

[NOTE.—The Forty-second Congress, first session, met March 4, 1871, in accordance with the act of January 22, 1867.]

SPECIAL MESSAGES.

WASHINGTON, *March 17, 1871.*

To the Senate of the United States:

I transmit to the Senate, in compliance with its resolution of the 14th instant, a report from the Secretary of State, making known that official notice has been received at the Department of State of the ratification by the legislature of one, and only one, additional State—to wit, that of New Jersey—of the fifteenth amendment to the Constitution of the United States since the 30th of March, 1870, the date of his certificate that three-fourths of the whole number of States in the United States had ratified that amendment and that it had become valid to all intents and purposes as part of the Constitution of the United States.

U. S. GRANT.

WASHINGTON, D. C., *March 23, 1871.*

To the Senate and House of Representatives:

A condition of affairs now exists in some of the States of the Union rendering life and property insecure and the carrying of the mails and the collection of the revenue dangerous. The proof that such a condition of affairs exists in some localities is now before the Senate. That the power to correct these evils is beyond the control of the State authorities I do not doubt; that the power of the Executive of the United States, acting within the limits of existing laws, is sufficient for present emergencies is not clear.

Therefore I urgently recommend such legislation as in the judgment of Congress shall effectually secure life, liberty, and property and the enforcement of law in all parts of the United States.

It may be expedient to provide that such law as shall be passed in pursuance of this recommendation shall expire at the end of the next session of Congress.

There is no other subject upon which I would recommend legislation during the present session.

U. S. GRANT.

WASHINGTON, *March 28, 1871.*

To the Senate of the United States:

In answer to the resolution of the Senate of the 16th instant, I transmit a report from the Secretary of State and the papers* which accompanied it.

U. S. GRANT.

WASHINGTON, *March 30, 1871.*

To the Senate of the United States:

I transmit, for consideration with a view to its ratification, a treaty of commerce and navigation between the United States and the Kingdom of Italy, signed at Florence on the 26th of last month.

U. S. GRANT.

EXECUTIVE MANSION, *March 31, 1871.*

To the Senate of the United States:

In answer to your resolution of the 17th instant, requesting, "if not incompatible with the public service, the report recently made by a board of officers of the Engineer Department on the condition of the Mississippi River near Vicksburg, Miss., with such remarks, suggestions, or recommendations as may be made by the Chief Engineer of the Army," I herewith transmit a report, dated 28th instant, with accompanying papers, received from the Secretary of War.

U. S. GRANT.

EXECUTIVE MANSION, *April 5, 1871.*

To the Senate and House of Representatives:

I have the honor to submit herewith to the two Houses of Congress the report of the commissioners appointed in pursuance of joint resolution approved January 12, 1871.

It will be observed that this report more than sustains all that I have heretofore said in regard to the productiveness and healthfulness of the Republic of San Domingo, of the unanimity of the people for annexation to the United States, and of their peaceable character.

It is due to the public, as it certainly is to myself, that I should here give all the circumstances which first led to the negotiation of a treaty for the annexation of the Republic of San Domingo to the United States.

* Reports, communications, etc., relative to the International Statistical Congress held at The Hague in 1869.

When I accepted the arduous and responsible position which I now hold, I did not dream of instituting any steps for the acquisition of insular possessions. I believed, however, that our institutions were broad enough to extend over the entire continent as rapidly as other peoples might desire to bring themselves under our protection. I believed further that we should not permit any independent government within the limits of North America to pass from a condition of independence to one of ownership or protection under a European power.

Soon after my inauguration as President I was waited upon by an agent of President Baez with a proposition to annex the Republic of San Domingo to the United States. This gentleman represented the capacity of the island, the desire of the people, and their character and habits about as they have been described by the commissioners whose report accompanies this message. He stated further that, being weak in numbers and poor in purse, they were not capable of developing their great resources; that the people had no incentive to industry on account of lack of protection for their accumulations, and that if not accepted by the United States—with institutions which they loved above those of any other nation—they would be compelled to seek protection elsewhere. To these statements I made no reply and gave no indication of what I thought of the proposition. In the course of time I was waited upon by a second gentleman from San Domingo, who made the same representations, and who was received in like manner.

In view of the facts which had been laid before me, and with an earnest desire to maintain the "Monroe doctrine," I believed that I would be derelict in my duty if I did not take measures to ascertain the exact wish of the Government and inhabitants of the Republic of San Domingo in regard to annexation and communicate the information to the people of the United States. Under the attending circumstances I felt that if I turned a deaf ear to this appeal I might in the future be justly charged with a flagrant neglect of the public interests and an utter disregard of the welfare of a downtrodden race praying for the blessings of a free and strong government and for protection in the enjoyment of the fruits of their own industry.

Those opponents of annexation who have heretofore professed to be preeminently the friends of the rights of man I believed would be my most violent assailants if I neglected so clear a duty. Accordingly, after having appointed a commissioner to visit the island, who declined on account of sickness, I selected a second gentleman, in whose capacity, judgment, and integrity I had, and have yet, the most unbounded confidence.

He visited San Domingo, not to secure or hasten annexation, but, unprejudiced and unbiased, to learn all the facts about the Government, the people, and the resources of that Republic. He went certainly as well prepared to make an unfavorable report as a favorable one, if the facts warranted it. His report fully corroborated the views of previous commissioners, and upon its receipt I felt that a sense of duty and a due regard for our great national interests required me to negotiate a treaty for the acquisition of the Republic of San Domingo.

As soon as it became publicly known that such a treaty had been negotiated, the attention of the country was occupied with allegations calculated to prejudice the merits of the case and with aspersions upon those whose duty had connected them with it. Amid the public excitement thus created the treaty failed to receive the requisite two-thirds vote of the Senate, and was rejected; but whether the action of that body was based wholly upon the merits of the treaty, or might not have been in some degree influenced by such unfounded allegations, could not be known by the people, because the debates of the Senate in secret session are not published.

Under these circumstances I deemed it due to the office which I hold and due to the character of the agents who had been charged with the investigation that such proceedings should be had as would enable the people to know the truth. A commission was therefore constituted, under authority of Congress, consisting of gentlemen selected with special reference to their high character and capacity for the laborious work intrusted to them, who were instructed to visit the spot and report upon the facts. Other eminent citizens were requested to accompany the commission, in order that the people might have the benefit of their views. Students of science and correspondents of the press, without regard to political opinions, were invited to join the expedition, and their numbers were limited only by the capacity of the vessel.

The mere rejection by the Senate of a treaty negotiated by the President only indicates a difference of opinion between two coordinate departments of the Government, without touching the character or wounding the pride of either. But when such rejection takes place simultaneously with charges openly made of corruption on the part of the President or those employed by him the case is different. Indeed, in such case the honor of the nation demands investigation. This has been accomplished by the report of the commissioners herewith transmitted, and which fully vindicates the purity of the motives and action of those who represented the United States in the negotiation.

And now my task is finished, and with it ends all personal solicitude upon the subject. My duty being done, yours begins; and I gladly hand over the whole matter to the judgment of the American people and of their representatives in Congress assembled. The facts will now be spread before the country, and a decision rendered by that tribunal whose convictions so seldom err, and against whose will I have no policy to enforce. My opinion remains unchanged; indeed, it is confirmed by the report that the interests of our country and of San Domingo alike invite the annexation of that Republic.

In view of the difference of opinion upon this subject, I suggest that no action be taken at the present session beyond the printing and general dissemination of the report. Before the next session of Congress the people will have considered the subject and formed an intelligent opinion concerning it, to which opinion, deliberately made up, it will be the duty of every department of the Government to give heed; and no one will more cheerfully conform to it than myself. It is not only the theory of our Constitution that the will of the people, constitutionally expressed, is the supreme law, but I have ever believed that "all men are wiser than any one man;" and if the people, upon a full presentation of the facts, shall decide that the annexation of the Republic is not desirable, every department of the Government ought to acquiesce in that decision.

In again submitting to Congress a subject upon which public sentiment has been divided, and which has been made the occasion of acrimonious debates in Congress, as well as of unjust aspersions elsewhere, I may, I trust, be indulged in a single remark.

No man could hope to perform duties so delicate and responsible as pertain to the Presidential office without sometimes incurring the hostility of those who deem their opinions and wishes treated with insufficient consideration; and he who undertakes to conduct the affairs of a great government as a faithful public servant, if sustained by the approval of his own conscience, may rely with confidence upon the candor and intelligence of a free people whose best interests he has striven to subserve, and can bear with patience the censure of disappointed men.

U. S. GRANT.

WASHINGTON, *April 5, 1871.*

To the Senate of the United States:

I transmit confidentially, for the information and consideration of the Senate, a copy of a dispatch of the 25th of February last relative to the annexation of the Hawaiian Islands, addressed to the Department of State by Henry A. Pierce, minister resident of the United States at Honolulu. Although I do not deem it advisable to express any opinion or to make any recommendation in regard to the subject at this juncture, the views of the Senate, if it should be deemed proper to express them, would be very acceptable with reference to any future course which there might be a disposition to adopt.

U. S. GRANT.

WASHINGTON, *April 11, 1871.*

To the House of Representatives:

I transmit to the House of Representatives, in answer to their resolution of March 31, 1871, a report from the Secretary of State, with accompanying documents.*

U. S. GRANT.

* Dispatches from the United States minister at Florence relative to the occupation of Rome by the King of Italy.

[The following messages were sent to the special session of the Senate convened by proclamation (see pp. 133-134) of April 20, 1871.]

WASHINGTON, *May 10, 1871.*

To the Senate of the United States:

I transmit to the Senate, for consideration with a view to ratification, a treaty between the United States and Great Britain for the settlement of pending questions between the two countries, signed at Washington on the 8th instant by the commissioners of the United States and Great Britain, respectively.

Copies of the powers and instructions to the commissioners on the part of the United States and the protocols of the conferences are also transmitted.

U. S. GRANT.

WASHINGTON, *May 15, 1871.*

To the Senate of the United States:

I transmit to the Senate, in answer to their resolution of the 10th instant, a report * from the Secretary of State and the papers which accompanied it.

U. S. GRANT.

WASHINGTON, *May 17, 1871.*

To the Senate of the United States:

In answer to a resolution of the Senate of the 15th instant, I transmit herewith a report † from the Secretary of State.

U. S. GRANT.

PROCLAMATIONS.

BY THE PRESIDENT OF THE UNITED STATES OF AMERICA.

A PROCLAMATION.

Whereas it is provided in the Constitution of the United States that the United States shall protect every State in this Union, on application of the legislature, or of the executive (when the legislature can not be convened), against domestic violence; and

Whereas it is provided in the laws of the United States that in all cases of insurrection in any State or of obstruction to the laws thereof it shall be lawful for the President of the United States, on application of the legislature of such State, or of the executive (when the legislature can not be convened), to call forth the militia of any other State or States,

---

* Relating to claims of the subjects of foreign nations growing out of the War of the Rebellion.
† Relating to claims under the treaty of Washington of May 8, 1871.

or to employ such part of the land and naval force as shall be judged necessary for the purpose of suppressing such insurrection or of causing the laws to be duly executed; and

Whereas I have received information that combinations of armed men, unauthorized by law, are now disturbing the peace and safety of the citizens of the State of South Carolina and committing acts of violence in said State of a character and to an extent which render the power of the State and its officers unequal to the task of protecting life and property and securing public order therein; and

Whereas the legislature of said State is not now in session and can not be convened in time to meet the present emergency, and the executive of said State has therefore made application to me for such part of the military force of the United States as may be necessary and adequate to protect said State and the citizens thereof against the domestic violence hereinbefore mentioned and to enforce the due execution of the laws; and

Whereas the laws of the United States require that whenever it may be necessary, in the judgment of the President, to use the military force for the purpose aforesaid, he shall forthwith, by proclamation, command such insurgents to disperse and retire peaceably to their respective abodes within a limited time:

Now, therefore, I, Ulysses S. Grant, President of the United States, do hereby command the persons composing the unlawful combinations aforesaid to disperse and retire peaceably to their respective abodes within twenty days from this date.

In witness whereof I have hereunto set my hand and caused the seal of the United States to be affixed.

[SEAL.] Done at the city of Washington, this 24th day of March, A. D. 1871, and of the Independence of the United States the ninety-fifth.

U. S. GRANT.

By the President:
HAMILTON FISH,
Secretary of State.

BY THE PRESIDENT OF THE UNITED STATES OF AMERICA.

A PROCLAMATION.

Whereas objects of interest to the United States require that the Senate should be convened at 12 o'clock on Wednesday, the 10th day of May next, to receive and act upon such communications as may be made to it on the part of the Executive:

Now, therefore, I, Ulysses S. Grant, President of the United States, have considered it to be my duty to issue this my proclamation, declaring that an extraordinary occasion requires the Senate of the United States to convene for the transaction of business at the Capitol, in the city of Washington, on Wednesday, the 10th day of May next, at 12 o'clock on that day, of which all who shall at that time be entitled to act as members of that body are hereby required to take notice.

Given under my hand and the seal of the United States, at Washington, the 20th day of April, A. D. 1871, and of the Independence of the United States of America the ninety-fifth.

[SEAL.]

U. S. GRANT.

By the President:
   HAMILTON FISH,
         Secretary of State.

BY THE PRESIDENT OF THE UNITED STATES OF AMERICA.

A PROCLAMATION.

The act of Congress entitled "An act to enforce the provisions of the fourteenth amendment to the Constitution of the United States, and for other purposes," approved April 20, A. D. 1871, being a law of extraordinary public importance, I consider it my duty to issue this my proclamation, calling the attention of the people of the United States thereto, enjoining upon all good citizens, and especially upon all public officers, to be zealous in the enforcement thereof, and warning all persons to abstain from committing any of the acts thereby prohibited.

This law of Congress applies to all parts of the United States and will be enforced everywhere to the extent of the powers vested in the Executive. But inasmuch as the necessity therefor is well known to have been caused chiefly by persistent violations of the rights of citizens of the United States by combinations of lawless and disaffected persons in certain localities lately the theater of insurrection and military conflict, I do particularly exhort the people of those parts of the country to suppress all such combinations by their own voluntary efforts through the agency of local laws and to maintain the rights of all citizens of the United States and to secure to all such citizens the equal protection of the laws.

Fully sensible of the responsibility imposed upon the Executive by the act of Congress to which public attention is now called, and reluctant to call into exercise any of the extraordinary powers thereby conferred upon me except in cases of imperative necessity, I do, nevertheless, deem it my duty to make known that I will not hesitate to exhaust the powers thus vested in the Executive whenever and wherever it shall become necessary to do so for the purpose of securing to all citizens of the United States the peaceful enjoyment of the rights guaranteed to them by the Constitution and laws.

It is my earnest wish that peace and cheerful obedience to law may prevail throughout the land and that all traces of our late unhappy civil strife may be speedily removed. These ends can be easily reached by acquiescence in the results of the conflict, now written in our Constitution, and by the due and proper enforcement of equal, just, and impartial laws in every part of our country.

The failure of local communities to furnish such means for the attainment of results so earnestly desired imposes upon the National Government the duty of putting forth all its energies for the protection of its citizens of every race and color and for the restoration of peace and order throughout the entire country.

In testimony whereof I have hereunto set my hand and caused the seal of the United States to be affixed.

[SEAL.]   Done at the city of Washington, this 3d day of May, A. D. 1871, and of the Independence of the United States the ninety-fifth.

U. S. GRANT.

By the President:

HAMILTON FISH, *Secretary of State.*

BY THE PRESIDENT OF THE UNITED STATES OF AMERICA.

A PROCLAMATION.

Whereas unlawful combinations and conspiracies have long existed and do still exist in the State of South Carolina for the purpose of depriving certain portions and classes of the people of that State of the rights, privileges, immunities, and protection named in the Constitution of the United States and secured by the act of Congress approved April 20, 1871, entitled "An act to enforce the provisions of the fourteenth amendment to the Constitution of the United States;" and

Whereas in certain parts of said State, to wit, in the counties of Spartanburg, York, Marion, Chester, Laurens, Newberry, Fairfield, Lancaster, and Chesterfield, such combinations and conspiracies do so obstruct and hinder the execution of the laws of said State and of the United States as to deprive the people aforesaid of the rights, privileges, immunities, and protection aforesaid and do oppose and obstruct the laws of the United States and their due execution and impede and obstruct the due course of justice under the same; and

Whereas the constituted authorities of said State are unable to protect the people aforesaid in such rights within the said counties; and

Whereas the combinations and conspiracies aforesaid, within the counties aforesaid, are organized and armed and are so numerous and powerful as to be able to defy the constituted authorities of said State and of the United States within the said State, and by reason of said causes the conviction of such offenders and the preservation of the public peace and safety have become impracticable in said counties:

Now, therefore, I, Ulysses S. Grant, President of the United States of

America, do hereby command all persons composing the unlawful combinations and conspiracies aforesaid to disperse and to retire peaceably to their homes within five days of the date hereof, and to deliver either to the marshal of the United States for the district of South Carolina, or to any of his deputies, or to any military officer of the United States within said counties, all arms, ammunition, uniforms, disguises, and other means and implements used, kept, possessed, or controlled by them for carrying out the unlawful purposes for which the combinations and conspiracies are organized.

In witness whereof I have hereunto set my hand and caused the seal of the United States to be affixed.

[SEAL.]   Done at the city of Washington, this 12th day of October, A. D. 1871, and of the Independence of the United States of America the ninety-sixth.

U. S. GRANT.

By the President:

HAMILTON FISH,
Secretary of State.

BY THE PRESIDENT OF THE UNITED STATES OF AMERICA.

A PROCLAMATION.

Whereas by an act of Congress entitled "An act to enforce the provisions of the fourteenth amendment to the Constitution of the United States, and for other purposes," approved the 20th day of April, A. D. 1871, power is given to the President of the United States, when in his judgment the public safety shall require it, to suspend the privileges of the writ of *habeas corpus* in any State or part of a State whenever combinations and conspiracies exist in such State or part of a State for the purpose of depriving any portion or class of the people of such State of the rights, privileges, immunities, and protection named in the Constitution of the United States and secured by the act of Congress aforesaid; and whenever such combinations and conspiracies do so obstruct and hinder the execution of the laws of any such State and of the United States as to deprive the people aforesaid of the rights, privileges, immunities, and protection aforesaid, and do oppose and obstruct the laws of the United States and their due execution, and impede and obstruct the due course of justice under the same; and whenever such combinations shall be organized and armed, and so numerous and powerful as to be able by violence either to overthrow or to set at defiance the constituted authorities of said State and of the United States within such State; and whenever by reason of said causes the conviction of such offenders and the preservation of the public peace shall become in such State or part of a State impracticable; and

Whereas such unlawful combinations and conspiracies for the purposes aforesaid are declared by the act of Congress aforesaid to be rebellion against the Government of the United States; and

Whereas by said act of Congress it is provided that before the President shall suspend the privileges of the writ of *habeas corpus* he shall first have made proclamation commanding such insurgents to disperse; and

Whereas on the 12th day of the present month of October the President of the United States did issue his proclamation, reciting therein, among other things, that such combinations and conspiracies did then exist in the counties of Spartanburg, York, Marion, Chester, Laurens, Newberry, Fairfield, Lancaster, and Chesterfield, in the State of South Carolina, and commanding thereby all persons composing such unlawful combinations and conspiracies to disperse and retire peaceably to their homes within five days from the date thereof, and to deliver either to the marshal of the United States for the district of South Carolina, or to any of his deputies, or to any military officer of the United States within said counties, all arms, ammunition, uniforms, disguises, and other means and implements used, kept, possessed, or controlled by them for carrying out the unlawful purposes for which the said combinations and conspiracies are organized; and

Whereas the insurgents engaged in such unlawful combinations and conspiracies within the counties aforesaid have not dispersed and retired peaceably to their respective homes, and have not delivered to the marshal of the United States, or to any of his deputies, or to any military officer of the United States within said counties, all arms, ammunition, uniforms, disguises, and other means and implements used, kept, possessed, or controlled by them for carrying out the unlawful purposes for which the combinations and conspiracies are organized, as commanded by said proclamation, but do still persist in the unlawful combinations and conspiracies aforesaid:

Now, therefore, I, Ulysses S. Grant, President of the United States of America, by virtue of the authority vested in me by the Constitution of the United States and the act of Congress aforesaid, do hereby declare that in my judgment the public safety especially requires that the privileges of the writ of *habeas corpus* be suspended, to the end that such rebellion may be overthrown, and do hereby suspend the privileges of the writ of *habeas corpus* within the counties of Spartanburg, York, Marion, Chester, Laurens, Newberry, Fairfield, Lancaster, and Chesterfield, in said State of South Carolina, in respect to all persons arrested by the marshal of the United States for the said district of South Carolina, or by any of his deputies, or by any military officer of the United States, or by any soldier or citizen acting under the orders of said marshal, deputy, or such military officer within any one of said counties, charged with any violation of the act of Congress aforesaid, during the continuance of such rebellion.

In witness whereof I have hereunto set my hand and caused the seal
of the United States to be affixed.

[SEAL.]   Done at the city of Washington, this 17th day of October,
A. D. 1871, and of the Independence of the United States of
America the ninety-sixth.

U. S. GRANT.

By the President:

J. C. BANCROFT DAVIS,
Acting Secretary of State.

BY THE PRESIDENT OF THE UNITED STATES OF AMERICA.

A PROCLAMATION.

The process of the seasons has again enabled the husbandman to garner
the fruits of successful toil.   Industry has been generally well rewarded.
We are at peace with all nations, and tranquillity, with few exceptions,
prevails at home.   Within the past year we have in the main been free
from ills which elsewhere have afflicted our kind.   If some of us have
had calamities, these should be an occasion for sympathy with the sufferers, of resignation on their part to the will of the Most High, and of
rejoicing to the many who have been more favored.

I therefore recommend that on Thursday, the 30th day of November
next, the people meet in their respective places of worship and there
make the usual annual acknowledgments to Almighty God for the blessings He has conferred upon them, for their merciful exemption from
evils, and invoke His protection and kindness for their less fortunate
brethren, whom in His wisdom He has deemed it best to chastise.

In witness whereof I have hereunto set my hand and caused the seal
of the United States to be affixed.

[SEAL.]   Done at the city of Washington, this 28th day of October,
A. D. 1871, and of the Independence of the United States the
ninety-sixth.

U. S. GRANT.

By the President:

HAMILTON FISH, *Secretary of State.*

BY THE PRESIDENT OF THE UNITED STATES OF AMERICA.

A PROCLAMATION.

Whereas in my proclamation of the 12th day of October, in the year
1871, it was recited that certain unlawful combinations and conspiracies
existed in certain counties in the State of South Carolina for the purpose
of depriving certain portions and classes of the people of that State of
the rights, privileges, and immunities and protection named in the Constitution of the United States and secured by the act of Congress approved
April 20, 1871, entitled "An act to enforce the provisions of the four-

teenth amendment to the Constitution of the United States," and the persons composing such combinations and conspiracies were commanded to disperse and to retire peaceably to their homes within five days from said date; and

Whereas by my proclamation of the 17th day of October, in the year 1871, the privileges of the writ of *habeas corpus* were suspended in the counties named in said proclamation; and

Whereas the county of Marion was named in said proclamations as one of the counties in which said unlawful combinations and conspiracies for the purposes aforesaid existed, and in which the privileges of the writ of *habeas corpus* were suspended; and

Whereas it has been ascertained that in said county of Marion said combinations and conspiracies do not exist to the extent recited in said proclamations; and

Whereas it has been ascertained that unlawful combinations and conspiracies of the character and to the extent and for the purposes described in said proclamations do exist in the county of Union in said State:

Now, therefore, I, Ulysses S. Grant, President of the United States of America, do hereby revoke, as to the said county of Marion, the suspension of the privileges of the writ of *habeas corpus* directed in my said proclamation of the 17th day of October, 1871.

And I do hereby command all persons in the said county of Union composing the unlawful combinations and conspiracies aforesaid to disperse and to retire peaceably to their homes within five days of the date hereof, and to deliver either to the marshal of the United States for the district of South Carolina, or to any of his deputies, or to any military officer of the United States within said county, all arms, ammunition, uniforms, disguises, and other means and implements used, kept, possessed, or controlled by them for carrying out the unlawful purposes for which the combinations and conspiracies are organized.

In witness whereof I have hereunto set my hand and caused the seal of the United States to be affixed.

[SEAL.] Done at the city of Washington, this 3d day of November, A. D. 1871, and of the Independence of the United States of America the ninety-sixth.

U. S. GRANT.

By the President:

HAMILTON FISH, *Secretary of State.*

BY THE PRESIDENT OF THE UNITED STATES OF AMERICA.

A PROCLAMATION.

Whereas by an act of Congress entitled "An act to enforce the provisions of the fourteenth amendment to the Constitution of the United States, and for other purposes," approved the 20th day of April, A. D.

1871, power is given to the President of the United States, when in his judgment the public safety shall require it, to suspend the privileges of the writ of *habeas corpus* in any State or part of a State whenever combinations and conspiracies exist in such State or part of a State for the purpose of depriving any portion or class of the people of such State of the rights, privileges, immunities, and protection named in the Constitution of the United States and secured by the act of Congress aforesaid; and whenever such combinations and conspiracies do so obstruct and hinder the execution of the laws of any such State and of the United States as to deprive the people aforesaid of the rights, privileges, immunities, and protection aforesaid, and do oppose and obstruct the laws of the United States and their due execution, and impede and obstruct the due course of justice under the same; and whenever such combinations shall be organized and armed and so numerous and powerful as to be able by violence either to overthrow or to set at defiance the constituted authorities of said State and of the United States within such State; and whenever by reason of said causes the conviction of such offenders and the preservation of the public peace shall become in such State or part of a State impracticable; and

Whereas such unlawful combinations and conspiracies for the purposes aforesaid are declared by the act of Congress aforesaid to be rebellion against the Government of the United States; and

Whereas by said act of Congress it is provided that before the President shall suspend the privileges of the writ of *habeas corpus* he shall first have made proclamation commanding such insurgents to disperse; and

Whereas on the 3d day of the present month of November the President of the United States did issue his proclamation, reciting therein, among other things, that such combinations and conspiracies did then exist in the county of Union, in the State of South Carolina, and commanding thereby all persons composing such unlawful combinations and conspiracies to disperse and retire peaceably to their homes within five days from the date thereof, and to deliver either to the marshal of the United States for the district of South Carolina, or to any of his deputies, or to any military officer of the United States within said county, all arms, ammunition, uniforms, disguises, and other means and implements used, kept, possessed, or controlled by them for carrying out the unlawful purposes for which the said combinations and conspiracies are organized; and

Whereas the insurgents engaged in such unlawful combinations and conspiracies within the county aforesaid have not dispersed and retired peaceably to their respective homes, and have not delivered to the marshal of the United States, or to any of his deputies, or to any military officer of the United States within said county, all arms, ammunition, uniforms, disguises, and other means and implements used, kept, possessed, or controlled by them for carrying out the unlawful purposes for which the combinations and conspiracies are organized, as commanded by said proclamation, but do still persist in the unlawful combinations and conspiracies aforesaid:

Now, therefore, I, Ulysses S. Grant, President of the United States of America, by virtue of the authority vested in me by the Constitution of the United States and the act of Congress aforesaid, do hereby declare that in my judgment the public safety especially requires that the privileges of the writ of *habeas corpus* be suspended, to the end that such rebellion may be overthrown, and do hereby suspend the privileges of the writ of *habeas corpus* within the county of Union, in said State of South Carolina, in respect to all persons arrested by the marshal of the United States for the said district of South Carolina, or by any of his deputies, or by any military officer of the United States, or by any soldier or citizen acting under the orders of said marshal, deputy, or such military officer within said county, charged with any violation of the act of Congress aforesaid, during the continuance of such rebellion.

In witness whereof I have hereunto set my hand and caused the seal of the United States to be affixed.

[SEAL.]   Done at the city of Washington, this 10th day of November, A. D. 1871, and of the Independence of the United States of America the ninety-sixth.

U. S. GRANT.

By the President:
    HAMILTON FISH,
        Secretary of State.

EXECUTIVE ORDER.

BY THE PRESIDENT OF THE UNITED STATES.

EXECUTIVE ORDER.

WASHINGTON, *March 31, 1871.*

The act of June 15, 1852, section 1 (10 U. S. Statutes at Large, p. 10), provides:

That whenever any officer of either of the Territories of the United States shall be absent therefrom and from the duties of his office no salary shall be paid him during the year in which such absence shall occur, unless good cause therefor shall be shown to the President of the United States, who shall officially certify his opinion of such cause to the proper accounting officer of the Treasury, to be filed in his office.

It has been the practice under this law for the Territorial officers who have desired to be absent from their respective Territories to apply for leaves to the head of the proper Department at Washington, and when such leave has been given the required certificate of the President has been granted as a matter of course.

The unusual number of applications for leave of absence which have been lately made by Territorial officers has induced the President to announce that he expects the gentlemen who hold those offices to stay in their respective Territories and to attend strictly to their official duties. They have been appointed for service in the Territory and for the benefit and convenience of the Territorial population. He expects them by their personal presence to identify themselves with the people and acquire local information, without which their duties can not be well performed. Frequent or long absence makes them in some degree strangers, and therefore less acceptable to the people. Their absence, no matter with what substitution, must often put the people to inconvenience. Executive officers may be required for emergencies which could not be foreseen. Judges should be at hand, not only when the courts are in session, but for matters of bail, *habeas corpus*, orders in equity, examination of persons charged with crime, and other similar business, which often arises in vacation.

These and similar considerations no doubt induced Congress to pass the law above quoted.

It is therefore directed that in future the heads of Departments shall grant leaves of absence to Territorial officers only for reasons of the most urgent character, and then only for the shortest possible time.

By order of the President:

HAMILTON FISH,
Secretary of State.

THIRD ANNUAL MESSAGE.

EXECUTIVE MANSION, *December 4, 1871.*

To the Senate and House of Representatives:

In addressing my third annual message to the law-making branch of the Government it is gratifying to be able to state that during the past year success has generally attended the effort to execute all laws found upon the statute books. The policy has been not to inquire into the wisdom of laws already enacted, but to learn their spirit and intent and to enforce them accordingly.

The past year has, under a wise Providence, been one of general prosperity to the nation. It has, however, been attended with more than usual chastisements in the loss of life and property by storm and fire. These disasters have served to call forth the best elements of human nature in our country and to develop a friendship for us on the part of foreign nations which goes far toward alleviating the distresses occasioned by these calamities. The benevolent, who have so generously shared their means with the victims of these misfortunes, will reap their reward in the consciousness of having performed a noble act and in receiving the grateful thanks of men, women, and children whose sufferings they have relieved.

The relations of the United States with foreign powers continue to be friendly. The year has been an eventful one in witnessing two great nations, speaking one language and having one lineage, settling by peaceful arbitration disputes of long standing and liable at any time to bring those nations into bloody and costly conflict. An example has thus been set which, if successful in its final issue, may be followed by other civilized nations, and finally be the means of returning to productive industry millions of men now maintained to settle the disputes of nations by the bayonet and the broadside.

I transmit herewith a copy of the treaty alluded to, which has been concluded since the adjournment of Congress with Her Britannic Majesty, and a copy of the protocols of the conferences of the commissioners by whom it was negotiated. This treaty provides methods for adjusting the questions pending between the two nations.

Various questions are to be adjusted by arbitration. I recommend Congress at an early day to make the necessary provision for the tribunal at Geneva and for the several commissioners on the part of the United States called for by the treaty.

His Majesty the King of Italy, the President of the Swiss Confederation, and His Majesty the Emperor of Brazil have each consented, on the joint request of the two powers, to name an arbiter for the tribunal at Geneva. I have caused my thanks to be suitably expressed for the readiness with which the joint request has been complied with, by the appointment of gentlemen of eminence and learning to these important positions.

His Majesty the Emperor of Germany has been pleased to comply with the joint request of the two Governments, and has consented to act as the arbitrator of the disputed water boundary between the United States and Great Britain.

The contracting parties in the treaty have undertaken to regard as between themselves certain principles of public law, for which the United States have contended from the commencement of their history. They have also agreed to bring those principles to the knowledge of the other maritime powers and to invite them to accede to them. Negotiations are going on as to the form of the note by which the invitation is to be extended to the other powers.

I recommend the legislation necessary on the part of the United States to bring into operation the articles of the treaty relating to the fisheries and to the other matters touching the relations of the United States toward the British North American possessions, to become operative so soon as the proper legislation shall be had on the part of Great Britain and its possessions. It is much to be desired that this legislation may become operative before the fishermen of the United States begin to make their arrangements for the coming season.

I have addressed a communication, of which a copy is transmitted herewith, to the governors of New York, Pennsylvania, Ohio, Indiana, Michigan, Illinois, and Wisconsin, urging upon the governments of those States, respectively, the necessary action on their part to carry into effect the object of the article of the treaty which contemplates the use of the canals, on either side, connected with the navigation of the lakes and rivers forming the boundary, on terms of equality, by the inhabitants of both countries. It is hoped that the importance of the object and the benefits to flow therefrom will secure the speedy approval and legislative sanction of the States concerned.

I renew the recommendation for an appropriation for determining the true position of the forty-ninth parallel of latitude where it forms the boundary between the United States and the British North American possessions, between the Lake of the Woods and the summit of the Rocky Mountains. The early action of Congress on this recommendation would put it in the power of the War Department to place a force in the field during the next summer.

The resumption of diplomatic relations between France and Germany has enabled me to give directions for the withdrawal of the protection extended to Germans in France by the diplomatic and consular representatives of the United States in that country. It is just to add that the delicate duty of this protection has been performed by the minister and the consul-general at Paris, and the various consuls in France under the supervision of the latter, with great kindness as well as with prudence and tact. Their course has received the commendation of the German Government, and has wounded no susceptibility of the French.

The Government of the Emperor of Germany continues to manifest a friendly feeling toward the United States, and a desire to harmonize with the moderate and just policy which this Government maintains in its relations with Asiatic powers, as well as with the South American Republics. I have given assurances that the friendly feelings of that Government are fully shared by the United States.

The ratifications of the consular and naturalization conventions with the Austro-Hungarian Empire have been exchanged.

I have been officially informed of the annexation of the States of the Church to the Kingdom of Italy, and the removal of the capital of that Kingdom to Rome. In conformity with the established policy of the United States, I have recognized this change. The ratifications of the new treaty of commerce between the United States and Italy have been exchanged. The two powers have agreed in this treaty that private property at sea shall be exempt from capture in case of war between the two powers. The United States have spared no opportunity of incorporating this rule into the obligation of nations.

The Forty-first Congress, at its third session, made an appropriation for the organization of a mixed commission for adjudicating upon the claims of citizens of the United States against Spain growing out of the insurrection in Cuba. That commission has since been organized. I transmit herewith the correspondence relating to its formation and its jurisdiction. It is to be hoped that this commission will afford the claimants a complete remedy for their injuries.

It has been made the agreeable duty of the United States to preside over a conference at Washington between the plenipotentiaries of Spain and the allied South American Republics, which has resulted in an armistice, with the reasonable assurance of a permanent peace.

The intimate friendly relations which have so long existed between the United States and Russia continue undisturbed. The visit of the third son of the Emperor is a proof that there is no desire on the part of his Government to diminish the cordiality of those relations. The hospitable reception which has been given to the Grand Duke is a proof that on our side we share the wishes of that Government. The inexcusable course of the Russian minister at Washington rendered it necessary to ask his recall and to decline to longer receive that functionary as a diplomatic representative. It was impossible, with self-respect or with a just regard to the dignity of the country, to permit Mr. Catacazy to continue to hold intercourse with this Government after his personal abuse of Government officials, and during his persistent interferences, through various means, with the relations between the United States and other powers. In accordance with my wishes, this Government has been relieved of further intercourse with Mr. Catacazy, and the management of the affairs of the imperial legation has passed into the hands of a gentleman entirely unobjectionable.

With Japan we continue to maintain intimate relations. The cabinet of the Mikado has since the close of the last session of Congress selected citizens of the United States to serve in offices of importance in several departments of Government. I have reason to think that this selection is due to an appreciation of the disinterestedness of the policy which the United States have pursued toward Japan. It is our desire to continue to maintain this disinterested and just policy with China as well as Japan. The correspondence transmitted herewith shows that there is no disposition on the part of this Government to swerve from its established course.

Prompted by a desire to put an end to the barbarous treatment of our shipwrecked sailors on the Korean coast, I instructed our minister at Peking to endeavor to conclude a convention with Korea for securing the safety and humane treatment of such mariners.

Admiral Rodgers was instructed to accompany him with a sufficient force to protect him in case of need.

A small surveying party sent out, on reaching the coast was treacherously attacked at a disadvantage. Ample opportunity was given for explanation and apology for the insult. Neither came. A force was then landed. After an arduous march over a rugged and difficult country, the forts from which the outrages had been committed were reduced by a gallant assault and were destroyed. Having thus punished the criminals, and having vindicated the honor of the flag, the expedition returned, finding it impracticable under the circumstances to conclude the desired convention. I respectfully refer to the correspondence relating thereto, herewith submitted, and leave the subject for such action as Congress may see fit to take.

The Republic of Mexico has not yet repealed the very objectionable laws establishing what is known as the "free zone" on the frontier of the United States. It is hoped that this may yet be done, and also that more stringent measures may be taken by that Republic for restraining lawless persons on its frontiers. I hope that Mexico by its own action will soon relieve this Government of the difficulties experienced from these causes.

Our relations with the various Republics of Central and South America continue, with one exception, to be cordial and friendly.

I recommend some action by Congress regarding the overdue installments under the award of the Venezuelan Claims Commission of 1866. The internal dissensions of this Government present no justification for the absence of effort to meet their solemn treaty obligations.

The ratification of an extradition treaty with Nicaragua has been exchanged.

It is a subject for congratulation that the great Empire of Brazil has taken the initiatory step toward the abolition of slavery. Our relations with that Empire, always cordial, will naturally be made more so by this act. It is not too much to hope that the Government of Brazil may hereafter find it for its interest, as well as intrinsically right, to advance toward entire emancipation more rapidly than the present act contemplates.

The true prosperity and greatness of a nation is to be found in the elevation and education of its laborers.

It is a subject for regret that the reforms in this direction which were voluntarily promised by the statesmen of Spain have not been carried out in its West India colonies. The laws and regulations for the apparent abolition of slavery in Cuba and Porto Rico leave most of the laborers in bondage, with no hope of release until their lives become a burden to their employers.

I desire to direct your attention to the fact that citizens of the United States, or persons claiming to be citizens of the United States, are large holders in foreign lands of this species of property, forbidden by the fundamental law of their alleged country. I recommend to Congress to provide by stringent legislation a suitable remedy against the holding, owning, or dealing in slaves, or being interested in slave property, in foreign lands, either as owners, hirers, or mortgagors, by citizens of the United States.

It is to be regretted that the disturbed condition of the island of Cuba continues to be a source of annoyance and of anxiety. The existence of a protracted struggle in such close proximity to our own territory, without apparent prospect of an early termination, can not be other than an object of concern to a people who, while abstaining from interference in the affairs of other powers, naturally desire to see every country in the undisturbed enjoyment of peace, liberty, and the blessings of free institutions.

Our naval commanders in Cuban waters have been instructed, in case it should become necessary, to spare no effort to protect the lives and property of *bona fide* American citizens and to maintain the dignity of the flag.

It is hoped that all pending questions with Spain growing out of the affairs in Cuba may be adjusted in the spirit of peace and conciliation which has hitherto guided the two powers in their treatment of such questions.

To give importance to and to add to the efficiency of our diplomatic relations with Japan and China, and to further aid in retaining the good opinion of those peoples, and to secure to the United States its share of the commerce destined to flow between those nations and the balance of the commercial world, I earnestly recommend that an appropriation be made to support at least four American youths in each of those countries, to serve as a part of the official family of our ministers there. Our representatives would not even then be placed upon an equality with the representatives of Great Britain and of some other powers. As now situated, our representatives in Japan and China have to depend for interpreters and translators upon natives of those countries who know our language imperfectly, or procure for the occasion the services of employees in foreign business houses or the interpreters to other foreign ministers.

I would also recommend liberal measures for the purpose of supporting the American lines of steamers now plying between San Francisco and Japan and China, and the Australian line—almost our only remaining lines of ocean steamers—and of increasing their services.

The national debt has been reduced to the extent of $86,057,126.80 during the year, and by the negotiation of national bonds at a lower rate of interest the interest on the public debt has been so far diminished that now the sum to be raised for the interest account is nearly $17,000,000 less than on the 1st of March, 1869. It was highly desirable that this rapid diminution should take place, both to strengthen the credit of the country and to convince its citizens of their entire ability to meet every dollar of liability without bankrupting them. But in view of the accomplishment of these desirable ends; of the rapid development of the resources of the country; its increasing ability to meet large demands, and the amount already paid, it is not desirable that the present resources of the country should continue to be taxed in order to continue this rapid payment. I therefore recommend a modification of both the tariff and internal-tax law. I recommend that all taxes from internal sources be abolished, except those collected from spirituous, vinous, and malt liquors, tobacco in its various forms, and from stamps.

In readjusting the tariff I suggest that a careful estimate be made of the amount of surplus revenue collected under the present laws, after providing for the current expenses of the Government, the interest account, and a sinking fund, and that this surplus be reduced in such a manner as to afford the greatest relief to the greatest number. There are many articles not produced at home, but which enter largely into general consumption through articles which are manufactured at home, such as medicines compounded, etc., etc., from which very little revenue is derived, but which enter into general use. All such articles I recommend to be placed on the "free list." Should a further reduction prove advisable, I would then recommend that it be made upon those articles which can best bear it without disturbing home production or reducing the wages of American labor.

I have not entered into figures, because to do so would be to repeat what will be laid before you in the report of the Secretary of the Treasury The present laws for collecting revenue pay collectors of customs small salaries, but provide for moieties (shares in all seizures), which, at principal ports of entry particularly, raise the compensation of those officials to a large sum. It has always seemed to me as if this system must at times work perniciously. It holds out an inducement to dishonest men, should such get possession of those offices, to be lax in their scrutiny of goods entered, to enable them finally to make large seizures. Your attention is respectfully invited to this subject.

Continued fluctuations in the value of gold, as compared with the national currency, has a most damaging effect upon the increase and development of the country, in keeping up prices of all articles necessary in everyday life. It fosters a spirit of gambling, prejudicial alike to national morals and the national finances. If the question can be met as to how to get a fixed value to our currency, that value constantly and uniformly approaching par with specie, a very desirable object will be gained.

For the operations of the Army in the past year, the expense of maintaining it, the estimate for the ensuing year, and for continuing seacoast and other improvements conducted under the supervision of the War Department, I refer you to the accompanying report of the Secretary of War.

I call your attention to the provisions of the act of Congress approved March 3, 1869, which discontinues promotions in the staff corps of the Army until provided for by law. I recommend that the number of officers in each grade in the staff corps be fixed, and that whenever the number in any one grade falls below the number so fixed, that the vacancy may be filled by promotion from the grade below. I also recommend that when the office of chief of a corps becomes vacant the place may be filled by selection from the corps in which the vacancy exists.

The report of the Secretary of the Navy shows an improvement in the number and efficiency of the naval force, without material increase in the expense of supporting it. This is due to the policy which has been adopted, and is being extended as fast as our material will admit, of using smaller vessels as cruisers on the several stations. By this means we have been enabled to occupy at once a larger extent of cruising grounds, to visit more frequently the ports where the presence of our flag is desirable, and generally to discharge more efficiently the appropriate duties of the Navy in time of peace, without exceeding the number of men or the expenditure authorized by law.

During the past year the Navy has, in addition to its regular service, supplied the men and officers for the vessels of the Coast Survey, and has completed the surveys authorized by Congress of the isthmuses of Darien and Tehuantepec, and, under like authority, has sent out an expedition, completely furnished and equipped, to explore the unknown ocean of the north.

The suggestions of the report as to the necessity for increasing and improving the *matériel* of the Navy, and the plan recommended for reducing the *personnel* of the service to a peace standard, by the gradual abolition of certain grades of officers, the reduction of others, and the employment of some in the service of the commercial marine, are well considered and deserve the thoughtful attention of Congress.

I also recommend that all promotions in the Navy above the rank of captain be by selection instead of by seniority. This course will secure in the higher grades greater efficiency and hold out an incentive to young officers to improve themselves in the knowledge of their profession.

The present cost of maintaining the Navy, its cost compared with that of the preceding year, and the estimates for the ensuing year are contained in the accompanying report of the Secretary of the Navy.

The enlarged receipts of the Post-Office Department, as shown by the accompanying report of the Postmaster-General, exhibit a gratifying increase in that branch of the public service. It is the index of the growth of education and of the prosperity of the people, two elements highly conducive to the vigor and stability of republics. With a vast territory like ours, much of it sparsely populated, but all requiring the services of the mail, it is not at present to be expected that this Department can be made self-sustaining. But a gradual approach to this end from year to year is confidently relied on, and the day is not far distant when the Post-Office Department of the Government will prove a much greater blessing to the whole people than it is now.

The suggestions of the Postmaster-General for improvements in the

Department presided over by him are earnestly recommended to your special attention. Especially do I recommend favorable consideration of the plan for uniting the telegraphic system of the United States with the postal system. It is believed that by such a course the cost of tele- graphing could be much reduced, and the service as well, if not better, rendered. It would secure the further advantage of extending the tele- graph through portions of the country where private enterprise will not construct it. Commerce, trade, and, above all, the efforts to bring a peo- ple widely separated into a community of interest are always benefited by a rapid intercommunication. Education, the groundwork of repub- lican institutions, is encouraged by increasing the facilities to gather speedy news from all parts of the country. The desire to reap the bene- fit of such improvements will stimulate education. I refer you to the report of the Postmaster-General for full details of the operations of last year and for comparative statements of results with former years.

There has been imposed upon the executive branch of the Govern- ment the execution of the act of Congress approved April 20, 1871, and commonly known as the Kuklux law, in a portion of the State of South Carolina. The necessity of the course pursued will be demonstrated by the report of the Committee to Investigate Southern Outrages. Under the provisions of the above act I issued a proclamation* calling the atten- tion of the people of the United States to the same, and declaring my reluctance to exercise any of the extraordinary powers thereby conferred upon me, except in case of imperative necessity, but making known my purpose to exercise such powers whenever it should become necessary to do so for the purpose of securing to all citizens of the United States the peaceful enjoyment of the rights guaranteed to them by the Constitution and the laws.

After the passage of this law information was received from time to time that combinations of the character referred to in this law existed and were powerful in many parts of the Southern States, particularly in certain counties in the State of South Carolina.

Careful investigation was made, and it was ascertained that in nine counties of that State such combinations were active and powerful, em- bracing a sufficient portion of the citizens to control the local authority, and having, among other things, the object of depriving the emancipated class of the substantial benefits of freedom and of preventing the free political action of those citizens who did not sympathize with their own views. Among their operations were frequent scourgings and occasional assassinations, generally perpetrated at night by disguised persons, the victims in almost all cases being citizens of different political sentiments from their own or freed persons who had shown a disposition to claim equal rights with other citizens. Thousands of inoffensive and well- disposed citizens were the sufferers by this lawless violence.

* See pp. 4088–4089.

KU KLUX AND RECONSTRUCTION TROUBLES

THE KU KLUX KLAN

"The Ku Klux Klan was a secret organization in several of the Southern States soon after the Civil War. Its object was to suppress the negro as a factor in politics, by means of intimidation and terrorization, and for a time many of the most prominent and respectable citizens of the Southern States belonged to it; but later the more respectable element withdrew and the organization outran its original purpose. In many localities gross disorders and crimes were committed by persons in disguise, who were either members of the Klan or who were using the disguise and methods of the order for evil purposes."

Quoted from the article entitled "Ku Klux Klan" in the encyclopedic index (volume eleven).

The upper panel shows New Orleans, the center of reconstruction troubles at about 1870; the central panel reproduces a daguerreotype of three captured Ku Klux Klansmen in the disguises they wore when apprehended; and the lower panel represents an anti-negro riot in New Orleans, where General Sheridan was stationed with an army.

Thereupon, on the 12th of October, 1871, a proclamation* was issued, in terms of the law, calling upon the members of those combinations to disperse within five days and to deliver to the marshal or military officers of the United States all arms, ammunition, uniforms, disguises, and other means and implements used by them for carrying out their unlawful purposes.

This warning not having been heeded, on the 17th of October another proclamation† was issued, suspending the privileges of the writ of *habeas corpus* in nine counties in that State.

Direction was given that within the counties so designated persons supposed, upon creditable information, to be members of such unlawful combinations should be arrested by the military forces of the United States and delivered to the marshal, to be dealt with according to law. In two of said counties, York and Spartanburg, many arrests have been made. At the last account the number of persons thus arrested was 168. Several hundred, whose criminality was ascertained to be of an inferior degree, were released for the present. These have generally made confessions of their guilt.

Great caution has been exercised in making these arrests, and, notwithstanding the large number, it is believed that no innocent person is now in custody. The prisoners will be held for regular trial in the judicial tribunals of the United States.

As soon as it appeared that the authorities of the United States were about to take vigorous measures to enforce the law, many persons absconded, and there is good ground for supposing that all of such persons have violated the law. A full report of what has been done under this law will be submitted to Congress by the Attorney-General.

In Utah there still remains a remnant of barbarism, repugnant to civilization, to decency, and to the laws of the United States. Territorial officers, however, have been found who are willing to perform their duty in a spirit of equity and with a due sense of the necessity of sustaining the majesty of the law. Neither polygamy nor any other violation of existing statutes will be permitted within the territory of the United States. It is not with the religion of the self-styled Saints that we are now dealing, but with their practices. They will be protected in the worship of God according to the dictates of their consciences, but they will not be permitted to violate the laws under the cloak of religion.

It may be advisable for Congress to consider what, in the execution of the laws against polygamy, is to be the status of plural wives and their offspring. The propriety of Congress passing an enabling act authorizing the Territorial legislature of Utah to legitimize all children born prior to a time fixed in the act might be justified by its humanity to these innocent children. This is a suggestion only, and not a recommendation.

* See pp. 4089–4090.　　　　　† See pp. 4090–4092.

The policy pursued toward the Indians has resulted favorably, so far as can be judged from the limited time during which it has been in operation. Through the exertions of the various societies of Christians to whom has been intrusted the execution of the policy, and the board of commissioners authorized by the law of April 10, 1869, many tribes of Indians have been induced to settle upon reservations, to cultivate the soil, to perform productive labor of various kinds, and to partially accept civilization. They are being cared for in such a way, it is hoped, as to induce those still pursuing their old habits of life to embrace the only opportunity which is left them to avoid extermination.

I recommend liberal appropriations to carry out the Indian peace policy, not only because it is humane, Christianlike, and economical, but because it is right.

I recommend to your favorable consideration also the policy of granting a Territorial government to the Indians in the Indian Territory west of Arkansas and Missouri and south of Kansas. In doing so every right guaranteed to the Indian by treaty should be secured. Such a course might in time be the means of collecting most of the Indians now between the Missouri and the Pacific and south of the British possessions into one Territory or one State. The Secretary of the Interior has treated upon this subject at length, and I commend to you his suggestions.

I renew my recommendation that the public lands be regarded as a heritage to our children, to be disposed of only as required for occupation and to actual settlers. Those already granted have been in great part disposed of in such a way as to secure access to the balance by the hardy settler who may wish to avail himself of them, but caution should be exercised even in attaining so desirable an object.

Educational interest may well be served by the grant of the proceeds of the sale of public lands to settlers. I do not wish to be understood as recommending in the least degree a curtailment of what is being done by the General Government for the encouragement of education.

The report of the Secretary of the Interior submitted with this will give you all the information collected and prepared for publication in regard to the census taken during the year 1870; the operations of the Bureau of Education for the year; the Patent Office; the Pension Office; the Land Office, and the Indian Bureau.

The report of the Commissioner of Agriculture gives the operations of his Department for the year. As agriculture is the groundwork of our prosperity, too much importance can not be attached to the labors of this Department. It is in the hands of an able head, with able assistants, all zealously devoted to introducing into the agricultural productions of the nation all useful products adapted to any of the various climates and soils of our vast territory, and to giving all useful information as to the method of cultivation, the plants, cereals, and other products adapted to particular localities. Quietly but surely the Agricultural Bureau is working a great national good, and if liberally supported the more widely its influence will be extended and the less dependent we shall be upon the products of foreign countries.

The subject of compensation to the heads of bureaus and officials holding positions of responsibility, and requiring ability and character to fill properly, is one to which your attention is invited. But few of the officials receive a compensation equal to the respectable support of a family, while their duties are such as to involve millions of interest. In private life services demand compensation equal to the services rendered; a wise economy would dictate the same rule in the Government service.

I have not given the estimates for the support of Government for the ensuing year, nor the comparative statement between the expenditures for the year just passed and the one just preceding, because all these figures are contained in the accompanying reports or in those presented directly to Congress. These estimates have my approval.

More than six years having elapsed since the last hostile gun was fired between the armies then arrayed against each other—one for the perpetuation, the other for the destruction, of the Union—it may well be considered whether it is not now time that the disabilities imposed by the fourteenth amendment should be removed. That amendment does not exclude the ballot, but only imposes the disability to hold offices upon certain classes. When the purity of the ballot is secure, majorities are sure to elect officers reflecting the views of the majority. I do not see the advantage or propriety of excluding men from office merely because they were before the rebellion of standing and character sufficient to be elected to positions requiring them to take oaths to support the Constitution, and admitting to eligibility those entertaining precisely the same views, but of less standing in their communities. It may be said that the former violated an oath, while the latter did not; the latter did not have it in their power to do so. If they had taken this oath, it can not be doubted they would have broken it as did the former class. If there are any great criminals, distinguished above all others for the part they took in opposition to the Government, they might, in the judgment of Congress, be excluded from such an amnesty.

This subject is submitted for your careful consideration.

The condition of the Southern States is, unhappily, not such as all true patriotic citizens would like to see. Social ostracism for opinion's sake, personal violence or threats toward persons entertaining political views opposed to those entertained by the majority of the old citizens, prevents immigration and the flow of much-needed capital into the States lately in rebellion. It will be a happy condition of the country when the old citizens of these States will take an interest in public affairs, promulgate ideas honestly entertain d, vote for men representing their views, and tolerate the same freedom of expression and ballot in those entertaining different political convictions.

Under the provisions of the act of Congress approved February 21, 1871, a Territorial government was organized in the District of Columbia. Its results have thus far fully realized the expectations of its advocates. Under the direction of the Territorial officers, a system of improvements has been inaugurated by means of which Washington is rapidly becoming a city worthy of the nation's capital. The citizens of the District having voluntarily taxed themselves to a large amount for the purpose of contributing to the adornment of the seat of Government, I recommend liberal appropriations on the part of Congress, in order that the Government may bear its just share of the expense of carrying out a judicious system of improvements.

By the great fire in Chicago the most important of the Government buildings in that city were consumed. Those burned had already become inadequate to the wants of the Government in that growing city, and, looking to the near future, were totally inadequate. I recommend, therefore, that an appropriation be made immediately to purchase the remainder of the square on which the burned buildings stood, provided it can be purchased at a fair valuation, or provided that the legislature of Illinois will pass a law authorizing its condemnation for Government purposes; and also an appropriation of as much money as can properly be expended toward the erection of new buildings during this fiscal year.

The number of immigrants ignorant of our laws, habits, etc., coming into our country annually has become so great and the impositions practiced upon them so numerous and flagrant that I suggest Congressional action for their protection. It seems to me a fair subject of legislation by Congress. I can not now state as fully as I desire the nature of the complaints made by immigrants of the treatment they receive, but will endeavor to do so during the session of Congress, particularly if the subject should receive your attention.

It has been the aim of the Administration to enforce honesty and efficiency in all public offices. Every public servant who has violated the trust placed in him has been proceeded against with all the rigor of the law. If bad men have secured places, it has been the fault of the system established by law and custom for making appointments, or the fault of those who recommend for Government positions persons not sufficiently well known to them personally, or who give letters indorsing the characters of office seekers without a proper sense of the grave responsibility which such a course devolves upon them. A civil-service reform which can correct this abuse is much desired. In mercantile pursuits the business man who gives a letter of recommendation to a friend to enable him to obtain credit from a stranger is regarded as morally responsible for the integrity of his friend and his ability to meet his obligations. A reformatory law which would enforce this principle against all indorsers of persons for public place would insure great caution in making recommendations. A salutary lesson has been taught the careless and the dishonest public servant in the great number of prosecutions and convictions of the last two years.

It is gratifying to notice the favorable change which is taking place throughout the country in bringing to punishment those who have proven recreant to the trusts confided to them and in elevating to public office none but those who possess the confidence of the honest and the virtuous, who, it will always be found, comprise the majority of the community in which they live.

In my message to Congress one year ago I urgently recommended a reform in the civil service of the country. In conformity with that recommendation Congress, in the ninth section of "An act making appropriations for sundry civil expenses of the Government, and for other purposes," approved March 3, 1871, gave the necessary authority to the Executive to inaugurate a civil-service reform, and placed upon him the responsibility of doing so. Under the authority of said act I convened a board of gentlemen eminently qualified for the work to devise rules and regulations to effect the needed reform. Their labors are not yet complete, but it is believed that they will succeed in devising a plan that can be adopted to the great relief of the Executive, the heads of Departments, and members of Congress, and which will redound to the true interest of the public service. At all events, the experiment shall have a fair trial.

I have thus hastily summed up the operations of the Government during the last year, and made such suggestions as occur to me to be proper for your consideration. I submit them with a confidence that your combined action will be wise, statesmanlike, and in the best interests of the whole country.

U. S. GRANT.

SPECIAL MESSAGES.

EXECUTIVE MANSION, *December 4, 1871.*

To the House of Representatives:

In compliance with section 2 of the act making appropriations for the consular and diplomatic expenses of the Government for the year ending June 30, 1871, approved July 11, 1870, I herewith transmit the names and reports of and the amounts paid to consular agents of the United States.

U. S. GRANT.

WASHINGTON, *December 4, 1871.*

To the Senate and House of Representatives:

I transmit herewith to Congress a report, dated November 8, 1871, received from the Secretary of State, in compliance with the requirement of the act of March 3, 1871, making appropriations, among other things, for the increase of expenses and compensation of certain diplomatic and consular officers of the United States on account of the late war between France and Prussia. The expenditures therein mentioned have been made on my approval.

                                                              U. S. GRANT.

WASHINGTON, *December 4, 1871.*

To the Senate and House of Representatives:

I herewith transmit to Congress a report, dated the 4th instant, with the accompanying papers,* received from the Secretary of State, in compliance with the requirements of the eighteenth section of the act entitled "An act to regulate the diplomatic and consular systems of the United States," approved August 18, 1856.

                                                              U. S. GRANT.

WASHINGTON, *December 5, 1871.*

To the Senate and House of Representatives:

In pursuance of the provisions of the second section of the act approved June 20, 1864, entitled "An act making appropriations for the consular and diplomatic expenses of the Government for the year ending the 30th of June, 1865, and for other purposes," I inform Congress that William Heine, a consular clerk, was on the 30th of August last removed from office for the following cause, viz: Insubordination, disobedience of orders, and disrespectful conduct toward his superiors.

                                                              U. S. GRANT.

WASHINGTON, *December 6, 1871.*

To the Senate of the United States:

I transmit to the Senate, in answer to their resolution of the 5th instant, a report from the Secretary of State, with accompanying papers.†

                                                              U. S. GRANT.

EXECUTIVE MANSION, *December 19, 1871.*

To the Senate and House of Representatives:

In accordance with the act of Congress approved March 3, 1871, I convened a commission of eminent gentlemen to devise rules and regulations for the purpose of reforming the civil service. Their labors are

---

* Report of fees collected, etc., by consular officers of the United States for 1870, and tariff of consular fees prescribed by the President October 1, 1870.

† Correspondence relative to the retirement of Constantin de Catacazy, minister from Russia to the United States.

now completed, and I transmit herewith their report,* together with the rules which they recommend for my action. These rules have been adopted and will go into effect on the 1st day of January, 1872.

Under the law referred to, as I interpret it, the authority is already invested in the Executive to enforce these regulations, with full power to abridge, alter, or amend them, at his option, when changes may be deemed advisable.

These views, together with the report of the commissioners, are submitted for your careful consideration as to whether further legislation may be necessary in order to carry out an effective and beneficial civil-service reform. If left to me, without further Congressional action, the rules prescribed by the commission, under the reservation already mentioned, will be faithfully executed; but they are not binding, without further legislation, upon my successors.

Being desirous of bringing this subject to the attention of Congress before the approaching recess, I have not time to sufficiently examine the accompanying report to enable me to suggest definite legislative action to insure the support which may be necessary in order to give a thorough trial to a policy long needed.

I ask for all the strength which Congress can give me to enable me to carry out the reforms in the civil.service recommended by the commission, and adopted to take effect, as before stated, on January 1, 1872.

The law which provides for the convening of a commission to devise rules and regulations for reforming the civil service authorizes, I think, the permanent organization of a primary board under whose general direction all examinations of applicants for public office shall be conducted. There is no appropriation to continue such a board beyond the termination of its present labors. I therefore recommend that a proper appropriation be made to continue the services of the present board for another year, and in view of the fact that three members of the board hold positions in the public service, which precludes them from receiving extra compensation, under existing laws, that they be authorized to receive a fair compensation for extra services rendered by them in the performance of this duty.

U. S. GRANT.

RULES FOR THE CIVIL SERVICE.

1. No person shall be admitted to any position in the civil service within the appointment of the President or the heads of Departments who is not a citizen of the United States; who shall not have furnished satisfactory evidence in regard to character, health, and age, and who shall not have passed a satisfactory examination in speaking, reading, and writing the English language.

2. An advisory board of suitable persons, to be employed by the President under the ninth section of the act of March 3, 1871, entitled "An act making appropriations for sundry civil expenses of the Government for the fiscal year ending June 30, 1872,

*Omitted.

and for other purposes," shall, so far as practicable, group the positions in each branch of the civil service according to the character of the duties to be performed, and shall grade each group from lowest to highest for the purpose of promotion within the group. Admission to the civil service shall always be to the lowest grade of any group; and to such positions as can not be grouped or graded admission shall be determined as provided for the lowest grade.

3. A vacancy occurring in the lowest grade of any group of offices shall be filled, after due public notice, from all applicants who shall present themselves, and who shall have furnished the evidence and satisfied the preliminary examination already mentioned, and who shall have passed a public competitive examination to test knowledge, ability, and special qualifications for the performance of the duties of the office. The board conducting such competitive examination shall prepare, under the supervision of the Advisory Board, a list of the names of the applicants in the order of their excellence as proved by such examination, beginning with the highest, and shall then certify to the nominating or appointing power, as the case may be, the names standing at the head of such list, not exceeding three, and from the names thus certified the appointment shall be made.

4. A vacancy occurring in any grade of a group of offices above the lowest shall be filled by a competitive examination of applicants from the other grades of that group, and the list of names from which the appointment is to be made shall be prepared and certified as provided in the preceding rule; but if no such applicants are found competent the appointment shall be made upon an examination of all applicants, conducted in accordance with the provisions for admission to the lowest grade.

5. Applicants certified as otherwise qualified for appointment as cashiers of collectors of customs, cashiers of assistant treasurers, cashiers of postmasters, superintendents of money-order divisions in post-offices, and such other custodians of large sums of money as may hereafter be designated by the Advisory Board, and for whose pecuniary fidelity another officer is responsible, shall, nevertheless, not be appointed except with the approval of such other officer.

6. Postmasters whose annual salary is less than $200 may be appointed upon the written request of applicants, with such evidence of character and fitness as shall be satisfactory to the head of the Department.

7. The appointment of all persons entering the civil service in accordance with these regulations, excepting persons appointed by the President by and with the advice and consent of the Senate, postmasters, and persons appointed to any position in a foreign country, shall be made for a probationary term of six months, during which the conduct and capacity of such persons shall be tested; and if at the end of said probationary term satisfactory proofs of their fitness shall have been furnished by the board of examiners to the head of the Department in which they shall have been employed during said term, they shall be reappointed.

8. The President will designate three persons in each Department of the public service to serve as a board of examiners, which, under the supervision of the Advisory Board and under regulations to be prescribed by it, and at such times and places as it may determine, shall conduct, personally or by persons approved by the Advisory Board, all investigations and examinations for admission into said Departments or for promotion therein.

9. Any person who, after long and faithful service in a Department, shall be incapacitated by mental or bodily infirmity for the efficient discharge of the duties of his position may be appointed by the head of the Department, at his discretion, to a position of less responsibility in the same Department.

10. Nothing in these rules shall prevent the appointment of aliens to positions in the consular service which by reason of small compensation or of other sufficient cause are, in the judgment of the appointing power, necessarily so filled, nor the appointment of such persons within the United States as are indispensable to a proper

discharge of the duties of certain positions, but who may not be familiar with the English language or legally capable of naturalization.

11. No head of a Department nor any subordinate officer of the Government shall, as such officer, authorize or permit or assist in levying any assessment of money for political purposes, under the form of voluntary contributions or otherwise, upon any person employed under his control, nor shall any such person pay any money so assessed.

12. The Advisory Board shall at any time recommend to the President such changes in these rules as it may consider necessary to secure the greater efficiency of the civil service.

13. From these rules are excepted the heads of Departments, Assistant Secretaries of Departments, Assistant Attorneys-General, and First Assistant Postmaster-General, Solicitor-General, Solicitor of the Treasury, Naval Solicitor, Solicitor of Internal Revenue, examiner of claims in the State Department, Treasurer of the United States, Register of the Treasury, First and Second Comptrollers of the Treasury, judges of the United States courts, district attorneys, private secretary of the President, ambassadors and other public ministers, Superintendent of the Coast Survey, Director of the Mint, governors of Territories, special commissioners, special counsel, visiting and examining boards, persons appointed to positions without compensation for services, dispatch agents, and bearers of dispatches.

EXECUTIVE MANSION, *December 20, 1871.*

To the House of Representatives:

In answer to the resolution of the House of Representatives of the 6th instant, requesting information in regard to certain measures with reference to the Spanish West Indies, I transmit reports from the Secretary of State and of the Navy, with the documents by which they were accompanied.

U. S. GRANT.

WASHINGTON, *January 8, 1872.*

To the House of Representatives:

In answer to a resolution of the House of Representatives of the 6th of December, requesting to be informed if any further action is necessary by Congress to secure the immediate temporary preservation of the archives or public records now in the State Department, I transmit a report and accompanying papers from the Secretary of State.

U. S. GRANT.

WASHINGTON, *January 9, 1872.*

To the Senate:

In answer to the resolution of the Senate of the 19th of December last, calling for certain correspondence relating to the subject of international coinage not heretofore furnished, I transmit herewith a report from the Secretary of State, with the papers which accompanied it.

U. S. GRANT.

WASHINGTON, *January 15, 1872.*

To the Senate of the United States:

I transmit, for the consideration of the Senate with a view to ratification, a convention between the United States and His Majesty the Emperor of Austria-Hungary, relative to the protection of trade-marks.

U. S. GRANT.

WASHINGTON, *January 15, 1872.*

To the Senate of the United States:

I transmit, for the consideration of the Senate with a view to ratification, a convention between the United States and His Majesty the Emperor of Germany, relative to the rights, privileges, and duties of consuls and to the protection of trade-marks, signed at Berlin on the 11th ultimo.

A copy of the dispatch of the 11th ultimo from Mr. Bancroft, which accompanied the convention, is also transmitted for the information of the Senate.

U. S. GRANT.

WASHINGTON, *January 16, 1872.*

To the Senate of the United States:

In answer to the resolution of the Senate of the 16th of May last, calling for papers, correspondence, and information relating to the case of the ship *Hudson* and schooner *Washington*,* I transmit reports from the Secretaries of State and of the Navy and the papers by which they were accompanied.

U. S. GRANT.

WASHINGTON, *January 30, 1872.*

To the House of Representatives:

In answer to a resolution of the House of Representatives of the 15th instant, calling for certain correspondence relating to the release of the Fenian prisoner William G. Halpine, I transmit herewith a report of the Secretary of State.

U. S. GRANT.

WASHINGTON, *February 2, 1872.*

To the Senate of the United States:

I transmit to the Senate, in answer to their resolution of the 16th ultimo, a report from the Secretary of State, with accompanying papers.†

U. S. GRANT.

---

* Seized by British authorities at the Falkland Islands in 1854.

† Correspondence relative to the seizure and detention of the American steamers *Hero*, *Dudley Buck*, *Nutrias*, and *San Fernando*, property of the Venezuela Steam Transportation Company, and the virtual imprisonment of the officers of those vessels.

WASHINGTON, *February 13, 1872.*

To the Senate of the United States:

In answer to the resolution adopted by the Senate on the 19th of December last, relative to questions with Spain growing out of affairs in Cuba and to instructions to our naval commanders in Cuban waters, I transmit reports from the Secretaries of State and of the Navy.

U. S. GRANT.

WASHINGTON, *February 13, 1872.*

To the Senate of the United States:

In answer to the resolution of the Senate of the 8th instant, I transmit a report from the Secretary of State and the copy of the case of the United States presented to the tribunal of arbitration at Geneva, which accompanied it.

U. S. GRANT.

WASHINGTON, *February 23, 1872.*

To the Senate of the United States:

I transmit herewith, for the consideration of the Senate, a preliminary report of Dr. E. C. Wines, appointed under a joint resolution of Congress of the 7th of March, 1871, as commissioner of the United States to the international congress on the prevention and repression of crime, including penal and reformatory treatment.

U. S. GRANT.

WASHINGTON, *March 11, 1872.*

To the House of Representatives:

I transmit herewith a report,* dated the 5th instant, received from the Secretary of State, in compliance with the resolution of the House of Representatives of the 28th of February ultimo.

U. S. GRANT.

EXECUTIVE MANSION, *March 15, 1872.*

To the Senate and House of Representatives:

I have the honor herewith to transmit to Congress a recommendation from Hon. M. D. Leggett, Commissioner of Patents, for the reorganization of his office, and also the letter of the Secretary of the Interior accompanying it.

I concur with the Secretary of the Interior in the views expressed in his letter, and recommend the careful consideration of Congress to the subject of this communication, and action which will secure a more efficient performance of the duties of the Patent Office than is practicable under present legislation.

U. S. GRANT.

* Relative to the number of consular and commercial agents of the United States abroad who speak or write the language of the country in which their districts are situated.

WASHINGTON, *March 16, 1872.*

To the House of Representatives:

I transmit herewith a report,* dated the 16th instant, received from the Secretary of State, in compliance with the resolution of the House of Representatives of the 7th instant.

U. S. GRANT.

WASHINGTON, *March 19, 1872.*

To the Senate of the United States:

I transmit to the Senate, for consideration with a view to its ratification, a "general convention of friendship, commerce, and extradition" between the United States and the Orange Free State, signed at Bloemfontein on the 22d of December last by W. W. Edgcomb, consul of the United States at Cape Town, acting on behalf of this Government, and by Mr. F. K. Höhne on behalf of the Orange Free State.

U. S. GRANT.

WASHINGTON, *March 20, 1872.*

To the House of Representatives:

I transmit herewith a report,† dated the 20th instant, received from the Secretary of State, to whom was referred the resolution of the House of Representatives of the 28th ultimo.

U. S. GRANT.

WASHINGTON, *March 23, 1872.*

To the House of Representatives of the United States:

In answer to a resolution of the House of Representatives of the 20th instant, I transmit a report from the Secretary of State, with a list of the newspapers ‡ which accompanied it.

U. S. GRANT.

WASHINGTON, *March 28, 1872.*

To the House of Representatives:

I transmit to the House of Representatives, in answer to their resolution of the 19th instant, a report of the Secretary of State and the papers § which accompany the same.

U. S. GRANT.

* Stating that there are no papers in the Department of State to show that the inhabitants of the Navigators Islands, in the Pacific Ocean, have made application to have the protection of the United States extended over said islands.

† Transmitting a translation of the Spanish royal decree of July 6, 1860, prescribing regulations for the introduction of Chinese laborers into Cuba, and translation of a decree of Count Valmaseda, Captain-General of Cuba, of December 13, 1871, relative to the decree of July 6, 1860.

‡ Selected to publish the laws of the United States for the second session of the Forty-second Congress.

§ Correspondence relative to the imprisonment by Spanish authorities of Dr. J. E. Houard, a citizen of the United States, charged with complicity in the insurrection in Cuba.

WASHINGTON, *April 2, 1872.*

To the Senate of the United States:

In answer to the resolution of the Senate of the 18th of January last, relating to British light-house dues, I transmit herewith a report from the Secretary of State and the documents which accompanied it.

U. S. GRANT.

WASHINGTON, *April 4, 1872.*

To the House of Representatives:

In answer to the resolution of the House of Representatives of the 14th of January last, I transmit herewith a report* of the Secretary of State.

U. S. GRANT.

EXECUTIVE MANSION, *April 19, 1872.*

To the House of Representatives:

In answer to the resolution of the House of Representatives of the 25th of January last, I have the honor to submit the following, accompanied by the report of the Attorney-General, to whom the resolution was referred:

Representations having been made to me that in certain portions of South Carolina a condition of lawlessness and terror existed, I requested the then Attorney-General (Akerman) to visit that State, and after personal examination to report to me the facts in relation to the subject. On the 16th of October last he addressed me a communication from South Carolina, in which he stated that in the counties of Spartanburg, York, Chester, Union, Laurens, Newberry, Fairfield, Lancaster, and Chesterfield there were combinations for the purpose of preventing the free political action of citizens who were friendly to the Constitution and the Government of the United States, and of depriving emancipated classes of the equal protection of the laws.

"These combinations embrace at least two-thirds of the active white men of those counties, and have the sympathy and countenance of a majority of the one-third. They are connected with similar combinations in other counties and States, and no doubt are part of a grand system of criminal associations pervading most of the Southern States. The members are bound to obedience and secrecy by oaths which they are taught to regard as of higher obligation than the lawful oaths taken before civil magistrates.

"They are organized and armed. They effect their objects by personal violence, often extending to murder. They terrify witnesses; they control juries in the State courts, and sometimes in the courts of the United States. Systematic perjury is one of the means by which prosecutions of the members are defeated. From information given by officers

---

*Stating that the report of Richard D. Cutts on the marketable products of the sea was transmitted with the message of President Johnson of February 17, 1869.

of the State and of the United States and by credible private citizens I am justified in affirming that the instances of criminal violence perpetrated by these combinations within the last twelve months in the above-named counties could be reckoned by thousands.''

I received information of a similar import from various other sources, among which were the Joint Select Committee of Congress upon Southern Outrages, the officers of the State, the military officers of the United States on duty in South Carolina, the United States attorney and marshal, and other civil officers of the Government, repentant and abjuring members of those unlawful organizations, persons specially employed by the Department of Justice to detect crimes against the United States, and from other credible persons.

Most, if not all, of this information, except what I derived from the Attorney-General, came to me orally, and was to the effect that said counties were under the sway of powerful combinations, properly known as ''Kuklux Klans,'' the objects of which were by force and terror to prevent all political action not in accord with the views of the members; to deprive colored citizens of the right to bear arms and of the right to a free ballot; to suppress schools in which colored children were taught, and to reduce the colored people to a condition closely akin to that of slavery; that these combinations were organized and armed, and had rendered the local laws ineffectual to protect the classes whom they desired to oppress; that they had perpetrated many murders and hundreds of crimes of minor degree, all of which were unpunished; and that witnesses could not safely testify against them unless the more active members were placed under restraint.

U. S. GRANT.

WASHINGTON, *April 20, 1872.*

To the House of Representatives:

I transmit, for the information of the House of Representatives, a report from the Secretary of State and the copy of the counter case of the United States in the matter of the claims against Great Britain, as presented to the board of arbitration at Geneva, which accompanies it.

U. S. GRANT.

[The same message was sent to the Senate.]

WASHINGTON, *April 24, 1872.*

To the House of Representatives of the United States:

In answer to a resolution of the 22d instant, I transmit to the House of Representatives a report from the Secretary of State, with the British case* and papers which accompanied it.

U. S. GRANT.

* Presented to the board of arbitration at Geneva.

To the House of Representatives:

In answer to a resolution of the House of Representatives of yester-day, I transmit a report of the Secretary of State and copies of the British counter case,* and the volumes of appendixes to the British case which accompany it.

U. S. GRANT.

APRIL 29, 1872.

EXECUTIVE MANSION, *April 30, 1872.*

To the Senate and House of Representatives:

I have the honor to transmit herewith the annual report of the board of public works of the District of Columbia, submitted to me for that purpose by the governor of the Territory in accordance with section 37 of "An act to provide a government for the District of Columbia," approved February 21, 1871.

U. S. GRANT.

WASHINGTON, D. C., *May 7, 1872.*

To the House of Representatives:

In answer to a resolution of the House of Representatives of the 15th of March last, I transmit herewith a report of the Secretary of State and the papers† which accompanied it.

U. S. GRANT.

WASHINGTON, *May 7, 1872.*

To the Senate of the United States:

I transmit, for the consideration of the Senate with a view to its ratification, a convention between the United States and the Republic of Ecuador for the purpose of regulating the citizenship of persons who emigrate from the one country to the other, which instrument was signed in this city on the 6th instant.

U. S. GRANT.

WASHINGTON, *May 7, 1872.*

To the Senate of the United States:

I herewith communicate to the Senate a report from the Acting Secretary of the Interior of this date, in answer to the resolution of that body adopted on the 23d ultimo, calling for information relative to the recent affray at the court-house in Going Snake district, Indian Territory.

In view of the feeling of hostility which exists between the Cherokees and the United States authorities of the western district of Arkansas, it seems to be necessary that Congress should adopt such measures as will tend to allay that feeling and at the same time secure the enforcement of the laws in that Territory.

---

* Presented to the board of arbitration at Geneva.

† Correspondence relative to the claim of the owners of the steamer *Aroostook* for compensation for the use of that vessel in searching for bodies and property lost in the United States steamer *Oneida*, wrecked in the Bay of Yedo in 1870.

I therefore concur with the Acting Secretary of the Interior in suggesting the adoption of a pending bill for the erection of a judicial district within the Indian Territory, as a measure which will afford the most immediate remedy for the existing troubles.

U. S. GRANT.

[A similar message, dated May 10, was sent to the House of Representatives, in answer to a resolution of that body of April 29.]

WASHINGTON, *May 13, 1872.*

To the Senate of the United States:

I transmit herewith the correspondence which has recently taken place respecting the differences of opinion which have arisen between this Government and that of Great Britain with regard to the powers of the tribunal of arbitration created under the treaty signed at Washington May 8, 1871.

I respectfully invite the attention of the Senate to the proposed article submitted by the British Government with the object of removing the differences which seem to threaten the prosecution of the arbitration, and request an expression by the Senate of their disposition in regard to advising and consenting to the formal adoption of an article such as is proposed by the British Government.

The Senate is aware that the consultation with that body in advance of entering into agreements with foreign states has many precedents. In the early days of the Republic General Washington repeatedly asked their advice upon pending questions with such powers. The most important recent precedent is that of the Oregon boundary treaty, in 1846.

The importance of the results hanging upon the present state of the treaty with Great Britain leads me to follow these former precedents and to desire the counsel of the Senate in advance of agreeing to the proposal of Great Britain.

U. S. GRANT.

EXECUTIVE MANSION, *May 14, 1872.*

To the Senate and House of Representatives of the United States:

In my message to Congress at the beginning of its present session allusion was made to the hardships and privations inflicted upon poor immigrants on shipboard and upon arrival on our shores, and a suggestion was made favoring national legislation for the purpose of effecting a radical cure of the evil.

Promise was made that a special message on this subject would be presented during the present session should information be received which would warrant it. I now transmit to the two Houses of Congress all that has been officially received since that time bearing upon the subject, and recommend that such legislation be had as will secure, first, such room and accommodation on shipboard as is necessary for health and comfort, and such privacy and protection as not to compel immigrants to be the unwilling witnesses to so much vice and misery; and, second, legislation to protect them upon their arrival at our seaports from the knaves who are ever ready to despoil them of the little all which they are able to bring with them. Such legislation will be in the interests of humanity, and seems to be fully justifiable. The immigrant is not a citizen of any State or Territory upon his arrival, but comes here to become a citizen of a great Republic, free to change his residence at will, to enjoy the blessings of a protecting Government, where all are equal before the law, and to add to the national wealth by his industry.

On his arrival he does not know States or corporations, but confides implicitly in the protecting arm of the great, free country of which he has heard so much before leaving his native land. It is a source of serious disappointment and discouragement to those who start with means sufficient to support them comfortably until they can choose a residence and begin employment for a comfortable support to find themselves subject to ill treatment and every discomfort on their passage here, and at the end of their journey seized upon by professed friends, claiming legal right to take charge of them for their protection, who do not leave them until all their resources are exhausted, when they are abandoned in a strange land, surrounded by strangers, without employment and ignorant of the means of securing it. Under the present system this is the fate of thousands annually, the exposures on shipboard and the treatment on landing driving thousands to lives of vice and shame who, with proper humane treatment, might become useful and respectable members of society.

I do not advise national legislation in affairs that should be regulated by the States; but I see no subject more national in its character than provision for the safety and welfare of the thousands who leave foreign lands to become citizens of this Republic.

When their residence is chosen, they may then look to the laws of their locality for protection and guidance.

The mass of immigrants arriving upon our shores, coming, as they do, on vessels under foreign flags, makes treaties with the nations furnishing these immigrants necessary for their complete protection. For more than two years efforts have been made on our part to secure such treaties, and there is now reasonable ground to hope for success.

U. S. GRANT.

WASHINGTON, *May 14, 1872.*

To the Senate of the United States:

In answer to a resolution of the Senate of the 28th of March last, I transmit herewith copies of the correspondence between the Department of State and the consul of the United States at Bucharest relative to the persecution and oppression of the Israelites in the Principality of Roumania.

                                                U. S. GRANT.

WASHINGTON, *May 15, 1872.*

To the House of Representatives:

I transmit herewith, for the information of the House of Representatives, the correspondence which has recently taken place respecting the differences of opinion which have arisen between this Government and that of Great Britain with regard to the powers of the tribunal of arbitration created under the treaty signed at Washington May 8, 1871, and which has led to certain negotiations, still pending, between the two Governments.

                                                U. S. GRANT.

WASHINGTON, *May 17, 1872.*

To the Senate of the United States:

I herewith transmit to the Senate a communication of this date from the Acting Secretary of the Interior, and the papers therein described, containing information * called for in the Senate resolution of the 23d ultimo, which was answered in part on the 8th [7th] instant.

                                                U. S. GRANT.

WASHINGTON, *May 21, 1872.*

To the House of Representatives:

In answer to the resolution of the House of Representatives of the 14th instant, requesting information in regard to the commerce between the United States and certain British colonial possessions, I transmit a report from the Secretary of State and the documents by which it was accompanied.

                                                U. S. GRANT.

WASHINGTON, *May 22, 1872.*

To the House of Representatives:

In answer to a resolution of the House of Representatives of the 20th instant, requesting me to join the Italian Government in a protest against the intolerant and cruel treatment of the Jews in Roumania, I transmit a report from the Secretary of State relative to the subject.

                                                U. S. GRANT.

WASHINGTON, *May 22, 1872.*

To the Senate of the United States:

I transmit to the Senate, for its consideration, an agreement between the Great Chief of the island of Tutuila, one of the Samoan group, in the

* Relating to acts of United States marshals and deputy marshals in that portion of the western district of Arkansas comprising the Indian country.

South Pacific, and Commander R. W. Meade, commanding the United States steamer *Narragansett*, bearing date the 17th of February last. This instrument proposes to confer upon this Government the exclusive privilege of establishing a naval station in the dominions of that chief for the equivalent of protecting those dominions.

A copy of a letter of the 15th instant, and of its accompaniment, addressed by the Secretary of the Navy to the Secretary of State, descriptive of Tutuila and of other islands of the group, and of a letter in the nature of a protest from a person claiming to be consul of the North German Confederation in that quarter, are also herewith transmitted. No report has yet been received from Commander Meade on the subject. Although he was without special instructions or authority to enter into such agreement, the advantages of the concession which it proposes to make are so great, in view of the advantageous position of Tutuila, especially as a coaling station for steamers between San Francisco and Australia, that I should not hesitate to recommend its approval but for the protection on the part of the United States which it seems to imply. With some modification of the obligation of protection which the agreement imports, it is recommended to the favorable consideration of the Senate.   U. S. GRANT.

EXECUTIVE MANSION, *May 23, 1872.*

To the Senate of the United States:

I have the honor to transmit herewith, in answer to the resolution of the Senate of March 12, requesting to be informed of "the amount of money expended by the Government of the United States during the last three years for telegraphing by ocean cables," reports from the different Departments of the Government, to which the resolution was referred.

U. S. GRANT.

EXECUTIVE MANSION, *May 24, 1872.*

To the Senate and House of Representatives:

In compliance with section 2 of the act approved July 11, 1870, entitled "An act making appropriations for the consular and diplomatic expenses of the Government for the year ending June 30, 1871, and for other purposes," I have the honor to transmit herewith the report of D. B. R. Keim, agent to examine consular affairs.   U. S. GRANT.

EXECUTIVE MANSION, *May 28, 1872.*

To the House of Representatives:

In further answer to the resolution of the 14th instant of the House of Representatives, wherein information in regard to commerce between the United States and certain British colonial possessions is requested, I transmit a report from the Postmaster-General and the document by which it was accompanied.

U. S. GRANT.

WASHINGTON, *May 28, 1872.*

To the House of Representatives:

In answer to the resolution of the House of Representatives of the 7th instant, requesting copies of correspondence in regard to an extradition treaty with Belgium, I transmit a report from the Secretary of State and the documents by which it was accompanied.

U. S. GRANT.

EXECUTIVE MANSION, *May 31, 1872.*

To the Senate and House of Representatives:

I have the honor to respectfully call the attention of Congress to an act approved July 14, 1870, directing the Secretary of War to place at the disposal of the President certain bronze ordnance, to aid in the erection of an equestrian statue of the late General John A. Rawlins, and to the facts that no appropriation of money to pay for the statue is made by the resolution and no artist is named or party designated to whom the ordnance is to be delivered. In view of the ambiguity of the statute, I would recommend that Congress signify what action is desired as to the selection of the artist, and that the necessary sum required for the erection of the monument be appropriated. A board of officers should also be named to designate the location of the monument.

U. S. GRANT.

VETO MESSAGES.

EXECUTIVE MANSION, *March 28, 1872.*

To the House of Representatives:

I herewith return, for the further consideration of Congress, without my approval, House bill No. 1550, "An act for the relief of the estate of Dr. John F. Hanks," for the reason that the records of the Treasury Department show that the current moneys taken by Colonel S. B. Holabird from the Louisiana State Bank of New Orleans in the month of August, 1862, were accounted for by that officer to the Treasury Department, and the names of the depositors given, and that the name of Dr. John F. Hanks does not appear among them.

It also appears from the records of the Treasury Department that among the effects taken from the Louisiana State Bank of New Orleans was the sum of $1,729 of Confederate money, and that the said sum stood upon the books of said bank to the credit of J. F. Hanks. It is but justice, however, to the executors of the estate of Dr. Hanks to state that there is every reason to believe that the money deposited by Dr. Hanks in the Louisiana State Bank was in current funds, and that when application was made to Congress for the recovery of the same they believed, and had evidence to satisfy them, that such funds had found their way into the Treasury of the United States. There has unquestionably been a mistake made, either by the officers of the Louisiana State Bank or the persons engaged in removing the funds of that bank, by which the estate of Dr. Hanks is loser to the amount of relief afforded by House bill No. 1550.

Accompanying this I send the statement furnished by the Secretary of the Treasury of the funds covered into his Department, and accounted for through it, arising from the seizure of funds of the Louisiana State Bank of New Orleans in the month of August, 1862.

U. S. GRANT.

EXECUTIVE MANSION, April 1, 1872.

To the House of Representatives:

I return herewith, for the further consideration of Congress, House bill No. 1867, "An act for the relief of James T. Johnston," without my approval, for the reason that the records of the Treasury Department show that the lot sold in the name of J. T. Johnston, situate on Prince street, Alexandria, Va., for taxes due the United States, is numbered 162, instead of 163, as represented in this bill. With the exception of this discrepancy in the number of the lot there is no reason why the bill should not receive my approval.

U. S. GRANT.

WASHINGTON, April 10, 1872.

To the House of Representatives:

I have received and taken into consideration the bill entitled "An act for the relief of the children of John M. Baker, deceased," and, pursuant to the duty required of me by the Constitution, I return the same with my objections to the House of Representatives, in which it originated.

The bill proposes to pay a sum of money to the children of John M. Baker, deceased, late United States consul at Rio Janeiro, for services of that person as acting chargé d'affaires of the United States in the year 1834. So far as it can be ascertained it is apprehended that the bill may have received the sanction of Congress through some inadvertence, for upon inquiry at the proper Department it appears that Mr. Baker never did act as chargé d'affaires of the United States at Rio Janeiro, and that he was not authorized so to act, but, on the contrary, was expressly forbidden to enter into diplomatic correspondence with the Government of Brazil.

The letter of the 8th of February, 1854, a copy of which is annexed, addressed by William L. Marcy, then Secretary of State, to James M.

Mason, chairman of the Committee on Foreign Relations of the Senate, specifies objections to the claim, which it is believed have not since diminished, and in which I fully concur.

U. S. GRANT.

EXECUTIVE MANSION, *April 15, 1872.*

To the Senate of the United States:

I return without my approval an act entitled "An act granting a pension to Abigail Ryan, widow of Thomas A. Ryan." The name of Mrs. Ryan is now borne upon the pension rolls, pursuant to an act of Congress entitled "An act for the relief of Mrs. Abigail Ryan," approved June 15, 1866 (14 U. S. Statutes at Large, p. 590).

U. S. GRANT.

EXECUTIVE MANSION, *April 22, 1872.*

To the House of Representatives:

I return herewith House resolution No. 622, entitled "An act granting a pension to Richard B. Crawford," without my approval, for the reason that said Crawford is now drawing a pension as a private soldier, the wound on account of which he was pensioned having been received before his promotion to a lieutenancy.

U. S. GRANT.

EXECUTIVE MANSION, *May 14, 1872.*

To the Senate of the United States:

I have the honor to return herewith the bill (S. 955) entitled "An act granting a pension to Mary Ann Montgomery, widow of William W. Montgomery, late captain in Texas Volunteers," without my approval, inasmuch as the concluding phrase, "and in respect to her minor children under 16 years of age," has obviously no meaning whatsoever. If it were the intention of the framer of the bill that the pension thereby granted should revert to said minor children upon the remarriage or death of the widow, the phrase referred to should read as follows: "And in the event of her remarriage or death, to her minor children under 16 years of age." I therefore return the bill for proper action.

U. S. GRANT.

WASHINGTON, *June 1, 1872.*

To the Senate of the United States:

I have examined the bill entitled "An act for the relief of J. Milton Best," and, being unable to give it my approval, return the same to the Senate, the House in which it originated, without my signature.

The bill appropriates the sum of $25,000 to compensate Dr. J. Milton Best for the destruction of his dwelling house and its contents by order of the commanding officer of the United States military forces at Paducah, Ky., on the 26th day of March, 1864. It appears that this house was one of a considerable number destroyed for the purpose of giving open range to the guns of a United States fort. On the day preceding the destruction the houses had been used as a cover for rebel troops attacking the fort, and, apprehending a renewal of the attack, the commanding officer caused the destruction of the houses. This, then, is a claim for compensation on account of the ravages of war. It can not be denied that the payment of this claim would invite the presentation of demands for very large sums of money; and such is the supposed magnitude of the claims that may be made against the Government for necessary and unavoidable destruction of property by the Army that I deem it proper to return this bill for reconsideration.

It is a general principle of both international and municipal law that all property is held subject not only to be taken by the Government for public uses, in which case, under the Constitution of the United States, the owner is entitled to just compensation, but also subject to be temporarily occupied, or even actually destroyed, in times of great public danger, and when the public safety demands it; and in this latter case governments do not admit a legal obligation on their part to compensate the owner. The temporary occupation of, injuries to, and destruction of property caused by actual and necessary military operations are generally considered to fall within the last-mentioned principle. If a government makes compensation under such circumstances, it is a matter of bounty rather than of strict legal right.

If it be deemed proper to make compensation for such losses, I suggest for the consideration of Congress whether it would not be better, by general legislation, to provide some means for the ascertainment of the damage in all similar cases, and thus save to claimants the expense, inconvenience, and delay of attendance upon Congress, and at the same time save the Government from the danger of having imposed upon it fictitious or exaggerated claims supported wholly by *ex parte* proof. If the claimant in this case ought to be paid, so ought all others similarly situated; and that there are many such can not be doubted. Besides, there are strong reasons for believing that the amount of damage in this case has been greatly overestimated. If this be true, it furnishes an illustration of the danger of trusting entirely to *ex parte* testimony in such matters.

U. S. GRANT.

EXECUTIVE MANSION, *June 7, 1872.*
To the Senate of the United States:

I have the honor to return herewith Senate bill No. 569, an act entitled "An act for the relief of Thomas B. Wallace, of Lexington, in the State of Missouri," without my approval.

This claim, for which $11,250 are appropriated by this bill, is of the same nature and character as the claim of Dr. J. Milton Best, which was returned to the Senate on the 1st instant without my signature.

The same reasons which prompted the return of that bill for reconsideration apply in this case, which also is a claim for compensation on account of the ravages of war, and comes under the same general principle of both international and municipal law, that all property is held subject not only to be taken by the Government for public uses, in which case, under the Constitution of the United States, the owner is entitled to just compensation, but also subject to be temporarily occupied, or even actually destroyed, in times of great public danger, and when the public safety demands it; and in the latter case governments do not admit a legal obligation on their part to compensate the owner.

The temporary occupation of, injuries to, and destruction of property caused by actual and necessary military operations are generally considered to fall within the last-mentioned principle, and if a government makes compensation under such circumstances it is a matter of bounty rather than of strict legal right. If it be deemed proper to make compensation for such losses, I renew my recommendation that provision be made by general legislation for all similar cases.

U. S. GRANT.

PROCLAMATIONS.

By the President of the United States of America.

A PROCLAMATION.

Whereas satisfactory information has been received by me, through Don Mauricio Lopez Roberts, envoy extraordinary and minister plenipotentiary of His Majesty the King of Spain, that the Government of that country has abolished discriminating duties heretofore imposed on merchandise imported from all other countries, excepting the islands of Cuba and Porto Rico, into Spain and the adjacent islands in vessels of the United States, said abolition to take effect from and after the 1st day of January next:

Now, therefore, I, Ulysses S. Grant, President of the United States of America, by virtue of the authority vested in me by an act of Congress of the 7th day of January, 1824, and by an act in addition thereto of the 24th day of May, 1828, do hereby declare and proclaim that on and after the said 1st day of January next, so long as merchandise imported from any other country, excepting the islands of Cuba and Porto Rico, into the ports of Spain and the islands adjacent thereto in vessels belonging to citizens of the United States shall be exempt from discriminating duties, any such duties on merchandise imported into the United States in Spanish vessels, excepting from the islands of Cuba and Porto Rico, shall be discontinued and abolished.

In testimony whereof I have hereunto set my hand and caused the seal of the United States to be affixed.

[SEAL.]   Done at the city of Washington, this 19th day of December, A. D. 1871, and of the Independence of the United States of America the ninety-sixth.   **U. S. GRANT.**

By the President:
> HAMILTON FISH,
> *Secretary of State.*

BY THE PRESIDENT OF THE UNITED STATES OF AMERICA.

A PROCLAMATION.

Whereas, pursuant to the first section of the act of Congress approved the 11th day of June, 1864, entitled "An act to provide for the execution of treaties between the United States and foreign nations respecting consular jurisdiction over the crews of vessels of such foreign nations in the waters and ports of the United States," it is provided that before that act shall take effect as to the ships and vessels of any particular nation having such treaty with the United States the President of the United States shall have been satisfied that similar provisions have been made for the execution of such treaty by the other contracting party and shall have issued his proclamation to that effect, declaring that act to be in force as to such nation; and

Whereas due inquiry having been made and a satisfactory answer having been received that similar provisions are in force in the United Kingdoms of Sweden and Norway:

Now, therefore, be it known that I, Ulysses S. Grant, President of the United States of America, do hereby proclaim the same accordingly.

Done at the city of Washington, this 11th day of May, A. D. 1872, and of the Independence of the United States of America the ninety-sixth.   [SEAL.]

U. S. GRANT.

By the President:
> HAMILTON FISH,
> *Secretary of State.*

BY THE PRESIDENT OF THE UNITED STATES OF AMERICA.

A PROCLAMATION.

Whereas the act of Congress approved June 25, 1868, constituted, on and after that date, eight hours a day's work for all laborers, workmen, and mechanics employed by or on behalf of the Government of the United States; and

Whereas on the 19th day of May, A. D. 1869, by Executive proclamation it was directed that from and after that date no reduction should be made in the wages paid by the Government by the day to such laborers, workmen, and mechanics on account of such reduction of the hours of labor; and

Whereas it is now represented to me that the act of Congress and the proclamation aforesaid have not been strictly observed by all officers of the Government having charge of such laborers, workmen, and mechanics:

Now, therefore, I, Ulysses S. Grant, President of the United States, do hereby again call attention to the act of Congress aforesaid, and direct all officers of the executive department of the Government having charge of the employment and payment of laborers, workmen, or mechanics employed by or on behalf of the Government of the United States to make no reduction in the wages paid by the Government by the day to such laborers, workmen, and mechanics on account of the reduction of the hours of labor.

In testimony whereof I have hereunto set my hand and caused the seal of the United States to be affixed.

[SEAL.]   Done at the city of Washington, this 11th day of May, A. D. 1872, and of the Independence of the United States the ninety-sixth.

U. S. GRANT.

By the President:
    HAMILTON FISH,
            Secretary of State.

BY THE PRESIDENT OF THE UNITED STATES OF AMERICA.

A PROCLAMATION.

Whereas the act of Congress approved May 22, 1872, removes all political disabilities imposed by the third section of the fourteenth article of amendments to the Constitution of the United States from all persons whomsoever except Senators and Representatives of the Thirty-sixth and Thirty-seventh Congresses and officers in the judicial, military, and naval service of the United States, heads of Departments, and foreign ministers of the United States; and

Whereas it is represented to me that there are now pending in the several circuit and district courts of the United States proceedings by *quo warranto* under the fourteenth section of the act of Congress approved May 31, 1870, to remove from office certain persons who are alleged to hold said offices in violation of the provisions of said article of amendment to the Constitution of the United States, and also penal prosecutions against such persons under the fifteenth section of the act of Congress aforesaid:

Now, therefore, I, Ulysses S. Grant, President of the United States, do hereby direct all district attorneys having charge of such proceedings and prosecutions to dismiss and discontinue the same, except as to persons who may be embraced in the exceptions named in the act of Congress first above cited.

In testimony whereof I have hereunto set my hand and caused the seal of the United States to be affixed.

[SEAL.]   Done at the city of Washington, this 1st day of June, A. D. 1872, and of the Independence of the United States of America the ninety-sixth.   U. S. GRANT.

By the President:

HAMILTON FISH,
Secretary of State.

BY THE PRESIDENT OF THE UNITED STATES OF AMERICA.

A PROCLAMATION.

Whereas satisfactory information has been received by me from His Majesty the Emperor of Japan, through an official communication of Mr. Arinori Mori, His Majesty's chargé d'affaires, under date of the 2d instant, that no other or higher duties of tonnage or impost are imposed or levied in the ports of the Empire of Japan upon vessels wholly belonging to citizens of the United States or upon the produce, manufactures, or merchandise imported in the same from the United States or from any foreign country than are levied on Japanese ships and their cargoes in the same ports under like circumstances:

Now, therefore, I, Ulysses S. Grant, President of the United States of America, by virtue of the authority vested in me by an act of Congress of the 24th day of May, 1828, do hereby declare and proclaim that from and after the said 2d instant, so long as vessels of the United States and their cargoes shall be exempt from discriminating duties as aforesaid, any such duties on Japanese vessels entering the ports of the United States, or on the produce, manufactures, or merchandise imported in such vessels, shall be discontinued and abolished.

In testimony whereof I have hereunto set my hand and caused the seal of the United States to be affixed.

[SEAL.]   Done at the city of Washington, the 4th day of September, A. D. 1872, and of the Independence of the United States the ninety-seventh.   U. S. GRANT.

By the President:

CHARLES HALE,
Acting Secretary of State.

BY THE PRESIDENT OF THE UNITED STATES OF AMERICA.

A PROCLAMATION.

Whereas the revolution of another year has again brought the time when it is usual to look back upon the past and publicly to thank the Almighty for His mercies and His blessings; and

Whereas if any one people has more occasion than another for such thankfulness it is the citizens of the United States, whose Government is their creature, subject to their behests; who have reserved to themselves ample civil and religious freedom and equality before the law; who during the last twelvemonth have enjoyed exemption from any grievous or general calamity, and to whom prosperity in agriculture, manufactures, and commerce has been vouchsafed:

Now, therefore, by these considerations, I recommend that on Thursday, the 28th day of November next, the people meet in their respective places of worship and there make their acknowledgments to God for His kindness and bounty.

In witness whereof I have hereunto set my hand and caused the seal of the United States to be affixed.

[SEAL.] Done at the city of Washington, this 11th day of October, A. D. 1872, and of the Independence of the United States the ninety-seventh.

U. S. GRANT.

By the President:

HAMILTON FISH, *Secretary of State*

BY THE PRESIDENT OF THE UNITED STATES OF AMERICA.

A PROCLAMATION.

Whereas upon information received by me from His Majesty the Emperor of the French that discriminating duties before the date of said information levied in French ports upon merchandise imported from the countries of its origin in vessels of the United States were discontinued and abolished, and in pursuance of the provisions of an act of Congress of the 7th of January, 1824, and of an act in addition thereto of the 24th of May, 1828, I did, on the 12th day of June, 1869, issue my proclamation* declaring that the discriminating duties before that date levied upon merchandise imported from the countries of its origin into ports of the United States in French vessels were thereby discontinued and abolished; and

Whereas upon information subsequently received by me that the levying of such duties on all merchandise imported into France in vessels of the United States, whether from the country of its origin or from other countries, had been discontinued, I did, on the 20th of November, 1869,

* See pp. 3969-3970.

in pursuance of the provisions of the said acts of Congress and by the authority in me vested thereby, issue my proclamation* declaring that the discriminating duties before that date levied upon merchandise imported into the United States in French vessels, either from the countries of its origin or from any other country, were thereby discontinued and abolished; and

Whereas by the provisions of the said acts of Congress of January 7, 1824, and of the 24th of May, 1828, as well as by the terms of the said proclamations of the 12th of June, 1869, and of the 20th of November, 1869, the said suspension of discriminating duties upon merchandise imported into the United States in French vessels was granted by the United States on condition that, and to continue so long as, merchandise imported into France in vessels of the United States should be admitted into the ports of France on the same terms of exemption from the payment of such discriminating duties; and

Whereas information has been received by me that by a law of the French Republic passed on the 30th of January, 1872, and published on the 3d of February, 1872, merchandise imported into France in vessels of the United States from countries other than the United States is (with the exception of certain articles enumerated in said law) subjected to discriminating duties; and

Whereas by the operation of said law of the French Republic of the 30th of January, 1872, the exemption of French vessels and their cargoes granted by the terms of the said proclamations of the 12th of June, 1869, and of the 20th of November, 1869, in accordance with the provisions of the acts of Congress aforesaid, has ceased to be reciprocal on the part of France toward vessels owned by citizens of the United States and their cargoes:

Now, therefore, I, Ulysses S. Grant, President of the United States of America, by virtue of the authority vested in me by an act of Congress of the 7th day of January, 1824, and by an act in addition thereto of the 24th day of May, 1828, do hereby declare and proclaim that on and after this date the said suspension of the collection of discriminating duties upon merchandise imported into the United States in French vessels from countries other than France, provided for by my said proclamations of the 12th day of June, 1869, and the 20th day of November, 1869, shall cease and determine, and all the provisions of the acts imposing discriminating foreign tonnage and import duties in the United States are hereby revived, and shall henceforth be and remain in full force as relates to goods and merchandise imported into the United States in French vessels from countries other than France, so long as any discriminating duties shall continue to be imposed by France upon goods and merchandise imported into France in vessels of the United States from countries other than the United States.

* See p. 3973.

In testimony whereof I have hereunto set my hand and caused the seal of the United States to be affixed.

[SEAL.]   Done at the city of Washington, this 30th day of October, A. D. 1872, and of the Independence of the United States the ninety-seventh.

U. S. GRANT.

By the President:

HAMILTON FISH,
Secretary of State.

EXECUTIVE ORDERS

WASHINGTON, *April 16, 1872.*

The Advisory Board of the civil service, having completed the grouping contemplated by the rules already adopted, have recommended certain provisions for carrying the rules into effect.

The recommendations as herewith published are approved, and the provisions will be enforced as rapidly as the proper arrangements can be made; and the thirteenth of the rules adopted on the 19th day of December last is amended to read as published herewith.

The utmost fidelity and diligence will be expected of all officers in every branch of the public service. Political assessments, as they are called, have been forbidden within the various Departments; and while the right of all persons in official position to take part in politics is acknowledged, and the elective franchise is recognized as a high trust to be discharged by all entitled to its exercise, whether in the employment of the Government or in private life, honesty and efficiency, not political activity, will determine the tenure of office.

U. S. GRANT.

By the President:

HAMILTON FISH,
Secretary of State.

[For rules for the civil service promulgated by the President December 19, 1871, see pp. 4111–4113.]

[Rule 13, as amended.]

13. From these rules are excepted the heads of Departments, Assistant Secretaries of Departments, Assistant Attorneys-General, Assistant Postmasters-General, Solicitor-General, Solicitor of the Treasury, Naval Solicitor, Solicitor of Internal Revenue, examiner of claims in the State Department, Treasurer of the United States, Register of the Treasury, First and Second Comptrollers of the Treasury, other heads of bureaus in the several Departments, judges of the United States courts, district attorneys, private secretary of the President, ambassadors and other public ministers, Superintendent of the Coast Survey, Director of the Mint, governors of Territories, special commissioners, special counsel, visiting and examining boards, persons appointed to positions without compensation for services, dispatch agents, and bearers of dispatches.

REGULATIONS AND CLASSIFICATION.

1. No person will be appointed to any position in the civil service who shall not have furnished satisfactory evidence of his fidelity to the Union and the Constitution of the United States.

2. The evidence in regard to character, health, age, and knowledge of the English language required by the first rule shall be furnished in writing, and if such evidence shall be satisfactory to the head of the Department in which the appointment is to be made the applicant shall be notified when and where to appear for examination; but when the applicants are so numerous that the examination of all whose preliminary papers are satisfactory is plainly impracticable, the head of the Department shall select for examination a practicable number of those who are apparently best qualified.

3. Examinations to fill vacancies in any of the Executive Departments in Washington shall be held not only at the city of Washington, but also, when directed by the head of the Department in which the vacancy may exist, in the several States, either at the capital or other convenient place.

4. The appointment of persons to be employed exclusively in the secret service of the Government, also of persons to be employed as translators, stenographers, or private secretaries, or to be designated for secret service, to fill vacancies in clerkships in either of the Executive Departments at Washington, may be excepted from the operation of the rules.

5. When a vacancy occurs in a consular office of which the lawful annual compensation is $3,000 or more, it will be filled, at the discretion of the President, either by the transfer of some person already in the service or by a new appointment, which may be excepted from the operation of the rules. But if the vacancy occur in an office of which the lawful annual compensation, by salary or by fees ascertained by the last official returns, is more than $1,000 and less than $3,000, and it is not filled by transfer, applications will be addressed to the Secretary of State, inclosing proper certificates of character, responsibility, and capacity, and the Secretary will notify the applicant who upon investigation appears to be most suitable and competent to attend for examination; and if he shall be found qualified he will be nominated for confirmation, but if not found qualified, or if his nomination be not confirmed by the Senate, the Secretary will proceed in like manner with the other applicants who appear to him to be qualified. If, however, no applicants under this regulation shall be found suitable and qualified, the vacancy will be filled at discretion. The appointment of commercial agents and of consuls whose annual compensation is $1,000 or less (if derived from fees, the amount to be ascertained by the last official returns), of vice-consuls, deputy consuls, and of consular agents and other officers who are appointed upon the nomination of the principal officer, and for whom he is responsible upon his official bond, may be, until otherwise ordered, excepted from the operation of the rules.

6. When a vacancy occurs in the office of collector of the customs, naval officer, appraiser, or surveyor of the customs in the customs districts of New York, Boston and Charlestown, Baltimore, San Francisco, New Orleans, Philadelphia, Vermont (Burlington), Oswego, Niagara, Buffalo Creek, Champlain, Portland and Falmouth, Corpus Christi, Oswegatchie, Mobile, Brazos de Santiago (Brownsville), Texas (Galveston, etc.), Savannah, Charleston, Chicago, or Detroit, the Secretary of the Treasury shall ascertain if any of the subordinates in the customs districts in which such vacancy occurs are suitable persons qualified to discharge efficiently the duties of the office to be filled; and if such persons be found he shall certify to the President the name or names of those subordinates, not exceeding three, who in his judgment are best qualified for the position, from which the President will make the nomination to fill the vacancy; but if no such subordinate be found qualified, or if the nomination

be not confirmed, the nomination will be made at the discretion of the President. Vacancies occurring in such positions in the customs service in the said districts as are included in the subjoined classification will be filled in accordance with the rules. Appointments to all other positions in the customs service in said districts may be, until otherwise ordered, excepted from the operation of the rules.

7. When a vacancy occurs in the office of collector, appraiser, surveyor, or other chief officer in any customs district not specified in the preceding regulation, applications in writing from any subordinate or subordinates in the customs service of the district, or from other person or persons residing within the said district, may be addressed to the Secretary of the Treasury, inclosing proper certificates of character, responsibility, and capacity; and if any of the subordinates so applying shall be found suitable and qualified, the name or names, not exceeding three, of the best qualified shall be certified by the board of examiners to the Secretary, and from this list the nomination or appointment will be made; but if no such subordinate be found qualified, the said board shall certify to the Secretary the name or names, not exceeding three, of the best qualified among the other applicants, and from this list the nomination or appointment will be made. If, however, no applicants under this regulation shall be found suitable and qualified, the vacancy will be filled at discretion. Appointments to all other positions in the customs service in said districts may be, until otherwise ordered, excepted from the operation of the rules.

8. When a vacancy occurs in the office of postmaster in cities having, according to the census of 1870, a population of 20,000 or more, the Postmaster-General shall ascertain if any of the subordinates in such office are suitable persons qualified to discharge efficiently the duties of postmaster, and if such are found he shall certify to the President the name or names of those subordinates, not exceeding three in number, who in his judgment are best qualified for the position, from which list the President will make the nomination to fill the vacancy; but if no such subordinate be found so qualified, or if the nomination be not confirmed by the Senate, the nomination will be made at the discretion of the President. Vacancies occurring in such positions in the said post-office as are included in the subjoined classification will be filled in accordance with the rules. Appointments to all other positions in the said post-offices may be, until otherwise ordered, excepted from the operation of the rules.

9. When a vacancy occurs in the office of postmaster of a class not otherwise provided for, applications for the position from any subordinate or subordinates in the office, or from other persons residing within the delivery of the office, may be addressed to the Postmaster-General, inclosing proper certificates of character, responsibility, and capacity; and if any of the subordinates so applying shall be found suitable and qualified, the name or names of the best qualified, not exceeding three, shall be certified by the board of examiners to the Postmaster-General, and from them the nomination or appointment shall be made; but if no subordinate be found qualified, the said board shall certify to the Postmaster-General the name or names, not exceeding three, of the best qualified among the other applicants, and from them the nomination or appointment shall be made. If, however, no applicants under this regulation shall be found suitable and qualified, the vacancy will be filled at discretion. Appointments to all other positions in the said post-offices may be, until otherwise ordered, excepted from the operation of the rules.

10. Special agents of the Post-Office Department shall be appointed by the Postmaster-General at discretion from persons already in the postal service, and who shall have served therein for a period of not less than one year immediately preceding the appointment; but if no person within the service shall, in the judgment of the Postmaster-General, be suitable and qualified, the appointment shall be made from all applicants under the rules.

11. Mail-route messengers shall be appointed in the manner provided for the appointment of postmasters whose annual salary is less than $200.

12. When a vacancy occurs in the office of register or receiver of the land office, or of pension agent, applications in writing from residents in the district in which the

vacancy occurs may be addressed to the Secretary of the Interior, inclosing proper certificates of character, responsibility, and capacity; and if any of the applicants shall be found suitable and qualified, the name or names, not exceeding three, of the best qualified shall be certified by the board of examiners to the Secretary, and from this list the nomination will be made. If, however, no applicants under this regulation shall be found suitable and qualified, the nomination will be made at discretion.

13. When a vacancy occurs in the office of United States marshal, applications in writing from residents in the district in which the vacancy occurs may be addressed to the Attorney-General of the United States, inclosing proper certificates of character, responsibility, and capacity; and if any of the applicants shall be found suitable and qualified, the name or names, not exceeding three, of the best qualified shall be certified by the board of examiners to the Attorney-General, and from this list the nomination will be made. If, however, no applicants under this regulation shall be found suitable and qualified, the nomination will be made at discretion.

14. Appointments to fill vacancies occurring in offices in the several Territories, excepting those of judges of the United States courts, Indian agents, and superintendents, will be made from suitable and qualified persons domiciled in the Territory in which the vacancy occurs, if any such are found.

15. It shall be the duty of the examining board in each of the Departments to report to the Advisory Board such modifications in the rules and regulations as in the judgment of such examining board are required for appointments to certain positions to which, by reason of distance, or of difficult access, or of other sufficient cause, the rules and regulations can not be applied with advantage; and if the reason for such modifications shall be satisfactory to the Advisory Board, said board will recommend them for approval.

16. Nothing in these rules and regulations shall prevent the reappointment at discretion of the incumbents of any office the term of which is fixed by law, and when such reappointment is made no vacancy within the meaning of the rules shall be deemed to have occurred.

17. Appointments to all positions in the civil service not included in the subjoined classification, nor otherwise specially provided for by the rules and regulations, may, until otherwise ordered, be excepted from the operation of the rules.

EXECUTIVE MANSION,
Washington, D. C., May 27, 1872.

SIR:* The President directs me to say that the several Departments of the Government will be closed on the 30th instant, in order to enable the employees of the Government to participate, in connection with the Grand Army of the Republic, in the decoration of the graves of the soldiers who fell during the rebellion.

I am, sir, your obedient servant,

HORACE PORTER, *Secretary.*

DEPARTMENT OF STATE,
Washington, October 11, 1872.

The undersigned is charged by the President with the painful duty of announcing to the people of the United States the death of an illustrious citizen.

William Henry Seward, distinguished for faithful and eminent service in varied public trusts during a long series of years, died at Auburn, in the

* Addressed to the heads of the Executive Departments, etc.

State of New York, yesterday, October 10. Charged with the administration of the Department of State at a most critical period in the history
of the nation, Mr. Seward brought to the duties of that office exalted
patriotism, unwearied industry, and consummate ability. A grateful
nation will cherish his name, his fame, and his memory.

The several Executive Departments will cause appropriate honors to
be rendered to the memory of the deceased statesman at home and abroad.

HAMILTON FISH,

Secretary of State.

FOURTH ANNUAL MESSAGE.

EXECUTIVE MANSION, *December 2, 1872.*

To the Senate and House of Representatives:

In transmitting to you this my fourth annual message it is with thankfulness to the Giver of All Good that as a nation we have been blessed
for the past year with peace at home, peace abroad, and a general prosperity vouchsafed to but few peoples.

With the exception of the recent devastating fire which swept from the
earth with a breath, as it were, millions of accumulated wealth in the city
of Boston, there has been no overshadowing calamity within the year to
record. It is gratifying to note how, like their fellow-citizens of the
city of Chicago under similar circumstances a year earlier, the citizens of
Boston are rallying under their misfortunes, and the prospect that their
energy and perseverance will overcome all obstacles and show the same
prosperity soon that they would had no disaster befallen them. Otherwise we have been free from pestilence, war, and calamities, which often
overtake nations; and, as far as human judgment can penetrate the
future, no cause seems to exist to threaten our present peace.

When Congress adjourned in June last, a question had been raised by
Great Britain, and was then pending, which for a time seriously imperiled
the settlement by friendly arbitration of the grave differences between
this Government and that of Her Britannic Majesty, which by the treaty
of Washington had been referred to the tribunal of arbitration which
had met at Geneva, in Switzerland.

The arbitrators, however, disposed of the question which had jeop-
arded the whole of the treaty and threatened to involve the two nations
in most unhappy relations toward each other in a manner entirely satisfactory to this Government and in accordance with the views and the
policy which it had maintained.

The tribunal, which had convened at Geneva in December, concluded
its laborious session on the 14th day of September last, on which day,

having availed itself of the discretionary power given to it by the treaty to award a sum in gross, it made its decision, whereby it awarded the sum of $15,500,000 in gold as the indemnity to be paid by Great Britain to the United States for the satisfaction of all the claims referred to its consideration.

This decision happily disposes of a long-standing difference between the two Governments, and, in connection with another award, made by the German Emperor under a reference to him by the same treaty, leaves these two Governments without a shadow upon the friendly relations which it is my sincere hope may forever remain equally unclouded.

The report of the agent of the United States appointed to attend the Geneva tribunal, accompanied by the protocols of the proceedings of the arbitrators, the arguments of the counsel of both Governments, the award of the tribunal, and the opinions given by the several arbitrators, is transmitted herewith.

I have caused to be communicated to the heads of the three friendly powers who complied with the joint request made to them under the treaty the thanks of this Government for the appointment of arbitrators made by them respectively, and also my thanks to the eminent personages named by them, and my appreciation of the dignity, patience, impartiality, and great ability with which they discharged their arduous and high functions.

Her Majesty's Government has communicated to me the appreciation by Her Majesty of the ability and indefatigable industry displayed by Mr. Adams, the arbitrator named on the part of this Government during the protracted inquiries and discussions of the tribunal. I cordially unite with Her Majesty in this appreciation.

It is due to the agent of the United States before the tribunal to record my high appreciation of the marked ability, unwearied patience, and the prudence and discretion with which he has conducted the very responsible and delicate duties committed to him, as it is also due to the learned and eminent counsel who attended the tribunal on the part of this Government to express my sense of the talents and wisdom which they brought to bear in the attainment of the result so happily reached.

It will be the province of Congress to provide for the distribution among those who may be entitled to it of their respective shares of the money to be paid. Although the sum awarded is not payable until a year from the date of the award, it is deemed advisable that no time be lost in making a proper examination of the several cases in which indemnification may be due. I consequently recommend the creation of a board of commissioners for the purpose.

By the thirty-fourth article of the treaty of Washington the respective claims of the United States and of Great Britain in their construction of the treaty of the 15th of June, 1846, defining the boundary line between their respective territories, were submitted to the arbitration and award of His Majesty the Emperor of Germany, to decide which of those claims is most in accordance with the true interpretation of the treaty of 1846.

His Majesty the Emperor of Germany, having been pleased to undertake the arbitration, has the earnest thanks of this Government and of the people of the United States for the labor, pains, and care which he has devoted to the consideration of this long-pending difference. I have caused an expression of my thanks to be communicated to His Majesty. Mr. Bancroft, the representative of this Government at Berlin, conducted the case and prepared the statement on the part of the United States with the ability that his past services justified the public in expecting at his hands. As a member of the Cabinet at the date of the treaty which has given rise to the discussion between the two Governments, as the minister to Great Britain when the construction now pronounced unfounded was first advanced, and as the agent and representative of the Government to present the case and to receive the award, he has been associated with the question in all of its phases, and in every stage has manifested a patriotic zeal and earnestness in maintenance of the claim of the United States. He is entitled to much credit for the success which has attended the submission.

After a patient investigation of the case and of the statements of each party, His Majesty the Emperor, on the 21st day of October last, signed his award in writing, decreeing that the claim of the Government of the United States, that the boundary line between the territories of Her Britannic Majesty and the United States should be drawn through the Haro Channel, is most in accordance with the true interpretation of the treaty concluded on the 15th of June, 1846, between the Governments of Her Britannic Majesty and of the United States.

Copies of the "case" presented on behalf of each Government, and of the "statement in reply" of each, and a translation of the award, are transmitted herewith.

This award confirms the United States in their claim to the important archipelago of islands lying between the continent and Vancouvers Island, which for more than twenty-six years (ever since the ratification of the treaty) Great Britain has contested, and leaves us, for the first time in the history of the United States as a nation, without a question of disputed boundary between our territory and the possessions of Great Britain on this continent.

It is my grateful duty to acknowledge the prompt, spontaneous action of Her Majesty's Government in giving effect to the award. In anticipation of any request from this Government, and before the reception in the United States of the award signed by the Emperor, Her Majesty had given instructions for the removal of her troops which had been stationed there and for the cessation of all exercise or claim of jurisdiction, so as to leave the United States in the exclusive possession of the lately disputed territory. I am gratified to be able to announce that the orders for the removal of the troops have been executed, and that the military joint occupation of San Juan has ceased. The islands are now in the exclusive possession of the United States.

It now becomes necessary to complete the survey and determination of that portion of the boundary line (through the Haro Channel) upon which the commission which determined the remaining part of the line were unable to agree. I recommend the appointment of a commission to act jointly with one which may be named by Her Majesty for that purpose.

Experience of the difficulties attending the determination of our admitted line of boundary, after the occupation of the territory and its settlement by those owing allegiance to the respective Governments, points to the importance of establishing, by natural objects or other monuments, the actual line between the territory acquired by purchase from Russia and the adjoining possessions of Her Britannic Majesty. The region is now so sparsely occupied that no conflicting interests of individuals or of jurisdiction are likely to interfere to the delay or embarrassment of the actual location of the line. If deferred until population shall enter and occupy the territory, some trivial contest of neighbors may again array the two Governments in antagonism. I therefore recommend the appointment of a commission, to act jointly with one that may be appointed on the part of Great Britain, to determine the line between our Territory of Alaska and the conterminous possessions of Great Britain.

In my last annual message I recommended the legislation necessary on the part of the United States to bring into operation the articles of the treaty of Washington of May 8, 1871, relating to the fisheries and to other matters touching the relations of the United States toward the British North American possessions, to become operative so soon as the proper legislation should be had on the part of Great Britain and its possessions.

That legislation on the part of Great Britain and its possessions had not then been had, and during the session of Congress a question was raised which for the time raised a doubt whether any action by Congress in the direction indicated would become important. This question has since been disposed of, and I have received notice that the Imperial Parliament and the legislatures of the provincial governments have passed laws to carry the provisions of the treaty on the matters referred to into operation. I therefore recommend your early adoption of the legislation in the same direction necessary on the part of this Government.

The joint commission for determining the boundary line between the United States and the British possessions between the Lake of the Woods and the Rocky Mountains has organized and entered upon its work. It is desirable that the force be increased, in order that the completion of the survey and determination of the line may be the sooner attained. To this end I recommend that a sufficient appropriation be made.

With France, our earliest ally; Russia, the constant and steady friend of the United States; Germany, with whose Government and people we have so many causes of friendship and so many common sympathies, and the other powers of Europe, our relations are maintained on the most friendly terms.

Since my last annual message the exchange has been made of the ratifications of a treaty with the Austro-Hungarian Empire relating to naturalization; also of a treaty with the German Empire respecting consuls and trade-marks; also of a treaty with Sweden and Norway relating to naturalization; all of which treaties have been duly proclaimed.

Congress at its last session having made an appropriation to defray the expense of commissioners on the part of the United States to the International Statistical Congress at St. Petersburg, the persons appointed in that character proceeded to their destination and attended the sessions of the congress. Their report shall in due season be laid before you. This congress meets at intervals of about three years, and has held its sessions in several of the countries of Europe. I submit to your consideration the propriety of extending an invitation to the congress to hold its next meeting in the United States. The Centennial Celebration to be held in 1876 would afford an appropriate occasion for such meeting.

Preparations are making for the international exposition to be held during the next year in Vienna, on a scale of very great magnitude. The tendency of these expositions is in the direction of advanced civilization, and of the elevation of industry and of labor, and of the increase of human happiness, as well as of greater intercourse and good will between nations. As this exposition is to be the first which will have been held in eastern Europe, it is believed that American inventors and manufacturers will be ready to avail themselves of the opportunity for the presentation of their productions if encouraged by proper aid and protection.

At the last session of Congress authority was given for the appointment of one or more agents to represent this Government at the exposition. The authority thus given has been exercised, but, in the absence of any appropriation, there is danger that the important benefits which the occasion offers will in a large degree be lost to citizens of the United States. I commend the subject strongly to your consideration, and recommend that an adequate appropriation be made for the purpose.

To further aid American exhibitors at the Vienna Exposition, I would recommend, in addition to an appropriation of money, that the Secretary of the Navy be authorized to fit up two naval vessels to transport between our Atlantic cities and Trieste, or the most convenient port to Vienna, and back, their articles for exhibition.

Since your last session the President of the Mexican Republic, distinguished by his high character and by his services to his country, has died. His temporary successor has now been elected with great unanimity by the people—a proof of confidence on their part in his patriotism and wisdom which it is believed will be confirmed by the results of his administration. It is particularly desirable that nothing should be left undone by the Government of either Republic to strengthen their relations as neighbors and friends.

It is much to be regretted that many lawless acts continue to disturb the quiet of the settlements on the border between our territory and that of Mexico, and that complaints of wrongs to American citizens in various parts of the country are made. The revolutionary condition in which the neighboring Republic has so long been involved has in some degree contributed to this disturbance. It is to be hoped that with a more settled rule of order through the Republic, which may be expected from the present Government, the acts of which just complaint is made will cease.

The proceedings of the commission under the convention with Mexico of the 4th of July, 1868, on the subject of claims, have, unfortunately, been checked by an obstacle, for the removal of which measures have been taken by the two Governments which it is believed will prove successful.

The commissioners appointed, pursuant to the joint resolution of Congress of the 7th of May last, to inquire into depredations on the Texan frontier have diligently made investigations in that quarter. Their report upon the subject will be communicated to you. Their researches were necessarily incomplete, partly on account of the limited appropriation made by Congress. Mexico, on the part of that Government, has appointed a similar commission to investigate these outrages. It is not announced officially, but the press of that country states that the fullest investigation is desired, and that the cooperation of all parties concerned is invited to secure that end. I therefore recommend that a special appropriation be made at the earliest day practicable, to enable the commissioners on the part of the United States to return to their labors without delay.

It is with regret that I have again to announce a continuance of the disturbed condition of the island of Cuba. No advance toward the pacification of the discontented part of the population has been made. While the insurrection has gained no advantages and exhibits no more of the elements of power or of the prospects of ultimate success than were exhibited a year ago, Spain, on the other hand, has not succeeded in its repression, and the parties stand apparently in the same relative attitude which they have occupied for a long time past.

This contest has lasted now for more than four years. Were its scene at a distance from our neighborhood, we might be indifferent to its result, although humanity could not be unmoved by many of its incidents wherever they might occur. It is, however, at our door.

I can not doubt that the continued maintenance of slavery in Cuba is among the strongest inducements to the continuance of this strife. A terrible wrong is the natural cause of a terrible evil. The abolition of slavery and the introduction of other reforms in the administration of government in Cuba could not fail to advance the restoration of peace and order. It is greatly to be hoped that the present liberal Government of Spain will voluntarily adopt this view.

The law of emancipation, which was passed more than two years since, has remained unexecuted in the absence of regulations for its enforcement. It was but a feeble step toward emancipation, but it was the recognition of right, and was hailed as such, and exhibited Spain in harmony with sentiments of humanity and of justice and in sympathy with the other powers of the Christian and civilized world.

Within the past few weeks the regulations for carrying out the law of emancipation have been announced, giving evidence of the sincerity of intention of the present Government to carry into effect the law of 1870. I have not failed to urge the consideration of the wisdom, the policy, and the justice of a more effective system for the abolition of the great evil which oppresses a race and continues a bloody and destructive contest close to our border, as well as the expediency and the justice of conceding reforms of which the propriety is not questioned.

Deeply impressed with the conviction that the continuance of slavery is one of the most active causes of the continuance of the unhappy condition in Cuba, I regret to believe that citizens of the United States, or those claiming to be such, are large holders in Cuba of what is there claimed as property, but which is forbidden and denounced by the laws of the United States. They are thus, in defiance of the spirit of our own laws, contributing to the continuance of this distressing and sickening contest. In my last annual message I referred to this subject, and I again recommend such legislation as may be proper to denounce, and, if not prevent, at least to discourage American citizens from holding or dealing in slaves.

It is gratifying to announce that the ratifications of the convention concluded under the auspices of this Government between Spain on the one part and the allied Republics of the Pacific on the other, providing for an armistice, have been exchanged. A copy of the instrument is herewith submitted. It is hoped that this may be followed by a permanent peace between the same parties.

The differences which at one time threatened the maintenance of peace between Brazil and the Argentine Republic it is hoped are in the way of satisfactory adjustment.

With these States, as with the Republics of Central and of South America, we continue to maintain the most friendly relations.

It is with regret, however, I announce that the Government of Venezuela has made no further payments on account of the awards under the convention of the 25th of April, 1866. That Republic is understood to be now almost, if not quite, tranquilized. It is hoped, therefore, that it will lose no time in providing for the unpaid balance of its debt to the

United States, which, having originated in injuries to our citizens by Venezuelan authorities, and having been acknowledged, pursuant to a treaty, in the most solemn form known among nations, would seem to deserve a preference over debts of a different origin and contracted in a different manner. This subject is again recommended to the attention of Congress for such action as may be deemed proper.

Our treaty relations with Japan remain unchanged. An imposing embassy from that interesting and progressive nation visited this country during the year that is passing, but, being unprovided with powers for the signing of a convention in this country, no conclusion in that direction was reached. It is hoped, however, that the interchange of opinions which took place during their stay in this country has led to a mutual appreciation of the interests which may be promoted when the revision of the existing treaty shall be undertaken.

In this connection I renew my recommendation of one year ago, that—

To give importance to and to add to the efficiency of our diplomatic relations with Japan and China, and to further aid in retaining the good opinion of those peoples, and to secure to the United States its share of the commerce destined to flow between those nations and the balance of the commercial world, an appropriation be made to support at least four American youths in each of those countries, to serve as a part of the official family of our ministers there. Our representatives would not even then be placed upon an equality with the representatives of Great Britain and of some other powers. As now situated, our representatives in Japan and China have to depend for interpreters and translators upon natives of those countries, who know our language imperfectly, or procure for the occasion the services of employees in foreign business houses or the interpreters to other foreign ministers.

I renew the recommendation made on a previous occasion, of the transfer to the Department of the Interior, to which they seem more appropriately to belong, of all the powers and duties in relation to the Territories with which the Department of State is now charged by law or by custom.

Congress from the beginning of the Government has wisely made provision for the relief of distressed seamen in foreign countries. No similar provision, however, has hitherto been made for the relief of citizens in distress abroad other than seamen. It is understood to be customary with other governments to authorize consuls to extend such relief to their citizens or subjects in certain cases. A similar authority and an appropriation to carry it into effect are recommended in the case of citizens of the United States destitute or sick under such circumstances. It is well known that such citizens resort to foreign countries in great numbers. Though most of them are able to bear the expenses incident to locomotion, there are some who, through accident or otherwise, become penniless, and have no friends at home able to succor them. Persons in this situation must either perish, cast themselves upon the charity of foreigners, or be relieved at the private charge of our own officers, who usually, even with the most benevolent dispositions, have nothing to spare for such purposes.

Should the authority and appropriation asked for be granted, care will be taken so to carry the beneficence of Congress into effect that it shall not be unnecessarily or unworthily bestowed.

TREASURY.

The moneys received and covered into the Treasury during the fiscal year ended June 30, 1872, were:

From customs	$216,370,286.77
From sales of public lands	2,575,714.19
From internal revenue	130,642,177.72
From tax on national-bank circulation, etc.	6,523,396.39
From Pacific railway companies	749,861.87
From customs fines, etc.	1,136,442.34
From fees—consular, patent, land, etc.	2,284,095.92
From miscellaneous sources	4,412,254.71
Total ordinary receipts	364,694,229.91
From premium on sales of coin	9,412,637.65
Total net receipts	374,106,867.56
Balance in Treasury June 30, 1871 (including $18,228.35 received from "unavailable")	109,935,705.59
Total available cash	484,042,573.15

The net expenditures by warrants during the same period were:

For civil expenses	$16,187,059.20
For foreign intercourse	1,839,369.14
For Indians	7,061,728.82
For pensions	28,533,402.76
For military establishment, including fortifications, river and harbor improvements, and arsenals	35,372,157.20
For naval establishment, including vessels and machinery and improvements at navy-yards	21,249,809.99
For miscellaneous civil, including public buildings, light-houses, and collecting the revenue	42,958,329.08
For interest on the public debt	117,357,839.72
Total, exclusive of principal and premium on the public debt	270,559,695.91
For premium on bonds purchased $6,958,266.76	
For redemption of the public debt 99,960,253.54	
	106,918,520.30
Total net disbursements	377,478,216.21
Balance in Treasury June 30, 1872	106,564,356.94
Total	484,042,573.15

From the foregoing statement it appears that the net reduction of the principal of the debt during the fiscal year ending June 30, 1872, was $99,960,253.54.

The source of this reduction is as follows:

Net ordinary receipts during the year	$364,694,229.91
Net ordinary expenditures, including interest on the public debt	270,559,695.91
Leaving surplus revenue	94,134,534.00
Add amount received from premium on sales of gold, in excess of the premium paid on bonds purchased	2,454,370.89
Add the amount of the reduction of the cash balance at the close of the year, accompanied with same at commencement of the year	3,371,348.65
Total	99,960,253.54

This statement treats solely of the principal of the public debt.

By the monthly statement of the public debt, which adds together the principal, interest due and unpaid, and interest accrued to date, not due, and deducts the cash in the Treasury as ascertained on the day of publication, the reduction was $100,544,491.28.

The source of this reduction is as follows:

Reduction in principal account	$99,960,003.54
Reduction in unpaid-interest account	3,330,952.96
	103,290,956.50
Reduction in cash on hand	2,746,465.22
	100,544,491.28

On the basis of the last table the statements show a reduction of the public debt from the 1st of March, 1869, to the present time as follows:

From March 1, 1869, to March 1, 1870	$87,134,782.84
From March 1, 1870, to March 1, 1871	117,619,630.25
From March 1, 1871, to March 1, 1872	94,895,348.94
From March 1, 1872, to November 1, 1872 (eight months)	64,047,237.84
Total	363,696,999.87

With the great reduction of taxation by the acts of Congress at its last session, the expenditure of the Government in collecting the revenue will be much reduced for the next fiscal year. It is very doubtful, however, whether any further reduction of so vexatious a burden upon any people will be practicable for the present. At all events, as a measure of justice to the holders of the nation's certificates of indebtedness, I would recommend that no more legislation be had on this subject, unless it be to correct errors of omission or commission in the present laws, until sufficient time has elapsed to prove that it can be done and still leave sufficient revenue to meet current expenses of Government, pay interest on the public debt, and provide for the sinking fund established by law. The preservation of our national credit is of the highest importance; next in importance to this comes a solemn duty to provide a national currency of fixed, unvarying value as compared with gold, and as soon as practicable, having due regard for the interests of the debtor class and the vicissitudes of trade and commerce, convertible into gold at par.

WAR DEPARTMENT.

The report of the Secretary of War shows the expenditures of the War Department for the fiscal year ending June 30, 1871, to be $35,799,991.82, and for the fiscal year ending June 30, 1872, to be $35,372,157.20, showing a reduction in favor of the last fiscal year of $427,834.62.

The estimates for military appropriations for the next fiscal year, ending June 30, 1874, are $33,801,378.78.

The estimates of the Chief of Engineers are submitted separately for fortifications, river and harbor improvements, and for public buildings and grounds and the Washington Aqueduct.

The affairs of the Freedmen's Bureau have all been transferred to the War Department, and regulations have been put into execution for the speedy payment of bounty, pay, etc., due colored soldiers, properly coming under that Bureau. All war accounts, for money and property, prior to 1871 have been examined and transmitted to the Treasury for final settlement.

During the fiscal year there has been paid for transportation on railroads $1,300,000, of which $800,857 was over the Pacific railroads; for transportation by water $626,373.52, and by stage $48,975.84; for the purchase of transportation animals, wagons, hire of teamsters, etc., $924,650.64.

About $370,000 have been collected from Southern railroads during the year, leaving about $4,000,000 still due.

The Quartermaster has examined and transmitted to the accounting officers for settlement $367,172.72 of claims by loyal citizens for quartermaster stores taken during the war.

Subsistence supplies to the amount of $89,048.12 have been issued to Indians.

The annual average mean strength of the Army was 24,101 white and 2,494 colored soldiers. The total deaths for the year reported were 367 white and 54 colored.

The distribution of the Medical and Surgical History of the War is yet to be ordered by Congress.

There exists an absolute necessity for a medical corps of the full number established by act of Congress of July 28, 1866, there being now fifty-nine vacancies, and the number of successful candidates rarely exceeds eight or ten in any one year.

The river and harbor improvements have been carried on with energy and economy. Though many are only partially completed, the results have saved to commerce many times the amount expended. The increase of commerce, with greater depths of channels, greater security in navigation, and the saving of time, adds millions to the wealth of the country and increases the resources of the Government.

The bridge across the Mississippi River at Rock Island has been completed, and the proper site has been determined upon for the bridge at La Crosse.

The able and exhaustive report made by the commission appointed to investigate the Sutro Tunnel has been transmitted to Congress.

The observations and reports of the Signal Office have been continued. Stations have been maintained at each of the principal lake, seaport, and river cities. Ten additional stations have been established in the United States, and arrangements have been made for an exchange of reports with Canada, and a similar exchange of observations is contemplated with the West India Islands.

The favorable attention of Congress is invited to the following recommendations of the Secretary of War:

A discontinuance of the appointment of extra lieutenants to serve as adjutants and quartermasters; the adoption of a code providing specific penalties for well-defined offenses, so that the inequality of sentences adjudged by courts-martial may be adjusted; the consolidation of accounts under which expenditures are made, as a measure of economy; a reappropriation of the money for the construction of a depot at San Antonio, the title to the site being now perfected; a special act placing the cemetery at the City of Mexico on the same basis as other national cemeteries; authority to purchase sites for military posts in Texas; the appointment of commissary sergeants from noncommissioned officers, as a measure for securing the better care and protection of supplies; an appropriation for the publication of the catalogue and tables of the anatomical section of the Army Medical Museum; a reappropriation of the amount for the manufacture of breech-loading arms, should the selection be so delayed by the board of officers as to leave the former appropriation unexpended at the close of the fiscal year; the sale of such arsenals east of the Mississippi as can be spared, and the proceeds applied to the establishment of one large arsenal of construction and repair upon the Atlantic Coast and the purchase of a suitable site for a proving and experimental ground for heavy ordnance; the abrogation of laws which deprive inventors in the United States service from deriving any benefit from their inventions; the repeal of the law prohibiting promotions in the staff corps; a continuance of the work upon coast defenses; the repeal of the seventh section of the act of July 13, 1866, taking from engineer soldiers the per diem granted to other troops; a limitation of time for presentation of old war claims for subsistence supplies under act of July 4, 1864; and a modification in the mode of the selection of cadets for the Military Academy, in order to enhance the usefulness of the Academy, which is impaired by reason of the large amount of time necessarily expended in giving new cadets a thorough knowledge of the more elementary branches of learning, which they should acquire before entering the Academy. Also an appropriation for philosophical apparatus and an increase in the numbers and pay of the Military Academy band.

The attention of Congress will be called during its present session to various enterprises for the more certain and cheaper transportation of the constantly increasing surplus of Western and Southern products to the Atlantic Seaboard. The subject is one that will force itself upon the legislative branch of the Government sooner or later, and I suggest, therefore, that immediate steps be taken to gain all available information to insure equable and just legislation.

One route to connect the Mississippi Valley with the Atlantic, at Charleston, S. C., and Savannah, Ga., by water, by the way of the Ohio and Tennessee rivers, and canals and slack-water navigation to the Savannah and Ocmulgee rivers, has been surveyed, and report made by an accomplished engineer officer of the Army. Second and third new routes will be proposed for the consideration of Congress, namely, by an extension of the Kanawha and James River Canal to the Ohio, and by extension of the Chesapeake and Ohio Canal.

I am not prepared to recommend Government aid to these or other enterprises until it is clearly shown that they are not only of national interest, but that when completed they will be of a value commensurate with their cost.

That production increases more rapidly than the means of transportation in our country has been demonstrated by past experience. That the unprecedented growth in population and products of the whole country will require additional facilities—and cheaper ones for the more bulky articles of commerce to reach tide water and a market will be demanded in the near future—is equally demonstrable. I would therefore suggest either a committee or a commission to be authorized to consider this whole question, and to report to Congress at some future day for its better guidance in legislating on this important subject.

The railroads of the country have been rapidly extended during the last few years to meet the growing demands of producers, and reflect much credit upon the capitalists and managers engaged in their construction.

In addition to these, a project to facilitate commerce by the building of a ship canal around Niagara Falls, on the United States side, which has been agitated for many years, will no doubt be called to your attention at this session.

Looking to the great future growth of the country and the increasing demands of commerce, it might be well while on this subject not only to have examined and reported upon the various practicable routes for connecting the Mississippi with tide water on the Atlantic, but the feasibility of an almost continuous landlocked navigation from Maine to the Gulf of Mexico. Such a route along our coast would be of great value at all times, and of inestimable value in case of a foreign war. Nature has provided the greater part of this route, and the obstacles to overcome are easily within the skill of the engineer.

I have not alluded to this subject with the view of having any further expenditure of public money at this time than may be necessary to procure and place all the necessary information before Congress in an authentic form, to enable it hereafter, if deemed practicable and worthy, to legislate on the subject without delay.

NAVY DEPARTMENT.

The report of the Secretary of the Navy herewith accompanying explains fully the condition of that branch of the public service, its wants and deficiencies, expenses incurred during the past year, and appropriations for the same. It also gives a complete history of the services of the Navy for the past year in addition to its regular service.

It is evident that unless early steps are taken to preserve our Navy

THE GREAT CHICAGO FIRE

This conflagration occurred October 9 and 10, 1871. By it the city was almost entirely destroyed. More than two hundred million dollars' worth of property was destroyed, and one hundred thousand people were made homeless.

The effect of this event on the country was depressing, and the ablest, calmest and most conservative men of the Nation predicted it would usher in hard times. The optimistic and courageous spirit of the people of Chicago in immediately planning and commencing to build their city contributed more to dispel the gloom than any other factor. No more striking example of the real unity of these United States could be given than the promptness with which all sections join in relieving the distressed after a calamity like the Chicago, Boston and San Francisco fires.

in a very few years the United States will be the weakest nation upon the ocean, of all great powers. With an energetic, progressive, business people like ours, penetrating and forming business relations with every part of the known world, a navy strong enough to command the respect of our flag abroad is necessary for the full protection of their rights.

I recommend careful consideration by Congress of the recommendations made by the Secretary of the Navy.

POST-OFFICE DEPARTMENT.

The accompanying report of the Postmaster-General furnishes a full and satisfactory exhibit of the operations of the Post-Office Department during the year. The ordinary revenues of the Department for the fiscal year ending June 30, 1872, amounted to $21,915,426.37, and the expenditures to $26,658,192.31. Compared with the previous fiscal year the increase of revenue was $1,878,330.95, or 9.37 per cent, and the increase of expenditures $2,268,088.23, or 9.29 per cent. Adding to the ordinary revenues the annual appropriation of $700,000 for free matter and the amounts paid to the subsidized mail steamship lines from special appropriations, the deficiency paid out of the General Treasury was $3,317,-765.94, an excess of $389,707.28 over the deficiency for the year 1871.

Other interesting statistical information relating to our rapidly extending postal service is furnished in this report. The total length of railroad mail routes on the 30th of June, 1872, was 57,911 miles, 8,077 additional miles of such service having been put into operation during the year. Eight new lines of railway post-offices have been established, with an aggregate length of 2,909 miles. The number of letters exchanged in the mails with foreign countries was 24,362,500, an increase of 4,066,502, or 20 per cent, over the number in 1871; and the postage thereon amounted to $1,871,257.25. The total weight of the mails exchanged with European countries exceeded 820 tons. The cost of the United States transatlantic mail steamship service was $220,301.70. The total cost of the United States ocean steamship service, including the amounts paid to the subsidized lines of mail steamers, was $1,027,020.97.

The following are the only steamship lines now receiving subsidies for mail service under special acts of Congress: The Pacific Mail Steamship Company receive $500,000 per annum for conveying a monthly mail between San Francisco, Japan, and China, which will be increased to $1,000,000 per annum for a semimonthly mail on and after October 1, 1873; the United States and Brazil Mail Steamship Company receive $150,000 per annum for conveying a monthly mail between New York and Rio de Janeiro, Brazil; and the California, Oregon and Mexican Steamship Company receive $75,000 per annum for conveying a monthly mail between San Francisco and Honolulu (Hawaiian Islands), making the total amount of mail steamship subsidies at present $725,000 per annum.

Our postal communications with all parts of the civilized world have been placed upon a most advantageous footing by the improved postal conventions and arrangements recently concluded with the leading commercial countries of Europe and America, and the gratifying statement is made that with the conclusion of a satisfactory convention with France, the details of which have been definitely agreed to by the head of the French postal department, subject to the approval of the minister of finance, little remains to be accomplished by treaty for some time to come with respect either to reduction of rates or improved facilities of postal intercourse.

Your favorable consideration is respectfully invited to the recommendations made by the Postmaster-General for an increase of service from monthly to semimonthly trips on the mail steamship route to Brazil; for a subsidy in aid of the establishment of an American line of mail steamers between San Francisco, New Zealand, and Australia; for the establishment of post-office savings banks, and for the increase of the salaries of the heads of bureaus. I have heretofore recommended the abolition of the franking privilege, and see no reason now for changing my views on that subject. It not having been favorably regarded by Congress, however, I now suggest a modification of that privilege to correct its glaring and costly abuses. I would recommend also the appointment of a committee or commission to take into consideration the best method (equitable to private corporations who have invested their time and capital in the establishment of telegraph lines) of acquiring the title to all telegraph lines now in operation, and of connecting this service with the postal service of the nation. It is not probable that this subject could receive the proper consideration during the limits of a short session of Congress, but it may be initiated, so that future action may be fair to the Government and to private parties concerned.

There are but three lines of ocean steamers—namely, the Pacific Mail Steamship Company, between San Francisco, China, and Japan, with provision made for semimonthly service after October 1, 1873; the United States and Brazil line, monthly; and the California, New Zealand, and Australian line, monthly—plying between the United States and foreign ports, and owned and operated under our flag. I earnestly recommend that such liberal contracts for carrying the mails be authorized with these lines as will insure their continuance.

If the expediency of extending the aid of Government to lines of steamers which hitherto have not received it should be deemed worthy of the consideration of Congress, political and commercial objects make it advisable to bestow such aid on a line under our flag between Panama and the western South American ports. By this means much trade now diverted to other countries might be brought to us, to the mutual advantage of this country and those lying in that quarter of the continent of America.

The report of the Secretary of the Treasury will show an alarming falling off in our carrying trade for the last ten or twelve years, and even for the past year. I do not believe that public treasure can be better expended in the interest of the whole people than in trying to recover this trade. An expenditure of $5,000,000 per annum for the next five years, if it would restore to us our proportion of the carrying trade of the world, would be profitably expended.

The price of labor in Europe has so much enhanced within the last few years that the cost of building and operating ocean steamers in the United States is not so much greater than in Europe; and I believe the time has arrived for Congress to take this subject into serious consideration.

DEPARTMENT OF JUSTICE.

Detailed statements of the disbursements through the Department of Justice will be furnished by the report of the Attorney-General, and though these have been somewhat increased by the recent acts of Congress "to enforce the rights of citizens of the United States to vote in the several States of the Union," and "to enforce the provisions of the fourteenth amendment to the Constitution of the United States," and the amendments thereto, I can not question the necessity and salutary effect of those enactments. Reckless and lawless men, I regret to say, have associated themselves together in some localities to deprive other citizens of those rights guaranteed to them by the Constitution of the United States, and to that end have committed deeds of blood and violence; but the prosecution and punishment of many of these persons have tended greatly to the repression of such disorders. I do not doubt that a great majority of the people in all parts of the country favor the full enjoyment by all classes of persons of those rights to which they are entitled under the Constitution and laws, and I invoke the aid and influence of all good citizens to prevent organizations whose objects are by unlawful means to interfere with those rights. I look with confidence to the time, not far distant, when the obvious advantages of good order and peace will induce an abandonment of all combinations prohibited by the acts referred to, and when it will be unnecessary to carry on prosecutions or inflict punishment to protect citizens from the lawless doings of such combinations.

Applications have been made to me to pardon persons convicted of a violation of said acts, upon the ground that clemency in such cases would tend to tranquilize the public mind, and to test the virtue of that policy I am disposed, as far as my sense of justice will permit, to give to these applications a favorable consideration; but any action thereon is not to be construed as indicating any change in my determination to enforce with vigor such acts so long as the conspiracies and combinations therein named disturb the peace of the country.

It is much to be regretted, and is regretted by no one more than myself, that a necessity has ever existed to execute the "enforcement act.'' No one can desire more than I that the necessity of applying it may never again be demanded.

INTERIOR DEPARTMENT.

The Secretary of the Interior reports satisfactory improvement and progress in each of the several bureaus under the control of the Interior Department. They are all in excellent condition. The work which in some of them for some years has been in arrears has been brought down to a recent date, and in all the current business is being promptly dispatched.

INDIANS.

The policy which was adopted at the beginning of this Administration with regard to the management of the Indians has been as successful as its most ardent friends anticipated within so short a time. It has reduced the expense of their management; decreased their forays upon the white settlements; tended to give the largest opportunity for the extension of the great railways through the public domain and the pushing of settlements into more remote districts of the country, and at the same time improved the condition of the Indians. The policy will be maintained without any change excepting such as further experience may show to be necessary to render it more efficient.

The subject of converting the so-called Indian Territory south of Kansas into a home for the Indian, and erecting therein a Territorial form of government, is one of great importance as a complement of the existing Indian policy. The question of removal to that Territory has within the past year been presented to many of the tribes resident upon other and less desirable portions of the public domain, and has generally been received by them with favor. As a preliminary step to the organization of such a Territory, it will be necessary to confine the Indians now resident therein to farms of proper size, which should be secured to them in fee; the residue to be used for the settlement of other friendly Indians. Efforts will be made in the immediate future to induce the removal of as many peaceably disposed Indians to the Indian Territory as can be settled properly without disturbing the harmony of those already there. There is no other location now available where a people who are endeavoring to acquire a knowledge of pastoral and agricultural pursuits can be as well accommodated as upon the unoccupied lands in the Indian Territory. A Territorial government should, however, protect the Indians from the inroads of whites for a term of years, until they become sufficiently advanced in the arts and civilization to guard their own rights, and from the disposal of the lands held by them for the same period.

LANDS.

During the last fiscal year there were disposed of out of the public lands 11,864,975 acres, a quantity greater by 1,099,270 acres than was disposed of the previous year. Of this amount 1,370,320 acres were sold for cash, 389,460 acres located with military warrants, 4,671,332 acres taken for homesteads, 693,613 acres located with college scrip, 3,554,887 acres granted to railroads, 465,347 acres granted to wagon roads, 714,255 acres given to States as swamp land, 5,760 acres located by Indian scrip. The cash receipts from all sources in the Land Office amounted to $3,218,100. During the same period 22,016,608 acres of the public lands were surveyed, which, added to the quantity before surveyed, amounts to 583,364,780 acres, leaving 1,257,633,628 acres of the public lands still unsurveyed.

The reports from the subordinates of the Land Office contain interesting information in regard to their respective districts. They uniformly mention the fruitfulness of the soil during the past season and the increased yields of all kinds of produce. Even in those States and Territories where mining is the principal business agricultural products have exceeded the local demand, and liberal shipments have been made to distant points.

PATENTS.

During the year ending September 30, 1872, there were issued from the Patent Office 13,626 patents, 233 extensions, and 556 certificates and registries of trade-marks. During the same time 19,587 applications for patents, including reissues and designs, have been received and 3,100 caveats filed. The fees received during the same period amounted to $700,954.86, and the total expenditures to $623,553.90, making the net receipts over the expenditures $77,400.96.

Since 1836 200,000 applications for patents have been filed and about 133,000 patents issued. The office is being conducted under the same laws and general organization as were adopted at its original inauguration, when only from 100 to 500 applications were made per annum. The Commissioner shows that the office has outgrown the original plan, and that a new organization has become necessary. This subject was presented to Congress in a special communication in February last, with my approval and the approval of the Secretary of the Interior, and the suggestions contained in said communication were embraced in the bill that was reported to the House by the Committee on Patents at the last session. The subject of the reorganization of the Patent Office, as contemplated by the bill referred to, is one of such importance to the industrial interests of the country that I commend it to the attention of Congress.

The Commissioner also treats the subject of the separation of the Patent Office from the Department of the Interior. This subject is also embraced in the bill heretofore referred to. The Commissioner complains of the want of room for the model gallery and for the working force and necessary files of the office. It is impossible to transact the business of the office properly without more room in which to arrange files and drawings, that must be consulted hourly in the transaction of business. The whole of the Patent Office building will soon be needed, if it is not already, for the accommodation of the business of the Patent Office.

PENSIONS.

The amount paid for pensions in the last fiscal year was $30,169,340, an amount larger by $3,708,434 than was paid during the preceding year. Of this amount $2,313,409 were paid under the act of Congress of February 17, 1871, to survivors of the War of 1812. The annual increase of pensions by the legislation of Congress has more than kept pace with the natural yearly losses from the rolls. The act of Congress of June 8, 1872, has added an estimated amount of $750,000 per annum to the rolls, without increasing the number of pensioners. We can not, therefore, look for any substantial decrease in the expenditures of this Department for some time to come, or so long as Congress continues to so change the rates of pension.

The whole number of soldiers enlisted in the War of the Rebellion was 2,688,523. The total number of claims for invalid pensions is 176,000, being but 6 per cent of the whole number of enlisted men. The total number of claims on hand at the beginning of the year was 91,689; the number received during the year was 26,574; the number disposed of was 39,178, making a net gain of 12,604. The number of claims now on file is 79,085. .

On the 30th of June, 1872, there were on the rolls the names of 95,405 invalid military pensioners, 113,518 widows, orphans, and dependent relatives, making an aggregate of 208,923 army pensioners. At the same time there were on the rolls the names of 1,449 navy pensioners and 1,730 widows, orphans, and dependent relatives, making the whole number of naval pensioners 3,179. There have been received since the passage of the act to provide pensions for the survivors of the War of 1812 36,551 applications, prior to June 30, 1872. Of these there were allowed during the last fiscal year 20,126 claims; 4,845 were rejected during the year, leaving 11,580 claims pending at that date. The number of pensions of all classes granted during the last fiscal year was 33,838. During that period there were dropped from the rolls, for various causes, 9,104 names, leaving a grand total of 232,229 pensioners on the rolls on the 30th of June, 1872.

It is thought that the claims for pensions on account of the War of 1812 will all be disposed of by the 1st of May, 1873. It is estimated that $30,480,000 will be required for the pension service during the next fiscal year.

THE CENSUS.

The Ninth Census is about completed. Its early completion is a subject of congratulation, inasmuch as the use to be made of the statistics therein contained depends very greatly on the promptitude of publication.

The Secretary of the Interior recommends that a census be taken in 1875, which recommendation should receive the early attention of Congress. The interval at present established between the Federal census is so long that the information obtained at the decennial period as to the material condition, wants, and resources of the nation is of little practical value after the expiration of the first half of that period. It would probably obviate the constitutional provision regarding the decennial census if a census taken in 1875 should be divested of all political character and no reapportionment of Congressional representation be made under it. Such a census, coming, as it would, in the last year of the first century of our national existence, would furnish a noble monument of the progress of the United States during that century.

EDUCATION.

The rapidly increasing interest in education is a most encouraging feature in the current history of the country, and it is no doubt true that this is due in a great measure to the efforts of the Bureau of Education. That office is continually receiving evidences, which abundantly prove its efficiency, from the various institutions of learning and educators of all kinds throughout the country.

The report of the Commissioner contains a vast amount of educational details of great interest. The bill now pending before Congress, providing for the appropriation of the net proceeds of the sales of public lands for educational purposes, to aid the States in the general education of their rising generation, is a measure of such great importance to our real progress and is so unanimously approved by the leading friends of education that I commend it to the favorable attention of Congress.

TERRITORIES.

Affairs in the Territories are generally satisfactory. The energy and business capacity of the pioneers who are settling up the vast domains not yet incorporated into States are keeping pace in internal improvements and civil government with the older communities. In but one of them (Utah) is the condition of affairs unsatisfactory, except so far as the quiet of the citizen may be disturbed by real or imaginary danger of Indian hostilities. It has seemed to be the policy of the legislature of Utah to evade all responsibility to the Government of the United States, and even to hold a position in hostility to it.

I recommend a careful revision of the present laws of the Territory by Congress, and the enactment of such a law (the one proposed in Congress at its last session, for instance, or something similar to it) as will secure peace, the equality of all citizens before the law, and the ultimate extinguishment of polygamy.

Since the establishment of a Territorial government for the District of Columbia the improvement of the condition of the city of Washington and surroundings and the increased prosperity of the citizens are observable to the most casual visitor. The nation, being a large owner of property in the city, should bear, with the citizens of the District, its just share of the expense of these improvements.

I recommend, therefore, an appropriation to reimburse the citizens for the work done by them along and in front of public grounds during the past year, and liberal appropriations in order that the improvements and embellishments of the public buildings and grounds may keep pace with the improvements made by the Territorial authorities.

AGRICULTURE.

The report of the Commissioner of Agriculture gives a very full and interesting account of the several divisions of that Department—the horticultural, agricultural, statistical, entomological, and chemical—and the benefits conferred by each upon the agricultural interests of the country. The whole report is a complete history, in detail, of the workings of that Department in all its branches, showing the manner in which the farmer, merchant, and miner is informed, and the extent to which he is aided in his pursuits.

The Commissioner makes one recommendation—that measures be taken by Congress to protect and induce the planting of forests—and suggests that no part of the public lands should be disposed of without the condition that one-tenth of it should be reserved in timber where it exists, and where it does not exist inducements should be offered for planting it.

CENTENNIAL CELEBRATION.

In accordance with the terms of the act of Congress approved March 3, 1871, providing for the celebration of the one hundredth anniversary of American independence, a commission has been organized, consisting of two members from each of the States and Territories. This commission has held two sessions, and has made satisfactory progress in the organization and in the initiatory steps necessary for carrying out the provisions of the act, and for executing also the provisions of the act of June 1, 1872, creating a centennial board of finance. A preliminary report of progress has been received from the president of the commission, and is herewith transmitted. It will be the duty of the commission at your coming session to transmit a full report of the progress made, and to lay before you the details relating to the exhibition of American and foreign arts, products, and manufactures, which by the terms of the act is to be held under the auspices of the Government of the United States in the city of Philadelphia in the year 1876.

This celebration will be looked forward to by American citizens with great interest, as marking a century of greater progress and prosperity than is recorded in the history of any other nation, and as serving a further good purpose in bringing together on our soil peoples of all the commercial nations of the earth in a manner calculated to insure international good feeling.

CIVIL SERVICE.

An earnest desire has been felt to correct abuses which have grown up in the civil service of the country through the defective method of making appointments to office. Heretofore Federal offices have been regarded too much as the reward of political services. Under authority of Congress rules have been established to regulate the tenure of office and the mode of appointments. It can not be expected that any system of rules can be entirely effective and prove a perfect remedy for the existing evils until they have been thoroughly tested by actual practice and amended according to the requirements of the service. During my term of office it shall be my earnest endeavor to so apply the rules as to secure the greatest possible reform in the civil service of the Government, but it will require the direct action of Congress to render the enforcement of the system binding upon my successors; and I hope that the experience of the past year, together with appropriate legislation by Congress, may reach a satisfactory solution of this question and secure to the public service for all time a practical method of obtaining faithful and efficient officers and employees.   U. S. GRANT.

SPECIAL MESSAGES.

WASHINGTON, *December 2, 1872.*

To the Senate and House of Representatives:

I transmit herewith a report, dated the 2d instant, received from the Secretary of State, supplementary to the report submitted by him under date of the 8th of November, 1871, with reference to the expenditures authorized by the fourth and fifth paragraphs of the act of March 3, 1871, and by the act of May 18, 1872, making appropriations for the increased expenses and compensation for extraordinary services of certain diplomatic and consular officers of the United States by reason of the late war between France and Prussia. These expenditures have been made on my approval.   U. S. GRANT.

WASHINGTON, *December 3, 1872.*

To the Senate and House of Representatives:

I transmit herewith to Congress a report, dated the 2d instant, with the accompanying papers,* received from the Secretary of State, in com-

* Report of fees collected, etc., by consular officers of the United States for 1871, and tariff of consular fees.

pliance with the requirements of the eighteenth section of the act entitled "An act to regulate the diplomatic and consular systems of the United States," approved August 18, 1856.

U. S. GRANT.

WASHINGTON, *December 3, 1872.*

To the Senate of the United States:

I transmit to the Senate, for its consideration with a view to ratification, a convention between the United States of America and the United States of Mexico, signed in this city on the 27th ultimo, further extending the time fixed by the convention between the same parties of the 4th of July, 1868, for the duration of the joint commission on the subject of claims.

U. S. GRANT.

WASHINGTON, *December 3, 1872.*

To the Senate of the United States:

I transmit to the Senate, for its consideration with a view to ratification, a treaty between the United States of America and the Republic of Ecuador, providing for the mutual surrender of fugitive criminals, signed at Quito on the 28th of June last.

U. S. GRANT.

WASHINGTON, *December 3, 1872.*

To the Senate of the United States:

I transmit, for the consideration of the Senate with a view to ratification, a convention between the United States and His Majesty the King of Denmark, relating to naturalization.

U. S. GRANT.

WASHINGTON, *December 9, 1872.*

To the Senate of the United States:

In answer to the resolution of the Senate of the 5th instant, I transmit herewith a report* from the Secretary of State.

U. S. GRANT.

EXECUTIVE MANSION, *December 12, 1872.*

To the House of Representatives:

In compliance with section 2 of the act making appropriations for the consular and diplomatic expenses of the Government for the year ended June 30, 1871, and for other purposes, I herewith transmit a report received from the Secretary of the Treasury, giving the name of, the report made by, and the amount paid to the single consular agent of the United States.†

U. S. GRANT.

---

*Stating that the correspondence relative to the existence of slavery on the coast of Africa and to the action taken by Great Britain and other countries for its suppression was transmitted with the annual message of the President on the 2d instant.

† De B. Randolph Keim.

WASHINGTON, *December 16, 1872.*

To the Senate and House of Representatives:

I transmit to Congress a report from the Secretary of State, accompanied by that of the commissioners for inquiring into depredations upon the frontier of the State of Texas, appointed pursuant to the joint resolution of the 7th of May last. U. S. GRANT.

WASHINGTON, *January 5, 1873.*

To the Senate of the United States:

I transmit, for the consideration of the Senate with a view to ratification, a convention for the surrender of criminals between the United States of America and the Republic of Honduras, which was signed at Comayagua on the 4th day of June, 1873. U. S. GRANT.

WASHINGTON, *January 13, 1873.*

To the House of Representatives:

In answer to resolution of the House of Representatives of the 16th of December last, calling for information relative to the condition of affairs in Louisiana, and what, if any, action has been taken in regard thereto, I herewith transmit the report of the Attorney-General and the papers by which it is accompanied. U. S. GRANT.

WASHINGTON, *January 22, 1873.*

To the Senate of the United States:

I transmit herewith to the Senate, for its consideration with a view to ratification, an additional article to the treaty between the United States and Her Britannic Majesty of the 8th of May, 1871.

U. S. GRANT.

EXECUTIVE MANSION, *January 31, 1873.*

To the Senate and House of Representatives:

In compliance with section 2 of the act approved July 11, 1870, entitled "An act making appropriations for the consular and diplomatic expenses of the Government for the year ending June 30, 1871, and for other purposes," I have the honor to submit herewith a letter of the Secretary of the Treasury relative to the consular agent* appointed under authority of said act, together with the amounts paid such agent, and to transmit the report of the said agent upon the consular service of the United States. U. S. GRANT.

* De L. Randolph Keim.

WASHINGTON, *February 8, 1873.*

To the House of Representatives:

In answer to the resolution of the House of Representatives of the 29th of January, requesting information in relation to the case of Bernhard Bernstein,* I transmit herewith a report from the Secretary of State upon that subject, with accompanying documents.

U. S. GRANT.

WASHINGTON, *February 13, 1873.*

To the Senate and House of Representatives:

I transmit herewith a report from the Secretary of State and accompanying papers.†

U. S. GRANT.

EXECUTIVE MANSION, *February 14, 1873.*

To the Senate and House of Representatives:

I consider it my duty to call the attention of Congress to the condition of affairs in the Territory of Utah, and to the dangers likely to arise if it continues during the coming recess, from a threatened conflict between the Federal and Territorial authorities.

No discussion is necessary in regard to the general policy of Congress respecting the Territories of the United States, and I only wish now to refer to so much of that policy as concerns their judicial affairs and the enforcement of law within their borders.

No material differences are found in respect to these matters in the organic acts of the Territories, but an examination of them will show that it has been the invariable policy of Congress to place and keep their civil and criminal jurisdiction, with certain limited exceptions, in the hands of persons nominated by the President and confirmed by the Senate, and that the general administration of justice should be as prescribed by Congressional enactment. Sometimes the power given to the Territorial legislatures has been somewhat larger and sometimes somewhat smaller than the powers generally conferred. Never, however, have powers been given to a Territorial legislature inconsistent with the idea that the general judicature of the Territory was to be under the direct supervision of the National Government.

Accordingly, the organic law creating the Territory of Utah, passed September 9, 1850, provided for the appointment of a supreme court, the judges of which are judges of the district courts; a clerk, marshal, and an attorney, and to these Federal officers is confided jurisdiction in all important matters; but, as decided recently by the Supreme Court, the

* Claim against Russia for illegal arrest and imprisonment.

† Report of the United States commissioner to the International Penitentiary Congress of London, and appendix containing summary of proceedings of the National Prison Congress of Baltimore.

act requires jurors to serve in these courts to be selected in such manner as the Territorial legislature sees fit to prescribe. It has undoubtedly been the desire of Congress, so far as the same might be compatible with the supervisory control of the Territorial government, to leave the minor details connected with the administration of law to regulation by local authority; but such a desire ought not to govern when the effect will be, owing to the peculiar circumstances of the case, to produce a conflict between the Federal and the Territorial authorities, or to impede the enforcement of law, or in any way to endanger the peace and good order of the Territory.

Evidently it was never intended to intrust the Territorial legislature with power which would enable it, by creating judicatures of its own or increasing the jurisdiction of courts appointed by Territorial authority, although recognized by Congress, to take the administration of the law out of the hands of the judges appointed by the President or to interfere with their action.

Several years of unhappy experience make it apparent that in both of these respects the Territory of Utah requires special legislation by Congress.

Public opinion in that Territory, produced by circumstances too notorious to require further notice, makes it necessary, in my opinion, in order to prevent the miscarriage of justice and to maintain the supremacy of the laws of the United States and of the Federal Government, to provide that the selection of grand and petit jurors for the district courts, if not put under the control of Federal officers, shall be placed in the hands of persons entirely independent of those who are determined not to enforce any act of Congress obnoxious to them, and also to pass some act which shall deprive the probate courts, or any court created by the Territorial legislature, of any power to interfere with or impede the action of the courts held by the United States judges.

I am convinced that so long as Congress leaves the selection of jurors to the local authorities it will be futile to make any effort to enforce laws not acceptable to a majority of the people of the Territory, or which interfere with local prejudices or provide for the punishment of polygamy or any of its affiliated vices or crimes.

I presume that Congress, in passing upon the subject, will provide all reasonable and proper safeguards to secure honest and impartial jurors, whose verdicts will command confidence and be a guaranty of equal protection to all good and law-abiding citizens, and at the same time make it understood that crime can not be committed with impunity.

I have before said that while the laws creating the several Territories have generally contained uniform provisions in respect to the judiciary, yet Congress has occasionally varied these provisions in minor details, as the circumstances of the Territory affected seemed to demand; and in creating the Territory of Utah Congress evidently thought that circumstances there might require judicial remedies not necessary in other Territories, for by section 9 of the act creating that Territory it is provided that a writ of error may be brought from the decision of any judge of the supreme or district court of the Territory to the Supreme Court of the United States upon any writ of *habeas corpus* involving the question of personal freedom—a provision never inserted in any other Territorial act except that creating the Territory of New Mexico.

This extraordinary provision shows that Congress intended to mold the organic law to the peculiar necessities of the Territory, and the legislation which I now recommend is in full harmony with the precedent thus established.

I am advised that United States courts in Utah have been greatly embarrassed by the action of the Territorial legislature in conferring criminal jurisdiction and the power to issue writs of *habeas corpus* on the probate courts in the Territory, and by their consequent interference with the administration of justice. Manifestly the legislature of the Territory can not give to any court whatever the power to discharge by *habeas corpus* persons held by or under process from the courts created by Congress, but complaint is made that persons so held have been discharged in that way by the probate courts. I can not doubt that Congress will agree with me that such a state of things ought not longer to be tolerated, and that no class of persons anywhere should be allowed to treat the laws of the United States with open defiance and contempt.

Apprehensions are entertained that if Congress adjourns without any action upon this subject turbulence and disorder will follow, rendering military interference necessary—a result I should greatly deprecate; and in view of this and other obvious considerations, I earnestly recommend that Congress, at the present session, pass some act which will enable the district courts of Utah to proceed with independence and efficiency in the administration of law and justice.

U. S. GRANT.

WASHINGTON, *February 17, 1873.*

To the Senate of the United States:

In answer to a resolution of the Senate of the 14th instant, adopted in executive session, requiring of the Secretary of State information touching the business before the late mixed commission on claims under the convention with Mexico, I transmit a report from the Secretary of State and the papers by which it was accompanied.

U. S. GRANT.

WASHINGTON, *February 24, 1873.*

To the Senate and House of Representatives:

In my annual message to Congress at the opening of the second session of the present Congress in December, 1871, I recommended the legislation necessary on the part of the United States to bring into operation the articles of the treaty of Washington of May 8, 1871, relative to the fisheries and to other matters touching the relations of the United States toward the British North American possessions, to become operative so soon as the proper legislation should be had on the part of Great Britain and its possessions. That legislation on the part of Great Britain and its possessions had not then been had.

Having, prior to the meeting of Congress in December last, received official information of the consideration by Great Britain and its possessions of the legislation necessary on their part to bring those articles into operation, I communicated that fact to Congress in my annual message at the opening of the present session, and renewed the recommendation for your early adoption of the legislation in the same direction necessary on the part of this Government.

The near approach of the end of the session induces me again to urgently call your attention to the importance of this legislation on the part of Congress.

It will be remembered that the treaty of Washington resulted from an overture on the part of Great Britain to treat with reference to the fisheries on the coast of Her Majesty's possessions in North America and other questions between them affecting the relations of the United States toward these possessions. To this overture a reply was made on the part of this Government that while appreciating the importance of a friendly and complete understanding between the two Governments with reference to the subject specially suggested by the British Government, it was thought that the removal of the differences growing out of what were generically known as the Alabama claims was essential to the restoration of cordial and amicable relations between the two Governments, and the assent of this Government to treat on the subject of the fisheries was made dependent on the assent of Great Britain to allow the joint commission which it had prepared on the questions suggested by that Government to treat also and settle the differences growing out of the Alabama claims.

Great Britain assented to this, and the treaty of Washington proposed a settlement of both classes of questions.

Those relating to the Alabama claims and to the northwestern water boundary, commonly known as the San Juan question, have been disposed of in pursuance of the terms of the treaty.

Those relating to the fisheries were made by the terms of the treaty to depend upon the legislation which the constitutions of the respective Governments made necessary to carry those provisions into effect.

Great Britain and her possessions have on their part enacted the necessary legislation.

This Government is now enjoying the advantages of those provisions of the treaty which were the result of the condition of its assent to treat upon the questions which Great Britain had submitted.

The tribunal at Geneva has made an award in favor of the United States on the Alabama claims, and His Majesty the Emperor of Germany has decided in favor of the contention of the United States on the north-western boundary line.

I can not urge too strongly the importance of your early consideration of the legislation that may be necessary on the part of this Government.

In addition to the claim that Great Britain may have upon the good faith of this Government to consider the legislation necessary in connection with the questions which that Government presented as the subject of a negotiation which has resulted so favorably to this Government upon the other questions in which the United States felt so much interest, it is of importance that the rights of the American fishermen, as provided for under the treaty, should be determined before the now approaching fishing season opens, and that the serious difficulties to the fishing interests and the grave questions between the two Governments that may arise therefrom be averted.

U. S. GRANT.

EXECUTIVE MANSION, *February 25, 1873.*

To the Senate and House of Representatives:

Your attention is respectfully invited to the condition of affairs in the State of Louisiana.

Grave complications have grown out of the election there on the 6th of November last, chiefly attributable, it is believed, to an organized attempt on the part of those controlling the election officers and returns to defeat in that election the will of a majority of the electors of the State. Different persons are claiming the executive offices, two bodies are claiming to be the legislative assembly of the State, and the confusion and uncertainty produced in this way fall with paralyzing effect upon all its interests.

Controversy arose as soon as the election occurred over its proceedings and results, but I declined to interfere until suit involving this controversy to some extent was brought in the circuit court of the United States under and by virtue of the act of May 31, 1870, entitled "An act to enforce the right of citizens of the United States to vote in the several States of the Union, and for other purposes."

Finding that resistance was made to judicial process in that suit, without any opportunity, and, in my judgment, without any right, to review the judgment of the court upon the jurisdictional or other questions arising in the case, I directed the United States marshal to enforce such process and to use, if necessary, troops for that purpose, in accordance with the thirteenth section of said act, which provides that "it shall be lawful for the President of the United States to employ such part of the land or naval forces of the United States or of the militia as shall be necessary to aid in the execution of judicial process under this act.''

Two bodies of persons claimed to be the returning board for the State, and the circuit court in that case decided that the one to which Lynch belonged, usually designated by his name, was the lawful returning board; and this decision has been repeatedly affirmed by the district and supreme courts of the State. Having no opportunity or power to canvass the votes, and the exigencies of the case demanding an immediate decision, I conceived it to be my duty to recognize those persons as elected who received and held their credentials to office from what then appeared to me to be, and has since been decided by the supreme court of the State to be, the legal returning board.

Conformably to the decisions of this board, a full set of State officers has been installed and a legislative assembly organized, constituting, if not a *de jure,* at least a *de facto* government, which, since some time in December last, has had possession of the offices and been exercising the usual powers of government; but opposed to this has been another government claiming to control the affairs of the State, and which has to some extent been *pro forma* organized.

Recent investigation into said election has developed so many frauds and forgeries as to make it doubtful what candidates received a majority of the votes actually cast, and in view of these facts a variety of action has been proposed. I have no specific recommendation to make upon the subject, but if there is any practicable way of removing these difficulties by legislation, then I earnestly request that such action may be taken at the present session of Congress.

It seems advisable that I should state now what course I shall feel bound to pursue in reference to the matter in the event of no action by Congress at this time. Subject to any satisfactory arrangement that may be made by the parties to the controversy, which of all things is the most desirable, it will be my duty, so far as it may be necessary for me to act, to adhere to that government heretofore recognized by me. To judge of the election and qualifications of its members is the exclusive province of the Senate, as it is also the exclusive province of the House to judge of the election and qualifications of its members; but as to State offices, filled and held under State laws, the decisions of the State judicial tribunals, it seems to me, ought to be respected.

I am extremely anxious to avoid any appearance of undue interference in State affairs, and if Congress differs from me as to what ought to be done I respectfully urge its immediate decision to that effect; otherwise I shall feel obliged, as far as I can by the exercise of legitimate authority, to put an end to the unhappy controversy which disturbs the peace and prostrates the business of Louisiana, by the recognition and support of that government which is recognized and upheld by the courts of the State.

U. S. GRANT.

VETO MESSAGES.

EXECUTIVE MANSION, *January 6, 1873.*
To the House of Representatives:

I return herewith, for the further consideration of Congress, House bill No. 2291, entitled "An act for the relief of Edmund Jussen," to which I have not appended my approval, for the following reasons:

The bill directs the accounting officers to transfer from Mr. Jussen's account to that of his successor all indebtedness arising from the loss or destruction or nontaking of warehouse bonds on certain spirits destroyed by fire. This provision would be wholly ineffective in so far as it proposes to increase the liability of Mr. Jussen's successor, he having been appointed subsequently to the destruction of the spirits. It might operate to relieve Mr. Jussen, but it seems probable that he is already relieved by the act of May 27, 1872, passed since the introduction of this bill. That act provides for the rebatement of taxes on distilled spirits destroyed by fire, except in cases where the owners of such spirits may be indemnified against tax by a valid claim of insurance. The relief of the taxpayers of course includes the relief of collectors from liability caused by failure to take bonds. It does not appear whether there was any insurance in this case. If not, the applicant is already relieved; but if there was an insurance the effect of this bill, if it became a law, might be to except Mr. Jussen from the operation of the general rule established by the proviso of the act of May 27, 1872. If such exception be proper, it should not be confined to an individual case, but extended to all. If there was an insurance, this bill would relieve Mr. Jussen from the liability with which it is very doubtful if his successor could be legally charged, or with which he ought to be charged.

U. S. GRANT.

EXECUTIVE MANSION, *January 22, 1873.*
The SPEAKER OF THE HOUSE OF REPRESENTATIVES.

SIR: I herewith return to the House of Representatives, in which it originated, H. R. No. 630, entitled "An act in relation to new trials in the Court of Claims," without my approval.

The object of the bill is to reduce from two years to six months the time in which a new trial, upon motion of the United States, may be granted in the Court of Claims.

Great difficulties are now experienced in contesting fraudulent and unjust claims against the Government prosecuted in said court, and the effect of this bill, if it becomes a law, will be to increase those difficulties. Persons sue in this court generally with the advantage of a personal knowledge of the circumstances of the case, and are prompted by personal interest to activity in its preparation for trial, which consists sometimes in the production of false testimony and the suppression of the truth, while the United States are dependent for defense upon such inquiries as the officers of the Government, generally strangers to the transaction, are enabled to make, not infrequently in remote parts of the country and among those not averse to depredations upon the National Treasury. Instances have occurred where the existing opportunities for a new trial have enabled the Government to discover and defeat claims that ought not to have been allowed, after judgments thereon had been rendered by the Court of Claims.

By referring to the act which it is proposed to modify it will be seen that the payment of judgments recovered is not necessarily suspended for two years; but where the proofs are doubtful or suspicious the Government may appeal to the Supreme Court, and in the meantime may avail itself of any discovery or revelation of new evidence touching the facts of the case.

I fail to see the necessity or advantages of the proposed change in the law, and whatever may be the purposes of the bill, its effect, if passed, I am apprehensive will be to facilitate the prosecution of fraudulent claims against the United States. Believing that justice can and will be done to honest claimants in the Court of Claims as the law now stands, and believing also that the proposed change in the law will remove a valuable safeguard to the Treasury, I must for these reasons respectfully withhold my assent to the bill.

U. S. GRANT.

EXECUTIVE MANSION, *January 29, 1873.*

To the Senate of the United States:

I have the honor to return herewith Senate bill No. 490, entitled "An act for the relief of the East Tennessee University," without my approval.

This claim, for which $18,500 are appropriated out of the moneys of the United States, arises in part for the destruction of property by troops in time of war, and therefore the same objections attach to it as were expressed in my message of June 1, 1872, returning the Senate bill awarding $25,000 to J. Milton Best.

If the precedent is once established that the Government is liable for the ravages of war, the end of demands upon the public Treasury can not be forecast.

The loyalty of the people of the section in which the university is located, under circumstances of personal danger and trials, thus entitling them to the most favorable construction of the obligation of the Government toward them, is admitted, and nothing but regard for my duty to the whole people, in opposing a principle which, if allowed, will entail greater burdens upon the whole than the relief which will be afforded to a part by allowing this bill to become a law, could induce me to return it with objections.

Recognizing the claims of these citizens to sympathy and the most favorable consideration of their claims by the Government, I would heartily favor a donation of the amount appropriated by this bill for their relief.

U. S. GRANT.

WASHINGTON, *February 8, 1873.*

To the House of Representatives:

I have the honor to return herewith House bill (H. R. 2852) entitled "An act for the relief of James A. McCullah, late collector of the fifth district of Missouri," without my approval, for the following reasons:

It is provided in section 34 of the act of June 30, 1864, as amended by the act of July 13, 1866, that it shall be proved to the satisfaction of the Commissioner of Internal Revenue that due diligence was used by the collector, who shall certify the facts to the First Comptroller. This bill, should it become a law, clearly excuses Mr. McCullah, late collector, from showing that he used due diligence for the collection of the tax in question while the lists remained in his hands.

U. S. GRANT.

EXECUTIVE MANSION, *February 11, 1873.*

To the Senate of the United States:

I return herewith without my approval Senate bill No. 161, entitled "An act for the relief of those suffering from the destruction of salt works near Manchester, Ky., pursuant to the order of Major-General Carlos Buell."

All the objections made by me to the bill for the relief of J. Milton Best, and also of the East Tennessee University, apply with equal force to this bill.

According to the official report of Brigadier-General Craft, by whose immediate command the property in question was destroyed, there was a large rebel force in the neighborhood, who were using the salt works and had carried away a considerable quantity of salt, and were preparing to take more as soon as the necessary transportation could be procured; and he further states "that the leaders of the rebellion calculated upon their supply of salt to come from these works," and that in his opinion their destruction was a military necessity. I understand him to say, in effect, that the salt works were captured from the rebels; that it was impracticable to hold them, and that they were demolished so as to be of no further use to the enemy.

I can not agree that the owners of property destroyed under such circumstances are entitled to compensation therefor from the United States. Whatever other view may be taken of the subject, it is incontrovertible that these salt works were destroyed by the Union Army while engaged in regular military operations, and that the sole object of their destruction was to weaken, cripple, or defeat the armies of the so-called Southern Confederacy.

I am greatly apprehensive that the allowance of this claim could and would be construed into the recognition of a principle binding the United States to pay for all property which their military forces destroyed in the late war for the Union. No liability by the Government to pay for property destroyed by the Union forces in conducting a battle or siege has yet been claimed, but the precedent proposed by this bill leads directly and strongly in that direction, for it is difficult upon any ground of reason or justice to distinguish between a case of that kind and the one under consideration. Had General Craft and his command destroyed the salt works by shelling out the enemy found in their actual occupancy, the case would not have been different in principle from the one presented in this bill. What possible difference can it make in the rights of owners or the obligations of the Government whether the destruction was in driving the enemy out or in keeping them out of the possession of the salt works?

This bill does not present a case where private property is taken for public use in any sense of the Constitution. It was not taken from the owners, but from the enemy; and it was not then used by the Government, but destroyed. Its destruction was one of the casualties of war, and, though not happening in actual conflict, was perhaps as disastrous to the rebels as would have been a victory in battle.

Owners of property destroyed to prevent the spread of a conflagration, as a general rule, are not entitled to compensation therefor; and for reasons equally strong the necessary destruction of property found in the hands of the public enemy, and constituting a part of their military supplies, does not entitle the owner to indemnity from the Government for damages to him in that way.

I fully appreciate the hardship of the case, and would be glad if my convictions of duty allowed me to join in the proposed relief; but I can not consent to the doctrine which is found in this bill, as it seems to me, by which the National Treasury is exposed to all claims for property injured or destroyed by the armies of the United States in the late protracted and destructive war in this country.

U. S. GRANT.

PROCLAMATION.

By the President of the United States of America.

A PROCLAMATION.

Whereas objects of interest to the United States require that the Senate should be convened at 12 o'clock on the 4th of March next, to receive and act upon such communications as may be made to it on the part of the Executive:

Now, therefore, I, Ulysses S. Grant, President of the United States, have considered it to be my duty to issue this my proclamation, declaring that an extraordinary occasion requires the Senate of the United States to convene for the transaction of business at the Capitol, in the city of Washington, on the 4th day of March next, at 12 o'clock at noon on that day, of which all who shall at that time be entitled to act as members of that body are hereby required to take notice.

Given under my hand and the seal of the United States, at Washington, [SEAL.] the 21st day of February, A. D. 1873, and of the Independence of the United States of America the ninety-seventh.

U. S. GRANT.

By the President:
HAMILTON FISH,
Secretary of State.

EXECUTIVE ORDERS.

BY THE PRESIDENT OF THE UNITED STATES.

EXECUTIVE ORDER.

WASHINGTON, *January 17, 1873.*

Whereas it has been brought to the notice of the President of the United States that many persons holding civil office by appointment from him or otherwise under the Constitution and laws of the United States, while holding such Federal positions, accept offices under the authority of the States and Territories in which they reside, or of municipal corporations under the charters and ordinances of such corporations, thereby assuming the duties of the State, Territorial, or municipal office at the same time that they are charged with the duties of the civil office held under Federal authority; and

Whereas it is believed that, with few exceptions, the holding of two such offices by the same person is incompatible with a due and faithful discharge of the duties of either office; that it frequently gives rise to great inconvenience, and often results in detriment to the public service, and, moreover, is not in harmony with the genius of the Government:

In view of the premises, therefore, the President has deemed it proper thus and hereby to give public notice that from and after the 4th day of March, A. D. 1873 (except as herein specified), persons holding any Federal civil office by appointment under the Constitution and laws of the United States will be expected, while holding such office, not to accept or hold any office under any State or Territorial government or under the charter or ordinances of any municipal corporation; and further, that the acceptance or continued holding of any such State, Territorial, or municipal office, whether elective or by appointment, by any person holding civil office as aforesaid under the Government of the United States, other than judicial offices under the Constitution of the United States, will be deemed a vacation of the Federal office held by such person, and will be taken to be and will be treated as a resignation by such Federal officer of his commission or appointment in the service of the United States.

The offices of justices of the peace, of notaries public, and of commissioners to take the acknowledgment of deeds, of bail, or to administer oaths shall not be deemed within the purview of this order, and are excepted from its operation and may be held by Federal officers.

The appointment of deputy marshal of the United States may be conferred upon sheriffs or deputy sheriffs; and deputy postmasters the emoluments of whose office do not exceed $600 per annum are also excepted from the operations of this order, and may accept and hold appointments under State, Territorial, or municipal authority, provided the same be found not to interfere with the discharge of their duties as postmaster.

Heads of Departments and other officers of the Government who have the appointment of subordinate officers are required to take notice of this order, and to see to the enforcement of its provisions and terms within the sphere of their respective Departments or offices and as relates to the several persons holding appointments under them, respectively.

By order of the President:

HAMILTON FISH,
Secretary of State.

DEPARTMENT OF STATE,
Washington, January 28, 1873.

Inquiries having been made from various quarters as to the application of the Executive order issued on the 17th January, relating to the holding of State or municipal offices by persons holding civil offices under the Federal Government, the President directs the following reply to be made:

It has been asked whether the order prohibits a Federal officer from holding also the office of an alderman or of a common councilman in a city, or of a town councilman of a town or village, or of appointments under city, town, or village governments. By some it has been suggested that there may be distinction made in case the office be with or without salary or compensation. The city or town offices of the description referred to, by whatever names they may be locally known, whether held by election or by appointment, and whether with or without salary or compensation, are of the class which the Executive order intends not to be held by persons holding Federal offices.

It has been asked whether the order prohibits Federal officers from holding positions on boards of education, school committees, public libraries, religious or eleemosynary institutions incorporated or established or sustained by State or municipal authority. Positions and service on such boards or committees and professorships in colleges are not regarded as "offices" within the contemplation of the Executive order, but as employments or service in which all good citizens may be engaged without incompatibility, and in many cases without necessary interference with any position which they may hold under the Federal Government. Officers of the Federal Government may therefore engage in such service, provided the attention required by such employment does not interfere with the regular and efficient discharge of the duties of their office under the Federal Government. The head of the Department under whom the Federal office is held will in all cases be the sole judge whether or not the employment does thus interfere.

The question has also been asked with regard to officers of the State militia. Congress having exercised the power conferred by the Constitution to provide for organizing the militia, which is liable to be called forth to be employed in the service of the United States, and is thus in some sense under the control of the General Government, and is, moreover, of the greatest value to the public, the Executive order of the 17th January is not considered as prohibiting Federal officers from being officers of the militia in the States and Territories.

It has been asked whether the order prohibits persons holding office under the Federal Government being members of local or municipal fire departments; also whether it applies to mechanics employed by the day in the armories, arsenals, and navy-yards, etc., of the United States. Unpaid service in local or municipal fire departments is not regarded as an office within the intent of the Executive order, and may be performed by Federal officers, provided it does not interfere with the regular and efficient discharge of the duties of the Federal office, of which the head of the Department under which the office is held will in each case be the judge. Employment by the day as mechanics and laborers in the armories, arsenals, navy-yards, etc., does not constitute an office of any kind, and those thus employed are not within the contemplation of the Executive order. Master workmen and others who hold appointments from the Government or from any Department, whether for a fixed time or at the pleasure of the appointing power, are embraced within the operation of the order.

By order of the President:

HAMILTON FISH,
Secretary of State.

SECOND INAUGURAL ADDRESS.

FELLOW-CITIZENS: Under Providence I have been called a second time to act as Executive over this great nation. It has been my endeavor in the past to maintain all the laws, and, so far as lay in my power, to act for the best interests of the whole people. My best efforts will be given in the same direction in the future, aided, I trust, by my four years' experience in the office.

When my first term of the office of Chief Executive began, the country had not recovered from the effects of a great internal revolution, and three of the former States of the Union had not been restored to their Federal relations.

It seemed to me wise that no new questions should be raised so long as that condition of affairs existed. Therefore the past four years, so far as I could control events, have been consumed in the effort to restore harmony, public credit, commerce, and all the arts of peace and progress. It is my firm conviction that the civilized world is tending toward republicanism, or government by the people through their chosen representatives, and that our own great Republic is destined to be the guiding star to all others.

Under our Republic we support an army less than that of any European power of any standing and a navy less than that of either of at least five of them. There could be no extension of territory on the continent which would call for an increase of this force, but rather might such extension enable us to diminish it.

The theory of government changes with general progress. Now that the telegraph is made available for communicating thought, together with rapid transit by steam, all parts of a continent are made contiguous for all purposes of government, and communication between the extreme limits of the country made easier than it was throughout the old thirteen States at the beginning of our national existence.

The effects of the late civil strife have been to free the slave and make him a citizen. Yet he is not possessed of the civil rights which citizenship should carry with it. This is wrong, and should be corrected. To this correction I stand committed, so far as Executive influence can avail.

Social equality is not a subject to be legislated upon, nor shall I ask that anything be done to advance the social status of the colored man, except to give him a fair chance to develop what there is good in him, give him access to the schools, and when he travels let him feel assured that his conduct will regulate the treatment and fare he will receive.

The States lately at war with the General Government are now happily rehabilitated, and no Executive control is exercised in any one of them that would not be exercised in any other State under like circumstances.

In the first year of the past Administration the proposition came up for the admission of Santo Domingo as a Territory of the Union. It was not a question of my seeking, but was a proposition from the people of Santo Domingo, and which I entertained. I believe now, as I did then, that it was for the best interest of this country, for the people of Santo Domingo, and all concerned that the proposition should be received favorably. It was, however, rejected constitutionally, and therefore the subject was never brought up again by me.

In future, while I hold my present office, the subject of acquisition of territory must have the support of the people before I will recommend any proposition looking to such acquisition. I say here, however, that I do not share in the apprehension held by many as to the danger of governments becoming weakened and destroyed by reason of their extension of territory. Commerce, education, and rapid transit of thought and matter by telegraph and steam have changed all this. Rather do I believe that our Great Maker is preparing the world, in His own good time, to become one nation, speaking one language, and when armies and navies will be no longer required.

My efforts in the future will be directed to the restoration of good feeling between the different sections of our common country; to the restoration of our currency to a fixed value as compared with the world's standard of values—gold—and, if possible, to a par with it; to the construction of cheap routes of transit throughout the land, to the end that the products of all may find a market and leave a living remuneration to the producer; to the maintenance of friendly relations with all our neighbors and with distant nations; to the reestablishment of our commerce and share in the carrying trade upon the ocean; to the encouragement of such manufacturing industries as can be economically pursued in this country, to the end that the exports of home products and industries may pay for our imports—the only sure method of returning to and permanently maintaining a specie basis; to the elevation of labor; and, by a humane course, to bring the aborigines of the country under the benign influences of education and civilization. It is either this or war of extermination. Wars of extermination, engaged in by people pursuing commerce and all industrial pursuits, are expensive even against the weakest people, and are demoralizing and wicked. Our superiority of strength and advantages of civilization should make us lenient toward the Indian. The wrong inflicted upon him should be taken into account and the balance placed to his credit. The moral view of the question should be considered and the question asked, Can not the Indian be made a useful and productive member of society by proper teaching and treatment? If the effort is made in good faith, we will stand better before the civilized nations of the earth and in our own consciences for having made it.

All these things are not to be accomplished by one individual, but they will receive my support and such recommendations to Congress as will in my judgment best serve to carry them into effect. I beg your support and encouragement.

It has been, and is, my earnest desire to correct abuses that have grown up in the civil service of the country. To secure this reformation rules regulating methods of appointment and promotions were established and have been tried. My efforts for such reformation shall be continued to the best of my judgment. The spirit of the rules adopted will be maintained.

I acknowledge before this assemblage, representing, as it does, every section of our country, the obligation I am under to my countrymen for the great honor they have conferred on me by returning me to the highest office within their gift, and the further obligation resting on me to render to them the best services within my power. This I promise, looking forward with the greatest anxiety to the day when I shall be released from responsibilities that at times are almost overwhelming, and from which I have scarcely had a respite since the eventful firing upon Fort Sumter, in April, 1861, to the present day. My services were then tendered and accepted under the first call for troops growing out of that event.

I did not ask for place or position, and was entirely without influence or the acquaintance of persons of influence, but was resolved to perform my part in a struggle threatening the very existence of the nation. I performed a conscientious duty, without asking promotion or command, and without a revengeful feeling toward any section or individual.

Notwithstanding this, throughout the war, and from my candidacy for my present office in 1868 to the close of the last Presidential campaign, I have been the subject of abuse and slander scarcely ever equaled in political history, which to-day I feel that I can afford to disregard in view of your verdict, which I gratefully accept as my vindication.

MARCH 4, 1873.

PROCLAMATIONS.

BY THE PRESIDENT OF THE UNITED STATES OF AMERICA.

A PROCLAMATION.

Whereas, under the pretense that William P. Kellogg, the present executive of Louisiana, and the officers associated with him in the State administration were not duly elected, certain turbulent and disorderly persons have combined together with force and arms to resist the laws and constituted authorities of said State; and

Whereas it has been duly certified by the proper local authorities and judicially determined by the inferior and supreme courts of said State that said officers are entitled to hold their offices, respectively, and execute and discharge the functions thereof; and

Whereas Congress, at its late session, upon a due consideration of the subject, tacitly recognized the said executive and his associates, then as now in office, by refusing to take any action with respect thereto; and

Whereas it is provided in the Constitution of the United States that the United States shall protect every State in this Union, on application of the legislature, or of the executive when the legislature can not be convened, against domestic violence; and

Whereas it is provided in the laws of the United States that in all cases of insurrection in any State or of obstruction to the laws thereof it shall be lawful for the President of the United States, on application of the legislature of such State, or of the executive when the legislature can not be convened, to call forth the militia of any other State or States, or to employ such part of the land and naval forces as shall be judged necessary, for the purpose of suppressing such insurrection or causing the laws to be duly executed; and

Whereas the legislature of said State is not now in session, and can not be convened in time to meet the present emergency, and the executive of said State, under section 4 of Article IV of the Constitution of the United States and the laws passed in pursuance thereof, has therefore made application to me for such part of the military force of the United States as may be necessary and adequate to protect said State and the citizens thereof against domestic violence and to enforce the due execution of the laws; and

Whereas it is required that whenever it may be necessary, in the judgment of the President, to use the military force for the purpose aforesaid, he shall forthwith, by proclamation, command such insurgents to disperse and retire peaceably to their respective homes within a limited time:

Now, therefore, I, Ulysses S. Grant, President of the United States, do hereby make proclamation and command said turbulent and disorderly persons to disperse and retire peaceably to their respective abodes within twenty days from this date, and hereafter to submit themselves to the laws and constituted authorities of said State; and I invoke the aid and cooperation of all good citizens thereof to uphold law and preserve the public peace.

In witness whereof I have hereunto set my hand and caused the seal of the United States to be affixed.

[SEAL.]   Done at the city of Washington, this 22d day of May, A. D. 1873, and of the Independence of the United States the ninety-seventh.

U. S. GRANT.

By the President:
    J. C. BANCROFT DAVIS,
        Acting Secretary of State.

BY THE PRESIDENT OF THE UNITED STATES OF AMERICA.

A PROCLAMATION.

Whereas by the thirty-third article of a treaty concluded at Washington on the 8th day of May, 1871, between the United States and Her Britannic Majesty it was provided that—

Articles XVIII to XXV, inclusive, and Article XXX of this treaty shall take effect as soon as the laws required to carry them into operation shall have been passed by the Imperial Parliament of Great Britain, by the parliament of Canada, and by the legislature of Prince Edwards Island on the one hand, and by the Congress of the United States on the other.

And whereas by the first section of an act entitled "An act to carry into effect the provisions of the treaty between the United States and Great Britain signed in the city of Washington the 8th day of May, 1871, relating to the fisheries," it is provided—

That whenever the President of the United States shall receive satisfactory evidence that the Imperial Parliament of Great Britain, the parliament of Canada, and the legislature of Prince Edwards Island have passed laws on their part to give full effect to the provisions of the treaty between the United States and Great Britain signed at the city of Washington on the 8th day of May, 1871, as contained in articles eighteenth to twenty-fifth, inclusive, and article thirtieth of said treaty, he is hereby authorized to issue his proclamation declaring that he has such evidence.

And whereas the Secretary of State of the United States and Her Britannic Majesty's envoy extraordinary and minister plenipotentiary at Washington have recorded in a protocol a conference held by them at the Department of State, in Washington, on the 7th day of June, 1873, in the following language:

PROTOCOL OF A CONFERENCE HELD AT WASHINGTON ON THE 7TH DAY OF JUNE, 1873.

Whereas it is provided by Article XXXIII of the treaty between Her Majesty the Queen of the United Kingdom of Great Britain and Ireland and the United States of America signed at Washington on the 8th of May, 1871, as follows:

"ARTICLE XXXIII.

"The foregoing Articles XVIII to XXV, inclusive, and Article XXX of this treaty shall take effect as soon as the laws required to carry them into operation shall have been passed by the Imperial Parliament of Great Britain, by the parliament of Canada, and by the legislature of Prince Edwards Island on the one hand, and by the Congress of the United States on the other. Such assent having been given, the said articles shall remain in force for the period of ten years from the date at which they may come into operation, and, further, until the expiration of two years after either of the high contracting parties shall have given notice to the other of its wish to terminate the same; each of the high contracting parties being at liberty to give such notice to the other at the end of the said period of ten years or at any time afterwards;" and

Whereas, in accordance with the stipulations of the above-recited article, an act was passed by the Imperial Parliament of Great Britain in the thirty-fifth and thirty-sixth years of the reign of Queen Victoria, intituled "An act to carry into effect a treaty between Her Majesty and the United States of America;" and

Whereas an act was passed by the senate and house of commons of Canada in the fifth session of the first parliament held in the thirty-fifth year of Her Majesty's reign and assented to in Her Majesty's name by the Governor-General on the 14th day of June, 1872, intituled "An act relating to the treaty of Washington, 1871;" and

Whereas an act was passed by the legislature of Prince Edwards Island and assented to by the lieutenant-governor of that colony on the 29th day of June, 1872, intituled "An act relating to the treaty of Washington, 1871;" and

Whereas an act was passed by the Senate and House of Representatives of the United States of America in Congress assembled, and approved on the 1st day of March, 1873, by the President of the United States, intituled "An act to carry into effect the provisions of the treaty between the United States and Great Britain signed in the city of Washington the 8th day of May, 1871, relating to fisheries:"

The undersigned, Hamilton Fish, Secretary of State of the United States, and the Right Hon. Sir Edward Thornton, one of Her Majesty's most honorable privy council, knight commander of the most honorable Order of the Bath, Her Britannic Majesty's envoy extraordinary and minister plenipotentiary to the United States of America, duly authorized for this purpose by their respective Governments, having met together at Washington, and having found that the laws required to carry the Articles XVIII to XXV, inclusive, and Article XXX of the treaty aforesaid into operation have been passed by the Imperial Parliament of Great Britain, by the parliament of Canada, and by the legislature of Prince Edwards Island on the one part, and by the Congress of the United States on the other, hereby declare that Articles XVIII to XXV, inclusive, and Article XXX of the treaty between Her Britannic Majesty and the United States of America of the 8th of May, 1871, will take effect on the 1st day of July next.

In witness whereof the undersigned have signed this protocol and have hereunto affixed their seals.

Done in duplicate at Washington, this 7th day of June, 1873.

[SEAL.]   (Signed)   HAMILTON FISH.

[SEAL.]   (Signed)   EDWD. THORNTON.

Now, therefore, I, Ulysses S. Grant, President of the United States of America, in pursuance of the premises, do hereby declare that I have received satisfactory evidence that the Imperial Parliament of Great Britain, the parliament of Canada, and the legislature of Prince Edwards Island have passed laws on their part to give full effect to the provisions of the said treaty as contained in articles eighteenth to twenty-fifth, inclusive, and article thirtieth of said treaty.

In testimony whereof I have hereunto set my hand and caused the seal of the United States to be affixed.

[SEAL.]   Done at the city of Washington, this 1st day of July, A. D. 1873, and of the Independence of the United States of America the ninety-seventh.

U. S. GRANT.

By the President:

HAMILTON FISH,
Secretary of State.

BY THE PRESIDENT OF THE UNITED STATES OF AMERICA.

A PROCLAMATION.

Whereas by the act of Congress approved March 3, 1871, providing for a national celebration of the one hundredth anniversary of the independence of the United States by the holding of an International Exhibition of Arts, Manufactures, and Products of the Soil and Mine in the city of Philadelphia in the year 1876, it is provided as follows:

That whenever the President shall be informed by the governor of the State of Pennsylvania that provision has been made for the erection of suitable buildings for the purpose, and for the exclusive control by the commission herein provided for of the proposed exhibition, the President shall, through the Department of State, make proclamation of the same, setting forth the time at which the exhibition will open and the place at which it will be held; and he shall communicate to the diplomatic representatives of all nations copies of the same, together with such regulations as may be adopted by the commissioners, for publication in their respective countries.

And whereas his excellency the governor of the said State of Pennsylvania did, on the 24th day of June, 1873, inform me that provision has been made for the erection of said buildings and for the exclusive control by the commission provided for in the said act of the proposed exhibition; and

Whereas the president of the United States Centennial Commission has officially informed me of the dates fixed for the opening and closing of the said exhibition and the place at which it is to be held:

Now, therefore, be it known that I, Ulysses S. Grant, President of the United States, in conformity with the provisions of the act of Congress aforesaid, do hereby declare and proclaim that there will be held at the city of Philadelphia, in the State of Pennsylvania, an International Exhibition of Arts, Manufactures, and Products of the Soil and Mine, to be opened on the 19th day of April, A. D. 1876, and to be closed on the 19th day of October, in the same year.

And in the interest of peace, civilization, and domestic and international friendship and intercourse, I commend the celebration and exhibition to the people of the United States, and in behalf of this Government and people I cordially commend them to all nations who may be pleased to take part therein.

In testimony whereof I have hereunto set my hand and caused the seal of the United States to be affixed.

[SEAL.]   Done at the city of Washington, this 3d day of July, 1873, and of the Independence of the United States the ninety-seventh.

U. S. GRANT.

By the President:
    HAMILTON FISH,
        Secretary of State.

By the President of the United States of America.

A PROCLAMATION.

Whereas satisfactory evidence was given me on the 13th day of September current by the Marquis de Noailles, envoy extraordinary and minister plenipotentiary from the French Republic, that on and after the 1st day of October next merchandise imported into France in vessels of the United States, from whatever country, will be subject to no other duties or imposts than those which shall be collected upon merchandise imported into France from countries of its origin or from any other country in French vessels:

Now, therefore, I, Ulysses S. Grant, President of the United States of America, by virtue of the authority vested in me by law, do hereby declare and proclaim that on and after the 1st day of October next, so long as merchandise imported into France in vessels of the United States, whether from the countries of its origin or from other countries, shall be admitted into the ports of France on the terms aforesaid, the discriminating duties heretofore levied upon merchandise imported into the United States in French vessels, either from the countries of its origin or from any other country, shall be and are discontinued and abolished.

In testimony whereof I have hereunto set my hand and caused the seal of the United States to be affixed.

[SEAL.] Done at the city of Washington, this 22d day of September, A. D. 1873, and of the Independence of the United States of America the ninety-eighth.

U. S. GRANT.

By the President:

J. C. Bancroft Davis,
Acting Secretary of State.

By the President of the United States of America.

A PROCLAMATION.

The approaching close of another year brings with it the occasion for renewed thanksgiving and acknowledgment to the Almighty Ruler of the Universe for the unnumbered mercies which He has bestowed upon us.

Abundant harvests have been among the rewards of industry. With local exceptions, health has been among the many blessings enjoyed. Tranquillity at home and peace with other nations have prevailed.

Frugal industry is regaining its merited recognition and its merited rewards.

Gradually but, under the providence of God, surely, as we trust, the nation is recovering from the lingering results of a dreadful civil strife.

For these and all the other mercies vouchsafed it becomes us as a people to return heartfelt and grateful acknowledgments, and with our thanksgiving for blessings we may unite prayers for the cessation of local and temporary sufferings.

I therefore recommend that on Thursday, the 27th day of November next, the people meet in their respective places of worship to make their acknowledgments to Almighty God for His bounties and His protection, and to offer to Him prayers for their continuance.

In witness whereof I have hereunto set my hand and caused the seal of the United States to be affixed.

[SEAL.]   Done at the city of Washington, this 14th day of October, A. D. 1873, and of the Independence of the United States the ninety-eighth.   U. S. GRANT.

By the President:

HAMILTON FISH, *Secretary of State.*

EXECUTIVE ORDERS.

WASHINGTON, *March 14, 1873.*

In consequence of the peculiar and confidential relations which from the nature of the service must exist and be maintained between the Department of State and its clerks, rules 2, 3, and 4 of the rules and regulations for the civil service promulgated by the President 19th of December, 1871, as amended by the Executive order 16th of April, 1872, shall in their application to that Department be modified as follows, namely:

Vacancies occurring in any grade of consulates or clerkships in the Department may be filled either by transfer from some other grade or service—clerical, consular, or diplomatic—under the Department of State, or by the appointment of some person who has previously served under the Department of State to its satisfaction, or by the appointment of some person who has made application to the Secretary of State, with proper certificates of character, responsibility, and capacity, in the manner provided for applications for consulates of which the lawful annual compensation is more than $1,000 and less than $3,000, and who has on examination been found qualified for the position.

U. S. GRANT.

[From the New-York Daily Tribune, May 10, 1873.]

WASHINGTON, *May 9, 1873.*

The President announces with deep regret the death of the Hon. Salmon P. Chase, Chief Justice of the United States, who closed a life of long public service, in the city of New York, on the 7th instant, having filled the offices of Senator of the United States, governor of Ohio, Secretary of the Treasury, and crowning a long career in the exalted position of Chief Justice of the United States. The President directs that the public offices in Washington be closed on Saturday, the 10th instant, the day of his funeral, and that they be draped in mourning for the period of thirty days, and that the flags be displayed at half-mast on the public buildings and forts and on the national vessels on the day of the funeral, in honor of the memory of the illustrious dead.

By order of the President:

HAMILTON FISH,
Secretary of State.

EXECUTIVE MANSION,
Washington, D. C., May 21, 1873.

SIR:* The President directs me to say that the several Departments of the Government will be closed on the 30th instant, in order to enable the employees of the Government to participate, in connection with the Grand Army of the Republic, in the decoration of the graves of the soldiers who fell during the rebellion.

I am, sir, your obedient servant,

O. E. BABCOCK,
Secretary.

WASHINGTON, *August 5, 1873.*

The Civil Service Commission, at its session at Washington which terminated June 4, 1873, recommended certain further rules to be prescribed by the President for the government of the civil service of the United States. These rules as herewith published are approved, and their provisions will be enforced as rapidly as the proper arrangements can be made.

U. S. GRANT.

By the President:

HAMILTON FISH,
Secretary of State.

FURTHER RULES FOR PROMOTING THE EFFICIENCY OF THE CIVIL SERVICE OF THE UNITED STATES.

Rule 1.—It being essential to the public welfare to maintain in the Executive the exercise of the power of nomination and appointment vested by the Constitution, and thereby to secure that measure of independence and separate responsibility which is contemplated by that instrument; and it being needful, in making such nominations and appointments, that the appointing power should obtain and in the proper Department preserve the evidence of fitness in reference to which all such nominations and appointments should be made: Therefore recommendations concerning any nomination or appointment to office or place in the civil service can not

* Addressed to the heads of the Executive Departments, etc.

be considered unless made in writing, signed by the person making them, setting forth the character of the person recommended and his qualifications for the office in reference to which the recommendation is made; nor, when the recommendation is by a person holding an office or station in or under the Government of the United States, can such written recommendation, except when made in response to a written request by the officer making the appointment, or in the discharge of an official duty imposed by the Constitution or the laws, be considered as entitled to any greater weight than if made by such person as a private individual. But this rule shall not apply to recommendations made by officers as to their own subordinates.

Rule 2.—While it is not the purpose of the rules and regulations prescribed for the government of the civil service either to restrict the power of removal or to extend the tenure of service, such power will not be exercised arbitrarily, and therefore applications must not be entertained by any authority having the duty of nomination or appointment for the removal of any person in the civil service, nor will any person be removed for the mere purpose of making a place for any other person.

Rule 3.—To prevent any misapprehension in the public mind in regard to the functions of the members of the Civil Service Commission and of the members of any board of examiners, it is declared not to be any part of the duty or authority of any such member to act upon, take part in, or in any way entertain any recommendation, application, or question concerning appointments or removals in respect of the civil service, otherwise than in the strict discharge of their respective duties as prescribed by the rules and regulations; and for the same purpose it is further declared that the functions of the members of said Commission as to the matters aforesaid extend only to the question of the proper rules and regulations to be made and to supervising their application, and that the functions of the examiners as to said matters extend only to preparing for, conducting, rating, and making reports concerning examinations required to be made under such rules and regulations.

Rule 4.—The grouping heretofore made for the Executive Departments at Washington is hereby modified by striking out the words "female clerks, copyists, and counters, at $900 a year," these places being below the grade of clerkships of class 1; and all applicants for such positions shall be examined in (1) penmanship, (2) copying, (3) elements of English grammar, chiefly orthography, and (4) fundamental rules of arithmetic, except that mere counters may be examined only in the fundamental rules of arithmetic and as to their facility in counting money; and those found competent by such examination shall be reported in the order of their excellence as eligible for appointment, and selections may be made by the appointing power, at discretion, from the list of those so reported, being at liberty to give preference to such as may be justly regarded as having the highest claims to public consideration by reason of loss of support or of property occasioned by the death or disability of any person in the defense of the Union in war or in other public service of the Government. And in the notices of the examination of females to fill vacancies among those last mentioned it shall be stated as follows: "That from among all those who shall pass a satisfactory examination the head of the Department will be at liberty to select such persons for the vacancies as may be justly regarded as having the highest claims to public consideration."

Rule 5.—The notices to appear at any examinations other than those referred to in the fourth rule of this series, so far as practicable and necessary to prevent misapprehension, shall advise female applicants to whom they may be sent of any limitation which the law or the necessities of the public service impose upon such applicants entering the vacancies for which the examinations are to take place.

Rule 6.—That it shall be the duty of the respective boards of examiners, on the written request of heads of Departments, to hold examinations in anticipation of vacancies, as well as to fill vacancies, and to prepare lists showing the results of competition, so that when any such vacancy may happen there shall be those thus shown to be eligible to nomination or appointment, from whom the proper selection shall be made according to the provisions of the rules and regulations relating to competitive examination; and examinations upon like request shall be held in reference to vacancies to be filled under the fourth rule of this series.

Rule 7.—Applicants for appointment as cashiers of collectors of customs, cashiers of assistant treasurers, cashiers of postmasters, superintendents of money-order divisions in post-offices, and other custodians of large sums of public money for whose fidelity another officer has given official bonds may be appointed at discretion; but this rule shall not apply to any appointment to a position grouped below the grade of assistant teller.

Rule 8.—In cases of defalcation or embezzlement of public money, or other emergency calling for immediate action, where the public service would be materially injured unless the vacancy is promptly filled without resorting to the methods of selection and appointment prescribed by the rules and regulations, or when a vacancy happens at a place remote and difficult of access and the methods prescribed for filling it can not be applied without causing delay injurious to the public service, the appointment may be made at discretion; but this rule shall not apply to any place which is provided to be filled under the rules of competitive examination.

Rule 9.—For the purpose of bringing the examinations for the civil service as near to the residences of those desiring to be examined as the appropriation at the command of the President will warrant, and for the further purpose of facilitating as far as practicable the making of selections for such service equably from the several portions of the Union, while at the same time preserving the principle of promoting merit as tested by fair competition, it is provided as follows:

(1) That the several States and Territories are grouped into five divisions, to be designated as civil-service districts, the said districts to be numbered consecutively from one to five, as follows:

I. The first district embraces the States of Maine, New Hampshire, Massachusetts, Vermont, Connecticut, Rhode Island, and New York; and the examinations therein shall be held alternately at the city of New York and the city of Boston, but first at the city of New York.

II. The second district embraces the States of New Jersey, Pennsylvania, Delaware, Maryland, North Carolina, Virginia, West Virginia, and the District of Columbia; and the examinations therein shall be held at Washington.

III. The third district embraces the States of Ohio, Michigan, Indiana, Wisconsin, and Kentucky; and the examinations therein shall be held alternately at Cincinnati and Detroit, but first at Cincinnati.

IV. The fourth district embraces the States of Illinois, Missouri, Minnesota, Iowa, Kansas, Nebraska, Nevada, California, and Oregon, and also all the Territories except New Mexico and the District of Columbia; and the examinations therein shall be held at St. Louis.

V. The fifth district embraces the States of South Carolina, Georgia, Florida, Alabama, Mississippi, Arkansas, Louisiana, Texas, and Tennessee, together with the Territory of New Mexico; and the examinations therein shall be held alternately at the city of Savannah and the city of Memphis, but first at the city of Savannah.

(2) That in each of said districts examinations for admission to the civil service at Washington shall be conducted as hereinafter provided; and those whose residence is within any such district at the time of filing the application for examination shall be regarded as belonging to such district in reference both to competition and to appointments; and each district shall be treated as a sphere of competition, and those so residing therein, wherever examined, shall be regarded as competing only with each other; but a person residing in any district may be allowed or notified to be examined in any other district.

(3) All applications for examination for service at Washington must be addressed

to the head of the Department at that city which the applicant desires to enter, and be in conformity to the previous rules and regulations so far as the same are not modified by this series; and every such application must be dated, must give the town or municipality as well as the State or Territory where the applicant has his legal residence, and also his post-office address.

(4) Each of the heads of Departments will cause to be kept in permanent form a register of all such applicants for his Department, to be called a "Register of applicants," and will cause such applications to be preserved on file for convenient reference.

(5) The provisions of the former rules and regulations in reference to the examining boards in the Departments and in the other local offices in the various cities, so far as consistent herewith, are continued until otherwise ordered.

(6) The President will employ or designate a suitable person to be chief examiner, whose duty it will be, subject to the supervision of the Civil Service Commission, to promote uniformity in preparing for, conducting, reporting, and grading the examinations by said boards at Washington, and to prepare for, attend, supervise, and report the examinations herein provided to be held elsewhere than at Washington.

(7) The several heads of Departments must also cause to be made in permanent form and to be preserved a "Record of persons eligible for appointment," arranging under separate headings those resident in each separate district, wherein shall be entered the names of the persons who have been examined within twelve months now last past, and who are still eligible to nomination or appointment; and to such record must from time to time be added the names of those persons who shall hereafter pass an examination which shall show them to be so eligible for nomination or appointment. And such "Record of persons eligible for appointment" shall be so kept and the names therein be so classified that all those whose residences appearing as aforesaid to be in the same districts shall be tabulated together, so as to show their relative excellence in each said district, except that the names of all those examined under the fourth rule of this series shall be separately entered upon the "Record of persons eligible for appointment" for each Department, so as to show where they reside.

(8) That the officer having the power of making nomination or appointment may resort for that purpose to those so entered in the "Record of persons eligible for appointment" as residing in either of said civil-service districts; but (except in respect of those examined under said rule 4) the method of competition heretofore provided must be regarded as applying among those so registered as residing in any such district, and as requiring the nomination and appointment to be made from some one of the three persons graded as the highest on some one of said five several arrangements of persons so eligible.

(9) At a reasonable time before any examination is to take place each head of Department will furnish the chief examiner with a list of those to be examined, and ten days before any examination is to take place in any said district, elsewhere than at Washington, notice shall be sent by mail by such chief examiner to all such applicants residing or allowed to be examined in such district, stating the time and place of such examination and the other matters of which the rules and regulations require notice to be given.

(10) For the purpose of the examinations last mentioned the said chief examiner shall receive from the several heads of Departments at Washington and from the head of any local office which may request to have any examinations made of persons for said offices the names of those who are to be examined at any place outside of Washington, and shall make a list of the same, showing the date of the filing of each application, which he shall produce at the place of examination; and the examination shall be held of all those on such list who shall duly appear and submit thereto, provided the number be not so great, in the opinion of the examining board,

as to render the examination of the whole impracticable, in which event only a reasonable number, to be selected in the order of the date of the filing of their applications, need be examined.

(11) For each place outside of Washington where such examination is to be held the President will designate persons, to be, when practicable, suitable officers of the United States, who, together with such chief examiner, or some substituted departmental examiner from Washington to be sent in his place when such chief examiner can not attend, shall constitute the board for such examination; and by said persons, or a majority thereof, of whom such chief examiner or said substitute shall be one, such examinations shall be held and certified in a uniform manner; and the time occupied by each person examined shall be noted on the examination papers. The questions to be put to those examined as applicants through the request of either head of Department or head of local office shall be such as may be provided and as might be put if all such examinations were, or were to be, conducted under the rules and regulations by the examining boards of any such Department in Washington or by any such local board.

(12) The chief examiner or his substitute shall make reports to each Department and local office separately in respect of all such persons as either said head of Department or of a local office requested to be examined, and said reports, respectively, shall be accompanied by the examination papers of those so separately reported; and the board of examiners in each Department or local office shall make up and state the excellence of each person so reported as examined, and such excellence, being not below the minimum grade of 70 per cent, shall be duly entered in the "Record of persons eligible for appointment" in the proper district or local office.

(13) The district examinations herein provided for shall be held not more than twice in any one year in the same district, except in Washington, where an examination may be held in respect of each Department as frequently as the head of such Department, subject to the approval of the President, may direct; and all persons so examined in Washington, wherever they may reside, shall be entered on the "Record of persons eligible for appointment" equally as if examined elsewhere.

(14) Whenever the entry of the name of any person has been on the "Record of persons eligible for appointment" during eighteen consecutive months, such entry shall be marked "Time expired," and such name shall not again be placed thereon except as the result of another examination.

(15) Persons who may be required to be examined for any custom-house, post-office, or other local office or place of service other than Washington may be notified by the head of such office to appear and be examined at any examination provided for under this rule; and the result of such examination shall be reported by the chief examiner or his substitute to the proper examining board for such office or place, or to the head of the local office; and such board shall enter the name, with the proper indication of the grade of excellence, among those who are to compete at any such place or office, and from whom selection, on the basis of competition, shall be made.

(16) But where the result of any examination aforesaid shall show the excellence of any such applicant to be below the minimum grade of 70 per cent (on the basis of 100 as perfect), the only entry thereof to be made in registers of the Department or of local office shall be of the words "Not eligible," which shall be written against the name of such person in the register of applicants; and such applicant shall not be again examined for any Department or office within six months of the date of the former examination.

(17) The provisions of this rule do not apply to examinations for promotion, nor do they apply to the State Department, in which examinations will be conducted under the provisions of the Executive order of March 14, 1873.

(18) Subject to the other provisions of this rule, the times of holding the exami-

nations herein provided for in the first, third, fourth, and fifth districts, respectively, shall be fixed by the chief examiner after consultation with the heads of Departments at Washington. One examination, however, shall be held in each of the last-mentioned districts prior to the 1st day of November next, and the chief examiner shall on or before that date make a report in writing to the Civil Service Commission, setting forth generally the facts in regard to the examinations referred to in this rule and appropriate suggestions for increasing their usefulness.

Rule 10.—So many of the persons employed by the President under the ninth section of the act of March 3, 1871, as are referred to in the opinion of the Attorney-General of the date of August 31, 1871, under the name of the Civil Service Commission, and are still in such employment, together with the successors of those who have resigned, and their successors, shall hereafter be regarded as composing and shall be designated as "The Civil Service Commission;" and the use of the designation "Advisory Board," as referring to such persons, will be hereafter discontinued.

GENERAL ORDERS, No. 102.

WAR DEPARTMENT,
ADJUTANT-GENERAL'S OFFICE,
Washington, October 10, 1873.

The President of the United States commands it to be made known that all soldiers who have deserted their colors, and who shall, on or before the 1st day of January, 1874, surrender themselves at any military station, shall receive a full pardon, only forfeiting the pay and allowances due them at the time of desertion, and shall be restored to duty without trial or punishment on condition that they faithfully serve through the term of their enlistment.

By order of the Secretary of War:

E. D. TOWNSEND,
Adjutant-General.

FIFTH ANNUAL MESSAGE.

EXECUTIVE MANSION, *December 1, 1873.*
To the Senate and House of Representatives:

The year that has passed since the submission of my last message to Congress has, especially during the latter part of it, been an eventful one to the country. In the midst of great national prosperity a financial crisis has occurred that has brought low fortunes of gigantic proportions; political partisanship has almost ceased to exist, especially in the agricultural regions; and, finally, the capture upon the high seas of a vessel bearing our flag has for a time threatened the most serious consequences, and has agitated the public mind from one end of the country to the other. But this, happily, now is in the course of satisfactory adjustment, honorable to both nations concerned.

The relations of the United States, however, with most of the other powers continue to be friendly and cordial. With France, Germany, Russia, Italy, and the minor European powers; with Brazil and most of the South American Republics, and with Japan, nothing has occurred during the year to demand special notice. The correspondence between the Department of State and various diplomatic representatives in or from those countries is transmitted herewith.

In executing the will of Congress, as expressed in its joint resolution of the 14th of February last, and in accordance with the provisions of the resolution, a number of "practical artisans," of "scientific men," and of "honorary commissioners" were authorized to attend the exposition at Vienna as commissioners on the part of the United States. It is believed that we have obtained the object which Congress had in view when it passed the joint resolution—"in order to enable the people of the United States to participate in the advantages of the International Exhibition of the Products of Agriculture, Manufactures, and the Fine Arts to be held at Vienna." I take pleasure in adding that the American exhibitors have received a gratifying number of diplomas and of medals.

During the exposition a conference was held at Vienna for the purpose of consultation on the systems prevailing in different countries for the protection of inventions. I authorized a representative from the Patent Office to be present at Vienna at the time when this conference was to take place, in order to aid as far as he might in securing any possible additional protection to American inventors in Europe. The report of this agent will be laid before Congress.

It is my pleasant duty to announce to Congress that the Emperor of China, on attaining his majority, received the diplomatic representatives of the Western powers in person. An account of these ceremonies and of the interesting discussions which preceded them will be found in the documents transmitted herewith. The accompanying papers show that some advance, although slight, has been made during the past year toward the suppression of the infamous Chinese cooly trade. I recommend Congress to inquire whether additional legislation be not needed on this subject.

The money awarded to the United States by the tribunal of arbitration at Geneva was paid by Her Majesty's Government a few days in advance of the time when it would have become payable according to the terms of the treaty. In compliance with the provisions of the act of March 3, 1873, it was at once paid into the Treasury, and used to redeem, so far as it might, the public debt of the United States; and the amount so redeemed was invested in a 5 per cent registered bond of the United States for $15,500,000, which is now held by the Secretary of State, subject to the future disposition of Congress.

I renew my recommendation, made at the opening of the last session of Congress, that a commission be created for the purpose of auditing and determining the amounts of the several "direct losses growing out of the destruction of vessels and their cargoes" by the *Alabama*, the *Florida*, or the *Shenandoah* after leaving Melbourne, for which the sufferers have received no equivalent or compensation, and of ascertaining the names of the persons entitled to receive compensation for the same, making the computations upon the basis indicated by the tribunal of arbitration at Geneva; and that payment of such losses be authorized to an extent not to exceed the awards of the tribunal at Geneva.

By an act approved on the 14th day of February last Congress made provision for completing, jointly with an officer or commissioner to be named by Her Britannic Majesty, the determination of so much of the boundary line between the territory of the United States and the possessions of Great Britain as was left uncompleted by the commissioners appointed under the act of Congress of August 11, 1856. Under the provisions of this act the northwest water boundary of the United States has been determined and marked in accordance with the award of the Emperor of Germany. A protocol and a copy of the map upon which the line was thus marked are contained in the papers submitted herewith.

I also transmit a copy of the report of the commissioner for marking the northern boundary between the United States and the British possessions west of the Lake of the Woods, of the operations of the commission during the past season. Surveys have been made to a point 497 miles west of the Lake of the Woods, leaving about 350 miles to be surveyed, the field work of which can be completed during the next season.

The mixed commission organized under the provisions of the treaty of Washington for settling and determining the claims of citizens of either power against the other arising out of acts committed against their persons or property during the period between April 13, 1861, and April 9, 1865, made its final award on the 25th day of September last. It was awarded that the Government of the United States should pay to the Government of Her Britannic Majesty, within twelve months from the date of the award, the sum of $1,929,819 in gold. The commission disallowed or dismissed all other claims of British subjects against the United States. The amount of the claims presented by the British Government, but disallowed or dismissed, is understood to be about $93,000,000. It also disallowed all the claims of citizens of the United States against Great Britain which were referred to it.

I recommend the early passage of an act appropriating the amount necessary to pay this award against the United States.

I have caused to be communicated to the Government of the King of Italy the thanks of this Government for the eminent services rendered by Count Corti as the third commissioner on this commission. With dignity, learning, and impartiality he discharged duties requiring great labor and constant patience, to the satisfaction, I believe, of both Governments. I recommend legislation to create a special court, to consist of three judges, who shall be empowered to hear and determine all claims of aliens upon the United States arising out of acts committed against their persons or property during the insurrection. The recent reference under the treaty of Washington was confined to claims of British subjects arising during the period named in the treaty; but it is understood that there are other British claims of a similar nature, arising after the 9th of April, 1865, and it is known that other claims of a like nature are advanced by citizens or subjects of other powers. It is desirable to have these claims also examined and disposed of.

Official information being received from the Dutch Government of a state of war between the King of the Netherlands and the Sultan of Acheen, the officers of the United States who were near the seat of the war were instructed to observe an impartial neutrality. It is believed that they have done so.

The joint commission under the convention with Mexico of 1868, having again been legally prolonged, has resumed its business, which, it is hoped, may be brought to an early conclusion. The distinguished representative of Her Britannic Majesty at Washington has kindly consented, with the approval of his Government, to assume the arduous and responsible duties of umpire in this commission, and to lend the weight of his character and name to such decisions as may not receive the acquiescence of both the arbitrators appointed by the respective Governments.

The commissioners appointed pursuant to the authority of Congress to examine into the nature and extent of the forays by trespassers from that country upon the herds of Texas have made a report, which will be submitted for your consideration.

The Venezuelan Government has been apprised of the sense of Congress in regard to the awards of the joint commission under the convention of 25th April, 1866, as expressed in the act of the 25th of February last.

It is apprehended that that Government does not realize the character of its obligations under that convention. As there is reason to believe, however, that its hesitancy in recognizing them springs, in part at least, from real difficulty in discharging them in connection with its obligations to other governments, the expediency of further forbearance on our part is believed to be worthy of your consideration.

The Ottoman Government and that of Egypt have latterly shown a disposition to relieve foreign consuls of the judicial powers which heretofore they have exercised in the Turkish dominions, by organizing other tribunals. As Congress, however, has by law provided for the discharge of judicial functions by consuls of the United States in that quarter under the treaty of 1830, I have not felt at liberty formally to accept the proposed change without the assent of Congress, whose decision upon the subject at as early a period as may be convenient is earnestly requested.

I transmit herewith, for the consideration and determination of Congress, an application of the Republic of Santo Domingo to this Government to exercise a protectorate over that Republic.

Since the adjournment of Congress the following treaties with foreign powers have been proclaimed: A naturalization convention with Denmark; a convention with Mexico for renewing the Claims Commission; a convention of friendship, commerce, and extradition with the Orange Free State, and a naturalization convention with Ecuador.

I renew the recommendation made in my message of December, 1870, that Congress authorize the Postmaster-General to issue all commissions to officials appointed through his Department.

I invite the earnest attention of Congress to the existing laws of the United States respecting expatriation and the election of nationality by individuals. Many citizens of the United States reside permanently abroad with their families. Under the provisions of the act approved February 10, 1855, the children of such persons are to be deemed and taken to be citizens of the United States, but the rights of citizenship are not to descend to persons whose fathers never resided in the United States.

It thus happens that persons who have never resided within the United States have been enabled to put forward a pretension to the protection of the United States against the claim to military service of the government under whose protection they were born and have been reared. In some cases even naturalized citizens of the United States have returned to the land of their birth, with intent to remain there, and their children, the issue of a marriage contracted there after their return, and who have never been in the United States, have laid claim to our protection when the lapse of many years had imposed upon them the duty of military service to the only government which had ever known them personally.

Until the year 1868 it was left, embarrassed by conflicting opinions of courts and of jurists, to determine how far the doctrine of perpetual allegiance derived from our former colonial relations with Great Britain was applicable to American citizens. Congress then wisely swept these doubts away by enacting that—

Any declaration, instruction, opinion, order, or decision of any officer of this Government which denies, restricts, impairs, or questions the right of expatriation is inconsistent with the fundamental principles of this Government.

But Congress did not indicate in that statute, nor has it since done so, what acts are to be deemed to work expatriation. For my own guidance in determining such questions I required (under the provisions of the Constitution) the opinion in writing of the principal officer in each of the Executive Departments upon certain questions relating to this subject. The result satisfies me that further legislation has become necessary. I therefore commend the subject to the careful consideration of

Congress, and I transmit herewith copies of the several opinions of the principal officers of the Executive Departments, together with other correspondence and pertinent information on the same subject.

The United States, who led the way in the overthrow of the feudal doctrine of perpetual allegiance, are among the last to indicate how their own citizens may elect another nationality. The papers submitted herewith indicate what is necessary to place us on a par with other leading nations in liberality of legislation on this international question. We have already in our treaties assented to the principles which would need to be embodied in laws intended to accomplish such results. We have agreed that citizens of the United States may cease to be citizens and may voluntarily render allegiance to other powers. We have agreed that residence in a foreign land without intent to return, shall of itself work expatriation. We have agreed in some instances upon the length of time necessary for such continued residence to work a presumption of such intent. I invite Congress now to mark out and define when and how expatriation can be accomplished; to regulate by law the condition of American women marrying foreigners; to fix the status of children born in a foreign country of American parents residing more or less permanently abroad, and to make rules for determining such other kindred points as may seem best to Congress.

In compliance with the request of Congress, I transmitted to the American minister at Madrid, with instructions to present it to the Spanish Government, the joint resolution approved on the 3d of March last, tendering to the people of Spain, in the name and on the behalf of the American people, the congratulations of Congress upon the efforts to consolidate in Spain the principles of universal liberty in a republican form of government.

The existence of this new Republic was inaugurated by striking the fetters from the slaves in Porto Rico. This beneficent measure was followed by the release of several thousand persons illegally held as slaves in Cuba. Next, the Captain-General of that colony was deprived of the power to set aside the orders of his superiors at Madrid, which had pertained to the office since 1825. The sequestered estates of American citizens, which had been the cause of long and fruitless correspondence, were ordered to be restored to their owners. All these liberal steps were taken in the face of a violent opposition directed by the reactionary slaveholders of Havana, who are vainly striving to stay the march of ideas which has terminated slavery in Christendom, Cuba only excepted. Unhappily, however, this baneful influence has thus far succeeded in defeating the efforts of all liberal-minded men in Spain to abolish slavery in Cuba, and in preventing the promised reform in that island. The struggle for political supremacy continues there.

The proslavery and aristocratic party in Cuba is gradually arraigning itself in more and more open hostility and defiance of the home government, while it still maintains a political connection with the Republic in the peninsula; and although usurping and defying the authority of the home government whenever such usurpation or defiance tends in the direction of oppression or of the maintenance of abuses, it is still a power in Madrid, and is recognized by the Government. Thus an element more dangerous to continued colonial relations between Cuba and Spain than that which inspired the insurrection at Yara—an element opposed to granting any relief from misrule and abuse, with no aspirations after freedom, commanding no sympathies in generous breasts, aiming to rivet still stronger the shackles of slavery and oppression—has seized many of the emblems of power in Cuba, and, under professions of loyalty to the mother country, is exhausting the resources of the island, and is doing acts which are at variance with those principles of justice, of liberality, and of right which give nobility of character to a republic. In the interests of humanity, of civilization, and of progress, it is to be hoped that this evil influence may be soon averted.

The steamer *Virginius* was on the 26th day of September, 1870, duly registered at the port of New York as a part of the commercial marine of the United States. On the 4th of October, 1870, having received the certificate of her register in the usual legal form, she sailed from the port of New York and has not since been within the territorial jurisdiction of the United States. On the 31st day of October last, while sailing under the flag of the United States on the high seas, she was forcibly seized by the Spanish gunboat *Tornado*, and was carried into the port of Santiago de Cuba, where fifty-three of her passengers and crew were inhumanly, and, so far at least as relates to those who were citizens of the United States, without due process of law, put to death.

It is a well-established principle, asserted by the United States from the beginning of their national independence, recognized by Great Britain and other maritime powers, and stated by the Senate in a resolution passed unanimously on the 16th of June, 1858, that—

American vessels on the high seas in time of peace, bearing the American flag, remain under the jurisdiction of the country to which they belong, and therefore any visitation, molestation, or detention of such vessel by force, or by the exhibition of force, on the part of a foreign power is in derogation of the sovereignty of the United States.

In accordance with this principle, the restoration of the *Virginius* and the surrender of the survivors of her passengers and crew, and a due reparation to the flag, and the punishment of the authorities who had been guilty of the illegal acts of violence, were demanded. The Spanish Government has recognized the justice of the demand, and has arranged for the immediate delivery of the vessel, and for the surrender of the survivors of the passengers and crew, and for a salute to the flag, and for proceedings looking to the punishment of those who may be proved to have been guilty of illegal acts of violence toward citizens of the United States, and also toward indemnifying those who may be shown to be entitled to indemnity. A copy of a protocol of a conference between the Secretary of State and the Spanish minister, in which the terms of this arrangement were agreed to, is transmitted herewith.

The correspondence on this subject with the legation of the United States in Madrid was conducted in cipher and by cable, and needs the verification of the actual text of the correspondence. It has seemed to me to be due to the importance of the case not to submit this correspondence until the accurate text can be received by mail. It is expected shortly, and will be submitted when received.

In taking leave of this subject for the present I wish to renew the expression of my conviction that the existence of African slavery in Cuba is a principal cause of the lamentable condition of the island. I do not doubt that Congress shares with me the hope that it will soon be made to disappear, and that peace and prosperity may follow its abolition.

The embargoing of American estates in Cuba, cruelty to American citizens detected in no act of hostility to the Spanish Government, the murdering of prisoners taken with arms in their hands, and, finally, the capture upon the high seas of a vessel sailing under the United States flag and bearing a United States registry have culminated in an outburst of indignation that has seemed for a time to threaten war. Pending negotiations between the United States and the Government of Spain on the subject of this capture, I have authorized the Secretary of the Navy to put our Navy on a war footing, to the extent, at least, of the entire annual appropriation for that branch of the service, trusting to Congress and the public opinion of the American people to justify my action.

Assuming from the action of the last Congress in appointing a Committee on Privileges and Elections to prepare and report to this Congress a constitutional amendment to provide a better method of electing the President and Vice-President of the United States, and also from the necessity of such an amendment, that there will be submitted to the State legislatures for ratification such an improvement in our Constitution, I suggest two others for your consideration:

First. To authorize the Executive to approve of so much of any measure passing the two Houses of Congress as his judgment may dictate, without approving the whole, the disapproved portion or portions to be subjected to the same rules as now, to wit, to be referred back to the House in which the measure or measures originated, and, if passed by a two-thirds vote of the two Houses, then to become a law without the approval of the President. I would add to this a provision that there should be no legislation by Congress during the last twenty-four hours of its sitting, except upon vetoes, in order to give the Executive an opportunity to examine and approve or disapprove bills understandingly.

Second. To provide by amendment that when an extra session of

Congress is convened by Executive proclamation legislation during the continuance of such extra session shall be confined to such subjects as the Executive may bring before it from time to time in writing.

The advantages to be gained by these two amendments are too obvious for me to comment upon them. One session in each year is provided for by the Constitution, in which there are no restrictions as to the subjects of legislation by Congress. If more are required, it is always in the power of Congress, during their term of office, to provide for sessions at any time. The first of these amendments would protect the public against the many abuses and waste of public moneys which creep into appropriation bills and other important measures passing during the expiring hours of Congress, to which otherwise due consideration can not be given.

TREASURY DEPARTMENT.

The receipts of the Government from all sources for the last fiscal year were $333,738,204, and expenditures on all accounts $290,345,245, thus showing an excess of receipts over expenditures of $43,392,959. But it is not probable that this favorable exhibit will be shown for the present fiscal year. Indeed, it is very doubtful whether, except with great economy on the part of Congress in making appropriations and the same economy in administering the various Departments of Government, the revenues will not fall short of meeting actual expenses, including interest on the public debt.

I commend to Congress such economy, and point out two sources where it seems to me it might commence, to wit, in the appropriations for public buildings in the many cities where work has not yet been commenced; in the appropriations for river and harbor improvement in those localities where the improvements are of but little benefit to general commerce, and for fortifications.

There is a still more fruitful source of expenditure, which I will point out later in this message. I refer to the easy method of manufacturing claims for losses incurred in suppressing the late rebellion.

I would not be understood here as opposing the erection of good, substantial, and even ornamental buildings by the Government wherever such buildings are needed. In fact, I approve of the Government owning its own buildings in all sections of the country, and hope the day is not far distant when it will not only possess them, but will erect in the capital suitable residences for all persons who now receive commutation for quarters or rent at Government expense, and for the Cabinet, thus setting an example to the States which may induce them to erect buildings for their Senators. But I would have this work conducted at a time when the revenues of the country would abundantly justify it.

The revenues have materially fallen off for the first five months of the present fiscal year from what they were expected to produce, owing to the general panic now prevailing, which commenced about the middle of September last. The full effect of this disaster, if it should not prove a "blessing in disguise," is yet to be demonstrated. In either event it is your duty to heed the lesson and to provide by wise and well-considered legislation, as far as it lies in your power, against its recurrence, and to take advantage of all benefits that may have accrued.

My own judgment is that, however much individuals may have suf-fered, one long step has been taken toward specie payments; that we can never have permanent prosperity until a specie basis is reached; and that a specie basis can not be reached and maintained until our exports, exclusive of gold, pay for our imports, interest due abroad, and other specie obligations, or so nearly so as to leave an appreciable accumulation of the precious metals in the country from the products of our mines.

The development of the mines of precious metals during the past year and the prospective development of them for years to come are gratify-ing in their results. Could but one-half of the gold extracted from the mines be retained at home, our advance toward specie payments would be rapid.

To increase our exports sufficient currency is required to keep all the industries of the country employed. Without this national as well as individual bankruptcy must ensue. Undue inflation, on the other hand, while it might give temporary relief, would only lead to inflation of prices, the impossibility of competing in our own markets for the prod-ucts of home skill and labor, and repeated renewals of present expe-riences. Elasticity to our circulating medium, therefore, and just enough of it to transact the legitimate business of the country and to keep all industries employed, is what is most to be desired. The exact medium is specie, the recognized medium of exchange the world over. That obtained, we shall have a currency of an exact degree of elasticity. If there be too much of it for the legitimate purposes of trade and com-merce, it will flow out of the country. If too little, the reverse will result. To hold what we have and to appreciate our currency to that standard is the problem deserving of the most serious consideration of Congress.

The experience of the present panic has proven that the currency of the country, based, as it is, upon the credit of the country, is the best that has ever been devised. Usually in times of such trials currency has become worthless, or so much depreciated in value as to inflate the values of all the necessaries of life as compared with the currency. Everyone holding it has been anxious to dispose of it on any terms. Now we wit-ness the reverse. Holders of currency hoard it as they did gold in former experiences of a like nature.

It is patent to the most casual observer that much more currency, or money, is required to transact the legitimate trade of the country during the fall and winter months, when the vast crops are being removed, than during the balance of the year. With our present system the amount in the country remains the same throughout the entire year, resulting in an accumulation of all the surplus capital of the country in a few centers when not employed in the moving of crops, tempted there by the offer of interest on call loans. Interest being paid, this surplus capital must earn this interest paid with a profit. Being subject to "call," it can not be loaned, only in part at best, to the merchant or manufacturer for a fixed term. Hence, no matter how much currency there might be in the country, it would be absorbed, prices keeping pace with the volume, and panics, stringency, and disasters would ever be recurring with the autumn. Elasticity in our monetary system, therefore, is the object to be attained first, and next to that, as far as possible, a prevention of the use of other people's money in stock and other species of speculation. To prevent the latter it seems to me that one great step would be taken by prohibiting the national banks from paying interest on deposits, by requiring them to hold their reserves in their own vaults, and by forcing them into resumption, though it would only be in legal-tender notes. For this purpose I would suggest the establishment of clearing houses for your consideration.

To secure the former many plans have been suggested, most, if not all, of which look to me more like inflation on the one hand, or compelling the Government, on the other, to pay interest, without corresponding benefits, upon the surplus funds of the country during the seasons when otherwise unemployed.

I submit for your consideration whether this difficulty might not be overcome by authorizing the Secretary of the Treasury to issue at any time to national banks of issue any amount of their own notes below a fixed percentage of their issue (say 40 per cent), upon the banks' depositing with the Treasurer of the United States an amount of Government bonds equal to the amount of notes demanded, the banks to forfeit to the Government, say, 4 per cent of the interest accruing on the bonds so pledged during the time they remain with the Treasurer as security for the increased circulation, the bonds so pledged to be redeemable by the banks at their pleasure, either in whole or in part, by returning their own bills for cancellation to an amount equal to the face of the bonds withdrawn. I would further suggest for your consideration the propriety of authorizing national banks to diminish their standing issue at pleasure, by returning for cancellation their own bills and withdrawing so many United States bonds as are pledged for the bills returned.

In view of the great actual contraction that has taken place in the currency and the comparative contraction continuously going on, due to the increase of population, increase of manufactories and all the industries, I do not believe there is too much of it now for the dullest period of the year. Indeed, if clearing houses should be established, thus forcing redemption, it is a question for your consideration whether banking should not be made free, retaining all the safeguards now required to secure bill holders. In any modification of the present laws regulating national banks, as a further step toward preparing for resumption of specie payments, I invite your attention to a consideration of the propriety of exacting from them the retention as a part of their reserve either the whole or a part of the gold interest accruing upon the bonds pledged as security for their issue. I have not reflected enough on the bearing this might have in producing a scarcity of coin with which to pay duties on imports to give it my positive recommendation. But your attention is invited to the subject.

During the last four years the currency has been contracted, directly, by the withdrawal of 3 per cent certificates, compound-interest notes, and "seven-thirty" bonds outstanding on the 4th of March, 1869, all of which took the place of legal-tenders in the bank reserves to the extent of $63,000,000.

During the same period there has been a much larger comparative contraction of the currency. The population of the country has largely increased. More than 25,000 miles of railroad have been built, requiring the active use of capital to operate them. Millions of acres of land have been opened to cultivation, requiring capital to move the products. Manufactories have multiplied beyond all precedent in the same period of time, requiring capital weekly for the payment of wages and for the purchase of material; and probably the largest of all comparative contraction arises from the organizing of free labor in the South. Now every laborer there receives his wages, and, for want of savings banks, the greater part of such wages is carried in the pocket or hoarded until required for use.

These suggestions are thrown out for your consideration, without any recommendation that they shall be adopted literally, but hoping that the best method may be arrived at to secure such an elasticity of the currency as will keep employed all the industries of the country and prevent such an inflation as will put off indefinitely the resumption of specie payments, an object so devoutly to be wished for by all, and by none more earnestly than the class of people most directly interested—those who "earn their bread by the sweat of their brow." The decisions of Congress on this subject will have the hearty support of the Executive.

In previous messages I have called attention to the decline in American shipbuilding and recommended such legislation as would secure to us our proportion of the carrying trade. Stimulated by high rates and abundance of freight, the progress for the last year in shipbuilding has been very satisfactory. There has been an increase of about 3 per cent in the amount transported in American vessels over the amount of last year. With the reduced cost of material which has taken place, it may reasonably be hoped that this progress will be maintained, and even increased. However, as we pay about $80,000,000 per annum to foreign vessels for the transportation to a market of our surplus products, thus increasing the balance of trade against us to this amount, the subject is one worthy of your serious consideration.

"Cheap transportation" is a subject that has attracted the attention of both producers and consumers for the past few years, and has contributed to, if it has not been the direct cause of, the recent panic and stringency.

As Congress, at its last session, appointed a special committee to investigate this whole subject during the vacation and report at this session, I have nothing to recommend until their report is read.

There is one work, however, of a national character, in which the greater portion of the East and the West, the North and the South, are equally interested, to which I will invite your attention.

The State of New York has a canal connecting Lake Erie with tide water on the Hudson River. The State of Illinois has a similar work connecting Lake Michigan with navigable water on the Illinois River, thus making water communication inland between the East and the West and South. These great artificial water courses are the property of the States through which they pass, and pay toll to those States. Would it not be wise statesmanship to pledge these States that if they will open these canals for the passage of large vessels the General Government will look after and keep in navigable condition the great public highways with which they connect, to wit, the Overslaugh on the Hudson, the St. Clair Flats, and the Illinois and Mississippi rivers? This would be a national work; one of great value to the producers of the West and South in giving them cheap transportation for their produce to the seaboard and a market, and to the consumers in the East in giving them cheaper food, particularly of those articles of food which do not find a foreign market, and the prices of which, therefore, are not regulated by foreign demands. The advantages of such a work are too obvious for argument. I submit the subject to you, therefore, without further comment.

In attempting to regain our lost commerce and carrying trade I have heretofore called attention to the States south of us offering a field where much might be accomplished. To further this object I suggest that a small appropriation be made, accompanied with authority for the Secretary of the Navy to fit out a naval vessel to ascend the Amazon River to the mouth of the Madeira; thence to explore that river and its tributaries into Bolivia, and to report to Congress at its next session, or as soon as practicable, the accessibility of the country by water, its resources, and the population so reached. Such an exploration would cost but little; it can do no harm, and may result in establishing a trade of value to both nations.

In further connection with the Treasury Department I would recommend a revision and codification of the tariff laws and the opening of more mints for coining money, with authority to coin for such nations as may apply.

WAR DEPARTMENT.

The attention of Congress is invited to the recommendations contained in the report of the Secretary of War herewith accompanying.

The apparent great cost of supporting the Army is fully explained by this report, and I hope will receive your attention.

While inviting your general attention to all the recommendations made by the Secretary of War, there are two which I would especially invite you to consider: First, the importance of preparing for war in time of peace by providing proper armament for our seacoast defenses. Proper armament is of vastly more importance than fortifications. The latter can be supplied very speedily for temporary purposes when needed; the former can not. The second is the necessity of reopening promotion in the staff corps of the Army. Particularly is this necessity felt in the Medical, Pay, and Ordnance departments.

At this time it is necessary to employ "contract surgeons" to supply the necessary medical attendance required by the Army.

With the present force of the Pay Department it is now difficult to make the payments to troops provided for by law. Long delays in payments are productive of desertions and other demoralization, and the law prohibits the payment of troops by other than regular army paymasters.

There are now sixteen vacancies in the Ordnance Department, thus leaving that branch of the service without sufficient officers to conduct the business of the different arsenals on a large scale if ever required.

NAVY DEPARTMENT.

During the past year our Navy has been depleted by the sale of some vessels no longer fit for naval service and by the condemnation of others not yet disposed of. This, however, has been more than compensated for by the repair of six of the old wooden ships and by the building of eight new sloops of war, authorized by the last Congress. The building of these latter has occurred at a doubly fortunate time. They are about being completed at a time when they may possibly be much needed, and the work upon them has not only given direct employment to thousands of men, but has no doubt been the means of keeping open establishments for other work at a time of great financial distress.

Since the commencement of the last month, however, the distressing occurrences which have taken place in the waters of the Caribbean Sea, almost on our very seaboard, while they illustrate most forcibly the necessity always existing that a nation situated like ours should maintain in a state of possible efficiency a navy adequate to its responsibilities, has at the same time demanded that all the effective force we really have

WAR VESSELS OF 1874

THE NAVY IN 1874

For a brief interval at the end of the Civil War, the monitors made our Navy the most powerful in the world. Then Congressional parsimony prevented the construction of new vessels and by denying the money necessary to make repairs, sent the war-worn veterans to the scrapheap. Before 1874 our Navy was the laughingstock of the world. Our naval weakness explains the several embroglios we got into with Cuban and Spanish authorities, who seized our vessels, arrested our consuls and shot our citizens with impunity. These incidents and the continual agitation of the subject by naval authorities at last converted the public. The Secretary of the Navy appointed a Board, of which John Rodgers was the head, to consider and report on the state of the Navy. That Board reported that the situation of the United States required a force of twenty-one battle-ships, seventy cruisers and numerous rams and torpedo-boats. Congress, profoundly moved, ordered the construction of one ram, which proved to be useless. The people were not satisfied, and Congress was forced to vote money for two cruisers. This disclosed the fact that the country did not contain a shipyard, a steel mill or rifling plant capable of doing the work. It was not until 1890 that we really began to build the new Navy, for in that year the lamented *Maine* was launched.

The story of the Navy is told in the article entitled " Navy," and " Navy Department," in the index (volume eleven). Our Presidents have always recognized the folly of unpreparedness and their recommendations regarding our naval power are especially valuable. The article, " Virginius, The," relates an incident of Spanish effrontery that occurred in 1873.

shall be put in immediate readiness for warlike service. This has been and is being done promptly and effectively, and I am assured that all the available ships and every authorized man of the American Navy will be ready for whatever action is required for the safety of our citizens or the maintenance of our honor. This, of course, will require the expenditure in a short time of some of the appropriations which were calculated to extend through the fiscal year, but Congress will, I doubt not, understand and appreciate the emergency, and will provide adequately not only for the present preparation, but for the future maintenance of our naval force. The Secretary of the Navy has during the past year been quietly putting some of our most effective monitors in condition for service, and thus the exigency finds us in a much better condition for work than we could possibly have been without his action.

POST-OFFICE DEPARTMENT.

A complete exhibit is presented in the accompanying report of the Postmaster-General of the operations of the Post-Office Department during the year. The ordinary postal revenues for the fiscal year ended June 30, 1873, amounted to $22,996,741.57, and the expenditures of all kinds to $29,084,945.67. The increase of revenues over 1872 was $1,081,315.20, and the increase of expenditures $2,426,753.36.

Independent of the payments made from special appropriations for mail steamship lines, the amount drawn from the General Treasury to meet deficiencies was $5,265,475. The constant and rapid extension of our postal service, particularly upon railways, and the improved facilities for the collection, transmission, distribution, and delivery of the mails which are constantly being provided account for the increased expenditures of this popular branch of the public service.

The total number of post-offices in operation on June 30, 1873, was 33,244, a net increase of 1,381 over the number reported the preceding year. The number of Presidential offices was 1,363, an increase of 163 during the year. The total length of railroad mail routes at the close of the year was 63,457 miles, an increase of 5,546 miles over the year 1872. Fifty-nine railway post-office lines were in operation June 30, 1873, extending over 14,866 miles of railroad routes and performing an aggregate service of 34,925 miles daily.

The number of letters exchanged with foreign countries was 27,459,-185, an increase of 3,096,685 over the previous year, and the postage thereon amounted to $2,021,310.86. The total weight of correspondence exchanged in the mails with European countries exceeded 912 tons, an increase of 92 tons over the previous year. The total cost of the United States ocean steamship service, including $725,000 paid from special appropriations to subsidized lines of mail steamers, was $1,047,271.35.

New or additional postal conventions have been concluded with Sweden, Norway, Belgium, Germany, Canada, Newfoundland, and Japan, reducing postage rates on correspondence exchanged with those countries; and further efforts have been made to conclude a satisfactory postal convention with France, but without success.

I invite the favorable consideration of Congress to the suggestions and recommendations of the Postmaster-General for an extension of the free-delivery system in all cities having a population of not less than 10,000; for the prepayment of postage on newspapers and other printed matter of the second class; for a uniform postage and limit of weight on miscellaneous matter; for adjusting the compensation of all postmasters not appointed by the President, by the old method of commissions on the actual receipts of the office, instead of the present mode of fixing the salary in advance upon special returns; and especially do I urge favorable action by Congress on the important recommendations of the Postmaster-General for the establishment of United States postal savings depositories.

Your attention is also again called to a consideration of the question of postal telegraphs and the arguments adduced in support thereof, in the hope that you may take such action in connection therewith as in your judgment will most contribute to the best interests of the country.

DEPARTMENT OF JUSTICE.

Affairs in Utah require your early and special attention. The Supreme Court of the United States, in the case of Clinton *vs.* Englebrecht, decided that the United States marshal of that Territory could not lawfully summon jurors for the district courts; and those courts hold that the Territorial marshal can not lawfully perform that duty, because he is elected by the legislative assembly, and not appointed as provided for in the act organizing the Territory. All proceedings at law are practically abolished by these decisions, and there have been but few or no jury trials in the district courts of that Territory since the last session of Congress. Property is left without protection by the courts, and crimes go unpunished. To prevent anarchy there it is absolutely necessary that Congress provide the courts with some mode of obtaining jurors, and I recommend legislation to that end, and also that the probate courts of the Territory, now assuming to issue writs of injunction and *habeas corpus* and to try criminal cases and questions as to land titles, be denied all jurisdiction not possessed ordinarily by courts of that description.

I have become impressed with the belief that the act approved March 2, 1867, entitled "An act to establish a uniform system of bankruptcy throughout the United States," is productive of more evil than good at this time. Many considerations might be urged for its total repeal, but, if this is not considered advisable, I think it will not be seriously questioned that those portions of said act providing for what is called involuntary bankruptcy operate to increase the financial embarrassments of the country. Careful and prudent men very often become involved in debt in the transaction of their business, and though they may possess ample property, if it could be made available for that purpose, to meet all their liabilities, yet, on account of the extraordinary scarcity of money, they may be unable to meet all their pecuniary obligations as they become due, in consequence of which they are liable to be prostrated in their business by proceedings in bankruptcy at the instance of unrelenting creditors. People are now so easily alarmed as to monetary matters that the mere filing of a petition in bankruptcy by an unfriendly creditor will necessarily embarrass, and oftentimes accomplish the financial ruin, of a responsible business man. Those who otherwise might make lawful and just arrangements to relieve themselves from difficulties produced by the present stringency in money are prevented by their constant exposure to attack and disappointment by proceedings against them in bankruptcy, and, besides, the law is made use of in many cases by obdurate creditors to frighten or force debtors into a compliance with their wishes and into acts of injustice to other creditors and to themselves. I recommend that so much of said act as provides for involuntary bankruptcy on account of the suspension of payment be repealed.

Your careful attention is invited to the subject of claims against the Government and to the facilities afforded by existing laws for their prosecution. Each of the Departments of State, Treasury, and War has demands for many millions of dollars upon its files, and they are rapidly accumulating. To these may be added those now pending before Congress, the Court of Claims, and the Southern Claims Commission, making in the aggregate an immense sum. Most of these grow out of the rebellion, and are intended to indemnify persons on both sides for their losses during the war; and not a few of them are fabricated and supported by false testimony. Projects are on foot, it is believed, to induce Congress to provide for new classes of claims, and to revive old ones through the repeal or modification of the statute of limitations, by which they are now barred. I presume these schemes, if proposed, will be received with little favor by Congress, and I recommend that persons having claims against the United States cognizable by any tribunal or Department thereof be required to present them at an early day, and that legislation be directed as far as practicable to the defeat of unfounded and unjust demands upon the Government; and I would suggest, as a means of preventing fraud, that witnesses be called upon to appear in person to testify before those tribunals having said claims before them for adjudication. Probably the largest saving to the National Treasury can be secured by timely legislation on these subjects of any of the economic measures that will be proposed.

You will be advised of the operations of the Department of Justice by the report of the Attorney-General, and I invite your attention to the amendments of existing laws suggested by him, with the view of reducing the expenses of that Department.

DEPARTMENT OF THE INTERIOR.

The policy inaugurated toward the Indians at the beginning of the last Administration has been steadily pursued, and, I believe, with beneficial results. It will be continued with only such modifications as time and experience may demonstrate as necessary.

With the encroachment of civilization upon the Indian reservations and hunting grounds, disturbances have taken place between the Indians and whites during the past year, and probably will continue to do so until each race appreciates that the other has rights which must be respected.

The policy has been to collect the Indians as rapidly as possible on reservations, and as far as practicable within what is known as the Indian Territory, and to teach them the arts of civilization and self-support. Where found off their reservations, and endangering the peace and safety of the whites, they have been punished, and will continue to be for like offenses.

The Indian Territory south of Kansas and west of Arkansas is sufficient in area and agricultural resources to support all the Indians east of the Rocky Mountains. In time, no doubt, all of them, except a few who may elect to make their homes among white people, will be collected there. As a preparatory step for this consummation, I am now satisfied that a Territorial form of government should be given them, which will secure the treaty rights of the original settlers and protect their homesteads from alienation for a period of twenty years.

The operations of the Patent Office are growing to such a magnitude and the accumulation of material is becoming so great that the necessity of more room is becoming more obvious day by day. I respectfully invite your attention to the reports of the Secretary of the Interior and Commissioner of Patents on this subject.

The business of the General Land Office exhibits a material increase in all its branches during the last fiscal year. During that time there were disposed of out of the public lands 13,030,606 acres, being an amount greater by 1,165,631 acres than was disposed of during the preceding year. Of the amount disposed of, 1,626,266 acres were sold for cash, 214,940 acres were located with military land warrants, 3,793,612 acres were taken for homesteads, 653,446 acres were located with agricultural-college scrip, 6,083,536 acres were certified by railroads, 76,576 acres were granted to wagon roads, 238,548 acres were approved to States as swamp lands, 138,681 acres were certified for agricultural colleges, common schools, universities, and seminaries, 190,775 acres were approved to States for internal improvements, and 14,222 acres were located with Indian scrip. The cash receipts during the same time were $3,408,-515.50, being $190,415.50 in excess of the receipts of the previous year. During the year 30,488,132 acres of public land were surveyed, an increase over the amount surveyed the previous year of 1,037,193 acres, and, added to the area previously surveyed, aggregates 616,554,895 acres which have been surveyed, leaving 1,218,443,505 acres of the public land still unsurveyed.

The increased and steadily increasing facilities for reaching our unoccupied public domain and for the transportation of surplus products enlarge the available field for desirable homestead locations, thus stimulating settlement and extending year by year in a gradually increasing ratio the area of occupation and cultivation.

The expressed desire of the representatives of a large colony of citizens of Russia to emigrate to this country, as is understood, with the consent of their Government, if certain concessions can be made to enable them to settle in a compact colony, is of great interest, as going to show the light in which our institutions are regarded by an industrious, intelligent, and wealthy people, desirous of enjoying civil and religious liberty; and the acquisition of so large an immigration of citizens of a superior class would without doubt be of substantial benefit to the country. I invite attention to the suggestion of the Secretary of the Interior in this behalf.

There was paid during the last fiscal year for pensions, including the expense of disbursement, $29,185,289.62, being an amount less by $984,050.98 than was expended for the same purpose the preceding year. Although this statement of expenditures would indicate a material reduction in amount compared with the preceding year, it is believed that the changes in the pension laws at the last session of Congress will absorb that amount the current year. At the close of the last fiscal year there were on the pension rolls 99,804 invalid military pensioners and 112,088 widows, orphans, and dependent relatives of deceased soldiers, making a total of that class of 211,892; 18,266 survivors of the War of 1812 and 5,053 widows of soldiers of that war pensioned under the act of Congress of February 14, 1871, making a total of that class of 23,319; 1,430 invalid navy pensioners and 1,770 widows, orphans, and dependent relatives of deceased officers, sailors, and marines of the Navy, making a total of navy pensioners of 3,200, and a grand total of pensioners of all classes of 238,411, showing a net increase during the last fiscal year of 6,182. During the last year the names of 16,405 pensioners were added to the rolls, and 10,223 names were dropped therefrom for various causes.

The system adopted for the detection of frauds against the Government in the matter of pensions has been productive of satisfactory results, but legislation is needed to provide, if possible, against the perpetration of such frauds in future.

The evidently increasing interest in the cause of education is a most encouraging feature in the general progress and prosperity of the country, and the Bureau of Education is earnest in its efforts to give proper direction to the new appliances and increased facilities which are being offered to aid the educators of the country in their great work.

The Ninth Census has been completed, the report thereof published and distributed, and the working force of the Bureau disbanded. The Secretary of the Interior renews his recommendation for a census to be taken in 1875, to which subject the attention of Congress is invited. The original suggestion in that behalf has met with the general approval of the country; and even if it be not deemed advisable at present to provide for a regular quinquennial census, a census taken in 1875, the report of which could be completed and published before the one hundredth anniversary of our national independence, would be especially interesting and valuable, as showing the progress of the country during the first century of our national existence. It is believed, however, that a regular census every five years would be of substantial benefit to the country, inasmuch as our growth hitherto has been so rapid that the results of the decennial census are necessarily unreliable as a basis of estimates for the latter years of a decennial period.

DISTRICT OF COLUMBIA.

Under the very efficient management of the governor and the board of public works of this District the city of Washington is rapidly assuming the appearance of a capital of which the nation may well be proud. From being a most unsightly place three years ago, disagreeable to pass through in summer in consequence of the dust arising from unpaved streets, and almost impassable in the winter from the mud, it is now one of the most sightly cities in the country, and can boast of being the best paved. The work has been done systematically, the plans, grades, location of sewers, water and gas mains being determined upon before the work was commenced, thus securing permanency when completed. I question whether so much has ever been accomplished before in any American city for the same expenditures. The Government having large reservations in the city, and the nation at large having an interest in their capital, I recommend a liberal policy toward the District of Columbia, and that the Government should bear its just share of the expense of these improvements. Every citizen visiting the capital feels a pride in its growing beauty, and that he too is part owner in the investments made here.

I would suggest to Congress the propriety of promoting the establishment in this District of an institution of learning, or university of the highest class, by the donation of lands. There is no place better suited for such an institution than the national capital. There is no other place in which every citizen is so directly interested.

CIVIL-SERVICE REFORM.

In three successive messages to Congress I have called attention to the subject of "civil-service reform."

Action has been taken so far as to authorize the appointment of a board to devise rules governing methods of making appointments and promotions, but there never has been any action making these rules, or any rules, binding, or even entitled to observance, where persons desire the appointment of a friend or the removal of an official who may be disagreeable to them.

To have any rules effective they must have the acquiescence of Congress as well as of the Executive. I commend, therefore, the subject to your attention, and suggest that a special committee of Congress might confer with the Civil-Service Board during the present session for the purpose of devising such rules as can be maintained, and which will secure the services of honest and capable officials, and which will also protect them in a degree of independence while in office.

Proper rules will protect Congress, as well as the Executive, from much needless persecution, and will prove of great value to the public at large.

I would recommend for your favorable consideration the passage of an enabling act for the admission of Colorado as a State in the Union. It possesses all the elements of a prosperous State, agricultural and mineral, and, I believe, has a population now to justify such admission. In connection with this I would also recommend the encouragement of a canal for purposes of irrigation from the eastern slope of the Rocky Mountains to the Missouri River. As a rule I am opposed to further donations of public lands for internal improvements owned and controlled by private corporations, but in this instance I would make an exception. Between the Missouri River and the Rocky Mountains there is an arid belt of public land from 300 to 500 miles in width, perfectly valueless for the occupation of man, for the want of sufficient rain to secure the growth of any product. An irrigating canal would make productive a belt as wide as the supply of water could be made to spread over across this entire country, and would secure a cordon of settlements connecting the present population of the mountain and mining regions with that of the older States. All the land reclaimed would be clear gain. If alternate sections are retained by the Government, I would suggest that the retained sections be thrown open to entry under the homestead laws, or sold to actual settlers for a very low price.

I renew my previous recommendation to Congress for general amnesty. The number engaged in the late rebellion yet laboring under disabilities is very small, but enough to keep up a constant irritation. No possible danger can accrue to the Government by restoring them to eligibility to hold office.

I suggest for your consideration the enactment of a law to better secure the civil rights which freedom should secure, but has not effectually secured, to the enfranchised slave.

U. S. GRANT.

SPECIAL MESSAGES.

WASHINGTON, *December 2, 1873.*

To the Senate and House of Representatives:

I herewith transmit to Congress a report, dated the 2d instant, with accompanying papers,* received from the Secretary of State, in compliance with the requirements of the sixteenth and eighteenth sections of the act entitled "An act to regulate the diplomatic and consular systems of the United States," approved August 18, 1856.

U. S. GRANT.

WASHINGTON, *January 5, 1874.*

To the Senate of the United States:

I transmit, for the consideration of the Senate with a view to ratification, a convention for the surrender of criminals between the United States of America and the Republic of Honduras, which was signed at Comayagua on the 4th day of June, 1873.

U. S. GRANT.

WASHINGTON, *January 5, 1874.*

To the Senate and House of Representatives:

In my annual message of December last I gave reason to expect that when the full and accurate text of the correspondence relating to the steamer *Virginius*, which had been telegraphed in cipher, should be received the papers concerning the capture of the vessel, the execution of a part of its passengers and crew, and the restoration of the ship and the survivors would be transmitted to Congress.

In compliance with the expectations then held out, I now transmit the papers and correspondence on that subject.

On the 26th day of September, 1870, the *Virginius* was registered in the custom-house at New York as the property of a citizen of the United States, he having first made oath, as required by law, that he was "the true and only owner of the said vessel, and that there was no subject or citizen of any foreign prince or state, directly or indirectly, by way of trust, confidence, or otherwise, interested therein."

Having complied with the requisites of the statute in that behalf, she cleared in the usual way for the port of Curaçoa, and on or about the 4th day of October, 1870, sailed for that port. It is not disputed that she made the voyage according to her clearance, nor that from that day to this she has not returned within the territorial jurisdiction of the United States. It is also understood that she preserved her American papers,

---

* Report of fees collected, etc., by consular officers of the United States for 1872, list of consular officers and their official residences, and tariff of consular fees.

and that when within foreign ports she made the practice of putting forth a claim to American nationality, which was recognized by the authorities at such ports.

When, therefore, she left the port of Kingston, in October last, under the flag of the United States, she would appear to have had, as against all powers except the United States, the right to fly that flag and to claim its protection, as enjoyed by all regularly documented vessels registered as part of our commercial marine.

No state of war existed conferring upon a maritime power the right to molest and detain upon the high seas a documented vessel, and it can not be pretended that the *Virginius* had placed herself without the pale of all law by acts of piracy against the human race.

If her papers were irregular or fraudulent, the offense was one against the laws of the United States, justiciable only in their tribunals.

When, therefore, it became known that the *Virginius* had been captured on the high seas by a Spanish man-of-war; that the American flag had been hauled down by the captors; that the vessel had been carried to a Spanish port, and that Spanish tribunals were taking jurisdiction over the persons of those found on her, and exercising that jurisdiction upon American citizens, not only in violation of the rules of international law, but in contravention of the provisions of the treaty of 1795, I directed a demand to be made upon Spain for the restoration of the vessel and for the return of the survivors to the protection of the United States, for a salute to the flag, and for the punishment of the offending parties.

The principles upon which these demands rested could not be seriously questioned, but it was suggested by the Spanish Government that there were grave doubts whether the *Virginius* was entitled to the character given her by her papers, and that therefore it might be proper for the United States, after the surrender of the vessel and the survivors, to dispense with the salute to the flag, should such fact be established to their satisfaction.

This seemed to be reasonable and just. I therefore assented to it, on the assurance that Spain would then declare that no insult to the flag of the United States had been intended.

I also authorized an agreement to be made that should it be shown to the satisfaction of this Government that the *Virginius* was improperly bearing the flag proceedings should be instituted in our courts for the punishment of the offense committed against the United States. On her part Spain undertook to proceed against those who had offended the sovereignty of the United States, or who had violated their treaty rights.

The surrender of the vessel and the survivors to the jurisdiction of the tribunals of the United States was an admission of the principles upon which our demands had been founded. I therefore had no hesitation in agreeing to the arrangement finally made between the two Governments—an arrangement which was moderate and just, and calculated to cement the good relations which have so long existed between Spain and the United States.

Under this agreement the *Virginius*, with the American flag flying, was delivered to the Navy of the United States at Bahia Honda, in the island of Cuba, on the 16th ultimo. She was then in an unseaworthy condition. In the passage to New York she encountered one of the most tempestuous of our winter storms. At the risk of their lives the officers and crew placed in charge of her attempted to keep her afloat. Their efforts were unavailing, and she sank off Cape Fear. The prisoners who survived the massacres were surrendered at Santiago de Cuba on the 18th ultimo, and reached the port of New York in safety.

The evidence submitted on the part of Spain to establish the fact that the *Virginius* at the time of her capture was improperly bearing the flag of the United States is transmitted herewith, together with the opinion of the Attorney-General thereon and a copy of the note of the Spanish minister, expressing on behalf of his Government a disclaimer of an intent of indignity to the flag of the United States.

U. S. GRANT.

WASHINGTON, *January 5, 1874.*

To the Senate of the United States:

I transmit, for the consideration of the Senate with a view to ratification, a convention between the United States of America and the Republic of Salvador, which was signed at San Salvador on the 12th of May last, stipulating for an extension of the period for exchanging the ratifications of the treaty of amity, commerce, and consular privileges concluded between the two countries on the 6th December, 1870.

U. S. GRANT.

WASHINGTON, *January 5, 1874.*

To the Senate of the United States:

I transmit, for the consideration of the Senate with a view to ratification, a convention between the United States of America and the Republic of Salvador, which was signed at San Salvador on the 12th of May last, for an extension of the period for exchanging the ratifications of the treaty for the extradition of criminals concluded between the two countries on the 23d of May, 1870.

U. S. GRANT.

WASHINGTON, *January 6, 1874.*

To the Senate of the United States:

I transmit to the Senate an "agreement," signed at Lima on the 5th of June last by Mr. Francis Thomas, envoy extraordinary and minister plenipotentiary of the United States, and Mr. José de la Riva Aguero, minister for foreign affairs of Peru, providing for an extension of the time for the exchange of the ratifications of the treaty of friendship, commerce, and navigation and the treaty of extradition between the United States and Peru of the 6th and 12th of September, 1870, respectively. The limit of the proposed extension is to be nine months from the time when the Senate of the United States may approve thereof. The expediency of this approval is consequently submitted to the consideration of the Senate. The instruments themselves were approved by that body on the 31st of March, 1871, and they were ratified by me in order that our ratifications might be ready for exchange for those of Peru. The omission of the latter seasonably to perform that act is understood to have been occasioned solely by the delay in the meeting of the Congress of that Republic, whose sanction, pursuant to its constitution, was necessary.   U. S. GRANT.

EXECUTIVE MANSION,
Washington, January 7, 1874.

To the House of Representatives:

In reply to the resolution of the House of Representatives of the 15th of last December, requesting a revision of the estimates for the expenses of the Government for the fiscal year ending June 30, 1875, I have the honor to transmit herewith amended estimates and replies from the several Departments.   U. S. GRANT.

EXECUTIVE MANSION, *January 8, 1874.*

To the Senate and House of Representatives:

In compliance with the act of Congress approved March 3, 1873, entitled "An act to authorize inquiries into the causes of steam-boiler explosions," I directed the Secretaries of the Treasury and Navy Departments to create a commission to conduct the experiments and collect the information contemplated by the act. Such a commission was created, and I have the honor to submit herewith a report of the result of their labors to the present time.   U. S. GRANT.

EXECUTIVE MANSION, *January 13, 1874.*

To the Senate of the United States:

Since nominating the Hon. Caleb Cushing for Chief Justice of the Supreme Court of the United States information has reached me which induces me to withdraw him from nomination as the highest judicial officer of the Government, and I do therefore hereby withdraw said nomination.   U. S. GRANT.

EXECUTIVE MANSION, *January 19, 1874.*
To the Senate of the United States:

In reply to the resolution of the Senate of the 8th instant, requesting information "relative to any unauthorized occupation or invasion of or encroachment upon the Indian Territory, so called, by individuals or bodies of men, in violation of treaty stipulations," I have the honor to submit herewith the reply of the Secretary of the Interior, to whom the resolution was referred.

U. S. GRANT.

WASHINGTON, *January 27, 1874.*
To the Senate of the United States:

I transmit, for the consideration of the Senate with a view to its ratification, a protocol relative to a claim on the Government of Chile in the case of the ship *Good Return.*

U. S. GRANT.

WASHINGTON, *February 6, 1874.*
To the House of Representatives:

I transmit to the House of Representatives, in answer to their resolution of the 16th ultimo, a report from the Secretary of State, with accompanying papers.*

U. S. GRANT.

WASHINGTON, *February 6, 1874.*
To the Senate and House of Representatives:

I transmit herewith a copy of a communication, dated the 22d ultimo, received from the governor of the State of New York, in which it is announced that, in accordance with the invitation of Congress as expressed in the act approved July 2, 1864, that State now presents for acceptance a bronze statue of George Clinton, deceased, one of its distinguished citizens.

U. S. GRANT.

EXECUTIVE MANSION,
Washington, February 9, 1874.
To the House of Representatives:

I have the honor to transmit herewith the report of the Secretary of the Department of the Interior, to whom was referred the resolution of the House of Representatives of January 7, requesting "a statement of the extent and nature of the contracts, purchases, and expenditures for the Indian service made since July 1, 1873, setting forth which, if any, of them were made or entered into without conference with the Board of Indian

---

* Correspondence relative to the refusal of the United States consul at Cadiz, Spain, to certify invoices of wine shipped from that port, etc

Commissioners appointed by the President, and the extent and description of contracts and vouchers objected to by said board, stating to what extent payments have been made thereon against their remonstrance.''

U. S. GRANT.

EXECUTIVE MANSION,
Washington, February 10, 1874.

To the House of Representatives:

I have the honor to transmit herewith reports from the Secretaries of the War Department and Department of the Interior, to whom were referred the resolutions of the House of Representatives of the 7th of January last, requesting ''copies of all the correspondence between the different Departments of the Government and the peace commissioners during the war with the Modoc Indians in southern Oregon and northern California during the years 1872 and 1873; also copies of all the correspondence with and orders issued to the military authorities engaged in said war up to the period of the removal of said Modoc Indians from the States of Oregon and California.''

U. S. GRANT.

WASHINGTON, *February 17, 1874.*

To the Senate and House of Representatives:

I transmit herewith a communication from the Secretary of State and accompanying papers.*

U. S. GRANT.

EXECUTIVE MANSION, *February 19, 1874.*

To the Senate and House of Representatives:

I have the honor to transmit herewith a memorial upon the ''cultivation of timber and the preservation of forests,'' and a draft of a joint resolution prepared by the American Association for the Advancement of Science, together with a communication from the Commissioner of the General Land Office upon the same subject.

U. S. GRANT.

EXECUTIVE MANSION,
Washington, February 25, 1874.

To the Senate and House of Representatives:

I have the honor herewith to submit the report of the Centennial Commissioners, and to add a word in the way of recommendation.

There have now been international expositions held by three of the great powers of Europe. It seems fitting that the one hundredth anniversary of our independence should be marked by an event that will

---

*Report of John M. Thacher, United States delegate to the International Patent Congress held at Vienna in August, 1873, and exhibits.

display to the world the growth and progress of a nation devoted to free, dom and to the pursuit of fame, fortune, and honors by the lowest citizen as well as the highest. A failure in this enterprise would be deplorable. Success can be assured by arousing public opinion to the importance of the occasion.

To secure this end, in my judgment, Congressional legislation is neces, sary to make the exposition both national and international.

The benefits to be derived from a successful international exposition are manifold. It will necessarily be accompanied by expenses beyond the receipts from the exposition itself, but they will be compensated for many fold by the commingling of people from all sections of our own country; by bringing together the people of different nationalities; by bringing into juxtaposition, for ready examination, our own and foreign skill and progress in manufactures, agriculture, art, science, and civilization.

The selection of the site for the exposition seems to me appropriate, from the fact that one hundred years before the date fixed for the exposition the Declaration of Independence, which launched us into the galaxy of nations as an independent people, emanated from the same spot.

We have much in our varied climate, soil, mineral products, and skill of which advantage can be taken by other nationalities to their profit. In return they will bring to our shores works of their skill and familiarize our people with them, to the mutual advantage of all parties.

Let us have a complete success in our Centennial Exposition or suppress it in its infancy, acknowledging our inability to give it the international character to which our self-esteem aspires.

U. S. GRANT.

EXECUTIVE MANSION,
Washington, D. C., March 4, 1874.

To the House of Representatives:

I have the honor to transmit herewith replies from the several Departments, in answer to a resolution of the House of Representatives of the 16th of January last, requesting a list of all expenses incurred by the various Departments for transportation of any matter which before the abolition of the franking privilege was carried in the mails.

U. S. GRANT.

WASHINGTON, *March 20, 1874.*

To the Senate of the United States:

I transmit herewith, for the consideration of the Senate and with a view to its ratification, a convention concluded between the United States and Belgium on the 19th March, 1874, concerning extradition.

U. S. GRANT

EXECUTIVE MANSION, *March 23, 1874.*

To the Senate and House of Representatives:

I have the honor to transmit herewith the report of the board of commissioners on the irrigation of the San Joaquin, Tulare, and Sacramento valleys, of the State of California, and also the original maps accompanying said report.

U. S. GRANT.

EXECUTIVE MANSION, *Washington, April 18, 1874.*

To the Senate and House of Representatives:

Herewith I transmit the report of the Civil Service Commission authorized by the act of Congress of March 3, 1871, and invite your special attention thereto.

If sustained by Congress, I have no doubt the rules can, after the experience gained, be so improved and enforced as to still more materially benefit the public service and relieve the Executive, members of Congress, and the heads of Departments from influences prejudicial to good administration.

The rules, as they have heretofore been enforced, have resulted beneficially, as is shown by the opinions of the members of the Cabinet and their subordinates in the Departments, and in that opinion I concur; but rules applicable to officers who are to be appointed by and with the advice and consent of the Senate are in great measure impracticable, except in so far as they may be sustained by the action of that body. This must necessarily remain so unless the direct sanction of the Senate is given to the rules.

I advise for the present only such appropriation as may be adequate to continue the work in its present form, and would leave to the future to determine whether the direct sanction of Congress should be given to rules that may, perhaps, be devised for regulating the method of selection of appointees, or a portion of them, who need to be confirmed by the Senate.

The same amount appropriated last year would be adequate for the coming year, but I think the public interest would be promoted by authority in the Executive for allowing a small compensation for special service performed beyond usual office hours, under the act of 1871, to persons already in the service of the Government.

U. S. GRANT.

WASHINGTON, *April 21, 1874.*

To the Senate and House of Representatives:

I transmit herewith to the Senate and House of Representatives a communication from the Secretary of State and the report by which it is accompanied, upon Samoan or Navigators Islands.

U. S. GRANT.

EXECUTIVE MANSION,
Washington, April 23, 1874.

To the House of Representatives:

I transmit herewith the papers called for by the resolution of the House of Representatives of the 20th instant, requesting all correspondence by telegraph or otherwise between the persons claiming to be governor of Arkansas and myself relating to the troubles in that State, together with copies of any order or directions given by me or under my direction to the military officer in charge of the garrison or in command of the United States troops at Little Rock.

U. S. GRANT.

EXECUTIVE MANSION,
Washington, April 28, 1874.

To the House of Representatives:

I have the honor to transmit herewith additional correspondence received since my communication of the 23d instant, in reply to the resolution of the House of Representatives of the 20th instant, requesting copies of correspondence between persons claiming to be governor of Arkansas and myself relating to troubles in that State.

U. S. GRANT.

EXECUTIVE MANSION,
Washington, April 30, 1874.

To the House of Representatives:

In pursuance of the resolution of the House of Representatives of the 15th instant, requesting to be informed "what geographical and geological surveys under different Departments and branches of the Government are operating in the same and contiguous areas of territory west of the Mississippi River, and whether it be not practicable to consolidate them under one Department or to define the geographical limits to be embraced by each," I have the honor to transmit herewith the views of the officers of the War and Interior Departments on the subjects named in the said resolution, and invite attention thereto.

Where surveys are made with the view of sectionizing the public lands, preparatory to opening them for settlement or entry, there is no question but such surveys and all work connected therewith should be under the direct control of the Interior Department or the Commissioner of the General Land Office, subject to the supervision of the Secretary of the Interior. But where the object is to complete the map of the country; to determine the geographical, astronomical, geodetic, topographic, hydrographic, meteorological, geological, and mineralogical features of the country—in other words, to collect full information of the unexplored or but partially known portions of the country—it seems to me a matter of no importance as to which Department of the Government should have control of the work. The conditions which should control this subject are, in my judgment, first, which Department is prepared to do the work best; second, which can do it the most expeditiously and economically.

As the country to be explored is occupied in great part by uncivilized Indians, all parties engaged in the work at hand must be supplied with escorts from the Army, thus placing a large portion of the expense upon the War Department; and as the Engineer Corps of the Army is composed of scientific gentlemen, educated and practiced for just the kind of work to be done, and as they are under pay whether employed in this work or not, it would seem that the second condition named would be more fully complied with by employing them to do the work. There is but little doubt that they will accomplish it as promptly and as well, and much more economically.

U. S. GRANT.

WASHINGTON, *May 19, 1874.*

To the House of Representatives:

I transmit herewith, in answer to the resolution of the House of Representatives of the 9th instant, a report* from the Secretary of State, with accompanying papers.

U. S. GRANT.

WASHINGTON, *May 25, 1874.*

To the Senate and House of Representatives:

In response to the resolution of the Senate of the 15th instant, I have the honor to transmit herewith "all papers and correspondence relating to the troubles in the State of Arkansas not heretofore communicated to either House of Congress."

U. S. GRANT.

WASHINGTON, *May 25, 1874.*

To the Senate and House of Representatives:

I have the honor to transmit, in response to the resolution of the Senate of the 18th instant, requesting "the answers in full received by the Civil Service Commission in reply to their circular addressed to the various heads of Departments and bureaus requesting a report as to the operation and effect of the civil-service rules in the several Departments and offices," a copy of a letter received from the chairman of the Civil Service Commission, to whom the resolution was referred.

U. S. GRANT.

*Relating to the involuntary deportation to the United States of foreign convicts, paupers, idiots, insane persons, etc., and transmitting correspondence relative thereto.

WASHINGTON, *May 26, 1874.*

To the Senate of the United States:

I transmit herewith a report from the Secretary of State, and accompanying it copies of all papers on file or on record in the Department of State respecting the claim on Brazil concerning the *Caroline.*

U. S. GRANT.

WASHINGTON, *May 26, 1874.*

To the Senate and House of Representatives:

I transmit to the Senate and House of Representatives a communication from the Secretary of State and a copy of the report of the commissioners to inquire into depredations on the frontiers of Texas, by which it is accompanied.

U. S. GRANT.

WASHINGTON, *June 15, 1874.*

To the Senate of the United States:

I transmit, for the consideration of the Senate with a view to ratification, a declaration respecting trade-marks between the United States and the Emperor of Russia, concluded and signed at St. Petersburg on the 16/28 day of March last.

U. S. GRANT.

WASHINGTON, *June 18, 1874.*

To the Senate of the United States:

The plenipotentiaries of Her Britannic Majesty at Washington have submitted to the Secretary of State, for my consideration, a draft of a treaty for the reciprocal regulation of the commerce and trade between the United States and Canada, with provisions for the enlargement of the Canadian canals and for their use by United States vessels on terms of equality with British vessels. I transmit herewith a report from the Secretary of State, with a copy of the draft thus proposed.

I am of the opinion that a proper treaty for such purposes would result beneficially for the United States. It would not only open or enlarge markets for our products, but it would increase the facilities of transportation from the grain-growing States of the West to the seaboard.

The proposed draft has many features to commend it to our favorable consideration; but whether it makes all the concessions which could justly be required of Great Britain, or whether it calls for more concessions from the United States than we should yield, I am not prepared to say.

Among its provisions are articles proposing to dispense with the arbitration respecting the fisheries, which was provided for by the treaty of Washington, in the event of the conclusion and ratification of a treaty and the passage of all the necessary legislation to enforce it.

These provisions, as well as other considerations, make it desirable that this subject should receive attention before the close of the present session. I therefore express an earnest wish that the Senate may be able to consider and determine before the adjournment of Congress whether it will give its constitutional concurrence to the conclusion of a treaty with Great Britain for the purposes already named, either in such form as is proposed by the British plenipotentiaries or in such other more acceptable form as the Senate may prefer.

U. S. GRANT.

WASHINGTON, *June 18, 1874.*

To the Senate and House of Representatives:

I transmit herewith a report from the Secretary of State and its accompanying papers.*

U. S. GRANT.

EXECUTIVE MANSION, *Washington, June 20, 1874.*

To the Senate and House of Representatives:

I respectfully invite the attention of Congress to one feature of the bill entitled "An act for the government of the District of Columbia, and for other purposes." Provision is therein made for the payment of the debts of the District in bonds to be issued by the sinking-fund commissioners, running fifty years and bearing interest at the rate of 3.65 per cent per annum, with the payment of the principal and interest guaranteed by the United States.

The government by which these debts were created is abolished, and no other provision seems to be made for their payment. Judging from the transactions in other bonds, there are good grounds, in my opinion, for the apprehension that bonds bearing this rate of interest when issued will be worth much less than their equivalent in the current money of the United States. This appears to me to be unjust to those to whom these bonds are to be paid, and, to the extent of the difference between their face and real value, looks like repudiating the debts of the District. My opinion is that to require creditors of the District of Columbia to receive these bonds at par when it is apparent that to be converted into money they must be sold at a large discount will not only prove greatly injurious to the credit of the District, but will reflect unfavorably upon the credit and good faith of the United States.

I would recommend, therefore, that provision be made at the present session of Congress to increase the interest upon these bonds, so that when sold they will bring an equivalent in money, and that the Secretary of the Treasury be authorized to negotiate the sale of these bonds at not less than par and pay the proceeds thereof to those who may be ascertained to have valid claims against the District of Columbia.

U. S. GRANT.

*Report of the United States delegates to the eighth session of the International Statistical Congress, held at St. Petersburg, Russia, in August, 1872, and appendix.

VETO MESSAGES.

EXECUTIVE MANSION,
Washington, *April 10, 1874.*

To the House of Representatives:

I have the honor to herewith return to you without my approval House bill No. 1224, entitled "An act for the relief of William H. Denniston, late an acting second lieutenant, Seventieth New York Volunteers," for the reasons set forth in the accompanying letter of the Secretary of War.

U. S. GRANT.

WAR DEPARTMENT,
Washington, D. C., *April 8, 1874.*

The PRESIDENT.

SIR: I have the honor to return House bill No. 1224, "for the relief of William H. Denniston, late an acting second lieutenant, Seventieth New York Volunteers," with the remark that the name of William H. Denniston, as an officer or private, is not borne on any rolls of the Seventieth New York Volunteers on file in the Department. Of this fact the Committee on Military Affairs of the House of Representatives was informed by letter from the Adjutant-General's Office dated December 19, 1873.

No vacancy existed in Company D (the company claimed) of this regiment for a second lieutenant during the period claimed, Second Lieutenant J. B. Zeigler having filled that position to May 6, 1862, and Second Lieutenant James Stevenson from that date to June 25, 1862. On regimental return for July, 1862, Edward Shields is reported promoted second lieutenant June 15, 1862.

There is no evidence in the Department that he actually served as a second lieutenant for the time covered by the bill herewith, and it is therefore respectfully recommended that the bill be returned to the House of Representatives without approval.

When the records of the War Department, prepared under laws and regulations having in view the establishment and preservation of data necessary to the protection of the public interests as well as that of the claimants, fail to show service, it is a subject of importance to legalize a claim wherein the military department of the Government has not seen the order under which the alleged service may have been claimed. A precedent of the kind is beyond doubt an injury to the public interest, and will tend to other special acts of relief under which thousands of muster rolls certified at the date, under the Articles of War, as exhibiting the true state of the command will be invalidated, and large appropriations of money will be required to settle claims the justness of which can not always be determined at a date so remote from their origin.

Very respectfully, your obedient servant,

WM. W. BELKNAP,
Secretary of War.

EXECUTIVE MANSION, *April 22, 1874.*

To the Senate of the United States:

Herewith I return Senate bill No. 617, entitled "An act to fix the amount of United States notes and the circulation of national banks, and for other purposes," without my approval.

In doing so I must express my regret at not being able to give my assent to a measure which has received the sanction of a majority of the legislators chosen by the people to make laws for their guidance, and I have studiously sought to find sufficient arguments to justify such assent, but unsuccessfully.

Practically it is a question whether the measure under discussion would give an additional dollar to the irredeemable paper currency of the country or not, and whether by requiring three-fourths of the reserve to be retained by the banks and prohibiting interest to be received on the balance it might not prove a contraction.

But the fact can not be concealed that theoretically the bill increases the paper circulation $100,000,000, less only the amount of reserves restrained from circulation by the provision of the second section. The measure has been supported on the theory that it would give increased circulation. It is a fair inference, therefore, that if in practice the measure should fail to create the abundance of circulation expected of it the friends of the measure, particularly those out of Congress, would clamor for such inflation as would give the expected relief.

The theory, in my belief, is a departure from true principles of finance, national interest, national obligations to creditors, Congressional promises, party pledges (on the part of both political parties), and of personal views and promises made by me in every annual message sent to Congress and in each inaugural address.

In my annual message to Congress in December, 1869, the following passages appear:

Among the evils growing out of the rebellion, and not yet referred to, is that of an irredeemable currency. It is an evil which I hope will receive your most earnest attention. It is a duty, and one of the highest duties, of Government to secure to the citizen a medium of exchange of fixed, unvarying value. This implies a return to a specie basis, and no substitute for it can be devised. It should be commenced now and reached at the earliest practicable moment consistent with a fair regard to the interests of the debtor class. Immediate resumption, if practicable, would not be desirable. It would compel the debtor class to pay, beyond their contracts, the premium on gold at the date of their purchase, and would bring bankruptcy and ruin to thousands. Fluctuation, however, in the paper value of the measure of all values (gold) is detrimental to the interests of trade. It makes the man of business an involuntary gambler, for in all sales where future payment is to be made both parties speculate as to what will be the value of the currency to be paid and received. I earnestly recommend to you, then, such legislation as will insure a gradual return to specie payments and put an immediate stop to fluctuations in the value of currency.

I still adhere to the views then expressed.

As early as December 4, 1865, the House of Representatives passed a resolution, by a vote of 144 yeas to 6 nays, concurring "in the views of the Secretary of the Treasury in relation to the necessity of a contraction of the currency, with a view to as early a resumption of specie payments as the business interests of the country will permit," and pledging "cooperative action to this end as speedily as possible."

The first act passed by the Forty-first Congress, [approved] on the 18th day of March, 1869, was as follows:

AN ACT to strengthen the public credit.

Be it enacted, etc., That in order to remove any doubt as to the purpose of the Government to discharge all just obligations to the public creditors, and to settle conflicting questions and interpretations of the law by virtue of which such obligations have been contracted, it is hereby provided and declared that the faith of the United States is solemnly pledged to the payment in coin or its equivalent of all the obligations of the United States not bearing interest, known as United States notes, and all the interest-bearing obligations of the United States, except in cases where the law authorizing the issue of any such obligation has expressly provided that the same may be paid in lawful money or in other currency than gold and silver; but none of the said interest-bearing obligations not already due shall be redeemed or paid before maturity unless at such time United States notes shall be convertible into coin at the option of the holder, or unless at such time bonds of the United States bearing a lower rate of interest than the bonds to be redeemed can be sold at par in coin. And the United States also solemnly pledges its faith to make provision at the earliest practicable period for the redemption of the United States notes in coin.

This act still remains as a continuing pledge of the faith of the United States "to make provision at the earliest practicable period for the redemption of the United States notes in coin."

A declaration contained in the act of June 30, 1864, created an obligation that the total amount of United States notes issued or to be issued should never exceed $400,000,000. The amount in actual circulation was actually reduced to $356,000,000, at which point Congress passed the act of February 4, 1868, suspending the further reduction of the currency. The forty-four millions have ever been regarded as a reserve, to be used only in case of emergency, such as has occurred on several occasions, and must occur when from any cause revenues suddenly fall below expenditures; and such a reserve is necessary, because the fractional currency, amounting to fifty millions, is redeemable in legal tender on call.

It may be said that such a return of fractional currency for redemption is impossible; but let steps be taken for a return to a specie basis and it will be found that silver will take the place of fractional currency as rapidly as it can be supplied, when the premium on gold reaches a sufficiently low point. With the amount of United States notes to be issued permanently fixed within proper limits and the Treasury so strengthened as to be able to redeem them in coin on demand it will then be safe to inaugurate a system of free banking with such provisions as to make compulsory redemption of the circulating notes of the banks in coin, or in United States notes, themselves redeemable and made equivalent to coin.

As a measure preparatory to free banking, and for placing the Government in a condition to redeem its notes in coin "at the earliest practicable period," the revenues of the country should be increased so as to pay current expenses, provide for the sinking fund required by law, and also a surplus to be retained in the Treasury in gold.

I am not a believer in any artificial method of making paper money equal to coin when the coin is not owned or held ready to redeem the promises to pay, for paper money is nothing more than promises to pay, and is valuable exactly in proportion to the amount of coin that it can be converted into. While coin is not used as a circulating medium, or the currency of the country is not convertible into it at par, it becomes an article of commerce as much as any other product. The surplus will seek a foreign market as will any other surplus. The balance of trade has nothing to do with the question. Duties on imports being required in coin creates a limited demand for gold. About enough to satisfy that demand remains in the country. To increase this supply I see no way open but by the Government hoarding through the means above given, and possibly by requiring the national banks to aid.

It is claimed by the advocates of the measure herewith returned that there is an unequal distribution of the banking capital of the country. I was disposed to give great weight to this view of the question at first, but on reflection it will be remembered that there still remains $4,000,000 of authorized bank-note circulation assigned to States having less than their quota not yet taken. In addition to this the States having less than their quota of bank circulation have the option of twenty-five millions more to be taken from those States having more than their proportion. When this is all taken up, or when specie payments are fully restored or are in rapid process of restoration, will be the time to consider the question of "more currency."

U. S. GRANT.

EXECUTIVE MANSION,
Washington, May 12, 1874.

To the House of Representatives:

I return herewith without my signature House bill No. 1331, entitled "An act for the relief of Joab Spencer and James R. Mead for supplies furnished the Kansas tribe of Indians." I withheld my approval of said bill for reasons which satisfy me the claim should not be allowed for the entire amount stated in the bill, and which are set forth in the letter of the Secretary of the Interior of the 7th instant, a copy of which, with the accompanying papers, is herewith transmitted.

U. S. GRANT.

DEPARTMENT OF THE INTERIOR,
Washington, D. C., May 7, 1874.

The PRESIDENT.

SIR: I have the honor to return herewith engrossed bill H. R. 1331, entitled "An act for the relief of Joab Spencer and James R. Mead for supplies furnished the Kansas tribe of Indians," and to state that said bill was the subject of a report made to the Department by the Commissioner of Indian Affairs on the 11th ultimo, with which he submitted letters from Enoch Hoag, superintendent of Indian affairs, and Mahlon Stubbs, Indian agent, representing that the justness and correctness of the claim of Spencer & Mead had not been established, and suggesting that further proceedings in the premises be deferred until a thorough investigation of the facts and circumstances of the case could be had.

The suggestion of the Indian agent received the concurrence of the Commissioner of Indian Affairs and the approval of this Department, and on the 17th ultimo the attention of Congress was invited to the subject in a letter addressed to the Speaker of the House of Representatives by the Secretary of the Interior. At the latter date the bill appears to have been pending in the Senate, of which fact this Department at that time was not informed.

On the 5th instant the engrossed bill (H. R. No. 1331) was received by reference from the Executive Office, and forwarded to the Commissioner of Indian Affairs for a further report on the subject, and on the 6th instant that officer returned said bill to this Department with a letter presenting his views in relation to the matter and suggesting that the rights of the Indians and of Messrs. Spencer & Mead would be fully protected by a modification of the bill authorizing the Secretary of the Interior to pay such amount of their claim as might be found to be due. The suggestion meets the approval of this Department.

Copies of the papers connected with this claim are herewith submitted.*

I have the honor to be, very respectfully, your obedient servant,

B. R. COWEN,
Acting Secretary.

PROCLAMATIONS.

By the President of the United States of America.

A PROCLAMATION.

Whereas certain turbulent and disorderly persons, pretending that Elisha Baxter, the present executive of Arkansas, was not elected, have combined together with force and arms to resist his authority as such executive and other authorities of said State; and

Whereas said Elisha Baxter has been declared duly elected by the general assembly of said State, as provided in the constitution thereof, and has for a long period been exercising the functions of said office, into which he was inducted according to the constitution and laws of said State, and ought by its citizens to be considered as the lawful executive thereof; and

Whereas it is provided in the Constitution of the United States that the United States shall protect every State in the Union, on application of the legislature, or of the executive when the legislature can not be convened, against domestic violence; and

Whereas said Elisha Baxter, under section 4 of Article IV of the Constitution of the United States and the laws passed in pursuance thereof,

*Omitted.

has heretofore made application to me to protect said State and the citizens thereof against domestic violence; and

Whereas the general assembly of said State was convened in extra session at the capital thereof on the 11th instant, pursuant to a call made by said Elisha Baxter, and both houses thereof have passed a joint resolution also applying to me to protect the State against domestic violence; and

Whereas it is provided in the laws of the United States that in all cases of insurrection in any State or of obstruction to the laws thereof it shall be lawful for the President of the United States, on application of the legislature of such State, or of the executive when the legislature can not be convened, to employ such part of the land and naval forces as shall be judged necessary for the purpose of suppressing such insurrection or causing the laws to be duly executed; and

Whereas it is required that whenever it may be necessary, in the judgment of the President, to use the military force for the purpose aforesaid, he shall forthwith, by proclamation, command such insurgents to disperse and retire peaceably to their respective homes within a limited time:

Now, therefore, I, Ulysses S. Grant, President of the United States, do hereby make proclamation and command all turbulent and disorderly persons to disperse and retire peaceably to their respective abodes within ten days from this date, and hereafter to submit themselves to the lawful authority of said executive and the other constituted authorities of said State; and I invoke the aid and cooperation of all good citizens thereof to uphold law and preserve public peace.

In witness whereof I have hereunto set my hand and caused the seal of the United States to be affixed.

[SEAL.] Done at the city of Washington, this 15th day of May, A. D. 1874, and of the Independence of the United States the ninety-eighth.

U. S. GRANT.

By the President:

HAMILTON FISH, *Secretary of State.*

BY THE PRESIDENT OF THE UNITED STATES OF AMERICA.

A PROCLAMATION.

Whereas by the thirty-third article of a treaty concluded at Washington on the 8th day of May, 1871, between the United States and Her Britannic Majesty, it was provided that—

Articles XVIII to XXV, inclusive, and Article XXX of this treaty shall take effect as soon as the laws required to carry them into operation shall have been passed by the Imperial Parliament of Great Britain, by the parliament of Canada, and by the legislature of Prince Edwards Island on the one hand, and by the Congress of the United States on the other.

And whereas it is provided by Article XXXII of the treaty aforesaid that—

The provisions and stipulations of Articles XVIII to XXV of this treaty, inclusive, shall extend to the colony of Newfoundland so far as they are applicable. But if the Imperial Parliament, the legislature of Newfoundland, or the Congress of the United States shall not embrace the colony of Newfoundland in their laws enacted for carrying the foregoing articles into effect, then this article shall be of no effect; but the omission to make provision by law to give it effect, by either of the legislative bodies aforesaid, shall not in any way impair any other articles of this treaty.

And whereas by the second section of an act entitled "An act to carry into effect the provisions of the treaty between the United States and Great Britain signed in the city of Washington the 8th day of May, 1871, relating to the fisheries," it is provided—

That whenever the colony of Newfoundland shall give its consent to the application of the stipulations and provisions of the said articles eighteenth to twenty-fifth of said treaty, inclusive, to that colony, and the legislature thereof and the Imperial Parliament shall pass the necessary laws for that purpose, the above-enumerated articles, being the produce of the fisheries of the colony of Newfoundland, shall be admitted into the United States free of duty from and after the date of a proclamation by the President of the United States declaring that he has satisfactory evidence that the said colony of Newfoundland has consented, in a due and proper manner, to have the provisions of the said articles eighteenth to twenty-fifth, inclusive, of the said treaty extended to it, and to allow the United States the full benefits of all the stipulations therein contained, and shall be so admitted free of duty so long as the said articles eighteenth to twenty-fifth, inclusive, and article thirtieth of said treaty shall remain in force according to the terms and conditions of article thirty-third of said treaty.

And whereas the Secretary of State of the United States and Her Britannic Majesty's envoy extraordinary and minister plenipotentiary at Washington have recorded in a protocol of a conference held by them at the Department of State in Washington on the 28th day of May, 1874, in the following language:

PROTOCOL OF A CONFERENCE HELD AT WASHINGTON ON THE 28TH DAY OF
MAY, 1874.

Whereas it is provided by Article XXXII of the treaty between the United States of America and Her Majesty the Queen of the United Kingdom of Great Britain and Ireland signed at Washington on the 8th of May, 1871, as follows:

"ARTICLE XXXII.

"It is further agreed that the provisions and stipulations of Articles XVIII to XXV of this treaty, inclusive, shall extend to the colony of Newfoundland so far as they are applicable. But if the Imperial Parliament, the legislature of Newfoundland, or the Congress of the United States shall not embrace the colony of Newfoundland in their laws enacted for carrying the foregoing articles into effect, then this article shall be of no effect; but the omission to make provision by law to give it effect, by either of the legislative bodies aforesaid, shall not in any way impair any other articles of this treaty;" and

Whereas an act was passed by the Senate and House of Representatives of the

United States of America in Congress assembled, and approved on the 1st day of March, 1873, by the President of the United States, entitled "An act to carry into effect the provisions of the treaty between the United States and Great Britain signed in the city of Washington the 8th of May, 1871, relating to fisheries," by which act it is provided:

"SEC. 2. That whenever the colony of Newfoundland shall give its consent to the application of the stipulations and provisions of the said articles eighteenth to twenty-fifth of said treaty, inclusive, to that colony, and the legislature thereof and the Imperial Parliament shall pass the necessary laws for that purpose, the above-enumerated articles, being the produce of the fisheries of the colony of Newfoundland, shall be admitted into the United States free of duty from and after the date of a proclamation by the President of the United States declaring that he has satisfactory evidence that the said colony of Newfoundland has consented, in a due and proper manner, to have the provisions of the said articles eighteenth to twenty-fifth, inclusive, of the said treaty extended to it, and to allow the United States the full benefits of all the stipulations therein contained, and shall be so admitted free of duty so long as the said articles eighteenth to twenty-fifth, inclusive, and article thirtieth of said treaty shall remain in force according to the terms and conditions of article thirty-third of said treaty;" and

Whereas an act was passed by the governor, legislative council, and assembly of Newfoundland, in legislative session convened, in the thirty-seventh year of Her Majesty's reign, and assented to by Her Majesty on the 12th day of May, 1874, intituled "An act to carry into effect the provisions of the treaty of Washington as far as they relate to this colony:"

The undersigned, Hamilton Fish, Secretary of State of the United States, and the Right Hon. Sir Edward Thornton, one of Her Majesty's most honorable privy council, knight commander of the most honorable Order of the Bath, Her Britannic Majesty's envoy extraordinary and minister plenipotentiary to the United States of America, duly authorized for this purpose by their respective Governments, having met together at Washington, and having found that the laws required to carry the Articles XVIII to XXV, inclusive, and Articles XXX and XXXII of the treaty aforesaid into operation have been passed by the Congress of the United States on the one part, and by the Imperial Parliament of Great Britain, by the parliament of Canada, and by the legislature of Prince Edwards Island and the legislature of Newfoundland on the other, hereby declare that Articles XVIII to XXV, inclusive, and Article XXX of the treaty between the United States of America and Her Britannic Majesty shall take effect in accordance with Article XXXIII of said treaty between the citizens of the United States of America and Her Majesty's subjects in the colony of Newfoundland on the 1st day of June next.

In witness whereof the undersigned have signed this protocol and have hereunto affixed their seals.

Done in duplicate at Washington, this 28th day of May, 1874.

| [SEAL.] | HAMILTON FISH. |
| [SEAL.] | EDWD. THORNTON. |

Now, therefore, I, Ulysses S. Grant, President of the United States of America, in pursuance of the premises, do hereby declare that I have received satisfactory evidence that the Imperial Parliament of Great Britain and the legislature of Newfoundland have passed laws on their part to give full effect to the provisions of the said treaty as contained in articles eighteenth to twenty-fifth, inclusive, and article thirtieth of said treaty.

In testimony whereof I have hereunto set my hand and caused the seal of the United States to be affixed.

[SEAL.]   Done at the city of Washington, this 29th day of May, A. D. 1874, and of the Independence of the United States of America the ninety-eighth.

U. S. GRANT.

By the President:

HAMILTON FISH, *Secretary of State.*

BY THE PRESIDENT OF THE UNITED STATES OF AMERICA.

A PROCLAMATION.

Whereas it has been satisfactorily represented to me that turbulent and disorderly persons have combined together with force and arms to overthrow the State government of Louisiana and to resist the laws and constituted authorities of said State: and

Whereas it is provided in the Constitution of the United States that the United States shall protect every State in this Union, on application of the legislature, or of the executive when the legislature can not be convened, against domestic violence; and

Whereas it is provided in the laws of the United States that in all cases of insurrection in any State or of obstruction to the laws thereof it shall be lawful for the President of the United States, on application of the legislature of such State, or of the executive when the legislature can not be convened, to call forth the militia of any other State or States, or to employ such part of the land and naval forces as shall be judged necessary, for the purpose of suppressing such insurrection or causing the laws to be duly executed; and

Whereas the legislature of said State is not now in session and can not be convened in time to meet the present emergency, and the executive of said State, under section 4 of Article IV of the Constitution of the United States and the laws passed in pursuance thereof, has therefore made application to me for such part of the military force of the United States as may be necessary and adequate to protect said State and the citizens thereof against domestic violence and to enforce the due execution of the laws; and

Whereas it is required that whenever it may be necessary, in the judgment of the President, to use the military force for the purpose aforesaid, he shall forthwith, by proclamation, command such insurgents to disperse and retire peaceably to their respective homes within a limited time:

Now, therefore, I, Ulysses S. Grant, President of the United States, do hereby make proclamation and command said turbulent and disorderly persons to disperse and retire peaceably to their respective abodes within five days from this date, and hereafter to submit themselves to the laws and constituted authorities of said State; and I invoke the aid and cooperation of all good citizens thereof to uphold law and preserve the public peace.

In witness whereof I have hereunto set my hand and caused the seal of the United States to be affixed.

[SEAL.]   Done at the city of Washington, this 15th day of September, A. D. 1874, and of the Independence of the United States the ninety-ninth.

U. S. GRANT.

By the President:

HAMILTON FISH, *Secretary of State.*

BY THE PRESIDENT OF THE UNITED STATES OF AMERICA.

A PROCLAMATION.

We are reminded by the changing seasons that it is time to pause in our daily avocations and offer thanks to Almighty God for the mercies and abundance of the year which is drawing to a close.

The blessings of free government continue to be vouchsafed to us; the earth has responded to the labor of the husbandman; the land has been free from pestilence; internal order is being maintained, and peace with other powers has prevailed.

It is fitting that at stated periods we should cease from our accustomed pursuits and from the turmoil of our daily lives and unite in thankfulness for the blessings of the past and in the cultivation of kindly feelings toward each other.

Now, therefore, recognizing these considerations, I, Ulysses S. Grant, President of the United States, do recommend to all citizens to assemble in their respective places of worship on Thursday, the 26th day of November next, and express their thanks for the mercy and favor of Almighty God, and, laying aside all political contentions and all secular occupations, to observe such day as a day of rest, thanksgiving, and praise.

In witness whereof I have hereunto set my hand and caused the seal of the United States to be affixed.

[SEAL.]   Done at the city of Washington, this 27th day of October, A. D. 1874, and of the Independence of the United States the ninety-ninth.

U. S. GRANT.

By the President:

HAMILTON FISH, *Secretary of State.*

BY THE PRESIDENT OF THE UNITED STATES OF AMERICA.

A PROCLAMATION.

Whereas, pursuant to the second section of the act of Congress approved the 23d of March last, entitled "An act to authorize the President to accept for citizens of the United States the jurisdiction of certain tribunals in the Ottoman dominions and Egypt, established or to be established under the authority of the Sublime Porte and of the Government of Egypt,'' the President is authorized, for the benefit of American citizens residing in the Turkish dominions, to accept the recent law of the Ottoman Porte ceding the right of foreigners possessing immovable property in said dominions; and

Whereas, pursuant to the authority thus in me vested, I have authorized George H. Boker, accredited as minister resident of the United States to the Ottoman Porte, to sign on behalf of this Government the protocol accepting the law aforesaid of the said Ottoman Porte, which protocol and law are, word for word, as follows:

[Translation.]

The United States of America and His Majesty the Sultan being desirous to establish by a special act the agreement entered upon between them regarding the admission of American citizens to the right of holding real estate granted to foreigners by the law promulgated on the 7th of Sepher, 1284 (January 18, 1867), have authorized:

The President of the United States of America, George H. Boker, minister resident of the United States of America near the Sublime Porte, and

His Imperial Majesty the Sultan, His Excellency A. Aarifi Pasha, his minister of foreign affairs, to sign the protocol which follows:

PROTOCOL.

The law granting foreigners the right of holding real estate does not interfere with the immunities specified by the treaties, and which will continue to protect the person and the movable property of foreigners who may become owners of real estate.

As the exercise of this right of possessing real property may induce foreigners to establish themselves in larger numbers in the Ottoman Empire, the Imperial Government thinks it proper to anticipate and to prevent the difficulties to which the application of this law may give rise in certain localities. Such is the object of the arrangements which follow:

The domicile of any person residing upon the Ottoman soil being inviolable, and as no one can enter it without the consent of the owner, except by virtue of orders emanating from competent authority and with the assistance of the magistrate or functionary invested with the necessary powers, the residence of foreigners is inviolable on the same principle, in conformity with the treaties, and the agents of the public force can not enter it without the assistance of the consul or of the delegate of the consul of the power on which the foreigner depends.

By residence we understand the house of inhabitation and its dependencies; that is to say, the outhouses, courts, gardens, and neighboring inclosures, to the exclusion of all other parts of the property.

In the localities distant by less than nine hours' journey from the consular residence, the agents of the public force can not enter the residence of a foreigner without the assistance of a consul, as was before said.

On his part the consul is bound to give his immediate assistance to the local authority so as not to let six hours elapse between the moment which he may be informed and the moment of his departure or the departure of his delegate, so that the action of the authorities may never be suspended more than twenty-four hours.

In the localities distant by nine hours or more than nine hours of travel from the residence of the consular agent, the agents of the public force may, on the request of the local authority, and with the assistance of three members of the council of the elders of the commune, enter into the residence of a foreigner without being assisted by the consular agent, but only in case of urgency and for the search and the proof of the crime of murder, of attempt at murder, of incendiarism, of armed robbery either with infraction or by night in an inhabited house, of armed rebellion, and of the fabrication of counterfeit money; and this entry may be made whether the crime was committed by a foreigner or by an Ottoman subject, and whether it took place in the residence of a foreigner or not in his residence, or in any other place.

These regulations are not applicable but to the parts of the real estate which constitute the residence, as it has been heretofore defined.

Beyond the residence the action of the police shall be exercised freely and without reserve; but in case a person charged with crime or offense should be arrested, and the accused shall be a foreigner, the immunities attached to his person shall be observed in respect to him.

The functionary or the officer charged with the accomplishment of a domiciliary visit in the exceptional circumstances determined before, and the members of the council of elders who shall assist him, will be obliged to make out a *procès verbal* of the domiciliary visit and to communicate it immediately to the superior authority under whose jurisdiction they are, and the latter shall transmit it to the nearest consular agent without delay.

A special regulation will be promulgated by the Sublime Porte to determine the mode of action of the local police in the several cases provided heretofore.

In localities more distant than nine hours' travel from the residence of the consular agent, in which the law of the judicial organization of the *velayet* may be in force, foreigners shall be tried without the assistance of the consular delegate by the council of elders fulfilling the function of justices of the peace, and by the tribunal of the canton, as well for actions not exceeding 1,000 piasters as for offenses entailing a fine of 500 piasters only at the maximum.

Foreigners shall have in any case the right of appeal to the tribunal of the arrondissement against the judgments issued as above stated, and the appeal shall be followed and judged with the assistance of the consul in conformity with the treaties.

The appeal shall always suspend the execution of a sentence.

In all cases the forcible execution of the judgments, issued on the conditions determined heretofore, shall not take place without the cooperation of the consul or of his delegate.

The Imperial Government will enact a law which shall determine the rules of procedure to be observed by the parties in the application of the preceding regulations.

Foreigners, in whatever locality they may be, may freely submit themselves to the jurisdiction of the council of elders or of the tribunal of the canton without the assistance of the consul in cases which do not exceed the competency of these councils or tribunals, reserving always the right of appeal before the tribunal of the arrondissement, where the case may be brought and tried with the assistance of the consul or his delegate.

The consent of a foreigner to be tried as above stated, without the assistance of his consul, shall always be given in writing and in advance of all procedure.

It is well understood that all these restrictions do not concern cases which have for their object questions of real estate, which shall be tried and determined under the conditions established by the law.

The right of defense and the publicity of the hearings shall be assured in all cases to foreigners who may appear before the Ottoman tribunals, as well as to Ottoman subjects.

The preceding dispositions shall remain in force until the revision of the ancient treaties, a revision which the Sublime Porte reserves to itself the right to bring about hereafter by an understanding between it and the friendly powers.

In witness whereof the respective plenipotentiaries have signed the protocol and have affixed thereto their seals.

Done at Constantinople the 11th of August, 1874.

[SEAL.]   (Signed)   A. AARIFI.
[SEAL.]   (Signed)   GEO. H. BOKER.

[Translation.]

LAW CONCEDING TO FOREIGNERS THE RIGHT OF HOLDING REAL ESTATE IN THE OTTOMAN EMPIRE.

Imperial Rescript.—Let it be done in conformity with the contents.   7 Sepher, 1284 (January 18, 1867).

With the object of developing the prosperity of the country, to put an end to the difficulties, to the abuses, and to the uncertainties which have arisen on the subject of the right of foreigners to hold property in the Ottoman Empire, and to complete in accordance with a precise regulation, the safeguards which are due to financial interests and to administrative action, the following legislative enactments have been promulgated by the order of His Imperial Majesty the Sultan:

ARTICLE I. Foreigners are admitted by the same privilege as Ottoman subjects, and without any other restriction, to enjoy the right of holding real estate, whether in the city or the country, throughout the Empire, with the exception of the Province of the Hédjaz, by submitting themselves to the laws and the regulations which govern Ottoman subjects as is hereafter stated.

This arrangement does not concern subjects of Ottoman birth who have changed their nationality, who shall be governed in this matter by a special law.

ART. II. Foreigners, proprietors of real estate in town or in country, are in consequence placed upon terms of equality with Ottoman subjects in all things that concern their landed property.

The legal effect of this equality is—

First. To oblige them to conform to all the laws and regulations of the police or of the municipality which govern at present or may govern hereafter the enjoyment, the transmission, the alienation, and the hypothecation of landed property.

Second. To pay all charges and taxes, under whatever form or denomination they may be, that are levied, or may be levied hereafter, upon city or country property.

Third. To render them directly amenable to the Ottoman civil tribunals in all questions relating to landed property and in all real actions, whether as plaintiffs or as defendants, even when either party is a foreigner. In short, they are in all things to hold real estate by the same title, on the same condition, and under the same forms as Ottoman owners, and without being able to avail themselves of their personal nationality, except under the reserve of the immunities attached to their persons and their movable goods, according to the treaties.

ART. III. In case of the bankruptcy of a foreigner possessing real estate, the assignees of the bankrupt may apply to the authorities and to the Ottoman civil tribunals requiring the sale of the real estate possessed by the bankrupt, and which by its nature and according to law is responsible for the debts of the owner.

The same course shall be followed when a foreigner shall have obtained against another foreigner owning real estate a judgment of condemnation before a foreign tribunal.

For the execution of this judgment against the real estate of his debtor he shall apply to the competent Ottoman authorities in order to obtain the sale of that real estate which is responsible for the debts of the owner; and this judgment shall be executed by the Ottoman authorities and tribunals only after they have decided that the real estate of which the sale is required really belongs to the category of that property which may be sold for the payment of debt.

ART. IV. Foreigners have the privilege to dispose, by donation or by testament, of that real estate of which such disposition is permitted by law.

As to that real estate of which they may not have disposed or of which the law does not permit them to dispose by gift or testament, its succession shall be governed in accordance with Ottoman law.

ART. V. All foreigners shall enjoy the privileges of the present law as soon as the powers on which they depend shall agree to the arrangements proposed by the Sublime Porte for the exercise of the right to hold real estate.

Now, therefore, be it known that I, Ulysses S. Grant, President of the United States of America, have caused the said protocol and law to be made public for the information and guidance of citizens of the United States.

In witness whereof I have hereunto set my hand and caused the seal of the United States to be affixed.

[SEAL.]   Done at the city of Washington, this 29th day of October, A. D. 1874, and of the Independence of the United States of America the ninety-ninth.

U. S. GRANT.

By the President:
    HAMILTON FISH,
        Secretary of State.

EXECUTIVE ORDERS.

BY THE PRESIDENT OF THE UNITED STATES.

EXECUTIVE ORDER.

WASHINGTON, *January 23, 1874.*

Whereas it has been brought to the notice of the President of the United States that in the International Exhibition of Arts, Manufactures, and Products of the Soil and Mine to be held in the city of Philadelphia in the year 1876 for the purpose of celebrating the one hundredth anniversary of the independence of the United States it is desirable that from the Executive Departments of the Government of the United States in which there may be articles suitable for the purpose intended there should appear such articles and materials as will, when presented in a collective exhibition, illustrate the functions and administrative faculties of the Government in time of peace and its resources as a war power, and thereby serve to demonstrate the nature of our institutions and their adaptations to the wants of the people:

Now, for the purpose of securing a complete and harmonious arrangement of the articles and materials designed to be exhibited from the

Executive Departments of the Government, it is ordered that a board to be composed of one person to be named by the head of each of the Executive Departments which may have articles and materials to be exhibited, and also of one person to be named in behalf of the Smithsonian Institution and one to be named in behalf of the Department of Agriculture, be charged with the preparation, arrangement, and safe-keeping of such articles and materials as the heads of the several Departments and the Commissioner of Agriculture and the Director of the Smithsonian Institution may respectively decide shall be embraced in the collection; that one of the persons thus named, to be designated by the President, shall be chairman of such board, and that the board appoint from their own number such other officers as they may think necessary; and that the said board when organized be authorized, under the direction of the President, to confer with the executive officers of the Centennial Exhibition in relation to such matters connected with the subject as may pertain to the respective Departments having articles and materials on exhibition; and that the names of the persons thus selected by the heads of the several Departments, the Commissioner of Agriculture, and the Director of the Smithsonian Institution shall be submitted to the President for designation.

By order of the President:

HAMILTON FISH,
Secretary of State.

GENERAL ORDERS, No. 22.

WAR DEPARTMENT,
ADJUTANT-GENERAL'S OFFICE,
Washington, March 9, 1874.

I. The following order has been received from the President of the United States:

EXECUTIVE MANSION,
Washington, March 9, 1874.

It is with deep regret that the President announces to the people of the United States the death of Millard Fillmore, one of his honored predecessors, who died at Buffalo, N. Y., last evening.

The long-continued and useful public service and eminent purity of character of the deceased ex-President will be remembered beyond the days of mourning in which a nation will be thrown by the event which is thus announced.

As a mark of respect to his memory, it is ordered that the Executive Mansion and the several Departments at Washington be draped in mourning until the close of the day on which the funeral shall take place, and that all business be suspended on the day of the funeral.

It is further ordered that the War and Navy Departments cause suitable military and naval honors to be paid on the occasion to the memory of the eminent citizen whose life is now closed. U. S. GRANT.

By the President:

HAMILTON FISH, *Secretary of State.*

II. In compliance with the President's instructions, the troops will be paraded at 10 o'clock a. m. on the day after the receipt of this order at each military post, when the order will be read to them, and the labors of that day will thereafter cease.

The national flag will be displayed at half-staff.

At dawn of day thirteen guns will be fired, and afterwards at intervals of thirty minutes between the rising and setting sun a single gun, and at the close of the day a national salute of thirty-seven guns.

The officers of the Army will wear crape on the left arm and on their swords and the colors of the several regiments will be put in mourning for the period of thirty days.

By order of the Secretary of War:

E. D. TOWNSEND, *Adjutant-General.*

SPECIAL ORDER.

NAVY DEPARTMENT,
Washington, March 9, 1874.

The President of the United States announces the death of ex-President Millard Fillmore in the following order:

[For order see preceding page.]

In pursuance of the foregoing order, it is hereby directed that the ensign at each naval station and of each vessel of the United States Navy in commission be hoisted at half-mast from sunrise to sunset, and that a gun be fired at intervals of every half hour from sunrise to sunset at each naval station and on board of flagships and of vessels acting singly, on Thursday, the 12th instant, the day of the funeral, where this order may be received in time, otherwise on the day after its receipt.

The officers of the Navy and Marine Corps will wear the usual badge of mourning attached to the sword hilt and on the left arm for the period of thirty days.

GEO. M. ROBESON,
Secretary of the Navy.

EXECUTIVE MANSION,
Washington, D. C., May 27, 1874.

SIR:* The President directs me to say that the several Departments of the Government will be closed on the 30th instant, in order to enable the

*Addressed to the heads of the Executive Departments, etc.

employees to participate in the decoration of the graves of the soldiers who fell during the rebellion.

I am, sir, your obedient servant,   O. E. BABCOCK,
Secretary.

WASHINGTON, *May 29, 1874.*

The Civil Service Commission, at its sessions at Washington, having recommended certain rules* to be prescribed by the President for the government of the Light-House Service of the United States, these rules as herewith published are approved, and their provisions will be enforced by the proper officers.   U. S. GRANT.

AUGUST 31, 1874.

It appearing to me from their trial at Washington and at the city of New York that the further extension of the civil-service rules will promote the efficiency of the public service, it is ordered that such rules be, and they are hereby, extended to the several Federal offices at the city and in the customs district of Boston, and that the proper measures be taken for carrying this order into effect.   U. S. GRANT.

SIXTH ANNUAL MESSAGE.

EXECUTIVE MANSION, *December 7, 1874.*

To the Senate and House of Representatives:

Since the convening of Congress one year ago the nation has undergone a prostration in business and industries such as has not been witnessed with us for many years. Speculation as to the causes for this prostration might be indulged in without profit, because as many theories would be advanced as there would be independent writers—those who expressed their own views without borrowing—upon the subject. Without indulging in theories as to the cause of this prostration, therefore, I will call your attention only to the fact, and to some plain questions as to which it would seem there should be no disagreement.

During this prostration two essential elements of prosperity have been most abundant—labor and capital. Both have been largely unemployed. Where security has been undoubted, capital has been attainable at very moderate rates. Where labor has been wanted, it has been found in abundance, at cheap rates compared with what—of necessaries and comforts of life—could be purchased with the wages demanded. Two great

* Omitted.

elements of prosperity, therefore, have not been denied us. A third might be added: Our soil and climate are unequaled, within the limits of any contiguous territory under one nationality, for its variety of products to feed and clothe a people and in the amount of surplus to spare to feed less favored peoples. Therefore, with these facts in view, it seems to me that wise statesmanship, at this session of Congress, would dictate legislation ignoring the past; directing in proper channels these great elements of prosperity to any people. Debt, debt abroad, is the only element that can, with always a sound currency, enter into our affairs to cause any continued depression in the industries and prosperity of our people.

A great conflict for national existence made necessary, for temporary purposes, the raising of large sums of money from whatever source attainable. It made it necessary, in the wisdom of Congress—and I do not doubt their wisdom in the premises, regarding the necessity of the times—to devise a system of national currency which it proved to be impossible to keep on a par with the recognized currency of the civilized world. This begot a spirit of speculation involving an extravagance and luxury not required for the happiness or prosperity of a people, and involving, both directly and indirectly, foreign indebtedness. The currency, being of fluctuating value, and therefore unsafe to hold for legitimate transactions requiring money, became a subject of speculation within itself. These two causes, however, have involved us in a foreign indebtedness, contracted in good faith by borrower and lender, which should be paid in coin, and according to the bond agreed upon when the debt was contracted—gold or its equivalent. The good faith of the Government can not be violated toward creditors without national disgrace. But our commerce should be encouraged; American shipbuilding and carrying capacity increased; foreign markets sought for products of the soil and manufactories, to the end that we may be able to pay these debts. Where a new market can be created for the sale of our products, either of the soil, the mine, or the manufactory, a new means is discovered of utilizing our idle capital and labor to the advantage of the whole people. But, in my judgment, the first step toward accomplishing this object is to secure a currency of fixed, stable value; a currency good wherever civilization reigns; one which, if it becomes superabundant with one people, will find a market with some other; a currency which has as its basis the labor necessary to produce it, which will give to it its value. Gold and silver are now the recognized medium of exchange the civilized world over, and to this we should return with the least practicable delay. In view of the pledges of the American Congress when our present legal-tender system was adopted, and debt contracted, there should be no delay—certainly no unnecessary delay—in fixing by legislation a method by which we will return to specie. To the accomplishment of this end I invite your special attention. I believe firmly that there can be no prosperous and permanent revival of business and industries until a policy is adopted—with legislation to carry it out—looking to a return to a specie basis. It is easy to conceive that the debtor and speculative classes may think it of value to them to make so-called money abundant until they can throw a portion of their burdens upon others. But even these, I believe, would be disappointed in the result if a course should be pursued which will keep in doubt the value of the legal-tender medium of exchange. A revival of productive industry is needed by all classes; by none more than the holders of property, of whatever sort, with debts to liquidate from realization upon its sale. But admitting that these two classes of citizens are to be benefited by expansion, would it be honest to give it? Would not the general loss be too great to justify such relief? Would it not be just as honest and prudent to authorize each debtor to issue his own legal-tenders to the extent of his liabilities? Than to do this, would it not be safer, for fear of overissues by unscrupulous creditors, to say that all debt obligations are obliterated in the United States, and now we commence anew, each possessing all he has at the time free from incumbrance? These propositions are too absurd to be entertained for a moment by thinking or honest people. Yet every delay in preparation for final resumption partakes of this dishonesty, and is only less in degree as the hope is held out that a convenient season will at last arrive for the good work of redeeming our pledges to commence. It will never come, in my opinion, except by positive action by Congress, or by national disasters which will destroy, for a time at least, the credit of the individual and the State at large. A sound currency might be reached by total bankruptcy and discredit of the integrity of the nation and of individuals. I believe it is in the power of Congress at this session to devise such legislation as will renew confidence, revive all the industries, start us on a career of prosperity to last for many years and to save the credit of the nation and of the people. Steps toward the return to a specie basis are the great requisites to this devoutly to be sought for end. There are others which I may touch upon hereafter.

A nation dealing in a currency below that of specie in value labors under two great disadvantages: First, having no use for the world's acknowledged medium of exchange, gold and silver, these are driven out of the country because there is no need for their use; second, the medium of exchange in use being of a fluctuating value—for, after all, it is only worth just what it will purchase of gold and silver, metals having an intrinsic value just in proportion to the honest labor it takes to produce them—a larger margin must be allowed for profit by the manufacturer and producer. It is months from the date of production to the date of realization. Interest upon capital must be charged, and risk of fluctuation in the value of that which is to be received in payment added. Hence high prices, acting as a protection to the foreign producer, who receives nothing in exchange for the products of his skill and labor except a currency good, at a stable value, the world over   It seems to me that nothing is clearer than that the greater part of the burden of exist-ing prostration, for the want of a sound financial system, falls upon the working man, who must after all produce the wealth, and the salaried man, who superintends and conducts business. The burden falls upon them in two ways—by the deprivation of employment and by the de-creased purchasing power of their salaries. It is the duty of Congress to devise the method of correcting the evils which are acknowledged to exist, and not mine. But I will venture to suggest two or three things which seem to me as absolutely necessary to a return to specie payments, the first great requisite in a return to prosperity. The legal-tender clause to the law authorizing the issue of currency by the National Gov-ernment should be repealed, to take effect as to all contracts entered into after a day fixed in the repealing act—not to apply, however, to payments of salaries by Government, or for other expenditures now provided by law to be paid in currency, in the interval pending between repeal and final resumption. Provision should be made by which the Secretary of the Treasury can obtain gold as it may become necessary from time to time from the date when specie redemption commences. To this might and should be added a revenue sufficiently in excess of expenses to insure an accumulation of gold in the Treasury to sustain permanent redemption.

I commend this subject to your careful consideration, believing that a favorable solution is attainable, and if reached by this Congress that the present and future generations will ever gratefully remember it as their deliverer from a thraldom of evil and disgrace.

With resumption, free banking may be authorized with safety, giving the same full protection to bill holders which they have under existing laws. Indeed, I would regard free banking as essential. It would give proper elasticity to the currency. As more currency should be required for the transaction of legitimate business, new banks would be started, and in turn banks would wind up their business when it was found that there was a superabundance of currency. The experience and judgment of the people can best decide just how much currency is required for the transaction of the business of the country. It is unsafe to leave the set-tlement of this question to Congress, the Secretary of the Treasury, or the Executive. Congress should make the regulation under which banks may exist, but should not make banking a monopoly by limiting the amount of redeemable paper currency that shall be authorized. Such importance do I attach to this subject, and so earnestly do I commend it to your attention, that I give it prominence by introducing it at the beginning of this message.

During the past year nothing has occurred to disturb the general friendly and cordial relations of the United States with other powers.

The correspondence submitted herewith between this Government and its diplomatic representatives, as also with the representatives of other countries, shows a satisfactory condition of all questions between the

United States and the most of those countries, and with few exceptions, to which reference is hereafter made, the absence of any points of difference to be adjusted.

The notice directed by the resolution of Congress of June 17, 1874 to be given to terminate the convention of July 17, 1858, between the United States and Belgium has been given, and the treaty will accordingly terminate on the 1st day of July, 1875. This convention secured to certain Belgian vessels entering the ports of the United States exceptional privileges which are not accorded to our own vessels. Other features of the convention have proved satisfactory, and have tended to the cultivation of mutually beneficial commercial intercourse and friendly relations between the two countries. I hope that negotiations which have been invited will result in the celebration of another treaty which may tend to the interests of both countries.

Our relations with China continue to be friendly. During the past year the fear of hostilities between China and Japan, growing out of the landing of an armed force upon the island of Formosa by the latter, has occasioned uneasiness. It is earnestly hoped, however, that the difficulties arising from this cause will be adjusted, and that the advance of civilization in these Empires may not be retarded by a state of war. In consequence of the part taken by certain citizens of the United States in this expedition, our representatives in those countries have been instructed to impress upon the Governments of China and Japan the firm intention of this country to maintain strict neutrality in the event of hostilities, and to carefully prevent any infraction of law on the part of our citizens.

In connection with this subject I call the attention of Congress to a generally conceded fact—that the great proportion of the Chinese immigrants who come to our shores do not come voluntarily, to make their homes with us and their labor productive of general prosperity, but come under contracts with headmen, who own them almost absolutely. In a worse form does this apply to Chinese women. Hardly a perceptible percentage of them perform any honorable labor, but they are brought for shameful purposes, to the disgrace of the communities where settled and to the great demoralization of the youth of those localities. If this evil practice can be legislated against, it will be my pleasure as well as duty to enforce any regulation to secure so desirable an end.

It is hoped that negotiations between the Government of Japan and the treaty powers, looking to the further opening of the Empire and to the removal of various restrictions upon trade and travel, may soon produce the results desired, which can not fail to inure to the benefit of all the parties. Having on previous occasions submitted to the consideration of Congress the propriety of the release of the Japanese Government from the further payment of the indemnity under the convention of October 22, 1864, and as no action had been taken thereon, it became my duty to regard the obligations of the convention as in force; and as the other powers interested had received their portion of the indemnity in full, the minister of the United States in Japan has, in behalf of this Government, received the remainder of the amount due to the United States under the convention of Simonosaki. I submit the propriety of applying the income of a part, if not of the whole, of this fund to the education in the Japanese language of a number of young men to be under obligations to serve the Government for a specified time as interpreters at the legation and the consulates in Japan. A limited number of Japanese youths might at the same time be educated in our own vernacular, and mutual benefits would result to both Governments. The importance of having our own citizens, competent and familiar with the language of Japan, to act as interpreters and in other capacities connected with the legation and the consulates in that country can not readily be overestimated.

The amount awarded to the Government of Great Britain by the mixed commission organized under the provisions of the treaty of Washington in settlement of the claims of British subjects arising from acts committed between April 13, 1861, and April 9, 1865, became payable, under the terms of the treaty, within the past year, and was paid upon the 21st day of September, 1874. In this connection I renew my recommendation, made at the opening of the last session of Congress, that a special court be created to hear and determine all claims of aliens against the United States arising from acts committed against their persons or property during the insurrection. It appears equitable that opportunity should be offered to citizens of other states to present their claims, as well as to those British subjects whose claims were not admissible under the late commission, to the early decision of some competent tribunal. To this end I recommend the necessary legislation to organize a court to dispose of all claims of aliens of the nature referred to in an equitable and satisfactory manner, and to relieve Congress and the Departments from the consideration of these questions.

The legislation necessary to extend to the colony of Newfoundland certain articles of the treaty of Washington of the 8th day of May, 1871, having been had, a protocol to that effect was signed in behalf of the United States and of Great Britain on the 28th day of May last, and was duly proclaimed on the following day. A copy of the proclamation* is submitted herewith.

A copy of the report of the commissioner appointed under the act of March 19, 1872, for surveying and marking the boundary between the United States and the British possessions from the Lake of the Woods to the summit of the Rocky Mountains is herewith transmitted. I am happy to announce that the field work of the commission has been completed, and the entire line from the northwest corner of the Lake of the Woods to the summit of the Rocky Mountains has been run and marked

*See pp. 4227-4230.

upon the surface of the earth. It is believed that the amount remaining unexpended of the appropriation made at the last session of Congress will be sufficient to complete the office work. I recommend that the authority of Congress be given to the use of the unexpended balance of the appropriation in the completion of the work of the commission in making its report and preparing the necessary maps.

The court known as the Court of Commissioners of Alabama Claims, created by an act of Congress of the last session, has organized and commenced its work, and it is to be hoped that the claims admissible under the provisions of the act may be speedily ascertained and paid.

It has been deemed advisable to exercise the discretion conferred upon the Executive at the last session by accepting the conditions required by the Government of Turkey for the privilege of allowing citizens of the United States to hold real estate in the former country, and by assenting to a certain change in the jurisdiction of courts in the latter. A copy of the proclamation * upon these subjects is herewith communicated.

There has been no material change in our relations with the independent States of this hemisphere which were formerly under the dominion of Spain. Marauding on the frontiers between Mexico and Texas still frequently takes place, despite the vigilance of the civil and military authorities in that quarter. The difficulty of checking such trespasses along the course of a river of such length as the Rio Grande, and so often fordable, is obvious. It is hoped that the efforts of this Government will be seconded by those of Mexico to the effectual suppression of these acts of wrong.

From a report upon the condition of the business before the American and Mexican Joint Claims Commission, made by the agent on the part of the United States, and dated October 28, 1874, it appears that of the 1,017 claims filed on the part of citizens of the United States, 483 had been finally decided and 75 were in the hands of the umpire, leaving 462 to be disposed of; and of the 998 claims filed against the United States, 726 had been finally decided, 1 was before the umpire, and 271 remained to be disposed of. Since the date of such report other claims have been disposed of, reducing somewhat the number still pending; and others have been passed upon by the arbitrators. It has become apparent, in view of these figures and of the fact that the work devolving on the umpire is particularly laborious, that the commission will be unable to dispose of the entire number of claims pending prior to the 1st day of February, 1875— the date fixed for its expiration. Negotiations are pending looking to the securing of the results of the decisions which have been reached and to a further extension of the commission for a limited time, which it is confidently hoped will suffice to bring all the business now before it to a final close.

The strife in the Argentine Republic is to be deplored, both on account

* See pp. 4231–4235.

of the parties thereto and from the probable effects on the interests of those engaged in the trade to that quarter, of whom the United States are among the principal. As yet, so far as I am aware, there has been no violation of our neutrality rights, which, as well as our duties in that respect, it shall be my endeavor to maintain and observe.

It is with regret I announce that no further payment has been received from the Government of Venezuela on account of awards in favor of citizens of the United States. Hopes have been entertained that if that Republic could escape both foreign and civil war for a few years its great natural resources would enable it to honor its obligations. Though it is now understood to be at peace with other countries, a serious insurrection is reported to be in progress in an important region of that Republic. This may be taken advantage of as another reason to delay the payment of the dues of our citizens.

The deplorable strife in Cuba continues without any marked change in the relative advantages of the contending forces. The insurrection continues, but Spain has gained no superiority. Six years of strife give to the insurrection a significance which can not be denied. Its duration and the tenacity of its adherence, together with the absence of manifested power of suppression on the part of Spain, can not be controverted, and may make some positive steps on the part of other powers a matter of self-necessity. I had confidently hoped at this time to be able to announce the arrangement of some of the important questions between this Government and that of Spain, but the negotiations have been protracted. The unhappy intestine dissensions of Spain command our profound sympathy, and must be accepted as perhaps a cause of some delay. An early settlement, in part at least, of the questions between the Governments is hoped. In the meantime, awaiting the results of immediately pending negotiations, I defer a further and fuller communication on the subject of the relations of this country and Spain.

I have again to call the attention of Congress to the unsatisfactory condition of the existing laws with reference to expatriation and the election of nationality. Formerly, amid conflicting opinions and decisions, it was difficult to exactly determine how far the doctrine of perpetual allegiance was applicable to citizens of the United States. Congress by the act of the 27th of July, 1868, asserted the abstract right of expatriation as a fundamental principle of this Government. Notwithstanding such assertion and the necessity of frequent application of the principle, no legislation has been had defining what acts or formalities shall work expatriation or when a citizen shall be deemed to have renounced or to have lost his citizenship. The importance of such definition is obvious. The representatives of the United States in foreign countries are continually called upon to lend their aid and the protection of the United States to persons concerning the good faith or the reality of whose citizenship there is at least great question. In some cases the provisions of the treaties furnish some guide; in others it seems left to the person claiming the benefits of citizenship, while living in a foreign country, contributing in no manner to the performance of the duties of a citizen of the United States, and without intention at any time to return and undertake those duties, to use the claims to citizenship of the United States simply as a shield from the performance of the obligations of a citizen elsewhere.

The status of children born of American parents residing in a foreign country, of American women who have married aliens, of American citizens residing abroad where such question is not regulated by treaty, are all sources of frequent difficulty and discussion. Legislation on these and similar questions, and particularly defining when and under what circumstances expatriation can be accomplished or is to be presumed, is especially needed. In this connection I earnestly call the attention of Congress to the difficulties arising from fraudulent naturalization. The United States wisely, freely, and liberally offers its citizenship to all who may come in good faith to reside within its limits on their complying with certain prescribed reasonable and simple formalities and conditions. Among the highest duties of the Government is that to afford firm, sufficient, and equal protection to all its citizens, whether native born or naturalized. Care should be taken that a right carrying with it such support from the Government should not be fraudulently obtained, and should be bestowed only upon full proof of a compliance with the law; and yet frequent instances are brought to the attention of the Government of illegal and fraudulent naturalization and of the unauthorized use of certificates thus improperly obtained. In some cases the fraudulent character of the naturalization has appeared upon the face of the certificate itself; in others examination discloses that the holder had not complied with the law, and in others certificates have been obtained where the persons holding them not only were not entitled to be naturalized, but had not even been within the United States at the time of the pretended naturalization. Instances of each of these classes of fraud are discovered at our legations, where the certificates of naturalization are presented either for the purpose of obtaining passports or in demanding the protection of the legation. When the fraud is apparent on the face of such certificates, they are taken up by the representatives of the Government and forwarded to the Department of State. But even then the record of the court in which the fraudulent naturalization occurred remains, and duplicate certificates are readily obtainable. Upon the presentation of these for the issue of passports or in demanding protection of the Government, the fraud sometimes escapes notice, and such certificates are not infrequently used in transactions of business to the deception and injury of innocent parties. Without placing any additional obstacles in the way of the obtainment of citizenship by the worthy and well-intentioned foreigner who comes in good faith to cast his lot with ours, I earnestly recommend further legislation to punish fraudulent naturalization and to secure the ready cancellation of the record of every naturalization made in fraud.

Since my last annual message the exchange has been made of the ratification of treaties of extradition with Belgium, Ecuador, Peru, and Salvador; also of a treaty of commerce and navigation with Peru, and one of commerce and consular privileges with Salvador; all of which have been duly proclaimed, as has also a declaration with Russia with reference to trade-marks.

The report of the Secretary of the Treasury, which by law is made directly to Congress, and forms no part of this message, will show the receipts and expenditures of the Government for the last fiscal year, the amount received from each source of revenue, and the amount paid out for each of the Departments of Government. It will be observed from this report that the amount of receipts over expenditures has been but $2,344,882.30 for the fiscal year ending June 30, 1874, and that for the current fiscal year the estimated receipts over expenditures will not much exceed $9,000,000. In view of the large national debt existing and the obligation to add 1 per cent per annum to the sinking fund, a sum amounting now to over $34,000,000 per annum, I submit whether revenues should not be increased or expenditures diminished to reach this amount of surplus. Not to provide for the sinking fund is a partial failure to comply with the contracts and obligations of the Government. At the last session of Congress a very considerable reduction was made in rates of taxation and in the number of articles submitted to taxation; the question may well be asked, whether or not, in some instances, unwisely. In connection with this subject, too, I venture the opinion that the means of collecting the revenue, especially from imports, have been so embarrassed by legislation as to make it questionable whether or not large amounts are not lost by failure to collect, to the direct loss of the Treasury and to the prejudice of the interests of honest importers and taxpayers.

The Secretary of the Treasury in his report favors legislation looking to an early return to specie payments, thus supporting views previously expressed in this message. He also recommends economy in appropriations; calls attention to the loss of revenue from repealing the tax on tea and coffee, without benefit to the consumer; recommends an increase of 10 cents a gallon on whisky, and, further, that no modification be made in the banking and currency bill passed at the last session of Congress, unless modification should become necessary by reason of the adoption of measures for returning to specie payments. In these recommendations I cordially join.

I would suggest to Congress the propriety of readjusting the tariff so as to increase the revenue, and at the same time decrease the number of articles upon which duties are levied. Those articles which enter into our manufactures and are not produced at home, it seems to me, should be entered free. Those articles of manufacture which we produce a constituent part of, but do not produce the whole, that part which we do not produce should enter free also. I will instance fine wool, dyes, etc. These articles must be imported to form a part of the manufacture of the higher grades of woolen goods. Chemicals used as dyes, compounded in medicines, and used in various ways in manufactures come under this class. The introduction free of duty of such wools as we do not produce would stimulate the manufacture of goods requiring the use of those we do produce, and therefore would be a benefit to home production. There are many articles entering into "home manufactures" which we do not produce ourselves the tariff upon which increases the cost of producing the manufactured article. All corrections in this regard are in the direction of bringing labor and capital in harmony with each other and of supplying one of the elements of prosperity so much needed.

The report of the Secretary of War herewith attached, and forming a part of this message, gives all the information concerning the operations, wants, and necessities of the Army, and contains many suggestions and recommendations which I commend to your special attention.

There is no class of Government employees who are harder worked than the Army—officers and men; none who perform their tasks more cheerfully and efficiently and under circumstances of greater privations and hardships.

Legislation is desirable to render more efficient this branch of the public service. All the recommendations of the Secretary of War I regard as judicious, and I especially commend to your attention the following: The consolidation of Government arsenals; the restoration of mileage to officers traveling under orders; the exemption of money received from the sale of subsistence stores from being covered into the Treasury; the use of appropriations for the purchase of subsistence stores without waiting for the beginning of the fiscal year for which the appropriation is made; for additional appropriations for the collection of torpedo material; for increased appropriations for the manufacture of arms; for relieving the various States from indebtedness for arms charged to them during the rebellion; for dropping officers from the rolls of the Army without trial for the offense of drawing pay more than once for the same period; for the discouragement of the plan to pay soldiers by check, and for the establishment of a professorship of rhetoric and English literature at West Point. The reasons for these recommendations are obvious, and are set forth sufficiently in the reports attached. I also recommend that the status of the staff corps of the Army be fixed, where this has not already been done, so that promotions may be made and vacancies filled as they occur in each grade when reduced below the number to be fixed by law. The necessity for such legislation is specially felt now in the Pay Department. The number of officers in that department is below the number adequate to the performance of the duties required of them by law.

The efficiency of the Navy has been largely increased during the last year. Under the impulse of the foreign complications which threatened us at the commencement of the last session of Congress, most of our efficient wooden ships were put in condition for immediate service, and the repairs of our ironclad fleet were pushed with the utmost vigor. The result is that most of these are now in an effective state and need only to be manned and put in commission to go at once into service.

Some of the new sloops authorized by Congress are already in commission, and most of the remainder are launched and wait only the completion of their machinery to enable them to take their places as part of our effective force.

Two iron torpedo ships have been completed during the last year, and four of our large double-turreted ironclads are now undergoing repairs. When these are finished, everything that is useful of our Navy, as now authorized, will be in condition for service, and with the advance in the science of torpedo warfare the American Navy, comparatively small as it is, will be found at any time powerful for the purposes of a peaceful nation.

Much has been accomplished during the year in aid of science and to increase the sum of general knowledge and further the interests of commerce and civilization. Extensive and much-needed soundings have been made for hydrographic purposes and to fix the proper routes of ocean telegraphs. Further surveys of the great Isthmus have been undertaken and completed, and two vessels of the Navy are now employed, in conjunction with those of England, France, Germany, and Russia, in observations connected with the transit of Venus, so useful and interesting to the scientific world.

The estimates for this branch of the public service do not differ materially from those of last year, those for the general support of the service being somewhat less and those for permanent improvements at the various stations rather larger than the corresponding estimate made a year ago. The regular maintenance and a steady increase in the efficiency of this most important arm in proportion to the growth of our maritime intercourse and interests is recommended to the attention of Congress.

The use of the Navy in time of peace might be further utilized by a direct authorization of the employment of naval vessels in explorations and surveys of the supposed navigable waters of other nationalities on this continent, especially the tributaries of the two great rivers of South America, the Orinoco and the Amazon. Nothing prevents, under existing laws, such exploration, except that expenditures must be made in such expeditions beyond those usually provided for in the appropriations. The field designated is unquestionably one of interest and one capable of large development of commercial interests—advantageous to the peoples reached and to those who may establish relations with them.

Education of the people entitled to exercise the right of franchise I regard essential to general prosperity everywhere, and especially so in republics, where birth, education, or previous condition does not enter into account in giving suffrage. Next to the public school, the post-office is the great agent of education over our vast territory. The rapidity with which new sections are being settled, thus increasing the carrying of mails in a more rapid ratio than the increase of receipts, is not alarming. The report of the Postmaster-General herewith attached shows that there was an increase of revenue in his Department in 1873 over the previous year of $1,674,411, and an increase of cost of carrying the mails and paying employees of $3,041,468.91. The report of the Postmaster-General gives interesting statistics of his Department, and compares them with the corresponding statistics of a year ago, showing a growth in every branch of the Department.

A postal convention has been concluded with New South Wales, an exchange of postal cards established with Switzerland, and the negotiations pending for several years past with France have been terminated in a convention with that country, which went into effect last August.

An international postal congress was convened in Berne, Switzerland, in September last, at which the United States was represented by an officer of the Post-Office Department of much experience and of qualification for the position. A convention for the establishment of an international postal union was agreed upon and signed by the delegates of the countries represented, subject to the approval of the proper authorities of those countries.

I respectfully direct your attention to the report of the Postmaster-General and to his suggestions in regard to an equitable adjustment of the question of compensation to railroads for carrying the mails.

Your attention will be drawn to the unsettled condition of affairs in some of the Southern States.

On the 14th of September last the governor of Louisiana called upon me, as provided by the Constitution and laws of the United States, to aid in suppressing domestic violence in that State. This call was made in view of a proclamation issued on that day by D. B. Penn, claiming that he was elected lieutenant-governor in 1872, and calling upon the militia of the State to arm, assemble, and drive from power the usurpers, as he designated the officers of the State government. On the next day I issued my proclamation * commanding the insurgents to disperse within five days from the date thereof, and subsequently learned that on that day they had taken forcible possession of the statehouse. Steps were taken by me to support the existing and recognized State government, but before the expiration of the five days the insurrectionary movement was practically abandoned, and the officers of the State government, with some minor exceptions, resumed their powers and duties. Consid-

* See pp. 4230-4231.

ering that the present State administration of Louisiana has been the only government in that State for nearly two years; that it has been tacitly acknowledged and acquiesced in as such by Congress, and more than once expressly recognized by me, I regarded it as my clear duty, when legally called upon for that purpose, to prevent its overthrow by an armed mob under pretense of fraud and irregularity in the election of 1872. I have heretofore called the attention of Congress to this subject, stating that on account of the frauds and forgeries committed at said election, and because it appears that the returns thereof were never legally canvassed, it was impossible to tell thereby who were chosen; but from the best sources of information at my command I have always believed that the present State officers received a majority of the legal votes actually cast at that election. I repeat what I said in my special message of February 23, 1873, that in the event of no action by Congress I must continue to recognize the government heretofore recognized by me.

I regret to say that with preparations for the late election decided indications appeared in some localities in the Southern States of a determination, by acts of violence and intimidation, to deprive citizens of the freedom of the ballot because of their political opinions. Bands of men, masked and armed, made their appearance; White Leagues and other societies were formed; large quantities of arms and ammunition were imported and distributed to these organizations; military drills, with menacing demonstrations, were held, and with all these murders enough were committed to spread terror among those whose political action was to be suppressed, if possible, by these intolerant and criminal proceedings. In some places colored laborers were compelled to vote according to the wishes of their employers, under threats of discharge if they acted otherwise; and there are too many instances in which, when these threats were disregarded, they were remorselessly executed by those who made them. I understand that the fifteenth amendment to the Constitution was made to prevent this and a like state of things, and the act of May 31, 1870, with amendments, was passed to enforce its provisions, the object of both being to guarantee to all citizens the right to vote and to protect them in the free enjoyment of that right. Enjoined by the Constitution "to take care that the laws be faithfully executed," and convinced by undoubted evidence that violations of said act had been committed and that a widespread and flagrant disregard of it was contemplated, the proper officers were instructed to prosecute the offenders, and troops were stationed at convenient points to aid these officers, if necessary, in the performance of their official duties. Complaints are made of this interference by Federal authority; but if said amendment and act do not provide for such interference under the circumstances as above stated, then they are without meaning, force, or effect, and the whole scheme of colored enfranchisement is worse than mockery and little better than a crime. Possibly Congress

may find it due to truth and justice to ascertain, by means of a committee, whether the alleged wrongs to colored citizens for political purposes
are real or the reports thereof were manufactured for the occasion.

The whole number of troops in the States of Louisiana, Alabama,
Georgia, Florida, South Carolina, North Carolina, Kentucky, Tennessee,
Arkansas, Mississippi, Maryland, and Virginia at the time of the election
was 4,082. This embraces the garrisons of all the forts from the Delaware to the Gulf of Mexico.

Another trouble has arisen in Arkansas. Article 13 of the constitution of that State (which was adopted in 1868, and upon the approval
of which by Congress the State was restored to representation as one of
the States of the Union) provides in effect that before any amendments
proposed to this constitution shall become a part thereof they shall be
passed by two successive assemblies and then submitted to and ratified
by a majority of the electors of the State voting thereon. On the 11th of
May, 1874, the governor convened an extra session of the general assembly of the State, which on the 18th of the same month passed an act providing for a convention to frame a new constitution. Pursuant to this
act, and at an election held on the 30th of June, 1874, the convention was
approved, and delegates were chosen thereto, who assembled on the 14th
of last July and framed a new constitution, the schedule of which provided
for the election of an entire new set of State officers in a manner contrary
to the then existing election laws of the State. On the 13th of October,
1874, this constitution, as therein provided, was submitted to the people
for their approval or rejection, and according to the election returns was
approved by a large majority of those qualified to vote thereon; and at
the same election persons were chosen to fill all the State, county, and
township offices. The governor elected in 1872 for the term of four years
turned over his office to the governor chosen under the new constitution,
whereupon the lieutenant-governor, also elected in 1872 for a term of four
years, claiming to act as governor, and alleging that said proceedings by
which the new constitution was made and a new set of officers elected
were unconstitutional, illegal, and void, called upon me, as provided in
section 4, Article IV, of the Constitution, to protect the State against
domestic violence. As Congress is now investigating the political affairs
of Arkansas, I have declined to interfere.

The whole subject of Executive interference with the affairs of a State
is repugnant to public opinion, to the feelings of those who, from their
official capacity, must be used in such interposition, and to him or those
who must direct. Unless most clearly on the side of law, such interference becomes a crime; with the law to support it, it is condemned without
a hearing. I desire, therefore, that all necessity for Executive direction
in local affairs may become unnecessary and obsolete. I invite the attention, not of Congress, but of the people of the United States, to the causes
and effects of these unhappy questions. Is there not a disposition on one

side to magnify wrongs and outrages, and on the other side to belittle them or justify them? If public opinion could be directed to a correct survey of what is and to rebuking wrong and aiding the proper authorities in punishing it, a better state of feeling would be inculcated, and the sooner we would have that peace which would leave the States free indeed to regulate their own domestic affairs. I believe on the part of our citizens of the Southern States—the better part of them—there is a disposition to be law abiding, and to do no violence either to individuals or to the laws existing. But do they do right in ignoring the existence of violence and bloodshed in resistance to constituted authority? I sympathize with their prostrate condition, and would do all in my power to relieve them, acknowledging that in some instances they have had most trying governments to live under, and very oppressive ones in the way of taxation for nominal improvements, not giving benefits equal to the hardships imposed. But can they proclaim themselves entirely irresponsible for this condition? They can not. Violence has been rampant in some localities, and has either been justified or denied by those who could have prevented it. The theory is even raised that there is to be no further interference on the part of the General Government to protect citizens within a State where the State authorities fail to give protection. This is a great mistake. While I remain Executive all the laws of Congress and the provisions of the Constitution, including the recent amendments added thereto, will be enforced with rigor, but with regret that they should have added one jot or tittle to Executive duties or powers. Let there be fairness in the discussion of Southern questions, the advocates of both or all political parties giving honest, truthful reports of occurrences, condemning the wrong and upholding the right, and soon all will be well. Under existing conditions the negro votes the Republican ticket because he knows his friends are of that party. Many a good citizen votes the opposite, not because he agrees with the great principles of state which separate parties, but because, generally, he is opposed to negro rule. This is a most delusive cry. Treat the negro as a citizen and a voter, as he is and must remain, and soon parties will be divided, not on the color line, but on principle. Then we shall have no complaint of sectional interference.

The report of the Attorney-General contains valuable recommendations relating to the administration of justice in the courts of the United States, to which I invite your attention.

I respectfully suggest to Congress the propriety of increasing the number of judicial districts in the United States to eleven (the present number being nine) and the creation of two additional judgeships. The territory to be traversed by the circuit judges is so great and the business of the courts so steadily increasing that it is growing more and more impossible for them to keep up with the business requiring their attention. Whether this would involve the necessity of adding two more justices of the Supreme Court to the present number I submit to the judgment of Congress.

The attention of Congress is invited to the report of the Secretary of the Interior and to the legislation asked for by him. The domestic interests of the people are more intimately connected with this Department than with either of the other Departments of Government. Its duties have been added to from time to time until they have become so onerous that without the most perfect system and order it will be impossible for any Secretary of the Interior to keep trace of all official transactions having his sanction and done in his name, and for which he is held personally responsible.

The policy adopted for the management of Indian affairs, known as the peace policy, has been adhered to with most beneficial results. It is confidently hoped that a few years more will relieve our frontiers from danger of Indian depredations.

I commend the recommendation of the Secretary for the extension of the homestead laws to the Indians and for some sort of Territorial government for the Indian Territory. A great majority of the Indians occupying this Territory are believed yet to be incapable of maintaining their rights against the more civilized and enlightened white man. Any Territorial form of government given them, therefore, should protect them in their homes and property for a period of at least twenty years, and before its final adoption should be ratified by a majority of those affected.

The report of the Secretary of the Interior herewith attached gives much interesting statistical information, which I abstain from giving an abstract of, but refer you to the report itself.

The act of Congress providing the oath which pensioners must subscribe to before drawing their pensions cuts off from this bounty a few survivors of the War of 1812 residing in the Southern States. I recommend the restoration of this bounty to all such. The number of persons whose names would thus be restored to the list of pensioners is not large. They are all old persons, who could have taken no part in the rebellion, and the services for which they were awarded pensions were in defense of the whole country.

The report of the Commissioner of Agriculture herewith contains suggestions of much interest to the general public, and refers to the approaching Centennial and the part his Department is ready to take in it. I feel that the nation at large is interested in having this exposition a success, and commend to Congress such action as will secure a greater general interest in it. Already many foreign nations have signified their intention to be represented at it, and it may be expected that every civilized nation will be represented.

The rules adopted to improve the civil service of the Government have been adhered to as closely as has been practicable with the opposition with which they meet. The effect, I believe, has been beneficial on the whole, and has tended to the elevation of the service. But it is impracticable to maintain them without direct and positive support of Congress. Generally the support which this reform receives is from those who give it their support only to find fault when the rules are apparently departed from. Removals from office without preferring charges against parties removed are frequently cited as departures from the rules adopted, and the retention of those against whom charges are made by irresponsible persons and without good grounds is also often condemned as a violation of them. Under these circumstances, therefore, I announce that if Congress adjourns without positive legislation on the subject of "civil-service reform" I will regard such action as a disapproval of the system, and will abandon it, except so far as to require examinations for certain appointees, to determine their fitness. Competitive examinations will be abandoned.

The gentlemen who have given their services, without compensation, as members of the board to devise rules and regulations for the government of the civil service of the country have shown much zeal and earnestness in their work, and to them, as well as to myself, it will be a source of mortification if it is to be thrown away. But I repeat that it is impossible to carry this system to a successful issue without general approval and assistance and positive law to support it.

I have stated that three elements of prosperity to the nation—capital, labor, skilled and unskilled, and products of the soil—still remain with us. To direct the employment of these is a problem deserving the most serious attention of Congress. If employment can be given to all the labor offering itself, prosperity necessarily follows. I have expressed the opinion, and repeat it, that the first requisite to the accomplishment of this end is the substitution of a sound currency in place of one of a fluctuating value. This secured, there are many interests that might be fostered to the great profit of both labor and capital. How to induce capital to employ labor is the question. The subject of cheap transportation has occupied the attention of Congress. Much new light on this question will without doubt be given by the committee appointed by the last Congress to investigate and report upon this subject.

A revival of shipbuilding, and particularly of iron steamship building, is of vast importance to our national prosperity. The United States is now paying over $100,000,000 per annum for freights and passage on foreign ships—to be carried abroad and expended in the employment and support of other peoples—beyond a fair percentage of what should go to foreign vessels, estimating on the tonnage and travel of each respectively. It is to be regretted that this disparity in the carrying trade exists, and to correct it I would be willing to see a great departure from the usual course of Government in supporting what might usually be termed private enterprise. I would not suggest as a remedy direct subsidy to American steamship lines, but I would suggest the direct offer of ample compensation for carrying the mails between Atlantic Seaboard cities and the Continent on American-owned and American-built steamers, and would extend this liberality to vessels carrying the mails to South American States and to Central America and Mexico, and would pursue the same policy from our Pacific seaports to foreign seaports on the Pacific. It might be demanded that vessels built for this service should come up to a standard fixed by legislation in tonnage, speed, and all other qualities, looking to the possibility of Government requiring them at some time for war purposes. The right also of taking possession of them in such emergency should be guarded.

I offer these suggestions, believing them worthy of consideration, in all seriousness, affecting all sections and all interests alike. If anything better can be done to direct the country into a course of general prosperity, no one will be more ready than I to second the plan.

Forwarded herewith will be found the report of the commissioners appointed under an act of Congress approved June 20, 1874, to wind up the affairs of the District government. It will be seen from the report that the net debt of the District of Columbia, less securities on hand and available, is:

Bonded debt issued prior to July 1, 1874	$8,883,940.43
3.65 bonds, act of Congress June 20, 1874	2,088,168.73
Certificates of the board of audit	4,770,558.45
	15,742,667.61

Less special-improvement assessments (chargeable to private property) in excess of any demand against such assessments	$1,614,054.37	
Less Chesapeake and Ohio Canal bonds	75,000.00	
And Washington and Alexandria Railroad bonds	59,000.00	
In the hands of the commissioners of the sinking fund		1,748,054.37
Leaving actual debt, less said assets		13,994,613.24

In addition to this there are claims preferred against the government of the District amounting, in the estimated aggregate reported by the board of audit, to $3,147,787.48, of which the greater part will probably be rejected. This sum can with no more propriety be included in the debt account of the District government than can the thousands of claims against the General Government be included as a portion of the national debt. But the aggregate sum thus stated includes something more than the funded debt chargeable exclusively to the District of Columbia. The act of Congress of June 20, 1874, contemplates an apportionment between the United States Government and the District of Columbia in respect of the payment of the principal and interest of the 3.65 bonds. Therefore in computing with precision the bonded debt of the District the aggregate sums above stated as respects 3.65 bonds now issued, the outstanding certificates of the board of audit, and the unadjusted claims pending before that board should be reduced to the extent of the amount to be apportioned to the United States Government in the manner indicated in the act of Congress of June 20, 1874.

I especially invite your attention to the recommendations of the commissioners of the sinking fund relative to the ambiguity of the act of June 20, 1874, the interest on the District bonds, and the consolidation of the indebtedness of the District.

I feel much indebted to the gentlemen who consented to leave their private affairs and come from a distance to attend to the business of this District, and for the able and satisfactory manner in which it has been conducted. I am sure their services will be equally appreciated by the entire country.

It will be seen from the accompanying full report of the board of health that the sanitary condition of the District is very satisfactory.

In my opinion the District of Columbia should be regarded as the grounds of the national capital, in which the entire people are interested. I do not allude to this to urge generous appropriations to the District, but to draw the attention of Congress, in framing a law for the government of the District, to the magnificent scale on which the city was planned by the founders of the Government; the manner in which, for ornamental purposes, the reservations, streets, and avenues were laid out, and the proportion of the property actually possessed by the General Government. I think the proportion of the expenses of the government and improvements to be borne by the General Government, the cities of Washington and Georgetown, and the county should be carefully and equitably defined.

In accordance with section 3, act approved June 23, 1874, I appointed a board to make a survey of the mouth of the Mississippi River with a view to determine the best method of obtaining and maintaining a depth of water sufficient for the purposes of commerce, etc.; and in accordance with an act entitled "An act to provide for the appointment of a commission of engineers to investigate and report a permanent plan for the reclamation of the alluvial basin of the Mississippi River subject to inundation," I appointed a commission of engineers. Neither board has yet completed its labors. When their reports are received, they will be forwarded to Congress without delay. U. S. GRANT.

SPECIAL MESSAGES.

WASHINGTON, *December 8, 1874.*

To the Senate of the United States:

In answer to the resolution of the Senate of the 3d of February, 1873, I transmit herewith a report from the Secretary of State, together with the papers* which accompanied it. U. S. GRANT.

*Dispatches in regard to the records and public documents of the Mexican Government relative to the lands embraced within the Territories of Arizona and New Mexico.

WASHINGTON, *December 8, 1874.*

To the Senate of the United States:

I transmit to the Senate, for consideration with a view to ratification, a convention between the United States of America and the Ottoman Empire, relative to the extradition of criminals fugitives from justice, signed by their respective plenipotentiaries at Constantinople on the 11th of August last.

U. S. GRANT.

WASHINGTON, *December 8, 1874.*

To the Senate of the United States:

I transmit to the Senate, for consideration with a view to ratification, a convention concluded between the United States of America and the Mexican Republic on the 20th of November last, for further extending the time for the duration of the joint commission respecting claims, originally fixed by the convention between the United States and Mexico signed on the 4th of July, 1868, and extended by those of the 19th of April, 1871, and 27th of November, 1872, between the same parties.

U. S. GRANT.

WASHINGTON, *December 8, 1874.*

To the Senate of the United States:

I transmit to the Senate, for consideration with a view to ratification, a convention between the United States of America and the Ottoman Empire, relative to the naturalization of citizens and subjects of the two countries, signed by their respective plenipotentiaries at Constantinople on the 11th of August last. A copy of the correspondence which accompanied the convention on the subject is herewith transmitted.

U. S. GRANT.

WASHINGTON, *December 8, 1874.*

To the Senate and House of Representatives:

I transmit herewith a report, dated the 8th instant, with accompanying papers,* from the Secretary of State, in compliance with the requirements of section 208 of the Revised Statutes of the United States.

U. S. GRANT.

EXECUTIVE MANSION, *December 22, 1874.*

The SPEAKER OF THE HOUSE OF REPRESENTATIVES:

I have the honor to transmit herewith, for the information of Congress, a memorial† forwarded to me by a convention of colored citizens assembled in the city of Montgomery, Ala., on the 2d of this month.

U. S. GRANT.

---

* Report of fees collected, etc., by consular officers of the United States for 1873. list of consular officers, and tariff of consular fees prescribed by the President September 1, 1874.
† Asking all the rights of citizenship.

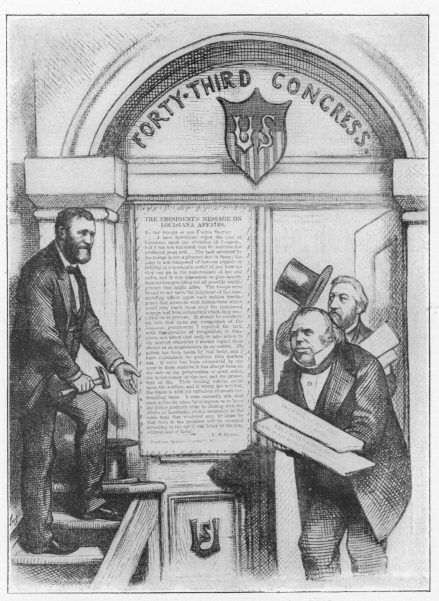

THE EFFECT OF GRANT'S MESSAGE OF JAN. 13, 1875

LOUISIANA AFFAIRS AND RECONSTRUCTION

The condition of Louisiana from 1868 to 1876 under the rule of corrupt rascals from the North and their allies, the negroes, was pitiful. On the one hand, the clever crooks from the North, by selling blocks of negro votes in the legislative assemblies, amassed fortunes, while negro politicians and legislators, who but a few years before were slaves, drove magnificent horses, lived in expensive state, and conspicuously wore huge diamonds. On the other hand, the landed and working classes were plundered into bankruptcy. The State tax grew from 29 cents on $100 in 1861, to 52½ cents in 1868, and to $2.15 in 1872. The people of New Orleans paid this State tax and a local tax of $3 on $100. The State debt grew from $14,000,000 in 1868, to $40,000,000 in 1874. Misgovernment meant confiscation. An estate in New Orleans was worth in 1867 $1,000,000 and produced an income of $70,000 annually. In 1872 the same estate did not fetch enough rent to cover the taxes, insurance and usual repairs. The cartoon shows Congress responding to Grant's message of January 13, 1875, regarding Louisiana affairs.

The rehabilitation of the South forms one of the most important and interesting chapters in our history. The article entitled "Reconstruction" in the index (volume eleven), presents a summary on which the Presidents have discussed the ways and means of reviving the life of the war-worn States of the South. In the index, under the name of each President, appears a history of his administration.

EXECUTIVE MANSION, *January 5, 1875.*

To the Senate of the United States:

In answer to the resolution of the Senate of the 21st December last, requesting the return of its resolution of the 17th of the same month, advising and consenting to the appointment of J. C. S. Colby to be consul of the United States at Chin-Kiang, I have the honor to state that Mr. Colby's commission was signed on the 17th day of December, and upon inquiry at the Department of State it was found that it had been forwarded to him by mail before the receipt of the resolution of recall.

U. S. GRANT.

EXECUTIVE MANSION, *January 12, 1875.*

To the Senate and House of Representatives:

In accordance with the requirements of the joint resolution approved March 25, 1874, authorizing an inquiry into and report upon the causes of epidemic cholera, I have the honor to transmit herewith reports upon the subject from the Secretaries of the Treasury and War Departments.

U. S. GRANT.

EXECUTIVE MANSION, *January 13, 1875.*

To the Senate of the United States:

I have the honor to make the following answer to a Senate resolution of the 8th instant, asking for information as to any interference by any military officer or any part of the Army of the United States with the organization or proceedings of the general assembly of the State of Louisiana, or either branch thereof; and also inquiring in regard to the existence of armed organizations in that State hostile to the government thereof and intent on overturning such government by force.

To say that lawlessness, turbulence, and bloodshed have characterized the political affairs of that State since its reorganization under the reconstruction acts is only to repeat what has become well known as a part of its unhappy history; but it may be proper here to refer to the election of 1868, by which the Republican vote of the State, through fraud and violence, was reduced to a few thousands, and the bloody riots of 1866 and 1868, to show that the disorders there are not due to any recent causes or to any late action of the Federal authorities.

Preparatory to the election of 1872 a shameful and undisguised conspiracy was formed to carry that election against the Republicans, without regard to law or right, and to that end the most glaring frauds and forgeries were committed in the returns, after many colored citizens had been denied registration and others deterred by fear from casting their ballots.

When the time came for a final canvass of the votes, in view of the foregoing facts William P. Kellogg, the Republican candidate for governor, brought suit upon the equity side of the United States circuit court for

Louisiana, and against Warmoth and others, who had obtained possession of the returns of the election, representing that several thousand voters of the State had been deprived of the elective franchise on account of their color, and praying that steps might be taken to have said votes counted and for general relief. To enable the court to inquire as to the truth of these allegations, a temporary restraining order was issued against the defendants, which was at once wholly disregarded and treated with contempt by those to whom it was directed. These proceedings have been widely denounced as an unwarrantable interference by the Federal judiciary with the election of State officers; but it is to be remembered that by the fifteenth amendment to the Constitution of the United States the political equality of colored citizens is secured, and under the second section of that amendment, providing that Congress shall have power to enforce its provisions by appropriate legislation, an act was passed on the 31st of May, 1870, and amended in 1871, the object of which was to prevent the denial or abridgment of suffrage to citizens on account of race, color, or previous condition of servitude; and it has been held by all the Federal judges before whom the question has arisen, including Justice Strong, of the Supreme Court, that the protection afforded by this amendment and these acts extends to State as well as other elections. That it is the duty of the Federal courts to enforce the provisions of the Constitution of the United States and the laws passed in pursuance thereof is too clear for controversy.

Section 15 of said act, after numerous provisions therein to prevent an evasion of the fifteenth amendment, provides that the jurisdiction of the circuit court of the United States shall extend to all cases in law or equity arising under the provisions of said act and of the act amendatory thereof. Congress seems to have contemplated equitable as well as legal proceedings to prevent the denial of suffrage to colored citizens; and it may be safely asserted that if Kellogg's bill in the above-named case did not present a case for the equitable interposition of the court, that no such case can arise under the act. That the courts of the United States have the right to interfere in various ways with State elections so as to maintain political equality and rights therein, irrespective of race or color, is comparatively a new, and to some seems to be a startling, idea, but it results as clearly from the fifteenth amendment to the Constitution and the acts that have been passed to enforce that amendment as the abrogation of State laws upholding slavery results from the thirteenth amendment to the Constitution. While the jurisdiction of the court in the case of Kellogg *vs.* Warmoth and others is clear to my mind, it seems that some of the orders made by the judge in that and the kindred case of Antoine were illegal. But while they are so held and considered, it is not to be forgotten that the mandate of his court had been contemptuously defied, and they were made while wild scenes of anarchy were sweeping away all restraint of law and order. Doubtless the judge of this court made grave mistakes; but the law allows the chancellor great latitude, not only in punishing those who contemn his orders and injunctions, but in preventing the consummation of the wrong which he has judicially forbidden. Whatever may be said or thought of those matters, it was only made known to me that process of the United States court was resisted, and as said act especially provides for the use of the Army and Navy when necessary to enforce judicial process arising thereunder, I considered it my duty to see that such process was executed according to the judgment of the court.

Resulting from these proceedings, through various controversies and complications, a State administration was organized with William P. Kellogg as governor, which, in the discharge of my duty under section 4, Article IV, of the Constitution, I have recognized as the government of the State.

It has been bitterly and persistently alleged that Kellogg was not elected. Whether he was or not is not altogether certain, nor is it any more certain that his competitor, McEnery, was chosen. The election was a gigantic fraud, and there are no reliable returns of its result. Kellogg obtained possession of the office, and in my opinion has more right to it than his competitor.

On the 20th of February, 1873, the Committee on Privileges and Elections of the Senate made a report in which they say they were satisfied by testimony that the manipulation of the election machinery by Warmoth and others was equivalent to 20,000 votes; and they add that to recognize the McEnery government "would be recognizing a government based upon fraud, in defiance of the wishes and intention of the voters of the State." Assuming the correctness of the statements in this report (and they seem to have been generally accepted by the country), the great crime in Louisiana, about which so much has been said, is that one is holding the office of governor who was cheated out of 20,000 votes, against another whose title to the office is undoubtedly based on fraud and in defiance of the wishes and intentions of the voters of the State.

Misinformed and misjudging as to the nature and extent of this report, the supporters of McEnery proceeded to displace by force in some counties of the State the appointees of Governor Kellogg, and on the 13th of April, in an effort of that kind, a butchery of citizens was committed at Colfax, which in bloodthirstiness and barbarity is hardly surpassed by any acts of savage warfare.

To put this matter beyond controversy I quote from the charge of Judge Woods, of the United States circuit court, to the jury in the case of The United States *vs.* Cruikshank and others, in New Orleans in March, 1874. He said:

In the case on trial there are many facts not in controversy. I proceed to state some of them in the presence and hearing of counsel on both sides; and if I state as a conceded fact any matter that is disputed, they can correct me.

After stating the origin of the difficulty, which grew out of an attempt of white persons to drive the parish judge and sheriff, appointees of Kellogg, from office, and their attempted protection by colored persons, which led to some fighting, in which quite a number of negroes were killed, the judge states:

Most of those who were not killed were taken prisoners. Fifteen or sixteen of the blacks had lifted the boards and taken refuge under the floor of the court-house. They were all captured. About thirty-seven men were taken prisoners. The number is not definitely fixed. They were kept under guard until dark. They were led out, two by two, and shot. Most of the men were shot to death. A few were wounded, not mortally, and by pretending to be dead were afterwards, during the night, able to make their escape. Among them was the Levi Nelson named in the indictment.

The dead bodies of the negroes killed in this affair were left unburied until Tuesday, April 15, when they were buried by a deputy marshal and an officer of the militia from New Orleans. These persons found fifty-nine dead bodies. They showed pistol-shot wounds, the great majority in the head, and most of them in the back of the head. In addition to the fifty-nine dead bodies found, some charred remains of dead bodies were discovered near the court-house. Six dead bodies were found under a warehouse, all shot in the head but one or two, which were shot in the breast.

The only white men injured from the beginning of these troubles to their close were Hadnot and Harris. The court-house and its contents were entirely consumed.

There is no evidence that anyone in the crowd of whites bore any lawful warrant for the arrest of any of the blacks. There is no evidence that either Nash or Cazabat, after the affair, ever demanded their offices, to which they had set up claim, but Register continued to act as parish judge and Shaw as sheriff.

These are facts in this case as I understand them to be admitted.

To hold the people of Louisiana generally responsible for these atrocities would not be just, but it is a lamentable fact that insuperable obstructions were thrown in the way of punishing these murderers; and the so-called conservative papers of the State not only justified the massacre, but denounced as Federal tyranny and despotism the attempt of the United States officers to bring them to justice. Fierce denunciations ring through the country about office holding and election matters in Louisiana, while every one of the Colfax miscreants goes unwhipped of justice, and no way can be found in this boasted land of civilization and Christianity to punish the perpetrators of this bloody and monstrous crime.

Not unlike this was the massacre in August last. Several Northern young men of capital and enterprise had started the little and flourishing town of Coushatta. Some of them were Republicans and office-holders under Kellogg. They were therefore doomed to death. Six of them were seized and carried away from their homes and murdered in cold blood. No one has been punished, and the conservative press of the State denounced all efforts to that end and boldly justified the crime.

Many murders of a like character have been committed in individual cases, which can not here be detailed. For example, T. S. Crawford, judge, and P. H. Harris, district attorney, of the twelfth judicial district of the State, on their way to court were shot from their horses by men in ambush on the 8th of October, 1873; and the widow of the former, in a communication to the Department of Justice, tells a piteous tale of the persecutions of her husband because he was a Union man, and of the efforts made to screen those who had committed a crime which, to use her own language, "left two widows and nine orphans desolate."

To say that the murder of a negro or a white Republican is not considered a crime in Louisiana would probably be unjust to a great part of the people, but it is true that a great number of such murders have been committed and no one has been punished therefor; and manifestly, as to them, the spirit of hatred and violence is stronger than law.

Representations were made to me that the presence of troops in Louisiana was unnecessary and irritating to the people, and that there was no danger of public disturbance if they were taken away. Consequently early in last summer the troops were all withdrawn from the State, with the exception of a small garrison at New Orleans Barracks. It was claimed that a comparative state of quiet had supervened. Political excitement as to Louisiana affairs seemed to be dying out. But the November election was approaching, and it was necessary for party purposes that the flame should be rekindled.

Accordingly, on the 14th of September D. P. Penn, claiming that he was elected lieutenant-governor in 1872, issued an inflammatory proclamation calling upon the militia of the State to arm, assemble, and drive from power the usurpers, as he designated the officers of the State. The White Leagues, armed and ready for the conflict, promptly responded.

On the same day the governor made a formal requisition upon me, pursuant to the act of 1795 and section 4, Article IV, of the Constitution, to aid in suppressing domestic violence. On the next day I issued my proclamation* commanding the insurgents to disperse within five days from the date thereof; but before the proclamation was published in New Orleans the organized and armed forces recognizing a usurping governor had taken forcible possession of the statehouse and temporarily subverted the government. Twenty or more people were killed, including a number of the police of the city. The streets of the city were stained with blood. All that was desired in the way of excitement had been accomplished, and, in view of the steps taken to repress it, the revolution is apparently, though it is believed not really, abandoned, and the cry of Federal usurpation and tyranny in Louisiana was renewed with redoubled energy. Troops had been sent to the State under this requisition of the governor, and as other disturbances seemed imminent they were allowed to remain there to render the executive such aid as might become necessary to enforce the laws of the State and repress the continued violence which seemed inevitable the moment Federal support should be withdrawn.

* See pp. 4230–4231.

Prior to, and with a view to, the late election in Louisiana white men associated themselves together in armed bodies called "White Leagues," and at the same time threats were made in the Democratic journals of the State that the election should be carried against the Republicans at all hazards, which very naturally greatly alarmed the colored voters. By section 8 of the act of February 28, 1871, it is made the duty of United States marshals and their deputies at polls where votes are cast for Representatives in Congress to keep the peace and prevent any violations of the so-called enforcement acts and other offenses against the laws of the United States; and upon a requisition of the marshal of Louisiana, and in view of said armed organizations and other portentous circumstances, I caused detachments of troops to be stationed in various localities in the State, to aid him in the performance of his official duties. That there was intimidation of Republican voters at the election, notwithstanding these precautions, admits of no doubt. The following are specimens of the means used:

On the 14th of October eighty persons signed and published the following at Shreveport:

We, the undersigned, merchants of the city of Shreveport, in obedience to a request of the Shreveport Campaign Club, agree to use every endeavor to get our employees to vote the People's ticket at the ensuing election, and in the event of their refusal so to do, or in case they vote the Radical ticket, to refuse to employ them at the expiration of their present contracts.

On the same day another large body of persons published in the same place a paper in which they used the following language:

We, the undersigned, merchants of the city of Shreveport, alive to the great importance of securing good and honest government to the State, do agree and pledge ourselves not to advance any supplies or money to any planter the coming year who will give employment or rent lands to laborers who vote the Radical ticket in the coming election.

I have no information of the proceedings of the returning board for said election which may not be found in its report, which has been published; but it is a matter of public information that a great part of the time taken to canvass the votes was consumed by the arguments of lawyers, several of whom represented each party before the board. I have no evidence that the proceedings of this board were not in accordance with the law under which they acted. Whether in excluding from their count certain returns they were right or wrong is a question that depends upon the evidence they had before them; but it is very clear that the law gives them the power, if they choose to exercise it, of deciding that way, and, *prima facie*, the persons whom they return as elected are entitled to the offices for which they were candidates.

Respecting the alleged interference by the military with the organization of the legislature of Louisiana on the 4th instant, I have no knowledge or information which has not been received by me since that time and published. My first information was from the papers of the morning

of the 5th of January. I did not know that any such thing was anticipated, and no orders nor suggestions were ever given to any military officer in that State upon that subject prior to the occurrence. I am well
aware that any military interference by the officers or troops of the United
States with the organization of the State legislature or any of its proceedings, or with any civil department of the Government, is repugnant to
our ideas of government. I can conceive of no case, not involving rebellion or insurrection, where such interference by authority of the General
Government ought to be permitted or can be justified. But there are circumstances connected with the late legislative imbroglio in Louisiana
which seem to exempt the military from any intentional wrong in that
matter. Knowing that they had been placed in Louisiana to prevent
domestic violence and aid in the enforcement of the State laws, the officers and troops of the United States may well have supposed that it was
their duty to act when called upon by the governor for that purpose.

Each branch of a legislative assembly is the judge of the election and
qualifications of its own members; but if a mob or a body of unauthorized persons seize and hold the legislative hall in a tumultuous and riotous manner, and so prevent any organization by those legally returned as
elected, it might become the duty of the State executive to interpose, if
requested by a majority of the members elect, to suppress the disturbance
and enable the persons elected to organize the house.

Any exercise of this power would only be justifiable under most extraordinary circumstances, and it would then be the duty of the governor to
call upon the constabulary or, if necessary, the military force of the State.
But with reference to Louisiana, it is to be borne in mind that any attempt
by the governor to use the police force of that State at this time would
have undoubtedly precipitated a bloody conflict with the White League,
as it did on the 14th of September.

There is no doubt but that the presence of the United States troops upon
that occasion prevented bloodshed and the loss of life. Both parties appear
to have relied upon them as conservators of the public peace.

The first call was made by the Democrats, to remove persons obnoxious
to them from the legislative halls; and the second was from the Republicans, to remove persons who had usurped seats in the legislature without legal certificates authorizing them to seats, and in sufficient number
to change the majority.

Nobody was disturbed by the military who had a legal right at that
time to occupy a seat in the legislature. That the Democratic minority
of the house undertook to seize its organization by fraud and violence;
that in this attempt they trampled under foot law; that they undertook
to make persons not returned as elected members, so as to create a majority; that they acted under a preconcerted plan, and under false pretenses
introduced into the hall a body of men to support their pretensions by
force if necessary, and that conflict, disorder, and riotous proceedings

followed are facts that seem to be well established; and I am credibly informed that these violent proceedings were a part of a premeditated plan to have the house organized in this way, recognize what has been called the McEnery senate, then to depose Governor Kellogg, and so revolutionize the State government.

Whether it was wrong for the governor, at the request of the majority of the members returned as elected to the house, to use such means as were in his power to defeat these lawless and revolutionary proceedings is perhaps a debatable question; but it is quite certain that there would have been no trouble if those who now complain of illegal interference had allowed the house to be organized in a lawful and regular manner. When those who inaugurate disorder and anarchy disavow such proceedings, it will be time enough to condemn those who by such means as they have prevent the success of their lawless and desperate schemes.

Lieutenant-General Sheridan was requested by me to go to Louisiana to observe and report the situation there, and, if in his opinion necessary, to assume the command, which he did on the 4th instant, after the legislative disturbances had occurred, at 9 o'clock p. m., a number of hours after the disturbances. No party motives nor prejudices can reasonably be imputed to him; but honestly convinced by what he has seen and heard there, he has characterized the leaders of the White Leagues in severe terms and suggested summary modes of procedure against them, which, though they can not be adopted, would, if legal, soon put an end to the troubles and disorders in that State. General Sheridan was looking at facts, and possibly, not thinking of proceedings which would be the only proper ones to pursue in time of peace, thought more of the utterly lawless condition of society surrounding him at the time of his dispatch and of what would prove a sure remedy. He never proposed to do an illegal act nor expressed determination to proceed beyond what the law in the future might authorize for the punishment of the atrocities which have been committed, and the commission of which can not be successfully denied. It is a deplorable fact that political crimes and murders have been committed in Louisiana which have gone unpunished, and which have been justified or apologized for, which must rest as a reproach upon the State and country long after the present generation has passed away.

I have no desire to have United States troops interfere in the domestic concerns of Louisiana or any other State.

On the 9th of December last Governor Kellogg telegraphed to me his apprehensions that the White League intended to make another attack upon the statehouse, to which, on the same day, I made the following answer, since which no communication has been sent to him:

Your dispatch of this date just received. It is exceedingly unpalatable to use troops in anticipation of danger. Let the State authorities be right, and then proceed with their duties without apprehension of danger. If they are then molested, the question will be determined whether the United States is able to maintain law and order within its limits or not.

I have deplored the necessity which seemed to make it my duty under the Constitution and laws to direct such interference. I have always refused except where it seemed to be my imperative duty to act in such a manner under the Constitution and laws of the United States. I have repeatedly and earnestly entreated the people of the South to live together in peace and obey the laws; and nothing would give me greater pleasure than to see reconciliation and tranquillity everywhere prevail, and thereby remove all necessity for the presence of troops among them. I regret, however, to say that this state of things does not exist, nor does its existence seem to be desired, in some localities; and as to those it may be proper for me to say that to the extent that Congress has conferred power upon me to prevent it neither Kuklux Klans, White Leagues, nor any other association using arms and violence to execute their unlawful purposes can be permitted in that way to govern any part of this country; nor can I see with indifference Union men or Republicans ostracized, persecuted, and murdered on account of their opinions, as they now are in some localities.

I have heretofore urged the case of Louisiana upon the attention of Congress, and I can not but think that its inaction has produced great evil.

To summarize: In September last an armed, organized body of men, in the support of candidates who had been put in nomination for the offices of governor and lieutenant-governor at the November election in 1872, and who had been declared not elected by the board of canvassers, recognized by all the courts to which the question had been submitted, undertook to subvert and overthrow the State government that had been recognized by me in accordance with previous precedents. The recognized governor was driven from the statehouse, and but for his finding shelter in the United States custom-house, in the capital of the State of which he was governor, it is scarcely to be doubted that he would have been killed.

From the statehouse, before he had been driven to the custom-house, a call was made, in accordance with the fourth section, fourth article, of the Constitution of the United States, for the aid of the General Government to suppress domestic violence. Under those circumstances, and in accordance with my sworn duties, my proclamation* of the 15th of September, 1874, was issued. This served to reinstate Governor Kellogg to his position nominally, but it can not be claimed that the insurgents have to this day surrendered to the State authorities the arms belonging to the State, or that they have in any sense disarmed. On the contrary, it is known that the same armed organizations that existed on the 14th of September, 1874, in opposition to the recognized State government, still retain their organization, equipments, and commanders, and can be called out at any hour to resist the State government. Under these

* See pp. 4230–4231.

circumstances the same military force has been continued in Louisiana as was sent there under the first call, and under the same general instructions. I repeat that the task assumed by the troops is not a pleasant one to them; that the Army is not composed of lawyers, capable of judging at a moment's notice of just how far they can go in the maintenance of law and order, and that it was impossible to give specific instructions providing for all possible contingencies that might arise. The troops were bound to act upon the judgment of the commanding officer upon each sudden contingency that arose, or wait instructions which could only reach them after the threatened wrongs had been committed which they were called on to prevent. It should be recollected, too, that upon my recognition of the Kellogg government I reported the fact, with the grounds of recognition, to Congress, and asked that body to take action in the matter; otherwise I should regard their silence as an acquiescence in my course. No action has been taken by that body, and I have maintained the position then marked out.

If error has been committed by the Army in these matters, it has always been on the side of the preservation of good order, the maintenance of law, and the protection of life. Their bearing reflects credit upon the soldiers, and if wrong has resulted the blame is with the turbulent element surrounding them.

I now earnestly ask that such action be taken by Congress as to leave my duties perfectly clear in dealing with the affairs of Louisiana, giving assurance at the same time that whatever may be done by that body in the premises will be executed according to the spirit and letter of the law, without fear or favor.

I herewith transmit copies of documents containing more specific information as to the subject-matter of the resolution.

U. S. GRANT.

EXECUTIVE MANSION, *January 14, 1875.*
To the Senate of the United States:

Senate bill No. 1044, "to provide for the resumption of specie payments," is before me, and this day receives my signature of approval.

I venture upon this unusual method of conveying the notice of approval to the "House in which the measure originated" because of its great importance to the country at large and in order to suggest further legislation which seems to me essential to make this law effective.

It is a subject of congratulation that a measure has become law which fixes a date when specie resumption shall commence and implies an obligation on the part of Congress, if in its power, to give such legislation as may prove necessary to redeem this promise.

To this end I respectfully call your attention to a few suggestions:

First. The necessity of an increased revenue to carry out the obligation of adding to the sinking fund annually 1 per cent of the public debt, amounting now to about $34,000,000 per annum, and to carry out the promises of this measure to redeem, under certain contingencies, eighty millions of the present legal-tenders, and, without contingency, the fractional currency now in circulation.

How to increase the surplus revenue is for Congress to devise, but I will venture to suggest that the duty on tea and coffee might be restored without permanently enhancing the cost to the consumers, and that the 10 per cent horizontal reduction of the tariff on articles specified in the law of June 6, 1872, be repealed. The supply of tea and coffee already on hand in the United States would in all probability be advanced in price by adopting this measure. But it is known that the adoption of free entry to those articles of necessity did not cheapen them, but merely added to the profits of the countries producing them, or of the middlemen in those countries, who have the exclusive trade in them.

Second. The first section of the bill now under consideration provides that the fractional currency shall be redeemed in silver coin as rapidly as practicable. There is no provision preventing the fluctuation in the value of the paper currency. With gold at a premium of anything over 10 per cent above the currency in use, it is probable, almost certain, that silver would be bought up for exportation as fast as it was put out, or until change would become so scarce as to make the premium on it equal to the premium on gold, or sufficiently high to make it no longer profitable to buy for export, thereby causing a direct loss to the community at large and great embarrassment to trade.

As the present law commands final resumption on the 1st day of January, 1879, and as the gold receipts by the Treasury are larger than the gold payments and the currency receipts are smaller than the currency payments, thereby making monthly sales of gold necessary to meet current currency expenses, it occurs to me that these difficulties might be remedied by authorizing the Secretary of the Treasury to redeem legal-tender notes, whenever presented in sums of not less than $100 and multiples thereof, at a premium for gold of 10 per cent, less interest at the rate of 2½ per cent per annum from the 1st day of January, 1875, to the date of putting this law into operation, and diminishing this premium at the same rate until final resumption, changing the rate of premium demanded from time to time as the interest amounts to one-quarter of 1 per cent. I suggest this rate of interest because it would bring currency at par with gold at the date fixed by law for final resumption. I suggest 10 per cent as the demand premium at the beginning because I believe this rate would insure the retention of silver in the country for change.

The provisions of the third section of the act will prevent combinations being made to exhaust the Treasury of coin.

With such a law it is presumable that no gold would be called for not required for legitimate business purposes. When large amounts of coin should be drawn from the Treasury, correspondingly large amounts of currency would be withdrawn from circulation, thus causing a sufficient stringency in currency to stop the outward flow of coin.

The advantages of a currency of a fixed known value would also be reached. In my opinion, by the enactment of such a law business and industries would revive and the beginning of prosperity on a firm basis would be reached.

Other means of increasing revenue than those suggested should probably be devised, and also other legislation.

In fact, to carry out the first section of the act another mint becomes a necessity. With the present facilities for coinage, it would take a period probably beyond that fixed by law for final specie resumption to coin the silver necessary to transact the business of the country.

There are now smelting furnaces, for extracting the silver and gold from the ores brought from the mountain territories, in Chicago, St. Louis, and Omaha—three in the former city—and as much of the change required will be wanted in the Mississippi Valley States, and as the metals to be coined come from west of those States, and, as I understand, the charges for transportation of bullion from either of the cities named to the mint in Philadelphia or to New York City amount to $4 for each $1,000 worth, with an equal expense for transportation back, it would seem a fair argument in favor of adopting one or more of those cities as the place or places for the establishment of new coining facilities.

I have ventured upon this subject with great diffidence, because it is so unusual to approve a measure—as I most heartily do this, even if no further legislation is attainable at this time—and to announce the fact by message. But I do so because I feel that it is a subject of such vital importance to the whole country that it should receive the attention of and be discussed by Congress and the people through the press, and in every way, to the end that the best and most satisfactory course may be reached of executing what I deem most beneficial legislation on a most vital question to the interests and prosperity of the nation.

U. S. GRANT.

EXECUTIVE MANSION, *January 20, 1875.*

To the House of Representatives:

I have the honor to transmit herewith a report from a board composed of one person named by the head of each Executive Department and of the Department of Agriculture and Smithsonian Institution, for the purpose of securing a complete and harmonious arrangement of the articles and materials designed to be exhibited from the Executive Departments of the Government at the international exhibition to be held in the city of Philadelphia in the year 1876 for the purpose of celebrating the one hundredth anniversary of the independence of the United States. The report gives a statement of what is proposed to be exhibited by each Department, together with an estimate of the expense which will have to be incurred. Submitting to Congress the estimate made by the board,

I recommend that Congress make a suitable appropriation to enable the different Departments to make a complete and creditable showing of the articles and materials designed to be exhibited by the Government, and which will undoubtedly form one of the most interesting features of the exhibition.

U. S. GRANT.

EXECUTIVE MANSION, *January 20, 1875.*

To the Senate and House of Representatives:

In my annual message of December 1, 1873, while inviting general attention to all the recommendations made by the Secretary of War, your special consideration was invited to "the importance of preparing for war in time of peace by providing proper armament for our seacoast defenses. Proper armament is of vastly more importance than fortifications. The latter can be supplied very speedily for temporary purposes when needed; the former can not."

These views gain increased strength and pertinence as the years roll by, and I have now again the honor to call special attention to the condition of the "armament of our fortifications" and the absolute necessity for immediate provision by Congress for the procurement of heavy cannon. The large expenditures required to supply the number of guns for our forts is the strongest argument that can be adduced for a liberal annual appropriation for their gradual accumulation. In time of war such preparations can not be made; cannon can not be purchased in open market nor manufactured at short notice; they must be the product of years of experience and labor.

I herewith inclose copies of a report of the Chief of Ordnance and of a board of ordnance officers on the trial of an 8-inch rifle converted from a 10-inch smoothbore, which shows very conclusively an economical means of utilizing these useless smoothbores and making them into 8-inch rifles, capable of piercing 7 inches of iron. The 1,294 10-inch Rodman guns should, in my opinion, be so utilized, and the appropriation requested by the Chief of Ordnance of $250,000 to commence these conversions is urgently recommended.

While convinced of the economy and necessity of these conversions, the determination of the best and most economical method of providing guns of still larger caliber should no longer be delayed. The experience of other nations, based on the new conditions of defense brought prominently forward by the introduction of ironclads into every navy afloat, demands heavier metal and rifle guns of not less than 12 inches in caliber. These enormous masses, hurling a shot of 700 pounds, can alone meet many of the requirements of the national defenses. They must be provided, and experiments on a large scale can alone give the data necessary for the determination of the question. A suitable proving ground, with all the facilities and conveniences referred to by the Chief of Ordnance, with a liberal annual appropriation, is an undoubted necessity.

The guns now ready for trial can not be experimented with without funds, and the estimate of $250,000 for the purpose is deemed reasonable and is strongly recommended.

The constant appeals for legislation on the "armament of fortifications" ought no longer to be disregarded if Congress desires in peace to prepare the important material without which future wars must inevitably lead to disaster.

This subject is submitted with the hope that the consideration it deserves may be given it at the present session.

U. S. GRANT.

EXECUTIVE MANSION, *January 25, 1875.*
To the Senate and House of Representatives:

I have the honor to transmit herewith the report of the commission of engineers appointed in compliance with the act of Congress approved June 22, 1874, to investigate and report a permanent plan for the reclamation of the alluvial basin of the Mississippi River subject to inundation.

U. S. GRANT.

EXECUTIVE MANSION, *January 26, 1875.*
To the Senate and House of Representatives:

I have the honor to transmit herewith, for the information of Congress, a report of the progress made to this date by the United States Centennial Commission appointed in accordance with the requirements of the act approved June 1, 1872.

U. S. GRANT.

WASHINGTON, *February 1, 1875.*
To the Senate of the United States:

I transmit to the Senate, for consideration with a view to ratification, a treaty concluded on the 30th ultimo between this Government and His Hawaiian Majesty, on the subject of commercial reciprocity. I also transmit, for the information of the Senate, the papers mentioned in the subjoined list, relating to the commerce between the United States and the Hawaiian Islands.

U. S. GRANT.

EXECUTIVE MANSION, *February 3, 1875.*
To the Senate and House of Representatives:

I have the honor to lay before Congress a communication of the Secretary of War relative to the action taken in issuing certain supplies to the suffering people in Kansas and Nebraska, in consequence of the drought and grasshopper plague, and to respectfully request that such action be approved.

U. S. GRANT.

EXECUTIVE MANSION, *February 8, 1875.*

To the Senate of the United States:

Herewith I have the honor to send, in accordance with the resolution of the Senate of the 3d instant, all the information in my possession not heretofore furnished relating to affairs in the State of Arkansas.

I will venture to express the opinion that all the testimony shows that in the election of 1872 Joseph Brooks was lawfully elected governor of that State; that he has been unlawfully deprived of the possession of his office since that time; that in 1874 the constitution of the State was by violence, intimidation, and revolutionary proceedings overthrown and a new constitution adopted and a new State government established.

These proceedings, if permitted to stand, practically ignore all rights of minorities in all the States. Also, what is there to prevent each of the States recently readmitted to Federal relations on certain conditions changing their constitutions and violating their pledges if this action in Arkansas is acquiesced in?

I respectfully submit whether a precedent so dangerous to the stability of State government, if not of the National Government also, should be recognized by Congress. I earnestly ask that Congress will take definite action in this matter to relieve the Executive from acting upon questions which should be decided by the legislative branch of the Government.

U. S. GRANT.

EXECUTIVE MANSION, *February 19, 1875.*

To the Senate and House of Representatives:

Under the requirements of section 6 of the "act for the government of the District of Columbia, and for other purposes," approved June 20, 1874, I have the honor to submit herewith the report of the board of audit upon the amount equitably chargeable to the street-railroad companies pursuant to the charters of said companies or the acts of Congress relating thereto, together with the reasons therefor.

U. S. GRANT.

VETO MESSAGES.

EXECUTIVE MANSION, *January 30, 1875.*

To the House of Representatives:

I have the honor to return herewith House bill No. 4462, entitled "An act for the relief of Alexander Burtch," from which I withhold my approval for the reasons given in the accompanying letter of the Secretary of War.

U. S. GRANT.

WAR DEPARTMENT,
Washington City, January 28, 1875.

The PRESIDENT.

SIR: I have the honor to return House bill No. 4462, "for the relief of Alexander Burtch."

It appears from the records of this office that Alexander Burtch, Company H, First Indiana Artillery, enlisted July 24, 1861, for three years, reenlisted as a veteran January 1, 1864, and deserted at Fort Gaines, Ala., September 25, 1865, and was a deserter at large at date of muster-out of his company, January 10, 1866.

This Department emphatically objects to this bill becoming a law upon the ground of its great injustice to every soldier who served honorably until his services were no longer required by the Government.

Very respectfully, your obedient servant,

WM. W. BELKNAP,
Secretary of War.

EXECUTIVE MANSION, *February 12, 1875.*

To the House of Representatives:

I have the honor to return herewith House bill No. 2352, entitled "An act granting a pension to Lewis Hinely," from which I withhold my approval for the reasons given in the accompanying letter of the Secretary of the Interior.

U. S. GRANT.

DEPARTMENT OF THE INTERIOR,
Washington, February 11, 1875

The PRESIDENT.

SIR: I have the honor to return herewith House bill No. 2352, "granting a pension to Lewis Hinely."

I am informed by the Commissioner of Pensions that the act does not designate the person for whose benefit it was passed. His true name, as verified by his own signature to papers on file in the Pension Office, is Louis Heinlig, and as there were several soldiers in the company and regiment named in the act whose names are similar to that specified therein, a correction appears to be necessary in order that the beneficiary of the act may be properly identified should the bill become a law.

I have the honor to be, very respectfully, your obedient servant,

C. DELANO, *Secretary.*

WASHINGTON, *March 3, 1875.*

To the House of Representatives: *

House bill No. 3341 † is herewith returned without my approval, for the reasons, first, that it appropriates from the Treasury a large sum of money at a time when the revenue is insufficient for current wants and this proposed further drain on the Treasury. The issue of bonds, authorized by the bill to a very large and indefinite amount, would seriously embarrass the refunding operations now progressing, whereby the interest of the bonded debt of the United States is being largely reduced. Second, I do not believe that any considerable portion of the ex-soldiers

---

* Pocket veto. This message was written in the President's room at the Capitol, but failed to reach the House of Representatives before the final adjournment of Congress. The original is filed at the Executive Mansion.

† "An act to equalize the bounties of soldiers who served in the late war for the Union."

who, it is supposed, will be beneficiaries of this appropriation are applicants for it, but, rather, it would result more in a measure for the relief of claim agents and middlemen who would intervene to collect or discount the bounties granted by it. The passage of this bill at this time is inconsistent with the measures of economy now demanded by the necessities of the country.

U. S. GRANT.

[The following messages were sent to the special session of the Senate convened by proclamation (see p. 4278.) of February 17, 1875.]

SPECIAL MESSAGES.

WASHINGTON, *March 8, 1875.*

To the Senate of the United States:

I nominate in the Medical Department, Army of the United States, Benjamin F. Pope, assistant surgeon, to rank from May 14, 1867.

NOTE.—October 5, 1870, Assistant Surgeon B. F. Pope, United States Army, applied for discharge to date December 31, 1870, under section 3, act of July 15, 1870.

By letter from the Adjutant-General's Office, War Department, November 2, 1870, he was informed he could not be discharged as requested, as the President had decided staff officers did not come under the provisions of the act.

Subsequently the President decided that staff officers who applied and could be spared could go out under the act. Accordingly, Assistant Surgeon Pope was discharged, on his original application, to date December 31, 1870, by special order of that date, this because time did not permit to communicate with him, and the belief that his desire to leave the service was unchanged.

He drew a year's pay and mileage under the order, came to Washington, and on May 19, 1871, applied for revocation of the order of discharge on the ground that, having been officially notified of disapproval, he had made arrangements to remain in service. Forwarded by the Surgeon-General recommended. Disapproved by the Secretary of War May 23, 1871.

June 17, 1871, the order of discharge was revoked. Assistant-Surgeon Pope then refunded the year's pay and mileage and drew pay for continuous service.

U. S. GRANT.

WASHINGTON, *March 9, 1875.*

To the Senate of the United States:

Pursuant to the authority conferred upon me by the joint resolution of Congress approved on the 17th of June last, due notice was, on the 1st day of July last, given to the Government of Belgium, through the minister of the United States at Brussels, of the desire of this Government to terminate the treaty between the United States and His Majesty the King of the Belgians of the 17th of July, 1858. It being deemed advisable, however, that another instrument, with provisions more consonant with the interests of this country, should be entered into with that Government, I directed that negotiations should be set on foot for the purpose. They have resulted in the treaty* between the same parties of the 8th instant, which is now transmitted for the consideration of the Senate with a view to its ratification.

U. S. GRANT.

WASHINGTON, *March 15, 1875.*

To the Senate:

In answer to the resolution of the Senate of the 12th of March instant, I herewith transmit a report† from the Secretary of State, with accompanying correspondence.

U. S. GRANT.

EXECUTIVE MANSION, *March 17, 1875.*

To the Senate of the United States:

I have the honor to transmit herewith communications from the Secretaries of War and the Interior, in answer to the resolution of the Senate of the 15th instant, requesting "any information in my possession in regard to the proposed emigration to the Black Hills country, in the Sioux Indian Reservation; whether such emigration is with the consent of the Indian tribes holding said country under the treaty of February 24, 1869, and, if not, what measures will be taken in relation to the same."

U. S. GRANT.

PROCLAMATIONS.

BY THE PRESIDENT OF THE UNITED STATES OF AMERICA.

A PROCLAMATION.

Whereas it is provided in the Constitution of the United States that the United States shall protect every State in the Union, on application of the legislature, or of the executive (when the legislature can not be convened), against domestic violence; and

Whereas it is provided by the laws of the United States that in all cases of insurrection in any State or of obstruction to the laws thereof it shall be lawful for the President of the United States, on application of the legislature of such State, or of the executive (when the legislature

---

* Of commerce and navigation.

† Stating that the question of indemnity demanded from Spain for the execution or detention of a portion of the crew of the steamer *Virginius* and for the execution of passengers, citizens of the United States, had been disposed of by an agreement between the two countries, and transmitting correspondence connected therewith.

can not be convened), to call forth the militia of any other State or States, or to employ such part of the land and naval force as shall be judged necessary, for the purpose of suppressing such insurrection or of causing the laws to be duly executed; and

Whereas the legislature of the State of Mississippi, now in session, have represented to me, in a concurrent resolution of that body, that several of the legally elected officers of Warren County, in said State, are prevented from executing the duties of their respective offices by force and violence; that the public buildings and records of said county have been taken into the possession of and are now held by lawless and unauthorized persons; that many peaceable citizens of said county have been killed, and others have been compelled to abandon and remain away from their homes and families; that illegal and riotous seizures and imprisonments have been made by such lawless persons; and, further, that a large number of armed men from adjacent States have invaded Mississippi to aid such lawless persons, and are still ready to give them such aid; and

Whereas it is further represented as aforesaid by said legislature that the courts of said county can not be held, and that the governor of said State has no sufficient force at his command to execute the laws thereof in said county and suppress said violence without causing a conflict of races and endangering life and property to an alarming extent; and

Whereas the said legislature as aforesaid have made application to me for such part of the military force of the United States as may be necessary and adequate to protect said State and the citizens thereof against the domestic violence hereinbefore mentioned and to enforce the due execution of the laws; and

Whereas the laws of the United States require that whenever it may be necessary, in the judgment of the President, to use the military force for the purposes aforesaid, he shall forthwith, by proclamation, command such insurgents to disperse and retire peaceably to their respective abodes within a limited time:

Now, therefore, I, Ulysses S. Grant, President of the United States, do hereby command said disorderly and turbulent persons to disperse and retire peaceably to their respective abodes within five days from the date hereof, and that they refrain from forcible resistance to the laws and submit themselves peaceably to the lawful authorities of said county and State.

In witness whereof I have hereunto set my hand and caused the seal of the United States to be affixed.

[SEAL.] Done at the city of Washington, this 21st day of December, A. D. 1874, and of the Independence of the United States the ninety-ninth.

U. S. GRANT.

By the President:

HAMILTON FISH, *Secretary of State.*

BY THE PRESIDENT OF THE UNITED STATES OF AMERICA.

A PROCLAMATION.

Whereas objects of interest to the United States require that the Senate should be convened at 12 o'clock on the 5th day of March next to receive and act upon such communications as may be made to it on the part of the Executive:

Now, therefore, I, Ulysses S. Grant, President of the United States, have considered it to be my duty to issue this my proclamation, declaring that an extraordinary occasion requires the Senate of the United States to convene for the transaction of business at the Capitol, in the city of Washington, on the 5th day of March next, at 12 o'clock at noon on that day, of which all who shall at that time be entitled to act as members of that body are hereby required to take notice.

Given under my hand and the seal of the United States, at Washington, the 17th day of February, A. D. 1875, and of the Independence of the United States of America the ninety-ninth.

[SEAL.]

U. S. GRANT.

By the President:

HAMILTON FISH,
Secretary of State.

BY THE PRESIDENT OF THE UNITED STATES OF AMERICA.

A PROCLAMATION.

Whereas by the eighth section of the act of Congress entitled "An act for the creation of a court for the adjudication and disposition of certain moneys received into the Treasury under an award made by the tribunal of arbitration constituted by virtue of the first article of the treaty concluded at Washington the 8th of May, A. D. 1871, between the United States of America and the Queen of Great Britain," approved June 23, 1874, it is provided—

That the judges of the court created by this act shall convene in the city of Washington as soon as conveniently may be after their appointment; and the said court shall exist for one year from the date of its first convening and organizing; and should it be found impracticable to complete the work of the said court before the expiration of the said one year, the President may by proclamation extend the time of the duration thereof to a period not more than six months beyond the expiration of the said one year; and in such case all the provisions of this act shall be taken and held to be the same as though the continuance of the said court had been originally fixed by this act at the limit to which it may be thus extended.

And whereas it has been made satisfactorily to appear to me that the said court convened on the 22d of July, 1874, and that a large portion of the business of said court still remains undisposed of, and that it is found impracticable to complete the work of the said court before the expiration of the said one year from its first convening and organizing:

Now, therefore, be it known that I, Ulysses S. Grant, President of the United States of America, by virtue of the authority vested in me by the provisions of the said eighth section of the act of Congress aforesaid, do hereby extend the time of the duration of said "Court of Commissioners of Alabama Claims" for a period of six months from and after the 22d day of July, A. D. 1875.

In testimony whereof I have hereunto signed my name and have caused the seal of the United States to be affixed.

[SEAL.]   Done at the city of Washington, this 2d day of June, A. D. 1875, and of the Independence of the United States the ninety-ninth.

U. S. GRANT.

By the President:
HAMILTON FISH,
Secretary of State.

BY THE PRESIDENT OF THE UNITED STATES OF AMERICA.

A PROCLAMATION.

In accordance with a practice at once wise and beautiful, we have been accustomed, as the year is drawing to a close, to devote an occasion to the humble expression of our thanks to Almighty God for the ceaseless and distinguished benefits bestowed upon us as a nation and for His mercies and protection during the closing year.

Amid the rich and free enjoyment of all our advantages, we should not forget the source from whence they are derived and the extent of our obligation to the Father of All Mercies.

We have full reason to renew our thanks to Almighty God for favors bestowed upon us during the past year.

By His continuing mercy civil and religious liberty have been maintained, peace has reigned within our borders, labor and enterprise have produced their merited rewards; and to His watchful providence we are indebted for security from pestilence and other national calamity.

Apart from national blessings, each individual among us has occasion to thoughtfully recall and devoutly recognize the favors and protection which he has enjoyed.

Now, therefore, I, Ulysses S. Grant, President of the United States, do recommend that on Thursday, the 25th day of November, the people of the United States, abstaining from all secular pursuits and from their accustomed avocations, do assemble in their respective places of worship, and, in such form as may seem most appropriate in their own hearts, offer to Almighty God their acknowledgments and thanks for all His mercies and their humble prayers for a continuance of His divine favor.

In witness whereof I have hereunto set my hand and caused the seal of the United States to be affixed.

[SEAL.]   Done at the city of Washington, this 27th day of October, A. D. 1875, and of the Independence of the United States the one hundredth.

U. S. GRANT.

By the President:

HAMILTON FISH, *Secretary of State.*

EXECUTIVE ORDERS.

EXECUTIVE MANSION, *March 9, 1875.*

In order to carry out the provisions of the fifth section of the act of Congress entitled "An act making appropriations for sundry civil expenses of the Government for the fiscal year ending June 30, 1876, and for other purposes," approved March 3, 1875, the board heretofore appointed to take charge of the articles and materials to be exhibited by the several Executive Departments, the Smithsonian Institution, and the Agricultural Department at the International Exhibition of 1876 is hereby continued under the following regulations and distribution of duties, viz:

The funds appropriated by the above-named section will be drawn from the Treasury upon the requisition of the chairman of the board, and be disbursed as are other public moneys under the existing laws relating to disbursing officers.

An officer of the Army will be detailed by the Secretary of War as disbursing officer of the board.

Each representative of an Executive Department and the representatives of the Smithsonian Institution, of the Agricultural Department, and the United States Commissioner of Food Fishes will have charge of the matters pertaining to his respective Department, subject to the general advisement of the board; and all bills will be paid by the disbursing officer upon vouchers certified by such representative and countersigned by the chairman of the board.

The disbursing officer will render monthly accounts current of all advances to and disbursements by him to the First Auditor of the Treasury for audit and settlement in the same manner as are other accounts of disbursing officers of the Government.

Each representative will be held responsible to the head of his respective Department for all public property of the United States furnished by the head of such Department or otherwise coming to his hands for the purposes of the exhibition, and will render proper accounts of the same to such head of Department until the property is returned.

U. S. GRANT,
President United States.

TREASURY DEPARTMENT, *March 9, 1875.*

The BOARD OF EXAMINERS,
    Treasury Department:

By direction of the President, the rules and regulations known as the civil-service rules, etc., governing appointments and promotions under the Treasury Department are hereby abolished, and hereafter all appointments will be made as provided for by section 164, Revised Statutes, enacted June 22, 1874.

You are instructed and directed to transfer all books, papers, records, and public property in your possession to the chief clerk of the Department, and notify all sub-boards of the promulgation of this order.

The clerks and other employees now on duty under the direction of the board of examiners will report to the chief clerk for assignment to duty.

I am, very respectfully,

B. H. BRISTOW, *Secretary.*

[A similar order was, by direction of the President, issued by the heads of the other Executive Departments.]

EXECUTIVE MANSION, *March 25, 1875.*

In pursuance of the fourth section of the act entitled "An act making appropriations for sundry civil expenses of the Government for the fiscal year ending June 30, 1876, and for other purposes," approved March 3, 1875, a board is hereby appointed, to consist of Lieutenant-Colonel T. T. S. Laidley, Ordnance Department, United States Army, president of the board; Commander L. A. Beardslee, United States Navy; Lieutenant-Colonel Q. A. Gillmore, Engineer Department, United States Army; David Smith, Chief Engineer, United States Navy; W. Sooy Smith, civil engineer; A. S. Holly, civil engineer; R. H. Thurston, civil engineer, who will convene at the Watertown Arsenal, Mass., on April 15, 1875, or as soon thereafter as practicable, for the purpose of determining by actual tests the strength and value of all kinds of iron, steel, and other metals which may be submitted to them or by them procured, and to prepare tables which will exhibit the strength and value of said materials for constructive and mechanical purposes, and to provide for the building of a suitable machine for establishing such tests, the machine to be set up and maintained at the Watertown Arsenal.

The funds appropriated for the purposes of these tests will be disbursed under the Ordnance Department of the Army, and the board will receive instructions from and make its report to the Chief of Ordnance.

Mr. R. H. Thurston, civil engineer, is designated as secretary of the board, at an annual compensation of $1,200.

Actual traveling expenses, as provided by law, will be allowed the members of the board.

U. S. GRANT.

EXECUTIVE MANSION,
Washington, May 24, 1875.

SIR:* The President directs me to say that the several Departments of the Government will be closed on Saturday, the 29th instant, in order to enable the employees to participate in the decoration of the graves of the soldiers who fell during the rebellion.

I am, sir, your obedient servant,

O. E. BABCOCK, *Secretary.*

TREASURY DEPARTMENT,
Washington, D. C., July 3, 1875.

To Collectors of Customs:

The importation of breech-loading rifles, and fixed ammunition suitable therefor, into the Territory of Alaska, and the shipment of such rifles or ammunition to any port or place in the Territory of Alaska, are hereby forbidden, and collectors of customs are instructed to refuse clearance of any vessel having on board any such arms or ammunition destined for any port or place in said Territory.

If, however, any vessel intends to touch or trade at a port in Alaska Territory or to pass within the waters thereof, but shall be ultimately destined for some port or place not within the limits of said Territory, and shall have on board any such firearms or ammunition, the master or chief officer thereof will be required to execute and deliver to the collector of customs at the port of clearance a good and sufficient bond, with two sureties, in double the value of such merchandise, conditioned that such arms or ammunition, or any part thereof, shall not be landed or disposed of within the Territory of Alaska. Such bond shall be taken for such time as the collector shall deem proper, and may be satisfied upon proofs similar to those required to satisfy ordinary export bonds, showing that such arms have been landed at some foreign port; or, if such merchandise is landed at any port of the United States not within the limits of the Territory of Alaska, the bond may be satisfied upon production of a certificate to that effect from the collector of the port where it is so landed.

CHAS. F. CONANT, *Acting Secretary.*

Approved:

U. S. GRANT, *President.*

EXECUTIVE MANSION, *July 27, 1875.*

In conformity to provisions contained in the river and harbor act approved March 3, 1875, granting to James B. Eads and his associates authority to use, for the construction of jetties at the mouth of the Mississippi River, any materials on the public lands of the United States that shall be suitable for and may be needed in said works, under such

---

* Addressed to the heads of the Executive Departments, etc.

regulations as the Secretary of War shall prescribe, it is hereby ordered and directed—

1. That the general supervision of all matters properly appertaining to the grant therein made is placed in the officer of engineers, Major C. B. Comstock, detailed by the Secretary of War, under the provisions of the said act, to report to him "the depth of water and width of channel secured and maintained from time to time in said channel, together with such other information as the Secretary of War may direct."

2. *Protection of the interests of the United States so far as the taking of material is concerned.*—Said Eads and his associates shall, prior to taking material from any public lands, obtain authority to do so from the Secretary of War, their applications specifying the kinds and amounts of material they wish to take from each subdivision of the public lands; and they shall at once cease from such taking on being notified that the authority is withdrawn.

3. *Protection of the interests of the United States so far as structures are concerned.*—Said Eads and his associates and contractors are authorized to erect, at their own expense, such shops, dwellings, storehouses, and wharves on the military reservation at the mouth of the Mississippi as may be necessary for the prosecution of the work, and shall furnish a list and plan showing the location of the same to the Secretary of War; but these shall be erected in such a way and at such places as not unnecessarily to interfere with navigation or any other interest in which the United States is concerned, whereof the Secretary of War shall be the judge. At his direction any such structure shall be at once removed.

4. *Protection of James B. Eads's interests.*—No person save said Eads and his contractors shall erect any building, tent, or other habitation on the military reservation at the mouth of the Mississippi River. Any person so doing may be summarily ejected by the United States marshal or his deputy. But as authority has already been given to James B. Eads by the Secretary of War to collect the material aforesaid until he should be furnished with the regulations as now herein given, the said Eads is authorized to continue collecting materials under that authority until the 1st day of September, 1875, after which time these regulations will go into effect.

U. S. GRANT.

GENERAL ORDERS, No. 73.

WAR DEPARTMENT,
ADJUTANT-GENERAL'S OFFICE,
Washington, August 2, 1875.

I. The following order has been received from the President of the United States:

EXECUTIVE MANSION, *Washington, July 31, 1875.*

It becomes the painful duty of the President to announce to the people of the United States the death of Andrew Johnson, the last survivor of his honored predecessors, which occurred in Carter County, East Tennessee, at an early hour this morning.

The solemnity of the occasion which called him to the Presidency, with the varied nature and length of his public services, will cause him to be long remembered and occasion mourning for the death of a distinguished public servant.

As a mark of respect for the memory of the deceased, it is ordered that the Executive Mansion and several Departments of the Government at Washington be draped in mourning until the close of the day designated for his funeral, and that all public business be suspended on that day.

It is further ordered that the War and Navy Departments cause suitable honors to be paid on the occasion to the memory of the illustrious dead.

U. S. GRANT.

By the President:
  JOHN L. CADWALADER,
    Acting Secretary of State.

II. In compliance with the President's instructions, the troops will be paraded at 10 o'clock a. m. on the day after the receipt of this order at each military post, when the order will be read to them, and the labors of that day will thereafter cease.

The national flag will be displayed at half-staff.

At dawn of day thirteen guns will be fired, and afterwards at intervals of thirty minutes between the rising and setting sun a single gun, and at the close of the day a national salute of thirty-seven guns.

The officers of the Army will wear crape on the left arm and on their swords and the colors of the several regiments will be put in mourning for the period of thirty days.

By order of the Secretary of War:
    E. D. TOWNSEND,
      Adjutant-General.

SPECIAL ORDER.

NAVY DEPARTMENT,
Washington, August 2, 1875.

The President of the United States announces the death of ex-President Andrew Johnson in the following order:

[For order see preceding page.]

In pursuance of the foregoing order, it is hereby directed that the ensign at each naval station and of each vessel of the United States Navy in commission be hoisted at half-mast from sunrise to sunset, and that a gun be fired at intervals of every half hour from sunrise to sunset at each naval station and on board of flagships and of vessels acting singly, on

Tuesday, the 3d instant, the day of the funeral, where this order may be received in time, otherwise on the day after its receipt.

The officers of the Navy and Marine Corps will wear the usual badge of mourning attached to the sword hilt and on the left arm for the period of thirty days.

DANIEL AMMEN,
Acting Secretary of the Navy.

GENERAL ORDERS, No. 97.

WAR DEPARTMENT,
ADJUTANT-GENERAL'S OFFICE,
Washington, November 22, 1875.

I. The following order announces the decease of Henry Wilson, Vice-President of the United States:

EXECUTIVE MANSION,
Washington, November 22, 1875.

It is with profound sorrow that the President has to announce to the people of the United States the death of the Vice-President, Henry Wilson, who died in the Capitol of the nation this morning.

The eminent station of the deceased, his high character, his long career in the service of his State and of the Union, his devotion to the cause of freedom, and the ability which he brought to the discharge of every duty stand conspicuous and are indelibly impressed on the hearts and affections of the American people.

In testimony of respect for this distinguished citizen and faithful public servant the various Departments of the Government will be closed on the day of the funeral, and the Executive Mansion and all the Executive Departments in Washington will be draped with badges of mourning for thirty days.

The Secretaries of War and of the Navy will issue orders that appropriate military and naval honors be rendered to the memory of one whose virtues and services will long be borne in recollection by a grateful nation.

U. S. GRANT.

By the President:
    HAMILTON FISH,
       Secretary of State.

II. On the day next succeeding the receipt of this order at each military post the troops will be paraded at 10 o'clock a. m. and this order read to them.

The national flag will be displayed at half-staff.

At dawn of day thirteen guns will be fired. Commencing at 12 o'clock noon seventeen minute guns will be fired, and at the close of the day the national salute of thirty-seven guns.

The usual badge of mourning will be worn by officers of the Army and the colors of the several regiments will be put in mourning for the period of three months.

By order of the Secretary of War:

E. D. TOWNSEND, *Adjutant-General.*

SPECIAL ORDER.

NAVY DEPARTMENT,
Washington, November 23, 1875.

The President of the United States announces the death of Vice-President Henry Wilson in the following order:

[For order see preceding page.]

In pursuance of the foregoing order, it is hereby directed that upon the day following the receipt of this the ensign at each United States naval station and of each United States naval vessel in commission be hoisted at half-mast from sunrise to sunset, and that thirteen guns be fired at sunrise, nineteen minute guns at meridian, and a national salute at sunset at each United States naval station and on board flagships and vessels acting singly, at home or abroad.

The officers of the Navy and Marine Corps will wear the usual badge of mourning for three months.

GEO. M. ROBESON,
Secretary of the Navy.

SEVENTH ANNUAL MESSAGE.

EXECUTIVE MANSION, *December 7, 1875.*

To the Senate and House of Representatives:

In submitting my seventh annual message to Congress, in this centennial year of our national existence as a free and independent people, it affords me great pleasure to recur to the advancement that has been made from the time of the colonies, one hundred years ago. We were then a people numbering only 3,000,000. Now we number more than 40,000,000. Then industries were confined almost exclusively to the tillage of the soil. Now manufactories absorb much of the labor of the country.

Our liberties remain unimpaired; the bondmen have been freed from slavery; we have become possessed of the respect, if not the friendship, of all civilized nations. Our progress has been great in all the arts—in science, agriculture, commerce, navigation, mining, mechanics, law, medicine, etc.; and in general education the progress is likewise encouraging.

Our thirteen States have become thirty-eight, including Colorado (which has taken the initiatory steps to become a State), and eight Territories, including the Indian Territory and Alaska, and excluding Colorado, making a territory extending from the Atlantic to the Pacific. On the south we have extended to the Gulf of Mexico, and in the west from the Mississippi to the Pacific.

One hundred years ago the cotton gin, the steamship, the railroad, the telegraph, the reaping, sewing, and modern printing machines, and numerous other inventions of scarcely less value to our business and happiness were entirely unknown.

In 1776 manufactories scarcely existed even in name in all this vast erritory. In 1870 more than 2,000,000 persons were employed in manufactories, producing more than $2,100,000,000 of products in amount annually, nearly equal to our national debt. From nearly the whole of the population of 1776 being engaged in the one occupation of agriculture, in 1870 so numerous and diversified had become the occupation of our people that less than 6,000,000 out of more than 40,000,000 were so engaged. The extraordinary effect produced in our country by a resort to diversified occupations has built a market for the products of fertile lands distant from the seaboard and the markets of the world.

The American system of locating various and extensive manufactories next to the plow and the pasture, and adding connecting railroads and steamboats, has produced in our distant interior country a result noticeable by the intelligent portions of all commercial nations. The ingenuity and skill of American mechanics have been demonstrated at home and abroad in a manner most flattering to their pride. But for the extraordinary genius and ability of our mechanics, the achievements of our agriculturists, manufacturers, and transporters throughout the country would have been impossible of attainment.

The progress of the miner has also been great. Of coal our production was small; now many millions of tons are mined annually. So with iron, which formed scarcely an appreciable part of our products half a century ago, we now produce more than the world consumed at the beginning of our national existence. Lead, zinc, and copper, from being articles of import, we may expect to be large exporters of in the near future. The development of gold and silver mines in the United States and Territories has not only been remarkable, but has had a large influence upon the business of all commercial nations. Our merchants in the last hundred years have had a success and have established a reputation for enterprise, sagacity, progress, and integrity unsurpassed by peoples of older nationalities. This "good name" is not confined to their homes, but goes out upon every sea and into every port where commerce enters. With equal pride we can point to our progress in all of the learned professions.

As we are now about to enter upon our second centennial— commencing our manhood as a nation—it is well to look back upon the past and

study what will be best to preserve and advance our future greatness
From the fall of Adam for his transgression to the present day no nation
has ever been free from threatened danger to its prosperity and happiness. We should look to the dangers threatening us, and remedy them
so far as lies in our power. We are a republic whereof one man is as
good as another before the law. Under such a form of government it
is of the greatest importance that all should be possessed of education
and intelligence enough to cast a vote with a right understanding of its
meaning. A large association of ignorant men can not for any considerable period oppose a successful resistance to tyranny and oppression
from the educated few, but will inevitably sink into acquiescence to the
will of intelligence, whether directed by the demagogue or by priestcraft.
Hence the education of the masses becomes of the first necessity for the
preservation of our institutions. They are worth preserving, because
they have secured the greatest good to the greatest proportion of the
population of any form of government yet devised. All other forms
of government approach it just in proportion to the general diffusion of
education and independence of thought and action. As the primary
step, therefore, to our advancement in all that has marked our progress
in the past century, I suggest for your earnest consideration, and most
earnestly recommend it, that a constitutional amendment be submitted to
the legislatures of the several States for ratification, making it the duty
of each of the several States to establish and forever maintain free public
schools adequate to the education of all the children in the rudimentary
branches within their respective limits, irrespective of sex, color, birth-
place, or religions; forbidding the teaching in said schools of religious,
atheistic, or pagan tenets; and prohibiting the granting of any school
funds or school taxes, or any part thereof, either by legislative, municipal, or other authority, for the benefit or in aid, directly or indirectly, of
any religious sect or denomination, or in aid or for the benefit of any
other object of any nature or kind whatever.

In connection with this important question I would also call your
attention to the importance of correcting an evil that, if permitted to
continue, will probably lead to great trouble in our land before the close
of the nineteenth century. It is the accumulation of vast amounts of
untaxed church property.

In 1850, I believe, the church property of the United States which
paid no tax, municipal or State, amounted to about $83,000,000. In
1860 the amount had doubled; in 1875 it is about $1,000,000,000. By
1900, without check, it is safe to say this property will reach a sum
exceeding $3,000,000,000. So vast a sum, receiving all the protection
and benefits of Government without bearing its proportion of the burdens and expenses of the same, will not be looked upon acquiescently by
those who have to pay the taxes. In a growing country, where real
estate enhances so rapidly with time as in the United States, there is

scarcely a limit to the wealth that may be acquired by corporations, religious or otherwise, if allowed to retain real estate without taxation. The contemplation of so vast a property as here alluded to, without taxation, may lead to sequestration without constitutional authority and through blood.

I would suggest the taxation of all property equally, whether church or corporation, exempting only the last resting place of the dead and possibly, with proper restrictions, church edifices.

Our relations with most of the foreign powers continue on a satisfactory and friendly footing.

Increased intercourse, the extension of commerce, and the cultivation of mutual interests have steadily improved our relations with the large majority of the powers of the world, rendering practicable the peaceful solution of questions which from time to time necessarily arise, leaving few which demand extended or particular notice.

The correspondence of the Department of State with our diplomatic representatives abroad is transmitted herewith.

I am happy to announce the passage of an act by the General Cortes of Portugal, proclaimed since the adjournment of Congress, for the abolition of servitude in the Portuguese colonies. It is to be hoped that such legislation may be another step toward the great consummation to be reached, when no man shall be permitted, directly or indirectly, under any guise, excuse, or form of law, to hold his fellow-man in bondage. I am of opinion also that it is the duty of the United States, as contributing toward that end, and required by the spirit of the age in which we live, to provide by suitable legislation that no citizen of the United States shall hold slaves as property in any other country or be interested therein.

Chile has made reparation in the case of the whale ship *Good Return*, seized without sufficient cause upward of forty years ago. Though she had hitherto denied her accountability, the denial was never acquiesced in by this Government, and the justice of the claim has been so earnestly contended for that it has been gratifying that she should have at last acknowledged it.

The arbitrator in the case of the United States steamer *Montijo*, for the seizure and detention of which the Government of the United States of Colombia was held accountable, has decided in favor of the claim. This decision has settled a question which had been pending for several years, and which, while it continued open, might more or less disturb the good understanding which it is desirable should be maintained between the two Republics.

A reciprocity treaty with the King of the Hawaiian Islands was concluded some months since. As it contains a stipulation that it shall not take effect until Congress shall enact the proper legislation for that purpose, copies of the instrument are herewith submitted, in order that, if such should be the pleasure of Congress, the necessary legislation upon the subject may be adopted.

In March last an arrangement was made, through Mr. Cushing, our minister in Madrid, with the Spanish Government for the payment by the latter to the United States of the sum of $80,000 in coin, for the purpose of the relief of the families or persons of the ship's company and certain passengers of the *Virginius*. This sum was to have been paid in three installments at two months each. It is due to the Spanish Government that I should state that the payments were fully and spontaneously anticipated by that Government, and that the whole amount was paid within but a few days more than two months from the date of the agreement, a copy of which is herewith transmitted. In pursuance of the terms of the adjustment, I have directed the distribution of the amount among the parties entitled thereto, including the ship's company and such of the passengers as were American citizens. Payments are made accordingly, on the application by the parties entitled thereto.

The past year has furnished no evidence of an approaching termination of the ruinous conflict which has been raging for seven years in the neighboring island of Cuba. The same disregard of the laws of civilized warfare and of the just demands of humanity which has heretofore called forth expressions of condemnation from the nations of Christendom has continued to blacken the sad scene. Desolation, ruin, and pillage are pervading the rich fields of one of the most fertile and productive regions of the earth, and the incendiary's torch, firing plantations and valuable factories and buildings, is the agent marking the alternate advance or retreat of contending parties.

The protracted continuance of this strife seriously affects the interests of all commercial nations, but those of the United States more than others, by reason of close proximity, its larger trade and intercourse with Cuba, and the frequent and intimate personal and social relations which have grown up between its citizens and those of the island. Moreover, the property of our citizens in Cuba is large, and is rendered insecure and depreciated in value and in capacity of production by the continuance of the strife and the unnatural mode of its conduct. The same is true, differing only in degree, with respect to the interests and people of other nations; and the absence of any reasonable assurance of a near termination of the conflict must of necessity soon compel the States thus suffering to consider what the interests of their own people and their duty toward themselves may demand.

I have hoped that Spain would be enabled to establish peace in her colony, to afford security to the property and the interests of our citizens, and allow legitimate scope to trade and commerce and the natural productions of the island. Because of this hope, and from an extreme reluctance to interfere in the most remote manner in the affairs of another and a friendly nation, especially of one whose sympathy and friendship in the struggling infancy of our own existence must ever be remembered with gratitude, I have patiently and anxiously waited the progress of events. Our own civil conflict is too recent for us not to consider the difficulties which surround a government distracted by a dynastic rebellion at home at the same time that it has to cope with a separate insurrection in a distant colony. But whatever causes may have produced the situation which so grievously affects our interests, it exists, with all its attendant evils operating directly upon this country and its people. Thus far all the efforts of Spain have proved abortive, and time has marked no improvement in the situation. The armed bands of either side now occupy nearly the same ground as in the past, with the difference, from time to time, of more lives sacrificed, more property destroyed, and wider extents of fertile and productive fields and more and more of valuable property constantly wantonly sacrificed to the incendiary's torch.

In contests of this nature, where a considerable body of people who have attempted to free themselves of the control of the superior government have reached such point in occupation of territory, in power, and in general organization as to constitute in fact a body politic; having a government in substance as well as in name; possessed of the elements of stability and equipped with the machinery for the administration of internal policy and the execution of its laws; prepared and able to administer justice at home, as well as in its dealings with other powers, it is within the province of those other powers to recognize its existence as a new and independent nation. In such cases other nations simply deal with an actually existing condition of things, and recognize as one of the powers of the earth that body politic which, possessing the necessary elements, has in fact become a new power. In a word, the creation of a new state is a fact.

To establish the condition of things essential to the recognition of this fact there must be a people occupying a known territory, united under some known and defined form of government, acknowledged by those subject thereto, in which the functions of government are administered by usual methods, competent to mete out justice to citizens and strangers, to afford remedies for public and for private wrongs, and able to assume the correlative international obligations and capable of performing the corresponding international duties resulting from its acquisition of the rights of sovereignty. A power should exist complete in its organization, ready to take and able to maintain its place among the nations of the earth.

While conscious that the insurrection in Cuba has shown a strength and endurance which make it at least doubtful whether it be in the power of Spain to subdue it, it seems unquestionable that no such civil organization exists which may be recognized as an independent government capable of performing its international obligations and entitled to be treated as one of the powers of the earth. A recognition under such circumstances would be inconsistent with the facts, and would compel the power granting it soon to support by force the government to which it had really given its only claim of existence. In my judgment the United States should adhere to the policy and the principles which have heretofore been its sure and safe guides in like contests between revolted colonies and their mother country, and, acting only upon the clearest evidence, should avoid any possibility of suspicion or of imputation.

A recognition of the independence of Cuba being, in my opinion, impracticable and indefensible, the question which next presents itself is that of the recognition of belligerent rights in the parties to the contest.

In a former message to Congress I had occasion to consider this question, and reached the conclusion that the conflict in Cuba, dreadful and devastating as were its incidents, did not rise to the fearful dignity of war. Regarding it now, after this lapse of time, I am unable to see that any notable success or any marked or real advance on the part of the insurgents has essentially changed the character of the contest. It has acquired greater age, but not greater or more formidable proportions. It is possible that the acts of foreign powers, and even acts of Spain herself, of this very nature, might be pointed to in defense of such recognition. But now, as in its past history, the United States should carefully avoid the false lights which might lead it into the mazes of doubtful law and of questionable propriety, and adhere rigidly and sternly to the rule, which has been its guide, of doing only that which is right and honest and of good report. The question of according or of withholding rights of belligerency must be judged in every case in view of the particular attending facts. Unless justified by necessity, it is always, and justly, regarded as an unfriendly act and a gratuitous demonstration of moral support to the rebellion. It is necessary, and it is required, when the interests and rights of another government or of its people are so far affected by a pending civil conflict as to require a definition of its relations to the parties thereto. But this conflict must be one which will be recognized in the sense of international law as war. Belligerence, too, is a fact. The mere existence of contending armed bodies and their occasional conflicts do not constitute war in the sense referred to. Applying to the existing condition of affairs in Cuba the tests recognized by publicists and writers on international law, and which have been observed by nations of dignity, honesty, and power when free from sensitive or selfish and unworthy motives, I fail to find in the insurrection the existence of such a substantial political organization, real, palpable, and manifest to the world, having the forms and capable of the ordinary functions of government toward its own people and to other states, with courts for the administration of justice, with a local habitation, possessing such organization of force, such material, such occupation of territory, as to take the contest out of the category of a mere rebellious insurrection or occasional skirmishes and place it on the terrible footing of war, to which a recognition of belligerency would aim to elevate it. The contest, moreover, is solely on land; the insurrection has not possessed itself of a single seaport whence it may send forth its flag, nor has it any means of communication with foreign powers except through the military lines of its adversaries. No apprehension of any of those sudden and difficult complications which a war upon the ocean is apt to precipitate upon the vessels, both commercial and national, and upon the consular officers of other powers calls for the definition of their relations to the parties to the contest. Considered as a question of expediency, I regard the accordance of belligerent rights still to be as unwise and premature as I regard it to be, at present, indefensible as a measure of right. Such recognition entails upon the country according the rights which flow from it difficult and complicated duties, and requires the exaction from the contending parties of the strict observance of their rights and obligations; it confers the right of search upon the high seas by vessels of both parties; it would subject the carrying of arms and munitions of war, which now may be transported freely and without interruption in the vessels of the United States, to detention and to possible seizure; it would give rise to countless vexatious questions, would release the parent Government from responsibility for acts done by the insurgents, and would invest Spain with the right to exercise the supervision recognized by our treaty of 1795 over our commerce on the high seas, a very large part of which, in its traffic between the Atlantic and the Gulf States and between all of them and the States on the Pacific, passes through the waters which wash the shores of Cuba. The exercise of this supervision could scarce fail to lead, if not to abuses, certainly to collisions perilous to the peaceful relations of the two States. There can be little doubt to what result such supervision would before long draw this nation. It would be unworthy of the United States to inaugurate the possibilities of such result by measures of questionable right or expediency or by any indirection. Apart from any question of theoretical right, I am satisfied that while the accordance of belligerent rights to the insurgents in Cuba might give them a hope and an inducement to protract the struggle, it would be but a delusive hope, and would not remove the evils which this Government and its people are experiencing, but would draw the United States into complications which it has waited long and already suffered much to avoid. The recognition of independence or of belligerency being thus, in my judgment, equally inadmissible, it remains to consider what course shall be adopted should the conflict not soon be brought to an end by acts of the parties themselves, and should the evils which result therefrom, affecting all nations, and particularly the United States, continue. In such event I am of opinion that other nations will be compelled to assume the responsibility which devolves upon them, and to seriously consider the only remaining measures possible—mediation and intervention.

Owing, perhaps, to the large expanse of water separating the island from the peninsula, the want of harmony and of personal sympathy between the inhabitants of the colony and those sent thither to rule them, and want of adaptation of the ancient colonial system of Europe to the present times and to the ideas which the events of the past century have developed, the contending parties appear to have within themselves no depository of common confidence to suggest wisdom when passion and excitement have their sway and to assume the part of peacemaker. In this view in the earlier days of the contest the good offices of the United States as a mediator were tendered in good faith, without any selfish purpose, in the interest of humanity and in sincere friendship for both parties, but were at the time declined by Spain, with the declaration, nevertheless, that at a future time they would be indispensable. No intimation has been received that in the opinion of Spain that time has been reached. And yet the strife continues, with all its dread horrors and all its injuries to the interests of the United States and of other nations. Each party seems quite capable of working great injury and damage to the other, as well as to all the relations and interests dependent on the existence of peace in the island; but they seem incapable of reaching any adjustment, and both have thus far failed of achieving any success whereby one party shall possess and control the island to the exclusion of the other. Under these circumstances the agency of others, either by mediation or by intervention, seems to be the only alternative which must, sooner or later, be invoked for the termination of the strife. At the same time, while thus impressed I do not at this time recommend the adoption of any measure of intervention. I shall be ready at all times, and as the equal friend of both parties, to respond to a suggestion that the good offices of the United States will be acceptable to aid in bringing about a peace honorable to both. It is due to Spain, so far as this Government is concerned, that the agency of a third power, to which I have adverted, shall be adopted only as a last expedient. Had it been the desire of the United States to interfere in the affairs of Cuba, repeated opportunities for so doing have been presented within the last few years; but we have remained passive, and have performed our whole duty and all international obligations to Spain with friendship, fairness, and fidelity, and with a spirit of patience and forbearance which negatives every possible suggestion of desire to interfere or to add to the difficulties with which she has been surrounded.

The Government of Spain has recently submitted to our minister at Madrid certain proposals which it is hoped may be found to be the basis, if not the actual submission, of terms to meet the requirements of the particular griefs of which this Government has felt itself entitled to complain. These proposals have not yet reached me in their full text. On their arrival they will be taken into careful examination, and may, I hope, lead to a satisfactory adjustment of the questions to which they refer and remove the possibility of future occurrences such as have given rise to our just complaints.

It is understood also that renewed efforts are being made to introduce reforms in the internal administration of the island. Persuaded, however, that a proper regard for the interests of the United States and of its citizens entitles it to relief from the strain to which it has been subjected by the difficulties of the questions and the wrongs and losses which arise from the contest in Cuba, and that the interests of humanity itself demand the cessation of the strife before the whole island shall be laid waste and larger sacrifices of life be made, I shall feel it my duty, should my hopes of a satisfactory adjustment and of the early restoration of peace and the removal of future causes of complaint be, unhappily, disappointed, to make a further communication to Congress at some period not far remote, and during the present session, recommending what may then seem to me to be necessary.

The free zone, so called, several years since established by the Mexican Government in certain of the States of that Republic adjacent to our frontier, remains in full operation. It has always been materially injurious to honest traffic, for it operates as an incentive to traders in Mexico to supply without customs charges the wants of inhabitants on this side of the line, and prevents the same wants from being supplied by merchants of the United States, thereby to a considerable extent defrauding our revenue and checking honest commercial enterprise.

Depredations by armed bands from Mexico on the people of Texas near the frontier continue. Though the main object of these incursions is robbery, they frequently result in the murder of unarmed and peaceably disposed persons, and in some instances even the United States post-offices and mail communications have been attacked. Renewed remonstrances upon this subject have been addressed to the Mexican Government, but without much apparent effect. The military force of this Government disposable for service in that quarter is quite inadequate to effectually guard the line, even at those points where the incursions are usually made. An experiment of an armed vessel on the Rio Grande for that purpose is on trial, and it is hoped that, if not thwarted by the shallowness of the river and other natural obstacles, it may materially contribute to the protection of the herdsmen of Texas.

The proceedings of the joint commission under the convention between the United States and Mexico of the 4th of July, 1868, on the subject of claims, will soon be brought to a close. The result of those proceedings will then be communicated to Congress.

I am happy to announce that the Government of Venezuela has, upon further consideration, practically abandoned its objection to pay to the United States that share of its revenue which some years since it allotted toward the extinguishment of the claims of foreigners generally. In thus reconsidering its determination that Government has shown a just sense of self-respect which can not fail to reflect credit upon it in the eyes of all disinterested persons elsewhere. It is to be regretted, however, that its payments on account of claims of citizens of the United States are still so meager in amount, and that the stipulations of the treaty in regard to the sums to be paid and the periods when those payments were to take place should have been so signally disregarded.

Since my last annual message the exchange has been made of the ratification of a treaty of commerce and navigation with Belgium, and of conventions with the Mexican Republic for the further extension of the joint commission respecting claims; with the Hawaiian Islands for commercial reciprocity, and with the Ottoman Empire for extradition; all of which have been duly proclaimed.

The Court of Commissioners of Alabama Claims has prosecuted its important duties very assiduously and very satisfactorily. It convened and was organized on the 22d day of July, 1874, and by the terms of the act under which it was created was to exist for one year from that date. The act provided, however, that should it be found impracticable to complete the work of the court before the expiration of the year the President might by proclamation extend the time of its duration to a period not more than six months beyond the expiration of the one year.

Having received satisfactory evidence that it would be impracticable to complete the work within the time originally fixed, I issued a proclamation* (a copy of which is presented herewith) extending the time of duration of the court for a period of six months from and after the 22d day of July last.

A report made through the clerk of the court (communicated herewith) shows the condition of the calendar on the 1st of November last and the large amount of work which has been accomplished. One thousand three hundred and eighty-two claims have been presented, of which 682 had been disposed of at the date of the report. I am informed that 170 cases were decided during the month of November. Arguments are being made and decisions given in the remaining cases with all the dispatch consistent with the proper consideration of the questions submitted. Many of these claims are in behalf of mariners, or depend on the evidence of mariners, whose absence has delayed the taking or the return of the necessary evidence.

It is represented to me that it will be impracticable for the court to finally dispose of all the cases before it within the present limit of its duration. Justice to the parties claimant, who have been at large expense in preparing their claims and obtaining the evidence in their support, suggests a short extension, to enable the court to dispose of all of the claims which have been presented.

I recommend the legislation which may be deemed proper to enable the court to complete the work before it.

* See pp. 4278-4279.

I recommend that some suitable provision be made, by the creation of a special court or by conferring the necessary jurisdiction upon some appropriate tribunal, for the consideration and determination of the claims of aliens against the Government of the United States which have arisen within some reasonable limitation of time, or which may hereafter arise, excluding all claims barred by treaty provisions or otherwise. It has been found impossible to give proper consideration to these claims by the Executive Departments of the Government. Such a tribunal would afford an opportunity to aliens other than British subjects to present their claims on account of acts committed against their persons or property during the rebellion, as also to those subjects of Great Britain whose claims, having arisen subsequent to the 9th day of April, 1865, could not be presented to the late commission organized pursuant to the provisions of the treaty of Washington.

The electric telegraph has become an essential and indispensable agent in the transmission of business and social messages. Its operation on land, and within the limit of particular states, is necessarily under the control of the jurisdiction within which it operates. The lines on the high seas, however, are not subject to the particular control of any one government.

In 1869 a concession was granted by the French Government to a company which proposed to lay a cable from the shores of France to the United States. At that time there was a telegraphic connection between the United States and the continent of Europe (through the possessions of Great Britain at either end of the line), under the control of an association which had, at large outlay of capital and at great risk, demonstrated the practicability of maintaining such means of communication. The cost of correspondence by this agency was great, possibly not too large at the time for a proper remuneration for so hazardous and so costly an enterprise. It was, however, a heavy charge upon a means of communication which the progress in the social and commercial intercourse of the world found to be a necessity, and the obtaining of this French concession showed that other capital than that already invested was ready to enter into competition, with assurance of adequate return for their outlay. Impressed with the conviction that the interests, not only of the people of the United States, but of the world at large, demanded, or would demand, the multiplication of such means of communication between separated continents, I was desirous that the proposed connection should be made; but certain provisions of this concession were deemed by me to be objectionable, particularly one which gave for a long term of years the exclusive right of telegraphic communication by submarine cable between the shores of France and the United States. I could not concede that any power should claim the right to land a cable on the shores of the United States and at the same time deny to the United States, or to its citizens or grantees, an equal right to land a cable on its shores. The right to control the conditions for the laying of a cable within the jurisdictional waters of the United States, to connect our shores with those of any foreign state, pertains exclusively to the Government of the United States, under such limitations and conditions as Congress may impose. In the absence of legislation by Congress I was unwilling, on the one hand, to yield to a foreign state the right to say that its grantees might land on our shores while it denied a similar right to our people to land on its shores, and, on the other hand, I was reluctant to deny to the great interests of the world and of civilization the facilities of such communication as were proposed. I therefore withheld any resistance to the landing of the cable on condition that the offensive monopoly feature of the concession be abandoned, and that the right of any cable which may be established by authority of this Government to land upon French territory and to connect with French land lines and enjoy all the necessary facilities or privileges incident to the use thereof upon as favorable terms as any other company be conceded. As the result thereof the company in question renounced the exclusive privilege, and the representative of France was informed that, understanding this relinquishment to be construed as granting the entire reciprocity and equal facilities which had been demanded, the opposition to the landing of the cable was withdrawn. The cable, under this French concession, was landed in the month of July, 1869, and has been an efficient and valuable agent of communication between this country and the other continent. It soon passed under the control, however, of those who had the management of the cable connecting Great Britain with this continent, and thus whatever benefit to the public might have ensued from competition between the two lines was lost, leaving only the greater facilities of an additional line and the additional security in case of accident to one of them. But these increased facilities and this additional security, together with the control of the combined capital of the two companies, gave also greater power to prevent the future construction of other lines and to limit the control of telegraphic communication between the two continents to those possessing the lines already laid. Within a few months past a cable has been laid, known as the United States Direct Cable Company, connecting the United States directly with Great Britain. As soon as this cable was reported to be laid and in working order the rates of the then existing consolidated companies were greatly reduced. Soon, however, a break was announced in this new cable, and immediately the rates of the other line, which had been reduced, were again raised. This cable being now repaired, the rates appear not to be reduced by either line from those formerly charged by the consolidated companies.

There is reason to believe that large amounts of capital, both at home and abroad, are ready to seek profitable investment in the advancement of this useful and most civilizing means of intercourse and correspondence.

They await, however, the assurance of the means and conditions on which they may safely be made tributary to the general good.

As these cable telegraph lines connect separate states, there are questions as to their organization and control which probably can be best, if not solely, settled by conventions between the respective states. In the absence, however, of international conventions on the subject, municipal legislation may secure many points which appear to me important, if not indispensable for the protection of the public against the extortions which may result from a monopoly of the right of operating cable telegrams or from a combination between several lines:

I. No line should be allowed to land on the shores of the United States under the concession from another power which does not admit the right of any other line or lines, formed in the United States, to land and freely connect with and operate through its land lines.

II. No line should be allowed to land on the shores of the United States which is not, by treaty stipulation with the government from whose shores it proceeds, or by prohibition in its charter, or otherwise to the satisfaction of this Government, prohibited from consolidating or amalgamating with any other cable telegraph line, or combining therewith for the purpose of regulating and maintaining the cost of telegraphing.

III. All lines should be bound to give precedence in the transmission of the official messages of the governments of the two countries between which it may be laid.

IV. A power should be reserved to the two governments, either conjointly or to each, as regards the messages dispatched from its shores, to fix a limit to the charges to be demanded for the transmission of messages.

I present this subject to the earnest consideration of Congress.

In the meantime, and unless Congress otherwise direct, I shall not oppose the landing of any telegraphic cable which complies with and assents to the points above enumerated, but will feel it my duty to prevent the landing of any which does not conform to the first and second points as stated, and which will not stipulate to concede to this Government the precedence in the transmission of its official messages and will not enter into a satisfactory arrangement with regard to its charges.

Among the pressing and important subjects to which, in my opinion, the attention of Congress should be directed are those relating to fraudulent naturalization and expatriation.

The United States, with great liberality, offers its citizenship to all who in good faith comply with the requirements of law. These requirements are as simple and upon as favorable terms to the emigrant as the high privilege to which he is admitted can or should permit. I do not propose any additional requirements to those which the law now demands; but the very simplicity and the want of unnecessary formality in our law have made fraudulent naturalization not infrequent, to the discredit and injury of all honest citizens, whether native or naturalized. Cases of this character are continually being brought to the notice of the Government by our representatives abroad, and also those of persons resident in other countries, most frequently those who, if they have remained in this country long enough to entitle them to become naturalized, have generally not much overpassed that period, and have returned to the country of their origin, where they reside, avoiding all duties to the United States by their absence, and claiming to be exempt from all duties to the country of their nativity and of their residence by reason of their alleged naturalization. It is due to this Government itself and to the great mass of the naturalized citizens who entirely, both in name and in fact, become citizens of the United States that the high privilege of citizenship of the United States should not be held by fraud or in derogation of the laws and of the good name of every honest citizen. On many occasions it has been brought to the knowledge of the Government that certificates of naturalization are held and protection or interference claimed by parties who admit that not only they were not within the United States at the time of the pretended naturalization, but that they have never resided in the United States; in others the certificate and record of the court show on their face that the person claiming to be naturalized had not resided the required time in the United States; in others it is admitted upon examination that the requirements of law have not been complied with; in some cases, even, such certificates have been matter of purchase. These are not isolated cases, arising at rare intervals, but of common occurrence, and which are reported from all quarters of the globe. Such occurrences can not, and do not, fail to reflect upon the Government and injure all honest citizens. Such a fraud being discovered, however, there is no practicable means within the control of the Government by which the record of naturalization can be vacated; and should the certificate be taken up, as it usually is, by the diplomatic and consular representatives of the Government to whom it may have been presented, there is nothing to prevent the person claiming to have been naturalized from obtaining a new certificate from the court in place of that which has been taken from him.

The evil has become so great and of such frequent occurrence that I can not too earnestly recommend that some effective measures be adopted to provide a proper remedy and means for the vacating of any record thus fraudulently made, and of punishing the guilty parties to the transaction.

In this connection I refer also to the question of expatriation and the election of nationality.

The United States was foremost in upholding the right of expatriation, and was principally instrumental in overthrowing the doctrine of perpetual allegiance. Congress has declared the right of expatriation to be a natural and inherent right of all people ; but while many other nations have enacted laws providing what formalities shall be necessary to work a change of allegiance, the United States has enacted no provisions of law and has in no respect marked out how and when expatriation may be accomplished by its citizens. Instances are brought to the attention of the Government where citizens of the United States, either naturalized or native born, have formally become citizens or subjects of foreign powers, but who, nevertheless, in the absence of any provisions of legislation on this question, when involved in difficulties or when it seems to be their interest, claim to be citizens of the United States and demand the intervention of a Government which they have long since abandoned and to which for years they have rendered no service nor held themselves in any way amenable.

In other cases naturalized citizens, immediately after naturalization, have returned to their native country; have become engaged in business; have accepted offices or pursuits inconsistent with American citizenship, and evidence no intent to return to the United States until called upon to discharge some duty to the country where they are residing, when at once they assert their citizenship and call upon the representatives of the Government to aid them in their unjust pretensions. It is but justice to all *bona fide* citizens that no doubt should exist on such questions, and that Congress should determine by enactment of law how expatriation may be accomplished and change of citizenship be established.

I also invite your attention to the necessity of regulating by law the status of American women who may marry foreigners, and of defining more fully that of children born in a foreign country of American parents who may reside abroad; and also of some further provision regulating or giving legal effect to marriages of American citizens contracted in foreign countries. The correspondence submitted herewith shows a few of the constantly occurring questions on these points presented to the consideration of the Government. There are few subjects to engage the attention of Congress on which more delicate relations or more important interests are dependent.

In the month of July last the building erected for the Department of State was taken possession of and occupied by that Department. I am happy to announce that the archives and valuable papers of the Government in the custody of that Department are now safely deposited and properly cared for.

The report of the Secretary of the Treasury shows the receipts from customs for the fiscal year ending June 30, 1874, to have been $163,-103,833.69, and for the fiscal year ending June 30, 1875, to have been $157,167,722.35, a decrease for the last fiscal year of $5,936,111.34. Receipts from internal revenue for the year ending the 30th of June, 1874, were $102,409,784.90, and for the year ending June 30, 1875, $110,007,493.58; increase, $7,597,708.68.

The report also shows a complete history of the workings of the Department for the last year, and contains recommendations for reforms and for legislation which I concur in, but can not comment on so fully as I should like to do if space would permit, but will confine myself to a few suggestions which I look upon as vital to the best interests of the whole people—coming within the purview of "Treasury;" I mean specie resumption. Too much stress can not be laid upon this question, and I hope Congress may be induced, at the earliest day practicable, to insure the consummation of the act of the last Congress, at its last session, to bring about specie resumption "on and after the 1st of January, 1879," at furthest. It would be a great blessing if this could be consummated even at an earlier day.

Nothing seems to me more certain than that a full, healthy, and permanent reaction can not take place in favor of the industries and financial welfare of the country until we return to a measure of values recognized throughout the civilized world. While we use a currency not equivalent to this standard the world's recognized standard, specie, becomes a commodity like the products of the soil, the surplus seeking a market wherever there is a demand for it.

Under our present system we should want none, nor would we have any, were it not that customs dues must be paid in coin and because of the pledge to pay interest on the public debt in coin. The yield of precious metals would flow out for the purchase of foreign productions and leave the United States "hewers of wood and drawers of water," because of wiser legislation on the subject of finance by the nations with whom we have dealings. I am not prepared to say that I can suggest the best legislation to secure the end most heartily recommended. It will be a source of great gratification to me to be able to approve any measure of Congress looking effectively toward securing "resumption."

Unlimited inflation would probably bring about specie payments more speedily than any legislation looking to redemption of the legal-tenders in coin; but it would be at the expense of honor. The legal-tenders would have no value beyond settling present liabilities, or, properly speaking, repudiating them. They would buy nothing after debts were all settled.

There are a few measures which seem to me important in this connection and which I commend to your earnest consideration:

A repeal of so much of the legal-tender act as makes these notes receivable for debts contracted after a date to be fixed in the act itself, say not later than the 1st of January, 1877. We should then have quotations at real values, not fictitious ones. Gold would no longer be at a premium, but currency at a discount. A healthy reaction would set in at once, and with it a desire to make the currency equal to what it purports to be. The merchants, manufacturers, and tradesmen of every calling could do business on a fair margin of profit, the money to be received having an unvarying value. Laborers and all classes who work for stipulated pay or salary would receive more for their income, because extra profits would no longer be charged by the capitalists to compensate for the risk of a downward fluctuation in the value of the currency.

Second. That the Secretary of the Treasury be authorized to redeem, say, not to exceed $2,000,000 monthly of legal-tender notes, by issuing in their stead a long bond, bearing interest at the rate of 3.65 per cent per annum, of denominations ranging from $50 up to $1,000 each. This would in time reduce the legal-tender notes to a volume that could be kept afloat without demanding redemption in large sums suddenly.

Third. That additional power be given to the Secretary of the Treasury to accumulate gold for final redemption, either by increasing revenue, curtailing expenses, or both (it is preferable to do both); and I recommend that reduction of expenditures be made wherever it can be done without impairing Government obligations or crippling the due execution thereof. One measure for increasing the revenue—and the only one I think of—is the restoration of the duty on tea and coffee. These duties would add probably $18,000,000 to the present amount received from imports, and would in no way increase the prices paid for those articles by the consumers.

These articles are the products of countries collecting revenue from exports, and as we, the largest consumers, reduce the duties they proportionately increase them. With this addition to the revenue, many duties now collected, and which give but an insignificant return for the cost of collection, might be remitted, and to the direct advantage of consumers at home.

I would mention those articles which enter into manufactures of all sorts. All duty paid upon such articles goes directly to the cost of the article when manufactured here, and must be paid for by the consumers. These duties not only come from the consumers at home, but act as a protection to foreign manufacturers of the same completed articles in our own and distant markets.

I will suggest or mention another subject bearing upon the problem of "how to enable the Secretary of the Treasury to accumulate balances." It is to devise some better method of verifying claims against the Government than at present exists through the Court of Claims, especially those claims growing out of the late war. Nothing is more certain than that a very large percentage of the amounts passed and paid are either wholly fraudulent or are far in excess of the real losses sustained. The large amount of losses proven—on good testimony according to existing laws, by affidavits of fictitious or unscrupulous persons—to have been sustained on small farms and plantations are not only far beyond the possible yield of those places for any one year, but, as everyone knows who has had experience in tilling the soil and who has visited the scenes of these spoliations, are in many instances more than the individual claimants were ever worth, including their personal and real estate.

The report of the Attorney-General, which will be submitted to Congress at an early day, will contain a detailed history of awards made and of claims pending of the class here referred to.

The report of the Secretary of War, accompanying this message, gives a detailed account of Army operations for the year just passed, expenses for maintenance, etc., with recommendations for legislation to which I respectfully invite your attention. To some of these I invite special attention:

First. The necessity of making $300,000 of the appropriation for the Subsistence Department available before the beginning of the next fiscal year. Without this provision troops at points distant from supply production must either go without food or existing laws must be violated. It is not attended with cost to the Treasury.

Second. His recommendation for the enactment of a system of annuities for the families of deceased officers by voluntary deductions from the monthly pay of officers. This again is not attended with burden upon the Treasury, and would for the future relieve much distress which every old army officer has witnessed in the past—of officers dying suddenly or being killed, leaving families without even the means of reaching their friends, if fortunate enough to have friends to aid them.

Third. The repeal of the law abolishing mileage, and a return to the old system.

Fourth. The trial with torpedoes under the Corps of Engineers, and appropriation for the same. Should war ever occur between the United States and any maritime power, torpedoes will be among if not the most effective and cheapest auxiliary for the defense of harbors, and also in aggressive operations, that we can have. Hence it is advisable to learn by experiment their best construction and application, as well as effect.

Fifth. A permanent organization for the Signal-Service Corps. This service has now become a necessity of peace as well as war, under the advancement made by the present able management.

Sixth. A renewal of the appropriation for compiling the official records of the war, etc.

The condition of our Navy at this time is a subject of satisfaction. It does not contain, it is true, any of the powerful cruising ironclads which make so much of the maritime strength of some other nations, but neither our continental situation nor our foreign policy requires that we should have a large number of ships of this character, while this situation and the nature of our ports combine to make those of other nations little dangerous to us under any circumstances.

Our Navy does contain, however, a considerable number of ironclads of the monitor class, which, though not properly cruisers, are powerful and effective for harbor defense and for operations near our own shores. Of these all the single-turreted ones, fifteen in number, have been substantially rebuilt, their rotten wooden beams replaced with iron, their hulls strengthened, and their engines and machinery thoroughly repaired, so that they are now in the most efficient condition and ready for sea as soon as they can be manned and put in commission.

The five double-turreted ironclads belonging to our Navy, by far the most powerful of our ships for fighting purposes, are also in hand undergoing complete repairs, and could be ready for sea in periods varying from four to six months. With these completed according to the present design and our two iron torpedo boats now ready, our ironclad fleet will be, for the purposes of defense at home, equal to any force that can readily be brought against it.

Of our wooden navy also cruisers of various sizes, to the number of about forty, including those now in commission, are in the Atlantic, and could be ready for duty as fast as men could be enlisted for those not already in commission. Of these, one-third are in effect new ships, and though some of the remainder need considerable repairs to their boilers and machinery, they all are, or can readily be made, effective.

This constitutes a fleet of more than fifty war ships, of which fifteen are ironclad, now in hand on the Atlantic coast. The Navy has been brought to this condition by a judicious and practical application of what could be spared from the current appropriations of the last few years and from that made to meet the possible emergency of two years ago. It has been done quietly, without proclamation or display, and though it has necessarily straitened the Department in its ordinary expenditure, and, as far as the ironclads are concerned, has added nothing to the cruising force of the Navy, yet the result is not the less satisfactory because it is to be found in a great increase of real rather than apparent force. The expenses incurred in the maintenance of an effective naval force in all its branches are necessarily large, but such force is essential to our position, relations, and character, and affects seriously the weight of our principles and policy throughout the whole sphere of national responsibilities.

The estimates for the regular support of this branch of the service for the next year amount to a little less in the aggregate than those made for the current year; but some additional appropriations are asked for objects not included in the ordinary maintenance of the Navy, but believed to be of pressing importance at this time. It would, in my opinion, be wise at once to afford sufficient means for the immediate completion of the five double-turreted monitors now undergoing repairs, which must otherwise advance slowly, and only as money can be spared from current expenses. Supplemented by these, our Navy, armed with the destructive weapons of modern warfare, manned by our seamen, and in charge of our instructed officers, will present a force powerful for the home purposes of a responsible though peaceful nation.

The report of the Postmaster-General herewith transmitted gives a full history of the workings of the Department for the year just past. It will be observed that the deficiency to be supplied from the General Treasury is increased over the amount required for the preceding year. In a country so vast in area as the United States, with large portions sparsely settled, it must be expected that this important service will be more or less a burden upon the Treasury for many years to come. But there is no branch of the public service which interests the whole people more than that of cheap and rapid transmission of the mails to every inhabited part of our territory. Next to the free school, the post-office is the great educator of the people, and it may well receive the support of the General Government.

The subsidy of $150,000 per annum given to vessels of the United States for carrying the mails between New York and Rio de Janeiro having ceased on the 30th day of September last, we are without direct mail facilities with the South American States. This is greatly to be regretted, and I do not hesitate to recommend the authorization of a renewal of that contract, and also that the service may be increased from monthly to semi-monthly trips. The commercial advantages to be gained by a direct line of American steamers to the South American States will far outweigh the expense of the service.

By act of Congress approved March 3, 1875, almost all matter, whether properly mail matter or not, may be sent any distance through the mails, in packages not exceeding 4 pounds in weight, for the sum of 16 cents per pound. So far as the transmission of real mail matter goes, this would seem entirely proper; but I suggest that the law be so amended as to exclude from the mails merchandise of all descriptions, and limit this transportation to articles enumerated, and which may be classed as mail matter proper.

The discovery of gold in the Black Hills, a portion of the Sioux Reservation, has had the effect to induce a large emigration of miners to that point. Thus far the effort to protect the treaty rights of the Indians to that section has been successful, but the next year will certainly witness a large increase of such emigration. The negotiations for the relinquishment of the gold fields having failed, it will be necessary for Congress to adopt some measures to relieve the embarrassment growing out of the causes named. The Secretary of the Interior suggests that the supplies now appropriated for the sustenance of that people, being no longer obligatory under the treaty of 1868, but simply a gratuity, may be issued or withheld at his discretion.

The condition of the Indian Territory, to which I have referred in several of my former annual messages, remains practically unchanged. The Secretary of the Interior has taken measures to obtain a full report of the condition of that Territory, and will make it the subject of a special report at an early day. It may then be necessary to make some further recommendation in regard to legislation for the government of that Territory.

The steady growth and increase of the business of the Patent Office indicates in some measure the progress of the industrial activity of the country. The receipts of the office are in excess of its expenditures, and the office generally is in a prosperous and satisfactory condition.

The report of the General Land Office shows that there were 2,459,601 acres less disposed of during this than during the last year. More than one-half of this decrease was in lands disposed of under the homestead and timber-culture laws. The cause of this decrease is supposed to be found in the grasshopper scourge and the droughts which prevailed so extensively in some of the frontier States and Territories during that time as to discourage and deter entries by actual settlers. The cash receipts were less by $690,322.23 than during the preceding year.

The entire surveyed area of the public domain is 680,253,094 acres, of which 26,077,531 acres were surveyed during the past year, leaving 1,154,471,762 acres still unsurveyed.

The report of the Commissioner presents many interesting suggestions in regard to the management and disposition of the public domain and the modification of existing laws, the apparent importance of which should insure for them the careful consideration of Congress.

The number of pensioners still continues to decrease, the highest number having been reached during the year ending June 30, 1873. During the last year 11,557 names were added to the rolls, and 12,977 were dropped therefrom, showing a net decrease of 1,420. But while the number of pensioners has decreased, the annual amount due on the pension rolls has increased $44,733.13. This is caused by the greatly increased average rate of pensions, which, by the liberal legislation of Congress, has increased from $90.26 in 1872 to $103.91 in 1875 to each invalid pensioner, an increase in the average rate of 15 per cent in the three years. During the year ending June 30, 1875, there was paid on account of pensions, including the expenses of disbursement, $29,683,116, being $910,632 less than was paid the preceding year. This reduction in amount of expenditures was produced by the decrease in the amount of arrearages due on allowed claims and on pensions the rate of which was increased by the legislation of the preceding session of Congress. At the close of the last fiscal year there were on the pension rolls 234,821 persons, of whom 210,363 were army pensioners, 105,478 being invalids and 104,885 widows and dependent relatives; 3,420 were navy pensioners, of whom 1,636 were invalids and 1,784 widows and dependent relatives; 21,038 were pensioners of the War of 1812, 15,875 of whom were survivors and 5,163 were widows.

It is estimated that $29,535,000 will be required for the payment of pensions for the next fiscal year, an amount $965,000 less than the estimate for the present year.

The geological explorations have been prosecuted with energy during the year, covering an area of about 40,000 square miles in the Territories of Colorado, Utah, and New Mexico, developing the agricultural and mineral resources and furnishing interesting scientific and topographical details of that region.

The method for the treatment of the Indians adopted at the beginning of my first term has been steadily pursued, and with satisfactory and encouraging results. It has been productive of evident improvement in the condition of that race, and will be continued, with only such modifications as further experience may indicate to be necessary.

The board heretofore appointed to take charge of the articles and materials pertaining to the War, the Navy, the Treasury, the Interior, and the Post-Office Departments, and the Department of Agriculture, the Smithsonian Institution, and the Commission of Food Fishes, to be contributed, under the legislation of last session, to the international exhibition to be held at Philadelphia during the centennial year 1876, has been diligent in the discharge of the duties which have devolved upon it; and the preparations so far made with the means at command give assurance that the governmental contribution will be made one of the marked characteristics of the exhibition. The board has observed commendable economy in the matter of the erection of a building for the governmental exhibit, the expense of which it is estimated will not exceed, say, $80,000. This amount has been withdrawn, under the law, from the appropriations of five of the principal Departments, which leaves some of those Departments without sufficient means to render their respective practical exhibits complete and satisfactory. The exhibition being an international one, and the Government being a voluntary contributor, it is my opinion that its contribution should be of a character, in quality and extent, to sustain the dignity and credit of so distinguished a contributor. The advantages to the country of a creditable display are, in an international point of view, of the first importance, while an indifferent or uncreditable participation by the Government would be humiliating to the patriotic feelings of our people themselves. I commend the estimates of the board for the necessary additional appropriations to the favorable consideration of Congress.

The powers of Europe almost without exception, many of the South American States, and even the more distant Eastern powers have manifested their friendly sentiments toward the United States and the interest of the world in our progress by taking steps to join with us in celebrating the centennial of the nation, and I strongly recommend that a more national importance be given to this exhibition by such legislation and by such appropriation as will insure its success. Its value in bringing to our shores innumerable useful works of art and skill, the commingling of the citizens of foreign countries and our own, and the interchange of ideas and manufactures will far exceed any pecuniary outlay we may make.

I transmit herewith the report of the Commissioner of Agriculture, together with the reports of the Commissioners, the board of audit, and the board of health of the District of Columbia, to all of which I invite your attention.

The Bureau of Agriculture has accomplished much in disseminating useful knowledge to the agriculturist, and also in introducing new and useful productions adapted to our soil and climate, and is worthy of the continued encouragement of the Government.

The report of the Commissioner of Education, which accompanies the report of the Secretary of the Interior, shows a gratifying progress in educational matters.

In nearly every annual message that I have had the honor of transmitting to Congress I have called attention to the anomalous, not to say scandalous, condition of affairs existing in the Territory of Utah, and have asked for definite legislation to correct it. That polygamy should exist in a free, enlightened, and Christian country, without the power to punish so flagrant a crime against decency and morality, seems preposterous. True, there is no law to sustain this unnatural vice; but what is needed is a law to punish it as a crime, and at the same time to fix the status of the innocent children, the offspring of this system, and of the possibly innocent plural wives. But as an institution polygamy should be banished from the land.

While this is being done I invite the attention of Congress to another, though perhaps no less an evil—the importation of Chinese women, but few of whom are brought to our shores to pursue honorable or useful occupations.

Observations while visiting the Territories of Wyoming, Utah, and Colorado during the past autumn convinced me that existing laws regulating the disposition of public lands, timber, etc., and probably the mining laws themselves, are very defective and should be carefully amended, and at an early day. Territory where cultivation of the soil can only be followed by irrigation, and where irrigation is not practicable the lands can only be used as pasturage, and this only where stock can reach water (to quench its thirst), can not be governed by the same laws as to entries as lands every acre of which is an independent estate by itself.

Land must be held in larger quantities to justify the expense of conducting water upon it to make it fruitful, or to justify utilizing it as pasturage. The timber in most of the Territories is principally confined to the mountain regions, which are held for entry in small quantities only, and as mineral lands. The timber is the property of the United States, for the disposal of which there is now no adequate law. The settler must become a consumer of this timber, whether he lives upon the plain or engages in working the mines. Hence every man becomes either a tres٭passer himself or knowingly a patron of trespassers.

My opportunities for observation were not sufficient to justify me in recommending specific legislation on these subjects, but I do recommend that a joint committee of the two Houses of Congress, sufficiently large to be divided into subcommittees, be organized to visit all the mining States and Territories during the coming summer, and that the committee shall report to Congress at the next session such laws or amendments to laws as it may deem necessary to secure the best interests of the Government and the people of these Territories, who are doing so much for their development.

I am sure the citizens occupying the territory described do not wish to be trespassers, nor will they be if legal ways are provided for them to become owners of these actual necessities of their position.

As this will be the last annual message which I shall have the honor of transmitting to Congress before my successor is chosen, I will repeat or recapitulate the questions which I deem of vital importance which may be legislated upon and settled at this session:

First. That the States shall be required to afford the opportunity of a good common-school education to every child within their limits.

Second. No sectarian tenets shall ever be taught in any school supported in whole or in part by the State, nation, or by the proceeds of any tax levied upon any community. Make education compulsory so far as to deprive all persons who can not read and write from becoming voters after the year 1890, disfranchising none, however, on grounds of illiteracy who may be voters at the time this amendment takes effect.

Third. Declare church and state forever separate and distinct, but each free within their proper spheres; and that all church property shall bear its own proportion of taxation.

Fourth. Drive out licensed immorality, such as polygamy and the importation of women for illegitimate purposes. To recur again to the centennial year, it would seem as though now, as we are about to begin the second century of our national existence, would be a most fitting time for these reforms.

Fifth. Enact such laws as will insure a speedy return to a sound currency, such as will command the respect of the world.

Believing that these views will commend themselves to the great majority of the right-thinking and patriotic citizens of the United States, I submit the rest to Congress.   U. S. GRANT.

SPECIAL MESSAGES.

EXECUTIVE MANSION, *January 6, 1876.*
To the Senate of the United States:

In reply to the resolution of the Senate of the 27th of February last, requesting the President to institute inquiries as to the proper place for the establishment of a branch mint at some point in the Western States or in the Mississippi Valley, I transmit herewith the report, and accompanying papers, of the Director of the Mint, who was charged with the duty of making the inquiries called for by said resolution.

                                             U. S. GRANT.

WASHINGTON, *January 21, 1876.*

To the House of Representatives:

I transmit to the House of Representatives, in answer to their resolution of the 17th instant, a report from the Secretary of State, with accompanying documents.*

U. S. GRANT.

WASHINGTON, *January 25, 1876.*

To the House of Representatives:

In answer to the resolution of the House of Representatives of the 22d of January instant, I herewith transmit a report† from the Secretary of State.

U. S. GRANT.

EXECUTIVE MANSION, *February 3, 1876.*

To the Senate of the United States:

In answer to the resolution of the Senate of the 19th of January instant, requesting the examination, with a view to ascertaining their suitableness for the purposes of a mint, of the building and grounds situated in Columbus, Ohio, known as the "Capital University," and proposed to be donated to the United States by F. Michel, of said city, I have the honor to transmit herewith the report of the Director of the Mint, accompanied by a diagram of the building and lot.

U. S. GRANT.

EXECUTIVE MANSION, *February, 1876.*

To the House of Representatives:

In answer to the resolution of the 6th of January of the House of Representatives, requesting to be informed "of the number of Indian agents, regular and special, clerks, and other employees in the Indian service, except those on duty in the office of the Secretary of the Interior, and the amounts paid to each as salaries and expenses," I have the honor to transmit herewith a copy of a report, dated the 31st ultimo, from the Commissioner of Indian Affairs, together with the statements therein referred to.

U. S. GRANT.

WASHINGTON, *February 8, 1876.*

To the Senate of the United States:

I transmit to the Senate, in answer to the resolution‡ of that body of the 18th ultimo, a report from the Secretary of State, with accompanying papers.

U. S. GRANT.

* Correspondence with Spain relative to Cuba.
† Stating that no correspondence had taken place during the year 1875 with any European Government other than Spain relative to Cuba.
‡ Calling for correspondence with any government or its representatives relative to the Centennial celebration to be held in Philadelphia.

EXECUTIVE MANSION, *February 28, 1876.*

To the Senate and House of Representatives:

I lay before you herewith a communication from the Secretary of the Interior, of date 26th instant, upon the subject of the deficiency of supplies at the Red Cloud Agency, Nebr.

This matter has already been presented to you by the Secretary, and the House of Representatives has requested an investigation by a military officer of the cause of this deficiency. I have taken proper steps to comply with this request of the House, but the present need of supplies is not disputed. A prolonged delay in furnishing provisions to these Indians will cause great distress and be likely to provoke raids on white settlements, and possibly lead to general outbreak and hostilities.

I therefore deem it proper to invite your attention to the importance of early and favorable action upon the estimates heretofore and herewith submitted.

These estimates and the views of the Secretary in regard to this emergency meet with my full concurrence, and I recommend that the appropriations asked for be made at the earliest day practicable.

U. S. GRANT.

WASHINGTON, *March 3, 1876.*

To the House of Representatives:

In answer to the resolution of the House of Representatives of the 21st ultimo, I transmit herewith a report from the Secretary of State, and accompanying papers,* together with a report from the Secretary of the Treasury.

U. S. GRANT.

EXECUTIVE MANSION, *March 6, 1876.*

To the Senate of the United States:

In answer to the resolution of the Senate of the 7th of January last, requesting a "statement of the number of military arrests made in the Territory of Alaska during the past five years, together with the date of each, the charge on which made in each case, the names of the persons arrested, and the period and character of the imprisonment of each in that Territory before trial or surrender to the civil authorities for trial," I have the honor to submit herewith the report of the Acting Secretary of War.

U. S. GRANT.

WASHINGTON, *March 10, 1876.*

To the Senate of the United States:

I transmit to the Senate, for consideration with a view to ratification, a metric convention between the United States and certain foreign gov-

---

* Correspondence relative to the mode of transferring to the United States the Alabama indemnity of $15,500,000, and correspondence and papers showing the payment of the indemnity, the form of receipt given therefor, and the disposition of the indemnity.

ernments, signed at Paris on the 20th of May, 1875, by Mr. E. B. Washburne, the minister of the United States at that capital, acting on behalf of this Government, and by the representatives acting on behalf of the foreign powers therein mentioned.

A copy of certain papers on the subject, mentioned in the subjoined list, is also transmitted for the information of the Senate.

U. S. GRANT.

WASHINGTON, *March 22, 1876.*

To the House of Representatives:

In answer to a resolution* of the House of Representatives of the 23d of February ultimo, I transmit herewith a report of the Secretary of State and the papers which accompany it. U. S. GRANT.

EXECUTIVE MANSION, *March 23, 1876.*

To the House of Representatives:

In answer to the resolution of the House of Representatives of the 3d of February last, requesting the President "to require a competent, experienced military officer of the United States to execute the duties of an Indian agent so far as to repair to the Red Cloud Agency, and, in his discretion, other Sioux agencies, with instructions to inquire into the causes of" the exhaustion of the appropriation for the subsistence and support of the Sioux Indians for the present fiscal year; "as also his opinion as to whether any further and what amount should be appropriated for the subsistence and support of said Indians for the remainder of the current fiscal year," I have the honor to transmit herewith the report of Lieutenant-Colonel Merritt, of the Ninth Cavalry, who was charged by the Secretary of War with the duty of making the inquiries called for by said resolution. U. S. GRANT.

EXECUTIVE MANSION, *March 24, 1876.*

To the Senate of the United States:

In further answer to the resolution of the Senate of the 7th of January last, requesting to be furnished "with a statement of the number of military arrests made in the Territory of Alaska during the past five years, together with the date of each, the charge on which made in each case, the names of the persons arrested, and the period and character of the imprisonment of each in that Territory before trial or surrender to the civil authorities for trial," I have the honor to transmit herewith the report of the Secretary of War. U. S. GRANT.

* Calling for information or facts relative to the charges against George F. Seward, United States minister to China.

EXECUTIVE MANSION, *March 27, 1876.*

To the House of Representatives:

In further answer to the resolution of the House of the 6th of January last, with regard to certain expenditures and employees in the Indian service, except those on duty in the office of the Secretary of the Interior, etc., I have the honor to transmit to you a supplementary report received from the Secretary of the Interior, respecting and explaining a clerical error to be found in that portion of the statement of the Interior Department which relates to the expenditures of the Board of Indian Commissioners, and to ask its consideration in connection with the papers which accompanied my message of the 3d of February last.

U. S. GRANT.

EXECUTIVE MANSION, *March 27, 1876.*

To the House of Representatives:

I have the honor to transmit herewith a communication received from the chairman of the board on behalf of the United States Executive Departments, containing in detail the operations of the board and setting forth the present embarrassments under which it is now laboring in the endeavor to conduct the participation of the Government in the Centennial Exhibition, and showing very clearly the necessity of additional funds to carry out the undertaking in a creditable manner.

U. S. GRANT.

EXECUTIVE MANSION, *April 3, 1876.*

To the House of Representatives:

I have the honor to transmit herewith, for your information, a communication from the Secretary of the Interior of this date, upon the urgent necessities of the Pawnee Indians.

This tribe has recently been removed to the Indian Territory, and is without means of subsistence except as supplied by the Government. Its members have evinced a disposition to become self-supporting, and it is believed that only temporary aid will be required by them. The sums advanced by the United States for this purpose it is expected will be refunded from the proceeds of the sale of the Pawnee Reservation in Nebraska.

The present destitute condition of these Indians would seem to call for immediate relief, and I recommend the subject to your early and favorable consideration.

U. S. GRANT.

EXECUTIVE MANSION, *April 6, 1876.*

To the Senate of the United States:

In further answer to the resolution of the Senate of the 7th of January last (partial answers having been transmitted on the 6th and 24th ultimo), calling for a statement of "the number of military arrests in the Territory of Alaska during the past five years," etc., I have the honor to submit herewith a report, with accompanying papers, received from the Secretary of War.

U. S. GRANT.

EXECUTIVE MANSION, *April 19, 1876.*

To the Senate and House of Representatives:

I have the honor to transmit herewith to Congress the final report of the board of audit constituted by section 6 of the "act for the government of the District of Columbia, and for other purposes," approved June 20, 1874, and abolished by the joint resolution approved March 14, 1876, and to call your attention to the statements therein presented.

U. S. GRANT.

WASHINGTON, *May 1, 1876.*

To the Senate:

I transmit herewith, for the information of Congress, a report of the president of the Centennial Commission upon the ceremonies to be observed at the opening of the exhibition on the 10th instant. It will be observed that an invitation is therein extended to Senators and Representatives to be present on that occasion.

U. S. GRANT.

[The same message was sent to the House of Representatives.]

WASHINGTON, *May 1, 1876.*

To the Senate:

I transmit herewith, for the consideration of the Senate with a view to its ratification by that body, a treaty between the United States and Mexico, concluded on the 29th ultimo.

U. S. GRANT.

WASHINGTON, *May 1, 1876.*

To the House of Representatives:

I transmit herewith, in answer to the resolution of the House of Representatives of 15th March last, a report* from the Secretary of State and accompanying papers.

U. S. GRANT.

WASHINGTON, *May 4, 1876.*

To the House of Representatives:

I have given very attentive consideration to a resolution of the House of Representatives passed on the 3d of April, requesting the President of the United States to inform the House whether any executive offices

---

* Explanatory of the object, intent, and character of the power conferred upon A. B. Steinberger, special agent to the Samoan or Navigators Islands, and transmitting correspondence relative to the object, operation, and result of his agency.

acts, or duties, and, if any, what, have within a specified period been per-formed at a distance from the seat of Government established by law, etc.

I have never hesitated and shall not hesitate to communicate to Congress, and to either branch thereof, all the information which the Constitution makes it the duty of the President to give, or which my judgment may suggest to me or a request from either House may indicate to me will be useful in the discharge of the appropriate duties confided to them. I fail, however, to find in the Constitution of the United States the authority given to the House of Representatives (one branch of the Congress, in which is vested the legislative power of the Government) to require of the Executive, an independent branch of the Government, coordinate with the Senate and House of Representatives, an account of his discharge of his appropriate and purely executive offices, acts, and duties, either as to when, where, or how performed.

What the House of Representatives may require as a right in its demand upon the Executive for information is limited to what is necessary for the proper discharge of its powers of legislation or of impeachment.

The inquiry in the resolution of the House as to where executive acts have within the last seven years been performed and at what distance from any particular spot or for how long a period at any one time, etc., does not necessarily belong to the province of legislation. It does not profess to be asked for that object.

If this information be sought through an inquiry of the President as to his executive acts in view or in aid of the power of impeachment vested in the House, it is asked in derogation of an inherent natural right, recognized in this country by a constitutional guaranty which protects every citizen, the President as well as the humblest in the land, from being made a witness against himself.

During the time that I have had the honor to occupy the position of President of this Government it has been, and while I continue to occupy that position it will continue to be, my earnest endeavor to recognize and to respect the several trusts and duties and powers of the coordinate branches of the Government, not encroaching upon them nor allowing encroachments upon the proper powers of the office which the people of the United States have confided to me, but aiming to preserve in their proper relations the several powers and functions of each of the coordinate branches of the Government, agreeably to the Constitution and in accordance with the solemn oath which I have taken to "preserve, protect, and defend" that instrument.

In maintenance of the rights secured by the Constitution to the executive branch of the Government I am compelled to decline any specific or detailed answer to the request of the House for information as to "any executive offices, acts, or duties, and, if any, what, have been performed at a distance from the seat of Government established by law, and for how long a period at any one time and in what part of the United States."

If, however, the House of Representatives desires to know whether during the period of upward of seven years during which I have held the office of President of the United States I have been absent from the seat of Government, and whether during that period I have performed or have neglected to perform the duties of my office, I freely inform the House that from the time of my entrance upon my office I have been in the habit, as were all of my predecessors (with the exception of one, who lived only one month after assuming the duties of his office, and one whose continued presence in Washington was necessary from the existence at the time of a powerful rebellion), of absenting myself at times from the seat of Government, and that during such absences I did not neglect or forego the obligations or the duties of my office, but continued to discharge all of the executive offices, acts, and duties which were required of me as the President of the United States. I am not aware that a failure occurred in any one instance of my exercising the functions and powers of my office in every case requiring their discharge, or of my exercising all necessary executive acts, in whatever part of the United States I may at the time have been. Fortunately, the rapidity of travel and of mail communication and the facility of almost instantaneous correspondence with the offices at the seat of Government, which the telegraph affords to the President in whatever section of the Union he may be, enable him in these days to maintain as constant and almost as quick intercourse with the Departments at Washington as may be maintained while he remains at the capital.

The necessity of the performance of executive acts by the President of the United States exists and is devolved upon him, wherever he may be within the United States, during his term of office by the Constitution of the United States.

His civil powers are no more limited or capable of limitation as to the place where they shall be exercised than are those which he might be required to discharge in his capacity of Commander in Chief of the Army and Navy, which latter powers it is evident he might be called upon to exercise, possibly, even without the limits of the United States. Had the efforts of those recently in rebellion against the Government been successful in driving a late President of the United States from Washington, it is manifest that he must have discharged his functions, both civil and military, elsewhere than in the place named by law as the seat of Government.

No act of Congress can limit, suspend, or confine this constitutional duty. I am not aware of the existence of any act of Congress which assumes thus to limit or restrict the exercise of the functions of the Executive. Were there such acts, I should nevertheless recognize the superior authority of the Constitution, and should exercise the powers required thereby of the President.

The act to which reference is made in the resolution of the House relates to the establishing of the seat of Government and the providing of suitable buildings and removal thereto of the offices attached to the Government, etc. It was not understood at its date and by General Washington to confine the President in the discharge of his duties and powers to actual presence at the seat of Government. On the 30th of March, 1791, shortly after the passage of the act referred to, General Washington issued an Executive proclamation having reference to the subject of this very act from Georgetown, a place remote from Philadelphia, which then was the seat of Government, where the act referred to directed that "all offices attached to the seat of Government" should for the time remain.

That none of his successors have entertained the idea that their executive offices could be performed only at the seat of Government is evidenced by the hundreds upon hundreds of such acts performed by my predecessors in unbroken line from Washington to Lincoln, a memorandum of the general nature and character of some of which acts is submitted herewith; and no question has ever been raised as to the validity of those acts or as to the right and propriety of the Executive to exercise the powers of his office in any part of the United States.

U. S. GRANT.

Memorandum of absences of the Presidents of the United States from the national capital during each of the several Administrations, and of public and executive acts performed during the time of such absences.

President Washington was frequently absent from the capital; he appears to have been thus absent at least one hundred and eighty-one days during his term.

During his several absences he discharged official and executive duties; among them—

In March, 1791, he issued a proclamation, dated at Georgetown, in reference to running the boundary for the territory of the permanent seat of the Government.

From Mount Vernon he signed an official letter to the Emperor of Morocco, and from the same place the commission of Oliver Wolcott as Comptroller of the Treasury and the proclamation respecting the whisky insurrection in Pennsylvania; also various sea letters, the proclamation of the treaty of 1795 between the United States and Spain, the Executive order of August 4, 1792, relative to the duties on distilled spirits, etc.

When at Germantown he signed the commission of John Breckenridge as attorney of the United States for Kentucky, and that of engineer of the United States Mint.

He proposed to have Mr. Yrujo officially presented, as envoy extraordinary and minister plenipotentiary from Spain, to him at Mount Vernon; but although Mr. Yrujo went there for the purpose, the ceremony of presentation was prevented by Mr. Yrujo's having accidentally left his credentials.

President John Adams was absent from the capital during his term of four years, on various occasions, three hundred and eighty-five days. He discharged official duties and performed the most solemn public acts at Quincy in the same manner as when at the seat of Government. In 1797 (August 25) he forwarded to the Secretary of State a number of passports which he had signed at Quincy. He issued at Quincy commissions to numerous officers of various grades, civil and military. On the 28th of September, 1797, he forwarded to the Secretary of State a commission for a justice or the Supreme Court, signed in blank at Quincy, instructing the Secretary to fill it with the name of John Marshall if he would accept, and, if not, Bushrod Washington. He issued a proclamation opening trade with certain ports of St. Domingo, and signed warrants for the execution of two soldiers and for a pardon.

President Jefferson was absent from the seat of Government during his two terms of office seven hundred and ninety-six days, more than one-fourth of the whole official period. During his absence he signed and issued from Monticello seventy-five commissions, one letter to the Emperor of Russia, and nine letters of credence to diplomatic agents of the United States accredited to other governments.

President Madison was absent from the seat of Government during his two Presidential terms six hundred and thirty-seven days. He signed and issued from Montpelier during his absence from the capital seventy-one commissions, one proclamation, and nine letters of credence to ministers, accrediting them to foreign governments, and, as it appears, transacted generally all the necessary routine business incident to the Executive office.

President Monroe was absent from the capital during his Presidential service of eight years seven hundred and eight days, independent of the year 1824 and the two months of 1825, for which period no data are found. He transacted public business wherever he happened to be, sometimes at his farm in Virginia, again at his summer resort on the Chesapeake, and sometimes while traveling. He signed and issued from these several places, away from the capital, numerous commissions to civil officers of the Government, exequaturs to foreign consuls, letters of credence, two letters to sovereigns, and thirty-seven pardons.

President John Q. Adams was absent from the capital during his Presidential term of four years two hundred and twenty-two days. During such absence he performed official and public acts, signing and issuing commissions, exequaturs, pardons, proclamations, etc. Referring to his absence in August and September, 1827, Mr. Adams, in his memoirs, volume 8, page 75, says: "I left with him [the chief clerk] some blank signatures, to be used when necessary for proclamations, remission of penalties, and commissions of consuls, taking of him a receipt for the number and kind of blanks left with him, with directions to return to me when I came back all the signed blanks remaining unused and to keep and give me an account of all those that shall have been disposed of. This has been my constant practice with respect to signed blanks of this description. I do the same with regard to patents and land grants."

President Jackson was absent from the capital during his Presidential service of eight years five hundred and two days. He also performed executive duties and public acts while absent. He appears to have signed and issued while absent from the capital very many public papers, embracing commissions, letters of credence, exequaturs, pardons, and among them four Executive proclamations. On the 26th of June, 1833, he addressed a letter from Boston to Mr. Duane, Secretary of the Treasury, giving his views at large on the removal of the "deposits" from the United States Bank and placing them in the State banks, directing that the change, with all its arrangements, should be, if possible, completed by the 15th September following, and recommending that Amos Kendall should be appointed an agent of the Treasury Department to make the necessary arrangements with the State banks. Soon after, September 23, a paper signed by the President and purporting to have been read to the Cabinet was published in the newspapers of the day. Early in the next session of Congress a resolution passed the Senate inquiring of the President whether the paper was genuine or not and if it was published by his authority, and requesting that a copy be laid before that body. The President replied, avowing the genuineness of the paper and that it was published by his authority, but declined to furnish a copy to the Senate on the ground that it was purely executive business, and that the request of the Senate was an undue interference with the independence of the Executive, a coordinate branch of the Government. In January, 1837 (26th), he refused the privilege to a committee under a resolution of the House of Representatives to make a general investigation of the Executive Departments without specific charges, on the ground, among others, that the use of the books, papers, etc., of the Departments for such purpose would interfere with the discharge of the public duties devolving upon the heads of the different Departments, and necessarily disarrange and retard the public business.

President Van Buren was absent from the capital during his Presidential term one hundred and thirty-one days. He discharged executive duties and performed official and public acts during these absences. Among the papers signed by President Van Buren during his absence from the seat of Government are commissions (one of these being for a United States judge of a district court), pardons, etc.

President Tyler was absent from the capital during his Presidential term one hundred and sixty-three days, and performed public acts and duties during such absences, signing public papers and documents to the number of twenty-eight, in which were included commissions, exequaturs, letters of credence, pardons, and one proclamation making public the treaty of 1842 between the United States and Ecuador.

President Polk was absent from the capital during his Presidential term thirty-seven days, and appears to have signed but two official public papers during such absence.

President Taylor was absent from the capital during the time he served as President thirty-one days, and while absent signed two commissions, three "full powers," two exequaturs, and the proclamation of August 11, 1849, relative to a threatened invasion of Cuba or some of the Provinces of Mexico.

President Fillmore was absent from the capital during the time he served as President sixty days. During such absence he signed pardons, commissions, exequaturs, etc.

President Pierce was absent from the capital in all during his Presidential term fifty-seven days. The several periods of absence which make up this aggregate were each brief, and it does not appear that during these absences the President signed any public official documents, except one pardon.

President Buchanan was absent from the capital during his Presidential term fifty-seven days, and the official papers which he is shown to have signed during such absence are three exequaturs and one letter of credence.

In addition to the public documents and papers executed by the several Presidents during their absences from the seat of Government, constant official correspondence was maintained by each with the heads of the different Executive Departments.

WASHINGTON, *May 15, 1876.*

To the House of Representatives:

In answer to the resolution of the House of Representatives of the 10th ultimo, I transmit herewith a report and accompanying papers upon the subject* from the Secretary of State.

U. S. GRANT.

WASHINGTON, *May 16, 1876.*

To the House of Representatives:

In answer to a resolution of the House of Representatives of the 5th instant, requesting information as to payments by the Government of

* Course pursued to enforce the provisions of the convention with Venezuela of April 25, 1866, and the payment of adjudicated claims under act approved February 25, 1873.

Venezuela on account of claims of citizens of the United States under the convention of the 25th of April, 1866, I transmit a report from the Secretary of State, to whom the resolution was referred.

U. S. GRANT.

WASHINGTON, *May 19, 1876.*

To the Senate:

I transmit herewith, in answer to a resolution of the Senate of the 27th March last, a report* from the Secretary of State and an accompanying paper.

U. S. GRANT.

WASHINGTON, *May 31, 1876.*

To the House of Representatives:

I transmit, in answer to a resolution of the House of Representatives of the 22d instant, a report of the Secretary of State, with its accompanying papers.†

U. S. GRANT.

EXECUTIVE MANSION, *June 7, 1876.*

To the Senate and House of Representatives:

I herewith transmit the report of the board appointed to test iron, steel, and other metals, in accordance with the provisions of section 4 of "An act making appropriations for sundry civil expenses of the Government for the fiscal year ending June 30, 1876, and for other purposes," approved March 3, 1875.

This board is to determine by actual tests the strength and value of all metals, and to prepare tables which will exhibit their strength and value for all constructions.

The accompanying memorials and resolutions of scientific associations, colleges, and schools strongly advocate the continuation of this board, which is national in its character and general in its investigations.

The board asks for an appropriation of $50,000 for the ensuing year, and that any unexpended balances remaining on hand on the 30th of June, 1876, may be reappropriated.

This recommendation is submitted for favorable action, in the belief that the labors of the board will, in the benefits accruing to important industrial interests, more than repay to the country at large any money that may be so expended.

U. S. GRANT.

WASHINGTON, *June 10, 1876.*

To the House of Representatives:

I transmit herewith, in answer to the resolution of the House of Representatives of the 30th day of March last, a report from the Secretary of

---

*Relating to amount of money in the custody of the Department of State to the credit of the awards of the mixed commission under the treaty with Venezuela of April 25, 1866.

† Relating to the steps taken for the protection of American citizens in the Ottoman dominions.

State, with accompanying papers, which presents the correspondence and condition of the question* up to the day of its date.

U. S. GRANT.

To the Senate: WASHINGTON, *June 14, 1876.*

In answer to the resolution of the Senate of the 26th April ultimo, I herewith transmit a report† from the Secretary of State, with accompanying documents.

U. S. GRANT.

EXECUTIVE MANSION, *June 17, 1876.*

To the Senate and House of Representatives:

The near approach of a new fiscal year and the failure of Congress up to this time to provide the necessary means to continue all the functions of Government make it my duty to call your attention to the embarrassments that must ensue if the fiscal year is allowed to close without remedial action on your part.

Article I, section 9, of the Constitution declares:

No money shall be drawn from the Treasury but in consequence of appropriations made by law.

To insure economy of expenditure and security of the public treasure Congress has from time to time enacted laws to restrain the use of public moneys, except for the specific purpose for which appropriated and within the time for which appropriated; and to prevent contracting debts in anticipation of appropriate appropriations, Revised Statutes, section 3679, provides:

No Department of the Government shall expend in any one fiscal year any sum in excess of appropriations made by Congress for that fiscal year, or involve the Government in any contract for the future payment of money in excess of such appropriations.

Section 3732 provides:

No contract or purchase on behalf of the United States shall be made unless the same is authorized by law or is under an appropriation adequate to its fulfillment, except in the War and Navy Departments, for clothing, subsistence, forage, fuel, quarters, or transportation, which, however, shall not exceed the necessities of the current year.

Section 3678, as follows:

All sums appropriated for the various branches of expenditure in the public service shall be applied solely to the objects for which they are respectively made, and for no others.

---

* The refusal of Great Britain to surrender certain fugitive criminals in accordance with the extradition clause of the treaty of August 9, 1842.

† Relating to claims before and judgments rendered by the Alabama Claims Commission arising from captures by the rebel cruiser *Shenandoah.*

Section 3690, that—

All balances of appropriations contained in the annual appropriation bills, and made specifically for the service of any fiscal year, and remaining unexpended at the expiration of such fiscal year, shall only be applied to the payment of expenses properly incurred during that year or to the fulfillment of contracts properly made within that year; and balances not needed for such purposes shall be carried to the surplus fund. This section, however, shall not apply to appropriations known as permanent or indefinite appropriations.

The effect of the laws quoted, taken in connection with the constitutional provision referred to, is, as above stated, to prohibit any outlay of public money toward defraying even the current and necessary expenses of Government after the expiration of the year for which appropriated, excepting when those expenses are provided for by some permanent appropriation, and excepting in the War and Navy Departments, under section 3732.

The number of permanent appropriations are very limited, and cover but few of the necessary expenditures of the Government. They are nearly all, if not quite all, embraced in sections 3687, 3688, and 3689 of the Revised Statutes. That contained in section 3687 is applicable to *expenses of collecting the revenue from customs*, that in section 3688 to the payment of interest on the *public debt*, and that in section 3689 to various objects too numerous to detail here.

It will be observed that while section 3679, quoted above, provides that *no* Department shall in any one fiscal year involve the Government in any contract for the future payment of money in excess of the appropriation for that year, section 3732, also quoted above, confers, by clear implication, upon the heads of the War and Navy Departments full authority, even in the absence of any appropriation, to purchase or contract for clothing, subsistence, forage, fuel, quarters, or transportation not exceeding the necessities of the current year. The latter provision is special and exceptional in its character, and is to be regarded as excluded from the operation of the former more general one. But if any of the appropriation bills above enumerated should fail to be matured before the expiration of the current fiscal year, the Government would be greatly embarrassed for want of the necessary funds to carry on the service. Precluded from expending money not appropriated, the Departments would have to suspend the service so far as the appropriations for it should have failed to be made.

A careful examination of this subject will demonstrate the embarrassed condition all branches of the Government will be in, and especially the executive, if there should be a failure to pass the necessary appropriation bills before the 1st of July, or otherwise provide.

I commend this subject most earnestly to your consideration, and urge that some measure be speedily adopted to avert the evils which would result from nonaction by Congress. I will venture the suggestion, by way of remedy, that a joint resolution, properly guarded, might be passed through the two Houses of Congress, extending the provisions of all appropriations for the present fiscal year to the next in all cases where there is a failure on the 1st of July to supply such appropriation; each appropriation so extended to hold good until Congress shall have passed a corresponding appropriation applicable to the new fiscal year, when all moneys expended under laws enacted for this fiscal year shall be deducted from the corresponding appropriation for the next.

To make my ideas on this subject more clear, I have caused to be drawn up a joint resolution embodying them more fully.

U. S. GRANT.

JOINT RESOLUTION to provide for defraying temporarily the ordinary and necessary expenses of the public service.

Whereas the ordinary and necessary expenses of the public service in its various branches, comprising among others the expenses which especially pertain to the legislative, executive, and judicial departments of the Government, to the consular and diplomatic service, to the postal service, to the support of the Army, and to the maintenance of the Navy, are generally met by annual appropriations which expire at the end of the current fiscal year; and

Whereas no public funds will be available to defray these expenses as the same shall accrue after that period unless appropriations shall have been previously made therefor by law; and

Whereas, to avoid the great embarrassment to the public service that might otherwise ensue, it is expedient to make provision for defraying temporarily such of these expenses as would be unprovided for in case some one of the usual annual appropriation bills designed to provide therefor should fail to be matured by the end of the fiscal year now current: Therefore,

Resolved by the Senate and House of Representatives of the United States of America in Congress assembled, That in case any of the following appropriation bills for the fiscal year ending June 30, 1877, shall not have passed by the commencement of such year, so that the funds to be appropriated thereby may then be available for expenditure—that is to say, the bill providing for the legislative, executive, and judicial expenses; the bill providing for the consular and diplomatic expenses; the bill providing for the service of the Post-Office Department; the bill providing for the support of the Army, and the bill providing for the naval service—the appropriation act for the current fiscal year corresponding in its general description and object to such appropriation bill shall extend to the fiscal year next ensuing until such appropriation bill is enacted and takes effect, to the end that the provisions of such appropriation act which apply to the ordinary and necessary expenses of the public service for the current fiscal year shall in like manner be applicable to similar expenses which may accrue during the period intervening between the end of the current fiscal year and the time when such appropriation bill for the next ensuing fiscal year shall be enacted and take effect.

WASHINGTON, *June 20, 1876.*

To the Senate and House of Representatives:

By the tenth article of the treaty between the United States and Great Britain signed in Washington on the 9th day of August, 1842, it was agreed that the two Governments should, upon mutual requisitions respectively made, deliver up to justice all persons who, being charged with certain crimes therein enumerated, committed within the jurisdiction of either, should seek an asylum or be found within the territories of the other.

The only condition or limitation contained in the treaty to the reciprocal obligation thus to deliver up the fugitive was that it should be done only upon such evidence of criminality as, according to the laws of the place where the fugitive or person so charged should be found, would justify his apprehension and commitment for trial if the crime or offense had there been committed.

In the month of February last a requisition was duly made, in pursuance of the provisions of the treaty, by this Government upon that of Great Britain for the surrender of one Ezra D. Winslow, charged with extensive forgeries and the utterance of forged paper, committed within the jurisdiction of the United States, who had sought an asylum and was found within the territories of Her Britannic Majesty and was apprehended in London. The evidence of the criminality of the fugitive was duly furnished and heard, and, being found sufficient to justify his apprehension and commitment for trial if the crimes had been committed in Great Britain, he was held and committed for extradition.

Her Majesty's Government, however, did not deliver up the fugitive in accordance with the terms of the treaty, notwithstanding every requirement thereof had been met on the part of the United States, but, instead of surrendering the fugitive, demanded certain assurances or stipulations not mentioned in the treaty, but foreign to its provisions, as a condition of the performance by Great Britain of her obligations under the treaty.

In a recent communication to the House of Representatives, and in answer to a call from that body for information on this case, I submitted the correspondence which has passed between the two Governments with reference thereto. It will be found in Executive Document No. 173 of the House of Representatives of the present session, and I respectfully refer thereto for more detailed information bearing on the question.

It appears from the correspondence that the British Government bases its refusal to surrender the fugitive and its demand for stipulations or assurances from this Government on the requirements of a purely domestic enactment of the British Parliament, passed in the year 1870.

This act was brought to the notice of this Government shortly after its enactment, and Her Majesty's Government was advised that the United States understood it as giving continued effect to the existing engagements under the treaty of 1842 for the extradition of criminals; and with this knowledge on its part, and without dissent from the declared views of the United States as to the unchanged nature of the reciprocal rights and obligations of the two powers under the treaty, Great Britain has continued to make requisitions and to grant surrenders in numerous instances, without suggestion that it was contemplated to depart from the practice under the treaty which has obtained for more than thirty years, until now, for the first time, in this case of Wins-low, it is assumed that under this act of Parliament Her Majesty may require a stipulation or agreement not provided for in the treaty as a condition to the observance by her Government of its treaty obligations toward this country.

This I have felt it my duty emphatically to repel.

In addition to the case of Winslow, requisition was also made by this Government on that of Great Britain for the surrender of Charles J. Brent, also charged with forgery, committed in the United States, and found in Great Britain. The evidence of criminality was duly heard and the fugitive committed for extradition.

A similar stipulation to that demanded in Winslow's case was also asked in Brent's, and was likewise refused.

It is with extreme regret that I am now called upon to announce to you that Her Majesty's Government has finally released both of these fugitives, Winslow and Brent, and set them at liberty, thus omitting to comply with the provisions and requirements of the treaty under which the extradition of fugitive criminals is made between the two Governments.

The position thus taken by the British Government, if adhered to, can not but be regarded as the abrogation and annulment of the article of the treaty on extradition.

Under these circumstances it will not, in my judgment, comport with the dignity or self-respect of this Government to make demands upon that Government for the surrender of fugitive criminals, nor to entertain any requisition of that character from that Government under the treaty.

It will be a cause of deep regret if a treaty which has been thus far beneficial in its practical operation, which has worked so well and so efficiently, and which, notwithstanding the exciting and at times violent political disturbances of which both countries have been the scene during its existence, has given rise to no complaints on the part of either Government against either its spirit or its provisions, should be abruptly terminated.

It has tended to the protection of society and to the general interests of both countries. Its violation or annulment would be a retrograde step in international intercourse.

I have been anxious and have made the effort to enlarge its scope and to make a new treaty which would be a still more efficient agent for the punishment and prevention of crime. At the same time, I have felt it my duty to decline to entertain a proposition made by Great Britain, pending its refusal to execute the existing treaty, to amend it by practically conceding by treaty the identical conditions which that Government demands under its act of Parliament. In addition to the impossibility of the United States entering upon negotiations under the menace of an intended violation or a refusal to execute the terms of an existing treaty i deemed it inadvisable to treat of only the one amendment proposed by Great Britain while the United States desires an enlargement of the list of crimes for which extradition may be asked, and other improvements which experience has shown might be embodied in a new treaty.

It is for the wisdom of Congress to determine whether the article of the treaty relating to extradition is to be any longer regarded as obligatory on the Government of the United States or as forming part of the supreme law of the land. Should the attitude of the British Government remain unchanged, I shall not, without an expression of the wish of Congress that I should do so, take any action either in making or granting requisitions for the surrender of fugitive criminals under the treaty of 1842.

Respectfully submitted.

U. S. GRANT.

EXECUTIVE MANSION, *July 8, 1876.*

To the Senate of the United States:

I have the honor to transmit herewith a report* from General W. T. Sherman [J. D. Cameron, Secretary of War], together with the most recent reports received from Brigadier-General A. H. Terry, as a response to the resolution of the Senate of the 7th instant, a copy of which is attached to this message.

U. S. GRANT.

WASHINGTON, *July 13, 1876.*

To the House of Representatives:

I transmit herewith, in answer to a resolution of the House of Representatives of the 1st ultimo, a report† from the Secretary of State upon the subject.

U. S. GRANT.

WASHINGTON, *July 19, 1876.*

To the House of Representatives:

I transmit a report from the Secretary of State, in answer to the resolution of the House of Representatives of the 1st of April last, on the subject of commercial intercourse with Mexico and Central America.

U. S. GRANT.

EXECUTIVE MANSION, *July 31, 1876.*

To the House of Representatives:

The act making appropriations for sundry civil expenses of the Government for the fiscal year ending June 30, 1877, is so defective in what

---

* Relating to hostile demonstrations of the Sioux Indians and the disaster to the forces under General Custer.

† Stating that no correspondence has taken place with Great Britain relative to the sequestration of the lands and property in New Zealand claimed by William Webster, an American citizen.

it omits to provide for that I can not announce its approval without at the same time pointing out what seems to me to be its defects. It makes but inadequate provision for the service at best, and in some instances fails to make any provision whatever.

Notably among the first class is the reduction in the ordinary annual appropriations for the Revenue-Cutter Service, to the prejudice of the customs revenue.

The same may be said of the Signal Service, as also the failure to provide for the increased expense devolved upon the mints and assay offices by recent legislation, and thus tending to defeat the objects of that legislation.

Of this class also are public buildings, for the protection, preservation, and completion of which there is no adequate appropriation, while the sum of $100,000 only is appropriated for the repairs of the different navy yards and stations and the preservation of the same, the ordinary and customary appropriations for which are not less than $1,000,000.

A similar reduction is made in the expenses for armories and arsenals.

The provision for the ordinary judicial expenses is much less than the estimated amount for that important service, the actual expenditures of the last fiscal year, and the certain demands of the current year.

The provision for the expenses of the surveys of public lands is less than one-half of the usual appropriation for that service and what are understood to be its actual demands.

Reduction in the expenditures for light-houses, beacons, and fog stations is also made in similar proportion.

Of the class for which no appropriation is made, among the most noticeable, perhaps, is that portion of the general expenses of the District of Columbia on behalf of the United States, as appropriated in former years, and the judgments of the Court of Claims. The failure to make a reasonable contribution to the expenses of the nation's capital is an apparent dereliction on the part of the United States and rank injustice to the people here who bear the burdens, while to refuse or neglect to provide for the payment of solemn judgments of its own courts is apparently to repudiate. Of a different character, but as prejudicial to the Treasury, is the omission to make provision to enable the Secretary of the Treasury to have the rebel archives and records of captured and abandoned property examined and information furnished therefrom for the use of the Government.

Finally, without further specification of detail, it may be said that the act which in its title purports to make provision for a diverse and greatly extended civil service unhappily appropriates an amount not more than 65 per cent of its ordinary demands.

The legislative department establishes and defines the service, and devolves upon the Executive Departments the obligation of submitting annually the needful estimates of expenses of such service. Congress properly exacts implicit obedience to the requirements of the law in the administration of the public service and rigid accountability in the expenditures therefor. It is submitted that a corresponding responsibility and obligation rest upon it to make the adequate appropriations to render possible such administration and tolerable such exaction. Anything short of an ample provision for a specified service is necessarily fraught with disaster to the public interests and is a positive injustice to those charged with its execution.

To appropriate and to execute are corresponding obligations and duties, and the adequacy of the former is the necessary measure of the efficiency of the execution.

In this eighth month of the present session of Congress—nearly one month of the fiscal year to which this appropriation applies having passed—I do not feel warranted in vetoing an absolutely necessary appropriation bill; but in signing it I deem it a duty to show where the responsibility belongs for whatever embarrassments may arise in the execution of the trust confided to me.

U. S. GRANT.

EXECUTIVE MANSION, *July 31, 1876.*

To the Senate of the United States:

In response to the resolution of the Senate of July 20, 1876, calling upon the President to communicate to the Senate, if in his opinion not incompatible with the public interest, any information in regard to the slaughter of American citizens at Hamburg, S. C., I have the honor to submit the following inclosures, to wit:

No. 1. Letter of the 22d of July, 1876, from Governor D. H. Chamberlain, of South Carolina, to me.

No. 2. My reply thereto.

No. 3. Report of Hon. William Stone, attorney-general of South Carolina.

No. 4. Report of General H. W. Purvis, adjutant and inspector general of South Carolina.

No. 5. Copy of evidence taken before a coroner's jury investigating facts relating to the Hamburg massacre.

No. 6. Printed copy of statement by M. C. Butler, of South Carolina.

No. 7. Printed letter from the same to the editors of the Journal of Commerce.

No. 8. Copy of letter from Governor Chamberlain to the Hon. T. J. Robertson.

No. 9. An address to the American people by the colored citizens of Charleston, S. C.

No. 10. An address by a committee appointed at a convention of leading representatives of Columbia, S. C.

No. 11. Copy of letter of July 15, 1876, from the district attorney of Mississippi to the Attorney-General of the United States.

No. 12. Letter from same to same.

No. 13. Copy of report of a grand jury lately in session in Oxford, Miss.

These inclosures embrace all the information in my possession touching the late disgraceful and brutal slaughter of unoffending men at the town of Hamburg, S. C. My letter to Governor Chamberlain contains all the comments I wish to make on the subject. As allusion is made in that letter to the condition of other States, and particularly to Louisiana and Mississippi, I have added to the inclosures letters and testimony in regard to the lawless condition of a portion of the people of the latter State.

In regard to Louisiana affairs, murders and massacres of innocent men for opinion's sake or on account of color have been of too recent date and of too frequent occurrence to require recapitulation or testimony here. All are familiar with their horrible details, the only wonder being that so many justify them or apologize for them.

But recently a committee of the Senate of the United States visited the State of Mississippi to take testimony on the subject of frauds and violence in elections. Their report has not yet been made public, but I await its forthcoming with a feeling of confidence that it will fully sustain all that I have stated relating to fraud and violence in the State of Mississippi.

U. S. GRANT.

EXECUTIVE MANSION, *August 11, 1876.*

To the Senate and House of Representatives:

I transmit herewith a telegram of the 5th of August instant from Lieutenant-General Sheridan to General Sherman, a letter of the 11th of the present month from General Sherman to the Secretary of War, and a letter from the latter of the same date to me, all setting forth the possible needs of the Army in consequence of existing hostilities.

I would strongly urge upon Congress the necessity for making some provision for a contingency which may arise during the vacation—for more troops in the Indian country than it is now possible to send.

It would seem to me to be much more economical and better to authorize an increase of the present cavalry force by 2,500 privates, but if this is not deemed advisable, then that the President be authorized to call out not exceeding five regiments, 1,000 strong each, of volunteers, to serve for a period not exceeding six months.

Should this latter authority be given, I would not order out any volunteers unless in my opinion, based upon reports from the scene of war, I deemed it absolutely necessary, and then only the smallest number considered sufficient to meet the emergency.

U. S. GRANT.

EXECUTIVE MANSION, *August 14, 1876.*

To the House of Representatives:

In affixing my signature to the river and harbor bill, No. 3822, I deem it my duty to announce to the House of Representatives my objections to some features of the bill, and the reason I sign it. If it was obligatory upon the Executive to expend all the money appropriated by Congress, I should return the river and harbor bill with my objections, notwithstanding the great inconvenience to the public interests resulting therefrom and the loss of expenditures from previous Congresses upon incompleted works. Without enumerating, many appropriations are made for works of purely private or local interest, in no sense national. I can not give my sanction to these, and will take care that during my term of office no public money shall be expended upon them.

There is very great necessity for economy of expenditures at this time, growing out of the loss of revenue likely to arise from a deficiency of appropriations to insure a thorough collection of the same. The reduction of revenue districts, diminution of special agents, and total abolition of supervisors may result in great falling off of the revenue. It may be a question to consider whether any expenditure can be authorized under the river and harbor appropriation further than to protect works already done and paid for. Under no circumstances will I allow expenditures upon works not clearly national.

U. S. GRANT.

WASHINGTON, *August 14, 1876.*

To the House of Representatives:

In announcing, as I do, that I have attached my signature of official approval to the "Act making appropriations for the consular and diplomatic service of the Government for the year ending June 30, 1877, and for other purposes," it is my duty to call attention to a provision in the act directing that notice be sent to certain of the diplomatic and consular officers of the Government "to close their offices."

In the literal sense of this direction it would be an invasion of the constitutional prerogatives and duty of the Executive.

By the Constitution the President "shall have power, by and with the advice and consent of the Senate, to make treaties, provided two-thirds of the Senators present concur; and he shall nominate, and, by and with the advice and consent of the Senate, shall appoint, ambassadors, other public ministers, and consuls," etc.

It is within the power of Congress to grant or withhold appropriation of money for the payment of salaries and expenses of the foreign representatives of the Government.

In the early days of the Government a sum in gross was appropriated, leaving it to the Executive to determine the grade of the officers and the countries to which they should be sent.

Latterly, for very many years, specific sums have been appropriated for designated missions or employments, and as a rule the omission by Congress to make an appropriation for any specific port has heretofore been accepted as an indication of a wish on the part of Congress which the executive branch of the Government respected and complied with.

In calling attention to the passage which I have indicated I assume that the intention of the provision is only to exercise the constitutional prerogative of Congress over the expenditures of the Government and to fix a time at which the compensation of certain diplomatic and consular officers shall cease, and not to invade the constitutional rights of the Executive, which I should be compelled to resist; and my present object is not to discuss or dispute the wisdom of failing to appropriate for several offices, but to guard against the construction that might possibly be placed on the language used, as implying a right in the legislative branch to direct the closing or discontinuing of any of the diplomatic or consular offices of the Government.

U. S. GRANT.

[For message of August 15, 1876, withdrawing objections to Senate bill No. 779, see p. 4342.]

WASHINGTON, *August 15, 1876.*

To the Senate of the United States:

I transmit to the Senate, in answer to its resolution of the 24th ultimo, a report from the Secretary of State, with its accompanying statement.*

U. S. GRANT.

VETO MESSAGES.

EXECUTIVE MANSION, *February 3, 1876.*

To the House of Representatives:

I have the honor to return herewith without my approval House bill No. 1561, entitled "An act transferring the custody of certain Indian trust funds from the Secretary of the Interior to the Treasurer of the United States," for the reasons set forth in the accompanying communication from the Secretary of the Interior.

U. S. GRANT.

DEPARTMENT OF THE INTERIOR,
Washington, February 2, 1876.

The PRESIDENT.

SIR: I acknowledge the receipt of your communication of the 29th ultimo, transmitting House bill No. 1561 and requesting this Department to report whether any objections to its becoming a law are known to exist.

---

*Aggregate number of civil officers in or connected with the Department of State from 1859 to 1875, inclusive.

in reply I have the honor to state that I am fearful that the act is not sufficiently definite in terms to accomplish the end desired, namely, the mere transfer of the custody of said trust funds, enabling this Department to receive the interest from the custodian and apply it as heretofore without the intervention of Congress. The nature of the guardianship and control over the Indians exercised by me as Secretary and trustee is such as to require this Department to keep an account of the funds to their credit or held in trust for them, and to receive the interest on their trust funds promptly when due. I am fearful that this ·bill may not allow me to do so, and to guard against any danger of embarrassment in the transaction of this business I inclose a draft of a bill* which, if substituted for the one already passed, will, it is believed, obviate the difficulties which may arise if the present bill should become a law.

Very respectfully, your obedient servant,

Z. CHANDLER, *Secretary.*

EXECUTIVE MANSION, *March 27, 1876.*

To the House of Representatives:

I have the honor to return herewith without my approval the bill (H. R. No. 83) entitled "An act for the relief of James A. Hile, of Lewis County, Mo.," for the reasons set forth in the accompanying communication of the Secretary of War.

U. S. GRANT.

WAR DEPARTMENT,
Washington City, March 25, 1876.

The PRESIDENT.

SIR: I have the honor to return act H. R. 83, with the following report from the Adjutant-General:

"It appears from the records of this office that James A. Hile, private Company F, Twenty-first Missouri Volunteers, enlisted July 15, 1861; deserted June 14, 1862; returned August 2, 1862; was restored to duty by special order No. 38, headquarters District of Columbus, Department of Tennessee, dated Columbus, Ky., February 26, 1863. He reenlisted February 28, 1864, as a veteran volunteer; was tried by general court-martial for absence without leave from November 25, 1864, to December 13, 1864, and sentenced to forfeit all pay and allowances for time absent by general order No. 48, headquarters Second Division, Sixteenth Army Corps, dated May 22, 1865.

"On the muster-out roll of company dated April 19, 1866, he is reported, 'Deserted March 1, 1866, at Bladen Springs, Ala.'

"This man, in his application to this office for discharge, stated under oath (affidavit dated July 27, 1870) that he left his command without leave and returned to his home February 28, 1866, having previously applied for a furlough, which was refused.

"This man, according to his own statement under oath, did desert as reported, and if this bill becomes a law it will be an injustice to every soldier who served honorably with his command until his services were no longer required by the Government, in addition to falsifying the record, as the bill directs the record shall be made to show he is *no deserter.*

"This is only one of many similar cases."

The remarks of the Adjutant-General adverse to the passage of the bill are concurred in.

Very respectfully, your obedient servant,

ALPHONSO TAFT,
Secretary of War.

* Omitted.

EXECUTIVE MANSION, *March 31, 1876.*

To the Senate of the United States:

For the reasons set forth in the accompanying communication from the Secretary of the Treasury, I have the honor to return herewith without my approval Senate bill No. 489, entitled "An act for the relief of G. B. Tyler and E. H. Luckett, assignees of William T. Cheatham."

U. S. GRANT.

TREASURY DEPARTMENT, *March 30, 1876.*

The PRESIDENT:

Referring to the letter of the 25th instant, written by your direction, transmitting Senate bill No. 489, "for the relief of G. B. Tyler and E. H. Luckett, assignees of William T. Cheatham," and requesting my opinion as to the propriety of its approval by you, I have to say that there are no data on file in the Department, so far as I can learn, which indicate that the amount it is proposed by this bill to refund to the assignees of Mr. Cheatham was wrongfully collected or that the amount should be refunded.

The Commissioner of Internal Revenue, in his report to me in reference to the matter, says:

"The reimbursement to the United States by said Cheatham of the salary paid to this storekeeper by the collector of internal revenue for the months of December, 1869, and January, 1870, was in accordance with the provisions of joint resolution of March 29, 1869 (16 U. S. Statutes at Large, p. 52), and there appears to be no reason for the refunding by the United States to the assignees of said Cheatham the salary of this storekeeper that would not apply with equal force to similar payments by all other distillers who were operating their distilleries or had spirits in their warehouses at that time."

The facts above stated are considered by this office valid and serious objections to the approval of this bill, and they would have been communicated to the Congressional committee before the passage of the bill had they called the attention of this office to the subject.

The bill is herewith returned.

I have the honor to be, very respectfully, your obedient servant,

B. H. BRISTOW,
Secretary.

EXECUTIVE MANSION, *April 18, 1870.*

To the Senate of the United States:

Herewith I return Senate bill No. 172, entitled "An act fixing the salary of the President of the United States," without my approval.

I am constrained to this course from a sense of duty to my successors in office, to myself, and to what is due to the dignity of the position of Chief Magistrate of a nation of more than 40,000,000 people.

When the salary of the President of the United States, pursuant to the Constitution, was fixed at $25,000 per annum, we were a nation of but 3,000,000 people, poor from a long and exhaustive war, without commerce or manufactures, with but few wants and those cheaply supplied. The salary must then have been deemed small for the responsibilities and dignity of the position, but justifiably so from the impoverished condition of the Treasury and the simplicity it was desired to cultivate in the Republic.

The salary of Congressmen under the Constitution was first fixed at $6 per day for the time actually in session—an average of about one hundred and twenty days to each session—or $720 per year, or less than one-thirtieth of the salary of the President.

Congress have legislated upon their own salaries from time to time since, until finally it reached $5,000 per annum, or one-fifth that of the President, before the salary of the latter was increased.

No one having a knowledge of the cost of living at the national capital will contend that the present salary of Congressmen is too high, unless it is the intention to make the office one entirely of honor, when the salary should be abolished—a proposition repugnant to our republican ideas and institutions.

I do not believe the citizens of this Republic desire their public servants to serve them without a fair compensation for their services. Twenty-five thousand dollars does not defray the expenses of the Executive for one year, or has not in my experience. It is not now one-fifth in value of what it was at the time of the adoption of the Constitution in supplying demands and wants.

Having no personal interest in this matter, I have felt myself free to return this bill to the House in which it originated with my objections, believing that in doing so I meet the wishes and judgment of the great majority of those who indirectly pay all the salaries and other expenses of Government.

U. S. GRANT.

EXECUTIVE MANSION, *May 26, 1876.*

To the House of Representatives:

I return herewith without my approval House bill No. 1922, entitled "An act providing for the recording of deeds, mortgages, and other conveyances affecting real estate in the District of Columbia."

The objection to affixing my signature to this bill may be found in the communication addressed to me by the Attorney-General, and which accompanies this message.

U. S. GRANT.

DEPARTMENT OF JUSTICE,
Washington, May 23, 1876.

The PRESIDENT.

SIR: In reply to your note of the 19th instant, in which you request me to report whether there are objections to your approval of "An act providing for the recording of deeds, mortgages, and other conveyances affecting real estate in the District of Columbia," being House bill No. 1922, I have the honor to state that the bill seems to me objectionable because of indefiniteness and uncertainty as to the time whic it purports to fix when deeds of trust, mortgages, etc., shall take effect and be valid as to creditors and subsequent purchasers for valuable consideration without notice.

Although there is no constitutional objection to the act, yet for the reason above stated I hesitate to advise its approval.

Very respectfully, your obedient servant,

EDWARDS PIERREPONT, *Attorney-General.*

EXECUTIVE MANSION, *June 9, 1876.*

To the Senate of the United States:

I return herewith without my approval Senate bill No. 165, entitled "An act for the relief of Michael W. Brock, of Meigs County, Tenn., late a private in Company D, Tenth Tennessee Volunteers."

The objection to affixing my signature to this bill may be found in the indorsement (which accompanies this message) by the Adjutant-General of the Army.

U. S. GRANT.

WAR DEPARTMENT,
ADJUTANT-GENERAL'S OFFICE,
Washington, June 8, 1876.

Respectfully returned to the Secretary of War.

The records of this office show that Michael W. Brock, Company D, Tenth Tennessee Volunteers, deserted November 24, 1864, due United States for horse and horse equipments, carbine, saber, and pistol, all complete.

He presented satisfactory evidence of his having left the service by proper authority, and the charge of desertion has been removed and the soldier furnished an honorable discharge.

No evidence has been presented to this office to establish that he was erroneously charged with Government property.

If satisfactory evidence is furnished showing conclusively that this soldier was erroneously charged with Government property, taken at time of his reported desertion, the charge will be removed, and in that case the inclosed act for his relief will be unnecessary.

E. D. TOWNSEND, *Adjutant-General.*

EXECUTIVE MANSION, *June 30, 1876.*

To the Senate of the United States:

I return herewith without my approval Senate bill No. 692, entitled "An act to amend chapter 166 of the laws of the second session of the Forty-third Congress."

The objections to affixing my signature to this bill may be found in the report, which accompanies this message, of the Chief of Engineers of the Army to the Secretary of War.

U. S. GRANT.

WAR DEPARTMENT,
Washington City, June 28, 1876.

The PRESIDENT:

SIR: I have the honor to return herewith Senate bill No. 692, "to amend chapter 66 of the laws of the second session of the Forty-third Congress," and beg to invite your attention to the report of the Chief of Engineers dated the 27th instant, copy inclosed, and for the reasons stated in said report it is believed the bill should not become a law.

Very respectfully, your obedient servant,

J. D. CAMERON,
Secretary of War.

OFFICE OF THE CHIEF OF ENGINEERS, *June 27, 1876.*

Respectfully returned to the honorable the Secretary of War.

"An act to aid in the improvement of the Fox and Wisconsin rivers, in the State of Wisconsin," approved March 3, 1875, contains the following clause:

"In case any lands or other property is now or shall be flowed or injured by means of any part of the works of said improvement heretofore or hereafter constructed, for which compensation is now or shall become legally owing, and in the opinion of the officer in charge it is not prudent that the dam or dams be lowered, the amount of such compensation may be ascertained in like manner," etc.

The dams referred to in the above clause are at the outlets of Lake Winnebago, known as the Neenah or Menasha channels of the Lower Fox River.

The officer of the Department of Justice appointed under the provisions of the act referred to to represent the interests of the United States in legal proceedings "for flowage damages hereinbefore described," acting apparently under the assumption that because the dams in question had not been lowered it was the opinion of the officer in charge that they should not be lowered, has had such surveys, investigations, etc., made as were deemed necessary by him to protect the interests of the United States, and under this action it is understood that, at the instance of claimants, judges of the circuit court have appointed commissioners to decide on the amount of compensation due, and the judges have fixed the rate of compensation the commissioners are to receive. These commissioners are not appointed at the instance of the United States.

In this way the awards for damages have already been made to the amount of $70,000, and ultimately a much larger sum will be claimed to be due from the United States.

The officer of engineers in charge of the improvement of the Fox and Wisconsin rivers reports that the dams which have occasioned the flowage were not constructed by the canal companies, and are not at all necessary for the purposes of navigation, and so far as that is concerned could not only be lowered, but entirely dispensed with.

They were built by private parties solely for their own use and profit and for water-power purposes, and have raised the water level and caused the flowage, for which they should be held liable.

In view of the preceding facts, and for the additional reason that the subject of the liability of the United States is now being investigated by the Department of Justice, it is respectfully suggested that the inclosed act to amend chapter 166 of the laws of the second session of the Forty-third Congress (S. 692) should not become a law.

A. A. HUMPHREYS,
Brigadier-General and Chief of Engineers.

EXECUTIVE MANSION, *July 11, 1876.*

To the House of Representatives:

For the reasons set forth in the accompanying report of the Secretary of War, I have the honor to return herewith without my approval House bill No. 1337, entitled "An act for the relief of Nelson Tiffany."

U. S. GRANT.

WAR DEPARTMENT, *June 7, 1876.*

The PRESIDENT.

SIR: I have the honor to return House bill No. 1337, "for the relief of Nelson Tiffany."

The Adjutant-General, to whom the bill was referred, reports as follows:

"Nelson Tiffany, private, Company A, Twenty-fifth Massachusetts Volunteers, deserted October 10, 1864, and remained absent until April 25, 1865, when he surrendered under the President's proclamation, thereby acknowledging his desertion.

"If this bill becomes a law, it will not only falsify the records of this Department, but will be an injustice to every man who served honorably during the War of the Rebellion."

*   *   *   *   *   *   *

Very respectfully, your obedient servant,

J. D. CAMERON,
Secretary of War.

EXECUTIVE MANSION, *July 13, 1876.*

To the House of Representatives:

For the reasons stated in the accompanying report by the Commissioner of Pensions to the Secretary of the Interior, I have the honor to return without my approval House bill No. 11, entitled "An act granting a pension to Eliza Jane Blumer."

U. S. GRANT.

DEPARTMENT OF THE INTERIOR,
Washington, July 8, 1876.

The PRESIDENT.

SIR: I have the honor to return herewith a bill (H. R. 11) entitled "An act granting a pension to Eliza Jane Blumer," and to invite your attention to the inclosed copy of a communication addressed to me on the 7th instant by the Commissioner of Pensions, relating to said bill.

In the opinion of this Department the misdescription of the soldier in the bill is of such a character as would render it difficult, if not impossible, to carry the provisions of the bill into effect should it become a law.

I have the honor to be, with great respect, your obedient servant,

CHAS. T. GORHAM,
Acting Secretary.

DEPARTMENT OF THE INTERIOR,
Washington, D. C., July 7, 1876.

The Honorable SECRETARY OF THE INTERIOR.

SIR: I have the honor to return herewith engrossed House bill No. 11, giving to Eliza Jane Blumer a pension as a widow of Henry A. Blumer, private of Company A, Forty-seventh Pennsylvania Volunteers, with the suggestion that if the bill is intended to pension Eliza Blumer, whose application, No. 46382, on file in this office, has been rejected, it should designate the soldier as of Company B of said regiment, it failing to appear from the records of the War Department that he served in any other company than that last named.

I am, sir, very respectfully, your obedient servant,

J. A. BENTLEY,
Commissioner.

EXECUTIVE MANSION, *July 20, 1876.*

To the House of Representatives:

I have the honor to return herewith without my approval House bill No. 2684, entitled "An act to amend sections 3946, 3951, and 3954 of the Revised Statutes."

It is the judgment of the Postmaster-General, whose report accompanies this message, that if this bill should become a law in its present form it would fail to give effect to its provisions. The remedial suggestions in his report are respectfully recommended to your attention.

U. S. GRANT.

POST-OFFICE DEPARTMENT,
Washington, D. C., July 19, 1876.

The PRESIDENT OF THE UNITED STATES,
Washington, D. C.

SIR: I have the honor to return herewith House bill No. 2684, "to amend sections 3946, 3951, and 3954 of the Revised Statutes," with the following objections thereto:

The sections of the Revised Statutes which this bill proposes to amend were substantially repealed by the twelfth section of the act entitled "An act making appropriations for the service of the Post-Office Department for the fiscal year ending June 30, 1875, and for other purposes," approved June 23, 1874. The sections of the Revised Statutes numbered as indicated in the bill were enacted as sections 246 and 251 of the "act to revise, consolidate, and amend the statutes relating to the Post-Office Department," approved June 8, 1872. These sections were subsequently embodied in the revision of the statutes.

If the accompanying bill should become a law in its present form, it would, in my judgment, fail to give effect to its provisions. The bill is a very important one for the service of the Post-Office Department. Efforts have been made for four or five years past to induce Congress to pass just such a law. To break up the vicious system of straw bidding, this bill would be very valuable, and I regret exceedingly that a mistake should have been made in the title and enacting clause which will render its provisions inoperative.

I therefore suggest that the attention of the House in which it originated shall be called to the defects in the bill explained above; and to enable that body to understand very fully what, in my judgment, would be required to perfect it, I would suggest that the title should read "A bill to amend subsections 246 and 251 of section 12 of an act entitled 'An act making appropriations for the service of the Post-Office Department for the fiscal year ending June 30, 1875, and for other purposes,' approved June 23, 1874, and also to amend section 3954 of the Revised Statutes," and that the enacting clause of the bill should be changed in conformity therewith.

I have the honor to be, with great respect, your obedient servant,

JAS. N. TYNER, *Postmaster-General.*

EXECUTIVE MANSION, *August 14, 1876.*

To the House of Representatives:

For the reason stated in the accompanying communication, submitted to me by the Secretary of War, I have the honor to return herewith without my approval House bill No. 36, entitled "An act to restore the name of Captain Edward S. Meyer to the active list of the Army."

U. S. GRANT.

WAR DEPARTMENT,
Washington, D. C., August 4, 1876.

The PRESIDENT.

SIR: I have the honor to return House bill No. 36, "to restore the name of Captain Edward S. Meyer to the active list of the Army," and beg to invite your attention to the inclosed report of the Adjutant-General of this date, stating objections to the approval of the bill.

Very respectfully, your obedient servant,

J. D. CAMERON,
Secretary of War.

ADJUTANT-GENERAL'S OFFICE, *August 4, 1876.*

Respectfully returned to the Secretary of War.

Edward S. Meyer served as a private in the Fourth Ohio Volunteers (three months) from May 4, 1861, to August 18, 1861. He again enlisted as private, Nineteenth Ohio Volunteers, September 10, 1861; was promoted first lieutenant November 1, 1861, and resigned September 27, 1862. He was commissioned captain, One hundred and seventh Ohio Volunteers, November 11, 1862; was wounded at Chancellorsville, Va., May 2, 1863, and discharged for physical disability January 1, 1865. He was again mustered into service February 8, 1865, as major, Fifth United States Veteran Volunteers (Hancock's Corps), and mustered out March 20, 1866. Was brevetted lieutenant-colonel, colonel, and brigadier-general of volunteers March 13, 1865.

He was appointed captain, Thirty-fifth United States Infantry, July 28, 1866; became unassigned August 12, 1869; assigned to Nineteenth Infantry August 5, 1870, and transferred to Ninth Cavalry January 1, 1871. Retired August 24, 1872.

July 8, 1869, Captain Meyer applied for retirement on account of wounds received at Chancellorsville May 2, 1863, by which he was incapacitated for active service. No action was then had on the request, pending action by Congress reducing the Army.

October 6, 1869, he asked to be placed on waiting orders, being unfit for duty, and no possibility of improvement without going North. He was accordingly relieved from duty and ordered home to await orders.

December 18, 1869, he called on the Secretary of War and asked to be assigned to duty.

January 4, 1870, he again applied to be assigned to duty with some regiment on the frontier, stating that his wound had healed, etc., and asking to withdraw his previous request for retirement. This was accompanied by a similar request from his father, Mr. S. Meyer, of Ohio.

July 29, 1870, he applied the third time to withdraw application for retirement and to be assigned to duty. On January 1, 1871, in accordance with his repeated requests to be assigned to duty, he was assigned to the Ninth Cavalry, serving in Texas. He joined the regiment, and on March 4, 1872, he renewed his former request to be ordered before a retiring board, stating that he found his injuries would not allow him to remain on duty on the frontier; that his disability was constantly increasing, etc. The medical director of the department approved the request, and added that Captain Meyer's wounds certainly unfitted him for service on the frontier.

April 13, 1872, Senator Sherman joined in requesting retirement of Captain Meyer. He was ordered before the retiring board and on August 20, 1872, was examined.

The board found Captain Meyer "incapacitated for active service, and that said incapacity results from a gunshot wound received in his lower jaw at the battle of Chancellorsville, Va., May 2, 1863," when captain in One hundred and seventh Ohio Volunteers. He was retired in accordance with the finding.

March 21 and December 6, 1873, Captain Meyer asked restoration to active service and reappointment as a captain of cavalry, which application was disapproved by the General of the Army.

Pending the action on the bill before Congress no reports were called for as to the official facts of record in the War Department, and no evidence has been filed in this office showing that he has sufficiently recovered.

The absence of such evidence and the fact that after one assignment to active duty he has failed to be sufficiently recovered are submitted as objections why the bill should not be approved.

E. D. TOWNSEND,
Adjutant-General.

EXECUTIVE MANSION, *August 15, 1876.*

To the House of Representatives:

I herewith return House bill No. 4085 without my approval. The repeal of the clause in the original bill for paving Pennsylvania avenue fixing the time for the completion of the work by December 1, 1876, is objectionable in this, that it fixes no date when the work is to be completed.

Experience shows that where contractors have unlimited time to complete any given work they consult their own convenience, and not the public good. Should Congress deem it proper to amend the present bill in such manner as to fix the date for the completion of the work to be done by any date between December 1 and the close of my official term, it will receive my approval.

U. S. GRANT.

EXECUTIVE MANSION, *August 15, 1876.*

To the Senate of the United States:

For the reasons stated in the accompanying communication, submitted to me by the Acting Secretary of the Interior, I have the honor to return herewith without my approval Senate bill No. 779, entitled "An act to provide for the sale of a portion of the reservation of the confederated Otoe and Missouria and the Sacs and Foxes of the Missouri tribes of Indians, in the States of Kansas and Nebraska."

U. S. GRANT.

DEPARTMENT OF THE INTERIOR,
Washington, D. C., August 14, 1876.

The PRESIDENT.

SIR: I have the honor to return herewith the bill (S. No. 779) entitled "An act to provide for the sale of a portion of the reservation of the confederated Otoe and Missouria and the Sacs and Foxes of the Missouri tribes of Indians, in the States of Kansas and Nebraska," and to invite your attention to the inclosed copy of a letter this day addressed to me by the Commissioner of Indian Affairs, stating that the bill, in his opinion, should not become a law.

I fully concur in the opinion expressed by the Commissioner, and for the reasons stated in his letter do not feel at liberty to recommend your approval of the bill.

I have the honor to be, with great respect, your obedient servant,

CHAS. T. GORHAM,
Acting Secretary.

DEPARTMENT OF THE INTERIOR,
OFFICE OF INDIAN AFFAIRS,
Washington, D. C., August 14, 1876.

The Honorable SECRETARY OF THE INTERIOR.

SIR: I have the honor to return herewith, in accordance with your verbal request, a bill entitled "An act to provide for the sale of a portion of the reservation of the confederated Otoe and Missouria and the Sacs and Foxes of the Missouri tribes of Indians, in the States of Kansas and Nebraska," with my views thereon, the same having passed both Houses of Congress and now awaits the approval of the President.

Your attention is respectfully invited to the act of June 10, 1872 (17 U. S. Statutes at Large, p. 391), which provides for the sale of these reservations, or a portion of them. The whole of both these reservations has been surveyed, a portion in accordance with this act of Congress and the remainder with a view to the allotment of lands to the Indians.

The second section of the bill provides for the appraisement of the whole reservation, while the third section authorizes the sale of a portion not exceeding 120,000 acres, a portion of which is in Kansas.

The bill authorizes the sale of that portion lying in Kansas through the land office located at Beatrice, Nebr. No provision is made for the relief of such Indians, if any there be, who may have settled upon the portion authorized to be sold, and who may have made improvements thereon. Moreover, in fulfillment of treaty obligations, the assent of the Indians to the operations of the whole bill, and not simply to the first section, should be required, as in the case of the Menominees (16 U. S. Statutes at Large, p. 410). In my opinion, this bill should not receive the approval of the President.

I have the honor to be, very respectfully, your obedient servant,

J. Q. SMITH, *Commissioner.*

[The Senate proceeded, as the Constitution prescribes, to reconsider the said bill returned by the President of the United States with his objections, and pending the question, Shall the bill pass, the objections of the President of the United States to the contrary notwithstanding? the following message was received:]

EXECUTIVE MANSION, *August 15, 1876.*

To the Senate of the United States:

Upon further investigation I am convinced that my message of this date, withholding my signature from Senate bill No. 779, entitled "An act to provide for the sale of a portion of the reservation of the confederated Otoe and Missouria and the Sacs and Foxes of the Missouri tribes of Indians, in the States of Kansas and Nebraska," was premature, and I request, therefore, that the bill may be returned, in order that I may affix my signature to it.

U. S. GRANT.

[A motion to refer the last message to the Committee on Privileges and Elections was, after debate, determined in the negative; and the question recurring, Shall the bill pass, the objections of the President of the United States to the contrary notwithstanding? it was determined in the affirmative—yeas 36, nays 0.]

EXECUTIVE MANSION, *August 15, 1876.*

To the Senate of the United States:

For the reasons presented in the accompanying communications, submitted by the Secretary of War, I have the honor to return herewith without my approval Senate bill No. 561, entitled "An act for the relief of Major Junius T. Turner."

U. S. GRANT.

WAR DEPARTMENT,
Washington City, August 14, 1876.

The PRESIDENT.

SIR: I have the honor to return Senate bill 561, "for the relief of Major Junius T. Turner," with copy of the report of the Adjutant-General of this date, stating objections to the approval of the bill.

Very respectfully, your obedient servant,

J. D. CAMERON,
Secretary of War.

WAR DEPARTMENT, ADJUTANT-GENERAL'S OFFICE,
August 14, 1876.

Respectfully returned to the Secretary of War.

The following objections exist to this bill becoming a law:

The bill as passed both Houses awards "such sum as shall equal the travel pay of a captain of volunteers from Washington, D. C., to San Francisco, Cal.," whereas at the date of the discharge of Junius T. Turner he was a private of Company E, California Battalion, Second Massachusetts Cavalry, and not a commissioned officer.

Aside from this, under the established regulations and rulings of the Treasury and War Departments, "a soldier, on receiving and accepting a commission as a company officer, is not entitled to traveling allowances." A departure from this rule, heretofore adhered to, would open up a very wide field for similar claims.

Private Junius T. Turner, Second Massachusetts Cavalry, was discharged by way of favor March 28, 1864, to accept promotion as second lieutenant, Third Maryland Cavalry, and was mustered as of that grade in said regiment March 29, 1864.

He was honorably discharged September 7, 1865, as captain, Third Maryland Cavalry, as set forth in the inclosed official copy of a letter* from this office, dated June 7, 1876, to Hon. C. D. MacDougall, M. C., of Committee on Military Affairs, House of Representatives.

E. D. TOWNSEND,
Adjutant-General.

[The Senate proceeded, as the Constitution prescribes, to reconsider the said bill returned by the President of the United States with his objections, and pending the question, Shall the bill pass, the objections of the President of the United States to the contrary notwithstanding? it was ordered that the message be referred to the Committee on Military Affairs. At the next (second) session of the Forty-fourth Congress the following message was received:]

EXECUTIVE MANSION, *January 12, 1877.*

To the Senate of the United States:

On the eve of the adjournment of the last session of Congress I returned to the Senate bill No. 561, entitled "An act for the relief of Major Junius T.

*Omitted.

Turner," with my objections to its becoming a law. I now desire to withdraw those objections, as I am satisfied they were made under a misapprehension of the facts.

U. S. GRANT.

[This message was also referred to the Committee on Military Affairs. which committee, on February 13, 1877, reported to the Senate a recommendation that the bill do pass, the objections of the President of the United States to the contrary notwithstanding. No action was taken.]

PROCLAMATIONS.

BY THE PRESIDENT OF THE UNITED STATES OF AMERICA.

A PROCLAMATION.

Whereas by the first section of an act entitled "An act to authorize the President to accept for citizens of the United States the jurisdiction of certain tribunals in the Ottoman dominions and Egypt, established or to be established under the authority of the Sublime Porte and of the Government of Egypt," approved March 23, 1874, it was enacted as follows:

That whenever the President of the United States shall receive satisfactory information that the Ottoman Government or that of Egypt has organized other tribunals on a basis likely to secure to citizens of the United States in their domains the same impartial justice which they now enjoy there under the judicial functions exercised by the minister, consuls, and other functionaries of the United States pursuant to the act of Congress approved the 22d of June, 1860, entitled "An act to carry into effect provisions of the treaties between the United States, China, Persia, and other countries giving certain judicial powers to ministers and consuls or other functionaries of the United States in those countries, and for other purposes," he is hereby authorized to suspend the operations of said acts as to the dominions in which such tribunals may be organized so far as the jurisdiction of said tribunals may embrace matters now cognizable by the minister, consuls, or other functionaries of the United States in said dominions, and to notify the Government of the Sublime Porte, or that of Egypt, or either of them, that the United States during such suspension will, as aforesaid, accept for their citizens the jurisdiction of the tribunals aforesaid over citizens of the United States which has heretofore been exercised by the minister, consuls, or other functionaries of the United States.

And whereas satisfactory information has been received by me that the Government of Egypt has organized other tribunals on a basis likely to secure to citizens of the United States in the dominions subject to such Government the impartial justice which they now enjoy there under the judicial functions exercised by the minister, consul, or other functionaries of the United States pursuant to the said act of Congress approved June 22, 1860:

Now, therefore, I, Ulysses S. Grant, President of the United States of

America, by virtue of the power and authority conferred upon me by the said act approved March 23, 1874, do hereby suspend during the pleasure of the President the operation of the said act approved June 22, 1860, as to the said dominions subject to the Government of Egypt in which such tribunals have been organized, so far as the jurisdiction of said tribunals may embrace matters now cognizable by the minister, consuls, or other functionaries of the United States in said dominions, except as to cases actually commenced before the date hereof.

In witness whereof I have hereunto set my hand and caused the seal of the United States to be affixed.

[SEAL.] Done at the city of Washington, this 27th day of March, A. D. 1876, and of the Independence of the United States of America the one hundredth.

U. S. GRANT.

By the President:
HAMILTON FISH,
Secretary of State.

BY THE PRESIDENT OF THE UNITED STATES.

A PROCLAMATION.

Whereas a joint resolution of the Senate and House of Representatives of the United States was duly approved on the 13th day of March last, which resolution is as follows:

Be it resolved by the Senate and House of Representatives of the United States of America in Congress assembled, That it be, and is hereby, recommended by the Senate and House of Representatives to the people of the several States that they assemble in their several counties or towns on the approaching centennial anniversary of our national independence, and that they cause to have delivered on such day an historical sketch of said county or town from its formation, and that a copy of said sketch may be filed, in print or manuscript, in the clerk's office of said county, and an additional copy, in print or manuscript, be filed in the office of the Librarian of Congress, to the intent that a complete record may thus be obtained of the progress of our institutions during the first centennial of their existence.

And whereas it is deemed proper that such recommendation be brought to the notice and knowledge of the people of the United States:

Now, therefore, I, Ulysses S. Grant, President of the United States, do hereby declare and make known the same, in the hope that the object of such resolution may meet the approval of the people of the United States and that proper steps may be taken to carry the same into effect.

Given under my hand, at the city of Washington, the 25th day of May,

[SEAL.] A. D. 1876, and of the Independence of the United States the one hundredth.

U. S. GRANT.

By the President:
HAMILTON FISH,
Secretary of State.

BY THE PRESIDENT OF THE UNITED STATES OF AMERICA.

A PROCLAMATION.

The centennial anniversary of the day on which the people of the United States declared their right to a separate and equal station among the powers of the earth seems to demand an exceptional observance.

The founders of the Government, at its birth and in its feebleness, invoked the blessings and the protection of a Divine Providence, and the thirteen colonies and three millions of people have expanded into a nation of strength and numbers commanding the position which then was asserted and for which fervent prayers were then offered.

It seems fitting that on the occurrence of the hundredth anniversary of our existence as a nation a grateful acknowledgment should be made to Almighty God for the protection and the bounties which He has vouchsafed to our beloved country.

I therefore invite the good people of the United States, on the approaching 4th day of July, in addition to the usual observances with which they are accustomed to greet the return of the day, further, in such manner and at such time as in their respective localities and religious associations may be most convenient, to mark its recurrence by some public religious and devout thanksgiving to Almighty God for the blessings which have been bestowed upon us as a nation during the century of our existence, and humbly to invoke a continuance of His favor and of His protection.

In witness whereof I have hereunto set my hand and caused the seal of the United States to be affixed.

[SEAL.]   Done at the city of Washington, this 26th day of June, A. D. 1876, and of the Independence of the United States of America the one hundredth.

U. S. GRANT.

By the President:
    HAMILTON FISH,
        Secretary of State.

BY THE PRESIDENT OF THE UNITED STATES OF AMERICA.

A PROCLAMATION.

Whereas the Congress of the United States did, by an act approved on the 3d day of March, 1875, authorize the inhabitants of the Territory of Colorado to form for themselves out of said Territory a State government with the name of the State of Colorado, and for the admission of such State into the Union on an equal footing with the original States upon certain conditions in said act specified; and

Whereas it was provided by said act of Congress that the convention elected by the people of said Territory to frame a State constitution should, when assembled for that purpose and after organization, declare on behalf of the people that they adopt the Constitution of the United States, and should also provide by an ordinance, irrevocable without the consent of the United States and the people of said State, that perfect toleration of religious sentiment shall be secured and that no inhabitant of said State shall ever be molested in person or property on account of his or her mode of religious worship, and that the people inhabiting said Territory do agree and declare that they forever disclaim all right and title to the unappropriated public lands lying within said Territory and that the same shall be and remain at the sole and entire disposition of the United States, and that the lands belonging to citizens of the United States residing without the said State shall never be taxed higher than the lands belonging to residents thereof, and that no taxes shall be imposed by the State on lands or property therein belonging to or which may hereafter be purchased by the United States; and

Whereas it was further provided by said act that the constitution thus formed for the people of the Territory of Colorado should, by an ordinance of the convention forming the same, be submitted to the people of said Territory for ratification or rejection at an election to be held in the month of July, 1876, at which election the lawful voters of said new State should vote directly for or against the proposed constitution, and the returns of said election should be made to the acting governor of the Territory, who, with the chief justice and United States attorney of said Territory, or any two of them, should canvass the same, and, if a majority of legal votes should be cast for said constitution in said proposed State the said acting governor should certify the same to the President of the United States, together with a copy of said constitution and ordinances, whereupon it should be the duty of the President of the United States to issue his proclamation declaring the State admitted into the Union on an equal footing with the original States, without any further action whatever on the part of Congress; and

Whereas it has been certified to me by the acting governor of said Territory of Colorado that within the time prescribed by said act of Congress a constitution for said proposed State has been adopted and the same ratified by a majority of the legal voters of said proposed new State, in accordance with the conditions prescribed by said act of Congress; and

Whereas a duly authenticated copy of said constitution and of the declaration and ordinance required by said act has been received by me:

Now, therefore, I, Ulysses S. Grant, President of the United States of America, do, in accordance with the provisions of the act of Congress aforesaid, declare and proclaim the fact that the fundamental conditions imposed by Congress on the State of Colorado to entitle that State to admission to the Union have been ratified and accepted, and that the admission of the said State into the Union is now complete.

In testimony whereof I have hereunto set my hand and have caused the seal of the United States to be affixed.

[SEAL.] Done at the city of Washington, this 1st day of August, A. D. 1876, and of the Independence of the United States of America the one hundred and first.

U. S. GRANT.

By the President:

HAMILTON FISH,
Secretary of State.

BY THE PRESIDENT OF THE UNITED STATES OF AMERICA.

A PROCLAMATION.

Whereas by Article V of a convention concluded at Washington upon the 30th day of January, 1875, between the United States of America and His Majesty the King of the Hawaiian Islands it was provided as follows, viz:

The present convention shall take effect as soon as it shall have been approved and proclaimed by His Majesty the King of the Hawaiian Islands and shall have been ratified and duly proclaimed on the part of the Government of the United States, but not until a law to carry it into operation shall have been passed by the Congress of the United States of America. Such assent having been given and the ratifications of the convention having been exchanged as provided in Article VI, the convention shall remain in force for seven years from the date at which it may come into operation, and, further, until the expiration of twelve months after either of the high contracting parties shall give notice to the other of its wish to terminate the same, each of the high contracting parties being at liberty to give such notice to the other at the end of the said term of seven years or at any time thereafter.

And whereas such convention has been approved and proclaimed by His Majesty the King of the Hawaiian Islands and has been ratified and duly proclaimed on the part of the United States, and a law to carry the same into operation has been passed by the Congress of the United States, and the ratifications of the convention have been exchanged as provided in Article VI thereof; and

Whereas the Acting Secretary of State of the United States and His Majesty's envoy extraordinary and minister plenipotentiary at Washington have recorded in a protocol a conference held by them at Washington on the 9th day of September, 1876, in the following language:

Whereas it is provided by Article V of the convention between the United States of America and His Majesty the King of the Hawaiian Islands concerning commercial reciprocity, signed at Washington on the 30th day of January, 1875, as follows:

"ART. V. The present convention shall take effect as soon as it shall have been approved and proclaimed by His Majesty the King of the Hawaiian Islands and shall have been ratified and duly proclaimed on the part of the Government of the United States, but not until the law to carry it into operation shall have been passed by the

Congress of the United States of America. Such assent having been given and the ratifications of the convention having been exchanged as provided in Article VI, the convention shall remain in force for seven years from the date at which it may come into operation, and, further, until the expiration of twelve months after either of the high contracting parties shall give notice to the other of its wish to terminate the same, each of the high contracting parties being at liberty to give such notice to the other at the end of the said term of seven years or at any time thereafter;" and

Whereas the said convention has been approved and proclaimed by His Majesty the King of the Hawaiian Islands, and has been ratified and duly proclaimed on the part of the Government of the United States; and

Whereas an act was passed by the Senate and House of Representatives of the United States of America in Congress assembled, entitled "An act to carry into effect a convention between the United States of America and His Majesty the King of the Hawaiian Islands signed on the 30th day of January, 1875," which was approved on the 15th day of August, in the year 1876; and

Whereas an act was passed by the Legislative Assembly of the Hawaiian Islands entitled "An act to carry into effect a convention between His Majesty the King and the United States of America signed at Washington on the 30th day of January, 1875," which was duly approved on the 18th day of July, in the year 1876; and

Whereas the ratifications of the said convention have been exchanged as provided in Article VI:

The undersigned, William Hunter, Acting Secretary of State of the United States of America, and the Hon. Elisha H. Allen, chief justice of the supreme court, chancellor of the Kingdom, member of the privy council of state, and His Majesty's envoy extraordinary and minister plenipotentiary to the United States of America, duly authorized for this purpose by their respective Governments, have met together at Washington, and, having found the said convention has been approved and proclaimed by His Majesty the King of the Hawaiian Islands and has been ratified and duly proclaimed on the part of the Government of the United States, and that the laws required to carry the said treaty into operation have been passed by the Congress of the United States of America on the one part and by the Legislative Assembly of the Hawaiian Islands on the other, hereby declare that the convention aforesaid, concluded between the United States of America and His Majesty the King of the Hawaiian Islands on the 30th day of January, 1875, will take effect on the date hereof.

Now, therefore, I, Ulysses S. Grant, President of the United States of America, in pursuance of the premises, do declare that the said convention has been approved and proclaimed by His Majesty the King of the Hawaiian Islands and been ratified and duly proclaimed on the part of the Government of the United States, and that the necessary legislation has been passed to carry the same into effect, and that the ratifications of the convention have been exchanged as provided in Article VI.

In testimony whereof I have hereunto set my hand and caused the seal of the United States to be affixed.

[SEAL.]   Done in the city of Washington, this 9th day of September, A. D. 1876, and of the Independence of the United States of America the one hundred and first.

U. S. GRANT.

By the President:

W. HUNTER,
Acting Secretary of State.

By the President of the United States of America.

A PROCLAMATION.

Whereas it has been satisfactorily shown to me that insurrection and domestic violence exist in several counties of the State of South Carolina, and that certain combinations of men against law exist in many counties of said State known as "rifle clubs," who ride up and down by day and night in arms, murdering some peaceable citizens and intimidating others, which combinations, though forbidden by the laws of the State, can not be controlled or suppressed by the ordinary course of justice; and

Whereas it is provided in the Constitution of the United States that the United States shall protect every State in this Union, on application of the legislature, or of the executive (when the legislature can not be convened), against domestic violence; and

Whereas by laws in pursuance of the above it is provided (in the laws of the United States) that in all cases of insurrection in any State or of obstruction to the laws thereof it shall be lawful for the President of the United States, on application of the legislature of such State, or of the executive (when the legislature can not be convened), to call forth the militia of any other State or States, or to employ such part of the land and naval forces as shall be judged necessary, for the purpose of suppressing such insurrection or causing the laws to be duly executed; and

Whereas the legislature of said State is not now in session and can not be convened in time to meet the present emergency, and the executive of said State, under section 4 of Article IV of the Constitution of the United States and the laws passed in pursuance thereof, has therefore made due application to me in the premises for such part of the military force of the United States as may be necessary and adequate to protect said State and the citizens thereof against domestic violence and to enforce the due execution of the laws; and

Whereas it is required that whenever it may be necessary, in the judgment of the President, to use the military force for the purpose aforesaid, he shall forthwith, by proclamation, command such insurgents to disperse and retire peaceably to their respective homes within a limited time:

Now, therefore, I, Ulysses S. Grant, President of the United States, do hereby make proclamation and command all persons engaged in said unlawful and insurrectionary proceedings to disperse and retire peaceably to their respective abodes within three days from this date, and hereafter abandon said combinations and submit themselves to the laws and constituted authorities of said State.

And I invoke the aid and cooperation of all good citizens thereof to uphold the laws and preserve the public peace.

In witness whereof I have hereunto set my hand and caused the seal of the United States to be affixed.

[SEAL.]   Done at the city of Washington, this 17th day of October, A. D. 1876, and of the Independence of the United States one hundred and one.

U. S. GRANT.

By the President:

JOHN L. CADWALADER,
        Acting Secretary of State.

BY THE PRESIDENT OF THE UNITED STATES OF AMERICA.

A PROCLAMATION.

From year to year we have been accustomed to pause in our daily pursuits and set apart a time to offer our thanks to Almighty God for the special blessings He has vouchsafed to us, with our prayers for a continuance thereof.

We have at this time equal reason to be thankful for His continued protection and for the many material blessings which His bounty has bestowed.

In addition to these favors accorded to us as individuals, we have especial occasion to express our hearty thanks to Almighty God that by His providence and guidance our Government, established a century ago, has been enabled to fulfill the purpose of its founders in offering an asylum to the people of every race, securing civil and religious liberty to all within its borders, and meting out to every individual alike justice and equality before the law.

It is, moreover, especially our duty to offer our humble prayers to the Father of All Mercies for a continuance of His divine favor to us as a nation and as individuals.

By reason of all these considerations, I, Ulysses S. Grant, President of the United States, do recommend to the people of the United States to devote the 30th day of November next to the expression of their thanks and prayers to Almighty God, and, laying aside their daily avocations and all secular occupations, to assemble in their respective places of worship and observe such day as a day of thanksgiving and rest.

In witness whereof I have hereunto set my hand and caused the seal of the United States to be affixed.

[SEAL.]   Done at the city of Washington, this 26th day of October, A. D. 1876, and of the Independence of the United States of America the one hundred and first.

U. S. GRANT.

By the President:

HAMILTON FISH,
        Secretary of State.

EXECUTIVE ORDERS.

EXECUTIVE MANSION,
Washington, May 20, 1876.

SIR:* The President directs me to say that the several Departments of the Government will be closed on Tuesday, the 30th instant, to enable the employees to participate in the decoration of the graves of the soldiers who fell during the rebellion.

I am, sir, your obedient servant,

C. C. SNIFFEN, *Secretary.*

WAR DEPARTMENT,
Washington City, August 10, 1876.

By direction of the President, General W. T. Sherman and Brigadier-General M. C. Meigs, Quartermaster-General United States Army, are appointed members of the commission to examine "the whole subject of reform and reorganization of the Army of the United States," as provided by section 4, act approved July 24, 1876, "making appropriations for the support of the Army for the fiscal year ending June 30, 1877, and for other purposes."

J. D. CAMERON, *Secretary of Wa.*

WASHINGTON, *August 21, 1876.*

It is with extreme pain that the President announces to the people of the United States the death of the Speaker of the House of Representatives, the Hon. Michael C. Kerr, of Indiana.

A man of great intellectual endowments, large culture, great probity and earnestness in his devotion to the public interests, has passed from the position, power, and usefulness to which he had been recently called.

The body over which he had been selected to preside not being in session to render its tribute of affection and respect to the memory of the deceased, the President invites the people of the United States to a solemn recognition of the public and private worth and the services of a pure and eminent character.

U. S. GRANT.

By the President:

JOHN L. CADWALADER, *Acting Secretary of State.*

EXECUTIVE MANSION, *November 23, 1876.*

A joint resolution adopted by Congress August 5, 1876, declares that—

Whereas it is ascertained that the hostile Indians of the Northwest are largely equipped with arms which require special metallic cartridges, and that such special

---

* Addressed to the heads of the Executive Departments, etc.

ammunition is in large part supplied to such hostile Indians, directly or indirectly, through traders and others in the Indian country: Therefore,

Resolved by the Senate and House of Representatives of the United States of America in Congress assembled, That the President of the United States is hereby authorized and requested to take such measures as in his judgment may be necessary to prevent such special metallic ammunition being conveyed to such hostile Indians, and is further authorized to declare the same contraband of war in such district of country as he may designate during the continuance of hostilities.

To carry into effect the above-cited resolution, the sale of fixed ammunition or metallic cartridges by any trader or other person in any district of the Indian country occupied by hostile Indians, or over which they roam, is hereby prohibited; and all such ammunition or cartridges introduced into said country by traders or other persons, and that are liable in any way or manner, directly or indirectly, to be received by such hostile Indians, shall be deemed contraband of war, seized by any military officer and confiscated; and the district of country to which this prohibition shall apply during the continuance of hostilities is hereby designated as that which embraces all Indian country, or country occupied by Indians or subject to their visits, lying within the Territories of Montana, Dakota, and Wyoming and the States of Nebraska and Colorado.

U. S. GRANT.

EIGHTH ANNUAL MESSAGE.

EXECUTIVE MANSION, *December 5, 1876.*

To the Senate and House of Representatives:

In submitting my eighth and last annual message to Congress it seems proper that I should refer to and in some degree recapitulate the events and official acts of the past eight years.

It was my fortune, or misfortune, to be called to the office of Chief Executive without any previous political training. From the age of 17 I had never even witnessed the excitement attending a Presidential campaign but twice antecedent to my own candidacy, and at but one of them was I eligible as a voter.

Under such circumstances it is but reasonable to suppose that errors of judgment must have occurred. Even had they not, differences of opinion between the Executive, bound by an oath to the strict performance of his duties, and writers and debaters must have arisen. It is not necessarily evidence of blunder on the part of the Executive because there are these differences of views. Mistakes have been made, as all can see and I admit, but it seems to me oftener in the selections made of the assistants appointed to aid in carrying out the various duties of administering the

Government—in nearly every case selected without a personal acquaintance with the appointee, but upon recommendations of the representatives chosen directly by the people. It is impossible, where so many trusts are to be allotted, that the right parties should be chosen in every instance. History shows that no Administration from the time of Washington to the present has been free from these mistakes. But I leave comparisons to history, claiming only that I have acted in every instance from a conscientious desire to do what was right, constitutional, within the law, and for the very best interests of the whole people. Failures have been errors of judgment, not of intent.

My civil career commenced, too, at a most critical and difficult time. Less than four years before, the country had emerged from a conflict such as no other nation had ever survived. Nearly one-half of the States had revolted against the Government, and of those remaining faithful to the Union a large percentage of the population sympathized with the rebellion and made an "enemy in the rear" almost as dangerous as the more honorable enemy in the front. The latter committed errors of judgment, but they maintained them openly and courageously; the former received the protection of the Government they would see destroyed, and reaped all the pecuniary advantage to be gained out of the then existing state of affairs, many of them by obtaining contracts and by swindling the Government in the delivery of their goods.

Immediately on the cessation of hostilities the then noble President, who had carried the country so far through its perils, fell a martyr to his patriotism at the hands of an assassin.

The intervening time to my first inauguration was filled up with wranglings between Congress and the new Executive as to the best mode of "reconstruction," or, to speak plainly, as to whether the control of the Government should be thrown immediately into the hands of those who had so recently and persistently tried to destroy it, or whether the victors should continue to have an equal voice with them in this control. Reconstruction, as finally agreed upon, means this and only this, except that the late slave was enfranchised, giving an increase, as was supposed, to the Union-loving and Union-supporting votes. If *free* in the full sense of the word, they would not disappoint this expectation. Hence at the beginning of my first Administration the work of reconstruction, much embarrassed by the long delay, virtually commenced. It was the work of the legislative branch of the Government. My province was wholly in approving their acts, which I did most heartily, urging the legislatures of States that had not yet done so to ratify the fifteenth amendment to the Constitution. The country was laboring under an enormous debt, contracted in the suppression of rebellion, and taxation was so oppressive as to discourage production. Another danger also threatened us—a foreign war. The last difficulty had to be adjusted and was adjusted without a war and in a manner highly hon-

EARLY MINING SCENES IN COLORADO

EARLY GOLD MINING SCENES IN COLORADO

In 1858 gold was discovered in Colorado. Remembering the similar event of ten years before in California, when early comers made from $50 to $500 a day, the adventurous spirits of the country went prospecting in the hills. The first panel reproduces a photograph of a typical party of gold hunters, while the lower panel reproduces one of a representative pioneer mining camp. The central vignette shows the placer method of mining. Gold containing dirt was carried in buckets to a cradle, where it was thrown on a sieve. A rush of water carried off the pebbles while the dirt and gold particles would fall through the sieve and be retained. The earth would then be allowed to dry, and was separated from the gold dust by blowing it away with the breath.

The article entitled "Gold" in the encyclopedic index (volume eleven) tells the story of the most precious of metals.

orable to all parties concerned. Taxes have been reduced within the last seven years nearly $300,000,000, and the national debt has been reduced in the same time over $435,000,000. By refunding the 6 per cent bonded debt for bonds bearing 5 and 4½ per cent interest, respectively, the annual interest has been reduced from over $130,000,000 in 1869 to but little over $100,000,000 in 1876. The balance of trade has been changed from over $130,000,000 against the United States in 1869 to more than $120,000,000 in our favor in 1876.

It is confidently believed that the balance of trade in favor of the United States will increase, not diminish, and that the pledge of Congress to resume specie payments in 1879 will be easily accomplished, even in the absence of much-desired further legislation on the subject.

A policy has been adopted toward the Indian tribes inhabiting a large portion of the territory of the United States which has been humane and has substantially ended Indian hostilities in the whole land except in a portion of Nebraska, and Dakota, Wyoming, and Montana Territories— the Black Hills region and approaches thereto. Hostilities there have grown out of the avarice of the white man, who has violated our treaty stipulations in his search for gold. The question might be asked why the Government has not enforced obedience to the terms of the treaty prohibiting the occupation of the Black Hills region by whites. The answer is simple: The first immigrants to the Black Hills were removed by troops, but rumors of rich discoveries of gold took into that region increased numbers. Gold has actually been found in paying quantity, and an effort to remove the miners would only result in the desertion of the bulk of the troops that might be sent there to remove them. All difficulty in this matter has, however, been removed—subject to the approval of Congress—by a treaty ceding the Black Hills and approaches to settlement by citizens.

The subject of Indian policy and treatment is so fully set forth by the Secretary of the Interior and the Commissioner of Indian Affairs, and my views so fully expressed therein, that I refer to their reports and recommendations as my own.

The relations of the United States with foreign powers continue on a friendly footing.

Questions have arisen from time to time in the foreign relations of the Government, but the United States have been happily free during the past year from the complications and embarrassments which have surrounded some of the foreign powers.

The diplomatic correspondence submitted herewith contains information as to certain of the matters which have occupied the Government.

The cordiality which attends our relations with the powers of the earth has been plainly shown by the general participation of foreign nations in the exhibition which has just closed and by the exertions made by distant powers to show their interest in and friendly feelings toward the United States in the commemoration of the centennial of the nation. The Government and people of the United States have not only fully appreciated this exhibition of kindly feeling, but it may be justly and fairly expected that no small benefits will result both to ourselves and other nations from a better acquaintance, and a better appreciation of our mutual advantages and mutual wants.

Congress at its last session saw fit to reduce the amount usually appropriated for foreign intercourse by withholding appropriations for representatives of the United States in certain foreign countries and for certain consular officers, and by reducing the amounts usually appropriated for certain other diplomatic posts, and thus necessitating a change in the grade of the representatives. For these reasons, immediately upon the passage of the bill making appropriations for the diplomatic and consular service for the present fiscal year, instructions were issued to the representatives of the United States at Bolivia, Ecuador, and Colombia, and to the consular officers for whom no appropriation had been made, to close their respective legations and consulates and cease from the performance of their duties; and in like manner steps were immediately taken to substitute chargés d'affaires for ministers resident in Portugal, Denmark, Greece, Switzerland, and Paraguay.

While thoroughly impressed with the wisdom of sound economy in the foreign service, as in other branches of the Government, I can not escape the conclusion that in some instances the withholding of appropriations will prove an expensive economy, and that the small retrenchment secured by a change of grade in certain diplomatic posts is not an adequate consideration for the loss of influence and importance which will attend our foreign representatives under this reduction. I am of the opinion that a reexamination of the subject will cause a change in some instances in the conclusions reached on these subjects at the last session of Congress.

The Court of Commissioners of Alabama Claims, whose functions were continued by an act of the last session of Congress until the 1st day of January, 1877, has carried on its labors with diligence and general satisfaction. By a report from the clerk of the court, transmitted herewith, bearing date November 14, 1876, it appears that within the time now allowed by law the court will have disposed of all the claims presented for adjudication. This report also contains a statement of the general results of the labors of the court to the date thereof. It is a cause of satisfaction that the method adopted for the satisfaction of the classes of claims submitted to the court, which are of long standing and justly entitled to early consideration, should have proved successful and acceptable.

It is with satisfaction that I am enabled to state that the work of the joint commission for determining the boundary line between the United States and British possessions from the northwest angle of the Lake of the Woods to the Rocky Mountains, commenced in 1872, has been completed. The final agreements of the commissioners, with the maps, have been duly signed, and the work of the commission is complete.

The fixing of the boundary upon the Pacific coast by the protocol of March 10, 1873, pursuant to the award of the Emperor of Germany by Article XXXIV of the treaty of Washington, with the termination of the work of this commission, adjusts and fixes the entire boundary between the United States and the British possessions, except as to the portion of territory ceded by Russia to the United States under the treaty of 1867. The work intrusted to the commissioner and the officers of the Army attached to the commission has been well and satisfactorily performed. The original of the final agreement of the commissioners, signed upon the 29th of May, 1876, with the original official "lists of astronomical stations observed," the original official "list of monuments marking the international boundary line," and the maps, records, and general reports relating to the commission, have been deposited in the Department of State. The official report of the commissioner on the part of the United States, with the report of the chief astronomer of the United States, will be submitted to Congress within a short time.

I reserve for a separate communication to Congress a statement of the condition of the questions which lately arose with Great Britain respecting the surrender of fugitive criminals under the treaty of 1842.

The Ottoman Government gave notice, under date of January 15, 1874, of its desire to terminate the treaty of 1862, concerning commerce and navigation, pursuant to the provisions of the twenty-second article thereof. Under this notice the treaty terminated upon the 5th day of June, 1876. That Government has invited negotiations toward the conclusion of a new treaty.

By the act of Congress of March 23, 1874, the President was authorized, when he should receive satisfactory information that the Ottoman Government or that of Egypt had organized new tribunals likely to secure to citizens of the United States the same impartial justice enjoyed under the exercise of judicial functions by diplomatic and consular officers of the United States, to suspend the operation of the act of June 22, 1860, and to accept for citizens of the United States the jurisdiction of the new tribunals. Satisfactory information having been received of the organization of such new tribunals in Egypt, I caused a proclamation* to be issued upon the 27th of March last, suspending the operation of the act of June 22, 1860, in Egypt, according to the provisions of the act. A copy of the proclamation accompanies this message. The United States has united with the other powers in the organization of these courts. It is hoped that the jurisdictional questions which have arisen may be readily adjusted, and that this advance in judicial reform may be hindered by no obstacles.

* See pp. 4344-4345.

The necessary legislation to carry into effect the convention respect ing commercial reciprocity concluded with the Hawaiian Islands in 1875 having been had, the proclamation to carry into effect the convention, as provided by the act approved August 15, 1876, was duly issued upon the 9th day of September last. A copy thereof accompanies this message.*

The commotions which have been prevalent in Mexico for some time past, and which, unhappily, seem to be not yet wholly quieted, have led to complaints of citizens of the United States of injuries by persons in authority. It is hoped. however, that these will ultimately be adjusted to the satisfaction of both Governments. The frontier of the United States in that quarter has not been exempt from acts of violence by citizens of one Republic on those of the other. The frequency of these is supposed to be increased and their adjustment made more difficult by the considerable changes in the course of the lower part of the Rio Grande River, which river is a part of the boundary between the two countries. These changes have placed on either side of that river portions of land which by existing conventions belong to the jurisdiction of the Government on the opposite side of the river. The subject of adjustment of this cause of difficulty is under consideration between the two Republics.

The Government of the United States of Colombia has paid the award in the case of the steamer *Montijo*, seized by authorities of that Government some years since, and the amount has been transferred to the claimants.

It is with satisfaction that I am able to announce that the joint commission for the adjustment of claims between the United States and Mexico under the convention of 1868, the duration of which has been several times extended, has brought its labors to a close. From the report of the agent of the United States, which accompanies the papers transmitted herewith, it will be seen that within the time limited by the commission 1,017 claims on the part of citizens of the United States against Mexico were referred to the commission. Of these claims 831 were dismissed or disallowed, and in 186 cases awards were made in favor of the claimants against the Mexican Republic, amounting in the aggregate to $4,125,622.20. Within the same period 998 claims on the part of citizens of the Mexican Republic against the United States were referred to the commission. Of these claims 831 were dismissed or disallowed, and in 167 cases awards were made in favor of the claimants against the United States, amounting in the aggregate to $150,498.41.

By the terms of the convention the amount of these awards is to be deducted from the amount awarded in favor of our citizens against Mexico, and the balance only to be paid by Mexico to the United States, leaving the United States to make provision for this proportion of the awards in favor of its own citizens.

I invite your attention to the legislation which will be necessary to provide for the payment.

* See pp. 4348-4349.

In this connection I am pleased to be able to express the acknowledgments due to Sir Edward Thornton, the umpire of the commission, who has given to the consideration of the large number of claims submitted to him much time, unwearied patience, and that firmness and intelligence which are well known to belong to the accomplished representative of Great Britain, and which are likewise recognized by the representative in this country of the Republic of Mexico.

Monthly payments of a very small part of the amount due by the Government of Venezuela to citizens of the United States on account of claims of the latter against that Government continue to be made with reasonable punctuality. That Government has proposed to change the system which it has hitherto pursued in this respect by issuing bonds for part of the amount of the several claims. The proposition, however, could not, it is supposed, properly be accepted, at least without the consent of the holders of certificates of the indebtedness of Venezuela. These are so much dispersed that it would be difficult, if not impossible, to ascertain their disposition on the subject.

In former messages I have called the attention of Congress to the necessity of legislation with regard to fraudulent naturalization and to the subject of expatriation and the election of nationality.

The numbers of persons of foreign birth seeking a home in the United States, the ease and facility with which the honest emigrant may, after the lapse of a reasonable time, become possessed of all the privileges of citizenship of the United States, and the frequent occasions which induce such adopted citizens to return to the country of their birth render the subject of naturalization and the safeguards which experience has proved necessary for the protection of the honest naturalized citizen of paramount importance. The very simplicity in the requirements of law on this question affords opportunity for fraud, and the want of uniformity in the proceedings and records of the various courts and in the forms of the certificates of naturalization issued affords a constant source of difficulty.

I suggest no additional requirements to the acquisition of citizenship beyond those now existing, but I invite the earnest attention of Congress to the necessity and wisdom of some provisions regarding uniformity in the records and certificates, and providing against the frauds which frequently take place and for the vacating of a record of naturalization obtained in fraud.

These provisions are needed in aid and for the protection of the honest citizen of foreign birth, and for the want of which he is made to suffer not infrequently. The United States has insisted upon the right of expatriation, and has obtained, after a long struggle, an admission of the principle contended for by acquiescence therein on the part of many foreign powers and by the conclusion of treaties on that subject. It is, however, but justice to the government to which such naturalized citizens have formerly owed allegiance, as well as to the United States, that certain fixed and definite rules should be adopted governing such cases and providing how expatriation may be accomplished.

While emigrants in large numbers become citizens of the United States, it is also true that persons, both native born and naturalized, once citizens of the United States, either by formal acts or as the effect of a series of facts and circumstances, abandon their citizenship and cease to be entitled to the protection of the United States, but continue on convenient occasions to assert a claim to protection in the absence of provisions on these questions.

And in this connection I again invite your attention to the necessity of legislation concerning the marriages of American citizens contracted abroad, and concerning the status of American women who may marry foreigners and of children born of American parents in a foreign country.

The delicate and complicated questions continually occurring with reference to naturalization, expatriation, and the status of such persons as I have above referred to induce me to earnestly direct your attention again to these subjects.

In like manner I repeat my recommendation that some means be provided for the hearing and determination of the just and subsisting claims of aliens upon the Government of the United States within a reasonable limitation, and of such as may hereafter arise. While by existing provisions of law the Court of Claims may in certain cases be resorted to by an alien claimant, the absence of any general provisions governing all such cases and the want of a tribunal skilled in the disposition of such cases upon recognized fixed and settled principles, either provides no remedy in many deserving cases or compels a consideration of such claims by Congress or the executive department of the Government.

It is believed that other governments are in advance of the United States upon this question, and that the practice now adopted is entirely unsatisfactory.

Congress, by an act approved the 3d day of March, 1875, authorized the inhabitants of the Territory of Colorado to form a State government, with the name of the State of Colorado, and therein provided for the admission of said State, when formed, into the Union upon an equal footing with the original States.

A constitution having been adopted and ratified by the people of that State, and the acting governor having certified to me the facts as provided by said act, together with a copy of such constitution and ordinances as provided for in the said act, and the provisions of the said act of Congress having been duly complied with, I issued a proclamation* upon the 1st of August, 1876, a copy of which is hereto annexed.

The report of the Secretary of War shows that the Army has been actively employed during the year in subduing, at the request of the Indian Bureau, certain wild bands of the Sioux Indian Nation and in

* See pp. 4346–4348.

preserving the peace at the South during the election. The commission constituted under the act of July 24, 1876, to consider and report on the "whole subject of the reform and reorganization of the Army" met in August last, and has collected a large mass of statistics and opinions bearing on the subject before it. These are now under consideration, and their report is progressing. I am advised, though, by the president of the commission that it will be impracticable to comply with the clause of the act requiring the report to be presented, through me, to Congress on the first day of this session, as there has not yet been time for that mature deliberation which the importance of the subject demands. Therefore I ask that the time of making the report be extended to the 29th day of January, 1877.

In accordance with the resolution of August 15, 1876, the Army regulations prepared under the act of March 1, 1875, have not been promulgated, but are held until after the report of the above-mentioned commission shall have been received and acted on.

By the act of August 15, 1876, the cavalry force of the Army was increased by 2,500 men, with the proviso that they should be discharged on the expiration of hostilities. Under this authority the cavalry regiments have been strengthened, and a portion of them are now in the field pursuing the remnants of the Indians with whom they have been engaged during the summer.

The estimates of the War Department are made up on the basis of the number of men authorized by law, and their requirements as shown by years of experience, and also with the purpose on the part of the bureau officers to provide for all contingencies that may arise during the time for which the estimates are made. Exclusive of engineer estimates (presented in accordance with acts of Congress calling for surveys and estimates for improvements at various localities), the estimates now presented are about six millions in excess of the appropriations for the years 1874–75 and 1875–76. This increase is asked in order to provide for the increased cavalry force (should their services be necessary), to prosecute economically work upon important public buildings, to provide for armament of fortifications and manufacture of small arms, and to replenish the working stock in the supply departments. The appropriations for these last named have for the past few years been so limited that the accumulations in store will be entirely exhausted during the present year, and it will be necessary to at once begin to replenish them.

I invite your special attention to the following recommendations of the Secretary of War:

First. That the claims under the act of July 4. 1864, for supplies taken by the Army during the war be removed from the offices of the Quartermaster and Commissary Generals and transferred to the Southern Claims Commission. These claims are of precisely similar nature to those now before the Southern Claims Commission, and the War Department bureaus have not the clerical force for their examination nor proper machinery for investigating the loyalty of the claimants.

Second. That Congress sanction the scheme of an annuity fund for the benefit of the families of deceased officers, and that it also provide for the permanent organization of the Signal Service, both of which were recommended in my last annual message.

Third. That the manufacturing operations of the Ordnance Department be concentrated at three arsenals and an armory, and that the remaining arsenals be sold and the proceeds applied to this object by the Ordnance Department.

The appropriations for river and harbor improvements for the current year were $5,015,000. With my approval, the Secretary of War directed that of this amount $2,000,000 should be expended, and no new works should be begun and none prosecuted which were not of national importance. Subsequently this amount was increased to $2,237,600, and the works are now progressing on this basis.

The improvement of the South Pass of the Mississippi River, under James B. Eads and his associates, is progressing favorably. At the present time there is a channel of 20.3 feet in depth between the jetties at the mouth of the pass and 18.5 feet at the head of the pass. Neither channel, however, has the width required before payments can be made by the United States. A commission of engineer officers is now examining these works, and their reports will be presented as soon as received.

The report of the Secretary of the Navy shows that branch of the service to be in condition as effective as it is possible to keep it with the means and authority given the Department. It is, of course, not possible to rival the costly and progressive establishments of great European powers with the old material of our Navy, to which no increase has been authorized since the war, except the eight small cruisers built to supply the place of others which had gone to decay. Yet the most has been done that was possible with the means at command; and by substantially rebuilding some of our old ships with durable material and completely repairing and refitting our monitor fleet the Navy has been gradually so brought up that, though it does not maintain its relative position among the progressive navies of the world, it is now in a condition more powerful and effective than it ever has been in time of peace.

The complete repairs of our five heavy ironclads are only delayed on account of the inadequacy of the appropriations made last year for the working bureaus of the Department, which were actually less in amount than those made before the war, notwithstanding the greatly enhanced price of labor and materials and the increase in the cost of the naval service growing out of the universal use and great expense of steam machinery. The money necessary for these repairs should be provided at once, that they may be completed without further unnecessary delay and expense.

When this is done, all the strength that there is in our Navy will be developed and useful to its full capacity, and it will be powerful for purposes of defense, and also for offensive action, should the necessity for that arise within a reasonable distance from our shores.

The fact that our Navy is not more modern and powerful than it is has been made a cause of complaint against the Secretary of the Navy by persons who at the same time criticise and complain of his endeavors to bring the Navy that we have to its best and most effiicent condition; but the good sense of the country will understand that it is really due to his practical action that we have at this time any effective naval force at command.

The report of the Postmaster-General shows the excess of expenditures (excluding expenditures on account of previous years) over receipts for the fiscal year ended June 30, 1876, to be $4,151,988.66.

Estimated expenditures for the fiscal year ending June 30, 1878, are $36,723,432.43.

Estimated revenue for same period is $30,645,165, leaving estimated excess of expenditure, to be appropriated as a deficiency, of $6,078,267.43.

The Postmaster-General, like his predecessor, is convinced that a change in the basis of adjusting the salaries of postmasters of the fourth class is necessary for the good of the service as well as for the interests of the Government, and urgently recommends that the compensation of the class of postmasters above mentioned be based upon the business of their respective offices, as ascertained from the sworn returns to the Auditor of stamps canceled.

A few postmasters in the Southern States have expressed great apprehension of their personal safety on account of their connection with the postal service, and have specially requested that their reports of apprehended danger should not be made public lest it should result in the loss of their lives. But no positive testimony of interference has been submitted, except in the case of a mail messenger at Spartanburg, in South Carolina, who reported that he had been violently driven away while in charge of the mails on account of his political affiliations. An assistant superintendent of the Railway Mail Service investigated this case and reported that the messenger had disappeared from his post, leaving his work to be performed by a substitute. The Postmaster-General thinks this case is sufficiently suggestive to justify him in recommending that a more severe punishment should be provided for the offense of assaulting any person in charge of the mails or of retarding or otherwise obstructing them by threats of personal injury.

"A very gratifying result is presented in the fact that the deficiency of this Department during the last fiscal year was reduced to $4,081,790.18, as against $6,169,938.88 of the preceding year. The difference can be traced to the large increase in its ordinary receipts (which greatly exceed the estimates therefor) and a slight decrease in its expenditures."

The ordinary *receipts* of the Post-Office Department for the past seven fiscal years have increased at an average of over 8 per cent per annum, while the increase of *expenditures* for the same period has been but about 5.50 per cent per annum, and the *decrease* of *deficiency* in the revenues has been at the rate of nearly 2 per cent per annum.

The report of the Commissioner of Agriculture accompanying this message will be found one of great interest, marking, as it does, the great progress of the last century in the variety of products of the soil; increased knowledge and skill in the labor of producing, saving, and manipulating the same to prepare them for the use of man; in the improvements in machinery to aid the agriculturist in his labors, and in a knowledge of those scientific subjects necessary to a thorough system of economy in agricultural production, namely, chemistry, botany, entomology, etc. A study of this report by those interested in agriculture and deriving their support from it will find it of value in pointing out those articles which are raised in greater quantity than the needs of the world require, and must sell, therefore, for less than the cost of production, and those which command a profit over cost of production because there is not an over-production.

I call special attention to the need of the Department for a new gallery for the reception of the exhibits returned from the Centennial Exhibition, including the exhibits donated by very many foreign nations, and to the recommendations of the Commissioner of Agriculture generally.

The reports of the District Commissioners and the board of health are just received—too late to read them and to make recommendations thereon—and are herewith submitted.

The international exhibition held in Philadelphia this year, in com-memoration of the one hundredth anniversary of American independ-ence, has proven a great success, and will, no doubt, be of enduring advantage to the country. It has shown the great progress in the arts, sciences, and mechanical skill made in a single century, and demon-strated that we are but little behind older nations in any one branch, while in some we scarcely have a rival. It has served, too, not only to bring peoples and products of skill and labor from all parts of the world together, but in bringing together people from all sections of our own country, which must prove a great benefit in the information imparted and pride of country engendered.

It has been suggested by scientists interested in and connected with the Smithsonian Institution, in a communication herewith, that the Gov-ernment exhibit be removed to the capital and a suitable building be erected or purchased for its accommodation as a permanent exhibit. I earnestly recommend this; and believing that Congress would second this view, I directed that all Government exhibits at the Centennial Exhibition should remain where they are, except such as might be in-jured by remaining in a building not intended as a protection in inclement weather, or such as may be wanted by the Department furnishing them, until the question of permanent exhibition is acted on.

Although the moneys appropriated by Congress to enable the participation of the several Executive Departments in the International Exhibition of 1876 were not sufficient to carry out the undertaking to the full extent at first contemplated, it gives me pleasure to refer to the very efficient and creditable manner in which the board appointed from these several Departments to provide an exhibition on the part of the Government have discharged their duties with the funds placed at their command. Without a precedent to guide them in the preparation of such a display, the success of their labors was amply attested by the sustained attention which the contents of the Government building attracted during the period of the exhibition from both foreign and native visitors.

I am strongly impressed with the value of the collection made by the Government for the purposes of the exhibition, illustrating, as it does, the mineral resources of the country, the statistical and practical evidences of our growth as a nation, and the uses of the mechanical arts and the applications of applied science in the administration of the affairs of Government.

Many nations have voluntarily contributed their exhibits to the United States to increase the interest in any permanent exhibition Congress may provide for. For this act of generosity they should receive the thanks of the people, and I respectfully suggest that a resolution of Congress to that effect be adopted.

The attention of Congress can not be too earnestly called to the necessity of throwing some greater safeguard over the method of choosing and declaring the election of a President. Under the present system there seems to be no provided remedy for contesting the election in any one State. The remedy is partially, no doubt, in the enlightenment of electors. The compulsory support of the free school and the disfranchisement of all who can not read and write the English language, after a fixed probation, would meet my hearty approval. I would not make this apply, however, to those already voters, but I would to all becoming so after the expiration of the probation fixed upon. Foreigners coming to this country to become citizens, who are educated in their own language, should acquire the requisite knowledge of ours during the necessary residence to obtain naturalization. If they did not take interest enough in our language to acquire sufficient knowledge of it to enable them to study the institutions and laws of the country intelligently, I would not confer upon them the right to make such laws nor to select those who do.

I append to this message, for convenient reference, a synopsis of administrative events and of all recommendations to Congress made by me during the last seven years. Time may show some of these recommendations not to have been wisely conceived, but I believe the larger part will do no discredit to the Administration. One of these recommendations met with the united opposition of one political party in the Senate and with a strong opposition from the other, namely, the treaty for the annexation of Santo Domingo to the United States, to which I will specially refer, maintaining, as I do, that if my views had been concurred in the country would be in a more prosperous condition to-day, both politically and financially.

Santo Domingo is fertile, and upon its soil may be grown just those tropical products of which the United States use so much, and which are produced or prepared for market now by slave labor almost exclusively, namely, sugar, coffee, dyewoods, mahogany, tropical fruits, tobacco, etc. About 75 per cent of the exports of Cuba are consumed in the United States. A large percentage of the exports of Brazil also find the same market. These are paid for almost exclusively in coin, legislation, particularly in Cuba, being unfavorable to a mutual exchange of the products of each country. Flour shipped from the Mississippi River to Havana can pass by the very entrance to the city on its way to a port in Spain. there pay a duty fixed upon articles to be reexported, transferred to a Spanish vessel and brought back almost to the point of starting, paying a second duty, and still leave a profit over what would be received by direct shipment. All that is produced in Cuba could be produced in Santo Domingo. Being a part of the United States, commerce between the island and mainland would be free. There would be no export duties on her shipments nor import duties on those coming here. There would be no import duties upon the supplies, machinery, etc., going from the States. The effect that would have been produced upon Cuban commerce, with these advantages to a rival, is observable at a glance. The Cuban question would have been settled long ago in favor of "free Cuba." Hundreds of American vessels would now be advantageously used in transporting the valuable woods and other products of the soil of the island to a market and in carrying supplies and emigrants to it. The island is but sparsely settled, while it has an area sufficient for the profitable employment of several millions of people. The soil would have soon fallen into the hands of United States capitalists. The products are so valuable in commerce that emigration there would have been encouraged; the emancipated race of the South would have found there a congenial home, where their civil rights would not be disputed and where their labor would be so much sought after that the poorest among them could have found the means to go. Thus in cases of great oppression and cruelty, such as has been practiced upon them in many places within the last eleven years, whole communities would have sought refuge in Santo Domingo. I do not suppose the whole race would have gone, nor is it desirable that they should go. Their labor is desirable—indispensable almost—where they now are. But the possession of this territory would have left the negro "master of the situation," by enabling him to demand his rights at home on pain of finding them elsewhere.

By the President of the United States.

A Proclamation.

Whereas a Joint Resolution of the Senate and House of Representatives of the United States was duly approved on the 13th day of March, last, which Resolution is as follows:

" Be it resolved by the Senate and House " of Representatives of the United States of Amer- " -ica in Congress assembled, That it be, and " is hereby recommended by the Senate and House " of Representatives to the people of the several " States that they assemble in their several " counties or towns on the approaching Cen- " -tennial Anniversary of our National Inde- " -pendence, and that they cause to have deliv- " -ered on such day an historical sketch of " said county or town from its formation, and that

PRESIDENT GRANT'S CENTENNIAL PROCLAMATION.

Given under my hand at the City of Washington, the twenty-fifth day of May, in the year of Our Lord, one thousand eight hundred and seventy six, and of the Independence of the United States the One Hundredth.

U. S. Grant

By the President:
Hamilton Fish,
Secretary of State.

PRESIDENT GRANT'S SIGNATURE TO CENTENNIAL
PROCLAMATION.

I do not present these views now as a recommendation for a renewal of the subject of annexation, but I do refer to it to vindicate my previous action in regard to it.

With the present term of Congress my official life terminates. It is not probable that public affairs will ever again receive attention from me further than as a citizen of the Republic, always taking a deep interest in the honor, integrity, and prosperity of the whole land.

U. S. GRANT.

SPECIAL MESSAGES.

EXECUTIVE MANSION, *December 6, 1876.*

To the Senate and House of Representatives:

I have the honor to transmit herewith a letter (accompanied by testimony) addressed to me by Hon. John Sherman and other distinguished citizens, in regard to the canvass of the vote for electors in the State of Louisiana.

U. S. GRANT.

EXECUTIVE MANSION, *December 14, 1876.*

To the House of Representatives:

In answer to a resolution of the 7th instant of the House of Representatives, asking to be informed whether any, and what, negotiations have or are being made with the Sioux Indians for their removal to the Indian Territory, and under what authority the same has been and is being done, I submit herewith a report received from the Secretary of the Interior, which contains, it is believed, all the information in possession of his Department touching the matter of the resolution.

U. S. GRANT.

EXECUTIVE MANSION, *December 14, 1876.*

To the Senate of the United States:

In answer to the resolution of the Senate of the 6th instant, requesting information "as to whether troops of the United States were stationed at the city of Petersburg, in the State of Virginia, on the 7th of November, 1876, and, if so, under what authority and for what purpose," I submit the inclosed letters from the Secretary of War, to whom the resolution was referred, together with the report of the General of the Army and accompanying papers.

These inclosures will give all the information called for by the resolution, and I confidently believe will justify the action taken. It is well understood that the presence of United States troops at polling places never prevented the free exercise of the franchise by any citizen, of whatever political faith. If, then, they have had any effect whatever upon the ballot cast, it has been to insure protection to the citizen casting it, in giving it to the candidate of his unbiased choice, without fear, and thus securing the very essence of liberty. It may be the presence of twenty-four United States soldiers, under the command of a captain and lieutenant, quartered in the custom-house at Petersburg, Va., on the 7th of November, at a considerable distance from any polling place, without any interference on their part whatever, and without going near the polls during the election, *may have secured a different result from what would have been obtained if they had not been there* (to maintain the peace in case of riot) *on the face of the returns;* but if such is the case it is only proof that in this one Congressional district in the State of Virginia the legal and constitutional voters have been able to return as elected the candidate of their choice.

U. S. GRANT.

EXECUTIVE MANSION, *December 22, 1876.*
To the Senate and House of Representatives:

I have the honor to transmit herewith a letter, submitted by the Secretary of the Interior, from the Commissioner of Indian Affairs, accompanied by the report and journal of proceedings of the commission appointed on the 24th day of August last to obtain certain concessions from the Sioux Indians, in accordance with the provisions contained in the Indian appropriation act for the current fiscal year.

I ask your special consideration of these articles of agreement, as among other advantages to be gained by them is the clear right of citizens to go into a country of which they have taken possession and from which they can not be excluded.

U. S. GRANT.

EXECUTIVE MANSION, *December 22, 1876.*
To the Senate and House of Representatives:

I have the honor to transmit herewith a report (and papers which accompanied it) of the progress of the work committed to their charge, addressed to me by the commissioners appointed under the act of Congress approved July 19, 1876, authorizing the repavement of Pennsylvania avenue.

U. S. GRANT.

WASHINGTON, *December 23, 1876.*
To the House of Representatives:

When Congress adjourned in August last the execution of the extradition article of the treaty of 1842 between the United States and Great Britain had been interrupted.

The United States had demanded of Her Majesty's Government the surrender of certain fugitives from justice charged with crimes committed within the jurisdiction of the United States, who had sought asylum and were found within the territories of Her British Majesty, and had, in due compliance with the requirements of the treaty, furnished the evidence of the criminality of the fugitives, which had been found sufficient to justify their apprehension and commitment for trial, as required by the treaty, and the fugitives were held and committed for extradition.

Her Majesty's Government, however, demanded from the United States certain assurances or stipulations as a condition for the surrender of these fugitives.

As the treaty contemplated no such conditions to the performance of the obligations which each Government had assumed, the demand for stipulations on the part of this Government was repelled.

Her Majesty's Government thereupon, in June last, released two of the fugitives (Ezra D. Winslow and Charles J. Brent), and subsequently released a third (one William E. Gray), and, refusing to surrender, set them at liberty.

In a message to the two Houses of Congress on the 20th day of June last, in view of the condition of facts as above referred to, I said:

The position thus taken by the British Government, if adhered to, can not but be regarded as the abrogation and annulment of the article of the treaty on extradition.

Under these circumstances it will not, in my judgment, comport with the dignity or self-respect of this Government to make demands upon that Government for the surrender of fugitive criminals, nor to entertain any requisition of that character from that Government under the treaty.

Article XI of the treaty of 1842 provided that "the tenth article [that relating to extradition] should continue in force until one or the other of the parties should signify its wish to terminate it, and no longer."

In view, however, of the great importance of an extradition treaty, especially between two states as intimately connected in commercial and social relations as are the United States and Great Britain, and in the hope that Her Majesty's Government might yet reach a different decision from that then attained, I abstained from recommending any action by Congress terminating the extradition article of the treaty. I have, however, declined to take any steps under the treaty toward extradition.

It is with great satisfaction that I am able now to announce to Congress and to the country that by the voluntary act of Her Majesty's Government the obstacles which had been interposed to the execution of the extradition article of the treaty have been removed.

On the 27th of October last Her Majesty's representative at this capital, under instructions from Lord Derby, informed this Government that Her Majesty's Government would be prepared, as a temporary measure, until a new extradition treaty can be concluded, to put in force all powers vested in it for the surrender of accused persons to the Government of the United States under the treaty of 1842, without asking for any engagement as to such persons not being tried in the United States for other than the offenses for which extradition had been demanded.

I was happy to greet this announcement as the removal of the obstacles which had arrested the execution of the extradition treaty between the two countries.

In reply to the note of Her Majesty's representative, after referring to the applications heretofore made by the United States for the surrender of the fugitives referred to in the correspondence which was laid before Congress at its last session, it was stated that on an indication of readiness to surrender these persons an agent would be authorized to receive them, and I would be ready to respond to requisitions which may be made on the part of Her Majesty's Government under the tenth article of the treaty of 1842, which I would then regard as in full force until such time as either Government shall avail itself of the right to terminate it provided by the eleventh article, or until a more comprehensive arrangement can be reached between the two Governments in regard to the extradition of criminals—an object to which the attention of this Government would gladly be given, with an earnest desire for a mutually satisfactory result.

A copy of the correspondence between Her Majesty's representative at this capital and the Secretary of State on the subject is transmitted herewith.

It is with great satisfaction that I have now to announce that Her Majesty's Government, while expressing its desire not to be understood to recede from the interpretation which in its previous correspondence it has put upon the treaty, but having regard to the prospect of a new treaty and the power possessed by either party of spontaneously denouncing the old one, caused the rearrest on the 4th instant of Brent, one of the fugitives who had been previously discharged, and, after awaiting the requisite time within which the fugitive is entitled to appeal or to apply for his discharge, on the 21st instant surrendered him to the agent appointed on behalf of this Government to receive and to convey him to the United States.

Her Majesty's Government has expressed an earnest desire to rearrest and to deliver up Winslow and Gray, the other fugitives who had been arrested and committed on the requisition of the United States, but were released because of the refusal of the United States to give the assurances and stipulations then required by Great Britain. These persons, however, are believed to have escaped from British jurisdiction; a diligent search has failed to discover them.

As the surrender of Brent without condition or stipulation of any kind being asked removes the obstacle which interrupted the execution of the treaty, I shall no longer abstain from making demands upon Her Majesty's Government for the surrender of fugitive criminals, nor from entertaining requisitions of that character from that Government under the treaty of 1842, but will again regard the treaty as operative, hoping to be able before long to conclude with Her Majesty's Government a new treaty of a broader and more comprehensive nature.

U. S. GRANT.

WASHINGTON, *January 8, 1877.*

To the House of Representatives:

In answer to the resolution of the House of Representatives of the 19th ultimo, I transmit herewith the report of the Secretary of State, together with the papers* which accompanied it.

U. S. GRANT.

[For message of January 12, 1877, withdrawing objections to Senate bill No. 561, see pp. 4343-4344.]

EXECUTIVE MANSION, *January 12, 1877.*

To the House of Representatives:

In reply to a resolution of inquiry dated December 23, 1876, of the House of Representatives, respecting the expenditure of certain moneys appropriated by the act of August 14, 1876, for river and harbor improvements, I have the honor to transmit herewith, for your information, a report and accompanying papers received from the Secretary of War, to whom the resolution was referred.

U. S. GRANT.

EXECUTIVE MANSION, *January 15, 1877.*

To the House of Representatives:

The joint resolution authorizing the Secretary of War to supply blankets to the Reform School in the District of Columbia is before me.

I am in entire sympathy with the purpose of the resolution, but before taking any action upon it I deem it my duty to submit for your consideration the accompanying letter, received from the Secretary of War, embodying a report, made in anticipation of the passage of the resolution, by the Quartermaster-General of the Army, in which, among other facts, it is stated that—

The appropriation for clothing for the Army for this fiscal year is much smaller than usual, and the supply of blankets which it will allow us to purchase is so small that none can properly be spared for other purposes than the supply of the Army.

If it be thought by Congress worth while to cause the supply of blankets for the institution referred to to be procured through the War Department, it is respectfully suggested that provision to meet the expense be made by special appropriation.

U. S. GRANT.

* Correspondence relative to the Venezuelan mixed commission held under the convention of April 25, 1866, for the settlement of claims against Venezuela.

EXECUTIVE MANSION, *January 19, 1877.*

To the House of Representatives:

At the request of the Attorney-General, I have the honor to transmit herewith a report in answer to the resolution of the House adopted on the 1st of August, 1876, relative to certain matters occurring in the administration of the provisional government of the District of Columbia, and chiefly affecting the Commissioners and the late board of audit.

U. S. GRANT.

WASHINGTON, *January 20, 1877.*

To the Senate of the United States:

Herewith I transmit a report from the Secretary of State, with accompanying papers, relating to the Court of Commissioners of Alabama Claims.

U. S. GRANT.

EXECUTIVE MANSION, *January 22, 1877.*

To the House of Representatives:

In answer to the resolution of the House of Representatives of the 8th of December last, inquiring whether any increase in the cavalry force of the army on the Mexican frontier of Texas has been made, as authorized by the act of July 24, 1876, and whether any troops have been removed from the frontier of Texas and from the post of Fort Sill, on the Kiowa and Comanche Reservation, and whether, if so, their places have been supplied by other forces, I have the honor to transmit a report received from the Secretary of War.

U. S. GRANT.

EXECUTIVE MANSION, *January 22, 1877.*

To the House of Representatives:

On the 9th day of December, 1876, the following resolution of the House of Representatives was received, namely:

Resolved, That the President be requested, if not incompatible with the public interest, to transmit to this House copies of any and all orders or directions emanating from him or from either of the Executive Departments of the Government to any military commander or civil officer with reference to the service of the Army, or any portion thereof, in the States of Virginia, South Carolina, Louisiana, and Florida since the 1st of August last, together with reports by telegraph or otherwise from either or any of said military commanders or civil officers.

It was immediately or soon thereafter referred to the Secretary of War and the Attorney-General, the custodians of all retained copies of "orders or directions" given by the Executive Departments of the Government covered by the above inquiry, together with all information upon which such "orders or directions" were given.

The information, it will be observed, is voluminous, and, with the limited clerical force in the Department of Justice, has consumed the time up to the present. Many of the communications accompanying this have been already made public in connection with messages heretofore sent to Congress. This class of information includes the important documents received from the governor of South Carolina and sent to Congress with my message on the subject of the Hamburg massacre; also the documents accompanying my response to the resolution of the House of Representatives in regard to the soldiers stationed at Petersburg.

There have also come to me and to the Department of Justice, from time to time, other earnest written communications from persons holding public trusts and from others residing in the South, some of which I append hereto as bearing upon the precarious condition of the public peace in those States. These communications I have reason to regard as made by respectable and responsible men. Many of them deprecate the publication of their names as involving danger to them personally.

The reports heretofore made by committees of Congress of the results of their inquiries in Mississippi and Louisiana, and the newspapers of several States recommending "the Mississippi plan," have also furnished important data for estimating the danger to the public peace and order in those States.

It is enough to say that these different kinds and sources of evidence have left no doubt whatever in my mind that intimidation has been used, and actual violence, to an extent requiring the aid of the United States Government, where it was practicable to furnish such aid, in South Carolina, in Florida, and in Louisiana, as well as in Mississippi, in Alabama, and in Georgia.

The troops of the United States have been but sparingly used, and in no case so as to interfere with the free exercise of the right of suffrage. Very few troops were available for the purpose of preventing or suppressing the violence and intimidation existing in the States above named. In no case, except that of South Carolina, was the number of soldiers in any State increased in anticipation of the election, saving that twenty-four men and an officer were sent from Fort Foote to Petersburg, Va., where disturbances were threatened prior to the election.

No troops were stationed at the voting places. In Florida and in Louisiana, respectively, the small number of soldiers already in the said States were stationed at such points in each State as were most threatened with violence, where they might be available as a posse for the officer whose duty it was to preserve the peace and prevent intimidation of voters. Such a disposition of the troops seemed to me reasonable and justified by law and precedent, while its omission would have been inconsistent with the constitutional duty of the President of the United States "to take care that the laws be faithfully executed." The statute expressly forbids the bringing of troops to the polls "except where it is necessary to keep the peace," implying that to keep the peace it may be done. But this even, so far as I am advised, has not in any case been done. The stationing of a company or part of a company in the vicinity, where they would be available to prevent riot, has been the only use made of troops prior to and at the time of the elections. Where so stationed, they could be called in an emergency requiring it by a marshal or deputy marshal as a posse to aid in suppressing unlawful violence. The evidence which has come to me has left me no ground to doubt that if there had been more military force available it would have been my duty to have disposed of it in several States with a view to the prevention of the violence and intimidation which have undoubtedly contributed to the defeat of the election law in Mississippi, Alabama, and Georgia, as well as in South Carolina, Louisiana, and Florida.

By Article IV, section 4, of the Constitution—

The United States shall guarantee to every State in this Union a republican form of government, and shall protect each of them against invasion, and on application of the legislature, or of the executive (when the legislature can not be convened), against domestic violence.

By act of Congress (U. S. Revised Statutes, secs. 1034, 1035) the President, in case of "insurrection in any State" or of "unlawful obstruction to the enforcement of the laws of the United States by the ordinary course of judicial proceedings," or whenever "domestic violence in any State so obstructs the execution of the laws thereof and of the United States as to deprive any portion of the people of such State" of their civil or political rights, is authorized to employ such parts of the land and naval forces as he may deem necessary to enforce the execution of the laws and preserve the peace and sustain the authority of the State and of the United States. Acting under this title (69) of the Revised Statutes United States, I accompanied the sending of troops to South Carolina with a proclamation* such as is therein prescribed.

The President is also authorized by act of Congress "to employ such part of the land or naval forces of the United States * * * as shall be necessary to prevent the violation and to enforce the due execution of the provisions" of title 24 of the Revised Statutes of the United States, for the protection of the civil rights of citizens, among which is the provision against conspiracies "to prevent, by force, intimidation, or threat, any citizen who is lawfully entitled to vote from giving his support or advocacy in a legal manner toward or in favor of the election of any lawfully qualified person as an elector for President or Vice-President or as a member of Congress of the United States." (U. S. Revised Statutes, sec. 1989.)

In cases falling under this title I have not considered it necessary to issue a proclamation to precede or accompany the employment of such part of the Army as seemed to be necessary.

* See pp. 4350–435

In case of insurrection against a State government or against the Government of the United States a proclamation is appropriate; but in keeping the peace of the United States at an election at which Members of Congress are elected no such call from the State or proclamation by the President is prescribed by statute or required by precedent.

In the case of South Carolina insurrection and domestic violence against the State government were clearly shown, and the application of the governor founded thereon was duly presented, and I could not deny his constitutional request without abandoning my duty as the Executive of the National Government.

The companies stationed in the other States have been employed to secure the better execution of the laws of the United States and to preserve the peace of the United States.

After the election had been had, and where violence was apprehended by which the returns from the counties and precincts might be destroyed, troops were ordered to the State of Florida, and those already in Louisiana were ordered to the points in greatest danger of violence.

I have not employed troops on slight occasions, nor in any case where it has not been necessary to the enforcement of the laws of the United States. In this I have been guided by the Constitution and the laws which have been enacted and the precedents which have been formed under it.

It has been necessary to employ troops occasionally to overcome resistance to the internal-revenue laws from the time of the resistance to the collection of the whisky tax in Pennsylvania, under Washington, to the present time.

In 1854, when it was apprehended that resistance would be made in Boston to the seizure and return to his master of a fugitive slave, the troops there stationed were employed to enforce the master's right under the Constitution, and troops stationed at New York were ordered to be in readiness to go to Boston if it should prove to be necessary.

In 1859, when John Brown, with a small number of men, made his attack upon Harpers Ferry, the President ordered United States troops to assist in the apprehension and suppression of him and his party without a formal call of the legislature or governor of Virginia and without proclamation of the President.

Without citing further instances in which the Executive has exercised his power, as Commander of the Army and Navy, to prevent or suppress resistance to the laws of the United States, or where he has exercised like authority in obedience to a call from a State to suppress insurrection, I desire to assure both Congress and the country that it has been my purpose to administer the executive powers of the Government fairly, and in no instance to disregard or transcend the limits of the Constitution.

U. S. GRANT.

WASHINGTON, *January 23, 1877.*

To the Senate of the United States:

I transmit, in answer to a resolution of the Senate of the 16th instant a report of the Secretary of State, with its accompanying papers.*

U. S. GRANT.

WASHINGTON, *January 25, 1877.*

To the Senate of the United States:

I transmit to the Senate, for consideration with a view to ratification, a treaty between the United States and His Majesty the King of Spain, in relation to the extradition of criminals, signed on the 5th of January, 1877.

U. S. GRANT.

EXECUTIVE MANSION, *January 29, 1877.*

To the Senate and House of Representatives:

I have the honor to transmit herewith the proceedings of the commission appointed to examine "the whole subject of reform and reorganization of the Army of the United States," under the provisions of the act of Congress approved July 24, 1876.

The commission report that so fully has their time been occupied by other important duties that they are not at this time prepared to submit a plan or make proper recommendations.

U. S. GRANT.

EXECUTIVE MANSION, *January 29, 1877.*

To the House of Representatives:

I have the honor to transmit herewith reports and accompanying papers received from the Secretaries of State and War, in answer to the resolution of the House of Representatives of the 9th instant, relative "to the imprisonment and detention by the Mexican authorities at Matamoras of John Jay Smith, an American citizen, and also to the wounding and robbing by Mexican soldiers at New Laredo of Dr. Samuel Huggins, an American citizen."

U. S. GRANT.

EXECUTIVE MANSION, *January 29, 1877.*

To the Senate of the United States:

I follow the example heretofore occasionally permitted of communicating in this mode my approval of the "act to provide for and regulate the counting of votes for President and Vice-President, and the decision of questions arising thereon, for the term commencing March 4, A. D. 1877," because of my appreciation of the imminent peril to the institutions of

---

* Correspondence with diplomatic officers of the United States in Turkey relative to atrocities and massacres by Turks in Bulgaria.

the country from which, in my judgment, the act affords a wise and constitutional means of escape.

For the first time in the history of our country, under the Constitution as it now is, a dispute exists with regard to the result of the election of the Chief Magistrate of the nation.

It is understood that upon the disposition of disputes touching the electoral votes cast at the late election by one or more of the States depends the question whether one or the other of the candidates for the Presidency is to be the lawful Chief Magistrate. The importance of having clearly ascertained, by a procedure regulated by law, which of the two citizens has been elected, and of having the right to this high office recognized and cheerfully agreed in by all the people of the Republic, can not be overestimated, and leads me to express to Congress and to the nation my great satisfaction at the adoption of a measure that affords an orderly means of decision of a gravely exciting question.

While the history of our country in its earlier periods shows that the President of the Senate has counted the votes and declared their standing, our whole history shows that in no instance of doubt or dispute has he exercised the power of deciding, and that the two Houses of Congress have disposed of all such doubts and disputes, although in no instance hitherto have they been such that their decision could essentially have affected the result.

For the first time the Government of the United States is now brought to meet the question as one vital to the result, and this under conditions not the best calculated to produce an agreement or to induce calm feeling in the several branches of the Government or among the people of the country. In a case where, as now, the result is involved, it is the highest duty of the lawmaking power to provide in advance a constitutional, orderly, and just method of executing the Constitution in this most interesting and critical of its provisions. The doing so, far from being a compromise of right, is an enforcement of right and an execution of powers conferred by the Constitution on Congress.

I think that this orderly method has been secured by the bill, which, appealing to the Constitution and the law as the guide in ascertaining rights, provides a means of deciding questions of single returns through the direct action of Congress, and in respect to double returns by a tribunal of inquiry, whose decisions stand unless both Houses of Congress shall concur in determining otherwise, thus securing a definite disposition of all questions of dispute, in whatever aspect they may arise. With or without this law, as all of the States have voted, and as a tie vote is impossible, it must be that one of the two candidates has been elected; and it would be deplorable to witness an irregular controversy as to which of the two should receive or which should continue to hold the office. In all periods of history controversies have arisen as to the succession or choice of the chiefs of states, and no party or citizens loving their country and its free institutions can sacrifice too much of mere feeling in preserving through the upright course of law their country from the smallest danger to its peace on such an occasion; and it can not be impressed too firmly in the hearts of all the people that true liberty and real progress can exist only through a cheerful adherence to constitutional law.

The bill purports to provide only for the settlement of questions arising from the recent elections. The fact that such questions can arise demonstrates the necessity, which I can not doubt will before long be supplied, of permanent general legislation to meet cases which have not been contemplated in the Constitution or laws of the country.

The bill may not be perfect, and its provisions may not be such as would be best applicable to all future occasions, but it is calculated to meet the present condition of the question and of the country.

The country is agitated. It needs and it desires peace and quiet and harmony between all parties and all sections. Its industries are arrested, labor unemployed, capital idle, and enterprise paralyzed by reason of the doubt and anxiety attending the uncertainty of a double claim to the Chief Magistracy of the nation. It wants to be assured that the result of the election will be accepted without resistance from the supporters of the disappointed candidate, and that its highest officer shall not hold his place with a questioned title of right. Believing that the bill will secure these ends, I give it my signature.

U. S. GRANT.

EXECUTIVE MANSION, *January 30, 1877.*

To the Senate and House of Representatives:

I desire to call the attention of Congress to the importance of providing for the continuance of the board for testing iron, steel, and other metals, which by the sundry civil appropriation act of last year was ordered to be discontinued at the end of the present fiscal year. This board, consisting of engineers and other scientific experts from the Army, the Navy, and from civil life (all of whom, except the secretary, give their time and labors to this object without compensation), was organized by authority of Congress in the spring of 1875, and immediately drafted a comprehensive plan for its investigations and contracted for a testing machine of 400 tons capacity, which would enable it to properly conduct the experiments. Meanwhile the subcommittees of the board have devoted their time to such experiments as could be made with the smaller testing machines already available. This large machine is just now completed and ready for erection at the Watertown Arsenal, and the real labors of the board are therefore just about to be commenced. If the board is to be discontinued at the end of the present fiscal year, the money already appropriated and the services of the gentlemen who have given so much time to the subject will be unproductive of any results.

The importance of these experiments can hardly be overestimated when we consider the almost endless variety of purposes for which iron and steel are employed in this country and the many thousands of lives which daily depend on the soundness of iron structures. I need hardly refer to the recent disaster at the Ashtabula bridge, in Ohio, and the conflicting theories of experts as to the cause of it, as an instance of what might have been averted by a more thorough knowledge of the properties of iron and the best modes of construction. These experiments can not properly be conducted by private firms, not only on account of the expense, but because the results must rest upon the authority of disinterested persons. They must therefore be undertaken under the sanction of the Government. Compared with their great value to the industrial interests of the country, the expense is very slight.

The board recommend an appropriation of $40,000 for the next fiscal year, and I earnestly commend their request to the favorable consideration of Congress. I also recommend that the board be required to conduct their investigations under the direction of the Secretary of War, and to make full report of their progress to that officer in time to be incorporated in his annual report.   U. S. GRANT.

WASHINGTON, *February 2, 1877.*

To the Senate of the United States:

I transmit, in answer to a resolution of the Senate of the 10th ultimo, a report of the Secretary of State, with its accompanying papers.*

U. S. GRANT.

EXECUTIVE MANSION, *February 3, 1877.*

To the Senate and House of Representatives:

By the act of Congress approved January 14, 1875, "to provide for the resumption of specie payments," the 1st of January, 1879, is fixed as the date when such resumption is to begin. It may not be desirable to fix an earlier date when it shall actually become obligatory upon the Government to redeem its outstanding legal-tender notes in coin on presentation, but it is certainly most desirable, and will prove most beneficial to every pecuniary interest of the country, to hasten the day when the paper circulation of the country and the gold coin shall have equal values.

At a later day, if currency and coin should retain equal values, it might become advisable to authorize or direct resumption. I believe the time has come when by a simple act of the legislative branch of the Government this most desirable result can be attained. I am strengthened in this view by the course trade has taken in the last two years and by the strength of the credit of the United States at home and abroad.

*Preliminary and final reports of J. Hubley Ashton, agent of the United States before the United States and Mexican Claims Commission.

For the fiscal year ending June 30, 1876, the exports of the United States exceeded the imports by $120,213,102; but our exports include $40,569,621 of specie and bullion in excess of imports of the same commodities. For the six months of the present fiscal year from July 1, 1876, to January 1, 1877, the excess of exports over imports amounted to $107,544,869, and the import of specie and bullion exceeded the export of the precious metals by $6,192,147 in the same time. The actual excess of exports over imports for the six months, exclusive of specie and bullion, amounted to $113,737,040, showing for the time being the accumulation of specie and bullion in the country amounting to more than $6,000,000, in addition to the national product of these metals for the same period—a total increase of gold and silver for the six months not far short of $60,000,000. It is very evident that unless this great increase of the precious metals can be utilized at home in such a way as to make it in some manner remunerative to the holders it must seek a foreign market as surely as would any other product of the soil or the manufactory. Any legislation which will keep coin and bullion at home will, in my judgment, soon bring about practical resumption, and will add the coin of the country to the circulating medium, thus securing a healthy "inflation" of a sound currency, to the great advantage of every legitimate business interest.

The act to provide for the resumption of specie payments authorizes the Secretary of the Treasury to issue bonds of either of the descriptions named in the act of Congress approved July 14, 1870, entitled "An act to authorize the refunding of the national debt," for not less than par in gold. With the present value of the $4\frac{1}{2}$ per cent bonds in the markets of the world, they could be exchanged at par for gold, thus strengthening the Treasury to meet final resumption and to keep the excess of coin over demand, pending its permanent use as a circulating medium, at home. All that would be further required would be to reduce the volume of legal-tender notes in circulation. To accomplish this I would suggest an act authorizing the Secretary of the Treasury to issue 4 per cent bonds, with forty years to run before maturity, to be exchanged for legal-tender notes whenever presented in sums of $50 or any multiple thereof, the whole amount of such bonds, however, not to exceed $150,000,000. To increase the home demand for such bonds I would recommend that they be available for deposit in the United States Treasury for banking purposes under the various provisions of law relating to national banks.

I would suggest further that national banks be required to retain a certain percentage of the coin interest received by them from the bonds deposited with the Treasury to secure their circulation.

I would also recommend the repeal of the third section of the joint resolution "for the issue of silver coin," approved July 22, 1876, limiting the subsidiary coin and fractional currency to $50,000,000.

I am satisfied that if Congress will enact some such law as will accomplish the end suggested they will give a relief to the country instant in its effects. and for which they will receive the gratitude of the whole people.

U. S. GRANT.

EXECUTIVE MANSION, *February 9, 1877.*

To the Senate and House of Representatives:

The accompanying memorial is transmitted to Congress at the request of a committee, composed of many distinguished citizens of New York, recently appointed to cooperate with a generous body of French citizens who design to erect in the harbor of New York a colossal statue of "Liberty Enlightening the World." Very little is asked of us to do, and I hope that the wishes of the memorialists may receive your very favorable consideration.

U. S. GRANT.

EXECUTIVE MANSION, *February 9, 1877.*

To the Senate and House of Representatives:

I transmit herewith the catalogues and report of the board on behalf of the Executive Departments at the International Exhibition of 1876, with their accompanying illustrations.

The labors performed by the members of the board, as evinced by the voluminous mass of information found in the various papers from the officers charged with their preparation, have been in the highest degree commendable, and believing that the publication of these papers will form an interesting memorial of the greatest of international exhibitions and of the centennial anniversary of the independence of our country, I recommend that they be printed in a suitable form for distribution and preservation.

The letter of the chairman of the board will give to Congress the history of its organization, the law and Executive orders under which it has acted, and the steps which have been taken to preserve the large and instructive collections made, with a view to their forming a part of a national museum, should Congress make the necessary appropriations for such a desirable object.

U. S. GRANT.

WASHINGTON, *February 15, 1877.*

To the Senate of the United States:

I transmit herewith, in answer to the resolution of the Senate of the 13th instant, a report from the Secretary of State, with accompanying papers.*

U. S. GRANT.

* Statements of appropriations and expenditures of the Department of State from March 4, 1789, to June 30, 1876, inclusive.

WASHINGTON, *February 23, 1877.*

To the Senate and House of Representatives:

I transmit herewith a report from the Secretary of State, bearing date the 20th instant, with its accompaniments, being the report of the commissioner of the United States and of the officers of engineers attached to the commission appointed to determine the boundary line between the United States and the possessions of Great Britain from the northwest angle of the Lake of the Woods to the summit of the Rocky Mountains. These reports announce the completion of the labors of this commission, whereby the entire boundary line between the United States and the possessions of Great Britain is marked and determined, except as to that part of the territory of the United States which was ceded by Russia under the treaty of 1867.

U. S. GRANT.

WASHINGTON, *February 24, 1877.*

To the House of Representatives:

I transmit herewith, in answer to the resolution of the House of Representatives of the 25th ultimo, a report from the Secretary of State, with accompanying papers.*

U. S. GRANT.

EXECUTIVE MANSION, *February 26, 1877.*

To the Senate of the United States:

I have the honor to return herewith Senate bill No. 234, entitled "An act to allow a pension of $37 per month to soldiers who have lost both an arm and a leg." Under existing law soldiers who have lost both an arm and a leg are entitled to draw a monthly pension of $18. As the object of this bill is to allow them $18 per month for each of these disabilities, or $36 in all, it is returned simply for an amendment of title which shall agree with its provisions. When this shall have been done, I will very gladly give it my immediate approval.

U. S. GRANT

WASHINGTON, *February 28, 1877.*

To the Senate of the United States:

In answer to the resolution† of the Senate of the 27th instant, I transmit herewith a report of the Secretary of State, together with the papers which accompanied it.

U. S. GRANT.

* Correspondence, etc., connected with the agency of A. B. Steinberger in the Samoan Islands.
† Directing the Secretary of State to transmit any communication demanding the payment of moneys claimed to be due the Dominican Government from the United States.

VETO MESSAGES.

EXECUTIVE MANSION, *January 15, 1877.*

To the House of Representatives:

For the reasons set forth in the accompanying communication addressed to the Secretary of the Interior by the Commissioner of the General Land Office, I have the honor to return herewith without my signature the bill (H. R. 2041) entitled "An act to amend section 2291 of the Revised Statutes of the United States, in relation to proof required in homestead entries."

U. S. GRANT.

DEPARTMENT OF THE INTERIOR,
Washington, D. C., January 12, 1877.

The PRESIDENT.

SIR: I have the honor to return herewith enrolled bill H. R. No. 2041, entitled "An act to amend section 2291 of the Revised Statutes of the United States, in relation to proof required in homestead entries," which accompanied your letter of the 10th instant, requesting to be informed whether any objection was known to this Department why the same should not become a law.

The matter was referred to the Commissioner of the General Land Office, and I transmit herewith a copy of a letter from him suggesting certain amendments to the second section of said act.

I concur in the recommendations made by the Commissioner.

I have the honor to be, with great respect, your obedient servant,

Z. CHANDLER,
Secretary.

DEPARTMENT OF THE INTERIOR,
GENERAL LAND OFFICE,
Washington, D. C., January 11, 1877.

The Honorable SECRETARY OF THE INTERIOR.

SIR: I am in receipt, by your reference of yesterday's date, of "An act to amend section 2291 of the Revised Statutes of the United States, in relation to proof required in homestead entries," which has passed both Houses of Congress and now awaits the signature of the President.

The purpose of the act is to enable parties seeking title under the homestead law to make final proof before a judge or clerk of court in the county or district where the lands are situated.

Its provisions are in conformity with the views and recommendations of this office, and I see no objection to them in so far as relates to the taking of the testimony.

I observe, however, that the second section provides that the proofs, affidavits, and oaths shall be filed in the office of the register, and no provision is made for the transmission of either the original papers or duplicates to this office, in order that patents may properly issue thereon, the provisions relating to certification for the purposes of evidence seeming to require that they shall remain on file in the district office. There is, therefore, no opportunity for the supervisory control of the Commissioner over entries so made to be exercised under the statutes, and thus the express requirements of existing law, as well as the essential harmony of the land system, are interfered with by its provisions. To remedy this defect in the proposed law I recommend that the act be returned to the legislative body with the request for an enactment in lieu of the second section which shall provide for the regular transmission of the papers to this office, as in other cases, or the simple striking out of the section altogether, as the provisions of existing law would then cover the case, and require the same disposal of this class of entries as obtains under present regulations so far as relates to the transmission of papers and proof to this office and the certification of the same by the Commissioner, under seal, for purposes of evidence.

I observe in section 3, line 4, the omission of the word "he" after the word "corrupt," which destroys the grammatical construction of the language and was probably a clerical error.

I return herewith the act referred to.

> Very respectfully, your obedient servant,
>
> A. WILLIAMSON,
> *Commissioner.*

EXECUTIVE MANSION, *January 23, 1877.*

To the House of Representatives:

I return herewith House bill (No. 4350) to abolish the board of com- missioners of the Metropolitan police of the District of Columbia and to transfer its duties to the Commissioners of the District of Columbia, without my approval.

It is my judgment that the police commissioners, while appointed by the Executive, should report to and receive instructions from the Dis- trict Commissioners. Under other circumstances than those existing at present I would have no objection to the entire abolition of the board and seeing the duties devolved directly upon the District Commissioners. The latter should, in my opinion, have supervision and control over the acts of the police commissioners under any circumstances; but as recent events have shown that gross violations of law have existed in this Dis- trict for years directly under the eyes of the police, it is highly desirable that the board of police commissioners should be continued in some form until the evil complained of is eradicated and until the police force is put on a footing to prevent, if possible, a recurrence of the evil. The board of police commissioners have recently been charged with the direct object of accomplishing this end.

U. S. GRANT.

WASHINGTON, *January 26, 1877.*

To the House of Representatives:

I return to the House of Representatives, in which they originated two joint resolutions, the one entitled "Joint resolution relating to con- gratulations from the Argentine Republic," the other entitled "Joint resolution in reference to congratulations from the Republic of Pretoria, South Africa."

The former of these resolutions purports to direct the Secretary of State to acknowledge a dispatch of congratulation from the Argentine Repub- lic and the high appreciation of Congress of the compliment thus con- veyed. The other directs the Secretary of State to communicate to the

Republic of Pretoria the high appreciation of Congress of the complimentary terms in which said Republic has referred to the first centennial of our national independence.

Sympathizing, as I do, in the spirit of courtesy and friendly recognition which has prompted the passage of these resolutions, I can not escape the conviction that their adoption has inadvertently involved the exercise of a power which infringes upon the constitutional rights of the Executive.

The usage of governments generally confines their correspondence and interchange of opinion and of sentiments of congratulation, as well as of discussion, to one certain established agency. To allow correspondence or interchange between states to be conducted by or with more than one such agency would necessarily lead to confusion, and possibly to contradictory presentation of views and to international complications.

The Constitution of the United States, following the established usage of nations, has indicated the President as the agent to represent the national sovereignty in its intercourse with foreign powers and to receive all official communications from them. It gives him the power, by and with the advice and consent of the Senate, to make treaties and to appoint embassadors and other public ministers; it intrusts to him solely "to receive embassadors and other public ministers," thus vesting in him the origination of negotiations and the reception and conduct of all correspondence with foreign states, making him, in the language of one of the most eminent writers on constitutional law, "the constitutional organ of communication with foreign states."

No copy of the addresses which it is proposed to acknowledge is furnished. I have no knowledge of their tone, language, or purport. From the tenor of the two joint resolutions it is to be inferred that these communications are probably purely congratulatory. Friendly and kindly intentioned as they may be, the presentation by a foreign state of any communication to a branch of the Government not contemplated by the Constitution for the reception of communications from foreign states might, if allowed to pass without notice, become a precedent for the address by foreigners or by foreign states of communications of a different nature and with wicked designs.

If Congress can direct the correspondence of the Secretary of State with foreign governments, a case very different from that now under consideration might arise, when that officer might be directed to present to the same foreign government entirely different and antagonistic views or statements.

By the act of Congress establishing what is now the Department of State, then known as the Department of Foreign Affairs, the Secretary is to "perform and execute such duties as shall from time to time be enjoined on or intrusted to him by the President of the United States, agreeably to the Constitution, relative to correspondence, commissions, or instructions to or with public ministers or consuls from the United States, or to negotiations with public ministers from foreign states or princes, or to memorials or other applications from foreign public minis- ters or other foreigners, or to such other matters respecting foreign affairs as the President of the United States shall assign to the said Depart- ment; and furthermore, the said principal officer [the Secretary of State] shall conduct the business of the said Department in such manner as the President of the United States shall from time to time order or instruct."

This law, which remains substantially unchanged, confirms the view that the whole correspondence of the Government with and from foreign states is intrusted to the President; that the Secretary of State conducts such correspondence exclusively under the orders and instructions of the President, and that no communication or correspondence from foreign- ers or from a foreign state can properly be addressed to any branch or Department of the Government except that to which such correspondence has been committed by the Constitution and the laws.

I therefore feel it my duty to return the joint resolutions without my approval to the House of Representatives, in which they originated.

In addition to the reasons already stated for withholding my constitu- tional approval from these resolutions is the fact that no information is furnished as to the terms or purport of the communications to which acknowledgments are desired; no copy of the communications accompa- nies the resolutions, nor is the name even of the officer or of the body to whom an acknowledgment could be addressed given; it is not known whether these congratulatory addresses proceed from the head of the state or from legislative bodies; and as regards the resolution relating to the Republic of Pretoria, I can not learn that any state or government of that name exists.

U. S. GRANT.

EXECUTIVE MANSION, *January 26, 1877.*

To the Senate of the United States:

I have the honor to return herewith without my approval Senate bill No. 685, entitled "An act to place the name of Daniel H. Kelly upon the muster roll of Company F, Second Tennessee Infantry."

The reasons for withholding my signature to this bill may be found in the accompanying report received from the Secretary of War.

U. S. GRANT.

The PRESIDENT. WAR DEPARTMENT, *January 24, 1877.*

SIR: I have the honor to return herewith Senate bill 685, "to place the name of Daniel H. Kelly upon the muster roll of Company F, Second Tennessee Infantry," with the report of the Adjutant-General, as follows:

"The inclosed act directs the Secretary of War to place the name of Daniel H. Kelly upon the muster roll of Company F, Second Tennessee Infantry, to date

December 1, 1861. There is no record of the enlistment, service, or death of this man on file in this office, and if this act becomes a law as it now reads it will be of no benefit to the heirs."

I have the honor to be, sir, with great respect, your obedient servant,

J. D. CAMERON,
Secretary of War.

EXECUTIVE MANSION, *February 14, 1877.*

To the House of Representatives:

I have the honor to return herewith without my approval House bill No. 3367, entitled "An act to remove the charge of desertion from the military record of Alfred Rouland."

The reasons for withholding my signature may be found in the accompanying report received from the Secretary of War.

U. S. GRANT.

WAR DEPARTMENT,
Washington City, February 8, 1877.

The PRESIDENT.

SIR: I have the honor to return House bill 3367, "to remove the charge of desertion from the military record of Alfred Rouland," and inclose copy of the report of the Adjutant-General, dated the 8th instant, who recommends that the bill be not approved.

In this connection I would invite attention to reports of the Military Committees of the House and Senate (House Report No. 461, Forty-fourth Congress, first session; Senate Report No. 578, Forty-fourth Congress, second session) in the case, of which copies are herewith.

I have the honor to be, very respectfully, your obedient servant,

J. D. CAMERON,
Secretary of War.

WAR DEPARTMENT,
Adjutant-General's Office, February 8, 1877.

Respectfully returned to the Secretary of War.

This man is reported on the muster-out roll of his company as having "deserted at Wilmington, N. C., April 16, 1866."

In his petition of December 28, 1874, on file in this office, occurs the following language:

"I was transferred to the Twenty-eighth Michigan Volunteers, and performed duty with that regiment from the 28th June, 1865, until the 16th day of April, 1866, when, being in a reduced and weak condition from continued chills and fever, and being in great fear of smallpox, which had become very prevalent at Wilmington, N. C., where my company was then stationed, I left my command without leave and returned to Michigan." * * *

This man is consequently a deserter in fact, and should this bill, restoring to an honorable status an admitted deserter, become a law, it will defeat every end of military discipline and justice, besides working a great injustice to every soldier who served faithfully and honorably.

It is therefore strongly recommended that it be not approved.

E. D. TOWNSEND,
Adjutant-General

EXECUTIVE MANSION, *February 14, 1877.*

To the House of Representatives:

I return the House bill No. 3155, entitled "An act to perfect the revision of the statutes of the United States," without my approval. My objection is to the single provision which amends section 3823 of the Revised Statutes.

That section is as follows:

SEC. 3823. The Clerk of the House of Representatives shall select in Virginia, South Carolina, North Carolina, Georgia, Florida, Alabama, Mississippi, Louisiana, Texas, and Arkansas one or more newspapers, not exceeding the number allowed by law, in which such treaties and laws of the United States as may be ordered for publication in newspapers according to law shall be published, and in some one or more of which so selected all such advertisements as may be ordered for publication in said districts by any United States court or judge thereof, or by any officer of such courts, or by any executive officer of the United States, shall be published, the compensation for which and other terms of publication shall be fixed by said Clerk at a rate not exceeding $2 per page for the publication of treaties and laws, and not exceeding $1 per square of eight lines of space for the publication of advertisements, the accc unts for which shall be adjusted by the proper accounting officers and paid in the manner now authorized by law in the like cases.

The bill proposes to amend this section as follows:

By striking out all after the word "in" in the first line to the word "one" in the third line, and inserting therefor the words "each State and Territory of the United States."

Prior to 1867 the advertising of the Executive Departments had been subject to the direction of the heads of those Departments, and had been published in newspapers selected by them and on terms fixed by them. In the year 1867 (14 U. S. Statutes at Large, pp. 466, 467), when the ten States above named were yet unrestricted, and when there existed a radical difference of opinion between the executive and legislative departments as to the administration of the Government in those States, this provision was enacted. Subsequently, during the same year (15 U. S. Statutes at Large, p. 8), so much of this provision "as relates to the publication of the laws and treaties of the United States" was extended to all the States and Territories, leaving the advertisements ordered by Congress and by the Executive Departments unaffected thereby. The continuance of this provision after the reconstruction acts had taken effect and the bringing it forward into the Revised Statutes were probably through inadvertence.

The existence of this section (3823) of the Revised Statutes seems to have been ignored by Congress itself in the adoption of section 3941, authorizing the Postmaster-General to advertise in such newspapers as he may choose. But the present act, if it should go into effect, would compel him and the other heads of the Executive Departments, as well as all the courts, to publish all their advertisements in newspapers selected by the Clerk of the House of Representatives. It would make general in its operation a provision which was exceptional and temporary in its origin and character. This, in my judgment, would be unwise, if not also an actual encroachment upon the constitutional rights of the executive branch of the Government. The person who should be appointed by law to select all the newspapers throughout the country to which the patronage of all branches of the Government of the United States should be given, if not an officer of the United States under Article II, section 2, clause 2, of the Constitution, would certainly have powers and duties which have hitherto been regarded as official.

But without reference to the question of its constitutionality, I am satisfied that this provision would not operate usefully or fairly. I am constrained, therefore, to withhold from it my approval. I regret that my objection to this one clause of the act can not be made available without withholding my approval from the entire act, which is otherwise unobjectionable.

U. S. GRANT.

EXECUTIVE MANSION, *February 28, 1877.*

To the Senate of the United States:

I have the honor to return herewith without my approval Senate bill No. 691, entitled "An act for the relief of Edward A. Leland." The reasons for withholding my approval may be found in the accompanying communication received from the Secretary of the Interior.

U. S. GRANT.

DEPARTMENT OF THE INTERIOR,
Washington, February 27, 1877.

The PRESIDENT.

SIR: I have the honor to return herewith the bill (S. 691) entitled "An act for the relief of Edward A. Leland," accompanied by a copy of a letter from the Commissioner of Patents suggesting an objection to the bill in its present form, and to recommend that it be returned to Congress for amendment in accordance with the suggestions of the Commissioner.

I have the honor to be, very respectfully,

Z. CHANDLER,
Secretary.

DEPARTMENT OF THE INTERIOR,
UNITED STATES PATENT OFFICE,
Washington, D. C., February 27, 1877.

Hon. Z. CHANDLER,
     Secretary of the Interior.

SIR: In the matter of the enrolled bill (S. 691) extending letters patent of Edward A. Leland, I have the honor to report that said letters patent were granted for an improved paint can August 14, 1860, for the term of fourteen years; that they consequently expired on the 14th day of August, 1874, whereupon the invention became the property of the public.

The present act proposes to extend the term of the patent seven years from said 14th day of August, 1874, and give to it the same effect in law as if it had been originally granted for the term of twenty-one years.

It will be seen, therefore, that those who have innocently used and purchased the invention since the expiration of the letters patent on the 14th of August, 1874, under the impression that the invention was the property of the public, will, by the retroactive terms of the bill, be liable for damages for such use upon suits for infringement.

This hardship is generally, if not always, provided against by a proviso to such bills, setting forth in terms "that no person shall be held liable for the infringement of said patent, if extended, for making use of said invention since the expiration of the original term of said patent and prior to the date of its extension."

Unless such a proviso is incorporated into the present bill, the injustice alluded to may be done.

Very respectfully, your obedient servant,

ELLIS SPEAR,
Commissioner of Patents.

PROCLAMATION.

By the President of the United States of America.

A PROCLAMATION.

Whereas objects of interest to the United States require that the Senate should be convened at 12 o'clock on the 5th day of March next to receive and act upon such communications as may be made to it on the part of the Executive:

Now, therefore, I, Ulysses S. Grant, President of the United States, have considered it to be my duty to issue this my proclamation, declaring that an extraordinary occasion requires the Senate of the United States to convene for the transaction of business at the Capitol, in the city of Washington, on the 5th day of March next, at 12 o'clock at noon on that day, of which all who shall at that time be entitled to act as members of that body are hereby required to take notice.

Given under my hand and the seal of the United States, at Washington, the 2d day of March, A. D. 1877, and of the Independence of the United States of America the one hundred and first.

[SEAL.]

U. S. GRANT.

By the President:
HAMILTON FISH,
Secretary of State.

Rutherford B. Hayes

March 4, 1877, to March 4, 1881

SEE VOLUME XI.

Volume eleven is not only an index to the other volumes, not only a key that unlocks the treasures of the entire publication, but it is in itself an alphabetically arranged brief history or story of the great controlling events constituting the History of the United States.

Under its proper alphabetical classification the story is told of every great subject referred to by any of the Presidents in their official Messages, and at the end of each story the official utterances of the Presidents themselves are cited upon the subject, so that you may readily turn to the page in the body of the work itself for this original information.

Next to the possession of knowledge is the ability to turn at will to where knowledge is to be found.

RUTHERFORD B. HAYES

With official portrait engraved from copy of original in steel.

RUTHERFORD B. HAYES

With official portrait engraved from copy of original in steel

Rutherford B. Hayes

RUTHERFORD B. HAYES was born in Delaware. Ohio, October 4, 1822. His father had died in July, 1822, leaving his mother in modest circumstances. He attended the common schools, and began early the study of Latin and Greek with Judge Sherman Finch, of Delaware. Prepared for college at an academy at Norwalk, Ohio, and at a school in Middletown, Conn. In the autumn of 1838 entered Kenyon College, at Gambier, Ohio. Excelled in logic, mental and moral philosophy, and mathematics, and also made his mark as a debater in the literary societies. On his graduation, in August, 1842, was awarded the valedictory oration, with which he won much praise. Soon afterwards began the study of law in the office of Thomas Sparrow, at Columbus, Ohio, and then attended a course of law lectures at Harvard University, entering the law school August 22, 1843, and finishing his studies there in January, 1845. As a law student he had the advantage of friendly intercourse with Judge Story and Professor Greenleaf, and also attended the lectures of Longfellow on literature and of Agassiz on natural science, pursuing at the same time the study of French and German. In May, 1845, was admitted to practice in the courts of Ohio as an attorney and counselor at law. Established himself first at Lower Sandusky (now Fremont), where in April, 1846, he formed a law partnership with Ralph P. Buckland, then a Member of Congress. In the winter of 1849–50 established himself at Cincinnati. His practice at first being light, continued his studies in law and literature, and also became identified with various literary societies, among them the literary club of Cincinnati, where he met Salmon P. Chase, Thomas Ewing, Thomas Corwin, Stanley Matthews, Moncure D. Conway, Manning F. Force, and others of note. December 30, 1852, married Miss Lucy Ware Webb, daughter of Dr. James Webb, a physician of Chillicothe, Ohio. In January, 1854, formed a law partnership with H. W. Corwine and William K. Rogers. In 1856 was nominated for the office of common pleas judge, but declined. In 1858 was elected city solicitor by the city council of Cincinnati to fill a vacancy, and in the following year was elected to the same office at a popular election, but was defeated for reelection in 1861. After becoming a voter he acted with the Whig party, voting for Henry Clay in 1844, for General Taylor in 1848, and for General Scott in 1852. Having from his youth cherished antislavery feelings, he joined the Republican party as soon as it was organized, and earnestly advocated the election of Frémont in 1856 and of Lincoln in 1860. At a great mass meeting held in Cincinnati immediately after the firing on Fort Sumter was made chairman of a committee on resolutions. His literary club formed a military company, of which he was elected captain. June 7, 1861, was appointed by the governor of Ohio major of the Twenty-third Ohio Volunteers. September 19, 1861, was appointed by General Rosecrans judge-advocate of the Department of the Ohio. October 24, 1861, was promoted to the rank of lieutenant-colonel. In the battle of South Mountain, September 14, 1862, distinguished himself by gallant conduct in leading a charge and in holding a position at the head of his troops after being severely wounded in his left arm. October 24, 1862, was appointed colonel of the Twenty-third Ohio. In July, 1863, while with the army in southwestern Virginia, caused an expedition of two regiments and a section of artillery under his command to be dispatched to Ohio for the purpose of checking the raid of the Confederate general John Morgan, and aided materially in preventing the raiders from recrossing the Ohio River and in compelling Morgan to surrender. In the spring of 1864 commanded a brigade in General Crook's expedition to cut the principal lines of communication between Richmond and the Southwest. Distinguished himself by conspicuous bravery at the head of his brigade in storming a fortified position on the crest of Cloyd Mountain. Commanded a brigade in the first battle of Winchester. Took a creditable part in the engagement at Berryville, and at the second battle of Winchester, September 19, 1864, performed a feat of great bravery. Leading an assault upon a battery on an eminence, he found in his way a morass over 50 yards wide. Being at the head of his brigade, he plunged in first, and, his horse becoming mired at once, he dismounted and waded across alone under the enemy's fire. Signaled his men to come over, and when about 40 had joined him he rushed upon the battery and captured it after a hand-to-hand fight. At Fishers Hill, September 22, 1864, being then in command of a division, executed a brilliant flank movement over mountains and through woods, took many pieces of artillery, and routed the enemy. At the battle of Cedar Creek, October 19, 1864, his conduct attracted so much attention that his commander, General Crook, commended him, saying, ''Colonel, from this day you will be a brigadier-general.'' The commission reached him a few days afterwards. March 13, 1865, received the rank of brevet major-general ''for gallant and distinguished services during the campaign of 1864 in West Virginia, and particularly at the battles of Fishers Hill and Cedar Creek, Virginia.'' In August, 1864, while in the field, was nominated for Congress and elected. After the war, returned to civil life, and took his seat in Congress December 4, 1865. Voted with his party on questions connected with the reconstruction of the Southern States; supported a resolution declaring the sacredness of the public debt and denouncing repudiation, and also one commending President Johnson for declining to accept presents and condemning the practice; opposed a resolution favoring an increase of pay of members of Congress; introduced in a Republican caucus resolutions declaring that the only mode of obtaining from the States lately in rebellion irreversible guaranties was by constitutional amendment, and that an amendment basing representation upon voters instead of population ought to be acted upon without delay. In August, 1866, was renominated for Congress by acclamation, and was reelected. Supported the impeachment of President Johnson. In June, 1867, was nominated for governor of Ohio, and at the election defeated Judge Allen G. Thurman. In June, 1869, was again nominated for governor, and at the election defeated George H. Pendleton. At the expiration of his term as governor declined to be a candidate for the United States Senate against John Sherman. In 1872 was again nominated for Congress, but at the election was defeated. Declined the office of assistant treasurer of the United States at Cincinnati. In 1873 established his home at Fremont with the intention of retiring from public life. In 1875 was again nominated for governor of Ohio, and at the election defeated William Allen. Was nominated for President of the United States at the national Republican convention at Cincinnati on June 16, 1876. The Democrats selected as their candidate Samuel J. Tilden, of New York. The result of the election became the subject of acrimonious dispute. Each party charged fraud upon the other, and both parties claimed to have carried the States of Louisiana, South Carolina, and Florida. To avoid a deadlock, which might have happened if the canvass of the electoral votes had been left to the two Houses of Congress (the Senate having a Republican and the House of Representatives a Democratic majority), an act, advocated by members of both parties, was passed to refer all contested cases to a commission composed of five Senators, five Representatives, and five Justices of the Supreme Court, the decision of this commission to be final unless set aside by a concurrent vote of the two Houses of Congress. The commission, refusing to go behind the certificates of the governors, decided in each contested case by a vote of 8 to 7 in favor of the Republican electors, beginning with Florida on February 7, and on March 2 Mr. Hayes was declared duly elected President of the United States. Was inaugurated March 5, 1877. At the expiration of his term returned to his home at Fremont, Ohio. Was the recipient of various distinctions. The degree of LL. D. was conferred upon him by Kenyon College, Harvard University, Yale College, and Johns Hopkins University. Was made senior vice-commander of the Military Order of the Loyal Legion, commander of the Ohio commandery of the same order, first president of the Society of the Army of West

Virginia, and president of the Twenty-third Regiment Ohio Volunteers Association. Was president of the trustees of the John F. Slater education fund; one of the trustees of the Peabody education fund; president of the National Prison Reform Association; an active member of the National Conference of Corrections and Charities; a trustee of the Western Reserve University, at Cleveland, Ohio, of the Wesleyan University, of Delaware, Ohio, of Mount Union College, at Alliance, Ohio, and of the Ohio State University. He died at Fremont, Ohio, January 17, 1893, and was buried there.

INAUGURAL ADDRESS.

FELLOW-CITIZENS: We have assembled to repeat the public ceremonial, begun by Washington, observed by all my predecessors, and now a time-honored custom, which marks the commencement of a new term of the Presidential office. Called to the duties of this great trust, I proceed, in compliance with usage, to announce some of the leading principles, on the subjects that now chiefly engage the public attention, by which it is my desire to be guided in the discharge of those duties. I shall not undertake to lay down irrevocably principles or measures of administration, but rather to speak of the motives which should animate us, and to suggest certain important ends to be attained in accordance with our institutions and essential to the welfare of our country.

At the outset of the discussions which preceded the recent Presidential election it seemed to me fitting that I should fully make known my sentiments in regard to several of the important questions which then appeared to demand the consideration of the country. Following the example, and in part adopting the language, of one of my predecessors, I wish now, when every motive for misrepresentation has passed away, to repeat what was said before the election, trusting that my countrymen will candidly weigh and understand it, and that they will feel assured that the sentiments declared in accepting the nomination for the Presidency will be the standard of my conduct in the path before me, charged, as I now am, with the grave and difficult task of carrying them out in the practical administration of the Government so far as depends, under the Constitution and laws, on the Chief Executive of the nation.

The permanent pacification of the country upon such principles and by such measures as will secure the complete protection of all its citizens in the free enjoyment of all their constitutional rights is now the one subject in our public affairs which all thoughtful and patriotic citizens regard as of supreme importance.

Many of the calamitous effects of the tremendous revolution which has passed over the Southern States still remain. The immeasurable benefits which will surely follow, sooner or later, the hearty and generous acceptance of the legitimate results of that revolution have not yet been realized. Difficult and embarrassing questions meet us at the threshold of this subject. The people of those States are still impoverished, and the inestimable blessing of wise, honest, and peaceful local self-government is not fully enjoyed. Whatever difference of opinion may exist as to the cause of this condition of things, the fact is clear that in the progress of events the time has come when such government is the imperative necessity required by all the varied interests, public and private, of those States. But it must not be forgotten that only a local government which recognizes and maintains inviolate the rights of all is a true self-government.

With respect to the two distinct races whose peculiar relations to each other have brought upon us the deplorable complications and perplexities which exist in those States, it must be a government which guards the interests of both races carefully and equally. It must be a government which submits loyally and heartily to the Constitution and the laws—the laws of the nation and the laws of the States themselves—accepting and obeying faithfully the whole Constitution as it is.

Resting upon this sure and substantial foundation, the superstructure of beneficent local governments can be built up, and not otherwise. In furtherance of such obedience to the letter and the spirit of the Constitution, and in behalf of all that its attainment implies, all so-called party interests lose their apparent importance, and party lines may well be permitted to fade into insignificance. The question we have to consider for the immediate welfare of those States of the Union is the question of government or no government; of social order and all the peaceful industries and the happiness that belong to it, or a return to barbarism. It is a question in which every citizen of the nation is deeply interested, and with respect to which we ought not to be, in a partisan sense, either Republicans or Democrats, but fellow-citizens and fellow-men, to whom the interests of a common country and a common humanity are dear.

The sweeping revolution of the entire labor system of a large portion of our country and the advance of 4,000,000 people from a condition of servitude to that of citizenship, upon an equal footing with their former masters, could not occur without presenting problems of the gravest moment, to be dealt with by the emancipated race, by their former masters, and by the General Government, the author of the act of emancipation. That it was a wise, just, and providential act, fraught with good for all concerned, is now generally conceded throughout the country. That a moral obligation rests upon the National Government to employ its constitutional power and influence to establish the rights of the people it has emancipated, and to protect them in the enjoyment of those rights when they are infringed or assailed, is also generally admitted.

The evils which afflict the Southern States can only be removed or remedied by the united and harmonious efforts of both races, actuated by motives of mutual sympathy and regard; and while in duty bound and fully determined to protect the rights of all by every constitutional means at the disposal of my Administration, I am sincerely anxious to use every legitimate influence in favor of honest and efficient local *self-government* as the true resource of those States for the promotion of the contentment and prosperity of their citizens. In the effort I shall make to accomplish this purpose I ask the cordial cooperation of all who cherish an interest in the welfare of the country, trusting that party ties and the prejudice of race will be freely surrendered in behalf of the great purpose to be accomplished. In the important work of restoring the South it is not the political situation alone that merits attention. The material development of that section of the country has been arrested by the social and political revolution through which it has passed, and now needs and deserves the considerate care of the National Government within the just limits prescribed by the Constitution and wise public economy.

But at the basis of all prosperity, for that as well as for every other part of the country, lies the improvement of the intellectual and moral condition of the people. Universal suffrage should rest upon universal education. To this end, liberal and permanent provision should be made for the support of free schools by the State governments, and, if need be, supplemented by legitimate aid from national authority.

Let me assure my countrymen of the Southern States that it is my earnest desire to regard and promote their truest interests—the interests of the white and of the colored people both and equally—and to put forth my best efforts in behalf of a civil policy which will forever wipe out in our political affairs the color line and the distinction between North and South, to the end that we may have not merely a united North or a united South, but a united country.

I ask the attention of the public to the paramount necessity of reform in our civil service—a reform not merely as to certain abuses and practices of so-called official patronage which have come to have the sanction of usage in the several Departments of our Government, but a change in the system of appointment itself; a reform that shall be thorough, radical, and complete; a return to the principles and practices of the founders of the Government. They neither expected nor desired from public officers any partisan service. They meant that public officers should owe their whole service to the Government and to the people. They meant that the officer should be secure in his tenure as long as his personal character remained untarnished and the performance of his duties satisfactory. They held that appointments to office were not to be made nor expected merely as rewards for partisan services, nor merely on the nomination of members of Congress, as being entitled in any respect to the control of such appointments.

The fact that both the great political parties of the country, in declaring their principles prior to the election, gave a prominent place to the subject of reform of our civil service, recognizing and strongly urging its necessity, in terms almost identical in their specific import with those I have here employed, must be accepted as a conclusive argument in behalf of these measures. It must be regarded as the expression of the united voice and will of the whole country upon this subject, and both political parties are virtually pledged to give it their unreserved support.

The President of the United States of necessity owes his election to office to the suffrage and zealous labors of a political party, the members of which cherish with ardor and regard as of essential importance the principles of their party organization; but he should strive to be always mindful of the fact that he serves his party best who serves the country best.

In furtherance of the reform we seek, and in other important respects a change of great importance, I recommend an amendment to the Constitution prescribing a term of six years for the Presidential office and forbidding a reelection.

With respect to the financial condition of the country, I shall not attempt an extended history of the embarrassment and prostration which we have suffered during the past three years. The depression in all our varied commercial and manufacturing interests throughout the country, which began in September, 1873, still continues. It is very gratifying, however, to be able to say that there are indications all around us of a coming change to prosperous times.

Upon the currency question, intimately connected, as it is, with this topic, I may be permitted to repeat here the statement made in my letter of acceptance, that in my judgment the feeling of uncertainty inseparable from an irredeemable paper currency, with its fluctuation of values, is one of the greatest obstacles to a return to prosperous times. The only safe paper currency is one which rests upon a coin basis and is at all times and promptly convertible into coin.

I adhere to the views heretofore expressed by me in favor of Congressional legislation in behalf of an early resumption of specie payments, and I am satisfied not only that this is wise, but that the interests, as well as the public sentiment, of the country imperatively demand it.

Passing from these remarks upon the condition of our own country to consider our relations with other lands, we are reminded by the international complications abroad, threatening the peace of Europe, that our traditional rule of noninterference in the affairs of foreign nations has proved of great value in past times and ought to be strictly observed.

The policy inaugurated by my honored predecessor, President Grant, of submitting to arbitration grave questions in dispute between ourselves and foreign powers points to a new, and incomparably the best, instrumentality for the preservation of peace, and will, as I believe, become a beneficent example of the course to be pursued in similar emergencies by other nations.

If, unhappily, questions of difference should at any time during the period of my Administration arise between the United States and any foreign government, it will certainly be my disposition and my hope to aid in their settlement in the same peaceful and honorable way, thus securing to our country the great blessings of peace and mutual good offices with all the nations of the world.

Fellow-citizens, we have reached the close of a political contest marked by the excitement which usually attends the contests between great political parties whose members espouse and advocate with earnest faith their respective creeds. The circumstances were, perhaps, in no respect extraordinary save in the closeness and the consequent uncertainty of the result.

For the first time in the history of the country it has been deemed best, in view of the peculiar circumstances of the case, that the objections and questions in dispute with reference to the counting of the electoral votes should be referred to the decision of a tribunal appointed for this purpose.

That tribunal—established by law for this sole purpose; its members, all of them, men of long-established reputation for integrity and intelligence, and, with the exception of those who are also members of the supreme judiciary, chosen equally from both political parties; its deliberations enlightened by the research and the arguments of able counsel—was entitled to the fullest confidence of the American people. Its decisions have been patiently waited for, and accepted as legally conclusive by the general judgment of the public. For the present, opinion will widely vary as to the wisdom of the several conclusions announced by that tribunal. This is to be anticipated in every instance where matters of dispute are made the subject of arbitration under the forms of law. Human judgment is never unerring, and is rarely regarded as otherwise than wrong by the unsuccessful party in the contest.

The fact that two great political parties have in this way settled a dispute in regard to which good men differ as to the facts and the law no less than as to the proper course to be pursued in solving the question in controversy is an occasion for general rejoicing.

Upon one point there is entire unanimity in public sentiment—that conflicting claims to the Presidency must be amicably and peaceably adjusted, and that when so adjusted the general acquiescence of the nation ought surely to follow.

It has been reserved for a government of the people, where the right of suffrage is universal, to give to the world the first example in history of a great nation, in the midst of the struggle of opposing parties for power, hushing its party tumults to yield the issue of the contest to adjustment according to the forms of law.

Looking for the guidance of that Divine Hand by which the destinies

of nations and individuals are shaped, I call upon you, Senators, Representatives, judges, fellow-citizens, here and everywhere, to unite with me
in an earnest effort to secure to our country the blessings, not only of
material prosperity, but of justice, peace, and union—a union depending
not upon the constraint of force, but upon the loving devotion of a free
people; "and that all things may be so ordered and settled upon the
best and surest foundations that peace and happiness, truth and justice,
religion and piety, may be established among us for all generations."

MARCH 5, 1877.

PROCLAMATIONS.

BY THE PRESIDENT OF THE UNITED STATES OF AMERICA.

A PROCLAMATION.

Whereas the final adjournment of the Forty-fourth Congress without
making the usual appropriations for the support of the Army for the
fiscal year ending June 30, 1878, presents an extraordinary occasion
requiring the President to exercise the power vested in him by the Constitution to convene the Houses of Congress in anticipation of the day
fixed by law for their next meeting:

Now, therefore, I, Rutherford B. Hayes, President of the United States,
do, by virtue of the power to this end in me vested by the Constitution,
convene both Houses of Congress to assemble at their respective chambers at 12 o'clock noon on Monday, the 15th day of October next, then
and there to consider and determine such measures as in their wisdom
their duty and the welfare of the people may seem to demand.

In witness whereof I have hereunto set my hand and caused the seal
of the United States to be affixed.

[SEAL.]   Done at the city of Washington, this 5th day of May, A. D.
1877, and of the Independence of the United States of America
the one hundred and first.   R. B. HAYES.

By the President:
WM. M. EVARTS, *Secretary of State.*

BY THE PRESIDENT OF THE UNITED STATES OF AMERICA.

A PROCLAMATION.

Whereas it is provided in the Constitution of the United States that
the United States shall protect every State in this Union, on application
of the legislature, or of the executive (when the legislature can not be
convened), against domestic violence ; and

Whereas the governor of the State of West Virginia has represented
that domestic violence exists in said State at Martinsburg, and at various

other points along the line of the Baltimore and Ohio Railroad in said State, which the authorities of said State are unable to suppress; and

Whereas the laws of the United States require that in all cases of insurrection in any State or of obstruction to the laws thereof, whenever it may be necessary, in the judgment of the President, he shall forthwith, by proclamation, command such insurgents to disperse and retire peaceably to their respective abodes within a limited time:

Now, therefore, I, Rutherford B. Hayes, President of the United States, do hereby admonish all good citizens of the United States and all persons within the territory and jurisdiction of the United States against aiding, countenancing, abetting, or taking part in such unlawful proceedings; and I do hereby warn all persons engaged in or connected with said domestic violence and obstruction of the laws to disperse and retire peaceably to their respective abodes on or before 12 o'clock noon of the 19th day of July instant.

In testimony whereof I have hereunto set my hand and caused the seal of the United States to be affixed.

[SEAL.] Done at the city of Washington, this 18th day of July, A. D. 1877, and of the Independence of the United States of America the one hundred and second.

R. B. HAYES.

By the President:

F. W. SEWARD, *Acting Secretary of State.*

BY THE PRESIDENT OF THE UNITED STATES OF AMERICA.

A PROCLAMATION.

Whereas it is provided in the Constitution of the United States that the United States shall protect every State in this Union, on application of the legislature, or of the executive (when the legislature can not be convened), against domestic violence; and

Whereas the governor of the State of Maryland has represented that domestic violence exists in said State at Cumberland, and along the line of the Baltimore and Ohio Railroad in said State, which the authorities of said State are unable to suppress; and

Whereas the laws of the United States require that in all cases of insurrection in any State or of obstruction to the laws thereof, whenever, in the judgment of the President, it becomes necessary to use the military forces to suppress such insurrection or obstruction to the laws, he shall forthwith, by proclamation, command such insurgents to disperse and retire peaceably to their respective abodes within a limited time:

Now, therefore, I, Rutherford B. Hayes, President of the United States, do hereby admonish all good citizens of the United States and all persons within the territory and jurisdiction of the United States against aiding, countenancing, abetting, or taking part in such unlawful proceedings; and I do hereby warn all persons engaged in or connected with said domestic violence and obstruction of the laws to disperse and retire peaceably to their respective abodes on or before noon of the 22d day of July instant.

In testimony whereof I have hereunto set my hand and caused the seal of the United States to be affixed.

[SEAL.] Done ~ he city of Washington, this 21st day of July, A. D. 1877, and of the Independence of the United States of America the one hundred and second.

R. B. HAYES.

By the President:

WM. M. EVARTS,
Secretary of State.

BY THE PRESIDENT OF THE UNITED STATES OF AMERICA.

A PROCLAMATION.

Whereas it is provided in the Constitution of the United States that the United States shall protect every State in this Union, on application of the legislature, or of the executive (when the legislature can not be convened), against domestic violence; and

Whereas the governor of the State of Pennsylvania has represented that domestic violence exists in said State which the authorities of said State are unable to suppress; and

Whereas the laws of the United States require that in all cases of insurrection in any State or of obstruction to the laws thereof, whenever, in the judgment of the President, it becomes necessary to use the military forces to suppress such insurrection or obstruction to the laws, he shall forthwith, by proclamation, command such insurgents to disperse and retire peaceably to their respective abodes within a limited time:

Now, therefore, I, Rutherford B. Hayes, President of the United States, do hereby admonish all good citizens of the United States and all persons within the territory and jurisdiction of the United States against aiding, countenancing, abetting, or taking part in such unlawful proceedings; and I do hereby warn all persons engaged in or connected with said domestic violence and obstruction of the laws to disperse and retire peaceably to their respective abodes on or before 12 o'clock noon of the 24th day of July instant.

In testimony whereof I have hereunto set my hand and caused the seal of the United States to be affixed.

[SEAL.] Done at the city of Washington, this 23d day of July, A. D. 1877, and of the Independence of the United States of America the one hundred and second.

R. B. HAYES.

By the President:

WM. M. EVARTS,
Secretary of State.

EXECUTIVE ORDERS.

EXECUTIVE MANSION,
Washington, May 9, 1877.

SIR:* The President directs me to say that the several Departments of the Government will be closed on Wednesday, the 30th instant, to enable the employees to participate in the decoration of the graves of the soldiers who fell during the rebellion.

I am, sir, your obedient servant,

W. K. ROGERS,
Secretary.

EXECUTIVE MANSION,
Washington, May 26, 1877.

Hon. JOHN SHERMAN,
Secretary of the Treasury.

MY DEAR SIR: I have read the partial report of the commission appointed to examine the New York custom-house. I concur with the commission in their recommendations. It is my wish that the collection of the revenues should be free from partisan control, and organized on a strictly business basis, with the same guaranties for efficiency and fidelity in the selection of the chief and subordinate officers that would be required by a prudent merchant. Party leaders should have no more influence in appointments than other equally respectable citizens. No assessments for political purposes on officers or subordinates should be allowed. No useless officer or employee should be retained. No officer should be required or permitted to take part in the management of political organizations, caucuses, conventions, or election campaigns. Their right to vote and to express their views on public questions, either orally or through the press, is not denied, provided it does not interfere with the discharge of their official duties.

Respectfully,

R. B. HAYES.

EXECUTIVE MANSION,
Washington, June 22, 1877.

SIR:† I desire to call your attention to the following paragraph in a letter addressed by me to the Secretary of the Treasury on the conduct to be observed by officers of the General Government in relation to the elections:

No officer should be required or permitted to take part in the management of political organizations, caucuses, conventions, or election campaigns. Their right

---

*Addressed to the heads of the Executive Departments, etc.
†Addressed to Federal officers generally.

to vote and to express their views on public questions, either orally or through the press, is not denied, provided it does not interfere with the discharge of their official duties. No assessment for political purposes on officers or subordinates should be allowed.

This rule is applicable to every department of the civil service. It should be understood by every officer of the General Government that he is expected to conform his conduct to its requirements.

Very respectfully,

R. B. HAYES.

EXECUTIVE MANSION, *August 7, 1877.*

By virtue of authority conferred upon the President of the United States by the provisions of section 2132, Revised Statutes of the United States, as follows:

The President is authorized, whenever in his opinion the public interest may require the same, to prohibit the introduction of goods, or of any particular article, into the country belonging to any Indian tribe, and to direct all licenses to trade with such tribe to be revoked and all applications therefor to be rejected. No trader to any other tribe shall, so long as such prohibition may continue, trade with any Indians of or for the tribe against which such prohibition is issued—

the introduction into the Indian country, for the purpose of sale or exchange to or with Indians, of any breech-loading firearms, and of any special ammunition adapted to such arms, and the sale and exchange to Indians in the Indian country of any such arms or ammunition, is hereby prohibited; and it is hereby directed that all authority under any license to trade in such arms or ammunition is hereby revoked.

The introduction into the country or district occupied by any tribe of hostile Indians, for the purpose of sale or exchange to them, of arms or ammunition of any description, and the sale or exchange thereof to or with such Indians, is hereby prohibited; and it is hereby directed that all license to trade in arms or ammunition of any description with such tribe be revoked.

By virtue of section 2150, Revised Statutes, as follows:

The military forces of the United States may be employed in such manner and under such regulations as the President may direct—

*　　　*　　　*　　　*　　　*　　　*　　　*

Third. In preventing the introduction of persons and property into the Indian country contrary to law, which persons and property shall be proceeded against according to law.

*　　　*　　　*　　　*　　　*　　　*　　　*

all military commanders are hereby charged with the duty of assisting in the execution of the above order and of Executive order of November 23, 1876,* the provisions of which are extended to include all Indian country within the Territories of Idaho, Utah, and Washington and the States of Nevada and Oregon.

R. B. HAYES.

* See pp. 4352-4353.

SPECIAL SESSION MESSAGE.

WASHINGTON, *October 15, 1877.*

Fellow-Citizens of the Senate and House of Representatives:

The adjournment of the last Congress without making appropriations for the support of the Army for the present fiscal year has rendered necessary a suspension of payments to the officers and men of the sums due them for services rendered after the 30th day of June last. The Army exists by virtue of statutes which prescribe its numbers, regulate its organization and employment, and which fix the pay of its officers and men and declare their right to receive the same at stated periods. These statutes, however, do not authorize the payment of the troops in the absence of specific appropriations therefor. The Constitution has wisely provided that "no money shall be drawn from the Treasury but in consequence of appropriations made by law;" and it has also been declared by statute that "no department of the Government shall expend in any one fiscal year any sum in excess of appropriations made by Congress for that fiscal year." We have, therefore, an Army in service, authorized by law and entitled to be paid, but no funds available for that purpose.

It may also be said, as an additional incentive to prompt action by Congress, that since the commencement of the fiscal year the Army, though without pay, has been constantly and actively employed in arduous and dangerous service, in the performance of which both officers and men have discharged their duty with fidelity and courage and without complaint. These circumstances, in my judgment, constituted an extraordinary occasion requiring that Congress be convened in advance of the time prescribed by law for your meeting in regular session. The importance of speedy action upon this subject on the part of Congress is so manifest that I venture to suggest the propriety of making the necessary appropriations for the support of the Army for the current year at its present maximum numerical strength of 25,000 men, leaving for future consideration all questions relating to an increase or decrease of the number of enlisted men. In the event of the reduction of the Army by subsequent legislation during the fiscal year, the excess of the appropriation could not be expended; and in the event of its enlargement the additional sum required for the payment of the extra force could be provided in due time. It would be unjust to the troops now in service, and whose pay is already largely in arrears, if payment to them should be further postponed until after Congress shall have considered all the questions likely to arise in the effort to fix the proper limit to the strength of the Army.

Estimates of appropriations for the support of the military establishment for the fiscal year ending June 30, 1878, were transmitted to Congress by the former Secretary of the Treasury at the opening of its session in December last. These estimates, modified by the present Secretary so as to conform to present requirements, are now renewed, amounting to $32,436,764.98, and, having been transmitted to both Houses of Congress, are submitted for your consideration.

There is also required by the Navy Department $2,003,861.24. This sum is made up of $1,446,688.16 due to officers and enlisted men for the last quarter of the last fiscal year; $311,953.50 due for advances made by the fiscal agent of the Government in London for the support of the foreign service; $50,000 due to the naval-hospital fund; $150,000 due for arrearages of pay to officers, and $45,219.58 for the support of the Marine Corps.

There will also be needed an appropriation of $262,535.22 to defray the unsettled expenses of the United States courts for the fiscal year ending June 30 last, now due to attorneys, clerks, commissioners, and marshals, and for rent of court rooms, the support of prisoners, and other deficiencies.

A part of the building of the Interior Department was destroyed by fire on the 24th of last month. Some immediate repairs and temporary structures have in consequence become necessary, estimates for which will be transmitted to Congress immediately, and an appropriation of the requisite funds is respectfully recommended.

The Secretary of the Treasury will communicate to Congress, in connection with the estimates for the appropriations for the support of the Army for the current fiscal year, estimates for such other deficiencies in the different branches of the public service as require immediate action and can not without inconvenience be postponed until the regular session.

I take this opportunity also to invite your attention to the propriety of adopting at your present session the necessary legislation to enable the people of the United States to participate in the advantages of the International Exhibition of Agriculture, Industry, and the Fine Arts which is to be held at Paris in 1878, and in which this Government has been invited by the Government of France to take part.

This invitation was communicated to this Government in May, 1876, by the minister of France at this capital, and a copy thereof was submitted to the proper committees of Congress at its last session, but no action was taken upon the subject.

The Department of State has received many letters from various parts of the country expressing a desire to participate in the exhibition, and numerous applications of a similar nature have also been made at the United States legation at Paris.

The Department of State has also received official advice of the strong desire on the part of the French Government that the United States should participate in this enterprise, and space has hitherto been and still is reserved in the exhibition buildings for the use of exhibitors from the United States, to the exclusion of other parties who have been applicants therefor.

In order that our industries may be properly represented at the exhibition, an appropriation will be needed for the payment of salaries and expenses of commissioners, for the transportation of goods, and for other purposes in connection with the object in view; and as May next is the time fixed for the opening of the exhibition, if our citizens are to share the advantages of this international competition for the trade of other nations the necessity of immediate action is apparent.

To enable the United States to cooperate in the international exhibition which was held at Vienna in 1873, Congress then passed a joint resolution making an appropriation of $200,000 and authorizing the President to appoint a certain number of practical artisans and scientific men who should attend the exhibition and report their proceedings and observations to him. Provision was also made for the appointment of a number of honorary commissioners.

I have felt that prompt action by Congress in accepting the invitation of the Government of France is of so much interest to the people of this country and so suitable to the cordial relations between the Governments of the two countries that the subject might properly be presented for attention at your present session.

The Government of Sweden and Norway has addressed an official invitation to this Government to take part in the International Prison Congress to be held at Stockholm next year. The problem which the congress proposes to study—how to diminish crime—is one in which all civilized nations have an interest in common, and the congress of Stockholm seems likely to prove the most important convention ever held for the study of this grave question. Under authority of a joint resolution of Congress approved February 16, 1875, a commissioner was appointed by my predecessor to represent the United States upon that occasion, and the Prison Congress having been, at the earnest desire of the Swedish Government, postponed to 1878, his commission was renewed by me. An appropriation of $8,000 was made in the sundry civil act of 1875 to meet the expenses of the commissioner. I recommend the reappropriation of that sum for the same purpose, the former appropriation having been covered into the Treasury and being no longer available for the purpose without further action by Congress. The subject is brought to your attention at this time in view of circumstances which render it highly desirable that the commissioner should proceed to the discharge of his important duties immediately.

As the several acts of Congress providing for detailed reports from the different Departments of the Government require their submission at the beginning of the regular annual session, I defer until that time any further reference to subjects of public interest.

R. B. HAYES

SPECIAL MESSAGES.

EXECUTIVE MANSION,
Washington, D. C., October 17, 1877.

To the Senate and House of Representatives:

I have the honor to transmit herewith the report of a board of inquiry appointed by the Secretary of the Interior to examine into the causes of the fire which destroyed a part of the Interior Department building on the 24th of last month.

R. B. HAYES.

EXECUTIVE MANSION,
Washington, D. C., October 17, 1877.

To the Senate and House of Representatives:

I have the honor to transmit herewith a report of the Secretary of the Navy, setting forth the particulars with reference to the existing deficiencies in the Navy Department.

R. B. HAYES.

WASHINGTON, *November 12, 1877.*

To the House of Representatives:

In answer to the resolution of the House of Representatives of the 1st instant, I transmit herewith reports from the Secretary of State and the Secretary of War, with their accompanying papers.*

R. B. HAYES.

WASHINGTON, *November 12, 1877.*

To the House of Representatives:

In answer to the resolution of the House of Representatives of the 5th instant, I transmit herewith reports from the Secretary of State and the Secretary of the Treasury, with their accompanying documents.†

R. B. HAYES.

EXECUTIVE MANSION, *November 12, 1877.*

To the Senate of the United States:

In compliance with the resolution of the Senate of the 16th of October, 1877, I have the honor to transmit herewith a statement of the appropriations and expenditures by the Navy Department from the 4th of March, 1789, to June 30, 1876.

A similar statement for the War Department is being prepared as

---

* Correspondence relative to Mexican border troubles.

† Correspondence relative to the imposition of a differential duty of 50 cents per ton upon Spanish vessels entering ports of the United States.

rapidly as the limited clerical force in the Treasury Department will permit, and when completed will be transmitted to the Senate.

R. B. HAYES.

EXECUTIVE MANSION, *November 12, 1877.*
To the Senate of the United States:

In compliance with the resolution of the Senate of the 30th of October, 1877, I have the honor to transmit herewith a statement of the annual appropriations and expenditures for army and navy pensions, showing also the repayments, the amounts carried to the surplus fund, and the net expenditures under each appropriation from March 4, 1789, to June 30, 1876.

R. B. HAYES.

WASHINGTON, *November 14, 1877.*
To the Senate of the United States:

In answer to the resolution of the Senate of the 8th instant, I transmit herewith a report * from the Secretary of State.

R. B. HAYES.

WASHINGTON, D. C., *November 15, 1877.*
To the House of Representatives:

I transmit to the House of Representatives, in answer to its resolution of the 12th instant, a report † from the Secretary of State.

R. B. HAYES.

WASHINGTON, *November 20, 1877.*
To the House of Representatives:

In answer to a joint resolution of the House of Representatives of the 6th instant, requesting the opinions of the heads of the Departments respecting the obligatory use of the metrical system of weights and measures, I transmit herewith a report from the Secretary of State.

R. B. HAYES.

WASHINGTON, *November 27, 1877.*
To the Senate of the United States:

I transmit to the Senate, for its consideration with a view to ratification, a declaration between the United States and the Government of Her Majesty the Queen of the United Kingdom of Great Britain and Ireland, for the reciprocal protection of the marks of manufacture and trade in the two countries, signed on the 24th of October, 1877.

R. B. HAYES.

* Stating that the information relative to the forcible rescue of two prisoners from the jail of Starr County, Tex., by an armed band of Mexicans had been transmitted by the President to the House of Representatives on the 12th instant.

† Relating to the indemnity paid by Spain on account of the execution of General Ryan and others at Santiago de Cuba.

PROCLAMATION.

BY THE PRESIDENT OF THE UNITED STATES OF AMERICA.

A PROCLAMATION.

The completed circle of summer and winter, seedtime and harvest, has brought us to the accustomed season at which a religious people celebrates with praise and thanksgiving the enduring mercy of Almighty God. This devout and public confession of the constant dependence of man upon the divine favor for all the good gifts of life and health and peace and happiness, so early in our history made the habit of our people, finds in the survey of the past year new grounds for its joyful and grateful manifestation.

In all the blessings which depend upon benignant seasons, this has indeed been a memorable year. Over the wide territory of our country, with all its diversity of soil and climate and products, the earth has yielded a bountiful return to the labor of the husbandman. The health of the people has been blighted by no prevalent or widespread diseases. No great disasters of shipwreck upon our coasts or to our commerce on the seas have brought loss and hardship to merchants or mariners and clouded the happiness of the community with sympathetic sorrow.

In all that concerns our strength and peace and greatness as a nation; in all that touches the permanence and security of our Government and the beneficent institutions on which it rests; in all that affects the character and dispositions of our people and tests our capacity to enjoy and uphold the equal and free condition of society, now permanent and universal throughout the land, the experience of the last year is conspicuously marked by the protecting providence of God and is full of promise and hope for the coming generations.

Under a sense of these infinite obligations to the Great Ruler of Times and Seasons and Events, let us humbly ascribe it to our own faults and frailties if in any degree that perfect concord and happiness, peace and justice, which such great mercies should diffuse through the hearts and lives of our people do not altogether and always and everywhere prevail. Let us with one spirit and with one voice lift up praise and thanksgiving to God for His manifold goodness to our land, His manifest care for our nation.

Now, therefore, I, Rutherford B. Hayes, President of the United States, do appoint Thursday, the 29th day of November next, as a day of national thanksgiving and prayer; and I earnestly recommend that, withdrawing themselves from secular cares and labors, the people of the United States do meet together on that day in their respective places of worship, there to give thanks and praise to Almighty God for His mercies and to devoutly beseech their continuance.

In witness whereof I have hereunto set my hand and caused the seal of the United States to be affixed.

[SEAL.]   Done at the city of Washington, this 29th day of October, A. D. 1877, and of the Independence of the United States the one hundred and second.

R. B. HAYES.

By the President:

WM. M. EVARTS,
Secretary of State.

EXECUTIVE ORDER.

EXECUTIVE MANSION,
Washington, D. C., November 2, 1877.

I lament the sad occasion which makes it my duty to testify the public respect for the eminent citizen and distinguished statesman whose death yesterday at his home in Indianapolis has been made known to the people by telegraphic announcement.

The services of Oliver P. Morton to the nation in the difficult and responsible administration of the affairs of the State of Indiana as its governor at a critical juncture of the civil war can never be overvalued by his countrymen. His long service in the Senate has shown his great powers as a legislator and as a leader and chief counselor of the political party charged with the conduct of the Government during that period.

In all things and at all times he has been able, strenuous, and faithful in the public service, and his fame with his countrymen rests upon secure foundations.

The several Executive Departments will be closed on the day of his funeral, and appropriate honors should be paid to the memory of the deceased statesman by the whole nation.

R. B. HAYES.

FIRST ANNUAL MESSAGE.

DECEMBER 3, 1877.

Fellow-Citizens of the Senate and House of Representatives:

With devout gratitude to the bountiful Giver of All Good, I congratulate you that at the beginning of your first regular session you find our country blessed with health and peace and abundant harvests, and with encouraging prospects of an early return of general prosperity.

To complete and make permanent the pacification of the country continues to be, and until it is fully accomplished must remain, the most important of all our national interests. The earnest purpose of good citizens generally to unite their efforts in this endeavor is evident. It found decided expression in the resolutions announced in 1876 by the national conventions of the leading political parties of the country. There was a widespread apprehension that the momentous results in our progress as a nation marked by the recent amendments to the Constitution were in imminent jeopardy; that the good understanding which prompted their adoption, in the interest of a loyal devotion to the general welfare, might prove a barren truce, and that the two sections of the country, once engaged in civil strife, might be again almost as widely severed and disunited as they were when arrayed in arms against each other.

The course to be pursued, which, in my judgment, seemed wisest in the presence of this emergency, was plainly indicated in my inaugural address. It pointed to the time, which all our people desire to see, when a genuine love of our whole country and of all that concerns its true welfare shall supplant the destructive forces of the mutual animosity of races and of sectional hostility. Opinions have differed widely as to the measures best calculated to secure this great end. This was to be expected. The measures adopted by the Administration have been subjected to severe and varied criticism. Any course whatever which might have been entered upon would certainly have encountered distrust and opposition. These measures were, in my judgment, such as were most in harmony with the Constitution and with the genius of our people, and best adapted, under all the circumstances, to attain the end in view. Beneficent results, already apparent, prove that these endeavors are not to be regarded as a mere experiment, and should sustain and encourage us in our efforts. Already, in the brief period which has elapsed, the immediate effectiveness, no less than the justice, of the course pursued is demonstrated, and I have an abiding faith that time will furnish its ample vindication in the minds of the great majority of my fellow-citizens. The discontinuance of the use of the Army for the purpose of upholding local governments in two States of the Union was no less a constitutional duty and requirement, under the circumstances existing at the time, than it was a much-needed measure for the restoration of local self-government and the promotion of national harmony. The withdrawal of the troops from such employment was effected deliberately, and with solicitous care for the peace and good order of society and the protection of the property and persons and every right of all classes of citizens.

The results that have followed are indeed significant and encouraging. All apprehension of danger from remitting those States to local self-government is dispelled, and a most salutary change in the minds of the people has begun and is in progress in every part of that section of the country once the theater of unhappy civil strife, substituting for suspicion, distrust, and aversion, concord, friendship, and patriotic attachment to the Union. No unprejudiced mind will deny that the terrible and often fatal collisions which for several years have been of frequent occurrence and have agitated and alarmed the public mind have almost entirely ceased, and that a spirit of mutual forbearance and hearty national interest has succeeded. There has been a general reestablishment of order and of the orderly administration of justice. Instances of remaining lawlessness have become of rare occurrence; political turmoil and turbulence have disappeared; useful industries have been resumed; public credit in the Southern States has been greatly strengthened, and the encouraging benefits of a revival of commerce between the sections of the country lately embroiled in civil war are fully enjoyed. Such are some of the results already attained, upon which the country is to be congratulated. They are of such importance that we may with confidence patiently await the desired consummation that will surely come with the natural progress of events.

It may not be improper here to say that it should be our fixed and unalterable determination to protect by all available and proper means under the Constitution and the laws the lately emancipated race in the enjoyment of their rights and privileges; and I urge upon those to whom heretofore the colored people have sustained the relation of bondmen the wisdom and justice of humane and liberal local legislation with respect to their education and general welfare. A firm adherence to the laws, both national and State, as to the civil and political rights of the colored people, now advanced to full and equal citizenship; the immediate repression and sure punishment by the national and local authorities, within their respective jurisdictions, of every instance of lawlessness and violence toward them, is required for the security alike of both races, and is justly demanded by the public opinion of the country and the age. In this way the restoration of harmony and good will and the complete protection of every citizen in the full enjoyment of every constitutional right will surely be attained. Whatever authority rests with me to this end I shall not hesitate to put forth.

Whatever belongs to the power of Congress and the jurisdiction of the courts of the Union, they may confidently be relied upon to provide and perform; and to the legislatures, the courts, and the executive authorities of the several States I earnestly appeal to secure, by adequate, appropriate, and seasonable means, within their borders, these common and uniform rights of a united people which loves liberty, abhors oppression, and reveres justice. These objects are very dear to my heart. I shall continue most earnestly to strive for their attainment. The cordial cooperation of all classes, of all sections of the country and of both races, is required for this purpose; and with these blessings assured, and not otherwise, we may safely hope to hand down our free institutions of government unimpaired to the generations that will succeed us.

Among the other subjects of great and general importance to the people of this country, I can not be mistaken, I think, in regarding as preeminent the policy and measures which are designed to secure the restoration of the currency to that normal and healthful condition in which, by the resumption of specie payments, our internal trade and foreign commerce may be brought into harmony with the system of exchanges which is based upon the precious metals as the intrinsic money of the world. In the public judgment that this end should be sought and compassed as speedily and securely as the resources of the people and the wisdom of their Government can accomplish, there is a much greater degree of unanimity than is found to concur in the specific measures which will bring the country to this desired end or the rapidity of the steps by which it can be safely reached.

Upon a most anxious and deliberate examination, which I have felt it my duty to give to the subject, I am but the more confirmed in the opinion which I expressed in accepting the nomination for the Presidency, and again upon my inauguration, that the policy of resumption should be pursued by every suitable means, and that no legislation would be wise that should disparage the importance or retard the attainment of that result. I have no disposition, and certainly no right, to question the sincerity or the intelligence of opposing opinions, and would neither conceal nor undervalue the considerable difficulties, and even occasional distresses, which may attend the progress of the nation toward this primary condition to its general and permanent prosperity. I must, however, adhere to my most earnest conviction that any wavering in purpose or unsteadiness in methods, so far from avoiding or reducing the inconvenience inseparable from the transition from an irredeemable to a redeemable paper currency, would only tend to increased and prolonged disturbance in values, and unless retrieved must end in serious disorder, dishonor, and disaster in the financial affairs of the Government and of the people.

The mischiefs which I apprehend and urgently deprecate are confined to no class of the people, indeed, but seem to me most certainly to threaten the industrious masses, whether their occupations are of skilled or common labor. To them, it seems to me, it is of prime importance that their labor should be compensated in money which is itself fixed in exchangeable value by being irrevocably measured by the labor necessary to its production. This permanent quality of the money of the people is sought for, and can only be gained by the resumption of specie payments. The rich, the speculative, the operating, the money-dealing classes may not always feel the mischiefs of, or may find casual profits in, a variable currency, but the misfortunes of such a currency to those who are paid salaries or wages are inevitable and remediless.

Closely connected with this general subject of the resumption of specie payments is one of subordinate, but still of grave, importance; I mean the readjustment of our coinage system by the renewal of the silver dollar as an element in our specie currency, endowed by legislation with the quality of legal tender to a greater or less extent.

As there is no doubt of the power of Congress under the Constitution "to coin money and regulate the value thereof," and as this power covers the whole range of authority applicable to the metal, the rated value and the legal-tender quality which shall be adopted for the coinage, the considerations which should induce or discourage a particular measure connected with the coinage, belong clearly to the province of legislative discretion and of public expediency. Without intruding upon this province of legislation in the least, I have yet thought the subject of such critical importance, in the actual condition of our affairs, as to present an occasion for the exercise of the duty imposed by the Constitution on the President of recommending to the consideration of Congress "such measures as he shall judge necessary and expedient."

Holding the opinion, as I do, that neither the interests of the Government nor of the people of the United States would be promoted by disparaging silver as one of the two precious metals which furnish the coinage of the world, and that legislation which looks to maintaining the volume of intrinsic money to as full a measure of both metals as their relative commercial values will permit would be neither unjust nor inexpedient, I must ask your indulgence to a brief and definite statement of certain essential features in any such legislative measure which I feel it my duty to recommend.

I do not propose to enter the debate, represented on both sides by such able disputants in Congress and before the people and in the press, as to the extent to which the legislation of any one nation can control this question, even within its own borders, against the unwritten laws of trade or the positive laws of other governments. The wisdom of Congress in shaping any particular law that may be presented for my approval may wholly supersede the necessity of my entering into these considerations, and I willingly avoid either vague or intricate inquiries. It is only certain plain and practical traits of such legislation that I desire to recommend to your attention.

In any legislation providing for a silver coinage, regulating its value, and imparting to it the quality of legal tender, it seems to me of great importance that Congress should not lose sight of its action as operating in a twofold capacity and in two distinct directions. If the United States Government were free from a public debt, its legislative dealing with the question of silver coinage would be purely sovereign and governmental, under no restraints but those of constitutional power and the public good as affected by the proposed legislation. But in the actual circumstances of the nation, with a vast public debt distributed very widely among our own citizens and held in great amounts also abroad, the nature of the silver-coinage measure, as affecting this relation of the Government to the holders of the public debt, becomes an element, in any proposed legislation, of the highest concern. The obligation of the public faith transcends all questions of profit or public advantage otherwise. Its unquestionable maintenance is the dictate as well of the highest expediency as of the most necessary duty, and will ever be carefully guarded by Congress and people alike.

The public debt of the United States to the amount of $729,000,000 bears interest at the rate of 6 per cent, and $708,000,000 at the rate of 5 per cent, and the only way in which the country can be relieved from the payment of these high rates of interest is by advantageously refunding the indebtedness. Whether the debt is ultimately paid in gold or in silver coin is of but little moment compared with the possible reduction of interest one-third by refunding it at such reduced rate. If the United States had the unquestioned right to pay its bonds in silver coin, the little benefit from that process would be greatly overbalanced by the injurious effect of such payment if made or proposed against the honest convictions of the public creditors.

All the bonds that have been issued since February 12, 1873, when gold became the only unlimited legal-tender metallic currency of the country, are justly payable in gold coin or in coin of equal value. During the time of these issues the only dollar that could be or was received by the Government in exchange for bonds was the gold dollar. To require the public creditors to take in repayment any dollar of less commercial value would be regarded by them as a repudiation of the full obligation assumed. The bonds issued prior to 1873 were issued at a time when the gold dollar was the only coin in circulation or contemplated by either the Government or the holders of the bonds as the coin in which they were to be paid. It is far better to pay these bonds in that coin than to seem to take advantage of the unforeseen fall in silver bullion to pay in a new issue of silver coin thus made so much less valuable. The power of the United States to coin money and to regulate the value thereof ought never to be exercised for the purpose of enabling the Government to pay its obligations in a coin of less value than that contemplated by the parties when the bonds were issued. Any attempt to pay the national indebtedness in a coinage of less commercial value than the money of the world would involve a violation of the public faith and work irreparable injury to the public credit.

It was the great merit of the act of March, 1869, in strengthening the public credit, that it removed all doubt as to the purpose of the United States to pay their bonded debt in coin. That act was accepted as a pledge of public faith. The Government has derived great benefit from it in the progress thus far made in refunding the public debt at low rates of interest. An adherence to the wise and just policy of an exact observance of the public faith will enable the Government rapidly to reduce the burden of interest on the national debt to an amount exceeding

$20,000,000 per annum, and effect an aggregate saving to the United States of more than $300,000,000 before the bonds can be fully paid.

In adapting the new silver coinage to the ordinary uses of currency in the everyday transactions of life and prescribing the quality of legal tender to be assigned to it, a consideration of the first importance should be so to adjust the ratio between the silver and the gold coinage, which now constitutes our specie currency, as to accomplish the desired end of maintaining the circulation of the two metallic currencies and keeping up the volume of the two precious metals as our intrinsic money. It is a mixed question, for scientific reasoning and historical experience to determine, how far and by what methods a practical equilibrium can be maintained which will keep both metals in circulation in their appropriate spheres of common use.

An absolute equality of commercial value, free from disturbing fluctuations, is hardly attainable, and without it an unlimited legal tender for private transactions assigned to both metals would irresistibly tend to drive out of circulation the dearer coinage and disappoint the principal object proposed by the legislation in view. I apprehend, therefore, that the two conditions of a near approach to equality of commercial value between the gold and silver coinage of the same denomination and of a limitation of the amounts for which the silver coinage is to be a legal tender are essential to maintaining both in circulation. If these conditions can be successfully observed, the issue from the mint of silver dollars would afford material assistance to the community in the transition to redeemable paper money, and would facilitate the resumption of specie payment and its permanent establishment. Without these conditions I fear that only mischief and misfortune would flow from a coinage of silver dollars with the quality of unlimited legal tender, even in private transactions.

Any expectation of temporary ease from an issue of silver coinage to pass as a legal tender at a rate materially above its commercial value is, I am persuaded, a delusion. Nor can I think that there is any substantial distinction between an original issue of silver dollars at a nominal value materially above their commercial value and the restoration of the silver dollar at a rate which once was, but has ceased to be, its commercial value. Certainly the issue of our gold coinage, reduced in weight materially below its legal-tender value, would not be any the less a present debasement of the coinage by reason of its equaling, or even exceeding, in weight a gold coinage which at some past time had been commercially equal to the legal-tender value assigned to the new issue.

In recommending that the regulation of any silver coinage which may be authorized by Congress should observe these conditions of commercial value and limited legal tender, I am governed by the feeling that every possible increase should be given to the volume of metallic money which can be kept in circulation, and thereby every possible aid afforded to the people in the process of resuming specie payments. It is because of my firm conviction that a disregard of these conditions would frustrate the good results which are desired from the proposed coinage, and embarrass with new elements of confusion and uncertainty the business of the country, that I urge upon your attention these considerations.

I respectfully recommend to Congress that in any legislation providing for a silver coinage and imparting to it the quality of legal tender there be impressed upon the measure a firm provision exempting the public debt heretofore issued and now outstanding from payment, either of principal or interest, in any coinage of less commercial value than the present gold coinage of the country.

The organization of the civil service of the country has for a number of years attracted more and more of the public attention. So general has become the opinion that the methods of admission to it and the conditions of remaining in it are unsound that both the great political parties have agreed in the most explicit declarations of the necessity of reform and in the most emphatic demands for it. I have fully believed these declarations and demands to be the expression of a sincere conviction of the intelligent masses of the people upon the subject, and that they should be recognized and followed by earnest and prompt action on the part of the legislative and executive departments of the Government, in pursuance of the purpose indicated.

Before my accession to office I endeavored to have my own views distinctly understood, and upon my inauguration my accord with the public opinion was stated in terms believed to be plain and unambiguous. My experience in the executive duties has strongly confirmed the belief in the great advantage the country would find in observing strictly the plan of the Constitution, which imposes upon the Executive the sole duty and responsibility of the selection of those Federal officers who by law are appointed, not elected, and which in like manner assigns to the Senate the complete right to advise and consent to or to reject the nominations so made, whilst the House of Representatives stands as the public censor of the performance of official duties, with the prerogative of investigation and prosecution in all cases of dereliction. The blemishes and imperfections in the civil service may, as I think, be traced in most cases to a practical confusion of the duties assigned to the several Departments of the Government. My purpose in this respect has been to return to the system established by the fundamental law, and to do this with the heartiest cooperation and most cordial understanding with the Senate and House of Representatives.

The practical difficulties in the selection of numerous officers for posts of widely varying responsibilities and duties are acknowledged to be very great. No system can be expected to secure absolute freedom from mistakes, and the beginning of any attempted change of custom is quite likely to be more embarrassed in this respect than any subsequent period.

It is here that the Constitution seems to me to prove its claim to the great wisdom accorded to it. It gives to the Executive the assistance of the knowledge and experience of the Senate, which, when acting upon nominations as to which they may be disinterested and impartial judges, secures as strong a guaranty of freedom from errors of importance as is perhaps possible in human affairs.

In addition to this, I recognize the public advantage of making all nominations, as nearly as possible, impersonal, in the sense of being free from mere caprice or favor in the selection; and in those offices in which special training is of greatly increased value I believe such a rule as to the tenure of office should obtain as may induce men of proper qualifications to apply themselves industriously to the task of becoming proficients. Bearing these things in mind, I have endeavored to reduce the number of changes in subordinate places usually made upon the change of the general administration, and shall most heartily cooperate with Congress in the better systematizing of such methods and rules of admission to the public service and of promotion within it as may promise to be most successful in making thorough competency, efficiency, and character the decisive tests in these matters.

I ask the renewed attention of Congress to what has already been done by the Civil Service Commission, appointed, in pursuance of an act of Congress, by my predecessor, to prepare and revise civil-service rules. In regard to much of the departmental service, especially at Washington, it may be difficult to organize a better system than that which has thus been provided, and it is now being used to a considerable extent under my direction. The Commission has still a legal existence, although for several years no appropriation has been made for defraying its expenses. Believing that this Commission has rendered valuable service and will be a most useful agency in improving the administration of the civil service, I respectfully recommend that a suitable appropriation, to be immediately available, be made to enable it to continue its labors.

It is my purpose to transmit to Congress as early as practicable a report by the chairman of the Commission, and to ask your attention to such measures on this subject as in my opinion will further promote the improvement of the civil service.

During the past year the United States have continued to maintain peaceful relations with foreign powers.

The outbreak of war between Russia and Turkey, though at one time attended by grave apprehension as to its effect upon other European nations, has had no tendency to disturb the amicable relations existing between the United States and each of the two contending powers. An attitude of just and impartial neutrality has been preserved, and I am gratified to state that in the midst of their hostilities both the Russian and the Turkish Governments have shown an earnest disposition to adhere to the obligations of all treaties with the United States and to give due regard to the rights of American citizens.

By the terms of the treaty defining the rights, immunities, and privileges of consuls, between Italy and the United States, ratified in 1868, either Government may, after the lapse of ten years, terminate the existence of the treaty by giving twelve months' notice of its intention. The Government of Italy, availing itself of this faculty, has now given the required notice, and the treaty will accordingly end on the 17th of September, 1878. It is understood, however, that the Italian Government wishes to renew it in its general scope, desiring only certain modifications in some of its articles. In this disposition I concur, and shall hope that no serious obstacles may intervene to prevent or delay the negotiation of a satisfactory treaty.

Numerous questions in regard to passports, naturalization, and exemption from military service have continued to arise in cases of emigrants from Germany who have returned to their native country. The provisions of the treaty of February 22, 1868, however, have proved to be so ample and so judicious that the legation of the United States at Berlin has been able to adjust all claims arising under it, not only without detriment to the amicable relations existing between the two Governments, but, it is believed, without injury or injustice to any duly naturalized American citizen. It is desirable that the treaty originally made with the North German Union in 1868 should now be extended so as to apply equally to all the States of the Empire of Germany.

The invitation of the Government of France to participate in the Exposition of the Products of Agriculture, Industry, and the Fine Arts to be held at Paris during the coming year was submitted for your consideration at the extra session. It is not doubted that its acceptance by the United States, and a well-selected exhibition of the products of American industry on that occasion, will tend to stimulate international commerce and emigration, as well as to promote the traditional friendship between the two countries.

A question arose some time since as to the proper meaning of the extradition articles of the treaty of 1842 between the United States and Great Britain. Both Governments, however, are now in accord in the belief that the question is not one that should be allowed to frustrate the ends of justice or to disturb the friendship between the two nations. No serious difficulty has arisen in accomplishing the extradition of criminals when necessary. It is probable that all points of disagreement will in due time be settled, and, if need be, more explicit declarations be made in a new treaty.

The Fishery Commission under Articles XVIII to XXV of the treaty of Washington has concluded its session at Halifax. The result of the deliberations of the commission, as made public by the commissioners, will be communicated to Congress.

A treaty for the protection of trade-marks has been negotiated with Great Britain, which has been submitted to the Senate for its consideration.

The revolution which recently occurred in Mexico was followed by the accession of the successful party to power and the installation of its chief,

General Porfirio Diaz, in the Presidential office. It has been the custom of the United States, when such changes of government have heretofore occurred in Mexico, to recognize and enter into official relations with the *de facto* government as soon as it should appear to have the approval of the Mexican people and should manifest a disposition to adhere to the obligations of treaties and international friendship. In the present case such official recognition has been deferred by the occurrences on the Rio Grande border, the records of which have been already communicated to each House of Congress in answer to their respective resolutions of inquiry. Assurances have been received that the authorities at the seat of the Mexican Government have both the disposition and the power to prevent and punish such unlawful invasions and depredations. It is earnestly to be hoped that events may prove these assurances to be well founded. The best interests of both countries require the maintenance of peace upon the border and the development of commerce between the two Republics.

It is gratifying to add that this temporary interruption of official relations has not prevented due attention by the representatives of the United States in Mexico to the protection of American citizens, so far as practicable; nor has it interfered with the prompt payment of the amounts due from Mexico to the United States under the treaty of July 4, 1868, and the awards of the joint commission. While I do not anticipate an interruption of friendly relations with Mexico, yet I can not but look with some solicitude upon a continuance of border disorders as exposing the two countries to initiations of popular feeling and mischances of action which are naturally unfavorable to complete amity. Firmly determined that nothing shall be wanting on my part to promote a good understanding between the two nations, I yet must ask the attention of Congress to the actual occurrences on the border, that the lives and property of our citizens may be adequately protected and peace preserved.

Another year has passed without bringing to a close the protracted contest between the Spanish Government and the insurrection in the island of Cuba. While the United States have sedulously abstained from any intervention in this contest, it is impossible not to feel that it is attended with incidents affecting the rights and interests of American citizens. Apart from the effect of the hostilities upon trade between the United States and Cuba, their progress is inevitably accompanied by complaints, having more or less foundation, of searches, arrests, embargoes, and oppressive taxes upon the property of American residents, and of unprovoked interference with American vessels and commerce. It is due to the Government of Spain to say that during the past year it has promptly disavowed and offered reparation for any unauthorized acts of unduly zealous subordinates whenever such acts have been brought to its attention. Nevertheless, such occurrences can not but tend to excite feelings of annoyance, suspicion, and resentment, which are greatly to be deprecated, between the respective subjects and citizens of two friendly powers.

Much delay (consequent upon accusations of fraud in some of the awards) has occurred in respect to the distribution of the limited amounts received from Venezuela under the treaty of April 25, 1866, applicable to the awards of the joint commission created by that treaty. So long as these matters are pending in Congress the Executive can not assume either to pass upon the questions presented or to distribute the fund received. It is eminently desirable that definite legislative action should be taken, either affirming the awards to be final or providing some method for reexamination of the claims. Our relations with the Republics of Central and South America and with the Empire of Brazil have continued without serious change, further than the temporary interruption of diplomatic intercourse with Venezuela and with Guatemala. Amicable relations have already been fully restored with Venezuela, and it is not doubted that all grounds of misunderstanding with Guatemala will speedily be removed. From all these countries there are favorable indications of a disposition on the part of their Governments and people to reciprocate our efforts in the direction of increased commercial intercourse.

The Government of the Samoan Islands has sent an envoy, in the person of its secretary of state, to invite the Government of the United States to recognize and protect their independence, to establish commercial relations with their people, and to assist them in their steps toward regulated and responsible government. The inhabitants of these islands, having made considerable progress in Christian civilization and the development of trade, are doubtful of their ability to maintain peace and independence without the aid of some stronger power. The subject is deemed worthy of respectful attention, and the claims upon our assistance by this distant community will be carefully considered.

The long commercial depression in the United States has directed attention to the subject of the possible increase of our foreign trade and the methods for its development, not only with Europe, but with other countries, and especially with the States and sovereignties of the Western Hemisphere. Instructions from the Department of State were issued to the various diplomatic and consular officers of the Government, asking them to devote attention to the question of methods by which trade between the respective countries of their official residence and the United States could be most judiciously fostered. In obedience to these instructions, examinations and reports upon this subject have been made by many of these officers and transmitted to the Department, and the same are submitted to the consideration of Congress.

The annual report of the Secretary of the Treasury on the state of the finances presents important questions for the action of Congress, upon some of which I have already remarked.

The revenues of the Government during the fiscal year ending June 30, 1877, were $269,000,586.62; the total expenditures for the same period were $238,660,008.93, leaving a surplus revenue of $30,340,-577.69. This has substantially supplied the requirements of the sinking fund for that year. The estimated revenues of the current fiscal year are $265,500,000, and the estimated expenditures for the same period are $232,430,643.72. If these estimates prove to be correct, there will be a surplus revenue of $33,069,356.28—an amount nearly sufficient for the sinking fund for that year. The estimated revenues for the next fiscal year are $269,250,000. It appears from the report that during the last fiscal year the revenues of the Government, compared with the previous year, have largely decreased. This decrease, amounting to the sum of $18,481,452.54, was mainly in customs duties, caused partly by a large falling off of the amount of imported dutiable goods and partly by the general fall of prices in the markets of production of such articles as pay *ad valorem* taxes.

While this is felt injuriously in the diminution of the revenue, it has been accompanied with a very large increase of exportations. The total exports during the last fiscal year, including coin, have been $658,637,457, and the imports have been $492,097,540, leaving a balance of trade in favor of the United States amounting to the sum of $166,539,917, the beneficial effects of which extend to all branches of business.

The estimated revenue for the next fiscal year will impose upon Congress the duty of strictly limiting appropriations, including the requisite sum for the maintenance of the sinking fund, within the aggregate estimated receipts.

While the aggregate of taxes should not be increased, amendments might be made to the revenue laws that would, without diminishing the revenue, relieve the people from unnecessary burdens. A tax on tea and coffee is shown by the experience not only of our own country, but of other countries, to be easily collected, without loss by undervaluation or fraud, and largely borne in the country of production. A tax of 10 cents a pound on tea and 2 cents a pound on coffee would produce a revenue exceeding $12,000,000, and thus enable Congress to repeal a multitude of annoying taxes yielding a revenue not exceeding that sum. The internal-revenue system grew out of the necessities of the war, and most of the legislation imposing taxes upon domestic products under this system has been repealed. By the substitution of a tax on tea and coffee all forms of internal taxation may be repealed, except that on whisky, spirits, tobacco, and beer. Attention is also called to the necessity of enacting more vigorous laws for the protection of the revenue and for the punishment of frauds and smuggling. This can best be done by judicious provisions that will induce the disclosure of attempted fraud by undervaluation and smuggling. All revenue laws should be simple in their provisions and easily understood. So far as practicable, the tates of taxation should be in the form of specific duties, and not *ad valorem*, requiring the judgment of experienced men to ascertain values and exposing the revenue to the temptation of fraud.

My attention has been called during the recess of Congress to abuses existing in the collection of the customs, and strenuous efforts have been made for their correction by Executive orders. The recommendations submitted to the Secretary of the Treasury by a commission appointed to examine into the collection of customs duties at the port of New York contain many suggestions for the modification of the customs laws, to which the attention of Congress is invited.

It is matter of congratulation that notwithstanding the severe burdens caused by the war the public faith with all creditors has been preserved, and that as the result of this policy the public credit has continuously advanced and our public securities are regarded with the highest favor in the markets of the world. I trust that no act of the Government will cast a shadow upon its credit.

The progress of refunding the public debt has been rapid and satisfactory. Under the contract existing when I entered upon the discharge of the duties of my office, bonds bearing interest at the rate of 4½ per cent were being rapidly sold, and within three months the aggregate sales of these bonds had reached the sum of $200,000,000. With my sanction the Secretary of the Treasury entered into a new contract for the sale of 4 per cent bonds, and within thirty days after the popular subscription for such bonds was opened subscriptions were had amounting to $75,496,550, which were paid for within ninety days after the date of subscription. By this process, within but little more than one year, the annual interest on the public debt was reduced in the sum of $3,775,000.

I recommended that suitable provision be made to enable the people to easily convert their savings into Government securities, as the best mode in which small savings may be well secured and yield a moderate interest. It is an object of public policy to retain among our own people the securities of the United States. In this way our country is guarded against their sudden return from foreign countries, caused by war or other disturbances beyond our limits.

The commerce of the United States with foreign nations, and especially the export of domestic productions, has of late years largely increased; but the greater portion of this trade is conducted in foreign vessels. The importance of enlarging our foreign trade, and especially by direct and speedy interchange with countries on this continent, can not be overestimated; and it is a matter of great moment that our own shipping interest should receive, to the utmost practical extent, the benefit of our commerce with other lands. These considerations are forcibly urged by all the large commercial cities of the country, and public attention is generally and wisely attracted to the solution of the problems they present. It is not doubted that Congress will take them up in the broadest spirit of liberality and respond to the public demand by practical legislation upon this important subject.

The report of the Secretary of War shows that the Army has been actively employed during the year, and has rendered very important service in suppressing hostilities in the Indian country and in preserving peace and protecting life and property in the interior as well as along the Mexican border. A long and arduous campaign has been prosecuted, with final complete success, against a portion of the Nez Percé tribe of Indians. A full account of this campaign will be found in the report of the General of the Army. It will be seen that in its course several severe battles were fought, in which a number of gallant officers and men lost their lives. I join with the Secretary of War and the General of the Army in awarding to the officers and men employed in the long and toilsome pursuit and in the final capture of these Indians the honor and praise which are so justly their due.

The very serious riots which occurred in several of the States in July last rendered necessary the employment of a considerable portion of the Army to preserve the peace and maintain order. In the States of West Virginia, Maryland, Pennsylvania, and Illinois these disturbances were so formidable as to defy the local and State authorities, and the National Executive was called upon, in the mode provided by the Constitution and laws, to furnish military aid. I am gratified to be able to state that the troops sent in response to these calls for aid in the suppression of domestic violence were able, by the influence of their presence in the disturbed regions, to preserve the peace and restore order without the use of force. In the discharge of this delicate and important duty both officers and men acted with great prudence and courage, and for their services deserve the thanks of the country.

Disturbances along the Rio Grande in Texas, to which I have already referred, have rendered necessary the constant employment of a military force in that vicinity. A full report of all recent military operations in that quarter has been transmitted to the House of Representatives in answer to a resolution of that body, and it will therefore not be necessary to enter into details. I regret to say that these lawless incursions into our territory by armed bands from the Mexican side of the line, for the purpose of robbery, have been of frequent occurrence, and in spite of the most vigilant efforts of the commander of our forces the marauders have generally succeeded in escaping into Mexico with their plunder. In May last I gave orders for the exercise of the utmost vigilance on the part of our troops for the suppression of these raids and the punishment of the guilty parties, as well as the recapture of property stolen by them. General Ord, commanding in Texas, was directed to invite the cooperation of the Mexican authorities in efforts to this end, and to assure them that I was anxious to avoid giving the least offense to Mexico. At the

RAILROAD STRIKE SCENES

RAILROAD STRIKE SCENES

The drawings on the other side, depicting incidents in the railroad strike of 1877, vividly recall to mind the numerous similar scenes which have been enacted since then. The reader who desires to familiarize himself with all phases of the labor question could find no higher source of information than the Presidents of the United States. The great majority of them were born in poverty and obscurity, and by merit hewed their way to fame. Not unmindful of the days when their own hands guided the plow, held the tailor's needle, rowed the flatboat, or drove the tow-path mule, they have endeavored to do exact justice to the laboring man. At the same time they have considered the interests of the whole country in their relation to the interests of the laborer, and have frankly and fully analyzed the matter in their messages to the American people. Presidents Roosevelt and Taft have both devoted a great deal of space to labor subjects, the latter's discussion of the boycott and injunction being particularly thorough and judicial. The use of United States troops or militia in the suppression of riots, as shown in two of the panels, is another phase which has received close attention, from Cleveland especially. See "Army," paragraph headed "Militia," in the encyclopedic index in volume eleven. The encyclopedic index (volume eleven) contains many articles regarding labor topics, among them "Arbitration," "Labor," "Boycott," "Injunction." For references to presidential utterances concerning it, see "Labor."

same time, he was directed to give notice of my determination to put an end to the invasion of our territory by lawless bands intent upon the plunder of our peaceful citizens, even if the effectual punishment of the outlaws should make the crossing of the border by our troops in their pursuit necessary. It is believed that this policy has had the effect to check somewhat these depredations, and that with a considerable increase of our force upon that frontier and the establishment of several additional military posts along the Rio Grande, so as more effectually to guard that extensive border, peace may be preserved and the lives and property of our citizens in Texas fully protected.

Prior to the 1st day of July last the Army was, in accordance with law, reduced to the maximum of 25,000 enlisted men, being a reduction of 2,500 below the force previously authorized. This reduction was made, as required by law, entirely from the infantry and artillery branches of the service, without any reduction of the cavalry. Under the law as it now stands it is necessary that the cavalry regiments be recruited to 100 men in each company for service on the Mexican and Indian frontiers. The necessary effect of this legislation is to reduce the infantry and artillery arms of the service below the number required for efficiency, and I concur with the Secretary of War in recommending that authority be given to recruit all companies of infantry to at least 50 men and all batteries of artillery to at least 75 men, with the power, in case of emergency, to increase the former to 100 and the latter to 122 men each.

I invite your special attention to the following recommendations of the Secretary of War:

First. That provision be made for supplying to the Army a more abundant and better supply of reading matter.

Second. That early action be taken by Congress looking to a complete revision and republication of the Army Regulations.

Third. That section 1258 of the Revised Statutes, limiting the number of officers on the retired list, be repealed.

Fourth. That the claims arising under the act of July 4, 1864, for supplies taken by the Army during the war, be taken from the offices of the Quartermaster and Commissary Generals and transferred to the Southern Claims Commission, or some other tribunal having more time and better facilities for their prompt investigation and decision than are possessed by these officers.

Fifth. That Congress provide for an annuity fund for the families of deceased soldiers, as recommended by the Paymaster-General of the Army.

The report of the Secretary of the Navy shows that we have six squadrons now engaged in the protection of our foreign commerce and other duties pertaining to the naval service. The condition and operations of the Department are also shown. The total expenditures for the fiscal year ending June 30, 1877, were $16,077,974.54. There are unpaid claims against the Department chargeable to the last year, which are presented to the consideration of Congress by the report of the Secretary. The estimates for the fiscal year commencing July 1, 1878, are $16,233,234.40, exclusive of the sum of $2,314,231 submitted for new buildings, repairs, and improvements at the several navy-yards. The appropriations for the present fiscal year, commencing July 1, 1877, are $13,592,932.90. The amount drawn from the Treasury from July 1 to November 1, 1877, is $5,343,037.40, of which there is estimated to be yet available $1,029,528.30, showing the amount of actual expenditure during the first four months of the present fiscal year to have been $4,313,509.10.

The report of the Postmaster-General contains a full and clear statement of the operations and condition of the Post-Office Department. The ordinary revenues of the Department for the fiscal year ending June 30, 1877, including receipts from the money-order business and from official stamps and stamped envelopes, amounted to the sum of $27,531,585.26. The additional sum of $7,013,000 was realized from appropriations from the general Treasury for various purposes, making the receipts from all sources $34,544,885.26. The total expenditures during the fiscal year amounted to $33,486,322.44, leaving an excess of total receipts over total expenditures of $1,058,562.82, and an excess of total expenditures over ordinary receipts of $5,954,737.18. Deducting from the total receipts the sum of $63,261.84, received from international money orders of the preceding fiscal year, and deducting from the total expenditures the sum of $1,163,818.20, paid on liabilities incurred in previous fiscal years, the expenditures and receipts appertaining, to the business of the last fiscal year were as follows:

Expenditures..	$32,322,504.24
Receipts (ordinary, from money-order business and from official postage stamps)..	27,468,323.42
Excess of expenditures	4,854,180.82

The ordinary revenues of the Post-Office Department for the year ending June 30, 1879, are estimated at an increase of 3 per cent over those of 1877, making $29,034,098.28, and the expenditures for the same year are estimated at $36,427,771, leaving an estimated deficiency for the year 1879 of $7,393,672.72. The additional legislation recommended by the Postmaster-General for improvements of the mail service and to protect the postal revenues from the abuses practiced under existing laws is respectfully commended to the careful consideration of Congress.

The report of the Attorney-General contains several suggestions as to the administration of justice, to which I invite your attention. The pressure of business in the Supreme Court and in certain circuit courts of the United States is now such that serious delays, to the great injury, and even oppression, of suitors, occur, and a remedy should be sought for this condition of affairs. Whether it will be found in the plan briefly sketched in the report, of increasing the number of judges of the circuit courts, and, by means of this addition to the judicial force, of creating an intermediate court of errors and appeals, or whether some other mode can be devised for obviating the difficulties which now exist, I leave to your mature consideration.

The present condition of the Indian tribes in the territory of the United States and our relations with them are fully set forth in the reports of the Secretary of the Interior and the Commissioner of Indian Affairs. After a series of most deplorable conflicts—the successful termination of which, while reflecting honor upon the brave soldiers who accomplished it, can not lessen our regret at their occurrence—we are now at peace with all the Indian tribes within our borders. To preserve that peace by a just and humane policy will be the object of my earnest endeavors. Whatever may be said of their character and savage propensities, of the difficulties of introducing among them the habits of civilized life, and of the obstacles they have offered to the progress of settlement and enterprise in certain parts of the country, the Indians are certainly entitled to our sympathy and to a conscientious respect on our part for their claims upon our sense of justice. They were the aboriginal occupants of the land we now possess. They have been driven from place to place. The purchase money paid to them in some cases for what they called their own has still left them poor. In many instances, when they had settled down upon land assigned to them by compact and begun to support themselves by their own labor, they were rudely jostled off and thrust into the wilderness again. Many, if not most, of our Indian wars have had their origin in broken promises and acts of injustice upon our part, and the advance of the Indians in civilization has been slow because the treatment they received did not permit it to be faster and more general. We can not expect them to improve and to follow our guidance unless we keep faith with them in respecting the rights they possess, and unless, instead of depriving them of their opportunities, we lend them a helping hand.

I cordially approve the policy regarding the management of Indian affairs outlined in the reports of the Secretary of the Interior and of the Commissioner of Indian Affairs. The faithful performance of our promises is the first condition of a good understanding with the Indians. I can not too urgently recommend to Congress that prompt and liberal provision be made for the conscientious fulfillment of all engagements entered into by the Government with the Indian tribes. To withhold the means necessary for the performance of a promise is always false economy, and is apt to prove disastrous in its consequences. Especial care is recommended to provide for Indians settled on their reservations cattle and agricultural implements, to aid them in whatever efforts they may make to support themselves, and by the establishment and maintenance of schools to bring them under the control of civilized influences.

I see no reason why Indians who can give satisfactory proof of having by their own labor supported their families for a number of years, and who are willing to detach themselves from their tribal relations, should not be admitted to the benefit of the homestead act and the privileges of citizenship, and I recommend the passage of a law to that effect. It will be an act of justice as well as a measure of encouragement. Earnest efforts are being made to purify the Indian service, so that every dollar appropriated by Congress shall redound to the benefit of the Indians, as intended. Those efforts will have my firm support. With an improved service and every possible encouragement held out to the Indians to better their condition and to elevate themselves in the scale of civilization, we may hope to accomplish at the same time a good work for them and for ourselves.

I invite the attention of Congress to the importance of the statements and suggestions made by the Secretary of the Interior concerning the depredations committed on the timber lands of the United States and the necessity for the preservation of forests. It is believed that the measures taken in pursuance of existing laws to arrest those depredations will be entirely successful if Congress, by an appropriation for that purpose, renders their continued enforcement possible. The experience of other nations teaches us that a country can not be stripped of its forests with impunity, and we shall expose ourselves to the gravest consequences unless the wasteful and improvident manner in which the forests in the United States are destroyed be effectually checked. I earnestly recommend that the measures suggested by the Secretary of the Interior for the suppression of depredations on the public timber lands of the United States, for the selling of timber from the public lands, and for the preservation of forests be embodied in a law, and that, considering the urgent necessity of enabling the people of certain States and Territories to purchase timber from the public lands in a legal manner, which at present they can not do, such a law be passed without unavoidable delay. I would also call the attention of Congress to the statements made by the Secretary of the Interior concerning the disposition that might be made of the desert lands, not irrigable, west of the one hundredth meridian. These lands are practically unsalable under existing laws, and the suggestion is worthy of consideration that a system of leasehold tenure would make them a source of profit to the United States, while at the same time legalizing the business of cattle raising which is at present carried on upon them.

The report of the Commissioner of Agriculture contains the gratifying announcement of the extraordinary success which has rewarded the agricultural industry of the country for the past year. With the fair prices which obtain for the products of the soil, especially for the surplus which our people have to export, we may confidently turn to this as the most important of all our resources for the revival of the depressed industries of the country. The report shows our agricultural progress during the year, and contains a statement of the work done by this Department for the advancement of agricultural industry, upon which the prosperity of our people so largely depends. Matters of information are included of great interest to all who seek, by the experience of others, to improve their own methods of cultivation. The efforts of the Department to increase the production of important articles of consumption will, it is hoped, improve the demand for labor and advance the business of the country, and eventually result in saving some of the many millions that are now annually paid to foreign nations for sugar and other staple products which habitual use has made necessary in our domestic everyday life.

The board on behalf of the United States Executive Departments at the International Exhibition of 1876 has concluded its labors. The final report of the board was transmitted to Congress by the President near the close of the last session. As these papers are understood to contain interesting and valuable information, and will constitute the only report emanating from the Government on the subject of the exhibition, I invite attention to the matter and recommend that the report be published for general information.

Congress is empowered by the Constitution with the authority of exclusive legislation over the District of Columbia, in which the seat of Government of the nation is located. The interests of the District, having no direct representation in Congress, are entitled to especial consideration and care at the hands of the General Government. The capital of the United States belongs to the nation, and it is natural that the American people should take pride in the seat of their National Government and desire it to be an ornament to the country. Much has been done to render it healthful, convenient, and attractive, but much remains to be done, which its permanent inhabitants are not able and ought not to be expected to do. To impose upon them a large proportion of the cost required for public improvements, which are in a great measure planned and executed for the convenience of the Government and of the many thousands of visitors from all parts of the country who temporarily reside at the capital of the nation, is an evident injustice. Special attention is asked by the Commissioners of the District in their report, which is herewith transmitted, to the importance of a permanent adjustment by Congress of the financial relations between the United States and the District, involving the regular annual contribution by the United States of its just proportion of the expenses of the District government and of the outlay for all needed public improvements, and such measure of relief from the burden of taxation now resting upon the people of the District as in the wisdom of Congress may be deemed just.

The report of the Commissioners shows that the affairs of the District are in a condition as satisfactory as could be expected in view of the heavy burden of debt resting upon it and its very limited means for necessary expenses.

The debt of the District is as follows:

Old funded debt	$8,379,691.96
3.65 bonds, guaranteed by the United States	13,743,250.00
Total bonded debt	22,122,941.96
To which should be added certain outstanding claims, as explained in the report of the Commissioners	1,187,204.52
Making the total debt of the District	23,310,146.48

The Commissioners also ask attention to the importance of the improvement of the Potomac River and the reclamation of the marshes bordering the city of Washington, and their views upon this subject are concurred in by the members of the board of health, whose report is also herewith transmitted. Both the commercial and sanitary interests of the District will be greatly promoted, I doubt not, by this improvement.

Your attention is invited to the suggestion of the Commissioners and of the board of health for the organization of a board of charities, to have supervision and control of the disbursement of all moneys for charitable purposes from the District treasury. I desire also to ask your especial attention to the need of adding to the efficiency of the public schools of the District by supplemental aid from the National Treasury. This is especially just, since so large a number of those attending these schools are children of employees of the Government. I earnestly commend to your care the interests of the people of the District, who are so intimately associated with the Government establishments, and to whose enterprise the good order and attractiveness of the capital are largely due; and I ask your attention to the request of the Commissioners for legislation in behalf of the interests intrusted to their care. The appropriations asked for the care of the reservations belonging to the Government within the city, by the Commissioner of Public Buildings and Grounds, are also commended to your favorable consideration.

The report of the joint commission created by the act approved 2d of August, 1876, entitled "An act providing for the completion of the Washington Monument," is also herewith transmitted, with accompanying documents. The board of engineer officers detailed to examine the monument, in compliance with the second section of the act, have reported that the foundation is insufficient. No authority exists for making the expenditure necessary to secure its stability. I therefore recommend that the commission be authorized to expend such portion of the sum appropriated by the act as may be necessary for the purpose. The present unfinished condition of the monument, begun so long ago, is a reproach to the nation. It can not be doubted that the patriotic sense of the country will warmly respond to such prompt provision as may be made for its completion at an early day, and I urge upon Congress the propriety and necessity of immediate legislation for this purpose.

The wisdom of legislation upon the part of Congress, in aid of the States, for the education of the whole people in those branches of study which are taught in the common schools of the country is no longer a question. The intelligent judgment of the country goes still further, regarding it as also both constitutional and expedient for the General Government to extend to technical and higher education such aid as is deemed essential to the general welfare and to our due prominence among the enlightened and cultured nations of the world. The ultimate settlement of all questions of the future, whether of administration or finance or of true nationality of sentiment, depends upon the virtue and intelligence of the people. It is vain to hope for the success of a free government without the means of insuring the intelligence of those who are the source of power. No less than one-seventh of the entire voting population of our country are yet unable to read and write.

It is encouraging to observe, in connection with the growth of frater-nal feeling in those States in which slavery formerly existed, evidences of increasing interest in universal education, and I shall be glad to give my approval to any appropriate measures which may be enacted by Con-gress for the purpose of supplementing with national aid the local sys-tems of education in those States and in all the States; and, having already invited your attention to the needs of the District of Columbia with respect to its public-school system, I here add that I believe it desirable, not so much with reference to the local wants of the District, but to the great and lasting benefit of the entire country, that this sys-tem should be crowned with a university in all respects in keeping with the national capital, and thereby realize the cherished hopes of Wash-ington on this subject.

I also earnestly commend the request of the Regents of the Smith-sonian Institution that an adequate appropriation be made for the estab-lishment and conduct of a national museum under their supervision.

The question of providing for the preservation and growth of the Library of Congress is also one of national importance. As the deposi-tory of all copyright publications and records, this library has outgrown the provisions for its accommodation; and the erection, on such site as the judgment of Congress may approve, of a fireproof library build-ing, to preserve the treasures and enlarge the usefulness of this valuable collection, is recommended. I recommend also such legislation as will render available and efficient for the purposes of instruction, so far as is consistent with the public service, the cabinets or museums of inven-tion, of surgery, of education, and of agriculture, and other collections the property of the National Government.

The capital of the nation should be something more than a mere polit-ical center. We should avail ourselves of all the opportunities which

Providence has here placed at our command to promote the general intelligence of the people and increase the conditions most favorable to the success and perpetuity of our institutions.

R. B. HAYES.

SPECIAL MESSAGES

EXECUTIVE MANSION, *December 10, 1877.*

To the Senate and House of Representatives:

I transmit herewith, for the information of Congress, a copy of the report of the commission appointed by me on the 27th of September, 1877, to examine the several public buildings in this city and determine the nature and extent of their security against conflagrations and the measures to be taken to guard the buildings and their contents from destruction or damage by fire.

The records of the Government constitute a most valuable collection for the country, whether we consider their pecuniary value or their historical importance; and it becomes my duty to call your attention to the means suggested for securing these valuable archives, as well as the buildings in which they are stored. The commissioners have performed their duties intelligently and faithfully. Their recommendations are fully concurred in by me and commended to the favorable consideration of Congress.

R. B. HAYES.

EXECUTIVE MANSION, *December 10, 1877.*

To the Senate and House of Representatives:

I have the honor to transmit herewith an additional report (and an accompanying statement) addressed to me by the commissioners appointed under the act of Congress approved July 19, 1876, authorizing the repavement of that part of Pennsylvania avenue lying between the Treasury Department and the Capitol Grounds.

R. B. HAYES.

EXECUTIVE MANSION, *December 13, 1877.*

To the House of Representatives:

I transmit herewith a special report upon the subject of forestry by the Commissioner of Agriculture, with the accompanying documents.

R. B. HAYES.

[A similar message was sent to the Senate.]

WASHINGTON, *January 11, 1878.*

To the House of Representatives:

In answer to the resolution of the House of Representatives of the 3d ultimo, requesting to be furnished with the correspondence between the

Government of Venezuela and that of the United States had since the adjournment of the first session of the Forty-fourth Congress in relation to the Venezuela Mixed Claims Commission, I transmit the report of the Secretary of State, together with its accompanying documents.

R. B. HAYES.

EXECUTIVE MANSION,
Washington, January 14, 1878.

To the Senate of the United States:

I have received the following resolution of the Senate:

IN EXECUTIVE SESSION, SENATE OF THE UNITED STATES,
December 11, 1877.

Resolved, That the President be respectfully requested to inform the Senate, with the view to the transaction of its executive business, whether in any of the instances of nominations hitherto sent to the Senate stated to be for appointment in place of officers removed such removals had been made at the time of sending such nominations to the Senate.

In reply I would respectfully inform the Senate that in the instances referred to removals had not been made at the time the nominations were sent to the Senate. The form used for such nominations was one found to have been in existence and heretofore used in some of the Departments, and was intended to inform the Senate that if the nomination proposed were approved it would operate to remove an incumbent whose name was indicated.

R. B. HAYES.

EXECUTIVE MANSION, *January 17, 1878.*

To the Senate of the United States:

In response to the resolution of the Senate of the 13th November last calling for information concerning the cause, numbers engaged, number of lives lost, and probable cost of the late so-called Nez Percé War, I have the honor to submit the accompanying communication from the General of the Army and an extract from the annual report of that officer. Upon the subject of the cost of the Nez Percé War, I submit reports from the Quartermaster-General and the Commissary-General of Subsistence.

R. B. HAYES.

WASHINGTON, *January 18, 1878.*

To the Senate of the United States:

I transmit to the Senate, for its consideration with a view to ratification, a treaty of friendship and commerce between the United States and the Government of the Samoan Islands, signed on the 17th instant.

R. B. HAYES

EXECUTIVE MANSION, *January 18, 1878.*

To the Senate of the United States:

In answer to the resolution of the Senate of December 6, 1877, I inclose a report made to me by the Attorney-General, the results of which seem to be correct, and which affords the information * requested.

R. B. HAYES.

[A similar message was sent to the House of Representatives, in answer to a resolution of that body of November 27, 1877.]

EXECUTIVE MANSION, *January 23, 1878.*

To the Senate of the United States:

In answer to the resolution of the Senate of November 16, 1877, I transmit reports † made to me by the Attorney-General and the Secretary of the Navy.

R. B. HAYES.

EXECUTIVE MANSION, *January 29, 1878.*

To the Senate of the United States:

In response to a resolution of the Senate of the 10th ultimo, I transmit herewith copies of reports ‡ of the Commissioners of Indian Affairs and General Land Office, dated 9th and 21st instant, respectively.

R. B. HAYES.

EXECUTIVE MANSION, *February 4, 1878.*

To the Senate and House of Representatives:

The commission appointed under the act of Congress approved March 3, 1873, entitled "An act to authorize inquiries into the causes of steam-boiler explosions," have addressed a report of progress, made to date thereof, to the Secretaries of the Treasury and Navy Departments, which has been transmitted to me by these officers. The commission also presented a copy of a report dated February 27, 1877, which they say "was mislaid and did not reach the President." These reports are respectfully submitted for the information of Congress.

R. B. HAYES.

WASHINGTON, *February 6, 1878.*

To the Senate:

I transmit herewith, in compliance with a resolution of the Senate of the 6th of December last, a report from the Secretary of State and its accompanying papers.§

R. B. HAYES.

---

*Operation of the Union Pacific Railroad and its branches.

†Relating to the seizure of logs, lumber, and naval stores suspected of having been taken from the public lands.

‡Relating to the payments to the Ute Indians under the fourth article of the agreement of September 13, 1873, and to the occupancy of lands ceded by said Indians.

§Correspondence relative to the Franco–German War.

EXECUTIVE MANSION, *February 11, 1878.*

To the Senate and House of Representatives:

In compliance with the resolution of Congress entitled "Joint resolution accepting a painting* tendered to Congress by Mrs. Elizabeth Thompson," approved by me on the 1st instant, I have this day caused a copy of the resolution to be delivered to Mrs. Thompson.

R. B. HAYES.

EXECUTIVE MANSION, *February 20, 1878.*

To the Senate of the United States:

In response to the resolution of the Senate of January 30, 1878, I transmit herewith a report,† dated the 16th instant, from the Commissioner of Indian Affairs.

R. B. HAYES.

EXECUTIVE MANSION, *February 20, 1878.*

To the Senate of the United States:

In answer to the resolution of the Senate dated December 7, 1877, I transmit herewith reports from the General of the Army, the Quartermaster-General, the Commissary-General of Subsistence, and the Chief of Ordnance, showing what has been the cost (estimated) of the late war with the Sioux Indians, and what the casualties of rank and file among the soldiers engaged in said Sioux War.

R. B. HAYES.

EXECUTIVE MANSION, *February 27, 1878.*

To the Senate of the United States:

I transmit herewith, for the information of the Senate, the reply of the Commissioner of Agriculture to a resolution of the Senate of the 20th instant, "relative to the disease prevailing among swine," etc.

R. B. HAYES.

WASHINGTON, *March 21, 1878.*

To the Senate:

In answer to the resolution of the Senate of the 11th of March instant, I herewith transmit a report from the Secretary of State, with accompanying documents.‡

R. B. HAYES.

*Carpenter's painting of President Lincoln and his Cabinet at the time of his first reading of the Proclamation of Emancipation.

† Relating to the survey of lands in the Indian Territory, etc.

‡ Correspondence relative to the appointment of a third commissioner under the twenty-third article of the treaty with Great Britain of May 8, 1871, on the question of the fisheries.

EXECUTIVE MANSION, *March 25, 1878.*
To the Senate of the United States:

In further answer to the resolution of the Senate of December 7, 1877, as to the cost of the Sioux War, I transmit copies of additional reports on the subject received from the Military Division of the Missouri.

R. B. HAYES.

WASHINGTON, D. C., *March 27, 1878.*
To the Senate of the United States:

In answer to the Senate's resolution of the 14th ultimo, requesting to be furnished with a copy of correspondence between the Government of the United States and that of China respecting the "Ward" claims and the claim of Charles E. Hill, I herewith submit a letter from the Secretary of State, together with its accompanying papers.

R. B. HAYES.

WASHINGTON, *March 29, 1878.*
To the House of Representatives:

I transmit herewith, in compliance with a resolution of the House of Representatives of the 21st ultimo, a report from the Secretary of State and its accompanying papers.*

R. B. HAYES.

EXECUTIVE MANSION, *May 2, 1878.*
To the Senate of the United States:

In answer to the resolution of the Senate of April 16, 1878, I transmit herewith reports† made to me by the Secretary of the Treasury and the Attorney-General.

R. B. HAYES.

WASHINGTON, *May 10, 1878.*
To the Senate of the United States:

I transmit to the Senate, for its consideration with a view to ratification, a convention defining the rights, immunities, and privileges of consular officers, between the United States and His Majesty the King of Italy, signed on the 8th instant.

R. B. HAYES.

---

*Correspondence with Spain relative to the seizure of the steamer *Virginius*, etc.
† Relating to the defalcations of William R. Whitaker while collector of internal revenue for the first district of Louisiana and while assistant treasurer of the United States at New Orleans.

WASHINGTON, *May 14, 1878.*

To the Senate of the United States:

In answer to the resolution of the Senate of the 29th ultimo, I transmit herewith a report from the Secretary of State, with its accompanying papers.*

R. B. HAYES.

EXECUTIVE MANSION, *May 17, 1878.*

To the Senate and House of Representatives:

I herewith transmit, for your appropriate action, a communication from the Secretary of State, on the subject of the result of the deliberations of the Fishery Commission appointed under certain provisions of the treaty of Washington, with the accompanying documents.

Article XXII of the treaty provides that any sum of money which the commissioners may award shall be paid by the United States Government in a gross sum within twelve months after such award shall have been given.

The commission announced the result of its deliberations on the 23d day of November last year, and an appropriation at the present session of Congress will be necessary to enable the Government to make the payment provided for in the treaty.

I respectfully submit to the consideration of Congress the record of the transaction as presented upon the papers, and recommend an appropriation of the necessary sum, with such discretion to the executive government in regard to its payment as in the wisdom of Congress the public interests may seem to require.

R. B. HAYES.

WASHINGTON, *May 25, 1878.*

To the Senate of the United States:

I transmit to the Senate, for its consideration with a view to its ratification, a consular convention between the United States and the Netherlands, signed on the 23d instant.

R. B. HAYES.

WASHINGTON, *June 11, 1878.*

To the House of Representatives:

In answer to a resolution of the House of Representatives of the 27th May ultimo, I transmit the response of the Secretary of State, accompanied by a copy of the papers† called for by the resolution.

R. B. HAYES.

---

*Correspondence relative to the terms and conditions under which the Cuban insurgents surrendered and to the policy of Spain in the government of Cuba.

†Relating to the convention of May 20, 1875, for the establishment of an international bureau of weights and measures.

EXECUTIVE MANSION, *June 12, 1878.*

To the Senate and House of Representatives:

In transmitting herewith to Congress a communication from the Secretary of State on the subject of the conference provided for in the act of February 28, 1878, entitled "An act to authorize the coinage of the standard silver dollar and to restore its legal-tender character," I respectfully recommend that an adequate appropriation be made for certain expenses of the conference and of the commissioners attending the same on behalf of the United States, as suggested in the communication of the Secretary of State.

R. B. HAYES.

EXECUTIVE MANSION, *June 15, 1878.*

To the House of Representatives:

I have the honor to transmit herewith the report of the board for testing iron, steel, and other metals, as requested in the resolution of the House of Representatives dated April 27, 1878.

R. B. HAYES.

To the Senate:　　　　　　　　　　　WASHINGTON, *June 17, 1878.*

In answer to the resolution of the Senate of the 27th of May ultimo, I herewith transmit a report from the Secretary of State, with accompanying documents.*

R. B. HAYES.

VETO MESSAGES.

EXECUTIVE MANSION, *February 28, 1878.*

To the House of Representatives:

After a very careful consideration of the House bill No. 1093, entitled "An act to authorize the coinage of the standard silver dollar and to restore its legal-tender character," I feel compelled to return it to the House of Representatives, in which it originated, with my objections to its passage.

Holding the opinion, which I expressed in my annual message, that "neither the interests of the Government nor of the people of the United States would be promoted by disparaging silver as one of the two precious metals which furnish the coinage of the world, and that legislation which looks to maintaining the volume of intrinsic money to as full a measure of both metals as their relative commercial values will permit would be neither unjust nor inexpedient," it has been my earnest desire

---

* Correspondence, etc., relative to the selection of M. Maurice Delfosse as one of the commissioners under the treaty with Great Britain of May 8, 1871, on the fisheries question.

to concur with Congress in the adoption of such measures to increase the silver coinage of the country as would not impair the obligation of contracts, either public or private, nor injuriously affect the public credit. It is only upon the conviction that this bill does not meet these essential requirements that I feel it my duty to withhold from it my approval.

My present official duty as to this bill permits only an attention to the specific objections to its passage which seem to me so important as to justify me in asking from the wisdom and duty of Congress that further consideration of the bill for which the Constitution has in such cases provided.

The bill provides for the coinage of silver dollars of the weight of 412½ grains each, of standard silver, to be a legal tender at their nominal value for all debts and dues, public and private, except where otherwise expressly stipulated in the contract. It is well known that the market value of that number of grains of standard silver during the past year has been from 90 to 92 cents as compared with the standard gold dollar. Thus the silver dollar authorized by this bill is worth 8 to 10 per cent less than it purports to be worth, and is made a legal tender for debts contracted when the law did not recognize such coins as lawful money.

The right to pay duties in silver or in certificates for silver deposits will, when they are issued in sufficient amount to circulate, put an end to the receipt of revenue in gold, and thus compel the payment of silver for both the principal and interest of the public debt. One billion one hundred and forty-three million four hundred and ninety-three thousand four hundred dollars of the bonded debt now outstanding was issued prior to February, 1873, when the silver dollar was unknown in circulation in this country, and was only a convenient form of silver bullion for exportation; $583,440,350 of the funded debt has been issued since February, 1873, when gold alone was the coin for which the bonds were sold, and gold alone was the coin in which both parties to the contract understood that the bonds would be paid. These bonds entered into the markets of the world. They were paid for in gold when silver had greatly depreciated, and when no one would have bought them if it had been understood that they would be paid in silver. The sum of $225,000,000 of these bonds has been sold during my Administration for gold coin, and the United States received the benefit of these sales by a reduction of the rate of interest to 4 per cent. During the progress of these sales a doubt was suggested as to the coin in which payment of these bonds would be made. The public announcement was thereupon authorized that it was "not to be anticipated that any future legislation of Congress or any action of any department of the Government would sanction or tolerate the redemption of the principal of these bonds or the payment of the interest thereon in coin of less value than the coin authorized by law at the time of the issue of the bonds, being the coin exacted by the Government in exchange for the same." In view of these facts it will be justly regarded as a grave breach of the public faith to undertake to pay these bonds, principal or interest, in silver coin worth in the market less than the coin received for them.

It is said that the silver dollar made a legal tender by this bill will under its operation be equivalent in value to the gold dollar. Many supporters of the bill believe this, and would not justify an attempt to pay debts, either public or private, in coin of inferior value to the money of the world. The capital defect of the bill is that it contains no provision protecting from its operation preexisting debts in case the coinage which it creates shall continue to be of less value than that which was the sole legal tender when they were contracted. If it is now proposed, for the purpose of taking advantage of the depreciation of silver in the payment of debts, to coin and make a legal tender a silver dollar of less commercial value than any dollar, whether of gold or paper, which is now lawful money in this country, such measure, it will hardly be questioned, will, in the judgment of mankind, be an act of bad faith. As to all debts heretofore contracted, the silver dollar should be made a legal tender only at its market value. The standard of value should not be changed without the consent of both parties to the contract. National promises should be kept with unflinching fidelity. There is no power to compel a nation to pay its just debts. Its credit depends on its honor. The nation owes what it has led or allowed its creditors to expect. I can not approve a bill which in my judgment authorizes the violation of sacred obligations. The obligation of the public faith transcends all questions of profit or public advantage. Its unquestionable maintenance is the dictate as well of the highest expediency as of the most necessary duty, and should ever be carefully guarded by the Executive, by Congress, and by the people.

It is my firm conviction that if the country is to be benefited by a silver coinage it can be done only by the issue of silver dollars of full value, which will defraud no man. A currency worth less than it purports to be worth will in the end defraud not only creditors, but all who are engaged in legitimate business, and none more surely than those who are dependent on their daily labor for their daily bread.

R. B. HAYES.

EXECUTIVE MANSION, *March 6, 1878.*

To the House of Representatives:

I return herewith House bill No. 3072, entitled "An act to authorize a special term of the circuit court of the United States for the southern district of Mississippi to be held at Scranton, in Jackson County," with the following objections to its becoming a law:

The act provides that a special term of the circuit court of the United States for the southern district of Mississippi shall be held at Scranton, in Jackson County, Miss., to begin on the second Monday in March, 1878, and directs the clerk of said court to "cause notice of said special term of said court to be published in a newspaper in Jackson, Miss., and also in a newspaper in Scranton, at least ten days before the beginning thereof."

The act can not be executed, inasmuch as there is not sufficient time to give the notice of the holding of the special term which Congress thought proper to require.

The number of suits to be tried at the special term in which the United States is interested is forty-nine, and the amount involved exceeds $200,000. The Government can not prepare for trial at said special term, because no fund appropriated by Congress can be made available for that purpose. If, therefore, the Government is compelled to go to trial at the special term provided for by this bill, the United States must be defeated for want of time and means to make preparation for the proper vindication of its rights.

The bill is therefore returned for the further consideration of Congress.

R. B. HAYES.

PROCLAMATIONS.

BY THE PRESIDENT OF THE UNITED STATES OF AMERICA.

A PROCLAMATION.

Whereas it is provided in the laws of the United States that whenever by reason of unlawful obstructions, combinations or assemblages of persons, or rebellion against the authority of the Government of the United States, it shall become impracticable, in the judgment of the President, to enforce by the ordinary course of judicial proceedings the laws of the United States within any State or Territory, it shall be lawful for the President to call forth the militia of any or all the States and to employ such parts of the land and naval forces of the United States as he may deem necessary to enforce the faithful execution of the laws of the United States or to suppress such rebellion, in whatever State or Territory thereof the laws of the United States may be forcibly opposed or the execution thereof forcibly obstructed; and

Whereas it has been made to appear to me that, by reason of unlawful combinations and assemblages of persons in arms, it has become impracticable to enforce by the ordinary course of judicial proceedings the laws of the United States within the Territory of New Mexico, and especially within Lincoln County therein, and that the laws of the United States have been therein forcibly opposed and the execution thereof forcibly resisted; and

Whereas the laws of the United States require that whenever it may be necessary, in the judgment of the President, to use the military force for the purpose of enforcing the faithful execution of the laws of the United States, he shall forthwith, by proclamation, command such insurgents to disperse and retire peaceably to their respective abodes within a limited time:

Now, therefore, I, Rutherford B. Hayes, President of the United States, do hereby admonish all good citizens of the United States, and especially of the Territory of New Mexico, against aiding, countenancing, abetting, or taking part in any such unlawful proceedings; and I do hereby warn all persons engaged in or connected with said obstruction of the laws to disperse and retire peaceably to their respective abodes on or before noon of the 13th day of October instant.

In witness whereof I have hereunto set my hand and caused the seal of the United States to be affixed.

[SEAL.]   Done at the city of Washington, this 7th day of October, A. D. 1878, and of the Independence of the United States the one hundred and third.

                                                    R. B. HAYES.

By the President:

F. W. SEWARD, *Acting Secretary of State.*

BY THE PRESIDENT OF THE UNITED STATES OF AMERICA.

A PROCLAMATION.

The recurrence of that season at which it is the habit of our people to make devout and public confession of their constant dependence upon the divine favor for all the good gifts of life and happiness and of public peace and prosperity exhibits in the record of the year abundant reasons for our gratitude and thanksgiving.

Exuberant harvests, productive mines, ample crops of the staples of trade and manufactures, have enriched the country.

The resources thus furnished to our reviving industry and expanding commerce are hastening the day when discords and distresses through the length and breadth of the land will, under the continued favor of Providence, have given way to confidence and energy and assured prosperity.

Peace with all nations has been maintained unbroken, domestic tranquillity has prevailed, and the institutions of liberty and justice which the wisdom and virtue of our fathers established remain the glory and defense of their children.

The general prevalence of the blessings of health through our wide land has made more conspicuous the sufferings and sorrows which the dark shadow of pestilence has cast upon a portion of our people. This heavy affliction even the Divine Ruler has tempered to the suffering communities in the universal sympathy and succor which have flowed to their relief, and the whole nation may rejoice in the unity of spirit in our people by which they cheerfully share one another's burdens.

Now, therefore, I, Rutherford B. Hayes, President of the United States, do appoint Thursday, the 28th day of November next, as a day of national thanksgiving and prayer; and I earnestly recommend that, withdrawing themselves from secular cares and labors, the people of the United States do meet together on that day in their respective places of worship, there to give thanks and praise to Almighty God for His mercies and to devoutly beseech their continuance.

In witness whereof I have hereunto set my hand and caused the seal of the United States to be affixed.

[SEAL.] Done at the city of Washington, this 30th day of October, A. D. 1878, and of the Independence of the United States the one hundred and third. R. B. HAYES.

By the President:
WM. M. EVARTS, *Secretary of State.*

EXECUTIVE ORDERS.

EXECUTIVE MANSION,
Washington, December 31, 1877.

JAMES H. COGGESHALL, Esq.,
*Marshal of the United States for the
District of Rhode Island, Providence, R. I.*

SIR: By virtue of the authority conferred upon me by section 5287 of the Revised Statutes of the United States. and in execution of the same, you are hereby empowered and directed to take possession of the steamer *Estelle*, now or lately lying at Bristol, in Rhode Island, and to detain the same until further orders from me concerning the same, and to employ such portion of the land and naval forces of the United States as may be necessary for that purpose. R. B. HAYES.

EXECUTIVE MANSION,
Washington, May 27, 1878.

SIR:* I am directed by the President to say that the several Departments of the Government will be closed on Thursday, the 30th instant, in respect to the memory of those who fell in defense of the Union, and to enable the employees to participate in the commemorative ceremonies of the day.

Very respectfully, your obedient servant,
W. K. ROGERS, *Private Secretary.*

*Addressed to the heads of the Executive Departments, etc.

SECOND ANNUAL MESSAGE.

EXECUTIVE MANSION, *December 2, 1878.*
Fellow-Citizens of the Senate and House of Representatives:

Our heartfelt gratitude is due to the Divine Being who holds in His hands the destinies of nations for the continued bestowal during the last year of countless blessings upon our country.

We are at peace with all other nations. Our public credit has greatly improved, and is perhaps now stronger than ever before. Abundant harvests have rewarded the labors of those who till the soil, our manufacturing industries are reviving, and it is believed that general prosperity, which has been so long anxiously looked for, is at last within our reach.

The enjoyment of health by our people generally has, however, been interrupted during the past season by the prevalence of a fatal pestilence (the yellow fever) in some portions of the Southern States, creating an emergency which called for prompt and extraordinary measures of relief. The disease appeared as an epidemic at New Orleans and at other places on the Lower Mississippi soon after midsummer. It was rapidly spread by fugitives from the infected cities and towns, and did not disappear until early in November. The States of Louisiana, Mississippi, and Tennessee have suffered severely. About 100,000 cases are believed to have occurred, of which about 20,000, according to intelligent estimates, proved fatal. It is impossible to estimate with any approach to accuracy the loss to the country occasioned by this epidemic It is to be reckoned by the hundred millions of dollars. The suffering and destitution that resulted excited the deepest sympathy in all parts of the Union. Physicians and nurses hastened from every quarter to the assistance of the afflicted communities. Voluntary contributions of money and supplies, in every needed form, were speedily and generously furnished. The Government was able to respond in some measure to the call for help, by providing tents, medicines, and food for the sick and destitute, the requisite directions for the purpose being given in the confident expectation that this action of the Executive would receive the sanction of Congress. About 1,800 tents, and rations of the value of about $25,000, were sent to cities and towns which applied for them, full details of which will be furnished to Congress by the proper Department.

The fearful spread of this pestilence has awakened a very general public sentiment in favor of national sanitary administration, which shall not only control quarantine, but have the sanitary supervision of internal commerce in times of epidemics, and hold an advisory relation to the State and municipal health authorities, with power to deal with whatever endangers the public health, and which the municipal and

State authorities are unable to regulate. The national quarantine act approved April 29, 1878, which was passed too late in the last session of Congress to provide the means for carrying it into practical operation during the past season, is a step in the direction here indicated. In view of the necessity for the most effective measures, by quarantine and otherwise, for the protection of our seaports and the country generally from this and other epidemics, it is recommended that Congress give to the whole subject early and careful consideration.

The permanent pacification of the country by the complete protection of all citizens in every civil and political right continues to be of paramount interest with the great body of our people. Every step in this direction is welcomed with public approval, and every interruption of steady and uniform progress to the desired consummation awakens general uneasiness and widespread condemnation. The recent Congressional elections have furnished a direct and trustworthy test of the advance thus far made in the practical establishment of the right of suffrage secured by the Constitution to the liberated race in the Southern States. All disturbing influences, real or imaginary, had been removed from all of these States.

The three constitutional amendments which conferred freedom and equality of civil and political rights upon the colored people of the South were adopted by the concurrent action of the great body of good citizens who maintained the authority of the National Government and the integrity and perpetuity of the Union at such a cost of treasure and life, as a wise and necessary embodiment in the organic law of the just results of the war. The people of the former slaveholding States accepted these results, and gave in every practicable form assurances that the thirteenth, fourteenth, and fifteenth amendments, and laws passed in pursuance thereof, should in good faith be enforced, rigidly and impartially, in letter and spirit, to the end that the humblest citizen, without distinction of race or color, should under them receive full and equal protection in person and property and in political rights and privileges. By these constitutional amendments the southern section of the Union obtained a large increase of political power in Congress and in the electoral college, and the country justly expected that elections would proceed, as to the enfranchised race, upon the same circumstances of legal and constitutional freedom and protection which obtained in all the other States of the Union. The friends of law and order looked forward to the conduct of these elections as offering to the general judgment of the country an important opportunity to measure the degree in which the right of suffrage could be exercised by the colored people and would be respected by their fellow-citizens; but a more general enjoyment of freedom of suffrage by the colored people and a more just and generous protection of that freedom by the communities of which they form a part were generally anticipated than the record of the elections discloses. In some of those States in which the colored people have been unable to make their opinions felt in the elections the result is mainly due to influences not easily measured or remedied by legal protection; but in the States of Louisiana and South Carolina at large, and in some particular Congressional districts outside of those States, the records of the elections seem to compel the conclusion that the rights of the colored voters have been overridden and their participation in the elections not permitted to be either general or free.

It will be for the Congress for which these elections were held to make such examinations into their conduct as may be appropriate to determine the validity of the claims of members to their seats. In the meanwhile it becomes the duty of the executive and judicial departments of the Government, each in its province, to inquire into and punish violations of the laws of the United States which have occurred. I can but repeat what I said in this connection in my last message, that whatever author-ity rests with me to this end I shall not hesitate to put forth; and I am unwilling to forego a renewed appeal to the legislatures, the courts, the executive authorities, and the people of the States where these wrongs have been perpetrated to give their assistance toward bringing to justice the offenders and preventing a repetition of the crimes. No means within my power will be spared to obtain a full and fair investigation of the alleged crimes and to secure the conviction and just punishment of the guilty.

It is to be observed that the principal appropriation made for the Department of Justice at the last session contained the following clause:

And for defraying the expenses which may be incurred in the enforcement of the act approved February 28, 1871, entitled "An act to amend an act approved May 31, 1870, entitled 'An act to enforce the rights of citizens of the United States to vote in the several States of this Union, and for other purposes,'" or any acts amendatory thereof or supplementary thereto.

It is the opinion of the Attorney-General that the expenses of these proceedings will largely exceed the amount which was thus provided, and I rely confidently upon Congress to make adequate appropriations to enable the executive department to enforce the laws.

I respectfully urge upon your attention that the Congressional elections, in every district, in a very important sense, are justly a matter of political interest and concern throughout the whole country. Each State, every political party, is entitled to the share of power which is conferred by the legal and constitutional suffrage. It is the right of every citizen possessing the qualifications prescribed by law to cast one unintimidated ballot and to have his ballot honestly counted. So long as the exercise of this power and the enjoyment of this right are common and equal, practically as well as formally, submission to the results of the suffrage will be accorded loyally and cheerfully, and all the departments of Government will feel the true vigor of the popular will thus expressed.

No temporary or administrative interests of Government, however urgent or weighty, will ever displace the zeal of our people in defense of the primary rights of citizenship. They understand that the protection of liberty requires the maintenance in full vigor of the manly methods of free speech, free press, and free suffrage, and will sustain the full authority of Government to enforce the laws which are framed to preserve these inestimable rights. The material progress and welfare of the States depend on the protection afforded to their citizens. There can be no peace without such protection, no prosperity without peace, and the whole country is deeply interested in the growth and prosperity of all its parts.

While the country has not yet reached complete unity of feeling and reciprocal confidence between the communities so lately and so seriously estranged, I feel an absolute assurance that the tendencies are in that direction, and with increasing force. The power of public opinion will override all political prejudices and all sectional or State attachments in demanding that all over our wide territory the name and character of citizen of the United States shall mean one and the same thing and carry with them unchallenged security and respect.

Our relations with other countries continue peaceful. Our neutrality in contests between foreign powers has been maintained and respected.

The Universal Exposition held at Paris during the past summer has been attended by large numbers of our citizens. The brief period allowed for the preparation and arrangement of the contributions of our citizens to this great exposition was well employed in energetic and judicious efforts to overcome this disadvantage. These efforts, led and directed by the commissioner-general, were remarkably successful, and the exhibition of the products of American industry was creditable and gratifying in scope and character. The reports of the United States commissioners, giving its results in detail, will be duly laid before you. Our participation in this international competition for the favor and the trade of the world may be expected to produce useful and important results—in promoting intercourse, friendship, and commerce with other nations.

In accordance with the provisions of the act of February 28, 1878, three commissioners were appointed to an international conference on the subject of adopting a common ratio between gold and silver, for the purpose of establishing internationally the use of bimetallic money and securing fixity of relative value between those metals.

Invitations were addressed to the various governments which had expressed a willingness to participate in its deliberations. The conference held its meetings in Paris in August last. The report of the commissioners, herewith submitted, will show its results. No common ratio between gold and silver could be agreed upon by the conference. The general conclusion was reached that it is necessary to maintain in the world the monetary functions of silver as well as of gold, leaving the selection of the use of one or the other of these two metals, or of both, to be made by each state.

Congress having appropriated at its last session the sum of $5,500,000 to pay the award of the joint commission at Halifax, if, after correspondence with the British Government on the subject of the conformity of the award to the requirements of the treaty and to the terms of the question thereby submitted to the commission, the President shall deem it his duty to make the payment, communications upon these points were addressed to the British Government through the legation of the United States at London. Failing to obtain the concurrence of the British Government in the views of this Government respecting the award, I have deemed it my duty to tender the sum named within the year fixed by the treaty, accompanied by a notice of the grounds of the payment and a protest against any other construction of the same. The correspondence upon this subject will be laid before you.

The Spanish Government has officially announced the termination of the insurrection in Cuba and the restoration of peace throughout that island. Confident expectations are expressed of a revival of trade and prosperity, which it is earnestly hoped may prove well founded. Numerous claims of American citizens for relief for injuries or restoration of property have been among the incidents of the long-continued hostilities. Some of these claims are in process of adjustment by Spain, and the others are promised early and careful consideration.

The treaty made with Italy in regard to reciprocal consular privileges has been duly ratified and proclaimed.

No questions of grave importance have arisen with any other of the European powers.

The Japanese Government has been desirous of a revision of such parts of its treaties with foreign powers as relate to commerce, and it is understood has addressed to each of the treaty powers a request to open negotiations with that view. The United States Government has been inclined to regard the matter favorably. Whatever restrictions upon trade with Japan are found injurious to that people can not but affect injuriously nations holding commercial intercourse with them. Japan, after a long period of seclusion, has within the past few years made rapid strides in the path of enlightenment and progress, and, not unreasonably, is looking forward to the time when her relations with the nations of Europe and America shall be assimilated to those which they hold with each other. A treaty looking to this end has been made, which will be submitted for the consideration of the Senate.

After an interval of several years the Chinese Government has again sent envoys to the United States. They have been received, and a permanent legation is now established here by that Government. It is not doubted that this step will be of advantage to both nations in promoting friendly relations and removing causes of difference.

The treaty with the Samoan Islands, having been duly ratified and accepted on the part of both Governments, is now in operation, and a survey and soundings of the harbor of Pago-Pago have been made by a naval vessel of the United States, with a view of its occupation as a naval station if found desirable to the service.

Since the resumption of diplomatic relations with Mexico correspondence has been opened and still continues between the two Governments upon the various questions which at one time seemed to endanger their relations. While no formal agreement has been reached as to the troubles on the border, much has been done to repress and diminish them. The effective force of United States troops on the Rio Grande, by a strict and faithful compliance with instructions, has done much to remove the sources of dispute, and it is now understood that a like force of Mexican troops on the other side of the river is also making an energetic movement against the marauding Indian tribes. This Government looks with the greatest satisfaction upon every evidence of strength in the national authority of Mexico, and upon every effort put forth to prevent or to punish incursions upon our territory. Reluctant to assume any action or attitude in the control of these incursions by military movements across the border not imperatively demanded for the protection of the lives and property of our own citizens, I shall take the earliest opportunity consistent with the proper discharge of this plain duty to recognize the ability of the Mexican Government to restrain effectively violations of our territory. It is proposed to hold next year an international exhibition in Mexico, and it is believed that the display of the agricultural and manufacturing products of the two nations will tend to better understanding and increased commercial intercourse between their people.

With Brazil and the Republics of Central and South America some steps have been taken toward the development of closer commercial intercourse. Diplomatic relations have been resumed with Colombia and with Bolivia. A boundary question between the Argentine Republic and Paraguay has been submitted by those Governments for arbitration to the President of the United States, and I have, after careful examination, given a decision upon it.

A naval expedition up the Amazon and Madeira rivers has brought back information valuable both for scientific and commercial purposes. A like expedition is about visiting the coast of Africa and the Indian Ocean. The reports of diplomatic and consular officers in relation to the development of our foreign commerce have furnished many facts that have proved of public interest and have stimulated to practical exertion the enterprise of our people.

The report of the Secretary of the Treasury furnishes a detailed statement of the operations of that Department of the Government and of the condition of the public finances.

The ordinary revenues from all sources for the fiscal year ended June 30, 1878, were $257,763,878.70; the ordinary expenditures for the same period were $236,964,326.80, leaving a surplus revenue for the year of $20,799,551.90. The receipts for the present fiscal year, ending June 30, 1879, actual and estimated, are as follows: Actual receipts for the first quarter, commencing July 1, 1878, $73,389,743.43; estimated receipts for the remaining three quarters of the year, $191,110,256.57; total receipts for the current fiscal year, actual and estimated, $264,500,000. The expenditures for the same period will be, actual and estimated, as follows: For the quarter commencing July 1, 1878, actual expenditures, $73,344,573.27; and for the remaining three quarters of the year the expenditures are estimated at $166,755,426.73, making the total expenditures $240,100,000, and leaving an estimated surplus revenue for the year ending June 30, 1879, of $24,400,000. The total receipts during the next fiscal year, ending June 30, 1880, estimated according to existing laws, will be $264,500,000, and the estimated ordinary expenditures for the same period will be $236,320,412.68, leaving a surplus of $28,179,587.32 for that year.

In the foregoing statements of expenditures, actual and estimated, no amount is allowed for the sinking fund provided for by the act approved February 25, 1862, which requires that 1 per cent of the entire debt of the United States shall be purchased or paid within each fiscal year, to be set apart as a sinking fund. There has been, however, a substantial compliance with the conditions of the law. By its terms the public debt should have been reduced between 1862 and the close of the last fiscal year $518,361,806.28; the actual reduction of the ascertained debt in that period has been $720,644,739.61, being in excess of the reduction required by the sinking fund act $202,282,933.33.

The amount of the public debt, less cash in the Treasury, November 1, 1878, was $2,024,200,083.18, a reduction since the same date last year of $23,150,617.39.

The progress made during the last year in refunding the public debt at lower rates of interest is very gratifying. The amount of 4 per cent bonds sold during the present year prior to November 23, 1878, is $100,270,900, and 6 per cent bonds, commonly known as five-twenties, to an equal amount, have been or will be redeemed as calls mature.

It has been the policy of the Department to place the 4 per cent bonds within easy reach of every citizen who desires to invest his savings, whether small or great, in these securities. The Secretary of the Treasury recommends that the law be so modified that small sums may be invested, and that through the post-offices or other agents of the Government the freest opportunity may be given in all parts of the country for such investments.

The best mode suggested is that the Department be authorized to issue certificates of deposit, of the denomination of $10, bearing interest at the rate of 3.65 per cent per annum and convertible at any time within one year after their issue into the 4 per cent bonds authorized by the refunding act, and to be issued only in exchange for United States notes sent to the Treasury by mail or otherwise. Such a provision of law, supported by suitable regulations, would enable any person readily, without cost or risk, to convert his money into an interest-bearing security of the United States, and the money so received could be applied to the redemption of 6 per cent bonds.

The coinage of gold during the last fiscal year was $52,798,980. The coinage of silver dollars under the act passed February 28, 1878, amounted on the 23d of November, 1878, to $19,814,550, of which amount $4,984,947 are in circulation, and the balance, $14,829,603, is still in the possession of the Government.

With views unchanged with regard to the act under which the coinage of silver proceeds, it has been the purpose of the Secretary faithfully to execute the law and to afford a fair trial to the measure.

In the present financial condition of the country I am persuaded that the welfare of legitimate business and industry of every description will be best promoted by abstaining from all attempts to make radical changes in the existing fina cial legislation. Let it be understood that during the coming year the business of the country will be undisturbed by governmental interference with the laws affecting it, and we may confidently expect that the resumption of specie payments, which will take place at the appointed time, will be successfully and easily maintained, and that it. will be followed by a healthful and enduring revival of business prosperity.

Let the healing influence of time, the inherent energies of our people, and the boundless resources of our country have a fair opportunity, and relief from present difficulties will surely follow.

The report of the Secretary of War shows that the Army has been well and economically supplied; that our small force has been actively employed and has faithfully performed all the service required of it. The morale of the Army has improved and the number of desertions has materially decreased during the year.

The Secretary recommends—

1. That a pension be granted to the widow of the late Lieutenant Henry H. Benner, Eighteenth Infantry, who lost his life by yellow fever while in command of the steamer *J. M. Chambers*, sent with supplies for the relief of sufferers in the South from that disease.

2. The establishment of the annuity scheme for the benefit of the heirs of deceased officers, as suggested by the Paymaster-General.

3. The adoption by Congress of a plan for the publication of the records of the War of the Rebellion, now being prepared for that purpose.

4. The increase of the extra per diem of soldier teachers employed in post schools, and liberal appropriations for the erection of buildings for schools and libraries at the different posts.

5. The repeal or amendment of the act of June 18, 1878, forbidding the use of the Army "as a *posse comitatus*, or otherwise, for the purpose of executing the laws, except in such cases and under such circumstances as such employment of said force may be expressly authorized by the Constitution or by act of Congress."

6. The passage of a joint resolution of Congress legalizing the issues of rations, tents, and medicines which were made for the relief of sufferers from yellow fever.

7. That provision be made for the erection of a fireproof building for the preservation of certain valuable records, now constantly exposed to destruction by fire.

These recommendations are all commended to your favorable consideration.

The report of the Secretary of the Navy shows that the Navy has improved during the last fiscal year. Work has been done on seventy-five vessels, ten of which have been thoroughly repaired and made ready for sea. Two others are in rapid progress toward completion. The total expenditures of the year, including the amount appropriated for the deficiencies of the previous year, were $17,468,392.65. The actual expenses chargeable to the year, exclusive of those deficiencies, were $13,306,914.09, or $767,199.18 less than those of the previous year, and $4,928,677.74 less than the expenses including the deficiencies. The estimates for the fiscal year ending June 30, 1880, are $14,562,381.45, exceeding the appropriations of the present year only $33,949.75, which excess is occasioned by the demands of the Naval Academy and the Marine Corps, as explained in the Secretary's report. The appropriations for the present fiscal year are $14,528,431.70, which, in the opinion of the Secretary, will be ample for all the current expenses of the Department during the year. The amount drawn from the Treasury from July 1 to November 1, 1878, is $4,740,544.14, of which $70,980.75 has been refunded, leaving as the expenditure for that period $4,669,563.39, or $520,899.24 less than the corresponding period of the last fiscal year.

The report of the Postmaster-General embraces a detailed statement of the operations of the Post-Office Department. The expenditures of that Department for the fiscal year ended June 30, 1878, were $34,165,084.49. The receipts, including sales of stamps, money-order business, and official stamps, were $29,277,516.95. The sum of $290,436.90, included in the foregoing statement of expenditures, is chargeable to preceding years, so that the actual expenditures for the fiscal year ended June 30, 1878, are $33,874,647.59. The amount drawn from the Treasury on appropriations, in addition to the revenues of the Department, was $5,307,652.82. The expenditures for the fiscal year ending June 30, 1880, are estimated at $36,571,900 and the receipts from all sources at $30,664,023.90, leaving a deficiency to be appropriated out of the Treasury of $5,907,876.10. The report calls attention to the fact that the compensation of postmasters and of railroads for carrying the mail is regulated by law, and that the failure of Congress to appropriate the amounts required for these purposes does not relieve the Government of responsibility, but necessarily increases the deficiency bills which Congress will be called upon to pass.

In providing for the postal service the following questions are presented: Should Congress annually appropriate a sum for its expenses largely in excess of its revenues, or should such rates of postage be established as will make the Department self-sustaining? Should the postal service be reduced by excluding from the mails matter which does not pay its way? Should the number of post routes be diminished? Should other methods be adopted which will increase the revenues or diminish the expenses of the postal service?

The International Postal Congress which met at Paris May 1, 1878, and continued in session until June 4 of the same year, was composed of delegates from nearly all the civilized countries of the world. It adopted a new convention (to take the place of the treaty concluded at Berne October 9, 1874), which goes into effect on the 1st of April, 1879, between the countries whose delegates have signed it. It was ratified and approved, by and with the consent of the President, August 13, 1878. A synopsis of this Universal Postal Convention will be found in the report of the Postmaster-General, and the full text in the appendix thereto. In its origin the Postal Union comprised twenty-three countries, having a population of 350,000,000 people. On the 1st of April next it will comprise forty-three countries and colonies, with a population of more than 650,000,000 people, and will soon, by the accession of the few remaining countries and colonies which maintain organized postal services, constitute in fact as well as in name, as its new title indicates, a universal union, regulating, upon a uniform basis of cheap postage rates, the postal intercourse between all civilized nations.

Some embarrassment has arisen out of the conflict between the customs laws of this country and the provisions of the Postal Convention in regard to the transmission of foreign books and newspapers to this country by mail. It is hoped that Congress will be able to devise some means of reconciling the difficulties which have thus been created, so as to do justice to all parties involved.

The business of the Supreme Court and of the courts in many of the circuits has increased to such an extent during the past year that additional legislation is imperative to relieve and prevent the delay of justice and possible oppression to suitors which is thus occasioned. The encumbered condition of these dockets is presented anew in the report of the Attorney-General, and the remedy suggested is earnestly urged for Congressional action. The creation of additional circuit judges, as proposed, would afford a complete remedy, and would involve an expense, at the present rate of salaries, of not more than $60,000 a year.

The annual reports of the Secretary of the Interior and of the Commissioner of Indian Affairs present an elaborate account of the present condition of the Indian tribes and of that branch of the public service which ministers to their interests. While the conduct of the Indians generally has been orderly and their relations with their neighbors friendly and peaceable, two local disturbances have occurred, which were deplorable in their character, but remained, happily, confined to a comparatively small number of Indians. The discontent among the Bannocks, which led first to some acts of violence on the part of some members of the tribe and finally to the outbreak, appears to have been caused by an insufficiency of food on the reservation, and this insufficiency to have been owing to the inadequacy of the appropriations made by Congress to the wants of the Indians at a time when the Indians were prevented from supplying the deficiency by hunting. After an arduous pursuit by the troops of the United States, and several engagements, the hostile Indians were reduced to subjection, and the larger part of them surrendered themselves as prisoners. In this connection I desire to call attention to the recommendation made by the Secretary of the Interior, that a sufficient fund be placed at the disposal of the Executive, to be used, with proper accountability, at discretion, in sudden emergencies of the Indian service.

The other case of disturbance was that of a band of Northern Cheyennes, who suddenly left their reservation in the Indian Territory and marched rapidly through the States of Kansas and Nebraska in the direction of their old hunting grounds, committing murders and other crimes on their way. From documents accompanying the report of the Secretary of the Interior it appears that this disorderly band was as fully supplied with the necessaries of life as the 4,700 other Indians who remained quietly on the reservation, and that the disturbance was caused by men of a restless and mischievous disposition among the Indians themselves. Almost the whole of this band have surrendered to the military authorities; and it is a gratifying fact that when some of them had taken refuge in the camp of the Red Cloud Sioux, with whom they had been in friendly relations, the Sioux held them as prisoners and readily gave them up to the officers of the United States, thus giving new proof of the loyal spirit which, alarming rumors to the contrary notwithstanding, they have uniformly shown ever since the wishes they expressed at the council of September, 1877, had been complied with.

Both the Secretary of the Interior and the Secretary of War unite in the recommendation that provision be made by Congress for the organization of a corps of mounted "Indian auxiliaries," to be under the control of the Army and to be used for the purpose of keeping the Indians on their reservations and preventing or repressing disturbance on their part. I earnestly concur in this recommendation. It is believed that the organization of such a body of Indian cavalry, receiving a moderate pay from the Government, would considerably weaken the restless element among the Indians by withdrawing from it a number of young men and giving them congenial employment under the Government, it being a matter of experience that Indians in our service almost without exception are faithful in the performance of the duties assigned to them. Such an organization would materially aid the Army in the accomplishment of a task for which its numerical strength is sometimes found insufficient.

But while the employment of force for the prevention or repression of Indian troubles is of occasional necessity, and wise preparation should be made to that end, greater reliance must be placed on humane and civilizing agencies for the ultimate solution of what is called the Indian problem. It may be very difficult and require much patient effort to curb the unruly spirit of the savage Indian to the restraints of civilized life, but experience shows that it is not impossible. Many of the tribes which are now quiet and orderly and self-supporting were once as savage as any that at present roam over the plains or in the mountains of the far West, and were then considered inaccessible to civilizing influences. It may be impossible to raise them fully up to the level of the white population of the United States; but we should not forget that they are the aborigines of the country, and called the soil their own on which our people have grown rich, powerful, and happy. We owe it to them as a moral duty to help them in attaining at least that degree of civilization which they may be able to reach. It is not only our duty, it is also our interest to do so. Indians who have become agriculturists or herdsmen, and feel an interest in property, will thenceforth cease to be a warlike and disturbing element. It is also a well-authenticated fact that Indians are apt to be peaceable and quiet when their children are at school, and I am gratified to know, from the expressions of Indians themselves and from many concurring reports, that there is a steadily increasing desire, even among Indians belonging to comparatively wild tribes, to have their children educated. I invite attention to the reports of the Secretary of the Interior and the Commissioner of Indian Affairs touching the experiment recently inaugurated, in taking fifty Indian children, boys and girls, from different tribes, to the Hampton Normal Agricultural Institute in Virginia, where they are to receive an elementary English education and training in agriculture and other useful works, to be returned to their tribes, after the completed course, as interpreters, instructors, and examples. It is reported that the officer charged with the selection of those children might have had thousands of young Indians sent with him had it been possible to make provision for them. I agree with the Secretary of the Interior in saying that "the result of this interesting experiment, if favorable, may be destined to become an important factor in the advancement of civilization among the Indians."

The question whether a change in the control of the Indian service should be made was at the last session of Congress referred to a committee for inquiry and report. Without desiring to anticipate that report, I venture to express the hope that in the decision of so important a question the views expressed above may not be lost sight of, and that the decision, whatever it may be, will arrest further agitation of this subject, such agitation being apt to produce a disturbing effect upon the service, as well as on the Indians themselves.

In the enrollment of the bill making appropriations for sundry civil expenses, at the last session of Congress, that portion which provided for the continuation of the Hot Springs Commission was omitted. As the commission had completed the work of taking testimony on the many conflicting claims, the suspension of their labors, before determining the rights of claimants, threatened for a time to embarrass the interests, not only of the Government, but also of a large number of the citizens of Hot Springs, who were waiting for final action on their claims before beginning contemplated improvements. In order to prevent serious difficulties, which were apprehended, and at the solicitation of many leading citizens of Hot Springs and others interested in the welfare of the town, the Secretary of the Interior was authorized to request the late commissioners to take charge of the records of their proceedings and to perform such work as could properly be done by them under such circumstances to facilitate the future adjudication of the claims at an early day and to preserve the status of the claimants until their rights should be finally determined. The late commissioners complied with that request, and report that the testimony in all the cases has been written out, examined, briefed, and so arranged as to facilitate an early settlement when authorized by law. It is recommended that the requisite authority be given at as early a day in the session as possible, and that a fair compensation be allowed the late commissioners for the expense incurred and the labor performed by them since the 25th of June last.

I invite the attention of Congress to the recommendations made by the Secretary of the Interior with regard to the preservation of the timber on the public lands of the United States. The protection of the public property is one of the first duties of the Government. The Department of the Interior should therefore be enabled by sufficient appropriations to enforce the laws in that respect. But this matter appears still more important as a question of public economy. The rapid destruction of our forests is an evil fraught with the gravest consequences, especially in the mountainous districts, where the rocky slopes, once denuded of their trees, will remain so forever. There the injury, once done, can not be repaired. I fully concur with the Secretary of the Interior in the opinion that for this reason legislation touching the public timber in the mountainous States and Territories of the West should be especially well considered, and that existing laws in which the destruction of the forests is not sufficiently guarded against should be speedily modified. A general law concerning this important subject appears to me to be a matter of urgent public necessity.

From the organization of the Government the importance of encouraging by all possible means the increase of our agricultural productions has been acknowledged and urged upon the attention of Congress and the people as the surest and readiest means of increasing our substantial and enduring prosperity.

The words of Washington are as applicable to-day as when, in his eighth annual message, he said:

It will not be doubted that, with reference either to individual or national welfare, agriculture is of primary importance. In proportion as nations advance in population and other circumstances of maturity this truth becomes more apparent, and renders the cultivation of the soil more and more an object of public patronage. Institutions for promoting it grow up, supported by the public purse; and to what object can it be dedicated with greater propriety? Among the means which have been employed to this end none have been attended with greater success than the establishment of boards (composed of proper characters) charged with collecting and diffusing information, and enabled by premiums and small pecuniary aids to encourage and assist a spirit of discovery and improvement. This species of establishment contributes doubly to the increase of improvement, by stimulating to enterprise and experiment, and by drawing to a common center the results everywhere of individual skill and observation and spreading them thence over the whole nation. Experience accordingly hath shewn that they are very cheap instruments of immense national benefits.

The preponderance of the agricultural over any other interest in the United States entitles it to all the consideration claimed for it by Washington. About one-half of the population of the United States is engaged in agriculture. The value of the agricultural products of the United States for the year 1878 is estimated at $3,000,000,000. The exports of agricultural products for the year 1877, as appears from the report of the Bureau of Statistics, were $524,000,000. The great extent of our country, with its diversity of soil and climate, enables us to produce within our own borders and by our own labor not only the necessaries, but most of the luxuries, that are consumed in civilized countries. Yet, notwithstanding our advantages of soil, climate, and intercommunication, it appears from the statistical statements in the report of the Commissioner of Agriculture that we import annually from foreign lands many millions of dollars worth of agricultural products which could be raised in our own country.

Numerous questions arise in the practice of advanced agriculture which can only be answered by experiments, often costly and sometimes fruitless, which are beyond the means of private individuals and are a just and proper charge on the whole nation for the benefit of the nation. It is good policy, especially in times of depression and uncertainty in other business pursuits, with a vast area of uncultivated, and hence unproductive, territory, wisely opened to homestead settlement, to encourage by every proper and legitimate means the occupation and tillage of the soil. The efforts of the Department of Agriculture to stimulate old and introduce new agricultural industries, to improve the quality and increase the quantity of our products, to determine the value of old or establish the importance of new methods of culture, are worthy of your careful and favorable consideration, and assistance by such appropriations of money and enlargement of facilities as may seem to be demanded by the present favorable conditions for the growth and rapid development of this important interest.

The abuse of animals in transit is widely attracting public attention. A national convention of societies specially interested in the subject has recently met at Baltimore, and the facts developed, both in regard to cruelties to animals and the effect of such cruelties upon the public health, would seem to demand the careful consideration of Congress and the enactment of more efficient laws for the prevention of these abuses.

The report of the Commissioner of the Bureau of Education shows very gratifying progress throughout the country in all the interests committed to the care of this important office. The report is especially encouraging with respect to the extension of the advantages of the common-school system in sections of the country where the general enjoyment of the privilege of free schools is not yet attained.

To education more than to any other agency we are to look as the resource for the advancement of the people in the requisite knowledge and appreciation of their rights and responsibilities as citizens, and I desire to repeat the suggestion contained in my former message in behalf of the enactment of appropriate measures by Congress for the purpose of supplementing with national aid the local systems of education in the several States.

Adequate accommodations for the great library, which is overgrowing the capacity of the rooms now occupied at the Capitol, should be provided without further delay. This invaluable collection of books, manuscripts, and illustrative art has grown to such proportions, in connection with the copyright system of the country, as to demand the prompt and careful attention of Congress to save it from injury in its present crowded and insufficient quarters. As this library is national in its character, and must from the nature of the case increase even more rapidly in the future than in the past, it can not be doubted that the people will sanction any wise expenditure to preserve it and to enlarge its usefulness.

The appeal of the Regents of the Smithsonian Institution for the means to organize, exhibit, and make available for the public benefit the articles now stored away belonging to the National Museum I heartily recommend to your favorable consideration.

The attention of Congress is again invited to the condition of the river front of the city of Washington. It is a matter of vital importance to the health of the residents of the national capital, both temporary and permanent, that the lowlands in front of the city, now subject to tidal overflow, should be reclaimed. In their present condition these flats obstruct the drainage of the city and are a dangerous source of malarial poison. The reclamation will improve the navigation of the river by restricting, and consequently deepening, its channel, and is also of importance when considered in connection with the extension of the public ground and the enlargement of the park west and south of the Washington Monument. The report of the board of survey, heretofore ordered by act of Congress, on the improvement of the harbor of Washington and Georgetown, is respectfully commended to consideration.

The report of the Commissioners of the District of Columbia presents a detailed statement of the affairs of the District.

The relative expenditures by the United States and the District for local purposes is contrasted, showing that the expenditures by the people of the District greatly exceed those of the General Government. The exhibit is made in connection with estimates for the requisite repair of the defective pavements and sewers of the city, which is a work of immediate necessity; and in the same connection a plan is presented for the permanent funding of the outstanding securities of the District.

The benevolent, reformatory, and penal institutions of the District are all entitled to the favorable attention of Congress. The Reform School needs additional buildings and teachers. Appropriations which will place all of these institutions in a condition to become models of usefulness and beneficence will be regarded by the country as liberality wisely bestowed.

The Commissioners, with evident justice, request attention to the discrimination made by Congress against the District in the donation of land for the support of the public schools, and ask that the same liberality that has been shown to the inhabitants of the various States and Territories of the United States may be extended to the District of Columbia.

The Commissioners also invite attention to the damage inflicted upon public and private interests by the present location of the depots and switching tracks of the several railroads entering the city, and ask for legislation looking to their removal. The recommendations and suggtions contained in the report will, I trust, receive the careful consideration of Congress.

Sufficient time has, perhaps, not elapsed since the reorganization of the government of the District under the recent legislation of Congress for the expression of a confident opinion as to its successful operation, but the practical results already attained are so satisfactory that the friends of the new government may well urge upon Congress the wisdom of its continuance, without essential modification, until by actual experience its advantages and defects may be more fully ascertained.

R. B. HAYES.

SPECIAL MESSAGES.

WASHINGTON, *December 4, 1878.*
To the Senate of the United States:

I transmit, for the consideration of the Senate with a view to ratification, a declaration respecting trade-marks between the United States and Brazil, concluded and signed at Rio de Janeiro on the 24th day of September last.

R. B. HAYES.

WASHINGTON, *December 4, 1878.*
To the Senate of the United States:

I transmit, for the consideration of the Senate with a view to ratification, a convention revising certain portions of existing commercial treaties and further extending commercial intercourse between the United States and Japan, concluded and signed at Washington on the 25th day of July last.

R. B. HAYES.

WASHINGTON, *December 9, 1878.*
To the Senate of the United States:

I transmit herewith a report from the Secretary of State, together with the copies of papers* therein referred to, in compliance with the resolution of the Senate of the 27th of May last.

R. B. HAYES.

WASHINGTON, *December 16, 1878.*
To the House of Representatives:

In answer to the resolution of the House of Representatives of the 5th instant, I transmit herewith a report from the Secretary of State, with its accompanying papers.†

R. B. HAYES.

EXECUTIVE MANSION, *December 17, 1878.*
To the Senate of the United States:

In answer to the resolution of the Senate of the 5th instant, requesting the transmission to the Senate of "any information which may have been received by the Departments concerning postal and commercial intercourse between the United States and South American countries, together with any recommendations desirable to be submitted of measures to be adopted for facilitating and improving such intercourse," I

---

*Correspondence relative to claims of United States citizens against Nicaragua.

†Correspondence relative to the expulsion from the German Empire of Julius Baumer, a naturalized citizen of the United States.

transmit herewith reports from the Secretary of State and the Postmaster-General, with accompanying papers.

The external commerce of the United States has for many years been the subject of solicitude because of the outward drain of the precious metals it has caused. For fully twenty years previous to 1877 the shipment of gold was constant and heavy—so heavy during the entire period of the suspension of specie payments as to preclude the hope of resumption safely during its continuance. In 1876, however, vigorous efforts were made by enterprising citizens of the country, and have since been continued, to extend our general commerce with foreign lands, especially in manufactured articles, and these efforts have been attended with very marked success.

The importation of manufactured goods was at the same time reduced in an equal degree, and the result has been an extraordinary reversal of the conditions so long prevailing and a complete cessation of the outward drain of gold. The official statement of the values represented in foreign commerce will show the unprecedented magnitude to which the movement has attained, and the protection thus secured to the public interests at the time when commercial security has become indispensable.

The agencies through which this change has been effected must be maintained and strengthened if the future is to be made secure. A return to excessive imports or to a material decline in export trade would render possible a return to the former condition of adverse balances, with the inevitable outward drain of gold as a necessary consequence. Every element of aid to the introduction of the products of our soil and manufactures into new markets should be made available. At present such is the favor in which many of the products of the United States are held that they obtain a remunerative distribution, notwithstanding positive differences of cost resulting from our defective shipping and the imperfection of our arrangements in every respect, in comparison with those of our competitors, for conducting trade with foreign markets.

If we have equal commercial facilities, we need not fear competition anywhere.

The laws have now directed a resumption of financial equality with other nations, and have ordered a return to the basis of coin values. It is of the greatest importance that the commercial condition now fortunately attained shall be made permanent, and that our rapidly increasing export trade shall not be allowed to suffer for want of the ordinary means of communication with other countries.

The accompanying reports contain a valuable and instructive summary of information with respect to our commercial interests in South America, where an inviting field for the enterprise of our people is presented. They are transmitted with the assurance that any measures that may be enacted in furtherance of these important interests will meet with my cordial approval

R. B. HAYES.

EXECUTIVE MANSION,
Washington, January 7, 1879.

To the House of Representatives:

In answer to the resolution of the House of Representatives of the 4th of December last, I transmit herewith a report from the Secretary of State, with its accompanying papers.*

R. B. HAYES.

WASHINGTON, *January 13, 1879.*

To the Senate of the United States:

In answer to a resolution of the Senate of the 3d of June last, requesting a copy of correspondence between this Government and that of Her Britannic Majesty in regard to inviting other maritime powers to accede to the three rules of neutrality laid down in Article VI of the treaty of May 8, 1871, I transmit herewith a report of the Secretary of State, together with its accompanying papers.

R. B. HAYES.

EXECUTIVE MANSION, *January 13, 1879.*

To the Senate of the United States:

In answer to a resolution of the Senate of the 17th of June last, requesting the Commissioner of Agriculture to send to the Senate certain reports on sheep husbandry, copies of the same, with accompanying papers, received from the Commissioner of Agriculture for this purpose, are herewith transmitted.

R. B. HAYES.

EXECUTIVE MANSION, *January 20, 1879.*

To the House of Representatives:

In answer to resolution of the House of Representatives of the 16th instant, requesting the Commissioner of Agriculture to forward to the House any facts or statistics in his office on the subject of forestry not heretofore reported, copies of the same, with accompanying papers, received from the Commissioner for this purpose, are herewith transmitted.

R. B. HAYES.

WASHINGTON, D. C., *January 23, 1879.*

To the House of Representatives:

In answer to a resolution of the 25th of May last, requesting information respecting the claim of Messrs. Carlos Butterfield & Co. against the Government of Denmark, I transmit herewith to the House of Representatives a report of the Secretary of State and its accompanying papers.

R. B. HAYES.

*Correspondence relative to commercial relations with Mexico.

WASHINGTON, *January 24, 1879.*

To the House of Representatives:

In answer to a resolution of the House of Representatives of the 7th instant, I transmit herewith a report* from the Secretary of State, with its accompanying papers.

R. B. HAYES.

EXECUTIVE MANSION, *January 24, 1879.*

To the Senate and House of Representatives:

I transmit herewith, for the consideration of Congress, copies of a report and accompanying papers received from the Secretary of the Interior, upon a communication addressed to the President of the United States in behalf of a certain claim of the Choctaw Nation arising under the provisions of the Choctaw and Chickasaw treaty of June 22, 1855.

R. B. HAYES.

EXECUTIVE MANSION, *January 31, 1879.*

To the Senate of the United States:

I transmit herewith a letter of the Secretary of the Treasury, in relation to the suspension of the late collector and naval officer of the port of New York, with accompanying documents.

In addition thereto I respectfully submit the following observations:

The custom-house in New York collects more than two-thirds of all the customs revenues of the Government. Its administration is a matter not of local interest merely, but is of great importance to the people of the whole country. For a long period of time it has been used to manage and control political affairs.

The officers suspended by me are and for several years have been engaged in the active personal management of the party politics of the city and State of New York. The duties of the offices held by them have been regarded as of subordinate importance to their partisan work. Their offices have been conducted as part of the political machinery under their control. They have made the custom-house a center of partisan political management. The custom-house should be a business office. It should be conducted on business principles. General James, the postmaster of New York City, writing on this subject, says:

The post-office is a business institution, and should be run as such. It is my deliberate judgment that I and my subordinates can do more for the party of our choice by giving the people of this city a good and efficient postal service than by controlling primaries or dictating nominations.

The New York custom-house should be placed on the same footing with the New York post-office. But under the suspended officers the custom-house would be one of the principal political agencies in the State

---

*Relating to the claim of John C. Landreau against the Government of Peru.

of New York. To change this, they profess to believe, would be, in the language of Mr. Cornell in his response, " to surrender their personal and political rights."

Convinced that the people of New York and of the country generally wish the New York custom-house to be administered solely with a view to the public interest, it is my purpose to do all in my power to introduce into this great office the reforms which the country desires.

With my information of the facts in the case, and with a deep sense of the responsible obligation imposed upon me by the Constitution " to take care that the laws be faithfully executed," I regard it as my plain duty to suspend the officers in question and to make the nominations now before the Senate, in order that this important office may be honestly and efficiently administered.

R. B. HAYES.

WASHINGTON, *February 6, 1879.*
To the Senate of the United States:

I transmit herewith, for the information of Congress, a report from the Secretary of State, with the accompanying papers therein referred to, in relation to the proceedings of the International Monetary Conference held at Paris in August, 1878.

R. B. HAYES.

EXECUTIVE MANSION, *February 8, 1879.*
To the Senate and House of Representatives:

I transmit herewith, for the consideration of Congress, the report of the commission appointed under the provisions of the act approved May 3, 1878, entitled "An act authorizing the President of the United States to make certain negotiations with the Ute Indians in the State of Colorado," with copies of letters from the Secretary of the Interior and the Commissioner of Indian Affairs, and accompanying documents.

R. B. HAYES.

WASHINGTON, D. C., *February 15, 1879.*
To the Senate and House of Representatives:

I transmit herewith report from the Secretary of State, and accompanying papers, in relation to proceedings of the International Prison Congress of Stockholm, held in August last.

R. B. HAYES.

WASHINGTON, D. C., *February 18, 1879.*
To the House of Representatives:

I transmit herewith a report from the Secretary of State, dated the 17th instant, in relation to the destruction of the bark *Forest Belle* in

Chinese waters in March last, submitted in compliance with the resolution of the House of Representatives of February 4, 1879.

R. B. HAYES.

EXECUTIVE MANSION,
February 21, 1879.

To the Senate and House of Representatives:

Referring to my communication to Congress under date of the 8th instant, transmitting the report of the commission appointed under the act entitled "An act authorizing the President of the United States to make certain negotiations with the Ute Indians in the State of Colorado," I submit herewith a copy of a letter from the Secretary of the Interior and additional papers upon the same subject.

R. B. HAYES.

WASHINGTON, *February 28, 1879.*

To the Senate of the United States:

I transmit herewith a report from the Secretary of State, with its accompanying papers, submitted in pursuance of a resolution of the Senate of the 20th instant, in relation to railroads in Mexico.

R. B. HAYES.

WASHINGTON, *March 3, 1879.*

To the Senate and House of Representatives:

I have received from the United States Centennial Commission their final report, presenting a full exhibit of the result of the United States Centennial Celebration and Exhibition of 1876, as required by the act of June 1, 1872.

In transmitting this report for the consideration of Congress, I express, I believe, the general judgment of the country, as well as my own, in assigning to this exhibition a measure of success gratifying to the pride and patriotism of our people and full of promise to the great industrial and commercial interests of the nation. The very ample and generous contributions which the foreign nations made to the splendor and usefulness of the exhibition and the cordiality with which their representatives took part in our national commemoration deserve our profound acknowledgments. At this close of the great services rendered by the United States Centennial Commission and the Centennial board of finance, it gives me great pleasure to commend to your attention and that of the people of the whole country the laborious, faithful, and prosperous performances of their duties which have marked the administration of their respective trusts.

R. B. HAYES.

VETO MESSAGE.

EXECUTIVE MANSION, *March 1, 1879.*

To the House of Representatives:

After a very careful consideration of House bill 2423, entitled "An act to restrict the immigration of Chinese to the United States," I herewith return it to the House of Representatives, in which it originated, with my objections to its passage.

The bill, as it was sent to the Senate from the House of Representatives, was confined in its provisions to the object named in its title, which is that of "An act to restrict the immigration of Chinese to the United States." The only means adopted to secure the proposed object was the limitation on the number of Chinese passengers which might be brought to this country by any one vessel to fifteen; and as this number was not fixed in any proportion to the size or tonnage of the vessel or by any consideration of the safety or accommodation of these passengers, the simple purpose and effect of the enactment were to repress this immigration to an extent falling but little short of its absolute exclusion.

The bill, as amended in the Senate and now presented to me, includes an independent and additional provision which aims at and in terms requires the abrogation by this Government of Articles V and VI of the treaty with China commonly called the Burlingame treaty, through the action of the Executive enjoined by this provision of the act.

The Burlingame treaty, of which the ratifications were exchanged at Peking November 23, 1869, recites as the occasion and motive of its negotiation by the two Governments that "since the conclusion of the treaty between the United States of America and the Ta Tsing Empire (China) of the 18th of June, 1858, circumstances have arisen showing the necessity of additional articles thereto," and proceeds to an agreement as to said additional articles. These negotiations, therefore, ending by the signature of the additional articles July 28, 1868, had for their object the completion of our treaty rights and obligations toward the Government of China by the incorporation of these new articles as thenceforth parts of the principal treaty to which they are made supplemental. Upon the settled rules of interpretation applicable to such supplemental negotiations the text of the principal treaty and of these "additional articles thereto" constitute one treaty from the conclusion of the new negotiations, in all parts of equal and concurrent force and obligation between the two Governments, and to all intents and purposes as if embraced in one instrument.

The principal treaty, of which the ratifications were exchanged August 16, 1859, recites that "the United States of America and the Ta Tsing Empire, desiring to maintain firm, lasting, and sincere friendship, have resolved to renew, in a manner clear and positive, by means of a treaty or general convention of peace, amity, and commerce, the rules which shall in future be mutually observed in the intercourse of their respective countries," and proceeds in its thirty articles to lay out a careful and comprehensive system for the commercial relations of our people with China. The main substance of all the provisions of this treaty is to define and secure the rights of our people in respect of access to, residence and protection in, and trade with China. The actual provisions in our favor in these respects were framed to be, and have been found to be, adequate and appropriate to the interests of our commerce; and by the concluding article we receive the important guaranty that—

Should at any time the Ta Tsing Empire grant to any nation, or the merchants or citizens of any nation, any right, privilege, or favor, connected either with navigation, commerce, political or other intercourse, which is not conferred by this treaty, such right, privilege, and favor shall at once freely inure to the benefit of the United States, its public officers, merchants, and citizens.

Against this body of stipulations in our favor and this permanent engagement of equality in respect of all future concessions to foreign nations the general promise of permanent peace and good offices on our part seems to be the only equivalent. For this the first article undertakes as follows:

There shall be, as there have always been, peace and friendship between the United States of America and the Ta Tsing Empire, and between their people respectively. They shall not insult or oppress each other for any trifling cause, so as to produce an estrangement between them; and if any other nation should act unjustly or oppressively, the United States will exert their good offices, on being informed of the case, to bring about an amicable arrangement of the question, thus showing their friendly feelings.

At the date of the negotiation of this treaty our Pacific possessions had attracted a considerable Chinese emigration, and the advantages and the inconveniences felt or feared therefrom had become more or less manifest; but they dictated no stipulations on the subject to be incorporated in the treaty. The year 1868 was marked by the striking event of a spontaneous embassy from the Chinese Empire, headed by an American citizen, Anson Burlingame, who had relinquished his diplomatic representation of his own country in China to assume that of the Chinese Empire to the United States and the European nations. By this time the facts of the Chinese immigration and its nature and influences, present and prospective, had become more noticeable and were more observed by the population immediately affected and by this Government. The principal feature of the Burlingame treaty was its attention to and its treatment of the Chinese immigration and the Chinese as forming, or as they should form, a part of our population. Up to this time our uncovenanted hospitality to immigration, our fearless liberality of citizenship, our equal and comprehensive justice to all inhabitants, whether they abjured their foreign nationality or not, our civil freedom, and our religious toleration had made all comers welcome, and under these pro-tections the Chinese in considerable numbers had made their lodgment upon our soil.

The Burlingame treaty undertakes to deal with this situation, and its fifth and sixth articles embrace its most important provisions in this regard and the main stipulations in which the Chinese Government has secured an obligatory protection of its subjects within our territory. They read as follows:

ART. V. The United States of America and the Emperor of China cordially recognize the inherent and inalienable right of man to change his home and allegiance, and also the mutual advantage of the free migration and emigration of their citizens and subjects respectively from the one country to the other for purposes of curiosity, of trade, or as permanent residents. The high contracting parties therefore join in reprobating any other than an entirely voluntary emigration for these purposes. They consequently agree to pass laws making it a penal offense for a citizen of the United States or Chinese subjects to take Chinese subjects either to the United States or to any other foreign country, or for a Chinese subject or citizen of the United States to take citizens of the United States to China or to any other foreign country, without their free and voluntary consent, respectively.

ART. VI. Citizens of the United States visiting or residing in China shall enjoy the same privileges, immunities, or exemptions in respect to travel or residence as may there be enjoyed by the citizens or subjects of the most favored nation, and, reciprocally, Chinese subjects visiting or residing in the United States shall enjoy the same privileges, immunities, and exemptions in respect to travel or residence as may there be enjoyed by the citizens or subjects of the most favored nation. But nothing herein contained shall be held to confer naturalization upon citizens of the United States in China, nor upon the subjects of China in the United States.

An examination of these two articles in the light of the experience then influential in suggesting their "necessity" will show that the fifth article was framed in hostility to what seemed the principal mischief to be guarded against, to wit, the introduction of Chinese laborers by methods which should have the character of a forced and servile importation, and not of a voluntary emigration of freemen seeking our shores upon motives and in a manner consonant with the system of our institutions and approved by the experience of the nation. Unquestionably the adhesion of the Government of China to these liberal principles of freedom in emigration, with which we were so familiar and with which we were so well satisfied, was a great advance toward opening that Empire to our civilization and religion, and gave promise in the future of greater and greater practical results in the diffusion throughout that great population of our arts and industries, our manufactures, our material improvements, and the sentiments of government and religion which seem to us so important to the welfare of mankind. The first clause of this article secures this acceptance by China of the American doctrines of free migration to and fro among the peoples and races of the earth.

The second clause, however, in its reprobation of "any other than an entirely voluntary emigration" by both the high contracting parties, and in the reciprocal obligations whereby we secured the solemn and unqualified engagement on the part of the Government of China "to pass laws making it a penal offense for a citizen of the United States or Chinese subjects to take Chinese subjects either to the United States or to any other foreign country without their free and voluntary consent," constitutes the great force and value of this article. Its importance both in principle and in its practical service toward our protection against servile importation in the guise of immigration can not be overestimated. It commits the Chinese Government to active and efficient measures to suppress this iniquitous system, where those measures are most necessary and can be most effectual. It gives to this Government the footing of a treaty right to such measures and the means and opportunity of insisting upon their adoption and of complaint and resentment at their neglect. The fifth article, therefore, if it fall short of what the pressure of the later experience of our Pacific States may urge upon the attention of this Government as essential to the public welfare, seems to be in the right direction and to contain important advantages which once relinquished can not be easily recovered.

The second topic which interested the two Governments under the actual condition of things which prompted the Burlingame treaty was adequate protection, under the solemn and definite guaranties of a treaty, of the Chinese already in this country and those who should seek our shores. This was the object, and forms the subject of the sixth article, by whose reciprocal engagement the citizens and subjects of the two Governments, respectively, visiting or residing in the country of the other are secured the same privileges, immunities, or exemptions there enjoyed by the citizens or subjects of the most favored nations. The treaty of 1858, to which these articles are made supplemental, provides for a great amount of privilege and protection, both of person and property, to American citizens in China, but it is upon this sixth article that the main body of the treaty rights and securities of the Chinese already in this country depends. Its abrogation, were the rest of the treaty left in force, would leave them to such treatment as we should voluntarily accord them by our laws and customs. Any treaty obligation would be wanting to restrain our liberty of action toward them, or to measure or sustain the right of the Chinese Government to complaint or redress in their behalf.

The lapse of ten years since the negotiation of the Burlingame treaty has exhibited to the notice of the Chinese Government, as well as to our own people, the working of this experiment of immigration in great numbers of Chinese laborers to this country, and their maintenance here of all the traits of race, religion, manners, and customs, habitations, mode of life, segregation here, and the keeping up of the ties of their original home, which stamp them as strangers and sojourners, and not as incorporated elements of our national life and growth. This experience may naturally suggest the reconsideration of the subject as dealt with by the

Burlingame treaty, and may properly become the occasion of more direct and circumspect recognition, in renewed negotiations, of the difficulties surrounding this political and social problem. It may well be that, to the apprehension of the Chinese Government no less than our own, the simple provisions of the Burlingame treaty may need to be replaced by more careful methods, securing the Chinese and ourselves against a larger and more rapid infusion of this foreign race than our system of industry and society can take up and assimilate with ease and safety. This ancient Government, ruling a polite and sensitive people, distinguished by a high sense of national pride, may properly desire an adjustment of their relations with us which would in all things confirm and in no degree endanger the permanent peace and amity and the growing commerce and prosperity which it has been the object and the effect of our existing treaties to cherish and perpetuate.

I regard the very grave discontents of the people of the Pacific States with the present working of the Chinese immigration, and their still graver apprehensions therefrom in the future, as deserving the most serious attention of the people of the whole country and a solicitous interest on the part of Congress and the Executive. If this were not my own judgment, the passage of this bill by both Houses of Congress would impress upon me the seriousness of the situation, when a majority of the representatives of the people of the whole country had thought fit to justify so serious a measure of relief.

The authority of Congress to terminate a treaty with a foreign power by expressing the will of the nation no longer to adhere to it is as free from controversy under our Constitution as is the further proposition that the power of making new treaties or modifying existing treaties is not lodged by the Constitution in Congress, but in the President, by and with the advice and consent of the Senate, as shown by the concurrence of two-thirds of that body. A denunciation of a treaty by any government is confessedly justifiable only upon some reason both of the highest justice and of the highest necessity. The action of Congress in the matter of the French treaties in 1798, if it be regarded as an abrogation by this nation of a subsisting treaty, strongly illustrates the character and degree of justification which was then thought suitable to such a proceeding. The preamble of the act recites that the—

Treaties concluded between the United States and France have been repeatedly violated on the part of the French Government, and the just claims of the United States for reparation of the injuries so committed have been refused, and their attempts to negotiate an amicable adjustment of all complaints between the two nations have been repelled with indignity.

And that—

Under authority of the French Government there is yet pursued against the United States a system of predatory violence, infracting the said treaties and hostile to the rights of a free and independent nation.

The enactment, as a logical consequence of these recited facts, declares—

That the United States are of right freed and exonerated from the stipulations of the treaties and of the consular convention heretofore concluded between the United

By the President of the United States
of America

A Proclamation.

Whereas it is provided in the Constitution of the United States that the United States shall protect every State in the Union on application of the Legislature, or of the Executive (when the Legislature cannot be convened) against domestic violence:

And whereas the Governor of the State of Maryland has represented that domestic violence exists in said state, at Cumberland, and along the line of the Baltimore and Ohio Rail Road in said state, which the authorities of said state are unable to suppress:

And whereas the laws of the United States require that in all cases of insurrection

FIRST PAGE OF PRESIDENT HAYES' PROCLAMATION TO SUPPRESS RAILROAD STRIKE IN MARYLAND.

or before noon of the twenty second day of July, instant:

In testimony whereof I have hereunto set my hand and caused the seal of the United States to be affixed.

Done at the City of Washington, this twenty first day of July, in the year of our Lord, one thousand eight hundred and seventy seven, and of the Independence of the United States of America the One Hundred and Second.

R. B. Hayes

By the President;
Wm. Evarts
Secretary of State

LAST PAGE AND SIGNATURE OF PRESIDENT HAYES' PROC-
LAMATION TO SUPPRESS MARYLAND RAILROAD STRIKE.

States and France, and that the same shall not henceforth be regarded as legally obligatory on the Government or citizens of the United States.

The history of the Government shows no other instance of an abrogation of a treaty by Congress.

Instances have sometimes occurred where the ordinary legislation of Congress has, by its conflict with some treaty obligation of the Government toward a foreign power, taken effect as an *infraction* of the treaty, and been judicially declared to be operative to that result; but neither such legislation nor such judicial sanction of the same has been regarded as an *abrogation*, even for the moment, of the treaty. On the contrary, the treaty in such case still subsists between the governments, and the casual infraction is repaired by appropriate satisfaction in maintenance of the treaty.

The bill before me does not enjoin upon the President the abrogation of the entire Burlingame treaty, much less of the principal treaty of which it is made the supplement. As the power of modifying an existing treaty, whether by adding or striking out provisions, is a part of the treaty-making power under the Constitution, its exercise is not competent for Congress, nor would the assent of China to this partial abrogation of the treaty make the action of Congress in thus procuring an amendment of a treaty a competent exercise of authority under the Constitution. The importance, however, of this special consideration seems superseded by the principle that a denunciation of a part of a treaty not made by the terms of the treaty itself separable from the rest is a denunciation of the whole treaty. As the other high contracting party has entered into no treaty obligations except such as include the part denounced, the denunciation by one party of the part necessarily liberates the other party from the whole treaty.

I am convinced that, whatever urgency might in any quarter or by any interest be supposed to require an instant suppression of further immigration from China, no reasons can require the immediate withdrawal of our treaty protection of the Chinese already in this country, and no circumstances can tolerate an exposure of our citizens in China, merchants or missionaries, to the consequences of so sudden an abrogation of their treaty protection. Fortunately, however, the actual recession in the flow of the emigration from China to the Pacific Coast, shown by trustworthy statistics, relieves us from any apprehension that the treatment of the subject in the proper course of diplomatic negotiations will introduce any new features of discontent or disturbance among the communities directly affected. Were such delay fraught with more inconveniences than have ever been suggested by the interests most earnest in promoting this legislation, I can not but regard the summary disturbance of our existing treaties with China as greatly more inconvenient to much wider and more permanent interests of the country.

I have no occasion to insist upon the more general considerations of interest and duty which sacredly guard the faith of the nation, in whatever form of obligation it may have been given. These sentiments animate the deliberations of Congress and pervade the minds of our whole people. Our history gives little occasion for any reproach in this regard; and in asking the renewed attention of Congress to this bill I am persuaded that their action will maintain the public duty and the public honor.

R. B. HAYES

PROCLAMATION.

By the President of the United States of America

A PROCLAMATION.

Whereas the final adjournment of the Forty-fifth Congress without making the usual and necessary appropriations for the legislative, executive, and judicial expenses of the Government for the fiscal year ending June 30, 1880, and without making the usual and necessary appropriations for the support of the Army for the same fiscal year, presents an extraordinary occasion requiring the President to exercise the power vested in him by the Constitution to convene the Houses of Congress in anticipation of the day fixed by law for their next meeting:

Now, therefore, I, Rutherford B. Hayes, President of the United States, do, by virtue of the power to this end in me vested by the Constitution, convene both Houses of Congress to assemble at their respective chambers at 12 o'clock noon on Tuesday, the 18th day of March instant, then and there to consider and determine such measures as in their wisdom their duty and the welfare of the people may seem to demand.

In witness whereof I have hereunto set my hand and caused the seal of the United States to be affixed.

[SEAL.]   Done at the city of Washington, this 4th day of March, A. D. 1879, and of the Independence of the United States of America the one hundred and third.

R. B. HAYES.

By the President:

WM. M. EVARTS, *Secretary of State.*

SPECIAL SESSION MESSAGE.

WASHINGTON, *March 19, 1879.*

Fellow-Citizens of the Senate and House of Representatives:

The failure of the last Congress to make the requisite appropriations for legislative and judicial purposes, for the expenses of the several Executive Departments of the Government, and for the support of the Army has made it necessary to call a special session of the Forty-sixth Congress.

The estimates of the appropriations needed which were sent to Congress by the Secretary of the Treasury at the opening of the last session are renewed, and are herewith transmitted to both the Senate and the House of Representatives.

Regretting the existence of the emergency which requires a special session of Congress at a time when it is the general judgment of the country that the public welfare will be best promoted by permanency in our legislation and by peace and rest, I commend these few necessary measures to your considerate attention.

RUTHERFORD B. HAYES.

SPECIAL MESSAGES.

WASHINGTON, *March 20, 1879.*

To the Senate of the United States:

In compliance with the resolution of the Senate of the 3d instant, calling for the reports of Gustavus Goward on the Samoan Islands, I transmit herewith a report from the Secretary of State, with the accompanying papers.

R. B. HAYES.

EXECUTIVE MANSION, *April 18, 1879.*

To the Senate of the United States:

In compliance with a resolution of the Senate of the 15th instant, I transmit herewith a copy of the report of the commission appointed by the President on the 15th of March, 1872, relating to the different interoceanic canal surveys and the practicability of the construction of a ship canal across this continent.

R. B. HAYES.

EXECUTIVE MANSION, *May 15, 1879.*

To the Senate of the United States:

In response to a resolution of the Senate of the 7th instant, requesting information in reference to an alleged occupation of a portion of the Indian Territory by white settlers, etc., I transmit herewith a copy of my proclamation dated April 26, 1879;* also copies of the correspondence and papers on file and of record in the Department of the Interior and the War Department touching the subject of the resolution.

R. B. HAYES.

* See pp. 4499-4500.

EXECUTIVE MANSION, *May 26, 1879.*

To the Senate of the United States:

In response to a resolution of the Senate of the 14th instant, I transmit herewith a communication* from the Secretary of the Interior and accompanying papers.
R. B. HAYES.

EXECUTIVE MANSION, *June 5, 1879.*

To the Senate and House of Representatives:

I transmit herewith the "proceedings and report" of the board of officers convened by Special Orders, No. 78, Headquarters of the Army, Washington, April 12, 1878, in the case of Fitz John Porter. The report of the board was made in March last, but the official record of the proceedings did not reach me until the 3d instant.

I have given to this report such examination as satisfies me that I ought to lay the proceedings and conclusions of the board before Congress. As I am without power, in the absence of legislation, to act upon the recommendations of the report further than by submitting the same to Congress, the proceedings and conclusions of the board are transmitted for the information of Congress and such action as in your wisdom shall seem expedient and just.
R. B. HAYES.

WASHINGTON, *June 13, 1879.*

To the House of Representatives:

I transmit herewith, in compliance with the resolution of the House of Representatives of the 29th ultimo, a report of the Secretary of State relative to the steps taken by this Government to promote the establishment of an interoceanic canal across or near the Isthmus of Darien.
R. B. HAYES.

WASHINGTON, *June 23, 1879.*

To the Senate of the United States:

I transmit herewith to the Senate a report from the Secretary of State, in response to a resolution of that body of the 20th instant, calling for the proceedings and accompanying papers of the International Silver Conference held in Paris in 1878.
R. B. HAYES.

EXECUTIVE MANSION, *June 30, 1879.*

To the Senate and House of Representatives:

The bill making provision for the payment of the fees of United States marshals and their general deputies, which I have this day returned to

---

*Relating to lands in the Indian Territory acquired by the treaties of 1866.

the House of Representatives, in which it originated, with my objections,* having upon its reconsideration by that body failed to become a law, I respectfully call your attention to the immediate necessity of making some adequate provision for the due and efficient execution by the marshals and deputy marshals of the United States of the constant and important duties enjoined upon them by the existing laws. All appropriations to provide for the performance of these indispensable duties expire to-day. Under the laws prohibiting public officers from involving the Government in contract liabilities beyond actual appropriations, it is apparent that the means at the disposal of the executive department for executing the laws through the regular ministerial officers will after to-day be left inadequate. The suspension of these necessary functions in the orderly administration of the first duties of government for the shortest period is inconsistent with the public interests, and at any moment may prove inconsistent with the public safety.

It is impossible for me to look without grave concern upon a state of things which will leave the public service thus unprovided for and the public interests thus unprotected, and I earnestly urge upon your attention the necessity of making immediate appropriations for the maintenance of the service of the marshals and deputy marshals for the fiscal year which commences to-morrow.

RUTHERFORD B. HAYES.

WASHINGTON, *July 1, 1879.*

To the Senate of the United States:

In answer to a resolution of the Senate of the 28th June, 1879, requesting a copy of any correspondence which may have passed between the Department of State and the Republic of Mexico in regard to the proposed Austin-Topolovampo Railroad survey across the northern States of that country, I transmit herewith the report of the Secretary of State upon the subject.

R. B. HAYES.

VETO MESSAGES.

EXECUTIVE MANSION, *April 29, 1879.*

To the House of Representatives:

I have maturely considered the important questions presented by the bill entitled "An act making appropriations for the support of the Army for the fiscal year ending June 30, 1880, and for other purposes," and I now return it to the House of Representatives, in which it originated, with my objections to its approval.

The bill provides in the usual form for the appropriations required

* See pp. 4497–4499.

for the support of the Army during the next fiscal year. If it contained no other provisions, it would receive my prompt approval. It includes, however, further legislation, which, attached, as it is, to appropriations which are requisite for the efficient performance of some of the most necessary duties of the Government, involves questions of the gravest character. The sixth section of the bill is amendatory of the statute now in force in regard to the authority of persons in the civil, military, and naval service of the United States "at the place where any general or special election is held in any State." This statute was adopted February 25, 1865, after a protracted debate in the Senate, and almost without opposition in the House of Representatives, by the concurrent votes of both of the leading political parties of the country, and became a law by the approval of President Lincoln. It was reenacted in 1874 in the Revised Statutes of the United States, sections 2002 and 5528, which are as follows:

SEC. 2002. No military or naval officer, or other person engaged in the civil, military, or naval service of the United States, shall order, bring, keep, or have under his authority or control any troops or armed men at the place where any general or special election is held in any State, unless it be necessary to repel the armed enemies of the United States or to keep the peace at the polls.

SEC. 5528. Every officer of the Army or Navy, or other person in the civil, military, or naval service of the United States, who orders, brings, keeps, or has under his authority or control any troops or armed men at any place where a general or special election is held in any State, unless such force be necessary to repel armed enemies of the United States or to keep the peace at the polls, shall be fined not more than $5,000 and suffer imprisonment at hard labor not less than three months nor more than five years.

The amendment proposed to this statute in the bill before me omits from both of the foregoing sections the words "or to keep the peace at the polls." The effect of the adoption of this amendment may be considered—

First. Upon the right of the United States Government to use military force to keep the peace at the elections for Members of Congress; and

Second. Upon the right of the Government, by civil authority, to protect these elections from violence and fraud.

In addition to the sections of the statute above quoted, the following provisions of law relating to the use of the military power at the elections are now in force:

SEC. 2003. No officer of the Army or Navy of the United States shall prescribe or fix, or attempt to prescribe or fix, by proclamation, order, or otherwise, the qualifications of voters in any State, or in any manner interfere with the freedom of any election in any State, or with the exercise of the free right of suffrage in any State.

SEC. 5529. Every officer or other person in the military or naval service who, by force, threat, intimidation, order, advice, or otherwise, prevents, or attempts to prevent, any qualified voter of any State from freely exercising the right of suffrage at any general or special election in such State shall be fined not more than $5,000 and imprisoned at hard labor not more than five years.

SEC. 5530. Every officer of the Army or Navy who prescribes or fixes, or attempts to prescribe or fix, whether by proclamation, order, or otherwise, the qualifications of voters at any election in any State shall be punished as provided in the preceding section.

SEC. 5531. Every officer or other person in the military or naval service who, by force, threat, intimidation, order, or otherwise, compels, or attempts to compel, any officer holding an election in any State to receive a vote from a person not legally qualified to vote, or who imposes, or attempts to impose, any regulations for conducting any general or special election in a State different from those prescribed by law, or who interferes in any manner with any officer of an election in the discharge of his duty, shall be punished as provided in section 5529.

SEC. 5532. Every person convicted of any of the offenses specified in the five preceding sections shall, in addition to the punishments therein severally prescribed, be disqualified from holding any office of honor, profit, or trust under the United States; but nothing in those sections shall be construed to prevent any officer, soldier, sailor, or marine from exercising the right of suffrage in any election district to which he may belong, if otherwise qualified according to the laws of the State in which he offers to vote.

The foregoing enactments would seem to be sufficient to prevent military interference with the elections. But the last Congress, to remove all apprehension of such interference, added to this body of law section 15 of an act entitled "An act making appropriations for the support of the Army for the fiscal year ending June 30, 1879, and for other purposes," approved June 18, 1878, which is as follows:

SEC. 15. From and after the passage of this act it shall not be lawful to employ any part of the Army of the United States, as a *posse comitatus* or otherwise, for the purpose of executing the laws, except in such cases and under such circumstances as such employment of said force may be expressly authorized by the Constitution or by act of Congress; and no money appropriated by this act shall be used to pay any of the expenses incurred in the employment of any troops in violation of this section; and any person willfully violating the provisions of this section shall be deemed guilty of a misdemeanor, and on conviction thereof shall be punished by fine not exceeding $10,000 or imprisonment not exceeding two years, or by both such fine and imprisonment.

This act passed the Senate, after full consideration, without a single vote recorded against it on its final passage, and, by a majority of more than two-thirds, it was concurred in by the House of Representatives.

The purpose of the section quoted was stated in the Senate by one of its supporters as follows:

Therefore I hope, without getting into any controversy about the past, but acting wisely for the future, that we shall take away the idea that the Army can be used by a general or special deputy marshal, or any marshal, merely for election purposes, as a posse, ordering them about the polls or ordering them anywhere else, when there is an election going on, to prevent disorders or to suppress disturbances that should be suppressed by the peace officers of the State; or, if they must bring others to their aid they should summon the unorganized citizens, and not summon the officers and men of the Army as a *posse comitatus* to quell disorders, and thus get up a feeling which will be disastrous to peace among the people of the country.

In the House of Representatives the object of the act of 1878 was stated by the gentleman who had it in charge in similar terms. He said:

But these are all minor points and insignificant questions compared with the great principle which was incorporated by the House in the bill in reference to the use of the Army in time of peace. The Senate had already conceded what they called and what we might accept as the principle, but they had stricken out the penalty, and had stricken out the word "*expressly*," so that the Army might be used in all cases where *implied* authority might be inferred. The House committee planted themselves firmly upon the doctrine that rather than yield this fundamental principle, for which for three years this House had struggled, they would allow the bill to fail, notwithstanding the reforms which we had secured, regarding these reforms as of but little consequence alongside the great principle that the Army of the United States, in time of peace, should be under the control of Congress and obedient to its laws. After a long and protracted negotiation, the Senate committee have conceded that principle in all its length and breadth, including the penalty, which the Senate had stricken out. We bring you back, therefore, a report, with the alteration of a single word, which the lawyers assure me is proper to be made, restoring to this bill the principle for which we have contended so long, and which is so vital to secure the rights and liberties of the people.

  *   *   *   *   *   *

Thus have we this day secured to the people of this country the same great protection against a standing army which cost a struggle of two hundred years for the Commons of England to secure for the British people.

From this brief review of the subject it sufficiently appears that under existing laws there can be no military interference with the elections. No case of such interference has, in fact, occurred since the passage of the act last referred to. No soldier of the United States has appeared under orders at any place of election in any State. No complaint even of the presence of United States troops has been made in any quarter. It may therefore be confidently stated that there is no necessity for the enactment of section 6 of the bill before me to prevent military interference with the elections. The laws already in force are all that is required for that end.

But that part of section 6 of this bill which is significant and vitally important is the clause which, if adopted, will deprive the civil authorities of the United States of all power to keep the peace at the Congressional elections. The Congressional elections in every district, in a very important sense, are justly a matter of political interest and concern throughout the whole country. Each State, every political party, is entitled to the share of power which is conferred by the legal and constitutional suffrage. It is the right of every citizen possessing the qualifications prescribed by law to cast one unintimidated ballot and to have his ballot honestly counted. So long as the exercise of this power and the enjoyment of this right are common and equal, practically as well as formally, submission to the results of the suffrage will be accorded loyally and cheerfully, and all the departments of Government will feel the true vigor of the popular will thus expressed.

Two provisions of the Constitution authorize legislation by Congress for the regulation of the Congressional elections.

Section 4 of Article I of the Constitution declares—

The times, places, and manner of holding elections for Senators and Representatives shall be prescribed in each State by the legislature thereof; but the Congress may at any time, by law, make or alter such regulations, except as to the places of choosing Senators.

The fifteenth amendment of the Constitution is as follows:

SEC. 1. The right of citizens of the United States to vote shall not be denied or abridged by the United States or by any State on account of race, color, or previous condition of servitude.

SEC. 2. The Congress shall have power to enforce this article by appropriate legislation.

The Supreme Court has held that this amendment invests the citizens of the United States with a new constitutional right which is within the protecting power of Congress. That right the court declares to be exemption from discrimination in the exercise of the elective franchise on account of race, color, or previous condition of servitude. The power of Congress to protect this right by appropriate legislation is expressly affirmed by the court.

National legislation to provide safeguards for free and honest elections is necessary, as experience has shown, not only to secure the right to vote to the enfranchised race at the South, but also to prevent fraudulent voting in the large cities of the North. Congress has therefore exercised the power conferred by the Constitution, and has enacted certain laws to prevent discriminations on account of race, color, or previous condition of servitude, and to punish fraud, violence, and intimidation at Federal elections. Attention is called to the following sections of the Revised Statutes of the United States, viz:

Section 2004, which guarantees to all citizens the right to vote, without distinction on account of race, color, or previous condition of servitude.

Sections 2005 and 2006, which guarantee to all citizens equal opportunity, without discrimination, to perform all the acts required by law as a prerequisite or qualification for voting.

Section 2022, which authorizes the United States marshal and his deputies to keep the peace and preserve order at the Federal elections.

Section 2024, which expressly authorizes the United States marshal and his deputies to summon a *posse comitatus* whenever they or any of them are forcibly resisted in the execution of their duties under the law or are prevented from executing such duties by violence.

Section 5522, which provides for the punishment of the crime of interfering with the supervisors of elections and deputy marshals in the discharge of their duties at the elections of Representatives in Congress.

These are some of the laws on this subject which it is the duty of the executive department of the Government to enforce. The intent and effect of the sixth section of this bill is to prohibit all the civil officers of the United States, under penalty of fine and imprisonment, from employing any adequate civil force for this purpose at the place where their enforcement is most necessary, namely, at the places where the Congressional elections are held. Among the most valuable enactments to which I have referred are those which protect the supervisors of Federal elections in the discharge of their duties at the polls. If the proposed legislation should become the law, there will be no power vested in any officer of the Government to protect from violence the officers of the United States engaged in the discharge of their duties. Their rights and duties under the law will remain, but the National Government will be powerless to enforce its own statutes. The States may employ both military and civil power to keep the peace and to enforce the laws at State elections. It is now proposed to deny to the United States even the necessary civil authority to protect the national elections. No sufficient reason has been given for this discrimination in favor of the State and against the national authority. If well-founded objections exist against the present national election laws, all good citizens should unite in their amendment. The laws providing the safeguards of the elections should be impartial, just, and efficient. They should, if possible, be so nonpartisan and fair in their operation that the minority— the party out of power—will have no just grounds to complain. The present laws have in practice unquestionably conduced to the prevention of fraud and violence at the elections. In several of the States members of different political parties have applied for the safeguards which they furnish. It is the right and duty of the National Government to enact and enforce laws which will secure free and fair Congressional elections. The laws now in force should not be repealed except in connection with the enactment of measures which will better accomplish that important end. Believing that section 6 of the bill before me will weaken, if it does not altogether take away, the power of the National Government to protect the Federal elections by the civil authorities, I am forced to the conclusion that it ought not to receive my approval.

This section is, however, not presented to me as a separate and independent measure, but is, as has been stated, attached to the bill making the usual annual appropriations for the support of the Army. It makes a vital change in the election laws of the country, which is in no way connected with the use of the Army. It prohibits, under heavy penalties, any person engaged in the civil service of the United States from having any force at the place of any election, prepared to preserve order, to make arrests, to keep the peace, or in any manner to enforce the laws. This is altogether foreign to the purpose of an Army appropriation bill. The practice of tacking to appropriation bills measures not pertinent to such bills did not prevail until more than forty years after the adoption of the Constitution. It has become a common practice. All parties when in power have adopted it. Many abuses and great waste of public money have in this way crept into appropriation bills. The public opinion of the country is against it. The States which have recently adopted constitutions have generally provided a remedy for the evil by enacting that no law shall contain more than one subject, which shall be plainly expressed in its title. The constitutions of more than half of the States contain substantially this provision. The public welfare will be promoted in many ways by a return to the early practice of the Government and to the true principle of legislation, which requires that every measure shall stand or fall according to its own merits. If it were understood that to attach to an appropriation bill a measure irrelevant to the general object of the bill would imperil and probably prevent its final passage and approval, a valuable reform in the parliamentary practice of Congress would be accomplished. The best justification that has been offered for attaching irrelevant riders to appropriation bills is that it is done for convenience' sake, to facilitate the passage of measures which are deemed expedient by all the branches of Government which participate in legislation. It can not be claimed that there is any such reason for attaching this amendment of the election laws to the Army appropriation bill. The history of the measure contradicts this assumption. A majority of the House of Representatives in the last Congress was in favor of section 6 of this bill. It was known that a majority of the Senate was opposed to it, and that as a separate measure it could not be adopted. It was attached to the Army appropriation bill to compel the Senate to assent to it. It was plainly announced to the Senate that the Army appropriation bill would not be allowed to pass unless the proposed amendments of the election laws were adopted with it. The Senate refused to assent to the bill on account of this irrelevant section. Congress thereupon adjourned without passing an appropriation bill for the Army, and the present extra session of the Forty-sixth Congress became necessary to furnish the means to carry on the Government.

The ground upon which the action of the House of Representatives is defended has been distinctly stated by many of its advocates. A week before the close of the last session of Congress the doctrine in question was stated by one of its ablest defenders as follows:

It is our duty to repeal these laws. It is not worth while to attempt the repeal except upon an appropriation bill. The Republican Senate would not agree to nor the Republican President sign a bill for such repeal. Whatever objection to legislation upon appropriation bills may be made in ordinary cases does not apply where free elections and the liberty of the citizens are concerned. * * * We have the power to vote money; let us annex conditions to it, and insist upon the redress of grievances.

By another distinguished member of the House it was said:

The right of the Representatives of the people to withhold supplies is as old as English liberty. History records numerous instances where the Commons, feeling that the people were oppressed by laws that the Lords would not consent to repeal by the ordinary methods of legislation, obtained redress at last by refusing appropriations unless accompanied by relief measures.

That a question of the gravest magnitude, and new in this country, was raised by this course of proceeding, was fully recognized also by its defenders in the Senate. It was said by a distinguished Senator:

Perhaps no greater question, in the form we are brought to consider it, was ever considered by the American Congress in time of peace; for it involves not merely the merits or demerits of the laws which the House bill proposes to repeal, but involves the rights, the privileges, the powers, the duties of the two branches of Congress and of the President of the United States. It is a vast question; it is a question whose importance can scarcely be estimated; it is a question that never yet has been brought so sharply before the American Congress and the American people as it may be now. It is a question which sooner or later must be decided, and the decision must determine what are the powers of the House of Representatives under the Constitution, and what is the duty of that House in the view of the framers of that Constitution, according to its letter and its spirit.

Mr. President, I should approach this question, if I were in the best possible condition to speak and to argue it, with very grave diffidence, and certainly with the utmost anxiety; for no one can think of it as long and as carefully as I have thought of it without seeing that we are at the beginning, perhaps, of a struggle that may last as long in this country as a similar struggle lasted in what we are accustomed to call the mother land. There the struggle lasted for two centuries before it was ultimately decided. It is not likely to last so long here, but it may last until every man in this chamber is in his grave. It is the question whether or no the House of Representatives has a right to say, "We will grant supplies only upon condition that grievances are redressed. We are the representatives of the taxpayers of the Republic. We, the House of Representatives, alone have the right to originate money bills. We, the House of Representatives, have alone the right to originate bills which grant the money of the people. The Senate represents States; we represent the taxpayers of the Republic. We, therefore, by the very terms of the Constitution, are charged with the duty of originating the bills which grant the money of the people. We claim the right, which the House of Commons in England established after two centuries of contest, to say that we will not grant the money of the people unless there is a redress of grievances."

Upon the assembling of this Congress, in pursuance of a call for an extra session, which was made necessary by the failure of the Forty-fifth Congress to make the needful appropriations for the support of the Government, the question was presented whether the attempt made in the last Congress to ingraft by construction a new principle upon the Constitution should be persisted in or not. This Congress has ample opportunity and time to pass the appropriation bills, and also to enact any political measures which may be determined upon in separate bills by the usual and orderly methods of proceeding. But the majority of both Houses have deemed it wise to adhere to the principles asserted and maintained in the last Congress by the majority of the House of Representatives. That principle is that the House of Representatives has the sole right to originate bills for raising revenue, and therefore has the right to withhold appropriations upon which the existence of the Government may depend unless the Senate and the President shall give their assent to any legislation which the House may see fit to attach to appropriation bills. To establish this principle is to make a radical, dangerous, and unconstitutional change in the character of our institutions. The various departments of the Government and the Army and the Navy are established by the Constitution or by laws passed in pursuance thereof. Their duties are clearly defined and their support is carefully provided for by law. The money required for this purpose has been collected from the people and is now in the Treasury, ready to be paid out as soon as the appropriation bills are passed. Whether appropriations are made cr not, the collection of the taxes will go on. The public money will accumulate in the Treasury. It was not the intention of the framers of the Constitution that any single branch of the Government should have the power to dictate conditions upon which this treasure should be applied to the purpose for which it was collected. Any such intention, if it had been entertained, would have been plainly expressed in the Constitution.

That a majority of the Senate now concurs in the claim of the House adds to the gravity of the situation, but does not alter the question at issue. The new doctrine, if maintained, will result in a consolidation of unchecked and despotic power in the House of Representatives. A bare majority of the House will become the Government. The Executive will no longer be what the framers of the Constitution intended—an equal and independent branch of the Government. It is clearly the constitutional duty of the President to exercise his discretion and judgment upon all bills presented to him without constraint or duress from any other branch of the Government. To say that a majority of either or both of the Houses of Congress may insist upon the approval of a bill under the penalty of stopping all of the operations of the Government for want of the necessary supplies is to deny to the Executive that share of the legislative power which is plainly conferred by the second section of the seventh article of the Constitution. It strikes from the Constitution the qualified negative of the President. It is said that this should be done because it is the peculiar function of the House of Representatives to represent the will of the people. But no single branch or department of the Government has exclusive authority to speak for the American people. The most authentic and solemn expression of their will is contained in the Constitution of the United States. By that Constitution they have ordained and established a Government whose powers are distributed among coordinate branches, which, as far as possible consistently with a harmonious cooperation, are absolutely independent of each other. The people of this country are unwilling to see the supremacy of the Constitution replaced by the omnipotence of any one department of the Government.

The enactment of this bill into a law will establish a precedent which will tend to destroy the equal independence of the several branches of the Government. Its principle places not merely the Senate and the Executive, but the judiciary also, under the coercive dictation of the House. The House alone will be the judge of what constitutes a grievance, and also of the means and measure of redress. An act of Congress to protect elections is now the grievance complained of; but the House may on the same principle determine that any other act of Congress, a treaty made by the President with the advice and consent of the Senate, a nomination or appointment to office, or that a decision or opinion of the Supreme Court is a grievance, and that the measure of redress is to withhold the appropriations required for the support of the offending branch of the Government.

Believing that this bill is a dangerous violation of the spirit and meaning of the Constitution, I am compelled to return it to the House in which it originated without my approval. The qualified negative with which the Constitution invests the President is a trust that involves a duty which he can not decline to perform. With a firm and conscientious purpose to do what I can to preserve unimpaired the constitutional powers and equal independence, not merely of the Executive, but of every branch of the Government, which will be imperiled by the adoption of the principle of this bill, I desire earnestly to urge upon the House of Representatives a return to the wise and wholesome usage of the earlier days of the Republic, which excluded from appropriation bills all irrelevant legislation. By this course you will inaugurate an important reform in the method of Congressional legislation; your action will be in harmony with the fundamental principles of the Constitution and the patriotic sentiment of nationality which is their firm support, and you will restore to the country that feeling of confidence and security and the repose which are so essential to the prosperity of all of our fellow-citizens.

RUTHERFORD B. HAYES.

To the House of Representatives:

After a careful consideration of the bill entitled "An act to prohibit military interference at elections," I return it to the House of Representatives, in which it originated, with the following objections to its approval:

In the communication sent to the House of Representatives on the 29th of last month, returning to the House without my approval the bill entitled "An act making appropriations for the support of the Army for the fiscal year ending June 30, 1880, and for other purposes," I endeavored to show, by quotations from the statutes of the United States now in force and by a brief statement of facts in regard to recent elections in the several States, that no additional legislation was necessary to prevent interference with the elections by the military or naval forces of the United States. The fact was presented in that communication that at the time of the passage of the act of June 18, 1878, in relation to the employment of the Army as a *posse comitatus* or otherwise, it was maintained by its friends that it would establish a vital and fundamental principle which would secure to the people protection against a standing army. The fact was also referred to that since the passage of this act Congressional, State, and municipal elections have been held throughout the Union, and that in no instance has complaint been made of the presence of United States soldiers at the polls.

Holding, as I do, the opinion that any military interference whatever at the polls is contrary to the spirit of our institutions and would tend to destroy the freedom of elections, and sincerely desiring to concur with Congress in all of its measures, it is with very great regret that I am forced to the conclusion that the bill before me is not only unnecessary to prevent such interference, but is a dangerous departure from long-settled and important constitutional principles.

The true rule as to the employment of military force at the elections is not doubtful. No intimidation or coercion should be allowed to control or influence citizens in the exercise of their right to vote, whether it appears in the shape of combinations of evil-disposed persons, or of armed bodies of the militia of a State, or of the military force of the United States.

The elections should be free from all forcible interference, and, as far as practicable, from all apprehensions of such interference. No soldiers, either of the Union or of the State militia, should be present at the polls to take the place or to perform the duties of the ordinary civil police force. There has been and will be no violation of this rule under orders from me during this Administration; but there should be no denial of the right of the National Government to employ its military force on any day and at any place in case such employment is necessary to enforce the Constitution and laws of the United States.

The bill before me is as follows:

Be it enacted, *etc.*, That it shall not be lawful to bring to or employ at any place where a general or special election is being held in a State any part of the Army or Navy of the United States, unless such force be necessary to repel the armed enemies of the United States or to enforce section 4, Article IV, of the Constitution of the United States and the laws made in pursuance thereof, on application of the legislature or executive of the State where such force is to be used; and so much of all laws as is inconsistent herewith is hereby repealed.

It will be observed that the bill exempts from the general prohibition against the employment of military force at the polls two specified cases. These exceptions recognize and concede the soundness of the principle that military force may properly and constitutionally be used at the place of elections when such use is necessary to enforce the Constitution and the laws; but the excepted cases leave the prohibition so extensive and far-reaching that its adoption will seriously impair the efficiency of the executive department of the Government.

The first act expressly authorizing the use of military power to execute the laws was passed almost as early as the organization of the Government under the Constitution, and was approved by President Washington May 2, 1792. It is as follows:

SEC. 2. *And be it further enacted*, That whenever the laws of the United States shall be opposed or the execution thereof obstructed in any State by combinations too powerful to be suppressed by the ordinary course of judicial proceedings or by the powers vested in the marshals by this act, the same being notified to the President of the United States by an associate justice or the district judge, it shall be lawful for the President of the United States to call forth the militia of such State to suppress such combinations and to cause the laws to be duly executed. And if the militia of a State where such combination may happen shall refuse or be insufficient to suppress the same, it shall be lawful for the President, if the Legislature of the United States be not in session, to call forth and employ such numbers of the militia of any other State or States most convenient thereto as may be necessary; and the use of militia so to be called forth may be continued, if necessary, until the expiration of thirty days after the commencement of the ensuing session.

In 1795 this provision was substantially reenacted in a law which repealed the act of 1792. In 1807 the following act became the law by the approval of President Jefferson:

That in all cases of insurrection or obstruction to the laws, either of the United States or of any individual State or Territory, where it is lawful for the President of the United States to call forth the militia for the purpose of suppressing such insurrection or of causing the laws to be duly executed, it shall be lawful for him to employ for the same purposes such part of the land or naval force of the United States as shall be judged necessary, having first observed all the prerequisites of the law in that respect.

By this act it will be seen that the scope of the law of 1795 was extended so as to authorize the National Government to use not only the militia, but the Army and Navy of the United States, in "causing the laws to be duly executed."

The important provision of the acts of 1792, 1795, and 1807, modified in its terms from time to time to adapt it to the existing emergency, remained in force until, by an act approved by President Lincoln July 29, 1861, it was reenacted substantially in the same language in which it is now found in the Revised Statutes, viz:

SEC. 5298. Whenever, by reason of unlawful obstructions, combinations, or assemblages of persons, or rebellion against the authority of the Government of the United States, it shall become impracticable, in the judgment of the President, to enforce by the ordinary course of judicial proceedings the laws of the United States within any State or Territory, it shall be lawful for the President to call forth the militia of any or all the States and to employ such parts of the land and naval forces of the United States as he may deem necessary to enforce the faithful execution of the laws of the United States or to suppress such rebellion, in whatever State or Territory thereof the laws of the United States may be forcibly opposed or the execution thereof forcibly obstructed.

This ancient and fundamental law has been in force from the foundation of the Government. It is now proposed to abrogate it on certain days and at certain places. In my judgment no fact has been produced which tends to show that it ought to be repealed or suspended for a single hour at any place in any of the States or Territories of the Union. All the teachings of experience in the course of our history are in favor of sustaining its efficiency unimpaired. On every occasion when the supremacy of the Constitution has been resisted and the perpetuity of our institutions imperiled the principle of this statute, enacted by the fathers, has enabled the Government of the Union to maintain its authority and to preserve the integrity of the nation.

At the most critical periods of our history my predecessors in the executive office have relied on this great principle. It was on this principle that President Washington suppressed the whisky rebellion in Pennsylvania in 1794.

In 1806, on the same principle, President Jefferson broke up the Burr conspiracy by issuing "orders for the employment of such force, either of the regulars or of the militia, and by such proceedings of the civil authorities, * * * as might enable them to suppress effectually the further progress of the enterprise." And it was under the same authority that President Jackson crushed nullification in South Carolina and that President Lincoln issued his call for troops to save the Union in 1861. On numerous other occasions of less significance, under probably every Administration, and certainly under the present, this power has been usefully exerted to enforce the laws, without objection by any party in the country, and almost without attracting public attention.

The great elementary constitutional principle which was the foundation of the original statute of 1792, and which has been its essence in the various forms it has assumed since its first adoption, is that the Government of the United States possesses under the Constitution, in full measure, the power of self-protection by its own agencies, altogether independent of State authority, and, if need be, against the hostility of State governments. It should remain embodied in our statutes unimpaired, as it has been from the very origin of the Government. It should be regarded as hardly less valuable or less sacred than a provision of the Constitution itself.

There are many other important statutes containing provisions that are liable to be suspended or annulled at the times and places of holding elections if the bill before me should become a law. I do not undertake to furnish a list of them. Many of them—perhaps the most of them—have been set forth in the debates on this measure. They relate to extradition, to crimes against the election laws, to quarantine regulations, to neutrality, to Indian reservations, to the civil rights of citizens, and to other subjects. In regard to them all it may be safely said that the meaning and effect of this bill is to take from the General Government an important part of its power to enforce the laws.

Another grave objection to the bill is its discrimination in favor of the State and against the national authority. The presence or employment of the Army or Navy of the United States is lawful under the terms of this bill at the place where an election is being held in a State to uphold the authority of a State government then and there in need of such military intervention, but unlawful to uphold the authority of the Government of the United States then and there in need of such military intervention. Under this bill the presence or employment of the Army or Navy of the United States would be lawful and might be necessary to maintain the conduct of a State election against the domestic violence that would overthrow it, but would be unlawful to maintain the conduct of a national election against the same local violence that would overthrow it. This discrimination has never been attempted in any previous legislation by Congress, and is no more compatible with sound principles of the Constitution or the necessary maxims and methods of our system of government on occasions of elections than at other times. In the early legislation of 1792 and of 1795, by which the militia of the States was the only military power resorted to for the execution of the constitutional powers in support of State or national authority, both functions of the Government were put upon the same footing. By the act of 1807 the employment of the Army and Navy was authorized for the performance of both constitutional duties in the same terms.

In all later statutes on the same subject-matter the same measure of authority to the Government has been accorded for the performance of both these duties. No precedent has been found in any previous legislation, and no sufficient reason has been given for the discrimination in favor of the State and against the national authority which this bill contains.

Under the sweeping terms of the bill the National Government is effectually shut out from the exercise of the right and from the discharge of the imperative duty to use its whole executive power whenever and wherever required for the enforcement of its laws at the places and times when and where its elections are held. The employment of its organized armed forces for any such purpose would be an offense against the law unless called for by, and therefore upon permission of, the authorities of the State in which the occasion arises. What is this but the substitution of the discretion of the State governments for the discretion of the Government of the United States as to the performance of its own duties? In my judgment this is an abandonment of its obligations by the National Government—a subordination of national authority and an intrusion of State supervision over national duties which amounts, in spirit and tendency, to State supremacy.

Though I believe that the existing statutes are abundantly adequate to completely prevent military interference with the elections in the sense in which the phrase is used in the title of this bill and is employed by the people of this country, I shall find no difficulty in concurring in any additional legislation limited to that object which does not interfere with the indispensable exercise of the powers of the Government under the Constitution and laws.

R. B. HAYES.

MAY 12, 1879.

EXECUTIVE MANSION, *May 29, 1879.*

To the House of Representatives:

After mature consideration of the bill entitled "An act making appropriations for the legislative, executive, and judicial expenses of the Government for the fiscal year ending June 30, 1880, and for other purposes,"

I herewith return it to the House of Representatives, in which it originated, with the following objections to its approval:

The main purpose of the bill is to appropriate the money required to support during the next fiscal year the several civil departments of the Government. The amount appropriated exceeds in the aggregate $18,000,000.

This money is needed to keep in operation the essential functions of all the great departments of the Government—legislative, executive, and judicial. If the bill contained no other provisions, no objection to its approval would be made. It embraces, however, a number of clauses, relating to subjects of great general interest, which are wholly unconnected with the appropriations which it provides for. The objections to the practice of tacking general legislation to appropriation bills, especially when the object is to deprive a coordinate branch of the Government of its right to the free exercise of its own discretion and judgment touching such general legislation, were set forth in the special message in relation to House bill No. 1, which was returned to the House of Representatives on the 29th of last month. I regret that the objections which were then expressed to this method of legislation have not seemed to Congress of sufficient weight to dissuade from this renewed incorporation of general enactments in an appropriation bill, and that my constitutional duty in respect of the general legislation thus placed before me can not be discharged without seeming to delay, however briefly, the necessary appropriations by Congress for the support of the Government. Without repeating these objections, I respectfully refer to that message for a statement of my views on the principle maintained in debate by the advocates of this bill, viz, that "to withhold appropriations is a constitutional means for the redress" of what the majority of the House of Representatives may regard as "a grievance."

The bill contains the following clauses, viz:

And provided further, That the following sections of the Revised Statutes of the United States, namely, sections 2016, 2018, and 2020, and all of the succeeding sections of said statutes down to and including section 2027, and also section 5522, be, and the same are hereby, repealed; * * * and that all the other sections of the Revised Statutes, and all laws and parts of laws authorizing the appointment of chief supervisors of elections, special deputy marshals of elections, or general deputy marshals having any duties to perform in respect to any election, and prescribing their duties and powers and allowing them compensation, be, and the same are hereby, repealed.

It also contains clauses amending sections 2017, 2019, 2028, and 2031 of the Revised Statutes.

The sections of the Revised Statutes which the bill, if approved, would repeal or amend are part of an act approved May 30, 1870, and amended February 28, 1871, entitled "An act to enforce the rights of citizens of the United States to vote in the several States of this Union, and for other purposes." All of the provisions of the above-named acts which it is proposed in this bill to repeal or modify relate to the Congressional elections. The remaining portion of the law, which will continue in force after the enactment of this measure, is that which provides for the appointment, by a judge of the circuit court of the United States, of two supervisors of election in each election district at any Congressional election, on due application of citizens who desire, in the language of the law, "to have such election *guarded* and *scrutinized*." The duties of the supervisors will be to attend at the polls at all Congressional elections, and to remain after the polls are open until every vote cast has been counted; but they will "have no authority to make arrests or to perform other duties than to be in the immediate presence of the officers holding the election and to witness all their proceedings, including the counting of the votes and the making of a return thereof." The part of the election law which will be repealed by the approval of this bill includes those sections which give authority to the supervisors of elections "to personally scrutinize, count, and canvass each ballot," and all the sections which confer authority upon the United States marshals and deputy marshals in connection with the Congressional elections. The enactment of this bill will also repeal section 5522 of the criminal statutes of the United States, which was enacted for the protection of United States officers engaged in the discharge of their duties at the Congressional elections. This section protects supervisors and marshals in the performance of their duties by making the obstruction or the assaulting of these officers, or any interference with them, by bribery or solicitation or otherwise, crimes against the United States.

The true meaning and effect of the proposed legislation are plain. The supervisors, with the authority to observe and witness the proceedings at the Congressional elections, will be left, but there will be no power to protect them, or to prevent interference with their duties, or to punish any violation of the law from which their powers are derived. If this bill is approved, only the shadow of the authority of the United States at the national elections will remain; the substance will be gone. The supervision of the elections will be reduced to a mere inspection, without authority on the part of the supervisors to do any act whatever to make the election a fair one. All that will be left to the supervisors is the permission to have such oversight of the elections as political parties are in the habit of exercising without any authority of law, in order to prevent their opponents from obtaining unfair advantages. The object of the bill is to destroy any control whatever by the United States over the Congressional elections.

The passage of this bill has been urged upon the ground that the election of members of Congress is a matter which concerns the States alone; that these elections should be controlled exclusively by the States; that there are and can be no such elections as national elections, and that the existing law of the United States regulating the Congressional elections is without warrant in the Constitution.

It is evident, however, that the framers of the Constitution regarded the election of members of Congress in every State and in every district as in a very important sense justly a matter of political interest and concern to the whole country. The original provision of the Constitution on this subject is as follows (sec. 4, Art. I):

The times, places, and manner of holding elections for Senators and Representatives shall be prescribed in each State by the legislature thereof; but the Congress may at any time, by law, make or alter such regulations, except as to the places of choosing Senators.

A further provision has been since added, which is embraced in the fifteenth amendment. It is as follows:

SEC. 1. The right of citizens of the United States to vote shall not be denied or abridged by the United States or by any State on account of race, color, or previous condition of servitude.

SEC. 2. The Congress shall have power to enforce this article by appropriate legislation.

Under the general provision of the Constitution (sec. 4, Art. I) Congress in 1866 passed a comprehensive law which prescribed full and detailed regulations for the election of Senators by the legislatures of the several States. This law has been in force almost thirteen years. In pursuance of it all the members of the present Senate of the United States hold their seats. Its constitutionality is not called in question. It is confidently believed that no sound argument can be made in support of the constitutionality of national regulation of Senatorial elections which will not show that the elections of members of the House of Representatives may also be constitutionally regulated by the national authority.

The bill before me itself recognizes the principle that the Congressional elections are not State elections, but national elections. It leaves in full force the existing statute under which supervisors are still to be appointed by national authority to "observe and witness" the Congressional elections whenever due application is made by citizens who desire said elections to be "guarded and scrutinized." If the power to supervise in any respect whatever the Congressional elections exists under section 4, Article I, of the Constitution, it is a power which, like every other power belonging to the Government of the United States, is paramount and supreme, and includes the right to employ the necessary means to carry it into effect.

The statutes of the United States which regulate the election of members of the House of Representatives, an essential part of which it is proposed to repeal by this bill, have been in force about eight years. Four Congressional elections have been held under them, two of which were at the Presidential elections of 1872 and 1876. Numerous prosecutions, trials, and convictions have been had in the courts of the United States in all parts of the Union for violations of these laws. In no reported case has their constitutionality been called in question by any judge of the courts of the United States. The validity of these laws is sustained by the uniform course of judicial action and opinion.

If it is urged that the United States election laws are not necessary, an ample reply is furnished by the history of their origin and of their results. They were especially prompted by the investigation and exposure of the frauds committed in the city and State of New York at the elections of 1868. Committees representing both of the leading political parties of the country have submitted reports to the House of Representatives on the extent of those frauds. A committee of the Fortieth Congress, after a full investigation, reached the conclusion that the number of fraudulent votes cast in the city of New York alone in 1868 was not less than 25,000. A committee of the Forty-fourth Congress in their report, submitted in 1877, adopted the opinion that for every 100 actual voters of the city of New York in 1868 108 votes were cast, when in fact the number of lawful votes cast could not have exceeded 88 per cent of the actual voters of the city. By this statement the number of fraudulent votes at that election in the city of New York alone was between thirty and forty thousand. These frauds completely reversed the result of the election in the State of New York, both as to the choice of governor and State officers and as to the choice of electors of President and Vice-President of the United States. They attracted the attention of the whole country. It was plain that if they could be continued and repeated with impunity free government was impossible. A distinguished Senator, in opposing the passage of the election laws, declared that he had "for a long time believed that our form of government was a comparative failure in the larger cities." To meet these evils and to prevent these crimes the United States laws regulating Congressional elections were enacted.

The framers of these laws have not been disappointed in their results. In the large cities, under their provisions, the elections have been comparatively peaceable, orderly, and honest. Even the opponents of these laws have borne testimony to their value and efficiency and to the necessity for their enactment. The committee of the Forty-fourth Congress, composed of members a majority of whom were opposed to these laws, in their report on the New York election of 1876, said:

The committee would commend to other portions of the country and to other cities this remarkable system, developed through the agency of both local and Federal authorities acting in harmony for an honest purpose. In no portion of the world and in no era of time where there has been an expression of the popular will through the forms of law has there been a more complete and thorough illustration of republican institutions. Whatever may have been the previous habit or conduct of elections in those cities, or howsoever they may conduct themselves in the future, this election of 1876 will stand as a monument of what good faith, honest endeavor, legal forms, and just authority may do for the protection of the electoral franchise.

This bill recognizes the authority and duty of the United States to appoint supervisors to guard and scrutinize the Congressional elections, but it denies to the Government of the United States all power to make its supervision effectual. The great body of the people of all parties want free and fair elections. They do not think that a free election means freedom from the wholesome restraints of law or that the place of election should be a sanctuary for lawlessness and crime. On the day of an election peace and good order are more necessary than on any other day of the year. On that day the humblest and feeblest citizens, the aged and the infirm, should be, and should have reason to feel that they are, safe in the exercise of their most responsible duty and their most sacred right as members of society—their duty and their right to vote. The constitutional authority to regulate the Congressional elections which belongs to the Government of the United States, and which it is necessary to exert to secure the right to vote to every citizen possessing the requisite qualifications, ought to be enforced by appropriate legislation. So far from public opinion in any part of the country favoring any relaxation of the authority of the Government in the protection of elections from violence and corruption, I believe it demands greater vigor both in the enactment and in the execution of the laws framed for that purpose. Any oppression, any partisan partiality, which experience may have shown in the working of existing laws may well engage the careful attention both of Congress and of the Executive, in their respective spheres of duty, for the correction of these mischiefs. As no Congressional elections occur until after the regular session of Congress will have been held, there seems to be no public exigency that would preclude a seasonable consideration at that session of any administrative details that might improve the present methods designed for the protection of all citizens in the complete and equal exercise of the right and power of the suffrage at such elections. But with my views, both of the constitutionality and of the value of the existing laws, I can not approve any measure for their repeal except in connection with the enactment of other legislation which may reasonably be expected to afford wiser and more efficient safeguards for free and honest Congressional elections.

RUTHERFORD B. HAYES.

EXECUTIVE MANSION, *June 23, 1879.*

To the House of Representatives:

After careful examination of the bill entitled "An act making appropriations for certain judicial expenses," I return it herewith to the House of Representatives, in which it originated, with the following objections to its approval:

The general purpose of the bill is to provide for certain judicial expenses of the Government for the fiscal year ending June 30, 1880, for which the sum of $2,690,000 is appropriated. These appropriations are required to keep in operation the general functions of the judicial department of the Government, and if this part of the bill stood alone there would be no objection to its approval. It contains, however, other provisions, to which I desire respectfully to ask your attention.

At the present session of Congress a majority of both Houses, favoring a repeal of the Congressional election laws embraced in title 26 of the Revised Statutes, passed a measure for that purpose, as part of a bill entitled "An act making appropriations for the legislative, executive, and judicial expenses of the Government for the fiscal year ending June 30, 1880, and for other purposes." Unable to concur with Congress in that measure, on the 29th of May last I returned the bill to the House of Representatives, in which it originated, without my approval, for that further consideration for which the Constitution provides. On reconsideration the bill was approved by less than two-thirds of the House, and failed to become a law. The election laws therefore remain valid enactments, and the supreme law of the land, binding not only upon all private citizens, but also alike and equally binding upon all who are charged with the duties and responsibilities of the legislative, the executive, and the judicial departments of the Government.

It is not sought by the bill before me to repeal the election laws. Its object is to defeat their enforcement. The last clause of the first section is as follows:

And no part of the money hereby appropriated is appropriated to pay any salaries, compensation, fees, or expenses under or in virtue of title 26 of the Revised Statutes, or of any provision of said title.

Title 26 of the Revised Statutes, referred to in the foregoing clause, relates to the elective franchise, and contains the laws now in force regulating the Congressional elections.

The second section of the bill reaches much further. It is as follows:

SEC. 2. That the sums appropriated in this act for the persons and public service embraced in its provisions are in full for such persons and public service for the fiscal year ending June 30, 1880; and no Department or officer of the Government shall during said fiscal year make any contract or incur any liability for the future payment of money under any of the provisions of title 26 of the Revised Statutes of the United States authorizing the appointment or payment of general or special deputy marshals for service in connection with elections or on election day until an appropriation sufficient to meet such contract or pay such liability shall have first been made by law.

This section of the bill is intended to make an extensive and essential change in the existing laws. The following are the provisions of the statutes on the same subject which are now in force:

SEC. 3679. No Department of the Government shall expend in any one fiscal year any sum in excess of appropriations made by Congress for that fiscal year, or involve the Government in any contract for the future payment of money in excess of such appropriations.

SEC. 3732. No contract or purchase on behalf of the United States shall be made unless the same is authorized by law or is under an appropriation adequate to its fulfillment, except in the War and Navy Departments, for clothing, subsistence, forage, fuel, quarters, or transportation, which, however, shall not exceed the necessities of the current year.

The object of these sections of the Revised Statutes is plain. It is, first, to prevent any money from being expended unless appropriations have been made therefor, and, second, to prevent the Government from being bound by any contract not previously authorized by law, except for certain necessary purposes in the War and Navy Departments.

Under the existing laws the failure of Congress to make the appropriations required for the execution of the provisions of the election laws would not prevent their enforcement. The right and duty to appoint the general and special deputy marshals which they provide for would still remain, and the executive department of the Government would also be empowered to incur the requisite liability for their compensation. But the second section of this bill contains a prohibition not found in any previous legislation. Its design is to render the election laws inoperative and a dead letter during the next fiscal year. It is sought to accomplish this by omitting to appropriate money for their enforcement and by expressly prohibiting any Department or officer of the Government from incurring any liability under any of the provisions of title 26 of the Revised Statutes authorizing the appointment or payment of general or special deputy marshals for service on election days until an appropriation sufficient to pay such liability shall have first been made.

The President is called upon to give his affirmative approval to positive enactments which in effect deprive him of the ordinary and necessary means of executing laws still left in the statute book and embraced within his constitutional duty to see that the laws are executed. If he approves the bill, and thus gives to such positive enactments the authority of law, he participates in the curtailment of his means of seeing that the law is faithfully executed, while the obligation of the law and of his constitutional duty remains unimpaired.

The appointment of special deputy marshals is not made by the statute a spontaneous act of authority on the part of any executive or judicial officer of the Government, but is accorded as a popular right of the citizens to call into operation this agency for securing the purity and freedom of elections in any city or town having 20,000 inhabitants or upward. Section 2021 of the Revised Statutes puts it in the power of any two citizens of such city or town to require of the marshal of the district the appointment of these special deputy marshals. Thereupon the duty of the marshal becomes imperative, and its nonperformance would expose him to judicial mandate or punishment or to removal from office by the President, as the circumstances of his conduct might require. The bill now before me neither revokes this popular right of the citizens, nor relieves the marshal of the duty imposed by law, nor the President of his duty to see that this law is faithfully executed.

I forbear to enter again upon any general discussion of the wisdom and necessity of the election laws or of the dangerous and unconstitutional principle of this bill—that the power vested in Congress to originate appropriations involves the right to compel the Executive to approve any legislation which Congress may see fit to attach to such bills, under the penalty of refusing the means needed to carry on essential functions of the Government. My views on these subjects have been sufficiently presented in the special messages sent by me to the House of Representatives during their present session. What was said in those messages I regard as conclusive as to my duty in respect to the bill before me. The arguments urged in those communications against the repeal of the election laws and against the right of Congress to deprive the Executive of that separate and independent discretion and judgment which the Constitution confers and requires are equally cogent in opposition to this bill. This measure leaves the powers and duties of the supervisors of elections untouched. The compensation of those officers is provided for under permanent laws, and no liability for which an appropriation is now required would therefore be incurred by their appointment. But the power of the National Government to protect them in the discharge of their duty at the polls would be taken away. The States may employ both civil and military power at the elections, but by this bill even the civil authority to protect Congressional elections is denied to the United States. The object is to prevent any adequate control by the United States over the national elections by forbidding the payment of deputy marshals, the officers who are clothed with authority to enforce the election laws.

The fact that these laws are deemed objectionable by a majority of both Houses of Congress is urged as a sufficient warrant for this legislation.

There are two lawful ways to overturn legislative enactments. One is their repeal; the other is the decision of a competent tribunal against their validity. The effect of this bill is to deprive the executive department of the Government of the means to execute laws which are not repealed, which have not been declared invalid, and which it is therefore the duty of the executive and of every other department of Government to obey and to enforce.

I have in my former message on this subject expressed a willingness to concur in suitable amendments for the improvement of the election laws; but I can not consent to their absolute and entire repeal, and I can not approve legislation which seeks to prevent their enforcement.

RUTHERFORD B. HAYES.

EXECUTIVE MANSION, *June 27, 1879.*
To the Senate of the United States:

I return without approval Senate bill No. 595,* with the following objection to its becoming a law:

Doubts have arisen upon consideration of the bill as to whether Major Collins will be required under it to refund to the United States the pay and allowances received by him at the time he was mustered out of the

* "An act to amend 'An act for the relief of Joseph B. Collins, approved March 3, 1879.'"

service. Believing that it was not the intention of Congress to require such repayment, the bill is returned without my signature to the House in which it originated.

R. B. HAYES.

EXECUTIVE MANSION, *June 30, 1879.*

To the House of Representatives:

I return to the House of Representatives, in which it originated, the bill entitled "An act making appropriations to pay fees of United States marshals and their general deputies," with the following objections to its becoming a law:

The bill appropriates the sum of $600,000 for the payment during the fiscal year ending June 30, 1880, of United States marshals and their general deputies. The offices thus provided for are essential to the faithful execution of the laws. They were created and their powers and duties defined by Congress at its first session after the adoption of the Constitution in the judiciary act which was approved September 24, 1789. Their general duties, as defined in the act which originally established them, were substantially the same as those prescribed in the statutes now in force.

The principal provision on the subject in the Revised Statutes is as follows:

SEC. 787. It shall be the duty of the marshal of each district to attend the district and circuit courts when sitting therein, and to execute throughout the district all lawful precepts directed to him and issued under the authority of the United States; and he shall have power to command all necessary assistance in the execution of his duty.

The original act was amended February 28, 1795, and the amendment is now found in the Revised Statutes in the following form:

SEC. 788. The marshals and their deputies shall have in each State the same powers in executing the laws of the United States as the sheriffs and their deputies in such State may have by law in executing the laws thereof.

By subsequent statutes additional duties have been from time to time imposed upon the marshals and their deputies, the due and regular performance of which are required for the efficiency of almost every branch of the public service. Without these officers there would be no means of executing the warrants, decrees, or other process of the courts, and the judicial system of the country would be fatally defective. The criminal jurisdiction of the courts of the United States is very extensive. The crimes committed within the maritime jurisdiction of the United States are all cognizable only in the courts of the United States. Crimes against public justice; crimes against the operations of the Government, such as forging or counterfeiting the money or securities of the United States; crimes against the postal laws; offenses against the elective franchise, against the civil rights of citizens, against the existence of the

Government: crimes against the internal-revenue laws, the customs laws, the neutrality laws; crimes against laws for the protection of Indians and of the public lands—all of these crimes and many others can be punished only under United States laws, laws which, taken together, constitute a body of jurisprudence which is vital to the welfare of the whole country, and which can be enforced only by means of the marshals and deputy marshals of the United States. In the District of Columbia all of the process of the courts is executed by the officers in question. In short, the execution of the criminal laws of the United States, the service of all civil process in cases in which the United States is a party, and the execution of the revenue laws, the neutrality laws, and many other laws of large importance depend on the maintenance of the marshals and their deputies. They are in effect the only police of the United States Government. Officers with corresponding powers and duties are found in every State of the Union and in every country which has a jurisprudence which is worthy of the name. To deprive the National Government of these officers would be as disastrous to society as to abolish the sheriffs, constables, and police officers in the several States. It would be a denial to the United States of the right to execute its laws—a denial of all authority which requires the use of civil force. The law entitles these officers to be paid. The funds needed for the purpose have been collected from the people and are now in the Treasury. No objection is, therefore, made to that part of the bill before me which appropriates money for the support of the marshals and deputy marshals of the United States.

The bill contains, however, other provisions which are identical in tenor and effect with the second section of the bill entitled "An act making appropriations for certain judicial expenses," which on the 23d of the present month was returned to the House of Representatives with my objections to its approval. The provisions referred to are as follows:

SEC. 2. That the sums appropriated in this act for the persons and public service embraced in its provisions are in full for such persons and public service for the fiscal year ending June 30, 1880; and no Department or officer of the Government shall during said fiscal year make any contract or incur any liability for the future payment of money under any of the provisions of title 26 mentioned in section 1 of this act until an appropriation sufficient to meet such contract or pay such liability shall have first been made by law.

Upon a reconsideration in the House of Representatives of the bill which contained these provisions it lacked a constitutional majority, and therefore failed to become a law. In order to secure its enactment, the same measure is again presented for my approval, coupled in the bill before me with appropriations for the support of marshals and their deputies during the next fiscal year. The object, manifestly, is to place before the Executive this alternative: Either to allow necessary functions of the public service to be crippled or suspended for want of the appropriations required to keep them in operation, or to approve legislation which in official communications to Congress he has declared would be a violation of his constitutional duty.   Thus in this bill the principle is clearly embodied that by virtue of the provision of the Constitution which requires that "all bills for raising revenue shall originate in the House of Representatives" a bare majority of the House of Representatives has the right to withhold appropriations for the support of the Government unless the Executive consents to approve any legislation which may be attached to appropriation bills.   I respectfully refer to the communications on this subject which I have sent to Congress during its present session for a statement of the grounds of my conclusions, and desire here merely to repeat that in my judgment to establish the principle of this bill is to make a radical, dangerous, and unconstitutional change in the character of our institutions.

RUTHERFORD B. HAYES.

PROCLAMATIONS.

BY THE PRESIDENT OF THE UNITED STATES OF AMERICA.

A PROCLAMATION.

Whereas it has become known to me that certain evil-disposed persons have within the territory and jurisdiction of the United States begun and set on foot preparations for an organized and forcible possession of and settlement upon the lands of what is known as the Indian Territory, west of the State of Arkansas, which Territory is designated, recognized, and described by the treaties and laws of the United States and by the executive authorities as Indian country, and as such is only subject to occupation by Indian tribes, officers of the Indian Department, military posts, and such persons as may be privileged to reside and trade therein under the intercourse laws of the United States; and

Whereas those laws provide for the removal of all persons residing and trading therein without express permission of the Indian Department and agents, and also of all persons whom such agents may deem to be improper persons to reside in the Indian country:

Now, therefore, for the purpose of properly protecting the interests of the Indian nations and tribes, as well as of the United States, in said Indian Territory, and of duly enforcing the laws governing the same, I, Rutherford B. Hayes, President of the United States, do admonish and warn all such persons so intending or preparing to remove upon said lands or into said Territory without permission of the proper agent of the Indian Department against any attempt to so remove or settle upon any of the lands of said Territory; and I do further warn and notify any and all such persons who may so offend that they will be speedily and immediately removed therefrom by the agent, according to the laws made and provided; and if necessary the aid and assistance of the military forces of the United States will be invoked to carry into proper execution the laws of the United States herein referred to.

In testimony whereof I have hereunto set my hand and caused the seal of the United States to be affixed.

[SEAL.] Done at the city of Washington, this 26th day of April, A. D. 1879, and of the Independence of the United States the one hundred and third.

RUTHERFORD B. HAYES.

By the President:

WM. M. EVARTS, *Secretary of State.*

BY THE PRESIDENT OF THE UNITED STATES OF AMERICA.

A PROCLAMATION.

At no recurrence of the season which the devout habit of a religious people has made the occasion for giving thanks to Almighty God and humbly invoking His continued favor has the material prosperity enjoyed by our whole country been more conspicuous, more manifold, or more universal.

During the past year, also, unbroken peace with all foreign nations, the general prevalence of domestic tranquillity, the supremacy and security of the great institutions of civil and religious freedom, have gladdened the hearts of our people and confirmed their attachment to their Government, which the wisdom and courage of our ancestors so fitly framed and the wisdom and courage of their descendants have so firmly maintained to be the habitation of liberty and justice to successive generations.

Now, therefore, I, Rutherford B. Hayes, President of the United States, do appoint Thursday, the 27th day of November instant, as a day of national thanksgiving and prayer; and I earnestly recommend that, withdrawing themselves from secular cares and labors, the people of the United States do meet together on that day in their respective places of worship, there to give thanks and praise to Almighty God for His mercies and to devoutly beseech their continuance.

In witness whereof I have hereunto set my hand and caused the seal of the United States to be affixed.

[SEAL.] Done at the city of Washington, this 3d day of November, A. D. 1879, and of the Independence of the United States the one hundred and fourth.

RUTHERFORD B. HAYES.

By the President:

WM. M. EVARTS, *Secretary of State.*

EXECUTIVE ORDERS.

[From the New-York Tribune, February 14, 1879.]

EXECUTIVE MANSION,
Washington, February 4, 1879.

General E. A. MERRITT.

MY DEAR GENERAL: I congratulate you on your confirmation. It is a great gratification to me, very honorable to you, and will prove, I believe, of signal service to the country. My desire is that the office be conducted on strictly business principles, and according to the rules for the civil service which were recommended by the Civil Service Commission in the Administration of General Grant. I want you to be perfectly independent of mere influence from any quarter. Neither my recommendation, nor that of Secretary Sherman, nor of any member of Congress or other influential person must be specially regarded. Let appointments and removals be made on business principles and according to rules. There must be, I assume, a few places filled by those you personally know to be trustworthy, but restrict the area of patronage to the narrowest limits. Let no man be put out merely because he is a friend to Mr. Arthur, and no man put in merely because he is our friend. The good of the service should be the sole end in view. The best means yet presented, it seems to me, are the rules recommended by the Civil Service Commission. I shall issue no new order on the subject at present. I am glad you approve of the message, and I wish you to see that all that is expressed or implied in it is faithfully carried out.

Again congratulating you, and assuring you of my entire confidence, I remain, sincerely,

R. B. HAYES.

REGULATIONS TO PREVENT THE INTRODUCTION OF THE "PLAGUE" INTO THE UNITED STATES.

TREASURY DEPARTMENT,
OFFICE OF THE SURGEON-GENERAL
UNITED STATES MARINE-HOSPITAL SERVICE,
Washington, D. C., March 3, 1879.

To Officers of the Customs Revenue, Medical Officers of the Marine-Hospital Service, and others whom it may concern:

The act approved April 29, 1878, entitled "An act to prevent the introduction of contagious or infectious diseases into the United States," provides that no vessel coming from any foreign port or country where any contagious or infectious disease exists, nor any vessel conveying infected merchandise, shall enter any port of the United States or pass the boundary line between the United States and any foreign country except in such manner as may be prescribed under said act.

Attention has been called to the prevalence of a dangerous epidemic disease in southern Russia known as the "plague," and its extremely virulent and contagious character, as manifested in the late outbreak, leaves no doubt that it is similar to, if not identical with, the "plague" which devastated the Old World in past centuries.

Because, therefore, of the danger which attaches to rags, furs, etc., as carriers of infection, the following regulations are framed, under the direction of the Secretary of the Treasury, and subject to the approval of the President, for the protection of the health of the people of the United States against the danger referred to:

Until further orders no vessel from any port of the Black Sea or the Sea of A 'of, conveying any rags, furs, skins, hair, feathers, boxed or baled clothing or bedding or any similar articles liable to convey infection, nor any vessel from any port of the Mediterranean or Red seas having on board such articles coming from southern Russia, shall enter any port of the United States until such articles shall have been removed from the vessel to open lighters or to some isolated locality and the vessel disinfected and thoroughly ventilated; and the suspected articles shall be disinfected, either by chemical agents and exposure to free currents of air or by burning, as shall be determined in each case by the Surgeon-General of the Marine-Hospital Service.

The certificate of the State or municipal quarantine officer of health may be accepted as satisfactory evidence of compliance with these regulations on the part of the vessel.

JNO. M. WOODWORTH,
Surgeon-General United States Marine-Hospital Service.

Approved: R. B. HAYES.

CUSTOM-HOUSE, NEW YORK CITY,
Collector's Office, February 26, 1879.

Hon. JOHN SHERMAN,
Secretary of the Treasury.

SIR: The President, by letter of 4th instant, having requested that appointments and promotions in this office should be made in accordance with the civil-service rules of 1872, and having also made a similar request of the naval officer, it has been deemed best to make, if practicable, the same rules applicable to all the offices in this city included in the order of the Treasury Department dated August 7, 1872.

With that view, and after several conferences, it has been agreed by the assistant treasurer, naval officer, appraiser, surveyor, and myself to submit the inclosed modifications of the rules of 1872, and should they meet approval to put in operation forthwith the rules so modified.

I am, very respectfully,   E. A. MERRITT, *Collector.*

[The modifications submitted with the above letter are omitted, and instead are inserted the following regulations, based upon said modifications, approved by the President March 6, 1879, and amended with his approval in January, 1880.]

REGULATIONS GOVERNING APPOINTMENTS AND PROMOTIONS IN THE CUSTOMS SERVICE AND SUBTREASURY IN THE CITY OF NEW YORK.

I. Every application for appointment to a vacancy in the lowest grade of any group in the offices of the collector and the surveyor of customs, the naval officer, the appraiser, and the assistant treasurer of the United States in the city of New York must be made in the handwriting of the applicant to the head of the office in which employment is desired. It must state: (1) The position to which the applicant desires to be appointed;* (2) place and date of birth; (3) legal residence, and how long it has been such; (4) education; (5) occupation, past and present; (6) whether ever employed in the civil service, and, if so, when, how long, in what branch and capacity, and reasons for leaving the service; (7) whether ever in the Regular or

* The positions for which applications may be made in the several offices are:
Collector's and surveyor's office: (1) Inspector, at salary of $4 per day; (2) clerk, at annual salary of $1,200; (3) weigher's clerk, at annual salary of $1,200; (4) gauger's clerk, at annual salary

Volunteer Army or Navy, and, if so, when and in what organization and capacity; (8) applicant's name in full.

II. The applicant must certify to having composed and written the application without assistance; to the truth of the statements which it contains; to being a citizen of the United States, and faithful to the Union and the Constitution; and, if ever in the Regular or Volunteer Army or Navy, to having been honorably discharged.

III. Every application must be accompanied by a certificate, signed by two trustworthy and responsible persons, well known in the community in which they reside, that the applicant is personally well known to them to be of good moral character and of temperate and industrious habits, and to be faithful to the Union and the Constitution of the United States.

IV. Every application must also be accompanied by the certificate of a practicing physician as to the applicant's general health and physical capacity to perform the duties of the position to which he desires to be appointed: *Provided, however*, That no appointment will be made to any position in active outdoor service unless a surgeon of the United States Marine-Hospital Service shall certify that he has made a physical examination of the applicant and found him fit for such position. Such surgeon's examination may be postponed until required by the nominating officer.

V. Applications filed previously to the adoption of these regulations must be renewed or perfected in accordance therewith to entitle them to consideration. No applications for appointment as day or night inspectors in the custom-house from persons under 21 years of age, or for other positions under these regulations from persons under 18 years of age, will be considered. In compliance with section 1031 of the Treasury Regulations now in force, persons over 45 years of age are not eligible to any group the lowest grade of which is confined to persons receiving an annual salary of less than $1,800. This prohibition, however, shall not be applied to those who have been honorably discharged from the service and are otherwise qualified.

VI. All applications upon their receipt will be carefully examined by the board of examiners, and those which do not conform in every particular to the foregoing requirements, and such as show that the applicants are manifestly not qualified for the duties of the position desired, will be rejected and the applicants so notified. All other applicants will be designated as eligible for examination, and will be so notified. Inasmuch as applications are to be made in writing and each case is to be decided upon its merits, personal importunity will have no weight.

VII. Not less than five days prior to each examination a notification to appear at a time and place to be stated will be mailed to the eligible candidates, unless it shall be found impracticable to examine all of them, in which case a practicable number will be selected under the second regulation* for the civil service promulgated April 16, 1872, and notified to appear for examination. Those not selected for examination will remain on the eligible list. If any person notified to appear shall be unable to do so on account of sickness or other causes, he must promptly advise the board of examiners, in person or by mail, of his inability to attend, and his name will remain upon the eligible list; but any person attending an examination will not be allowed to subsequently plead sickness or other disabling causes as an excuse for defects in examination.

of $1,200; (5) night inspector, at a salary of $2.50 per day, and clerk, at an annual salary of less than $1,200.

Naval office: (1) Clerk, at an annual salary of $1,200; (2) clerk, at an annual salary of less than $1,200.

Assistant treasurer's office: (1) Clerk, at an annual salary of $2,000; (2) clerk, at an annual salary of $1,200; (3) clerk, at an annual salary of less than $1,200.

Appraiser's office: (1) Examiner, at an annual salary of $1,800; (2) clerk, verifier, or sampler, at an annual salary of $1,200; (3) clerk, verifier, or sampler, at an annual salary of less than $1,200; (4) openers and packers, at a salary of $3 per day.

* See p. 4135.

VIII. All candidates for appointment to positions the annual salary of which is $1,200 or more, who shall appear in accordance with such notification, will be subjected to a competitive written examination upon the following subjects: (1) Copying from dictation; (2) arithmetic—fundamental rules, fractions, proportion, percentage and interest, reduction; (3) elements of accounts and bookkeeping; (4) geography, history, and government—general questions, principally such as relate to the United States; (5) elements of English grammar, chiefly orthography and syntax; (6) writing and briefing letters; and (7) penmanship.

Candidates for appointment to positions the salary of which is less than $1,200 will be examined in like manner upon the following subjects: (1) Penmanship; (2) copying; (3) elements of English grammar, chiefly orthography and syntax; and (4) fundamental rules of arithmetic.

Proficiency in penmanship, orthography, and punctuation will be determined principally by a review of the examination papers, and as far as possible the examination in all the branches will be confined to practical exercises.

In examinations for appointments to positions requiring special or technical knowledge such additions may be made by the board of examiners to the list of subjects as the nature of the case may require.

For temporary employment to meet casual exigencies in the public business, or for special services as experts, appointments may be made without examination; but no such appointment shall be made for a term exceeding three months, which may be specially extended for a similar term only; and no such appointment shall be made to any regular or permanent position.

IX. The various subjects of the examination may be subdivided, if thought desirable, into classes, and to each subject or class a relative weight, according to its importance in the examination, will be assigned by each board of examiners. The mode of ascertaining the result of the examination will be as follows: The degree of accuracy with which each question shall be answered will first be marked by the board on a scale of 100. The average of the marks given to the answers to the questions in each subject or class will next be ascertained. Each average will then be multiplied by the number indicating the relative weight of the subject or class, and the sum of the products will be divided by the sum of the relative weights. The quotient will determine the candidate's standing in the examination. Relative weight will be assigned not merely to the special qualifications of the candidates, but to their general aptitude, as shown in the course of examination. Candidates will be examined during office hours, and in no case will their examination be continued more than one day.

X. The board of examiners will prepare a list of the persons examined in the order of their excellence, as proved by such examination, beginning with the highest, and will then certify to the head of the office the names standing at the head of such list, not exceeding three. When more than one appointment is to be made, the vacancies will be numbered, and the first three names will be certified for the first vacancy, the remaining two and the fourth for the second vacancy, the remaining two and the fifth for the third vacancy, and so on for the whole number of vacancies; but if, after selecting one of any three certified for appointment, the head of the office shall object to another presentation of either of the remaining names, it shall not be again certified.

XI. The examination papers of any candidate who shall have passed a minimum standard of 75 per cent, but who shall fail to be appointed, will, if requested by the candidate, be brought into competition with those candidates who shall compete for vacancies of the same class and nature occurring within one year: *Provided, however*, That the candidate shall not have been specially objected to by the head of the office under the last preceding regulation. No candidate who upon examination has been marked below the minimum will be allowed to again compete within one year from the date of such examination, unless for admission to a lower group.

XII. All examination papers will be filed, and will at all times be open to the inspection of those interested, under such restrictions as may be imposed by the head of the office.

XIII. There shall be one examining board for all appointments and promotions under these rules in the offices of the collector, surveyor, and naval officer, which shall consist of the surveyor and one representative to be nominated each by the collector and the naval officer, and three alternates, to be nominated one each by the collector, the naval officer, and the surveyor: *Provided, however,* That in examinations for positions in the surveyor's office the surveyor's alternate shall act on such board. The examining boards in the offices of the assistant treasurer and the appraiser shall consist of three persons, with three alternates, to be nominated by the assistant treasurer and the appraiser, respectively. All nominations as members and alternates on the examining boards shall be submitted to the Secretary of the Treasury for his approval. The heads of the several offices shall constitute a board of revision and appeal, which, upon appeal from any person examined or from any member of an examining board, shall revise the decision of said board.

XIV. Whenever the head of an office shall notify the board of examiners for such office that a vacancy which he desires to fill exists in any grade above the lowest not excepted from the rules and regulations for the civil service, the board will fix a time for holding an examination for the purpose, and at least five days before the same is to take place will cause a notice to be posted in a conspicuous place in the office, stating the grade and group of the vacancy, the date of the examination, and that the vacancy is to be filled by a competitive examination of applicants from the next lower grade, unless none in such lower grade be found qualified, when those in the next lower grade may compete, or, if there be none in any of the lower grades qualified, competition will be open to applicants. In any examination for promotion, if the competitors from the next lower grade shall not exceed three in number, the board may, at its discretion, open the competition to the next lower grade or below, as they may deem best; and furthermore, if such promotion would probably occasion vacancies requiring other promotions, the board may combine in one the necessary examinations for such promotions. No person who has been examined in any grade for promotion and failed to receive such promotion shall again be admitted to examination within six months, but in the meantime his general average, as ascertained by such examination, may be brought into competition, as provided in Regulation XI.

XV. The examination will be held upon the general subjects fixed for examinations for admission to the lowest grade of the group and upon such other subjects as the general nature of the business of the office and the special nature of the position to be filled may seem to the board of examiners to require. Due weight will be given to the efficiency with which the several candidates shall have previously performed their duties in the office; but no one who shall fail to pass a minimum standard of 75 per cent in the written examination will be certified for appointment.

XVI. If no applicants from within the group shall be found competent, an examination will be held of all who shall make application in accordance with the regulations governing applications for admission to the office, after due public notice by the head of the office. The examination will be conducted in accordance with the provisions for admission to the office, as required by the fourth rule* for the civil service promulgated December 19, 1871, but the nature of the examination will be the same as in any previous examination for the same vacancy.

XVII. The list of names from which the appointment is to be made will be prepared and certified in the manner provided for admission to the lowest grade.

XVIII. Persons employed in any of the offices to which these rules are applicable may be transferred without examination from one office to a grade no higher

*See p. 4112.

in another office, with the consent of the heads of the respective offices and the approval of the Secretary of the Treasury.

XIX. Under the provisions of rule 2* of August 5, 1873, and the operation of these regulations, the power of suspension and of recommendation for discharge from the service shall remain with the nominating officer unrestricted. If, however, in his judgment it be deemed advisable, he may direct any person in his department to be cited before the regular examining board, and such board shall examine into and report upon the qualifications, efficiency, and general fitness for the position held, or for any position in the same or a lower grade, of the person so cited to appear; and furthermore, any person in the service engaged in active outdoor duties may be cited to appear before a surgeon of the United States Marine-Hospital Service and be examined by such surgeon as to the physical abilities of such person to perform the duties of the position occupied or of a position of less exposure, if otherwise qualified.

XX. The sessions of the examining boards shall not be open to the public, but the board of revision and appeal may select such number of prominent citizens as may be deemed advisable, who shall have free access to the examining rooms, and who shall take no part in the conduct of the examination, but may, by inspection and inquiry, assure themselves regarding its thoroughness and impartiality, and may publicly certify the results of their inspection.

[Seventh rule for the civil service under the Executive order of April 16, 1872.†]

The appointment of all persons entering the civil service in accordance with these regulations, excepting persons appointed by the President by and with the advice and consent of the Senate, postmasters, and persons appointed to any position in a foreign country, shall be made for a probationary term of six months, during which the conduct and capacity of such persons shall be tested; and if at the end of said probationary term satisfactory proofs of their fitness shall have been furnished by the board of examiners to the head of the Department in which they shall have been employed during said term, they shall be reappointed.

[Fourth regulation for the civil service under the Executive order of April 16, 1872.‡]

The appointment of persons to be employed exclusively in the secret service of the Government, also of persons to be employed as translators, stenographers, or private secretaries, * * * may be excepted from the operation of the rules.

[Ninth rule for the civil service under the Executive order of April 16, 1872.§]

Any person who, after long and faithful service in a Department, shall be incapacitated by mental or bodily infirmity for the efficient discharge of the duties of his position may be appointed by the head of the Department, at his discretion, to a position of less responsibility in the same Department.

[Seventh rule for the civil service under the Executive order of August 5, 1873.‖]

Applicants for appointment as cashiers of collectors of customs, cashiers of assistant treasurers, cashiers of postmasters, superintendents of money-order divisions in post-offices, and other custodians of large sums of public money for whose fidelity another officer has given official bonds may be appointed at discretion; but this rule shall not apply to any appointment to a position grouped below the grade of assistant teller.

The amendments of the New York custom-house rules seem proper.

R. B. H.

*See p. 4185. † See rule 7, promulgated December 19, 1871, p. 4112. ‡ See p. 4135.
§ See rule 9, promulgated December 19, 1871, p. 4112. ‖ See p. 4186.

MARCH 6, 1879.

General E. A. MERRITT,
Collector of Customs, New York.

SIR: Your letter of the 26th ultimo, inclosing a draft of modification of the civil-service rules, was duly received, and the rules have been considered and approved by the President. You may therefore act upon them.

Very respectfully,

JOHN SHERMAN,
Secretary.

RULES GOVERNING APPOINTMENT AND PROMOTION IN THE NEW YORK POST-OFFICE.

For the purpose of making it more certain that only persons of good character and adequate capacity shall be selected from among applicants too numerous for the postmaster to become informed of their individual merits by personal investigation, the following rules are established:

1. Hereafter all applications for clerical appointment at this post-office must be made in accordance with a prescribed form, a copy of which will be furnished to each applicant.

2. All appointments to clerical positions will be made to the lowest grade, and no applications from persons under 16 or over 25 years of age will be entertained.

3. On receipt of an application for appointment, and before further action is taken in regard to it, the applicant will be referred to the medical officer for examination as to his physical condition, as being adequate for the service; and if the report is unfavorable the application will be rejected. Should the report be favorable, the application will be filed and registered in its regular order.

4. Every application must be accompanied by a certificate, signed by not less than three nor more than five reputable citizens, stating the time for which each has been acquainted with the applicant, and testifying to his good character and reputation for integrity, sobriety, and industry, and to the willingness of the signers to furnish personally any further information they may possess concerning the applicant, if so requested by the postmaster or the board of examiners.

5. Applications not properly filled out as herein required, or which are found to contain false statements, or which in any other manner show the unfitness of the applicant for employment in the post-office, will be rejected and the applicant notified of such rejection.

6. All examination papers, with the markings showing the relative proficiency of the candidates, will be carefully preserved and filed.

7. The names of candidates which have been on the register for one year without being reached for examination will be regarded as removed, and will not be selected for examination unless again placed on the register by a new application, after which they will be selected when reached in order.

8. All applications duly received and filed shall, when reached in order, be referred to a board of examiners, which is hereby appointed, and which shall consist of the assistant postmaster, auditor, the general superintendents of the fourth, fifth, and sixth divisions, and the assistant general superintendent of the third division. The postmaster's private secretary shall also act as secretary of said board.

9. When vacancies occur in the lowest grade, the board of examiners shall notify such number of applicants, not less than twenty, of those first on the register of applicants to appear for a competitive examination.

10. The questions to be asked and answered at such examinations shall be such as

will show the relative proficiency of the candidates, first, in penmanship; second, in arithmetic; third, in geography; fourth, in English grammar; fifth, in the history of the United States and in matters of a public nature, to the extent that may be required adequately to test general capacity or special fitness for the postal service.

11. The board shall present to the postmaster a list of the names of the successful candidates in the order of their excellence, as shown by the examination, beginning with the highest; and the appointments will be made from the three highest names on the list.

12. All further details in methods of examination will be left to the discretion of the board, but subject to the instructions of the postmaster, in conformity herewith.

13. All vacancies that may occur in the higher grades of any department shall be filled by promotion from the lower grades by means of competitive examinations, to which shall be admitted as competitors such persons only as are already employed in the division in which the vacancy exists or in divisions having analogous duties. The questions in these examinations shall be restricted mainly to matters pertaining to the ordinary business of that department. The examinations shall be conducted by the general superintendent of the division to which the department is attached, assisted by such one or more other officers of the same as the postmaster may select; and they shall report the result to the postmaster in the manner provided in rule 11, and the vacancy will be filled by the promotion of some one of the three standing highest in the competition. But whenever the vacancy to be filled by promotion is that of a position requiring the exercise of administrative authority the board may add such questions as will test the degree to which the candidates possess special qualifications for such position.

14. For positions as porters the examination will be confined to questions intended to test the physical ability of the candidates and their proficiency in reading, penmanship, and elementary arithmetic only.

15. The postmaster reserves from the operation of the above rules for original appointment and promotion positions of especial pecuniary trust, as well as those involving confidential relations, as private secretary, etc.

THOMAS L. JAMES, *Postmaster.*

Approved. Let these rules go into effect May 1, 1879.

D. M. KEY, *Postmaster-General.*

APRIL 3, 1879.

The foregoing rules are approved.

R. B. HAYES.

[From the Evening Star, Washington, D. C., May 28, 1879.]

EXECUTIVE MANSION,
Washington, May 28, 1879.

SIR:* I am directed by the President to say that the several Departments of the Government will be closed on Friday, the 30th instant, in remembrance of those who fell in defense of the nation, and to enable the employees to participate in the commemorative ceremonies of the day.

Very respectfully, your obedient servant,

W. K. ROGERS, *Private Secretary.*

*Addressed to the heads of the Executive Departments, etc.

TREASURY DEPARTMENT,
OFFICE OF THE SURGEON-GENERAL
UNITED STATES MARINE-HOSPITAL SERVICE,
Washington, D. C., May 31, 1879.

To Medical Officers of the Marine-Hospital Service and others whom it may concern:

Official information having been received to the effect that the "plague" which existed in southern Russia is now almost extinct, the regulations issued March 3, 1879,* imposing certain restrictions upon the importation of rags, etc., into the United States, are hereby revoked.

By order of the Secretary of the Treasury:

J. B. HAMILTON,
Surgeon-General United States Marine-Hospital Service.

Approved:

R. B. HAYES.

EXECUTIVE MANSION,
Washington, November 1, 1879.

The sad intelligence of the death of Zachariah Chandler, late Secretary of the Interior, and during so many years a Senator from the State of Michigan, has been communicated to the Government and to the country, and in proper respect to his memory I hereby order that the several Executive Departments be closed to public business and their flags and those of their dependencies throughout the country be displayed at half-mast on the day of his funeral.

R. B. HAYES.

EXECUTIVE MANSION,
Washington, November 17, 1879.

DEAR SIR:† I am directed by the President to say that the several Departments of the Government will be closed on Wednesday, the 19th instant, to enable the employees to participate in the ceremonies attending the unveiling of the statue of the late General George H. Thomas.

Very truly, yours,

W. K. ROGERS, *Private Secretary.*

THIRD ANNUAL MESSAGE.

EXECUTIVE MANSION, *December 1, 1879.*

Fellow-Citizens of the Senate and House of Representatives:

The members of the Forty-sixth Congress have assembled in their first regular session under circumstances calling for mutual congratulation and grateful acknowledgment to the Giver of All Good for the large and unusual measure of national prosperity which we now enjoy.

The most interesting events which have occurred in our public affairs

*See pp. 4501-4502.   †Addressed to the heads of the Executive Departments, etc.

since my last annual message to Congress are connected with the financial operations of the Government, directly affecting the business interests of the country. I congratulate Congress on the successful execution of the resumption act. At the time fixed, and in the manner contemplated by law, United States notes began to be redeemed in coin. Since the 1st of January last they have been promptly redeemed on presentation, and in all business transactions, public and private, in all parts of the country, they are received and paid out as the equivalent of coin. The demand upon the Treasury for gold and silver in exchange for United States notes has been comparatively small, and the voluntary deposit of coin and bullion in exchange for notes has been very large. The excess of the precious metals deposited or exchanged for United States notes over the amount of United States notes redeemed is about $40,000,000.

The resumption of specie payments has been followed by a very great revival of business. With a currency equivalent in value to the money of the commercial world, we are enabled to enter upon an equal competition with other nations in trade and production. The increasing foreign demand for our manufactures and agricultural products has caused a large balance of trade in our favor, which has been paid in gold, from the 1st of July last to November 15, to the amount of about $59,000,000. Since the resumption of specie payments there has also been a marked and gratifying improvement of the public credit. The bonds of the Government bearing only 4 per cent interest have been sold at or above par, sufficient in amount to pay off all of the national debt which was redeemable under present laws. The amount of interest saved annually by the process of refunding the debt since March 1, 1877, is $14,297,177. The bonds sold were largely in small sums, and the number of our citizens now holding the public securities is much greater than ever before. The amount of the national debt which matures within less than two years is $792,121,700, of which $500,000,000 bear interest at the rate of 5 per cent, and the balance is in bonds bearing 6 per cent interest. It is believed that this part of the public debt can be refunded by the issue of 4 per cent bonds, and, by the reduction of interest which will thus be effected, about $11,000,000 can be annually saved to the Treasury. To secure this important reduction of interest to be paid by the United States further legislation is required, which it is hoped will be provided by Congress during its present session.

The coinage of gold by the mints of the United States during the last fiscal year was $40,986,912. The coinage of silver dollars since the passage of the act for that purpose up to November 1, 1879, was $45,000,850, of which $12,700,344 have been issued from the Treasury and are now in circulation, and $32,300,506 are still in the possession of the Government.

The pendency of the proposition for unity of action between the United States and the principal commercial nations of Europe to effect a permanent system for the equality of gold and silver in the recognized money of the world leads me to recommend that Congress refrain from new legislation on the general subject. The great revival of trade, internal and foreign, will supply during the coming year its own instructions, which may well be awaited before attempting further experimental measures with the coinage. I would, however, strongly urge upon Congress the importance of authorizing the Secretary of the Treasury to suspend the coinage of silver dollars upon the present legal ratio. The market value of the silver dollar being uniformly and largely less than the market value of the gold dollar, it is obviously impracticable to maintain them at par with each other if both are coined without limit. If the cheaper coin is forced into circulation, it will, if coined without limit, soon become the sole standard of value, and thus defeat the desired object, which is a currency of both gold and silver which shall be of equivalent value, dollar for dollar, with the universally recognized money of the world.

The retirement from circulation of United States notes with the capacity of legal tender in private contracts is a step to be taken in our progress toward a safe and stable currency which should be accepted as the policy and duty of the Government and the interest and security of the people. It is my firm conviction that the issue of legal-tender paper money based wholly upon the authority and credit of the Government, except in extreme emergency, is without warrant in the Constitution and a violation of sound financial principles. The issue of United States notes during the late civil war with the capacity of legal tender between private individuals was not authorized except as a means of rescuing the country from imminent peril. The circulation of these notes as paper money for any protracted period of time after the accomplishment of this purpose was not contemplated by the framers of the law under which they were issued. They anticipated the redemption and withdrawal of these notes at the earliest practicable period consistent with the attainment of the object for which they were provided.

The policy of the United States, steadily adhered to from the adoption of the Constitution, has been to avoid the creation of a national debt; and when, from necessity in time of war, debts have been created, they have been paid off, on the return of peace, as rapidly as possible. With this view, and for this purpose, it is recommended that the existing laws for the accumulation of a sinking fund sufficient to extinguish the public debt within a limited period be maintained. If any change of the objects or rates of taxation is deemed necessary by Congress, it is suggested that experience has shown that a duty can be placed on tea and coffee which will not enhance the price of those articles to the consumer, and which will add several millions of dollars annually to the Treasury.

The continued deliberate violation by a large number of the prominent and influential citizens of the Territory of Utah of the laws of the United

States for the prosecution and punishment of polygamy demands the attention of every department of the Government. This Territory has a population sufficient to entitle it to admission as a State, and the general interests of the nation, as well as the welfare of the citizens of the Territory, require its advance from the Territorial form of government to the responsibilities and privileges of a State. This important change will not, however, be approved by the country while the citizens of Utah in very considerable number uphold a practice which is condemned as a crime by the laws of all civilized communities throughout the world.

The law for the suppression of this offense was enacted with great unanimity by Congress more than seventeen years ago, but has remained until recently a dead letter in the Territory of Utah, because of the peculiar difficulties attending its enforcement. The opinion widely prevailed among the citizens of Utah that the law was in contravention of the constitutional guaranty of religious freedom. This objection is now removed. The Supreme Court of the United States has decided the law to be within the legislative power of Congress and binding as a rule of action for all who reside within the Territories. There is no longer any reason for delay or hesitation in its enforcement. It should be firmly and effectively executed. If not sufficiently stringent in its provisions, it should be amended; and in aid of the purpose in view I recommend that more comprehensive and more searching methods for preventing as well as punishing this crime be provided. If necessary to secure obedience to the law, the enjoyment and exercise of the rights and privileges of citizenship in the Territories of the United States may be withheld or withdrawn from those who violate or oppose the enforcement of the law on this subject.

The elections of the past year, though occupied only with State officers, have not failed to elicit in the political discussions which attended them all over the country new and decisive evidence of the deep interest which the great body of citizens take in the progress of the country toward a more general and complete establishment, at whatever cost, of universal security and freedom in the exercise of the elective franchise. While many topics of political concern demand great attention from our people, both in the sphere of national and State authority, I find no reason to qualify the opinion I expressed in my last annual message, that no temporary or administrative interests of government, however urgent or weighty, will ever displace the zeal of our people in defense of the primary rights of citizenship, and that the power of public opinion will override all political prejudices, and all sectional and State attachments in demanding that all over our wide territory the name and character of citizen of the United States shall mean one and the same thing and carry with them unchallenged security and respect. I earnestly appeal to the intelligence and patriotism of all good citizens of every part of the country, however much they may be divided in opinions on other political subjects, to unite in compelling obedience to existing laws aimed at the protection of the right of suffrage. I respectfully urge upon Congress to supply any defects in these laws which experience has shown and which it is within its power to remedy. I again invoke the cooperation of the executive and legislative authorities of the States in this great purpose. I am fully convinced that if the public mind can be set at rest on this paramount question of popular rights no serious obstacle will thwart or delay the complete pacification of the country or retard the general diffusion of prosperity.

In a former message I invited the attention of Congress to the subject of the reformation of the civil service of the Government, and expressed the intention of transmitting to Congress as early as practicable a report upon this subject by the chairman of the Civil Service Commission.

In view of the facts that during a considerable period the Government of Great Britain has been dealing with administrative problems and abuses in various particulars analogous to those presented in this country, and that in recent years the measures adopted were understood to have been effective and in every respect highly satisfactory, I thought it desirable to have fuller information upon the subject, and accordingly requested the chairman of the Civil Service Commission to make a thorough investigation for this purpose. The result has been an elaborate and comprehensive report.

The report sets forth the history of the partisan spoils system in Great Britain, and of the rise and fall of the parliamentary patronage, and of official interference with the freedom of elections. It shows that after long trials of various kinds of examinations those which are competitive and open on equal terms to all, and which are carried on under the superintendence of a single commission, have, with great advantage, been established as conditions of admission to almost every official place in the subordinate administration of that country and of British India. The completion of the report, owing to the extent of the labor involved in its preparation and the omission of Congress to make any provision either for the compensation or the expenses of the Commission, has been postponed until the present time. It is herewith transmitted to Congress.

While the reform measures of another government are of no authority for us, they are entitled to influence to the extent to which their intrinsic wisdom and their adaptation to our institutions and social life may commend them to our consideration. The views I have heretofore expressed concerning the defects and abuses in our civil administration remain unchanged, except in so far as an enlarged experience has deepened my sense of the duty both of officers and of the people themselves to cooperate for their removal. The grave evils and perils of a partisan spoils system of appointment to office and of office tenure are now generally recognized. In the resolutions of the great parties, in the reports of Departments, in the debates and proceedings of Congress, in the messages of Executives, the gravity of these evils has been pointed out and the need of their reform has been admitted.

To command the necessary support, every measure of reform must be based on common right and justice, and must be compatible with the healthy existence of great parties, which are inevitable and essential in a free state.

When the people have approved a policy at a national election, confidence on the part of the officers they have selected and of the advisers who, in accordance with our political institutions, should be consulted in the policy which it is their duty to carry into effect is indispensable. It is eminently proper that they should explain it before the people, as well as illustrate its spirit in the performance of their official duties.

Very different considerations apply to the greater number of those who fill the subordinate places in the civil service. Their responsibility is to their superiors in official position. It is their duty to obey the legal instructions of those upon whom that authority is devolved, and their best public service consists in the discharge of their functions irrespective of partisan politics. Their duties are the same whatever party is in power and whatever policy prevails. As a consequence it follows that their tenure of office should not depend on the prevalence of any policy or the supremacy of any party, but should be determined by their capacity to serve the people most usefully quite irrespective of partisan interests. The same considerations that should govern the tenure should also prevail in the appointment, discipline, and removal of these subordinates. The authority of appointment and removal is not a perquisite, which may be used to aid a friend or reward a partisan, but is a trust, to be exercised in the public interest under all the sanctions which attend the obligation to apply the public funds only for public purposes.

Every citizen has an equal right to the honor and profit of entering the public service of his country. The only just ground of discrimination is the measure of character and capacity he has to make that service most useful to the people. Except in cases where, upon just and recognized principles—as upon the theory of pensions—offices and promotions are bestowed as rewards for past services, their bestowal upon any theory which disregards personal merit is an act of injustice to the citizen, as well as a breach of that trust subject to which the appointing power is held.

In the light of these principles it becomes of great importance to provide just and adequate means, especially for every Department and large administrative office, where personal discrimination on the part of its head is not practicable, for ascertaining those qualifications to which appointments and removals should have reference. To fail to provide such means is not only to deny the opportunity of ascertaining the facts upon which the most righteous claim to office depends, but of necessity to discourage all worthy aspirants by handing over appointments and removals to mere influence and favoritism. If it is the right of the worthiest claimant to gain the appointment and the interest of the people to bestow it upon him, it would seem clear that a wise and just method of ascertaining personal fitness for office must be an important and permanent function of every just and wise government. It has long since become impossible in the great offices for those having the duty of nomination and appointment to personally examine into the individual qualifications of more than a small proportion of those seeking office. and with the enlargement of the civil service that proportion must continue to become less.

In the earlier years of the Government the subordinate offices were so few in number that it was quite easy for those making appointments and promotions to personally ascertain the merits of candidates. Party managers and methods had not then become powerful agencies of coercion, hostile to the free and just exercise of the appointing power.

A large and responsible part of the duty of restoring the civil service to the desired purity and efficiency rests upon the President, and it is my purpose to do what is within my power to advance such prudent and gradual measures of reform as will most surely and rapidly bring about that radical change of system essential to make our administrative methods satisfactory to a free and intelligent people. By a proper exercise of authority it is in the power of the Executive to do much to promote such a reform. But it can not be too clearly understood that nothing adequate can be accomplished without cooperation on the part of Congress and considerate and intelligent support among the people. Reforms which challenge the generally accepted theories of parties and demand changes in the methods of Departments are not the work of a day. Their permanent foundations must be laid in sound principles and in an experience which demonstrates their wisdom and exposes the errors of their adversaries. Every worthy officer desires to make his official action a gain and an honor to his country; but the people themselves, far more than their officers in public station, are interested in a pure, economical, and vigorous administration.

By laws enacted in 1853 and 1855, and now in substance incorporated in the Revised Statutes, the practice of arbitrary appointments to the several subordinate grades in the great Departments was condemned, and examinations as to capacity, to be conducted by departmental boards of examiners, were provided for and made conditions of admission to the public service. These statutes are a decision by Congress that examinations of some sort as to attainments and capacity are essential to the well-being of the public service. The important questions since the enactment of these laws have been as to the character of these examinations, and whether official favor and partisan influence or common right and merit were to control the access to the examinations. In practice these examinations have not always been open to worthy persons generally who might wish to be examined. Official favoritism and partisan influence, as a rule, appear to have designated those who alone were permitted to go before the examining boards, subjecting even the examiners to a pressure from the friends of the candidates very difficult to resist. As a consequence the standard of admission fell below that which the public interest demanded. It was also almost inevitable that a system which provided for various separate boards of examiners, with no common supervision or uniform method of procedure, should result in confusion, inconsistency, and inadequate tests of capacity, highly detrimental to the public interest. A further and more radical change was obviously required.

In the annual message of December, 1870, my predecessor declared that—

There is no duty which so much embarrasses the Executive and heads of Departments as that of appointments, nor is there any such arduous and thankless labor imposed on Senators and Representatives as that of finding places for constituents. The present system does not secure the best men, and often not even fit men, for public place. The elevation and purification of the civil service of the Government will be hailed with approval by the whole people of the United States.

Congress accordingly passed the act approved March 3, 1871, "to regulate the civil service of the United States and promote the efficiency thereof," giving the necessary authority to the Executive to inaugurate a civil-service reform.

Acting under this statute, which was interpreted as intended to secure a system of just and effectual examinations under uniform supervision, a number of eminently competent persons were selected for the purpose, who entered with zeal upon the discharge of their duties, prepared with an intelligent appreciation of the requirements of the service the regulations contemplated, and took charge of the examinations, and who in their capacity as a board have been known as the "Civil Service Commission." Congress for two years appropriated the money needed for the compensation and for the expense of carrying on the work of the Commission.

It appears from the report of the Commission submitted to the President in April, 1874, that examinations had been held in various sections of the country, and that an appropriation of about $25,000 would be required to meet the annual expenses, including salaries, involved in discharging the duties of the Commission. The report was transmitted to Congress by special message of April 18, 1874, with the following favorable comment upon the labors of the Commission:

If sustained by Congress, I have no doubt the rules can, after the experience gained, be so improved and enforced as to still more materially benefit the public service and relieve the Executive, members of Congress, and the heads of Departments from influences prejudicial to good administration. The rules, as they have hitherto been enforced, have resulted beneficially, as is shown by the opinions of the members of the Cabinet and their subordinates in the Departments, and in that opinion I concur.

And in the annual message of December of the same year similar views are expressed and an appropriation for continuing the work of the Commission again advised.

The appropriation was not made, and as a consequence the active work of the Commission was suspended, leaving the Commission itself still in existence. Without the means, therefore, of causing qualifications to be tested in any systematic manner or of securing for the public service the advantages of competition upon any extensive plan, I recommended in my annual message of December, 1877, the making of an appropriation for the resumption of the work of the Commission.

In the meantime, however, competitive examinations, under many embarrassments, have been conducted within limited spheres in the Executive Departments in Washington and in a number of the custom-houses and post-offices of the principal cities of the country, with a view to further test their effects, and in every instance they have been found to be as salutary as they are stated to have been under the Administration of my predecessor. I think the economy, purity, and efficiency of the public service would be greatly promoted by their systematic introduction, wherever practicable, throughout the entire civil service of the Government, together with ample provision for their general supervision in order to secure consistency and uniform justice.

Reports from the Secretary of the Interior, from the Postmaster-General, from the postmaster in the city of New York, where such examinations have been some time on trial, and also from the collector of the port, the naval officer, and the surveyor in that city, and from the postmasters and collectors in several of the other large cities, show that the competitive system, where applied, has in various ways contributed to improve the public service.

The reports show that the results have been salutary in a marked degree, and that the general application of similar rules can not fail to be of decided benefit to the service.

The reports of the Government officers, in the city of New York especially, bear decided testimony to the utility of open competitive examinations in their respective offices, showing that—

These examinations and the excellent qualifications of those admitted to the service through them have had a marked incidental effect upon the persons previously in the service, and particularly upon those aspiring to promotion. There has been on the part of these latter an increased interest in the work and a desire to extend acquaintance with it beyond the particular desk occupied, and thus the morale of the entire force has been raised. * * * The examinations have been attended by many citizens, who have had an opportunity to thoroughly investigate the scope and character of the tests and the method of determining the results, and those visitors have without exception approved the methods employed, and several of them have publicly attested their favorable opinion.

Upon such considerations I deem it my duty to renew the recommendation contained in my annual message of December, 1877, requesting Congress to make the necessary appropriation for the resumption of the work of the Civil Service Commission. Economy will be promoted by authorizing a moderate compensation to persons in the public service who may perform extra labor upon or under the Commission, as the Executive may direct.

I am convinced that if a just and adequate test of merit is enforced for admission to the public service and in making promotions such abuses as removals without good cause and partisan and official interference with the proper exercise of the appointing power will in large measure disappear.

There are other administrative abuses to which the attention of Congress should be asked in this connection. Mere partisan appointments and the constant peril of removal without cause very naturally lead to an absorbing and mischievous political activity on the part of those thus appointed, which not only interferes with the due discharge of official duty, but is incompatible with the freedom of elections. Not without warrant in the views of several of my predecessors in the Presidential office, and directly within the law of 1871, already cited, I endeavored, by regulation made on the 22d day of June, 1877, to put some reasonable limits to such abuses. It may not be easy, and it may never perhaps be necessary, to define with precision the proper limit of political action on the part of Federal officers. But while their right to hold and freely express their opinions can not be questioned, it is very plain that they should neither be allowed to devote to other subjects the time needed for the proper discharge of their official duties nor to use the authority of their office to enforce their own opinions or to coerce the political action of those who hold different opinions.

Reasons of justice and public policy quite analogous to those which forbid the use of official power for the oppression of the private citizen impose upon the Government the duty of protecting its officers and agents from arbitrary exactions. In whatever aspect considered, the practice of making levies for party purposes upon the salaries of officers is highly demoralizing to the public service and discreditable to the country. Though an officer should be as free as any other citizen to give his own money in aid of his opinions or his party, he should also be as free as any other citizen to refuse to make such gifts. If salaries are but a fair compensation for the time and labor of the officer, it is gross injustice to levy a tax upon them. If they are made excessive in order that they may bear the tax, the excess is an indirect robbery of the public funds.

I recommend, therefore, such a revision and extension of present statutes as shall secure to those in every grade of official life or public employment the protection with which a great and enlightened nation should guard those who are faithful in its service.

Our relations with foreign countries have continued peaceful.

With Great Britain there are still unsettled questions, growing out of the local laws of the maritime provinces and the action of provincial authorities deemed to be in derogation of rights secured by treaty to American fishermen. The United States minister in London has been instructed to present a demand for $105,305.02 in view of the damages received by American citizens at Fortune Bay on the 6th day of January, 1878. The subject has been taken into consideration by the British Government, and an early reply is anticipated.

Upon the completion of the necessary preliminary examinations the subject of our participation in the provincial fisheries, as regulated by treaty, will at once be brought to the attention of the British Government, with a view to an early and permanent settlement of the whole question, which was only temporarily adjusted by the treaty of Washington.

Efforts have been made to obtain the removal of restrictions found injurious to the exportation of cattle to the United Kingdom.

Some correspondence has also occurred with regard to the rescue and saving of life and property upon the Lakes, which has resulted in important modifications of the previous regulations of the Dominion government on the subject in the interest of humanity and commerce.

In accordance with the joint resolution of the last session of Congress, commissioners were appointed to represent the United States at the two international exhibitions in Australia, one of which is now in progress at Sydney, and the other to be held next year at Melbourne. A desire has been expressed by our merchants and manufacturers interested in the important and growing trade with Australia that an increased provision should be made by Congress for the representation of our industries at the Melbourne exhibition of next year, and the subject is respectfully submitted to your favorable consideration.

The assent of the Government has been given to the landing on the coast of Massachusetts of a new and independent transatlantic cable between France, by way of the French island of St. Pierre, and this country, subject to any future legislation of Congress on the subject. The conditions imposed before allowing this connection with our shores to be established are such as to secure its competition with any existing or future lines of marine cable and preclude amalgamation therewith, to provide for entire equality of rights to our Government and people with those of France in the use of the cable, and prevent any exclusive possession of the privilege as accorded by France to the disadvantage of any future cable communication between France and the United States which may be projected and accomplished by our citizens. An important reduction of the present rates of cable communication with Europe, felt to be too burdensome to the interests of our commerce, must necessarily flow from the establishment of this competing line.

The attention of Congress was drawn to the propriety of some general regulation by Congress of the whole subject of transmarine cables by my predecessor in his message of December 7, 1875, and I respectfully submit to your consideration the importance of Congressional action in the matter.

The questions of grave importance with Spain growing out of the incidents of the Cuban insurrection have been for the most part happily and honorably settled. It may reasonably be anticipated that the commission now sitting in Washington for the decision of private cases in this connection will soon be able to bring its labors to a conclusion.

The long-standing question of East Florida claims has lately been renewed as a subject of correspondence, and may possibly require Congressional action for its final disposition.

A treaty with the Netherlands with respect to consular rights and privileges similar to those with other powers has been signed and ratified, and the ratifications were exchanged on the 31st of July last. Negotiations for extradition treaties with the Netherlands and with Denmark are now in progress.

Some questions with Switzerland in regard to pauper and convict emigrants have arisen, but it is not doubted that they will be arranged upon a just and satisfactory basis. A question has also occurred with respect to an asserted claim by Swiss municipal authorities to exercise tutelage over persons and property of Swiss citizens naturalized in this country. It is possible this may require adjustment by treaty.

With the German Empire frequent questions arise in connection with the subjects of naturalization and expatriation, but the Imperial Government has constantly manifested a desire to strictly maintain and comply with all treaty stipulations in regard to them.

In consequence of the omission of Congress to provide for a diplomatic representative at Athens, the legation to Greece has been withdrawn. There is now no channel of diplomatic communication between the two countries, and the expediency of providing for one in some form is submitted to Congress.

Relations with Austria, Russia, Italy, Portugal, Turkey, and Belgium continue amicable, and marked by no incident of especial importance.

A change of the personal head of the Government of Egypt has taken place. No change, however, has occurred in the relations between Egypt and the United States. The action of the Egyptian Government in presenting to the city of New York one of the ancient obelisks, which possess such historic interest, is highly appreciated as a generous mark of international regard. If prosperity should attend the enterprise of its transportation across the Atlantic, its erection in a conspicuous position in the chief commercial city of the nation will soon be accomplished.

The treaty recently made between Japan and the United States in regard to the revision of former commercial treaties it is now believed will be followed by similar action on the part of other treaty powers. The attention of Congress is again invited to the subject of the indemnity funds received some years since from Japan and China, which, with their accumulated interest, now amount to considerable sums. If any part of these funds is justly due to American citizens, they should receive it promptly; and whatever may have been received by this Government in excess of strictly just demands should in some form be returned to the nations to whom it equitably belongs.

The Government of China has signified its willingness to consider the question of the emigration of its subjects to the United States with a dispassionate fairness and to cooperate in such measures as may tend to prevent injurious consequences to the United States. The negotiations are still proceeding, and will be pressed with diligence.

A question having arisen between China and Japan about the Lew Chew Islands, the United States Government has taken measures to inform those powers of its readiness to extend its good offices for the maintenance of peace if they shall mutually deem it desirable and find it practicable to avail themselves of the proffer.

It is a gratification to be able to announce that, through the judicious and energetic action of the military commanders of the two nations on each side of the Rio Grande, under the instructions of their respective Governments, raids and depredations have greatly decreased, and in the localities where formerly most destructive have now almost wholly ceased. In view of this result, I entertain a confident expectation that the prevalence of quiet on the border will soon become so assured as to justify a modification of the present orders to our military commanders as to crossing the border, without encouraging such disturbances as would endanger the peace of the two countries.

The third installment of the award against Mexico under the claims commission of July 4, 1868, was duly paid, and has been put in course of distribution in pursuance of the act of Congress providing for the same. This satisfactory situation between the two countries leads me to anticipate an expansion of our trade with Mexico and an increased contribution of capital and industry by our people to the development of the great resources of that country. I earnestly commend to the wisdom of Congress the provision of suitable legislation looking to this result.

Diplomatic intercourse with Colombia is again fully restored by the arrival of a minister from that country to the United States. This is especially fortunate in view of the fact that the question of an interoceanic canal has recently assumed a new and important aspect and is now under discussion with the Central American countries through whose territory the canal, by the Nicaragua route, would have to pass. It is trusted that enlightened statesmanship on their part will see that the early prosecution of such a work will largely inure to the benefit, not only of their own citizens and those of the United States, but of the commerce of the civilized world. It is not doubted that should the work be undertaken under the protective auspices of the United States, and upon satisfactory concessions for the right of way and its security by the

Central American Governments, the capital for its completion would be readily furnished from this country and Europe, which might, failing such guaranties, prove inaccessible.

Diplomatic relations with Chile have also been strengthened by the reception of a minister from that country.

The war between Peru, Bolivia, and Chile still continues. The United States have not deemed it proper to interpose in the matter further than to convey to all the Governments concerned the assurance that the friendly offices of the Government of the United States for the restoration of peace upon an honorable basis will be extended in case the belligerents shall exhibit a readiness to accept them.

Cordial relations continue with Brazil and the Argentine Republic, and trade with those countries is improving. A provision for regular and more frequent mail communication, in our own ships, between the ports of this country and the nations of South America seems to me to deserve the attention of Congress as an essential precursor of an enlargement of our commerce with them and an extension of our carrying trade.

A recent revolution in Venezuela has been followed by the establishment of a provisional government. This government has not yet been formally recognized, and it is deemed desirable to await the proposed action of the people which is expected to give it the sanction of constitutional forms.

A naval vessel has been sent to the Samoan Islands to make surveys and take possession of the privileges ceded to the United States by Samoa in the harbor of Pago-Pago. A coaling station is to be established there, which will be convenient and useful to United States vessels.

The subject of opening diplomatic relations with Roumania and Servia, now become independent sovereignties, is at present under consideration, and is the subject of diplomatic correspondence.

There is a gratifying increase of trade with nearly all European and American countries, and it is believed that with judicious action in regard to its development it can and will be still more enhanced and that American products and manufactures will find new and expanding markets. The reports of diplomatic and consular officers upon this subject, under the system now adopted, have resulted in obtaining much valuable information, which has been and will continue to be laid before Congress and the public from time to time.

The third article of the treaty with Russia of March 30, 1867, by which Alaska was ceded to the United States, provides that the inhabitants of the ceded territory, with the exception of the uncivilized native tribes, shall be admitted to the enjoyment of all the rights of citizens of the United States and shall be maintained and protected in the free enjoyment of their liberty, property, and religion. The uncivilized tribes are subject to such laws and regulations as the United States may from time to time adopt in regard to the aboriginal tribes of that country.

Both the obligations of this treaty and the necessities of the people require that some organized form of government over the Territory of Alaska be adopted.

There appears to be no law for the arrest of persons charged with common-law offenses, such as assault, robbery, and murder, and no magistrate authorized to issue or execute process in such cases. Serious difficulties have already arisen from offenses of this character, not only among the original inhabitants, but among citizens of the United States and other countries who have engaged in mining, fishing, and other business operations within the territory. A bill authorizing the appointment of justices of the peace and constables and the arrest and detention of persons charged with criminal offenses, and providing for an appeal to United States courts for the district of Oregon in suitable cases, will at a proper time be submitted to Congress.

The attention of Congress is called to the annual report of the Secretary of the Treasury on the condition of the public finances.

The ordinary revenues from all sources for the fiscal year ended June 30, 1879, were $273,827,184.46; the ordinary expenditures for the same period were $266,947,883.53, leaving a surplus revenue for the year of $6,879,300.93.

The receipts for the present fiscal year, ending June 30, 1880, actual and estimated, are as follows: Actual receipts for the first quarter, commencing July 1, 1879, $79,843,663.61; estimated receipts for the remaining three quarters of the year, $208,156,336.39; total receipts for the current fiscal year, actual and estimated, $288,000,000.

The expenditures for the same period will be, actual and estimated, as follows: For the quarter commencing July 1, 1879, actual expenditures, $91,683,385.10; and for the remaining three quarters of the year the expenditures are estimated at $172,316,614.90, making the total expenditures $264,000,000, and leaving an estimated surplus revenue for the year ending June 30, 1880, of $24,000,000. The total receipts during the next fiscal year, ending June 30, 1881, estimated according to existing laws, will be $288,000,000, and the estimated ordinary expenditures for the same period will be $278,097,364.39, leaving a surplus of $9,902,-635.61 for that year.

The large amount expended for arrears of pensions during the last and the present fiscal year, amounting to $21,747,249.60, has prevented the application of the full amount required by law to the sinking fund for the current year; but these arrears having been substantially paid, it is believed that the sinking fund can hereafter be maintained without any change of existing law.

The Secretary of War reports that the War Department estimates for the fiscal year ending June 30, 1881, are $40,380,428.93, the same being for a less sum of money than any annual estimate rendered to Congress from that Department during a period of at least twelve years.

He concurs with the General of the Army in recommending such legislation as will authorize the enlistment of the full number of 25,000 men for the line of the Army, exclusive of the 3,463 men required for detached duty, and therefore not available for service in the field.

He also recommends that Congress be asked to provide by law for the disposition of a large number of abandoned military posts and reservations, which, though very valuable in themselves, have been rendered useless for military purposes by the advance of civilization and settlement.

He unites with the Quartermaster-General in recommending that an appropriation be made for the construction of a cheap and perfectly fire-proof building for the safe storage of a vast amount of money accounts, vouchers, claims, and other valuable records now in the Quartermaster-General's Office, and exposed to great risk of total destruction by fire.

He also recommends, in conformity with the views of the Judge-Advocate-General, some declaratory legislation in reference to the military statute of limitations as applied to the crime of desertion.

In these several recommendations I concur.

The Secretary of War further reports that the work for the improvement of the South Pass of the Mississippi River, under contract with Mr. James B. Eads, made in pursuance of an act of Congress, has been prosecuted during the past year with a greater measure of success in the attainment of results than during any previous year. The channel through the South Pass, which at the beginning of operations in June, 1875, had a depth of only 7½ feet of water, had on the 8th of July, 1879, a minimum depth of 26 feet, having a width of not less than 200 feet and a central depth of 30 feet. Payments have been made in accordance with the statute, as the work progressed, amounting in the aggregate to $4,250,000; and further payments will become due, as provided by the statute, in the event of success in maintaining the channel now secured.

The reports of the General of the Army and of his subordinates present a full and detailed account of the military operations for the suppression of hostilities among the Indians of the Ute and Apache tribes, and praise is justly awarded to the officers and troops engaged for promptness, skill, and courage displayed.

The past year has been one of almost unbroken peace and quiet on the Mexican frontier, and there is reason to believe that the efforts of this Government and of Mexico to maintain order in that region will prove permanently successful.

This Department was enabled during the past year to find temporary, though crowded, accommodations and a safe depository for a portion of its records in the completed east wing of the building designed for the State, War, and Navy Departments. The construction of the north wing of the building, a part of the structure intended for the use of the War Department, is being carried forward with all possible dispatch, and the work should receive from Congress such liberal appropriations as will secure its speedy completion.

The report of the Secretary of the Navy shows continued improvement in that branch of the service during the last fiscal year. Extensive repairs have been made upon vessels, and two new ships have been completed and made ready for sea.

The total expenditures of the year ended June 30, 1879, including specific appropriations not estimated for by the Department, were $13,-555,710.09. The expenses chargeable to the year, after deducting the amount of these specific appropriations, were $13,343,317.79; but this is subject to a reduction of $283,725.99, that amount having been drawn upon warrants, but not paid out during the year. The amount of appropriations applicable to the last fiscal year was $14,538,646.17. There was, therefore, a balance of $1,479,054.37 remaining unexpended and to the credit of the Department on June 30, 1879. The estimates for the fiscal year ending June 30, 1881, are $14,864,147.95, which exceeds the appropriations for the present fiscal year $361,897.28. The reason for this increase is explained in the Secretary's report. The appropriations available for the present fiscal year are $14,502,250.67, which will, in the opinion of the Secretary, answer all the ordinary demands of the service. The amount drawn from the Treasury from July 1 to November 1, 1879 was $5,770,404.12, of which $1,095,440.33 has been refunded, leaving as the expenditure for that period $4,674,963.79. If the expenditures of the remaining two-thirds of the year do not exceed the proportion for these four months, there will remain unexpended at the end of the year $477,359.30 of the current appropriations. The report of the Secretary shows the gratifying fact that among all the disbursing officers of the Pay Corps of the Navy there is not one who is a defaulter to the extent of a single dollar. I unite with him in recommending the removal of the observatory to a more healthful location. That institution reflects credit upon the nation, and has obtained the approbation of scientific men in all parts of the world. Its removal from its present location would not only be conducive to the health of its officers and professors, but would greatly increase its usefulness.

The appropriation for judicial expenses, which has heretofore been made for the Department of Justice in gross, was subdivided at the last session of Congress, and no appropriation whatever was made for the payment of the fees of marshals and their deputies, either in the service of process or for the discharge of other duties; and since June 30 these officers have continued the performance of their duties without compensation from the Government, taking upon themselves the necessary incidental outlays, as well as rendering their own services. In only a few unavoidable instances has the proper execution of the process of the United States failed by reason of the absence of the requisite appropriation. This course of official conduct on the part of these officers, highly creditable to their fidelity, was advised by the Attorney-General, who informed them, however, that they would necessarily have to rely for their compensation upon the prospect of future legislation by Congress. I therefore especially recommend that immediate appropriation be made by Congress for this purpose.

The act making the principal appropriation for the Department of Justice at previous sessions has uniformly contained the following clause:

And for defraying the expenses which may be incurred in the enforcement of the act approved February 28, 1871, entitled "An act to amend an act approved May 31, 1870, entitled 'An act to enforce the rights of citizens of the United States to vote in the several States of this Union, and for other purposes,'" or any acts amendatory thereof or supplementary thereto.

No appropriation was made for this purpose for the current year. As no general election for Members of Congress occurred, the omission was a matter of little practical importance. Such election will, however, take place during the ensuing year, and the appropriation made for the pay of marshals and deputies should be sufficient to embrace compensation for the services they may be required to perform at such elections.

The business of the Supreme Court is at present largely in arrears. It can not be expected that more causes can be decided than are now disposed of in its annual session, or that by any assiduity the distinguished magistrates who compose the court can accomplish more than is now done. In the courts of many of the circuits also the business has increased to such an extent that the delay of justice will call the attention of Congress to an appropriate remedy. It is believed that all is done in each circuit which can fairly be expected from its judicial force. The evils arising from delay are less heavily felt by the United States than by private suitors, as its causes are advanced by the courts when it is seen that they involve the discussion of questions of a public character.

The remedy suggested by the Attorney-General is the appointment of additional circuit judges and the creation of an intermediate court of errors and appeals, which shall relieve the Supreme Court of a part of its jurisdiction, while a larger force is also obtained for the performance of circuit duties.

I commend this suggestion to the consideration of Congress. It would seem to afford a complete remedy, and would involve, if ten additional circuit judges are appointed, an expenditure, at the present rate of salaries, of not more than $60,000 a year, which would certainly be small in comparison with the objects to be attained.

The report of the Postmaster-General bears testimony to the general revival of business throughout the country. The receipts of the Post-Office Department for the fiscal year ended June 30, 1879, were $30,041,982.86, being $764,465.91 more than the revenues of the preceding year. The amount realized from the sale of postage stamps, stamped envelopes, and postal cards was $764,465.91 more than in the preceding year, and

$2,387,559.23 more than in 1877. The expenditures of the Department were $33,449,899.45, of which the sum of $376,461.63 was paid on liabilities incurred in preceding years.

The expenditures during the year were $801,209.77 less than in the preceding year. This reduction is to be attributed mainly to the operation of the law passed June 17, 1878, changing the compensation of postmasters from a commission on the value of stamps sold to a commission on stamps canceled.

The amount drawn from the Treasury on appropriations, in addition to the revenues of the Department, was $3,031,454.96, being $2,276,197.86 less than in the preceding year.

The expenditures for the fiscal year ending June 30, 1881, are estimated at $39,920,900 and the receipts from all sources at $32,210,000, leaving a deficiency to be appropriated for out of the Treasury of $7,710,900.

The relations of the Department with railroad companies have been harmonized, notwithstanding the general reduction by Congress of their compensation by the appropriation for special facilities, and the railway post-office lines have been greatly extended, especially in the Southern States. The interests of the Railway Mail Service and of the public would be greatly promoted and the expenditures could be more readily controlled by the classification of the employees of the Railway Mail Service as recommended by the Postmaster-General, the appropriation for salaries, with respect to which the maximum limit is already fixed by law, to be made in gross.

The Postmaster-General recommends an amendment of the law regulating the increase of compensation for increased service and increased speed on star routes, so as to enable him to advertise for proposals for such increased service and speed. He also suggests the advantages to accrue to the commerce of the country from the enactment of a general law authorizing contracts with American-built steamers, carrying the American flag, for transporting the mail between ports of the United States and ports of the West Indies and South America, at a fixed maximum price per mile, the amount to be expended being regulated by annual appropriations, in like manner with the amount paid for the domestic star service.

The arrangement made by the Postmaster-General and the Secretary of the Treasury for the collection of duty upon books received in the mail from foreign countries has proved so satisfactory in its practical operation that the recommendation is now made that Congress shall extend the provisions of the act of March 3, 1879, under which this arrangement was made, so as to apply to all other dutiable articles received in the mails from foreign countries.

The reports of the Secretary of the Interior and of the Commissioner of Indian Affairs, setting forth the present state of our relations with the Indian tribes on our territory, the measures taken to advance their civilization and prosperity, and the progress already achieved by them, will be found of more than ordinary interest. The general conduct of our Indian population has been so satisfactory that the occurrence of two disturbances, which resulted in bloodshed and destruction of property, is all the more to be lamented.

The history of the outbreak on the White River Ute Reservation, in western Colorado, has become so familiar by elaborate reports in the public press that its remarkable incidents need not be stated here in detail. It is expected that the settlement of this difficulty will lead to such arrangements as will prevent further hostile contact between the Indians and the border settlements in western Colorado.

The other disturbance occurred at the Mescalero Agency, in New Mexico, where Victoria, at the head of a small band of marauders, after committing many atrocities, being vigorously chased by a military force, made his way across the Mexican border and is now on foreign soil.

While these occurrences, in which a comparatively small number of Indians were engaged, are most deplorable, a vast majority of our Indian population have fully justified the expectations of those who believe that by humane and peaceful influences the Indian can be led to abandon the habits of savage life and to develop a capacity for useful and civilized occupations. What they have already accomplished in the pursuit of agricultural and mechanical work, the remarkable success which has attended the experiment of employing as freighters a class of Indians hitherto counted among the wildest and most intractable, and the general and urgent desire expressed by them for the education of their children may be taken as sufficient proof that they will be found capable of accomplishing much more if they continue to be wisely and fairly guided. The "Indian policy" sketched in the report of the Secretary of the Interior, the object of which is to make liberal provision for the education of Indian youth, to settle the Indians upon farm lots in severalty, to give them title in fee to their farms, inalienable for a certain number of years, and when their wants are thus provided for to dispose by sale of the lands on their reservations not occupied and used by them, a fund to be formed out of the proceeds for the benefit of the Indians which will gradually relieve the Government of the expenses now provided for by annual appropriations, must commend itself as just and beneficial to the Indians, and as also calculated to remove those obstructions which the existence of large reservations presents to the settlement and development of the country. I therefore earnestly recommend the enactment of a law enabling the Government to give Indians a title in fee, inalienable for twenty-five years, to the farm lands assigned to them by allotment. I also repeat the recommendation made in my first annual message, that a law be passed admitting Indians who can give satisfactory proof of having by their own labor supported their families for a number of years, and who are willing to detach themselves from their

EXTERMINATION OF CUSTER'S COMMAND—
GRAVES ON THE BATTLEFIELD

THE CUSTER MASSACRE

Sitting Bull, an inveterate hater of the white man, led his tribe, the Sioux, into hostilities with the Government on the question of obeying the Government's order to move into a new reservation. Being notified that the army would compel obedience, the Sioux took position in the Bad Lands of Montana. Three columns—Gibbon's, Crook's and Terry's—moved upon him from east, west and south. Custer's regiment, the Seventh Cavalry, was part of Terry's column. On June 22, 1876, Custer broke away from the column and rode South so as to take the Sioux in rear and complete the circle. Striking the trail, Custer divided his command, sending one portion under Reno down the Little Big Horn to assail the camp from the West while he attacked from the South. Reno was attacked and had to stand on the defensive and was prevented from executing his part of the plan. Custer, with about 200 men, charged the Sioux, who numbered 2,400, was encircled by the Indians, and fought until every man but one was dead. That one, a scout, wrapped himself in a Sioux blanket and escaped. Custer's body was spared from mutilation by the Indians, a remarkable evidence of respect.

See the articles, "Indian Tribes, Sioux," and "Custer Massacre," in the encyclopedic index (volume eleven).

tribal relations, to the benefit of the homestead act, and to grant them patents containing the same provision of inalienability for a certain period.

The experiment of sending a number of Indian children of both sexes to the Hampton Normal and Agricultural Institute, in Virginia, to receive an elementary English education and practical instruction in farming and other useful industries, has led to results so promising that it was thought expedient to turn over the cavalry barracks at Carlisle, in Pennsylvania, to the Interior Department for the establishment of an Indian school on a larger scale. This school has now 158 pupils, selected from various tribes, and is in full operation. Arrangements are also made for the education of a number of Indian boys and girls belonging to tribes on the Pacific Slope in a similar manner, at Forest Grove, in Oregon. These institutions will commend themselves to the liberality of Congress and to the philanthropic munificence of the American people.

Last spring information was received of the organization of an extensive movement in the Western States, the object of which was the occupation by unauthorized persons of certain lands in the Indian Territory ceded by the Cherokees to the Government for the purpose of settlement by other Indian tribes.

On the 26th of April I issued a proclamation* warning all persons against participation in such an attempt, and by the cooperation of a military force the invasion was promptly checked. It is my purpose to protect the rights of the Indian inhabitants of that Territory to the full extent of the executive power; but it would be unwise to ignore the fact that a territory so large and so fertile, with a population so sparse and with so great a wealth of unused resources, will be found more exposed to the repetition of such attempts as happened this year when the surrounding States are more densely settled and the westward movement of our population looks still more eagerly for fresh lands to occupy. Under such circumstances the difficulty of maintaining the Indian Territory in its present state will greatly increase, and the Indian tribes inhabiting it would do well to prepare for such a contingency. I therefore fully approve of the advice given to them by the Secretary of the Interior on a recent occasion, to divide among themselves in severalty as large a quantity of their lands as they can cultivate; to acquire individual title in fee instead of their present tribal ownership in common, and to consider in what manner the balance of their lands may be disposed of by the Government for their benefit. By adopting such a policy they would more certainly secure for themselves the value of their possessions, and at the same time promote their progress in civilization and prosperity, than by endeavoring to perpetuate the present state of things in the Territory.

The question whether a change in the control of the Indian service should be made was in the Forty-fifth Congress referred to a joint committee of both Houses for inquiry and report. In my last annual message

* See pp. 4400-4500.

I expressed the hope that the decision of that question, then in prospect, would "arrest further agitation of this subject, such agitation being apt to produce a disturbing effect upon the service as well as on the Indians themselves." Since then, the committee having reported, the question has been decided in the negative by a vote in the House of Representatives.

For the reasons here stated, and in view of the fact that further uncertainty on this point will be calculated to obstruct other much-needed legislation, to weaken the discipline of the service, and to unsettle salutary measures now in progress for the government and improvement of the Indians, I respectfully recommend that the decision arrived at by Congress at its last session be permitted to stand.

The efforts made by the Department of the Interior to arrest the depredations on the timber lands of the United States have been continued, and have met with considerable success. A large number of cases of trespass have been prosecuted in the courts of the United States; others have been settled, the trespassers offering to make payment to the Government for the value of the timber taken by them. The proceeds of these prosecutions and settlements turned into the Treasury far exceed in amount the sums appropriated by Congress for this purpose. A more important result, however, consists in the fact that the destruction of our public forests by depredation, although such cases still occur, has been greatly reduced in extent, and it is probable that if the present policy is vigorously pursued and sufficient provision to that end is made by Congress such trespasses, at least those on a large scale, can be entirely suppressed, except in the Territories, where timber for the daily requirements of the population can not, under the present state of the law, be otherwise obtained. I therefore earnestly invite the attention of Congress to the recommendation made by the Secretary of the Interior, that a law be enacted enabling the Government to sell timber from the public lands without conveying the fee, where such lands are principally valuable for the timber thereon, such sales to be so regulated as to conform to domestic wants and business requirements, while at the same time guarding against a sweeping destruction of the forests. The enactment of such a law appears to become a more pressing necessity every day.

My recommendations in former messages are renewed in favor of enlarging the facilities of the Department of Agriculture. Agriculture is the leading interest and the permanent industry of our people. It is to the abundance of agricultural production, as compared with our home consumption, and the largely increased and highly profitable market abroad which we have enjoyed in recent years, that we are mainly indebted for our present prosperity as a people. We must look for its continued maintenance to the same substantial resource. There is no branch of industry in which labor, directed by scientific knowledge, yields such increased production in comparison with unskilled labor, and no branch of the public service to which the encouragement of liberal appropriations can be more appropriately extended. The omission to render such aid is not a wise economy, but, on the contrary, undoubtedly results in losses of immense sums annually that might be saved through well-directed efforts by the Government to promote this vital interest.

The results already accomplished with the very limited means heretofore placed at the command of the Department of Agriculture is an earnest of what may be expected with increased appropriations for the several purposes indicated in the report of the Commissioner, with a view to placing the Department upon a footing which will enable it to prosecute more effectively the objects for which it is established.

Appropriations are needed for a more complete laboratory, for the establishment of a veterinary division and a division of forestry, and for an increase of force.

The requirements for these and other purposes, indicated in the report of the Commissioner under the head of the immediate necessities of the Department, will not involve any expenditure of money that the country can not with propriety now undertake in the interests of agriculture.

It is gratifying to learn from the Bureau of Education the extent to which educational privileges throughout the United States have been advanced during the year. No more fundamental responsibility rests upon Congress than that of devising appropriate measures of financial aid to education, supplemental to local action in the States and Territories and in the District of Columbia. The wise forethought of the founders of our Government has not only furnished the basis for the support of the common-school systems of the newer States, but laid the foundations for the maintenance of their universities and colleges of agriculture and the mechanic arts. Measures in accordance with this traditional policy, for the further benefit of all these interests and the extension of the same advantages to every portion of the country, it is hoped will receive your favorable consideration.

To preserve and perpetuate the national literature should be among the foremost cares of the National Legislature. The library gathered at the Capitol still remains unprovided with any suitable accommodations for its rapidly increasing stores. The magnitude and importance of the collection, increased as it is by the deposits made under the law of copyright, by domestic and foreign exchanges, and by the scientific library of the Smithsonian Institution, call for building accommodations which shall be at once adequate and fireproof. The location of such a public building, which should provide for the pressing necessities of the present and for the vast increase of the nation's books in the future, is a matter which addresses itself to the discretion of Congress. It is earnestly recommended as a measure which should unite all suffrages and which should no longer be delayed.

The joint commission created by the act of Congress of August 2, 1876, for the purpose of supervising and directing the completion of the

Washington National Monument, of which commission the President is a member, has given careful attention to this subject, and already the strengthening of the foundation has so far progressed as to insure the entire success of this part of the work. A massive layer of masonry has been introduced below the original foundation, widening the base, increasing the stability of the structure, and rendering it possible to carry the shaft to completion. It is earnestly recommended that such further appropriations be made for the continued prosecution of the work as may be necessary for the completion of this national monument at an early day.

In former messages, impressed with the importance of the subject, I have taken occasion to commend to Congress the adoption of a generous policy toward the District of Columbia. The report of the Commissioners of the District, herewith transmitted, contains suggestions and recommendations, to all of which I earnestly invite your careful attention. I ask your early and favorable consideration of the views which they express as to the urgent need of legislation for the reclamation of the marshes of the Potomac and its Eastern Branch within the limits of the city, and for the repair of the streets of the capital, heretofore laid with wooden blocks and now by decay rendered almost impassable and a source of imminent danger to the health of its citizens. The means at the disposal of the Commissioners are wholly inadequate for the accomplishment of these important works, and should be supplemented by timely appropriations from the Federal Treasury.

The filling of the flats in front of the city will add to the adjacent lands and parks now owned by the United States a large and valuable domain, sufficient, it is thought, to reimburse its entire cost, and will also, as an incidental result, secure the permanent improvement of the river for the purposes of navigation.

The Constitution having invested Congress with supreme and exclusive jurisdiction over the District of Columbia, its citizens must of necessity look to Congress alone for all needful legislation affecting their interests; and as the territory of this District is the common property of the people of the United States, who equally with its resident citizens are interested in the prosperity of their capital, I can not doubt that you will be amply sustained by the general voice of the country in any measures you may adopt for this purpose.

I also invite the favorable consideration of Congress to the wants of the public schools of this District, as exhibited in the report of the Commissioners. While the number of pupils is rapidly increasing, no adequate provision exists for a corresponding increase of school accommodation, and the Commissioners are without the means to meet this urgent need. A number of the buildings now used for school purposes are rented, and are in important particulars unsuited for the purpose. The cause of popular education in the District of Columbia is surely entitled to the same consideration at the hands of the National Government as in the several States and Territories, to which munificent grants of the public lands have been made for the endowment of schools and universities.

RUTHERFORD B. HAYES.

SPECIAL MESSAGES.

EXECUTIVE MANSION, *December 19, 1879.*

To the Senate and House of Representatives:

I have the honor to transmit herewith a draft of a bill submitted by the Board of Commissioners of the District of Columbia, entitled "A bill to provide for the reclamation of the marshes in the harbors of the cities of Washington and Georgetown, and for other purposes," together with the accompanying letter of the president of the board requesting its transmission to Congress.

The bill embraces a plan for the reclamation of the marshes of the Potomac River and its Eastern Branch within the limits of the city of Washington, and is carefully framed with a view to economy in the prosecution of the work. The attention of Congress is again invited to the urgent need of legislation for this important work, which has been so long delayed.

The improvement contemplated is essential to the health of those who reside, whether permanently or temporarily, at the capital, and to the safe and convenient navigation of the waters in its vicinity by vessels employed in the service of the Government and for the purposes of commerce. It is a measure of more than local benefit. The capital of the nation should be relieved from every disadvantage which it is practicable to remove, and should possess every attraction with which it can be invested by the intelligent and fostering care of those who are intrusted with its immediate supervision. The people of the country will sustain and approve the efforts of their representatives in the discharge of this responsibility.

R. B. HAYES.

EXECUTIVE MANSION, *January 7, 1880.*

To the Senate of the United States:

In reply to a resolution of the Senate of December 3, 1879, requesting the President of the United States to inform the Senate whether payments have been made to the Ute Indians in accordance with the fourth article of an agreement made with said Indians September 3, 1873, I transmit herewith a letter from the Secretary of the Interior and accompanying papers.

R. B. HAYES.

WASHINGTON, *January 12, 1880.*

To the House of Representatives:

In answer to resolution of the House of Representatives of the 3d of December, 1879, relative to the consulate at Hongkong, I transmit here-with a report from the Secretary of State, with its accompanying papers.

R. B. HAYES.

EXECUTIVE MANSION, *January 14, 1880.*

To the House of Representatives:

I have the honor herewith to transmit the final report of the board for testing iron, steel, and other metals, with the accompanying papers. These papers constitute the remainder of the reports made by the board, which were transmitted by me to the House of Representatives on the 15th of June, 1878 (House Ex. Doc. No. 98, Forty-fifth Congress, second session).

The United States testing machine at Watertown Arsenal, constructed for the board, is reported as being of great value in the determination of data and the solution of problems of interest to the people of the whole country, and the special attention of Congress is called to the necessity of an appropriation to enable the War Department to make use of it. An estimate of $20,000 for the purpose was submitted to Congress in the last Book of Estimates (see p. 82), and an appropriation of that sum is respectfully recommended.

The act of July 31, 1876 (19 U. S. Statutes at Large, ch. 246, p. 119), made an appropriation for completing the experiments in testing iron, steel, and other metals, and provided that the board should be discontinued from and after the expenditure of the amount appropriated. In accordance with this legislation, the board ceased to exist on the 30th of June, 1879.

R. B. HAYES.

EXECUTIVE MANSION,
Washington, January 21, 1880.

To the Senate of the United States:

I transmit, for the consideration of the Senate with a view to ratification, a convention between the United States of America and the French Republic for the settlement of certain claims of the citizens of either country against the other.

R. B. HAYES.

EXECUTIVE MANSION, *January 26, 1880.*

To the House of Representatives:

In reply to the resolution of the House of Representatives of the 21st instant, requesting the Commissioner of Agriculture to furnish all infor-mation which he may have in his possession bearing upon the culture of the sugar beet, etc., the accompanying letter and report, received from the Acting Commissioner of Agriculture for this purpose, are herewith transmitted.

R. B. HAYES.

EXECUTIVE MANSION, *February 5, 1880.*
To the House of Representatives:

In reply to a resolution of the House of Representatives of the 3d instant, requesting the Commissioner of Agriculture to forward any facts or statistics in his office on the subject of forestry not heretofore published from his Department, the following report, received from the Commissioner, upon this subject is hereby transmitted.

R. B. HAYES.

WASHINGTON, *February 16, 1880.*
To the House of Representatives of the United States:

In compliance with the resolution of the House of Representatives of the 5th instant, calling for any information which I may have received of the proceedings of the International Polar Congress convened in Hamburg, Germany, October 1, 1879, I transmit herewith a report from the Secretary of State on the subject.

R. B. HAYES.

WASHINGTON, *February 16, 1880.*
To the Senate of the United States:

In compliance with the resolution of the Senate of the 19th of January, 1880, calling for information in relation to claims before the American-Spanish Claims Commission and the proceedings of the commission, I transmit herewith a report from the Secretary of State upon the subject.

R. B. HAYES.

EXECUTIVE MANSION, *February 24, 1880.*
To the House of Representatives:

I herewith transmit a communication from the Attorney-General, with reference to the requisite appropriation for the current fiscal year for the compensation of the marshals of the United States, including their reimbursement for necessary expenditures in the discharge of their official duties.

R. B. HAYES.

EXECUTIVE MANSION, *February 25, 1880.*
To the Senate and House of Representatives:

I have the honor to transmit herewith a preliminary report and a draft of a bill submitted by the Public Lands Commission authorized by the act of Congress approved March 3, 1879.

The object of the report and of the bill accompanying it is of such importance that I respectfully commend it to the prompt and earnest consideration of Congress.

R. B. HAYES.

WASHINGTON, *February 27, 1880.*

To the Senate of the United States:

In answer to the resolution of the Senate of the 27th ultimo, I transmit herewith a report from the Secretary of State, with its papers, relating to the claim of Max. Bromberger against the Government of Mexico.

R. B. HAYES.

WASHINGTON, *February 27, 1880.*

To the Senate of the United States:

I transmit herewith to the Senate, for its consideration with a view to ratification, a treaty between the Government of the United States and His Highness Sultan Abdallah, King of Johanna, concerning commercial intercourse with that independent East African island, concluded at Johanna Town on the 4th day of October, 1879.

For your better understanding of the subject, I transmit also the correspondence of Commodore Shufeldt with the Navy Department, which accompanied the treaty, describing the condition and resources of the island of Johanna and narrating the progress of the negotiation, which was undertaken under the general instructions of the Department of State.

R. B. HAYES.

WASHINGTON, *March 1, 1880.*

To the Senate and House of Representatives:

I deem it proper to invite the attention of Congress to the subject of the unsettled claims of Spanish inhabitants of East Florida during the years of 1812 and 1813, generally known as the "East Florida claims," the settlement of which is provided for by a stipulation found in Article IX of the treaty of February, 1819, between the United States and Spain. The provision of the treaty in question which relates to the subject is the following:

The United States will cause satisfaction to be made for the injuries, if any, which by process of law shall be established to have been suffered by the Spanish officers and individual Spanish inhabitants by the late operations of the American army in Florida.

The act of Congress of the 3d of March, 1823 (3 U. S. Statutes at Large, p. 768), to carry into effect the ninth article of the treaty in question, provided for the examination and judicial ascertainment of the claims by the judges of the superior courts established at St. Augustine and Pensacola, and also made provision for the payment by the

Secretary of the Treasury of such claims as might be reported to him by the said judges, upon his being satisfied that such claims were just and equitable; and a subsequent act, approved the 26th of June, 1834 (6 U. S. Statutes at Large, p. 569), gave further directions for the payment, and also provided for the hearing and determination by the judge of the superior court of St. Augustine of such claims as had not then been already heard and determined. Under these acts of Congress I understand that all claims presented to the judges in Florida were passed upon and the result of the proceedings thus had reported to the Secretary of the Treasury. It also appears that in the computation of damages the judges adopted a rule of 5 per cent per annum on the ascertained actual loss from the date of that loss to the time of the rendition of their finding, and that the Secretary of the Treasury in 1836, when the first reports were presented to him, not deeming this portion of the claims covered by the 5 per cent rule just and equitable within the meaning of the treaty and the acts of Congress, refused to pay it, but did continue to pay the ascertained amounts of actual loss. The demand for payment of this rejected item has been pressed at various times and in various ways up to the present time, but Mr. Woodbury's successors in the Treasury Department have not felt at liberty to review that ruling.

Under these circumstances I have thought it proper to lay the subject before Congress for its consideration and such action as may be deemed necessary. The history of the proceedings already had in regard to the matter is of record in the Treasury Department, and will be furnished by the Secretary of the Treasury should Congress desire it.

R. B. HAYES.

To the Senate: EXECUTIVE MANSION, *March 8, 1880.*

I transmit herewith the report of the Secretary of State and the accompanying papers, in response to the resolution adopted by the Senate on the 11th day of February last, requesting copies of all correspondence between this Government and any foreign government since February, 1869, respecting a ship canal across the isthmus between North America and South America, together with copies of any *projet* of treaties respecting the same which the Department of State may have proposed or submitted since that date to any foreign power or its diplomatic representative.

In further compliance with the resolution of the Senate, I deem it proper to state briefly my opinion as to the policy of the United States with respect to the construction of an interoceanic canal by any route across the American Isthmus.

The policy of this country is a canal under American control. The United States can not consent to the surrender of this control to any

European power or to any combination of European powers. If existing treaties between the United States and other nations or if the rights of sovereignty or property of other nations stand in the way of this policy—a contingency which is not apprehended—suitable steps should be taken by just and liberal negotiations to promote and establish the American policy on this subject consistently with the rights of the nations to be affected by it.

The capital invested by corporations or citizens of other countries in such an enterprise must in a great degree look for protection to one or more of the great powers of the world. No European power can intervene for such protection without adopting measures on this continent which the United States would deem wholly inadmissible. If the protection of the United States is relied upon, the United States must exercise such control as will enable this country to protect its national interests and maintain the rights of those whose private capital is embarked in the work.

An interoceanic canal across the American Isthmus will essentially change the geographical relations between the Atlantic and Pacific coasts of the United States and between the United States and the rest of the world. It would be the great ocean thoroughfare between our Atlantic and our Pacific shores, and virtually a part of the coast line of the United States. Our merely commercial interest in it is greater than that of all other countries, while its relations to our power and prosperity as a nation, to our means of defense, our unity, peace, and safety, are matters of paramount concern to the people of the United States. No other great power would under similar circumstances fail to assert a rightful control over a work so closely and vitally affecting its interest and welfare.

Without urging further the grounds of my opinion, I repeat, in conclusion, that it is the right and the duty of the United States to assert and maintain such supervision and authority over any interoceanic canal across the isthmus that connects North and South America as will protect our national interests. This, I am quite sure, will be found not only compatible with but promotive of the widest and most permanent advantage to commerce and civilization.

RUTHERFORD B. HAYES.

[A similar message was sent to the House of Representatives, in answer to a resolution of that body of February 10.]

EXECUTIVE MANSION, *March 9, 1880.*

To the Senate and House of Representatives:

I have the honor to transmit herewith a report from the Secretary of the Interior, containing an agreement signed by the chiefs and headmen of the Ute Indians now present at the seat of Government. The stipulations of this agreement appear to me so reasonable and just and the object to be accomplished by its execution so eminently desirable to both the white people of the United States and the Indians that it has my cordial approval, and I earnestly commend it to Congress for favorable consideration and appropriate legislative action.

RUTHERFORD B. HAYES.

WASHINGTON, *March 9, 1880.*

To the Senate of the United States:

I transmit herewith to the Senate, for its consideration with a view to ratification, a convention between the United States and His Majesty the King of the Belgians, defining the rights, immunities, and privileges of consular officers, concluded this day at Washington.

R. B. HAYES.

EXECUTIVE MANSION, *March 11, 1880.*

To the House of Representatives:

I transmit herewith a report, dated on the 9th instant, from the Secretary of State, with the accompanying papers, in answer to a resolution of the House of Representatives of the 25th ultimo, requesting the President to transmit to that body, if not deemed incompatible with the public interest, copies of such dispatches as have recently been received by the Secretary of State from the consul-general at Shanghai upon the subject of slavery in China and those portions of the penal code of China which forbid expatriation.

R. B. HAYES.

WASHINGTON, *March 12, 1880.*

To the House of Representatives:

In answer to a resolution of the House of Representatives of March 2, 1880, requesting the Secretary of State to communicate to the House certain information in relation to the publication and circulation of commercial reports, I transmit herewith a report from the Secretary of State, with its accompanying papers.

R. B. HAYES.

WASHINGTON, *March 29, 1880.*

To the Senate of the United States:

In compliance with the resolution of the Senate of the 29th of January, 1880, calling for information in relation to the awards of the mixed commission organized under the provisions of the treaty of April 25, 1866, between the United States and Venezuela, I transmit herewith a report from the Secretary of State upon the subject.

R. B. HAYES.

WASHINGTON, *April 12, 1880.*

To the House of Representatives:

In response to the resolution of the House of Representatives of the 12th of February last, on the subject of negotiations concerning the immigration of Chinese to the United States, I transmit a report of the Secretary of State, to whom the matter was referred.

R. B. HAYES.

WASHINGTON, *April 15, 1880.*

To the Senate of the United States:

In response to the resolution of the Senate of the 27th of February last, concerning the action had by the Executive with respect to the investigation of certain cases in which awards were made by the late United States and Mexican Commission, I transmit herewith a report of the Secretary of State, to whom the matter was referred.

R. B. HAYES.

EXECUTIVE MANSION,
Washington, D. C., April 16, 1880.

To the House of Representatives:

The board for testing iron, steel, and other metals, appointed under the authority of "An act making appropriations for sundry civil expenses of the Government for the fiscal year ending June 30, 1876, and for other purposes," contracted with Mr. A. H. Emery, of New York, for a testing machine, to be paid out of the appropriation made for the purpose. That machine has been completed and accepted, and is now in position at the Watertown Arsenal, Mass. It is spoken of by the members composing the late board as the most perfect and reliable machine in the world, embodying new mechanical principles and combinations not heretofore used in any other constructions.

In designing, perfecting, and making this machine the contractor has expended large sums of money over and above the contract price, besides giving years of labor, for which he has received no compensation. He now appeals to Congress for relief, and the papers herewith exhibit a case that calls for Congressional action. It is respectfully submitted to the House of Representatives, recommending speedy and favorable consideration.

R. B. HAYES.

EXECUTIVE MANSION, *April 22, 1880.*

To the Senate and House of Representatives:

I have the honor to inform Congress that Mr. J. Randolph Coolidge, Dr. Algernon Coolidge, Mr. Thomas Jefferson Coolidge, and Mrs. Ellen Dwight, of Massachusetts, the heirs of the late Joseph Coolidge, jr., desire to present to the United States the desk on which the Declaration of Independence was written. It bears the following inscription in the handwriting of Thomas Jefferson:

Thomas Jefferson gives this writing desk to Joseph Coolidge, jr., as a memorial of his affection. It was made from a drawing of his own, by Ben. Randall, cabinet-maker of Philadelphia, with whom he first lodged on his arrival in that city in May, 1776, and is the identical one on which he wrote the Declaration of Independence.

Politics, as well as religion, has its superstitions. These, gaining strength with time, may one day give imaginary value to this relic for its association with the birth of the great charter of our independence.

MONTICELLO, *November 18, 1825.*

The desk was placed in my possession by Hon. Robert C. Winthrop, and is herewith transmitted to Congress with the letter of Mr. Winthrop expressing the wish of the donors "to offer it to the United States, so that it may henceforth have a place in the Department of State in connection with the immortal instrument which was written upon it in 1776."

I respectfully recommend that such action be taken by Congress as may be deemed appropriate with reference to a gift to the nation so precious in its history and for the memorable associations which belong to it.

RUTHERFORD B. HAYES.

WASHINGTON, D. C., *April 14, 1880.*

His Excellency RUTHERFORD B. HAYES,
President of the United States.

MY DEAR SIR: I have been privileged to bring with me from Boston, as a present to the United States, a very precious historical relic. It is the little desk on which Mr. Jefferson wrote the original draft of the Declaration of Independence.

This desk was given by Mr. Jefferson himself to my friend, the late Joseph Coolidge, of Boston, at the time of his marriage to Jefferson's granddaughter, Miss Randolph, and it bears an autograph inscription of singular interest, written by the illustrious author of the Declaration in the very last year of his life.

On the recent death of Mr. Coolidge, whose wife had died a year or two previously, the desk became the property of their children, Mr. J. Randolph Coolidge, Dr. Algernon Coolidge, Mr. Thomas Jefferson Coolidge, and Mrs. Ellen Dwight, who now desire to offer it to the United States, so that it may henceforth have a place in the Department of State in connection with the immortal instrument which was written upon it in 1776.

They have done me the honor to make me the medium of this distinguished gift, and I ask permission to place it in the hands of the Chief Magistrate of the nation in their name and at their request.

Believe me, dear Mr. President, with the highest respect, very faithfully, your obedient servant,

ROBT. C. WINTHROP.

WASHINGTON, *May 13, 1880.*

To the Senate of the United States:

I transmit herewith to the Senate, in response to their resolution of the 24th of March last, in relation to the fulfillment of the ninth article of the treaty of 1819 between the United States and Spain, a report of the Secretary of State on the correspondence asked for by the resolution, with its accompanying documents, and in connection therewith a previous report from the Secretary of State and an opinion of the Attorney-General on the subject of the East Florida claims.

R. B. HAYES.

WASHINGTON, *May 17, 1880.*

To the House of Representatives:

In compliance with the resolution of the House of Representatives of the 27th ultimo, calling for copies of the correspondence with the Government of Great Britain in regard to the alleged outrage upon American fishermen at Fortune Bay, in the Province of Newfoundland, I transmit herewith the correspondence called for and a report from the Secretary of State on the subject.

In transmitting this correspondence and the report I respectfully ask the immediate and careful attention of Congress to the failure of accord between the two Governments as to the interpretation and execution of the fishery articles of the treaty of Washington, as disclosed in this correspondence and elucidated by the exposition of the subject by the Secretary of State.

I concur in the opinions of this report as to the measures proper to be taken by this Government in maintenance of the rights accorded to our fishermen by the British concession of the treaty and in providing for suitable action toward securing an indemnity for the injury these interests have already suffered.

Accordingly, I recommend to Congress the adoption of these measures, with such attendant details of legislation as in the wisdom of Congress shall seem expedient.

R. B. HAYES.

[The same message was sent to the Senate, in answer to a resolution of that body of April 28.]

WASHINGTON, *May 24, 1880.*

To the Senate of the United States:

I submit to the Senate, for its consideration with a view to ratification, the accompanying convention for the extradition of criminals, concluded between the United States and the Government of His Majesty the King of the Netherlands on the 22d instant.

R. B. HAYES.

EXECUTIVE MANSION, *May 25, 1880.*

To the Senate and House of Representatives:

I have the honor to transmit herewith a communication from the Secretary of the Interior, with reference to the agreement made with the chiefs of the Ute Indians recently in Washington, a copy of which was submitted to Congress on the 9th of March last.

The special and immediate attention of Congress to the imminent danger attending the postponement of appropriate legislation to carry into effect the stipulations of this agreement is earnestly solicited.

R. B. HAYES.

EXECUTIVE MANSION, *June 5, 1880.*

To the Senate of the United States:

In response to a resolution of the Senate of the 31st ultimo, requesting the President "to communicate to the Senate whether any supervisor or supervisors of the census appointed by and with the advice and consent of the Senate have been removed from office by him or with his consent," etc., I transmit herewith a report from the Secretary of the Interior.

R. B. HAYES.

VETO MESSAGES.

EXECUTIVE MANSION, *May 4, 1880.*

To the House of Representatives:

After mature consideration of the bill entitled "An act making appropriations to supply certain deficiencies in the appropriations for the service of the Government for the fiscal year ending June 30, 1880, and for other purposes," I return it to the House of Representatives, in which it originated, with my objections to its passage.

The bill appropriates about $8,000,000, of which over $600,000 is for the payment of the fees of United States marshals and of the general and special deputy marshals earned during the current fiscal year, and their incidental expenses. The appropriations made in the bill are needed to carry on the operations of the Government and to fulfill its obligations for the payment of money long since due to its officers for services and expenses essential to the execution of their duties under the laws of the United States. The necessity for these appropriations is so urgent and they have been already so long delayed that if the bill before me contained no permanent or general legislation unconnected with these appropriations it would receive my prompt approval. It contains, however, provisions which materially change, and by implication repeal, important parts of the laws for the regulation of the United States elections. These laws have for several years past been the subject of vehement political controversy, and have been denounced as unnecessary, oppressive, and unconstitutional. On the other hand, it has been maintained with equal zeal and earnestness that the election laws are indispensable to fair and lawful elections, and are clearly warranted by the

Constitution. Under these circumstances, to attempt in an appropriation bill the modification or repeal of these laws is to annex a condition to the passage of needed and proper appropriations, which tends to deprive the Executive of that equal and independent exercise of discretion and judgment which the Constitution contemplates.

The objection to the bill, therefore, to which I respectfully ask your attention is that it gives a marked and deliberate sanction, attended by no circumstances of pressing necessity, to the questionable and, as I am clearly of opinion, the dangerous practice of tacking upon appropriation bills general and permanent legislation. This practice opens a wide door to hasty, inconsiderate, and sinister legislation. It invites attacks upon the independence and constitutional powers of the Executive by providing an easy and effective way of constraining Executive discretion. Although of late this practice has been resorted to by all political parties when clothed with power, it did not prevail until forty years after the adoption of the Constitution, and it is confidently believed that it is condemned by the enlightened judgment of the country. The States which have adopted new constitutions during the last quarter of a century have generally provided remedies for the evil. Many of them have enacted that no law shall contain more than one subject, which shall be plainly expressed in its title. The constitutions of more than half of the States contain substantially this provision, or some other of like intent and meaning. The public welfare will be promoted in many ways by a return to the early practice of the Government and to the true rule of legislation, which is that every measure should stand upon its own merits.

I am firmly convinced that appropriation bills ought not to contain any legislation not relevant to the application or expenditure of the money thereby appropriated, and that by a strict adherence to this principle an important and much needed reform will be accomplished.

Placing my objection to the bill on this feature of its frame, I forbear any comment upon the important general and permanent legislation which it contains, as matter for specific and independent consideration.

RUTHERFORD B. HAYES.

EXECUTIVE MANSION, *June 15, 1880.*
To the Senate of the United States:

After mature consideration of the bill entitled "An act regulating the pay and appointment of deputy marshals," I am constrained to withhold from it my approval, and to return it to the Senate, in which it originated, with my objections to its passage.

The laws now in force on the subject of the bill before me are contained in the following sections of the Revised Statutes:

SEC. 2021. Whenever an election at which Representatives or Delegates in Congress are to be chosen is held in any city or town of 20,000 inhabitants or upward, the marshal for the district in which the city or town is situated shall, on the application in writing of at least two citizens residing in such city or town, appoint special deputy marshals, whose duty it shall be, when required thereto, to aid and assist the supervisors of election in the verification of any list of persons who may have registered or voted; to attend in each election district or voting precinct at the times and places fixed for the registration of voters, and at all times or places when and where the registration may by law be scrutinized and the names of registered voters be marked for challenge; and also to attend, at all times for holding elections, the polls in such district or precinct.

SEC. 2022. The marshal and his general deputies, and such special deputies, shall keep the peace and support and protect the supervisors of election in the discharge of their duties, preserve order at such places of registration and at such polls, prevent fraudulent registration and fraudulent voting thereat, or fraudulent conduct on the part of any officer of election, and immediately, either at the place of registration or polling place, or elsewhere, and either before or after registering or voting, to arrest and take into custody, with or without process, any person who commits, or attempts or offers to commit, any of the acts or offenses prohibited herein, or who commits any offense against the laws of the United States; but no person shall be arrested without process for any offense not committed in the presence of the marshal or his general or special deputies, or either of them, or of the supervisors of election, or either of them; and for the purposes of arrest or the preservation of the peace the supervisors of election shall, in the absence of the marshal's deputies, or if required to assist such deputies, have the same duties and powers as deputy marshals; nor shall any person, on the day of such election, be arrested without process for any offense committed on the day of registration.

SEC. 2023. Whenever any arrest is made under any provision of this title, the person so arrested shall forthwith be brought before a commissioner, judge, or court of the United States for examination of the offenses alleged against him; and such commissioner, judge, or court shall proceed in respect thereto as authorized by law in case of crimes against the United States.

SEC. 2024. The marshal or his general deputies, or such special deputies as are thereto specially empowered by him in writing, and under his hand and seal, whenever he or either or any of them is forcibly resisted in executing their duties under this title, or shall by violence, threats, or menaces be prevented from executing such duties or from arresting any person who has committed any offense for which the marshal or his general or his special deputies are authorized to make such arrest, are, and each of them is, empowered to summon and call to his aid the bystanders or *posse comitatus* of his district.

SEC. 2028. No person shall be appointed a supervisor of election or a deputy marshal under the preceding provisions who is not at the time of his appointment a qualified voter of the city, town, county, parish, election district, or voting precinct in which his duties are to be performed.

SEC. 5521. If any person be appointed a supervisor of election or a special deputy marshal under the provisions of title "The elective franchise," and has taken the oath of office as such supervisor of election or such special deputy marshal, and thereafter neglects or refuses, without good and lawful excuse, to perform and discharge fully the duties, obligations, and requirements of such office until the expiration of the term for which he was appointed, he shall not only be subject to removal from office with loss of all pay or emoluments, but shall be punished by imprisonment for not less than six months nor more than one year, or by a fine of not less than $200 and not more than $500, or by both fine and imprisonment, and shall pay the costs of prosecution.

SEC. 5522. Every person, whether with or without any authority, power, or process, or pretended authority, power, or process, of any State, Territory, or municipality, who obstructs, hinders, assaults, or by bribery, solicitation, or otherwise interferes with or prevents the supervisors of election, or either of them, or the marshal or his general or special deputies, or either of them, in the performance of any duty required of them, or either of them, or which he or they, or either of them, may be authorized to perform by any law of the United States, in the execution of process or otherwise, or who by any of the means before mentioned hinders or prevents the free attendance and presence at such places of registration, or at such polls of election, or full and free access and egress to and from any such place of registration or poll of election, or in going to and from any such place of registration or poll of election, or to and from any room where any such registration or election or canvass of votes, or of making any returns or certificates thereof, may be had, or who molests, interferes with, removes, or ejects from any such place of registration or poll of election, or of canvassing votes cast thereat, or of making returns or certificates thereof, any supervisor of election, the marshal or his general or special deputies, or either of them, or who threatens, or attempts or offers so to do, or refuses or neglects to aid and assist any supervisor of election, or the marshal or his general or special deputies, or either of them, in the performance of his or their duties, when required by him or them, or either of them, to give such aid and assistance, shall be liable to instant arrest without process, and shall be punished by imprisonment not more than two years, or by a fine of not more than $3,000, or by both such fine and imprisonment, and shall pay the cost of the prosecution.

The Supreme Court of the United States, in the recent case of *Ex parte* Siebold and others, decided at the October term, 1879, on the question raised in the case as to the constitutionality of the sections of the Revised Statutes above quoted, uses the following language:

These portions of the Revised Statutes are taken from the act commonly known as the enforcement act, approved May 31, 1870, and entitled "An act to enforce the right of citizens of the United States to vote in the several States of this Union, and for other purposes," and from the supplement to that act, approved February 28, 1871. They relate to elections of members of the House of Representatives, and were an assertion on the part of Congress of a power to pass laws for regulating and superintending said elections and for securing the purity thereof and the rights of citizens to vote thereat peaceably and without molestation.

It must be conceded to be a most important power, and of a fundamental character. In the light of recent history and of the violence, fraud, corruption, and irregularity which have frequently prevailed at such elections, it may easily be conceived that the exertion of the power, if it exists, may be necessary to the stability of our form of government.

The greatest difficulty in coming to a just conclusion arises from mistaken notions with regard to the relations which subsist between the State and National Governments. * * * It seems to be often overlooked that a national constitution has been adopted in this country, establishing a real government therein, operating upon persons and territory and things, and which, moreover, is, or should be, as dear to every American citizen as his State government is. Whenever the true conception of the nature of this Government is once conceded, no real difficulty will arise in the just interpretation of its powers; but if we allow ourselves to regard it as a hostile organization, opposed to the proper sovereignty and dignity of the State governments, we shall continue to be vexed with difficulties as to its jurisdiction and authority. No greater jealousy is required to be exercised toward this Government in reference to the preservation of our liberties than is proper to be exercised toward the State governments. Its powers are limited in number and clearly defined, and its action within the scope of those powers is restrained by a sufficiently rigid bill of rights for the protection of its citizens from oppression. The true interests of the people of this country require that both the National and State Governments should be allowed, without jealous interference on either side, to exercise all the powers which respectively belong to them according to a fair and practical construction of the Constitution. State rights and the rights of the United States should be equally respected. Both are essential to the preservation of our liberties and the perpetuity of our institutions. But in endeavoring to vindicate the one we should not allow our zeal to nullify or impair the other. * * *

The true doctrine, as we conceive, is this, that while the States are really sovereign as to all matters which have not been granted to the jurisdiction and control of the United States, the Constitution and constitutional laws of the latter are, as we have already said, the supreme law of the land, and when they conflict with the laws of the States they are of paramount authority and obligation. This is the fundamental principle on which the authority of the Constitution is based, and unless it be conceded in practice as well as theory the fabric of our institutions, as it was contemplated by its founders, can not stand. The questions involved have respect not more to the autonomy and existence of the States than to the continued existence of the United States as a government to which every American citizen may look for security and protection in every part of the land. * * *

Why do we have marshals at all if they can not physically lay their hands on persons and things in the performance of their proper duties? What functions can they perform if they can not use force? In executing the process of the courts must they call on the nearest constable for protection? Must they rely on him to use the requisite compulsion and to keep the peace while they are soliciting and entreating the parties and bystanders to allow the law to take its course? This is the necessary consequence of the positions that are assumed. If we indulge in such impracticable views as these, and keep on refining and re-refining, we shall drive the National Government out of the United States and relegate it to the District of Columbia, or perhaps to some foreign soil. We shall bring it back to a condition of greater helplessness than that of the old Confederation.

The argument is based on a strained and impracticable view of the nature and powers of the National Government. It must execute its powers or it is no government. It must execute them on the land as well as on the sea, on things as well as on persons. And to do this it must necessarily have power to command obedience, preserve order, and keep the peace; and no person or power in this land has the right to resist or question its authority so long as it keeps within the bounds of its jurisdiction.

I have deemed it fitting and proper to quote thus largely from an important and elaborate opinion of the Supreme Court because the bill before me proceeds upon a construction of the Constitution as to the powers of the National Government which is in direct conflict with the judgment of the highest judicial tribunal of our country.

Under the sections of the present law above quoted officers of the United States are authorized, and it is their duty in the case of Congressional elections, to keep the peace at the polls and at the places of registration; to arrest immediately any person who is guilty of crimes against the United States election laws; to protect all officers of elections in the performance of their duties; and whenever an arrest is made to bring the person so arrested before a commissioner, judge, or court of the United States for examination of the offenses alleged against him. "Such special deputy marshals as are specially empowered thereto by the marshal in writing," if forcibly resisted, may call to their aid the bystanders or *posse comitatus*. It is made a crime punishable with fine or imprisonment to hinder, assault, or otherwise interfere with the marshal or "his special deputies," or to threaten or to attempt so to do. If any person appointed such special deputy marshal has taken the oath of office and thereafter neglects or refuses to fully discharge the duties of such office, he is punishable not only by removal from office, but by fine and imprisonment. The functions of the special deputy marshals now provided for by law being executive, they are placed under the authority of the well-known chief executive officer of the courts of the United States. They are in fact, and not merely in name, the deputies of the marshal, and he and his bondsmen are responsible for them. A civil force for the execution of the law is thus instituted in accordance with long-established and familiar usage, which is simple, effective, and under a responsible head. The necessity for the possession of these powers by appropriate officers will not be called in question by intelligent citizens who appreciate the importance of peaceable, orderly, and lawful elections. Similar powers are conferred and exercised under State laws with respect to State elections. The executive officers of the United States under the existing laws have no other or greater power to supervise and control the conduct of the Congressional elections than the State executive officers exercise in regard to State elections.

The bill before me changes completely the present law by substituting for the special deputy marshals of the existing statutes new officers hitherto unknown to the law, and who lack the power, responsibility, and protection which are essential to enable them to act efficiently as executive officers.

The bill under consideration is as follows:

Be it enacted by the Senate and House of Representatives of the United States of America in Congress assembled, That from and after the passage of this act the pay of all deputy marshals for services in reference to any election shall be $5 for each day of actual service, and no more.

SEC. 2. That all deputy marshals to serve in reference to any election shall be appointed by the circuit court of the United States for the district in which such marshals are to perform their duties in each year; and the judges of the several circuit courts of the United States are hereby authorized to open their respective courts at any time for that purpose; and in case the circuit courts shall not be open for that purpose at least ten days prior to a registration, if there be one, or, if no registration be required, then at least ten days before such election, the judges of the district courts of the United States are hereby respectively authorized to cause their courts to be opened for the purpose of appointing such deputy marshals, who shall be appointed by the said district courts; and the officers so appointed shall be in equal numbers from the different political parties, and shall be well-known citizens, of good moral character, and actual residents of the voting precincts in which their duties are to be performed, and shall not be candidates for any office at such election; and all laws and parts of laws inconsistent with this act are hereby repealed: *Provided*, That the marshals of the United States for whom deputies shall be appointed by the court under this act shall not be liable for any of the acts of such deputies.

It will be observed that the deputy marshals proposed by the bill before me are distinctly different officers from the special deputies of the marshal, as such officers are now provided for in the statutes. This bill does not connect the new officers with the existing laws relating to special deputy marshals so as to invest the proposed deputy marshals with the same powers, to impose upon them the same duties, and to give them the same protection by means of the criminal laws. When new officers are created, distinct in character and appointed by different authority, although similar in name to officers already provided for, such officers are not held by similar responsibilities to the criminal law, do not possess the same powers, and are not similarly protected unless it is expressly so provided by legislation.

The so-called deputy marshals provided for in this bill will have no executive head. The marshal can neither appoint nor remove them. He can not control them, and he is not responsible for them. They will have no authority to call to their aid, if resisted, the *posse comitatus.* They are protected by no criminal statutes in the performance of their duties. An assault upon one of these deputies with the intent to prevent a lawful election will be no more than an ordinary assault upon any other citizen. They can not keep the peace. They can not make arrests when crimes are committed in their presence. Whatever powers they have are confined to the precincts in which they reside. Outside of the precincts for which they are appointed the deputy marshals of this bill can not keep the peace, make arrests, hold prisoners, take prisoners before a proper tribunal for hearing, nor perform any other duty. No oaths of office are required of them, and they give no bond. They have no superior who is responsible for them, and they are not punishable for neglect of duty or misconduct in office. In all these respects this bill makes a radical change between the powers of the United States officers at national elections and the powers uniformly possessed and exercised by State officers at State elections. This discrimination against the authority of the United States is a departure from the usage of the Government established by precedents beginning with the earliest statutes on the subject, and violates the true principles of the Constitution. The Supreme Court, in the decision already referred to, says:

It is argued that the preservation of peace and good order in society is not within the powers confided to the Government of the United States, but belongs exclusively to the States. Here again we are met with the theory that the Government of the United States does not rest upon the soil and territory of the country. We think that this theory is founded on an entire misconception of the nature and powers of that Government. We hold it to be an incontrovertible principle that the Government of the United States may, by means of physical force, exercised through its official agents, execute on every foot of American soil the powers and functions that belong to it. This necessarily involves the power to command obedience to its laws, and hence the power to keep the peace to that extent.

This power to enforce its laws and to execute its functions in all places does not derogate from the power of the State to execute its laws at the same time and in the same places. The one does not exclude the other, except where both can not be executed at the same time. In that case the words of the Constitution itself show which is to yield. "This Constitution and all laws which shall be made in pursuance thereof * * * shall be the supreme law of the land."

In conclusion it is proper to say that no objection would be made to the appointment of officers to act with reference to the elections by the courts of the United States, and that I am in favor of appointing officers to supervise and protect the elections without regard to party; but the bill before me, while it recognizes the power and duty of the United States to provide officers to guard and scrutinize the Congressional elections, fails to adapt its provisions to the existing laws so as to secure efficient supervision and protection. It is therefore returned to the Senate, in which it originated, for that further consideration which is contemplated by the Constitution.

RUTHERFORD B. HAYES.

PROCLAMATIONS.

By the President of the United States of America.

A PROCLAMATION.

Whereas it has become known to me that certain evil-disposed persons have within the territory and jurisdiction of the United States begun and set on foot preparations for an organized and forcible possession of and settlement upon the lands of what is known as the Indian Territory, west of the State of Arkansas, which Territory is designated, recognized, and described by the treaties and laws of the United States and by the executive authorities as Indian country, and as such is only subject to occupation by Indian tribes, officers of the Indian Department, military posts, and such persons as may be privileged to reside and trade therein under the intercourse laws of the United States; and

Whereas those laws provide for the removal of all persons residing and trading therein without express permission of the Indian Department and agents, and also of all persons whom such agents may deem to be improper persons to reside in the Indian country; and

Whereas, in aid and support of such organized movement, it has been represented that no further action will be taken by the Government to prevent persons from going into said territory and settling therein, but such representations are wholly without authority:

Now, therefore, for the purpose of properly protecting the interests of the Indian nations and tribes, as well as of the United States, in said Indian Territory, and of duly enforcing the laws governing the same, I, Rutherford B. Hayes, President of the United States, do admonish and warn all such persons so intending or preparing to remove upon said lands or into said Territory without permission of the proper agent of the Indian Department against any attempt to so remove or settle upon any of the lands of said Territory; and I do further warn and notify any and all such persons who may so offend that they will be speedily and immediately removed therefrom by the agent, according to the laws made and provided, and that no efforts will be spared to prevent the invasion of said Territory, rumors spread by evil-disposed persons to the contrary notwithstanding; and if necessary the aid and assistance of the military forces of the United States will be invoked to carry into proper execution the laws of the United States herein referred to.

In testimony whereof I have hereunto set my hand and caused the seal of the United States to be affixed.

[SEAL.] Done at the city of Washington, this 12th day of February, A. D. 1880, and of the Independence of the United States the one hundred and fourth.

R. B. HAYES.

By the President:

WM. M. EVARTS, *Secretary of State.*

BY THE PRESIDENT OF THE UNITED STATES OF AMERICA.

A PROCLAMATION.

At no period in their history since the United States became a nation has this people had so abundant and so universal reasons for joy and gratitude at the favor of Almighty God or been subject to so profound an obligation to give thanks for His loving kindness and humbly to implore His continued care and protection.

Health, wealth, and prosperity throughout all our borders; peace, honor, and friendship with all the world; firm and faithful adherence by the great body of our population to the principles of liberty and justice which have made our greatness as a nation, and to the wise institutions and strong frame of government and society which will perpetuate it—for all these let the thanks of a happy and united people, as with one voice, ascend in devout homage to the Giver of All Good.

I therefore recommend that on Thursday, the 25th day of November next, the people meet in their respective places of worship to make their acknowledgments to Almighty God for His bounties and His protection and to offer to Him prayers for their continuance.

In witness whereof I have hereunto set my hand and caused the seal of the United States to be affixed.

[SEAL.] Done at the city of Washington, this 1st day of November, A. D. 1880, and of the Independence of the United States the one hundred and fifth.

R. B. HAYES

By the President:

WM. M. EVARTS, *Secretary of State.*

BY THE PRESIDENT OF THE UNITED STATES OF AMERICA.

A PROCLAMATION.

Whereas satisfactory evidence has been given to me by the Government of His Majesty the Emperor of China that no discriminating duties of tonnage or imposts are imposed or levied in the ports of that nation upon vessels wholly belonging to citizens of the United States, or upon the produce, manufactures, or merchandise imported in the same:

Therefore, I, Rutherford B. Hayes, President of the United States of America, by virtue of the authority in me vested by law, do hereby declare and proclaim that the foreign discriminating duties of tonnage and impost within the United States are and shall be suspended and discontinued so far as respects the vessels of China and the produce, manufactures, and merchandise imported therein into the United States from China, or from any other foreign country, so long as the exemption aforesaid on the part of China of vessels belonging to citizens of the United States and their cargoes shall be continued and no longer.

In testimony whereof I have hereunto set my hand and caused the seal of the United States to be affixed.

[SEAL.]   Done at the city of Washington, this 23d day of November, A. D. 1880, and of the Independence of the United States of America the one hundred and fifth.

R. B. HAYES.

By the President:
    WM. M. EVARTS,
        Secretary of State.

EXECUTIVE ORDER.

[From the Evening Star, Washington, D. C., May 27, 1880.]

EXECUTIVE MANSION,
Washington, D. C., May 27, 1880.

DEAR SIR:* I am directed by the President to say that the several Departments of the Government will be closed on Saturday, the 29th instant, in remembrance of those who fell in defense of the nation, and to enable the employees to participate in the commemorative ceremonies of the day.

Very respectfully, your obedient servant,

W. K. ROGERS,
Private Secretary.

* Addressed to the heads of the Executive Departments, etc.

FOURTH ANNUAL MESSAGE.

EXECUTIVE MANSION, *December 6, 1880.*
Fellow-Citizens of the Senate and House of Representatives:

I congratulate you on the continued and increasing prosperity of our country. By the favor of Divine Providence we have been blessed during the past year with health, with abundant harvests, with profitable employment for all our people, and with contentment at home, and with peace and friendship with other nations. The occurrence of the twenty-fourth election of Chief Magistrate has afforded another opportunity to the people of the United States to exhibit to the world a significant example of the peaceful and safe transmission of the power and authority of government from the public servants whose terms of office are about to expire to their newly chosen successors. This example can not fail to impress profoundly thoughtful people of other countries with the advantages which republican institutions afford. The immediate, general, and cheerful acquiescence of all good citizens in the result of the election gives gratifying assurance to our country and to its friends throughout the world that a government based on the free consent of an intelligent and patriotic people possesses elements of strength, stability, and permanency not found in any other form of government.

Continued opposition to the full and free enjoyment of the rights of citizenship conferred upon the colored people by the recent amendments to the Constitution still prevails in several of the late slaveholding States. It has, perhaps, not been manifested in the recent election to any large extent in acts of violence or intimidation. It has, however, by fraudulent practices in connection with the ballots, with the regulations as to the places and manner of voting, and with counting, returning, and canvassing the votes cast, been successful in defeating the exercise of the right preservative of all rights—the right of suffrage—which the Constitution expressly confers upon our enfranchised citizens.

It is the desire of the good people of the whole country that sectionalism as a factor in our politics should disappear. They prefer that no section of the country should be united in solid opposition to any other section. The disposition to refuse a prompt and hearty obedience to the equal-rights amendments to the Constitution is all that now stands in the way of a complete obliteration of sectional lines in our political contests. As long as either of these amendments is flagrantly violated or disregarded, it is safe to assume that the people who placed them in the Constitution, as embodying the legitimate results of the war for the Union, and who believe them to be wise and necessary, will continue to act together and to insist that they shall be obeyed. The paramount question still is as to the enjoyment of the right by every American citizen who has the requisite qualifications to freely cast his vote and to have it honestly counted. With this question rightly settled, the country will be relieved of the contentions of the past; bygones will indeed be bygones, and political and party issues, with respect to economy and efficiency of administration, internal improvements, the tariff, domestic taxation, education, finance, and other important subjects, will then receive their full share of attention; but resistance to and nullification of the results of the war will unite together in resolute purpose for their support all who maintain the authority of the Government and the perpetuity of the Union, and who adequately appreciate the value of the victory achieved. This determination proceeds from no hostile sentiment or feeling to any part of the people of our country or to any of their interests. The inviolability of the amendments rests upon the fundamental principle of our Government. They are the solemn expression of the will of the people of the United States.

The sentiment that the constitutional rights of all our citizens must be maintained does not grow weaker. It will continue to control the Government of the country. Happily, the history of the late election shows that in many parts of the country where opposition to the fifteenth amendment has heretofore prevailed it is diminishing, and is likely to cease altogether if firm and well-considered action is taken by Congress. I trust the House of Representatives and the Senate, which have the right to judge of the elections, returns, and qualifications of their own members, will see to it that every case of violation of the letter or spirit of the fifteenth amendment is thoroughly investigated, and that no benefit from such violation shall accrue to any person or party. It will be the duty of the Executive, with sufficient appropriations for the purpose, to prosecute unsparingly all who have been engaged in depriving citizens of the rights guaranteed to them by the Constitution.

It is not, however, to be forgotten that the best and surest guaranty of the primary rights of citizenship is to be found in that capacity for self-protection which can belong only to a people whose right to universal suffrage is supported by universal education. The means at the command of the local and State authorities are in many cases wholly inadequate to furnish free instruction to all who need it. This is especially true where before emancipation the education of the people was neglected or prevented, in the interest of slavery. Firmly convinced that the subject of popular education deserves the earnest attention of the people of the whole country, with a view to wise and comprehensive action by the Government of the United States, I respectfully recommend that Congress, by suitable legislation and with proper safeguards, supplement the local educational funds in the several States where the grave duties and responsibilities of citizenship have been devolved on uneducated people by devoting to the purpose grants of the public lands and, if necessary, by appropriations from the Treasury of the United States. Whatever

Government can fairly do to promote free popular education ought to be done. Wherever general education is found, peace, virtue, and social order prevail and civil and religious liberty are secure.

In my former annual messages I have asked the attention of Congress to the urgent necessity of a reformation of the civil-service system of the Government. My views concerning the dangers of patronage, or appointments for personal or partisan considerations, have been strengthened by my observation and experience in the Executive office, and I believe these dangers threaten the stability of the Government. Abuses so serious in their nature can not be permanently tolerated. They tend to become more alarming with the enlargement of administrative service, as the growth of the country in population increases the number of officers and placemen employed.

The reasons are imperative for the adoption of fixed rules for the regulation of appointments, promotions, and removals, establishing a uniform method having exclusively in view in every instance the attainment of the best qualifications for the position in question. Such a method alone is consistent with the equal rights of all citizens and the most economical and efficient administration of the public business.

Competitive examinations in aid of impartial appointments and promotions have been conducted for some years past in several of the Executive Departments and by my direction this system has been adopted in the custom-houses and post-offices of the larger cities of the country. In the city of New York over 2,000 positions in the civil service have been subject in their appointments and tenure of place to the operation of published rules for this purpose during the past two years. The results of these practical trials have been very satisfactory, and have confirmed my opinion in favor of this system of selection. All are subjected to the same tests, and the result is free from prejudice by personal favor or partisan influence. It secures for the position applied for the best qualifications attainable among the competing applicants. It is an effectual protection from the pressure of importunity, which under any other course pursued largely exacts the time and attention of appointing officers, to their great detriment in the discharge of other official duties, preventing the abuse of the service for the mere furtherance of private or party purposes, and leaving the employee of the Government, freed from the obligations imposed by patronage, to depend solely upon merit for retention and advancement, and with this constant incentive to exertion and improvement.

These invaluable results have been attained in a high degree in the offices where the rules for appointment by competitive examination have been applied.

A method which has so approved itself by experimental tests at points where such tests may be fairly considered conclusive should be extended to all subordinate positions under the Government. I believe that a strong and growing public sentiment demands immediate measures for securing and enforcing the highest possible efficiency in the civil service and its protection from recognized abuses, and that the experience referred to has demonstrated the feasibility of such measures.

The examinations in the custom-houses and post-offices have been held under many embarrassments and without provision for compensation for the extra labor performed by the officers who have conducted them, and whose commendable interest in the improvement of the public service has induced this devotion of time and labor without pecuniary reward. A continuance of these labors gratuitously ought not to be expected, and without an appropriation by Congress for compensation it is not practicable to extend the system of examinations generally throughout the civil service. It is also highly important that all such examinations should be conducted upon a uniform system and under general supervision. Section 1753 of the Revised Statutes authorizes the President to prescribe the regulations for admission to the civil service of the United States, and for this purpose to employ suitable persons to conduct the requisite inquiries with reference to "the fitness of each candidate, in respect to age, health, character, knowledge, and ability for the branch of service into which he seeks to enter;" but the law is practically inoperative for want of the requisite appropriation.

I therefore recommend an appropriation of $25,000 per annum to meet the expenses of a commission, to be appointed by the President in accordance with the terms of this section, whose duty it shall be to devise a just, uniform, and efficient system of competitive examinations and to supervise the application of the same throughout the entire civil service of the Government. I am persuaded that the facilities which such a commission will afford for testing the fitness of those who apply for office will not only be as welcome a relief to members of Congress as it will be to the President and heads of Departments, but that it will also greatly tend to remove the causes of embarrassment which now inevitably and constantly attend the conflicting claims of patronage between the legislative and executive departments. The most effectual check upon the pernicious competition of influence and official favoritism in the bestowal of office will be the substitution of an open competition of merit between the applicants, in which everyone can make his own record with the assurance that his success will depend upon this alone.

I also recommend such legislation as, while leaving every officer as free as any other citizen to express his political opinions and to use his means for their advancement, shall also enable him to feel as safe as any private citizen in refusing all demands upon his salary for political purposes. A law which should thus guarantee true liberty and justice to all who are engaged in the public service, and likewise contain stringent provisions against the use of official authority to coerce the political action of private citizens or of official subordinates, is greatly to be desired.

The most serious obstacle, however, to an improvement of the civil service, and especially to a reform in the method of appointment and removal, has been found to be the practice, under what is known as the spoils system, by which the appointing power has been so largely encroached upon by members of Congress. The first step in the reform of the civil service must be a complete divorce between Congress and the Executive in the matter of appointments. The corrupting doctrine that "to the victors belong the spoils" is inseparable from Congressional patronage as the established rule and practice of parties in power. It comes to be understood by applicants for office and by the people generally that Representatives and Senators are entitled to disburse the patronage of their respective districts and States. It is not necessary to recite at length the evils resulting from this invasion of the Executive functions. The true principles of Government on the subject of appointments to office, as stated in the national conventions of the leading parties of the country, have again and again been approved by the American people, and have not been called in question in any quarter. These authentic expressions of public opinion upon this all-important subject are the statement of principles that belong to the constitutional structure of the Government.

Under the Constitution the President and heads of Departments are to make nominations for office. The Senate is to advise and consent to appointments, and the House of Representatives is to accuse and prosecute faithless officers. The best interest of the public service demands that these distinctions be respected; that Senators and Representatives, who may be judges and accusers, should not dictate appointments to office.

To this end the cooperation of the legislative department of the Government is required alike by the necessities of the case and by public opinion. Members of Congress will not be relieved from the demands made upon them with reference to appointments to office until by legislative enactment the pernicious practice is condemned and forbidden.

It is therefore recommended that an act be passed defining the relations of members of Congress with respect to appointment to office by the President; and I also recommend that the provisions of section 1767 and of the sections following of the Revised Statutes, comprising the tenure-of-office act of March 2, 1867, be repealed.

Believing that to reform the system and methods of the civil service in our country is one of the highest and most imperative duties of statesmanship, and that it can be permanently done only by the cooperation of the legislative and executive departments of the Government, I again commend the whole subject to your considerate attention.

It is the recognized duty and purpose of the people of the United States to suppress polygamy where it now exists in our Territories and to prevent its extension. Faithful and zealous efforts have been made by the United States authorities in Utah to enforce the laws against it. Experience has shown that the legislation upon this subject, to be effective, requires extensive modification and amendment. The longer action is delayed the more difficult it will be to accomplish what is desired. Prompt and decided measures are necessary. The Mormon sectarian organization which upholds polygamy has the whole power of making and executing the local legislation of the Territory. By its control of the grand and petit juries it possesses large influence over the administration of justice. Exercising, as the heads of this sect do, the local political power of the Territory, they are able to make effective their hostility to the law of Congress on the subject of polygamy, and, in fact, do prevent its enforcement. Polygamy will not be abolished if the enforcement of the law depends on those who practice and uphold the crime. It can only be suppressed by taking away the political power of the sect which encourages and sustains it.

The power of Congress to enact suitable laws to protect the Territories is ample. It is not a case for halfway measures. The political power of the Mormon sect is increasing. It controls now one of our wealthiest and most populous Territories. It is extending steadily into other Territories. Wherever it goes it establishes polygamy and sectarian political power. The sanctity of marriage and the family relation are the corner stone of our American society and civilization. Religious liberty and the separation of church and state are among the elementary ideas of free institutions. To reestablish the interests and principles which polygamy and Mormonism have imperiled, and to fully reopen to intelligent and virtuous immigrants of all creeds that part of our domain which has been in a great degree closed to general immigration by intolerant and immoral institutions, it is recommended that the government of the Territory of Utah be reorganized.

I recommend that Congress provide for the government of Utah by a governor and judges, or commissioners, appointed by the President and confirmed by the Senate—a government analogous to the provisional government established for the territory northwest of the Ohio by the ordinance of 1787. If, however, it is deemed best to continue the existing form of local government, I recommend that the right to vote, hold office, and sit on juries in the Territory of Utah be confined to those who neither practice nor uphold polygamy. If thorough measures are adopted, it is believed that within a few years the evils which now afflict Utah will be eradicated, and that this Territory will in good time become one of the most prosperous and attractive of the new States of the Union.

Our relations with all foreign countries have been those of undisturbed peace, and have presented no occasion for concern as to their continued maintenance.

My anticipation of an early reply from the British Government to the demand of indemnity to our fishermen for the injuries suffered by that industry at Fortune Bay in January, 1878, which I expressed in my last annual message, was disappointed. This answer was received only in the latter part of April in the present year, and when received exhibited a failure of accord between the two Governments as to the measure of the inshore fishing privilege secured to our fishermen by the treaty of Washington of so serious a character that I made it the subject of a communication to Congress, in which I recommended the adoption of the measures which seemed to me proper to be taken by this Government in maintenance of the rights accorded to our fishermen under the treaty and toward securing an indemnity for the injury these interests had suffered. A bill to carry out these recommendations was under consideration by the House of Representatives at the time of the adjournment of Congress in June last.

Within a few weeks I have received a communication from Her Majesty's Government renewing the consideration of the subject, both of the indemnity for the injuries at Fortune Bay and of the interpretation of the treaty in which the previous correspondence had shown the two Governments to be at variance. Upon both these topics the disposition toward a friendly agreement is manifested by a recognition of our right to an indemnity for the transaction at Fortune Bay, leaving the measure of such indemnity to further conference, and by an assent to the view of this Government, presented in the previous correspondence, that the regulation of conflicting interests of the shore fishery of the provincial sea-coasts and the vessel fishery of our fishermen should be made the subject of conference and concurrent arrangement between the two Governments.

I sincerely hope that the basis may be found for a speedy adjustment of the very serious divergence of views in the interpretation of the fishery clauses of the treaty of Washington, which, as the correspondence between the two Governments stood at the close of the last session of Congress, seemed to be irreconcilable.

In the important exhibition of arts and industries which was held last year at Sydney, New South Wales, as well as in that now in progress at Melbourne, the United States have been efficiently and honorably represented. The exhibitors from this country at the former place received a large number of awards in some of the most considerable departments, and the participation of the United States was recognized by a special mark of distinction. In the exhibition at Melbourne the share taken by our country is no less notable, and an equal degree of success is confidently expected.

The state of peace and tranquillity now enjoyed by all the nations of the continent of Europe has its favorable influence upon our diplomatic and commercial relations with them. We have concluded and ratified a convention with the French Republic for the settlement of claims of the citizens of either country against the other. Under this convention a commission, presided over by a distinguished publicist, appointed in pursuance of the request of both nations by His Majesty the Emperor of Brazil, has been organized and has begun its sessions in this city. A congress to consider means for the protection of industrial property has recently been in session in Paris, to which I have appointed the ministers of the United States in France and in Belgium as delegates. The International Commission upon Weights and Measures also continues its work in Paris. I invite your attention to the necessity of an appropriation to be made in time to enable this Government to comply with its obligations under the metrical convention.

Our friendly relations with the German Empire continue without interruption. At the recent International Exhibition of Fish and Fisheries at Berlin the participation of the United States, notwithstanding the haste with which the commission was forced to make its preparations, was extremely successful and meritorious, winning for private exhibitors numerous awards of a high class and for the country at large the principal prize of honor offered by His Majesty the Emperor. The results of this great success can not but be advantageous to this important and growing industry. There have been some questions raised between the two Governments as to the proper effect and interpretation of our treaties of naturalization, but recent dispatches from our minister at Berlin show that favorable progress is making toward an understanding in accordance with the views of this Government, which makes and admits no distinction whatever between the rights of a native and a naturalized citizen of the United States. In practice the complaints of molestation suffered by naturalized citizens abroad have never been fewer than at present.

There is nothing of importance to note in our unbroken friendly relations with the Governments of Austria-Hungary, Russia, Portugal, Sweden and Norway, Switzerland, Turkey, and Greece.

During the last summer several vessels belonging to the merchant marine of this country, sailing in neutral waters of the West Indies, were fired at, boarded, and searched by an armed cruiser of the Spanish Government. The circumstances as reported involve not only a private injury to the persons concerned, but also seemed too little observant of the friendly relations existing for a century between this country and Spain. The wrong was brought to the attention of the Spanish Government in a serious protest and remonstrance, and the matter is undergoing investigation by the royal authorities with a view to such explanation or reparation as may be called for by the facts.

The commission sitting in this city for the adjudication of claims of our citizens against the Government of Spain is, I hope, approaching the termination of its labors.

The claims against the United States under the Florida treaty with Spain were submitted to Congress for its action at the late session, and

I again invite your attention to this long-standing question, with a view to a final disposition of the matter.

At the invitation of the Spanish Government, a conference has recently been held at the city of Madrid to consider the subject of protection by foreign powers of native Moors in the Empire of Morocco. The minister of the United States in Spain was directed to take part in the deliberations of this conference, the result of which is a convention signed on behalf of all the powers represented. The instrument will be laid before the Senate for its consideration. The Government of the United States has also lost no opportunity to urge upon that of the Emperor of Morocco the necessity, in accordance with the humane and enlightened spirit of the age, of putting an end to the persecutions, which have been so prevalent in that country, of persons of a faith other than the Moslem, and especially of the Hebrew residents of Morocco.

The consular treaty concluded with Belgium has not yet been officially promulgated, owing to the alteration of a word in the text by the Senate of the United States, which occasioned a delay, during which the time allowed for ratification expired. The Senate will be asked to extend the period for ratification.

The attempt to negotiate a treaty of extradition with Denmark failed on account of the objection of the Danish Government to the usual clause providing that each nation should pay the expense of the arrest of the persons whose extradition it asks.

The provision made by Congress at its last session for the expense of the commission which had been appointed to enter upon negotiations with the Imperial Government of China on subjects of great interest to the relations of the two countries enabled the commissioners to proceed at once upon their mission. The Imperial Government was prepared to give prompt and respectful attention to the matters brought under negotiation, and the conferences proceeded with such rapidity and success that on the 17th of November last two treaties were signed at Peking, one relating to the introduction of Chinese into this country and one relating to commerce. Mr. Trescot, one of the commissioners, is now on his way home bringing the treaties, and it is expected that they will be received in season to be laid before the Senate early in January.

Our minister in Japan has negotiated a convention for the reciprocal relief of shipwrecked seamen. I take occasion to urge once more upon Congress the propriety of making provision for the erection of suitable fireproof buildings at the Japanese capital for the use of the American legation and the court-house and jail connected with it. The Japanese Government, with great generosity and courtesy, has offered for this purpose an eligible piece of land.

In my last annual message I invited the attention of Congress to the subject of the indemnity funds received some years ago from China and Japan. I renew the recommendation then made that whatever portions of these runas are due to American citizens should be promptly paid and the residue returned to the nations, respectively, to which they justly and equitably belong.

The extradition treaty with the Kingdom of the Netherlands, which has been for some time in course of negotiation, has during the past year been concluded and duly ratified.

Relations of friendship and amity have been established between the Government of the United States and that of Roumania. We have sent a diplomatic representative to Bucharest, and have received at this capital the special envoy who has been charged by His Royal Highness Prince Charles to announce the independent sovereignty of Roumania. We hope for a speedy development of commercial relations between the two countries.

In my last annual message I expressed the hope that the prevalence of quiet on the border between this country and Mexico would soon become so assured as to justify the modification of the orders then in force to our military commanders in regard to crossing the frontier, without encouraging such disturbances as would endanger the peace of the two countries. Events moved in accordance with these expectations, and the orders were accordingly withdrawn, to the entire satisfaction of our own citizens and the Mexican Government. Subsequently the peace of the border was again disturbed by a savage foray under the command of the Chief Victoria, but by the combined and harmonious action of the military forces of both countries his band has been broken up and substantially destroyed.

There is reason to believe that the obstacles which have so long prevented rapid and convenient communication between the United States and Mexico by railways are on the point of disappearing, and that several important enterprises of this character will soon be set on foot, which can not fail to contribute largely to the prosperity of both countries.

New envoys from Guatemala, Colombia, Bolivia, Venezuela, and Nicaragua have recently arrived at this capital, whose distinction and enlightenment afford the best guaranty of the continuance of friendly relations between ourselves and these sister Republics.

The relations between this Government and that of the United States of Colombia have engaged public attention during the past year, mainly by reason of the project of an interoceanic canal across the Isthmus of Panama, to be built by private capital under a concession from the Colombian Government for that purpose. The treaty obligations subsisting between the United States and Colombia, by which we guarantee the neutrality of the transit and the sovereignty and property of Colombia in the Isthmus, make it necessary that the conditions under which so stupendous a change in the region embraced in this guaranty should be effected—transforming, as it would, this Isthmus from a barrier between the Atlantic and Pacific oceans into a gateway and thoroughfare between them for the navies and the merchant ships of the world—should receive the approval of this Government, as being compatible with the discharge of these obligations on our part and consistent with our interests as the principal commercial power of the Western Hemisphere. The views which I expressed in a special message to Congress in March last in relation to this project I deem it my duty again to press upon your attention. Subsequent consideration has but confirmed the opinion "that it is the right and duty of the United States to assert and maintain such supervision and authority over any interoceanic canal across the isthmus that connects North and South America as will protect our national interest."

The war between the Republic of Chile on the one hand and the allied Republics of Peru and Bolivia on the other still continues. This Government has not felt called upon to interfere in a contest that is within the belligerent rights of the parties as independent states. We have, however, always held ourselves in readiness to aid in accommodating their difference, and have at different times reminded both belligerents of our willingness to render such service.

Our good offices in this direction were recently accepted by all the belligerents, and it was hoped they would prove efficacious; but I regret to announce that the measures which the ministers of the United States at Santiago and Lima were authorized to take with the view to bring about a peace were not successful. In the course of the war some questions have arisen affecting neutral rights. In all of these the ministers of the United States have, under their instructions, acted with promptness and energy in protection of American interests.

The relations of the United States with the Empire of Brazil continue to be most cordial, and their commercial intercourse steadily increases, to their mutual advantage.

The internal disorders with which the Argentine Republic has for some time past been afflicted, and which have more or less influenced its external trade, are understood to have been brought to a close. This happy result may be expected to redound to the benefit of the foreign commerce of that Republic, as well as to the development of its vast interior resources.

In Samoa the Government of King Malietoa, under the support and recognition of the consular representatives of the United States, Great Britain, and Germany, seems to have given peace and tranquillity to the islands. While it does not appear desirable to adopt as a whole the scheme of tripartite local government which has been proposed, the common interests of the three great treaty powers require harmony in their relations to the native frame of government, and this may be best secured by a simple diplomatic agreement between them. It would be well if the consular jurisdiction of our representative at Apia were increased in extent and importance so as to guard American interests in the surrounding and outlying islands of Oceanica.

The obelisk generously presented by the Khedive of Egypt to the city of New York has safely arrived in this country, and will soon be erected in that metropolis. A commission for the liquidation of the Egyptian debt has lately concluded its work, and this Government, at the earnest solicitation of the Khedive, has acceded to the provisions adopted by it, which will be laid before Congress for its information. A commission for the revision of the judicial code of the reform tribunal of Egypt is now in session in Cairo. Mr. Farman, consul-general, and J. M. Batchelder, esq., have been appointed as commissioners to participate in this work. The organization of the reform tribunals will probably be continued for another period of five years.

In pursuance of the act passed at the last session of Congress, invitations have been extended to foreign maritime states to join in a sanitary conference in Washington, beginning the 1st of January. The acceptance of this invitation by many prominent powers gives promise of success in this important measure, designed to establish a system of international notification by which the spread of infectious or epidemic diseases may be more effectively checked or prevented. The attention of Congress is invited to the necessary appropriations for carrying into effect the provisions of the act referred to.

The efforts of the Department of State to enlarge the trade and commerce of the United States, through the active agency of consular officers and through the dissemination of information obtained from them, have been unrelaxed. The interest in these efforts, as developed in our commercial communities, and the value of the information secured by this means to the trade and manufactures of the country were recognized by Congress at its last session, and provision was made for the more frequent publication of consular and other reports by the Department of State. The first issue of this publication has now been prepared, and subsequent issues may regularly be expected. The importance and interest attached to the reports of consular officers are witnessed by the general demand for them by all classes of merchants and manufacturers engaged in our foreign trade. It is believed that the system of such publications is deserving of the approval of Congress, and that the necessary appropriations for its continuance and enlargement will commend itself to your consideration.

The prosperous energies of our domestic industries and their immense production of the subjects of foreign commerce invite, and even require, an active development of the wishes and interests of our people in that direction. Especially important is it that our commercial relations with the Atlantic and Pacific coasts of South America, with the West Indies and the Gulf of Mexico, should be direct, and not through the circuit of European systems, and should be carried on in our own bottoms. The full appreciation of the opportunities which our front on the Pacific Ocean gives to commerce with Japan, China, and the East Indies, with Australia and the island groups which lie along these routes of navigation, should inspire equal efforts to appropriate to our own shipping and to administer by our own capital a due proportion of this trade. Whatever modifications of our regulations of trade and navigation may be necessary or useful to meet and direct these impulses to the enlargement of our exchanges and of our carrying trade I am sure the wisdom of Congress will be ready to supply. One initial measure, however, seems to me so clearly useful and efficient that I venture to press it upon your earnest attention. It seems to be very evident that the provision of regular steam postal communication by aid from government has been the forerunner of the commercial predominance of Great Britain on all these coasts and seas, a greater share in whose trade is now the desire and the intent of our people. It is also manifest that the efforts of other European nations to contend with Great Britain for a share of this commerce have been successful in proportion with their adoption of regular steam postal communication with the markets whose trade they sought. Mexico and the States of South America are anxious to receive such postal communication with this country and to aid in their development. Similar cooperation may be looked for in due time from the Eastern nations and from Australia. It is difficult to see how the lead in this movement can be expected from private interests. In respect of foreign commerce quite as much as in internal trade postal communication seems necessarily a matter of common and public administration, and thus pertaining to Government. I respectfully recommend to your prompt attention such just and efficient measures as may conduce to the development of our foreign commercial exchanges and the building up of our carrying trade.

In this connection I desire also to suggest the very great service which might be expected in enlarging and facilitating our commerce on the Pacific Ocean were a transmarine cable laid from San Francisco to the Sandwich Islands, and thence to Japan at the north and Australia at the south. The great influence of such means of communication on these routes of navigation in developing and securing the due share of our Pacific Coast in the commerce of the world needs no illustration or enforcement. It may be that such an enterprise, useful, and in the end profitable, as it would prove to private investment, may need to be accelerated by prudent legislation by Congress in its aid, and I submit the matter to your careful consideration.

An additional and not unimportant, although secondary, reason for fostering and enlarging the Navy may be found in the unquestionable service to the expansion of our commerce which would be rendered by the frequent circulation of naval ships in the seas and ports of all quarters of the globe. Ships of the proper construction and equipment to be of the greatest efficiency in case of maritime war might be made constant and active agents in time of peace in the advancement and protection of our foreign trade and in the nurture and discipline of young seamen, who would naturally in some numbers mix with and improve the crews of our merchant ships. Our merchants at home and abroad recognize the value to foreign commerce of an active movement of our naval vessels, and the intelligence and patriotic zeal of our naval officers in promoting every interest of their countrymen is a just subject of national pride.

The condition of the financial affairs of the Government, as shown by the report of the Secretary of the Treasury, is very satisfactory. It is believed that the present financial situation of the United States, whether considered with respect to trade, currency, credit, growing wealth, or the extent and variety of our resources, is more favorable than that of any other country of our time, and has never been surpassed by that of any country at any period of its history. All our industries are thriving; the rate of interest is low; new railroads are being constructed; a vast immigration is increasing our population, capital, and labor; new enterprises in great number are in progress, and our commercial relations with other countries are improving.

The ordinary revenues from all sources for the fiscal year ended June 30, 1880, were—

From customs	$186,522,064.60
From internal revenue	124,009,373.92
From sales of public lands	1,016,506.60
From tax on circulation and deposits of national banks	7,014,971.44
From repayment of interest by Pacific Railway companies	1,707,367.18
From sinking fund for Pacific Railway companies	786,621.22
From customs fees, fines, penalties, etc	1,148,800.16
From fees—consular, letters patent, and lands	2,337,029.00
From proceeds of sales of Government property	282,616.50
From profits on coinage, etc	2,792,186.78
From revenues of the District of Columbia	1,809,469.70
From miscellaneous sources	4,099,603.88
Total ordinary receipts	333,526,610.98

The ordinary expenditures for the same period were—

For civil expenses	$15,693,963.55
For foreign intercourse	1,211,490.58
For Indians	5,945,457.09
For pensions (including $19,341,025.20 arrears of pensions)	56,777,174.44
For the military establishment, including river and harbor improvements and arsenals	38,116,916.22
For the naval establishment, including vessels, machinery, and improvements at navy-yards	13,536,984.74
For miscellaneous expenditures, including public buildings, light-houses, and collecting the revenue	34,535,691.00
For expenditures on account of the District of Columbia	3,272,384.63
For interest on the public debt	95,757,575.11
For premium on bonds purchased	2,795,320.42

leaving a surplus revenue of $65,883,653.20, which, with an amount drawn from the cash balance in Treasury of $8,084,434.21, making $73,968,087.41, was applied to the redemption—

Of bonds for the sinking fund	$73,652,900.00
Of fractional currency	251,717.41
Of the loan of 1858	40,000.00
Of temporary loan	100.00
Of bounty-land scrip	25.00
Of compound-interest notes	16,500.00
Of 7.30 notes of 1864-65	2,650.00
Of one and two year notes	3,700.00
Of old demand notes	495.00
Total	73,968,087.41

The amount due the sinking fund for this year was $37,931,643.55. There was applied thereto the sum of $73,904,617.41, being $35,972,- 973.86 in excess of the actual requirements for the year.

The aggregate of the revenues from all sources during the fiscal year ended June 30, 1880, was $333,526,610.98, an increase over the preceding year of $59,699,426.52. The receipts thus far of the current year, together with the estimated receipts for the remainder of the year, amount to $350,000,000, which will be sufficient to meet the estimated expenditures of the year and leave a surplus of $90,000,000.

It is fortunate that this large surplus revenue occurs at a period when it may be directly applied to the payment of the public debt soon to be redeemable. No public duty has been more constantly cherished in the United States than the policy of paying the nation's debt as rapidly as possible.

The debt of the United States, less cash in the Treasury and exclusive of accruing interest, attained its maximum of $2,756,431,571.43 in August, 1865, and has since that time been reduced to $1,886,019,504.65. Of the principal of the debt, $108,758,100 has been paid since March 1, 1877, effecting an annual saving of interest of $6,107,593. The burden of interest has also been diminished by the sale of bonds bearing a low rate of interest and the application of the proceeds to the redemption of bonds bearing a higher rate. The annual saving thus secured since March 1, 1877, is $14,290,453.50. Within a short period over six hundred millions of 5 and 6 per cent bonds will become redeemable. This presents a very favorable opportunity not only to further reduce the principal of the debt, but also to reduce the rate of interest on that which will remain unpaid. I call the attention of Congress to the views expressed on this subject by the Secretary of the Treasury in his annual report, and recommend prompt legislation to enable the Treasury Department to complete the refunding of the debt which is about to mature.

The continuance of specie payments has not been interrupted or endangered since the date of resumption. It has contributed greatly to the revival of business and to our remarkable prosperity. The fears that preceded and accompanied resumption have proved groundless. No considerable amount of United States notes have been presented for redemption, while very large sums of gold bullion, both domestic and imported, are taken to the mints and exchanged for coin or notes. The increase of coin and bullion in the United States since January 1, 1879, is estimated at $227,399,428.

There are still in existence, uncanceled, $346,681,016 of United States legal-tender notes. These notes were authorized as a war measure, made necessary by the exigencies of the conflict in which the United States was then engaged. The preservation of the nation's existence required, in the judgment of Congress, an issue of legal-tender paper money. That it served well the purpose for which it was created is not questioned, but the employment of the notes as paper money indefinitely, after the accomplishment of the object for which they were provided, was not contemplated by the framers of the law under which they were issued. These notes long since became, like any other pecuniary obligation of the Government, a debt to be paid, and when paid to be canceled as mere evidence of an indebtedness no longer existing. I therefore repeat what was said in the annual message of last year, that the retirement from circulation of United States notes with the capacity of legal tender in private contracts is a step to be taken in our progress toward a safe and stable currency which should be accepted as the policy and duty of the Government and the interest and security of the people.

At the time of the passage of the act now in force requiring the coinage of silver dollars, fixing their value, and giving them legal-tender character it was believed by many of the supporters of the measure that the silver dollar which it authorized would speedily become, under the operations of the law, of equivalent value to the gold dollar. There were other supporters of the bill, who, while they doubted as to the probability of this result, nevertheless were willing to give the proposed experiment a fair trial, with a view to stop the coinage if experience should prove that the silver dollar authorized by the bill continued to be of less commercial value than the standard gold dollar.

The coinage of silver dollars under the act referred to began in March. 1878, and has been continued as required by the act. The average rate per month to the present time has been $2,276,492. The total amount coined prior to the 1st of November last was $72,847,750. Of this amount $47,084,450 remain in the Treasury, and only $25,763,291 are in the hands of the people. A constant effort has been made to keep this currency in circulation, and considerable expense has been necessarily incurred for this purpose; but its return to the Treasury is prompt and sure. Contrary to the confident anticipation of the friends of the measure at the time of its adoption, the value of the silver dollar containing 412½ grains of silver has not increased. During the year prior to the passage of the bill authorizing its coinage the market value of the silver which it contained was from 90 to 92 cents as compared with the standard gold dollar. During the last year the average market value of the silver dollar has been 88½ cents.

It is obvious that the legislation of the last Congress in regard to silver, so far as it was based on an anticipated rise in the value of silver as a result of that legislation, has failed to produce the effect then predicted. The longer the law remains in force, requiring, as it does, the coinage of a nominal dollar which in reality is not a dollar, the greater becomes the danger that this country will be forced to accept a single metal as the sole legal standard of value in circulation, and this a standard of less value than it purports to be worth in the recognized money of the world.

The Constitution of the United States, sound financial principles, and our best interests all require that the country should have as its legal-tender money both gold and silver coin of an intrinsic value, as bullion, equivalent to that which upon its face it purports to possess. The Constitution in express terms recognizes both gold and silver as the only true legal-tender money. To banish either of these metals from our currency is to narrow and limit the circulating medium of exchange to the disparagement of important interests. The United States produces more silver than any other country, and is directly interested in maintaining it as one of the two precious metals which furnish the coinage of the world. It will, in my judgment, contribute to this result if Congress will repeal so much of existing legislation as requires the coinage of silver dollars containing only 412½ grains of silver, and in its stead will authorize the Secretary of the Treasury to coin silver dollars of equivalent value, as bullion, with gold dollars. This will defraud no man, and will be in accordance with familiar precedents. Congress on several occasions has altered the ratio of value between gold and silver, in order to establish it more nearly in accordance with the actual ratio of value between the two metals.

In financial legislation every measure in the direction of greater fidelity in the discharge of pecuniary obligations has been found by experience to diminish the rates of interest which debtors are required to pay and to increase the facility with which money can be obtained for every legitimate purpose. Our own recent financial history shows how surely money becomes abundant whenever confidence in the exact performance of moneyed obligations is established.

The Secretary of War reports that the expenditures of the War Department for the fiscal year ended June 30, 1880, were $39,924,773.03. The appropriations for this Department for the current fiscal year amount to $41,993,630.40.

With respect to the Army, the Secretary invites attention to the fact that its strength is limited by statute (U. S. Revised Statutes, sec. 1115) to not more than 30,000 enlisted men, but that provisos contained in appropriation bills have limited expenditures to the enlistment of but 25,000. It is believed the full legal strength is the least possible force at which the present organization can be maintained, having in view efficiency, discipline, and economy. While the enlistment of this force would add somewhat to the appropriation for pay of the Army, the saving made in other respects would be more than an equivalent for this additional outlay, and the efficiency of the Army would be largely increased.

The rapid extension of the railroad system west of the Mississippi River and the great tide of settlers which has flowed in upon new territory impose on the military an entire change of policy. The maintenance of small posts along wagon and stage routes of travel is no longer necessary. Permanent quarters at points selected, of a more substantial character than those heretofore constructed, will be required. Under existing laws permanent buildings can not be erected without the sanction of Congress, and when sales of military sites and buildings have been authorized the moneys received have reverted to the Treasury and could only become available through a new appropriation. It is recommended that provision be made by a general statute for the sale of such abandoned military posts and buildings as are found to be unnecessary and for the application of the proceeds to the construction of other posts. While many of the present posts are of but slight value for military purposes, owing to the changed condition of the country, their occupation is continued at great expense and inconvenience, because they afford the only available shelter for troops.

The absence of a large number of officers of the line, in active duty, from their regiments is a serious detriment to the maintenance of the service. The constant demand for small detachments, each of which should be commanded by a commissioned officer, and the various details of officers for necessary service away from their commands occasion a scarcity in the number required for company duties. With a view to lessening this drain to some extent, it is recommended that the law authorizing the detail of officers from the active list as professors of tactics and military science at certain colleges and universities be so amended as to provide that all such details be made from the retired list of the Army.

Attention is asked to the necessity of providing by legislation for organizing, arming, and disciplining the *active* militia of the country, and liberal appropriations are recommended in this behalf. The reports of the Adjutant-General of the Army and the Chief of Ordnance touching this subject fully set forth its importance.

The report of the officer in charge of education in the Army shows that there are 78 schools now in operation in the Army, with an aggregate attendance of 2,305 enlisted men and children. The Secretary recommends the enlistment of 150 schoolmasters, with the rank and pay of commissary-sergeants. An appropriation is needed to supply the judge-advocates of the Army with suitable libraries, and the Secretary recommends that the Corps of Judge-Advocates be placed upon the same footing as to promotion with the other staff corps of the Army. Under existing laws the Bureau of Military Justice consists of one officer (the Judge-Advocate-General), and the Corps of Judge-Advocates of eight officers of equal rank (majors), with a provision that the limit of the corps shall remain at four when reduced by casualty or resignation to that number. The consolidation of the Bureau of Military Justice and the Corps of Judge-Advocates upon the same basis with the other staff corps of the Army would remove an unjust discrimination against deserving officers and subserve the best interests of the service.

Especial attention is asked to the report of the Chief of Engineers upon the condition of our national defenses. From a personal inspection of many of the fortifications referred to, the Secretary is able to emphasize the recommendations made and to state that their incomplete and defenseless condition is discreditable to the country. While other nations have been increasing their means for carrying on offensive warfare and attacking maritime cities, we have been dormant in preparation for defense. Nothing of importance has been done toward strengthening and finishing our casemated works since our late civil war, during which the great guns of modern warfare and the heavy armor of modern fortifications and ships came into use among the nations; and our earthworks, left by a sudden failure of appropriations some years since in all stages of incompletion, are now being rapidly destroyed by the elements.

The two great rivers of the North American continent, the Mississippi and the Columbia, have their navigable waters wholly within the limits of the United States, and are of vast importance to our internal and foreign commerce. The permanency of the important work on the South Pass of the Mississippi River seems now to be assured. There has been no failure whatever in the maintenance of the maximum channel during the six months ended August 9 last. This experiment has opened a broad, deep highway to the ocean, and is an improvement upon the permanent success of which congratulations may be exchanged among people abroad and at home, and especially among the communities of the Mississippi Valley, whose commercial exchanges float in an unobstructed channel safely to and from the sea.

A comprehensive improvement of the Mississippi and its tributaries is a matter of transcendent importance. These great waterways comprise a system of inland transportation spread like network over a large portion of the United States, and navigable to the extent of many thousands of miles. Producers and consumers alike have a common interest in such unequaled facilities for cheap transportation. Geographically, commercially, and politically, they are the strongest tie between the various sections of the country. These channels of communication and interchange are the property of the nation. Its jurisdiction is paramount over their waters, and the plainest principles of public interest require their intelligent and careful supervision, with a view to their protection, improvement, and the enhancement of their usefulness.

The channel of the Columbia River for a distance of about 100 miles from its mouth is obstructed by a succession of bars, which occasion serious delays in navigation and heavy expense for lighterage and towage. A depth of at least 20 feet at low tide should be secured and maintained to meet the requirements of the extensive and growing inland and ocean commerce it subserves. The most urgent need, however, for this great waterway is a permanent improvement of the channel at the mouth of the river.

From Columbia River to San Francisco, a distance of over 600 miles, there is no harbor on our Pacific coast which can be approached during stormy weather. An appropriation of $150,000 was made by the Forty-fifth Congress for the commencement of a breakwater and harbor of refuge, to be located at some point between the Straits of Fuca and San Francisco at which the necessities of commerce, local and general, will be best accommodated. The amount appropriated is thought to be quite inadequate for the purpose intended. The cost of the work, when finished, will be very great, owing to the want of natural advantages for a site at any point on the coast between the designated limits, and it has not been thought to be advisable to undertake the work without a larger appropriation. I commend the matter to the attention of Congress.

The completion of the new building for the War Department is urgently needed, and the estimates for continuing its construction are especially recommended.

The collections of books, specimens, and records constituting the Army Medical Museum and Library are of national importance. The library now contains about 51,500 volumes and 57,000 pamphlets relating to medicine, surgery, and allied topics. The contents of the Army Medical Museum consist of 22,000 specimens, and are unique in the completeness with which both military surgery and the diseases of armies are illustrated. Their destruction would be an irreparable loss, not only to the United States, but to the world. There are filed in the Record and Pension Division over 16,000 bound volumes of hospital records, together with a great quantity of papers, embracing the original records of the hospitals of our armies during the civil war. Aside from their historical value, these records are daily searched for evidence needed in the settlement of large numbers of pension and other claims, for the protection of the Government against attempted frauds, as well as for the benefit of honest claimants. These valuable collections are now in a building which is peculiarly exposed to the danger of destruction by fire. It is therefore earnestly recommended that an appropriation be made for a new fireproof building, adequate for the present needs and reasonable future expansion of these valuable collections. Such a building should be absolutely fireproof; no expenditure for mere architectural display is required. It is believed that a suitable structure can be erected at a cost not to exceed $250,000.

I commend to the attention of Congress the great services of the Commander in Chief of our armies during the war for the Union, whose wise, firm, and patriotic conduct did so much to bring that momentous conflict to a close. The legislation of the United States contains many precedents for the recognition of distinguished military merit, authorizing rank and emoluments to be conferred for eminent services to the country. An act of Congress authorizing the appointment of a Captain-General of the Army, with suitable provisions relating to compensation, retirement, and other details, would, in my judgment, be altogether fitting and proper, and would be warmly approved by the country.

The report of the Secretary of the Navy exhibits the successful and satisfactory management of that Department during the last fiscal year. The total expenditures for the year were $12,916,639.45, leaving unexpended at the close of the year $2,141,682.23 of the amount of available appropriations. The appropriations for the present fiscal year, ending June 30, 1881, are $15,095,061.45, and the total estimates for the next fiscal year, ending June 30, 1882, are $15,953,751.61. The amount drawn by warrant from July 1, 1880, to November 1, 1880, is $5,041,570.45.

The recommendation of the Secretary of the Navy that provision be made for the establishment of some form of civil government for the people of Alaska is approved. At present there is no protection of persons or property in that Territory except such as is afforded by the officers of the United States ship *Jamestown*. This vessel was dispatched to Sitka because of the fear that without the immediate presence of the national authority there was impending danger of anarchy. The steps taken to restore order have been accepted in good faith by both white and Indian inhabitants, and the necessity for this method of restraint does not, in my opinion, now exist. If, however, the *Jamestown* should be withdrawn, leaving the people, as at present, without the ordinary judicial and administrative authority of organized local government, serious consequences might ensue.

The laws provide only for the collection of revenue, the protection of public property, and the transmission of the mails. The problem is to supply a local rule for a population so scattered and so peculiar in its origin and condition. The natives are reported to be teachable and self-supporting, and if properly instructed doubtless would advance rapidly in civilization, and a new factor of prosperity would be added to the national life. I therefore recommend the requisite legislation upon this subject.

The Secretary of the Navy has taken steps toward the establishment of naval coaling stations at the Isthmus of Panama, to meet the requirements of our commercial relations with Central and South America, which are rapidly growing in importance. Locations eminently suitable, both as regards our naval purposes and the uses of commerce, have been selected, one on the east side of the Isthmus, at Chiriqui Lagoon, in the Caribbean Sea, and the other on the Pacific coast, at the Bay of Golfito. The only safe harbors, sufficiently commodious, on the Isthmus are at these points, and the distance between them is less than 100 miles. The report of the Secretary of the Navy concludes with valuable suggestions with respect to the building up of our merchant marine service, which deserve the favorable consideration of Congress.

The report of the Postmaster-General exhibits the continual growth and the high state of efficiency of the postal service. The operations of no Department of the Government, perhaps, represent with greater exactness the increase in the population and the business of the country. In 1860 the postal receipts were $8,518,067.40; in 1880 the receipts were $33,315,479.34. All the inhabitants of the country are directly and personally interested in having proper mail facilities, and naturally watch the Post-Office very closely. This careful oversight on the part of the people has proved a constant stimulus to improvement. During the past year there was an increase of 2,134 post-offices, and the mail routes were extended 27,177 miles, making an additional annual transportation of 10,804,191 miles. The revenues of the postal service for the ensuing year are estimated at $38,845,174.10, and the expenditures at $42,475,932, leaving a deficiency to be appropriated out of the Treasury of $3,630,757.90.

The Universal Postal Union has received the accession of almost all the countries and colonies of the world maintaining organized postal services, and it is confidently expected that all the other countries and colonies now outside the union will soon unite therewith, thus realizing the grand idea and aim of the founders of the union of forming, for purposes of international mail communication, a single postal territory, embracing the world, with complete uniformity of postal charges and conditions of international exchange for all descriptions of correspondence. To enable the United States to do its full share of this great work, additional legislation is asked by the Postmaster-General, to whose recommendations especial attention is called.

The suggestion of the Postmaster-General that it would be wise to encourage, by appropriate legislation, the establishment of American lines of steamers by our own citizens to carry the mails between our own ports and those of Mexico, Central America, South America, and of transpacific countries is commended to the serious consideration of Congress.

The attention of Congress is also invited to the suggestions of the Postmaster-General in regard to postal savings.

The necessity for additional provision to aid in the transaction of the business of the Federal courts becomes each year more apparent. The dockets of the Supreme Court and of the circuit courts in the greater number of the circuits are encumbered with the constant accession of cases. In the former court, and in many instances in the circuit courts, years intervene before it is practicable to bring cases to hearing.

The Attorney-General recommends the establishment of an intermediate court of errors and appeals. It is recommended that the number of judges of the circuit court in each circuit, with the exception of the second circuit, should be increased by the addition of another judge; in the second circuit, that two should be added; and that an intermediate appellate court should be formed in each circuit, to consist of the circuit judges and the circuit justice, and that in the event of the absence of either of these judges the place of the absent judge should be supplied by the judge of one of the district courts in the circuit. Such an appel-

late court could be safely invested with large jurisdiction, and its decisions would satisfy suitors in many cases where appeals would still be
allowed to the Supreme Court. The expense incurred for this intermediate court will require a very moderate increase of the appropriations
for the expenses of the Department of Justice. This recommendation is
commended to the careful consideration of Congress.

It is evident that a delay of justice, in many instances oppressive and
disastrous to suitors, now necessarily occurs in the Federal courts, which
will in this way be remedied.

The report of the Secretary of the Interior presents an elaborate account of the operations of that Department during the past year. It
gives me great pleasure to say that our Indian affairs appear to be in a
more hopeful condition now than ever before. The Indians have made
gratifying progress in agriculture, herding, and mechanical pursuits.
Many who were a few years ago in hostile conflict with the Government are quietly settling down on farms where they hope to make their
permanent homes, building houses and engaging in the occupations of
civilized life. The introduction of the freighting business among them
has been remarkably fruitful of good results, in giving many of them
congenial and remunerative employment and in stimulating their ambition to earn their own support. Their honesty, fidelity, and efficiency
as carriers are highly praised. The organization of a police force of
Indians has been equally successful in maintaining law and order upon
the reservations and in exercising a wholesome moral influence among
the Indians themselves. I concur with the Secretary of the Interior
in the recommendation that the pay of this force be increased, as an
inducement to the best class of young men to enter it.

Much care and attention has been devoted to the enlargement of educational facilities for the Indians. The means available for this important
object have been very inadequate. A few additional boarding schools
at Indian agencies have been established and the erection of buildings
has been begun for several more; but an increase of the appropriations
for this interesting undertaking is greatly needed to accommodate the
large number of Indian children of school age. The number offered by
their parents from all parts of the country for education in the Government schools is much larger than can be accommodated with the means
at present available for that purpose. The number of Indian pupils at
the normal school at Hampton, Va., under the direction of General
Armstrong, has been considerably increased, and their progress is highly
encouraging. The Indian school established by the Interior Department
in 1879 at Carlisle, Pa., under the direction of Captain Pratt, has been
equally successful. It has now nearly 200 pupils of both sexes, representing a great variety of the tribes east of the Rocky Mountains. The
pupils in both these institutions receive not only an elementary English
education, but are also instructed in housework, agriculture, and useful

mechanical pursuits.   A similar school was established this year at Forest Grove, Oreg., for the education of Indian youth on the Pacific Coast.
In addition to this, thirty-six Indian boys and girls were selected from
the Eastern Cherokees and placed in boarding schools in North Carolina,
where they are to receive an elementary English education and training
in industrial pursuits.   The interest shown by Indian parents, even
among the so-called wild tribes, in the education of their children is
very gratifying, and gives promise that the results accomplished by the
efforts now making will be of lasting benefit.

The expenses of Indian education have so far been drawn from the permanent civilization fund at the disposal of the Department of the Interior,
but the fund is now so much reduced that the continuance of this beneficial work will in the future depend on specific appropriations by Congress for the purpose; and I venture to express the hope that Congress
will not permit institutions so fruitful of good results to perish for want
of means for their support.   On the contrary, an increase of the number of such schools appears to me highly advisable.

The past year has been unusually free from disturbances among the
Indian tribes.   An agreement has been made with the Utes by which
they surrender their large reservation in Colorado in consideration of an
annuity to be paid to them, and agree to settle in severalty on certain
lands designated for that purpose, as farmers, holding individual title to
their land in fee simple, inalienable for a certain period.   In this way a
costly Indian war has been avoided, which at one time seemed imminent,
and for the first time in the history of the country an Indian nation has
given up its tribal existence to be settled in severalty and to live as individuals under the common protection of the laws of the country.

The conduct of the Indians throughout the country during the past
year, with but few noteworthy exceptions, has been orderly and peaceful.
The guerrilla warfare carried on for two years by Victoria and his band
of Southern Apaches has virtually come to an end by the death of that
chief and most of his followers on Mexican soil.   The disturbances
caused on our northern frontier by Sitting Bull and his men, who had
taken refuge in the British dominions, are also likely to cease.   A large
majority of his followers have surrendered to our military forces, and the
remainder are apparently in progress of disintegration.

I concur with the Secretary of the Interior in expressing the earnest
hope that Congress will at this session take favorable action on the bill
providing for the allotment of lands on the different reservations in severalty to the Indians, with patents conferring fee-simple title inalienable
for a certain period, and the eventual disposition of the residue of the
reservations for general settlement, with the consent and for the benefit
of the Indians, placing the latter under the equal protection of the laws of
the country.   This measure, together with a vigorous prosecution of our
educational efforts, will work the most important and effective advance

toward the solution of the Indian problem, in preparing for the gradual merging of our Indian population in the great body of American citizenship.

A large increase is reported in the disposal of public lands for settlement during the past year, which marks the prosperous growth of our agricultural industry and a vigorous movement of population toward our unoccupied lands. As this movement proceeds, the codification of our land laws, as well as proper legislation to regulate the disposition of public lands, become of more pressing necessity, and I therefore invite the consideration of Congress to the report and the accompanying draft of a bill made by the Public Lands Commission, which were communicated by me to Congress at the last session. Early action upon this important subject is highly desirable.

The attention of Congress is again asked to the wasteful depredations committed on our public timber lands and the rapid and indiscriminate destruction of our forests. The urgent necessity for legislation to this end is now generally recognized. In view of the lawless character of the depredations committed and the disastrous consequences which will inevitably follow their continuance, legislation has again and again been recommended to arrest the evil and to preserve for the people of our Western States and Territories the timber needed for domestic and other essential uses.

The report of the Director of the Geological Survey is a document of unusual interest. The consolidation of the various geological and geographical surveys and exploring enterprises, each of which has heretofore operated upon an independent plan, without concert, can not fail to be of great benefit to all those industries of the country which depend upon the development of our mineral resources. The labors of the scientific men, of recognized merit, who compose the corps of the Geological Survey, during the first season of their field operations and inquiries, appear to have been very comprehensive, and will soon be communicated to Congress in a number of volumes. The Director of the Survey recommends that the investigations carried on by his bureau, which so far have been confined to the so-called public-land States and Territories, be extended over the entire country, and that the necessary appropriation be made for this purpose. This would be particularly beneficial to the iron, coal, and other mining interests of the Mississippi Valley and of the Eastern and Southern States. The subject is commended to the careful consideration of Congress.

The Secretary of the Interior asks attention to the want of room in the public buildings of the capital, now existing and in progress of construction, for the accommodation of the clerical force employed and of the public records. Necessity has compelled the renting of private buildings in different parts of the city for the location of public offices, for which a large amount of rent is annually paid, while the separation of offices belonging to the same Department impedes the transaction of current business. The Secretary suggests that the blocks surrounding Lafayette Square on the east, north, and west be purchased as the sites for new edifices for the accommodation of the Government offices, leaving the square itself intact, and that if such buildings were constructed upon a harmonious plan of architecture they would add much to the beauty of the national capital, and would, together with the Treasury and the new State, Navy, and War Department building, form one of the most imposing groups of public edifices in the world.

The Commissioner of Agriculture expresses the confident belief that his efforts in behalf of the production of our own sugar and tea have been encouragingly rewarded. The importance of the results attained have attracted marked attention at home and have received the special consideration of foreign nations. The successful cultivation of our own tea and the manufacture of our own sugar would make a difference of many millions of dollars annually in the wealth of the nation.

The report of the Commissioner asks attention particularly to the continued prevalence of an infectious and contagious cattle disease known and dreaded in Europe and Asia as cattle plague, or pleuro-pneumonia. A mild type of this disease in certain sections of our country is the occasion of great loss to our farmers and of serious disturbance to our trade with Great Britain, which furnishes a market for most of our live stock and dressed meats. The value of neat cattle exported from the United States for the eight months ended August 31, 1880, was more than $12,000,000, and nearly double the value for the same period in 1879— an unexampled increase of export trade. Your early attention is solicited to this important matter.

The Commissioner of Education reports a continued increase of public interest in educational affairs, and that the public schools generally throughout the country are well sustained. Industrial training is attracting deserved attention, and colleges for instruction, theoretical and practical, in agriculture and mechanic arts, including the Government schools recently established for the instruction of Indian youth, are gaining steadily in public estimation. The Commissioner asks special attention to the depredations committed on the lands reserved for the future support of public instruction, and to the very great need of help from the nation for schools in the Territories and in the Southern States. The recommendation heretofore made is repeated and urged, that an educational fund be set apart from the net proceeds of the sales of the public lands annually, the income of which and the remainder of the net annual proceeds to be distributed on some satisfactory plan to the States and the Territories and the District of Columbia.

The success of the public schools of the District of Columbia, and the progress made, under the intelligent direction of the board of education and the superintendent, in supplying the educational requirements of the

District with thoroughly trained and efficient teachers, is very gratifying. The acts of Congress, from time to time, donating public lands to the several States and Territories in aid of educational interests have proved to be wise measures of public policy, resulting in great and lasting benefit. It would seem to be a matter of simple justice to extend the benefits of this legislation, the wisdom of which has been so fully vindicated by experience, to the District of Columbia.

I again commend the general interests of the District of Columbia to the favorable consideration of Congress. The affairs of the District, as shown by the report of the Commissioners, are in a very satisfactory condition.

In my annual messages heretofore and in my special message of December 19, 1879, I have urged upon the attention of Congress the necessity of reclaiming the marshes of the Potomac adjacent to the capital, and I am constrained by its importance to advert again to the subject. These flats embrace an area of several hundred acres. They are an impediment to the drainage of the city and seriously impair its heal'h. It is believed that with this substantial improvement of its river front the capital would be in all respects one of the most attractive citi s in the world. Aside from its permanent population, this city is necessarily the place of residence of persons from every section of the country engaged in the public service. Many others reside here temporarily for the transaction of business with the Government.

It should not be forgotten that the land acquired will probably be worth the cost of reclaiming it and that the navigation of the river will be greatly improved. I therefore again invite the attention of Congress to the importance of prompt provision for this much needed and too long delayed improvement.

The water supply of the city is inadequate. In addition to the ordinary use throughout the city, the consumption by Government is necessarily very great in the navy-yard, arsenal, and the various Departments, and a large quantity is required for the proper preservation of the numerous parks and the cleansing of sewers. I recommend that this subject receive the early attention of Congress, and that in making provision for an increased supply such means be adopted as will have in view the future growth of the city. Temporary expedients for such a purpose can not but be wasteful of money, and therefore unwise. A more ample reservoir, with corresponding facilities for keeping it filled, should, in my judgment, be constructed. I commend again to the attention of Congress the subject of the removal from their present location of the depots of the several railroads entering the city; and I renew the recommendations of my former messages in behalf of the erection of a building for the Congressional Library, the completion of the Washington Monument, and of liberal appropriations in support of the benevolent, reformatory, and penal institutions of the District.

RUTHERFORD B. HAYES.

SPECIAL MESSAGES.

WASHINGTON, *December 9, 1880.*

To the Senate of the United States:

I transmit to the Senate, for its consideration with a view to ratification, a convention for the establishment, on fixed and uniform bases, of the exercise of the right of protection in Morocco, and for the settlement of certain questions connected therewith, between His Excellency the President of the United States of America; His Majesty the Emperor of Germany, King of Prussia; His Majesty the Emperor of Austria, King of Hungary; His Majesty the King of the Belgians; His Majesty the King of Denmark; His Majesty the King of Spain; His Excellency the President of the French Republic; Her Majesty the Queen of the United Kingdom of Great Britain and Ireland; His Majesty the King of Italy; His Majesty the Sultan of Morocco; His Majesty the King of the Netherlands; His Majesty the King of Portugal and the Algarves, and His Majesty the King of Sweden and Norway, signed at Madrid on the 3d day of July last.   R. B. HAYES.

EXECUTIVE MANSION, *December 13, 1880.*

To the Senate of the United States:

The accompanying documents, received from the Commissioner of Agriculture, are transmitted to the Senate in reply to the resolution of the 7th instant, relating to contagious diseases of cattle.

R. B. HAYES.

EXECUTIVE MANSION,
Washington, January 5, 1881.

To the Senate of the United States:

I transmit, for the consideration of the Senate with a view to ratification, a convention between the United States of America and the Empire of Japan, providing for the reimbursement of certain specified expenses which may be incurred by either country in consequence of the shipwreck on its coasts of the vessels of the other.   R. B. HAYES.

EXECUTIVE MANSION, *January 5, 1881.*

To the Senate of the United States:

In response to the resolution of the Senate of June 21, 1879, I herewith transmit reports* received from the Secretary of the Interior and the Secretary of War.   R. B. HAYES.

---

* Transmitting statements of the number of soldiers and civilians killed and wounded, number of Indians killed, value of property destroyed, and expenses incurred by the United States in certain Indian wars from 1865 to 1879.

EXECUTIVE MANSION,
Washington, January 10, 1881.

To the Senate of the United States:

I transmit herewith, for the consideration of the Senate, two treaties*
signed at Peking on the 17th of November, 1880, by the commissioners
plenipotentiary of the United States and China, respectively, together
with a letter of the Secretary of State in relation thereto, and accompanying papers.

R. B. HAYES.

EXECUTIVE MANSION,
Washington, January 10, 1881.

To the House of Representatives:

I submit herewith, for the information of the House of Representatives, copies of correspondence with the Department of State relating
to an invitation extended by the French Republic to this Government to
send one or more delegates to represent it at an international congress of
electricians to be held at Paris on the 15th day of September, 1881.
It appears from the same correspondence that an international exhibition of electricity is to be held at the palace of the Champs Élysées, in
Paris, from August 15, 1881, to the 15th of November following, and it
is therefore suggested by the French authorities that it might be well to
invest the delegates selected to take part in the international congress
with the additional character of commissioners to the international exhibition of electricity.

In view of the important scientific, industrial, and commercial interests designed to be promoted by the proposed international congress of
electricians and exhibition of electricity, I submit the subject to your
favorable consideration and recommend that a suitable appropriation be
made to enable this Government to accept the foregoing invitation by
appointing one or more delegates to attend the congress in question.

R. B. HAYES.

EXECUTIVE MANSION,
Washington, January 18, 1881.

To the Senate and House of Representatives:

I have the honor to submit herewith the report of the Public Lands
Commission, embracing the history and a codification of the public-land
laws; and I desire earnestly to invite the attention of Congress to this
important subject.

R. B. HAYES.

*(1) Regulation of Chinese immigration into the United States; (2) commercial intercourse and
judicial procedure.

EXECUTIVE MANSION,
Washington, January 20, 1881.

To the Senate of the United States:

I transmit herewith to the Senate a letter from the Secretary of State, with accompanying papers, in relation to the recent effort of the Government of the United States to bring about peace between Chile and Peru and Bolivia.

R. B. HAYES.

EXECUTIVE MANSION, *February 1, 1881.*

To the Senate and House of Representatives:

In compliance with the request of a large number of intelligent and benevolent citizens, and believing that it was warranted by the extraordinary circumstances of the case, on the 18th day of December, 1880, I appointed a commission consisting of George Crook and Nelson A. Miles, brigadier-generals in the Army; William Stickney, of the District of Columbia, and Walter Allen, of Massachusetts, and requested them to confer with the Ponca Indians in the Indian Territory, and, if in their judgment it was advisable, also with that part of the tribe which remained in Dakota, and "to ascertain the facts in regard to their removal and present condition so far as was necessary to determine the question as to what justice and humanity required should be done by the Government of the United States, and to report their conclusions and recommendations in the premises."

The commission, in pursuance of these instructions, having visited the Ponca Indians at their homes in the Indian Territory and in Dakota and made a careful investigation of the subject referred to them, have reported their conclusions and recommendations, and I now submit their report, together with the testimony taken, for the consideration of Congress. A minority report by Mr. Allen is also herewith submitted.

On the 27th of December, 1880, a delegation of Ponca chiefs from the Indian Territory presented to the Executive a declaration of their wishes, in which they stated that it was their desire "to remain on the lands now occupied by the Poncas in the Indian Territory" and "to relinquish all their right and interest in the lands formerly owned and occupied by the Ponca tribe in the State of Nebraska and the Territory of Dakota;" and the declaration sets forth the compensation which they will accept for the lands to be surrendered and for the injuries done to the tribe by their removal to the Indian Territory. This declaration, agreeably to the request of the chiefs making it, is herewith transmitted to Congress.

The public attention has frequently been called to the injustice and wrong which the Ponca tribe of Indians has suffered at the hands of the Government of the United States. This subject was first brought before

Congress and the country by the Secretary of the Interior in his annual report for the year 1877, in which he said:

The case of the Poncas seems entitled to especial consideration at the hands of Congress. They have always been friendly to the whites. It is said, and, as far as I have been able to learn, truthfully, that no Ponca ever killed a white man. The orders of the Government have always met with obedient compliance at their hands. Their removal from their old homes on the Missouri River was to them a great hardship. They had been born and raised there. They had houses there in which they lived according to their ideas of comfort. Many of them had engaged in agriculture and possessed cattle and agricultural implements. They were very reluctant to leave all this, but when Congress had resolved upon their removal they finally overcame that reluctance and obeyed. Considering their constant good conduct, their obedient spirit, and the sacrifices they have made, they are certainly entitled to more than ordinary care at the hands of the Government, and I urgently recommend that liberal provision be made to aid them in their new settlement.

In the same volume the report of E. A. Howard, the agent of the Poncas, is published, which contains the following:

*   *   *   *   *   *   *

I am of the opinion that the removal of the Poncas from the northern climate of Dakota to the southern climate of the Indian Territory at the season of the year it was done will prove a mistake, and that a great mortality will surely follow among the people when they shall have been here for a time and become poisoned with the malaria of the climate. Already the effects of the climate may be seen upon them in the *ennui* that seems to have settled upon each and in the large number now sick.

It is a matter of astonishment to me that the Government should have ordered the removal of the Ponca Indians from Dakota to the Indian Territory without having first made some provision for their settlement and comfort. Before their removal was carried into effect an appropriation should have been made by Congress sufficient to have located them in their new home, by building a comfortable house for the occupancy of every family of the tribe. As the case now is, no appropriation has been made by Congress, except for a sum but little more than sufficient to remove them; no houses have been built for their use, and the result is that these people have been placed on an uncultivated reservation to live in their tents as best they may, and await further legislative action.

*   *   *   *   *   *   *

These Indians claim that the Government had no right to move them from their reservation without first obtaining from them by purchase or treaty the title which they had acquired from the Government, and for which they rendered a valuable consideration. They claim that the date of the settlement of their tribe upon the land composing their old reservation is prehistoric; that they were all born there, and that their ancestors from generations back beyond their knowledge were born and lived upon its soil, and that they finally acquired a complete and perfect title from the Government by a treaty made with the "Great Father" at Washington, which they claim made it as legitimately theirs as is the home of the white man acquired by gift or purchase.

*   *   *   *   *   *   *

The subject was again referred to in similar terms in the annual report of the Interior Department for 1878, in the reports of the Commissioner of Indian Affairs and of the agent for the Poncas, and in 1879 the Secretary of the Interior said:

That the Poncas were grievously wronged by their removal from their location on the Missouri River to the Indian Territory, their old reservation having, by a mistake in making the Sioux treaty, been transferred to the Sioux, has been at length and repeatedly set forth in my reports, as well as those of the Commissioner of Indian Affairs. All that could be subsequently done by this Department in the absence of new legislation to repair that wrong and to indemnify them for their losses has been done with more than ordinary solicitude. They were permitted to select a new location for themselves in the Indian Territory, the Quapaw Reserve, to which they had first been taken, being objectionable to them. They chose a tract of country on the Arkansas River and the Salt Fork northwest of the Pawnee Reserve. I visited their new reservation personally to satisfy myself of their condition. The lands they now occupy are among the very best in the Indian Territory in point of fertility, well watered and well timbered, and admirably adapted for agriculture as well as stock raising. In this respect their new reservation is unquestionably superior to that which they left behind them on the Missouri River. Seventy houses have been built by and for them, of far better quality than the miserable huts they formerly occupied in Dakota, and the construction of a larger number is now in progress, so that, as the agent reports, every Ponca family will be comfortably housed before January. A very liberal allowance of agricultural implements and stock cattle has been given them, and if they apply themselves to agricultural work there is no doubt that their condition will soon be far more prosperous than it has ever been before. During the first year after their removal to the Indian Territory they lost a comparatively large number of their people by death, in consequence of the change of climate, which is greatly to be deplored; but their sanitary condition is now very much improved. The death rate among them during the present year has been very low, and the number of cases of sickness is constantly decreasing. It is thought that they are now sufficiently acclimated to be out of danger.

*   *   *   *   *   *   *

A committee of the Senate, after a very full investigation of the subject, on the 31st of May, 1880, reported their conclusions to the Senate, and both the majority and minority of the committee agreed that "a great wrong had been done to the Ponca Indians." The majority of the committee say:

*   *   *   *   *   *   *

Nothing can strengthen the Government in a just policy to the Indians so much as a demonstration of its willingness to do ample and complete justice whenever it can be shown that it has inflicted a wrong upon a weak and trusting tribe. It is impossible for the United States to hope for any confidence to be reposed in them by the Indians until there shall be shown on their part a readiness to do justice.

The minority report is equally explicit as to the duty of the Government to repair the wrong done the Poncas. It says:

*   *   *   *   *   *   *

We should be more prompt and anxious because they are weak and we are strong. In my judgment we should be liberal to the verge of lavishness in the expenditure of our money to improve their condition, so that they and all others may know that, although, like all nations and all men, we may do wrong, we are willing to make ample reparation.

The report of the commission appointed by me, of which General Crook was chairman, and the testimony taken by them and their investigations, add very little to what was already contained in the official reports of the Secretary of the Interior and the report of the Senate committee touching the injustice done to the Poncas by their removal to the Indian Territory. Happily, however, the evidence reported by the commission and their recommendations point out conclusively the true measures of redress which the Government of the United States ought now to adopt.

The commission in their conclusions omit to state the important facts as to the present condition of the Poncas in the Indian Territory, but the evidence they have reported shows clearly and conclusively that the Poncas now residing in that Territory, 521 in number, are satisfied with their new homes; that they are healthy, comfortable, and contented, and that they have freely and firmly decided to adhere to the choice announced in their letter of October 25, 1880, and in the declaration of December 27, 1880, to remain in the Indian Territory and not to return to Dakota.

The evidence reported also shows that the fragment of the Ponca tribe—perhaps 150 in number—which is still in Dakota and Nebraska prefer to remain on their old reservation.

In view of these facts I am convinced that the recommendations of the commission, together with the declaration of the chiefs of December last, if substantially followed, will afford a solution of the Ponca question which is consistent with the wishes and interests of both branches of the tribe, with the settled Indian policy of the Government, and, as nearly as is now practicable, with the demands of justice.

Our general Indian policy for the future should embrace the following leading ideas:

1. The Indians should be prepared for citizenship by giving to their young of both sexes that industrial and general education which is required to enable them to be self-supporting and capable of self-protection in a civilized community.

2. Lands should be allotted to the Indians in severalty, inalienable for a certain period.

3. The Indians should have a fair compensation for their lands not required for individual allotments, the amount to be invested, with suitable safeguards, for their benefit.

4. With these prerequisites secured, the Indians should be made citizens and invested with the rights and charged with the responsibilities of citizenship.

It is therefore recommended that legislation be adopted in relation to the Ponca Indians, authorizing the Secretary of the Interior to secure to the individual members of the Ponca tribe, in severalty, sufficient land for their support. inalienable for a term of years and until the restriction upon alienation may be removed by the President. Ample time and opportunity should be given to the members of the tribe freely to choose their allotments either on their old or their new reservation.

Full compensation should be made for the lands to be relinquished, for their losses by the Sioux depredations and by reason of their removal to the Indian Territory, the amount not to be less than the sums named in the declaration of the chiefs made December 27, 1880.

In short, nothing should be left undone to show to the Indians that the Government of the United States regards their rights as equally sacred with those of its citizens.

The time has come when the policy should be to place the Indians as rapidly as practicable on the same footing with the other permanent inhabitants of our country.

I do not undertake to apportion the blame for the injustice done to the Poncas. Whether the Executive or Congress or the public is chiefly in fault is not now a question of practical importance. As the Chief Executive at the time when the wrong was consummated, I am deeply sensible that enough of the responsibility for that wrong justly attaches to me to make it my particular duty and earnest desire to do all I can to give to these injured people that measure of redress which is required alike by justice and by humanity.

RUTHERFORD B. HAYES.

EXECUTIVE MANSION,
Washington, February 2, 1881.

To the House of Representatives:

I transmit herewith, for consideration and appropriate action by Congress, a letter from the Secretary of the Navy, in relation to the proposed establishment of naval stations of the United States on the American Isthmus. In this paper the current testimony of prominent officers of this Government for a long series of years, as to the feasibility and necessity of establishing such stations and the great advantage to flow therefrom to the naval and commercial interests of the United States, is clearly set forth, and the considerations adduced can not but commend themselves, I am confident, to the careful attention of Congress. Convinced of the wisdom and propriety of the suggestions thus presented, I recommend to Congress the appropriation of the sum named by the Secretary of the Navy, to be at his disposal at once, for expenditure as soon as suitable arrangements can be made to the proposed end.

R. B. HAYES.

EXECUTIVE MANSION, *February 4, 1881.*

To the Senate and House of Representatives:

I herewith transmit a communication from the Secretary of the Navy, with reference to the dispatch of a vessel for the relief of the *Jeannette* polar expedition, and commend the recommendations of the Secretary to the prompt and favorable action of Congress.

R. B. HAYES.

EXECUTIVE MANSION, *February 14, 1881.*
To the Senate and House of Representatives:

I herewith transmit the final report addressed to me by the commissioners appointed under the act of Congress approved July 19, 1876, authorizing the repavement of that part of Pennsylvania avenue lying between the Treasury Department and the Capitol Grounds.

R. B. HAYES.

WASHINGTON, *February 17, 1881.*
To the House of Representatives:

I transmit herewith a report of the Secretary of State, in response to the resolution addressed to him by the House of Representatives of the 31st of January ultimo, on the subject of international action for the restoration of silver to full use as money.

The prospect of an early international conference, promising valuable results in accordance with the interests of this country, is such that I recommend to the immediate attention of Congress an appropriation providing for the proper representation of this Government at such conference.

R. B. HAYES.

WASHINGTON, *February 21, 1881.*
To the Senate of the United States:

In compliance with the resolution of the Senate of 15th of June, 1880, requesting the Secretary of State to report to that body at its next regular session what changes, if any, of the laws regulating the management of the Department of State, or of the divisions and the bureaus thereof, are necessary or would be beneficial in promoting the efficiency or economy of its administration or management, and also to make report concerning the mode of keeping the departmental accounts, the checks and safeguards upon expenditures, and the administrative or clerical changes for the better which may suggest themselves as expedient, I transmit herewith a report from the Secretary of State upon the subjects embraced in that resolution so far as they touch the Department of State.

R. B. HAYES.

EXECUTIVE MANSION, *February 25, 1881.*
To the Senate of the United States:

I transmit herewith, for the consideration of the Senate with a view to advising and consenting to the ratification thereof, a convention for the extradition of criminals, between the United States of America and the United States of Colombia, signed at Bogotá on the 3d of January, 1881. I also transmit certain correspondence touching the negotiation of said convention.

R. B. HAYES.

EXECUTIVE MANSION,
Washington, February 25, 1881.

To the Senate of the United States:

I transmit herewith to the Senate, for its consideration with a view to ratification in due course, a convention supplementary to the consular convention of May 8, 1878, between the United States of America and His Majesty the King of Italy, concluded in the city of Washington on the 24th of February, 1881.

R. B. HAYES.

EXECUTIVE MANSION, *February 28, 1881.*

To the Senate of the United States:

I transmit herewith a copy of proclamation* for the convening of an extra session of the Senate of the United States at the Capitol, in the city of Washington, on the 4th day of March next, at noon.

R. B. HAYES.

EXECUTIVE MANSION, *February 28, 1881.*

To the Senate and House of Representatives:

I transmit herewith a copy of a letter addressed to the chairman of the Civil Service Commission on the 3d of December last, requesting to be furnished with a report upon the result in the post-office and custom-house in the city of New York of the application of the civil-service rules requiring open competitive examinations for appointments and promotions, together with the report of Hon. Dorman B. Eaton, the chairman of the Commission, in response.

The report presents a very gratifying statement of the results of the application of the rules referred to in the two largest and most important local offices in the civil service of the Government. The subject is one of great importance to the people of the whole country. I would commend the suggestions and recommendation of the chairman of the Commission to the careful consideration of Congress.

R. B. HAYES.

EXECUTIVE MANSION,
Washington, February 28, 1881.

To the Senate of the United States:

I transmit herewith, in answer to the resolution of the Senate of the 20th ultimo, a report from the Secretary of State, with accompanying papers.†

R. B. HAYES.

*See pp. 4591-4592.
†Correspondence relative to the sending to the United States by foreign governments of criminals, paupers, and insane persons.

EXECUTIVE MANSION, *March 3, 1881.*

To the Senate of the United States:

I have the honor to inform the Senate that Hon. Benjamin Harrison, Senator elect from the State of Indiana, has resigned his office as a member of the Commission for the Improvement of the Mississippi River, and the same has been accepted to take effect March 3, 1881.

R. B. HAYES.

EXECUTIVE MANSION, *March 3, 1881.*

To the Senate of the United States:

I have the honor to inform the Senate that Hon. John Sherman, Senator elect from the State of Ohio, has resigned the position of Secretary of the Treasury, and that said resignation has been accepted to take effect at the close of the present day.

R. B. HAYES.

VETO MESSAGE.

EXECUTIVE MANSION, *March 3, 1881.*

To the House of Representatives:

Having considered the bill entitled "An act to facilitate the refunding of the national debt," I am constrained to return it to the House of Representatives, in which it originated, with the following statement of my objections to its passage:

The imperative necessity for prompt action and the pressure of public duties in this closing week of my term of office compel me to refrain from any attempt to make a full and satisfactory presentation of the objections to the bill.

The importance of the passage at the present session of Congress of a suitable measure for the refunding of the national debt which is about to mature is generally recognized. It has been urged upon the attention of Congress by the Secretary of the Treasury and in my last annual message. If successfully accomplished, it will secure a large decrease in the annual interest payment of the nation, and I earnestly recommend, if the bill before me shall fail, that another measure for this purpose be adopted before the present Congress adjourns.

While, in my opinion, it would be unwise to authorize the Secretary of the Treasury, in his discretion, to offer to the public bonds bearing 3½ per cent interest in aid of refunding, I should not deem it my duty to interpose my constitutional objection to the passage of the present bill if it did not contain, in its fifth section, provisions which, in my judgment, seriously impair the value and tend to the destruction of the present national banking system of the country. This system has now been in operation almost twenty years. No safer or more beneficial banking system was ever established. Its advantages as a business are free to all who have the necessary capital. It furnishes a currency to the public which for convenience and security of the bill holder has probably never been equaled by that of any other banking system. Its notes are secured by the deposit with the Government of the interest-bearing bonds of the United States.

The section of the bill before me which relates to the national banking system, and to which objection is made, is not an essential part of a refunding measure. It is as follows:

SEC. 5. From and after the 1st day of July, 1881, the 3 per cent bonds authorized by the first section of this act shall be the only bonds receivable as security for national-bank circulation or as security for the safe-keeping and prompt payment of the public money deposited with such banks; but when any such bonds deposited for the purposes aforesaid shall be designated for purchase or redemption by the Secretary of the Treasury, the banking association depositing the same shall have the right to substitute other issues of the bonds of the United States in lieu thereof: *Provided*, That no bond upon which interest has ceased shall be accepted or shall be continued on deposit as security for circulation or for the safe-keeping of the public money; and in case bonds so deposited shall not be withdrawn, as provided by law, within thirty days after the interest has ceased thereon, the banking association depositing the same shall be subject to the liabilities and proceedings on the part of the Comptroller provided for in section 5234 of the Revised Statutes of the United States: *And provided further*, That section 4 of the act of June 20, 1874, entitled "An act fixing the amount of United States notes, providing for a redistribution of the national-bank currency, and for other purposes," be, and the same is hereby, repealed, and sections 5159 and 5160 of the Revised Statutes of the United States be, and the same are hereby, reenacted.

Under this section it is obvious that no additional banks will hereafter be organized, except possibly in a few cities or localities where the prevailing rates of interest in ordinary business are extremely low. No new banks can be organized and no increase of the capital of existing banks can be obtained except by the purchase and deposit of 3 per cent bonds. No other bonds of the United States can be used for the purpose. The one thousand millions of other bonds recently issued by the United States, and bearing a higher rate of interest than 3 per cent, and therefore a better security for the bill holder, can not after the 1st of July next be received as security for bank circulation. This is a radical change in the banking law. It takes from the banks the right they have heretofore had under the law to purchase and deposit as security for their circulation any of the bonds issued by the United States, and deprives the bill holder of the best security which the banks are able to give by requiring them to deposit bonds having the least value of any bonds issued by the Government.

The average rate of taxation of capital employed in banking is more than double the rate of taxation upon capital employed in other legitimate business. Under these circumstances, to amend the banking law so as to deprive the banks of the privilege of securing their notes by the most valuable bonds issued by the Government will, it is believed, in a large part of the country, be a practical prohibition of the organization of new banks and prevent the existing banks from enlarging their capital. The national banking system, if continued at all, will be a monopoly in the hands of those already engaged in it, who may purchase the Government bonds bearing a more favorable rate of interest than the 3 per cent bonds prior to next July.

To prevent the further organization of banks is to put in jeopardy the whole system, by taking from it that feature which makes it, as it now is, a banking system free upon the same terms to all who wish to engage in it. Even the existing banks will be in danger of being driven from business by the additional disadvantages to which they will be subjected by this bill. In short, I can not but regard the fifth section of the bill as a step in the direction of the destruction of the national banking system.

Our country, after a long period of business depression, has just entered upon a career of unexampled prosperity.

The withdrawal of the currency from circulation of the national banks, and the enforced winding up of the banks in consequence, would inevitably bring serious embarrassment and disaster to the business of the country. Banks of issue are essential instruments of modern commerce. If the present efficient and admirable system of banking is broken down, it will inevitably be followed by a recurrence to other and inferior methods of banking. Any measure looking to such a result will be a disturbing element in our financial system. It will destroy confidence and surely check the growing prosperity of the country.

Believing that a measure for refunding the national debt is not necessarily connected with the national banking law, and that any refunding act would defeat its own object if it imperiled the national banking system or seriously impaired its usefulness, and convinced that section 5 of the bill before me would, if it should become a law, work great harm, I herewith return the bill to the House of Representatives for that further consideration which is provided for in the Constitution.

RUTHERFORD B. HAYES.

PROCLAMATION.

BY THE PRESIDENT OF THE UNITED STATES OF AMERICA.

A PROCLAMATION.

Whereas objects of interest to the United States require that the Senate should be convened at 12 o'clock on the 4th of March next to receive and act upon such communications as may be made to it on the part of the Executive:

Now, therefore, I, Rutherford B. Hayes, President of the United States, have considered it to be my duty to issue this my proclamation, declaring that an extraordinary occasion requires the Senate of the United States to convene for the transaction of business at the Capitol, in the city of Washington, on the 4th day of March next, at 12 o'clock at noon on that day, of which all who shall **at** that time be entitled to act as members of that body are hereby required to take notice.

Given under my hand and the seal of the United States, at Washington, the 28th day of February, A. D. 1881, and of the Independence of the United States of America the one hundred and fifth.

[SEAL.]

R. B. HAYES.

By the President:

WM. M. EVARTS,
Secretary of State.

EXECUTIVE ORDER.

EXECUTIVE MANSION,
Washington, February 22, 1881.

The SECRETARY OF WAR:

In view of the well-known fact that the sale of intoxicating liquors in the Army of the United States is the cause of much demoralization among both officers and men, and that it gives rise to a large proportion of the cases before general and garrison courts-martial, involving great expense and serious injury to the service—

It is therefore directed, That the Secretary of War take suitable steps, as far as practicable consistently with vested rights, to prevent the sale of intoxicating liquors as a beverage at the camps, forts, and other posts of the Army.

R. B. HAYES.

O

James A. Garfield

March 4, 1881, to September 19, 1881

SEE VOLUME XI.

Volume eleven is not only an index to the other volumes, not only a key that unlocks the treasures of the entire publication, but it is in itself an alphabetically arranged brief history or story of the great controlling events constituting the History of the United States.

Under its proper alphabetical classification the story is told of every great subject referred to by any of the Presidents in their official Messages, and at the end of each story the official utterances of the Presidents themselves are cited upon the subject, so that you may readily turn to the page in the body of the work itself for this original information.

Next to the possession of knowledge is the ability to turn at will to where knowledge is to be found.

HOME, AT HIRAM, OHIO, OF

JAMES A. GARFIELD

With official portrait engraved from copy of original in steel

James A. Garfield

JAMES ABRAM GARFIELD was born in Orange, Cuyahoga County, Ohio, November 19, 1831. His father, Abram Garfield, was a native of New York, but of Massachusetts ancestry; descended from Edward Garfield, an English Puritan, who in 1630 was one of the founders of Watertown. His mother, Eliza Ballou, was born in New Hampshire, of a Huguenot family that fled from France to New England after the revocation of the Edict of Nantes in 1685. Garfield, therefore, was from lineage well represented in the struggles for civil and religious liberty, both in the Old and in the New World. His father moved to Ohio in 1830 and settled in what was then known as the "Wilderness," now as the "Western Reserve," which was occupied by Connecticut people. He died at the age of 33, leaving a widow and four small children, of whom James was the youngest. Mrs. Garfield brought up her family unaided, and impressed upon them a high standard of moral and intellectual worth. James attended school in a log hut at the age of 3 years, learned to read, and began that habit of omnivorous reading which ended only with his life. At 10 years of age was accustomed to manual labor, helping out his mother's meager income by work at home or on the farms of the neighbors. Attended the district school in the winter months, made good progress, and was conspicuous for his assiduity. At the age of 14 had a fair knowledge of arithmetic and grammar, and was particularly apt in the facts of American history. His imagination was especially kindled by tales of the sea, and he so far yielded to his love of adventure that in 1848 he went to Cleveland and proposed to ship as a sailor on board a lake schooner. Seeing that this life was not the romance he had conceived, he turned promptly from the lake; but loath to return home without adventure and without money, he drove some months for a boat on the Ohio Canal, when he was promoted from the towpath to the boat. Attended the Geauga Seminary at Chester, Ohio, during the winter of 1849–50. In the vacations learned and practiced the trade of a carpenter, helped at harvest, taught—did anything and everything to earn money to pay for his schooling. After the first term he asked and needed no aid from home; he had reached the point where he could support himself. Was converted under the instructions of a Christian preacher, was baptized and received into that denomination. As soon as he finished his studies in Chester entered (1851) the Hiram Eclectic Institute (now Hiram College), at Hiram, Portage County, Ohio, the principal educational institution of his church. He was not very quick of acquisition, but his perseverance was indomitable and he soon had an excellent knowledge of Latin and a fair acquaintance with algebra, natural philosophy, and botany. His superiority was easily recognized in the prayer meetings and debating societies of the college, where he was assiduous and conspicuous. Living here was inexpensive, and he readily made his expenses by teaching in the English departments, and also gave instruction in the ancient languages. Entered Williams College in the autumn of 1854, and graduated with the highest honors in the class of 1856. Returned to Ohio and resumed his place as a teacher of Latin and Greek at Hiram Institute, and the next year, being then only 26 years of age, was made its president. The regulations and practices of his church, known as the Christian Church, or Church of the Disciples, permitted him to preach, and he used the permission. He also pursued the study of law, entering his name in 1858 as a student in a law office in Cleveland, but studying in Hiram. Cast his first vote in 1856 for John C. Frémont, the first Republican candidate for the Presidency. Married Lucretia Rudolph November 11, 1858. In 1859 was chosen to represent the counties of Summit and Portage in the Ohio senate. In August, 1861, Governor William Dennison commissioned him lieutenant-colonel in the Forty-second Regiment Ohio Volunteers. Was promoted to the command of this regiment. In December, 1861, reported to General Buell in Louisville, Ky. Was given a brigade and assigned the difficult task of driving the Confederate general Humphrey Marshall from eastern Kentucky. General Garfield triumphed over the Confederate forces at the battle of Middle Creek, January 10, 1862, and in recognition of his services was made a brigadier-general by President Lincoln. During the campaign of the Big Sandy, while Garfield was engaged in breaking up some scattered Confederate encampments, his supplies gave out and he was threatened with starvation. Going himself to the Ohio River, he seized a steamer, loaded it with provisions, and on the refusal of any pilot to undertake the perilous voyage, because of a freshet that had swelled the river, he stood at the helm for forty-eight hours and piloted the craft through the dangerous channel. In order to surprise Marshall, then intrenched in Cumberland Gap, Garfield marched his soldiers 100 miles in four days through a blinding snowstorm. Returning to Louisville, he found that General Buell was away; overtook him at Columbia, Tenn., and was assigned to the command of the Twentieth Brigade. Reached Shiloh in time to take part in the second day's fight. Was engaged in all the operations in front of Corinth, and in June, 1862, rebuilt the bridges on the Memphis and Charleston Railroad, and exhibited noticeable engineering skill in repairing the fortifications of

Huntsville. Was granted leave of absence July 30, 1862, on account of ill health, and returned to Hiram, Ohio, where he lay ill for two months. Went to Washington on September 25, 1862, and was ordered on court-martial duty. November 25 was assigned to the case of General Fitz John Porter. In February, 1863, returned to duty under General Rose-crans, then in command of the Army of the Cumberland. Rosecrans made him his chief of staff, with responsibilities beyond those usually given to this office. In this field Garfield's influence on the campaign in middle Tennessee was most important. One familiar incident shows and justifies the great influence he wielded in its counsels. Before the battle of Chickamauga, June 24, 1863, General Rosecrans asked the written opinion of seventeen of his generals on the advisability of an immediate advance. All others opposed, but Garfield advised it, and his arguments were so convincing that Rosecrans determined to seek an engagement. General Garfield wrote out all the orders of that fateful day, September 19, excepting one, and that one was the blunder that lost the day. Garfield volunteered to take the news of the defeat on the right to General George H. Thomas, who held the left of the line. It was a bold ride, under constant fire, but he reached Thomas and gave the information that saved the Army of the Cumberland. For this action he was made a major-general September 19, 1863—promoted for gallantry on a field that was lost. Yielded to Mr. Lincoln's urgent request and on December 5, 1863, resigned his commission and hastened to Washington to sit in Congress, to which he had been chosen fifteen months before. Was offered a division in the Army of the Cumberland by General Thomas, but yielded to the representations of the President and Secretary Stanton that he would be more useful in the House of Representatives. Was placed on the Committee on Military Affairs, then the most important in Congress. In the Thirty-ninth Congress (1865) was changed, at his own request, from the Committee on Military Affairs to the Committee on Ways and Means. In the Fortieth Congress (1867) was restored to the Committee on Military Affairs and made its chairman. In the Forty-first Congress the Committee on Banking and Currency was created and he was made its chairman. Served also on the Select Committee on the Census and on the Committee on Rules. Was chairman of the Committee on Appropriations in the Forty-second and Forty-third Congresses. In the Forty-fourth, Forty-fifth, and Forty-sixth Congresses (the House being Democratic) was assigned to the Committee on Ways and Means. In 1876, at President Grant's request, went to New Orleans in company with Senators Sherman and Matthews and other Republicans, to watch the counting of the Louisiana vote. He made a special study of the West Feliciana Parish case, and embodied his views in a brief but significant report. In January, 1877, made two notable speeches in the House on the duty of Congress in a Presidential election, and claimed that the Vice-President had a constitutional right to count the electoral vote. Opposed the Electoral Commission, yet when the commission was ordered was chosen by acclamation to fill one of the two seats allotted to Republican Representatives. Mr. Blaine left the House for the Senate in 1877, and this made Mr. Garfield the undisputed leader of his party in the House. At this time and subsequently was its candidate for Speaker. Was elected to the United States Senate January 13, 1880. Attended the Republican convention which met at Chicago in June, 1880, where he opposed the renomination of President Grant and supported Senator Sherman. On the thirty-sixth ballot the delegates broke their ranks, and, rushing to General Garfield, he was unanimously nominated for President on June 8, 1880. Was elected November 2, 1880, receiving 214 electoral votes to 144 that were cast for Winfield S. Hancock. Was shot July 2, 1881, by an assassin in the Baltimore and Potomac Railroad station, in Washington, and died from the effects of the wound September 19 at Elberon, N. J. He was buried at Cleveland, Ohio.

INAUGURAL ADDRESS.

FELLOW-CITIZENS: We stand to-day upon an eminence which overlooks a hundred years of national life—a century crowded with perils, but crowned with the triumphs of liberty and law. Before continuing the onward march let us pause on this height for a moment to strengthen our faith and renew our hope by a glance at the pathway along which our people have traveled.

It is now three days more than a hundred years since the adoption of the first written constitution of the United States—the Articles of Confederation and Perpetual Union. The new Republic was then beset with danger on every hand. It had not conquered a place in the family of nations. The decisive battle of the war for independence, whose centennial anniversary will soon be gratefully celebrated at Yorktown, had not yet been fought. The colonists were struggling not only against the armies of a great nation, but against the settled opinions of mankind; for the world did not then believe that the supreme authority of government could be safely intrusted to the guardianship of the people themselves.

We can not overestimate the fervent love of liberty, the intelligent courage, and the sum of common sense with which our fathers made the great experiment of self-government. When they found, after a short trial, that the confederacy of States was too weak to meet the necessities of a vigorous and expanding republic, they boldly set it aside, and in its stead established a National Union, founded directly upon the will of the

GARFIELD READING HIS INAUGURAL ADDRESS

people, endowed with full power of self-preservation and ample authority for the accomplishment of its great object.

Under this Constitution the boundaries of freedom have been enlarged, the foundations of order and peace have been strengthened, and the growth of our people in all the better elements of national life has indicated the wisdom of the founders and given new hope to their descendants. Under this Constitution our people long ago made themselves safe against danger from without and secured for their mariners and flag equality of rights on all the seas. Under this Constitution twenty-five States have been added to the Union, with constitutions and laws, framed and enforced by their own citizens, to secure the manifold blessings of local self-government.

The jurisdiction of this Constitution now covers an area fifty times greater than that of the original thirteen States and a population twenty times greater than that of 1780.

The supreme trial of the Constitution came at last under the tremendous pressure of civil war. We ourselves are witnesses that the Union emerged from the blood and fire of that conflict purified and made stronger for all the beneficent purposes of good government.

And now, at the close of this first century of growth, with the inspirations of its history in their hearts, our people have lately reviewed the condition of the nation, passed judgment upon the conduct and opinions of political parties, and have registered their will concerning the future administration of the Government. To interpret and to execute that will in accordance with the Constitution is the paramount duty of the Executive.

Even from this brief review it is manifest that the nation is resolutely facing to the front, resolved to employ its best energies in developing the great possibilities of the future. Sacredly preserving whatever has been gained to liberty and good government during the century, our people are determined to leave behind them all those bitter controversies concerning things which have been irrevocably settled, and the further discussion of which can only stir up strife and delay the onward march.

The supremacy of the nation and its laws should be no longer a subject of debate. That discussion, which for half a century threatened the existence of the Union, was closed at last in the high court of war by a decree from which there is no appeal—that the Constitution and the laws made in pursuance thereof are and shall continue to be the supreme law of the land, binding alike upon the States and the people. This decree does not disturb the autonomy of the States nor interfere with any of their necessary rights of local self-government, but it does fix and establish the permanent supremacy of the Union.

The will of the nation, speaking with the voice of battle and through the amended Constitution, has fulfilled the great promise of 1776 by proclaiming "liberty throughout the land to all the inhabitants thereof."

The elevation of the negro race from slavery to the full rights of citizenship is the most important political change we have known since the adoption of the Constitution of 1787. No thoughtful man can fail to appreciate its beneficent effect upon our institutions and people. It has freed us from the perpetual danger of war and dissolution. It has added immensely to the moral and industrial forces of our people. It has liberated the master as well as the slave from a relation which wronged and enfeebled both. It has surrendered to their own guardianship the manhood of more than 5,000,000 people, and has opened to each one of them a career of freedom and usefulness. It has given new inspiration to the power of self-help in both races by making labor more honorable to the one and more necessary to the other. The influence of this force will grow greater and bear richer fruit with the coming years.

No doubt this great change has caused serious disturbance to our Southern communities. This is to be deplored, though it was perhaps unavoidable. But those who resisted the change should remember that under our institutions there was no middle ground for the negro race between slavery and equal citizenship. There can be no permanent disfranchised peasantry in the United States. Freedom can never yield its fullness of blessings so long as the law or its administration places the smallest obstacle in the pathway of any virtuous citizen.

The emancipated race has already made remarkable progress. With unquestioning devotion to the Union, with a patience and gentleness not born of fear, they have "followed the light as God gave them to see the light." They are rapidly laying the material foundations of self-support, widening their circle of intelligence, and beginning to enjoy the blessings that gather around the homes of the industrious poor. They deserve the generous encouragement of all good men. So far as my authority can lawfully extend, they shall enjoy the full and equal protection of the Constitution and the laws.

The free enjoyment of equal suffrage is still in question, and a frank statement of the issue may aid its solution. It is alleged that in many communities negro citizens are practically denied the freedom of the ballot. In so far as the truth of this allegation is admitted, it is answered that in many places honest local government is impossible if the mass of uneducated negroes are allowed to vote. These are grave allegations. So far as the latter is true, it is the only palliation that can be offered for opposing the freedom of the ballot. Bad local government is certainly a great evil, which ought to be prevented; but to violate the freedom and sanctities of the suffrage is more than an evil. It is a crime which, if persisted in, will destroy the Government itself. Suicide is not a remedy. If in other lands it be high treason to compass the death of the king, it shall be counted no less a crime here to strangle our sovereign power and stifle its voice.

It has been said that unsettled questions have no pity for the repose of nations. It should be said with the utmost emphasis that this question of the suffrage will never give repose or safety to the States or to the nation until each, within its own jurisdiction, makes and keeps the ballot free and pure by the strong sanctions of the law.

But the danger which arises from ignorance in the voter can not be denied. It covers a field far wider than that of negro suffrage and the present condition of the race. It is a danger that lurks and hides in the sources and fountains of power in every state. We have no standard by which to measure the disaster that may be brought upon us by ignorance and vice in the citizens when joined to corruption and fraud in the suffrage.

The voters of the Union, who make and unmake constitutions, and upon whose will hang the destinies of our governments, can transmit their supreme authority to no successors save the coming generation of voters, who are the sole heirs of sovereign power. If that generation comes to its inheritance blinded by ignorance and corrupted by vice, the fall of the Republic will be certain and remediless.

The census has already sounded the alarm in the appalling figures which mark how dangerously high the tide of illiteracy has risen among our voters and their children.

To the South this question is of supreme importance. But the responsibility for the existence of slavery did not rest upon the South alone. The nation itself is responsible for the extension of the suffrage, and is under special obligations to aid in removing the illiteracy which it has added to the voting population. For the North and South alike there is but one remedy. All the constitutional power of the nation and of the States and all the volunteer forces of the people should be surrendered to meet this danger by the savory influence of universal education.

It is the high privilege and sacred duty of those now living to educate their successors and fit them, by intelligence and virtue, for the inheritance which awaits them.

In this beneficent work sections and races should be forgotten and partisanship should be unknown. Let our people find a new meaning in the divine oracle which declares that ''a little child shall lead them,'' for our own little children will soon control the destinies of the Republic.

My countrymen, we do not now differ in our judgment concerning the controversies of past generations, and fifty years hence our children will not be divided in their opinions concerning our controversies. They will surely bless their fathers and their fathers' God that the Union was preserved, that slavery was overthrown, and that both races were made equal before the law. We may hasten or we may retard, but we can not prevent, the final reconciliation. Is it not possible for us now to make a truce with time by anticipating and accepting its inevitable verdict?

Enterprises of the highest importance to our moral and material well-being unite us and offer ample employment of our best powers. Let all our people, leaving behind them the battlefields of dead issues, move forward and in their strength of liberty and the restored Union win the grander victories of peace.

The prosperity which now prevails is without parallel in our history. Fruitful seasons have done much to secure it, but they have not done all. The preservation of the public credit and the resumption of specie payments, so successfully attained by the Administration of my predecessors, have enabled our people to secure the blessings which the seasons brought.

By the experience of commercial nations in all ages it has been found that gold and silver afford the only safe foundation for a monetary system. Confusion has recently been created by variations in the relative value of the two metals, but I confidently believe that arrangements can be made between the leading commercial nations which will secure the general use of both metals. Congress should provide that the compulsory coinage of silver now required by law may not disturb our monetary system by driving either metal out of circulation. If possible, such an adjustment should be made that the purchasing power of every coined dollar will be exactly equal to its debt-paying power in all the markets of the world.

The chief duty of the National Government in connection with the currency of the country is to coin money and declare its value. Grave doubts have been entertained whether Congress is authorized by the Constitution to make any form of paper money legal tender. The present issue of United States notes has been sustained by the necessities of war; but such paper should depend for its value and currency upon its convenience in use and its prompt redemption in coin at the will of the holder, and not upon its compulsory circulation. These notes are not money, but promises to pay money. If the holders demand it, the promise should be kept.

The refunding of the national debt at a lower rate of interest should be accomplished without compelling the withdrawal of the national-bank notes, and thus disturbing the business of the country.

I venture to refer to the position I have occupied on financial questions during a long service in Congress, and to say that time and experience have strengthened the opinions I have so often expressed on these subjects.

The finances of the Government shall suffer no detriment which it may be possible for my Administration to prevent.

The interests of agriculture deserve more attention from the Government than they have yet received. The farms of the United States afford homes and employment for more than one-half our people, and furnish much the largest part of all our exports. As the Government lights our coasts for the protection of mariners and the benefit of commerce, so it should give to the tillers of the soil the best lights of practical science and experience.

Our manufactures are rapidly making us industrially independent, and are opening to capital and labor new and profitable fields of employment. Their steady and healthy growth should still be matured. Our facilities for transportation should be promoted by the continued improvement of our harbors and great interior waterways and by the increase of our tonnage on the ocean.

The development of the world's commerce has led to an urgent demand for shortening the great sea voyage around Cape Horn by constructing ship canals or railways across the isthmus which unites the continents. Various plans to this end have been suggested and will need consideration, but none of them has been sufficiently matured to warrant the United States in extending pecuniary aid. The subject, however, is one which will immediately engage the attention of the Government with a view to a thorough protection to American interests. We will urge no narrow policy nor seek peculiar or exclusive privileges in any commercial route; but, in the language of my predecessor, I believe it to be the right "and duty of the United States to assert and maintain such supervision and authority over any interoceanic canal across the isthmus that connects North and South America as will protect our national interest."

The Constitution guarantees absolute religious freedom. Congress is prohibited from making any law respecting an establishment of religion or prohibiting the free exercise thereof. The Territories of the United States are subject to the direct legislative authority of Congress, and hence the General Government is responsible for any violation of the Constitution in any of them. It is therefore a reproach to the Government that in the most populous of the Territories the constitutional guaranty is not enjoyed by the people and the authority of Congress is set at naught. The Mormon Church not only offends the moral sense of manhood by sanctioning polygamy, but prevents the administration of justice through ordinary instrumentalities of law.

In my judgment it is the duty of Congress, while respecting to the uttermost the conscientious convictions and religious scruples of every citizen, to prohibit within its jurisdiction all criminal practices, especially of that class which destroy the family relations and endanger social order. Nor can any ecclesiastical organization be safely permitted to usurp in the smallest degree the functions and powers of the National Government.

The civil service can never be placed on a satisfactory basis until it is regulated by law. For the good of the service itself, for the protection of those who are intrusted with the appointing power against the waste of time and obstruction to the public business caused by the inordinate pressure for place, and for the protection of incumbents against intrigue and wrong, I shall at the proper time ask Congress to fix the tenure of the minor offices of the several Executive Departments and prescribe the grounds upon which removals shall be made during the terms for which incumbents have been appointed.

Finally, acting always within the authority and limitations of the Constitution, invading neither the rights of the States nor the reserved rights of the people, it will be the purpose of my Administration to maintain the authority of the nation in all places within its jurisdiction; to enforce obedience to all the laws of the Union in the interests of the people; to demand rigid economy in all the expenditures of the Government, and to require the honest and faithful service of all executive officers, remembering that the offices were created, not for the benefit of incumbents or their supporters, but for the service of the Government.

And now, fellow-citizens, I am about to assume the great trust which you have committed to my hands. I appeal to you for that earnest and thoughtful support which makes this Government in fact, as it is in law, a government of the people.

I shall greatly rely upon the wisdom and patriotism of Congress and of those who may share with me the responsibilities and duties of administration, and, above all, upon our efforts to promote the welfare of this great people and their Government I reverently invoke the support and blessings of Almighty God.

MARCH 4, 1881.

SPECIAL MESSAGES.

EXECUTIVE MANSION,
Washington, April 6, 1881.

To the Senate of the United States:

I transmit herewith, in response to the resolution of the Senate of the 18th ultimo, a report of the Secretary of State, with accompanying papers, in relation to the capitulations of the Ottoman Empire.

JAMES A. GARFIELD.

EXECUTIVE MANSION,
Washington, May 20, 1881.

To the Senate of the United States:

I transmit herewith a report of the Secretary of State, with accompanying papers, submitted in response to the Senate resolution of the 12th ultimo, touching the case of Michael P. Boyton.*

JAMES A. GARFIELD.

* Arrested and imprisoned by authorities of Great Britain.

To the Senate of the United States.

I transmit herewith a report of the Secretary of State, with accompanying papers, submitted in response to the Senate Resolution of the 12th ultimo touching the case of Michael P. Boyton.—

James A. Garfield.

Executive Mansion
Washington, May 20, 1881.

A NOTE TO THE SENATE BY PRESIDENT GARFIELD.

EXECUTIVE ORDER.

EXECUTIVE MANSION,
Washington, May 28, 1881.

DEAR SIR:* I am directed by the President to inform you that the several Departments of the Government will be closed on Monday, the 30th instant, to enable the employees to participate in the decoration of the graves of the soldiers who fell during the rebellion.

Very respectfully,
J. STANLEY BROWN, *Private Secretary.*

DEATH OF PRESIDENT GARFIELD.

ANNOUNCEMENT OF THE ASSASSINATION TO REPRESENTATIVES OF THE UNITED STATES ABROAD.

[From the Washington Post, July 3, 1881.]

DEPARTMENT OF STATE,
Washington, July 2, 1881.

JAMES RUSSELL LOWELL,
Minister, etc., London:

The President of the United States was shot this morning by an assassin named Charles Guiteau. The weapon was a large-sized revolver. The President had just reached the Baltimore and Potomac station, at about 9.20, intending, with a portion of his Cabinet, to leave on the limited express for New York. I rode in the carriage with him from the Executive Mansion and was walking by his side when he was shot. The assassin was immediately arrested, and the President was conveyed to a private room in the station building and surgical aid at once summoned. He has now, at 10.20, been removed to the Executive Mansion. The surgeons, on consultation, regard his wounds as very serious, though not necessarily fatal. His vigorous health gives strong hopes of his recovery. He has not lost consciousness for a moment. Inform our ministers in Europe.

JAMES G. BLAINE, *Secretary of State.*

PUBLIC ANNOUNCEMENT OF DEATH BY THE PHYSICIANS.

[From the New York Herald, September 20, 1881.]

ELBERON, N. J., *September 19—11.30 p. m.*

The President died at thirty-five minutes past 10 p. m. After the bulletin was issued at half past 5 this evening the President continued in much the same condition as during the afternoon, the pulse varying from 102 to 106, with rather increased force and volume. After taking

*Addressed to the heads of the Executive Departments, etc.

nourishment he fell into a quiet sleep about thirty-five minutes before his death, and while asleep his pulse ran to 120 and was somewhat more feeble. At ten minutes after 10 o'clock he awoke, complaining of severe pain over the region of the heart, and almost immediately became unconscious, and ceased to breathe at twenty-five minutes to 11.

D. W. BLISS.
FRANK H. HAMILTON.
D. HAYES AGNEW.

ANNOUNCEMENT TO THE VICE-PRESIDENT.

[From the New-York Times, September 20, 1881.]

[LONG BRANCH, N. J., *September 19, 1881.*]

Hon. CHESTER A. ARTHUR,
No. 123 Lexington Avenue, New York:

It becomes our painful duty to inform you of the death of President Garfield and to advise you to take the oath of office as President of the United States without delay. If it concur with your judgment, we will be very glad if you will come here on the earliest train to-morrow morning.

WILLIAM WINDOM,
Secretary of the Treasury.
WILLIAM H. HUNT,
Secretary of the Navy.
THOMAS L. JAMES,
Postmaster-General.
WAYNE MacVEAGH
Attorney-General
S. J. KIRKWOOD,
Secretary of the Interior.

[The Secretaries of State and of War were absent from Long Branch.]

REPLY OF THE VICE-PRESIDENT.

[From the Evening Star, Washington, September 20, 1881.]

NEW YORK, *September 20, 1881.**

I have your message announcing the death of President Garfield. Permit me to renew through you the expression of sorrow and sympathy which I have already telegraphed to Attorney-General MacVeagh. In accordance with your suggestion, I have taken the oath of office as President before the Hon. John R. Brady, justice of the supreme court of the State of New York. I will soon advise you further in regard to the other suggestion in your telegram.

C. A. ARTHUR.

* Addressed to the Cabinet.

ANNOUNCEMENT TO REPRESENTATIVES OF THE UNITED STATES ABROAD.

[From the Sun, New York, September 21, 1881.]

[LONG BRANCH, N. J., *September 20, 1881.*]

LOWELL, *Minister, London:*

James A. Garfield, President of the United States, died at Elberon, N. J., last night at ten minutes before 11 o'clock. For nearly eighty days he suffered great pain, and during the entire period exhibited extraordinary patience, fortitude, and Christian resignation. The sorrow throughout the country is deep and universal. Fifty millions of people stand as mourners by his bier. Today, at his residence in the city of New York, Chester A. Arthur, Vice-President, took the oath of office as President, to which he succeeds by virtue of the Constitution. President Arthur has entered upon the discharge of his duties. You will formally communicate these facts to the British Government and transmit this dispatch by telegraph to the American ministers on the Continent for like communication to the Governments to which they are respectively accredited.

BLAINE, *Secretary.*

ANNOUNCEMENT TO REPRESENTATIVES OF FOREIGN GOVERNMENTS IN THE UNITED STATES.

[From official records, Department of State.]

DEPARTMENT OF STATE,
Washington, September 20, 1881.

SIR: It is my sad duty to announce to you that the illness of the President of the United States, which you have followed with an anxiety similar of our own and a sympathy which you have repeatedly testified to this Department during the sorrowful period that has passed since he was shot by an assassin on the 2d of July, terminated last evening, when he expired at thirty-five minutes past 10 o'clock.

As soon as the order and details of the funeral ceremonies are arranged you will be duly informed thereof.

ROBERT R. HITT,
Acting Secretary.

ANNOUNCEMENT TO THE ARMY.

[From official records, War Department.]

GENERAL ORDERS, NO. 71.

HEADQUARTERS OF THE ARMY,
ADJUTANT-GENERAL'S OFFICE,
Washington, September 20, 1881.

I. The following order of the Secretary of War announces to the Army the death of James A. Garfield, President of the United States :

WAR DEPARTMENT, *September 20, 1881.*

With profound sorrow the Secretary of War announces to the Army that James A. Garfield, President of the United States, died at Elberon,

N. J., at twenty-five minutes before 11 in the evening of September 19, 1881.

The great grief which is felt by the nation at the untimely death of the President will be especially felt by the Army, in whose service he bore so distinguished a part during the War of the Rebellion. In him the Army has lost a beloved Commander in Chief, friend, and former comrade.

Proper honors will be paid to the memory of the late Chief Magistrate of the nation at headquarters of each military department and division and at each military station.

The General of the Army will give the necessary instructions for carrying this order into effect.

ROBT. T. LINCOLN, Secretary of War.

II. On the day after the receipt of this order at the headquarters of military commands in the field, and at each military station, and at the Military Academy at West Point, the troops and cadets will be paraded at 10 o'clock a. m. and the order read to them, after which all labor for the day will cease.

At dawn of day thirteen guns will be fired at each military post, and afterwards at intervals of thirty minutes between the rising and setting sun a single gun, and at the close of the day a national salute of thirty-eight guns.

The national flag will be displayed at half-staff at the headquarters of the several military divisions and departments and at all military stations until the remains of the late Chief Magistrate are consigned to their final resting place at Cleveland, Ohio, at 2 p. m. on the 26th instant.

The officers of the Army of the United States will wear the badge of mourning on the left arm and on their swords and the colors of the regiments will be draped in mourning for the period of six months.

III. The following officers of the Army will, with a like number of officers of the Navy selected for the purpose, compose the guard of honor and accompany the remains of their late Commander in Chief from the national capital to Cleveland, Ohio, and continue with them until they are consigned to their final resting place: The General of the Army, Major-General Winfield S. Hancock, Quartermaster-General M. C. Meigs, Adjutant-General R. C. Drum, Inspector-General D. B. Sacket.

By command of General Sherman:

R. C. DRUM, Adjutant-General.

[From official records, War Department.]

GENERAL ORDERS, No. 72.

HEADQUARTERS OF THE ARMY,
ADJUTANT-GENERAL'S OFFICE,
Washington, September 20, 1881.

The following order has been received from the War Department:

The Secretary of War announces to the Army that upon the death of James A. Garfield, President of the United States, Chester A. Arthur,

Vice-President, on the 20th day of September, 1881, at his residence in the city of New York, took the oath of office as President of the United States, to which office he succeeded by virtue of the Constitution. President Arthur has entered upon the discharge of his official duties.

ROBT. T. LINCOLN,
Secretary of War.

By command of General Sherman:

R. C. DRUM, *Adjutant-General.*

ANNOUNCEMENT TO THE NAVY.

[From official records, Navy Department.]

GENERAL ORDER.

NAVY DEPARTMENT,
Washington, September 20, 1881.

The officers and men of the Navy and of the Marine Corps of the United States are hereby notified that President Garfield died at Long Branch on the 19th instant at 10 o'clock and 40 minutes p. m. Under the Constitution and laws of the Government Chester A. Arthur, then Vice-President, duly took the oath as President of the United States, and has entered upon the duties of that office. As President and Commander in Chief of the Navy of the United States he will be obeyed and respected by all persons connected with this Department. It is becoming that at a time when the heart of the nation is heavy with grief a proper expression should be given to the respect and affection so sincerely and universally entertained for the memory of the wise, patriotic, and noble Chief Magistrate who has departed this life under circumstances so distressing. To this end the officers of the Navy will see to it that all honors and ceremonies befitting the occasion are observed by their respective commands in accordance with the regulations of the service.

The offices of the Department will remain closed for all business during the time the remains of the President shall lie in state at the Capitol.

WILLIAM H. HUNT,
Secretary of the Navy.

[From official records, Navy Department.]

SPECIAL ORDER.

NAVY DEPARTMENT,
Washington, September 23, 1881.

Struck down by the hand of a cowardly assassin, in the day of his vigor and usefulness, on the eve of departure from the capital in search of much-needed rest from the toils and cares of office, our Chief Magistrate, President, and Commander in Chief, James A. Garfield, after bearing with heroic fortitude untold suffering, succumbed to the dread summons and yielded up his life at Elberon, N. J., on the evening of the 19th instant. The nation mourns its loss. The funeral services will take place at Cleveland, Ohio, on Monday, the 26th instant. It is eminently fit and proper that special honors should be paid to the memory of the late President on that day, and the Department therefore directs that at all naval stations and on board all vessels in commission the flags shall be at half-mast from sunrise to sunset and a gun fired every half hour during that period. The period of mourning by half-masted colors will cease at sunset. On foreign stations this order will be carried out on the day after its receipt. The navy-yards will be closed and all work suspended during the day. Officers of the Navy and Marine Corps will, as a further mark of respect, wear crape on the left arm and sword hilt for six months from the 20th instant.

ED. T. NICHOLS,
Acting Secretary of the Navy.

ACTION OF SENATORS AND OF REPRESENTATIVES ELECT IN WASHINGTON.

The members of the Senate and members elect of the House of Representatives in Washington held meetings on September 22 and selected the following gentlemen to accompany the remains of the late President to Cleveland, Ohio:

Senators Henry B. Anthony, of Rhode Island; John Sherman, of Ohio; Thomas F. Bayard, of Delaware; John J. Ingalls, of Kansas; James L. Pugh, of Alabama; Henry W. Blair, of New Hampshire; Johnson N. Camden, of West Virginia, and John T. Morgan, of Alabama.

Representatives elect John Randolph Tucker, of Virginia; John A. Kasson, of Iowa; Samuel J. Randall, of Pennsylvania; Frank Hiscock, of New York; Benjamin Wilson, of West Virginia; John R. Thomas, of Illinois; Amos Townsend, of Ohio, and Charles M. Shelley, of Alabama.

ORDERS OF THE HEADS OF THE EXECUTIVE DEPARTMENTS.

[From the National Republican, Washington, September 21, 1881.]

LONG BRANCH, *September 20.**

It has been agreed here by all the heads of Departments that the Departments shall remain closed from this time until the conclusion of President Garfield's funeral ceremonies in Washington, and it is understood that you will notify the acting heads of all Departments of this arrangement. * * *

ROBERT T. LINCOLN,
Secretary of War.

* Sent to the chief clerk of the War Department.

THE SHOOTING OF GARFIELD BY GUITEAU

THE SHOOTING OF PRESIDENT GARFIELD

On July 2, 1881, Garfield, accompanied by his Secretary of State, entered the Pennsylvania Railroad station in Washington, planning to make a visit to Williams College, his alma mater. They had barely crossed the threshold when Charles J. Guiteau fired two bullets into the President's back. On September 19th, after a heroic struggle, the martyr died.

Guiteau declared he "removed the President as a political necessity, because on his death party dissensions would expire, and the Government would be saved from falling into the hands of the ex-rebels and their northern allies."

On June 30, 1882, after full and fair trial, during which his sanity was proven, Guiteau was executed in Washington, D. C. He had been preacher, editor, reformer and politician, and was a disappointed office-seeker. The event furthered the cause of civil-service reform.

[From official records, Treasury Department.]

ORDER.

TREASURY DEPARTMENT,
OFFICE OF THE SECRETARY,
Washington, D. C., September 20, 1881.

It is ordered, as a mark of respect to the memory of President Garfield, that the Treasury Department be closed during this day.

H. F. FRENCH,
Acting Secretary.

[From official records, Treasury Department.]

NOTICE.

TREASURY DEPARTMENT,
OFFICE OF THE SECRETARY,
Washington, D. C., September 21, 1881.

As a token of respect to the memory of the late President, James A. Garfield, the Treasury Department will be closed to public business to-day at 12 o'clock noon, and remain closed Thursday and Friday, the 22d and 23d instant.

H. F. FRENCH,
Acting Secretary.

[From official records, Treasury Department.]

ORDER.

TREASURY DEPARTMENT,
OFFICE OF THE SECRETARY,
Washington, D. C., September 24, 1881.

In accordance with the proclamation of the President* appointing Monday, the 26th day of September, as a day of humiliation and mourning, being the day of the burial of the late President, James A. Garfield, it is ordered that this Department be closed during that day.

H. F. FRENCH,
Acting Secretary.

[From official records, Post-Office Department.]

POST-OFFICE DEPARTMENT,
Washington, D. C., September 20, 1881.

Ordered, That, owing to the death of President James A. Garfield, this Department be closed for all public business until after the funeral party shall have left Washington for Ohio.

RICHD. A. ELMER,
Acting Postmaster-General.

*See p. 4621.

[From official records, Post-Office Department.]

POST-OFFICE DEPARTMENT,
Washington, D. C., September 24, 1881.

Ordered, That, in conformity with the action of other executive branches of the Government, this Department be closed on Monday next, the 26th instant, and that the day be fittingly observed by all persons connected therewith as the occasion of the consignment to their final resting place of the remains of the late beloved and honored Chief Magistrate of the United States, James A. Garfield.

RICHD. A. ELMER, *Acting Postmaster-General.*

[From official records, Interior Department.]

ORDER.

DEPARTMENT OF THE INTERIOR,
Washington, September 20, 1881.

As a token of respect to the memory of the late President, James A. Garfield, the Department of the Interior and the several bureaus and offices thereof will be closed to public business until Saturday, the 24th instant.

A. BELL, *Acting Secretary.*

[From official records, Interior Department.]

ORDER.

DEPARTMENT OF THE INTERIOR,
Washington, September 24, 1881.

In pursuance of the proclamation of the President of the United States* appointing Monday, the 26th instant, as a day of humiliation and mourning for the death of the late President, this Department and the several bureaus and offices thereof will be closed to business on that day.

A. BELL, *Acting Secretary.*

FUNERAL ANNOUNCEMENT TO THE PUBLIC.

[From the New-York Times, September 21, 1881.]

[ELBERON, N. J., *September 20, 1881.*]

The remains of the late President of the United States will be removed to Washington by special train on Wednesday, September 21, leaving Elberon at 10 a. m. and reaching Washington at 4 p. m. Detachments from the United States Army and from the marines of the Navy will be in attendance on arrival at Washington to perform escort duty. The remains will lie in state in the Rotunda of the Capitol on Thursday and

*See p. 4621.

Friday, and will be guarded by deputations from the Executive Departments and by officers of the Senate and House of Representatives.

Religious ceremonies will be observed in the Rotunda at 3 o'clock on Friday afternoon. At 5 o'clock the remains will be transferred to the funeral car and be removed to Cleveland, Ohio, *via* the Pennsylvania Railroad, arriving there Saturday at 2 p. m. In Cleveland the remains will lie in state until Monday at 2 p. m., and be then interred in Lakeview Cemetery. No ceremonies are expected in the cities and towns along the route of the funeral train beyond the tolling of bells. Detailed arrangements for final sepulture are committed to the municipal authorities of Cleveland, under the direction of the executive of the State of Ohio.

JAMES G. BLAINE,
Secretary of State.

OFFICIAL ARRANGEMENTS FOR THE FUNERAL.

[From official records, War Department.]

ORDER OF ARRANGEMENT FOR THE FUNERAL AT WASHINGTON CITY OF JAMES A. GARFIELD, LATE PRESIDENT OF THE UNITED STATES.

The remains of the late President will lie in state in the Rotunda of the Capitol until 3 o'clock p. m. on Friday, the 23d instant, when they will be borne to the depot of the Baltimore and Potomac Railroad and thence conveyed to their final resting place at Cleveland, Ohio.

ORDER OF PROCESSION.

FUNERAL ESCORT.
(Under command of Brevet Major-General R. B. Ayres.)
Battalion of District of Columbia Volunteers.
Battalion of marines.
Battalion of foot artillery.
Battery of light artillery.

CIVIC PROCESSION.
(Under command of Chief Marshal Colonel Robert Boyd.)
Clergymen in attendance.
Physicians who attended the late President.
Guard of honor.   Hearse.   Guard of honor.
Bearers.   Bearers.
(The officers of the Army, Navy, and Marine Corps in the city, and not on duty with the troops forming the escort, in full dress, will form, right in front, on either side of the hearse—the Army on the right and the Navy and Marine Corps on the left—and compose the guard of honor.)
Family of the late President.
Relatives of the late President.
Ex-Presidents of the United States
The President.
The Cabinet ministers.
The Diplomatic Corps.

The Chief Justice and Associate Justices of the Supreme Court of the United States.
The Senators of the United States.
Members of the United States House of Representatives.
Governors of States and Territories and Commissioners of the District of Columbia.
The judges of the Court of Claims, the judiciary of the District of Columbia, and judges of the United States courts.
The Assistant Secretaries of State, Treasury, and Interior Departments.
The Assistant Postmasters-General.
The Solicitor-General and the Assistant Attorneys-General.
Organized societies.
Citizens and strangers.

The troops designated to form the escort will assemble on the east side of the Capitol and form line fronting the eastern portico of the Capitol precisely at 2 o'clock p. m. on Friday, the 23d instant.

The procession will move on the conclusion of the religious services at the Capitol (appointed to commence at 3 o'clock), when minute guns will be fired at the navy-yard by the vessels of war which may be in port, at Fort Myer, and by the battery of artillery stationed near the Capitol for that purpose. At the same hour the bells of the several churches, fire-engine houses, and the schoolhouses will be tolled.

The civic procession will form in accordance with directions to be given by the chief marshal.

The officers of the Army and Navy selected to compose the guard of honor and accompany the remains to their final resting place will assemble at 4 p. m. at the Baltimore and Potomac Railroad depot, where they will receive the body of the late President and deposit it in the car prepared for the purpose.

ROBERT T. LINCOLN,
Secretary of War.

WILLIAM H. HUNT,
Secretary of the Navy.

J. DENT,
President Board of Commissioners District of Columbia.

[From the Washington Post, September 23, 1881.]

CIRCULAR.

HEADQUARTERS OF THE ARMY,
ADJUTANT-GENERAL'S OFFICE,
Washington, September 22, 1881.

The officers of the Army in this city not otherwise ordered for special duty on this occasion will assemble in full uniform at 3 p. m. on the 23d instant on the east front of the Capitol and form line, right in front, on the right of the hearse, to act as a guard of honor to the remains of the late President of the United States from the Capitol to the Baltimore and Potomac Railroad depot.

By command of General Sherman:

R. C. DRUM, *Adjutant-General*

GENERAL ORDERS, NO. 22.

ADJUTANT-GENERAL'S OFFICE,
DISTRICT OF COLUMBIA MILITIA,
September 21, 1881.

Pursuant to orders from the honorable Secretary of War, the troops comprising the militia of the District of Columbia will assemble in full-dress uniform at 3 p. m. on the 21st instant on Sixth street NW., the right resting on Pennsylvania avenue, the left extended south, to take part in and form a portion of the escort to the remains of the late President, and will also hold themselves in readiness to participate at the funeral ceremonies on Friday, the 23d instant. The formation will be as follows on both occasions:

Washington Light Infantry Corps, Captain W. G. Moore.
Union Veteran Corps, Captain S. E. Thomason.
National Rifles, Captain J. O. P. Burnside.
Washington Light Guards, Lieutenant F. S. Hodgson.
Butler Zouaves, Captain C. B. Fisher.
Capital City Guards, Captain W. S. Kelly.
Washington Cadets, Captain C. A. Dolan.

The officers of Light Battery A, District of Columbia Artillery, will report to adjutant-general District of Columbia Militia for duty as aids on both occasions.

A. WEBSTER,
Adjutant-General District of Columbia Militia.

GENERAL ORDER NO. 23.

ADJUTANT-GENERAL'S OFFICE,
DISTRICT OF COLUMBIA MILITIA,
September 22, 1881.

Pursuant to orders from the honorable Secretary of War, and in compliance with general order No. 22 from these headquarters, all the organizations comprising the militia of the District of Columbia will assemble in full-dress uniform at 2 p. m. on the 23d instant on the ground east of the Capitol, right resting on B street N., the left extending south, facing west. The formation will be the same as designated in general order No. 22. Upon their arrival on the ground designated each commanding officer will report in person to the commanding officer of the District Volunteers.

By order of the Commissioners of the District of Columbia:

AMOS WEBSTER,
Adjutant-General District of Columbia Militia, Commanding.

[From the Washington Post, September 23, 1881.]

SPECIAL ORDER.

NAVY DEPARTMENT,
Washington, September 22, 1881.

The officers of the Navy and Marine Corps on duty and resident in Washington will assemble to-morrow, the 23d instant, at 3 o'clock p. m., at the east front of the Capitol, in full dress, to accompany the remains of the late President Garfield to the Baltimore and Potomac Railroad depot.

Commander H. L. Howison, United States Navy, is hereby appointed adjutant, and will direct the formation of the officers of the Navy and Marine Corps.
ED. T. NICHOLS,
Acting Secretary of the Navy.

[From the Medical Record, New York, 1881, vol. 20, p. 364.]

OFFICIAL BULLETIN OF THE AUTOPSY ON THE BODY OF PRESIDENT GARFIELD.

The following official bulletin was prepared by the surgeons who have been in attendance upon the late President:

By previous arrangement a *post-mortem* examination of the body of President Garfield was made this afternoon in the presence and with the assistance of Drs. Hamilton, Agnew, Bliss, Barnes, Woodward, Reyburn, Andrew H. Smith, of Elberon, and Acting Assistant Surgeon D. S. Lamb, of the Army Medical Museum, of Washington. The operation was performed by Dr. Lamb. It was found that the ball, after fracturing the right eleventh rib, had passed through the spinal column in front of the spinal cord, fracturing the body of the first lumbar vertebra, driving a number of small fragments of bone into the adjacent soft parts, and lodging below the pancreas, about 2½ inches to the left of the spine and behind the peritoneum, where it had become completely encysted.

The immediate cause of death was secondary hemorrhage from one of the mesenteric arteries adjoining the track of the ball, the blood rupturing the peritoneum and nearly a pint escaping into the abdominal cavity. This hemorrhage is believed to have been the cause of the severe pain in the lower part of the chest complained of just before death. An abscess cavity 6 inches by 4 in dimensions was found in the vicinity of the gall bladder, between the liver and the transverse colon, which were strongly adherent. It did not involve the substance of the liver, and no communication was found between it and the wound.

A long suppurating channel extended from the external wound, between the loin muscles and the right kidney, almost to the right groin. This channel, now known to be due to the burrowing of pus from the wound, was supposed during life to have been the track of the ball.

On an examination of the organs of the chest evidences of severe bronchitis were found on both sides, with broncho-pneumonia of the lower portions of the right lung, and, though to a much less extent, of the left. The lungs contained no abscesses and the heart no clots. The liver was enlarged and fatty, but not from abscesses. Nor were any found in any other organ except the left kidney, which contained near its surface a small abscess about one-third of an inch in diameter.

In reviewing the history of the case in connection with the autopsy it is quite evident that the different suppurating surfaces, and especially the fractured, spongy tissue of the vertebræ, furnish a sufficient explanation of the septic condition which existed.

D. W. BLISS.

J. K. BARNES.

J. J. WOODWARD.

ROBERT REYBURN.

FRANK H. HAMILTON.

D. HAYES AGNEW.

ANDREW H. SMITH.

D. S. LAMB.

[SEPTEMBER 20, 1881.]

FORMAL OATH OF OFFICE ADMINISTERED TO PRESIDENT ARTHUR.

President Chester A. Arthur took the formal oath of office as President of the United States in the room of the Vice-President, in the Capitol, Thursday, September 22, 1881, at 12.10 o'clock p. m. Chief Justice Morrison R. Waite administered the oath prescribed by the Constitution in the presence of the members of the Cabinet, the Justices of the Supreme Court, ex-Presidents Grant and Hayes, General W. T. Sherman, and a number of Senators and Representatives.

[For Inaugural Address of President Arthur see pp. 33–34.]

ACTION OF CONGRESS.

President Arthur, in his first annual message to the first session of the Forty-seventh Congress, thus announced the death of his predecessor:

An appalling calamity has befallen the American people since their chosen representatives last met in the halls where you are now assembled. We might else recall with unalloyed content the rare prosperity with which throughout the year the nation has been blessed. Its harvests have been plenteous; its varied industries have thriven; the health of its people has been preserved; it has maintained with foreign governments the undisturbed relations of amity and peace. For these manifestations of His favor we owe to Him who holds our destiny in His hands the tribute of our grateful devotion.

To that mysterious exercise of His will which has taken from us the loved and illustrious citizen who was but lately the head of the nation we bow in sorrow and submission.

The memory of his exalted character, of his noble achievements, and of his patriotic life will be treasured forever as a sacred possession of the whole people.

The announcement of his death drew from foreign governments and peoples tributes of sympathy and sorrow which history will record as signal tokens of the kinship of nations and the federation of mankind.

The Senate on December 6, 1881, adopted the following resolution:

Resolved, That a committee of six Senators be appointed on the part of the Senate to join such committee as may be appointed on the part of the House to consider and report by what token of respect and affection it may be proper for the Congress of the United States to express the deep sensibility of the nation to the event of the decease of the late President, James A. Garfield, and that so much of the message of the President as relates to that melancholy event be referred to said committee.

The committee on the part of the Senate, having been subsequently increased to eight, comprised the following-named gentlemen:

John Sherman, of Ohio; George H. Pendleton, of Ohio; Henry L. Dawes, of Massachusetts; Elbridge G. Lapham, of New York; Thomas F. Bayard, of Delaware; John T. Morgan, of Alabama; Omar D. Conger, of Michigan, and Joseph E. Brown, of Georgia.

The House of Representatives on December 6, 1881, passed the following resolution:

Resolved, That a committee of one member from each State represented in this House be appointed on the part of the House to join such committee as may be appointed on the part of the Senate to consider and report by what token of respect and affection it may be proper for the Congress of the United States to express the deep sensibility of the nation to the event of the decease of their late President, James Abram Garfield, and that so much of the message of the President as refers to that melancholy event be referred to said committee.

The committee on the part of the House of Representatives comprised the following-named gentlemen:

William McKinley, jr., of Ohio; Romualdo Pacheco, of California; James B. Belford, of Colorado; John T. Wait, of Connecticut; William H. Forney, of Alabama; Poindexter Dunn, of Arkansas; Edward L. Martin, of Delaware; Robert H. M. Davidson, of Florida; Alexander H. Stephens, of Georgia; Joseph G. Cannon, of Illinois; Godlove S. Orth, of Indiana; John A. Kasson, of Iowa; John A. Anderson, of Kansas; John G. Carlisle, of Kentucky; Randall L. Gibson, of Louisiana; Nelson Dingley, jr., of Maine; Robert M. McLane, of Maryland; Benjamin W. Harris, of Massachusetts; Roswell G. Horr, of Michigan; Mark H. Dunnell, of Minnesota; Charles E. Hooker, of Mississippi; Nicholas Ford, of Missouri; Edward K. Valentine, of Nebraska; George W. Cassidy, of Nevada; Joshua G. Hall, of New Hampshire; John Hill, of New Jersey; Samuel S. Cox, of New York; Robert B. Vance, of North Carolina; Melvin C. George, of Oregon; Charles O'Neill, of Pennsylvania; Jonathan

Chace, of Rhode Island; D. Wyatt Aiken, of South Carolina; Augustus H. Pettibone, of Tennessee; Roger Q. Mills, of Texas; Charles H. Joyce, of Vermont; J. Randolph Tucker, of Virginia; Benjamin Wilson, of West Virginia, and Charles G. Williams, of Wisconsin.

The following concurrent resolutions were adopted by both Houses of Congress on December 21, 1881:

Whereas the melancholy event of the violent and tragic death of James Abram Garfield, late President of the United States, having occurred during the recess of Congress, and the two Houses sharing in the general grief and desiring to manifest their sensibility upon the occasion of the public bereavement: Therefore

Be it resolved by the House of Representatives (the Senate concurring), That the two Houses of Congress will assemble in the Hall of the House of Representatives on a day and hour to be fixed and announced by the joint committee, and that in the presence of the two Houses there assembled an address upon the life and character of James Abram Garfield, late President of the United States, be pronounced by Hon. James G. Blaine, and that the President of the Senate *pro tempore* and the Speaker of the House of Representatives be requested to invite the President and ex-Presidents of the United States, the heads of the several Departments, the judges of the Supreme Court, the representatives of the foreign governments near this Government, the governors of the several States, the General of the Army, and the Admiral of the Navy, and such officers of the Army and Navy as have received the thanks of Congress who may then be at the seat of Government to be present on the occasion.

And be it further resolved, That the President of the United States be requested to transmit a copy of these resolutions to Mrs. Lucretia R. Garfield, and to assure her of the profound sympathy of the two Houses of Congress for her deep personal affliction and of their sincere condolence for the late national bereavement.

February 1, 1882, both Houses of Congress adopted the following resolution:

Resolved by the House of Representatives (the Senate concurring), That Monday, the 27th day of February, 1882, be set apart for the memorial services upon the late President, James A. Garfield.

[For proclamation of President Arthur appointing, in consequence of the death of James Abram Garfield, late President of the United States, a day of humiliation and mourning, see p.4621.]

Chester A. Arthur

September 19, 1881, to March 4, 1885

SEE VOLUME XI.

Volume eleven is not only an index to the other volumes, not only a key that unlocks the treasures of the entire publication, but it is in itself an alphabetically arranged brief history or story of the great controlling events constituting the History of the United States.

Under its proper alphabetical classification the story is told of every great subject referred to by any of the Presidents in their official Messages, and at the end of each story the official utterances of the Presidents themselves are cited upon the subject, so that you may readily turn to the page in the body of the work itself for this original information.

Next to the possession of knowledge is the ability to turn at will to where knowledge is to be found.

HOME ON LEXINGTON AVENUE, NEW YORK CITY, OF
CHESTER A. ARTHUR
With official portrait engraved from copy of original in steel

HOME ON LEXINGTON AVENUE, NEW YORK CITY, OF

CHESTER A. ARTHUR

With official portrait engraved from copy of original in steel

Chester A. Arthur

CHESTER ALAN ARTHUR was born in Fairfield, Franklin County, Vt., October 5, 1830. He was the eldest son of Rev. William Arthur and Malvina Stone. His father, a Baptist minister, was born in Ireland and emigrated to the United States. Chester prepared for college at Union Village in Greenwich and at Schenectady, N. Y., and in 1845 entered the sophomore class of Union College. While in his sophomore year taught school for a term at Schaghticoke, Rensselaer County, and a second term at the same place during his last year in college. Joined the Psi Upsilon Society, and was one of six in a class of one hundred who were elected members of the Phi Beta Kappa Society, the condition of admission being high scholarship. After his graduation in 1848, at the age of 18, attended a law school at Ballston Spa, N. Y.; returned to Lansingburg, N. Y., where his father then resided, and continued his legal studies. Was principal of an academy at North Pownal, Bennington County, Vt., in 1851. In 1853 entered the law office of Erastus D. Culver in New York City as a student; was admitted to the bar during the same year, and at once became a member of the firm of Culver, Parker & Arthur. Having formed from early associations sentiments of hostility to slavery, as a law student and after his admission to the bar became an earnest advocate for the slaves. Became a Henry Clay Whig, and cast his first vote in 1852 for Winfield Scott for President. Participated in the first Republican State convention, at Saratoga, and took an active part in the Frémont campaign of 1856. October 29, 1859, married Ellen Lewis Herndon, of Fredericksburg, Va. January 1, 1861, was appointed on Governor Edwin D. Morgan's staff as engineer in chief, with the rank of brigadier-general. Had previously taken part in the organization of the State militia, and had been judge-advocate of the Second Brigade. When the civil war began, in April, 1861, he became acting quartermaster-general, and as such began in New York City the work of preparing and forwarding the State's quota of troops. Was called to Albany in December for consultation concerning the defenses of New York Harbor. Summoned a board of engineers on December 24, of which he became a member, and on January 18, 1862, submitted an elaborate report on the condition of the national forts both on the seacoast and on the inland border of the State. Was appointed inspector-general February 10, 1862, with the rank of brigadier-general, and in May inspected the New York troops at Fredericksburg and on the Chickahominy. In June, 1862, Governor Morgan ordered his return from the Army of the Potomac, and he acted as secretary of the meeting of the governors of the loyal States which was held June 28 in New York City. At Governor Morgan's request, General Arthur resumed his former work, resigned as inspector-general, and on July 10 was appointed quartermaster-general. Retired from the office December 31, 1862, when Horatio Seymour succeeded Governor Morgan. Between 1862 and 1872 was engaged in continuous and active law practice—in partnership with Henry G. Gardner from 1862 till 1867, then for five years alone, and on January 1, 1872, formed the firm of Arthur, Phelps & Knevals. Was for a short time counsel for the department of assessments and taxes, but resigned the place. Continued during all this period to take an active part in politics. Was chairman in 1868 of the Central Grant Club of New York, and became chairman of the executive committee of the Republican State committee in 1879. Was appointed collector of the port of New York by President Grant on November 20, 1871; was reappointed on December 17, 1875, and confirmed by the Senate on the same day without reference to a committee, a courtesy never before extended to an appointee who had not been a Senator; retained the office until July 11, 1878, when he was suspended by President Hayes. On retiring from the office of collector resumed the practice of law with the firm of Arthur, Phelps, Knevals & Ransom. Advocated in 1880 the nomination of General Grant to succeed President Hayes. Was a delegate at large to the Chicago convention, which met June 2, 1880. After the nomination of General Garfield for the Presidency a general desire arose in the convention to nominate for Vice-President some advocate of General Grant and a resident of New York State. The New York delegation indicated their preference for General Arthur, and he was nominated on the first ballot. Was elected Vice-President November 2, 1880; took the oath of office March 4, 1881, and presided over the extraordinary session of the Senate that then began, which was very exciting. That body being equally divided, he was frequently called upon to exercise the right of casting the controlling vote. President Garfield was shot July 2, 1881, and died September 19. His Cabinet announced his death to the Vice-President, then in New York, and at their suggestion he took the oath as President on the 20th at his residence in New York City before Judge John R. Brady, of the New York supreme court. On the 22d the oath was formally administered again in the Vice-President's room in the Capitol at Washington by Chief Justice Waite. President Arthur's name was presented to the Republican Presidential convention which met at Chicago June 3, 1884. On the first ballot he received 278 votes against 540 for all others, 276 on the second, 274 on the third, and 207 on the fourth, which resulted in the nomination of James G. Blaine. In the canvass which ensued Mr. Arthur rendered all possible assistance to the Republican cause and candidates. Died suddenly at his residence in New York City November 18, 1886, and was buried in Rural Cemetery at Albany.

INAUGURAL ADDRESS.

For the fourth time in the history of the Republic its Chief Magistrate has been removed by death. All hearts are filled with grief and horror at the hideous crime which has darkened our land, and the memory of the murdered President, his protracted sufferings, his unyielding fortitude, the example and achievements of his life, and the pathos of his death will forever illumine the pages of our history.

For the fourth time the officer elected by the people and ordained by the Constitution to fill a vacancy so created is called to assume the Executive chair. The wisdom of our fathers, foreseeing even the most dire possibilities, made sure that the Government should never be imperiled because of the uncertainty of human life. Men may die, but the fabrics of our free institutions remain unshaken. No higher or more assuring proof could exist of the strength and permanence of popular government than the fact that though the chosen of the people be struck down his constitutional successor is peacefully installed without shock or strain except the sorrow which mourns the bereavement. All the noble aspirations of my lamented predecessor which found expression in his life, the measures devised and suggested during his brief Administration to correct abuses, to enforce economy, to advance prosperity, and to promote the general welfare, to insure domestic security and maintain friendly and honorable relations with the nations of the earth, will be garnered in the hearts of the people; and it will be my earnest endeavor to profit, and to see that the nation shall profit, by his example and experience.

Prosperity blesses our country. Our fiscal policy is fixed by law, is well grounded and generally approved. No threatening issue mars our foreign intercourse, and the wisdom, integrity, and thrift of our people may be trusted to continue undisturbed the present assured career of peace, tranquillity, and welfare. The gloom and anxiety which have enshrouded the country must make repose especially welcome now. No demand for speedy legislation has been heard; no adequate occasion is apparent for an unusual session of Congress. The Constitution defines the functions and powers of the executive as clearly as those of either of the other two departments of the Government, and he must answer for the just exercise of the discretion it permits and the performance of the duties it imposes. Summoned to these high duties and responsibilities and profoundly conscious of their magnitude and gravity, I assume the trust imposed by the Constitution, relying for aid on divine guidance and the virtue, patriotism, and intelligence of the American people.

SEPTEMBER 22, 1881.

PROCLAMATIONS.

BY THE PRESIDENT OF THE UNITED STATES OF AMERICA.

A PROCLAMATION.

Whereas in His inscrutable wisdom it has pleased God to remove from us the illustrious head of the nation, James A. Garfield, late President of the United States; and

Whereas it is fitting that the deep grief which fills all hearts should manifest itself with one accord toward the throne of infinite grace, and that we should bow before the Almighty and seek from Him that consolation in our affliction and that sanctification of our loss which He is able and willing to vouchsafe:

Now, therefore, in obedience to sacred duty and in accordance with the desire of the people, I, Chester A. Arthur, President of the United States of America, do hereby appoint Monday next, the 26th day of September—on which day the remains of our honored and beloved dead will be consigned to their last resting place on earth—to be observed throughout the United States as a day of humiliation and mourning; and I earnestly recommend all the people to assemble on that day in their respective places of divine worship, there to render alike their tribute of sorrowful submission to the will of Almighty God and of reverence and love for the memory and character of our late Chief Magistrate.

In witness whereof I have hereunto set my hand and caused the seal of the United States to be affixed.

[SEAL.]   Done at the city of Washington, the 22d day of September, A. D. 1881, and of the Independence of the United States of America the one hundred and sixth.

CHESTER A. ARTHUR.

By the President:

JAMES G. BLAINE, *Secretary of State.*

BY THE PRESIDENT OF THE UNITED STATES OF AMERICA.

A PROCLAMATION.

Whereas objects of interest to the United States require that the Senate should be convened at an early day to receive and act upon such communications as may be made to it on the part of the Executive:

Now, therefore, I, Chester A. Arthur, President of the United States,

GARFIELD'S BODY LYING IN STATE IN CAPITOL

THE DEATH OF GARFIELD

" Great in life, he was surpassingly great in death. For no cause, in the very frenzy of wantonness, by the red hand of murder, he was thrust from the full tide of this world's interest, from its hopes, its aspirations, its victories, into the visible presence of death—and he did not quail. Not alone for one short moment in which, stunned and dazed, he could give up life, hardly aware of its relinquishment, but through days of deadly languor, through weeks of agony, that was not less agony because silently borne, with clear sight and calm courage, he looked into his open grave. . . . And his soul was not shaken. His countrymen were thrilled with instant, profound and universal sympathy. . . . He became the center of a nation's love, enshrined in the prayers of a world. But all the love and all the sympathy could not share with him his suffering. He trod the winepress alone. . . . As the end drew near his early craving for the sea returned. . . . Gently, silently, the love of a great people bore the pale sufferer to the longed-for healing of the sea. With wan, fevered face tenderly lifted to the cooling breeze, he looked out wistfully upon the ocean's changing wonders . . . on the serene and shining pathway of the stars. Let us think that his dying eyes read a mystic meaning which only the rapt and parting soul may know. Let us believe that in the silence of the receding world he heard the great waves breaking on a farther shore, and felt already upon his wasted brow the breath of the eternal morning."

From the Funeral Oration by James G. Blaine.

have considered it to be my duty to issue this my proclamation, declaring that an extraordinary occasion requires the Senate of the United States to convene for the transaction of business at the Capitol, in the city of Washington, on Monday, the 10th day of October next, at 12 o'clock noon on that day, of which all who shall at that time be entitled to act as members of that body are hereby required to take notice.

Given under my hand and the seal of the United States, at Washington, the 23d day of September, A. D. 1881, and of the Independence of the United States the one hundred and sixth.

[SEAL.]

CHESTER A. ARTHUR.

By the President:
JAMES G. BLAINE,
Secretary of State

SPECIAL MESSAGES.

WASHINGTON, *October 12, 1881.*

To the Senate of the United States:

I transmit herewith to the Senate a communication from the Secretary of State, submitting the text, in the English and French languages, of the proceedings of the International Sanitary Conference, provided for by the joint resolution of the Senate and House of Representatives of the United States of America, held at Washington in the early part of 1881.

CHESTER A. ARTHUR.

To the Senate.

I transmit herewith the report of the Secretary of State in answer to the resolution of the Senate of October 14, with accompanying document.*

CHESTER A. ARTHUR.

OCTOBER 24, 1881.

WASHINGTON, *October 26, 1881.*

To the Senate of the United States:

I transmit to the Senate, for its consideration with a view to ratification, a convention between the United States and His Majesty the King of Roumania, defining the rights, immunities, and privileges of consular officers, signed on the 17th day of June, 1881.

CHESTER A. ARTHUR.

* Letter of instruction to United States ministers in Europe relative to protecting the rights and interests of the United States in the projected interoceanic canal at Panama.

PROCLAMATION.

BY THE PRESIDENT OF THE UNITED STATES OF AMERICA

A PROCLAMATION.

It has long been the pious custom of our people, with the closing of the year, to look back upon the blessings brought to them in the changing course of the seasons and to return solemn thanks to the all-giving source from whom they flow. And although at this period, when the falling leaf admonishes us that the time of our sacred duty is at hand, our nation still lies in the shadow of a great bereavement, and the mourning which has filled our hearts still finds its sorrowful expression toward the God before whom we but lately bowed in grief and supplication, yet the countless benefits which have showered upon us during the past twelvemonth call for our fervent gratitude and make it fitting that we should rejoice with thankfulness that the Lord in His infinite mercy has most signally favored our country and our people. Peace without and prosperity within have been vouchsafed to us, no pestilence has visited our shores, the abundant privileges of freedom which our fathers left us in their wisdom are still our increasing heritage; and if in parts of our vast domain sore affliction has visited our brethren in their forest homes, yet even this calamity has been tempered and in a manner sanctified by the generous compassion for the sufferers which has been called forth throughout our land. For all these things it is meet that the voice of the nation should go up to God in devout homage.

Wherefore I, Chester A. Arthur, President of the United States, do recommend that all the people observe Thursday, the 24th day of November instant, as a day of national thanksgiving and prayer, by ceasing, so far as may be, from their secular labors and meeting in their several places of worship, there to join in ascribing honor and praise to Almighty God, whose goodness has been so manifest in our history and in our lives, and offering earnest prayers that His bounties may continue to us and to our children.

In witness whereof I have hereunto set my hand and caused the seal of the United States to be affixed.

[SEAL.] Done at the city of Washington, this 4th day of November, A. D. 1881, and of the Independence of the United States the one hundred and sixth.

CHESTER A. ARTHUR.

By the President:
JAMES G. BLAINE,
Secretary of State

EXECUTIVE ORDER.*

YORKTOWN, VA., *October 19, 1881.*

In recognition of the friendly relations so long and so happily subsisting between Great Britain and the United States, in the trust and confidence of peace and good will between the two countries for all the centuries to come, and especially as a mark of the profound respect entertained by the American people for the illustrious sovereign and gracious lady who sits upon the British throne

It is hereby ordered, That at the close of the ceremonies commemorative of the valor and success of our forefathers in their patriotic struggle for independence the British flag shall be saluted by the forces of the Army and Navy of the United States now at Yorktown.

The Secretary of War and the Secretary of the Navy will give orders accordingly.

CHESTER A. ARTHUR.

By the President:
JAMES G. BLAINE,
Secretary of State.

FIRST ANNUAL MESSAGE.

WASHINGTON, *December 6, 1881.*

To the Senate and House of Representatives of the United States:

An appalling calamity has befallen the American people since their chosen representatives last met in the halls where you are now assembled. We might else recall with unalloyed content the rare prosperity with which throughout the year the nation has been blessed. Its harvests have been plenteous; its varied industries have thriven; the health of its people has been preserved; it has maintained with foreign governments the undisturbed relations of amity and peace. For these manifestations of His favor we owe to Him who holds our destiny in His hands the tribute of our grateful devotion.

To that mysterious exercise of His will which has taken from us the loved and illustrious citizen who was but lately the head of the nation we bow in sorrow and submission.

The memory of his exalted character, of his noble achievements, and of his patriotic life will be treasured forever as a sacred possession of the whole people.

*Read by the Secretary of State before the people assembled to celebrate the Yorktown Centennial.

The announcement of his death drew from foreign governments and peoples tributes of sympathy and sorrow which history will record as signal tokens of the kinship of nations and the federation of mankind.

The feeling of good will between our own Government and that of Great Britain was never more marked than at present. In recognition of this pleasing fact I directed, on the occasion of the late centennial celebration at Yorktown, that a salute be given to the British flag.

Save for the correspondence to which I shall refer hereafter in relation to the proposed canal across the Isthmus of Panama, little has occurred worthy of mention in the diplomatic relations of the two countries.

Early in the year the Fortune Bay claims were satisfactorily settled by the British Government paying in full the sum of £15,000, most of which has been already distributed. As the terms of the settlement included compensation for injuries suffered by our fishermen at Aspee Bay, there has been retained from the gross award a sum which is deemed adequate for those claims.

The participation of Americans in the exhibitions at Melbourne and Sydney will be approvingly mentioned in the reports of the two exhibitions, soon to be presented to Congress. They will disclose the readiness of our countrymen to make successful competition in distant fields of enterprise.

Negotiations for an international copyright convention are in hopeful progress.

The surrender of Sitting Bull and his forces upon the Canadian frontier has allayed apprehension, although bodies of British Indians still cross the border in quest of sustenance. Upon this subject a correspondence has been opened which promises an adequate understanding. Our troops have orders to avoid meanwhile all collisions with alien Indians.

The presence at the Yorktown celebration of representatives of the French Republic and descendants of Lafayette and of his gallant compatriots who were our allies in the Revolution has served to strengthen the spirit of good will which has always existed between the two nations.

You will be furnished with the proceedings of the Bimetallic Conference held during the summer at the city of Paris. No accord was reached, but a valuable interchange of views was had, and the conference will next year be renewed.

At the Electrical Exhibition and Congress, also held at Paris, this country was creditably represented by eminent specialists, who, in the absence of an appropriation, generously lent their efficient aid at the instance of the State Department. While our exhibitors in this almost distinctively American field of achievement have won several valuable awards, I recommend that Congress provide for the repayment of the personal expenses incurred in the public interest by the honorary commissioners and delegates.

No new questions respecting the status of our naturalized citizens in

Germany have arisen during the year, and the causes of complaint, especially in Alsace and Lorraine, have practically ceased through the liberal action of the Imperial Government in accepting our often-expressed views on the subject. The application of the treaty of 1868 to the lately acquired Rhenish provinces has received very earnest attention, and a definite and lasting agreement on this point is confidently expected. The participation of the descendants of Baron von Steuben in the Yorktown festivities, and their subsequent reception by their American kinsmen, strikingly evinced the ties of good will which unite the German people and our own.

Our intercourse with Spain has been friendly. An agreement concluded in February last fixes a term for the labors of the Spanish and American Claims Commission. The Spanish Government has been requested to pay the late awards of that Commission, and will, it is believed, accede to the request as promptly and courteously as on former occasions.

By recent legislation onerous fines have been imposed upon American shipping in Spanish and colonial ports for slight irregularities in manifests. One case of hardship is specially worthy of attention. The bark *Masonic*, bound for Japan, entered Manila in distress, and is there sought to be confiscated under Spanish revenue laws for an alleged shortage in her transshipped cargo. Though efforts for her relief have thus far proved unavailing, it is expected that the whole matter will be adjusted in a friendly spirit.

The Senate resolutions of condolence on the assassination of the Czar Alexander II were appropriately communicated to the Russian Government, which in turn has expressed its sympathy in our late national bereavement. It is desirable that our cordial relations with Russia should be strengthened by proper engagements assuring to peaceable Americans who visit the Empire the consideration which is due to them as citizens of a friendly state. This is especially needful with respect to American Israelites, whose classification with the native Hebrews has evoked energetic remonstrances from this Government.

A supplementary consular agreement with Italy has been sanctioned and proclaimed, which puts at rest conflicts of jurisdiction in the case of crimes on shipboard.

Several important international conferences have been held in Italy during the year. At the Geographical Congress of Venice, the Beneficence Congress of Milan, and the Hygienic Congress of Turin this country was represented by delegates from branches of the public service or by private citizens duly accredited in an honorary capacity. It is hoped that Congress will give such prominence to the results of their participation as they may seem to deserve.

The abolition of all discriminating duties against such colonial productions of the Dutch East Indies as are imported hither from Holland has been already considered by Congress. I trust that at the present session the matter may be favorably concluded.

The insecurity of life and property in many parts of Turkey has given rise to correspondence with the Porte looking particularly to the better protection of American missionaries in the Empire. The condemned murderer of the eminent missionary Dr. Justin W. Parsons has not yet been executed, although this Government has repeatedly demanded that exemplary justice be done.

The Swiss Government has again solicited the good offices of our diplomatic and consular agents for the protection of its citizens in countries where it is not itself represented. This request has, within proper limits, been granted.

Our agents in Switzerland have been instructed to protest against the conduct of the authorities of certain communes in permitting the emigration to this country of criminals and other objectionable persons. Several such persons, through the cooperation of the commissioners of emigration at New York, have been sent back by the steamers which brought them. A continuance of this course may prove a more effectual remedy than diplomatic remonstrance.

Treaties of commerce and navigation and for the regulation of consular privileges have been concluded with Roumania and Servia since their admission into the family of European States.

As is natural with contiguous states having like institutions and like aims of advancement and development, the friendship of the United States and Mexico has been constantly maintained. This Government has lost no occasion of encouraging the Mexican Government to a beneficial realization of the mutual advantages which will result from more intimate commercial intercourse and from the opening of the rich interior of Mexico to railway enterprise. I deem it important that means be provided to restrain the lawlessness unfortunately so common on the frontier and to suppress the forays of the reservation Indians on either side of the Rio Grande.

The neighboring States of Central America have preserved internal peace, and their outward relations toward us have been those of intimate friendship. There are encouraging signs of their growing disposition to subordinate their local interests to those which are common to them by reason of their geographical relations.

The boundary dispute between Guatemala and Mexico has afforded this Government an opportunity to exercise its good offices for preventing a rupture between those States and for procuring a peaceable solution of the question. I cherish strong hope that in view of our relations of amity with both countries our friendly counsels may prevail.

A special envoy of Guatemala has brought to me the condolences of his Government and people on the death of President Garfield.

The Costa Rican Government lately framed an engagement with

Colombia for settling by arbitration the boundary question between those countries, providing that the post of arbitrator should be offered successively to the King of the Belgians, the King of Spain, and the President of the Argentine Confederation. The King of the Belgians has declined to act, but I am not as yet advised of the action of the King of Spain. As we have certain interests in the disputed territory which are protected by our treaty engagements with one of the parties, it is important that the arbitration should not without our consent affect our rights, and this Government has accordingly thought proper to make its views known to the parties to the agreement, as well as to intimate them to the Belgian and Spanish Governments.

The questions growing out of the proposed interoceanic waterway across the Isthmus of Panama are of grave national importance. This Government has not been unmindful of the solemn obligations imposed upon it by its compact of 1846 with Colombia, as the independent and sovereign mistress of the territory crossed by the canal, and has sought to render them effective by fresh engagements with the Colombian Republic looking to their practical execution. The negotiations to this end, after they had reached what appeared to be a mutually satisfactory solution here, were met in Colombia by a disavowal of the powers which its envoy had assumed and by a proposal for renewed negotiation on a modified basis.

Meanwhile this Government learned that Colombia had proposed to the European powers to join in a guaranty of the neutrality of the proposed Panama canal—a guaranty which would be in direct contravention of our obligation as the sole guarantor of the integrity of Colombian territory and of the neutrality of the canal itself. My lamented predecessor felt it his duty to place before the European powers the reasons which make the prior guaranty of the United States indispensable, and for which the interjection of any foreign guaranty might be regarded as a superfluous and unfriendly act.

Foreseeing the probable reliance of the British Government on the provisions of the Clayton-Bulwer treaty of 1850 as affording room for a share in the guaranties which the United States covenanted with Colombia four years before, I have not hesitated to supplement the action of my predecessor by proposing to Her Majesty's Government the modification of that instrument and the abrogation of such clauses thereof as do not comport with the obligations of the United States toward Colombia or with the vital needs of the two friendly parties to the compact.

This Government sees with great concern the continuance of the hostile relations between Chile, Bolivia, and Peru. An early peace between these Republics is much to be desired, not only that they may themselves be spared further misery and bloodshed, but because their continued antagonism threatens consequences which are, in my judgment, dangerous to the interests of republican government on this continent and cal-culated to destroy the best elements of our free and peaceful civilization.

As in the present excited condition of popular feeling in these countries there has been serious misapprehension of the position of the United States, and as separate diplomatic intercourse with each through independent ministers is sometimes subject, owing to the want of prompt reciprocal communication, to temporary misunderstanding, I have deemed it judicious at the present time to send a special envoy accredited to all and each of them, and furnished with general instructions which will, I trust, enable him to bring these powers into friendly relations.

The Government of Venezuela maintains its attitude of warm friendship and continues with great regularity its payment of the monthly quota of the diplomatic debt. Without suggesting the direction in which Congress should act, I ask its attention to the pending questions affecting the distribution of the sums thus far received.

The relations between Venezuela and France growing out of the same debt have been for some time past in an unsatisfactory state, and this Government, as the neighbor and one of the largest creditors of Venezuela, has interposed its influence with the French Government with the view of producing a friendly and honorable adjustment.

I regret that the commercial interests between the United States and Brazil, from which great advantages were hoped a year ago, have suffered from the withdrawal of the American lines of communication between the Brazilian ports and our own.

Through the efforts of our minister resident at Buenos Ayres and the United States minister at Santiago, a treaty has been concluded between the Argentine Republic and Chile, disposing of the long-pending Patagonian boundary question. It is a matter of congratulation that our Government has been afforded the opportunity of successfully exerting its good influence for the prevention of disagreements between these Republics of the American continent.

I am glad to inform you that the treaties lately negotiated with China have been duly ratified on both sides and the exchange made at Peking. Legislation is necessary to carry their provisions into effect. The prompt and friendly spirit with which the Chinese Government, at the request of the United States, conceded the modification of existing treaties should secure careful regard for the interests and susceptibilities of that Government in the enactment of any laws relating to Chinese immigration.

Those clauses of the treaties which forbid the participation of citizens or vessels of the United States in the opium trade will doubtless receive your approval. They will attest the sincere interest which our people and Government feel in the commendable efforts of the Chinese Government to put a stop to this demoralizing and destructive traffic.

In relation both to China and Japan some changes are desirable in our present system of consular jurisdiction. I hope at some future time to lay before you a scheme for its improvement in the entire East.

The intimacy between our own country and Japan, the most advanced of the Eastern nations, continues to be cordial. I am advised that the Emperor contemplates the establishment of full constitutional government, and that he has already summoned a parliamentary congress for the purpose of effecting the change. Such a remarkable step toward complete assimilation with the Western system can not fail to bring Japan into closer and more beneficial relationship with ourselves as the chief Pacific power.

A question has arisen in relation to the exercise in that country of the judicial functions conferred upon our ministers and consuls. The indictment, trial, and conviction in the consular court at Yokohama of John Ross, a merchant seaman on board an American vessel, have made it necessary for the Government to institute a careful examination into the nature and methods of this jurisdiction.

It appeared that Ross was regularly shipped under the flag of the United States, but was by birth a British subject. My predecessor felt it his duty to maintain the position that during his service as a regularly shipped seaman on board an American merchant vessel Ross was subject to the laws of that service and to the jurisdiction of the United States consular authorities.

I renew the recommendation which has been heretofore urged by the Executive upon the attention of Congress, that after the deduction of such amount as may be found due to American citizens the balance of the indemnity funds heretofore obtained from China and Japan, and which are now in the hands of the State Department, be returned to the Governments of those countries.

The King of Hawaii, in the course of his homeward return after a journey around the world, has lately visited this country. While our relations with that Kingdom are friendly, this Government has viewed with concern the efforts to seek replenishment of the diminishing population of the islands from outward sources, to a degree which may impair the native sovereignty and independence, in which the United States was among the first to testify a lively interest.

Relations of unimpaired amity have been maintained throughout the year with the respective Governments of Austria-Hungary, Belgium, Denmark, Hayti, Paraguay and Uruguay, Portugal, and Sweden and Norway. This may also be said of Greece and Ecuador, although our relations with those States have for some years been severed by the withdrawal of appropriations for diplomatic representatives at Athens and Quito. It seems expedient to restore those missions, even on a reduced scale, and I decidedly recommend such a course with respect to Ecuador, which is likely within the near future to play an important part among the nations of the Southern Pacific.

At its last extra session the Senate called for the text of the Geneva convention for the relief of the wounded in war. I trust that this action foreshadows such interest in the subject as will result in the adhesion of the United States to that humane and commendable engagement.

I invite your attention to the propriety of adopting the new code of international rules for the prevention of collisions on the high seas and of conforming the domestic legislation of the United States thereto, so that no confusion may arise from the application of conflicting rules in the case of vessels of different nationalities meeting in tidal waters. These international rules differ but slightly from our own. They have been adopted by the Navy Department for the governance of the war ships of the United States on the high seas and in foreign waters, and, through the action of the State Department in disseminating the rules and in acquainting shipmasters with the option of conforming to them without the jurisdictional waters of the United States, they are now very generally known and obeyed.

The State Department still continues to publish to the country the trade and manufacturing reports received from its officers abroad. The success of this course warrants its continuance and such appropriation as may be required to meet the rapidly increasing demand for these publications. With special reference to the Atlanta Cotton Exposition, the October number of the reports was devoted to a valuable collection of papers on the cotton-goods trade of the world.

The International Sanitary Conference for which, in 1879, Congress made provision assembled in this city early in January last, and its sessions were prolonged until March. Although it reached no specific conclusions affecting the future action of the participant powers, the interchange of views proved to be most valuable. The full protocols of the sessions have been already presented to the Senate.

As pertinent to this general subject, I call your attention to the operations of the National Board of Health. Established by act of Congress approved March 3, 1879, its sphere of duty was enlarged by the act of June 2 in the same year. By the last-named act the board was required to institute such measures as might be deemed necessary for preventing the introduction of contagious or infectious diseases from foreign countries into the United States or from one State into another.

The execution of the rules and regulations prepared by the board and approved by my predecessor has done much to arrest the progress of epidemic disease, and has thus rendered substantial service to the nation.

The International Sanitary Conference, to which I have referred, adopted a form of a bill of health to be used by all vessels seeking to enter the ports of the countries whose representatives participated in its deliberations. This form has since been prescribed by the National Board of Health and incorporated with its rules and regulations, which have been approved by me in pursuance of law.

The health of the people is of supreme importance. All measures looking to their protection against the spread of contagious diseases and to the increase of our sanitary knowledge for such purposes deserve attention of Congress.

The report of the Secretary of the Treasury presents in detail a highly satisfactory exhibit of the state of the finances and the condition of the various branches of the public service administered by that Department.

The ordinary revenues from all sources for the fiscal year ending June 30, 1881, were:

From customs	$198,159,676.02
From internal revenue	135,264,385.51
From sales of public lands	2,201,863.17
From tax on circulation and deposits of national banks	8,116,115.72
From repayment of interest by Pacific Railway companies	810,833.80
From sinking fund for Pacific Railway companies	805,180.54
From customs fees, fines, penalties, etc	1,225,514.86
From fees—consular, letters patent, and lands	2,244,983.98
From proceeds of sales of Government property	262,174.00
From profits on coinage	3,468,485.61
From revenues of the District of Columbia	2,016,199.23
From miscellaneous sources	6,206,880.13
Total ordinary receipts	360,782,292.57

The ordinary expenditures for the same period were:

For civil expenses	$17,941,177.19
For foreign intercourse	1,093,954.92
For Indians	6,514,161.09
For pensions	50,059,279.62
For the military establishment, including river and harbor improvements and arsenals	40,466,460.55
For the naval establishment, including vessels, machinery, and improvements at navy-yards	15,686,671.66
For miscellaneous expenditures, including public buildings, light-houses, and collecting the revenue	41,837,280.57
For expenditures on account of the District of Columbia	3,543,912.03
For interest on the public debt	82,508,741.18
For premium on bonds purchased	1,061,248.78
Total ordinary expenditures	260,712,887.59

Leaving a surplus revenue of $100,069,404.98, which was applied as follows:

To the redemption of—	
Bonds for the sinking fund	$74,371,200.00
Fractional currency for the sinking fund	109,001.05
Loan of February, 1861	7,418,000.00
Ten-forties of 1864	2,016,150.00
Five-twenties of 1862	18,300.00
Five-twenties of 1864	3,400.00
Five-twenties of 1865	37,300.00
Consols of 1865	143,150.00
Consols of 1867	959,150.00
Consols of 1868	337,400.00
Texan indemnity stock	1,000.00
Old demand, compound-interest, and other notes	18,330.00
And to the increase of cash in the Treasury	14,637,023.93
	100,069,404.98

The requirements of the sinking fund for the year amounted to $90,786,064.02, which sum included a balance of $49,817,128.78, not provided for during the previous fiscal year. The sum of $74,480,201.05 was applied to this fund, which left a deficit of $16,305,873.47. The increase of the revenues for 1881 over those of the previous year was $29,352,901.10. It is estimated that the receipts during the present fiscal year will reach $400,000,000 and the expenditures $270,000,000, leaving a surplus of $130,000,000 applicable to the sinking fund and the redemption of the public debt.

I approve the recommendation of the Secretary of the Treasury that provision be made for the early retirement of silver certificates and that the act requiring their issue be repealed. They were issued in pursuance of the policy of the Government to maintain silver at or near the gold standard, and were accordingly made receivable for all customs, taxes, and public dues. About sixty-six millions of them are now outstanding. They form an unnecessary addition to the paper currency, a sufficient amount of which may be readily supplied by the national banks.

In accordance with the act of February 28, 1878, the Treasury Department has monthly caused at least two millions in value of silver bullion to be coined into standard silver dollars. One hundred and two millions of these dollars have been already coined, while only about thirty-four millions are in circulation.

For the reasons which he specifies, I concur in the Secretary's recommendation that the provision for coinage of a fixed amount each month be repealed, and that hereafter only so much be coined as shall be necessary to supply the demand.

The Secretary advises that the issue of gold certificates should not for the present be resumed, and suggests that the national banks may properly be forbidden by law to retire their currency except upon reasonable notice of their intention so to do. Such legislation would seem to be justified by the recent action of certain banks on the occasion referred to in the Secretary's report.

Of the fifteen millions of fractional currency still outstanding, only about eighty thousand has been redeemed the past year. The suggestion that this amount may properly be dropped from future statements of the public debt seems worthy of approval.

So also does the suggestion of the Secretary as to the advisability of relieving the calendar of the United States courts in the southern district of New York by the transfer to another tribunal of the numerous suits there pending against collectors.

The revenue from customs for the past fiscal year was $198,159,676.02, an increase of $11,637,611.42 over that of the year preceding. One hundred and thirty-eight million ninety-eight thousand five hundred and sixty-two dollars and thirty-nine cents of this amount was collected at the port of New York, leaving $50,251,113.63 as the amount collected at all the other ports of the country. Of this sum $47,977,137.63 was collected on sugar, melado, and molasses; $27,285,624.78 on wool and its manufactures; $21,462,534.34 on iron and steel and manufactures thereof; $19,038,665.81 on manufactures of silk; $10,825,115.21 on manufactures of cotton, and $6,469,643.04 on wines and spirits, making a total revenue from these sources of $133,058,720.81.

The expenses of collection for the past year were $6,419,345.20, an increase over the preceding year of $387,410.04. Notwithstanding the increase in the revenue from customs over the preceding year, the gross value of the imports, including free goods, decreased over $25,000,000. The most marked decrease was in the value of unmanufactured wool, $14,023,682, and in that of scrap and pig iron, $12,810,671. The value of imported sugar, on the other hand, showed an increase of $7,457,474; of steel rails, $4,345,521; of barley, $2,154,204, and of steel in bars, ingots, etc., $1,620,046.

Contrasted with the imports during the last fiscal year, the exports were as follows:

Domestic merchandise	$883,925,947
Foreign merchandise	18,451,399
Total	902,377,346
Imports of merchandise	642,664,628
Excess of exports over imports of merchandise	259,712,718
Aggregate of exports and imports	1,545,041,974

Compared with the previous year, there was an increase of $66,738,688 in the value of exports of merchandise and a decrease of $25,290,118 in the value of imports. The annual average of the excess of imports of merchandise over exports thereof for ten years previous to June 30, 1873, was $104,706,922, but for the last six years there has been an excess of exports over imports of merchandise amounting to $1,180,668,105, an annual average of $196,778,017. The specie value of the exports of domestic merchandise was $376,616,473 in 1870 and $883,925,947 in 1881, an increase of $507,309,474, or 135 per cent. The value of imports was $435,958,408 in 1870 and $642,664,628 in 1881, an increase of $206,706,220, or 47 per cent.

During each year from 1862 to 1879, inclusive, the exports of specie exceeded the imports. The largest excess of such exports over imports was reached during the year 1864, when it amounted to $92,280,929. But during the year ended June 30, 1880, the imports of coin and bullion exceeded the exports by $75,891,391, and during the last fiscal year the excess of imports over exports was $91,168,650.

In the last annual report of the Secretary of the Treasury the attention of Congress was called to the fact that $469,651,050 in 5 per cent bonds and $203,573,750 in 6 per cent bonds would become redeemable during the year, and Congress was asked to authorize the refunding of these bonds at a lower rate of interest. The bill for such refunding having failed to become a law, the Secretary of the Treasury in April last notified the holders of the $195,690,400 6 per cent bonds then out-standing that the bonds would be paid at par on the 1st day of July following, or that they might be "continued" at the pleasure of the Government, to bear interest at the rate of 3½ per cent per annum.

Under this notice $178,055,150 of the 6 per cent bonds were continued at the lower rate and $17,635,250 were redeemed.

In the month of May a like notice was given respecting the redemption or continuance of the $439,841,350 of 5 per cent bonds then outstanding, and of these $401,504,900 were continued at 3½ per cent per annum and $38,336,450 redeemed.

The 6 per cent bonds of the loan of February 8, 1861, and of the Oregon war debt, amounting together to $14,125,800, having matured during the year, the Secretary of the Treasury gave notice of his intention to redeem the same, and such as have been presented have been paid from the surplus revenues. There have also been redeemed at par $16,179,100 of the 3½ per cent "continued" bonds, making a total of bonds redeemed or which have ceased to bear interest during the year of $123,969,650.

The reduction of the annual interest on the public debt through these transactions is as follows:

By reduction of interest to 3½ per cent	$10,473,952.25
By redemption of bonds	6,352,340.00
Total	16,826,292.25

The 3½ per cent bonds, being payable at the pleasure of the Government, are available for the investment of surplus revenues without the payment of premiums.

Unless these bonds can be funded at a much lower rate of interest than they now bear, I agree with the Secretary of the Treasury that no legislation respecting them is desirable.

It is a matter for congratulation that the business of the country has been so prosperous during the past year as to yield by taxation a large surplus of income to the Government. If the revenue laws remain unchanged, this surplus must year by year increase, on account of the reduction of the public debt and its burden of interest and because of the rapid increase of our population. In 1860, just prior to the institution of our internal-revenue system, our population but slightly exceeded 30,000,000; by the census of 1880 it is now found to exceed 50,000,000. It is estimated that even if the annual receipts and expenditures should continue as at present the entire debt could be paid in ten years.

In view, however, of the heavy load of taxation which our people have already borne, we may well consider whether it is not the part of wisdom to reduce the revenues, even if we delay a little the payment of the debt.

It seems to me that the time has arrived when the people may justly demand some relief from their present onerous burden, and that by due economy in the various branches of the public service this may readily be afforded.

I therefore concur with the Secretary in recommending the abolition of all internal-revenue taxes except those upon tobacco in its various forms and upon distilled spirits and fermented liquors, and except also the special tax upon the manufacturers of and dealers in such articles. The retention of the latter tax is desirable as affording the officers of the Government a proper supervision of these articles for the prevention of fraud. I agree with the Secretary of the Treasury that the law imposing a stamp tax upon matches, proprietary articles, playing cards, checks, and drafts may with propriety be repealed, and the law also by which banks and bankers are assessed upon their capital and deposits. There seems to be a general sentiment in favor of this course.

In the present condition of our revenues the tax upon deposits is especially unjust. It was never imposed in this country until it was demanded by the necessities of war, and was never exacted, I believe, in any other country even in its greatest exigencies. Banks are required to secure their circulation by pledging with the Treasurer of the United States bonds of the General Government. The interest upon these bonds, which at the time when the tax was imposed was 6 per cent, is now in most instances 3½ per cent. Besides, the entire circulation was originally limited by law and no increase was allowable. When the existing banks had practically a monopoly of the business, there was force in the suggestion that for the franchise to the favored grantees the Government might very properly exact a tax on circulation; but for years the system has been free and the amount of circulation regulated by the public demand.

The retention of this tax has been suggested as a means of reimbursing the Government for the expense of printing and furnishing the circulating notes. If the tax should be repealed, it would certainly seem proper to require the national banks to pay the amount of such expense to the Comptroller of the Currency.

It is perhaps doubtful whether the immediate reduction of the rate of taxation upon liquors and tobacco is advisable, especially in view of the drain upon the Treasury which must attend the payment of arrears of pensions. A comparison, however, of the amount of taxes collected under the varying rates of taxation which have at different times prevailed suggests the intimation that some reduction may soon be made without material diminution of the revenue.

The tariff laws also need revision; but, that a due regard may be paid to the conflicting interests of our citizens, important changes should be made with caution. If a careful revision can not be made at this session, a commission such as was lately approved by the Senate and is now recommended by the Secretary of the Treasury would doubtless lighten the labors of Congress whenever this subject shall be brought to its consideration.

The accompanying report of the Secretary of War will make known to you the operations of that Department for the past year.

He suggests measures for promoting the efficiency of the Army without adding to the number of its officers, and recommends the legislation necessary to increase the number of enlisted men to 30,000, the maximum allowed by law.

This he deems necessary to maintain quietude on our ever-shifting frontier; to preserve peace and suppress disorder and marauding in new settlements; to protect settlers and their property against Indians, and Indians against the encroachments of intruders; and to enable peaceable immigrants to establish homes in the most remote parts of our country.

The Army is now necessarily scattered over such a vast extent of territory that whenever an outbreak occurs reenforcements must be hurried from many quarters, over great distances, and always at heavy cost for transportation of men, horses, wagons, and supplies.

I concur in the recommendations of the Secretary for increasing the Army to the strength of 30,000 enlisted men.

It appears by the Secretary's report that in the absence of disturbances on the frontier the troops have been actively employed in collecting the Indians hitherto hostile and locating them on their proper reservations; that Sitting Bull and his adherents are now prisoners at Fort Randall; that the Utes have been moved to their new reservation in Utah; that during the recent outbreak of the Apaches it was necessary to reenforce the garrisons in Arizona by troops withdrawn from New Mexico; and that some of the Apaches are now held prisoners for trial, while some have escaped, and the majority of the tribe are now on their reservation.

There is need of legislation to prevent intrusion upon the lands set apart for the Indians. A large military force, at great expense, is now required to patrol the boundary line between Kansas and the Indian Territory. The only punishment that can at present be inflicted is the forcible removal of the intruder and the imposition of a pecuniary fine, which in most cases it is impossible to collect. There should be a penalty by imprisonment in such cases.

The separate organization of the Signal Service is urged by the Secretary of War, and a full statement of the advantages of such permanent organization is presented in the report of the Chief Signal Officer. A detailed account of the useful work performed by the Signal Corps and the Weather Bureau is also given in that report.

I ask attention to the statements of the Secretary of War regarding the requisitions frequently made by the Indian Bureau upon the Subsistence Department of the Army for the casual support of bands and tribes of Indians whose appropriations are exhausted. The War Department should not be left, by reason of inadequate provision for the Indian Bureau, to contribute for the maintenance of Indians.

The report of the Chief of Engineers furnishes a detailed account of the operations for the improvement of rivers and harbors.

I commend to your attention the suggestions contained in this report in regard to the condition of our fortifications, especially our coast defenses, and recommend an increase of the strength of the Engineer Battalion, by which the efficiency of our torpedo system would be improved.

I also call your attention to the remarks upon the improvement of the South Pass of the Mississippi River, the proposed free bridge over the Potomac River at Georgetown, the importance of completing at an early day the north wing of the War Department building, and other recommendations of the Secretary of War which appear in his report.

The actual expenditures of that Department for the fiscal year ending June 30, 1881, were $42,122,201.39. The appropriations for the year 1882 were $44,889,725.42. The estimates for 1883 are $44,541,276.91.

The report of the Secretary of the Navy exhibits the condition of that branch of the service and presents valuable suggestions for its improvement. I call your especial attention also to the appended report of the Advisory Board which he convened to devise suitable measures for increasing the efficiency of the Navy, and particularly to report as to the character and number of vessels necessary to place it upon a footing commensurate with the necessities of the Government.

I can not too strongly urge upon you my conviction that every consideration of national safety, economy, and honor imperatively demands a thorough rehabilitation of our Navy.

With a full appreciation of the fact that compliance with the suggestions of the head of that Department and of the Advisory Board must involve a large expenditure of the public moneys, I earnestly recommend such appropriations as will accomplish an end which seems to me so desirable.

Nothing can be more inconsistent with true public economy than withholding the means necessary to accomplish the objects intrusted by the Constitution to the National Legislature. One of those objects, and one which is of paramount importance, is declared by our fundamental law to be the provision for the "common defense." Surely nothing is more essential to the defense of the United States and of all our people than the efficiency of our Navy.

We have for many years maintained with foreign governments the relations of honorable peace, and that such relations may be permanent is desired by every patriotic citizen of the Republic. But if we heed the teachings of history we shall not forget that in the life of every nation emergencies may arise when a resort to arms can alone save it from dishonor.

No danger from abroad now threatens this people, nor have we any cause to distrust the friendly professions of other governments. But for avoiding as well as for repelling dangers that may threaten us in the future we must be prepared to enforce any policy which we think wise to adopt.

We must be ready to defend our harbors against aggression; to protect, by the distribution of our ships of war over the highways of commerce, the varied interests of our foreign trade and the persons and property of our citizens abroad; to maintain everywhere the honor of our flag and the distinguished position which we may rightfully claim among the nations of the world.

The report of the Postmaster-General is a gratifying exhibit of the growth and efficiency of the postal service.

The receipts from postage and other ordinary sources during the past fiscal year were $36,489,816.58. The receipts from the money-order business were $295,581.39, making a total of $36,785,397.97. The expenditure for the fiscal year was $39,251,736.46. The deficit supplied out of the general Treasury was $2,481,129.35, or 6.3 per cent of the amount expended. The receipts were $3,469,918.63 in excess of those of the previous year, and $4,575,397.97 in excess of the estimate made two years ago, before the present period of business prosperity had fairly begun.

The whole number of letters mailed in this country in the last fiscal year exceeded 1,000,000,000.

The registry system is reported to be in excellent condition, having been remodeled during the past four years with good results. The amount of registration fees collected during the last fiscal year was $712,882.20, an increase over the fiscal year ending June 30, 1877, of $345,443.40.

The entire number of letters and packages registered during the year was 8,338,919, of which only 2,061 were lost or destroyed in transit.

The operations of the money-order system are multiplying yearly under the impulse of immigration, of the rapid development of the newer States and Territories, and the consequent demand for additional means of intercommunication and exchange.

During the past year 338 additional money-order offices have been established, making a total of 5,499 in operation at the date of this report.

During the year the domestic money orders aggregated in value $105,075,769.35.

A modification of the system is suggested, reducing the fees for money orders not exceeding $5 from 10 cents to 5 cents and making the maximum limit $100 in place of $50.

Legislation for the disposition of unclaimed money orders in the possession of the Post-Office Department is recommended, in view of the fact that their total value now exceeds $1,000,000.

The attention of Congress is again invited to the subject of establishing a system of savings depositories in connection with the Post-Office Department.

The statistics of mail transportation show that during the past year railroad routes have been increased in length 6,249 miles and in cost

$1,114,382, while steamboat routes have been decreased in length 2,182 miles and in cost $134,054. The so-called star routes have been decreased in length 3,949 miles and in cost $364,144.

Nearly all of the more expensive routes have been superseded by railroad service. The cost of the star service must therefore rapidly decrease in the Western States and Territories.

The Postmaster-General, however, calls attention to the constantly increasing cost of the railway mail service as a serious difficulty in the way of making the Department self-sustaining.

Our postal intercourse with foreign countries has kept pace with the growth of the domestic service. Within the past year several countries and colonies have declared their adhesion to the Postal Union. It now includes all those which have an organized postal service except Bolivia, Costa Rica, New Zealand, and the British colonies in Australia.

As has been already stated, great reductions have recently been made in the expense of the star-route service. The investigations of the Department of Justice and the Post-Office Department have resulted in the presentation of indictments against persons formerly connected with that service, accusing them of offenses against the United States. I have enjoined upon the officials who are charged with the conduct of the cases on the part of the Government, and upon the eminent counsel who before my accession to the Presidency were called to their assistance, the duty of prosecuting with the utmost vigor of the law all persons who may be found chargeable with frauds upon the postal service.

The Acting Attorney-General calls attention to the necessity of modifying the present system of the courts of the United States—a necessity due to the large increase of business, especially in the Supreme Court. Litigation in our Federal tribunals became greatly expanded after the close of the late war. So long as that expansion might be attributable to the abnormal condition in which the community found itself immediately after the return of peace, prudence required that no change be made in the constitution of our judicial tribunals. But it has now become apparent that an immense increase of litigation has directly resulted from the wonderful growth and development of the country. There is no ground for belief that the business of the United States courts will ever be less in volume than at present. Indeed, that it is likely to be much greater is generally recognized by the bench and bar.

In view of the fact that Congress has already given much consideration to this subject, I make no suggestion as to detail, but express the hope that your deliberations may result in such legislation as will give early relief to our overburdened courts.

The Acting Attorney-General also calls attention to the disturbance of the public tranquillity during the past year in the Territory of Arizona. A band of armed desperadoes known as "Cowboys," probably numbering from fifty to one hundred men, have been engaged for months in committing acts of lawlessness and brutality which the local authorities have been unable to repress. The depredations of these "Cowboys" have also extended into Mexico, which the marauders reach from the Arizona frontier. With every disposition to meet the exigencies of the case, I am embarrassed by lack of authority to deal with them effectually. The punishment of crimes committed within Arizona should ordinarily, of course, be left to the Territorial authorities; but it is worthy consideration whether acts which necessarily tend to embroil the United States with neighboring governments should not be declared crimes against the United States. Some of the incursions alluded to may perhaps be within the scope of the law (U. S. Revised Statutes, sec. 5286) forbidding "military expeditions or enterprises" against friendly states; but in view of the speedy assembling of your body I have preferred to await such legislation as in your wisdom the occasion may seem to demand.

It may perhaps be thought proper to provide that the setting on foot within our own territory of brigandage and armed marauding expeditions against friendly nations and their citizens shall be punishable as an offense against the United States.

I will add that in the event of a request from the Territorial government for protection by the United States against "domestic violence" this Government would be powerless to render assistance.

The act of 1795, chapter 36, passed at a time when Territorial governments received little attention from Congress, enforced this duty of the United States only as to the State governments. But the act of 1807, chapter 39, applied also to Territories. This law seems to have remained in force until the revision of the statutes, when the provision for the Territories was dropped. I am not advised whether this alteration was intentional or accidental; but as it seems to me that the Territories should be offered the protection which is accorded to the States by the Constitution, I suggest legislation to that end.

It seems to me, too, that whatever views may prevail as to the policy of recent legislation by which the Army has ceased to be a part of the *posse comitatus*, an exception might well be made for permitting the military to assist the civil Territorial authorities in enforcing the laws of the United States. This use of the Army would not seem to be within the alleged evil against which that legislation was aimed. From sparseness of population and other circumstances it is often quite impracticable to summon a civil posse in places where officers of justice require assistance and where a military force is within easy reach.

The report of the Secretary of the Interior, with accompanying documents, presents an elaborate account of the business of that Department. A summary of it would be too extended for this place. I ask your careful attention to the report itself.

Prominent among the matters which challenge the attention of Congress at its present session is the management of our Indian affairs.

While this question has been a cause of trouble and embarrassment from the infancy of the Government, it is but recently that any effort has been made for its solution at once serious, determined, consistent, and promising success.

It has been easier to resort to convenient makeshifts for tiding over temporary difficulties than to grapple with the great permanent problem, and accordingly the easier course has almost invariably been pursued.

It was natural, at a time when the national territory seemed almost illimitable and contained many millions of acres far outside the bounds of civilized settlements, that a policy should have been initiated which more than aught else has been the fruitful source of our Indian complications.

I refer, of course, to the policy of dealing with the various Indian tribes as separate nationalities, of relegating them by treaty stipulations to the occupancy of immense reservations in the West, and of encouraging them to live a savage life, undisturbed by any earnest and well-directed efforts to bring them under the influences of civilization.

The unsatisfactory results which have sprung from this policy are becoming apparent to all.

As the white settlements have crowded the borders of the reservations, the Indians, sometimes contentedly and sometimes against their will, have been transferred to other hunting grounds, from which they have again been dislodged whenever their new-found homes have been desired by the adventurous settlers.

These removals and the frontier collisions by which they have often been preceded have led to frequent and disastrous conflicts between the races.

It is profitless to discuss here which of them has been chiefly responsible for the disturbances whose recital occupies so large a space upon the pages of our history.

We have to deal with the appalling fact that though thousands of lives have been sacrificed and hundreds of millions of dollars expended in the attempt to solve the Indian problem, it has until within the past few years seemed scarcely nearer a solution than it was half a century ago. But the Government has of late been cautiously but steadily feeling its way to the adoption of a policy which has already produced gratifying results, and which, in my judgment, is likely, if Congress and the Executive accord in its support, to relieve us ere long from the difficulties which have hitherto beset us.

For the success of the efforts now making to introduce among the Indians the customs and pursuits of civilized life and gradually to absorb them into the mass of our citizens, sharing their rights and holden to their responsibilities, there is imperative need for legislative action.

My suggestions in that regard will be chiefly such as have been already called to the attention of Congress and have received to some extent its consideration.

First. I recommend the passage of an act making the laws of the various States and Territories applicable to the Indian reservations within their borders and extending the laws of the State of Arkansas to the portion of the Indian Territory not occupied by the Five Civilized Tribes.

The Indian should receive the protection of the law. He should be allowed to maintain in court his rights of person and property. He has repeatedly begged for this privilege. Its exercise would be very valuable to him in his progress toward civilization.

Second. Of even greater importance is a measure which has been frequently recommended by my predecessors in office, and in furtherance of which several bills have been from time to time introduced in both Houses of Congress. The enactment of a general law permitting the allotment in severalty, to such Indians, at least, as desire it, of a reasonable quantity of land secured to them by patent, and for their own protection made inalienable for twenty or twenty-five years, is demanded for their present welfare and their permanent advancement.

In return for such considerate action on the part of the Government, there is reason to believe that the Indians in large numbers would be persuaded to sever their tribal relations and to engage at once in agricultural pursuits. Many of them realize the fact that their hunting days are over and that it is now for their best interests to conform their manner of life to the new order of things. By no greater inducement than the assurance of permanent title to the soil can they be led to engage in the occupation of tilling it.

The well-attested reports of their increasing interest in husbandry justify the hope and belief that the enactment of such a statute as I recommend would be at once attended with gratifying results. A resort to the allotment system would have a direct and powerful influence in dissolving the tribal bond, which is so prominent a feature of savage life, and which tends so strongly to perpetuate it.

Third. I advise a liberal appropriation for the support of Indian schools, because of my confident belief that such a course is consistent with the wisest economy.

Even among the most uncultivated Indian tribes there is reported to be a general and urgent desire on the part of the chiefs and older members for the education of their children. It is unfortunate, in view of this fact, that during the past year the means which have been at the command of the Interior Department for the purpose of Indian instruction have proved to be utterly inadequate.

The success of the schools which are in operation at Hampton, Carlisle, and Forest Grove should not only encourage a more generous provision for the support of those institutions, but should prompt the establishment of others of a similar character.

They are doubtless much more potent for good than the day schools upon the reservation, as the pupils are altogether separated from the surroundings of savage life and brought into constant contact with civilization.

There are many other phases of this subject which are of great interest, but which can not be included within the becoming limits of this communication. They are discussed ably in the reports of the Secretary of the Interior and the Commissioner of Indian Affairs.

For many years the Executive, in his annual message to Congress, has urged the necessity of stringent legislation for the suppression of polygamy in the Territories, and especially in the Territory of Utah. The existing statute for the punishment of this odious crime, so revolting to the moral and religious sense of Christendom, has been persistently and contemptuously violated ever since its enactment. Indeed, in spite of commendable efforts on the part of the authorities who represent the United States in that Territory, the law has in very rare instances been enforced, and, for a cause to which reference will presently be made, is practically a dead letter.

The fact that adherents of the Mormon Church, which rests upon polygamy as its corner stone, have recently been peopling in large numbers Idaho, Arizona, and other of our Western Territories is well calculated to excite the liveliest interest and apprehension. It imposes upon Congress and the Executive the duty of arraying against this barbarous system all the power which under the Constitution and the law they can wield for its destruction.

Reference has been already made to the obstacles which the United States officers have encountered in their efforts to punish violations of law. Prominent among these obstacles is the difficulty of procuring legal evidence sufficient to warrant a conviction even in the case of the most notorious offenders.

Your attention is called to a recent opinion of the Supreme Court of the United States, explaining its judgment of reversal in the case of Miles, who had been convicted of bigamy in Utah. The court refers to the fact that the secrecy attending the celebration of marriages in that Territory makes the proof of polygamy very difficult, and the propriety is suggested of modifying the law of evidence which now makes a wife incompetent to testify against her husband.

This suggestion is approved. I recommend also the passage of an act providing that in the Territories of the United States the fact that a woman has been married to a person charged with bigamy shall not disqualify her as a witness upon his trial for that offense. I further recommend legislation by which any person solemnizing a marriage in any of the Territories shall be required, under stringent penalties for neglect or refusal, to file a certificate of such marriage in the supreme court of the Territory.

Doubtless Congress may devise other practicable measures for obviating the difficulties which have hitherto attended the efforts to suppress this iniquity. I assure you of my determined purpose to cooperate with you in any lawful and discreet measures which may be proposed to that end.

Although our system of government does not contemplate that the nation should provide or support a system for the education of our people, no measures calculated to promote that general intelligence and virtue upon which the perpetuity of our institutions so greatly depends have ever been regarded with indifference by Congress or the Executive.

A large portion of the public domain has been from time to time devoted to the promotion of education.

There is now a special reason why, by setting apart the proceeds of its sales of public lands or by some other course, the Government should aid the work of education. Many who now exercise the right of suffrage are unable to read the ballot which they cast. Upon many who had just emerged from a condition of slavery were suddenly devolved the responsibilities of citizenship in that portion of the country most impoverished by war. I have been pleased to learn from the report of the Commissioner of Education that there has lately been a commendable increase of interest and effort for their instruction; but all that can be done by local legislation and private generosity should be supplemented by such aid as can be constitutionally afforded by the National Government.

I would suggest that if any fund be dedicated to this purpose it may be wisely distributed in the different States according to the ratio of illiteracy, as by this means those localities which are most in need of such assistance will reap its special benefits.

The report of the Commissioner of Agriculture exhibits the results of the experiments in which that Department has been engaged during the past year and makes important suggestions in reference to the agricultural development of the country.

The steady increase of our population and the consequent addition to the number of those engaging in the pursuit of husbandry are giving to this Department a growing dignity and importance. The Commissioner's suggestions touching its capacity for greater usefulness deserve attention, as it more and more commends itself to the interests which it was created to promote.

It appears from the report of the Commissioner of Pensions that since 1860 789,063 original pension claims have been filed; 450,949 of these have been allowed and inscribed on the pension roll; 72,539 have been rejected and abandoned, being 13+ per cent of the whole number of claims settled.

There are now pending for settlement 265,575 original pension claims, 227,040 of which were filed prior to July 1, 1880. These, when allowed, will involve the payment of arrears from the date of discharge in case of an invalid and from date of death or termination of a prior right in all other cases.

From all the data obtainable it is estimated that 15 per cent of the number of claims now pending will be rejected or abandoned. This would show the probable rejection of 34,040 cases and the probable admission of about 193,000 claims, all of which involve the payment of arrears of pension.

With the present force employed, the number of adjudications remaining the same and no new business intervening, this number of claims (193,000) could be acted upon in a period of six years; and taking January 1, 1884, as a near period from which to estimate in each case an average amount of arrears, it is found that every case allowed would require for the first payment upon it the sum of $1,350. Multiplying this amount by the whole number of probable admissions gives $250,-000,000 as the sum required for first payment. This represents the sum which must be paid upon claims which were filed before July 1, 1880, and are now pending and entitled to the benefits of the arrears act. From this amount ($250,000,000) may be deducted from ten to fifteen millions for cases where, the claimant dying, there is no person who under the law would be entitled to succeed to the pension, leaving $235,000,000 as the probable amount to be paid.

In these estimates no account has been taken of the 38,500 cases filed since June 30, 1880, and now pending, which must receive attention as current business, but which do not involve the payment of any arrears beyond the date of filing the claim. Of this number it is estimated that 86 per cent will be allowed.

As has been stated, with the present force of the Pension Bureau (675 clerks) it is estimated that it will take six years to dispose of the claims now pending.

It is stated by the Commissioner of Pensions that by an addition of 250 clerks (increasing the adjudicating force rather than the mechanical) double the amount of work could be accomplished, so that these cases could be acted upon within three years.

Aside from the considerations of justice which may be urged for a speedy settlement of the claims now on the files of the Pension Office, it is no less important on the score of economy, inasmuch as fully one-third of the clerical force of the office is now wholly occupied in giving attention to correspondence with the thousands of claimants whose cases have been on the files for the past eighteen years. The fact that a sum so enormous must be expended by the Government to meet demands for arrears of pensions is an admonition to Congress and the Executive to give cautious consideration to any similar project in the future. The great temptation to the presentation of fictitious claims afforded by the fact that the average sum obtained upon each application is $1,300 leads me to suggest the propriety of making some special appropriation for the prevention of fraud.

I advise appropriations for such internal improvements as the wisdom of Congress may deem to be of public importance. The necessity of improving the navigation of the Mississippi River justifies a special allusion to that subject. I suggest the adoption of some measure for the removal of obstructions which now impede the navigation of that great channel of commerce.

In my letter accepting the nomination for the Vice-Presidency I stated that in my judgment—

No man should be the incumbent of an office the duties of which he is for any cause unfit to perform; who is lacking in the ability, fidelity, or integrity which a proper administration of such office demands. This sentiment would doubtless meet with general acquiescence, but opinion has been widely divided upon the wisdom and practicability of the various reformatory schemes which have been suggested and of certain proposed regulations governing appointments to public office.

The efficiency of such regulations has been distrusted mainly because they have seemed to exalt mere educational and abstract tests above general business capacity and even special fitness for the particular work in hand. It seems to me that the rules which should be applied to the management of the public service may properly conform in the main to such as regulate the conduct of successful private business:

Original appointments should be based upon ascertained fitness.

The tenure of office should be stable.

Positions of responsibility should, so far as practicable, be filled by the promotion of worthy and efficient officers.

The investigation of all complaints and the punishment of all official misconduct should be prompt and thorough.

The views expressed in the foregoing letter are those which will govern my administration of the executive office. They are doubtless shared by all intelligent and patriotic citizens, however divergent in their opinions as to the best methods of putting them into practical operation.

For example, the assertion that "original appointments should be based upon ascertained fitness" is not open to dispute.

But the question how in practice such fitness can be most effectually ascertained is one which has for years excited interest and discussion. The measure which, with slight variations in its details, has lately been urged upon the attention of Congress and the Executive has as its principal feature the scheme of competitive examination. Save for certain exceptions, which need not here be specified, this plan would allow admission to the service only in its lowest grade, and would accordingly demand that all vacancies in higher positions should be filled by promotion alone. In these particulars it is in conformity with the existing civil-service system of Great Britain; and indeed the success which has attended that system in the country of its birth is the strongest argument which has been urged for its adoption here.

The fact should not, however, be overlooked that there are certain features of the English system which have not generally been received with favor in this country, even among the foremost advocates of civil-service reform.

PRESIDENT ARTHUR'S ANNOUNCEMENT OF PRESIDENT
GARFIELD'S DEATH.

PRESIDENT ARTHUR'S SIGNATURE TO OFFICIAL ANNOUNCE-
MENT OF PRESIDENT GARFIELD'S DEATH.

Among them are:

1. A tenure of office which is substantially a life tenure.

2. A limitation of the maximum age at which an applicant can enter the service, whereby all men in middle life or older are, with some exceptions, rigidly excluded.

3. A retiring allowance upon going out of office.

These three elements are as important factors of the problem as any of the others. To eliminate them from the English system would effect a most radical change in its theory and practice.

The avowed purpose of that system is to induce the educated young men of the country to devote their lives to public employment by an assurance that having once entered upon it they need never leave it, and that after voluntary retirement they shall be the recipients of an annual pension. That this system as an entirety has proved very successful in Great Britain seems to be generally conceded even by those who once opposed its adoption.

To a statute which should incorporate all its essential features I should feel bound to give my approval; but whether it would be for the best interests of the public to fix upon an expedient for immediate and extensive application which embraces certain features of the English system, but excludes or ignores others of equal importance, may be seriously doubted, even by those who are impressed, as I am myself, with the grave importance of correcting the evils which inhere in the present methods of appointment.

If, for example, the English rule which shuts out persons above the age of 25 years from a large number of public employments is not to be made an essential part of our own system, it is questionable whether the attainment of the highest number of marks at a competitive examination should be the criterion by which all applications for appointment should be put to test. And under similar conditions it may also be questioned whether admission to the service should be strictly limited to its lowest ranks.

There are very many characteristics which go to make a model civil servant. Prominent among them are probity, industry, good sense, good habits, good temper, patience, order, courtesy, tact, self-reliance, manly deference to superior officers, and manly consideration for inferiors. The absence of these traits is not supplied by wide knowledge of books, or by promptitude in answering questions, or by any other quality likely to be brought to light by competitive examination.

To make success in such a contest, therefore, an indispensable condition of public employment would very likely result in the practical exclusion of the older applicants, even though they might possess qualifications far superior to their younger and more brilliant competitors.

These suggestions must not be regarded as evincing any spirit of opposition to the competitive plan, which has been to some extent successfully employed already, and which may hereafter vindicate the claim of its most earnest supporters; but it ought to be seriously considered whether the application of the same educational standard to persons of mature years and to young men fresh from school and college would not be likely to exalt mere intellectual proficiency above other qualities of equal or greater importance.

Another feature of the proposed system is the selection by promotion of all officers of the Government above the lowest grade, except such as would fairly be regarded as exponents of the policy of the Executive and the principles of the dominant party.

To afford encouragement to faithful public servants by exciting in their minds the hope of promotion if they are found to merit it is much to be desired.

But would it be wise to adopt a rule so rigid as to permit no other mode of supplying the intermediate walks of the service?

There are many persons who fill subordinate positions with great credit, but lack those qualities which are requisite for higher posts of duty; and, besides; the modes of thought and action of one whose service in a governmental bureau has been long continued are often so cramped by routine procedure as almost to disqualify him from instituting changes required by the public interests. An infusion of new blood from time to time into the middle ranks of the service might be very beneficial in its results.

The subject under discussion is one of grave importance. The evils which are complained of can not be eradicated at once; the work must be gradual.

The present English system is a growth of years, and was not created by a single stroke of executive or legislative action.

Its beginnings are found in an order in council promulgated in 1855, and it was after patient and cautious scrutiny of its workings that fifteen years later it took its present shape.

Five years after the issuance of the order in council, and at a time when resort had been had to competitive examinations as an experiment much more extensively than has yet been the case in this country, a select committee of the House of Commons made a report to that House which, declaring its approval of the competitive plan, deprecated, nevertheless, any precipitancy in its general adoption as likely to endanger its ultimate success.

During this tentative period the results of the two methods of pass examination and competitive examination were closely watched and compared. It may be that before we confine ourselves upon this important question within the stringent bounds of statutory enactment we may profitably await the result of further inquiry and experiment.

The submission of a portion of the nominations to a central board of examiners selected solely for testing the qualifications of applicants may perhaps, without resort to the competitive test, put an end to the mischiefs which attend the present system of appointment, and it may be feasible to vest in such a board a wide discretion to ascertain the characteristics and attainments of candidates in those particulars which I have already referred to as being no less important than mere intellectual attainment.

If Congress should deem it advisable at the present session to establish competitive tests for admission to the service, no doubts such as have been suggested shall deter me from giving the measure my earnest support.

And I urgently recommend, should there be a failure to pass any other act upon this subject, that an appropriation of $25,000 per year may be made for the enforcement of section 1753 of the Revised Statutes.

With the aid thus afforded me I shall strive to execute the provisions of that law according to its letter and spirit.

I am unwilling, in justice to the present civil servants of the Government, to dismiss this subject without declaring my dissent from the severe and almost indiscriminate censure with which they have been recently assailed. That they are as a class indolent, inefficient, and corrupt is a statement which has been often made and widely credited; but when the extent, variety, delicacy, and importance of their duties are considered the great majority of the employees of the Government are, in my judgment, deserving of high commendation.

The continuing decline of the merchant marine of the United States is greatly to be deplored. In view of the fact that we furnish so large a proportion of the freights of the commercial world and that our shipments are steadily and rapidly increasing, it is cause of surprise that not only is our navigation interest diminishing, but it is less than when our exports and imports were not half so large as now, either in bulk or value. There must be some peculiar hindrance to the development of this interest, or the enterprise and energy of American mechanics and capitalists would have kept this country at least abreast of our rivals in the friendly contest for ocean supremacy.

The substitution of iron for wood and of steam for sail have wrought great revolutions in the carrying trade of the world; but these changes could not have been adverse to America if we had given to our navigation interests a portion of the aid and protection which have been so wisely bestowed upon our manufactures. I commend the whole subject to the wisdom of Congress, with the suggestion that no question of greater magnitude or farther reaching importance can engage their attention.

In 1875 the Supreme Court of the United States declared unconstitutional the statutes of certain States which imposed upon shipowners or consignees a tax of $1.50 for each passenger arriving from a foreign country, or in lieu thereof required a bond to indemnify the State and local authorities against expense for the future relief or support of such passenger. Since this decision the expense attending the care and supervision of immigrants has fallen on the States at whose ports they have landed. As a large majority of such immigrants, immediately upon their arrival, proceed to the inland States and the Territories to seek permanent homes, it is manifestly unjust to impose upon the State whose shores they first reach the burden which it now bears. For this reason, and because of the national importance of the subject, I recommend legislation regarding the supervision and transitory care of immigrants at the ports of debarkation.

I regret to state that the people of Alaska have reason to complain that they are as yet unprovided with any form of government by which life or property can be protected. While the extent of its population does not justify the application of the costly machinery of Territorial administration, there is immediate necessity for constituting such a form of government as will promote the education of the people and secure the administration of justice.

The Senate at its last session passed a bill providing for the construction of a building for the Library of Congress, but it failed to become a law. The provision of suitable protection for this great collection of books and for the copyright department connected with it has become a subject of national importance and should receive prompt attention.

The report of the Commissioners of the District of Columbia herewith transmitted will inform you fully of the condition of the affairs of the District.

They urge the vital importance of legislation for the reclamation and improvement of the marshes and for the establishment of the harbor lines along the Potomac River front.

It is represented that in their present condition these marshes seriously affect the health of the residents of the adjacent parts of the city, and that they greatly mar the general aspect of the park in which stands the Washington Monument. This improvement would add to that park and to the park south of the Executive Mansion a large area of valuable land, and would transform what is now believed to be a dangerous nuisance into an attractive landscape extending to the river front.

They recommend the removal of the steam railway lines from the surface of the streets of the city and the location of the necessary depots in such places as may be convenient for the public accommodation, and they call attention to the deficiency of the water supply, which seriously affects the material prosperity of the city and the health and comfort of its inhabitants.

I commend these subjects to your favorable consideration.

The importance of timely legislation with respect to the ascertainment and declaration of the vote for Presidential electors was sharply called to the attention of the people more than four years ago.

It is to be hoped that some well-defined measure may be devised before another national election which will render unnecessary a resort to any expedient of a temporary character for the determination of questions upon contested returns.

Questions which concern the very existence of the Government and the liberties of the people were suggested by the prolonged illness of the late President and his consequent incapacity to perform the functions of his office.

It is provided by the second article of the Constitution, in the fifth clause of its first section, that "in case of the removal of the President from office, or of his death, resignation, or inability to discharge the powers and duties of the said office, the same shall devolve on the Vice-President."

What is the intendment of the Constitution in its specification of "inability to discharge the powers and duties of the said office" as one of the contingencies which calls the Vice-President to the exercise of Presidential functions?

Is the inability limited in its nature to long-continued intellectual incapacity, or has it a broader import?

What must be its extent and duration?

How must its existence be established?

Has the President whose inability is the subject of inquiry any voice in determining whether or not it exists, or is the decision of that momentous and delicate question confided to the Vice-President, or is it contemplated by the Constitution that Congress should provide by law precisely what should constitute inability and how and by what tribunal or authority it should be ascertained?

If the inability proves to be temporary in its nature, and during its continuance the Vice-President lawfully exercises the functions of the Executive, by what tenure does he hold his office?

Does he continue as President for the remainder of the four years' term?

Or would the elected President, if his inability should cease in the interval, be empowered to resume his office?

And if, having such lawful authority, he should exercise it, would the Vice-President be thereupon empowered to resume his powers and duties as such?

I can not doubt that these important questions will receive your early and thoughtful consideration.

Deeply impressed with the gravity of the responsibilities which have so unexpectedly devolved upon me, it will be my constant purpose to cooperate with you in such measures as will promote the glory of the country and the prosperity of its people.

CHESTER A. ARTHUR.

SPECIAL MESSAGES.

EXECUTIVE MANSION,
Washington, December 12, 1881.

To the Senate of the United States:

I transmit herewith, in response to the resolution of the Senate of the 17th of May last, a report of the Secretary of State, with accompanying papers, touching the Geneva convention for the relief of the wounded in war.

CHESTER A. ARTHUR.

EXECUTIVE MANSION, *December 15, 1881.*

To the Senate and House of Representatives:

I transmit herewith a communication from the Secretary of the Interior, with accompanying papers, in reference to the applications of the Chicago, Texas and Mexican Central and the St. Louis and San Francisco Railway companies for a right of way across the lands of the Choctaw Nation in the Indian Territory for the building of a proposed railroad and telegraph line.

The matter is commended to the careful attention of Congress.

CHESTER A. ARTHUR.

EXECUTIVE MANSION, *December 15, 1881.*

To the Senate of the United States:

I transmit herewith, in response to a resolution of the Senate of the 12th instant, a report from the Secretary of State, with an accompanying paper, touching the proposed modification of the Clayton-Bulwer treaty of April 19, 1850, between the United States and Great Britain.

CHESTER A. ARTHUR.

WASHINGTON, *December 15, 1881.*

To the Senate of the United States:

I transmit to the Senate, for its consideration with a view to ratification, a treaty of peace, friendship, and commerce between the United States of America and the Kingdom of Madagascar, signed on the 13th day of May, 1881, together with certain correspondence relating thereto.

CHESTER A. ARTHUR.

WASHINGTON, *December 19, 1881.*

To the Senate of the United States:

I transmit herewith to the Senate a report from the Secretary of State, in response to its resolution of the 13th of October last, calling for the transmission to the Senate of papers on file in the Department of State relating to the seizure of one Vicenzo Rebello, an Italian, in the city of New Orleans, in June, 1881, by one James Mooney, under a warrant of arrest issued by John A. Osborn, United States commissioner in and for the city of New York.

CHESTER A. ARTHUR.

WASHINGTON, *December 19, 1881.*

To the Senate of the United States:

I transmit herewith to the Senate a report of the Secretary of State, in relation to the necessity of modifying the present system of consular jurisdiction of the United States in the countries of the East. I regard this subject, to which I have adverted in my general message to Congress, as one deserving the earnest attention of the National Legislature.

CHESTER A. ARTHUR.

[A similar message was sent to the House of Representatives.]

WASHINGTON, *December 19, 1881.*

To the House of Representatives:

I transmit herewith to the House of Representatives, for the consideration of Congress, a communication from the Secretary of State, setting forth the expediency of organizing a class of supernumerary secretaries of legation to meet the needs of our diplomatic service abroad.

CHESTER A. ARTHUR.

WASHINGTON, *December 19, 1881.*

To the Senate of the United States:

I transmit herewith, in reply to the resolution of the Senate of the 19th of May last, a report from the Secretary of State, with an accompanying paper.*

CHESTER A. ARTHUR.

EXECUTIVE MANSION, *December 21, 1881.*

To the House of Representatives:

I transmit herewith, for the consideration of Congress, a communication from the Secretary of the Interior, with an accompanying paper, in which he recommends a further appropriation for the payment of the expenses of the Tenth Census; also an appropriation of $2,000 to recompense the disbursing clerk of the Department of the Interior for his services in disbursing the appropriations for the Tenth Census.

CHESTER A. ARTHUR.

* List of officers, clerks, etc., in the Department of State.

EXECUTIVE MANSION, *December 21, 1881.*

To the Senate of the United States:

I transmit herewith, in response to a resolution of the Senate of the 6th instant, a letter from the Secretary of the Treasury and its accompanying papers.*

CHESTER A. ARTHUR.

EXECUTIVE MANSION, *January 6, 1882.*

To the Senate and House of Representatives:

I transmit a communication† received this day from the late Postmaster-General, to which I invite your careful attention.

Though the period limited for the reception of bids under the existing advertisement expires on the 7th instant, several weeks must necessarily elapse before they can be classified and examined and the actual letting take place.

If, therefore, Congress shall be of the opinion that a change in the law is needed, it may, I presume, be made immediately applicable.

CHESTER A. ARTHUR.

EXECUTIVE MANSION, *January 9, 1882.*

To the Senate of the United States:

I transmit herewith a communication from the Secretary of the Interior, with accompanying papers, in reference to the bill of the Choctaw Council approved November 10, 1881, granting a right of way through the Choctaw Nation to the St. Louis and San Francisco Railway Company, a bill (S. No. 60) for the ratification of which is now understood to be pending before your honorable body.

CHESTER A. ARTHUR.

EXECUTIVE MANSION, *January 11, 1882.*

To the Senate and House of Representatives:

I transmit herewith a communication from the Secretary of the Interior, with draft of a bill and accompanying papers, in reference to an agreement by the Shoshone and Bannock Indians with the United States for the disposal of certain of their lands in the Fort Hall Indian Reservation, in Idaho, for the use of the Utah and Northern Railway.

The matter is commended to the careful consideration of Congress.

CHESTER A. ARTHUR.

---

*Instructions to, and reports of certain, examiners of national banks.

†Relating to fraudulent bonds accompanying certain bids and contracts for carrying United States mail.

EXECUTIVE MANSION, *January 18, 1882.*

To the Senate and House of Representatives:

I transmit herewith a communication from the Secretary of the Interior, with draft of a bill to appropriate money to meet a deficiency in the Indian service for the fiscal year ending June 30, 1882.

A copy of report of the Commissioner of Indian Affairs, dated 13th instant, in regard to the bill is also inclosed.

The subject is commended to the attention of Congress.

CHESTER A. ARTHUR.

EXECUTIVE MANSION, *January 18, 1882.*

To the Senate and House of Representatives:

I transmit herewith a communication from the Secretary of the Interior, with draft of a bill and accompanying papers, amendatory of the act of March 3, 1880, for the sale of the Otoe and Missouria Indian Reservation, in the States of Nebraska and Kansas.

The subject is presented to the consideration of Congress.

CHESTER A. ARTHUR.

EXECUTIVE MANSION,
Washington, January 18, 1882.

To the Senate and House of Representatives:

I transmit herewith a letter from the Secretary of the Interior, forwarding copy of a letter addressed to him by the Commissioner of Indian Affairs, inclosing draft of a bill to create the office of medical inspector for the United States Indian service.

CHESTER A. ARTHUR.

EXECUTIVE MANSION, *January 18, 1882.*

To the Senate and House of Representatives:

I transmit herewith a communication from the Secretary of the Interior, with draft of bill and accompanying papers, providing for the improvement of the condition of Indians occupying reservations, and for other purposes.

The matter is commended to the consideration of Congress.

CHESTER A. ARTHUR.

EXECUTIVE MANSION, *January 18, 1882.*

To the Senate and House of Representatives:

I transmit herewith a communication from the Secretary of the Interior, and accompanying letter from the Commissioner of Indian Affairs, recommending a renewal of the appropriation of $10,000 heretofore made for defraying the expenses of the Board of Indian Commissioners.

The subject is commended to the consideration of Congress.

CHESTER A. ARTHUR.

EXECUTIVE MANSION, *January 18, 1882.*

To the Senate and House of Representatives:

I transmit herewith a communication from the Secretary of the Interior, with draft of a bill and accompanying papers, in reference to the settlement of the estate of deceased Kickapoo Indians in the State of Kansas, and for other purposes.

The matter is commended to the attention of Congress.

CHESTER A. ARTHUR.

EXECUTIVE MANSION, *January 18, 1882.*

To the Senate and House of Representatives:

I transmit herewith a communication from the Secretary of the Interior, with a draft of a bill and accompanying papers, to accept and ratify an agreement with the Crow Indians for the sale of a portion of their reservation in the Territory of Montana, required for the Northern Pacific Railroad, and to make the necessary appropriation for carrying the same into effect.

The subject is presented for the consideration of Congress.

CHESTER A. ARTHUR.

EXECUTIVE MANSION, *January 19, 1882.*

To the Senate and House of Representatives:

I transmit herewith, for the consideration of Congress, a communication from the Secretary of War, with accompanying papers, recommending an appropriation for the purchase of a site and the erection of a fireproof building to contain the records, library, and museum of the Surgeon-General's Office.

CHESTER A. ARTHUR.

OFFICE OF THE PRESIDENT OF THE UNITED STATES,
Washington, January 19, 1882.

To the Senate and House of Representatives:

I transmit herewith, for the consideration of Congress, a letter from the Secretary of War, inclosing a copy of one from the Chief Signal Officer of the Army, dated the 11th instant, setting forth the necessity for additional room for the Signal Office and recommending that Congress provide that of the amount estimated ($350,000) for ''observation and report of storms, 1883," the sum of $10,000 may be expended for the hire of a safe and suitable building in Washington City for the office of the Chief Signal Officer.

CHESTER A. ARTHUR.

OFFICE OF THE PRESIDENT OF THE UNITED STATES,
January 19, 1882.
To the Senate and House of Representatives:

I transmit herewith, for the consideration of Congress, a communication from the Secretary of War, dated the 14th instant, and accompanying letter from the Chief Signal Officer of the Army, recommending the passage of a joint resolution, in accordance with the inclosed draft, authorizing the printing and binding of 10,000 additional copies of the latter's annual report for the year 1881.

CHESTER A. ARTHUR.

WASHINGTON, *January 23, 1882.*
To the Senate of the United States:

I transmit to the Senate, for its consideration with a view to ratification, a treaty of commerce and navigation between the United States of America and His Majesty the King of Roumania, signed on the 11th day of April last.

CHESTER A. ARTHUR.

WASHINGTON, *January 24, 1882.*
To the Senate of the United States:

I transmit to the Senate, for its consideration with a view to ratification, a treaty of commerce between the United States and the Prince of Serbia, signed on the 14th of October last.

*   *   *   *   *   *   *

CHESTER A. ARTHUR.

WASHINGTON, *January 24, 1882.*
To the Senate of the United States:

I transmit to the Senate, for its consideration with a view to ratification, a convention defining the rights, immunities, and privileges of consular officers, between the United States and the Prince of Serbia, signed on the 14th of October last.

*   *   *   *   *   *   *

CHESTER A. ARTHUR.

EXECUTIVE MANSION, *January 24, 1882.*
To the Senate and House of Representatives:

I transmit herewith a communication from the Secretary of the Interior, with draft of a bill to increase the salary of the Commissioner of the

General Land Office and to create the offices of Assistant Commissioner of the General Land Office and inspectors of surveyors-general and district land officers.

The matter is commended to the attention of Congress.

CHESTER A. ARTHUR.

EXECUTIVE MANSION, *January 24, 1882.*

To the Senate and House of Representatives :

I transmit herewith a communication from the Secretary of the Interior, with draft of a bill for the per capita distribution of the sum of $2,000 to the band of Eastern Shawnee Indians at Quapaw Agency, Ind. T., with accompanying papers noted in said communication.

CHESTER A. ARTHUR.

EXECUTIVE MANSION, *January 24, 1882.*

To the Senate and House of Representatives:

I transmit herewith a communication from the Secretary of the Interior, with draft of a bill to increase the salary of the Commissioner of Indian Affairs and to create the office of Assistant Commissioner of Indian Affairs.

The matter is commended to the attention of Congress.

CHESTER A. ARTHUR.

EXECUTIVE MANSION, *January 24, 1882.*

To the Senate and House of Representatives:

I transmit herewith a communication from the Secretary of the Interior, with draft of a bill and accompanying papers, in reference to the proposition of the Creek Nation of Indians for the cession of certain of their lands in the Indian Territory occupied by the Seminole Indians.

The subject is commended to the consideration of Congress.

CHESTER A. ARTHUR.

EXECUTIVE MANSION, *January 24, 1882.*

To the Senate and House of Representatives:

I transmit herewith a communication from the Secretary of the Interior, with draft of a bill authorizing the sale of certain pine timber cut upon the Menomonee Reservation in Wisconsin, together with the accompanying papers noted in said communication.

CHESTER A. ARTHUR.

EXECUTIVE MANSION, *January 26, 1882.*

To the Senate and House of Representatives:

I transmit herewith, for the consideration of Congress, a communication from the Secretary of War, dated the 23d instant, and accompanying copies of letters from the Adjutant-General, Inspector-General, and Quartermaster-General of the Army, recommending the amendment of section 3 of the act approved May 15, 1872, entitled "An act to establish the pay of the enlisted men of the Army," so as to require a settlement of the clothing accounts of enlisted men at every bimonthly muster for pay.

CHESTER A. ARTHUR.

EXECUTIVE MANSION, *January 26, 1882.*

To the Senate and House of Representatives:

I transmit herewith, for the consideration of Congress, a communication from the Secretary of War, with plan and estimate of the cost of constructing five dining-rooms and kitchens at Jefferson Barracks, Mo.

CHESTER A. ARTHUR.

EXECUTIVE MANSION, *January 26, 1882.*

To the Senate and House of Representatives:

I transmit herewith a communication from the Secretary of the Interior, with draft of a bill for the per capita distribution of the sum of $5,000 to the band of Western Miami Indians at the Quapaw Agency, Ind. T., with accompanying papers noted in said communication.

CHESTER A. ARTHUR.

EXECUTIVE MANSION, *January 26, 1882.*

To the Senate and House of Representatives:

I transmit herewith, for the consideration of Congress, a communication from the Secretary of War, reporting a list of reservations which are no longer needed for military purposes and setting forth the necessity for such legislation as will provide for their disposal.

CHESTER A. ARTHUR.

EXECUTIVE MANSION, *January 26, 1882.*

To the Senate and House of Representatives:

I transmit herewith a communication from the Secretary of the Interior, with draft of an amendment to be inserted in the annual Indian appropriation bill now pending, providing for the disposal of certain bonds and funds held by the Treasurer of the United States as custodian in the name of the Ottawa and Chippewa Indians, together with accompanying papers noted in said communication.

The matter is presented for the consideration of Congress.

CHESTER A. ARTHUR.

EXECUTIVE MANSION, *January 26, 1882.*

To the Senate and House of Representatives:

I transmit herewith, for the consideration of Congress, a communication from the Secretary of War and its accompanying papers, setting forth the necessity for the erection of a new embankment wall on the creek bordering the grounds of the Frankford Arsenal, Pa., and recommending that an appropriation be made for that purpose.

CHESTER A. ARTHUR.

EXECUTIVE MANSION, *January 26, 1882.*

To the Senate and House of Representatives:

I transmit herewith, for the consideration of Congress, a letter from the Secretary of the Interior, concerning an appropriation for the improvement of the Hot Springs Reservation, in Garland County, Ark.

CHESTER A. ARTHUR.

EXECUTIVE MANSION, *January 26, 1882.*

To the Senate and House of Representatives:

I transmit herewith, for your consideration, a communication from the Secretary of the Interior, dated the 18th instant, touching the necessity for additional room for the clerical force of the Department of the Interior.

CHESTER A. ARTHUR.

EXECUTIVE MANSION, *January 26, 1882.*

To the Senate and House of Representatives:

I transmit herewith, for the information of Congress, the annual report of the Government directors of the Union Pacific Railway to the Secretary of the Interior for the year 1881.

CHESTER A. ARTHUR.

EXECUTIVE MANSION, *January 26, 1882.*

To the Senate and House of Representatives:

I transmit herewith a communication from the Secretary of the Interior, with draft of amendment to be inserted in the Indian appropriation bill, to carry into effect the provisions of the fifth section of the act of March 3, 1873, providing for the consolidation of funds belonging to the Miami Indians of Kansas.

The matter is presented for the consideration of Congress.

CHESTER A. ARTHUR.

EXECUTIVE MANSION,
Washington, January 26, 1882.

To the House of Representatives:

I transmit herewith a report of the Secretary of State, with accompanying papers, furnished in response to a resolution of the House of Representatives of the 24th instant, calling for correspondence touching the efforts of this Government to bring about peace between Chile and Peru and Bolivia, and touching claims against or contracts respecting either of the belligerent Governments.

CHESTER A. ARTHUR.

EXECUTIVE MANSION,
Washington, January 26, 1882.

To the Senate of the United States:

I transmit herewith a report of the Secretary of State and accompanying papers, furnished in response to the resolution of the Senate of the 13th ultimo, calling for correspondence touching affairs in or between Peru and Chile.

CHESTER A. ARTHUR.

EXECUTIVE MANSION, *January 27, 1882.*

To the Senate of the United States:

I transmit herewith, in further response to the Senate resolution of the 13th December, 1881, a report of the Secretary of State, embodying the purport of a recent telegram from the special envoy of the United States setting forth the conditions of peace presented by Chile.

CHESTER A. ARTHUR.

[A similar message was sent to the House of Representatives, in answer to a resolution of that body of January 24, 1882.]

EXECUTIVE MANSION, *January 28, 1882.*

To the Senate of the United States:

In further answer to the resolution of the Senate of December 12, 1881, I herewith transmit the remainder of the correspondence touching the desired modification of the Clayton-Bulwer treaty. The dispatch of the Secretary of State of November 29, 1881, was not sent to the

Senate with the former dispatches, because at that time no advice had been received that its contents had been communicated to the British Government.

CHESTER A. ARTHUR.

EXECUTIVE MANSION, *February 1, 1882.*

To the House of Representatives:

I transmit herewith a communication from the Secretary of the Interior, inclosing a letter from the Commissioner of Pensions, giving, in compliance with the resolution of the House of Representatives passed on the 26th of January, 1882, estimates of the amounts which will be required annually to pay pensions for the next twenty-five years, based on the presumed conditions stated in the resolution.

CHESTER A. ARTHUR.

EXECUTIVE MANSION, *February 2, 1882.*

To the Senate and House of Representatives:

I transmit herewith a letter from the Secretary of the Interior, with accompanying papers, relative to lawlessness which prevails in parts of Arizona, and in connection therewith call attention to that portion of my message of the 6th of December last in which suggestions were made as to legislation which seems to be required to enable the General Government to assist the local authorities of the Territory in restoring and maintaining order.

CHESTER A. ARTHUR.

EXECUTIVE MANSION, *February 2, 1882.*

To the Senate and House of Representatives:

I transmit herewith a communication from the Secretary of the Interior, with a draft of a bill authorizing the disposal of dead and damaged timber upon Indian reservations under the direction of the Interior Department, and correspondence noted by the Secretary.

The subject is presented for the consideration of Congress.

CHESTER A. ARTHUR.

EXECUTIVE MANSION,
Washington, February 2, 1882.

To the Senate and House of Representatives:

I transmit herewith a letter from the Secretary of the Interior, inclosing copy of a letter addressed to him by the Commissioner of the General Land Office, asking, for reasons stated therein, that Congress may be requested to make a special appropriation for a temporary increase of the clerical force of the General Land Office.

A draft of a bill for that purpose is herewith inclosed, and the subject is commended to the consideration of Congress.

CHESTER A. ARTHUR.

EXECUTIVE MANSION,
Washington, February 2, 1882.

To the Senate of the United States:

I transmit herewith, in further response to the resolution of the Senate of the 18th of March, 1881, a report of the Secretary of State, with its accompaniment, touching the capitulations of the Ottoman Empire.

CHESTER A. ARTHUR.

EXECUTIVE MANSION, *February 2, 1882.*

To the Senate and House of Representatives:

I transmit herewith, for the consideration of Congress, a communication from the Secretary of War, dated the 27th of January, 1882, and accompanying estimates for new buildings for the general recruiting service at Davids Island, New York Harbor, and Columbus Barracks, Ohio.

CHESTER A. ARTHUR.

EXECUTIVE MANSION, *February 2, 1882.*

To the Senate and House of Representatives:

I transmit herewith a communication from the Secretary of the Interior, with the draft of a bill to authorize the settlement of certain accounts for advertising the sale of Kansas Indian lands, with accompanying papers referred to in said communication.

The subject is commended to the consideration of Congress.

CHESTER A. ARTHUR.

EXECUTIVE MANSION, *February 2, 1882.*

To the Senate and House of Representatives:

I transmit herewith a communication from the Secretary of the Interior, with a draft of a bill for the payment of certain settlers in the State of Nevada for improvements on lands in Duck Valley, in said State, taken for the use and occupancy of the Shoshone Indians.

CHESTER A. ARTHUR.

EXECUTIVE MANSION, *February 2, 1882.*

To the Senate and House of Representatives:

I transmit herewith, tor the consideration of Congress, a communication from the Secretary of the Interior, dated January 31, 1882, upon the subject of additional legislation for the expenses of the Tenth Census, and inclose draft of an act supplemental to the act approved January 28, 1882.

CHESTER A. ARTHUR.

EXECUTIVE MANSION, *February 3, 1882.*

To the Senate and House of Representatives:

I transmit herewith, for the consideration of Congress, a communication of the Secretary of the Interior of the 27th ultimo, with accompanying papers, on the subject of the confirmation of the homestead entries of certain lands in Marquette district, Michigan, made by Hugh Foster and John Waishkey, jr.

CHESTER A. ARTHUR.

EXECUTIVE MANSION, *February 3, 1882.*

To the Senate and House of Representatives:

I transmit herewith a communication from the Secretary of the Interior, with a draft of a bill to prevent timber depredations on Indian reservations, and correspondence noted by the Secretary.

The subject is presented for the consideration of Congress.

CHESTER A. ARTHUR.

EXECUTIVE MANSION, *February 3, 1882.*

To the Senate of the United States:

I transmit herewith a report of the Secretary of State of this date, with accompanying papers, furnished in obedience to a resolution of the Senate of the 12th ultimo, calling for certain correspondence in the case of claim of Antonio Pelletier against the Government of Hayti.

CHESTER A. ARTHUR.

[A similar message was sent to the House of Representatives.]

EXECUTIVE MANSION, *February 8, 1882.*

To the Senate and House of Representatives:

I transmit herewith a communication of 1st instant from the Secretary of the Interior, covering information respecting the lands granted to the State of Oregon for the Willamette Valley and Cascade Mountain Wagon Road Company.

The subject is commended to the consideration of Congress.

CHESTER A. ARTHUR.

EXECUTIVE MANSION, *February 8, 1882.*

To the Senate and House of Representatives:

I transmit herewith, for the consideration of Congress, a communication from the Secretary of War, inclosing copies of papers relating to the site of Fort Bliss, at El Paso, Tex., with special reference to certain errors contained in the deeds conveying the land to the United States, and recommending the passage by Congress of an act, a draft of which is also inclosed, to rectify and establish the title of the United States to the site in question.

CHESTER A. ARTHUR.

EXECUTIVE MANSION, *February 8, 1882.*
To the Senate and House of Representatives:

I transmit herewith, for the consideration of Congress, a letter from the Secretary of War of the 6th instant, together with plans and esti mates for barracks and quarters in the Military Division of the Pacific and at Fort Monroe, Va., for the fiscal year ending June 30, 1883; also the correspondence accompanying the same.

CHESTER A. ARTHUR.

EXECUTIVE MANSION, *February 15, 1882.*
To the Senate and House of Representatives:

I transmit herewith, for the consideration of Congress, a letter from the Secretary of War, dated the 11th instant, covering plans and esti-mates for completing the new barracks at Fort Leavenworth, Kans., and for the erection of additional quarters for officers thereat, in con-nection with the School of Cavalry and Infantry; also the correspond-ence accompanying the same.

CHESTER A. ARTHUR.

EXECUTIVE MANSION, *February 15, 1882.*
To the Senate and House of Representatives:

I transmit herewith, for the information of Congress, the report of the Board of Indian Commissioners for the year 1881, accompanied by a let-ter from the Secretary of the Interior, dated the 9th instant, suggesting legislation regarding reports from said board. The report is sent with the message to the House of Representatives.

CHESTER A. ARTHUR.

EXECUTIVE MANSION, *February 15, 1882.*
To the Senate and House of Representatives:

I transmit herewith a communication from the Secretary of the Navy, dated the 8th instant, and accompanying copies of letters from Rear-Admiral John Rodgers, Superintendent of the Naval Observatory, Pro-fessor J. E. Nourse, United States Navy, and Hon. John Eaton, Com-missioner of Education, suggesting the publication of a second edition of the Second Arctic Expedition made by Captain C. F. Hall.

CHESTER A. ARTHUR.

EXECUTIVE MANSION, *February 15, 1882.*

To the Senate and House of Representatives :

I transmit herewith, for the consideration of Congress, a letter from the Secretary of the Interior, inclosing a letter from the Commissioner of Education, in which the recommendation is made that an appropriation of $50,000 be made for the purpose of education in Alaska.

CHESTER A. ARTHUR.

EXECUTIVE MANSION, *February 15, 1882.*

To the House of Representatives:

I transmit herewith the response of the Secretary of State to your resolution of the 30th ultimo, calling for certain information relative to the amount of fees collected by consuls of the United States from American vessels.

CHESTER A. ARTHUR.

EXECUTIVE MANSION, *February 17, 1882.*

To the House of Representatives:

In answer to the resolution of the House of Representatives of the 6th instant, requesting a further compliance with its call for correspondence respecting the war on the Pacific, I transmit herewith a report of the Secretary of State and its accompanying papers.

CHESTER A. ARTHUR.

EXECUTIVE MANSION, *February 17, 1882.*

To the Senate of the United States:

In answer to the resolution of the Senate of the 12th of December, 1881, respecting the Clayton-Bulwer treaty, I transmit herewith a further report by the Secretary of State, accompanied by copies of papers on the subject.

CHESTER A. ARTHUR.

EXECUTIVE MANSION, *February 17, 1882.*

To the Senate of the United States:

In answer to the resolution of the Senate of the 31st of January last, calling for the correspondence touching the relations of the United States with Guatemala and Mexico and their relations with each other, I transmit a report of the Secretary of State, which is accompanied by a copy of the papers called for by the resolution.

CHESTER A. ARTHUR.

EXECUTIVE MANSION, *February 21, 1882.*

To the Senate and House of Representatives:

I submit herewith, for the consideration of Congress, a letter from the Secretary of the Interior, and accompanying papers, in which he recommends that authority be given for the payment of certain damages which unexpectedly occurred to the property of private persons on the Government reservation at Hot Springs, Ark., in consequence of work performed under the direction of the superintendent in the performance of his duty.

CHESTER A. ARTHUR.

EXECUTIVE MANSION, *February 21, 1882.*

To the Senate and House of Representatives:

I transmit herewith, for the consideration of Congress, a communication from the Secretary of the Interior, inclosing a copy of a communication from the Commissioner of Pensions, in which he recommends that more adequate provision be made for the payment of the expenses of obtaining evidence of the extent of the disability of those pensioners of the United States and applicants for pension who reside in foreign countries.

CHESTER A. ARTHUR.

EXECUTIVE MANSION, *February 21, 1882.*

To the Senate and House of Representatives:

I transmit herewith, for the consideration of Congress, a communication from the Secretary of the Navy, with accompanying papers, asking, for reasons stated by him, that Congress may be requested to make a special appropriation for the payment of the claim of Isaac A. Sylvester against the Navy Department.

CHESTER A. ARTHUR.

EXECUTIVE MANSION, *February 21, 1882.*

To the Senate and House of Representatives:

I transmit herewith a communication of the Secretary of the Interior, dated the 16th instant, relative to the necessity for a deficiency appropriation for the payment of salaries of clerks and laborers in the Patent Office during the present fiscal year.

The subject is commended to the consideration of Congress.

CHESTER A. ARTHUR.

EXECUTIVE MANSION, *February 28, 1882.*

To the Senate and House of Representatives:

I transmit herewith a communication from the Secretary of the Navy, with a copy of a letter from the Superintendent of the United States

Naval Observatory, accompanied by a draft of a bill, with estimates for an observation of the transit of Venus on the 6th of December, 1882. The matter is commended to the consideration of Congress.

CHESTER A. ARTHUR.

EXECUTIVE MANSION, *February 28, 1882.*

To the Senate and House of Representatives:

I transmit herewith a letter from the Secretary of the Interior, inclosing a memorial and papers from the Seneca Nation of New York Indians embodying a resolution and remonstrance against the passage of Senate bill No. 19, "to provide for the allotment of lands in severalty to Indians on the various reservations," etc., together with a report thereon of the Commissioner of Indian Affairs, recommending an amendment to the seventh section thereof excluding the lands of said Indians.

The accompanying papers are transmitted with the message to the Senate.

CHESTER A. ARTHUR.

EXECUTIVE MANSION, *February 28, 1882.*

To the Senate and House of Representatives:

I submit herewith, for the consideration of Congress, a letter from the Secretary of the Interior, inclosing a petition of Mr. P. W. Norris for compensation for services rendered and expenses incurred by him as superintendent of the Yellowstone National Park from the 18th of April, 1877, to the 1st of July, 1878.

CHESTER A. ARTHUR.

EXECUTIVE MANSION, *February 28, 1882.*

To the Senate of the United States:

I transmit herewith a communication of the Secretary of the Interior of the 23d instant, with accompanying papers, furnished in obedience to a resolution of the Senate of the 30th ultimo, calling for certain information in relation to the Malheur Indian Reservation, in the State of Oregon.

CHESTER A. ARTHUR.

EXECUTIVE MANSION, *February 28, 1882.*

To the House of Representatives:

In reply to the resolution of the House of Representatives of the 24th ultimo, I transmit herewith copies of letters from the Secretary of the Treasury and the chairman of the Civil Service Commission, dated the 3d and 13th instant, respectively, from which it will be seen that the appropriation of $15,000 made at the last session of Congress for the promotion of efficiency in the different branches of the civil service is still unexpended, and that in order to execute the provisions of section 1753 of the Revised Statutes an annual appropriation of $25,000 would be necessary.

CHESTER A. ARTHUR.

WASHINGTON, *March 1, 1882.*

To the Senate of the United States:

I transmit herewith, in response to a resolution of the Senate of May 19, 1881, a communication, with accompanying papers, from the Secretary of State, respecting the collection by consular officers of certain official fees in connection with the authentication of invoices, and the compensation of such officers.

CHESTER A. ARTHUR.

EXECUTIVE MANSION, *March 1, 1882.*

To the Senate and House of Representatives:

I transmit herewith a communication, dated the 28th of February, 1882, from the Secretary of the Interior, with accompanying papers, in relation to the request of the Cherokee Indians of the Indian Territory for payment for lands belonging to them in said Territory ceded to the United States by the sixteenth article of their treaty of July 19, 1866, for the settlement of friendly Indians.

CHESTER A. ARTHUR.

EXECUTIVE MANSION, *March 2, 1882.*

To the Senate and House of Representatives:

I transmit herewith, for the consideration of Congress, a communication from the Secretary of War, dated the 18th ultimo, inclosing plans and estimates for the construction of the post of Fort Thornburg, in Utah Territory, and recommending an appropriation of $84,000 for that purpose and that the same be made available for immediate use.

CHESTER A. ARTHUR.

EXECUTIVE MANSION, *March 3, 1882.*

To the Senate and House of Representatives:

I transmit herewith, for the consideration of Congress, a communication from the Secretary of War, transmitting plans and estimates for the large military post proposed to be constructed at Fort Selden, N. Mex.

CHESTER A. ARTHUR.

WASHINGTON, *March 3, 1882.*

To the Senate of the United States:

I transmit to the Senate, for its action thereon, the accession of the United States to the convention concluded at Geneva on the 22d August,

1864, between various powers, for the amelioration of the wounded of armies in the field, and to the additional articles thereto, signed at Geneva on the 20th October, 1868.

CHESTER A. ARTHUR.

EXECUTIVE MANSION, *March 3, 1882.*

To the Senate and House of Representatives:

I transmit herewith a communication from the Secretary of the Interior, dated the 2d instant, with accompanying papers, submitting an estimate of appropriations for the payment of expenses of removal of certain Eastern Cherokee Indians to the Indian Territory.

The subject is presented for the consideration of Congress.

CHESTER A. ARTHUR.

EXECUTIVE MANSION, *March 7, 1882.*

To the Senate and House of Representatives:

I transmit a communication from the Secretary of the Navy, with a copy of a letter from the Chief of the Bureau of Equipment and Recruiting and a draft of a bill recommending an increase of 500 enlisted men for the naval service.

The matter is commended to the consideration of Congress.

CHESTER A. ARTHUR.

EXECUTIVE MANSION, *March 8, 1882.*

To the Senate and House of Representatives:

I transmit herewith a communication from the Secretary of the Interior, dated the 6th instant, with accompanying papers* from the Commissioner of Indian Affairs and draft of a bill to amend section 2135, Revised Statutes.

The subject is commended to the consideration of Congress.

CHESTER A. ARTHUR.

EXECUTIVE MANSION, *March 10, 1882.*

To the Senate and House of Representatives:

I transmit herewith, for the consideration of Congress, a communication from the Secretary of the Navy, with accompanying papers, asking, for reasons stated by him, that Congress may be requested to make a special appropriation for paving a portion of the roadway of Hanover street and curbing and paving the sidewalk of that street on the side next the Government property at the Naval Academy, Annapolis, Md.

CHESTER A. ARTHUR.

*Relating to the selling and trading of annuity goods by Lower Brulé Indians.

EXECUTIVE MANSION, *March 10, 1882.*

To the Senate and House of Representatives:

I transmit herewith a communication from the Secretary of the Interior of the 9th instant, submitting, with accompanying papers, an estimate of appropriation for the purpose of defraying the expenses of the Ute Commission, appointed under section 2 of the act of June 15, 1880.

The matter is commended to the early action of Congress.

CHESTER A. ARTHUR.

EXECUTIVE MANSION, *March 10, 1882.*

To the Senate and House of Representatives:

I transmit herewith, for the consideration of Congress, a communication from the Secretary of War of the 6th instant, and accompanying papers, recommending the passage of an act making certain debts incurred by soldiers a lien against their pay.

CHESTER A. ARTHUR.

EXECUTIVE MANSION, *March 10, 1882.*

To the House of Representatives:

I herewith transmit, in response to a resolution of the House of Representatives of the 7th ultimo, a report of the Secretary of State, touching the arrest and imprisonment in Mexico of Thomas Shields and two other American citizens, to which that resolution relates.

CHESTER A. ARTHUR.

EXECUTIVE MANSION, *March 10, 1882.*

To the House of Representatives:

I transmit herewith, in answer to the resolution of the House of Representatives of the 30th of January last, a report from the Secretary of State, with accompanying paper.*

CHESTER A. ARTHUR.

EXECUTIVE MANSION, *March 13, 1882.*

To the Senate and House of Representatives:

I transmit herewith a communication from the president of the National Board of Health, calling attention to the necessity for additional legislation to prevent the introduction of contagious and infectious diseases into the United States from foreign countries.

The subject is commended to the careful consideration of Congress.

CHESTER A. ARTHUR.

---

* List of promotions, removals, and appointments in the consular service since March 4, 1877.

EXECUTIVE MANSION, *March 14, 1882.*

To the House of Representatives:

I inclose herewith an amended estimate for an increase in the clerical force of the office of the Commissioner of Pensions, which I recommend to your consideration.

CHESTER A. ARTHUR.

[The same message was sent to the Senate.]

EXECUTIVE MANSION, *March 16, 1882.*

To the Senate of the United States:

I transmit herewith a report of the Secretary of State and an accompanying paper, in further response to the resolution of the Senate of the 13th of December last, calling for correspondence touching affairs in or between Peru and Chile.

CHESTER A ARTHUR.

EXECUTIVE MANSION, *March 17, 1882.*

To the Senate and House of Representatives:

I transmit herewith a communication from the Secretary of the Interior, with accompanying papers, covering the action of the Osage Indians declining to accede to the terms of the act of March 3, 1881, reducing the price of their lands in Kansas.

CHESTER A. ARTHUR.

EXECUTIVE MANSION, *March 18, 1882.*

To the House of Representatives:

In response to the resolution of the House of Representatives adopted March 16, 1882, in which the President is requested, if not incompatible with the public interests, to furnish to the House all the facts before him at the time he authorized the sending or employment of troops or military forces of the United States in the State of Nebraska during the present month, together with his reasons therefor, I have the honor to state that the employment of military forces of the United States as to which it is understood that information is desired by the House of Representatives was authorized on the 10th instant, and that all the facts before me at that time are set forth in telegraphic communications, dated the 9th and 10th instant, from the governor of the State of Nebraska and Brigadier-General Crook, commanding the Department of the Platte, of which copies are herewith submitted.

For the further information of the House of Representatives, I transmit copies of telegraphic correspondence had on the 9th, 10th, and 11th instant between the Secretary of War and the governor of Nebraska and the Secretary of War and the Lieutenant-General of the Army, of which the instructions issued by my direction for the employment of the military forces upon the application of the governor of Nebraska are a part.

From these papers it will be seen that the authority to employ troops was given upon the application of the governor of Nebraska in order to protect the State against domestic violence. The instructions were given in compliance with the requirements of that part of section 4 of Article IV of the Constitution which provides that the United States shall, on application of the legislature, or of the executive (when the legislature can not be convened), protect each of the States against domestic violence.

CHESTER A. ARTHUR.

EXECUTIVE MANSION, *March 20, 1882.*
To the Senate of the United States:

In compliance with a resolution of the Senate of the 9th instant, in structing the Secretary of State to ascertain and report to the Senate the cause for the alleged imprisonment by the British Government of Daniel McSweeney, a citizen of the United States, I transmit herewith a report on the subject from the Secretary of State, with its accompanying papers.

CHESTER A. ARTHUR.

EXECUTIVE MANSION, *March 21, 1882.*
To the Senate and House of Representatives:

I transmit herewith, for the consideration of Congress, a communication from the Secretary of War, dated the 18th instant, inclosing plans and estimates for a brick building for the post of Fort Leavenworth, Kans., to contain quarters for two companies of troops, to replace the one destroyed by fire on the 1st February last, and recommending an appropriation of $18,745.77, in accordance with the estimates.

CHESTER A. ARTHUR.

EXECUTIVE MANSION, *March 21, 1882.*
To the Senate and House of Representatives:

I transmit herewith, for the consideration of Congress, a communication from the Secretary of the Interior, dated the 6th instant, with accompanying paper, submitting draft of a bill "to authorize payment for Government transportation on certain railroads."

CHESTER A. ARTHUR.

EXECUTIVE MANSION, *March 21, 1882.*
To the Senate and House of Representatives:

I transmit herewith a communication from the Secretary of the Navy, calling attention to the necessity of appropriating the sum of $12,000 under the head of "Contingent equipment and recruiting," for immediate use, to defray accruing expenses during the remainder of the current fiscal year.

The matter is commended to the favorable consideration of Congress.

CHESTER A. ARTHUR.

WASHINGTON, *March 22, 1882.*

To the Senate and House of Representatives:

In compliance with section 4119 of the Revised Statutes (act of June 22, 1860), I transmit to Congress a copy of two additional regulations issued in accordance with the fifth section of that act by the envoy extraordinary and minister plenipotentiary of the United States accredited to the Government of China, and assented to by the several United States consular officers in that country, for the service of summonses on absent defendants in causes before the consular courts of the United States of America in China. These regulations, which are accompanied by a copy of the minister's dispatch on the subject, are commended to the consideration of Congress, with a view to their approval.

CHESTER A. ARTHUR.

EXECUTIVE MANSION, *March 23, 1882.*

To the Senate and House of Representatives:

I transmit herewith, for the consideration of Congress, a communication from the Secretary of War, dated March 23, 1882, with accompanying reports and estimates, recommending an increase in the clerical force in his office and in the offices of the Adjutant-General and Surgeon-General of the Army, in order that prompt replies may be made to the calls for information by the Commissioner of Pensions in pension cases under a proposed plan to accomplish the settlement of all such claims within a limited number of years; also an increased appropriation for contingent expenses for each of the offices mentioned.

CHESTER A. ARTHUR.

EXECUTIVE MANSION, *March 23, 1882.*

To the Senate and House of Representatives:

I transmit herewith a copy of a law* passed at the recent session of the legislature of the Territory of New Mexico, for the action of Congress under section 1850 of the Revised Statutes.

CHESTER A. ARTHUR.

* Providing a time for the commencement of the sessions of the legislative assembly of the Territory of New Mexico.

EXECUTIVE MANSION, *March 27, 1882.*

To the Senate and House of Representatives:

I transmit herewith a communication from the Secretary of the Interior, dated the 24th instant, and the accompanying letter of the Commissioner of Patents, submitting a supplemental estimate for an appropriation of $52,500 for the employment of twenty-five assistant principal examiners of patents, at an annual salary of $2,100 each.

The matter is commended to the consideration of Congress.

CHESTER A. ARTHUR.

EXECUTIVE MANSION, *March 28, 1882.*

To the Senate and House of Representatives:

I transmit herewith a communication from the Secretary of the Navy, with accompanying papers, on the subject of purchasing from the American Wood Preserving Company the machinery which was erected by that company at the navy-yard, Boston, under contract with the Navy Department, for the purpose of fully testing the company's process of preserving timber for use in the Navy.

The attention of Congress is invited to the subject.

CHESTER A. ARTHUR.

EXECUTIVE MANSION, *March 28, 1882.*

To the House of Representatives:

I transmit herewith, in response to the resolution of the House of Representatives of yesterday, the 27th instant, a report of the Secretary of State, with accompanying papers, touching the negotiations for the restoration of peace in South America.

CHESTER A. ARTHUR.

WASHINGTON, *March 28, 1882.*

To the Senate of the United States:

I transmit to the Senate, for its consideration with a view to ratification, a convention for the protection of trade-marks, concluded between the United States and His Majesty the King of Roumania on the 7th of October, 1881.

CHESTER A. ARTHUR.

EXECUTIVE MANSION, *March 29, 1882.*

To the Senate and House of Representatives:

I transmit herewith a communication from the Secretary of the Interior, dated 24th instant, in relation to the urgent necessity for action on the part of Congress for the prevention of trespasses upon Indian lands, with copy of report from Commissioner of Indian Affairs upon the subject and draft of bill for the object indicated.

The subject is commended to the consideration of Congress.

CHESTER A. ARTHUR.

EXECUTIVE MANSION, *March 29, 1882.*

To the Senate and House of Representatives:

I transmit herewith, for the consideration of Congress, a communication from the Secretary of War, dated March 25, 1882, with accompanying correspondence, plans, and estimates, in which he recommends an appropriation of $40,000 for the completion of the new post at Fort Lewis, Colo.

CHESTER A. ARTHUR.

EXECUTIVE MANSION, *March 30, 1882.*

To the Senate and House of Representatives:

I transmit herewith a communication from the Secretary of the Interior, dated the 28th instant, and the accompanying letter of the Superintendent of the Government Hospital for the Insane, submitting an estimate for a deficiency appropriation of $20,792.51 for the support of that institution for the remaining portion of the present fiscal year.

CHESTER A. ARTHUR.

EXECUTIVE MANSION, *March 30, 1882.*

To the Senate and House of Representatives:

I transmit herewith a letter from the Secretary of the Interior, inclosing draft of a bill to amend section 2056 of the Revised Statutes of the United States, relating to the term of office of Indian inspectors and Indian agents.

The subject is commended to the consideration of Congress.

CHESTER A. ARTHUR.

EXECUTIVE MANSION, *March 30, 1882.*

To the Senate and House of Representatives:

I transmit herewith a communication from the Secretary of the Interior, dated the 29th of March, and the accompanying letter of the Commissioner of the General Land Office, submitting an estimate for the additions of $34,200 and $20,000, respectively, to the appropriations for salaries, fees, and commissions of registers and receivers, and for contingent expenses, land offices, for the next fiscal year.

CHESTER A. ARTHUR.

EXECUTIVE MANSION, *March 30, 1882.*

To the House of Representatives:

I transmit herewith a report of the Secretary of State and accompanying documents, in response to a resolution of the House of Representatives of February 13, 1882, touching the protection of American citizens in Persia and the establishment of diplomatic relations with that country.

CHESTER A. ARTHUR.

EXECUTIVE MANSION, *April 3, 1882.*

To the Senate and House of Representatives:

I transmit herewith, for the consideration of Congress, a letter from the Secretary of the Interior, in which he sets forth the necessity which will exist for an appropriation for the payment of the commissioners to be appointed under the recent act of Congress entitled "An act to amend section 5352 of the Revised Statutes of the United States in reference to bigamy, and for other purposes," and also for the payment of the election officers to be appointed by said commissioners.

In this connection I submit to Congress that, in view of the important and responsible duties devolved upon the commissioners under this act, their compensation at $3,000 per annum, as provided therein, should be increased to a sum not less than $5,000 per annum.

Such increased compensation, in my judgment, would secure a higher order of ability in the persons to be selected and tend more effectually to carry out the objects of the act.

CHESTER A. ARTHUR.

EXECUTIVE MANSION, *April 3, 1882.*

To the House of Representatives:

I forward herewith, in compliance with a resolution of the House of Representatives of the 6th of February ultimo, calling for information in reference to the arrest and imprisonment in Mexico of certain American citizens, a further report from the Secretary of State and its accompanying paper, concerning the cases of Thomas Shields and Charles Weber, to which that resolution refers.

CHESTER A. ARTHUR.

EXECUTIVE MANSION, *April 4, 1882.*

To the House of Representatives:

In partial response to the resolution of the House of Representatives of the 31st of January last, on the subject of American citizens imprisoned in Ireland, I transmit herewith a report of the Secretary of State.

CHESTER A. ARTHUR.

EXECUTIVE MANSION, *April 4, 1882.*

To the Senate and House of Representatives:

I transmit herewith, for the consideration of Congress, a letter from the Secretary of War, dated March 31, 1882, and accompanying report from the Chief of Engineers, with its inclosures, relative to the construction of a bridge across the Potomac River at or near Georgetown, in the District of Columbia, under the provisions of the act approved February 23, 1881, in which he requests that an additional appropriation of $80,000 be made to give practical effect to the act referred to in accordance with the recommendations of the Chief of Engineers.

CHESTER A. ARTHUR.

EXECUTIVE MANSION, *April 5, 1882.*

To the Senate and House of Representatives:

I transmit herewith a communication from the Secretary of the Interior, setting forth the necessity for an increased number of law clerks in the office of the Assistant Attorney-General in the Department of the Interior, because of the growing amount of business in that office.

The matter is commended to the attention and favorable action of Congress.

CHESTER A. ARTHUR.

EXECUTIVE MANSION, *April 5, 1882.*

To the Senate and House of Representatives:

I transmit herewith a communication from the Secretary of the Interior of this date, with draft of bill for the relief of Pierre Garrieaux and correspondence in relation thereto.

CHESTER A. ARTHUR.

EXECUTIVE MANSION, *April 5, 1882.*

To the House of Representatives:

I transmit herewith, in reply to the resolution of the House of Representatives of the 31st of January last, a report from the Secretary of State, with accompanying papers.*

CHESTER A. ARTHUR.

WASHINGTON, *April 5, 1882.*

To the Senate:

I transmit herewith, in reply to the resolution of the Senate of the 29th of March last, the report of the Secretary of State, with accompanying papers.*

CHESTER A. ARTHUR.

---

*Correspondence, etc., relative to American citizens imprisoned in Ireland.

EXECUTIVE MANSION, *April 6, 1882.*

To the Senate and House of Representatives:

I transmit herewith, for the consideration of Congress, a letter from the Secretary of War, dated the 4th instant, inclosing plans and estimates for the completion of the post of Fort McKinney, Wyoming Territory, and recommending an appropriation of $50,000 for the purpose in accordance with the estimates.

CHESTER A. ARTHUR.

EXECUTIVE MANSION, *April 6, 1882.*

To the Senate and House of Representatives:

I transmit herewith, for the consideration of Congress, a communication from the Secretary of War, dated the 4th instant, inclosing estimates for deficiency in the appropriation for the transportation of the Army and its supplies for the fiscal year ending June 30, 1882, and recommending an appropriation in accordance therewith.

CHESTER A. ARTHUR.

EXECUTIVE MANSION, *April 11, 1882.*

To the Senate and House of Representatives:

I transmit herewith, for the consideration of Congress, a letter from the Secretary of War, dated the 6th instant, in which he recommends a reappropriation of the unexpended balances of two appropriations of $50,000 each, made in 1880 and 1881, "for continuing the improvement of the water-power pool" at the Rock Island Arsenal, and that the additional sum of $30,000 be granted for the same purpose; also the additional sum of $70,000 "for deepening the canal and for opening six waterways in connection with the water power."

CHESTER A. ARTHUR.

EXECUTIVE MANSION, *April 12, 1882.*

To the Senate and House of Representatives:

I transmit herewith a communication from the Secretary of the Interior, with the accompanying report from the Commissioner of Indian Affairs, dated 29th ultimo, recommending an increase of item for "transportation of Indian supplies for the fiscal year 1882" (deficiency), as designated in Senate Executive Document 57, Forty-seventh Congress, first session.

CHESTER A. ARTHUR.

EXECUTIVE MANSION, *April 12, 1882.*

To the Senate and House of Representatives:

I transmit herewith a communication from the Secretary of the Interior, inclosing draft of bill prepared in the Office of Indian Affairs, submitted with Commissioner's report of 27th ultimo, confirming to the

Cheyenne and Arapahoe Indians the lands in the Indian Territory set apart for their occupancy by an Executive order dated August 10, 1869, which lands are in lieu of those set apart for their use and occupancy by the second article of the treaty with said Indians concluded October 28, 1867.

CHESTER A. ARTHUR.

EXECUTIVE MANSION, *April 12, 1882.*

To the Senate and House of Representatives:

I transmit herewith, for the consideration of Congress, a letter from the Secretary of War, dated the 6th instant, inclosing one from the acting chief clerk of the War Department on the subject, recommending an additional appropriation of $2,000 for contingent expenses of the War Department for 1882; also that appropriation provided for the purpose for the next fiscal year be increased $10,000.

CHESTER A. ARTHUR.

OFFICE OF THE PRESIDENT OF THE UNITED STATES,
Washington, April 14, 1882.

To the Senate of the United States:

I transmit herewith, for the consideration of Congress, the inclosed letter and accompanying statement from the Secretary of the Navy, in relation to the necessity of building a new boiler shop at the navy-yard, New York, and repairing the caisson gate of the dry dock at that station, in which it is requested that an appropriation of $147,243.04 be made for these objects.

CHESTER A. ARTHUR.

[The same message was sent to the House of Representatives.]

EXECUTIVE MANSION, *April 14, 1882.*

To the House of Representatives:

I transmit herewith, with commendation to the attention of Congress, a report of the Secretary of State and its accompanying papers, concerning the proposed establishment of an international bureau of exchanges

CHESTER A. ARTHUR.

EXECUTIVE MANSION, *April 14, 1882.*

To the Senate and House of Representatives:

I transmit herewith a communication from the Secretary of the Interior, with correspondence, relative to right of way of the Republican Valley Railroad across the Otoe and Missouria Reservation in the State of Nebraska, and draft of an amendment to S. No. 930, "A bill to amend an act entitled 'An act to provide for the sale of the remainder of the reservation of the confederated Otoe and Missouria tribes of Indians in the States of Nebraska and Kansas, and for other purposes,' approved March 3, 1881."

CHESTER A. ARTHUR.

EXECUTIVE MANSION, *April 17, 1882.*

To the Senate and House of Representatives:

I transmit herewith a letter, dated the 29th ultimo, from the Secretary of War, inclosing copy of a communication from the Mississippi River Commission, in which the commission recommends that an appropriation may be made of $1,010,000 for "closing existing gaps in levees," in addition to the like sum for which an estimate has already been submitted.

The subject is one of such importance that I deem it proper to recommend early and favorable consideration of the recommendations of the commission. Having possession of and jurisdiction over the river, Congress, with a view of improving its navigation and protecting the people of the valley from floods, has for years caused surveys of the river to be made for the purpose of acquiring knowledge of the laws that control it and of its phenomena. By act approved June 28, 1879, the Mississippi River Commission was created, composed of able engineers. Section 4 of the act provides that—

It shall be the duty of said commission to take into consideration and mature such plan or plans and estimates as will correct, permanently locate, and deepen the channel and protect the banks of the Mississippi River; improve and give safety and ease to the navigation thereof; prevent destructive floods; promote and facilitate commerce, trade, and the postal service.

The constitutionality of a law making appropriations in aid of these objects can not be questioned. While the report of the commission submitted and the plans proposed for the river's improvement seem justified as well on scientific principles as by experience and the approval of the people most interested, I desire to leave it to the judgment of Congress to decide upon the best plan for the permanent and complete improvement of the navigation of the river and for the protection of the valley.

The immense losses and widespread suffering of the people dwelling near the river induce me to urge upon Congress the propriety of not only making an appropriation to close the gaps in the levees occasioned by the recent floods, as recommended by the commission, but that Congress should inaugurate measures for the permanent improvement of the navigation of the river and security of the valley. It may be that such a system of improvement would as it progressed require the appropriation of twenty or thirty millions of dollars. Even such an expenditure, extending, as it must, over several years, can not be regarded as extravagant in view of the immense interest involved. The safe and convenient navigation of the Mississippi is a matter of concern to all sections of the country, but to the Northwest, with its immense harvests, needing cheap transportation to the sea, and to the inhabitants of the river valley, whose lives and property depend upon the proper construction of the safeguards which protect them from the floods, it is of vital importance that a well-matured and comprehensive plan for improvement should be put into operation with as little delay as possible. The cotton product of the region subject to the devastating floods is a source of wealth to the nation and of great importance to keeping the balances of trade in our favor.

It may not be inopportune to mention that this Government has imposed and collected some $70,000,000 by a tax on cotton, in the production of which the population of the Lower Mississippi is largely engaged, and it does not seem inequitable to return a portion of this tax to those who contributed it, particularly as such an action will also result in an important gain to the country at large, and especially so to the great and rich States of the Northwest and the Mississippi Valley.

CHESTER A. ARTHUR.

EXECUTIVE MANSION, *April 17, 1882.*

To the Senate and House of Representatives:

I transmit herewith a communication, dated the 14th instant, from the Secretary of the Interior, with draft of bill, and accompanying papers, for the establishment of an Indian training school on the site of the old Fort Ripley Military Reservation, in the State of Minnesota.

The subject is commended to the consideration of Congress.

CHESTER A. ARTHUR.

EXECUTIVE MANSION, *April 17, 1882.*

To the Senate and House of Representatives:

I transmit herewith a communication from the Secretary of the Interior of the 12th instant, with accompanying papers, in relation to coal lands upon the San Carlos Reservation, in the Territory of Arizona.

The subject is presented for the consideration of Congress.

CHESTER A. ARTHUR.

To the Senate: EXECUTIVE MANSION, *April 17, 1882.*

I transmit herewith a report from the Secretary of State and its accompanying papers, concerning the international regulations for preventing collisions at sea, and I earnestly commend this important subject to the early and favorable consideration of Congress.

CHESTER A. ARTHUR.

[The same message was sent to the House of Representatives.]

EXECUTIVE MANSION, *April 18, 1882.*

To the Senate and House of Representatives:

I send herewith a copy of the circular invitation extended to all the independent countries of North and South America to participate in a general congress to be held in the city of Washington on the 22d of November next for the purpose of considering and discussing the methods of preventing war between the nations of America.

In giving this invitation I was not unaware that there existed differences between several of the Republics of South America which would militate against the happy results which might otherwise be expected from such an assemblage. The differences indicated are such as exist between Chile and Peru, between Mexico and Guatemala, and between the States of Central America.

It was hoped that these differences would disappear before the time fixed for the meeting of the congress. This hope has not been realized.

Having observed that the authority of the President to convene such a congress has been questioned, I beg leave to state that the Constitution confers upon the President the power, by and with the advice and consent of the Senate, to make treaties, and that this provision confers the power to take all requisite measures to initiate them, and to this end the President may freely confer with one or several commissioners or delegates from other nations. The congress contemplated by the invitation could only effect any valuable results by its conclusions eventually taking the form of a treaty of peace between the States represented; and, besides, the invitation to the States of North and South America is merely a preliminary act, of which constitutionality or the want of it can hardly be affirmed.

It has been suggested that while the international congress would have no power to affect the rights of nationalities there represented, still Congress might be unwilling to subject the existing treaty rights of the United States on the Isthmus and elsewhere on the continent to be clouded and rendered uncertain by the expression of the opinions of a congress composed largely of interested parties.

I am glad to have it in my power to refer to the Congress of the United States, as I now do, the propriety of convening the suggested international congress, that I may thus be informed of its views, which it will be my pleasure to carry out.

Inquiry having been made by some of the Republics invited whether it is intended that this international congress shall convene, it is important that Congress should at as early a day as is convenient inform me by resolution or otherwise of its opinion in the premises. My action will be in harmony with such expression.   CHESTER A. ARTHUR.

DEPARTMENT OF STATE, *Washington, November 29, 1881.*

SIR:* The attitude of the United States with respect to the question of general peace on the American continent is well known through its persistent efforts for years past to avert the evils of warfare, or, these efforts failing, to bring positive conflicts to an end through pacific counsels or the advocacy of impartial arbitration. This attitude has been consistently maintained, and always with such fairness as to leave no room for imputing to our Government any motive except the humane and disinterested one of saving the kindred States of the American continent from the burdens of war. The position of the United States as the leading power of the New World might well give to its Government a claim to authoritative utterance for the purpose of quieting discord among its neighbors, with all of whom the most friendly relations exist. Nevertheless, the good offices of this Government are not and have not at any time been tendered with a show of dictation or compulsion, but only as exhibiting the solicitous good will of a common friend.

For some years past a growing disposition has been manifested by certain States of Central and South America to refer disputes affecting grave questions of international relationship and boundaries to arbitration rather than to the sword. It has been on several such occasions a source of profound satisfaction to the Government of the United States to see that this country is in a large measure looked to by all the American powers as their friend and mediator.

The just and impartial counsel of the President in such cases has never been withheld, and his efforts have been rewarded by the prevention of sanguinary strife or angry contentions between peoples whom we regard as brethren.

The existence of this growing tendency convinces the President that the time is ripe for a proposal that shall enlist the good will and active cooperation of all the States of the Western Hemisphere, both north and south, in the interest of humanity and for the common weal of nations.

He conceives that none of the Governments of America can be less alive than our own to the dangers and horrors of a state of war, and especially of war between kinsmen. He is sure that none of the chiefs of Governments on the continent can be less sensitive than he is to the sacred duty of making every endeavor to do away with the chances of fratricidal strife. And he looks with hopeful confidence to such active assistance from them as will serve to show the broadness of our common humanity and the strength of the ties which bind us all together as a great and harmonious system of American Commonwealths.

Impressed by these views, the President extends to all the independent countries of North and South America an earnest invitation to participate in a general congress to be held in the city of Washington on the 24th day of November, 1882, for the purpose of considering and discussing the methods of preventing war between the nations of America. He desires that the attention of the congress shall be strictly confined to this one great object; that its sole aim shall be to seek a way of permanently averting the horrors of cruel and bloody combat between countries, oftenest of one blood and speech, or the even worse calamity of internal commotion and civil strife; that it shall regard the burdensome and far-reaching consequences of such struggles, the legacies of exhausted finances, of oppressive debt, of onerous taxation, of ruined

* Sent under the same date, *mutatis mutandis*, to the United States ministers in the Argentine Republic, Bolivia, Brazil, Central America, Chile, Colombia, Mexico, Paraguay and Uruguay, Peru, and Venezuela; also directly to the minister of foreign relations of Ecuador, in which country the United States had no diplomatic representative.

cities, of paralyzed industries, of devastated fields, of ruthless conscription, of the slaughter of men, of the grief of the widow and the orphan, of imbittered resentments that long survive those who provoked them and heavily afflict the innocent generations that come after.

The President is especially desirous to have it understood that in putting forth this invitation the United States does not assume the position of counseling, or attempting through the voice of the congress to counsel, any determinate solution of existing questions which may now divide any of the countries of America. Such questions can not properly come before the congress. Its mission is higher. It is to provide for the interests of all in the future, not to settle the individual differences of the present. For this reason especially the President has indicated a day for the assembling of the congress so far in the future as to leave good ground for hope that by the time named the present situation on the South Pacific coast will be happily terminated, and that those engaged in the contest may take peaceable part in the discussion and solution of the general question affecting in an equal degree the well-being of all.

It seems also desirable to disclaim in advance any purpose on the part of the United States to prejudge the issues to be presented to the congress. It is far from the intent of this Government to appear before the congress as in any sense the protector of its neighbors or the predestined and necessary arbitrator of their disputes. The United States will enter into the deliberations of the congress on the same footing as the other powers represented, and with the loyal determination to approach any proposed solution not merely in its own interest or with a view to asserting its own power, but as a single member among many coordinate and coequal States. So far as the influence of this Government may be potential, it will be exerted in the direction of conciliating whatever conflicting interests of blood or government or historical tradition may necessarily come together in response to a call embracing such vast and diverse elements.

You will present these views to the minister of foreign relations of Mexico, enlarging, if need be, in such terms as will readily occur to you, upon the great mission which it is within the power of the proposed congress to accomplish in the interest of humanity, and upon the firm purpose of the United States to maintain a position of the most absolute and impartial friendship toward all. You will thereupon, in the name of the President of the United States, tender to His Excellency the President of the Mexican Republic a formal invitation to send two commissioners to the congress, provided with such powers and instructions on behalf of their Government as will enable them to consider the questions brought before that body within the limit of submission contemplated by this invitation.

The United States as well as the other powers will in like manner be represented by two commissioners, so that equality and impartiality will be amply secured in the proceedings of the congress.

In delivering this invitation through the minister of foreign affairs you will read this dispatch to him and leave with him a copy, intimating that an answer is desired by this Government as promptly as the just consideration of so important a proposition will permit.

I am, sir, your obedient servant,   JAMES G. BLAINE.

EXECUTIVE MANSION, *April 18, 1882.*

To the Senate and House of Representatives:

I transmit herewith, for the consideration of Congress, a note addressed by the minister plenipotentiary of Mexico to the Secretary of State, proposing the conclusion of a convention between the two countries for defining the boundary between the United States and Mexico from the Rio Grande westward to the Pacific Ocean by the erection of durable monuments. I also lay before Congress a letter on the same subject, with its accompaniment, from the Secretary of War, to whom the proposition was referred by the Secretary of State for the expression of his views thereon.

I deem it important that the boundary line between the two countries, as defined by existing treaties and already once surveyed, should be run anew and defined by suitable permanent monuments. By so doing uncertainty will be prevented as to jurisdiction in criminal and municipal affairs, and questions be averted which may at any time in the near future arise with the growth of population on the border.

Moreover, I conceive that the willing and speedy assent of the Government of the United States to the proposal thus to determine the existing stipulated boundary with permanence and precision will be in some sense an assurance to Mexico that the unauthorized suspicion which of late years seems to have gained some credence in that Republic that the United States covets and seeks to annex neighboring territory is without foundation. That which the United States seeks, and which the definite settlement of the boundary in the proposed manner will promote, is a confiding and friendly feeling between the two nations, leading to advantageous commerce and closer commercial relations.

I have to suggest that in accepting this proposal suitable provision be made for an adequate military force on the frontier to protect the surveying parties from hostile Indians. The troops so employed will at the same time protect the settlers on the border and help to prevent marauding on both sides by the nomadic Indians.

CHESTER A. ARTHUR.

EXECUTIVE MANSION, *April 20, 1882.*
To the Senate and House of Representatives:

I transmit herewith, for the consideration of Congress, a letter from the Secretary of War of the 18th instant, inclosing plans and estimates for the completion of the post of Fort Maginnis, Montana Territory, and recommending an appropriation for the purpose of $25,000, as called for by the estimates.

CHESTER A. ARTHUR.

EXECUTIVE MANSION, *April 21, 1882.*
To the Senate and House of Representatives:

I transmit herewith a communication, dated the 15th instant, from the Secretary of the Interior, with draft of bill and accompanying papers, touching the amendment of section 2142 of the Revised Statutes of the United States.

The subject is presented for the consideration of Congress.

CHESTER A. ARTHUR.

OFFICE OF THE PRESIDENT OF THE UNITED STATES,
Washington, April 21, 1882.

To the Senate of the United States:

I transmit herewith a communication addressed to me by the Secretary of the Navy, with accompanying papers, in which an appropriation is asked for the purpose of observing the transit of Venus in 1882.

The matter is commended to the favorable action of Congress.

CHESTER A. ARTHUR.

[The same message was sent to the House of Representatives.]

EXECUTIVE MANSION, *April 25, 1882.*

To the House of Representatives:

I transmit herewith a report of the Secretary of State, presented in compliance with the request of the House of Representatives in a resolution of the 10th instant, asking for information touching the existing restrictions on the importation of American neat cattle into Great Britain.

CHESTER A. ARTHUR.

EXECUTIVE MANSION, *April 25, 1882.*

To the House of Representatives:

I transmit herewith, for the consideration of the House of Representatives, a report from the Secretary of State, in relation to the International Fisheries Exhibition which is to be held at London in May, 1883. Fully approving of the suggestions contained in the report, I would earnestly recommend that favorable action be taken upon the subject at the present session of Congress, in order that there may be ample time for making the appropriations necessary to enable this country to participate in the exhibition.

CHESTER A. ARTHUR.

EXECUTIVE MANSION, *April 26, 1882.*

To the Senate and House of Representatives:

By recent information received from official and other sources I am advised that an alarming state of disorder continues to exist within the

Territory of Arizona, and that lawlessness has already gained such head there as to require a resort to extraordinary means to repress it.

The governor of the Territory, under date of the 31st ultimo, reports that violence and anarchy prevail, particularly in Cochise County and along the Mexican border; that robbery, murder, and resistance to law have become so common as to cease causing surprise, and that the people are greatly intimidated and losing confidence in the protection of the law. I transmit his communication herewith and call especial attention thereto.

In a telegram from the General of the Army dated at Tucson, Ariz., on the 11th instant, herewith transmitted, that officer states that he hears of lawlessness and disorders which seem well attested, and that the civil officers have not sufficient force to make arrests and hold the prisoners for trial or punish them when convicted.

Much of this disorder is caused by armed bands of desperadoes known as "Cowboys," by whom depredations are not only committed within the Territory, but it is alleged predatory incursions are made therefrom into Mexico. In my message to Congress at the beginning of the present session I called attention to the existence of these bands and suggested that the setting on foot within our own territory of brigandage and armed marauding expeditions against friendly nations and their citizens be made punishable as an offense against the United States. I renew this suggestion.

To effectually repress the lawlessness prevailing within the Territory a prompt execution of the process of the courts and vigorous enforcement of the laws against offenders are needed. This the civil authorities there are unable to do without the aid of other means and forces than they can now avail themselves of. To meet the present exigencies the governor asks that provision be made by Congress to enable him to employ and maintain temporarily a volunteer militia force to aid the civil authorities, the members of which force to be invested with the same powers and authority as are conferred by the laws of the Territory upon peace officers thereof.

On the ground of economy as well as effectiveness, however, it appears to me to be more advisable to permit the cooperation with the civil authorities of a part of the Army as a *posse comitatus*. Believing that this, in addition to such use of the Army as may be made under the powers already conferred by section 5298, Revised Statutes, would be adequate to secure the accomplishment of the ends in view, I again call the attention of Congress to the expediency of so amending section 15 of the act of June 18, 1878, chapter 263, as to allow the military forces to be employed as a *posse comitatus* to assist the civil authorities within a Territory to execute the laws therein. This use of the Army, as I have in my former message observed, would not seem to be within the alleged evil against which that legislation was aimed.

CHESTER A. ARTHUR.

EXECUTIVE MANSION,
Washington, May 2, 1882.

To the House of Representatives:

In answer to a resolution of the House of Representatives of the 30th of January last, calling for correspondence respecting the condition of Israelites in Russia, I transmit herewith a report from the Secretary of State and its accompanying papers.

CHESTER A. ARTHUR.

EXECUTIVE MANSION,
Washington, May 2, 1882.

To the Senate and House of Representatives:

I transmit herewith, for the consideration of Congress, a letter from the Secretary of the Interior, in which he requests that an appropriation of $108,000 be made for constructing a fireproof roof over the south and east wings of the building occupied by the Department of the Interior.

CHESTER A. ARTHUR.

EXECUTIVE MANSION,
Washington, May 2, 1882.

To the Senate of the United States:

I transmit herewith, in response to the resolution of the Senate of the 18th ultimo, a report of the Secretary of State, with copies of certain diplomatic correspondence* with Spain in 1876, called for by that resolution.

CHESTER A. ARTHUR.

EXECUTIVE MANSION, *May 5, 1882.*

To the Senate and House of Representatives:

I transmit herewith a communication from the Secretary of the Interior of the 3d instant, with accompanying papers, in relation to a proposed amendment of the act of the 15th December, 1880, providing for the disposal of the Fort Dodge Military Reservation, Kans.

The subject is commended to the consideration of Congress.

CHESTER A. ARTHUR.

EXECUTIVE MANSION, *May 9, 1882.*

To the Senate and House of Representatives:

I transmit herewith, for the consideration of Congress, a communication from the Secretary of the Interior, inclosing a letter from the Superintendent of Census, submitting an estimate for an appropriation of $80,000 to defray the expenses of the Census Office during the remainder of the present fiscal year.

CHESTER A. ARTHUR.

---

*Relating to United States citizens condemned to death in Cuba, etc.

EXECUTIVE MANSION, *May 9, 1882.*

To the Senate and House of Representatives:

I transmit herewith, for the consideration of Congress, a communication from the Secretary of the Interior, inclosing a letter from the Commissioner of the General Land Office, submitting an estimate for a special appropriation of $3,200 for completing an exhibit of all the private land claims in the State of Louisiana.

CHESTER A. ARTHUR.

EXECUTIVE MANSION, *May 11, 1882.*

To the Senate and House of Representatives:

I submit herewith, for the consideration of Congress, a letter from the Secretary of the Interior, inclosing a copy of a letter from the governor of Arizona, in which he requests that an appropriation of $2,000 be made for the contingent expenses of the Territory for the next fiscal year.

CHESTER A. ARTHUR.

EXECUTIVE MANSION, *May 15, 1882.*

To the Senate and House of Representatives:

I transmit herewith a communication from the Secretary of the Interior, submitting a copy of a letter from the Commissioner of Pensions inviting attention to the fact that the "deficiency" appropriation of $16,000,000 to meet the June payment of army pensions should be available as early as the 25th instant if practicable, in order to avoid any delay in payment.

CHESTER A. ARTHUR.

EXECUTIVE MANSION, *May 15, 1882.*

To the Senate and House of Representatives:

I transmit herewith a communication, dated the 11th instant, from the Secretary of the Interior, together with estimate of appropriation and accompanying papers, to provide, in accordance with treaty stipulations and existing laws, for the payment of certain interest due the Osage Indians.

The subject is presented for the consideration of Congress.

CHESTER A. ARTHUR.

EXECUTIVE MANSION, *May 15, 1882.*

To the Senate of the United States:

I transmit herewith a report of the Secretary of State, with accompanying papers, submitted in response to the Senate resolution of the 21st of March last, requesting a copy of instructions given to Mr. George F.

Seward, when minister to China, concerning Chinese immigration, etc., and Mr. Seward's dispatches on that subject.

CHESTER A. ARTHUR.

EXECUTIVE MANSION, *May 18, 1882.*

To the House of Representatives:

I transmit herewith a concluding report from the Secretary of State of the 17th instant, and its accompanying papers, relative to Thomas Shields and Charles Weber, who were imprisoned at Apan, Mexico, and whose cases formed the subject of the resolution of the House of Representatives of February 6, 1882.

CHESTER A. ARTHUR.

EXECUTIVE MANSION,
Washington, May 18, 1882.

To the Senate of the United States:

I transmit herewith a letter from the Secretary of State, accompanied by a copy of the correspondence referred to in Senate resolution of the 26th ultimo, in relation to the Japanese indemnity.

CHESTER A. ARTHUR.

EXECUTIVE MANSION, *May 22, 1882.*

To the Senate and House of Representatives:

I transmit herewith a communication from the Secretary of the Interior, dated 18th instant, and accompanying report from the Commissioner of Indian Affairs, relative to the necessity for buildings at the Mescalero Agency, N. Mex., and for an appropriation for the support, civilization, etc., of the Apaches at the Mescalero and Jicarilla agencies, together with an estimate for the same, in the form of a proposed clause for insertion in the sundry civil bill now pending for consideration in committee.

The subject is presented for the consideration of Congress.

CHESTER A. ARTHUR.

EXECUTIVE MANSION, *May 22, 1882.*

To the Senate and House of Representatives:

I transmit herewith a communication from the Secretary of the Interior of the 18th instant, with accompanying papers, submitting the draft of a proposed clause for insertion in one of the pending appropriation bills, to provide for the payment for improvements made by certain settlers on the Round Valley Indian Reservation, in California, as appraised under the act approved March 3, 1873.

The subject is presented for the consideration of Congress.

CHESTER A. ARTHUR.

EXECUTIVE MANSION, *May 22, 1882.*

To ix House of Representatives:

I transmit herewith a letter from the Secretary of State and accompanying documents, submitted in compliance with resolution of the House of Representatives of the 20th ultimo, calling for additional information respecting cases of American citizens under arrest in Ireland.

CHESTER A. ARTHUR.

EXECUTIVE MANSION, *May 22, 1882.*

To the Senate and House of Representatives:

I transmit herewith a letter from the Secretary of War, dated the 18th instant, and accompanying papers from the Acting Chief Signal Officer, representing the necessity of a special appropriation being made not later than the 1st of June proximo for the purpose of dispatching a vessel, with men and supplies, for the relief of the expedition which was last year sent to Lady Franklin Bay, Grinnell Land.

CHESTER A. ARTHUR.

EXECUTIVE MANSION, *May 24, 1882.*

To the Senate of the United States:

In compliance with a resolution of the Senate of the 1st of March last, I transmit a communication from the Secretary of the Navy, accompanied by the report (with the exception of such parts thereof as it is deemed incompatible with the public interests to furnish) of Commodore R. W. Shufeldt, United States Navy, of his cruise around the world in the United States steamer *Ticonderoga.*

CHESTER A. ARTHUR.

EXECUTIVE MANSION,
Washington, May 25, 1882.

To the Senate and House of Representatives:

I transmit herewith a letter from the Secretary of State, concerning the awards made against Venezuela by the mixed commission under the convention of April 25, 1866. I earnestly invite the attention of Congress to this communication and the accompanying inclosures. In case neither House takes action upon it during the present Congress I shall feel it my duty to direct that this prolonged discussion be definitely terminated by recognizing the absolute validity of all the awards.

CHESTER A. ARTHUR.

EXECUTIVE MANSION, *May 26, 1882.*

To the House of Representatives:

In answer to the resolution of the House of Representatives of the 10th of April ultimo, calling upon the Secretary of State for information in regard to the restrictions imposed by the French Government upon pork exported from the United States, I transmit herewith a report of that officer and its accompanying papers.

CHESTER A. ARTHUR.

EXECUTIVE MANSION, *June 5, 1882.*

To the Senate and House of Representatives:

I transmit herewith a communication from the Secretary of the Interior of the 24th ultimo, with accompanying papers, submitting the draft of a proposed clause for insertion in one of the pending appropriation bills, to provide for the payment of certain legal services rendered to the Cherokee Indians in North Caroiina in 1881, amounting to $150.

The subject is presented for the consideration of Congress.

CHESTER A. ARTHUR.

EXECUTIVE MANSION,
Washington, June 5, 1882.

To the Senate of the United States:

In further answer to the Senate's resolution of the 12th of December last, I transmit herewith a report of the Secretary of State and its accompanying paper, in regard to the modification of the Clayton-Bulwer treaty.

CHESTER A. ARTHUR.

EXECUTIVE MANSION, *June 14, 1882.*

To the Senate and House of Representatives:

I transmit herewith a letter from the Secretary of the Interior, respecting the Louisiana private land claim of Antonio Vaca, deceased, to which, with the accompanying papers, I invite the attention of Congress.

CHESTER A. ARTHUR.

EXECUTIVE MANSION,
Washington, June 14, 1882.

To the Senate of the United States:

I transmit herewith, in response to the resolution of the Senate of the 5th instant, a report from the Secretary of State, submitting copies of the full correspondence between the Department of State and Hon. William Henry Trescot, special envoy extraordinary to the Republics of Peru, Chile, and Bolivia, and Walker Blaine, Third Assistant Secretary of State.

CHESTER A. ARTHUR.

EXECUTIVE MANSION, *June 16, 1882.*

To the Senate and House of Representatives:

I submit herewith, for the consideration of Congress, a communication from the Secretary of the Interior, in which he recommends that the sum of $245,000, the amount which the Superintendent estimates will be required to complete the work of the Tenth Census, be appropriated for the purpose.

CHESTER A. ARTHUR.

EXECUTIVE MANSION, *June 16, 1882.*

To the Senate and House of Representatives:

I transmit herewith, for the consideration of Congress, a letter from the Secretary of War, dated the 14th instant, covering plans and estimates for repairs, additions, and alterations to public buildings at the depot of the mounted recruiting service, Jefferson Barracks, Mo., and in which he recommends that the sum of $24,938.44 be appropriated for the purpose, in accordance with the estimates, during the present session of Congress.

CHESTER A. ARTHUR.

To the Senate: EXECUTIVE MANSION, *June 16, 1882.*

I transmit herewith a report from the Secretary of State and its accompanying papers, concerning the Smoke Abatement Exhibition which was held at South Kensington, London, last winter.

CHESTER A. ARTHUR.

WASHINGTON, *June 16, 1882.*

To the Senate of the United States:

I transmit herewith to the Senate, for its consideration with a view to ratification, a convention between the United States and His Majesty the King of the Belgians, touching the reciprocal surrender of fugitives from justice, signed on the 13th day of June, 1882, and intended to supersede the convention for extradition of criminals between both countries which was concluded on the 19th day of March, 1874.

CHESTER A. ARTHUR.

EXECUTIVE MANSION, *June 19, 1882.*

To the Senate and House of Representatives:

I transmit herewith a communication, dated the 16th instant, from the Secretary of the Interior, inclosing, with accompanying papers, a draft of a bill "to enlarge the Pawnee Indian Reservation in Indian Territory."

The subject is presented for the consideration of Congress.

CHESTER A. ARTHUR.

EXECUTIVE MANSION, *June 19, 1882.*

To the House of Representatives:

I transmit herewith a letter from the Secretary of State, referring a communication from the Mexican minister at this capital touching the arrest and imprisonment in Mexico of Thomas Shields and two other American citizens, to which the resolution of the House of Representatives of the 6th day of February last relates.

CHESTER A. ARTHUR.

WASHINGTON, *June 23, 1882.*

To the Senate of the United States:

I transmit herewith to the Senate, with a view to ratification, a convention between the United States and His Majesty the King of Spain, for securing reciprocal protection for the trade-marks and manufactured articles of their respective citizens and subjects within the dominions or territories of the other country, signed on the 19th day of June, 1882.

CHESTER A. ARTHUR.

EXECUTIVE MANSION, *June 26, 1882.*

To the Senate and House of Representatives:

I transmit herewith a communication from the Secretary of War, dated the 9th instant, and its accompanying copy of the telegram from the general commanding the Military Division of the Pacific and Department of California, relative to the construction of additional quarters, barracks, storehouses, etc., within the limits of the Military Department of Arizona.

The Secretary of War recommends that for the purpose of constructing the additional buildings referred to the sum of their estimated cost, $205,000, be appropriated during the present session of Congress.

CHESTER A. ARTHUR.

EXECUTIVE MANSION, *June 28, 1882.*

To the Senate and House of Representatives:

I transmit herewith a communication from the Secretary of the Interior of the 22d instant, with accompanying papers, submitting the draft of a proposed clause for insertion in one of the pending appropriation bills, to provide for the payment for improvements made by certain settlers on the Jicarilla Apache Indian Reservation, in New Mexico.

The subject is presented for the consideration of Congress.

CHESTER A. ARTHUR.

EXECUTIVE MANSION, *July 3, 1882.*

To the House of Representatives:

In answer to the resolution of the House of Representatives of the 25th of April last, calling for information in regard to the reassembling of the Paris Monetary Conference during the current year and other matters connected therewith, I transmit herewith a report on the subject and its accompanying papers.   CHESTER A. ARTHUR.

EXECUTIVE MANSION,
Washington, July 20, 1882.

To the Senate of the United States:

I transmit herewith a report of the Secretary of State and accompanying papers, furnished in response to the resolution of the Senate of December 21, 1881, calling for the correspondence with the Mexican Government in regard to the claims of Benjamin Weil and La Abra Silver Mining Company against Mexico.   CHESTER A. ARTHUR.

EXECUTIVE MANSION,
Washington, July 20, 1882.

To the Senate of the United States:

I transmit herewith to the Senate, for its consideration with a view to ratification, a convention between the United States and Mexico, providing for the reopening and retrying of the claims of Benjamin Weil and La Abra Silver Mining Company against Mexico, which was signed on the 13th instant.

A report of the Secretary of State, with its accompanying correspondence, transmitted to the Senate this day in response to the resolution of December 21, 1881, will show the antecedents of the negotiation which resulted in the accompanying convention.   In view of the accumulation of testimony presented by Mexico relative to these two claims, I have deemed it proper to avail myself of the authority given to the Executive by the Constitution, and of which authority the act of Congress of June 18, 1878, is declarative, to effect a rehearing of these cases.   I therefore empowered the Secretary of State to negotiate with the minister of Mexico a convention to that end.

The more important correspondence preliminary to the treaty is herewith transmitted.

It will be seen by the stipulations of the treaty that the rehearing will have no retroactive effect as to payments already distributed, that the *bona fide* interests of third parties are amply secured, and that the Government of the United States is fully guarded against any liability resulting from the rehearing.   CHESTER A. ARTHUR.

EXECUTIVE MANSION,
Washington, July 20, 1882.

To the Senate of the United States:

I transmit herewith to the Senate, for consideration with a view to ratification, a supplementary convention between the United States and the French Republic, signed at Washington on the 19th instant, extending the term of duration of the commission organized under the convention of January 15, 1880, between the two countries.

CHESTER A. ARTHUR.

EXECUTIVE MANSION,
Washington, July 29, 1882.

To the Senate of the United States:

I transmit herewith, in response to the Senate resolution of the 15th instant, a report of the Secretary of State and accompanying papers, relating to the Clayton-Bulwer treaty.

CHESTER A. ARTHUR.

EXECUTIVE MANSION,
Washington, July 29, 1882.

To the Senate of the United States:

I transmit herewith to the Senate, for consideration with a view to ratification, a treaty between the United States and the Kingdom of Korea, or Chosen, concluded on the 22d May last. For the information of the Senate the accompanying letter of the Secretary of State is also transmitted.

CHESTER A. ARTHUR.

EXECUTIVE MANSION,
Washington, August 1, 1882.

To the Senate of the United States:

I transmit herewith to the Senate, for consideration with a view to ratification, a convention concluded on the 29th of July, 1882, between the United States and Mexico, providing for an international boundary survey to relocate the existing frontier line between the two countries west of the Rio Grande.

CHESTER A. ARTHUR.

OFFICE OF THE PRESIDENT OF THE UNITED STATES,
Washington, August 4, 1882.

To the Senate of the United States:

In reply to a resolution of the Senate passed April 25, 1882, I transmit herewith a communication, with accompanying papers, from the Secretary of the Navy, in relation to the title by which the United States holds the land now occupied as a navy-yard at Boston, Mass.

CHESTER A. ARTHUR.

EXECUTIVE MANSION, *August 5, 1882.*

To the House of Representatives:

I transmit herewith a report of the Secretary of State, submitted in compliance with the resolution of the House of Representatives of the 28th of June, calling for additional information respecting the case of American citizens under arrest in Ireland.

CHESTER A. ARTHUR.

EXECUTIVE MANSION,
Washington, August 7, 1882.

To the Senate of the United States:

I transmit herewith to the Senate, with a view to ratification, a convention concluded this day between the United States of America and His Majesty the King of Spain, supplementary to the extradition convention concluded between said countries on the 5th day of January, 1877.

CHESTER A. ARTHUR.

VETO MESSAGES.

EXECUTIVE MANSION,
Washington, April 4, 1882.

To the Senate of the United States:

After careful consideration of Senate bill No. 71, entitled "An act to execute certain treaty stipulations relating to Chinese," I herewith return it to the Senate, in which it originated, with my objections to its passage.

A nation is justified in repudiating its treaty obligations only when they are in conflict with great paramount interests. Even then all possible reasonable means for modifying or changing those obligations by mutual agreement should be exhausted before resorting to the supreme right of refusal to comply with them.

These rules have governed the United States in their past intercourse with other powers as one of the family of nations. I am persuaded that if Congress can feel that this act violates the faith of the nation as pledged to China it will concur with me in rejecting this particular mode of regulating Chinese immigration, and will endeavor to find another which shall meet the expectations of the people of the United States without coming in conflict with the rights of China.

The present treaty relations between that power and the United States spring from an antagonism which arose between our paramount domestic interests and our previous relations.

The treaty commonly known as the Burlingame treaty conferred upon Chinese subjects the right of voluntary emigration to the United States for the purposes of curiosity or trade or as permanent residents, and was in all respects reciprocal as to citizens of the United States in China. It gave to the voluntary emigrant coming to the United States the right to travel there or to reside there, with all the privileges, immunities, or exemptions enjoyed by the citizens or subjects of the most favored nation.

Under the operation of this treaty it was found that the institutions of the United States and the character of its people and their means of obtaining a livelihood might be seriously affected by the unrestricted introduction of Chinese labor. Congress attempted to alleviate this condition by legislation, but the act which it passed proved to be in violation of our treaty obligations, and, being returned by the President with his objections, failed to become a law.

Diplomatic relief was then sought. A new treaty was concluded with China. Without abrogating the Burlingame treaty, it was agreed to modify it so far that the Government of the United States might regulate, limit, or suspend the coming of Chinese laborers to the United States or their residence therein, but that it should not absolutely prohibit them, and that the limitation or suspension should be reasonable and should apply only to Chinese who might go to the United States as laborers, other classes not being included in the limitations. This treaty is unilateral, not reciprocal. It is a concession from China to the United States in limitation of the rights which she was enjoying under the Burlingame treaty. It leaves us by our own act to determine when and how we will enforce those limitations. China may therefore fairly have a right to expect that in enforcing them we will take good care not to overstep the grant and take more than has been conceded to us.

It is but a year since this new treaty, under the operation of the Constitution, became part of the supreme law of the land, and the present act is the first attempt to exercise the more enlarged powers which it relinquishes to the United States.

In its first article the United States is empowered to decide whether the coming of Chinese laborers to the United States or their residence therein affects or threatens to affect our interests or to endanger good order, either within the whole country or in any part of it. The act recites that "in the opinion of the Government of the United States the coming of Chinese laborers to this country endangers the good order of certain localities thereof." But the act itself is much broader than the recital. It acts upon residence as well as immigration, and its provisions are effective throughout the United States. I think it may fairly be accepted as an expression of the opinion of Congress that the coming of such laborers to the United States or their residence here affects our interests and endangers good order throughout the country. On this point I should feel it my duty to accept the views of Congress.

The first article further confers the power upon this Government to regulate, limit, or suspend, but not actually to prohibit, the coming of such laborers to or their residence in the United States. The negotiators of the treaty have recorded with unusual fullness their understanding of the sense and meaning with which these words were used.

As to the class of persons to be affected by the treaty, the Americans inserted in their draft a provision that the words "Chinese laborers" signify all immigration other than that for "teaching, trade, travel, study, and curiosity." The Chinese objected to this that it operated to include artisans in the class of laborers whose immigration might be forbidden. The Americans replied that they "could" not consent that artisans shall be excluded from the class of Chinese laborers, for it is this very competition of skilled labor in the cities where the Chinese labor immigration concentrates which has caused the embarrassment and popular discontent. In the subsequent negotiations this definition dropped out, and does not appear in the treaty. Article II of the treaty confers the rights, privileges, immunities, and exemptions which are accorded to citizens and subjects of the most favored nation upon Chinese subjects proceeding to the United States as teachers, students, merchants, or from curiosity. The American commissioners report that the Chinese Government claimed that in this article they did by exclusion provide that nobody should be entitled to claim the benefit of the general provisions of the Burlingame treaty but those who might go to the United States in those capacities or for those purposes. I accept this as the definition of the word "laborers" as used in the treaty.

As to the power of legislating respecting this class of persons, the new treaty provides that we "may not absolutely prohibit" their coming or their residence. The Chinese commissioners gave notice in the outset that they would never agree to a prohibition of voluntary emigration. Notwithstanding this the United States commissioners submitted a draft, in which it was provided that the United States might "regulate, limit, suspend, or prohibit" it. The Chinese refused to accept this. The Americans replied that they were "willing to consult the wishes of the Chinese Government in preserving the principle of free intercourse between the people of the two countries, as established by existing treaties, provided that the right of the United States Government to use its discretion in guarding against any possible evils of immigration of Chinese laborers is distinctly recognized. Therefore if such concession removes all difficulty on the part of the Chinese commissioners (but only in that case) the United States commissioners will agree to remove the word 'prohibit' from their article and to use the words 'regulate, limit, or suspend.'" The Chinese reply to this can only be inferred from the fact that in the place of an agreement, as proposed by our commissioners, that we might prohibit the coming or residence of Chinese laborers, there was inserted in the treaty an agreement that we might not do it.

The remaining words, "regulate, limit, and suspend," first appear in the American draft. When it was submitted to the Chinese, they said:

We infer that of the phrases regulate, limit, suspend, or prohibit, the first is a general expression referring to the others. * * * We are entirely ready to negotiate with your excellencies to the end that a limitation either in point of time or of numbers may be fixed upon the emigration of Chinese laborers to the United States.

At a subsequent interview they said that "by limitation in number they meant, for example, that the United States, having, as they supposed, a record of the number of immigrants in each year, as well as the total number of Chinese now there, that no more should be allowed to go in any one year in future than either the greatest number which had gone in any year in the past, or that the total number should never be allowed to exceed the number now there. As to limitation of time they meant, for example, that Chinese should be allowed to go in alternate years, or every third year, or, for example, that they should not be allowed to go for two, three, or five years."

At a subsequent conference the Americans said:

The Chinese commissioners have in their project explicitly recognized the right of the United States to use some discretion, and have proposed a limitation as to time and number. This *is* the right to regulate, limit, or suspend.

In one of the conferences the Chinese asked the Americans whether they could give them any idea of the laws which would be passed to carry the powers into execution. The Americans answered that this could hardly be done; that the United States Government might never deem it necessary to exercise this power. It would depend upon circumstances. If Chinese immigration concentrated in cities where it threatened public order, or if it confined itself to localities where it was an injury to the interests of the American people, the Government of the United States would undoubtedly take steps to prevent such accumulations of Chinese. If, on the contrary, there was no large immigration, or if there were sections of the country where such immigration was clearly beneficial, then the legislation of the United States under this power would be adapted to such circumstances. For example, there might be a demand for Chinese labor in the South and a surplus of such labor in California, and Congress might legislate in accordance with these facts. In general the legislation would be in view of and depend upon the circumstances of the situation at the moment such legislation became necessary. The Chinese commissioners said this explanation was satisfactory; that they had not intended to ask for a draft of any special act, but for some general idea how the power would be exercised. What had just been said gave them the explanation which they wanted.

With this entire accord as to the meaning of the words they were about to employ and the object of the legislation which might be had in consequence, the parties signed the treaty, in Article I of which—

The Government of China agrees that the Government of the United States may regulate, limit, or suspend such coming or residence, but may not absolutely prohibit it. The limitation or suspension shall be reasonable, and shall apply only to Chinese who may go to the United States as laborers, other classes not being included in the limitations. Legislation taken in regard to Chinese laborers will be of such a character only as is necessary to enforce the regulation, limitation, or suspension of immigration.

The first section of the act provides that—

From and after the expiration of sixty days next after the passage of this act, and until the expiration of twenty years next after the passage of this act, the coming of Chinese laborers be, and the same is hereby, suspended; and during such suspension it shall not be lawful for any Chinese laborer to come, or, having so come after the expiration of said sixty days, to remain within the United States.

The examination which I have made of the treaty and of the declarations which its negotiators have left on record of the meaning of its language leaves no doubt in my mind that neither contracting party in concluding the treaty of 1880 contemplated the passage of an act prohibiting immigration for twenty years, which is nearly a generation, or thought that such a period would be a reasonable suspension or limitation, or intended to change the provisions of the Burlingame treaty to that extent. I regard this provision of the act as a breach of our national faith, and being unable to bring myself in harmony with the views of Congress on this vital point the honor of the country constrains me to return the act with this objection to its passage.

Deeply convinced of the necessity of some legislation on this subject, and concurring fully with Congress in many of the objects which are sought to be accomplished, I avail myself of the opportunity to point out some other features of the present act which, in my opinion, can be modified to advantage.

The classes of Chinese who still enjoy the protection of the Burlingame treaty are entitled to the privileges, immunities, and exemptions accorded to citizens and subjects of the most favored nation. We have treaties with many powers which permit their citizens and subjects to reside within the United States and carry on business under the same laws and regulations which are enforced against citizens of the United States. I think it may be doubted whether provisions requiring personal registration and the taking out of passports which are not imposed upon natives can be required of Chinese. Without expressing an opinion on that point, I may invite the attention of Congress to the fact that the system of personal registration and passports is undemocratic and hostile to the spirit of our institutions. I doubt the wisdom of putting an entering wedge of this kind into our laws. A nation like the United States, jealous of the liberties of its citizens, may well hesitate before it incorporates into its polity a system which is fast disappearing in Europe before the progress of liberal institutions. A wide experience has shown how futile such precautions are, and how easily passports may be borrowed, exchanged, or even forged by persons interested to do so.

If it is, nevertheless, thought that a passport is the most convenient way for identifying the Chinese entitled to the protection of the Burlingame treaty, it may still be doubted whether they ought to be required to register. It is certainly our duty under the Burlingame treaty to make their stay in the United States, in the operation of general laws upon them, as nearly like that of our own citizens as we can consistently with our right to shut out the laborers. No good purpose is served in requiring them to register.

My attention has been called by the Chinese minister to the fact that the bill as it stands makes no provision for the transit across the United States of Chinese subjects now residing in foreign countries. I think that this point may well claim the attention of Congress in legislating on this subject.

I have said that good faith requires us to suspend the immigration of Chinese laborers for a less period than twenty years; I now add that good policy points in the same direction.

Our intercourse with China is of recent date. Our first treaty with that power is not yet forty years old. It is only since we acquired California and established a great seat of commerce on the Pacific that we may be said to have broken down the barriers which fenced in that ancient Monarchy. The Burlingame treaty naturally followed. Under the spirit which inspired it many thousand Chinese laborers came to the United States. No one can say that the country has not profited by their work. They were largely instrumental in constructing the railways which connect the Atlantic with the Pacific. The States of the Pacific Slope are full of evidences of their industry. Enterprises profitable alike to the capitalist and to the laborer of Caucasian origin would have lain dormant but for them. A time has now come when it is supposed that they are not needed, and when it is thought by Congress and by those most acquainted with the subject that it is best to try to get along without them. There may, however, be other sections of the country where this species of labor may be advantageously employed without interfering with the laborers of our own race. In making the proposed experiment it may be the part of wisdom as well as of good faith to fix the length of the experimental period with reference to this fact.

Experience has shown that the trade of the East is the key to national wealth and influence. The opening of China to the commerce of the whole world has benefited no section of it more than the States of our own Pacific Slope. The State of California, and its great maritime port especially, have reaped enormous advantages from this source. Blessed with an exceptional climate, enjoying an unrivaled harbor, with the riches of a great agricultural and mining State in its rear and the wealth of the whole Union pouring into it over its lines of railway, San Francisco has before it an incalculable future if our friendly and amicable relations with Asia remain undisturbed. It needs no argument to show that the policy which we now propose to adopt must have a direct tendency to repel Oriental nations from us and to drive their trade and commerce into more friendly lands. It may be that the great and paramount interest of protecting our labor from Asiatic competition may justify us in a permanent adoption of this policy; but it is wiser in the first place to make a shorter experiment, with a view hereafter of maintaining permanently only such features as time and experience may commend.

I transmit herewith copies of the papers relating to the recent treaty with China, which accompanied the confidential message of President Hayes to the Senate of the 10th January, 1881, and also a copy of a memorandum respecting the act herewith returned, which was handed to the Secretary of State by the Chinese minister in Washington.

CHESTER A. ARTHUR.

EXECUTIVE MANSION, *July 1, 1882.*

To the House of Representatives of the United States:

Herewith I return House bill No. 2744, entitled "An act to regulate the carriage of passengers by sea," without my approval. In doing this I regret that I am not able to give my assent to an act which has received the sanction of the majority of both Houses of Congress.

The object proposed to be secured by the act is meritorious and philanthropic. Some correct and accurate legislation upon this subject is undoubtedly necessary. Steamships that bring large bodies of emigrants must be subjected to strict legal enactments, so as to prevent the passengers from being exposed to hardship and suffering; and such legislation should be made as will give them abundance of space and air and light, protecting their health by affording all reasonable comforts and conveniences and by providing for the quantity and quality of the food to be furnished and all of the other essentials of roomy, safe, and healthful accommodations in their passage across the sea.

A statute providing for all this is absolutely needed, and in the spirit of humane legislation must be enacted. The present act, by most of its provisions, will obtain and secure this protection for such passengers, and were it not for some serious errors contained in it it would be most willingly approved by me.

My objections are these: In the first section, in lines from 13 to 24, inclusive, it is provided "that the compartments or spaces," etc., "shall be of sufficient dimensions to allow for each and any passenger," etc., "100 cubic feet, if the compartment or space is located on the first deck next below the uppermost deck of the vessel," etc., "or 120 cubic feet for each passenger," etc., "if the compartment or space is located on the second deck below the uppermost deck of the vessel," etc. "It shall not be lawful to carry or bring passengers on any deck other than the two decks mentioned," etc.

Nearly all of the new and most of the improved ocean steamers have a spar deck, which is above the main deck. The main deck was in the old style of steamers the only uppermost deck. The spar deck is a comparatively new feature of the large and costly steamships, and is now practically the uppermost deck. Below this spar deck is the main deck. Because of the misuse of the words "uppermost deck" instead of the use of the words "main deck" by this act, the result will be to exclude nearly all of the large steamships from carrying passengers anywhere but on the main deck and on the deck below, which is the steerage deck, and to leave the orlop, or lower deck, heretofore used for passengers, useless and unoccupied by passengers. This objection, which is now presented in connection with others that will be presently explained, will, if this act is enforced as it is now phrased, render useless for passenger traffic and expose to heavy loss all of the great ocean steam lines; and it will also hinder emigration, as there will not be ships enough that could accept these conditions to carry all who may now wish to come.

The use of the new and the hitherto unknown term "uppermost deck" creates this difficulty, and I can not consent to have an abuse of terms like this to operate thus injuriously to these large fleets of ships. The passengers will not be benefited by such a statute, but emigration will be hindered, if not for a while almost prevented for many.

Again, the act in the first section, from line 31 to line 35, inclusive, provides: "And such passengers shall not be carried or brought in any between-decks, nor in any compartment," etc., "the clear height of which is less than 7 feet." Between the decks of all ships are the beams; they are about a foot in width. The legal method of ascertaining tonnage for the purpose of taxation is to measure between the beams from the floor to the ceiling. If this becomes a law the space required would be 8 feet from floor to ceiling, and this is impracticable, for in all ships the spaces between decks are adjusted in proportion to the dimensions of the ship; and if these spaces between decks are changed so as not to correspond in their proportions with the dimensions of the vessel, the ship will not work well in the sea, her sailing qualities will be injured, and she will be rendered unfit for service.

It is only in great ships of vast tonnage that the height between decks can be increased. All the ordinary-sized ships are necessarily constructed with 7 feet space in the interval between the beams from the floor to the ceiling. To adopt this act, with this provision, would be to drive out of the service of transporting passengers most all of the steamships now in such trade, and no practical good obtained by it, for really, with the exception of the narrow beam, the space between the decks is now 7 feet. The purpose of the space commanded by the act is to obtain sufficient air and ventilation, and that is actually now given to the passenger by the 7 feet that exists in all of these vessels between floor and ceiling.

There is also another objection that I must suggest. In section 12, from line 14 to line 24, it is provided: "Before such vessel shall be cleared or may lawfully depart," etc., "the master of said vessel shall furnish," etc, "a correct list of all passengers who have been or are intended to be taken on board the vessel, and shall specify," etc. This provision would prevent the clearing of the vessel. Steam vessels start at an appointed hour and with punctuality. Down almost to the very hour of their departure new passengers, other than those who have engaged their passage, constantly come on board. If this provision is to be the law, they must be rejected, for the ship can not, without incurring heavy penalties, take passengers whose names are not set forth on the list required before such vessel shall be cleared. They should be allowed to take such new passengers upon condition that they would furnish an additional list containing such persons' names. There are other points of objection of a minor character that might be presented for consideration if the bill could be reconsidered and amended, but the three that I have recited are conspicuous defects in a bill that ought to be a code for such a purpose, clear and explicit, free from all such objections. The practical result of this law would be to subject all of the competing lines of large ocean steamers to great losses. By restricting their carrying accommodations it would also stay the current of emigration that it is our policy to encourage as well as to protect. A good bill, correctly phrased, and expressing and naming in plain, well-known technical terms the proper and usual places and decks where passengers are and ought to be placed and carried, will receive my prompt and immediate assent as a public necessity and blessing.

CHESTER A. ARTHUR.

EXECUTIVE MANSION, *August 1, 1882.*

To the House of Representatives:

Having watched with much interest the progress of House bill No. 6242, entitled "An act making appropriations for the construction, repair, and preservation of certain works on rivers and harbors, and for other purposes," and having since it was received carefully examined it, after mature consideration I am constrained to return it herewith to the House of Representatives, in which it originated, without my signature and with my objections to its passage.

Many of the appropriations in the bill are clearly for the general welfare and most beneficent in their character. Two of the objects for which provision is made were by me considered so important that I felt it my duty to direct to them the attention of Congress. In my annual message in December last I urged the vital importance of legislation for the reclamation of the marshes and for the establishment of the harbor lines along the Potomac front. In April last, by special message, I recommended an appropriation for the improvement of the Mississippi River. It is not necessary that I say that when my signature would make the bill appropriating for these and other valuable national objects a law it is with great reluctance and only under a sense of duty that I withhold it.

My principal objection to the bill is that it contains appropriations for purposes not for the common defense or general welfare, and which do not promote commerce among the States. These provisions, on the contrary, are entirely for the benefit of the particular localities in which it is proposed to make the improvements. I regard such appropriation of the public money as beyond the powers given by the Constitution to Congress and the President.

I feel the more bound to withhold my signature from the bill because of the peculiar evils which manifestly result from this infraction of the Constitution. Appropriations of this nature, to be devoted purely to local objects, tend to an increase in number and in amount. As the citizens of one State find that money, to raise which they in common with the whole country are taxed, is to be expended for local improvements in another State, they demand similar benefits for themselves, and it is not unnatural that they should seek to indemnify themselves for such use of the public funds by securing appropriations for similar improvements in their own neighborhood. Thus as the bill becomes more objectionable it secures more support. This result is invariable and necessarily follows a neglect to observe the constitutional limitations imposed upon the lawmaking power.

The appropriations for river and harbor improvements have, under the influences to which I have alluded, increased year by year out of proportion to the progress of the country, great as that has been. In 1870 the aggregate appropriation was $3,975,900; in 1875, $6,648,517.50; in 1880, $8,976,500; and in 1881, $11,451,000; while by the present act there is appropriated $18,743,875.

While feeling every disposition to leave to the Legislature the responsibility of determining what amount should be appropriated for the purposes of the bill, so long as the appropriations are confined to objects indicated by the grant of power, I can not escape the conclusion that, as a part of the lawmaking power of the Government, the duty devolves upon me to withhold my signature from a bill containing appropriations which in my opinion greatly exceed in amount the needs of the country for the present fiscal year. It being the usage to provide money for these purposes by annual appropriation bills, the President is in effect directed to expend so large an amount of money within so brief a period that the expenditure can not be made economically and advantageously.

The extravagant expenditure of public money is an evil not to be measured by the value of that money to the people who are taxed for it.

They sustain a greater injury in the demoralizing effect produced upon those who are intrusted with official duty through all the ramifications of government.

These objections could be removed and every constitutional purpose readily attained should Congress enact that one-half only of the aggregate amount provided for in the bill be appropriated for expenditure during the fiscal year, and that the sum so appropriated be expended only for such objects named in the bill as the Secretary of War, under the direction of the President, shall determine; provided that in no case shall the expenditure for any one purpose exceed the sum now designated by the bill for that purpose.

I feel authorized to make this suggestion because of the duty imposed upon the President by the Constitution "to recommend to the consideration of Congress such measures as he shall judge necessary and expedient," and because it is my earnest desire that the public works which are in progress shall suffer no injury. Congress will also convene again in four months, when this whole subject will be open for their consideration.

CHESTER A. ARTHUR.

PROCLAMATIONS.

By the President of the United States of America.

A PROCLAMATION.

Whereas it is provided in the laws of the United States that—

Whenever, by reason of unlawful obstructions, combinations, or assemblages of persons or rebellion against the authority of the Government of the United States, it shall become impracticable, in the judgment of the President, to enforce by the ordinary course of judicial proceedings the laws of the United States within any State or Territory, it shall be lawful for the President to call forth the militia of any or all the States and to employ such parts of the land and naval forces of the United States as he may deem necessary to enforce the faithful execution of the laws of the United States or to suppress such rebellion, in whatever State or Territory thereof the laws of the United States may be forcibly opposed or the execution thereof forcibly obstructed.

And whereas it has been made to appear satisfactorily to me, by information received from the governor of the Territory of Arizona and from the General of the Army of the United States and other reliable sources, that in consequence of unlawful combinations of evil-disposed persons who are banded together to oppose and obstruct the execution of the laws it has become impracticable to enforce by the ordinary course of judicial proceedings the laws of the United States within that Territory, and that the laws of the United States have been therein forcibly op‧ posed and the execution thereof forcibly resisted; and

Whereas the laws of the United States require that whenever it may be necessary, in the judgment of the President, to use the military forces for the purpose of enforcing the faithful execution of the laws of the United States, he shall forthwith, by proclamation, command such insurgents to disperse and retire peaceably to their respective abodes within a limited time:

Now, therefore, I, Chester A. Arthur, President of the United States, do hereby admonish all good citizens of the United States, and especially of the Territory of Arizona, against aiding, countenancing, abetting, or taking part in any such unlawful proceedings; and I do hereby warn all persons engaged in or connected with said obstruction of the laws to disperse and retire peaceably to their respective abodes on or before noon of the 15th day of May.

In witness whereof I have hereunto set my hand and caused the seal of the United States to be affixed.

[SEAL.]   Done at the city of Washington, this 3d day of May, A. D. 1882, and of the Independence of the United States the one hundred and sixth.

CHESTER A. ARTHUR.

By the President:
FREDK. T. FRELINGHUYSEN,
Secretary of State.

BY THE PRESIDENT OF THE UNITED STATES OF AMERICA.

A PROCLAMATION.

In conformity with a custom the annual observance of which is justly held in honor by this people, I, Chester A. Arthur, President of the United States, do hereby set apart Thursday, the 30th day of November next, as a day of public thanksgiving.

The blessings demanding our gratitude are numerous and varied. For the peace and amity which subsist between this Republic and all the nations of the world; for the freedom from internal discord and violence; for the increasing friendship between the different sections of the land; for liberty, justice, and constitutional government; for the devotion of the people to our free institutions and their cheerful obedience to mild laws; for the constantly increasing strength of the Republic while extending its privileges to fellow-men who come to us; for the improved means of internal communication and the increased facilities of intercourse with other nations; for the general prevailing health of the year; for the prosperity of all our industries, the liberal return for the mechanic's toil affording a market for the abundant harvests of the husbandman;

for the preservation of the national faith and credit; for wise and gener-ous provision to effect the intellectual and moral education of our youth; for the influence upon the conscience of a restraining and transforming religion, and for the joys of home—for these and for many other bless-ings we should give thanks.

Wherefore I do recommend that the day above designated be observed throughout the country as a day of national thanksgiving and prayer, and that the people, ceasing from their daily labors and meeting in accordance with their several forms of worship, draw near to the throne of Almighty God, offering to Him praise and gratitude for the manifold goodness which He has vouchsafed to us and praying that His blessings and His mercies may continue.

And I do further recommend that the day thus appointed be made a special occasion for deeds of kindness and charity to the suffering and the needy, so that all who dwell within the land may rejoice and be glad in this season of national thanksgiving.

In witness whereof I have hereunto set my hand and caused the seal of the United States to be affixed.

[SEAL.]   Done at the city of Washington, this 25th day of October, A. D. 1882, and of the Independence of the United States the one hundred and seventh.

CHESTER A. ARTHUR.

By the President:

FREDK. T. FRELINGHUYSEN, *Secretary of State.*

EXECUTIVE ORDERS.

To Collectors of Customs: TREASURY DEPARTMENT, *March 30, 1882.*

Under the provisions of section 1955, Revised Statutes, so much of Department instructions of July 3, 1875,* approved by the President, as prohibits the importation and use of breech-loading rifles and suitable ammunition therefor into and within the limits of the Territory of Alaska is hereby amended and modified so as to permit emigrants who intend to become actual *bona fide* settlers upon the mainland to ship to the care of the collector of customs at Sitka, for their own personal protection and for the hunting of game, not exceeding one such rifle and suitable ammunition therefor to each male adult; also to permit actual *bona fide* residents of the mainland of Alaska (not including Indians or traders), upon application to the collector and with his approval, to order and ship for personal use such arms and ammunition to his care, not exceeding one rifle for each such person, and proper ammunition.

The sale of such arms and ammunition is prohibited except by persons about to leave the Territory, and then only to *bona fide* residents (excluding Indians and traders) upon application to and with the approval of the collector.

H. F. FRENCH, *Acting Secretary.*

Approved:

CHESTER A. ARTHUR.

*See Vol. VII, p. 4282.

CHESTER A. ARTHUR, PRESIDENT OF THE UNITED STATES OF
AMERICA.

To all to whom these presents shall come, greeting:

Whereas on the 10th day of January, 1863, Fitz John Porter, then
major-general of volunteers in the military service of the United States,
and also colonel of the Fifteenth Regiment of Infantry and brevet brigadier-general in the United States Army, was by a general court-martial,
for certain offenses of which he had been thereby convicted, sentenced
" to be cashiered and to be forever disqualified from holding any office of
trust or profit under the Government of the United States;" and

Whereas on the 21st day of January, 1863, that sentence was duly confirmed by the President of the United States, and by his order of the
same date carried into execution; and

Whereas so much of that sentence as forever disqualified the said Fitz
John Porter from holding office imposed upon him a continuing penalty and is still being executed; and

Whereas doubts have since arisen concerning the guilt of the said Fitz
John Porter of the offenses whereof he was convicted by the said court-
martial, founded upon the result of an investigation ordered on the 12th
day of April, 1878, by the President of the United States, which are
deemed by me to be of sufficient gravity to warrant the remission of that
part of said sentence which has not yet been completely executed:

Now, therefore, know ye that I, Chester A. Arthur, President of the
United States, by virtue of the power vested in me by the Constitution
of the United States and in consideration of the premises, do hereby
grant to the said Fitz John Porter full remission of the hereinbefore-
mentioned continuing penalty.

In witness whereof I have hereunto signed my name and caused the
seal of the United States to be affixed.

Done at the city of Washington, this 4th day of May, A. D. 1882, and
[SEAL.] of the Independence of the United States the one hundred and
sixth. CHESTER A. ARTHUR.

By the President:
FREDK. T. FRELINGHUYSEN, *Secretary of State.*

EXECUTIVE MANSION, *Washington, May 26, 1882.*

SIR:* I am directed by the President to inform you that the several
Departments of the Government will be closed on Tuesday, the 30th
instant, to enable the employees to participate in the decoration of the
graves of the soldiers who fell during the rebellion.

Very respectfully,
FRED. J. PHILLIPS, *Private Secretary.*

*Addressed to the heads of the Executive Departments, etc.

WAR DEPARTMENT,
Washington, July 13, 1882.

I. By direction of the President, the Military Department of West Point will be discontinued September 1, 1882.

II. By direction of the President, sections 1 and 2 of Article I of the general regulations for the United States Military Academy are hereby amended to read as follows:

1. The General of the Army, under the War Department, shall have supervision and charge of the United States Military Academy. He will watch over its administration and discipline and the instruction of the Corps of Cadets, and will make reports thereof to the Secretary of War.

2. The Superintendent, and in his absence the next in rank, shall have the immediate government and military command of the Academy, and shall be commandant of the military post of West Point. The Superintendent will render, through the Adjutant-General, to the General of the Army, for submission to the Secretary of War, all required reports, returns, and estimates concerning the Academy.

ROBERT T. LINCOLN,
Secretary of War.

SECOND ANNUAL MESSAGE.

WASHINGTON, *December 4, 1882.*

To the Senate and House of Representatives of the United States:

It is provided by the Constitution that the President shall from time to time give to the Congress information of the state of the Union and recommend to their consideration such measures as he shall judge necessary and expedient.

In reviewing the events of the year which has elapsed since the commencement of your sessions, I first call your attention to the gratifying condition of our foreign affairs. Our intercourse with other powers has continued to be of the most friendly character.

Such slight differences as have arisen during the year have been already settled or are likely to reach an early adjustment. The arrest of citizens of the United States in Ireland under recent laws which owe their origin to the disturbed condition of that country has led to a somewhat extended correspondence with the Government of Great Britain. A disposition to respect our rights has been practically manifested by the release of the arrested parties.

The claim of this nation in regard to the supervision and control of any interoceanic canal across the American Isthmus has continued to be the subject of conference.

It is likely that time will be more powerful than discussion in removing the divergence between the two nations whose friendship is so closely cemented by the intimacy of their relations and the community of their interests.

Our long-established friendliness with Russia has remained unshaken. It has prompted me to proffer the earnest counsels of this Government that measures be adopted for suppressing the proscription which the Hebrew race in that country has lately suffered. It has not transpired that any American citizen has been subjected to arrest or injury, but our courteous remonstrance has nevertheless been courteously received. There is reason to believe that the time is not far distant when Russia will be able to secure toleration to all faiths within her borders.

At an international convention held at Paris in 1880, and attended by representatives of the United States, an agreement was reached in respect to the protection of trade-marks, patented articles, and the rights of manufacturing firms and corporations. The formulating into treaties of the recommendations thus adopted is receiving the attention which it merits.

The protection of submarine cables is a subject now under consideration by an international conference at Paris. Believing that it is clearly the true policy of this Government to favor the neutralization of this means of intercourse, I requested our minister to France to attend the convention as a delegate. I also designated two of our eminent scientists to attend as our representatives at the meeting of an international committee at Paris for considering the adoption of a common unit to measure electric force.

In view of the frequent occurrence of conferences for the consideration of important matters of common interest to civilized nations, I respectfully suggest that the Executive be invested by Congress with discretionary powers to send delegates to such conventions, and that provision be made to defray the expenses incident thereto.

The difference between the United States and Spain as to the effect of a judgment and certificate of naturalization has not yet been adjusted, but it is hoped and believed that negotiations now in progress will result in the establishment of the position which seems to this Government so reasonable and just.

I have already called the attention of Congress to the fact that in the ports of Spain and its colonies onerous fines have lately been imposed upon vessels of the United States for trivial technical offenses against local regulations. Efforts for the abatement of these exactions have thus far proved unsuccessful.

I regret to inform you also that the fees demanded by Spanish consuls in American ports are in some cases so large, when compared with the value of the cargo, as to amount in effect to a considerable export duty, and that our remonstrances in this regard have not as yet received the attention which they seem to deserve.

The German Government has invited the United States to participate in an international exhibition of domestic cattle to be held at Hamburg in July, 1883. If this country is to be represented, it is important that in the early days of this session Congress should make a suitable appropriation for that purpose.

The death of Mr. Marsh, our late minister to Italy, has evoked from that Government expressions of profound respect for his exalted character and for his honorable career in the diplomatic service of his country. The Italian Government has raised a question as to the propriety of recognizing in his dual capacity the representative of this country recently accredited both as secretary of legation and as consul-general at Rome. He has been received as secretary, but his exequatur as consul-general has thus far been withheld.

The extradition convention with Belgium, which has been in operation since 1874, has been lately supplanted by another. The Senate has signified its approval, and ratifications have been duly exchanged between the contracting countries. To the list of extraditable crimes has been added that of the assassination or attempted assassination of the chief of the State.

Negotiations have been opened with Switzerland looking to a settlement by treaty of the question whether its citizens can renounce their allegiance and become citizens of the United States without obtaining the consent of the Swiss Government.

I am glad to inform you that the immigration of paupers and criminals from certain of the Cantons of Switzerland has substantially ceased and is no longer sanctioned by the authorities.

The consideration of this subject prompts the suggestion that the act of August 3, 1882, which has for its object the return of foreign convicts to their own country, should be so modified as not to be open to the interpretation that it affects the extradition of criminals on preferred charges of crime.

The Ottoman Porte has not yet assented to the interpretation which this Government has put upon the treaty of 1830 relative to its jurisdictional rights in Turkey. It may well be, however, that this difference will be adjusted by a general revision of the system of jurisdiction of the United States in the countries of the East, a subject to which your attention has been already called by the Secretary of State.

In the interest of justice toward China and Japan, I trust that the question of the return of the indemnity fund to the Governments of those countries will reach at the present session the satisfactory solution which I have already recommended, and which has recently been foreshadowed by Congressional discussion.

The treaty lately concluded with Korea awaits the action of the Senate.

During the late disturbance in Egypt the timely presence of American vessels served as a protection to the persons and property of many of our own citizens and of citizens of other countries, whose governments have expressed their thanks for this assistance.

The recent legislation restricting immigration of laborers from China has given rise to the question whether Chinese proceeding to or from another country may lawfully pass through our own.

Construing the act of May 6, 1882, in connection with the treaty of November 7, 1880, the restriction would seem to be limited to Chinese immigrants coming to the United States as laborers, and would not forbid a mere transit across our territory. I ask the attention of Congress to the subject, for such action, if any, as may be deemed advisable.

This Government has recently had occasion to manifest its interest in the Republic of Liberia by seeking to aid the amicable settlement of the boundary dispute now pending between that Republic and the British possession of Sierra Leone.

The reciprocity treaty with Hawaii will become terminable after September 9, 1883, on twelve months' notice by either party. While certain provisions of that compact may have proved onerous, its existence has fostered commercial relations which it is important to preserve. I suggest, therefore, that early consideration be given to such modifications of the treaty as seem to be demanded by the interests of our people.

In view of our increasing trade with both Hayti and Santo Domingo, I advise that provision be made for diplomatic intercourse with the latter by enlarging the scope of the mission at Port au Prince.

I regret that certain claims of American citizens against the Government of Hayti have thus far been urged unavailingly.

A recent agreement with Mexico provides for the crossing of the frontier by the armed forces of either country in pursuit of hostile Indians. In my message of last year I called attention to the prevalent lawlessness upon the borders and to the necessity of legislation for its suppression. I again invite the attention of Congress to the subject.

A partial relief from these mischiefs has been sought in a convention, which now awaits the approval of the Senate, as does also another touching the establishment of the international boundary between the United States and Mexico. If the latter is ratified, the action of Congress will be required for establishing suitable commissions of survey. The boundary dispute between Mexico and Guatemala, which led this Government to proffer its friendly counsels to both parties, has been amicably settled.

No change has occurred in our relations with Venezuela. I again invoke your action in the matter of the pending awards against that Republic, to which reference was made by a special message from the Executive at your last session.

An invitation has been received from the Government of Venezuela to send representatives in July, 1883, to Caracas for participating in the centennial celebration of the birth of Bolivar, the founder of South American independence. In connection with this event it is designed to commence the erection at Caracas of a statue of Washington and to conduct an industrial exhibition which will be open to American products. I recommend that the United States be represented and that suitable provision be made therefor.

The elevation of the grade of our mission in Central America to the plenipotentiary rank, which was authorized by Congress at its late session, has been since effected.

The war between Peru and Bolivia on the one side and Chile on the other began more than three years ago. On the occupation by Chile in 1880 of all the littoral territory of Bolivia, negotiations for peace were conducted under the direction of the United States. The allies refused to concede any territory, but Chile has since become master of the whole coast of both countries and of the capital of Peru. A year since, as you have already been advised by correspondence transmitted to you in January last, this Government sent a special mission to the belligerent powers to express the hope that Chile would be disposed to accept a money indemnity for the expenses of the war and to relinquish her demand for a portion of the territory of her antagonist.

This recommendation, which Chile declined to follow, this Government did not assume to enforce; nor can it be enforced without resort to measures which would be in keeping neither with the temper of our people nor with the spirit of our institutions.

The power of Peru no longer extends over its whole territory, and in the event of our interference to dictate peace would need to be supplemented by the armies and navies of the United States. Such interference would almost inevitably lead to the establishment of a protectorate—a result utterly at odds with our past policy, injurious to our present interests, and full of embarrassments for the future.

For effecting the termination of hostilities upon terms at once just to the victorious nation and generous to its adversaries, this Government has spared no efforts save such as might involve the complications which I have indicated.

It is greatly to be deplored that Chile seems resolved to exact such rigorous conditions of peace and indisposed to submit to arbitration the terms of an amicable settlement. No peace is likely to be lasting that is not sufficiently equitable and just to command the approval of other nations.

About a year since invitations were extended to the nations of this continent to send representatives to a peace congress to assemble at Washington in November, 1882. The time of meeting was fixed at a period then remote, in the hope, as the invitation itself declared, that in the meantime the disturbances between the South American Republics would be adjusted. As that expectation seemed unlikely to be realized, I asked in April last for an expression of opinion from the two Houses of Congress as to the advisability of holding the proposed convention at the time appointed. This action was prompted in part by doubts which mature reflection had suggested whether the diplomatic usage and traditions of the Government did not make it fitting that the Executive should consult the representatives of the people before pursuing a line of policy somewhat novel in its character and far reaching in its possible consequences. In view of the fact that no action was taken by Congress in the premises and that no provision had been made for necessary expenses, I subsequently decided to postpone the convocation, and so notified the several Governments which had been invited to attend.

I am unwilling to dismiss this subject without assuring you of my support of any measures the wisdom of Congress may devise for the promotion of peace on this continent and throughout the world, and I trust that the time is nigh when, with the universal assent of civilized peoples, all international differences shall be determined without resort to arms by the benignant processes of arbitration.

Changes have occurred in the diplomatic representation of several foreign powers during the past year. New ministers from the Argentine Republic, Austria-Hungary, Brazil, Chile, China, France, Japan, Mexico, the Netherlands, and Russia have presented their credentials. The missions of Denmark and Venezuela at this capital have been raised in grade. Switzerland has created a plenipotentiary mission to this Government, and an embassy from Madagascar and a minister from Siam will shortly arrive.

Our diplomatic intercourse has been enlarged by the establishment of relations with the new Kingdom of Servia, by the creation of a mission to Siam, and by the restoration of the mission to Greece. The Shah of Persia has expressed his gratification that a chargé d'affaires will shortly be sent to that country, where the rights of our citizens have been hitherto courteously guarded by the representatives of Great Britain.

I renew my recommendation of such legislation as will place the United States in harmony with other maritime powers with respect to the international rules for the prevention of collisions at sea.

In conformity with your joint resolution of the 3d of August last, I have directed the Secretary of State to address foreign governments in respect to a proposed conference for considering the subject of the universal adoption of a common prime meridian to be used in the reckoning of longitude and in the regulation of time throughout the civilized world. Their replies will in due time be laid before you.

An agreement was reached at Paris in 1875 between the principal powers for the interchange of official publications through the medium of their respective foreign departments.

The admirable system which has been built up by the enterprise of the Smithsonian Institution affords a practical basis for our cooperation in this scheme, and an arrangement has been effected by which that institution will perform the necessary labor, under the direction of the Department of State. A reasonable compensation therefor should be provided by law.

A clause in the act making appropriations for the diplomatic and consular service contemplates the reorganization of both branches of such service on a salaried basis, leaving fees to inure to the benefit of the Treasury. I cordially favor such a project, as likely to correct abuses in the present system. The Secretary of State will present to you at an early day a plan for such reorganization.

A full and interesting exhibit of the operations of the Treasury Department is afforded by the report of the Secretary.

It appears that the ordinary revenues from all sources for the fiscal year ended June 30, 1882, were as follows:

From customs	$220,410,730.25
From internal revenue	146,497,595.45
From sales of public lands	4,753,140.37
From tax on circulation and deposits of national banks	8,956,794.45
From repayment of interest by Pacific Railway companies	840,554.37
From sinking fund for Pacific Railway companies	796,271.42
From customs fees, fines, penalties, etc	1,343,348.00
From fees—consular, letters patent, and lands	2,638,990.97
From proceeds of sales of Government property	314,959.85
From profits on coinage, bullion deposits, and assays	4,116,693.73
From Indian trust funds	5,705,243.22
From deposits by individuals for surveying public lands	2,052,306.36
From revenues of the District of Columbia	1,715,176.41
From miscellaneous sources	3,383,445.43
Total ordinary receipts	403,525,250.28

The ordinary expenditures for the same period were—

For civil expenses	$18,042,386.42
For foreign intercourse	1,307,583.19
For Indians	9,736,747.40
For pensions	61,345,193.95
For the military establishment, including river and harbor improvements, and arsenals	43,570,494.19
For the naval establishment, including vessels, machinery, and improvements at navy-yards	15,032,046.26
For miscellaneous expenditures, including public buildings, light-houses, and collecting the revenue	34,539,237.50
For expenditures on account of the District of Columbia	3,330,543.87
For interest on the public debt	71,077,206.79
Total ordinary expenditures	257,981,439.57

Leaving a surplus revenue of $145,543,810.71, which, with an amount drawn from the cash balance in the Treasury of $20,737,694.84, making $166,281,505.55, was applied to the redemption—

Of bonds for the sinking fund	$60,079,150.00
Of fractional currency for the sinking fund	58,705.55
Of loan of July and August, 1861	62,572,050.00
Of loan of March, 1863	4,472,900.00
Of funded loan of 1881	37,194,450.00
Of loan of 1858	1,000.00
Of loan of February, 1861	303,000.00
Of five-twenties of 1862	2,100.00
Of five-twenties of 1864	7,400.00
Of five-twenties of 1865	6,500.00
Of ten-forties of 1864	254,550.00
Of consols of 1865	86,450.00
Of consols of 1867	408,250.00
Of consols of 1868	141,400.00
Of Oregon War debt	675,250.00
Of old demand, compound-interest, and other notes	18,350.00
	166,281,505.55

The foreign commerce of the United States during the last fiscal year, including imports and exports of merchandise and specie, was as follows:

Exports:
Merchandise... $750,542,257
Specie 49,417,479

Total.. 799,959,736

Imports:
Merchandise 724,639,574
Specie 42,472,390

Total 767,111,964

Excess of exports over imports of merchandise.............................. 25,902,683

This excess is less than it has been before for any of the previous six years, as appears by the following table:

Year ended June 30—	Excess of exports over imports of merchandise.
1876..	$79,643,481
1877..	151,152,094
1878..	257,814,234
1879..	264,661,666
1880..	167,683,912
1881..	259,712,718
1882..	25,902,683

During the year there have been organized 171 national banks, and of those institutions there are now in operation 2,269, a larger number than ever before. The value of their notes in active circulation on July 1, 1882, was $324,656,458.

I commend to your attention the Secretary's views in respect to the likelihood of a serious contraction of this circulation, and to the modes by which that result may, in his judgment, be averted.

In respect to the coinage of silver dollars and the retirement of silver certificates, I have seen nothing to alter but much to confirm the sentiments to which I gave expression last year.

A comparison between the respective amounts of silver-dollar circulation on November 1, 1881, and on November 1, 1882, shows a slight increase of a million and a half of dollars; but during the interval there had been in the whole number coined an increase of twenty-six millions. Of the one hundred and twenty-eight millions thus far minted, little more than thirty-five millions are in circulation. The mass of accumulated coin has grown so great that the vault room at present available for storage is scarcely sufficient to contain it. It is not apparent why it is desirable to continue this coinage, now so enormously in excess of the public demand.

As to the silver certificates, in addition to the grounds which seemed last year to justify their retirement may be mentioned the effect which is likely to ensue from the supply of gold certificates for whose issuance Congress recently made provision, and which are now in active circulation.

You can not fail to note with interest the discussion by the Secretary as to the necessity of providing by legislation some mode of freeing the Treasury of an excess of assets in the event that Congress fails to reach an early agreement for the reduction of taxation.

I heartily approve the Secretary's recommendation of immediate and extensive reductions in the annual revenues of the Government.

It will be remembered that I urged upon the attention of Congress at its last session the importance of relieving the industry and enterprise of the country from the pressure of unnecessary taxation. It is one of the tritest maxims of political economy that all taxes are burdensome, however wisely and prudently imposed; and though there have always been among our people wide differences of sentiment as to the best methods of raising the national revenues, and, indeed, as to the principles upon which taxation should be based, there has been substantial accord in the doctrine that only such taxes ought to be levied as are necessary for a wise and economical administration of the Government. Of late the public revenues have far exceeded that limit, and unless checked by appropriate legislation such excess will continue to increase from year to year. For the fiscal year ended June 30, 1881, the surplus revenue amounted to $100,000,000; for the fiscal year ended on the 30th of June last the surplus was more than one hundred and forty-five millions.

The report of the Secretary shows what disposition has been made of these moneys. They have not only answered the requirements of the sinking fund, but have afforded a large balance applicable to other reductions of the public debt.

But I renew the expression of my conviction that such rapid extinguishment of the national indebtedness as is now taking place is by no means a cause for congratulation; it is a cause rather for serious apprehension.

If it continues, it must speedily be followed by one of the evil results so clearly set forth in the report of the Secretary.

Either the surplus must lie idle in the Treasury or the Government will be forced to buy at market rates its bonds not then redeemable, and which under such circumstances can not fail to command an enormous premium, or the swollen revenues will be devoted to extravagant expenditure, which, as experience has taught, is ever the bane of an overflowing treasury.

It was made apparent in the course of the animated discussions which this question aroused at the last session of Congress that the policy of diminishing the revenue by reducing taxation commanded the general approval of the members of both Houses.

I regret that because of conflicting views as to the best methods by which that policy should be made operative none of its benefits have as yet been reaped.

In fulfillment of what I deem my constitutional duty, but with little hope that I can make valuable contribution to this vexed question, I shall proceed to intimate briefly my own views in relation to it.

Upon the showing of our financial condition at the close of the last fiscal year, I felt justified in recommending to Congress the abolition of all internal revenue taxes except those upon tobacco in its various forms and upon distilled spirits and fermented liquors, and except also the special tax upon the manufacturers of and dealers in such articles.

I venture now to suggest that unless it shall be ascertained that the probable expenditures of the Government for the coming year have been underestimated all internal taxes save those which relate to distilled spirits can be prudently abrogated.

Such a course, if accompanied by a simplification of the machinery of collection, which would then be easy of accomplishment, might reasonably be expected to result in diminishing the cost of such collection by at least $2,500,000 and in the retirement from office of from 1,500 to 2,000 persons.

The system of excise duties has never commended itself to the favor of the American people, and has never been resorted to except for supplying deficiencies in the Treasury when, by reason of special exigencies, the duties on imports have proved inadequate for the needs of the Government. The sentiment of the country doubtless demands that the present excise tax shall be abolished as soon as such a course can be safely pursued.

It seems to me, however, that, for various reasons, so sweeping a measure as the total abolition of internal taxes would for the present be an unwise step.

Two of these reasons are deserving of special mention:

First. It is by no means clear that even if the existing system of duties on imports is continued without modification those duties alone will yield sufficient revenue for all the needs of the Government. It is estimated that $100,000,000 will be required for pensions during the coming year, and it may well be doubted whether the maximum annual demand for that object has yet been reached. Uncertainty upon this question would alone justify, in my judgment, the retention for the present of that portion of the system of internal revenue which is least objectionable to the people.

Second. A total abolition of excise taxes would almost inevitably prove a serious if not an insurmountable obstacle to a thorough revision of the tariff and to any considerable reduction in import duties.

The present tariff system is in many respects unjust. It makes unequal distributions both of its burdens and its benefits. This fact was practically recognized by a majority of each House of Congress in the passage of the act creating the Tariff Commission. The report of that commission will be placed before you at the beginning of this session, and will, I trust, afford you such information as to the condition and prospects of the various commercial, agricultural, manufacturing, mining, and other interests of the country and contain such suggestions for statutory revision as will practically aid your action upon this important subject.

The revenue from customs for the fiscal year ended June 30, 1879, amounted to $137,000,000.

It has in the three succeeding years reached, first, $186,000,000, then $198,000,000, and finally, as has been already stated, $220,000,000.

The income from this source for the fiscal year which will end on June 30, 1883, will doubtless be considerably in excess of the sum last mentioned.

If the tax on domestic spirits is to be retained, it is plain, therefore, that large reductions from the customs revenue are entirely feasible. While recommending this reduction, I am far from advising the abandonment of the policy of so discriminating in the adjustment of details as to afford aid and protection to domestic labor. But the present system should be so revised as to equalize the public burden among all classes and occupations and bring it into closer harmony with the present needs of industry.

Without entering into minute detail, which under present circumstances is quite unnecessary, I recommend an enlargement of the free list so as to include within it the numerous articles which yield inconsiderable revenue, a simplification of the complex and inconsistent schedule of duties upon certain manufactures, particularly those of cotton, iron, and steel, and a substantial reduction of the duties upon those articles and upon sugar, molasses, silk, wool, and woolen goods.

If a general revision of the tariff shall be found to be impracticable at this session, I express the hope that at least some of the more conspicuous inequalities of the present law may be corrected before your final adjournment. One of them is specially referred to by the Secretary. In view of a recent decision of the Supreme Court, the necessity of amending the law by which the Dutch standard of color is adopted as the test of the saccharine strength of sugars is too obvious to require comment.

From the report of the Secretary of War it appears that the only outbreaks of Indians during the past year occurred in Arizona and in the southwestern part of New Mexico. They were promptly quelled, and the quiet which has prevailed in all other parts of the country has permitted such an addition to be made to the military force in the region endangered by the Apaches that there is little reason to apprehend trouble in the future.

Those parts of the Secretary's report which relate to our seacoast defenses and their armament suggest the gravest reflections. Our existing fortifications are notoriously inadequate to the defense of the great harbors and cities for whose protection they were built.

The question of providing an armament suited to our present necessities has been the subject of consideration by a board, whose report was transmitted to Congress at the last session. Pending the consideration of that report, the War Department has taken no steps for the manufacture or conversion of any heavy cannon, but the Secretary expresses the hope that authority and means to begin that important work will be soon provided. I invite the attention of Congress to the propriety of making more adequate provision for arming and equipping the militia than is afforded by the act of 1808, which is still upon the statute book. The matter has already been the subject of discussion in the Senate, and a bill which seeks to supply the deficiencies of existing laws is now upon its calendar.

The Secretary of War calls attention to an embarrassment growing out of the recent act of Congress making the retirement of officers of the Army compulsory at the age of 64. The act of 1878 is still in force, which limits to 400 the number of those who can be retired for disability or upon their own application. The two acts, when construed together, seem to forbid the relieving, even for absolute incapacity, of officers who do not fall within the purview of the later statute, save at such times as there chance to be less than 400 names on the retired list. There are now 420. It is not likely that Congress intended this result, and I concur with the Secretary that the law ought to be amended.

The grounds that impelled me to withhold my signature from the bill entitled "An act making appropriations for the construction, repair, and preservation of certain works on rivers and harbors," which became a law near the close of your last session, prompt me to express the hope that no similar measure will be deemed necessary during the present session of Congress. Indeed, such a measure would now be open to a serious objection in addition to that which was lately urged upon your attention. I am informed by the Secretary of War that the greater portion of the sum appropriated for the various items specified in that act remains unexpended.

Of the new works which it authorized, expenses have been incurred upon two only, for which the total appropriation was $210,000. The present available balance is disclosed by the following table:

Amount of appropriation by act of August 2, 1882	$18,738,875
Amount of appropriation by act of June 19, 1882	10,000
Amount of appropriation for payments to J. B. Eads	304,000
Unexpended balance of former appropriations	4,738,263
	23,791,138
Less amount drawn from Treasury between July 1, 1882, and November 30, 1882	6,056,194
	17,734,944

It is apparent by this exhibit that so far as concerns most of the items to which the act of August 2, 1882, relates there can be no need of further appropriations until after the close of the present session. If, however, any action should seem to be necessary in respect to particular objects, it will be entirely feasible to provide for those objects by appropriate legislation. It is possible, for example, that a delay until the assembling of the next Congress to make additional provision for the Mississippi River improvements might be attended with serious consequences. If such should appear to be the case, a just bill relating to that subject would command my approval.

This leads me to offer a suggestion which I trust will commend itself to the wisdom of Congress. Is it not advisable that grants of considerable sums of money for diverse and independent schemes of internal improvement should be made the subjects of separate and distinct legislative enactments? It will scarcely be gainsaid, even by those who favor the most liberal expenditures for such purposes as are sought to be accomplished by what is commonly called the river and harbor bill, that the practice of grouping in such a bill appropriations for a great diversity of objects, widely separated either in their nature or in the locality with which they are concerned, or in both, is one which is much to be deprecated unless it is irremediable. It inevitably tends to secure the success of the bill as a whole, though many of the items, if separately considered, could scarcely fail of rejection. By the adoption of the course I have recommended every member of Congress, whenever opportunity should arise for giving his influence and vote for meritorious appropriations, would be enabled so to do without being called upon to sanction others undeserving his approval. So also would the Executive be afforded thereby full opportunity to exercise his constitutional prerogative of opposing whatever appropriations seemed to him objectionable without imperiling the success of others which commended themselves to his judgment.

It may be urged in opposition to these suggestions that the number of works of internal improvement which are justly entitled to governmental aid is so great as to render impracticable separate appropriation bills therefor, or even for such comparatively limited number as make disposition of large sums of money. This objection may be well founded, and, whether it be or not, the advantages which would be likely to ensue from the adoption of the course I have recommended may perhaps be more effectually attained by another, which I respectfully submit to Congress as an alternative proposition.

It is provided by the constitutions of fourteen of our States that the executive may disapprove any item or items of a bill appropriating money, whereupon the part of the bill approved shall be law and the part disapproved shall fail to become law unless repassed according to the provisions prescribed for the passage of bills over the veto of the executive. The States wherein some such provision as the foregoing is a part of the fundamental law are Alabama, California, Colorado, Florida, Georgia, Louisiana, Minnesota, Missouri, Nebraska, New Jersey, New York, Pennsylvania, Texas, and West Virginia. I commend to your careful consideration the question whether an amendment of the Federal Constitution in the particular indicated would not afford the best remedy for what is often a grave embrassment both to members of Congress and to the Executive, and is sometimes a serious public mischief.

The report of the Secretary of the Navy states the movements of the various squadrons during the year, in home and foreign waters, where our officers and seamen, with such ships as we possess, have continued to illustrate the high character and excellent discipline of the naval organization.

On the 21st of December, 1881, information was received that the exploring steamer *Jeannette* had been crushed and abandoned in the Arctic Ocean. The officers and crew, after a journey over the ice, embarked in three boats for the coast of Siberia. One of the parties, under the command of Chief Engineer George W. Melville, reached the land, and, falling in with the natives, was saved. Another, under Lieutenant-Commander De Long, landed in a barren region near the mouth of the Lena River. After six weeks had elapsed all but two of the number had died from fatigue and starvation. No tidings have been received from the party in the third boat, under the command of Lieutenant Chipp, but a long and fruitless investigation leaves little doubt that all its members perished at sea. As a slight tribute to their heroism I give in this communication the names of the gallant men who sacrificed their lives on this expedition: Lieutenant-Commander George W. De Long, Surgeon James M. Ambler, Jerome J. Collins, Hans Halmer Erichsen, Heinrich H. Kaacke, George W. Boyd, Walter Lee, Adolph Dressler, Carl A. Görtz, Nelse Iverson, the cook Ah Sam, and the Indian Alexy. The officers and men in the missing boat were Lieutenant Charles W. Chipp, commanding; William Dunbar, Alfred Sweetman, Walter Sharvell, Albert C. Kuehne, Edward Star, Henry D. Warren, and Peter E. Johnson.

Lieutenant Giles B. Harber and Master Willliam H. Scheutze are now bringing home the remains of Lieutenant De Long and his comrades, in pursuance of the directions of Congress.

The *Rodgers*, fitted out for the releif of the *Jeannette* in accordance with the act of Congress of March 3, 1881, sailed from San Francisco June 16 under the command of Lieutenant Robert M. Berry. On November 30 she was accidentally destroyed by fire while in winter quarters in St. Lawrence Bay, but the officers and crew succeeded in escaping to the shore. Lieutenant Berry and one of his officers, after making a search for the *Jeannette* along the coast of Siberia, fell in with Chief Engineer Melville's party and returned home by way of Europe. The other officers and the crew of the *Rodgers* were brought from St. Lawrence Bay by the whaling steamer *North Star*. Master Charles F. Putnam, who had been placed in charge of a depot of supplies at Cape Serdze, returning to his post from St. Lawrence Bay across the ice in a blinding snow storm, was carried out to sea and lost, notwithstanding all efforts to rescue him.

It appears by the Secretary's report that the available naval force of the United States consists of 37 cruisers, 14 single-turreted monitors, built during the rebellion, a large number of smoothbore guns and Parrott rifles, and 87 rifled cannon.

The cruising vessels should be gradually replaced by iron or steel ships, the monitors by modern armored vessels, and the armament by high-power rifled guns.

The reconstruction of our Navy, which was recommended in my last message, was begun by Congress authorizing, in its recent act, the construction of two large unarmored steel vessels of the character recommended by the late Naval Advisory Board, and subject to the final approval of a new advisory board to be organized as provided by that act. I call your attention to the recommendation of the Secretary and the board that authority be given to construct two more cruisers of smaller dimensions and one fleet dispatch vessel, and that appropriations be made for high-power rifled cannon for the torpedo service and for other harbor defenses.

Pending the consideration by Congress of the policy to be hereafter adopted in conducting the eight large navy-yards and their expensive establishments, the Secretary advocates the reduction of expenditures therefor to the lowest possible amounts.

For the purpose of affording the officers and seamen of the Navy opportunities for exercise and discipline in their profession, under appropriate control and direction, the Secretary advises that the Light-House Service and Coast Survey be transferred, as now organized, from the Treasury to the Navy Department; and he also suggests, for the reasons which he assigns, that a similar transfer may wisely be made of the cruising revenue vessels.

The Secretary forcibly depicts the intimate connection and interdependence of the Navy and the commercial marine, and invites attention to the continued decadence of the latter and the corresponding transfer of our growing commerce to foreign bottoms.

This subject is one of the utmost importance to the national welfare. Methods of reviving American shipbuilding and of restoring the United States flag in the ocean carrying trade should receive the immediate attention of Congress. We have mechanical skill and abundant material for the manufacture of modern iron steamships in fair competition with our commercial rivals. Our disadvantage in building ships is the greater cost of labor, and in sailing them, higher taxes, and greater interest on capital, while the ocean highways are already monopolized by our formidable competitors. These obstacles should in some way be overcome, and for our rapid communication with foreign lands we should not continue to depend wholly upon vessels built in the yards of other countries and sailing under foreign flags. With no United States steamers on the principal ocean lines or in any foreign ports, our facilities for extending our commerce are greatly restricted, while the nations which build and sail the ships and carry the mails and passengers obtain thereby conspicuous advantages in increasing their trade.

The report of the Postmaster-General gives evidence of the satisfactory condition of that Department and contains many valuable data and accompanying suggestions which can not fail to be of interest.

The information which it affords that the receipts for the fiscal year have exceeded the expenditures must be very gratifying to Congress and to the people of the country.

As matters which may fairly claim particular attention, I refer you to his observations in reference to the advisability of changing the present basis for fixing salaries and allowances, of extending the money-order system, and of enlarging the functions of the postal establishment so as to put under its control the telegraph system of the country, though from this last and most important recommendation I must withhold my concurrence.

At the last session of Congress several bills were introduced into the House of Representatives for the reduction of letter postage to the rate of 2 cents per half ounce.

I have given much study and reflection to this subject, and am thoroughly persuaded that such a reduction would be for the best interests of the public.

It has been the policy of the Government from its foundation to defray as far as possible the expenses of carrying the mails by a direct tax in the form of postage. It has never been claimed, however, that this service ought to be productive of a net revenue.

As has been stated already, the report of the Postmaster-General shows that there is now a very considerable surplus in his Department and that henceforth the receipts are likely to increase at a much greater ratio than the necessary expenditures. Unless some change is made in the existing laws, the profits of the postal service will in a very few years swell the revenues of the Government many millions of dollars. The time seems auspicious, therefore, for some reduction in the rates of postage. In what shall that reduction consist?

A review of the legislation which has been had upon this subject during the last thirty years discloses that domestic letters constitute the only class of mail matter which has never been favored by a substantial reduction of rates. I am convinced that the burden of maintaining the service falls most unequally upon that class, and that more than any other it is entitled to present relief.

That such relief may be extended without detriment to other public interests will be discovered upon reviewing the results of former reductions.

Immediately prior to the act of 1845 the postage upon a letter composed of a single sheet was as follows :

If conveyed—	Cents.
30 miles or less	6
Between 30 and 80 miles	10
Between 80 and 150 miles	12½
Between 150 and 400 miles	18¾
Over 400 miles	25

By the act of 1845 the postage upon a single letter conveyed for any distance under 300 miles was fixed at 5 cents and for any greater distance at 10 cents.

By the act of 1851 it was provided that a single letter, if prepaid, should be carried any distance not exceeding 3,000 miles for 3 cents and any greater distance for 6 cents.

It will be noticed that both of these reductions were of a radical character and relatively quite as important as that which is now proposed.

In each case there ensued a temporary loss of revenue, but a sudden and large influx of business, which substantially repaired that loss within three years.

Unless the experience of past legislation in this country and elsewhere goes for naught, it may be safely predicted that the stimulus of 33⅓ per cent reduction in the tax for carriage would at once increase the number of letters consigned to the mails.

The advantages of secrecy would lead to a very general substitution of sealed packets for postal cards and open circulars, and in divers other ways the volume of first-class matter would be enormously augmented. Such increase amounted in England, in the first year after the adoption of penny postage, to more than 125 per cent.

As a result of careful estimates, the details of which can not be here set out, I have become convinced that the deficiency for the first year after the proposed reduction would not exceed 7 per cent of the expenditures, or $3,000,000, while the deficiency after the reduction of 1845 was more than 14 per cent, and after that of 1851 was 27 per cent.

Another interesting comparison is afforded by statistics furnished me by the Post-Office Department.

The act of 1845 was passed in face of the fact that there existed a deficiency of more than $30,000. That of 1851 was encouraged by the slight surplus of $132,000. The excess of revenue in the next fiscal year is likely to be $3,500,000.

If Congress should approve these suggestions, it may be deemed desirable to supply to some extent the deficiency which must for a time result by increasing the charge for carrying merchandise, which is now only 16 cents per pound ; but even without such an increase I am confident that the receipts under the diminished rates would equal the expenditures after the lapse of three or four years.

The report of the Department of Justice brings anew to your notice the necessity of enlarging the present system of Federal jurisprudence so as effectually to answer the requirements of the ever-increasing litigation with which it is called upon to deal.

The Attorney-General renews the suggestions of his predecessor that in the interests of justice better provision than the existing laws afford should be made in certain judicial districts for fixing the fees of witnesses and jurors.

In my message of December last I referred to pending criminal proceedings growing out of alleged frauds in what is known as the star-route service of the Post-Office Department, and advised you that I had enjoined upon the Attorney-General and associate counsel, to whom the interests of the Government were intrusted, the duty of prosecuting with the utmost vigor of the law all persons who might be found chargeable with those offenses. A trial of one of these cases has since occurred. It occupied for many weeks the attention of the supreme court of this District and was conducted with great zeal and ability. It resulted in a disagreement of the jury, but the cause has been again placed upon the calendar and will shortly be retried. If any guilty persons shall finally escape punishment for their offenses, it will not be for lack of diligent and earnest efforts on the part of the prosecution.

I trust that some agreement may be reached which will speedily enable Congress, with the concurrence of the Executive, to afford the commercial community the benefits of a national bankrupt law.

The report of the Secretary of the Interior, with its accompanying documents, presents a full statement of the varied operations of that Department. In respect to Indian affairs nothing has occurred which has changed or seriously modified the views to which I devoted much space in a former communication to Congress. I renew the recommendations therein contained as to extending to the Indian the protection of the law, allotting land in severalty to such as desire it, and making suitable provision for the education of youth. Such provision, as the Secretary forcibly maintains, will prove unavailing unless it is broad enough to include all those who are able and willing to make use of it, and should not solely relate to intellectual training, but also to instruction in such manual labor and simple industrial arts as can be made practically available.

Among other important subjects which are included within the Secretary's report, and which will doubtless furnish occasion for Congressional action, may be mentioned the neglect of the railroad companies to which large grants of land were made by the acts of 1862 and 1864 to take title thereto, and their consequent inequitable exemption from local taxation.

No survey of our material condition can fail to suggest inquiries as to the moral and intellectual progress of the people.

The census returns disclose an alarming state of illiteracy in certain portions of the country, where the provision for schools is grossly inadequate.

It is a momentous question for the decision of Congress whether immediate and substantial aid should not be extended by the General Government for supplementing the efforts of private beneficence and of State and Territorial legislation in behalf of education.

The regulation of interstate commerce has already been the subject of your deliberations. One of the incidents of the marvelous extension of the railway system of the country has been the adoption of such measures by the corporations which own or control the roads as have tended to impair the advantages of healthful competition and to make hurtful discriminations in the adjustment of freightage.

These inequalities have been corrected in several of the States by appropriate legislation, the effect of which is necessarily restricted to the limits of their own territory.

So far as such mischiefs affect commerce between the States or between any one of the States and a foreign country, they are subjects of national concern, and Congress alone can afford relief.

The results which have thus far attended the enforcement of the recent statute for the suppression of polygamy in the Territories are reported by the Secretary of the Interior. It is not probable that any additional legislation in this regard will be .deemed desirable until the effect of existing laws shall be more closely observed and studied.

I congratulate you that the commissioners under whose supervision those laws have been put in operation are encouraged to believe that the evil at which they are aimed may be suppressed without resort to such radical measures as in some quarters have been thought indispensable for success.

The close relation of the General Government to the Territories preparing to be great States may well engage your special attention. It is there that the Indian disturbances mainly occur and that polygamy has found room for its growth. I can not doubt that a careful survey of Territorial legislation would be of the highest utility. Life and property would become more secure. The liability of outbreaks between Indians and whites would be lessened. The public domain would be more securely guarded and better progress be made in the instruction of the young.

Alaska is still without any form of civil government. If means were provided for the education of its people and for the protection of their lives and property, the immense resources of the region would invite permanent settlements and open new fields for industry and enterprise.

The report of the Commissioner of Agriculture presents an account of the labors of that Department during the past year and includes information of much interest to the general public.

The condition of the forests of the country and the wasteful manner in which their destruction is taking place give cause for serious apprehension. Their action in protecting the earth's surface, in modifying the extremes of climate, and in regulating and sustaining the flow of springs and streams is now well understood, and their importance in relation to the growth and prosperity of the country can not be safely disregarded. They are fast disappearing before destructive fires and the legitimate requirements of our increasing population, and their total extinction can not be long delayed unless better methods than now prevail shall be adopted for their protection and cultivation. The attention of Congress is invited to the necessity of additional legislation to secure the preservation of the valuable forests still remaining on the public domain, especially in the extreme Western States and Territories, where the necessity for their preservation is greater than in less mountainous regions, and where the prevailing dryness of the climate renders their restoration, if they are once destroyed, well-nigh impossible.

The communication which I made to Congress at its first session, in December last, contained a somewhat full statement of my sentiments in relation to the principles and rules which ought to govern appointments to public service.

Referring to the various plans which had theretofore been the subject of discussion in the National Legislature (plans which in the main were modeled upon the system which obtains in Great Britain, but which lacked certain of the prominent features whereby that system is distinguished), I felt bound to intimate my doubts whether they, or any of them, would afford adequate remedy for the evils which they aimed to correct.

I declared, nevertheless, that if the proposed measures should prove acceptable to Congress they would receive the unhesitating support of the Executive.

Since these suggestions were submitted for your consideration there has been no legislation upon the subject to which they relate, but there has meanwhile been an increase in the public interest in that subject, and the people of the country, apparently without distinction of party, have in various ways and upon frequent occasions given expression to their earnest wish for prompt and definite action. In my judgment such action should no longer be postponed.

I may add that my own sense of its pressing importance has been quickened by observation of a practical phase of the matter, to which attention has more than once been called by my predecessors.

The civil list now comprises about 100,000 persons, far the larger part of whom must, under the terms of the Constitution, be selected by the President either directly or through his own appointees.

In the early years of the administration of the Government the personal direction of appointments to the civil service may not have been an irksome task for the Executive, but now that the burden has increased fully a hundredfold it has become greater than he ought to bear, and it necessarily diverts his time and attention from the proper discharge of other duties no less delicate and responsible, and which in the very nature of things can not be delegated to other hands.

In the judgment of not a few who have given study and reflection to this matter, the nation has outgrown the provisions which the Constitution has established for filling the minor offices in the public service.

But whatever may be thought of the wisdom or expediency of changing the fundamental law in this regard, it is certain that much relief may be afforded, not only to the President and to the heads of the Departments, but to Senators and Representatives in Congress, by discreet legislation. They would be protected in a great measure by the bill now pending before the Senate, or by any other which should embody its important features, from the pressure of personal importunity and from the labor of examining conflicting claims and pretensions of candidates.

I trust that before the close of the present session some decisive action may be taken for the correction of the evils which inhere in the present methods of appointment, and I assure you of my hearty cooperation in any measures which are likely to conduce to that end.

As to the most appropriate term and tenure of the official life of the subordinate employees of the Government, it seems to be generally agreed that, whatever their extent or character, the one should be definite and the other stable, and that neither should be regulated by zeal in the service of party or fidelity to the fortunes of an individual.

It matters little to the people at large what competent person is at the head of this department or of that bureau if they feel assured that the removal of one and the accession of another will not involve the retirement of honest and faithful subordinates whose duties are purely administrative and have no legitimate connection with the triumph of any political principles or the success of any political party or faction. It is to this latter class of officers that the Senate bill, to which I have already referred, exclusively applies.

While neither that bill nor any other prominent scheme for improving the civil service concerns the higher grade of officials, who are appointed by the President and confirmed by the Senate, I feel bound to correct a prevalent misapprehension as to the frequency with which the present Executive has displaced the incumbent of an office and appointed another in his stead.

It has been repeatedly alleged that he has in this particular signally departed from the course which has been pursued under recent Administrations of the Government. The facts are as follows:

The whole number of Executive appointments during the four years immediately preceding Mr. Garfield's accession to the Presidency was 2,696. Of this number 244, or 9 per cent, involved the removal of previous incumbents.

The ratio of removals to the whole number of appointments was much the same during each of those four years.

In the first year, with 790 appointments, there were 74 removals, or 9.3 per cent; in the second, with 917 appointments, there were 85 removals, or 8.5 per cent; in the third, with 480 appointments, there were 48 removals, or 10 per cent; in the fourth, with 429 appointments, there were 37 removals, or 8.6 per cent. In the four months of President Garfield's Administration there were 390 appointments and 89 removals, or 22.7 per cent. Precisely the same number of removals (89) has taken place in the fourteen months which have since elapsed, but they constitute only 7.8 per cent of the whole number of appointments (1,118) within that period and less than 2.6 of the entire list of officials (3,459), exclusive of the Army and Navy, which is filled by Presidential appointment.

I declare my approval of such legislation as may be found necessary for supplementing the existing provisions of law in relation to political assessments.

In July last I authorized a public announcement that employees of the Government should regard themselves as at liberty to exercise their pleasure in making or refusing to make political contributions, and that their action in that regard would in no manner affect their official status.

In this announcement I acted upon the view, which I had always maintained and still maintain, that a public officer should be as absolutely free as any other citizen to give or to withhold a contribution for the aid of the political party of his choice. It has, however, been urged, and doubtless not without foundation in fact, that by solicitation of official superiors and by other modes such contributions have at times been obtained from persons whose only motive for giving has been the fear of what might befall them if they refused. It goes without saying that such contributions are not voluntary, and in my judgment their collection should be prohibited by law. A bill which will effectually suppress them will receive my cordial approval.

I hope that, however numerous and urgent may be the demands upon your attention, the interests of this District will not be forgotten.

The denial to its residents of the great right of suffrage in all its relations to national, State, and municipal action imposes upon Congress the duty of affording them the best administration which its wisdom can devise.

The report of the District Commissioners indicates certain measures whose adoption would seem to be very desirable. I instance in particular those which relate to arrears of taxes, to steam railroads, and to assessments of real property.

Among the questions which have been the topic of recent debate in the halls of Congress none are of greater gravity than those relating to the ascertainment of the vote for Presidential electors and the intendment of the Constitution in its provisions for devolving Executive functions upon the Vice-President when the President suffers from inability to discharge the powers and duties of his office.

I trust that no embarrassments may result from a failure to determine these questions before another national election.

The closing year has been replete with blessings, for which we owe to the Giver of All Good our reverent acknowledgment. For the uninterrupted harmony of our foreign relations, for the decay of sectional animosities, for the exuberance of our harvests and the triumphs of our mining and manufacturing industries, for the prevalence of health, the spread of intelligence, and the conservation of the public credit, for the growth of the country in all the elements of national greatness—for these and countless other blessings we should rejoice and be glad. I trust that under the inspiration of this great prosperity our counsels may be harmonious, and that the dictates of prudence, patriotism, justice, and economy may lead to the adoption of measures in which the Congress and the Executive may heartily unite.   CHESTER A. ARTHUR.

SPECIAL MESSAGES.

EXECUTIVE MANSION. *December 6, 1882.*

To the Senate and House of Representatives:

I transmit herewith a communication from the Secretary of War, dated the 4th instant, and its accompanying papers, in which it is recommended that section 1216, Revised Statutes, be so amended as to include in its provisions the enlisted men of the Army, and that section 1285, Revised Statutes, be modified so as to read:

A certificate of merit granted to an enlisted man for distinguished service shall entitle him thereafter to additional pay, at the rate of $2 per month, while he is in the military service, although such service may not be continuous.

CHESTER A. ARTHUR.

EXECUTIVE MANSION, *December 6, 1882.*

To the Senate and House of Representatives:

I transmit herewith a communication from the Secretary of War, dated the 4th instant, setting forth certain facts respecting the title to the peninsula of Presque Isle, at Erie, Pa., and recommending that the subject be presented to Congress with the view of legislation by that body modifying the act of May 27, 1882, entitled "An act to authorize the Secretary of War to accept the peninsula in Lake Erie opposite the harbor of Erie, in the State of Pennsylvania" (17 U. S. Statutes at Large, p. 162), so as to authorize the Secretary of War to accept title to the said peninsula, proffered by the marine hospital of Pennsylvania pursuant to an act of the legislature of that State approved by the governor May 11, 1871.

CHESTER A. ARTHUR.

EXECUTIVE MANSION, *December 6, 1882.*

To the Senate and House of Representatives:

I transmit herewith, for the consideration of Congress, a communication from the Secretary of War, inclosing one from the commanding general Department of the Missouri, indorsed by the division commander, urging the advisability of prompt action in the matter of perfecting the title to the site of Fort Bliss, Tex.

Accompanying also is a copy of Senate Executive Document No. 96, Forty-seventh Congress, first session, which presents fully the facts in the case, as well as the character of the legislation necessary to secure to the United States proper title to the land in question.

The Secretary of War expresses his concurrence in the views of the military authorities as to the importance of this subject and urges that the requisite legislation be had by Congress at its present session.

CHESTER A. ARTHUR.

EXECUTIVE MANSION, *December 8, 1882.*

To the Senate and House of Representatives:

I transmit herewith a communication from the Secretary of the Interior, with a draft of a bill and accompanying papers, to accept and ratify an agreement made by the Pi-Ute Indians, and granting a right of way to the Carson and Colorado Railroad Company through the Walker River Reservation, in Nevada.

The subject is presented for the consideration of Congress.

CHESTER A. ARTHUR.

EXECUTIVE MANSION,
Washington, December 13, 1882.

To the House of Representatives:

In response to the resolution of the House of Representatives of the 30th of January, 1882, on the subject of the tariff of consular fees, I transmit herewith a report of the Secretary of State.

CHESTER A. ARTHUR.

EXECUTIVE MANSION, *December 15, 1882.*

To the Senate and House of Representatives:

I transmit herewith, for the consideration of Congress, a letter from the Secretary of the Interior, inclosing a copy of a letter from the acting governor of New Mexico, in which he sets forth reasons why authority should be given and provision made for holding a session of the Territorial legislature of New Mexico in January, 1883, or soon thereafter.

CHESTER A. ARTHUR.

EXECUTIVE MANSION, *December 19, 1882.*

To the Senate and House of Representatives:

I transmit herewith, for the consideration of Congress, a communication from the Secretary of War, upon the subject of abandoned military reservations, and renewing his former recommendation for such legislation as will provide for the disposal of military sites that are no longer needed for military purposes.

CHESTER A. ARTHUR.

EXECUTIVE MANSION, *December 21, 1882.*

To the Senate and House of Representatives:

I transmit herewith a communication from the Secretary of the Interior of the 18th instant, with accompanying papers, submitting a draft of a bill "for the relief of the Nez Percé Indians in the Territory of Idaho and of the allied tribes residing upon the Grande Ronde Indian Reservation, in the State of Oregon."

The subject is presented for the consideration of Congress.

CHESTER A. ARTHUR.

EXECUTIVE MANSION, *December 27, 1882.*

To the Senate and House of Representatives:

I submit herewith a letter from the Secretary of the Interior, inclosing a communication from the secretary of the Territory of New Mexico, who has custody of the public buildings at Santa Fe, in which are set forth reasons why an appropriation should be made for the completion of the capitol at Santa Fe, and commend the same to the consideration of Congress.

CHESTER A. ARTHUR.

EXECUTIVE MANSION, *January 5, 1883.*

To the Senate and House of Representatives:

I transmit herewith a communication from the Secretary of the Interior, together with a letter from the Superintendent of the Census, requesting an additional appropriation of $100,000 to complete the work of the Tenth Census, and recommend the same to Congress for its favorable consideration.

CHESTER A. ARTHUR.

EXECUTIVE MANSION, *January 5, 1883.*

To the Senate and House of Representatives:

I transmit herewith, for the consideration of Congress, a communication from the Secretary of War, dated the 2d instant, and inclosing one from Lieutenant Robert Craig, Fourth Artillery, indorsed by the Chief

Signal Officer of the Army, recommending that Congress authorize the printing and binding for the use of the Signal Office of 10,000 copies of the Annual Report of the Chief Signal Officer for the fiscal year 1882, and inclosing a draft of a joint resolution for the purpose.

CHESTER A. ARTHUR.

EXECUTIVE MANSION, *January 9, 1883.*

To the Senate and House of Representatives:

I transmit herewith a communication from the Secretary of the Interior, submitting a report, with accompanying papers, regarding the condition of the several libraries of said Department and the consolidation of the same.

CHESTER A. ARTHUR.

EXECUTIVE MANSION,
Washington, January 10, 1883.

To the Senate of the United States:

The Senate having by executive resolution of the 20th ultimo returned to me the supplemental convention of extradition signed August 7, 1882, in order that certain verbal changes therein might be made, as requested by the Spanish Government, as explained in the letter of the Secretary of State to the Committee on Foreign Relations of the Senate dated the 15th ultimo, I now lay the said convention so modified before the Senate, with a view to its ratification.

CHESTER A. ARTHUR.

EXECUTIVE MANSION, *January 11, 1883.*

To the Senate and House of Representatives:

I transmit herewith, for the consideration of Congress, a communication from the Secretary of War, dated the 10th instant, inclosing one from the Chief of Ordnance, together with one from Lieutenant-Colonel D. W. Flagler, commanding the Rock Island Arsenal, Ill., setting forth the insufficiency of the sum appropriated by the sundry civil appropriation act of August 7, 1882, for the deepening of the water-power tail-race canal at that arsenal, and recommending that a special appropriation of $20,000 be made for the completion of said work.

CHESTER A. ARTHUR.

EXECUTIVE MANSION, *January 12, 1883.*

To the House of Representatives:

I transmit herewith a report of the Secretary of State and accompanying papers, furnished in response to the resolution of the House of Representatives of July 15, 1882, calling for any information in the possession of the Department of State in reference to any change or modification of the stipulations which the French Cable Company made with the Government.

CHESTER A. ARTHUR.

EXECUTIVE MANSION, *January 19, 1883.*

To the Senate and House of Representatives:

I transmit herewith, for the consideration of Congress, a communication from the Secretary of War, dated the 17th instant, inclosing, with other papers on the subject, a petition of Thomas Mulvihill, of Pittsburg, Pa., praying for the repossession of certain shore lands at Pittsburg erroneously conveyed by him to the United States.

CHESTER A. ARTHUR.

EXECUTIVE MANSION, *January 19, 1883.*

To the Senate and House of Representatives:

I transmit herewith a communication, dated the 18th instant, from the Secretary of the Interior, with accompanying papers, in relation to the request of the Cherokee Indians in the Indian Territory for payment for lands in that Territory west of the ninety-sixth degree west longitude, the cession of which to the United States for the settlement of friendly Indians thereon is provided for in the sixteenth article of the treaty of July 19, 1866.

CHESTER A. ARTHUR.

EXECUTIVE MANSION, *January 19, 1883.*

To the Senate and House of Representatives:

I transmit herewith, for the consideration of Congress, a communication from the Secretary of War, dated the 17th instant, inclosing copies of letters respectively from the Chief of Engineers and Colonel A. F. Rockwell, in charge of public buildings and grounds in this city, urging the importance of an immediate appropriation of $1,000 for removing snow and ice from the walks and pavements in and around the various public reservations under his control during the remainder of the present fiscal year.

CHESTER A. ARTHUR.

EXECUTIVE MANSION, *January 19, 1883.*

To the Senate of the United States:

I have carefully considered the provisions of Senate bill No. 561, entitled " An act for the relief of Robert Stodart Wyld."

I am of the opinion that the general statute is sufficiently liberal to provide relief in all proper cases of destroyed United States bonds, and I believe that the act above referred to constitutes an evil precedent.

It is not, however, so objectionable as to call for my formal disapproval, and I have allowed it to become a law under the constitutional provision, contenting myself with communicating to the Senate, in which the bill originated, my disapproval of special legislation of this character.

CHESTER A. ARTHUR.

EXECUTIVE MANSION, *January 19, 1883.*
To the Senate and House of Representatives:

I transmit herewith, for the consideration of Congress, a communication from the Secretary of War, dated the 18th instant, inclosing an extract copy of a report of the Adjutant-General respecting the military reservation of Fort Cameron, Utah Territory, and recommending that authority be granted during the present session of Congress for the disposal of said reservation, it being no longer needed for military purposes.

CHESTER A. ARTHUR.

EXECUTIVE MANSION, *January 19, 1883.*
To the Senate and House of Representatives:

I transmit herewith a communication from the Secretary of the Interior, with a draft of a bill, and accompanying papers, to accept and ratify an agreement with the confederated tribes of Flathead, Kootenay, and Upper Pend d'Oreille Indians for the sale of a portion of their reservation in the Territory of Montana, required for the Northern Pacific Railroad, and to make the necessary appropriation for carrying the same into effect.

The subject is presented for the consideration of the Congress.

CHESTER A. ARTHUR.

EXECUTIVE MANSION,
Washington, January 23, 1883.
To the Senate of the United States:

In response to the resolution of the Senate of the United States dated January 5, 1883, requesting "that the Secretary of State be directed to transmit to the Senate copies of any letters on file in his Department from the consular service upon the subject of the shipment and discharge of seamen or payment of extra wages to seamen," I have to transmit a report of the Secretary of State on the subject.

CHESTER A. ARTHUR.

EXECUTIVE MANSION, *January 25, 1883.*
To the Senate and House of Representatives:

I transmit herewith a communication from the Secretary of State, concerning the character and condition of the library of the Department of State.

CHESTER A. ARTHUR.

EXECUTIVE MANSION, *January 26, 1883.*

To the House of Representatives:

It is hereby announced to the House of Congress in which it originated that the joint resolution (H. Res. 190) to refer certain claims to the Court of Claims has been permitted to become a law under the constitutional provision. Its apparent purpose is to allow certain bankers to sue in the Court of Claims for the amount of internal-revenue tax collected from them without lawful authority, upon showing as matter of excuse for not having brought their suits within the time limited by law that they had entered into an agreement with the district attorney which was in substance that they should be relieved of that necessity. I can not concur in the policy of setting aside the bar of the statute in those cases on such ground, but I have not deemed it necessary to return the joint resolution with my objections for reconsideration.

CHESTER A. ARTHUR.

EXECUTIVE MANSION, *January 30, 1883.*

To the Senate of the United States:

I transmit herewith a copy of a communication to me from the Secretary of the Treasury.*

I have acted in conformity with the recommendations, oral and written, which are therein set forth, concerning the action suggested to be that which would best effectuate the purpose of section 1768 of the Revised Statutes of the United States and be most considerate of the reputation and interests of the public officer to be affected and most subservient to the public interest.

CHESTER A. ARTHUR.

EXECUTIVE MANSION,
Washington, February 3, 1883.

To the Senate of the United States:

I transmit to the Senate, for consideration with a view to ratification, the treaty of commerce which was signed in duplicate January 20, 1883, by commissioners on the part of the United States and Mexico, with accompanying papers.

The attention of the Senate is called to the statement in the third protocol as to the insertion of the word "steel" in item No. (35) 66 of the list appended to article 2 of the treaty. No further information as to the possible correction therein referred to has yet reached me; but as the session of the Senate will soon terminate, I deem it advisable to transmit the treaty as signed, in the hope that its ratification may be assented to.

While the treaty does not contain all the provisions desired by the

_____
*Relating to the suspension of William H. Daniels, collector of customs for the district of Oswegatchie, N. Y.

United States, the difficulties in the way of a full and complete settlement of matters of common interest to the two countries were such as to make me willing to approve it as an important step toward a desirable result, not doubting that, as time shall show the advantages of the system thus inaugurated, the Government will be able by supplementary agreements to insert the word "steel" and to perfect what is lacking in the instrument.

CHESTER A. ARTHUR.

EXECUTIVE MANSION, *February 3, 1883.*

To the Senate and House of Representatives:

I transmit herewith a communication from the Secretary of the Interior of the 1st instant, submitting a report made by the commission appointed under the provisions of the act of August 7, 1882, to treat with the Sioux Indians for a modification of their existing treaties, together with a copy of the agreement negotiated by that commission.

The subject is presented for the favorable consideration of Congress.

CHESTER A. ARTHUR.

EXECUTIVE MANSION, *February 5, 1883.*

To the Senate and House of Representatives:

I transmit herewith, for the consideration of Congress, a communication from the Secretary of War, dated the 2d instant, in relation to the subject of invasion of the Indian Territory, and urging the importance of amending section 2148 of the Revised Statutes so as to impose a penalty of imprisonment for unlawful entry upon the Indian lands.

CHESTER A. ARTHUR.

EXECUTIVE MANSION,
Washington, February 5, 1883.

To the Senate of the United States:

Referring to my message to the Senate of the 3d instant, wherewith was transmitted, for consideration with a view to ratification, the treaty of commerce between Mexico and the United States which was signed at Washington on the 20th ultimo, I have now to inform the Senate that this Government is officially advised by that of Mexico, through its minister at this capital, that it assents to the insertion of the word "steel" in item No. (35) 66 of the list appended to article 2 of that treaty.

It is desired that the treaty be returned to me that the amendment may be made, after which it will be again sent to the Senate for final action.

CHESTER A. ARTHUR.

EXECUTIVE MANSION, *February 6, 1883.*

To the Senate of the United States:

I retransmit to the Senate the commercial treaty recently signed in this city by the commissioners of the United States and Mexico, as amended by the insertion of the word "steel" in item (35) 66 of the list appended to article 2 thereof.

CHESTER A. ARTHUR.

EXECUTIVE MANSION, *February 7, 1883.*

To the Senate and House of Representatives:

I transmit herewith a communication of the 3d instant, with accompanying papers, from the Secretary of the Interior, being a partial report upon the Cherokee Indian matters required under a clause in the sundry civil appropriation act of August 7, 1882.

CHESTER A. ARTHUR.

EXECUTIVE MANSION, *February 8, 1883.*

To the Senate and House of Representatives:

I transmit herewith a communication from the Secretary of the Interior of the 7th instant, with accompanying papers, setting forth the urgent necessity of stringent measures for the repression of the rapidly increasing evasions and violations of the laws relating to public lands, and of a special appropriation for the purpose both in the current and approaching fiscal years.

The subject is presented for the consideration of Congress.

CHESTER A. ARTHUR.

EXECUTIVE MANSION, *Washington, February 9, 1883.*

To the Senate of the United States:

I transmit herewith to the Senate, for its consideration with a view to ratification, a convention between the United States of America and the French Republic, for extending the term of the French and American claims convention, concluded at Washington on the 8th day of February, 1883.

CHESTER A. ARTHUR.

EXECUTIVE MANSION, *February 10, 1883.*

To the Senate and House of Representatives:

I transmit herewith, for the information of Congress, a copy of the report of the Board of Indian Commissioners for the year 1882. The report accompanies the message to the House of Representatives.

CHESTER A. ARTHUR.

EXECUTIVE MANSION, *February 10, 1883.*

To the House of Representatives:

I transmit herewith, in response to a resolution of the House of Representatives of the 25th ultimo, a report of the Secretary of State, in relation to export duties levied in foreign countries having commercial relations with the United States.

CHESTER A. ARTHUR.

EXECUTIVE MANSION, *February 12, 1883.*

To the Senate and House of Representatives:

I transmit herewith a communication of the 8th instant, with accompanying papers, from the Secretary of the Interior, comprising the further report in relation to matters of difference between the Eastern and Western bands of Cherokee Indians required by an item in the sundry civil act approved August 7, 1882 (pamphlet statutes, page 328).

CHESTER A. ARTHUR.

EXECUTIVE MANSION, *Washington, February 15, 1883.*

To the Senate of the United States:

I transmit herewith, in compliance with the resolution of the Senate of December 18, 1882, the report of Mr. George Earl Church upon Ecuador, which I have this day received from the Secretary of State.

CHESTER A. ARTHUR.

EXECUTIVE MANSION, *February 20, 1883.*

To the Senate and House of Representatives:

I transmit herewith, for the consideration of Congress, a letter from the Secretary of War, dated the 19th instant, inclosing a copy of one from Major George L. Gillespie, Corps of Engineers, dated the 15th instant, referring to the insufficiency of the sum ($39,000) appropriated by the sundry civil bill of August 7, 1882, for building the sea wall on Governors Island, New York Harbor, together with a copy of the indorsement of the Chief Engineer, showing the necessity for an additional appropriation of $15,000 for this purpose. The Secretary of War recommends that said additional sum of $15,000 be appropriated at the present session of Congress for the object stated.

CHESTER A. ARTHUR.

EXECUTIVE MANSION, *Washington, February 23, 1883.*

To the House of Representatives of the United States of America:

With reference to my message of the 12th ultimo on the same subject, I transmit herewith a further report of the Secretary of State, furnishing additional papers received since the date of his former report in response to a resolution of the House of Representatives of July 5, 1882, calling for any information in the possession of the Department of State in reference to any changes or modifications of the stipulations which the French Cable Company made with this Government.

CHESTER A. ARTHUR.

EXECUTIVE MANSION, *February 26, 1883.*

To the Senate and House of Representatives:

I transmit herewith, for the information of Congress, a copy of the annual report of the Government directors of the Union Pacific Railway Company, under date of the 19th instant.

The copy of the report referred to accompanies the message to the House of Representatives.

CHESTER A. ARTHUR.

EXECUTIVE MANSION, *February 27, 1883.*

To the Senate of the United States:

I transmit herewith a report of the Secretary of State, furnished in response to the resolution of the Senate of February 26, 1883, requesting information touching an alleged joint agreement between the ministers of the United States, of Great Britain, of France, and of Italy now serving in Peru.

CHESTER A. ARTHUR.

EXECUTIVE MANSION, *March 1, 1883.*

To the Senate of the United States:

Having approved the act recently passed by Congress "to regulate and improve the civil service of the United States," I deem it my duty to call your attention to the provision for the employment of a "chief examiner" contained in the third section of the act, which was the subject of consideration at the time of its approval.

I am advised by the Attorney-General that there is great doubt whether such examiner is not properly an officer of the United States because of the nature of his employment, its duration, emolument, and duties. If he be such, the provision for his employment (which involves an appointment by the Commission) is not in conformity with section 2, Article II of the Constitution. Assuming this to be the case, the result would be that the appointment of the chief examiner must be deemed to be vested in the President, by and with the advice and consent of the Senate, since in such case the appointment would not be otherwise provided for by law. Concurring in this opinion, I nominate Silas W. Burt, of New York, to be chief examiner of the Civil Service Commission.

CHESTER A. ARTHUR.

PROCLAMATIONS.

By the President of the United States of America.

A PROCLAMATION.

Whereas by the eighth section of an act entitled ''An act to encourage the holding of a World's Industrial and Cotton Centennial Exposition in the year 1884,'' approved February 10, 1883, it was enacted as follows:

That whenever the President shall be informed by the said board of management that provision has been made for suitable buildings, or the erection of the same, for the purposes of said exposition, the President shall, through the Department of State, make proclamation of the same, setting forth the time at which the exhibition will open and the place at which it will be held; and such board of management shall communicate to the diplomatic representatives of all nations copies of the same and a copy of this act, together with such regulations as may be adopted by said board of management, for publication in their respective countries.

And whereas the duly constituted board of managers of the aforesaid World's Industrial and Cotton Centennial Exposition has informed me that provision has been made for the erection of suitable buildings for the purposes of said exposition:

Now, therefore, I, Chester A. Arthur, President of the United States of America, by authority of and in fulfillment of the requirements of said act approved February 10, 1883, do hereby declare and make known that the World's Industrial and Cotton Centennial Exposition will be opened on the first Monday in December, 1884, at the city of New Orleans, in the State of Louisiana, and will there be holden continuously until the 31st day of May, 1885.

In testimony whereof I have hereunto set my hand and caused the seal of the United States to be affixed.

[SEAL.] Done at the city of Washington, this 10th day of September, 1883, and of the Independence of the United States the one hundred and eighth.

CHESTER A. ARTHUR.

By the President:
FREDK. T. FRELINGHUYSEN,
Secretary of State.

By the President of the United States of America.

A PROCLAMATION.

In furtherance of the custom of this people at the closing of each year to engage, upon a day set apart for that purpose, in a special festival of praise to the Giver of All Good, I, Chester A. Arthur, President of the

United States, do hereby designate Thursday, the 29th day of November next, as a day of national thanksgiving.

The year which is drawing to an end has been replete with evidences of divine goodness.

The prevalence of health, the fullness of the harvests, the stability of peace and order, the growth of fraternal feeling, the spread of intelligence and learning, the continued enjoyment of civil and religious liberty—all these and countless other blessings are cause for reverent rejoicing.

I do therefore recommend that on the day above appointed the people rest from their accustomed labors and, meeting in their several places of worship, express their devout gratitude to God that He hath dealt so bountifully with this nation and pray that His grace and favor abide with it forever.

In witness whereof I have hereunto set my hand and caused the seal of the United States to be affixed.

[SEAL.]   Done at the city of Washington, this 26th day of October, A. D. 1883, and of the Independence of the United States the one hundred and eighth.

CHESTER A. ARTHUR.

By the President:

FREDK. T. FRELINGHUYSEN,
Secretary of State.

EXECUTIVE ORDERS.

DEPARTMENT OF STATE,
Washington, March 26, 1883.

SIR:* It is my melancholy duty to inform you that the Hon. Timothy O. Howe, Postmaster-General, and lately a Senator of the United States, died yesterday at Kenosha, Wis., at 2 o'clock in the afternoon. By reason of this afflicting event the President directs that the Executive Departments of the Government and the offices dependent thereon throughout the country will be careful to manifest by all customary and appropriate observances due honor to the memory of one so eminent in successive offices of public esteem and trust and so distinguished and respected as a citizen.

To this end the President directs that the Post-Office Department and its dependencies in this capital shall be draped in mourning for a period of thirty days; that the several Executive Departments shall be closed on Wednesday next, the day of the funeral of the deceased, and that on

---

*Addressed to the heads of the Executive Departments, etc.

all public buildings of the Government throughout the United States the national flag shall be draped in mourning and displayed at half-mast.

I have the honor to be, sir, your obedient servant,

FREDK. T. FRELINGHUYSEN.

EXECUTIVE MANSION,
Washington, April 2, 1883.

Under the provisions of section 1 of the "act making appropriations for the naval service for the fiscal year ending June 30, 1884, and for other purposes," approved March 3, 1883, the following-named officers of the Army and Navy will constitute a board for the purpose of examining and reporting to Congress which of the navy-yards or arsenals owned by the Government has the best location and is best adapted for the establishment of a Government foundry, or what other method, if any, should be adopted for the manufacture of heavy ordnance adapted to modern warfare, for the use of the Army and Navy of the United States, the cost of all buildings, tools, and implements necessary to be used in the manufacture thereof, including the cost of a steam hammer or apparatus of sufficient size for the manufacture of the heaviest guns:

Commodore Edward Simpson, United States Navy; Captain Edmund O. Matthews, United States Navy; Colonel Thomas G. Baylor, Ordnance Department, United States Army; Lieutenant-Colonel Henry L. Abbot, Engineer Corps, United States Army; Major Samuel S. Elder, Second Artillery, United States Army; Lieutenant William H. Jacques, United States Navy.

CHESTER A. ARTHUR.

EXECUTIVE MANSION, *May 7, 1883.*

In the exercise of the power vested in the President by the Constitution, and by virtue of the seventeen hundred and fifty-third section of the Revised Statutes and of the civil-service act approved January 16, 1883, the following rules for the regulation and improvement of the executive civil service are hereby promulgated:

RULE I.

No person in said service shall use his official authority or influence either to coerce the political action of any person or body or to interfere with any election.

RULE II.

No person in the public service shall for that reason be under any obligations to contribute to any political fund or to render any political service, and he will not be removed or otherwise prejudiced for refusing to do so.

RULE III.

It shall be the duty of collectors, postmasters, assistant treasurers, naval officers, surveyors, appraisers, and custodians of public buildings at places where examinations are to be held to allow and arrange for the reasonable use of suitable rooms in the public buildings in their charge, and for heating, lighting, and furnishing the same for the purposes of such examinations; and all other executive officers shall in all legal and proper ways facilitate such examinations and the execution of these rules.

RULE IV.

1. All officials connected with any office where or for which any examination is to take place will give the Civil Service Commission and the chief examiner such information as may be reasonably required to enable the Commission to select competent and trustworthy examiners; and the examinations by those selected as examiners, and the work incident thereto, will be regarded as a part of the public business to be performed at such office.

2. It shall be the duty of every executive officer promptly to inform the Commission, in writing, of the removal or discharge from the public service of any examiner in his office or of the inability or refusal of any such examiner to act in that capacity.

RULE V.

There shall be three branches of the service classified under the civil-service act (not including laborers or workmen or officers required to be confirmed by the Senate), as follows:

1. Those classified in the Departments at Washington shall be designated "The classified departmental service."

2. Those classified under any collector, naval officer, surveyor, or appraiser in any customs district shall be designated "The classified customs service."

3. Those classified under any postmaster at any post-office, including that at Washington, shall be designated "The classified postal service."

4. The classified customs service shall embrace the several customs districts where the officials are as many as fifty, now the following: New York City, N. Y.; Boston, Mass.; Philadelphia, Pa.; San Francisco, Cal.; Baltimore, Md.; New Orleans, La.; Chicago, Ill.; Burlington, Vt.; Portland, Me.; Detroit, Mich.; Port Huron, Mich.

5. The classified postal service shall embrace the several post-offices where the officials are as many as fifty, now the following: Albany, N. Y.; Baltimore, Md.; Boston, Mass.; Brooklyn, N. Y.; Buffalo, N. Y.; Chicago, Ill.; Cincinnati, Ohio; Cleveland, Ohio; Detroit, Mich.; Indianapolis, Ind.; Kansas City, Mo.; Louisville, Ky.; Milwaukee, Wis.; Newark, N. J.; New Orleans, La.; New York City, N. Y.; Philadelphia, Pa.; Pittsburg, Pa.; Providence, R. I.; Rochester, N. Y.; St. Louis, Mo.; San Francisco, Cal.; Washington, D. C.

RULE VI.

1. There shall be open competitive examinations for testing the fitness of applicants for admission to the service. Such examinations shall be practical in their character and, so far as may be, shall relate to those matters which will fairly test the relative capacity and fitness of the persons examined to discharge the duties of the branch of the service which they seek to enter.

2. There shall also be competitive examinations of a suitable character to test the fitness of persons for promotion in the service.

RULE VII.

1. The general examinations under the first clause of Rule VI for admission to the service shall be limited to the following subjects: (1) Orthography, penmanship,

and copying; (2) arithmetic—fundamental rules, fractions, and percentage; (3) interest, discount, and elements of bookkeeping and of accounts; (4) elements of the English language, letter writing, and the proper construction of sentences; (5) elements of the geography, history, and government of the United States.

2. Proficiency in each of these subjects shall be credited in grading the standing of the persons examined in proportion to the value of a knowledge of such subjects in the branch or part of the service which the applicant seeks to enter.

3. No one shall be entitled to be certified for appointment whose standing upon a just grading in the general examination shall be less than 65 per cent of complete proficiency in the first three subjects mentioned in this rule, and that measure of proficiency shall be deemed adequate.

4. But for places in which a lower degree of education will suffice the Commission may limit the examinations to, first, penmanship, copying, and orthography; second, the fundamental rules of arithmetic; but no person shall be certified under this examination of a less grading than 65 per cent on each subject.

5. The Commission may also order examinations of a higher grade or upon additional or special subjects, to test the capacity and fitness which may be needed in any special place or branch of the service.

RULE VIII.

No question in any examination or proceeding by or under the Commission or examiners shall call for the expression or disclosure of any political or religious opinion or affiliation, nor shall any discrimination be made by reason thereof if known; and the Commission and its examiners shall discountenance all disclosure before either of them of such opinion by or concerning any applicants for examination or by or concerning anyone whose name is on any register awaiting appointment.

RULE IX.

All regular applications for the competitive examinations for admission to the classified service must be made on blanks in a form approved by the Commission. All requests for such blanks and all applications for examination must be addressed as follows: (1) If for the classified departmental service, to the United States Civil Service Commission, Washington, D. C.; (2) if for the classified postal service, to the postmaster under whom service is sought; (3) if for the classified customs service, to the head of either customs office in which service is sought. All officers receiving such applications will indorse thereon the date of the reception thereof and transmit the same to the proper examining board of the district or office where service is sought or, if in Washington, to the Civil Service Commission.

RULE X.

Every examining board shall keep such records and such papers on file and make such reports as the Commission shall require, and any such paper or record in the charge of any examining board or any officer shall at all times be open to examination as the Commission shall direct, and upon its request shall be forwarded to the Commission for inspection and revision.

RULE XI.

Every application, in order to entitle the applicant to appear for examination or to be examined, must state under oath the facts on the following subjects: (1) Full name, residence, and post-office address; (2) citizenship; (3) age; (4) place of birth; (5) health and physical capacity for the public service; (6) right of preference by reason of military or naval service; (7) previous employment in the public service; (8) business or employment and residence for the previous five years; (9) education. Such other information shall be furnished as the Commission may reasonably require touching the applicant's fitness for the public service. The applicant must also state the number of members of his family in the public service and where employed, and must also assert that he is not disqualified under section 3 of the civil-service act, which is as follows:

"That no person habitually using intoxicating beverages to excess shall be appointed to or retained in any office, appointment, or employment to which the provisions of this act are applicable."

RULE XII.

1. Every regular application must be supported by proper certificates of good moral character, health, and physical and mental capacity for doing the public work, the certificates to be in such form and number as the regulations of the Commission shall provide; but no certificate will be received which is inconsistent with the tenth section of the civil-service act.

2. No one shall be entitled to be examined for admission to the classified postal service if under 16 or over 35 years of age, or to the classified customs service or to the classified departmental service if under 18 or over 45 years of age; but no one shall be examined for appointment to any place in the classified customs service, except that of clerk or messenger, who is under 21 years of age; but these limitations of age shall not apply to honorably discharged soldiers and sailors of the last war who are otherwise duly qualified.

RULE XIII.

1. The date of the reception of all regular applications for the classified departmental service shall be entered of record by the Commission, and of all other regular applications by the proper examining boards of the district or office for which they are made; and applicants, when in excess of the number that can be examined at a single examination, shall be notified to appear in their order on the respective records. But any applicants in the several States and Territories for appointment in the classified departmental service may be notified to appear for examination at any place at which an examination is to be held, whether in any State or Territory or in Washington, which shall be deemed most convenient for them.

2. The Commission is authorized, in aid of the apportionment among the States and Territories, to hold examinations at places convenient for applicants from different States and Territories, or for those examination districts which it may designate and which the President shall approve.

RULE XIV.

Those examined shall be graded, and shall have their grade marked upon a register after those previously thereon, in the order of their excellence as shown by their examination papers, except that those from the same State or Territory may be entered upon the register together, in the order of relative excellence, to facilitate apportionment. Separate registers may be kept of those seeking to enter any part of the service in which special qualifications are required.

RULE XV.

The Commission may give a certificate to any person examined, stating the grade which such person attained and the proficiency in the several subjects, shown by the markings.

RULE XVI.

1. Whenever any officer having the power of appointment or employment shall so request, there shall be certified to him by the Commission or the proper examining board four names for the vacancy specified, to be taken from those graded highest on the proper register of those in his branch of the service and remaining eligible, regard being had to the apportionment of appointments to States and Territories; and from the said four a selection shall be made for the vacancy.

2. These certifications for the service at Washington shall be made in such order as to apportion, as nearly as may be practicable, the original appointments thereto among the States and Territories and the District of Columbia upon the basis of population as ascertained at the last preceding census.

3. In case the request for any such certification or any law or regulation shall call for those of either sex, the four highest of that sex shall be certified; otherwise sex shall be disregarded in such certification.

4. No person upon any register shall be certified more than three times to the same officer in the customs or postal service or more than twice to any department at Washington, unless upon request of the appointing officer; nor shall anyone remain eligible more than one year upon any register. And no person while remaining eligible on any register shall be admitted to a new examination of the same grade.

RULE XVII.

1. Every original appointment or employment in said classified service shall be for the probationary period of six months, at the end of which time, if the conduct and capacity of the person appointed have been found satisfactory, the probationer shall be absolutely appointed or employed, but otherwise be deemed out of the service.

2. Every officer under whom any probationer shall serve during any part of the probation provided for by these rules shall carefully observe the quality and value of the service rendered by such probationer, and shall report to the proper appointing officer, in writing, the facts observed by him, showing the character and qualifications of such probationer and of the service performed by him; and such reports shall be preserved on file.

3. Every false statement knowingly made by any person in his application for examination and every connivance by him at any false statement made in any certificate which may accompany his application shall be regarded as good cause for the removal or discharge of such person during his probation.

RULE XVIII.

Every head of a Department or office shall notify the Commission of the name of every person appointed to or employed in the classified service under him (giving the date of the appointment and the designation of the office or place) from those examined under the Commission, and shall also inform the Commission of the date of any rejection or final appointment or employment of any probationer and of the promotion, removal, discharge, resignation, transfer, or death of any such person after probation.

RULE XIX.

There are excepted from examination the following: (1) The confidential clerk or secretary of any head of a Department or office; (2) cashiers of collectors; (3) cashiers of postmasters; (4) superintendents of money-order divisions in post-offices; (5) the direct custodians of money for whose fidelity another officer is under official bond, but these exceptions shall not extend to any official below the grade of assistant cashier or teller; (6) persons employed exclusively in the secret service of the Government, or as translators or interpreters or stenographers; (7) persons whose employment is exclusively professional; (8) chief clerks, superintendents, and chiefs of divisions or bureaus. But no person so excepted shall be either transferred, appointed, or promoted, unless to some excepted place, without an examination under the Commission. Promotions may be made without examinations in offices where examinations for promotion are not now held until rules on the subject shall be promulgated.

RULE XX.

If the failure of competent persons to attend and be examined or the prevalence of contagious disease or other sufficient cause shall make it impracticable to supply in due season for any appointment the names of persons who have passed a competitive examination, the appointment may be made of a person who has passed a noncompetitive examination, which examination the Commission may provide for; but its next report shall give the reason for such resort to noncompetitive examination.

RULE XXI.

The Civil Service Commission will make appropriate regulations for carrying these rules into effect.

RULE XXII.

Every violation by any officer in the executive civil service of these rules or of the eleventh, twelfth, thirteenth, or fourteenth section of the civil-service act, relating to political assessments, shall be good cause for removal.

CHESTER A. ARTHUR.

EXECUTIVE MANSION, *May 21, 1883.*

Under the provisions of section 4 of the act approved March 3, 1883, it is hereby ordered that the several Executive Departments, the Department of Agriculture, and the Government Printing Office be closed on Wednesday, the 30th instant, to enable the employees to participate in the decoration of the graves of the soldiers who fell during the rebellion.

CHESTER A. ARTHUR.

WAR DEPARTMENT, *October 13, 1883.*

I.   The President, having acceded to the request of General William T. Sherman to be relieved from the command of the Army on the 1st of November, 1883, preparatory to his retirement from active service, directs the following changes and assignments to command:

General William T. Sherman will be relieved from the command of the Army on the above-mentioned date and will repair to his home, St. Louis, Mo., to await his retirement. The General will be attended prior to his retirement by those of his aids-de-camp whom he may designate to the Adjutant-General.

Lieutenant-General Philip H. Sheridan will proceed to Washington, and on the above-mentioned date assume command of the Army.

Major-General John M. Schofield will proceed to Chicago, Ill., and will on the above-mentioned date assume command of the Military Division of the Missouri.

Major-General John Pope will proceed to the Presidio of San Francisco, Cal., and will on the above-mentioned date assume command of the Military Division of the Pacific and of the Department of California.

Brigadier-General Christopher C. Augur will proceed to Fort Leavenworth, and will on the above-mentioned date assume command of the Department of the Missouri.

Brigadier-General Ranald S. Mackenzie will proceed to San Antonio, Tex., and will on the above-mentioned date assume command of the Department of Texas.

II. The Department of the South will on the 1st day of November, 1883, be merged in the Department of the East, under the command of Major-General Hancock, commanding the Military Division of the Atlantic and the Department of the East.

ROBERT T. LINCOLN,
Secretary of War.

In the exercise of the power vested in the President by the Constitution, and by virtue of the seventeen hundred and fifty-third section of the Revised Statutes and of the civil-service act approved January 16, 1883, the following rules for the regulation and improvement of the executive civil service are hereby amended and promulgated, as follows:

RULE VI.

1. There shall be open competitive examinations for testing the fitness of applicants for admission to the service. Such examinations shall be practical in their character and, so far as may be, shall relate to those matters which will fairly test the relative capacity and fitness of the persons examined to discharge the duties of the branch of the service which they seek to enter.

2. There shall, so far as they may be deemed useful, be competitive examinations of a suitable character to test the fitness of persons for promotion in the service.

RULE VII.

1. The general examinations under the first clause of Rule VI for admission to the service shall be limited to the following subjects: (1) Orthography, penmanship, and copying; (2) arithmetic—fundamental rules, fractions, and percentage; (3) interest, discount, and elements of bookkeeping and of accounts; (4) elements of the English language, letter writing, and the proper construction of sentences; (5) elements of the geography, history, and government of the United States.

2. Proficiency in each of these subjects shall be credited in grading the standing of the persons examined in proportion to the value of a knowledge of such subjects in the branch or part of the service which the applicant seeks to enter.

3. No one shall be entitled to be certified for appointment whose standing upon a just grading in the general examination shall be less than 65 per cent of complete proficiency in the first three subjects mentioned in this rule, and that measure of proficiency shall be deemed adequate.

4. But for places in which a lower degree of education will suffice the Commission may limit the examinations to less than the five subjects above mentioned; but no

person shall be certified for appointment under this clause whose grading shall be less than an average of 65 per cent on such of the first three subjects or parts thereof as the examination may embrace.

5. The Commission may also order examinations upon other subjects, of a technical or special character, to test the capacity which may be needed in any part of the classified service which requires peculiar information or skill. Examinations hereunder may be competitive or noncompetitive, and the maximum limitations of age contained in the twelfth rule shall not apply to applicants for the same. The application for and notice of these special examinations, the records thereof, and the certification of those found competent shall be such as the Commission may provide for. After consulting the head of any Department or office the Commission may from time to time designate, subject to the approval of the President, the positions therein for which applicants may be required to pass this special examination.

RULE VIII.

No question in any examination or proceeding by or under the Commission or examiners shall call for the expression or disclosure of any political or religious opinion or affiliation, and if such opinion or affiliation be known no discrimination shall be made by reason thereof by the examiners, the Commission, or the appointing power. The Commission and its examiners shall discountenance all disclosure before either of them of such opinion by or concerning any applicant for examination or by or concerning anyone whose name is on any register awaiting appointment.

RULE XI.

Every application, in order to entitle the applicant to appear for examination or to be examined, must state under oath the facts on the following subjects: (1) Full name, residence, and post-office address; (2) citizenship; (3) age; (4) place of birth; (5) health and physical capacity for the public service; (6) right of preference by reason of military or naval service; (7) previous employment in the public service; (8) business or employment and residence for the previous five years; (9) education. Such other information shall be furnished as the Commission may reasonably require touching the applicant's fitness for the public service. The applicant must also state the number of members of his family in the public service and where employed, and must also assert that he is not disqualified under section 8 of the civil-service act, which is as follows:

"That no person habitually using intoxicating beverages to excess shall be appointed to or retained in any office, appointment, or employment to which the provisions of this act are applicable."

No person under enlistment in the Army or Navy of the United States shall be examined under these rules.

RULE XIII.

1. The date of the reception of all regular applications for the classified departmental service shall be entered of record by the Commission, and of all other regular applications by the proper examining boards of the district or office for which they are made; and applicants, when in excess of the number that can be examined at a single examination, shall, subject to the needs of apportionment, be notified to appear in their order on the respective records. But any applicants in the several States and Territories for appointment in the classified departmental service may be notified to appear for examination at any place at which an examination is to be held, whether in any State or Territory or in Washington, which shall be deemed most convenient for them.

2. The Commission is authorized, in aid of the apportionment among the States

and Territories, to hold examinations at places convenient for applicants from different States and Territories, or for those examination districts which it may designate and which the President shall approve.

RULE XVI.

1. Whenever any officer having the power of appointment or employment shall so request, there shall be certified to him by the Commission or the proper examining board four names for the vacancy specified, to be taken from those graded highest on the proper register of those in his branch of the service and remaining eligible, regard being had to the apportionment of appointments to States and Territories; and from the said four a selection shall be made for the vacancy.

2. These certifications for the service at Washington shall be made in such order as to apportion, as nearly as may be practicable, the original appointments thereto among the States and Territories and the District of Columbia upon the basis of population as ascertained at the last preceding census.

3. In case the request for any such certification or any law or regulation shall call for those of either sex, the four highest of that sex shall be certified; otherwise sex shall be disregarded in such certification.

4. No person upon any register shall be certified more than four times to the same officer in the customs or postal service or more than twice to any Department at Washington, unless upon request of the appointing officer; nor shall anyone remain eligible more than one year upon any register. No person while remaining eligible on any register shall be admitted to a new examination, and no person having failed upon any examination shall within six months thereafter be admitted to another examination without the consent of the Commission; but these restrictions shall not extend to examinations under clause 5 of Rule VII.

RULE XVIII.

Every head of a Department or office shall notify the Commission of the name of every person appointed to or employed in the classified service under him (giving the date of the appointment and the designation of the office or place) from those examined under the Commission, and shall also inform the Commission of the date of any rejection or final appointment or employment of any probationer, and of the promotion, removal, discharge, resignation, transfer, or death of any such person after probation. Every head of an office in the postal or customs service shall give such information on these subjects to the board of examiners for his office as the regulations of the Commission may provide for.

RULE XIX.

There are excepted from examination the following: (1) The confidential clerk or secretary of any head of Department or office; (2) cashiers of collectors; (3) cashiers of postmasters; (4) superintendents of money-order divisions in post-offies; (5) the direct custodians of money for whose fidelity another officer is under official bond, but these exceptions shall not extend to any official below the grade of assistant cashier or teller; (6) persons employed exclusively in the secret service of the Government, or as translators or interpreters or stenographers; (7) persons whose employment is exclusively professional; (8) chief clerks, deputy collectors, and superintendents or chiefs of divisions or bureaus. But no person so excepted shall be either transferred, appointed, or promoted, unless to some excepted place, without an examination under the Commission. Promotions may be made without examinations in offices where examinations for promotion are not now held until rules on the subject shall be promulgated.

Approved, November 7, 1883.　　　　　**CHESTER A. ARTHUR.**

THIRD ANNUAL MESSAGE.

WASHINGTON, *December 4, 1883.*

To the Congress of the United States:

At the threshold of your deliberations I congratulate you upon the favorable aspect of the domestic and foreign affairs of this Government.

Our relations with other countries continue to be upon a friendly footing. With the Argentine Republic, Austria, Belgium, Brazil, Denmark, Hayti, Italy, Santo Domingo, and Sweden and Norway no incident has occurred which calls for special comment. The recent opening of new lines of telegraphic communication with Central America and Brazil permitted the interchange of messages of friendship with the Governments of those countries

During the year there have been perfected and proclaimed consular and commercial treaties with Servia and a consular treaty with Roumania, thus extending our intercourse with the Danubian countries, while our Eastern relations have been put upon a wider basis by treaties with Korea and Madagascar. The new boundary-survey treaty with Mexico, a trade-marks convention and a supplementary treaty of extradition with Spain, and conventions extending the duration of the Franco-American Claims Commission have also been proclaimed.

Notice of the termination of the fisheries articles of the treaty of Washington was duly given to the British Government, and the reciprocal privileges and exemptions of the treaty will accordingly cease on July 1, 1885. The fisheries industries, pursued by a numerous class of our citizens on the northern coasts, both of the Atlantic and Pacific oceans, are worthy of the fostering care of Congress. Whenever brought into competition with the like industries of other countries, our fishermen, as well as our manufacturers of fishing appliances and preparers of fish products, have maintained a foremost place. I suggest that Congress create a commission to consider the general question of our rights in the fisheries and the means of opening to our citizens, under just and enduring conditions, the richly stocked fishing waters and sealing grounds of British North America.

Question has arisen touching the deportation to the United States from the British Islands, by governmental or municipal aid, of persons unable there to gain a living and equally a burden on the community here. Such of these persons as fall under the pauper class as defined by law have been sent back in accordance with the provisions of our statutes. Her Majesty's Government has insisted that precautions have been taken before shipment to prevent these objectionable visitors from coming hither without guaranty of support by their relatives in this country. The action of the British authorities in applying measures for relief has, however, in so many cases proved ineffectual, and especially so in certain recent instances of needy emigrants reaching our territory through Canada, that a revision of our legislation upon this subject may be deemed advisable.

Correspondence relative to the Clayton-Bulwer treaty has been continued and will be laid before Congress.

The legislation of France against the importation of prepared swine products from the United States has been repealed. That result is due no less to the friendly representations of this Government than to a growing conviction in France that the restriction was not demanded by any real danger to health.

Germany still prohibits the introduction of all swine products from America. I extended to the Imperial Government a friendly invitation to send experts to the United States to inquire whether the use of those products was dangerous to health. This invitation was declined. I have believed it of such importance, however, that the exact facts should be ascertained and promulgated that I have appointed a competent commission to make a thorough investigation of the subject. Its members have shown their public spirit by accepting their trust without pledge of compensation, but I trust that Congress will see in the national and international bearings of the matter a sufficient motive for providing at least for reimbursement of such expenses as they may necessarily incur.

The coronation of the Czar at Moscow afforded to this Government an occasion for testifying its continued friendship by sending a special envoy and a representative of the Navy to attend the ceremony.

While there have arisen during the year no grave questions affecting the status in the Russian Empire of American citizens of other faith than that held by the national church, this Government remains firm in its conviction that the rights of its citizens abroad should be in no wise affected by their religious belief.

It is understood that measures for the removal of the restrictions which now burden our trade with Cuba and Puerto Rico are under consideration by the Spanish Government.

The proximity of Cuba to the United States and the peculiar methods of administration which there prevail necessitate constant discussion and appeal on our part from the proceedings of the insular authorities. I regret to say that the just protests of this Government have not as yet produced satisfactory results.

The commission appointed to decide certain claims of our citizens against the Spanish Government, after the recognition of a satisfactory rule as to the validity and force of naturalization in the United States, has finally adjourned. Some of its awards, though made more than two years ago, have not yet been paid. Their speedy payment is expected.

Claims to a large amount which were held by the late commission to be without its jurisdiction have been diplomatically presented to the

Spanish Government. As the action of the colonial authorities which has given rise to these claims was admittedly illegal, full reparation for the injury sustained by our citizens should be no longer delayed.

The case of the *Masonic* has not yet reached a settlement. The Manila court has found that the proceedings of which this Government has complained were unauthorized, and it is hoped that the Government of Spain will not withhold the speedy reparation which its sense of justice should impel it to offer for the unusual severity and unjust action of its subordinate colonial officers in the case of this vessel.

The Helvetian Confederation has proposed the inauguration of a class of international treaties for the referment to arbitration of grave questions between nations. This Government has assented to the proposed negotiation of such a treaty with Switzerland.

Under the treaty of Berlin liberty of conscience and civil rights are assured to all strangers in Bulgaria. As the United States have no distinct conventional relations with that country and are not a party to the treaty, they should, in my opinion, maintain diplomatic representation at Sofia for the improvement of intercourse and the proper protection of the many American citizens who resort to that country as missionaries and teachers. I suggest that I be given authority to establish an agency and consulate-general at the Bulgarian capital.

The United States are now participating in a revision of the tariffs of the Ottoman Empire. They have assented to the application of a license tax to foreigners doing business in Turkey, but have opposed the oppressive storage tax upon petroleum entering the ports of that country.

The Government of the Khedive has proposed that the authority of the mixed judicial tribunals in Egypt be extended so as to cover citizens of the United States accused of crime, who are now triable before consular courts. This Government is not indisposed to accept the change, but believes that its terms should be submitted for criticism to the commission appointed to revise the whole subject.

At no time in our national history has there been more manifest need of close and lasting relations with a neighboring state than now exists with respect to Mexico. The rapid influx of our capital and enterprise into that country shows, by what has already been accomplished, the vast reciprocal advantages which must attend the progress of its internal development. The treaty of commerce and navigation of 1848 has been terminated by the Mexican Government, and in the absence of conventional engagements the rights of our citizens in Mexico now depend upon the domestic statutes of that Republic. There have been instances of harsh enforcement of the laws against our vessels and citizens in Mexico and of denial of the diplomatic resort for their protection. The initial step toward a better understanding has been taken in the negotiation by the commission authorized by Congress of a treaty which is still before the Senate awaiting its approval.

The provisions for the reciprocal crossing of the frontier by the troops in pursuit of hostile Indians have been prolonged for another year. The operations of the forces of both Governments against these savages have been successful, and several of their most dangerous bands have been captured or dispersed by the skill and valor of United States and Mexican soldiers fighting in a common cause.

The convention for the resurvey of the boundary from the Rio Grande to the Pacific having been ratified and exchanged, the preliminary reconnoissance therein stipulated has been effected. It now rests with Congress to make provision for completing the survey and relocating the boundary monuments.

A convention was signed with Mexico on July 13, 1882, providing for the rehearing of the cases of Benjamin Weil and the Abra Silver Mining Company, in whose favor awards were made by the late American and Mexican Claims Commission. That convention still awaits the consent of the Senate. Meanwhile, because of those charges of fraudulent awards which have made a new commission necessary, the Executive has directed the suspension of payments of the distributive quota received from Mexico.

Our geographical proximity to Central America and our political and commercial relations with the States of that country justify, in my judgment, such a material increase of our consular corps as will place at each capital a consul-general.

The contest between Bolivia, Chile, and Peru has passed from the stage of strategic hostilities to that of negotiation, in which the counsels of this Government have been exercised. The demands of Chile for absolute cession of territory have been maintained and accepted by the party of General Iglesias to the extent of concluding a treaty of peace with the Government of Chile in general conformity with the terms of the protocol signed in May last between the Chilean commander and General Iglesias. As a result of the conclusion of this treaty General Iglesias has been formally recognized by Chile as President of Peru and his government installed at Lima, which has been evacuated by the Chileans. A call has been issued by General Iglesias for a representative assembly, to be elected on the 13th of January, and to meet at Lima on the 1st of March next. Meanwhile the provisional government of General Iglesias has applied for recognition to the principal powers of America and Europe. When the will of the Peruvian people shall be manifested, I shall not hesitate to recognize the government approved by them.

Diplomatic and naval representatives of this Government attended at Caracas the centennial celebration of the birth of the illustrious Bolivar. At the same time the inauguration of the statue of Washington in the Venezuelan capital testified to the veneration in which his memory is there held.

Congress at its last session authorized the Executive to propose to Venezuela a reopening of the awards of the mixed commission of Caracas. The departure from this country of the Venezuelan minister has delayed the opening of negotiations for reviving the commission. This Government holds that until the establishment of a treaty upon this subject the Venezuelan Government must continue to make the payments provided for in the convention of 1866.

There is ground for believing that the dispute growing out of the unpaid obligations due from Venezuela to France will be satisfactorily adjusted. The French cabinet has proposed a basis of settlement which meets my approval, but as it involves a recasting of the annual quotas of the foreign debt it has been deemed advisable to submit the proposal to the judgment of the cabinets of Berlin, Copenhagen, The Hague, London, and Madrid.

At the recent coronation of His Majesty King Kalakaua this Government was represented both diplomatically and by the formal visit of a vessel of war.

The question of terminating or modifying the existing reciprocity treaty with Hawaii is now before Congress. I am convinced that the charges of abuses and frauds under that treaty have been exaggerated, and I renew the suggestion of last year's message that the treaty be modified wherever its provisions have proved onerous to legitimate trade between the two countries. I am not disposed to favor the entire cessation of the treaty relations which have fostered good will between the countries and contributed toward the equality of Hawaii in the family of nations.

In pursuance of the policy declared by this Government of extending our intercourse with the Eastern nations, legations have during the past year been established in Persia, Siam, and Korea. It is probable that permanent missions of those countries will ere long be maintained in the United States. A special embassy from Siam is now on its way hither.

Treaty relations with Korea were perfected by the exchange at Seoul, on the 19th of May last, of the ratifications of the lately concluded convention, and envoys from the King of Tah Chosen have visited this country and received a cordial welcome. Korea, as yet unacquainted with the methods of Western civilization, now invites the attention of those interested in the advancement of our foreign trade, as it needs the implements and products which the United States are ready to supply. We seek no monopoly of its commerce and no advantages over other nations, but as the Chosenese, in reaching for a higher civilization, have confided in this Republic, we can not regard with indifference any encroachment on their rights.

China, by the payment of a money indemnity, has settled certain of the long-pending claims of our citizens, and I have strong hopes that the remainder will soon be adjusted.

Questions have arisen touching the rights of American and other foreign manufacturers in China under the provisions of treaties which permit aliens to exercise their industries in that country. On this specific point our own treaty is silent, but under the operation of the most-favored-nation clause we have like privileges with those of other powers. While it is the duty of the Government to see that our citizens have the full enjoyment of every benefit secured by treaty, I doubt the expediency of leading in a movement to constrain China to admit an interpretation which we have only an indirect treaty right to exact. The transference to China of American capital for the employment there of Chinese labor would in effect inaugurate a competition for the control of markets now supplied by our home industries.

There is good reason to believe that the law restricting the immigration of Chinese has been violated, intentionally or otherwise, by the officials of China upon whom is devolved the duty of certifying that the immigrants belong to the excepted classes.

Measures have been taken to ascertain the facts incident to this supposed infraction, and it is believed that the Government of China will cooperate with the United States in securing the faithful observance of the law.

The same considerations which prompted Congress at its last session to return to Japan the Simonoseki indemnity seem to me to require at its hands like action in respect to the Canton indemnity fund, now amounting to $300,000.

The question of the general revision of the foreign treaties of Japan has been considered in an international conference held at Tokyo, but without definite result as yet. This Government is disposed to concede the requests of Japan to determine its own tariff duties, to provide such proper judicial tribunals as may commend themselves to the Western powers for the trial of causes to which foreigners are parties, and to assimilate the terms and duration of its treaties to those of other civilized states.

Through our ministers at London and at Monrovia this Government has endeavored to aid Liberia in its differences with Great Britain touching the northwestern boundary of that Republic. There is a prospect of adjustment of the dispute by the adoption of the Mannah River as the line. This arrangement is a compromise of the conflicting territorial claims and takes from Liberia no country over which it has maintained effective jurisdiction.

The rich and populous valley of the Kongo is being opened to commerce by a society called the International African Association, of which the King of the Belgians is the president and a citizen of the United States the chief executive officer. Large tracts of territory have been ceded to the association by native chiefs, roads have been opened, steamboats placed on the river, and the nuclei of states established at twenty-two stations under one flag which offers freedom to commerce and prohibits the slave trade. The objects of the society are philanthropic. It does not aim at permanent political control, but seeks the neutrality of the valley. The United States can not be indifferent to this work nor to the interests of their citizens involved in it. It may become advisable for us to cooperate with other commercial powers in promoting the rights of trade and residence in the Kongo Valley free from the interference or political control of any one nation.

In view of the frequency of invitations from foreign governments to participate in social and scientific congresses for the discussion of important matters of general concern, I repeat the suggestion of my last message that provision be made for the exercise of discretionary power by the Executive in appointing delegates to such convocations. Able specialists are ready to serve the national interests in such capacity without personal profit or other compensation than the defrayment of expenses actually incurred, and this a comparatively small annual appropriation would suffice to meet.

I have alluded in my previous messages to the injurious and vexatious restrictions suffered by our trade in the Spanish West Indies. Brazil, whose natural outlet for its great national staple, coffee, is in and through the United States, imposes a heavy export duty upon that product. Our petroleum exports are hampered in Turkey and in other Eastern ports by restrictions as to storage and by onerous taxation. For these mischiefs adequate relief is not always afforded by reciprocity treaties like that with Hawaii or that lately negotiated with Mexico and now awaiting the action of the Senate. Is it not advisable to provide some measure of equitable retaliation in our relations with governments which discriminate against our own? If, for example, the Executive were empowered to apply to Spanish vessels and cargoes from Cuba and Puerto Rico the same rules of treatment and scale of penalties for technical faults which are applied to our vessels and cargoes in the Antilles, a resort to that course might not be barren of good results.

The report of the Secretary of the Treasury gives a full and interesting exhibit of the financial condition of the country.

It shows that the ordinary revenues from all sources for the fiscal year ended June 30, 1883, amounted to $398,287,581.95, whereof there was received—

From customs	$214,706,496.93
From internal revenue	144,720,368.98
From sales of public lands	7,955,864.42
From tax on circulation and deposits of national banks	9,111,008.85
From profits on coinage, bullion deposits, and assays	4,460,205.17
From other sources	17,333,637.60
Total	398,287,581.95

For the same period the ordinary expenditures were:

For civil expenses	$22,343,285.76
For foreign intercourse	2,419,275.24
For Indians	7,362,590.34

For pensions...	$66,012,573.64
For the military establishment, including river and harbor improvements and arsenals..	48,911,382.93
For the naval establishment, including vessels, machinery, and improvements at navy-yards..	15,283,437.17
For miscellaneous expenditures, including public buildings, light-houses, and collecting the revenue...	40,098,432.73
For expenditures on account of the District of Columbia.................	3,817,028.48
For interest on the public debt...	59,160,131.25
Total...	265,408,137.54

Leaving a surplus revenue of $132,879,444.41, which, with an amount drawn from the cash balance in the Treasury of $1,299,312.55, making $134,178,756.96, was applied to the redemption—

Of bonds for the sinking fund..	$44,850,700.00
Of fractional currency for the sinking fund..............................	46,556.96
Of funded loan of 1881, continued at 3½ per cent.......................	65,380,250.00
Of loan of July and August, 1861, continued at 3½ per cent.............	20,594,600.00
Of funded loan of 1907..	1,418,850.00
Of funded loan of 1881...	719,150.00
Of loan of February, 1861..	18,000.00
Of loan of July and August, 1861.......................................	266,600.00
Of loan of March, 1863...	116,850.00
Of loan of July, 1882..	47,650.00
Of five-twenties of 1862..	10,300.00
Of five-twenties of 1864..	7,050.00
Of five-twenties of 1865..	9,600.00
Of ten-forties of 1864..	133,550.00
Of consols of 1865...	40,800.00
Of consols of 1867...	235,700.00
Of consols of 1868...	154,650.00
Of Oregon War debt..	5,450.00
Of refunding certificates...	109,150.00
Of old demand, compound-interest, and other notes.....................	13,300.00
Total...	134,178,756.96

The revenue for the present fiscal year, actual and estimated, is as follows:

Source.	For the quarter ended September 30, 1883 (actual).	For the remaining three quarters of the year (estimated).
From customs.......................................	$57,402,975.67	$137,597,024.33
From internal revenue..............................	29,662,078.60	90,337,921.40
From sales of public lands..........................	2,932,635.17	5,067,364.83
From tax on circulation and deposits of national banks...	1,557,800.88	1,542,199.12
From repayment of interest and sinking fund, Pacific Railway companies.........................	521,059.51	1,478,940.49
From customs fees, fines, penalties, etc............	298,696.78	901,303.22
From fees—consular, letters patent, and lands...	863,209.80	2,436,790.20
From proceeds of sales of Government property.	112,562.23	167,437.77
From profits on coinage, etc.......................	950,229.46	3,149,770.54
From deposits for surveying public lands.......	172,461.31	327,538.69
From revenues of the District of Columbia......	256,017.99	1,643,982.01
From miscellaneous sources.......................	1,237,189.63	2,382,810.37
Total receipts..................................	95,966,917.03	247,033,082.97

The actual and estimated expenses for the same period are:

Object.	For the quarter ended September 30, 1883 (actual).	For the remaining three quarters of the year (estimated).
For civil and miscellaneous expenses, including public buildings, light-houses, and collecting the revenue....................................	$15,385,799.42	$51,114,200.58
For Indians.............................	2,623,390.54	4,126,609.46
For pensions....................................	16,285,261.98	53,714,738.02
For military establishment, including fortifications, river and harbor improvements, and arsenals..	13,512,204.33	26,487,795.67
For naval establishment, including vessels and machinery, and improvements at navy-yards..	4,199,299.69	12,300,700.31
For expenditures on account of the District of Columbia...........	1,138,836.41	2,611,163.59
For interest on the public debt..................	14,797,297.96	39,702,702.04
Total ordinary expenditures..............	67,942,090.33	190,057,909.67

Total receipts, actual and estimated.. $343,000,000.00
Total expenditures, actual and estimated............................... 258,000,000.00

                                                                           85,000,000.00
Estimated amount due the sinking fund............................... 45,816,741.07

Leaving a balance of... 39,183,258.93

If the revenue for the fiscal year which will end on June 30, 1885, be estimated upon the basis of existing laws, the Secretary is of the opinion that for that year the receipts will exceed by $60,000,000 the ordinary expenditures including the amount devoted to the sinking fund.

Hitherto the surplus, as rapidly as it has accumulated, has been devoted to the reduction of the national debt.

As a result the only bonds now outstanding which are redeemable at the pleasure of the Government are the 3 percents, amounting to about $305,000,000.

The 4½ percents, amounting to $250,000,000, and the $737,000,000 4 percents are not payable until 1891 and 1907, respectively.

If the surplus shall hereafter be as large as the Treasury estimates now indicate, the 3 per cent bonds may all be redeemed at least four years before any of the 4½ percents can be called in. The latter at the same rate of accumulation of surplus can be paid at maturity, and the moneys requisite for the redemption of the 4 percents will be in the Treasury many years before those obligations become payable.

There are cogent reasons, however, why the national indebtedness should not be thus rapidly extinguished. Chief among them is the fact that only by excessive taxation is such rapidity attainable.

In a communication to the Congress at its last session I recommended that all excise taxes be abolished except those relating to distilled spirits and that substantial reductions be also made in the revenues from customs. A statute has since been enacted by which the annual tax and tariff receipts of the Government have been cut down to the extent of at least fifty or sixty millions of dollars.

While I have no doubt that still further reductions may be wisely made, I do not advise the adoption at this session of any measures for large diminution of the national revenues. The results of the legislation of the last session of the Congress have not as yet become sufficiently apparent to justify any radical revision or sweeping modifications of existing law.

In the interval which must elapse before the effects of the act of March 3, 1883, can be definitely ascertained a portion at least of the surplus revenues may be wisely applied to the long-neglected duty of rehabilitating our Navy and providing coast defenses for the protection of our harbors. This is a matter to which I shall again advert.

Immediately associated with the financial subject just discussed is the important question what legislation is needed regarding the national currency.

The aggregate amount of bonds now on deposit in the Treasury to support the national-bank circulation is about $350,000,000. Nearly $200,000,000 of this amount consists of 3 percents, which, as already stated, are payable at the pleasure of the Government and are likely to be called in within less than four years unless meantime the surplus revenues shall be diminished.

The probable effect of such an extensive retirement of the securities which are the basis of the national-bank circulation would be such a contraction of the volume of the currency as to produce grave commercial embarrassments.

How can this danger be obviated? The most effectual plan, and one whose adoption at the earliest practicable opportunity I shall heartily approve, has already been indicated.

If the revenues of the next four years shall be kept substantially commensurate with the expenses, the volume of circulation will not be likely to suffer any material disturbance; but if, on the other hand, there shall be great delay in reducing taxation, it will become necessary either to substitute some other form of currency in place of the national-bank notes or to make important changes in the laws by which their circulation is now controlled.

In my judgment the latter course is far preferable. I commend to your attention the very interesting and thoughtful suggestions upon this subject which appear in the Secretary's report.

The objections which he urges against the acceptance of any other securities than the obligations of the Government itself as a foundation for national-bank circulation seem to me insuperable.

For averting the threatened contraction two courses have been suggested, either of which is probably feasible. One is the issuance of new bonds, having many years to run, bearing a low rate of interest, and exchangeable upon specified terms for those now outstanding. The other course, which commends itself to my own judgment as the better, is the enactment of a law repealing the tax on circulation and permitting the banks to issue notes for an amount equal to 90 per cent of the market value instead of, as now, the face value of their deposited bonds. I agree with the Secretary in the belief that the adoption of this plan would afford the necessary relief.

The trade dollar was coined for the purpose of traffic in countries where silver passed at its value as ascertained by its weight and fineness. It never had a legal-tender quality. Large numbers of these coins entered, however, into the volume of our currency. By common consent their circulation in domestic trade has now ceased, and they have thus become a disturbing element. They should not be longer permitted to embarrass our currency system. I recommend that provision be made for their reception by the Treasury and the mints, as bullion, at a small percentage above the current market price of silver of like fineness.

The Secretary of the Treasury advises a consolidation of certain of the customs districts of the country, and suggests that the President be vested with such power in relation thereto as is now given him in respect to collectors of internal revenue by section 3141 of the Revised Statutes. The statistics upon this subject which are contained in his report furnish of themselves a strong argument in defense of his views.

At the adjournment of Congress the number of internal-revenue collection districts was 126. By Executive order dated June 25, 1883, I directed that certain of these districts be consolidated. The result has been a reduction of one-third their number, which at present is but 83.

From the report of the Secretary of War it will be seen that in only a single instance has there been any disturbance of the quiet condition of our Indian tribes. A raid from Mexico into Arizona was made in March last by a small party of Indians, which was pursued by General Crook into the mountain regions from which it had come. It is confidently hoped that serious outbreaks will not again occur and that the Indian tribes which have for so many years disturbed the West will hereafter remain in peaceable submission.

I again call your attention to the present condition of our extended seacoast, upon which are so many large cities whose wealth and importance to the country would in time of war invite attack from modern armored ships, against which our existing defensive works could give no adequate protection. Those works were built before the introduction of modern heavy rifled guns into maritime warfare, and if they are not put in an efficient condition we may easily be subjected to humiliation by a hostile power greatly inferior to ourselves. As germane to this subject, I call your attention to the importance of perfecting our submarine-torpedo defenses. The board authorized by the last Congress to report upon the method which should be adopted for the manufacture of heavy ordnance adapted to modern warfare has visited the principal iron and steel works in this country and in Europe. It is hoped that its report will soon be made, and that Congress will thereupon be disposed to provide suitable facilities and plant for the manufacture of such guns as are now imperatively needed.

On several occasions during the past year officers of the Army have at the request of the State authorities visited their militia encampments for inspection of the troops. From the reports of these officers I am induced to believe that the encouragement of the State militia organizations by the National Government would be followed by very gratifying results, and would afford it in sudden emergencies the aid of a large body of volunteers educated in the performance of military duties.

The Secretary of the Navy reports that under the authority of the acts of August 5, 1882, and March 3, 1883, the work of strengthening our Navy by the construction of modern vessels has been auspiciously begun. Three cruisers are in process of construction—the *Chicago*, of 4,500 tons displacement, and the *Boston* and *Atlanta*, each of 2,500 tons. They are to be built of steel, with the tensile strength and ductility prescribed by law, and in the combination of speed, endurance, and armament are expected to compare favorably with the best unarmored war vessels of other nations. A fourth vessel, the *Dolphin*, is to be constructed of similar material, and is intended to serve as a fleet dispatch boat.

The double-turreted monitors *Puritan*, *Amphitrite*, and *Terror* have been launched on the Delaware River and a contract has been made for the supply of their machinery. A similar monitor, the *Monadnock*, has been launched in California.

The Naval Advisory Board and the Secretary recommend the completion of the monitors, the construction of four gunboats, and also of three additional steel vessels like the *Chicago*, *Boston*, and *Dolphin*.

As an important measure of national defense, the Secretary urges also the immediate creation of an interior coast line of waterways across the peninsula of Florida, along the coast from Florida to Hampton Roads, between the Chesapeake Bay and the Delaware River, and through Cape Cod.

I feel bound to impress upon the attention of Congress the necessity of continued progress in the reconstruction of the Navy. The condition of the public Treasury, as I have already intimated, makes the present an auspicious time for putting this branch of the service in a state of efficiency.

It is no part of our policy to create and maintain a Navy able to cope with that of the other great powers of the world.

We have no wish for foreign conquest, and the peace which we have long enjoyed is in no seeming danger of interruption.

But that our naval strength should be made adequate for the defense of our harbors, the protection of our commercial interests, and the maintenance of our national honor is a proposition from which no patriotic citizen can withhold his assent.

The report of the Postmaster-General contains a gratifying exhibit of the condition and prospects of the interesting branch of the public service committed to his care.

It appears that on June 30, 1883, the whole number of post-offices was 47,863, of which 1,632 were established during the previous fiscal year. The number of offices operating under the system of free delivery was 154.

At these latter offices the postage on local matter amounted to $4,195,230.52, a sum exceeding by $1,021,894.01 the entire cost of the carrier service of the country.

The rate of postage on drop letters passing through these offices is now fixed by law at 2 cents per half ounce or fraction thereof. In offices where the carrier system has not been established the rate is only half as large.

It will be remembered that in 1863, when free delivery was first established by law, the uniform single-rate postage upon local letters was 1 cent, and so it remained until 1872, when in those cities where carrier service was established it was increased in order to defray the expense of such service.

It seems to me that the old rate may now with propriety be restored, and that, too, even at the risk of diminishing, for a time at least, the receipts from postage upon local letters.

I can see no reason why that particular class of mail matter should be held accountable for the entire cost of not only its own collection and delivery, but the collection and delivery of all other classes; and I am confident, after full consideration of the subject, that the reduction of rate would be followed by such a growing accession of business as to occasion but slight and temporary loss to the revenues of the Post-Office. The Postmaster-General devotes much of his report to the consideration in its various aspects of the relations of the Government to the telegraph. Such reflection as I have been able to give to this subject since my last annual message has not led me to change the views which I there expressed in dissenting from the recommendation of the then Postmaster-General that the Government assume the same control over the telegraph which it has always exercised over the mail.

Admitting that its authority in the premises is as ample as has ever been claimed for it, it would not, in my judgment, be a wise use of that authority to purchase or assume the control of existing telegraph lines, or to construct others with a view of entering into general competition with private enterprise.

The objections which may be justly urged against either of those projects, and indeed against any system which would require an enormous increase in the civil-service list, do not, however, apply to some of the plans which have lately provoked public comment and discussion. It has been claimed, for example, that Congress might wisely authorize the Postmaster-General to contract with some private persons or corporation for the transmission of messages, or of a certain class of messages, at specified rates and under Government supervision. Various such schemes, of the same general nature, but widely differing in their special characteristics, have been suggested in the public prints, and the arguments by which they have been supported and opposed have doubtless attracted your attention.

It is likely that the whole subject will be considered by you at the present session.

In the nature of things it involves so many questions of detail that your deliberations would probably be aided slightly, if at all, by any particular suggestions which I might now submit.

I avow my belief, however, that the Government should be authorized by law to exercise some sort of supervision over interstate telegraphic communication, and I express the hope that for attaining that end some measure may be devised which will receive your approbation.

The Attorney-General criticises in his report the provisions of existing law fixing the fees of jurors and witnesses in the Federal courts. These provisions are chiefly contained in the act of February 26, 1853, though some of them were introduced into that act from statutes which had been passed many years previous. It is manifest that such compensation as might when these laws were enacted have been just and reasonable would in many instances be justly regarded at the present day as inadequate. I concur with the Attorney-General in the belief that the statutes should be revised by which these fees are regulated.

So, too, should the laws which regulate the compensation of district attorneys and marshals. They should be paid wholly by salaries instead of in part by fees, as is now the case.

The change would prove to be a measure of economy and would discourage the institution of needless and oppressive legal proceedings, which it is to be feared have in some instances been conducted for the mere sake of personal gain.

Much interesting and varied information is contained in the report of the Secretary of the Interior.

I particularly call your attention to his presentation of certain phases of the Indian question, to his recommendations for the repeal of the preemption and timber-culture acts, and for more stringent legislation to prevent frauds under the pension laws. The statutes which prescribe the definitions and punishments of crimes relating to pensions could doubtless be made more effective by certain amendments and additions which are pointed out in the Secretary's report.

I have previously referred to the alarming state of illiteracy in certain portions of the country, and again submit for the consideration of Congress whether some Federal aid should not be extended to public primary education wherever adequate provision therefor has not already been made.

The Utah Commission has submitted to the Secretary of the Interior its second annual report. As a result of its labors in supervising the recent election in that Territory, pursuant to the act of March 22, 1882, it appears that persons by that act disqualified to the number of about 12,000, were excluded from the polls. This fact, however, affords little cause for congratulation, and I fear that it is far from indicating any real and substantial progress toward the extirpation of polygamy. All the members elect of the legislature are Mormons. There is grave reason to believe that they are in sympathy with the practices that this Government is seeking to suppress, and that its efforts in that regard will be more likely to encounter their opposition than to receive their encouragement and support. Even if this view should happily be erroneous, the law under which the commissioners have been acting should be made more effective by the incorporation of some such stringent amendments as they recommend, and as were included in bill No. 2238 on the Calendar of the Senate at its last session.

I am convinced, however, that polygamy has become so strongly intrenched in the Territory of Utah that it is profitless to attack it with any but the stoutest weapons which constitutional legislation can fashion. I favor, therefore, the repeal of the act upon which the existing government depends, the assumption by the National Legislature of the entire political control of the Territory, and the establishment of a commission with such powers and duties as shall be delegated to it by law.

The Department of Agriculture is accomplishing much in the direction of the agricultural development of the country, and the report of the Commissioner giving the results of his investigations and experiments will be found interesting and valuable.

At his instance a convention of those interested in the cattle industry of the country was lately held at Chicago. The prevalence of pleuropneumonia and other contagious diseases of animals was one of the chief topics of discussion. A committee of the convention will invite your cooperation in investigating the causes of these diseases and providing methods for their prevention and cure.

I trust that Congress will not fail at its present session to put Alaska under the protection of law. Its people have repeatedly remonstrated against our neglect to afford them the maintenance and protection expressly guaranteed by the terms of the treaty whereby that Territory was ceded to the United States. For sixteen years they have pleaded in vain for that which they should have received without the asking.

They have no law for the collection of debts, the support of education,

SCENES TYPICAL OF OUR NORTHERNMOST TERRITORY, ALASKA

PURCHASE OF ALASKA

"Official communications passed between the United States and Russia concerning the purchase of Alaska, or, as it was then called, Russian America, as early as 1859. Russia was desirous of parting with the territory, and the fishing and trading interests favored the change of sovereignty. It was not until 1867, however, that definite steps were taken toward the transfer. In March of that year the Russian minister at Washington reopened negotiations, and on the 23d of that month Secretary Seward made an offer of $7,200,000 for the peninsula. A week later the minister communicated the Czar's acceptance, and at 4 o'clock on the morning of the 30th the treaty was signed, and later ratified by the Senate, and on Oct. 18th following the formal transfer was made at Sitka, Gen. Rousseau taking possession for the United States."

Quoted from the article "Alaska" in the encyclopedic index (volume eleven). Under the name of each State and Territory appears an article describing its position, resources, population, etc., and briefly reciting its history.

the conveyance of property, the administration of estates, or the enforcement of contracts; none, indeed, for the punishment of criminals, except such as offend against certain customs, commerce, and navigation acts.

The resources of Alaska, especially in fur, mines, and lumber, are considerable in extent and capable of large development, while its geographical situation is one of political and commercial importance.

The promptings of interest, therefore, as well as considerations of honor and good faith, demand the immediate establishment of civil government in that Territory.

Complaints have lately been numerous and urgent that certain corporations, controlling in whole or in part the facilities for the interstate carriage of persons and merchandise over the great railroads of the country, have resorted in their dealings with the public to divers measures unjust and oppressive in their character.

In some instances the State governments have attacked and suppressed these evils, but in others they have been unable to afford adequate relief because of the jurisdictional limitations which are imposed upon them by the Federal Constitution.

The question how far the National Government may lawfully interfere in the premises, and what, if any, supervision or control it ought to exercise, is one which merits your careful consideration.

While we can not fail to recognize the importance of the vast railway systems of the country and their great and beneficent influences upon the development of our material wealth, we should, on the other hand, remember that no individual and no corporation ought to be invested with absolute power over the interest of any other citizen or class of citizens. The right of these railway corporations to a fair and profitable return upon their investments and to reasonable freedom in their regulations must be recognized; but it seems only just that, so far as its constitutional authority will permit, Congress should protect the people at large in their interstate traffic against acts of injustice which the State governments are powerless to prevent.

In my last annual message I called attention to the necessity of protecting by suitable legislation the forests situated upon the public domain. In many portions of the West the pursuit of general agriculture is only made practicable by resort to irrigation, while successful irrigation would itself be impossible without the aid afforded by forests in contributing to the regularity and constancy of the supply of water.

During the past year severe suffering and great loss of property have been occasioned by profuse floods followed by periods of unusually low water in many of the great rivers of the country.

These irregularities were in great measure caused by the removal from about the sources of the streams in question of the timber by which the water supply had been nourished and protected.

The preservation of such portions of the forests on the national domain as essentially contribute to the equable flow of important water courses is of the highest consequence.

Important tributaries of the Missouri, the Columbia, and the Saskatchewan rise in the mountain region of Montana, near the northern boundary of the United States, between the Blackfeet and Flathead Indian reservations. This region is unsuitable for settlement, but upon the rivers which flow from it depends the future agricultural development of a vast tract of country. The attention of Congress is called to the necessity of withdrawing from public sale this part of the public domain and establishing there a forest preserve.

The industrial exhibitions which have been held in the United States during the present year attracted attention in many foreign countries, where the announcement of those enterprises had been made public through the foreign agencies of this Government. The Industrial Exhibition at Boston and the Southern Exposition at Louisville were largely attended by the exhibitors of foreign countries, notwithstanding the absence of any professed national character in those undertakings.

The Centennial Exposition to be held next year at New Orleans in commemoration of the centenary of the first shipment of cotton from a port of the United States bids fair to meet with like gratifying success. Under the act of Congress of the 10th of February, 1883, declaring that exposition to be national and international in its character, all foreign governments with which the United States maintain relations have been invited to participate.

The promoters of this important undertaking have already received assurances of the lively interest which it has excited abroad.

The report of the Commissioners of the District of Columbia is herewith transmitted. I ask for it your careful attention, especially for those portions which relate to assessments, arrears of taxes, and increase of water supply.

The commissioners who were appointed under the act of January 16, 1883, entitled "An act to regulate and improve the civil service of the United States," entered promptly upon the discharge of their duties.

A series of rules, framed in accordance with the spirit of the statute, was approved and promulgated by the President.

In some particulars wherein they seemed defective those rules were subsequently amended. It will be perceived that they discountenance any political or religious tests for admission to those offices of the public service to which the statute relates.

The act is limited in its original application to the classified clerkships in the several Executive Departments at Washington (numbering about 5,600) and to similar positions in customs districts and post-offices where as many as fifty persons are employed. A classification of these positions analogous to that existing in the Washington offices was duly made before the law went into effect. Eleven customs districts and twenty-three post-offices were thus brought under the immediate operation of the statute.

The annual report of the Civil Service Commission which will soon be submitted to Congress will doubtless afford the means of a more definite judgment than I am now prepared to express as to the merits of the new system. I am persuaded that its effects have thus far proved beneficial. Its practical methods appear to be adequate for the ends proposed, and there has been no serious difficulty in carrying them into effect. Since the 16th of July last no person, so far as I am aware, has been appointed to the public service in the classified portions thereof at any of the Departments, or at any of the post-offices and customs districts above named, except those certified by the Commission to be the most competent on the basis of the examinations held in conformity to the rules.

At the time when the present Executive entered upon his office his death, removal, resignation, or inability to discharge his duties would have left the Government without a constitutional head.

It is possible, of course, that a similar contingency may again arise unless the wisdom of Congress shall provide against its recurrence.

The Senate at its last session, after full consideration, passed an act relating to this subject, which will now, I trust, commend itself to the approval of both Houses of Congress.

The clause of the Constitution upon which must depend any law regulating the Presidential succession presents also for solution other questions of paramount importance.

These questions relate to the proper interpretation of the phrase "inability to discharge the powers and duties of said office," our organic law providing that when the President shall suffer from such inability the Presidential office shall devolve upon the Vice-President, who must himself under like circumstances give place to such officer as Congress may by law appoint to act as President.

I need not here set forth the numerous and interesting inquiries which are suggested by these words of the Constitution. They were fully stated in my first communication to Congress and have since been the subject of frequent deliberations in that body.

It is greatly to be hoped that these momentous questions will find speedy solution, lest emergencies may arise when longer delay will be impossible and any determination, albeit the wisest, may furnish cause for anxiety and alarm.

For the reasons fully stated in my last annual message I repeat my recommendation that Congress propose an amendment to that provision of the Constitution which prescribes the formalities for the enactment of laws, whereby, in respect to bills for the appropriation of public moneys, the Executive may be enabled, while giving his approval to particular items, to interpose his veto as to such others as do not commend themselves to his judgment.

The fourteenth amendment of the Constitution confers the rights of citizenship upon all persons born or naturalized in the United States and subject to the jurisdiction thereof. It was the special purpose of this amendment to insure to members of the colored race the full enjoyment of civil and political rights. Certain statutory provisions intended to secure the enforcement of those rights have been recently declared unconstitutional by the Supreme Court.

Any legislation whereby Congress may lawfully supplement the guaranties which the Constitution affords for the equal enjoyment by all the citizens of the United States of every right, privilege, and immunity of citizenship will receive my unhesitating approval.

CHESTER A. ARTHUR.

SPECIAL MESSAGES.

EXECUTIVE MANSION, *December 10, 1883.*
To the Senate and House of Representatives:

I transmit herewith a communication from the Secretary of the Interior of the 3d instant, submitting, with accompanying papers, draft of a bill to accept and ratify certain agreements made with the Sioux Indians and to grant a right of way to the Dakota Central Railway Company through the Sioux Reservation in Dakota.

The matter is presented for the consideration of the Congress.

CHESTER A. ARTHUR.

EXECUTIVE MANSION, *December 10, 1883.*
To the Senate and House of Representatives:

I transmit herewith a communication from the Secretary of the Interior of the 3d instant, with accompanying papers, submitting draft of a bill to prevent timber depredations on Indian reservations.

The subject is presented for the consideration of the Congress.

CHESTER A. ARTHUR.

EXECUTIVE MANSION, *December 10, 1883.*
To the Senate and House of Representatives:

I transmit herewith a communication of the 3d instant from the Secretary of the Interior, in relation to the urgent necessity of action on the part of the Congress for the more adequate prevention of trespasses upon Indian lands, with copy of report from the Commissioner of Indian Affairs upon the subject, draft of bill for the object indicated, and copy of correspondence from the Secretary of War recommending action in the premises.

The matter is commended to the consideration of the Congress.

CHESTER A. ARTHUR.

EXECUTIVE MANSION, *December 10, 1883.*

To the Senate and House of Representatives:

I transmit herewith a communication of the 3d instant from the Secretary of the Interior, with the draft of a bill "to accept and ratify an agreement made by the Pi-Ute Indians, and granting a right of way to the Carson and Colorado Railroad Company through the Walker River Reservation, in Nevada," and accompanying papers in relation to the subject.

The matter is presented for the consideration of the Congress.

CHESTER A. ARTHUR.

EXECUTIVE MANSION, *December 10, 1883.*

To the Senate and House of Representatives:

I transmit herewith a communication from the Secretary of the Interior of the 3d instant, with accompanying papers, submitting a draft of a bill "providing for the allotment of lands in severalty to certain Chippewa Indians of Lake Superior residing in the State of Wisconsin, and granting patents therefor."

The subject is presented for the consideration of the Congress.

CHESTER A. ARTHUR.

EXECUTIVE MANSION, *December 10, 1883.*

To the Senate and House of Representatives:

I transmit herewith a communication from the Secretary of the Interior of the 3d instant, with draft of bill for the payment of certain settlers in the State of Nevada for improvements on lands in Duck Valley, in that State, taken for the use and occupancy of the Shoshone Indians, with accompanying papers.

The subject is presented for the consideration of the Congress.

CHESTER A. ARTHUR.

EXECUTIVE MANSION, *December 10, 1883.*

To the Senate and House of Representatives:

I transmit herewith a communication from the Secretary of the Interior of the 3d instant, submitting, with accompanying papers, draft of a bill "to provide for the settlement of the estates of deceased Kickapoo Indians in the State of Kansas, and for other purposes."

The matter is presented for the consideration of the Congress.

CHESTER A. ARTHUR.

EXECUTIVE MANSION, *December 11, 1883.*

To the Senate and House of Representatives:

I transmit herewith a letter from the Secretary of the Interior, inclosing a communication from the Commissioner of Indian Affairs setting forth the necessity of a deficiency appropriation of $60,000 for the immediate wants of his Bureau.

CHESTER A. ARTHUR.

EXECUTIVE MANSION, *December 13, 1883.*

To the Senate and House of Representatives:

I transmit herewith, for the consideration of Congress, a letter from the Secretary of War, inclosing copies of official reports, etc., by the military authorities touching the necessity for the acquisition of additional land for the military reservation of Fort Preble, Me., and expressing his concurrence in the recommendation of the Lieutenant-General of the Army that the sum of $8,000 be appropriated by Congress for the purchase of such additional land.

CHESTER A. ARTHUR.

EXECUTIVE MANSION, *December 13, 1883.*

To the Senate and House of Representatives:

I transmit herewith, for the consideration of Congress, a communication from the Secretary of War, touching the question of the reconstruction of a bridge over the Republican River at or near Fort Riley, in the State of Kansas, and recommending such legislation as will authorize the reconstruction of said bridge by the United States in accordance with the terms and provisions of a joint resolution of the legislature of the State of Kansas approved March 6, 1883, a copy of which is herewith inclosed.

CHESTER A. ARTHUR.

EXECUTIVE MANSION, *December 13, 1883.*

To the Senate and House of Representatives:

I transmit herewith, for the consideration of Congress, a communication from the Secretary of War, dated the 4th instant, inclosing and commending to favorable consideration a letter from the board of commissioners of the Soldiers' Home, dated Washington, D. C., November 27, 1883, recommending such legislation as will confer upon said board of commissioners authority to advance a sum not exceeding $40,000 annually from funds found to be due the Soldiers' Home on settlements to be made in the offices of the Second Comptroller and Second Auditor, to pay for the services of extra clerks to be employed under the direction of the Secretary of the Treasury in making such settlements.

CHESTER A. ARTHUR.

EXECUTIVE MANSION, *December 13, 1883.*

To the Senate and House of Representatives:

I transmit herewith, for the consideration of Congress, a copy of a communication from the Secretary of War, dated the 8th instant, inclosing one from Captain S. M. Mills, Fifth Artillery, indorsed by the Chief Signal Officer of the Army, recommending that Congress authorize the printing and binding, for the use of the Signal Office, of 5,000 copies of the Annual Report of the Chief Signal Officer for the fiscal year 1882, and inclosing a draft of a joint resolution for that purpose.

CHESTER A. ARTHUR.

EXECUTIVE MANSION, *December 13, 1883.*

To the Senate and House of Representatives:

I transmit herewith, for the consideration of Congress, a letter from the Secretary of War, dated the 8th instant, and its accompanying papers, relative to the reconveyance to Mr. Thomas Mulvihill, of Pittsburg, Pa., of certain land erroneously conveyed by him to the United States, the particular facts regarding which are fully set forth in the inclosed copy of Senate Executive Document No. 46, Forty-seventh Congress, second session.

It appearing that the land in question was through error alone transferred to the United States, and that to retransfer the same to Mr. Mulvihill would be a measure of simple justice, it is recommended that such legislation be had as may be necessary to restore to Mr. Mulvihill his rights in the premises.

CHESTER A. ARTHUR.

EXECUTIVE MANSION, *December 17, 1883.*

To the Senate and House of Representatives:

I transmit herewith a communication from the Secretary of the Interior of the 4th instant, with accompanying papers, submitting a draft of a bill "to confirm the title to certain land in the Indian Territory to the Cheyennes and Arapahoes and the Wichitas and affiliated bands, to provide for the issuance of patents therefor, and for other purposes."

The subject is presented for the consideration of the Congress.

CHESTER A. ARTHUR.

EXECUTIVE MANSION, *December 17, 1883.*

To the Senate and House of Representatives:

I transmit herewith a communication of the 11th instant from the Secretary of the Interior, submitting, with accompanying papers, draft of a bill ''to provide for the issuance of patents for certain lands in the Indian Territory occupied by the Kickapoo, Iowa, and other Indians.''

The matter is presented for the consideration of the Congress.

CHESTER A. ARTHUR.

EXECUTIVE MANSION, *December 17, 1883.*

To the Senate and House of Representatives:

I transmit herewith a communication of the 6th instant from the Secretary of the Interior, submitting, with accompanying papers, a draft of a bill ''to accept and ratify an agreement with the confederated tribes of the Flathead, Kootenay, and Upper Pend d'Oreille Indians for the sale of a portion of their reservation in the Territory of Montana required for the use of the Northern Pacific Railroad, and for other purposes.''

The subject is presented for the consideration of the Congress.

CHESTER A. ARTHUR.

EXECUTIVE MANSION, *December 17, 1883.*

To the Senate and House of Representatives:

I transmit herewith a communication from the Secretary of the Interior of the 4th instant, submitting, with accompanying papers, draft of a bill ''to accept and ratify the agreement submitted by the Shoshones, Bannocks, and Sheepeaters of the Fort Hall and Lemhi reservations, in Idaho, May 14, 1880, for the sale of a portion of their land in said Territory and for other purposes, and to make the necessary appropriations for carrying out the same.''

The matter is presented for the consideration of the Congress.

CHESTER A. ARTHUR.

EXECUTIVE MANSION, *December 17, 1883.*

To the Senate and House of Representatives:

I transmit herewith a communication from the Secretary of the Interior, submitting a draft of a bill ''providing for allotment of lands in severalty to the Indians residing upon the Chehalis Reservation, in Washington Territory, and granting patents therefor,'' with accompanying report from the Commissioner of Indian Affairs upon the subject.

The matter is presented for the consideration of the Congress.

CHESTER A. ARTHUR.

EXECUTIVE MANSION, *December 17, 1883.*

To the Senate and House of Representatives:

I transmit herewith a communication from the Secretary of the Interior of the 3d instant, with accompanying papers, submitting a draft of a bill for the relief of the Nez Percé Indians in the Territory of Idaho and of the allied tribes residing on the Grande Ronde Indian Reservation, in the State of Oregon.

The subject is presented for the consideration of the Congress.

CHESTER A. ARTHUR.

EXECUTIVE MANSION, *December 17, 1883.*

To the Senate and House of Representatives:

I transmit herewith a communication from the Secretary of the Interior of the 4th instant, submitting, with accompanying papers, draft of a bill to accept and ratify certain agreements made with the Sioux Indians and to grant a right of way to the Chicago, Milwaukee, and St. Paul Railway Company through the Sioux Reservation in Dakota.

The matter is presented for the consideration of the Congress.

CHESTER A. ARTHUR.

EXECUTIVE MANSION, *December 17, 1883.*

To the Senate and House of Representatives:

I transmit herewith, for the consideration of Congress, a letter from the Secretary of War, dated December 13 instant, inclosing one from the Surgeon-General of the Army submitting a special estimate for funds in the sum of $200,000 for the erection in this city of a suitable fireproof building to contain the records, library, and museum of the Medical Department of the Army, together with preliminary plans for said building and copies of reports, etc., in relation to the subject.

CHESTER A. ARTHUR.

EXECUTIVE MANSION, *December 17, 1883.*

To the Senate and House of Representatives:

I transmit herewith, for the consideration of Congress, a communication from the Secretary of the Navy, dated the 10th instant, inclosing a letter from the Surgeon-General of the Navy respecting the advisability of providing for representation on the part of the United States in any international convention that may be organized for the purpose of establishing uniform standards of measure of color perception and acuteness of vision.

CHESTER A. ARTHUR.

EXECUTIVE MANSION, *December 17, 1883.*

To the Senate and House of Representatives:

I transmit herewith a communication of the 3d instant from the Secretary of the Interior, submitting, with accompanying papers, a draft of a bill for the payment of the value of certain improvements made by certain settlers on the Round Valley Indian Reservation, in the State of California, as appraised under the act approved March 3, 1873.

The subject is presented for the consideration of the Congress.

CHESTER A. ARTHUR.

EXECUTIVE MANSION, *December 17, 1883.*

To the Senate and House of Representatives:

I transmit herewith a communication of the 12th instant from the Secretary of the Interior, submitting a report of the Commissioner of Indian Affairs of December 8, 1883, and accompanying papers, on the subject of the "Old Settler" or "Western" Cherokees."

CHESTER A. ARTHUR.

EXECUTIVE MANSION, *December 17, 1883.*

To the Senate and House of Representatives:

I transmit herewith a communication of the 4th instant from the Secretary of the Interior, with draft of a bill to accept and ratify an agreement made with Chief Moses and other Indians for the relinquishment of certain lands in Washington Territory, and to make the necessary appropriations for carrying the same into effect, with accompanying papers.

The subject is presented for the consideration of the Congress.

CHESTER A. ARTHUR.

EXECUTIVE MANSION, *December 19, 1883.*

To the Senate and House of Representatives:

I transmit herewith, for the consideration of Congress, a letter from the Secretary of War, dated the 15th instant, inclosing one from the Quartermaster-General setting forth the necessity for the construction of a fireproof building in this city for the storage of the public records.

CHESTER A. ARTHUR.

EXECUTIVE MANSION, *December 19, 1883.*

To the Senate and House of Representatives:

I transmit herewith a letter from the Secretary of the Interior, inclosing a copy of a communication from the Commissioner of Indian Affairs setting forth the necessity of a deficiency appropriation of $78,110 for the purchase of supplies for the balance of the present fiscal year for the Crow Indians.

CHESTER A ARTHUR.

EXECUTIVE MANSION,
Washington, December 19, 1883.

To the Senate of the United States:

I transmit herewith, in response to the Senate resolution of the 18th instant, a report of the Secretary of State and accompanying papers, relating to the treaty between the United States and Great Britain signed April 19, 1850.

CHESTER A. ARTHUR.

EXECUTIVE MANSION, *December 19, 1883.*

To the Senate and House of Representatives:

I transmit herewith, for the consideration of Congress, a communication from the Secretary of War, dated December 14, 1883, upon the subject of abandoned military reservations, and renewing his former recommendation for such legislation as will provide for the disposal of military sites that are no longer needed for military purposes.

CHESTER A. ARTHUR.

EXECUTIVE MANSION,
Washington, December 19, 1883.

To the Senate of the United States of America:

I transmit herewith to the Senate, for its consideration with a view to ratification, a treaty of extradition between the United States of America and the Grand Duchy of Luxemburg, concluded at Berlin on the 29th of October, A. D. 1883.

CHESTER A. ARTHUR.

EXECUTIVE MANSION,
Washington, December 24, 1883.

To the House of Representatives:

The House of Representatives having adopted on the 19th instant a resolution in the following words—

Resolved, That the Secretary of State be, and he is hereby, requested to furnish for the information of this House, without delay, if not incompatible with the public service, all communications, documents, and papers in his possession relating to the trial, conviction, and execution of the late Patrick O'Donnell by the British Government—

I transmit herewith a report made to me by the Secretary of State, with the papers enumerated in the subjoined list, as answering said resolution.

CHESTER A. ARTHUR.

EXECUTIVE MANSION, *January 7, 1884.*

To the Senate and House of Representatives:

I transmit herewith a communication from the Secretary of the Interior of the 19th ultimo, submitting, with accompanying papers, a draft of a bill providing for the allotment of lands in severalty to the Arickaree, Gros Ventre, and Mandan Indians on the Fort Berthold Indian Reservation, in Dakota, and the granting of patents therefor, and for other purposes.

The matter is presented for the action of the Congress.

CHESTER A. ARTHUR.

EXECUTIVE MANSION, *January 7, 1884.*

To the Senate and House of Representatives:

I transmit herewith a communication from the Secretary of the Interior of the 19th ultimo, submitting, with accompanying papers, a draft of a bill "to allow Indian homestead entries in certain cases without the payment of fees and commissions."

The matter is presented for the consideration and action of the Congress.

CHESTER A. ARTHUR.

EXECUTIVE MANSION, *January 7, 1884.*

To the Senate and House of Representatives:

I transmit herewith, for the consideration of Congress, a letter from the Secretary of War, dated the 2d instant, inclosing copies of official correspondence, reports, etc., in relation to the military post of Fort Sullivan, Me., and recommending such legislation as will authorize the sale of the site to the highest bidder after public advertisement, the same being no longer needed for military purposes.

CHESTER A. ARTHUR.

EXECUTIVE MANSION, *January 8, 1884.*

To the Senate and House of Representatives:

I submit a communication from the governor of the State of Illinois, with a copy of an act of the general assembly of that State tendering to the United States the cession of the Illinois and Michigan Canal upon condition that it shall be enlarged and maintained as a national waterway for commercial purposes.

The proposed cession is an element of the subject which Congress had under consideration in directing by the act of August 2, 1882, a survey for a canal from a point on the Illinois River at or near the town of Hennepin by the most practicable route to the Mississippi River at or above the city of Rock Island, the canal to be not less than 70 feet wide at the water line and not less than 7 feet in depth of water, and with capacity for vessels of at least 280 tons burden; and also a survey of the Illinois and Michigan Canal and an estimate of the cost of enlarging it to the dimensions of the proposed canal between Hennepin and the Mississippi River.

The surveys ordered in the above act have been completed and the report upon them is included in the last annual report of the Secretary of War, and a copy is herewith submitted. It is estimated in the report that by the enlargement of the Illinois and Michigan Canal and the construction of the proposed canal by the shortest route between Hennepin and the Mississippi River a direct and convenient thoroughfare for vessels of 280 tons burden may be opened from the Mississippi River to Lake Michigan at a cost of $8,110,286.65, and that the annual charge for maintenance would be $138,600.

It appears from these papers that the estimated yield of corn, wheat, and oats for 1882 in the States of Illinois, Wisconsin, Iowa, Minnesota, Kansas, and Nebraska was more than 1,000,000,000 bushels. It is claimed that if the cheap water transportation route which is now continuous from the Atlantic Ocean to Chicago is extended to the Upper Mississippi by such a canal a great benefit in the reduction of freight charges would result to the people of the Upper Mississippi Valley, whose productions I have only partly noted, not only upon their own shipments, but upon the articles of commerce used by them, which are now taken from the Eastern States by water only as far as Chicago.

As a matter of great interest, especially to the citizens of that part of the country, I commend the general subject to your consideration.

CHESTER A. ARTHUR.

EXECUTIVE MANSION,
Washington, January 8, 1884.

To the House of Representatives:

In answer to the resolution of the House of Representatives of the 7th instant, respecting the alleged distribution of circulars in some of the Departments asking contributions for political purposes, I hereby transmit the reply of the Secretary of State.

CHESTER A. ARTHUR.

EXECUTIVE MANSION, *January 8, 1884.*
To the Senate and House of Representatives:

I transmit herewith to the House of Representatives a communication from the Secretary of War, submitting the annual report of the Mississippi River Commission.

I take this occasion to invite the early attention of Congress to the continuation of the work on the Mississippi River which is being carried on under the plans of the commission.   My sense of the importance of the improvement of this river, not only to the people of the Northwest, but especially to the inhabitants of the Lower Mississippi Valley, has already been expressed in a special communication to the last Congress.   The harvests of grain and cotton produced in the region bordering upon the Mississippi are so vast as to be of national importance, and the project now being executed for their cheap transportation should be sufficiently provided for.

The commission report that the results due to the still uncompleted works have been remarkable, and give the highest encouragement for expecting the ultimate success of the improvement.

The act of August 2, 1882, appropriated $4,123,000 for the work on that part of the river below Cairo.   The estimates of the commission already transmitted to Congress call for $3,000,000 for the continuation of the work below Cairo, and it appears from their report that all of the last appropriation available for active operations has been exhausted and that there is urgently needed an immediate appropriation of $1,000,-000 to continue the work without loss of time, in view of the approach of the flood season, with its attendant dangers.

I therefore recommend to Congress the early passage of a separate bill on this subject.

CHESTER A. ARTHUR.

EXECUTIVE MANSION, *January 9, 1884.*

To the Senate and House of Representatives:

I transmit herewith, for the consideration of Congress, a letter from the Secretary of War of the 7th instant, inclosing a copy of one from the Quartermaster-General of the Army submitting plans and estimates for the construction of walls, etc., at the Schuylkill Arsenal, Philadelphia, Pa., rendered necessary by the opening of Peltz street, and recommending that an appropriation be made of the amount estimated to be requisite for the work referred to.

CHESTER A. ARTHUR.

EXECUTIVE MANSION, *January 14, 1884.*

To the Senate and House of Representatives:

I transmit herewith a communication from the Secretary of the Interior, submitting, with accompanying papers, an estimate of appropriation in the sum of $25,000 for the settlement under existing treaties of certain freedmen and their descendants upon lands known as the Oklahoma district, within the Indian Territory.

The matter is presented for the consideration of the Congress.

CHESTER A. ARTHUR.

EXECUTIVE MANSION, *January 14, 1884.*

To the Senate and House of Representatives:

I transmit herewith a communication of the 11th instant from the Secretary of the Interior, submitting, with accompanying papers, an item of appropriation in the sum of $3,000 for the location and survey of boundary lines of certain lands purchased by the United States from the Creek Indians for the use of the Seminole Indians in the Indian Territory.

The matter is presented for the consideration of the Congress.

CHESTER A. ARTHUR.

EXECUTIVE MANSION, *January 14, 1884.*

To the Senate and House of Representatives:

I transmit herewith a communication from the Secretary of the Interior, submitting, with accompanying papers, a draft of a bill "for the relief of the Mission Indians in the State of California."

The subject is presented for the consideration of the Congress.

CHESTER A. ARTHUR.

EXECUTIVE MANSION,
Washington, January 15, 1884.

To the Senate of the United States:

In response to the resolution of the Senate of the 8th instant, calling for the correspondence on file upon the subject of discriminating duties upon commerce between the United States and Cuba and Puerto Rico, I transmit herewith a report made to me by the Secretary of State, with accompanying papers.

CHESTER A. ARTHUR.

EXECUTIVE MANSION, *January 16, 1884.*

To the Senate and House of Representatives:

I transmit herewith, for the consideration of Congress, a copy of a letter from the secretary of state of the State of Pennsylvania, dated November 26, 1883, inclosing a duly authenticated copy of an act of the legislature of that State entitled "An act to provide for the preservation, use, custody, and disposition of the marine hospital at Erie, and making an appropriation for the repair of the same," approved July 5, 1883, and tendering to the United States Government, on behalf of the governor, in pursuance of the provisions of the act, the said marine hospital for use as a soldiers' and sailors' home.

The papers having upon their receipt been referred by me to the Secretary of War, I inclose also a copy of his letter of the 12th instant returning the same, together with a copy of the report of Captain Edward

Maguire, Corps of Engineers, dated the 10th ultimo, giving a description of the property referred to and expressing his views as to its adaptability for a soldiers and sailors' home.

CHESTER A. ARTHUR.

EXECUTIVE MANSION, *January 16, 1884.*

To the Senate and House of Representatives:

I transmit herewith a letter from the Secretary of the Interior, dated the 11th instant, suggesting further action by Congress in the matter of granting leases of bath houses and bath-house sites at the Hot Springs Reservation, Ark.

The subject is presented for the consideration of the Congress.

CHESTER A. ARTHUR.

EXECUTIVE MANSION, *January 17, 1884.*

To the Senate and House of Representatives:

I transmit, for the consideration of Congress, a communication from the Secretary of War and the Secretary of the Navy, on the subject of an expedition for the relief of Lieutenant A. W. Greely and his party, composing what is known as the "Lady Franklin Bay Expedition," which was sent to the arctic regions in 1881 under the provisions of the acts of Congress approved May 1, 1880, and March 3, 1881.

In the plans for the relief of this party, as arranged with Lieutenant Greely, it was contemplated that an effort would be made to communicate with him and furnish him any needed assistance in 1882 and again in 1883.

Subsequently legislation was enacted which required the expedition of 1883 to bring the party home. It was a part of the arrangement that if communication should not be made with him on or before the 1st of September, 1883, he should, with his party, abandon his station at Lady Franklin Bay not later than the above-mentioned date and proceed southward, and would find a well-supplied relief station at the entrance to Smiths Sound, a point where it would not be difficult to reach him during a part of each year. The expeditions of 1882 and 1883 were sent, but neither one of them was able to communicate with Lieutenant Greely; and the last one failed to accomplish any part of its object beyond leaving a very small quantity of stores in the neighborhood of the entrance to Smiths Sound.

The situation of Lieutenant Greely and his party under these circumstances is one of great peril, and in presenting the preliminary views of the board appointed by me to take into consideration an expedition for their relief I urgently recommend prompt action by Congress to enable the recommendations of the Secretary of War and the Secretary of the Navy to be carried out without delay.

CHESTER A. ARTHUR.

EXECUTIVE MANSION, *January 22, 1884.*

To the House of Representatives:

I transmit herewith, in response to the resolution of the House dated January 11, 1883, a letter, dated the 21st instant, from the Secretary of War, together with a report submitted to him by the Chief of Engineers, embodying the information, so far as the same can be furnished from the records of his office, and a statement prepared in the Treasury Department, respecting the expenditures for rivers and harbors, called for by the said resolution.   CHESTER A. ARTHUR.

EXECUTIVE MANSION, *January 28, 1884.*

To the Senate and House of Representatives:

I transmit to Congress a communication from the Secretary of War, in relation to the necessity of an immediate appropriation of not less than $42,000 to enable the engineer in charge to make next autumn the explosion required for the removal of Flood Rock, in the East River, New York. The importance of the work is well known, and as it appears that without a speedy appropriation a delay of a year must follow, accompanied by large expenses to protect from injury the work already done, I commend the subject to the early and favorable consideration of Congress.

CHESTER A. ARTHUR.

EXECUTIVE MANSION,
Washington, January 30, 1884.

To the Senate of the United States:

In further response to the resolution of the Senate of the 8th instant, calling for the correspondence on file upon the subject of discriminating duties upon commerce between the United States and Cuba and Puerto Rico, I transmit certain papers additional to the papers which accompanied the report sent to you on the 15th instant.

CHESTER A. ARTHUR.

EXECUTIVE MANSION, *January 31, 1884.*

To the Senate and House of Representatives:

I transmit herewith a communication of the 29th instant from the Secretary of the Interior, submitting, with accompanying papers, a report of the Commissioner of Indian Affairs upon the subject of the right of way of the Chicago, Milwaukee and St. Paul Railway Company through the Lake Traverse Indian Reservation, in Dakota.

The subject is commended to the consideration of the Congress.

CHESTER A. ARTHUR.

EXECUTIVE MANSION, *January 31, 1884.*

To the House of Representatives of the United States:

I transmit herewith, in response to the resolutions of the House of Representatives, the following report of the Secretary of State, with accompanying papers, relative to the restrictions upon the importation of American hog products into Germany and France.

CHESTER A. ARTHUR.

EXECUTIVE MANSION, *February 6, 1884.*

To the Senate and House of Representatives:

I transmit herewith, for the consideration of Congress, a communication, under date of the 2d instant, from the Secretary of the Interior, transmitting the last annual report of the Government directors of the Union Pacific Railway Company.

The report accompanying the Secretary's communication has been sent to the House of Representatives.

CHESTER A. ARTHUR.

EXECUTIVE MANSION,
Washington, February 7, 1884.

To the House of Representatives:

I transmit herewith a report of the Secretary of State, in response to the resolution of the House of Representatives of the 16th ultimo, respecting the arrest and imprisonment of John E. Wheelock in Venezuela in 1879.

CHESTER A. ARTHUR.

EXECUTIVE MANSION,
Washington, February 7, 1884.

To the House of Representatives:

I transmit herewith, in response to a resolution of the House of Representatives of the 15th instant [ultimo], a report of the Secretary of State, with accompanying papers, in relation to the reported arrest at Lodz, in Russian Poland, of Reinhardt Wagner, a citizen of the United States.

CHESTER A. ARTHUR.

WASHINGTON, *February 7, 1884.*

To the Senate of the United States:

I transmit herewith to the Senate, for its consideration with a view to its ratification, an agreement concerning trade-marks between the United States and Italy, signed June 1, 1882, provided the terms thereof commend themselves to the Senate.

CHESTER A. ARTHUR.

EXECUTIVE MANSION, *February 11, 1884.*

To the Senate and House of Representatives:

I transmit a communication, under date of the 8th instant, addressed to me by the Secretary of the Navy, covering a report of Professor Simon Newcomb, United States Navy, on the subject of recent improvements in astronomical observatories, instruments, and methods of observations, as noted during his visit to the principal observatories of Europe in the year 1883, made in pursuance of orders of the Navy Department.

The request of the Secretary is commended to the consideration of Congress.

CHESTER A. ARTHUR.

EXECUTIVE MANSION,
Washington, February 12, 1884.

To the Senate of the United States:

I transmit herewith, for the consideration of the Senate in connection with the commercial convention of January 20, 1883, between the United States and Mexico, now pending before the Senate, a protocol of an agreement, signed on the 11th instant by the Secretary of State and the representative of Mexico at this capital, explaining and correcting an error of translation found in the Spanish text of said convention.

CHESTER A. ARTHUR.

EXECUTIVE MANSION, *February 13, 1884.*

To the Senate and House of Representatives:

I transmit herewith a communication of the 8th ultimo from the Secretary of the Interior, and the accompanying papers, relating to the establishment of the boundary line between the United States and the State of Texas.

The matter is presented for the consideration of the Congress.

CHESTER A. ARTHUR.

EXECUTIVE MANSION, *February 13, 1884.*

To the Senate of the United States:

In compliance with the resolution of the Senate of February 6, 1884, directing ''that the President be requested, if in his judgment not incompatible with the public interests, to communicate to the Senate the record of the proceedings, testimony, and findings of the court of inquiry in relation to the events connected with the loss of the steamer *Proteus* in the Arctic Ocean,'' I have the honor to transmit herewith a copy of the record, etc., called for in said resolution, together with the letter of the Secretary of War, dated the 12th instant, submitting the same to me.

CHESTER A. ARTHUR.

EXECUTIVE MANSION,
Washington, February 13, 1884.

To the Senate of the United States:

In reply to the resolution of the Senate of the 11th instant, I have the honor to inclose a communication* from the Secretary of State.

CHESTER A. ARTHUR.

EXECUTIVE MANSION, *February 18, 1884.*

To the Senate and House of Representatives:

I transmit herewith the report of a board of Army and Navy officers appointed by me in accordance with the act of Congress approved March 3, 1883, "for the purpose of examining and reporting to Congress which of the navy-yards or arsenals owned by the Government has the best location and is best adapted for the establishment of a Government foundry, or what other method, if any, should be adopted for the manufacture of heavy ordnance adapted to modern warfare, for the use of the Army and Navy of the United States, the cost of all buildings, tools, and implements necessary to be used in the manufacture thereof, including the cost of a steam hammer or apparatus of sufficient size for the manufacture of the heaviest guns."

CHESTER A. ARTHUR.

EXECUTIVE MANSION, *February 21, 1884.*

To the Senate and House of Representatives:

I transmit herewith a report of the Secretary of State of the 21st instant, whereby your honorable body, and through you the people of the United States, may become apprised of the generous contribution made by Her Britannic Majesty's Government toward the efforts for the relief of Lieutenant Greely's arctic exploring party by presenting to the United States the arctic steamship *Alert.*

CHESTER A. ARTHUR.

DEPARTMENT OF STATE,
Washington, February 21, 1884.

The PRESIDENT:

In the search for vessels suitable for the expedition now preparing to relieve Lieutenant Greely and his party, attention was early directed to the *Alert,* which is the property of the British Government, and was the advance ship of the expedition under Sir George Nares. It was desirable to secure this vessel, as she is peculiarly fitted for the intended service, and as the inspecting officers recommended her Mr. Lowell was therefore instructed to ask whether she could be spared for the service.

Information of the wish of this Government having previously and informally reached the British admiralty, a private intimation was conveyed to the United States minister to the effect that the British Government had not forgotten the very considerate conduct of this Government on the occasion of the recovery of the *Resolute,* and that should any suggestion be made that the vessel would be of use to the expedition she would be presented. The *Resolute,* a vessel, as the President remem-

*Relating to the demand of Mexico for the extradition of Alexander Trimble.

bers, formerly belonging to Her Majesty's navy, having been abandoned in the arctic region, was discovered and brought to the United States by American seamen, and thereupon was purchased by this Government of her sailors, repaired, and returned to Great Britain. On her arrival in England the vessel was received by the Queen in person, and the officers of the United States Navy who took the ship thither were treated with every official and personal courtesy.

The Government of Her Majesty has now given the *Alert* to the United States unconditionally, with her anchors, chains, and such of her equipment as can be utilized.

Recognizing this graceful and opportune act of courtesy on the part of Her Majesty's Government, the undersigned to-day instructed Mr. Lowell as follows, by telegraph:

"Her Majesty's Government having presented to the Government of the United States the ship *Alert* to aid in the relief of Lieutenant Greely and his party, you will inform the secretary of state for foreign affairs that the spirit which prompts this act of generosity, and this evidence of sympathy with the object in view, receives the highest appreciation of the President, as it will that of the people of the United States. The President sends his cordial thanks for the opportune gift of this vessel, which he accepts in the name of the United States, and which will be used in the humane enterprise for which it is so peculiarly adapted."

Respectfully submitted.   FREDK. T. FRELINGHUYSEN.

EXECUTIVE MANSION, *February 21, 1884.*

To the Senate and House of Representatives:

I transmit herewith, for the consideration of Congress, a letter from the Secretary of War, dated the 19th instant, submitting a letter from the Chief Signal Officer of the Army, dated the 2d instant, and its accompanying plan of a proposed meteorological observatory at Fort Myer, Va., together with an estimate of the cost of the same in the sum of $4,000 and a statement giving various reasons why the said observatory should be established.   CHESTER A. ARTHUR.

EXECUTIVE MANSION, *February 25, 1884.*

To the House of Representatives:

In answer to so much of the resolution of the House of Representatives of the 17th ultimo as calls for the correspondence with the Mexican Government respecting the payment of claims specified in the fifth section of the act of Congress approved June 17, 1878, I transmit herewith the report of the Secretary of State and its accompanying papers.

CHESTER A. ARTHUR.

EXECUTIVE MANSION, *February 29, 1884.*

To the Senate and House of Representatives:

In compliance with the act of Congress approved January 16, 1883, entitled "An act to regulate and improve the civil service of the United

States," the Civil Service Commission has made to the President its first annual report.

That report is herewith transmitted, together with communications from the heads of the several Executive Departments of the Government respecting the practical workings of the law under which the Commission has been acting.

Upon the good results which that law has already accomplished I congratulate Congress and the people, and I avow my conviction that it will henceforth prove to be of still more signal benefit to the public service.

I heartily commend the zeal and fidelity of the Commissioners and their suggestion for further legislation, and I advise the making of such an appropriation as shall be adequate for their needs.

CHESTER A. ARTHUR.

EXECUTIVE MANSION,
Washington, February 29, 1884.

To the Senate and House of Representatives:

I transmit herewith, for the consideration of Congress, a report of the Secretary of State, accompanying a report made by the commission lately designated by me to examine and report upon the asserted unhealthfulness of the swine products of this country. The views and conclusions of the commission deserve the most careful consideration of Congress, to the end that if any path be legitimately open for removing the prohibition which closes important foreign markets to those products it may be followed and appropriate legislation devised.

I earnestly recommend that Congress provide for reimbursing the expenses incurred by the commissioners in this praiseworthy service, and I should be glad also if some remunerative recognition of their public-spirited action in accepting the onerous and responsible duties imposed on them were to suggest itself to Congress. At all events, in view of the conflicting theories touching the origin and propagation of trichiniasis and the means of isolating and extirpating it among domestic swine, and considering the important bearing which precise knowledge on these points would have on the commercial aspects of the matter, I recommend provision for special research in this direction.

CHESTER A. ARTHUR.

EXECUTIVE MANSION,
Washington, March 5, 1884.

To the House of Representatives:

In further response to the resolution of the House of Representatives of the 15th January last, calling for copies of correspondence on file in the Department of State in relation to the reported arrest at Lodz, in Russia, of Reinhardt Wagner, a citizen of the United States, I transmit, in addition to the papers sent you on the 7th ultimo, a copy of a dispatch subsequently received.

CHESTER A. ARTHUR.

EXECUTIVE MANSION,
Washington, March 6, 1884.

To the House of Representatives of the United States:

I transmit herewith to the House of Representatives a report from the Secretary of State, in response to a resolution of that body of the 5th ultimo, calling for correspondence concerning the representations made to this Government in relation to the existing tariff discrimination against the works of foreign artists.

CHESTER A. ARTHUR.

EXECUTIVE MANSION,
Washington, March 10, 1884.

To the House of Representatives:

I transmit herewith the following documents, received from the Secretary of State, relative to the resolution of the House of Representatives upon the death of Mr. Edward Lasker.

CHESTER A. ARTHUR.

EXECUTIVE MANSION,
Washington, March 11, 1884.

To the Senate of the United States:

I submit herewith, for the consideration of the Senate with a view to obtaining its advice and consent thereto, a draft of a proclamation whereby the United States accede and adhere to an international convention for the protection of industrial property, signed at Paris March 20, 1883, and in explanation of the purport of that convention and the proposed mode of effecting the adhesion of the United States thereto I subjoin a report of the Secretary of State.

CHESTER A. ARTHUR.

EXECUTIVE MANSION, *March 14, 1884.*

To the Senate and House of Representatives:

I transmit herewith, for the consideration of Congress, a communication from the Secretary of War of the 12th instant, and accompanying papers, requesting an appropriation of $230,869.44 for the erection at the Presidio of San Francisco of additional buildings at headquarters Military Division of the Pacific, rendered necessary in consequence of the proposed increase of the garrison by removal of troops from points in San Francisco Harbor.

CHESTER A. ARTHUR.

EXECUTIVE MANSION, *March 18, 1884.*

To the Senate and House of Representatives:

I transmit herewith, for the consideration of Congress, a communication from the Secretaries of War and the Navy, concerning the expediency of offering rewards for the rescue of Lieutenant Greely and party by the independent efforts of private vessels, in addition to sending the three ships constituting the national relief expedition.

CHESTER A. ARTHUR.

EXECUTIVE MANSION,
Washington, March 18, 1884.

To the Senate of the United States:

In answer to the resolution of the Senate of the 15th of January last, respecting the discovery of phosphates upon the coast of Brazil by a citizen of the United States, I transmit herewith a report from the Secretary of State upon the subject, together with the accompanying papers.

CHESTER A. ARTHUR.

EXECUTIVE MANSION, *March 20, 1884.*

To the Senate and House of Representatives:

In accordance with the provisions of the act making appropriations for the diplomatic and consular service for the year ending June 30, 1883, I transmit herewith a communication from the Secretary of State in relation to the consular service.

CHESTER A. ARTHUR.

EXECUTIVE MANSION, *March 20, 1884.*

To the Senate and House of Representatives:

I transmit herewith a communication from the Secretary of War of the 18th instant, submitting a letter from Colonel A. F. Rockwell, United States Army, in charge of public buildings and grounds, embodying an estimate in the sum of $30,000 for a pedestal for the statue of General James A. Garfield, to be erected in the city of Washington by the Society of the Army of the Cumberland, together with a letter upon the subject from General Anson G. McCook, on behalf of the Society of the Army of the Cumberland, the object in view being the procurement of an appropriation by Congress of the amount of the accompanying estimate.

I commend the subject to the favorable consideration of Congress.

CHESTER A. ARTHUR.

EXECUTIVE MANSION, *March 26, 1884.*

To the Senate and House of Representatives:

In my annual message I impressed upon Congress the necessity of continued progress in the reconstruction of the Navy. The recommendations in this direction of the Secretary of the Navy and of the Naval Advisory Board were submitted by me unaccompanied by specific expressions of approval. I now deem it my duty to advise that appropriations be made at the present session toward designing and commencing the construction of at least the three additional steel cruisers and the four gunboats thus recommended, the cost of which, including their armament, will not exceed $4,283,000, of which sum one-half should be appropriated for the next fiscal year.

The *Chicago, Boston, Atlanta,* and *Dolphin* have been designed and are being built with care and skill, and there is every reason to believe that they will prove creditable and serviceable modern cruisers. Technical questions concerning the details of these or of additional vessels can not wisely be settled except by experts, and the Naval Advisory Board, organized by direction of Congress under the act of August 5, 1882, and consisting of three line officers, a naval constructor, and a naval engineer, selected "with reference only to character, experience, knowledge, and skill," and a naval architect and a marine engineer from civil life "of established reputation and standing as experts in naval or marine construction," is an appropriate authority to decide finally all such questions. I am unwilling to see the gradual reconstruction of our naval cruisers, now happily begun in conformity with modern requirements, delayed one full year for any unsubstantial reason.

Whatever conditions Congress may see fit to impose in order to secure judicious designs and honest and economical construction will be acceptable to me, but to relinquish or postpone the policy already deliberately declared will be, in my judgment, an act of national imprudence.

Appropriations should also be made without delay for finishing the four double-turreted monitors, the *Puritan, Amphitrite, Terror,* and *Monadnock,* and for procuring their armament and that of the *Miantonomoh.* Their hulls are built, and their machinery is under contract and approaching completion, except that of the *Monadnock,* on the Pacific coast. This should also be built, and the armor and heavy guns of all should be procured at the earliest practicable moment.

The total amount appropriated up to this time for the four vessels is $3,546,941.41. A sum not exceeding $3,838,769.62, including $866,725 for four powerful rifled cannon and for the remainder of the ordnance outfit, will complete and equip them for service. Of the sum required, only two millions need be appropriated for the next fiscal year. It is not expected that one of the monitors will be a match for the heaviest broadside ironclads which certain other Governments have constructed at a cost of four or five millions each. but they will be armored vessels of an approved and useful type, presenting limited surfaces for the shot of an enemy, and possessed of such seagoing capacity and offensive power as fully to answer our immediate necessities. Their completion having been determined upon in the recent legislation of Congress, no time should be lost in accomplishing the necessary object.

The Gun Foundry Board, appointed by direction of Congress, consisting of three army and three navy officers, has submitted its report, duly transmitted on the 20th day of February, 1884, recommending that the Government should promote the production at private steel works of the required material for heavy cannon, and that two Government factories, one for the Army and one for the Navy, should be established for the fabrication of guns from such material. An early consideration of the report is recommended, together with such action as will enable the Government to construct its ordnance upon its own territory and so to provide the armaments demanded by considerations which concern the national safety and honor.

CHESTER A. ARTHUR.

EXECUTIVE MANSION, *April 1, 1884.*

To the House of Representatives:

In response to a resolution of the House of Representatives of January 15, 1884, requesting the President to forward to the House information, including reports from consuls and others, concerning the undervaluation, false classification, and other irregular practices in the importation of foreign merchandise, and to recommend what legislation, if any, is needed to prevent such frauds on the revenue, I have the honor to transmit herewith a letter of the Secretary of the Treasury of the 28th ultimo, inclosing a draft of a bill on the subject, together with copies of reports taken from the files of the Treasury Department concerning the information desired.

CHESTER A. ARTHUR.

EXECUTIVE MANSION,
Washington, April 1, 1884.

To the House of Representatives:

I transmit herewith a report of the Secretary of State and accompanying papers, furnished in response to a resolution of the House of Representatives of January 16, 1884, calling for information as to the payments made by Spain in accordance with the terms of its treaty with the United States concluded February 17, 1834.

CHESTER A. ARTHUR.

EXECUTIVE MANSION, *April 2, 1884.*

To the Senate and House of Representatives:

I transmit to Congress a communication from the Secretary of War, embodying the views of the president of the Mississippi River Commission upon a report from Major Stickney, of the Engineer Corps, in relation to the protection of existing levees from destruction by the floods in the lower part of the Mississippi River. It appears that there is an urgent need of an appropriation of $100,000 to be used for this purpose, and that an enormous destruction of property may be thereby averted. I recommend an immediate appropriation of the sum required for the purpose, to be expended under the direction of the Mississippi River Commission.

CHESTER A. ARTHUR.

EXECUTIVE MANSION, *April 2, 1884.*

To the House of Representatives:

In response to the resolution of the House of Representatives of 5th of February last, respecting the arrest and imprisonment of certain American citizens by the authorities of Colombia, at Aspinwall, I transmit a report of the Secretary of State.

CHESTER A. ARTHUR.

EXECUTIVE MANSION, *April 11, 1884.*

To the Senate and House of Representatives:

The condition of our seacoast defenses and their armament has been brought to the attention of Congress in my annual messages, and I now submit a special estimate of the Chief of Ordnance, United States Army, transmitted by the Secretary of War, for a permanent annual appropriation of $1,500,000 to provide the necessary armament for our fortifications.

This estimate is founded upon the report of the Gun Foundry Board recently transmitted, to which I have heretofore invited the early attention of Congress.

In presenting this estimate I do not think it necessary to enumerate the considerations which make it of the highest importance that there should be no unnecessary delay in entering upon the work, which must be commensurate with the public interests to be guarded, and which will take much time.

CHESTER A. ARTHUR.

EXECUTIVE MANSION, *April 14, 1884.*

To the Senate and House of Representatives:

I transmit herewith, for the consideration of Congress, a communication from the Secretary of War of the 5th instant, submitting copies of certain papers, consisting of a letter, dated February 16 last, from Mr. Haughwout Howe, of New York City, presenting a proposition for the sale to the Government for the sum of $5,500 of certain hospital and other records pertaining to an association founded in New York City in April, 1862, for the purpose of extending relief to soldiers of the late war; a report of an examination made of these records by a representative of the War Department, and a report of the Adjutant-General stating that the records would prove of great value to the Department in the settlement of claims of deserving soldiers, as well as in detecting fraudulent claims, as the books, etc., contain information not now of record in the War Department.

The Secretary of War, it will be observed, recommends that an appropriation be made by Congress of the necessary sum for the purchase of the records referred to.

CHESTER A. ARTHUR.

EXECUTIVE MANSION,
Washington, April 14, 1884.

To the Senate of the United States of America:

I transmit herewith to the Senate, for its consideration with a view to ratification, a convention concluded between the United States of America and France and the twenty-four other powers named in said convention for the protection of submarine cables, concluded at Paris on the 14th day of March, A. D. 1884. I also inclose, for the information of the Senate, a copy of Mr. Morton's dispatch No. 518, of the 18th ultimo, in relation to the subject.

CHESTER A. ARTHUR.

WASHINGTON, *April 14, 1884.*

To the Senate of the United States:

I transmit to the Senate, for its consideration with a view to ratification, a convention concerning trade-marks and trade-labels between the United States and Belgium, signed on the 7th instant.

CHESTER A. ARTHUR.

EXECUTIVE MANSION,
Washington, April 18, 1884.

To the Senate and House of Representatives:

I transmit herewith a communication from the Secretary of State of the 16th instant, relative to the approaching visit of a special embassy from Siam to the United States, and recommend that the appropriation asked by the Secretary of State to suitably defray the expenses of such embassy while in this country be made.

CHESTER A. ARTHUR.

EXECUTIVE MANSION,
Washington, April 18, 1884.

To the House of Representatives:

I transmit herewith a copy of a report of the Secretary of State of the 16th instant, in relation to the final award made by the late French and

American Claims Commission against the United States for the sum of $625,566.35, for the payment of the claims of French citizens against this Government. I recommend that an appropriation of the above sum be made to enable the Government to fulfill its obligations under the treaty of January 15, 1880, between this country and France.

CHESTER A. ARTHUR.

EXECUTIVE MANSION,
Washington, April 18, 1884.

To the Senate and House of Representatives:

I transmit herewith a communication from the Secretary of State, dated the 16th instant, respecting the approaching international conference at Washington, D. C., for the purpose of fixing upon a meridian proper to be employed as a common zero of longitude and standard of time reckoning throughout the globe, and recommend that the sum of $10,000 be appropriated to enable the Secretary of State to meet the expenses of the same.

CHESTER A. ARTHUR.

EXECUTIVE MANSION,
Washington, April 18, 1884.

To the Senate of the United States:

In response to the resolution of the Senate of the 5th of December last, respecting the execution by the United States of the ninth article of the treaty of 1819 with Spain, I transmit herewith a report of the Secretary of State and its accompanying papers.

CHESTER A. ARTHUR.

EXECUTIVE MANSION,
Washington, April 22, 1884.

To the Senate of the United States:

I transmit herewith a report of the Secretary of State, in response to a resolution of the Senate of February 29, 1884, requesting information concerning the respective average production, consumption, exportation, and importation of wheat, rye, corn, and cotton in foreign countries, together with statistics showing the production and surplus or deficiency in the crops of the past two years in each of such countries, an estimate of the probable requirements of such products from the United States to meet the wants of these countries before the crops of the coming crop year are ready for market, and other available information concerning the questions to which the resolution refers.

CHESTER A. ARTHUR.

EXECUTIVE MANSION,
Washington, April 24, 1884.

To the House of Representatives:

I transmit herewith, in answer to a resolution of the House of Representatives of the 21st instant, a report of the Secretary of State, with the accompanying papers, in relation to the threatened confiscation of the American college at Rome by the Italian Government.

CHESTER A. ARTHUR.

EXECUTIVE MANSION,
Washington, April 28, 1884.

To the House of Representatives:

I transmit herewith a report of the Secretary of State, in relation to the bill for the support of the diplomatic and consular services.

CHESTER A. ARTHUR.

EXECUTIVE MANSION,
Washington, May 3, 1884.

To the House of Representatives:

I transmit herewith, for your consideration, a communication from the Secretary of State, recommending the appropriation of the sum of $22,500, or so much thereof as may be necessary, to meet the proper obligations of the Government on account of the courteous services of the various umpires of the late American-Spanish Commission.

CHESTER A. ARTHUR.

EXECUTIVE MANSION,
Washington, May 6, 1884.

To the Senate of the United States:

In answer to the resolution of the Senate of March 12, 1884, requesting to be furnished with a copy of correspondence between this Government and that of China respecting the Ward claims and the claim of Charles E. Hill, I herewith submit a letter of the Secretary of State, together with its accompanying papers.

CHESTER A. ARTHUR.

EXECUTIVE MANSION,
Washington, May 6, 1884.

To the Senate and House of Representatives:

I transmit herewith, for the information of Congress, a communication from the Secretary of the Interior, submitting a copy of the report of the Utah Commission.

CHESTER A. ARTHUR.

EXECUTIVE MANSION,
Washington, May 6, 1884.

To the Senate and House of Representatives:

I transmit herewith, for the information of Congress, a copy of the preliminary report of the board of management of the World's Industrial and Cotton Centennial Exposition, showing their operations and containing observations upon other matters concerning the project deemed of importance.

CHESTER A. ARTHUR.

EXECUTIVE MANSION, *May 6, 1884.*

To the House of Representatives:

In answer to that part of the resolution of the House of Representatives of the 17th of January last respecting the question of boundaries between the Republics of Mexico and Guatemala, I transmit herewith the report of the Secretary of State and its accompanying papers.

CHESTER A. ARTHUR.

EXECUTIVE MANSION,
Washington, May 12, 1884.

To the House of Representatives:

I transmit herewith, in answer to the resolution of the House of Representatives of the 6th of February last, a communication from the Secretary of State, respecting the extradition of criminals under the treaty of 1842 with Great Britain.

CHESTER A. ARTHUR.

EXECUTIVE MANSION,
Washington, May 12, 1884.

To the House of Representatives:

I transmit herewith a communication from the Secretary of State, transmitting a draft of a resolution providing for the presentation of a testimonial to Mr. E. L. Oxenham, British consul at Chin-Kiang, in acknowledgment of services rendered the United States.

CHESTER A. ARTHUR.

EXECUTIVE MANSION,
Washington, May 14, 1884.

To the Senate and House of Representatives:

I transmit herewith a communication from the Secretary of State of the 14th instant, with accompanying papers, relative to the necessity of an appropriation by Congress to enable this Government to execute the provisions of the convention between the United States and Mexico of

July 29, 1882, for the relocation of the monuments marking the boundary line between the two countries, and recommend that the amount asked, $224,556.75, be immediately provided.

CHESTER A. ARTHUR.

EXECUTIVE MANSION,
Washington, May 15, 1884.

To the Senate:

I transmit herewith to the Senate, for consideration with a view to advising and consenting thereto, an agreement, signed May 14, 1884, between the Secretary of State and the minister plenipotentiary of Siam, for the regulation of the liquor traffic in Siam when citizens of the United States engage in the importation or sale of liquors there.

CHESTER A. ARTHUR.

EXECUTIVE MANSION, *May 19, 1884.*

To the House of Representatives:

I transmit herewith, for such action as is deemed proper, a communication from the Secretary of State, recommending an additional appropriation of $6,000 for the construction of a wharf and roadway as a means of approach to the monument to be erected at Wakefield, Westmoreland County, Va., to mark the birthplace of George Washington.

I commend the matter to your favorable attention.

CHESTER A. ARTHUR.

EXECUTIVE MANSION, *May 19, 1884.*

To the House of Representatives:

I transmit herewith a report from the Secretary of State, with accompanying copies of correspondence, in further response to the resolution of the House of Representatives of January 16, 1884, respecting the arrest and imprisonment of John E. Wheelock in Venezuela in 1879.

CHESTER A. ARTHUR.

EXECUTIVE MANSION, *May 29, 1884.*

To the House of Representatives:

I transmit herewith, for such action as is deemed proper, a communication from the Secretary of State, accompanied by several inclosures, in which he recommends an appropriation for rewarding the services of the Osette Indians in rescuing and caring for the crew of the American steamer *Umatilla*, which vessel was wrecked in February last near the coast of Vancouvers Island.

CHESTER A. ARTHUR.

EXECUTIVE MANSION,
Washington, May 29, 1884.

To the Senate of the United States:

I transmit herewith, in response to the resolution of the Senate of March 10 last, a report from the Secretary of State, with accompanying papers, in regard to the claim of Edward H. Ladd against the Government of Colombia.

CHESTER A. ARTHUR.

EXECUTIVE MANSION,
Washington, June 9, 1884.

To the Senate and House of Representatives:

I transmit herewith, for the consideration of Congress, a letter and its accompanying estimate, submitted by the board charged with preparing a departmental exhibit for the World's Industrial and Cotton Centennial Exposition to be held at New Orleans, beginning December 1, 1884. This board was appointed by Executive order of May 13, 1884,* and is composed of representatives of the several Executive Departments, the Department of Agriculture, and the Smithsonian Institution. It is charged with the important and responsible duty of making arrangements for a complete and harmonious collection of the articles and materials deemed desirable to place on exhibition, in illustration of the resources of the country, its methods of governmental administration, and its means of offense and defense.

The board submits an estimate calling for an appropriation of $588,000 to accomplish the desired end. That amount is distributed among the Departments as shown in the table. The War, Navy, and Interior Departments call for the largest share, representing as they do the national defenses by land and sea, the progress of naval architecture and ordnance, the geological survey and mineral wealth of the Territories, the treatment of the Indians, and the education of the masses, all of which admit of varied and instructive exhibits. The Smithsonian Institution, having under its general care the National Museum and the Fish Commission, is prepared to make a display second in interest to none of modern days. The remaining Departments can present instructive and interesting exhibits, which will attract popular attention and convey an idea of their extensively ramified duties and of the many points where they beneficially affect the life of the people as a nation and as individuals.

The exhibit of the Government at the Centennial Exhibition held at Philadelphia in 1876 was admitted to be one of the most attractive features of that great national undertaking and a valuable addition to it. From men of intelligence and scientific attainments, at home and abroad, it received the highest encomiums, showing the interest it awakened

* See pp. 4817–4818.

among those whose lives are given to the improvement of the social and material condition of the people.

The reproduction of such a display now on a more extensive plan is rendered possible by the advancement of science and invention during the eight years that have passed since the Philadelphia exhibit was collected.

The importance, purposes, and benefits of the New Orleans Exhibition are continental in their scope. Standing at the threshold of the almost unopened markets of Spanish and Portuguese America, New Orleans is a natural gateway to their trade, and the exhibition offers to the people of Mexico and Central and South America an adequate knowledge of our farming implements, metal manufactures, cotton and woolen goods, and the like necessities of existence, in respect to which those countries are either deficient or supplied to a limited extent. The breaking down of the barriers which still separate us from the Republics of America whose productions so entirely complement our own will aid greatly in removing the disparity of commercial intercourse under which less than 10 per cent of our exports go to American countries.

I trust that Congress will realize the urgency of this recommendation and make its appropriation immediately available, so that the board may lose no time in undertaking the extensive preparations necessary to spread a more intimate knowledge of our Government institutions and national resources among the people of our country and of neighboring states in a way to command the respect due it in the family of nations.

CHESTER A. ARTHUR.

EXECUTIVE MANSION,
Washington, June 9, 1884.

To the Senate of the United States:

I transmit herewith, for consideration by the Senate and appropriate action thereon, a report of the Secretary of State, communicating the proposal of the King of Hawaii that the duration of the existing reciprocity treaty with the United States be extended for a further definite period of seven years.

The treaty having been heretofore under consideration by your honorable body, I deem it fitting to consult the Senate in the matter before directing the negotiations to proceed.

CHESTER A. ARTHUR.

EXECUTIVE MANSION,
Washington, June 11, 1884.

To the House of Representatives:

In compliance with the resolution of the House of Representatives of the 10th instant, I return House bill No. 2344, entitled "An act for the relief of Melissa G. Polar."

CHESTER A. ARTHUR.

EXECUTIVE MANSION,
Washington, June 11, 1884.

To the House of Representatives:

I transmit herewith to the House of Representatives, in response to a resolution of that body of the 21st of April last, a copy of the material correspondence on file in the Department of State relative to the claim of W. J. Hale against the Argentine Republic, and a list of the papers.

CHESTER A. ARTHUR.

EXECUTIVE MANSION,
Washington, June 12, 1884.

To the Senate of the United States:

I transmit herewith, in response to a resolution of the Senate dated May 2, 1884, the following report of the Secretary of State, with an accompanying paper, relative to the latest law of the Mexican Republic creating or modifying the *zona libre* in relation to importations of merchandise.

CHESTER A. ARTHUR.

EXECUTIVE MANSION,
Washington, June 13, 1884.

To the Senate:

I transmit to the Senate, for its consideration with a view to ratification, a convention signed on the 11th instant, supplementary to the extradition convention concluded between the United States and Italy on the 23d of March, 1868.

CHESTER A. ARTHUR.

EXECUTIVE MANSION,
Washington, June 19, 1884.

To the House of Representatives:

I transmit herewith, in answer to the resolution of the House of Representatives of the 31st of March last, a communication from the Secretary of State, with accompanying papers, concerning the rent of consular premises in China.

CHESTER A. ARTHUR.

EXECUTIVE MANSION, *June 21, 1884.*

To the Senate and House of Representatives:

I have permitted House bill No. 4689, entitled "An act for the relief of Eliza W. Patterson," to become a law by withholding action upon it for ten days after it was presented to me.

The affairs and interests of the District of Columbia are committed to Congress as its legislature. I do not question the constitutional right of Congress to pass a law relieving the family of an officer, in view of the services he had rendered his country, from the burdens of taxation, but I submit to Congress that this just gift of the nation to the family of such faithful officer should come from the National Treasury rather than from that of this District, and I therefore recommend that an appropriation be made to reimburse the District for the amount of taxes which would have been due to it had this act not become a law.

CHESTER A. ARTHUR.

EXECUTIVE MANSION,
Washington, June 24, 1884.

To the House of Representatives:

In answer to a resolution of the House of Representatives of the 7th instant, making an inquiry regarding the expenditure of moneys appropriated by Congress to meet the expenses of the French and American Claims Commission, I transmit herewith a report of the Secretary of State upon the subject.

CHESTER A. ARTHUR.

EXECUTIVE MANSION, *June 28, 1884.*

To the Senate and House of Representatives:

I transmit herewith a communication from the Secretary of the Interior, calling attention to certain omissions, etc., in the act (H. R. 1340) entitled "An act to establish a Bureau of Labor Statistics," and invite the attention of the Congress to the same.

CHESTER A. ARTHUR.

EXECUTIVE MANSION,
Washington, June 30, 1884.

To the House of Representatives:

I transmit herewith, in compliance with resolutions of the House of Representatives respectively dated March 22 and April 19, 1884, a report from the Secretary of State, communicating information in regard to moneys received from Venezuela under the treaty of April 25, 1866, and their distribution to holders of awards by the Department of State.

CHESTER A. ARTHUR.

EXECUTIVE MANSION,
Washington, July 3, 1884.

To the Senate of the United States:

I transmit herewith, in response to a resolution of the Senate of the 11th of February last, a report of the Secretary of State, relative to the papers on file in the Department of State touching the unsettled claims of citizens of the United States against France for spoliations prior to July 31, 1801.

CHESTER A. ARTHUR.

EXECUTIVE MANSION, *July 7, 1884.*

To the House of Representatives:

In compliance with the concurrent resolution of the Senate and House of Representatives of the 5th instant, I return herewith House bill 6770, entitled "An act making appropriations for the consular and diplomatic service of the Government for the fiscal year ending June 30, 1885, and for other purposes."

CHESTER A. ARTHUR.

VETO MESSAGE.

EXECUTIVE MANSION, *July 2, 1884.*

To the House of Representatives:

After careful consideration of the bill entitled "An act for the relief of Fitz John Porter," I herewith return it with my objections to that House of Congress in which it originated. Its enacting clause is in terms following:

That the President be, and he is hereby, authorized to nominate and, by and with the advice and consent of the Senate, to appoint Fitz John Porter, late a major-general of the United States Volunteers and a brevet brigadier-general and colonel of the Army, to the position of colonel in the Army of the United States, of the same grade and rank held by him at the time of his dismissal from the Army by sentence of court-martial promulgated January 27, 1863. * * *

It is apparent that should this bill become a law it will create a new office which can be filled by the appointment of the particular individual whom it specifies, and can not be filled otherwise; or it may be said with perhaps greater precision of statement that it will create a new office upon condition that the particular person designated shall be chosen to fill it. Such an act, as it seems to me, is either unnecessary and ineffective or it involves an encroachment by the legislative branch of the Government upon the authority of the Executive. As the Congress has no power under the Constitution to nominate or appoint an officer and can not lawfully impose upon the President the duty of nominating or appointing to office any particular individual of its own selection, this bill, if it can fairly be construed as requiring the President to make the nomination and, by and with the advice and consent of the Senate, the appointment which it authorizes, is in manifest violation of the Constitution. If such be not its just interpretation, it must be regarded as a mere enactment of advice and counsel, which lacks in the very nature of things the force of positive law and can serve no useful purpose upon the statute books.

There are other causes that deter me from giving this bill the sanction of my approval. The judgment of the court-martial by which more than twenty years since General Fitz John Porter was tried and convicted was pronounced by a tribunal composed of nine general officers of distinguished character and ability. Its investigation of the charges of which it found the accused guilty was thorough and conscientious, and its findings and sentence were in due course of law approved by Abraham

Lincoln, then President of the United States. Its legal competency, its jurisdiction of the accused and of the subject of the accusation, and the substantial regularity of all of its proceedings are matters which have never been brought into question. Its judgment, therefore, is final and conclusive in its character.

The Supreme Court of the United States has recently declared that a court-martial such as this was is the organism provided by law and clothed with the duty of administering justice in this class of cases. Its judgments, when approved, rest on the same basis and are surrounded by the same considerations which give conclusiveness to the judgments of other legal tribunals, including as well the lowest as the highest. It follows, accordingly, that when a lawfully constituted court-martial has duly declared its findings and its sentence and the same have been duly approved neither the President nor the Congress has any power to set them aside. The existence of such power is not openly asserted, nor perhaps is it necessarily implied, in the provisions of the bill which is before me, but when its enacting clauses are read in the light of the recitations of its preamble it will be seen that it seeks in effect the practical annulment of the findings and the sentence of a competent court-martial.

A conclusion at variance with these findings has been reached after investigation by a board consisting of three officers of the Army. This board was not created in pursuance of any statutory authority and was powerless to compel the attendance of witnesses or to pronounce a judgment which could have been lawfully enforced. The officers who constituted it, in their report to the Secretary of War, dated March 19, 1879, state that in their opinion—

Justice requires * * * such action as may be necessary to annul and set aside the findings and sentence of the court-martial in the case of Major-General Fitz John Porter and to restore him to the positions of which that sentence deprived him, such restoration to take effect from the date of his dismissal from the service.

The provisions of the bill now under consideration are avowedly based on the assumption that the findings of the court-martial have been discovered to be erroneous; but it will be borne in mind that the investigation which is claimed to have resulted in this discovery was made many years after the events to which that evidence related and under circumstances that made it impossible to reproduce the evidence on which they were based.

It seems to me that the proposed legislation would establish a dangerous precedent, calculated to imperil in no small measure the binding force and effect of the judgments of the various tribunals established under our Constitution and laws.

I have already, in the exercise of the pardoning power with which the President is vested by the Constitution, remitted the continuing penalty which had made it impossible for Fitz John Porter to hold any office of trust or profit under the Government of the United States; but I am unwilling to give my sanction to any legislation which shall practically annul and set at naught the solemn and deliberate conclusions of the tribunal by which he was convicted and of the President by whom its findings were examined and approved.

CHESTER A. ARTHUR.

PROCLAMATIONS.

BY THE PRESIDENT OF THE UNITED STATES OF AMERICA.

A PROCLAMATION.

Whereas both Houses of Congress did on the 20th instant request the commemoration, on the 23d instant, of the one hundredth anniversary of the surrender by George Washington, at Annapolis, of his commission as Commander in Chief of the patriot forces of America; and

Whereas it is fitting that this memorable act, which not only signalized the termination of the heroic struggle of seven years for independence, but also manifested Washington's devotion to the great principle that ours is a civic government of and by the people, should be generally observed throughout the United States:

Now, therefore, I, Chester A. Arthur, President of the United States, do hereby recommend that either by appropriate exercises in connection with the religious services of the 23d instant or by such public observances as may be deemed proper on Monday, the 24th instant, this signal event in the history of American liberty be commemorated; and further, I hereby direct that at 12 o'clock noon on Monday next the national salute be fired from all the forts throughout the country.

In witness whereof I have hereunto set my hand and caused the seal of the United States to be affixed.

[SEAL.]   Done this 21st day of December, A. D. 1883, and of the Independence of the United States the one hundred and eighth.

CHESTER A. ARTHUR

By the President:
  FREDK. T. FRELINGHUYSEN,
        Secretary of State.

BY THE PRESIDENT OF THE UNITED STATES OF AMERICA.

A PROCLAMATION.

Whereas by a memorandum of an agreement executed at Madrid on the 13th day of February, A. D. 1884, by and between the duly authorized agents and representatives of the Government of the United States of America and of the Government of His Majesty the King of Spain, satisfactory evidence has been given to me that the Government of that country has abolished the discriminating customs duty heretofore imposed upon the products of and articles proceeding from the United States of America imported into the islands of Cuba and Puerto Rico, said abolition to take effect on and after the 1st day of March next:

Now, therefore, I, Chester A. Arthur, President of the United States of America, by virtue of the authority vested in me by section 4228 of the Revised Statutes, do hereby declare and proclaim that on and after the said 1st day of March next, so long as the products of and articles proceeding from the United States imported into the islands of Cuba and Puerto Rico shall be exempt from discriminating customs duties, any such duties on the products of and articles proceeding from Cuba and Puerto Rico under the Spanish flag shall be suspended and discontinued.

In witness whereof I have hereunto set my hand and caused the seal of the United States to be affixed.

[SEAL.]   Done at the city of Washington, this 14th day of February, A. D. 1884, and of the Independence of the United States the one hundred and eighth.

CHESTER A. ARTHUR.

By the President:

FREDK. T. FRELINGHUYSEN, *Secretary of State.*

BY THE PRESIDENT OF THE UNITED STATES OF AMERICA.

A PROCLAMATION.

Whereas it is alleged that certain persons have within the territory and jurisdiction of the United States begun and set on foot preparations for an organized and forcible possession of and settlement upon the lands of what is known as the Oklahoma lands, in the Indian Territory, which Territory is designated, recognized, and described by the treaties and laws of the United States and by the executive authorities as Indian country, and as such is subject to occupation by Indian tribes only; and

Whereas the laws of the United States provide for the removal of all persons residing or being found in said Indian Territory without express permission of the Interior Department:

Now, therefore, for the purpose of properly protecting the interests of the Indian nations and tribes in said Territory, and that settlers may not be induced to go into a country, at great expense to themselves, where they can not be allowed to remain, I, Chester A. Arthur, President of the United States, do admonish and warn all such persons so intending or preparing to remove upon said lands or into said Territory against any attempt to so remove or settle upon any of the lands of said Territory; and I do further warn and notify any and all such persons who do so offend that they will be speedily and immediately removed therefrom by the proper officers of the Interior Department, and, if necessary, the aid and assistance of the military forces of the United States will be invoked to remove all such intruders from the said Indian Territory.

In testimony whereof I have hereunto set my hand and caused the seal of the United States to be affixed.

[SEAL.]   Done at the city of Washington, this 1st day of July, A. D. 1884, and of the Independence of the United States the one hundred and eighth.   CHESTER A. ARTHUR.

By the President:

FREDK. T. FRELINGHUYSEN, *Secretary of State.*

BY THE PRESIDENT OF THE UNITED STATES OF AMERICA.

A PROCLAMATION.

While quarantine regulations are committed to the several States, the General Government has reposed certain powers in the President, to be used at his discretion in preventing a threatened epidemic.

Feeling it my duty, I hereby call upon all persons who under existing systems in the several States are intrusted with the execution of quarantine regulations to be diligent and on the alert in order to prevent the introduction of the pestilence which we all regret to learn has made its appearance in some of the countries of Europe between which and the ports of the United States intercourse is direct and frequent.

I further advise that the cities and towns of the United States, whether on the coast or on the lines of interior communication, by sound sanitary regulations and the promotion of cleanliness, be prepared to resist the power of the disease and to mitigate its severity.

And I further direct the consuls of the United States in the ports where the pestilence has made or may make its appearance to exercise vigilance in carrying out the instructions heretofore given and in communicating to the Government of the United States any information of value relating to the progress or treatment of the disease.

Given under my hand and the seal of the United States, at the city of Washington, this 19th day of July, A. D. 1884, and of the Independence of the United States the one hundred and ninth.

[SEAL.]

CHESTER A. ARTHUR.

By the President:

FREDK. T. FRELINGHUYSEN, *Secretary of State.*

BY THE PRESIDENT OF THE UNITED STATES OF AMERICA.

A PROCLAMATION.

The season is nigh when it is the yearly wont of this people to observe a day appointed for that purpose by the President as an especial occasion for thanksgiving unto God.

Now, therefore, in recognition of this hallowed custom, I, Chester A. Arthur, President of the United States, do hereby designate as such day of general thanksgiving Thursday, the 27th day of this present November.

And I do recommend that throughout the land the people, ceasing from their accustomed occupations, do then keep holiday at their several homes and their several places of worship, and with heart and voice pay reverent acknowledgment to the Giver of All Good for the countless blessings wherewith He hath visited this nation.

In witness whereof I have hereunto set my hand and caused the seal of the United States to be affixed.

[SEAL.]   Done at the city of Washington, this 7th day of November, A. D. 1884, and of the Independence of the United States the one hundred and ninth.   CHESTER A. ARTHUR.

By the President:
    FREDK. T. FRELINGHUYSEN,
        Secretary of State.

EXECUTIVE ORDERS.

In the exercise of the power vested in the President by the Constitution, and by virtue of the seventeen hundred and fifty-third section of the Revised Statutes and of the civil-service act approved January 16, 1883, the following rule for the regulation and improvement of the executive civil service is hereby amended and promulgated, as follows:

RULE XII.

1. Every regular application must be supported by proper certificates of good moral character, health, and physical and mental capacity for doing the public work, the certificates to be in such form and number as the regulations of the Commission shall provide; but no certificate will be received which is inconsistent with the tenth section of the civil-service act.

2. No one shall be entitled to be examined for admission to the classified postal service if under 16 or over 35 years of age, or to the classified customs service or to the classified departmental service if under 18 or over 45 years of age; but no one shall be examined for appointment to any place in the classified customs service, except that of clerk or messenger, who is under 21 years of age; but these limitations of age shall not apply to persons honorably discharged from the military or naval service of the country who are otherwise duly qualified.

Approved, December 5, 1883.   CHESTER A. ARTHUR.

EXECUTIVE MANSION, *December 17, 1883.*

The following-named officers of the Army and Navy will constitute a board to consider an expedition to be sent for the relief of Lieutenant Greely and his party, composing what is known as the "Lady Franklin Bay Expedition," and to recommend to the Secretaries of War and the

Navy, jointly, the steps the board may consider necessary to be taken for the equipment and transportation of the relief expedition, and to suggest such plan for its control and conduct and for the organization of its personnel as may seem to them best adapted to accomplish its purpose:

Brigadier-General William B. Hazen, Chief Signal Officer, United States Army; Captain James A. Greer, United States Navy; Lieutenant-Commander B. H. McCalla, United States Navy; Captain George W. Davis, Fourteenth Infantry, United States Army.

The board will meet in Washington, D. C., on the 20th instant.

CHESTER A. ARTHUR.

In the exercise of the power vested in the President by the Constitution, and by virtue of the seventeen hundred and fifty-third section of the Revised Statutes and of the civil-service act approved January 16, 1883, the following rule and the amendment to Rule XVI for the regulation and improvement of the executive civil service are hereby promulgated:

RULE XXI.

1. No person shall be promoted, without examination under these rules, from any position for which an examination is not required to any position for which an examination is required under the rules; nor shall any person who has passed only a limited examination under clause 4 of Rule VII for the lower classes or grades in the departmental or customs service be promoted within two years after appointment to any position giving a salary of $1,000 or upward without first passing an examination under clause 1 of said rule, and such examination shall not be allowed within the first year after appointment.

2. But a person who has passed the examination under said clause 1 and has accepted a position giving a salary of $900 or less shall have the same right of promotion as if originally appointed to a position giving a salary of $1,000 or more.

3. The Commission may at any time certify for a $900 or any lower place in the classified service any person upon the register who has passed the examination under clause 1 of Rule VII if such person does not object before such certification is made.

II. The following words are added as a fifth clause at the end of Rule XVI, viz:

5. Any person appointed to or employed in any part of the classified service, after due certification for the same under these rules, who shall be dismissed or separated therefrom without fault or delinquency on his part may be reappointed or reemployed in the same part or grade of such service at the same office, within eight months next following such dismissal or separation, without further examination.

III. It is further ordered that the rule heretofore designated XXI be hereafter designated XXII, and XXII as Rule XXIII.

Approved, January 18, 1884.

CHESTER A. ARTHUR

EXECUTIVE MANSION, *February 8, 1884.*

General William T. Sherman, General of the Army, having this day reached the age of 64 years, is, in accordance with law, placed upon the retired list of the Army without reduction in his current pay and allowances.

The announcement of the severance from the command of the Army of one who has been for so many years its distinguished chief can but awaken in the minds, not only of the Army, but of the people of the United States, mingled emotions of regret and gratitude — regret at the withdrawal from active military service of an officer whose lofty sense of duty has been a model for all soldiers since he first entered the Army in July, 1840, and gratitude, freshly awakened, for the services, of incalculable value, rendered by him in the war for the Union, which his great military genius and daring did so much to end.

The President deems this a fitting occasion to give expression in this manner to the gratitude felt toward General Sherman by his fellow-citizens, and to the hope that Providence may grant him many years of health and happiness in the relief from the active duties of his profession.

CHESTER A. ARTHUR.

DEPARTMENT OF JUSTICE,
Washington, March 12, 1884.

To the District Attorneys and Marshals of the United States:

By direction of the President, I have to inform you it is reported that certain persons are aiding in the prosecution of heinous crimes by shipping to foreign ports explosives dangerous in the highest degree to life and property. No proof has been adduced that this rumor is founded upon fact, and the President can not believe its truth. The honor of this nation, however, requires that it should not be open to the imputation, unfounded though it be, of the slightest appearance of tolerating such crimes, whether to be committed against our people or those of other countries.

Your attention is therefore called to sections 5353, 5354, 5355, 4278, and 4279 of the Revised Statutes of the United States, which regulate the shipment of explosives and the punishment of those who infringe their provisions; and you are instructed to be diligent in your efforts to prevent the offenses described and to detect and prosecute those who have or may commit them.

Very respectfully,

BENJAMIN HARRIS BREWSTER,
Attorney-General.

BY THE PRESIDENT OF THE UNITED STATES.

EXECUTIVE ORDER.

Whereas it has been brought to the notice of the President of the United States that in the World's Industrial and Cotton Centennial Exhibition of Arts, Manufactures, and Products of the Soil and Mines, to be held in the city of New Orleans, commencing December 1, 1884, for the purpose of celebrating the one hundredth anniversary of the production, manufacture, and commerce of cotton, it is desirable that from the Executive Departments of the Government of the United States in which there may be articles suitable for the purpose intended there should appear such articles and materials as will, when presented in a collective exhibition, illustrate the functions and administrative faculties of the Government in time of peace and its resources as a war power, and thereby serve to demonstrate the nature of our institutions and their adaptation to the wants of the people:

Now, for the purpose of securing a complete and harmonious arrangement of the articles and materials designed to be exhibited from the Executive Departments of the Government, it is ordered that a board, to be composed of one person to be named by the head of each of the Executive Departments which may have articles and materials to be exhibited, and also of one person to be named in behalf of the Smithsonian Institution, and one to be named in behalf of the Department of Agriculture, and one to be named in behalf of the Bureau of Education, be charged with the preparation, arrangement, and safe-keeping of such articles and materials as the heads of the several Departments and the Commissioner of Agriculture, the Director of the Smithsonian Institution, and the Commissioner of Education may respectively decide shall be embraced in the collection; that one of the persons thus named, to be designated by the President, shall be chairman of such board, and that the board appoint from their number such other officers as they may think necessary; and that the said board, when organized, shall be authorized, under the direction of the President, to confer with the executive officers of the World's Industrial Cotton Centennial Exhibition in relation to such matters connected with the subject as may pertain to the respective Departments having articles and materials on exhibition, and that the names of the persons thus selected by the heads of the several Departments, the Commissioner of Agriculture, the Director of the Smithsonian Institution, and the Commissioner of Education shall be submitted to the President for designation.

Done at the city of Washington, this 9th day of April, 1884, and of the Independence of the United States the one hundred and eighth.

CHESTER A. ARTHUR.

By the President:
FREDK. T. FRELINGHUYSEN,
Secretary of State.

In the exercise of the power vested in the President by the Constitution and by virtue of the seventeen hundred and fifty-third section of the Revised Statutes and of the civil-service act approved January 16, 1883, the following rules for the regulation and improvement of the executive civil service are amended as stated below, and are hereby promulgated:

1. Rule XI is amended by adding thereto a second clause, as follows:

2. The Commission may by regulations, subject to change at any time by the President, declare the kind and measure of ill health, physical incapacity, misrepresentation, and bad faith which may properly exclude any person from the right of examination, grading, or certification under these rules. It may also provide for medical certificates of physical capacity in the proper cases, and for the appropriate certification of persons so defective in sight, speech, hearing, or otherwise as to be apparently disqualified for some of the duties of the part of the service which they seek to enter.

2. The second clause of Rule XII is amended by substituting for the first line and the second line thereof down to the word "age" therein (as printed in the annual report of the Commission) the following words:

No one shall be entitled to be examined for admission to the classified postal service if under 16 or over 35 years of age, excepting messengers, stampers, and other junior assistants, who must not be under 14 years of age.

3. Rule XXI, as printed in said report, is amended by substituting for the first two lines and the third line down to the word "rules" therein the following words:

No person, unless excepted under Rule XIX, shall be admitted into the classified civil service from any place not within said service without an examination and certification under the rules.

Approved, April 23, 1884.   CHESTER A. ARTHUR.

In the exercise of the power vested in the President by the Constitution, and by virtue of the seventeen hundred and fifty-third section of the Revised Statutes and of the civil-service act approved January 16, 1883, the following rule for the regulation and improvement of the executive civil service is amended as stated below, and is hereby promulgated:

Rule XI is amended by striking out the last sentence of said rule as printed in the annual report of the Commission and inserting in place thereof the following, namely:

No person under enlistment in the Army or Navy of the United States shall be examined under these rules except for some place in the Department under which he is enlisted requiring special qualifications, and with the consent in writing of the head of such Department.

Approved, April 23, 1884.   CHESTER A. ARTHUR.

BY THE PRESIDENT OF THE UNITED STATES.

EXECUTIVE ORDER.

In conformity with the Executive order directing the organization of a board, to be composed of one person to be named by the head of each of the Executive Departments which may have articles and materials to be exhibited at the World's Industrial and Cotton Centennial Exhibition, I hereby direct the persons who have been so designated, viz, Major and Brevet Lieutenant-Colonel Stephen C. Lyford, United States Army, of the War Department, president of the board; Charles S. Hill, of the Department of State; Lieutenant B. H. Buckingham, United States Navy, of the Navy Department; William F. McLennan, of the Treasury Department; Abraham D. Hazen, Assistant Postmaster-General; Benjamin Butterworth, of the Interior Department; Cecil Clay, of the Department of Justice; William Saunders, of the Agricultural Department; G. Brown Goode, of the Smithsonian Institution; Lyndon A. Smith, of the Bureau of Education, Interior Department, to assemble at the Department of State, in the city of Washington, at noon on the 17th day of May, 1884, and then and there to organize said board; and said board when so organized shall immediately proceed to the discharge of its duties.

I also designate W. A. De Caindry as the secretary of said board.

Done at the city of Washington, this 13th day of May, 1884, and of the Independence of the United States the one hundred and eighth.

CHESTER A. ARTHUR.

By the President:
FREDK. T. FRELINGHUYSEN,
Secretary of State.

EXECUTIVE MANSION,
Washington, May 26, 1884.

Under the provisions of section 4 of the act approved March 3, 1883, it is hereby ordered that the several Executive Departments, the Department of Agriculture, and the Government Printing Office be closed on Friday, the 30th instant, to enable the employees to participate in the decoration of the graves of the soldiers who fell during the rebellion.

CHESTER A. ARTHUR.

In the exercise of the power vested in the President by the Constitution, and by virtue of the seventeen hundred and fifty-third section of the Revised Statutes and of the civil-service act approved January 16, 1883, the following special rule for the regulation and improvement of the executive civil service is hereby promulgated:

SPECIAL RULE.

Any person who was employed on or before the 16th day of January, 1883, in any Executive Department at Washington in a position not included in the classified service in said Department, but who was at that date exclusively engaged in the duties of a clerk or copyist, and who has since been continuously so engaged, may, in the discretion of the head of the Department, be treated as within the classified service in the Department in a grade corresponding to such duties, provided such person has either already passed an examination under the civil-service rules or shall pass an appropriate competitive or noncompetitive examination thereunder at a grade of 65 per cent or upward.

Approved, June 12, 1884.

CHESTER A. ARTHUR.

EXECUTIVE MANSION, *July 8, 1884.*

In order to carry out the provisions of that portion of the act entitled "An act making appropriations for sundry civil expenses of the Government for the fiscal year ending June 30, 1885, and for other purposes," approved July 7, 1884, which contemplates the participation of the several Executive Departments, the Department of Agriculture, and the Smithsonian Institution in the World's Industrial and Cotton Centennial Exposition of 1884–85, the board heretofore appointed by Executive order to take charge of the articles and materials to be exhibited by these Departments, the Department of Agriculture, and the Smithsonian Institution is hereby continued under the following regulations and distribution of duties, viz:

The funds appropriated for such participation will be drawn from the Treasury upon the requisition of the president of the board, and will be disbursed and accounted for as are other public moneys under the existing laws and regulations relating to disbursing officers.

An officer of the Army will be detailed by the Secretary of War and an officer of the Navy will be detailed by the Secretary of the Navy to report to the president of the board for duty as disbursing officers of the board.

The representatives of the several Executive Departments, the representative of the Department of Agriculture, and the representative of the Smithsonian Institution will have charge of the matter pertaining to their respective Departments, subject to the general advisement of the board, and all bills will be paid by the disbursing officers upon vouchers certified by such representatives and countersigned by the president of the board.

The disbursing officers will render, through the president of the board, monthly accounts current of all advances and disbursements by them to the First Auditor of the Treasury for audit and settlement in the same manner as are other accounts of disbursing officers of the Government.

Each representative will be held responsible to the head of his respective Department for all public property of the United States furnished by the head of such Department or otherwise coming to his hands for the purposes of the exposition, and will render proper accounts of the same to such head of Department until the property is returned.

CHESTER A. ARTHUR.

EXECUTIVE MANSION, *July 10, 1884.*

The participation of the several Executive Departments, the Department of Agriculture, and the Smithsonian Institution in the Cincinnati

Industrial Exposition at Cincinnati, Ohio, and the Southern Exposition at Louisville, Ky., as contemplated by the "act making appropriations for sundry civil expenses of the Government for the fiscal year ending June 30, 1885, and for other purposes," is hereby placed under the management of the board referred to in Executive order of July 8, 1884, relating to the participation of said Departments and Institution in the World's Industrial and Cotton Centennial Exposition of 1884–85, the provisions of which order being hereby extended to embrace said Cincinnati and Louisville expositions.

CHESTER A. ARTHUR.

EXECUTIVE MANSION, *July 16, 1884.*

No appropriation having been specifically made for the participation of the Bureau of Education, Interior Department, in the World's Industrial and Cotton Centennial Exposition at New Orleans, La., the Industrial Exposition, Cincinnati, Ohio, or the Southern Exposition, Louisville, Ky., the representative on behalf of that Bureau in the board appointed by Executive order of May 13, 1884,* is relieved from further duty as a member of the board, and the display of that Bureau will be made as a part of the exhibit of the Interior Department out of the moneys appropriated for the participation of that Department in said expositions.

CHESTER A. ARTHUR.

In the exercise of the power vested in the President by the Constitution, and by virtue of the seventeen hundred and fifty-third section of the Revised Statutes and of the civil-service act approved January 16, 1883, the following special rule for the regulation and improvement of the executive civil service is hereby promulgated:

SPECIAL RULE.

The names of all persons who shall have successfully passed their examination under the civil-service rules previous to July 16, 1884, may remain on the register of persons eligible for appointment two years from the date of their respective registrations, unless sooner appointed.

Approved, July 18, 1884.

CHESTER A. ARTHUR.

In the exercise of the power vested in the President by the Constitution, and by virtue of the seventeen hundred and fifty-third section of the Revised Statutes and of the civil-service act approved January 16, 1883, the following special rule for the regulation and improvement of the executive civil service is hereby promulgated:

SPECIAL RULE NO. 3.

Appointments to the 150 places in the Pension Office provided to be filled by the act of July 7, 1884, except so far as they may be filled by promotions, must be

* See pp. 4817–4818.

separately apportioned by the appointing power in as near conformity to the second section of the act of January 16, 1883, as the need of filling them promptly and the residence and qualifications of the applicants will permit.

Approved, July 22, 1884.

CHESTER A. ARTHUR.

DEPARTMENT OF STATE,
Washington, September 5, 1884.

SIR:* With deep regret I announce to you that the Hon. Charles J. Folger, Secretary of the Treasury of the United States, yesterday died at his home in Geneva, State of New York.

Thus has closed the life of a distinguished and respected citizen, who by his services as an executive officer of the United States and as a legislator and judge of his own State won the esteem and regard of his fellow-countrymen.

The President directs that all Departments of the executive branch of the Government and the offices subordinate to them shall manifest due honor for the memory of this eminent citizen, in a manner consonant with the dignity of the office thus made vacant and with the upright character of him who held it.

To this end the President directs that the Treasury Department and its dependencies in this capital shall be draped in mourning for a period of thirty days, the several Executive Departments shall be closed on the day of the funeral of the deceased, and that on all public buildings of the Government throughout the United States the national flag shall be draped in mourning and displayed at half-mast.

I have the honor to be, sir, your obedient servant,

FREDK. T. FRELINGHUYSEN.

In the exercise of the power vested in the President by the Constitution, and by virtue of the seventeen hundred and fifty-third section of the Revised Statutes and of the civil-service act approved January 16, 1883, the following rule for the regulation and improvement of the executive civil service is hereby amended and promulgated:

RULE XIX.

There are excepted from examination the following: (1) The confidential clerk or secretary of any head of Department or office; (2) cashiers of collectors; (3) cashiers of postmasters; (4) superintendents of money-order divisions in post-offices; (5) the direct custodians of money for whose fidelity another officer is under official bond and disbursing officers having the custody of money who give bonds, but these exceptions shall not extend to any official below the grade of assistant cashier or teller; (6) persons employed exclusively in the secret service of the Government, or as translators or interpreters or stenographers; (7) persons whose employment is exclusively professional; (8) chief clerks, deputy collectors, and superintendents, or chiefs

* Addressed to the heads of the Executive Departments, etc.

of divisions and bureaus. But no person so excepted shall be either transferred, appointed, or promoted, unless to some excepted place, without an examination under the Commission. Promotions may be made without examination in offices where examinations for promotion are not now held until rules on this subject shall be promulgated.

Approved, November 10, 1884.   CHESTER A. ARTHUR.

FOURTH ANNUAL MESSAGE.

WASHINGTON, *December 1, 1884.*

To the Congress of the United States:

Since the close of your last session the American people, in the exercise of their highest right of suffrage, have chosen their Chief Magistrate for the four years ensuing.

When it is remembered that at no period in the country's history has the long political contest which customarily precedes the day of the national election been waged with greater fervor and intensity, it is a subject of general congratulation that after the controversy at the polls was over, and while the slight preponderance by which the issue had been determined was as yet unascertained, the public peace suffered no disturbance, but the people everywhere patiently and quietly awaited the result.

Nothing could more strikingly illustrate the temper of the American citizen, his love of order, and his loyalty to law. Nothing could more signally demonstrate the strength and wisdom of our political institutions.

Eight years have passed since a controversy concerning the result of a national election sharply called the attention of the Congress to the necessity of providing more precise and definite regulations for counting the electoral vote.

It is of the gravest importance that this question be solved before conflicting claims to the Presidency shall again distract the country, and I am persuaded that by the people at large any of the measures of relief thus far proposed would be preferred to continued inaction.

Our relations with all foreign powers continue to be amicable.

With Belgium a convention has been signed whereby the scope of present treaties has been so enlarged as to secure to citizens of either country within the jurisdiction of the other equal rights and privileges in the acquisition and alienation of property. A trade-marks treaty has also been concluded.

The war between Chile and Peru is at an end. For the arbitration of the claims of American citizens who during its continuance suffered through the acts of the Chilean authorities a convention will soon be negotiated.

The state of hostilities between France and China continues to be an embarrassing feature of our Eastern relations. The Chinese Government has promptly adjusted and paid the claims of American citizens whose property was destroyed in the recent riots at Canton. I renew the recommendation of my last annual message, that the Canton indemnity fund be returned to China.

The true interpretation of the recent treaty with that country permitting the restriction of Chinese immigration is likely to be again the subject of your deliberations. It may be seriously questioned whether the statute passed at the last session does not violate the treaty rights of certain Chinese who left this country with return certificates valid under the old law, and who now seem to be debarred from relanding for lack of the certificates required by the new.

The recent purchase by citizens of the United States of a large trading fleet heretofore under the Chinese flag has considerably enhanced our commercial importance in the East. In view of the large number of vessels built or purchased by American citizens in other countries and exclusively employed in legitimate traffic between foreign ports under the recognized protection of our flag, it might be well to provide a uniform rule for their registration and documentation, so that the *bona fide* property rights of our citizens therein shall be duly evidenced and properly guarded.

Pursuant to the advice of the Senate at the last session, I recognized the flag of the International Association of the Kongo as that of a friendly government, avoiding in so doing any prejudgment of conflicting territorial claims in that region. Subsequently, in execution of the expressed wish of the Congress, I appointed a commercial agent for the Kongo basin.

The importance of the rich prospective trade of the Kongo Valley has led to the general conviction that it should be open to all nations upon equal terms. At an international conference for the consideration of this subject called by the Emperor of Germany, and now in session at Berlin, delegates are in attendance on behalf of the United States. Of the results of the conference you will be duly advised.

The Government of Korea has generously aided the efforts of the United States minister to secure suitable premises for the use of the legation. As the conditions of diplomatic intercourse with Eastern nations demand that the legation premises be owned by the represented power, I advise that an appropriation be made for the acquisition of this property by the Government. The United States already possess valuable premises at Tangier as a gift from the Sultan of Morocco. As is stated hereafter, they have lately received a similar gift from the Siamese Government. The Government of Japan stands ready to present to us extensive grounds at Tokyo whereon to erect a suitable building for the legation, court-house, and jail, and similar privileges can probably be secured in China and Persia. The owning of such premises would not only effect a